INTRODUCTION TO
SOCIOLOGY

SEVENTH EDITION

Recent Sociology Titles from W. W. Norton

Code of the Streets by Elijah Anderson
Social Problems by Joel Best
The Contexts Reader edited by Jeff Goodwin and James M. Jasper
When Sex Goes to School by Kristin Luker
Inequality and Society edited by Jeff Manza and Michael Sauder
Readings for Sociology, 6th Edition, by Garth Massey
Sociology of Globalization by Saskia Sassen
The Sociology of News by Michael Schudson
The Social Construction of Sexuality by Steven Seidman
The Corrosion of Character by Richard Sennett
Biography and the Sociological Imagination by Michael J. Shanahan and Ross Macmillan
Six Degrees by Duncan J. Watts
More Than Just Race by William Julius Wilson

Norton Critical Editions

The Souls of Black Folk by W. E. B. Du Bois, edited by Henry Louis Gates Jr. and
    Terri Hume Oliver
The Communist Manifesto by Karl Marx, edited by Frederic L. Bender
Protestant Ethic and the Spirit of Capitalism by Max Weber, translated by Talcott Parsons
    and edited by Richard Swedberg

For more information on our publications in sociology, please visit wwnorton.com/college/soc

W. W. Norton & Company, Inc.
New York • London

INTRODUCTION TO
SOCIOLOGY

SEVENTH EDITION

Anthony Giddens
LONDON SCHOOL OF ECONOMICS

Mitchell Duneier
CITY UNIVERSITY OF NEW YORK
GRADUATE CENTER

PRINCETON UNIVERSITY

Richard P. Appelbaum
UNIVERSITY OF CALIFORNIA,
SANTA BARBARA

Deborah Carr
RUTGERS UNIVERSITY

W. W. Norton & Company has been independent since its founding in 1923, when William Warder Norton and Mary D. Herter Norton first published lectures delivered at the People's Institute, the adult education division of New York City's Cooper Union. The firm soon expanded its program beyond the Institute, publishing books by celebrated academics from America and abroad. By mid-century, the two major pillars of Norton's publishing program—trade books and college texts—were firmly established. In the 1950s, the Norton family transferred control of the company to its employees, and today—with a staff of four hundred and a comparable number of trade, college, and professional titles published each year—W. W. Norton & Company stands as the largest and oldest publishing house owned wholly by its employees.

Editor: Karl Bakeman
Assistant Editor: Kate Feighery
E-media editor: Eileen Connell
Ancillaries editor: Rachel Comerford
Project editors: Lory Frenkel and Christine D'Antonio
Photo editor: Stephanie Romeo
Photo researcher: Jennifer Bright
Design Director: Rubina Yeh
Composition and page layout: Brad Walrod/High Text Graphics, Inc.
Manufacturing: The Courier Companies—Kendallville, Indiana
Production manager: Benjamin Reynolds

Library of Congress Cataloging-in-Publication Data

Introduction to sociology/Anthony Giddens ... [et al.]—7th ed.
    p. cm.
Rev. ed. of: Introduction to sociology/Anthony Giddens, Mitchell Duneier, Richard P. Appelbaum.
    6th ed. © 2007.
Includes bibliographical references and index.
    ISBN: 978-0-393-93232-4 (pbk.)
    1. Sociology.   I. Giddens, Anthony.   II. Giddens, Anthony.   III. Introduction to sociology.

HM585.G53 2009
301—dc22   2008045588

W. W. Norton & Company, Inc., 500 Fifth Avenue, New York, N.Y. 10110
www.wwnorton.com

W. W. Norton & Company Ltd., Castle House, 75/76 Wells Street, London W1T 3QT

1 2 3 4 5 6 7 8 9 0

CONTENTS

Part Two: The Individual and Society 51

Chapter 6: Groups, Networks, and Organizations 135

Chapter 7: Conformity, Deviance, and Crime 171

Part Three: Structures of Power 203

Chapter 11: Ethnicity and Race 317

Chapter 12: Aging 355

Part Four: Social Institutions 421

Part Five: Social Change in the Modern World 563

Chapter 20: Globalization in a Changing World 655

PREFACE

We wrote this book with the belief that sociology plays a key role in modern intellectual culture and occupies a central place within the social sciences. We have aimed to write a book that combines classic theories of sociology with new cutting-edge studies and examples from real-life that reveal the basic issues of interest to sociologists today. In some places, we attempt to introduce the reader to a subject through the use of ethnographies written for this book. The book does not introduce overly sophisticated notions; nevertheless, ideas and findings drawn from the cutting edge of the discipline are incorporated throughout. We hope it is a fair and nonpartisan treatment; we endeavored to cover the major perspectives in sociology and the major findings of contemporary American research in an evenhanded, although not indiscriminate, way.

Major Themes

The book is constructed around a number of basic themes, each of which helps give the work a distinctive character. One of the central themes is the **micro and macro link**. At many points in the book, we show that interaction in micro-level contexts affects larger social processes and that such macro-level processes influence our day-to-day lives. We emphasize that one can better understand a social situation by analyzing it at both the micro and macro levels.

A second theme of the book is that of the **world in change.** Sociology was born of the transformations that wrenched the industrializing social order of the West away from the ways of life characteristic of earlier societies. The world created by these changes is the primary object of concern of sociological analysis. The pace of social change has continued to accelerate, and it is possible that we stand on the threshold of transitions as significant as those that occurred in the late eighteenth and nineteenth centuries. Sociology has prime responsibility for charting the transformations of the past and for grasping the major lines of development taking place today. To support this theme, visual sociologist, John Grady, has created new "World in Change" photo essays in eleven chapters, which use drawn art and photographs to explore the implications of large-scale social change on individual lives.

Another fundamental theme of the book is the **globalization of social life**. For far too long, sociology has been dominated by the view that societies can be studied as independent entities. But even in the past, societies never really existed in isolation. In current times, we can see a clear acceleration in processes of global integration. This is obvious, for example, in the expansion of international trade across the world. The emphasis on globalization also connects closely with the weight given to the interdependence of the industrialized and developing worlds today.

The book also focuses on the importance of **comparative study**. Sociology cannot be taught solely by understanding the institutions of any one particular society. Although we have slanted the discussion toward the United States, we have also balanced it with a rich variety of materials drawn from other cultures. These include research carried out in other Western countries as well as in Russia and eastern European societies, which are currently undergoing substantial changes. The book also includes much more material on developing countries than has been usual in introductory texts. In addition, we strongly emphasize the relationship between sociology and anthropology, whose concerns overlap comprehensively. Given the close connections that now mesh societies across the world and the virtual disappearance of traditional social systems, sociology and anthropology have increasingly become indistinguishable.

A fifth theme is the necessity of taking a **historical approach** to sociology. This involves more than just filling in the historical context within which events occur. One of the most important developments in sociology over the past few years has been an increasing emphasis on historical analysis. This should be understood not solely as applying a sociological outlook to the past but as a way of contributing to our understanding of institutions in the present. Recent work in historical sociology is discussed throughout the text and provides a framework for the interpretations offered in the chapters.

Throughout the text, particular attention is given to issues of **social class, gender, and race.** The study of social differentiation is ordinarily regarded as a series of specific fields within sociology as a whole—and this volume contains chapters that specifically explore thinking and research on each subject (Chapters 8, 10, and 11, respectively). However, questions about gender, race, and class relations are so fundamental to sociological analysis that they cannot simply be considered a subdivision. Thus many chapters contain sections concerned with the ways that multiple sources of social stratification shape the human experience.

The seventh theme, **public sociology**, is reflected in a series of boxes inspired by the 2004 annual meeting of the American Sociological Association. At this meeting, Michael Burawoy's pathbreaking presidential address called for the discipline to draw on the insights and methods of sociology to involve ordinary people in studying and solving the social problems that affect them. The book features twenty boxes that profile sociologists engaged in public sociology in diverse arenas—for example, Columbia sociology professor Diane Vaughan's influential research on the *Challenger* shuttle disaster, which helped shape subsequent governmental investigations; Douglas Massey's testimony before the U.S. Congress on immigration policy; and William Bielby's pathbreaking testimony as an expert witness in gender discrimination cases. These boxes do not simply celebrate public sociology, rather they seek to give students a nuanced sense of the benefits and burdens of the position of the discipline in the public realm. It is certainly our hope that the Public Sociology boxes will inspire students to draw on their sociological imaginations to become more publicly involved and will provide some useful ideas for instructors who wish to generate class projects that directly engage students in the real world. In his speech, Burawoy also emphasized that public sociology cannot exist without a professional sociology that develops a body of theoretical knowledge and empirical findings. The central task of the book is to explain what the discipline of sociology has to offer along these lines.

An eighth theme is that a strong grasp of **sociological research methods** is crucial for understanding the world around us. A new feature "Behind the Headlines" focuses on recent sociological studies that are reported (or misreported) in the mainstream media. A strong understanding of how social science research is conducted is crucial for interpreting and making sense of the many social "facts" that the media trumpets. These twenty boxes help young sociologists to peer behind the headlines and to scrutinize recent media claims such as "Day Care Makes Kids Behave Badly" (Chapter 4) and "Beware of Fat Friends" (Chapter 18). We hope that the Behind the Headlines boxes will encourage students to carefully scrutinize and interrogate the daily news headlines they see on television, print, and on the internet.

The final major theme is the relation between the **social and the personal**. Sociological thinking is a vital help to self-understanding, which in turn can be focused back on an improved understanding of the social world. Studying sociology should be a liberating experience: The field enlarges our sympathies and imagination, opens up new perspectives on the sources of our own behavior, and creates an awareness of cultural settings different from our own. Insofar as sociological ideas challenge dogma, teach appreciation of cultural variety, and allow us insight into the working of social institutions, the practice of sociology enhances the possibilities of human freedom.

All of the chapters in the book have been updated and revised to reflect the most recent available data. In addition, five chapters have received special attention: Chapter 5 ("Social Interaction and Everyday Life") now begins with a vignette revealing how a bar employee enacts Erving Goffman's concept of "civil inattention." It includes new material on how technology, ranging from iPods to e-mail, is reshaping the very ways that individuals communicate and interact with one another. Chapter 14 ("Work and Economic Life") opens by discussing the global community of Wal-Mart workers and showing how Wal-Mart may set the path for the future of the global economy. The chapter also provides new information on transnational corporations and outsourcing of jobs. Chapter 16 ("Education and the Mass Media") includes rich and controversial new information on the struggles that many students face in today's educational system, including the achievement gap between white males and all other students today. Chapter 18 ("The Sociology of the Body: Health and Illness and Sexuality") has expanded its focus on the body and reveals the important ways that both excessively high and low body weight create psychological and physical health problems for individuals, yet also reflect sweeping macrosocial changes in food production and social norms. Chapter 19 ("Urbanization, Population, and the Environment") now begins with a new section on China's rise as an industrial power and its effect on its population and environment. The chapter also describes the distinctive characteristics (and problems) facing urban, rural, and suburban residents in the United States.

Organization

There is little abstract discussion of basic sociological concepts at the beginning of this book. Instead, concepts are explained when they are introduced in the relevant chapters, and we have sought to illustrate them by means of concrete examples. Although these examples are usually taken from sociological research, we have also used material from other sources (such as newspaper articles). We have tried to keep the writing style as simple and direct as possible, while endeavoring to make the book lively and full of surprises.

The chapters follow a sequence designed to help students achieve a progressive mastery of the different fields of sociology, but we have taken care to ensure that the book can be used flexibly and is easy to adapt to the needs of individual courses. Chapters can be deleted or studied in a different order without much loss. Each has been written as a fairly autonomous unit, with cross-referencing to other chapters at relevant points.

Study Aids

The pedagogy in this book has been completely reconfigured for the Seventh Edition to facilitate critical thinking and reinforce important concepts. Each chapter begins with a chapter organizer, which highlights the learning objectives of each section and allows students to preview that chapter's discussion. This edition of *Introduction to Sociology* includes significantly expanded chapter review material, including keyword and concept-review questions and data exercises linking material in the text to real-world data on the Web.

Another helpful aid is the use of a globe icon to indicate examples of the changing world, the globalization process, or comparisons of U.S. society with other societies. Social change, the globalization of social life, and comparative analysis are all important themes of this text. The icon alerts readers to discussions of these themes.

We have also added a new feature, called "Concept Checks." Every chapter includes several review questions embedded throughout the chapters. These quizzes are designed to help students prepare for a test or to confirm for themselves that they comprehend the major topics in the book. Concept Checks range from reading comprehension to more advanced critical thinking skills.

Acknowledgments

During the writing of all seven editions of this book, many individuals offered comments and advice on particular chapters and, in some cases, large parts of the text. They helped us see issues in a different light, clarified some difficult points, and allowed us to take advantage of their specialized knowledge in their respective fields. We are deeply indebted to them. Special thanks go to Nick Ehrman for researching and writing fifteen boxes on public sociology; Neha Gondal, who worked assiduously to help us update data throughout the book and contributed significantly to the editing process; Todd Beer for his terrific work drafting questions for each of the book's figures; and Joe Conti, who drafted new end-of-chapter questions for the Seventh Edition.

Chris Baker, Walters State Community College
Mary Davidson, Columbia-Greene Community College
Mary Grigsby, University of Missouri
Lisa Handler, Community College of Philadelphia
Dawn Hall, Sinclair Community College
Clara Kim, University of Dayton
Amy Lane, University of Missouri
Gloria Lessan, Florida State University
Lillian Wallace, Pima College

We would like to thank the numerous readers of the text who have written with comments, criticisms, and suggestions for improvements. We have adopted many of their recommendations in this new edition.

We have many others to thank as well. We are especially grateful to Candace Levy, who did a marvelous job of copyediting the book and offered numerous suggestions for alterations and improvements that have contributed in important ways to the final form of the volume. We are also extremely grateful to project editors Lory Frenkel and Christine D'Antonio, production manager Ben Reynolds, and assistant editor Kate Feighery for managing the myriad details involved in producing this book. Eileen Connell, our electronic media editor, deserves special thanks for creating the elegant new website to accompany the book. Finally, Stephanie Romeo showed unusual flair and originality in the selections made for illustrating the book.

We are also grateful to our editors at Norton, Steve Dunn, Melea Seward, and Karl Bakeman, who have made many direct contributions to the various chapters, and have ensured that we have made reference to the very latest research. We would also like to register our thanks to a number of sociologists and sociology graduate students whose contributions have proved invaluable: Wendy Carter, Joe Conti, Audrey Devine-Eller, Neha Gondal, Neil Gross, Blackhawk Hancock, Paul LePore, Dmitry Khodyakov, Alair MacLean, Ann Meier, Susan Munkres, Josh Rossol, Sharmila Rudrappa, Christopher Wildeman, David Yamane, and Kathrin Zippel.

PART ONE

THE STUDY OF SOCIOLOGY

We live in a world today that is increasingly complex. Why are the conditions of our lives so different from those of earlier times? How will our lives change in the future? These types of questions lead to the study of sociology. As you read this text, you will encounter examples from different people's lives that will help answer these important questions.

In Chapter 1, we explore the scope of sociology and learn what insights the field can bring, such as the development of a global perspective and an understanding of social change. Sociology is not a body of theories everyone agrees on. As in any complex field, the questions we raise allow for different answers. In this chapter, we compare and contrast differing theoretical traditions.

Chapter 2 explores the tools of the trade and considers how sociologists do research. A number of basic methods of investigation are available to explore the social world. We must be sure that the information underlying sociological reasoning is as reliable and accurate as possible. The chapter examines the problems encountered when gathering such information and indicates how best to deal with them.

Learning Objectives

Developing a Sociological Perspective

Learn what sociology encompasses and how everyday topics like love and romance are shaped by social and historical forces.

Recognize that sociology involves not only acquiring knowledge but also developing a sociological imagination. Learn that we construct society through our actions and are constructed by it.

Understand that two key components of the sociological imagination are developing a global perspective and understanding social change.

The Development of Sociological Thinking

Learn how sociology originated and developed. Think about the theoretical issues that frame the study of sociology. Be able to identify some leading social theorists and their contributions to sociology. Learn the different theoretical approaches of modern sociologists.

Is Sociology a Science?

Understand how sociology is similar to and different from natural sciences.

How Can Sociology Help Us?

See the practical implications of sociology.

CHAPTER ONE

WHAT IS SOCIOLOGY?

have you ever known or heard of somebody with autism? In the past few decades, in the United States and in many other developed nations of the world, the incidence of autism—a profound developmental disorder—has increased rapidly, so much so that it appears as if we are in the midst of an autism epidemic. People with autism show less-than-normal competence in routine social interaction. They don't make normal eye contact, they have trouble taking turns in conversation, and they have difficulty establishing social solidarity by smiling in response to others. Although no one knows for sure, different studies suggest that as many as 1 in 150 children born in the United States today will be diagnosed with autism or a related disorder (Centers for Disease Control 2007).

Why would the incidence of autism have risen so rapidly? Since autism is a medical condition, you might be surprised to be reading about it in a sociology book. However, developing a sociological perspective can help us understand the causes of the rise in autism and thus help us design social policies that will stem it. No one knows what causes autism and no one knows what lies behind the rapid increase in cases. The search for a cause has produced hundreds of social and biological studies that have identified dozens of social and environmental factors and a host of possible genes as potentially related to the disease. In general, three theories compete for attention. What is important about these theories is that none of them argues that genetic influences alone can explain either autism risk or the rise in rates of autism. All of the theories indicate that social aspects of life must be carefully considered.

The first theory suggests that the increase is related to the changing ways in which we recognize its signs and symptoms. There is no medical test for autism, and our ability to determine that someone is autistic depends upon complicated criteria that require doctors to recognize particular social and interactional cues. In recent years, cues that were formerly not diagnosed as autism are now increasingly receiving this label. It is therefore possible that the number of people with the characteristics we associate with autism may have remained the same, but that the increasing number of cases is driven largely, if not wholly, by diagnostic changes and increasingly aggressive surveillance and screening policies. If this were true, it would mean that there has been no increase in the incidence of autism characteristics, just an increase in our discovery of and treatment of children with autism.

The second theory suggests that the epidemic is fueled by more toxic chemicals in the environment. There are many reasons to worry about how environmental changes could lead to more and more cases of autism. We know, for example, that many developmental disorders are caused by exposures to base metals, such as lead or the pesticides on private golf courses, or new metals in high-tech industrial sectors. Economic development and the pollution it causes may surely lead to a whole array of unanticipated health outcomes. The third theory is that the epidemic is being brought on by the increasing number of older men who are fathering children. This is because age of male sperm may be associated with developmental disorders such as autism.

To make sense of the autism epidemic, we need a strategy for disentangling the causes of the epidemic. In fact, the sociologists Peter Bearman and Marissa King have begun to tackle the causes of the epidemic by assembling an unusual data set that has begun to allow them to uniquely identify what part of the epidemic is caused by diagnostic process, genetic and/or family characteristics, and environmental change. By looking at every child born in California from 1992 to 2007, they have been able to show, for example, that almost one third of the autism epidemic is caused by changes in what doctors call "autism." This means, of course, that two out of every three cases of autism may be associated with other factors, perhaps other social factors, but perhaps other environmental and/or genetic factors.

These researchers also have shown that the communities where autism cases appear to arise from diagnostic processes are very different from those communities where they do not. The communities differ in ways that make sociological sense. Diagnostic change appears to be associated with community wealth. That is what we would expect, because treatment is

Fletcher Scott, a speech language pathologist and senior program therapist, works with Hannah Ishoo, 3, who has been diagnosed with autism, at the University of New Mexico Center for Development and Disability.

expensive and not many school districts have the economic resources to provide appropriate services for autistic children. Sociologists will not necessarily find the cure for autism, but their work is pointing the way for other scientists to narrow down the causes.

The imaginative research by Bearman and King exemplifies how sociology can teach us that what we regard as natural, inevitable, good, or true may not be such, and that the "givens" of our life—including things we take to be genetic or biological—are strongly influenced by historical and social forces. **Sociology** is the scientific study of human social life, groups, and societies. It is a dazzling and compelling enterprise, as its subject matter is our own behavior as social beings. The scope of sociological study is extremely wide, ranging from the analysis of how people establish social connections with one another in interactions to the investigation of global social processes such as the rise of Islamic fundamentalism.

Developing a Sociological Perspective

When we learn to think sociologically, not only can we understand large scale trends such as the rise of autism, we can also better understand the most intimate aspects of our own lives. For example, have you ever been in love? Almost certainly you have. Most people who are in their teens or older know what being in love is like. Love and romance provide some of the most intense feelings we ever experience. Why do people fall in love? The answer may seem obvious: Love expresses a mutual physical and personal attachment between two individuals. These days, we might not all think that love is "forever"; but falling in love, we might agree, is an experience arising from universal human emotions. It seems natural for a couple in love to want personal and sexual fulfillment in their relationship, perhaps through marriage. Yet this seemingly self-evident situation is in fact very unusual. Falling in love is *not* an experience most people across the world have—and where it does happen, it is rarely connected to marriage. The idea of romantic love did not become widespread until fairly recently in our society and has never even existed in many other cultures.

Only in modern times have love and sexuality become closely connected. In the Middle Ages and for centuries afterward, men and women married mainly to keep property in the hands of the family or to raise children to work the family farm—or, in the case of royalty, to seal political alliances. They may have become close companions after marriage, but not before. People sometimes had sexual affairs outside marriage, but these inspired few of the emotions we associate with love today. Romantic love was regarded at best as a weakness and at worst as a kind of sickness.

Romantic love developed in courtly circles as a characteristic of extramarital sexual adventures by members of the aristocracy. Until about two centuries ago, it was confined to such circles and kept separate from marriage. Relations between

What is the origin of romantic love? Originally, romantic love was limited to affairs for medieval aristocrats such as Tristan and Isolde, the subjects of a thirteenth-century court romance who inspired poems, operas, and films.

husband and wife among aristocratic groups were often cool and distant. Each spouse had his or her own bedroom and servants; they may rarely have seen each other in private. Sexual compatibility was not considered relevant to marriage. Among both rich and poor, the decision of whom to marry was made by family and kin; the individuals concerned had little or no say in the matter.

This remains true in many non-Western countries today. For example, in Afghanistan under the rule of the Taliban, men were prohibited from speaking to women they were not related or married to, and marriages were arranged by parents. If a girl and boy were seen by authorities to be speaking with one another, they would be whipped and left seriously injured, if not dead. The Taliban government saw romantic love as so offensive that it outlawed music and films. Like many in the non-Western world, the Taliban believed Afghanistan was being inundated by Hollywood movies and American rock music and videos, which are filled with sexual images. Osama bin Laden launched his terrorist attacks against the United States from Afghanistan, and the rhetoric of his followers has partly been aimed at criticizing such Western influences.

But it is not only in areas where Islamic fundamentalism has taken root that romantic love is considered unnatural. In India, for example, the majority of marriages are arranged by parents or other relatives. The opinions of prospective marriage partners are often—but not always—taken into account. A study of marriage in Kerala, a state in India, showed that just over half the young people thought that meeting the prospective spouse before marriage was relevant to marital happiness. Among parents, only 1 percent were willing to let their children choose marriage partners. Although romantic love is recognized, it is equated with temporary infatuation or seen as a barrier to a happy marriage.

Neither romantic love, then, nor its association with marriage can be understood as a natural feature of human life. Rather, such love has been shaped by social and historical influences. These are the influences sociologists study.

Most of us see the world in terms of the familiar features of our own lives. Sociology demonstrates the need for a much broader view of our nature and our actions. It teaches that what we regard as inevitable, good, or true may not be such and that the "natural" in our lives is strongly influenced by historical and social forces. Understanding the subtle yet profoundly complex ways in which our individual lives reflect the contexts of our social experience is basic to the sociological outlook.

Learning to think sociologically means cultivating the imagination. As sociologists, we need to imagine, for example, what the experience of sex and marriage is like for people who consider the ideals of romantic love to be alien or absurd. Sociology is *not* just a routine process of acquiring knowledge;

Three businessmen relax and chat over coffee. A group of workers on a hashish plantation smoke hash during a break. In both instances, the socially acceptable consumption of a drug serves as an occasion to socialize.

it requires breaking free from the immediacy of personal circumstances and putting things in a wider context. It requires what the American sociologist C. Wright Mills (1959b), in a famous phrase, called the **sociological imagination.**

The sociological imagination requires us, above all, to *"think ourselves away" from our daily routines to look at them anew.* Consider the simple act of drinking a cup of coffee. What might the sociological point of view illuminate about such apparently uninteresting behavior? An enormous amount. First, coffee possesses *symbolic value* as part of our daily social activities (see "Globalization and Everyday Life: The Sociology of Coffee"). Often the ritual associated with coffee drinking is much more important than the act itself. Two people who arrange to meet for coffee are probably more interested in getting together and chatting than in what they actually drink. Drinking and eating in all societies, in fact, promote social interaction and the enactment of rituals—rich subject matter for sociological study.

Second, coffee contains caffeine, a *drug* that stimulates the brain. In Western culture, coffee addicts are not regarded as drug users. Like alcohol, coffee is a socially acceptable drug, whereas marijuana, for instance, is not. Yet some societies tolerate the consumption of marijuana or even cocaine but frown on coffee and alcohol. Sociologists are interested in why these contrasts exist.

Third, an individual who drinks a cup of coffee is participating in a complicated set of *social and economic relationships* stretching across the world. The production, transport, and distribution of coffee require continuous transactions among people thousands of miles away from the coffee drinker. Studying such global transactions is an important task of sociology because many aspects of our lives are now affected by worldwide social influences and communications.

Finally, the act of sipping a cup of coffee presumes a process of *past social and economic development.* Along with other now-familiar items of Western diets—like tea, bananas, potatoes, and white sugar—widespread coffee consumption began only in the late 1800s under Western colonial expansion. Virtually all the coffee we drink today comes from areas (South America and Africa) that were colonized by Europeans; it is in no sense a "natural" part of the Western diet.

Studying Sociology

We all know a great deal about ourselves and the societies in which we live. We think we understand why we act as we do, without needing sociologists to tell us! And to some degree this is true. Yet there are boundaries to such self-knowledge, and one of the tasks of sociology is to reveal what these boundaries are.

The sociological imagination allows us to see that many events that seem to concern only the individual actually reflect larger social issues. Divorce, for instance, may be a very difficult process for an individual, but it is also a public issue in a society like the United States, where 43 percent of first marriages break up within fifteen years. Likewise, unemployment may be a highly personal and stressful experience for the individual, yet when millions of people in a society are in the same situation, unemployment is also a public issue expressing large social trends.

Try applying this outlook to your own life. Consider why you have decided to study sociology. You might be taking the course just to fulfill a requirement, or you might be enthusiastic to find out more about the subject. Whatever your motivations, you likely have a good deal in common, without knowing it, with others studying sociology. Your private decision reflects your position in the wider society.

Do the following characteristics apply to you? Are you young? White? From a professional or white-collar background? Have you done part-time work to boost your income? Do you want to find a good job when you leave school but not especially enjoy studying? Do you not really know what sociology is but think it involves the way people behave in groups? More than three quarters of you will answer yes to all these questions. College students are not typical of the population as a whole but tend to come from more privileged backgrounds. And their attitudes usually reflect those held by friends and acquaintances. Our social backgrounds strongly affect the kinds of decisions we think appropriate.

But suppose you answered no to one or more of these questions. You might come from a minority group or impoverished background. You may be middle-aged or older. If so, however, further conclusions probably follow. You likely had to struggle to get where you are; you might have faced hostile reactions when you told friends you were intending to go to college; or you might be combining school with full-time parenthood and/or work.

Although we are all influenced by social contexts, they don't strictly *determine* our behavior. We possess, and create, our own individuality. It is the business of sociology to investigate the connections between *what society makes of us and what we make of ourselves*. Our activities both structure our social world and at the same time are structured by it.

The concept of **social structure** is important in sociology. It refers to the fact that in our lives, social contexts are not random events but have distinct *patterns*. There are regularities in our behavior and our relationships. But social structure is not like a physical structure, such as a building, which exists independently of human actions. Human societies are always in the process of **structuration:** They are reconstructed at every moment by the very "building blocks" that compose them—human beings like you and me.

Consider again the case of coffee. A cup of coffee does not automatically arrive in your hands. You choose, for example, to go to a particular café, whether to drink your coffee black or light, and so forth. As you make these decisions, along with millions of other people, you shape the market for coffee and affect the lives of coffee producers living perhaps thousands of miles away on the other side of the world.

Developing a Global Perspective

All our local actions form part of larger social settings that extend around the globe. These connections have accelerated over the past thirty or forty years as a result of dramatic advances in communications, information technology, and transportation that enable people and goods to be continuously transported across the world. And the worldwide system of satellite communication, established only some thirty years ago, has made it possible for people to get in touch with each other instantaneously.

American society is influenced every moment of the day by **globalization**, the growth of world interdependence. Globalization not only involves worldwide networks but reflects local phenomena, too. For example, only a few years ago most Americans had limited choices for dining out. In many U.S. towns and cities today, however, a single street might feature Italian, Chinese, Japanese, Thai, French, and other types of restaurants, including fusion cuisine. In turn, our dietary decisions affect food producers on the other side of the world. For another example, look at the labels of your clothes and see how many countries they were manufactured in; this will show you globalization firsthand.

Do college students have a global perspective? By at least one measure, the answer is yes. Furthermore, their activist values suggest a sociological imagination. According to an annual survey of more than 263,710 first-year college students, a

"How would you like me to answer that question? As a member of my ethnic group, educational class, income group, or religious category?"

The Sociology of Coffee

The world drinks about 2.25 billion cups [of coffee] per day—the United States alone drinks one fifth of this. Coffee drinking is a cultural fixture that says as much about us as it does about the bean itself. Basically a habit forming stimulant, coffee is nonetheless associated with relaxation and sociability. In a society that combines buzzing overstimulation with soul-aching meaninglessness, coffee and its associated rituals are, for many of us, the lubricants that make it possible to go on.

Perhaps for this reason coffee occupies a distinctive niche in our cultural landscape. Along with alcohol, it is the only beverage to engender public houses devoted to its consumption. *** Uniquely, though, coffee is welcome in almost any situation, from the car to the boardroom, from the breakfast table to the public park, alone or in company of any kind. Since its adoption as a beverage, coffee has been offered as an antipode to alcohol—more so even than abstinence, perhaps in recognition of a human need for joyfully mood-altering substances and the convivial social interactions that go along with them.

Only a handful of consumer goods has fueled the passions of the public as much as coffee. *** [C]offee has inspired impassioned struggles on the battlefields of economics, human rights, politics, and religion, since its use first spread. Coffee

record 49.7 percent of all students who entered U.S. colleges in 2005 reported that they had "participated in organized demonstrations" concerned with social, political, and economic issues during the previous year (Hurtado 2006). The demonstrations involved a wide range of issues, including the growing power of global institutions such as the World Trade Organization and the World Bank, the production of clothing in overseas sweatshops, global warming, environmental destruction, and the right of workers to earn a living wage (Meatto 2000).

Developing a global perspective has great importance for sociology. It not only demonstrates how we are connected to people in other societies but also makes us more aware of problems the world faces at the beginning of the twenty-first century. The global perspective helps us see that our actions have consequences for others and that the world's problems have consequences for us.

Understanding Social Change

The changes in human ways of life over the last two hundred years, such as globalization, have been far reaching. For example, for virtually all of human history, the vast majority of people produced their own food and shelter and lived in tiny groups or small village communities. Even at the height of the most developed traditional civilizations—such as ancient Rome or traditional China—fewer than 10 percent of the population lived in urban areas; everyone else was engaged in food production in a rural setting. Today, in most industrialized societies, these proportions are almost completely reversed. Quite often, more than 90 percent of the people live in urban areas, and only 2 to 3 percent of the population work in agricultural production. Yet with changing conditions of economic activity central to the processes of globalization, the developing world may be a drink for sharing, but as a commodity it invites protectionism, oppression, and destruction. Its steamy past implicates the otherwise noble bean in early colonialism, various revolutions, the emergence of the bourgeoisie, international development, technological hubris, crushing global debt, and more. These forces, in turn, have shaped the way coffee has been incorporated into our culture and economy. Colonialism, for example, served as the primary reason for and vehicle of coffee's expansion throughout the globe; colonial powers dictated where coffee went and where it did not and established trading relationships that continue to this day.

The story of coffee also reveals how (and why) we interact with a plethora of other commodities, legal or not. Surprising similarities exist, for example, between coffee's early history and the current controversy over marijuana. Today's national debate over the merits of marijuana, although young by comparison, is the modern version of the strife surrounding coffee in other ages. The social acceptability of each has been affected by religious and political opinion, conflicting health claims, institutionalized cultural norms, and the monied interests of government and private industry. The evolution of coffee's social acceptability highlights the delicate dance of interests and "truths" that governs the ways in which we structure our societies.

Coffee is consumed with great fervor in rich countries such as the United States yet is grown with few exceptions in the poorest parts of the globe. In fact, it is the second most valuable item of legal international trade (after petroleum), and the largest food import of the United States by value. It is the principal source of foreign exchange for dozens of countries around

the world. The coffee in your cup is an immediate, tangible connection with the rural poor in some of the most destitute parts of the planet. It is a physical link across space and cultures from one end of the human experience to the other.

The coffee trading system that has evolved to bring all this about is an intricate knot of economics, politics, and sheer power—a bizarre arena trod *** by some of the world's largest transnational corporations, by enormous governments, and by vast trading cartels. The trip coffee takes from the crop to your cup turns out not to be so straightforward after all, but rather a turbulent and unpredictable ride through the waves and eddies of international commodity dynamics, where the product itself becomes secondary to the wash of money and power.

SOURCE: Gregory Dicum and Nina Luttinger, *The Coffee Book: Anatomy of an Industry from Crop to the Last Drop* (New York: The New Press, 1999), pp. ix–xi. Used with permission.

---

is urbanizing rapidly as well. By 2030, about 60 percent of the world population are expected to live in urban areas and in more developed regions; 81 percent will live in urban areas (United Nations 2006).

Furthermore, such transformations have radically altered the most personal and intimate side of our daily existence. To extend a previous example, the spread of ideals of romantic love was strongly conditioned by the transition from a rural to an urban, industrialized society. As people began to work in industrial production, marriage was no longer prompted by economic motives—by the need to control the inheritance of land and to work the land as a family unit. "Arranged" marriages became less common. Individuals increasingly initiated marriage relationships on the basis of emotional attraction and personal fulfillment. The idea of falling in love as a basis for contracting a marriage tie arose in this context.

Sociology developed through the attempts to understand the initial effect of these transformations that accompanied industrialization in the West. Our world today is radically different from that of former ages; sociology helps us understand this world and what its future is likely to hold.

☑ CONCEPT CHECKS

1. How does sociology help us understand the causes of violence?
2. What is the sociological imagination, according to C. Wright Mills?
3. How does the concept of social structure help sociologists better understand social phenomena?
4. What is globalization? How might it affect the lives of college students today?

The Development of Sociological Thinking

When students start studying sociology, many are puzzled by the diversity of approaches they encounter. Indeed, sociologists often disagree about how to study human behavior and how best to interpret research results. Why should this be so? Why can't sociologists agree more consistently, as natural scientists seem to do? The answer is bound up with the very nature of the field itself. Sociology is about our own lives and our own behavior, and studying ourselves is the most complex endeavor we can undertake.

Theories and Theoretical Approaches

Trying to understand something as complex as the effect of industrialization on society raises the importance of theory to sociology. Factual research shows *how* things occur. Yet sociology does not just consist of collecting facts; it also explores *why* things happen and thus requires constructing explanatory theories. For instance, we know that industrialization has influenced the emergence of modern societies. But what are the origins and preconditions of industrialization? Why are there differences among societies' industrialization processes? Why is industrialization associated with changes in criminal punishment or in family and marriage systems? To respond to such questions, we have to develop theoretical thinking.

A **theory** involves abstract interpretations that can explain a wide variety of situations. A theory about industrialization, for example, would identify the main, shared features of industrial development and would demonstrate which ones are most important in explaining such development. Of course, factual research and theories can never be completely separated. We can develop valid theoretical approaches only if we can test them out by means of factual research.

We need theories to help us make sense of facts, which do not speak for themselves. Many sociologists work primarily on factual research; but unless they are guided by some knowledge of theory, their work is unlikely to explain the complexity of modern societies. This is true even of research carried out with strictly practical objectives.

"Practical people" tend to be suspicious of theorists and may feel no need for abstract ideas, yet all practical decisions have some underlying theoretical assumptions. A manager of a business, for example, might have scant regard for theory. Nonetheless, every approach to business activity involves theoretical assumptions, even if unstated. Thus the manager might assume that employees are motivated to work hard mainly for money—the level of wages. This is not only a theoretical interpretation of human behavior but also a mistaken one, as research in industrial sociology demonstrates.

Without a **theoretical approach**, we would not know what to look for in beginning a study or in interpreting research results. However, the illumination of factual evidence is not the only reason for theory's prime position in sociology. Theoretical thinking must respond to general problems posed by the study of human social life, including philosophical issues. Deciding to what extent sociology should be modeled on the natural sciences is a question that does not yield easy solutions. This question has been addressed in different ways in the various theoretical approaches within the discipline.

Early Theorists

We human beings have always been curious about the sources of our behavior, but for thousands of years we have relied on ways of thinking passed down from generation to generation, often expressed in religious terms. (For example, before the rise of modern science, many people believed that natural events such as earthquakes were caused by gods or spirits.) Although early writers provided insights into human behavior and society, the systematic study of society began only in the late 1700s and early 1800s. The shattering of traditional ways of life wrought by the French Revolution and the emergence of the Industrial Revolution in Europe caused thinkers to pursue a new understanding of both the social and natural worlds.

A key development was the use of science instead of religion to understand the world. The types of questions facing nineteenth-century thinkers—What is human nature? Why is society structured like it is? How and why do societies change?—are the same ones facing sociologists today, even though the modern world is radically different from that of the past.

AUGUSTE COMTE

The French author Auguste Comte (1798–1857) invented the word *sociology*. He originally used the term *social physics,* but some of his intellectual rivals were also using that term. To distinguish his views from theirs, Comte introduced *sociology* to describe the subject he wished to establish.

Comte believed that this new field could produce knowledge of society based on scientific evidence. Sociology, he felt, should contribute to the welfare of humanity by using science to understand and therefore predict and control human behavior. Late in his career, Comte drew up ambitious plans for the

Auguste Comte
(1798–1857).

Émile Durkheim
(1858–1917).

reconstruction of French society in particular, and for human societies in general, based on scientific knowledge.

ÉMILE DURKHEIM

Although Émile Durkheim (1858–1917) drew on aspects of Comte's work, he thought that many of his predecessor's ideas were too speculative and vague and that Comte had not successfully carried out his program—to establish sociology on a scientific basis. To become scientific, according to Durkheim, sociology must study **social facts**, aspects of social life that shape our actions as individuals, such as the state of the economy or the influence of religion. His famous first principle of sociology was "Study social facts as *things!*" By this he meant that social life can be analyzed as rigorously as objects or events in nature.

Like a biologist studying the human body, Durkheim saw society as a set of independent parts, each of which could be studied separately. Each of a body's specialized parts (such as the brain, heart, lungs, and liver) contributes to sustaining the life of the organism. These work in harmony with one another; if they do not, the life of the organism is under threat. So it is, according to Durkheim, with society. For a society to have a continuing existence over time, its specialized institutions (such as the political system, the religion, the family, and the educational system) must function as an integrated whole. Durkheim referred to this social cohesion as **organic solidarity**. He argued that the continuation of a society depends on cooperation, which presumes a general consensus among its members over basic values and customs.

Another theme pursued by Durkheim, and by many others since, is that societies exert **social constraint** over their members' actions. Durkheim argued that society is far more than the sum of individual acts; when we analyze social structures, we study characteristics that have a "firmness" or "solidity" comparable to those of structures in the physical world. Think of a person standing in a room with several doors. The structure of the room constrains the range of the person's possible activities. The position of the walls and doors, for example, defines routes of exit and entry. Social structure, according to Durkheim, constrains our activities in a parallel way, limiting what we can do as individuals. It is "external" to us, just as the walls of the room are.

Durkheim's analysis of social change was based on the development of the **division of labor**; he saw it as gradually replacing religion as the basis of social cohesion and providing organic solidarity to modern societies. He argued that as the division of labor expands, people become more dependent on each other because each person needs goods and services that those in other occupations supply. Another of Durkheim's famous studies (1966; orig. 1897) analyzed suicide. Although suicide seems to be a personal act, the outcome of extreme personal unhappiness, Durkheim showed that social factors influence suicidal behavior—such as **anomie**, a feeling of aimlessness or despair provoked by modern social life. Suicide rates show regular patterns from year to year, he argued, and these patterns must be explained sociologically. According to Durkheim, processes of change in the modern world are so rapid and intense that they give rise to major social difficulties, which he linked to anomie. Traditional moral controls and standards, formerly supplied by religion, largely break down under modern social development, and this leaves many individuals feeling that their lives lack meaning. Durkheim later focused on the role of religion in social life. In his study of religious beliefs, practices, and rituals—*The Elementary Forms of the Religious Life* (1965; orig. 1912)—he explored the importance of religion in maintaining moral order in society.

KARL MARX

The ideas of Karl Marx (1818–1883) contrast sharply with those of Comte and Durkheim; however, Marx also sought to explain

Karl Marx
(1818–1883).

social changes arising from the Industrial Revolution. When he was a young man, his political activities brought him into conflict with the German authorities; after a brief stay in France, he settled in exile in Britain. Much of his writing concentrates on economic issues, but because he was always concerned with connecting economic problems to social institutions, his work is rich in sociological insights.

Marx's viewpoint was founded on what he called the **materialist conception of history**. According to this view, it is not the ideas or values human beings hold that are the main sources of social change, as Durkheim claimed. Rather, social change is prompted primarily by economic influences. The conflicts between classes—rich versus poor—provide the motivation for historical development. In Marx's words, "All human history thus far is the history of class struggles."

Though he wrote about various phases of history, Marx concentrated on change in modern times. For him, the most important changes related to the development of capitalism. Those who own capital—factories, machines, and large sums of money—form a ruling class. The mass of the population make up a class of wage workers, a working class, who do not own the means of their livelihood but must find employment provided by the owners of capital. **Capitalism** is thus a class system in which conflict is inevitable because it is in the interests of the ruling class to exploit the working class and in the interests of the workers to seek to overcome that exploitation.

According to Marx, in the future capitalism will be supplanted by a society with no divisions between rich and poor. He didn't mean that all inequalities will disappear. Rather, societies will no longer be split into a small class that monopolizes economic and political power and the large mass of people who benefit little from the wealth their work creates. The economic system will have communal ownership and will lead to a more equal society than we know at present.

Marx's work had a far-reaching effect on the twentieth-century world. Until recently, before the fall of Soviet communism, more than a third of the earth's population lived in societies whose governments derived inspiration from Marx's ideas. In addition, many sociologists have been influenced by Marx's ideas about class divisions.

MAX WEBER

Like Marx, the German-born Max Weber (pronounced "Vaber," 1864–1920) cannot be labeled simply a sociologist; his interests spanned many areas. His writings covered the fields of economics, law, philosophy, and comparative history as well as sociology, and much of his work also treated the development of modern capitalism. He was influenced by Marx but was also critical of some of Marx's major views. He rejected the materialist conception of history and saw class conflict as less significant than did Marx. In Weber's view, economic factors are important, but ideas and values have just as much effect on social change.

Some of Weber's most influential writings analyzed the distinctiveness of Western society compared with other major civilizations. He studied the religions of China, India, and the Near East, thereby making major contributions to the sociology of religion. Comparing the leading religious systems in China and India with those of the West, Weber concluded that certain aspects of Christian beliefs strongly influenced the rise of capitalism. He argued that the capitalist outlook of Western societies did not emerge, as Marx supposed, only from economic changes. In Weber's view, cultural ideas and values shape society and affect individual actions.

One of the most persistent concerns of Weber's work was the study of bureaucracy. A **bureaucracy** is a large organization that is divided into jobs based on specific functions and staffed by officials ranked according to a hierarchy. Industrial firms, government organizations, hospitals, and schools are examples of bureaucracies. Weber saw the advance of bureaucracy as an inevitable feature of our era. Bureaucracy

Max Weber
(1864–1920).

TABLE 1.1

Interpreting Modern Development

DURKHEIM
1. The main dynamic of modern development is the **division of labor** as a basis for social cohesion and **organic solidarity.**
2. Durkheim believed that sociology must study **social facts** as things, just as science would analyze the natural world. His study of suicide led him to stress the important influence of social factors, qualities of a society external to the individual, on a person's actions. Durkheim argued that society exerts **social constraint** over our actions.

MARX
1. The main dynamic of modern development is the expansion of **capitalism.** Rather than being cohesive, society is divided by class differences.
2. Marx believed that we must study the divisions within a society that are derived from the economic inequalities of capitalism.

WEBER
1. The main dynamic of modern development is the **rationalization** of social and economic life.
2. Weber focused on why Western societies developed so differently from other societies. He also emphasized the importance of cultural ideas and values on social change.

enables large organizations to run efficiently, but at the same time it poses problems for effective democratic participation in modern societies. Bureaucracy involves the rule of experts, who make decisions without consulting those whose lives are affected by them.

Some of Weber's writings also address the character of sociology itself. He was more cautious than either Durkheim or Marx in proclaiming sociology to be a science. According to Weber, it is misleading to imagine that we can study people by using the same procedures by which we investigate the physical world. Humans are thinking, reasoning beings; we attach meaning and significance to most of what we do, and any discipline that deals with human behavior must acknowledge this.

Neglected Founders

Although Comte, Durkheim, Marx, and Weber are foundational figures in sociology, other thinkers from the same period made important contributions. Very few women or members of racial minorities had the opportunity to become professional sociologists during the "classical" period of the late nineteenth and early twentieth centuries. In addition, the few that conducted sociological research of lasting importance have frequently been neglected by the field. These individuals deserve the attention of sociologists today.

HARRIET MARTINEAU

Harriet Martineau (1802–1876), born and educated in England, has been called the "first woman sociologist"; but like Marx and Weber, she cannot be thought of simply as a sociologist. She was the author of more than fifty books as well as numerous essays. Martineau is now credited with introducing sociology to England through her translation of Comte's founding treatise of the field, *Positive Philosophy* (Rossi 1973). In addition, she conducted a systematic study of American society during her extensive travels throughout the United States in the 1830s, which is the subject of her book *Society in*

Harriet Martineau (1802–1876).

America (1962; orig. 1837). Martineau is significant to sociologists today for several reasons. First, she argued that when one studies a society, one must focus on all its aspects, including key political, religious, and social institutions. Second, she insisted that an analysis of a society must include an understanding of women's lives. Third, she was the first to turn a sociological eye on previously ignored issues, including marriage, children, domestic and religious life, and race relations. Finally, she argued that sociologists should do more than just observe; they should also act in ways to benefit society. As a result, Martineau was an active proponent of women's rights and the emancipation of slaves.

W.E.B. DU BOIS

W.E.B. Du Bois (1868–1963) was the first African American to earn a doctorate at Harvard University. Among his many contributions to sociology, perhaps most important is the concept of "double consciousness," a way of talking about identity through the lens of the experiences of African Americans. He made a persuasive claim that one's sense of self and one's identity are greatly influenced by historical experiences and social circumstances—in the case of African Americans, the effect of slavery and, after emancipation, segregation and prejudice. Throughout his career, Du Bois focused on race relations in the United States; as he said in an often repeated quote, "the problem of the twentieth century is the problem of the color line" (Du Bois 1903). His influence on sociology today is evidenced by continued interest in the questions that he raised, particularly his concern that sociology must explain "the contact of diverse races of men" (Du Bois 1903). Du Bois was also the first social researcher to trace the problems faced by African Americans to their social and economic underpinnings, a connection that most sociologists now widely accept. Finally, he connected social analysis to social reform. He was one of the founding members of the National Association for the Advancement of Colored People (NAACP) and a long-time advocate for the collective struggle of African Americans.

Understanding the Modern World: The Sociological Debate

From Marx's time to the present, many sociological debates have centered on Marx's ideas about the influence of economics on the development of modern societies. According to Marx, the impulse behind social change in the modern era resides in the pressure toward constant economic transformation produced by the spread of *capitalist* production. Capitalism is a vastly more dynamic economic system than any other that preceded it. Capitalists compete to sell their goods to consumers; to survive in a competitive market, firms have to produce their wares as cheaply and efficiently as possible. This leads to constant technological innovation, because increasing the effectiveness of the technology used in a particular production process is one way in which companies can secure an edge over their rivals.

There are also strong incentives to seek new markets in which to sell goods, acquire cheap raw materials, and make use of cheap labor power. Capitalism, therefore, according to Marx, is a restlessly expanding system pushing outward across the world. This is how Marx explains the global spread of Western industry.

Subsequent Marxist authors have refined Marx's portrayal. However, numerous critics have set out to rebut Marx's view, offering alternative analyses of the influences shaping the modern world. Virtually everyone accepts that capitalism *has* played a major part, but other sociologists have argued that Marx exaggerated the effect of purely *economic* factors in producing change and that capitalism is *less central* to modern social development than he claimed. Most of these writers have also been skeptical of Marx's belief that a socialist system would eventually replace capitalism.

One of Marx's earliest and most acute critics was Max Weber, whose alternative position remains important today. According to Weber, noneconomic factors have played the key role in modern social development. Weber's celebrated work *The Protestant Ethic and the Spirit of Capitalism* (1977; orig. 1904) proposes that religious values—especially those associated with Puritanism—were of fundamental importance in creating a capitalistic outlook. This outlook did not emerge, as Marx supposed, only from economic changes.

Weber's understanding of the nature of modern societies, and the reasons for the spread of Western ways of life across the world, also contrasts substantially with that of Marx. According to Weber, capitalism—a distinct way of organizing

W.E.B. Du Bois
(1868–1963).

economic enterprise—is one among other major factors shaping social development in the modern period. Underlying capitalistic mechanisms, and in some ways more fundamental than them, is the effect of *science* and *bureaucracy*. Science has shaped modern technology and will presumably do so in any future society, whether socialist or capitalist. Bureaucracy is the only way of organizing large numbers of people effectively and therefore inevitably expands with economic and political growth. The developments of science, modern technology, and bureaucracy are examples of a general social process that Weber refers to collectively as rationalization. Rationalization means the organization of social, economic, and cultural life according to principles of efficiency, on the basis of technical knowledge.

Which interpretation of modern societies, that deriving from Marx or that coming from Weber, is correct? Scholars are divided on the issue. Moreover, within each camp there are variations, so not every theorist agrees with all the points of one interpretation. The contrasts between these two standpoints inform many areas of sociology.

Modern Theoretical Approaches

Although the origins of sociology were mainly European, over the last century the subject has become firmly established worldwide, and some of the most important developments have taken place in the United States.

SYMBOLIC INTERACTIONISM

The work of George Herbert Mead (1863–1931), a philosopher teaching at the University of Chicago, influenced the development of sociological thought, in particular through a perspective called **symbolic interactionism**. Mead placed particular importance on the study of *language* in analyzing the social world. According to him, language allows us to become self-conscious beings—aware of our own individuality. The key element in this process is the **symbol.** For example, the word *tree* is a symbol by which we represent the object tree. Once we have mastered such a concept, Mead argued, we can think of a tree even if none is visible. Symbolic thought frees us from being limited in our experience to what we actually see, hear, or feel.

Unlike animals, according to Mead, human beings live in a richly symbolic universe. This applies even to our sense of self. Each of us is a self-conscious being because we learn to look at ourselves as if from the outside—as others see us. When a child begins to use *I* to refer to that object (herself) whom others call "you," she is exhibiting the beginnings of self-consciousness.

All interactions among individuals, symbolic interactionists say, involve an exchange of symbols. When we interact with

George Herbert Mead (1863–1931).

others, we constantly look for clues to what type of behavior is appropriate in the context and how to interpret what others are up to. Symbolic interactionism directs our attention to the detail of interpersonal interaction and how that detail is used to make sense of what others say and do. For instance, suppose two people are on a first date. Each spends a good part of the evening sizing the other up and assessing how the relationship is likely to develop, if at all. Neither wishes to be seen doing this too openly, although each recognizes that it is going on. Both individuals are careful about their own behavior, being anxious to present themselves in a favorable light; but, knowing this, both are looking for aspects of the other's behavior that would reveal his or her true opinions. A complex and subtle process of symbolic interpretation shapes their interaction.

FUNCTIONALISM

Symbolic interactionism has been criticized for concentrating too much on things that are small in scope. Symbolic interactionists have found difficulty in dealing with larger-scale structures and processes—the very things that a rival tradition of thought, **functionalism**, emphasizes. Functionalist thinking in sociology was originally pioneered by Comte, who saw it as closely bound up with his overall view of the field.

To study the *function* of a social activity is to analyze its contribution to the continuation of the society as a whole. The best way to understand this idea is by analogy to the human body, a comparison Comte, Durkheim, and other functionalist authors made. To study an organ such as the heart, we need to show how it relates to other parts of the body. When we learn how the heart pumps blood, we understand its vital role in the continuation of the life of the organism. Similarly, analyzing the function of some aspect of society, such as religion, means showing its part in the continued existence and health of a society. Functionalism emphasizes the importance of *moral consensus* in maintaining order and stability in society. Moral consensus exists when most people share the same values. Functionalists regard order and balance as the normal state of society—this social equilibrium is grounded in a moral consensus among the members of society. According to Durkheim, for instance, religion reaffirms people's adherence to core social values, thereby helping to maintain social cohesion.

Functionalism became prominent in sociology through the writings of Talcott Parsons and Robert K. Merton, each of whom saw functionalist analysis as providing the key to the development of sociological theory and research. Merton's version of functionalism has been particularly influential.

Merton distinguished between manifest and latent functions. **Manifest functions** are those known to, and intended by, the participants in a social activity. **Latent functions** are consequences of that activity of which participants are unaware. Merton used the example of a rain dance performed by the Hopi tribe of Arizona and New Mexico. The Hopi believe that the ceremony will bring the rain they need for their crops (manifest function). This is why they organize and participate in it. But using Durkheim's theory of religion, Merton argued that the rain dance also promotes the cohesion of Hopi society (latent function). A major part of sociological explanation, according to Merton, consists in uncovering the latent functions of social activities and institutions.

Merton also distinguished between functions and dysfunctions. To look for the dysfunctional aspects of social behavior means focusing on features of social life that challenge the existing order. For example, it is mistaken to suppose that religion is always functional—that it contributes only to social cohesion. When two groups support different religions or different versions of the same religion, the result can be major social conflicts, causing widespread social disruption. Thus wars have often been fought between religious communities—as in the struggles between Protestants and Catholics in European history.

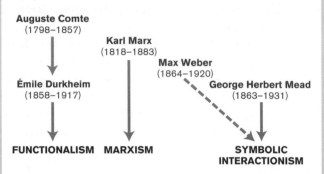

FIGURE 1.1

Theoretical Approaches in Sociology

The solid lines indicate direct influence; the dotted line, an indirect connection. Mead is not indebted to Weber, but Weber's views—stressing the meaningful, purposive nature of human action—have affinities with the themes of symbolic interactionism.

Auguste Comte
(1798–1857)

Karl Marx
(1818–1883)

Max Weber
(1864–1920)

Émile Durkheim
(1858–1917)

George Herbert Mead
(1863–1931)

FUNCTIONALISM **MARXISM** **SYMBOLIC INTERACTIONISM**

Why doesn't Weber follow Marx in sociological lineage? Name two influential founders of sociology who are not listed in this figure. What are the different areas of emphasis for functionalism and symbolic interactionism? Name two other sociologists who would be in line with Durkheim and who helped bring functionalist theory to prominence.

Robert K. Merton (1910–2003).

For a long while, functionalist thought was the leading theoretical tradition in sociology, particularly in the United States. In recent years, its popularity has declined. Although this was not true of Merton, many functionalist thinkers (Parsons is an example) unduly stressed factors leading to social cohesion at the expense of those producing division and conflict. In addition, many critics claim that functional analysis attributes to societies qualities they do not have. Functionalists often wrote as though societies had "needs" and "purposes," even though these concepts make sense only when applied to individual human beings. Figure 1.1 shows how functionalism relates to other theoretical approaches in sociology.

MARXISM AND CLASS CONFLICT

Functionalism and symbolic interactionism are not the only modern theoretical traditions of importance in sociology. A further influential approach is **Marxism**. Marxists, of course, all trace their views back to the writings of Karl Marx; but today there are schools of Marxist thought that take very different theoretical positions.

In all of its versions, Marxism differs from non-Marxist traditions of sociology in that its authors see it as a combination of sociological analysis and political reform. Marxism is supposed to generate a program of radical political change. Moreover, Marxists lay more emphasis on conflict, class divisions, power, and ideology than many non-Marxist sociologists do, especially those influenced by functionalism. The concept of **power**—and that of **ideology**—is of great importance to Marxist sociologists and to sociology in general. Power implies the capability of individuals or groups to make their own interests count, even when others resist. Power sometimes involves the direct use of force but is almost always accompanied by the development of ideas (ideologies), which are used to *justify* the actions of the powerful. Power, ideology, and conflict are always closely connected. Many conflicts are *about* power because of the rewards it can bring. Those who hold most power may depend on the influence of ideology to retain their dominance but are usually also able to use force if necessary.

FEMINISM AND FEMINIST THEORY

Feminist theory is one of the most prominent areas of contemporary sociology. This is a notable development because gender issues are scarcely central in the work of the major figures who established the discipline. The success of feminism's entry into sociology required a fundamental shift in the discipline's approach.

Many feminist theorists' experiences in the women's movement of the 1960s and 1970s influenced their work as sociologists. Like Marxism, feminism links sociological theory and political reform. Many feminist sociologists have been advocates for political and social action to remedy the inequalities between women and men in both the public and the private spheres.

Feminist sociologists argue that women's experiences are central to the study of society. Sociology, like most academic disciplines, has presumed a male point of view. Concerned with women's subordination in American society, feminist sociologists highlight gender relations and gender inequality as important determinants of social life in terms of both social interaction and social institutions such as the family, the workplace, and the educational system. Feminist theory emphasizes that gendered patterns and gendered inequalities are socially constructed. (We will cover this point in more detail in Chapter 10.)

Today, feminist sociology focuses on the intersection of gender, race, and class. A feminist approach to the study of inequality has influenced new fields of study, like men's studies, sexuality studies, and gay and lesbian studies.

RATIONAL CHOICE THEORY

The sociologist Max Weber thought that all behavior could be divided into four categories: (1) behavior oriented toward higher values, such as politics; (2) behavior oriented toward habit, such as walking to school on a familiar path; (3) behavior oriented toward affect (emotions), such as falling in love; and (4) behavior oriented toward self-interest, such as making money. Behavior in the last category is often called "instrumental" or "rational action." In recent years, many sociologists have adopted an approach that focuses on it. This has led numerous scholars to ask under what conditions human behavior can be said to constitute rational responses to opportunities and constraints.

The **rational choice approach** posits that if you could have only a single variable to explain society, self-interest would be the best one. A person who believes in this approach might even use it to explain things that seem irrational. One popular rational choice theory sees decisions to marry as maximizing self-interest in a marriage market; it might explain why marriage has declined the most in poor African American communities with low rates of employment. The explanation—that it is not in the self-interest of women to marry men who cannot support them (Wilson 1987)—goes against competing explanations suggesting that poor African Americans don't marry because they don't share mainstream values. The rational choice argument sees the decline as having little to do with values and much to do with self-interest under existing conditions. According to this theory, if employment rates for black men were to change, so would the number of "eligible" men and the desire of women to marry them.

Rational choice theorists find few irrational mysteries in life. One of the few some note is love, which they define as the irrational act of substituting another person's self-interest for one's own (Becker 1991). But such a definition makes it difficult to distinguish among basic altruism, friendship, and romantic love. Indeed, although a rational choice approach often can be useful, there are some aspects of life that it cannot explain. Consider an angry driver who tries to teach a tailgater a lesson by tailgating the tailgater. Self-interest does not explain this action because the "teacher" is unlikely to personally reap the benefits of a lesson well learned (Katz 1999).

POSTMODERN THEORY

Advocates of **postmodernism** claim that the classic social thinkers' idea that history has a shape—it "goes somewhere" and leads to progress—has collapsed. No longer do any "grand

For Public Sociology

On a Sunday evening in August 2004, Professor Michael Burawoy stood before more than five thousand of his colleagues at the American Sociological Association (ASA) conference to declare his vision for the future of public sociology. In attendance were not just professional sociologists but authors, activists, students, and journalists from both the United States and abroad. The ASA conference, held in downtown San Francisco, was the most heavily attended in years. Reflecting on Burawoy's speech, a reporter from London's *Guardian* (2004) newspaper would conclude that "something big is stirring in US academic life."

Titled "For Public Sociology," Burawoy's address sought to reawaken and celebrate the moral commitments of sociologists by connecting them to public engagement. Rather than stay isolated within the ivory tower, Burawoy (2004) called for "a sociology that seeks to bring sociology to publics beyond the academy, promoting dialogue about issues that affect the fate of society." Envisioning a collaborative relationship between sociologists and multiple publics, he described a future in which critical, policy, and public engagements would strengthen not just the profession but the fabric of civil society itself.

Founded as an academic discipline around a hundred years ago, sociology originally aspired to be "an angel of history" that sought order and justice in a rapidly changing world. Industrial transformations during the late nineteenth and early twentieth centuries had produced social dislocations on an unprecedented scale, inspiring scholars such as Karl

Michael Burawoy

Marx, Max Weber, Émile Durkheim, W.E.B. Du Bois, and Jane Addams to "salvage the promise of progress" from the forces that helped the few at the expense of the many. Although sociology by the mid-1900s was becoming more scientifically rigorous, this shift failed to keep alive sociology's "original passion for social justice, economic equality, human rights, sustainable environment, [and] political freedom" (Burawoy 2004). By becoming a profession, sociology was in danger of losing its soul.

narratives," or metanarratives—overall conceptions of history or society—make any sense (Lyotard 1985). In fact, there is no such thing as history. The postmodern world is not destined, as Marx hoped, to be a socialist one. Instead, it is dominated by the new media, which "take us out" of our past. Postmodern society is highly pluralistic and diverse. As countless films, videos, TV programs, and Web sites circulate images around the world, the many ideas and values we encounter have little connection with our local or personal histories. Everything seems constantly in flux: "[F]lexibility, diversity, differentiation, and mobility, communication, decentralization and internationalization are in the ascendant. In the process our own identities,

our sense of self, our own subjectivities are being transformed" (Hall et al. 1988).

One important theorist of postmodernity, Jean Baudrillard, believes that the electronic media have created a chaotic, empty world. Despite being influenced by Marxism in his early years, he argues that the spread of electronic communication and the mass media have reversed the Marxist theorem that economic forces shape society. Instead, he asserts, social life is influenced above all by signs and images.

In a media-dominated age, Baudrillard says, meaning is created by the flow of images, as in TV programs. Much of our world is now a make-believe universe in which we respond

"What would happen," Burawoy (2004) asks, "if, rather than repressing the moral moment of sociology, we were to give it room to breathe, recognize it rather than silence it, reflect on it rather than repress it? Would it enhance the legitimacy of sociology, or end its credibility?" These are critical questions with no easy answers; but if Burawoy is right, an active moral engagement with the publics beyond the classroom need not come at the expense of scientific integrity. Although some may disagree, providing the public with knowledge of what is while encouraging what ought to be allows public sociologists to reconnect with the moral impulses at the heart of the discipline.

Although sociology as a discipline has always been concerned with public issues, the resurgence of public sociology in recent years reflects a growing discomfort with levels of inequality in American society and throughout the world. In the face of "state despotism and market tyranny," public sociology is for Burawoy (2004) a way to regenerate the discipline's moral fiber. Whereas economics is mainly concerned with the virtues of the free market, and political science with political order and the state, the study of sociology "coincides with humanity's interest in opposing the erosion of civil liberties, the violation of human rights, the degradation of the environment, the impoverishment of working classes, the spread of disease, the exclusion of ever greater numbers from the means of their existence, and deepening inequalities—all forces that threaten the viability and resilience of civil society at home and abroad" (Burawoy et al. 2004). The role of sociology is to connect the burdens that people privately endure with the historical and contemporary conditions shaping the lives of hundreds, thousands, perhaps millions of people like them. The role of public sociology is to go a step further, to spark dialogue within and between multiple publics outside of academic classrooms by demonstrating how the sociological imagination can help us all better understand the world around us.

Burawoy's extensive fieldwork in eastern Europe, Africa, Russia, and the United States provides a view of that world from the bottom up. Inspired during the 1960s by prorevolutionary movements in the United States, Burawoy ventured to Zambia to study the integration of black and white workers as an employee at the Anglo American Mining Corporation. His book *The Colour of Class* (1972) documented how ideas about race allowed whites to be promoted over Zambian managers, providing a controversial reality check for the newly independent African state. His subsequent fieldwork at a Chicago machine shop (documented in *Manufacturing Consent,* 1979), the Lenin Steel Works in Hungary (described in *The Politics of Production,* 1985), and more recently at the Polar Furniture Enterprise in Syktyvkar, Russia, has allowed Burawoy to link personal experiences on the shop floor to patterns of class formation, cooperation, and dissent across settings (Byles 2001).

That "the world" is actually made up of multiple publics presents multiple opportunities for public sociology to thrive. Traditional routes of engagement have included authoring newspaper editorials, appearing on radio broadcasts, and testifying before government agencies (such as the local city council or the U.S. Congress). But public sociology also includes working in the trenches of civil society with publics such as labor movements, neighborhood associations, immigrant rights groups, and human rights organizations. Many of the categories that we now take for granted—women, gays, inner-city youth, people with AIDS—are themselves the social products of political actions taken by individuals, sociologists among them, who came together in moral opposition to the oppression of human beings in a country (and, increasingly, a world) dedicated to principles of equality and justice. Both of these forms of public sociology—the traditional and the organic—help "to make visible the invisible, to make the private public" (Burawoy 2004) and, in so doing, reaffirm the value of sociology in the conduct and creation of public life.

to media images rather than to real persons or places. Thus, when Diana, Princess of Wales, died in 1997, the worldwide outpouring of grief did not constitute mourning for a real person because Diana existed for most people only through the media. Her death was more like an event in a soap opera. Baudrillard (1983) speaks of "the dissolution of life into TV."

Theoretical Thinking in Sociology

So far we have been discussing theoretical approaches—broad orientations to the subject matter of sociology. However, there is a distinction between theoretical approaches and theories. Theories are more narrowly focused and attempt to explain particular social conditions or types of events. They are usually formed during the research process and suggest other problems for subsequent research. An example would be Durkheim's theory of suicide.

Some theories are more encompassing than others. Opinions vary about whether it is desirable or useful for sociologists to engage in very wide-ranging theoretical endeavors. Robert K. Merton (1957), for example, argues that sociologists should concentrate on what he calls *theories of the middle range.* Rather than attempting to create grand theoretical schemes (in the

"Male Teenage Athletes: The Violent and the Volatile"

High school and college athletes are often upheld as the stars of their schools—popular, physically fit leaders that their classmates look up to and admire. But the reputations of young male athletes have taken a serious hit in recent years. First, in 2006, three members of the Duke men's lacrosse team were accused of sexually assaulting a young woman at a team party held at the house of two of the team's captains. Although all charges were ultimately dropped and the rape accusations were found to be false, the reputations of athletes everywhere were called into question. Just months after the Duke story hit the evening news, the media reported the results from a new sociological study showing that "Contact Sports Lead to Aggression" (Women24 2007) and "Male Adolescent Athletes More Likely to Be Aggressors."

These headlines were reporting the results of a recent study that showed that

teenage boys who play football and other contact sports are often aggressive off the field, too. Do athletics promote violence? And if so, why? The answers can be found by closely examining the research of Penn State sociologist Derek

Members of the Duke University lacrosse team practice in Durham, North Carolina.

A. Kreager (2007), whose study "Unnecessary Roughness? School Sports, Peer Networks, and Male Adolescent Violence" was published in the *American Sociological Review*. Kreager analyzed data from a national sample of more

than 6,000 male high school students. The sample was taken from the National Longitudinal Study of Adolescent Health, a large multiyear survey of American secondary school students. The survey asked questions about school activities (including sports), grades, friendship networks, and troubled behavior—such as fighting and minor delinquency. Specifically, the students were asked whether they had gotten into a "serious physical fight" in the past twelve months.

The Kreager study showed that boys who were on the football or wrestling team were more likely than other male students to have gotten into a serious physical fight in the past year. Overall, 40 percent of the boys in the sample had a serious physical fight in the past year, but these proportions ranged from 45 percent of football players and 48 percent of wrestlers to just 38 percent of nonathletes. Boys in other sports, such as basketball

manner of Marx, for instance), we should develop more modest theories.

Middle-range theories are specific enough to be tested by empirical research, yet sufficiently general to cover a range of phenomena. Consider the theory of *relative deprivation,* which holds that how people evaluate their circumstances depends on whom they compare themselves to. Thus feelings of deprivation do not conform directly to the level of material poverty individuals experience. A family living in a small home in a poor area, where everyone is in similar circumstances, is likely

to feel less deprived than a family living in a similar house in a neighborhood where other homes are much larger and other people more affluent.

Indeed, the more wide ranging and ambitious a theory is, the more difficult it is to test empirically. Yet there seems no obvious reason that theoretical thinking in sociology should be confined to the "middle range."

Assessing theories, especially theoretical approaches, in sociology is a challenging and formidable task. The fact that no theoretical approach dominates the whole of sociology and baseball, however, did not have a heightened rate of physical fights.

Kreager also attempted to answer "why?" and found different explanations for the off-the-field aggressive behaviors of football players versus wrestlers. In the case of the wrestlers, he found that wrestling did not necessarily "cause" aggression. Rather, he found support for the "social selection" perspective. That means that boys who were more aggressive at the outset were more likely to join the wrestling team. In other words, aggressive tendencies led to joining the wrestling team, rather than the reverse.

In the case of football players, however, Kreager found that one's social ties mattered. Football players who associated off the field with other football players were more likely to get into fights. He speculated that "males in football groups have to demonstrate their masculinity to their friends by fighting." He also noted that groups of football players may find themselves in social settings that foster violence, such as parties with alcohol.

Kreager's work illustrates several important themes of sociology. First, he showed that it is possible to conduct a scientific study of a behavior that most people take for granted as "obvious"—the aggressive behavior of male athletes. Second, the study shows the importance of having a "sociological imagination," or having the ability to look beyond individualized explanations of human behavior and to consider the larger social context. Although parents and coaches may turn a blind eye to athletes' aggressive behavior, thinking that "boys will be boys" or that violent behavior reflects the personal problems of one particularly aggressive boy, sociologists like Kreager believe that context shapes human behavior.

It is important that Kreager found that it's not just male athletes who are aggressive. Although 48 percent of wrestlers had a fight in the prior year, the proportion of the overall sample who had a fight wasn't dramatically lower—40 percent had done so. That suggests that the culture of how young men are raised may encourage aggressive behavior. The culture of competitive sports, in particular, may foster aggression among high school male athletes. Kreager's study suggests that violence is not inevitable, and it can be lessened with thoughtful school practices. He suggests that "precluding problematic youth from playing contact sports, not tolerating athletic violence, fostering a more tolerant atmosphere ... [and] de-emphasizing the 'winning is everything' mentality" may help to lessen adolescent male violence.

Questions

- What proportions of football players and wrestlers reported having had a serious fight in the past year? How do these proportions differ from the proportion of nonathletes?
- What explanations did the study offer for the relatively high rate of aggression among football players versus the rate among wrestlers?
- Using your "sociological imagination," offer your own theory of why male athletes in contact sports are more likely than other males to behave aggressively.

FOR FURTHER EXPLORATION

Kreager, Derek A. 2007. "Unnecessary Roughness? School Sports, Peer Networks, and Male Adolescent Violence." *American Sociological Review* 72: 705–724.

Medindia Health Work. 2007. "Male Teenager Athletes: The Violent and the Volatile." www.medindia.net/news/view_main_print_new.asp (accessed January 17, 2008).

Norton, Amy. 2007. "Boys in Contact Sports More Prone to Fights." Reuters News (October 9, 2007). www.healthcentral.com/diet-exercise/news-161596–66_pf.html (accessed January 17, 2008).

Women24. 2007. "Contact Sports Lead to Aggression" (October 10, 2007). www.women24.com/Women24/PregnancyParenting/School/Article/0,,1-9-35_16102,00.html (accessed January 17, 2008).

might seem to be a sign of weakness in the subject. But this is not the case: The jostling of rival theoretical approaches and theories actually expresses the vitality of the sociological enterprise. In studying human beings—ourselves—theoretical variety rescues us from dogma. Because human behavior is so complicated, a single theoretical perspective could never cover all its aspects. Diversity in theoretical thinking provides a rich source of ideas for research and stimulates the imaginative capacities so essential to progress in sociological work.

Levels of Analysis: Microsociology and Macrosociology

An important distinction among theoretical perspectives involves the level of analysis each takes. The study of everyday behavior during face-to-face interaction is **microsociology**. **Macrosociology** is the analysis of large-scale social systems, like the political system or the economic order. It also includes analysis of long-term processes of change, such as the development of industrialism. Although micro analysis and macro analysis may seem distinct from one another, in fact the two are closely connected (Giddens 1984; Knorr-Cetina and Cicourel 1981).

Macro analysis is essential for understanding the institutional background of daily life, because people's lives are affected by the broader institutional framework. Consider a comparison of the daily cycle of activities in a medieval culture and in an industrialized urban environment. In modern societies, we are constantly in contact with strangers. This contact may be indirect and impersonal. However, no matter how many indirect or electronic relations we enter into, even the most complex societies require the presence of other people. While we may choose to send an acquaintance just an e-mail message, we can also choose to fly thousands of miles to spend the weekend with a friend.

Micro studies illuminate broad institutional patterns. Face-to-face interaction is the basis of all forms of social organization, no matter how large scale. In studying a business corporation, we could examine face-to-face behavior to analyze, for example, the interaction of directors in the boardroom, people working in various offices, or workers on the factory floor. We would not gain a picture of the whole corporation in this way because some of its business involves printed materials, letters, the telephone, and computers. Yet we could certainly contribute significantly to understanding how the organization works.

Later chapters will give further examples of how interaction in micro contexts affects larger social processes and how macro systems affect the more confined settings of social life.

☑ CONCEPT CHECKS

1. What role does theory play in sociological research?

2. According to Émile Durkheim, what makes sociology a social science? Why?
3. According to Karl Marx, what are the differences between the two classes that make up a capitalist society?
4. What are the differences between symbolic interactionism and functionalist approaches to the analysis of society?
5. How do rational choice theorists explain human behavior?
6. How are macro and micro analyses of society connected?

Is Sociology a Science?

Durkheim, Marx, and the other founders of sociology thought of the discipline as a science. But can we really study human social life in a scientific way? To answer this question, we must first understand what *science* means.

Science is the use of *systematic methods of empirical investigation, the analysis of data, theoretical thinking, and the logical assessment of arguments* to develop a body of knowledge about a subject matter. Sociology is a scientific endeavor, according to this definition. It involves systematic methods of empirical investigation, the analysis of data, and the assessment of theories in light of evidence and logical argument.

However, sociology is not equivalent to a natural science. Unlike objects in nature, humans are self-aware beings who confer sense and purpose on what they do. We can't even describe social life accurately unless we grasp the concepts that people apply in their behavior. For instance, to describe a death

Microsociology focuses on face-to-face interactions (*left*), while macrosociology analyzes large-scale social forces (*right*). How might a microsociologist and a macrosociologist analyze this food court differently?

as a suicide means knowing what the person intended when he died. Suicide can occur only when an individual has self-destruction actively in mind. If he accidentally steps in front of a car and is killed, he cannot be said to have committed suicide.

The fact that we cannot study human beings in the same way as objects in nature is an advantage to sociological researchers, who profit from being able to pose questions directly to those they study—other human beings. In other respects, sociology encounters difficulties not present in the natural sciences. People who are aware that their activities are being scrutinized may not behave normally; they may consciously or unconsciously portray themselves in a way that differs from their usual attitudes. They may even try to "assist" the researcher by giving the responses they believe he or she wants.

Is Sociology Merely a Restatement of the Obvious?

Because sociologists study things that you have some personal experience with, you will sometimes wonder if this subject is merely "a painful elaboration of the obvious" (Wright 2000). Is sociology merely the restatement, in more abstract jargon, of things we already know? Is it simply the tedious definition of social phenomena with which we are already familiar? Sociology at its worst can be all of these things, but it is never appropriate to judge any discipline by what its worst practitioners do. In fact, good sociology either sharpens our understanding of the obvious (Berger 1963) or completely transforms our common sense. In either event, good sociology is neither tedious nor a restatement of the obvious. In this text, we will sometimes begin with definitions of things that you may already understand. It is necessary for any academic discipline to define its terms. But when, for example, we define a family as a unit of people who are related to one another, we do so not as an endpoint but as a beginning. We know that you may not need a sociology text to tell you the definition of a family, yet we also know that if we do not begin by defining our terms, we cannot progress to sharper levels of understanding later on. Good sociology never defines terms as an end in itself.

☑ CONCEPT CHECKS

1. Name at least three defining characteristics of "science."
2. How is sociology distinct from the natural sciences?

How Can Sociology Help Us?

Sociology has practical implications, as C. Wright Mills emphasized when developing his idea of the sociological imagination.

Awareness of Cultural Differences

First, sociology allows us to see the social world from many perspectives. If we properly understand how others live, we better understand their problems. Practical policies that lack an informed awareness of the ways of life of people they affect have little chance of success. Thus a white social worker operating in an African American community won't gain the confidence of its members without having a sensitivity to the differences in social experience that separate white and black in the United States.

Assessing the Effects of Policies

Second, sociological research helps in assessing the results of policy initiatives. For example, a program of practical reform may fail to achieve its goals or may produce unintended negative consequences. Consider the large public-housing blocks built in city centers in many countries following World War II. The goal was to provide high standards of accommodation for low-income groups from slum areas and to offer shopping amenities and other civic services close at hand. However, research later showed that many people who had moved to the large apartment blocks felt isolated and unhappy. High-rise apartment blocks and shopping malls in poorer areas often became dilapidated and provided breeding grounds for muggings and other violent crimes.

Self-Enlightenment

Third, and perhaps most important, sociology can provide us with self-enlightenment—increased self understanding. The more we know about our own behavior and how our society works, the better chance we have to influence our futures. Sociology doesn't just help policy makers in making informed decisions. Those in power may not always consider the interests of the less powerful or underprivileged when making policies.

Self-enlightened groups can benefit from sociological research by using the information gleaned to respond to government policies or form policy initiatives of their own. Self-help groups such as Alcoholics Anonymous (AA) and social movements like the environmental movement are examples of social groups that have directly sought practical reforms, with some success.

The Sociologist's Role

Finally, many sociologists address practical matters in their work as professionals—as industrial consultants, urban planners, social workers, and personnel managers, among other jobs. An understanding of society also serves those working in law, journalism, business, and medicine.

Those who study sociology frequently develop a social conscience. Should sociologists themselves agitate for programs of reform or social change? Some argue that sociology can preserve its intellectual independence only if sociologists remain neutral in moral and political controversies. Yet are scholars who remain aloof more impartial in their assessment of sociological issues than others? No sociologically sophisticated person can be unaware of the inequalities, the lack of social justice, and the deprivations suffered by millions of people worldwide. It would be strange if sociologists did not take sides on practical issues, and it would be illogical to ban them from drawing on their expertise in so doing.

We have seen that sociology is a discipline in which we often set aside our personal view to explore the influences that shape our lives and those of others. Sociology emerged as an intellectual endeavor along with the development of modern societies, and the study of such societies remains its principal concern. But sociologists are also preoccupied with the nature of social interaction and human societies in general.

Sociology has major practical implications for people's lives. Learning to become a sociologist shouldn't be a dull academic endeavor! The best way to make sure of this is to approach the subject in an imaginative way and to relate sociological ideas and findings to your own life.

☑ CONCEPT CHECKS

1. Describe three ways that sociology can help us in our lives.
2. What skills and perspectives do sociologists bring to their work?

Study Outline

www.wwnorton.com/studyspace

Developing a Sociological Perspective

- *Sociology* is the systematic study of human societies with special emphasis on modern, industrialized systems. The subject arose as an attempt to understand the far-reaching changes in human societies over the past two to three centuries.
- Major social changes have impacted the most intimate and personal characteristics of people's lives. The development of romantic love as a basis for marriage is an example.
- The practice of sociology involves the ability to think imaginatively and to detach oneself from preconceived ideas about social relationships.

The Development of Sociological Thinking

- Sociology comprises a diversity of theoretical approaches. Because theoretical disputes are difficult to resolve even in the natural sciences, in sociology we face special difficulties because of the complex problems involved in studying our own behavior.
- Important early sociological theorists include Auguste Comte (1798–1857), Émile Durkheim (1858–1917), Karl Marx (1818–1883), and Max Weber (1864–1920). Many of their ideas remain important in sociology today.
- The main theoretical approaches in sociology are *symbolic interactionism, functionalism, Marxism, feminism, rational choice approach,* and *postmodernism.* To some extent, these approaches complement each other. However, there are also major contrasts among them.

Is Sociology a Science?

- The study of face-to-face interaction is usually called *microsociology*—in contrast to *macrosociology,* which studies larger groups, institutions, and social systems. Micro and macro analyses are very closely related; each complements the other.

How Can Sociology Help Us?

- Sociology is a *science* in that it involves systematic methods of investigation and the evaluation of theories in light of evidence and logical argument. But it cannot be modeled on the natural sciences, because studying human behavior is fundamentally different from studying the world of nature.

- Sociology has important practical implications for contributing to social criticism and social reform. First, the improved understanding of a given set of social circumstances offers a better chance of controlling them. Second, increased cultural sensitivities allow policies to be based on an awareness of divergent cultural values. Third, investigation of the consequences (intended and unintended) of particular policy programs can promote effective program change. Perhaps most important, sociology provides self-enlightenment, offering groups and individuals an increased opportunity to alter the conditions of their own lives.

Key Concepts

anomie (p. 11)
bureaucracy (p. 12)
capitalism (p. 12)
division of labor (p. 11)
feminist theory (p. 17)
functionalism (p. 15)
globalization (p. 7)
ideology (p. 17)
latent functions (p. 16)
macrosociology (p. 21)
manifest functions (p. 16)
Marxism (p. 16)
materialist conception of history (p. 12)
microsociology (p. 21)
organic solidarity (p. 11)
postmodernism (p. 17)
power (p. 17)
rational choice approach (p. 17)
rationalization (p. 13)
science (p. 22)
social constraint (p. 11)
social facts (p. 11)
social structure (p. 7)
sociological imagination (p. 6)
sociology (p. 4)
structuration (p. 7)
symbol (p. 15)
symbolic interactionism (p. 15)
theoretical approach (p. 10)
theory (p. 10)

Review Questions

1. What is the sociological imagination? Give an example of how it can be used. What are some things students of sociology can do to acquire the sociological imagination?
2. What are the main differences between the theories of Émile Durkheim, Karl Marx, and Max Weber?
3. Who are the neglected founders of sociology? What were some of their contributions to the development of sociology as a field of study?
4. What is symbolic interactionism? What are its strengths and weaknesses as a theoretical perspective?
5. What is functionalism? What were Robert Merton's contributions to functionalist theory?
6. What are the similarities and differences between Marxist and feminist theories?
7. What is the main argument of rational choice theory? What are some of aspects of social life that it cannot explain? Give an example.
8. What is postmodern theory?
9. What are the benefits and constraints of micro and macro approaches in sociology?
10. Is sociology a science? In what ways does it differ from the natural sciences?

Thinking Sociologically Exercises

1. Healthy older Americans often encounter exclusionary treatment when younger people assume they are feeble minded and thus overlook them for jobs they are fully capable of doing. How would functionalism, conflict theory, and symbolic interactionism explain the dynamics of prejudice against the elderly?
2. The text discusses the sociology of coffee, suggesting that coffee is more than a simple product designed to quench a person's thirst and fend off drowsiness. Discuss **five** sociological features of coffee consumption that show its "sociological" nature.

Learning Objectives

Sociological Questions

Name the different types of questions sociologists address in their research—factual, theoretical, comparative, and developmental.

The Research Process

Learn the steps of the research process and be able to complete the process yourself.

Understanding Cause and Effect

Differentiate between causation and correlation.

Research Methods

Familiarize yourself with the methods available to sociological researchers and know the advantages and disadvantages of each.

Research in the Real World: Methods, Problems, and Pitfalls

See how research methods were combined in a real study and recognize the problems the researcher faced.

CHAPTER TWO

ASKING AND ANSWERING SOCIOLOGICAL QUESTIONS

toward the end of a working day, the public restroom of a particular Saint Louis park is busier than one might expect. One man walks in clad in a gray suit; another has on a baseball cap, shorts, and a T-shirt; a third wears the mechanic's uniform from the gas station where he fixes cars. What are these men doing here? Surely there are more convenient places to use a restroom. Does some common interest besides the restroom bring them to this place?

None of these men have come to the public restroom to use the toilet. Instead, they are searching for "instant sex." Many men—married and unmarried, straight and gay—seek sex with strangers, hoping to experience sexual excitement but wanting to avoid involvement. They don't want any commitments beyond the encounters they will have in this public bathroom.

Until the 1970s, the phenomenon of impersonal sex persisted as a widespread but rarely studied form of human interaction. In the gay community, such public bathrooms were called "tearooms." Laud Humphreys, a sociologist, went to these public restrooms to be part of these scenes and then conducted surveys of the participants. He wrote about them in his book *Tearoom Trade* (1970). Humphreys's research cast a new light on the struggles of men who were forced to keep their sexual proclivities secret. He showed that many men with otherwise "normal" lives find ways to engage in potentially embarrassing behaviors that will not harm their careers or family lives. His research was conducted more than three decades ago, when the

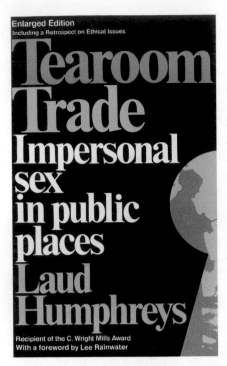

Laud Humphreys's groundbreaking study of anonymous gay sex in public bathrooms led to a deeper understanding of the consequences of the social stigma and legal persecution associated with gay lifestyles.

stigma associated with gay and lesbian identities was much greater than today and when police vigilantly enforced laws against such behavior. Many lives were ruined in the process of harsh enforcement.

Why Hang Out in Public Bathrooms?

Humphreys spent considerable time in such public bathrooms because an excellent way to understand social processes is to participate in and observe them. He also conducted survey interviews to gather more information than simple observation would have yielded. Humphreys's research illuminated an aspect of life that would shock many people and that certainly needed a deeper understanding. His work was based on systematic research, but it also carried a note of passion.

Humphreys argued that persecution against gay lifestyles leads men to live anguished existences in which they must resort to extreme secrecy and dangerous activities. His study predated the onset of AIDS; such activity would be much more dangerous today. He argued that tolerance for a gay subculture would enable gay men to provide one another with self-esteem, mutual support, and relief from torment.

Sociological Questions

The bathrooms under study in *Tearoom Trade* are perfect examples of phenomena that sociologists explore. For example, in looking at the bathrooms' surprising uses, Humphreys examined how society works in ways that differ from traditional expectations and how what we take to be natural—a public bathroom—is actually socially constructed, depending on how it is used.

Elements of modern theoretical approaches can help us understand the issues addressed by Humphreys's study. A *rational choice* approach would ask: How is behavior in the tearooms a rational response to opportunities and constraints? The answer is that the men who go to the tearooms have few other ways to fulfill their needs, so they must engage in behavior with intense risks. An *interactionist* might ask, How does this behavior occur through processes of interaction? What kinds of interactions take place? Humphreys found that people who frequent the tearooms learn from others to be silent. This is a response to the demand for privacy without involvement. Another finding is that men who do not respond to initial sexual advances in the tearoom are not approached further. Each party must cooperate to make a sexual situation occur. A *functionalist* approach might ask, What contribution does the tearoom make to the continuation of society as a whole? The answer is that it provides an outlet for sexual activity that, when carried out in secret, enables the participants and other members of society to conduct their "normal" lives without challenging the accepted order. A *Marxist* approach might ask, Is thinking about economic class relations apparent in the tearooms? Humphreys found that the impersonal sex of the tearooms had a democratic quality. Men of all social classes and races met in these places for sexual contact, a finding that has been verified by a study of Times Square in New York City (Delany 1999). Finally, a *feminist* approach might ask, How can women's lives be considered in this study of an all-male group? This approach was not dominant at the time of Humphreys's study, but a feminist today might ask how women—perhaps the men's unknowing wives—are affected by this secret behavior.

In the thirty-some years since *Tearoom Trade* was published, society has become more tolerant of gay identities and gay sex. Humphreys himself became part of the political movement—the gay rights movement—that made this change possible. He used his findings to convince courts and police that to alleviate the damaging side effects of covert sexual activity, they should ease up on prosecuting men for engaging in gay sex.

Sociological research should help us understand our social lives in a new way, as Humphreys's did. It should take us by surprise in its questions and its findings. The issues that concern sociologists, in both their theorizing and their research, are often similar to those that worry other people. But the results of such research frequently run counter to our commonsense beliefs.

What are the circumstances in which racial or sexual minorities live? How can mass starvation exist in a world that is wealthier than ever before? What effects will the increasing use of the Internet have on our lives? Is the family beginning to disintegrate as an institution? Sociologists try to answer these and many other questions, and their findings are by no means conclusive. Nevertheless, it is always the aim of sociological theorizing and research to move beyond ordinary speculation. Good sociological work phrases the questions as precisely as possible and gathers factual evidence before drawing conclusions. To accomplish this, we must know the most useful **research methods** to apply and how to best analyze the results.

Some of the questions that sociologists ask in their research studies are largely **factual questions**, or empirical questions. For example, many aspects of sexual behavior need direct and systematic sociological investigation. Thus we might ask, What kinds of occupations and domestic arrangements are most common among men who go to the tearooms? What proportion of tearoom participants are caught by the police? Factual questions of this kind are often difficult to answer, especially when official statistics do not exist. Even official statistics on crime may not reveal the real level of criminal activity, as researchers find that only about one half of all serious crimes are reported to the police.

Factual information about one society, of course, might indicate either an unusual case or a general set of influences. Thus sociologists often ask **comparative questions**, relating one social context within a society to another or contrasting examples from different societies. There are significant differences, for example, between the social and legal systems of the United States and of Canada. A typical comparative question might be, How much do patterns of criminal behavior and law enforcement vary between the two countries?

Sociologists also need to compare existing societies' present and past, so they ask **developmental questions**. After all, to understand the modern world, we have to examine previous forms of society and study the main direction of change. Thus we can investigate, for example, how the first prisons originated and what they are like today.

Factual investigations—that is, **empirical investigations**—concern how things occur. Yet sociology does not consist of just collecting facts; we always need to interpret what facts mean, and to do so we must pose **theoretical questions**. Many sociologists work primarily on empirical questions, but unless theory guides their research, their work is unlikely to be illuminating.

Also, sociologists strive not to attain theoretical knowledge for its own sake. A standard view is that although values should not bias conclusions, social research should be relevant to real-world concerns. In this chapter, we look further into such issues by asking whether it is possible to produce objective knowledge. First, we examine the stages involved in sociological research. Then, we compare the most widely used

---

TABLE 2.1

A Sociologist's Line of Questioning

Factual question	What happened?	During the 1980s, there was an increase in the proportion of women in their thirties bearing children for the first time.
Comparative question	Did this happen everywhere?	Was this a global phenomenon? Or did it occur just in the United States or only in a certain region of the United States?
Developmental question	Has this happened over time?	What have been the patterns of childbearing over time?
Theoretical question	What underlies this phenomenon?	Why are more women now waiting until their thirties to bear children? What factors should we look at to explain this change?

research methods as we consider some actual investigations. As we shall see, there are often significant differences between the way research should ideally be carried out and the way real-world studies are conducted.

☑ CONCEPT CHECKS

1. Why is sociology considered to be science?
2. Summarize the difference between comparative and developmental questions.

The Research Process

Let's look at the stages involved in research work, from the start of the investigation to the time its findings are published or made available in written form.

Defining the Research Problem

All research starts from a research problem. This may be an area of factual ignorance about, say, certain institutions, social processes, or cultures. A researcher might seek to answer such questions as, What proportion of the population holds strong religious beliefs? Are people today disaffected with "big government"? How far does the economic position of women lag behind that of men?

The best sociological research, however, begins with problems that are also puzzles. A puzzle is not just a lack of information, but a *gap in our understanding*. Much of the skill in producing worthwhile sociological research consists in correctly identifying puzzles.

Rather than simply answering the question, What is going on here? puzzle-solving research tries to illuminate *why* events happen as they do. Thus we might ask, Why are patterns of religious belief changing? What accounts for the recent decline in the proportions of the population voting in presidential elections? Why are women poorly represented in high-status jobs?

No piece of research stands alone. One project may lead to another because it raises issues the researcher had not previously considered. A sociologist may discover puzzles by reading the work of other researchers in books and professional journals or by being aware of social trends. For example, an increasing number of programs for treating the mentally ill encourage them to live in the community rather than being confined to asylums. Sociologists might be prompted to ask, What has caused this shift in attitude toward the mentally ill? What are the likely consequences for the patients themselves and the rest of the community?

Reviewing the Evidence

Once the problem is identified, the next step is to review the evidence in the field, because previous research might have already clarified the problem. If not, the sociologist must review

In looking at this painting by Brueghel, we can observe the number of people, what each is doing, the style of the buildings, or the colors the painter chose. But without the title, *Netherlandish Proverbs,* these facts tell us nothing about the picture's meaning. In the same way, sociologists need theory as a context for their observations.

related research: Have previous researchers spotted the same puzzle? How have they tried to resolve it? What aspects of the problem has their research left unanalyzed? Drawing on others' ideas helps the sociologist clarify the relevant issues and the appropriate research methods.

Making the Problem Precise

A third stage involves clearly formulating the research problem. If relevant literature already exists, the researcher might gain a good notion of how to approach the problem. Hunches sometimes become **hypotheses** at this stage. For the research to be effective, a hypothesis must be formulated in such a way that the factual material gathered will provide evidence either supporting or disproving it.

Working Out a Design

The researcher then decides *how* to collect the research materials, choosing from a range of methods according to the objectives of the study as well as the aspects of behavior under study. For some purposes, a survey (usually involving questionnaires) might be suitable. In other circumstances, interviews or an observational study might be appropriate.

Carrying Out the Research

During the actual research, unforeseen practical difficulties can occur. For example, it might prove impossible to contact certain questionnaire recipients or interview subjects. A business firm or government agency may not let the researcher carry out the work as planned. Such difficulties might bias the study results and lead to a false interpretation. For example, if the researcher is studying how business corporations have complied with affirmative-action programs for women, then companies that have not complied might not want to be studied.

Interpreting the Results

Once the material has been gathered for analysis, the researcher's troubles may be just beginning! Working out the implications of the data and relating them to the research problem are rarely easy tasks. Although it may be possible to reach a clear answer to the initial questions, many investigations are ultimately not fully conclusive.

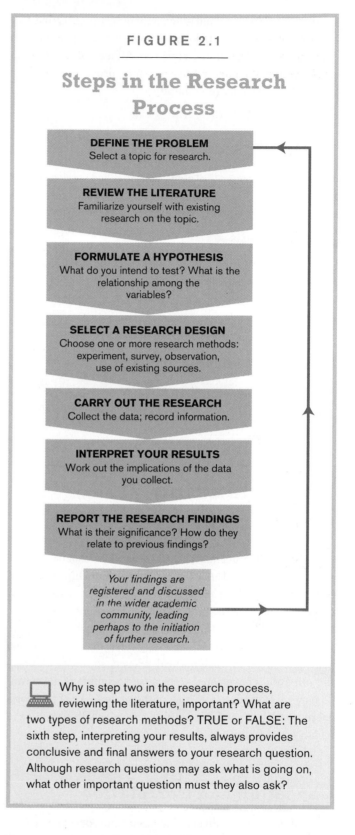

FIGURE 2.1

Steps in the Research Process

DEFINE THE PROBLEM
Select a topic for research.

REVIEW THE LITERATURE
Familiarize yourself with existing research on the topic.

FORMULATE A HYPOTHESIS
What do you intend to test? What is the relationship among the variables?

SELECT A RESEARCH DESIGN
Choose one or more research methods: experiment, survey, observation, use of existing sources.

CARRY OUT THE RESEARCH
Collect the data; record information.

INTERPRET YOUR RESULTS
Work out the implications of the data you collect.

REPORT THE RESEARCH FINDINGS
What is their significance? How do they relate to previous findings?

Your findings are registered and discussed in the wider academic community, leading perhaps to the initiation of further research.

Why is step two in the research process, reviewing the literature, important? What are two types of research methods? TRUE or FALSE: The sixth step, interpreting your results, always provides conclusive and final answers to your research question. Although research questions may ask what is going on, what other important question must they also ask?

Reporting the Findings

The research report, usually published as a journal article or book, relates the nature of the research and seeks to justify the conclusions. This is a final stage only in terms of the individual project. Most reports identify unanswered questions and suggest options for further research. All individual research investigations are part of the continuing process of research within the sociological community.

Reality Intrudes!

The preceding sequence of steps is a simplified version of what happens in actual research projects. These stages rarely succeed each other so neatly; the difference is like that between the recipes outlined in a cookbook and the actual process of preparing a meal. Experienced cooks often don't work from recipes at all, yet they might cook better than those who do. Following fixed schemes can be unduly restricting; much outstanding sociological research would not fit rigidly into this sequence, although most of the steps would be there.

☑ CONCEPT CHECKS

1. What are the seven steps of the research process?
2. How does the best sociological research solve a puzzle?

Understanding Cause and Effect

One of the main problems faced in research methodology is the analysis of cause and effect. A **causal relationship** is an association in which one event or situation produces another. If you release the parking brake in an automobile pointing downhill, the car will roll down the incline, gathering speed as it goes; you can explain why this happens by referring to the physical principles involved. Like natural science, sociology assumes that all events have causes. Because social life is not a random array of occurrences, one of the main tasks of sociological research—in combination with theoretical thinking—is to identify causes and effects.

Causation and Correlation

Causation cannot be directly inferred from **correlation**. Correlation means the existence of a regular relationship between two sets of occurrences or variables. A **variable** is any dimension along which individuals or groups differ—such as age, income, crime rate, or social class. When two variables are

Helsinki, Finland, uses bright light lamps in city buses to prevent depression during the winter. Why did Durkheim find a correlation between suicide and the seasons? Why were his conclusions problematic?

closely correlated, it might seem as if one caused the other; however, such is rarely the case. For example, since World War II a strong correlation has been seen between a decline in pipe smoking and a decrease in the number of people who regularly go to the movies. Clearly one change does not cause the other, and it would be difficult to discover even a remote causal connection between them.

Often, however, it is much less obvious that an observed correlation does not imply a causal relationship. Such correlations can lead to questionable or false conclusions. In his classic work *Suicide,* Émile Durkheim (1966; orig. 1897) found a correlation between rates of suicide and the seasons of the year. In the societies Durkheim studied, levels of suicide increased progressively from January to around June or July. Then they declined through the end of the year. One might suppose this demonstrates a causal relationship between temperature or climatic change and individuals' propensity to kill themselves. Perhaps as temperatures increase, people become more impulsive and hotheaded. However, the causal relation has nothing directly to do with temperature or climate. In spring and summer, most people have a more intensive social life than they do in winter. Individuals who are isolated or unhappy may experience an intensification of these feelings as the activity level of people around them rises; thus they may have acute suicidal tendencies more in spring and summer than in autumn and winter. We always have to be on guard in assessing whether correlation involves causation and in deciding in which direction causal relations run.

CAUSAL MECHANISM

Working out causal connections involved in correlations can be difficult. There is a strong correlation, for instance, between level of educational achievement and occupational success in modern societies. The better grades an individual gets in school, the better-paying job he or she is likely to get. What explains this correlation? Research shows that it is not mainly school experience itself but, rather, the home environment: Children from better-off homes, whose parents generally take a strong interest in their learning skills and where books are abundant, are more likely to do well than those whose homes lack these qualities. The causal mechanisms are the parents' attitudes and the facilities for learning in the home.

Causal connections in sociology are not entirely mechanical, however. People's attitudes and subjective reasons for acting as they do are causal factors in relationships among variables in social life.

CONTROLS

In assessing the cause or causes that explain a correlation, we need to distinguish independent variables from dependent variables. An **independent variable** is one that produces an effect on another variable. The variable affected is the **dependent variable**. In the example just mentioned, academic achievement is the independent variable and occupational success is the dependent variable. The distinction refers to the direction of the causal relation being investigated. The same factor may be an independent variable in one study and a dependent variable in another. If we were investigating the effects of differences in occupational success on lifestyles, occupational success would then be the independent variable.

To find out whether a correlation between variables is a causal connection, we use **controls**—that is, we hold some variables constant to look at the effects of others. This allows us to judge among explanations of observed correlations, separating causal from noncausal relationships. For example, child development researchers have posited a causal connection between maternal deprivation in infancy and serious personality problems in adulthood. (*Maternal deprivation* means that an infant is separated from his mother for several months or more.) To test whether there really is a causal relationship between maternal deprivation and later personality disorders, we would try to control, or "screen out," other influences that might explain the correlation.

Sometimes maternal deprivation occurs when an infant is admitted to a hospital for a lengthy period and has to be separated from his parents. Is it attachment to the mother, however, that really matters? Perhaps if a child receives love and attention from *other* people during infancy, he might subsequently be a stable person anyway. To investigate these possible causal connections, we would compare cases in which infants were deprived of regular care from anyone with other cases in which infants were separated from their mothers but

received love and care from someone else. If the first group developed severe personality difficulties but the second group did not, we would suspect that regular care from any one person in infancy is what matters, regardless of whether the caregiver is the mother. (In fact, infants do seem to prosper normally as long as they have a loving, stable relationship with a caregiver; this person does not have to be the mother.)

IDENTIFYING CAUSES

Many possible causes could explain any given correlation. How can we be sure we have covered them all? We cannot. We would never be able to satisfactorily carry out and interpret the results of any sociological research if we had to test for the influence of every potentially relevant causal factor. Thus, identifying causal relationships is normally guided by previous research. Without having some idea beforehand of the causal mechanisms involved in a correlation, we would find it very difficult to discover the real causal connections. We would not know what to test *for*.

Consider the history of studies of smoking and lung cancer. Research has consistently demonstrated a strong correlation between the two: Smokers are more likely to contract lung cancer than nonsmokers, and very heavy smokers more so than light smokers. The correlation can also be expressed the other way around: A high proportion of those who have lung cancer are smokers or have smoked for long periods in their past. So many studies have confirmed these correlations that a causal link is generally accepted, but the exact causal mechanisms remain largely unknown.

However much correlational work exists on any issue, other interpretations are always possible. It has been proposed, for instance, that people who are predisposed to get lung cancer are also predisposed to smoke. In this view, it may not be the smoking that causes lung cancer but rather some biological disposition to both smoking and getting cancer.

☑ CONCEPT CHECKS

1. Contrast correlation and causation.
2. Contrast independent and dependent variables.
3. What is the purpose of a control variable?

Research Methods

Let's look at the various research methods sociologists employ (Table 2.2).

TABLE 2.2

Three of the Main Methods Used in Sociological Research

RESEARCH METHOD	STRENGTHS	LIMITATIONS
Ethnography	Usually generates richer and more in-depth information than other methods.	Can be used to study only relatively small groups or communities.
	Ethnography can provide a broader understanding of social processes.	Findings might apply only to groups or communities studied; not easy to generalize on the basis of a single fieldwork study.
Surveys	Make possible the efficient collection of data on large numbers of individuals.	Material gathered may be superficial; if questionnaire is highly standardized, important differences among respondents' viewpoints may be glossed over.
	Allow for precise comparisons to be made among the answers of respondents.	Responses may be what people profess to believe rather than what they actually believe.
Experiments	Influence of specific variables can be controlled by the investigator.	Many aspects of social life cannot be brought into the laboratory.
	Are usually easier for subsequent researchers to repeat.	Responses of those studied may be affected by the experimental situation.

Ethnography

Ethnography involves firsthand studies of people, using **participant observation** or interviewing. The investigator works or lives with a group, organization, or community and perhaps participates in its activities. An ethnographer cannot just be present in the group she studies, but must justify her presence to its members. She must gain and sustain the cooperation of the community to achieve worthwhile results.

For a long while, research based on participant observation excluded accounts of the hazards or problems involved, but more recently field workers have been more open. Frequently, field workers experience feelings of loneliness and frustration, the latter occurring especially when group members refuse to talk frankly with the researcher. Some types of fieldwork may be physically dangerous; for instance, a researcher studying a delinquent gang might be seen as a police informer or might become unwittingly embroiled in conflicts with rival gangs.

In traditional works of ethnography, accounts provided little information about the observer because ethnographers were expected to present objective reports. More recently, ethnographers have increasingly spoken about their connection to the people under study. For example, it might be a matter of considering how one's race, class, or gender affected the work or how the power differences between observer and observed distorted the dialogue between them.

ADVANTAGES AND LIMITATIONS OF FIELDWORK

Successful ethnography provides information on the behavior of people in groups, organizations, and communities and how

Ethnographer David Redmon interviews a family in Mexico.

those people understand their own behavior. Once we look inside a given group, we can better understand not only that group but also broader social processes.

Yet fieldwork also has limitations. Only fairly small groups or communities can be studied. And much depends on the researcher's skill in gaining the confidence of the individuals involved. The reverse is also possible. A researcher could identify so closely with the group that he loses the perspective of an outside observer. Or a researcher may draw conclusions that are more about his own effects on the situation than he or his readers realize.

Surveys

Interpreting field studies usually involves problems of generalization, because we cannot be sure that what we find in one context will apply in other situations or even that two different researchers would draw the same conclusions when studying the same group. This is usually less problematic in **survey** research, in which questionnaires are sent or administered directly to a selected group of people. This group is called a **population**. Fieldwork is best suited for in-depth studies of small slices of social life; survey research produces information that is less detailed but that usually applies over a broad area.

STANDARDIZED AND OPEN-ENDED QUESTIONNAIRES

Two sorts of questionnaires are used in surveys. Some contain a standardized, or fixed-choice, set of questions to which only a fixed range of responses is possible—for instance, *Yes, No, Don't know* or *Very likely, Likely, Unlikely, Very unlikely*. In such surveys with a small number of categories, responses are easy to count and compare. However, because they do not allow for subtleties of opinion or verbal expression, they may yield restrictive, if not misleading, information.

Other questionnaires are open ended: Respondents have more opportunity to use their own words. Open-ended questionnaires typically provide more detailed information than standardized ones, and the researcher can follow up answers to probe more deeply into what the respondent thinks. However, the lack of standardization means that responses may be difficult to compare statistically.

Questionnaire items are normally listed so that a team of interviewers can ask the questions and record responses in the same order. All the items must be understandable to interviewers and interviewees alike. In the large national surveys undertaken by government agencies and research organizations, interviews occur more or less simultaneously across the country. Those who conduct the interviews and those who analyze the results could not work effectively if they constantly had to check with one another about ambiguities in the questions or answers.

Questionnaires should also accommodate the characteristics of respondents. Will they see the point of a particular question? Might it offend them? Do they have enough information to answer usefully? Will they answer at all? A questionnaire's terminology might be unfamiliar; for instance, "What is your marital status?" might baffle some people. It would be more appropriate to ask, "Are you single, married, separated, or divorced?" Most surveys are preceded by pilot studies that reveal problems not anticipated by the investigator. A **pilot study** is a trial run in which just a few people participate. Any difficulties can then be ironed out before the main survey takes place.

SAMPLING

Often, sociologists are interested in the characteristics of large numbers of individuals—for example, political attitudes of the American population as a whole. In such situations, researchers concentrate on a **sample**, or a small proportion of the overall group. Usually, the results from a properly chosen sample can be generalized to the total population. Studies of only two to three thousand voters, for instance, can accurately indicate the attitudes and voting intentions of the entire population. But to achieve such accuracy, the sample must be representative: The individuals studied must be typical of the population as a whole. Because **sampling** is highly complex, statisticians have developed rules for working out the correct size and nature of samples.

A particularly important procedure that ensures a **representative sample** is **random sampling**, in which every member of the sample population has the same probability of being included. The most sophisticated way of obtaining a random sample is to give each member of the population a number and then use a computer to generate a random list from which the sample is derived.

"THE PEOPLE'S CHOICE"

A famous early example of survey research was "The People's Choice," a study carried out by Paul Lazarsfeld and colleagues about half a century ago (Lazarsfeld et. al. 1948). This study, which investigated the voting intentions of residents of Erie County, Ohio, during the 1940 presidential campaign, pioneered several key techniques of survey research. To probe more deeply than a single questionnaire would, the investigators interviewed each member of a sample of voters on seven

"'Explosion' in the Gay and Lesbian Population?"

Was there an "explosion" in the number of gay and lesbian Americans during the last decade of the twentieth century? Anyone reading the newspapers in July 2001 would have answered yes. Headlines roared that the number of gay and lesbian households had "skyrocketed" (Gram 2001) and that the nuclear family was "fading" (*The Gazette* 2001) and "in meltdown" (Feder 2001). The evidence? These news reports focused on data from the 1990 and 2000 decennial censuses of the United States, which reported that the number of gay or lesbian couples living together increased drastically between 1990 and 2000.

For example, in the article "Jump in Reporting of Same-Sex Households in New York," writer Michael Hill reported that the census counted 13,748 same-sex partner households in New York State in 1990 and 46,490 such

households in 2000—more than a threefold increase. Similarly, the number of gay households in the United States also jumped more than threefold, from approximately 145,000 to 600,000. In the

A couple marches in the Chicago Gay Pride Parade.

article, Hill described a lesbian couple, Diana and Laurie Spencer, who felt comfortable living in a small town in upstate New York because of the feeling that as

the number of gay households increased acceptance of gays would increase as well.

While gay activists found these data to be affirming, conservative critics cited the census data as "evidence" that the traditional family, and morality more generally, were "unraveling before our eyes" (Dobson 2001). Demographers and survey researchers, however, were less concerned with the political implications and more concerned with figuring out whether these statistics were correct. Most concluded that the number of gay households probably had not increased substantially. Rather, the purported increase reflected changes in how the U.S. Bureau of the Census counts and classifies American households and their residents.

Every ten years, the Census Bureau obtains a full roster of information on all persons who live in a given household. For each household, a "householder" or

---

separate occasions. The aim was to trace and understand the reasons for changes in voting attitudes.

One of the researchers' hypotheses was that local relationships and events influence voting intentions more than distant world affairs, and the findings on the whole confirmed this. The researchers developed sophisticated measurement techniques for analyzing political attitudes, yet their work also contributed to theoretical thinking. The study showed that "opinion leaders" in a community shape the political opinions of those around them and that people's views are formed according to a "two-step flow of communication." In the first step, opinion leaders react to political events; in the second step, those

leaders influence their relatives, friends, and colleagues. The views expressed by opinion leaders, filtered through personal relationships, then influence the responses of other individuals toward political issues.

ADVANTAGES AND DISADVANTAGES OF SURVEYS

Surveys are widely used in sociological research for several reasons. Questionnaire responses can be more easily quantified and analyzed than material generated by most other research methods; large numbers of people can be studied; and, "head of household" is identified, and then all persons in the household are categorized in terms of their relationship to the householder. The Census Bureau also obtains information on the age and gender of all persons living in a household. Taken together, these data can be used to document patterns such as the number of grandchildren under age eighteen who are living with their grandparents or the number of adult siblings who are living together. However, the specific ways that the members of a household are described and classified have changed. In the 1990 census, if a person residing in a household reported being the "spouse" of the householder and being of the same sex as the householder, then census data analysts reclassified this person as a "boarder," or "roommate." In other cases, the Census Bureau recoded the person's gender, perhaps thinking that the gender was reported in error and that the couple was in fact an opposite-sex married couple (Beveridge 2007).

By the year 2000, however, that very same person—a person who indicated being of the same sex as the householder and being the "spouse" of the householder—would be classified as an "unmarried partner." Consequently, is it possible to definitively conclude that the number of gay households increased between 1990 and 2000, or would it be more accurate to conclude that the number of gay or lesbian households was undercounted in the 1990 census?

Experts believe that the latter is true. Angry gay and lesbian advocacy groups shared their concern with the Census Bureau, spurring the Census Bureau to publicly acknowledge its questionable analytic strategies on its Web site. The Census Bureau also urged data users to recognize that direct comparisons between the 1990 and 2000 censuses would be impossible. The Web site said, "As a result of [technical] changes in the processing routines, estimates of same-sex unmarried partners are not comparable between the 1990 and 2000 Census.... We believe 2000 estimates of this category are better estimates than those produced in 1990" (U.S. Bureau of the Census 2001). This incident illustrates an important issue in sociological research methods, particularly survey research methods. If the precise question or method used to measure a particular concept changes over time, then it is very difficult to determine whether social change is really happening or whether a social pattern has been stable but is simply being counted or described in a new way.

Questions

- According to early reports, by how much did the number of gay and lesbian households in the United States increase between 1990 and 2000?
- Were these initial estimates accurate? Why or why not?
- What lessons can survey researchers learn from the Census Bureau's error in counting and classifying gay and lesbian Americans?

FOR FURTHER EXPLORATION

Associated Press. 2001. "Census' Same-Sex Data Scrutinized." *Associated Press,* July 11, 2001.

Beveridge, Andrew. 2003. "Fun Findings and Non-Findings from Census 2000." Annual meetings of the American Association for Public Opinion Research (AAPOR), New York Chapter, February 27, 2003.

Dobson, James. 2001. *The State of the Family: July 2001 Newsletter.* Focus on the Family. www.ldolphin.org/family.html#14 (accessed January 10, 2008).

Feder, Don. 2001. "Nuclear Family in Meltdown." *Boston Herald,* May 23, 2001, p. 33.

The Gazette. 2001. "Nuclear Family Fading." *The Gazette,* May 15, 2001, p. A1.

Gram, David. 2001. "Census: Same-Sex Couples Increased." *Associated Press,* June 13, 2001.

U.S. Bureau of the Census. 2001. "Technical Note on Same-Sex Unmarried Partner Data from the 1990 and 2000 Censuses." www.census.gov/population/www/cen2000/samesex.html (accessed January 10, 2008).

given sufficient funds, researchers can employ a specialized agency to collect the responses. The scientific method is the model for this kind of research, as surveys give researchers a statistical measure of what they are studying.

However, many sociologists are critical of the survey method. They argue that findings whose accuracy may be dubious, given the relatively shallow nature of most survey responses, can nonetheless appear to be precise. Also, levels of nonresponse are sometimes high, especially when questionnaires travel through the mail. Furthermore, some studies are published based on results derived from little over half a sample, although normally there is an effort to recontact nonrespondents or to substitute other people. Although little is known about those who do not respond to surveys or who refuse to be interviewed, we do know that people often experience survey research as intrusive and time consuming.

Experiments

An **experiment** is an attempt to test a hypothesis under highly controlled conditions established by an investigator. Experiments are common in the natural sciences, where the researcher can control the conditions. In comparison, the scope

Graphing Evidence

Edward Tufte has written four path-breaking books—*The Visual Display of Quantitative Information* (1983); *Envisioning Information* (1990); *Visual Explanations* (1997); and *Beautiful Evidence* (2006)—where he argues that graphs and charts should tell a story, not just entertain us. Today too many of the charts that contain statistical data are little more than what Tufte calls "chartjunk," where precious little of the ink in the chart has any informative content.

Tufte believes that "chartjunk" is a problem for two reasons. First, it is a distraction, not an attraction. It distracts us from looking more carefully at the evidence, which is more or less nonexistent in the example below on the left. Second, such charts do not exploit the ability of our eyes to perceive and assess spatial relationships. Thus, they do not challenge our imaginations either to interpret or construct graphs or charts that really have a story to tell.

This example of chartjunk from Tufte shows two variables in the chart—the average price of a flawless one-carat diamond and the year. The graph is based on five data points, the exact values of which we can only guess. By the way, did you notice that there is an attractive woman in the figure? What did you notice first, the graph or the woman? Is presenting information in charts like this a problem, or should we just lighten up?

Tufte has made this 1861 graph by Charles Minard famous. The graph represents the number of soldiers lost during Napoleon's Russian campaign of 1812. The size of the band indicates the size of the army at each camp. Napoleon's retreat from Moscow is indicated by the darker band. By the time Napoleon made it to Poland, he had lost all but 10,000 troops. In addition to representing the size of the army, Minard charts the temperature scale, the movements of the auxiliary troops, and the direction of the army's movement. When this chart was first published in 1869 it provoked a massive outpouring of grief throughout France, more than fifty years after the event it depicted took place! Tufte considers this chart to be the greatest display of statistical data ever created. Do you agree?

DIAMONDS *WERE* A GIRL'S BEST FRIEND
Average price of a one-carat D-flawless

$60,000
$50,000
$40,000
$30,000
$20,000

1978 1979 1980 1981 1982

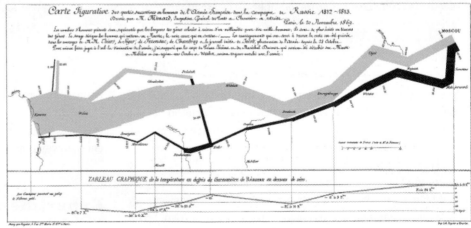

Created by John Grady.

Many spreadsheet programs have charting functions that can help a student design elegant and informative graphs while making choices about which design is best suited to the data being charted. Let's look at three charts of the same data using standard options available in Excel's Chart Wizard function and see which you find most satisfactory. We will graph data from a table reporting the number of times the most well-known civil rights organizations were cited in the *New York Times* from 1950 to 1979. Such data measure the salience of an organization: its prominence and, presumably, its influence. Which type of chart is the most informative? Could you use Excel's Chart Wizard to devise a better one?

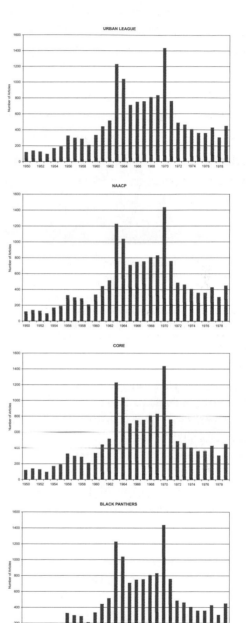

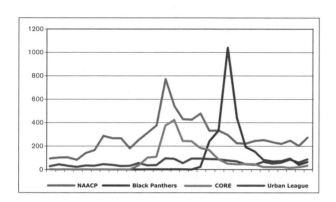

This line chart graphs the number of times each of four major civil rights groups was cited during this period. It has the advantage of allowing us to compare which organizations garnered the most press attention at a particular time.

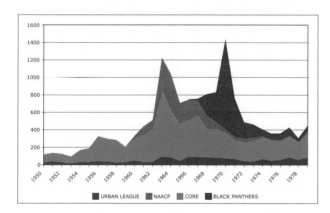

This shaded area chart graphs the contribution that each group's citations make to the total of all four groups. It has the advantage of showing us that this was a period of more intense concern with civil rights overall and that 1966 marked a turning point from non-violence to more militant resistance. However, it is harder to determine the ebb and flow of each group during the thirty-year period, with the exception of the Urban League at the bottom of the chart. It also requires informing the reader that the groups are stacked on top of one another and that none of the values for any given group is hidden by another group.

Tufte notes that there are times when it is better to have a series of similar charts—what he calls "small multiples"—to represent how values may vary, rather than trying to jam them all into one chart. These four charts are stacked bar graphs, each displaying only one group's contribution to the total number of citations in the *New York Times* during this period.

In Philip Zimbardo's make-believe jail, tension between students playing guards and students playing prisoners became dangerously real. From his experiment Zimbardo concluded that behavior in prisons is influenced more by the nature of the prison itself than the individual characteristics of those involved.

for experimentation in sociology is smaller. We can bring only small groups of individuals into a laboratory setting, and in such experiments people know they are being studied and may behave unnaturally.

Nevertheless, experimental methods can have useful applications in sociology. An example is the experiment carried out by Philip Zimbardo (1992), who set up a make-believe jail, randomly assigning some student volunteers to the role of guards and other volunteers to the role of prisoners. His aim was to see how the role playing would affect changes in attitude and behavior. The results shocked the investigators. Students who played guards quickly assumed an authoritarian manner; they displayed real hostility toward the prisoners, verbally abusing and bullying them. The prisoners, by contrast, showed a mixture of apathy and rebelliousness—a response often noted among inmates in real prisons. These effects were so marked and the level of tension so high that the experiment had to be called off at an early stage. The results, however, were important: Zimbardo concluded that behavior in prisons is more influenced by the nature of the prison situation than by the individual characteristics of those involved.

Life Histories

Life histories belong purely to sociology and the other social sciences; they have no place in natural science. Life histories consist of biographical material about particular individuals— usually as recalled by the individuals themselves. Other procedures of research don't usually yield as much information about the development of beliefs and attitudes over time. Life-historical studies rarely rely wholly on people's memories, however; they also use sources such as letters, contemporary reports, and newspaper descriptions to expand on and check the validity of the information individuals provide. Some sociologists feel that life histories are too unreliable to provide useful information, but others believe they offer sources of insight that few other research methods can match.

A celebrated early study incorporating life histories was *The Polish Peasant in Europe and America,* by W. I. Thomas and Florian Znaniecki (1966), first published in five volumes between 1918 and 1920. Thomas and Znaniecki developed a more sensitive and subtle account of the experience of migration than would have been possible without the interviews, letters, and newspaper articles they collected.

Comparative Research

Each research method just described is often applied in a comparative context. **Comparative research** is crucial in sociology because comparisons can clarify a particular area of research. Consider the American rate of divorce—the number of divorces granted each year. Divorce rates rose rapidly in the United States after World War II, reaching a peak in the early 1980s. Current trends suggest that one in five couples marrying today will divorce—a statistic expressing profound changes in the area of sexual relations and family life (U.S. Bureau of the Census 2007i). Do these changes reflect specific features of American society? We can find out by comparing divorce rates in the United States with those of other countries. The comparison reveals that although the U.S. rate is higher than that of most other Western societies, the overall trends are similar. Virtually all Western countries have experienced steadily climbing divorce rates over the past half century.

Historical Analysis

A historical perspective is often essential in sociological research to make sense of the material we collect.

Sociologists commonly want to investigate past events directly. Some periods of history can be studied in this way when survivors are still alive and can be interviewed about events

The Christmas Truce of 1914. German and British soldiers celebrate the holiday in No Man's Land on the Western Front.

they witnessed—such as the Holocaust during World War II. For earlier periods, sociologists depend on written records, which are often contained in the special collections of libraries or the National Archives.

An interesting example of the use of historical documents is sociologist Anthony Ashworth's (1980) study of trench warfare during World War I. Concerned with analyzing the experience of men who were under constant fire and crammed in close proximity for weeks on end, Ashworth drew on various documentary sources: official histories of the war, including those covering different military divisions and battalions; official publications of the time; informal notes and records kept by individual soldiers; and personal accounts of war experiences. By drawing on such varied sources, Ashworth discovered that most soldiers decided when to engage in combat with the enemy and often ignored the commands of their officers. For example, on Christmas Day, German and Allied soldiers suspended hostilities, and in one place the two sides even staged an informal soccer match.

Combining Comparative and Historical Research

Ashworth's research concentrated on a relatively short period. A study that investigated a much longer period and applied comparative research in a historical context was Theda Skocpol's *States and Social Revolutions* (1979), one of the best-known studies of social change. To produce a theory of the origins and nature of revolution grounded in detailed empirical study, Skocpol looked at processes of revolution in three historical contexts: the 1789 revolution in France, the 1917 revolution in Russia (which brought the communists to power and established the Soviet Union, which was eventually dissolved in 1989), and the revolution of 1949 in China (which created communist China).

By analyzing a variety of documentary sources, Skocpol was able to develop a powerful explanation of revolutionary change, one that emphasized the underlying social structural conditions. She showed that social revolutions are largely the result of unintended consequences. Before the Russian Revolution, for instance, various political groups were trying to overthrow the regime, but none of these—including the Bolsheviks (communists), who eventually came to power—anticipated the revolution that occurred. A series of clashes and confrontations gave rise to a process of social transformation that was much more radical than anyone had foreseen.

☑ CONCEPT CHECKS

1. What are the main advantages and limitations of ethnography as a research method?
2. Contrast the two types of questions commonly used in surveys.
3. What is a random sample?
4. Discuss the main strengths of experiments.
5. What are the similarities and differences between comparative and historical research?

The Sociological Imagination

In the decades following World War II, C. Wright Mills used his sociological imagination to explore the most pressing public issues of his time. Mills was formally affiliated with the Columbia University department of sociology but refused to confine his critiques of stratification systems, the cold war, and U.S. Latin American foreign policy to the narrow halls of academia. At the time, sociology as a discipline was in the process of becoming a more professional science, mainly by refining theory through the collection and statistical analysis of empirical data. Although he was a professional sociologist by training, Mills resisted the pressure to conform to what his colleagues were doing and the subjects they chose to study. Although he paid a price for this resistance (and perhaps because of it), Mills is remembered today as the most inspiring and courageous American public sociologist of the past fifty years.

Mills was preoccupied with how the experiences of private individuals are formed by the historical conditions in which they live. He wrote, "Men make their own history ... but they do not make it under the conditions of their own choice" (Mills 2000; orig. 1959). These conditions affect life chances, and despite a strong American cultural belief in free will, Mills believed that people are not completely autonomous actors capable of determining their own fate. His famous trilogy of books—*The New Men of Power* (1948), *White Collar* (1951), and *The Power Elite* (1956)—extends this theme to investigate how power has become consolidated in the hands of business, political, and military leaders in modern American society. His words remain eerily relevant today: "The more we understand

C. Wright Mills

what is happening in the world, the more frustrated we often become, for our knowledge leads to feelings of powerlessness. We feel that we are living in a world in which the citizen has become a mere spectator or a forced actor, and that our personal experience is politically useless and our political will a minor illusion" (Mills 2000; orig. 1959).

Mills was not, however, simply a pessimist bent on criticizing the world for its shortcomings. The fact that individual lives are constrained by social forces makes concerted social action all the more important. He sincerely believed in the

Research in the Real World: Methods, Problems, and Pitfalls

All research methods have advantages and limitations. Hence it is common to combine several methods in a single piece of research, using each to supplement and check on the others in a process known as **triangulation**. We can see the value of

combining methods—and, more generally, the problems and pitfalls of sociological research—by looking again at Humphreys's *Tearoom Trade*.

One of the questions that Humphreys wanted to answer was, What kinds of men came to the tearooms? It was very hard for him to find this out because all he could do was observe. The norm of silence in the restrooms made it difficult to ask questions or even to talk, and it would have been inappropriate to ask personal questions of people who wanted to be anonymous.

Humphreys's solution was to use survey methods. Standing by the door of the restrooms, he wrote down the license plate power of the sociological imagination to connect "personal troubles into public issues, and public issues into the terms of their human meaning" (Mills 2000; orig. 1959). As an exercise in using your sociological imagination, take educational performance as an example. Pretend that you are a teacher; during your first year of teaching you encounter among your twenty-seven students a twelve-year-old boy named Jonathan who reads below grade level. Some might guess that Jonathan's predicament rests in individual explanations of underperformance—he may have a learning disability or perhaps he hasn't applied himself in his schoolwork and should be held personally responsible.

On the other hand, what if you then learned that 70 percent of your students were reading below grade level? The sociological imagination requires a shift in perspective; we may want to ask different types of questions about the forces that affect the lives of students at school. Perhaps these students are members of a historically underprivileged community and have been attending school in substandard buildings. Perhaps they have grown up in a community characterized by high rates of poverty, violence, social disorder, and an absence of professional role models. Perhaps English is not their native language and they fell behind in their reading curricula as they worked to acquire a second language. Looking through a sociological lens, educational failure is a complex phenomenon involving a combination of multiple factors, some of which Jonathan may be capable of overcoming and some of which may remain beyond his control. For Mills, the sociological imagination is not just about asking certain types of questions but having the ability to shift from one perspective to another and back again, having "the capacity to range from the most impersonal and remote transformations to the most intimate features of the human self—and to see the relations between the two" (Mills 2000; orig. 1959).

As a writer, speaker, and countercultural icon, Mills used his public role to shed light on the social forces that governed people's lives, connect those forces to people's personal experiences, and advocate collective action as a means of protecting democracy from the reign of powerful elites. As his career progressed, Mills increasingly relished this role. In the final two years of his life, Mills became a well-known public figure. His *Listen, Yankee* appeared on the cover of *Harper's* magazine, and his "Letter to the New Left" inspired writings (such as the Port Huron Statement) that helped launch the civil rights movement. To reach a broad audience, Mills rid himself of "crippling academic prose" to develop an "intelligible way of communicating" to nonspecialized publics (Gitlin 2000). Unlike many of his colleagues, Mills believed that social science had a role to play in politics. By generating public discussion of issues rather than ingesting them whole as delivered by politicians, Mills (echoing Max Weber) believed that social scientists had an obligation to help repair damage done to democracy by the bureaucratization of the economy and the state. Mills was prophetic in recognizing the limits of both Marxism and liberalism to address the problems of developing countries; in his final years he began to focus attention on forms of international inequality that persist today.

If a passionate commitment to public sociology gave C. Wright Mills meaning in his professional life, it may also have helped hasten his untimely death. In December 1960, as Mills was preparing to debate foreign policy expert A. A. Berle Jr. on network television, he collapsed from a heart attack. In under fifteen months he was dead. Mills was only forty-five years old. He had produced an impressive body of work in a career that spanned just over a decade, and he relentlessly attacked "irresponsibility organized in high places," which he believed caused "those on the bottom—the forced actors who take the consequences—[to go] without leaders, without ideas of opposition" (Mills 2000; orig. 1959). Mills was not only a force of opposition but also a renegade leader who committed his considerable intellectual energy to the hope that democratic engagement would one day be revived.

numbers of people who pulled up to the parking lot and then entered the restrooms to seek sexual relations. He gave the plate numbers to a friend who worked at the Department of Motor Vehicles, securing the addresses of the men.

Months later, Washington University in Saint Louis was conducting a door-to-door survey of sexual habits. Humphreys asked the principal investigators if he could add the names and addresses of his sample of tearoom participants. Humphreys then disguised himself as one of the investigators and interviewed these men at their homes, supposedly just to ask the survey questions but actually also to learn more about their social backgrounds and daily lives. He found that most of the men were married and led very conventional lives. He often interviewed wives and other family members as well.

Human Subjects and Ethical Problems

All research involving human beings can pose ethical dilemmas. A key question for sociologists is whether the research poses risks to the subjects that are greater than the risks they face in their everyday lives.

In writing *Tearoom Trade,* Humphreys said he was less than truthful to those he was studying. Because Humphreys didn't reveal his identity as a sociologist when observing the tearoom, people assumed he was there for the same reasons they were and that his presence could be accepted at face value. While he did not tell any direct lies while observing the tearoom, he also did not reveal the real reason for his presence there. Was this aspect of his behavior ethical? The answer is that, on balance, it did not put any of his subjects at risk. On the basis of what he observed in the tearoom, Humphreys did not collect information that would have identified the men. At the same time, had Humphreys been frank at every stage, the research might not have gotten as far as it did. Indeed, some of the most valuable data collected by sociologists could have never been gathered if the researchers had first explained the project to each person encountered in the research process.

If this were the only dilemma posed by Humphreys's research project, it would not be notable in the ethics of social research. What raised more eyebrows was that Humphreys recorded the men's license plate numbers, obtained their home addresses from a friend at the Department of Motor Vehicles, and visited their homes in the guise of conducting a neutral survey. Even though Humphreys did not reveal to the men's families anything about their tearoom activities and even though he kept the data confidential, the knowledge he gained could have been damaging. Because Humphreys was documenting an illegal activity, police officers might have made him release information about the subjects' identities. A less skilled investigator might have slipped up when interviewing the subjects' families or Humphreys could have lost his notes, which someone else might have read. Considering the number of things that could go wrong in the research process, researchers do not consider projects of this kind to be legitimate.

Humphreys was one of the first sociologists to study the lives of gay men. His account was a humane treatment that went well beyond the existing knowledge on sexual communities. Although none of his subjects suffered as a result of his book, Humphreys later agreed with his critics on the key ethical controversy. He said that were he to do the study again, he would not trace license plates or go to people's homes. Instead, after gathering data in the tearooms, he might try to get to know a subset of the people well enough to inform them of his study and ask them to talk about the significance of these activities in their lives.

In recent years, the federal government has become increasingly strict with universities that use government grant money for research purposes. The National Science Foundation and the National Institutes of Health have strict requirements outlining how human subjects must be treated. In response, American universities now review all research that involves human subjects. The result has been both positive and negative. On the one hand, researchers are more aware of ethical considerations than ever before. On the other hand, many sociologists face increasing difficulty in getting their work done when institutional review boards require obtaining informed consent from research subjects before establishing a rapport with the subjects. There will likely never be easy solutions to problems of this kind.

The Influence of Sociology

The results of sociological research often go beyond the intellectual community and are disseminated throughout society. Remember, sociology is not just the *study* of modern societies; it is a significant element *in the continuing life* of those societies. Consider the transformations occurring in the United States in marriage, sexuality, and the family. Most people in modern societies have some knowledge of these changes as a result of the filtering down of sociological research. Our thinking and behavior are affected by sociological knowledge in complex and subtle ways, thus reshaping the very field of sociological investigation. Using the technical concepts of sociology, one can say that sociology stands in a reflexive relation to the human beings whose behavior is studied. **Reflexivity** describes the interchange between sociological research and human behavior. It's no surprise that sociological findings often correlate closely with common sense, because sociological research continually influences what our commonsense knowledge of society actually *is*.

☑ CONCEPT CHECKS

1. Why is it important to use triangulation in social research?
2. What ethical dilemmas did Humphreys's *Tearoom Trade* study pose?

Statistical Terms

Research in sociology often makes use of statistical techniques in the analysis of findings. Some are highly sophisticated and complex, but those most often used are easy to understand. The most common are **measures of central tendency** (ways of calculating averages) and **correlation coefficients** (measures of the degree to which one variable relates consistently to another).

There are three methods of calculating averages, each of which has certain advantages and shortcomings. Take as an example the amount of personal wealth (including all assets such as houses, cars, bank accounts, and investments) owned by thirteen individuals. Suppose the thirteen own the following amounts:

1	$	0	8	$	80,000
2	$	5,000	9	$	100,000
3	$	10,000	10	$	150,000
4	$	20,000	11	$	200,000
5	$	40,000	12	$	400,000
6	$	40,000	13	$	10,000,000
7	$	40,000			

The **mean** corresponds to the average, arrived at by adding together the personal wealth of all the people and dividing the result by the number of people in the sample (13). The total is $11,085,000; dividing this by 13, we calculate the mean to be $852,692.31. The mean is often a useful calculation because it is based on the whole range of data provided. However, the mean can be misleading when one or a small number of cases is very different from the majority. In this example, the mean is not in fact an appropriate measure of central tendency, because the presence of one very large figure, $10,000,000, skews the picture. One might get the impression when using the mean to summarize these data that most of the people own far more than they actually do.

In such instances, one of two other measures may be used. The **mode** is the figure that occurs most frequently in a given set of data. In our example, it is $40,000. The problem with the mode is that it doesn't take into account the *overall distribution* of the data—that is, the range of figures covered. The most frequently occurring case in a set of figures is not necessarily representative of the distribution as a whole and thus may not be a useful average. In this example, $40,000 is too close to the lower end of the figures.

The third measure is the **median**, which is the middle of any set of figures; here, this would be the seventh figure, again, $40,000. Our sample includes an odd number of figures, 13. If there had been an even number—for instance, 12—the median would be calculated by taking the mean of the two middle cases, figures 6 and 7. Like the mode, the median gives no indication of the actual *range* of the data measured.

Sometimes a researcher will use more than one measure of central tendency to avoid giving a deceptive picture of the average. More often, a researcher will calculate the **standard deviation** for the data in question. This is a way of calculating the **degree of dispersal**, or the range, of a set of figures—which in this case goes from $0 to $10,000,000.

Correlation coefficients offer a useful way of expressing how closely connected two (or more) variables are. When two variables correlate completely, we can speak of a perfect positive correlation, expressed as 1.0. When no relation is found between two variables—they have no consistent connection at all—the coefficient is 0. A perfect negative correlation, expressed as –1.0, exists when two variables are in a completely inverse relation to one another. Perfect correlations are never found in the social sciences. Correlations of the order of 0.6 or more, whether positive or negative, are usually regarded as indicating a strong degree of connection between whatever variables are being analyzed. Positive correlations on this level might be found between, say, social class background and voting behavior.

Reading a Table

You will often come across tables in reading sociological literature. They sometimes look complex but are easy to decipher if you follow the few basic steps listed here; with practice, these will become automatic. (See Table 2.3 as an example.) Do not succumb to the temptation to skip over tables; they contain information in concentrated form, which can be read more quickly than would be possible if the same material were expressed in words. By becoming skilled in the interpretation of tables, you will also be able to check how justified the conclusions a writer draws actually are.

1. Read the title in full. Tables frequently have long titles, which represent an attempt by the researcher to state accurately the nature of the information conveyed. The title of Table 2.3 gives first the *subject* of the data, second the fact that the table provides material for comparison, and third the fact that data are given only for a limited number of countries.

2. Look for explanatory comments, or *notes,* about the data. A footnote to Table 2.3 linked to the main column heading indicates that the data cover only licensed cars. This is important, because in some countries the proportion of vehicles properly licensed may be lower than in others. Footnotes may say how the material was collected or why it is displayed in a particular way. If the data have not been gathered by the researcher but are based on findings originally reported elsewhere, a source will be included. The source sometimes gives you some insight into how reliable the information is likely to be and tells you where to find the original data. In Table 2.3, the source note makes clear that the data have been taken from more than one source.

3. Read the *headings* along the top and left-hand side of the table. (Sometimes tables are arranged with "headings" at the foot rather than the top.) These tell you what type of information is contained in each row and column. In reading the table, keep in mind each set of headings as you scan the figures. In our example, the headings on the left name the countries involved, while those at the top refer to the levels of car ownership and the years for which numbers apply.

4. Identify the units used; the figures in the body of the table may represent cases, percentages, averages, or other measures. Sometimes it may be helpful to convert the figures to a form more useful to you: If percentages are not provided, for example, it may be worth calculating them.

5. Consider the conclusions that might be reached from the information in the table. Most tables are discussed by the author, and what he or she has to say should of course be borne in mind. But you should also ask what further issues or questions could be suggested by the data.

TABLE 2.3

Automobile Ownership: Comparisons of Several Selected Countries

Several interesting trends can be seen from the figures in this table. First, the level of car ownership varies considerably among different countries. The number of cars per 1,000 people is more than six times greater in the United States than in Brazil, for example. Second, there is a clear connection between car ownership ratios as a rough indicator of differences in prosperity. Third, in all the countries represented, the rate of car ownership increased between 1971 and 2002, but in some the rate of increase was higher than others—probably indicating differences in the degree to which countries have successfully generated economic growth or are catching up.

NUMBER OF CARS PER 1,000 OF THE ADULT POPULATION[a]

COUNTRY	1971	1981	1984	1989	1993	1996	2001	2002
Brazil	12	78	84	98	96	79	95	116
Chile	19	45	56	67	94	110	133	NA
Ireland	141	202	226	228	290	307	442	445
France	261	348	360	574	503	524	584	592
Greece	30	94	116	150	271	312	428	450
Italy	210	322	359	424	586	674	638	655
Japan	100	209	207	286	506	552	577	581
Sweden	291	348	445	445	445	450	497	500
United Kingdom	224	317	343	366	386	399	554	551
United States	448	536	540	607	747	767	785	789
West Germany[b]	247	385	312	479	470	528	583	588
China	NA	NA	NA	5[c]	6	8	12[d]	16

[a] Includes all licensed cars.

[b] Germany as a whole after 1989.

[c] Data for 1990.

[d] Data for 2000.

NA, not applicable.

SOURCES: Baltic 21 Secretariat; World Bank 1999; International Monetary Fund 2005; International Road Federation 1987; Organisation for Economic Co-operation and Development 2005; Statistical Office of the European Communities 1991; *The Economist* 1996; Toyota Corporation 2001; United Nations Economic Commission for Europe 2003; World Bank 2005.

Study Outline
www.wwnorton.com/studyspace

Sociological Questions

- Sociologists explore factual (i.e., empirical), comparative, developmental, and theoretical questions. Attempts to answer these four types of questions should not be biased by the researcher's values.

The Research Process

- Sociologists investigate social life by posing distinct questions and seeking answers via systematic research. These questions may be factual, comparative, developmental, or theoretical.
- All research begins from a research problem, which may be suggested by gaps in the existing literature, theoretical debates, or practical issues in the social world. There are clear steps in the development of research strategies—although these are rarely followed exactly in actual research.

Understanding Cause and Effect

- A causal relationship is one in which one event or situation brings about the other. Causation must be distinguished from correlation, which refers to the existence of a regular relationship between two variables (such as differences in age, income, or crime rates). An independent variable is one that produces an effect on another. The dependent variable is the one that is affected. Sociologists often use controls to ascertain a causal relationship.

Research Methods

- In fieldwork, or participant observation, the researcher spends lengthy periods with a group or community being studied. Survey research involves sending or administering questionnaires to samples of a larger population. Documentary research uses printed materials, from archives or other resources, as a source for information. Other research methods include experiments, the use of life histories, historical analysis, and comparative research.
- Because each research method has limitations, researchers often combine two or more methods, using each to check or supplement the material obtained from the others. This process is triangulation.

Research in the Real World: Methods, Problems, and Pitfalls

- Sociological research often poses ethical dilemmas. These may arise either where research subjects are deceived or where the published findings might adversely affect the subjects. There is no entirely satisfactory way to deal with these issues, but all researchers must be sensitive to the dilemmas they pose.

Key Concepts

causal relationship (p. 32)
causation (p. 32)
comparative questions (p. 29)
comparative research (p. 40)
controls (p. 33)
correlation (p. 32)
correlation coefficients (p. 45)
degree of dispersal (p. 45)
dependent variable (p. 33)
developmental questions (p. 29)
empirical investigations (p. 29)
ethnography (p. 34)
experiment (p. 37)
factual questions (p. 29)
hypotheses (p. 31)
independent variable (p. 33)
life histories (p. 40)
mean (p. 45)
measures of central tendency (p. 45)
median (p. 45)
mode (p. 45)
participant observation (p. 34)
pilot study (p. 35)
population (p. 35)
random sampling (p. 35)
reflexivity (p. 44)
representative sample (p. 35)
research methods (p. 29)
sample (p. 35)
sampling (p. 35)
standard deviation (p. 45)
survey (p. 35)
theoretical questions (p. 29)
triangulation (p. 42)
variable (p. 32)

Review Questions

1. Briefly describe the types of research questions sociologists ask and how they differ.
2. What are the seven basic steps of a sociological research project?
3. What is the difference between cause and correlation?
4. Why can it be difficult to establish causation?
5. What is a variable? What are independent and dependent variables?
6. For what kinds of research is ethnography a useful method? Give an example.
7. What are the strengths and weakness of experimental research for sociology?
8. What research methods did Laud Humphreys use in his research on tearooms?
9. While doing research, why is it important to take precautions to protect human subjects?
10. Briefly describe some elements that would characterize good quality sociological research.

Thinking Sociologically Exercises

1. Suppose the dropout rate in your local high school increased dramatically. Faced with such a serious problem, the board offers you a $500,000 grant to study the sudden increase. Following the recommended procedures outlined in the text, explain how you would conduct your research. What hypotheses might you test? How would you prove or disprove them?
2. Explain the advantages and disadvantages of documentary research. What will it yield that will be better than experimentation, surveys, and ethnographic fieldwork? What are its limitations compared with those approaches?

PART TWO

THE INDIVIDUAL AND SOCIETY

We start our exploration of sociology by looking at the connections between individual development and culture and by analyzing types of society from the past and present. Although our personalities and outlooks are influenced by our culture and society, we actively re-create and reshape the cultural and social contexts in which our activities occur.

Chapter 3 examines the unity and diversity of human culture. We consider how human beings resemble and differ from animals, and we analyze variations among human cultures.

Chapter 4 discusses socialization, concentrating on how the human infant develops into a social being. Because socialization continues throughout the life span, we also analyze the relationships among young, middle-aged, and older people.

Chapter 5 explores how people interact in everyday life and identifies the mechanisms people use to interpret what others say and do. The study of social interaction reveals a great deal about the larger social environment.

Chapter 6 focuses on social groups, networks, and organizations and how individuals interact in various settings. Chapter 7 looks at deviance and crime. We can learn about the way a population behaves by studying people whose behavior deviates from accepted patterns.

Learning Objectives

The Sociological Study of Culture

Know what culture consists of and recognize how it differs from society.

The Development of Human Culture

Understand that biological and cultural factors influence behavior. Learn the ideas of sociobiology and how some researchers refute them by emphasizing cultural differences.

Premodern Societies

Learn how societies have changed over time.

Societies in the Modern World

Recognize the processes that changed premodern societies—particularly industrialization and colonialism, and then global development. Know the differences among the first world, the second world, and the developing world (third world) and how they came about.

The Effect of Globalization

Recognize the effect of globalization on your own life and the lives of people around the world.

CHAPTER THREE

CULTURE AND SOCIETY

n the last decade of the twentieth century, French president Jacques Chirac was visiting France's new National Library when he reportedly viewed for the first time a computer mouse and expressed wonderment at the new technology (Cairncross 1997). The United States at that time ranked first among major countries in terms of Internet servers; France was not even among the top twenty-five (Starrs 1997).

France is no less modern than the United States, so why was it reluctant to come online? Could it be that in 1997, as today, the Internet was dominated by the United States and was thus a powerful source for spreading American culture and the English language? We know that the French are especially sensitive about the threat of American culture and the English language to their way of life: The French government spends $100 million a year promoting the country's language and culture (Jones 1998) and has actively sought to curb the "invasion" of English words such as *software* and *computer*. Many French people resent what they call American "cultural imperialism," seen as a form of conquest—one of values and attitudes—and including such unwelcome imports as McDonald's restaurants.

France is not alone in resisting the inroads of American culture. In Germany, for example, the Club for the Preservation of the German Language was founded to combat, in the words of its founder, "the colonization of German by English" (quoted in Jones 1998). As American culture spreads around the world, many people fear the erosion of their own cultures—even as they tune in to *The Simpsons,* sip Coke or Pepsi, and download music from the Web. Will modern technology eventually press the world's diverse cultures into a single mold? Or will it permit local cultures to flourish? These are some of the questions we explore in this chapter.

First, however, we consider what culture is and how it encourages conformity in thinking and acting. Then we examine the early development of human culture, emphasizing features that distinguish human behavior from that of other species and identifying aspects of culture that make it essential for human society. This leads to a discussion of cultural diversity, not only across different societies but also within a society such as the United States.

We also compare and contrast the main forms of society found in history, with the goal of closely relating (1) the different cultural values and products that human beings have developed and (2) the contrasting types of society in which such development has occurred. Throughout the chapter, we concentrate on how social change has affected cultural development. One example is the effect of technology and globalization, a topic we explore in the conclusion to this chapter.

Norms change across generations and time. Ryerson University student Chris Avenir helped run a Facebook study group for his chemistry class, and the professor accused him of cheating. Chris argued that it was the same as a traditional study group, but group interactions took place online. How is this situation an example of norms clashing?

The Sociological Study of Culture

The sociological study of culture began with Émile Durkheim in the nineteenth century and soon became the basis of *anthropology,* a social science that studies cultural differences and similarities among the world's many peoples. The work of early sociologists and anthropologists strongly reflected the beliefs and values of highly educated Europeans who assumed that "primitive" cultures were inferior and lagged behind modern European "civilization." However, two destructive world wars, fought largely between European countries that claimed to be the most "civilized" cultures on earth, helped discredit that belief. Sociologists and anthropologists now recognize that there are many different cultures, each with distinctive characteristics. The task of social science is to understand this cultural diversity, which is best done by avoiding value judgments.

What Is Culture?

Culture consists of the values the members of a group hold, the languages they speak, the symbols they revere, the norms they follow, and the material goods they create. Some elements of culture, especially people's beliefs and expectations about one another and about the world they inhabit, are a component of all social relations. **Values** are abstract ideals. For example,

being faithful to a single marriage partner is a prominent value in most Western societies, but in some other cultures a person may have several wives or husbands. **Norms** are principles or rules of social life that people are expected to observe. Norms of behavior in marriage include the way husbands and wives are supposed to behave toward their in-laws: In some societies, they are expected to develop a close relationship; in others, they keep a clear distance.

Norms, like the values they reflect, vary across cultures. Among most Americans, for example, one norm calls for direct eye contact between people during conversation; averting one's eyes is interpreted as a sign of weakness or rudeness. Yet among the Navajo, a cultural norm calls for averting one's eyes as a sign of respect. Direct eye contact, particularly between strangers, violates a norm of politeness and consequently seems insulting. When a Navajo and a Western tourist encounter one another for the first time, the Navajo may see the tourist as rude or vulgar, while the tourist may see the Navajo as disrespectful or deceptive. Such cultural misunderstandings may lead to unfair stereotypes and promote hostility. Values and norms shape behavior within a given culture. For example, in cultures that value learning, cultural norms encourage students to study and support parents in sacrificing for their children's education. In cultures that value hospitality, cultural norms guide expectations about gift giving or about the behaviors of guests and hosts.

Finally, **material goods** are the physical objects that a society creates and that influence the ways people live. They include consumer goods, from clothes to cars to houses; the tools and technologies used to make those goods, from sewing machines to computerized factories; and the towns and cities that serve as places for people to live and work. A central aspect of a society's material culture is technology.

Today, material culture is rapidly becoming globalized, largely through modern information technology such as the computer and the Internet. Although the United States has been in the forefront of this technological revolution, most other industrial countries are catching up. In fact, it no longer makes sense to speak of an exclusively "U.S. technology" any more than it makes sense to speak of a U.S. car. The "world car," with parts manufactured across the planet in a global assembly line, embodies technology developed in Japan, the United States, and Europe. Another example of the globalization of material culture is the way classrooms and department stores the world over increasingly resemble one another, and the fact that McDonald's restaurants are now found on nearly every continent.

Culture refers to the ways of life of individual members or groups within a society: how they dress, their marriage customs and family life, their patterns of work, their religious ceremonies, and their leisure pursuits. The concept also covers the goods they create—bows and arrows, plows, factories and machines, computers, books, dwellings. We should think of culture as a "design for living" or "tool kit" of practices, knowledge, and symbols acquired through learning rather than by instinct (Kluckhohn 1949; Swidler 1986).

How might we describe American culture? First, it involves a range of values shared by many, if not all, Americans—such as a belief in the merits of individual achievement or in equality of opportunity. Second, these values are connected to norms: For example, people are expected to work hard to achieve occupational success (Bellah et al. 1985; Parsons 1964). Third, it involves the use of material goods created mostly through modern industrial technology, such as cars, mass-produced food, clothing, and so forth.

Some cultures value individualism, whereas others emphasize shared needs. A simple example makes this clear. In the United States, copying from someone else's exam paper goes against core values of individual achievement, equality of opportunity, hard work, and respect for the rules. For Russian students, however, helping each other pass an exam reflects values of equality and collective problem solving in the face of authority. Think of your own reaction to this example. What does it say about the values of your society?

Even within one society or community, values may conflict. Some groups or individuals might value traditional religious beliefs, whereas others might favor progress and science. Some people might prefer lavish material comfort, whereas others might favor simplicity. In the modern age characterized by the global movement of people, ideas, goods, and information, cultural values will inevitably conflict. Sociological research suggests that such conflicts foster a sense of frustration and isolation in American society (Bellah et al. 1985).

Norms, like the values they reflect, also change over time. For example, beginning in 1964, with a U.S. Surgeon General's report that linked smoking with serious health problems, the U.S. government waged a highly effective campaign to

A woman looks at a dish of worms during the Taipei Chinese Food Festival in Taiwan (*left*). A shot of tequila served in a hollowed out cucumber accompanies a dish of sautéed maggots at a restaurant in Mexico City (*middle*). The chef at the Explorer's Club in New York City holds a calf eyeball with an olive in it for a martini (*right*).

discourage people from smoking. A strong social norm favoring smoking—once associated with independence, sex appeal, and glamour—has now given way to an equally strong social norm depicting smoking as unhealthful, unattractive, and selfish. Today, the percentage of American adults who smoke is only 21 percent (Centers for Disease Control and Prevention 2007b), which is half the rate of 1964, when the Surgeon General's report was issued.

Many norms that people take for granted—such as premarital sexual relations and unmarried couples living together—contradict values from only several decades ago. The values that guide our intimate relationships have evolved gradually over many years. But what about instances in which cultural norms and behaviors are altered in a deliberate way?

In January 2000, a Japanese government commission published a report outlining goals for Japan in the twenty-first century. In the face of economic recession, rising crime rates, and high unemployment, the commission found that Japanese citizens need to change some of their core values if their country is to overcome its current social ills. Concluding that Japanese culture overvalues conformity and equality, the commission called for action to reduce the excessive degree of homogeneity and uniformity. Among facets

The uniforms worn by these Tokyo schoolboys reflect the traditional Japanese value of conformity. A government commission proposed that holding on to such traditional values would prevent the Japanese people from aiming for the individual goals they believe will be necessary for success in the twenty-first century.

of Japanese life that reflect this conformity are the practices of Japanese schoolchildren wearing identical uniforms that mask signs of individuality and employees staying unnecessarily late at the office because of an unspoken rule that proscribes leaving early. These values, the commission reported, were preventing Japanese people from embracing notions of individual achievement that would be essential in the coming years. Although it is too early to say whether the government mandate will succeed, a common Japanese expression—"the nail that sticks up must be hammered down"—suggests that it will take time and effort to change traditional Japanese values of conformity and self-effacement.

Many behaviors and habits—such as movements, gestures, and expressions—are grounded in cultural norms. A good example is the way people smile, particularly in public contexts. Among the Inuit (Eskimos) of Greenland, for example, it is not common practice to smile at or exchange pleasantries with strangers. As the service industry has expanded in Greenland in recent years, however, some employers have tried to instill smiling and other "polite" attitudes toward customers as a cultural value that is essential to competitive business practices. Many supermarkets in Greenland make their staff watch training videos on friendly service techniques and may even send them abroad on training courses. The opening of fast-food restaurants like McDonald's has introduced Western-style service approaches that include greeting customers, introducing themselves, and smiling frequently. Initially the staff found the style insincere and artificial, but over time they have accepted the idea of public smiling—at least in the workplace.

Culture and Society

"Culture" can be distinguished from "society," but these notions are closely connected. A **society** is a *system of interrelationships* that connects individuals. No culture could exist without a society; no society could exist without culture. Without culture, we would have no language in which to express ourselves and no sense of self-consciousness; our ability to think or reason would be severely limited.

Culture also serves as an important source of conformity. For example, when you say that you subscribe to a particular value, you are probably voicing the beliefs of your family members, friends, teachers, or others who are significant in your life. When you choose a word to describe some personal experience, that word acquires its meaning in a language you learned from others. When you buy a seemingly unique article of clothing to express your individuality, that garment was likely created by the design department of a global manufacturer that studied the current tastes of consumers and then ordered the mass

Members of a 1960s commune pose together for a group portrait (*left*). Harajuku girls stroll down a street in Tokyo, Japan (*right*). Though their distinctive styles set them apart from mainstream society, these people are not as nonconformist as they may think they are. Both subcultures pictured here conform to the norms of their respective social groups.

production of your "unique" garment. When you listen to music, it is most likely the same kind that your friends listen to.

Cultures differ, however, in how much they value conformity. Research shows that Japanese culture lies at one extreme in terms of valuing conformity (Hofstede 1997), while at the other extreme lies American culture, ranking among the world's highest in cherishing individualism. Americans pride themselves on their independence of spirit, represented by the lone bald eagle, the U.S. national symbol.

American high school and college students often see themselves as especially nonconformist. Like the body piercers of today, the hippies of the 1960s and the punks of the 1980s all sported distinctive clothing styles, haircuts, and other forms of bodily adornment. Yet how individualistic are they? Are their styles actually "uniforms," just as navy blue suits or basic black are "uniforms" among conservative businesspeople? There is an aspect of conformity to their behavior—conformity to their own group.

One of the challenges for all cultures is to instill in people a willingness to conform. This is accomplished in two ways (Parsons 1964). First, members learn the norms of their culture starting from childhood, and parents play a key role. When learning is successful, the ingrained norms become unquestioned ways of thinking and acting; they appear "normal." (Note the similarity between the words *norm* and *normal.*)

Second, *social control* comes into play when a person fails to conform adequately to a culture's norms. Social control often involves informal punishment, such as rebuking friends for minor breaches of etiquette, gossiping behind their backs, or ostracizing them from the group. Formal forms of discipline might range from issuing parking tickets to imprisonment (Foucault 1979). Émile Durkheim, one of the founders of sociology (introduced in Chapter 1), argued that punishment not only helps guarantee conformity among those who would violate a culture's norms and values but also vividly reminds others what the norms and values are.

Culture and Change: A "Cultural Turn" in Sociology?

It is easy to assume that we are so thoroughly shaped by culture that we never escape its influence. In fact, that is how most sociologists thought about culture until recently (DiMaggio 1997). Most sociologists took for granted the importance of culture, without seriously considering how it works in daily life.

The phrase **cultural turn** describes sociology's recent emphasis on understanding the role of culture in daily life. One result has been to challenge the assumption that culture rigidly determines our values and behaviors. Instead, the sociologist Ann Swidler (1986) has characterized culture as a "tool kit" from which people select different understandings and behaviors. Thus some people can choose to dye their hair and wear nose rings and tattoo their bodies but still accept their parents' traditional ideas about sexual restraint. Because people participate in many different (and often conflicting) cultures, the tool kit can be quite large and its contents varied (Bourdieu 1990; Sewell 1992; Tilly 1992).

Our cultural tool kits include a variety of "scripts" that we can draw on—and even improvise on—to shape our beliefs, values, and actions. The more appropriate the script is to a particular set of circumstances, the more likely we will be to follow it—and recall events that conform to it long after they have occurred (D'Andrade 1995; DiMaggio 1997). For example, imagine that you are a woman walking alone in an unfamiliar city late at night and suddenly encounter a male stranger who begins to cross the street, stating as he approaches, "Excuse me, may I ask you a question?" Your choice of cultural script will shape your response. A popular cultural script—honed by film and television entertainment, reality TV, and politicians—is to fear such encounters, especially if you are female (Glassner 1999). As a result, instead of hearing him out, you quickly turn and head for the safety of a nearby all-night restaurant. Later, when retelling the story, you might recall the stranger as taller and more dangerous than he was, perhaps even that he was brandishing a weapon—traits consistent with American cultural scripts about such encounters.

Now imagine that you are the male in this encounter—perhaps an out-of-town businessman trying to find your hotel in an unfamiliar neighborhood. You see a woman walking on the other side of the street, and as you cross to ask directions, she turns and disappears into a restaurant. Your experience would be very different from that of the woman: You are concerned about the late hour, worried about being lost, and stunned by her sudden actions. Perhaps when you return home you will describe this event as evidence that people in this city are cold and indifferent to strangers.

In studying this case in light of the cultural turn, sociologists would attempt to understand the different cultural scripts involved and why each person might have chosen those scripts. How did physical appearance influence their different experiences? What words were spoken, and what meanings did they convey? What did the two people's "body language" communicate? Sociologists would also consider alternative scripts that might have altered the experience of each participant. For example, the woman might have chosen the script of "good Samaritan," viewing the approaching stranger as potentially in need of assistance and thereby offering to help. Or the man might have recognized that a lone woman would feel threatened and instead chosen a less confrontational script—perhaps remaining on his side of the street and beginning with a soft-spoken, "Excuse me, can you please tell me the way to my hotel? I seem to be lost."

The cultural turn in sociology reveals that there is no single "reality" to social encounters and that multiple cultural scripts can play out in any situation. The challenge of sociology is to understand people's differing realities, the scripts that they follow, and the reasons they choose one set of scripts over another (Bonnell and Hunt 1999; Chaney 1994; Glassner 1999; Hays 2000; Long 1997; Seidman 1997; Sewell 1999; Smith and West 2000; Swidler 2001).

☑ CONCEPT CHECKS

1. Describe the main elements of culture.
2. What roles does culture play in society?

The Development of Human Culture

Human culture and human biology are intertwined. Understanding how culture is related to the physical evolution of the human species can help us understand the central role of culture in shaping our lives.

Early Human Culture: Adaptation to Physical Environment

Given the archaeological evidence, as well as the similarities in blood chemistry and genetics between chimpanzees and humans, scientists believe that humans evolved from apelike creatures on the African continent some four million years ago. The first evidence of human-like culture dates back two million years. Early humans fashioned stone tools, hunted animals and gathered nuts and berries, harnessed the use of fire, and established a highly cooperative way of life. Because early humans planned their hunts, they must have had some ability for abstract thought.

Culture enabled early humans to compensate for their physical limitations, such as lack of claws, sharp teeth, and running speed, relative to other animals (Deacon 1998). It freed humans from dependence on the instinctual responses to the environment that are characteristic of other species. The larger, more complex human brain permitted greater adaptive learning

Cultures vary widely based on their environment. Compare the material culture in these photos of the Inuit building an igloo in Canada, a Yanomami man making a basket, and a Bedouin woman beside her tent in the Sahara desert.

in dealing with major environmental changes such as the Ice Age. For example, humans figured out how to build fires and sew clothing for warmth. Through greater flexibility, humans could survive unpredictable challenges in their surroundings and shape the world with their ideas and their tools. In an instant of geological time, we became the dominant species on the planet.

Yet early humans were closely tied to their physical environment because they lacked the technological ability to modify their surroundings significantly (Bennett 1976; Harris 1975, 1978, 1980). Their ability to secure food and make clothing and shelter depended on physical resources close at hand. Cultures in different environments varied widely according to geographic and climatic conditions, such as those found in deserts, rain forests, the frozen Arctic, and more temperate areas. Human inventiveness spawned a rich tapestry of cultures around the world. As you will see later in this chapter, however, modern technology and other forces of globalization pose both challenges and opportunities for future global cultural diversity.

Nature or Nurture?

Because humans evolved as part of the world of nature, one would assume that human thinking and behavior are the result of biology and evolution. In fact, one of the oldest controversies in the social sciences is the "nature/nurture" debate: Are we shaped by our biology, or are we products of learning through life's experiences—that is, of nurture? Whereas biologists and some psychologists emphasize biological factors, sociologists stress the role of learning and culture. They also argue that because human beings can make conscious choices, neither biology nor culture wholly determines human behavior.

The nature/nurture debate has raged for more than a century. For example, in the 1930s and 1940s, many social scientists focused on biological factors, with some seeking (unsuccessfully) to prove that a person's physique determined his or her personality. In the 1960s and 1970s, scholars in different fields emphasized culture. For example, social psychologists argued that even severe mental illness was the result of society labeling unusual behavior rather than of biochemical processes (Scheff 1966). Today, partly because of new understandings in genetics and brain neurophysiology, the pendulum is again swinging toward the side of biology.

The resurgence of biological explanations for human behavior began in 1975 when the evolutionary biologist Edward O. Wilson published *Sociobiology: The New Synthesis*. The term **sociobiology** refers to the application of biological principles to explain the social activities of animals, including human beings. Wilson argued that genes influence not only physical traits but also behavior. For instance, some species of animals perform elaborate courtship rituals leading to sexual union and reproduction. Human courtship and sexual behavior, according to sociobiologists, involve similar rituals. Also, in most species, males are larger and more aggressive than females. Some suggest that genetic factors explain why, in all known human societies, men tend to hold positions of greater authority than women.

One way in which sociobiologists illuminate the relations between the sexes is through the idea of "reproductive strategy." A reproductive strategy is a pattern of behavior developed through evolutionary selection that favors the chances of survival of offspring. The female body has a larger investment in its reproductive cells than the male—a fertilized human egg takes nine months to develop. Thus women will not squander that investment and are not driven to have sexual relations

"Tapping the Mood Gene"

What's the key to happiness? A quick glance of news headlines in 2003 would lead us to a simple answer: genetics. A study of young adults' depression was published in *Science,* and its findings were quickly picked up by the national media, who proclaimed that "Scientists Find Depression Gene" (BBC News 2003), "Vulnerability to Depression May Lie in Your DNA" (Doheny 2003), and "Gene Is Linked to Susceptibility to Depression" (Duenwald 2003). A closer inspection of the *Science* study, conducted by King's College psychologist Avshalom Caspi and his collaborators (2003), reveals that it takes more than just DNA to make someone depressed. Rather, both nature (or genetics) *and* nurture (social environment) affect our mental health.

Caspi and colleagues set out to investigate the ways that genes and stressful life events affect the chances that a young adult experiences depression and suicidal thoughts. The researchers focused on a cohort of 847 whites in New Zealand who were born in the early 1970s. They collected data on the cohort from birth through age twenty-six. These data included information on their families, economic resources, health, and the stressful

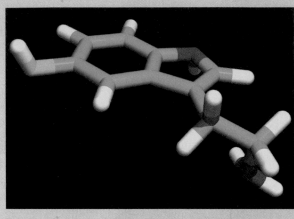

This computer model shows a molecule of serotonin, an important neurotransmitter in the brain. A lack of serotonin has been shown to cause depression.

experiences they encountered between the ages of twenty-one and twenty-six—such as parental divorce, school failure, economic troubles, and breaking up with a boyfriend or girlfriend. The study also obtained data on genetic factors. Specifically, the researchers measured which type of 5-HTT gene one had. The 5-HTT gene controls the ways that serotonin passes messages through brain cells, and it is considered a gene that may affect depression. The three possible 5-HTT gene varieties, or *genotypes,* were: two copies of a short allele, two copies of a long allele, and one short and one long allele. (An *allele* is a pair or series of genes.)

Three important findings emerged from the study. First, the more stressful events a young person experienced, the more likely that person was to become depressed. For example, those who experienced four or more stressful life events were nearly four times as likely to experience depression, compared to those who experienced no stressful events. Second, the researchers found *no statistical association* between the type of 5-HTT gene one had and that person's chances of being depressed. If

with many partners; their overriding aim is the care and protection of children. Men, on the other hand, desire to have sex with many partners, which is a sound strategy in terms of preserving the species. This view, it has been suggested, explains differences in sexual behavior and attitudes between men and women.

Sociobiologists do not argue that genes determine 100 percent of our behavior. For example, depending on the circumstances, men can choose to act in nonaggressive ways. Yet even though this argument seems to add culture as another explanatory factor in describing human behavior, social scientists have condemned sociobiology for claiming that a propensity for particular behaviors, such as violence, is somehow "genetically programmed" ("Seville Statement on Violence" 1990).

How Nature and Nurture Interact

Most sociologists today acknowledge a role for nature in determining attitudes and behavior, but with strong qualifications. For example, no one questions that newborn babies have basic human reflexes, such as "rooting" for the mother's nipple and responding to the human face (Cosmides and Tooby 1997; Johnson and Morton 1991). But it is a leap to conclude that genes had no effect on depression, how could reporters claim that a "depression gene" exists?

Although the scientists did not find a direct effect of genes on depression, they did find evidence of an "interaction effect." That means that the influence of one variable (such as stress) on depression is contingent upon a second variable (such as genetics). Specifically, the researchers found that the effects of life stress on depression were most severe for those young people who had a particular genetic makeup. Of the 15 percent of young people who had experienced four or more stressful life events, 33 percent of those who had a short allele became depressed—compared to just 17 percent of those who had two long alleles. Overall, these findings reveal that "nature" alone does not cause depression, but the interplay of both "nature" and "nurture" affects young people's chances of becoming depressed.

The media underplayed the importance of stressful life events yet overstated the influence of genes on depression. Rutgers University sociologist Allan Horwitz (2004) has argued that media attention on genetics draws attention away from important social influences on mental health. For example, many of the stressful life events considered in the study are events that are particularly common among economically disadvantaged young people, such as losing a job, being in debt, and having difficulty paying bills or covering medical expenses. By focusing on genetics only, the media and the scientific community may send the message that depression among young people can and should be treated through medications. However, Horwitz counters that an equally valuable strategy is to develop policies and practices that would help to reduce social inequalities and the stressors associated with these inequalities.

The media's portrayal of Caspi's study and Horwitz's critique of the media attention illustrate a key theme of "the sociological imagination." Sociologist C. Wright Mills claimed that the goal of sociology is to show how seemingly personal problems, like depression, may reflect underlying "public issues." The media's attention to individuals' genetic makeup, rather than to social context, suggests that Mills's message still has not been heard or heeded by all.

Questions

- What are the three key findings of the Caspi study of depression among young adults?
- What findings did the media pay most attention to? Why do you think the media focused only on selected findings?
- How does the Caspi study contribute to the "nature versus nurture" debate in sociology?

FOR FURTHER EXPLORATION

BBC News. 2003. "Scientists Find Depression Gene." www.news.bbc.co.uk/1/hi/health/30666065.stm (accessed July 17, 2003).

Caspi, Avshalom, Karen Sugden, Terrie E. Moffitt, Alan Taylor, Ian W. Craig, Hona-Lee Harrington, Joseph McClay, Jonathan Mill, Judy Martin, Antony Braithwaite, and Richie Poulton. 2003. "Influence of Life Stress on Depression: Moderation by a Polymorphism in the 5-HTT Gene." *Science, 301,* 386–389.

Doheny, Kathleen. 2003. "Vulnerability to Depression May Lie in Your DNA." www.healthfinder.gov/news/newsstory.asp?docID=514192 (accessed July 6, 2004).

Duenwald, Mary. 2003. "Gene Is Linked to Susceptibility to Depression." *New York Times,* July 18, 2003, A14.

Horwitz, Allan. 2004. "Media Portrayals and Health Inequalities: A Case Study of Characterizations of Gene X Environment Interactions." Paper presented at the Conference on Health Inequalities across the Life Course conference, Pennsylvania State University. June 6, 2004.

Kramer, Peter D. "Tapping the Mood Gene." *New York Times,* July 19, 2003, A13.

because babies have human reflexes, adult behavior is governed by **instincts**—biologically fixed patterns of action found in all cultures.

Sociologists now ask how nature and nurture interact to produce human behavior. But their main concern is with how behavior is learned through interactions with family, friends, schools, television, and every other facet of the social environment. For example, sociologists argue that it's not a biological disposition that makes American males feel attracted to a *particular* type of woman. Rather, it's their exposure to magazine ads, TV commercials, and film stars that transmit cultural standards of female beauty.

Early child rearing is especially relevant to this kind of learning. Human babies have a large brain, requiring birth relatively early in their fetal development while their heads can still pass through the birth canal. As a result, human babies must spend a number of years in the care of adults, during which time the child learns its society's culture.

Because humans think and act in many different ways, sociologists do not believe that "biology is destiny." If biology were all-important, we would expect all cultures to be similar, if not identical. Yet this is hardly the case. For example, pork is forbidden to religious Jews and Muslims, but it is a dietary staple in China. Americans greet one another with a casual "How are

The Sociology of Body Image

Victoria Pitts studies the human body. She is not a medical doctor. She is not a surgeon. She is not a nutritionist or a physical therapist or an exercise guru. Pitts is a sociologist who studies the ways that we evaluate and shape and mold our bodies in response to prevailing cultural standards. Although we may act as individuals, our actions are also responses to social messages. Currently, our culture views the body as something changeable, a pliable product under our control rather than a fixed entity that we are stuck with forever. Such messages are so strong we can hear them ringing in our ears. Although in different tones, they speak strongly to both men and women. We should lose weight. We should exercise regularly. We should tone our figures, lift weights, and buy vitamin supplements to look and feel healthy. We should search the Internet for health information; take action to prevent diseases; and take prescriptions to help us sleep, concentrate, or have sex. We should manage our appearance and health as well as create our personal style. Those messages are so prevalent they have come to resemble common sense. But they also create intense pressure to conform to social standards of beauty and, regardless of our choice of clothing or tattoo or hairstyle, to express our identities through our physical appearance.

"Consumer culture is obsessively body-oriented, and the media industries continue to capitalize on our fascination with both beautiful and anomalous bodies," says Pitts (2004). "Politically, the body continues to be a site of contest: cloning, genetic screening, [in vitro fertilization] treatments, abortion, contraception, drug use, sex work, pornography, body modification

Victoria Pitts

practices, and performance art . . . all raise important issues about the ownership and regulation of the body and body technologies. It now seems that embodiment is a site for a great deal of the 'action' in contemporary cultures."

Nowhere is that action more bizarre and spectacular than in those practicing *body modification* (BM), a form of self-expression popularized in San Francisco in the 1990s. BM includes not only tattoos and body piercings but also scarification, which is accomplished by cutting repeatedly with a

you?" But the Yanomamö living in the rain forests of Venezuela and Brazil greet one another with an exchange of gifts and would find the casual American greeting an insult.

This is not to say that human cultures have nothing in common. Extensive surveys have concluded that all known human cultures have such common characteristics as language, forms of emotional expression, rules for raising children or engaging in sexual behavior, and standards of beauty (Brown 1991). But there is enormous variety in *how* these common characteristics play out.

All cultures provide for childhood socialization, but the processes vary greatly from culture to culture. An American child learns the multiplication tables from a classroom teacher, whereas a child in the forests of Borneo learns to hunt with older members of the tribe. All cultures have standards of beauty and ornamentation, but what constitutes beauty in one culture may constitute the opposite in another (Elias 1987; Elias and Dunning 1987; Foucault 1988). For example, the half-starved body of a typical *Vogue* model or the bulked-up body of a weight lifter would be grossly unattractive to the Borneo forest dweller.

scalpel or a cauterizing (or burning) tool, and strike branding, which is akin to cattle branding. After cleaning the area and stenciling on the design, an artist begins cutting or burning the skin until the right depth is reached. "It can take 15 minutes, but I've also done pieces that took eight hours over two days," said Ryan Ouellette, a body-modification artist in Nashua, New Hampshire (quoted in Guynup 2004). Subdermal implants are a more shocking form of BM in which foreign objects are surgically implanted beneath the skin to create a raised or textured appearance. Now that tattoos, once having symbolized a refusal to conform to standard expectations of appearance, have become more mainstream, perhaps even normal, those seeking to make defiant statements through body practices are increasingly turning to body modification to express themselves in unique and shocking ways.

Although body modification may appear disturbing, the practice does not mean that individuals themselves are disturbed. Predominantly a middle-class, educated, and psychologically healthy group, body modifiers are consciously choosing to contradict and subvert the cultural sensibilities in which they feel trapped.

"Until recently, body modifiers were perceived as sick people in need of psychiatric, not sociological, attention," says Pitts, who was awarded an Advancement of the Discipline award from the American Sociological Association in 2002. Her first application to study the topic as a graduate student was met with rejection. The official report stated plainly that these people need to be studied by mental health professionals, not sociologists. But Pitts (2004) believes this interpretation is wrong: "It suggests both that the only healthy body is an unmarked one, and also that the surface body is a place where the 'truth' of an individual's depth psyche is revealed." Feminists also have been quick to reject body modification as a sign of internalized oppression or a form of self-hatred, creating intellectual land mines that Pitts has been able to avoid largely by using her sociological imagination. Indeed, many sociologists are now taking the view that the body is a "deeply meaningful space where sociality, culture and history are inscribed, reflected or produced" (Pitts 2004). Rather than seeing body modification as pathological, scholars are instead asking why individuals are moved to engage in particular body projects and how those projects create and respond to social forces regulating what we should and should not do to our own bodies.

One of Pitts's most difficult experiences as a public sociologist involved a court case in Vancouver, British Columbia, in which she was asked to testify as an expert witness. A young man who had performed scarification on the arm of his girlfriend had been charged with felony sexual assault after her parents discovered the marks and contacted police. Pitts felt conflicted about participating. She has never intended to glorify body modification as a cultural practice as much as she has tried to understand it sociologically. At the same time, it became clear to her that the young man would have difficulty getting a fair hearing if a sociological perspective on the cultures and subcultures of body modification was absent from the proceedings. Pitts decided to participate. The young man claimed in his trial that marking his girlfriend's arms was not in any way sexually abusive. It was perhaps foolish and extreme, but it was an attempt to express their identities as individuals and as a couple.

This book consistently forces you to wrestle with the theme of *social change*. Cultural norms of the body and how we assert our own identity within those norms are determined by a complex interaction of personal motives and the time and place in which we live. We all respond to cultural pressures. And the way we respond is conditioned by pressures largely beyond our control. But by focusing our attention on some of the most dramatic body projects occurring worldwide (her new work is on the rise of cosmetic surgery), Pitts helps us realize that by developing an understanding of "deviant" bodies, we arrive at a better understanding of ourselves.

Cultural Diversity

The study of cultural differences highlights the influence of cultural learning on behavior, which can vary widely from culture to culture. For example, in the modern West, we regard the deliberate killing of infants or young children as one of the worst of all crimes. Yet in traditional Chinese culture, female infants were sometimes strangled at birth because a daughter was regarded as a liability rather than an asset. In the West, we eat oysters but not kittens or puppies, both of which are regarded as delicacies in some other parts of the world. Jews and Muslims don't eat pork, whereas Hindus eat pork but avoid beef. Westerners regard kissing as a normal part of sexual behavior, but in other cultures the practice is either unknown or regarded as disgusting.

SUBCULTURES

Small societies tend to be culturally uniform, but industrialized societies involving numerous **subcultures** are themselves culturally diverse or multicultural. As processes such as slavery, colonialism, war, migration, and contemporary globalization have led to populations settling in new areas, societies have emerged that are cultural composites: Their population comprises groups from diverse cultural and linguistic backgrounds. In modern cities, for example, many subcultural communities live side by side.

Subcultures not only imply different cultural backgrounds or different languages within a larger society; they also include segments of the population that have different cultural patterns. Subcultures might include Goths, computer hackers, hippies, Rastafarians, and fans of hip-hop. Some people identify with a particular subculture, whereas others move among several.

Culture helps perpetuate the values and norms of a society, yet it also offers opportunities for creativity and change. Subcultures and countercultures—groups that reject prevailing values and norms—can promote views that represent alternatives to the dominant culture. Social movements or groups with common lifestyles are powerful forces of change within societies, allowing people to express and act on their opinions, hopes, and beliefs.

U.S. schoolchildren are frequently taught that the United States is a vast melting pot that assimilates subcultures. **Assimilation** is the process by which different cultures are absorbed into a mainstream culture. Although virtually all peoples living in the United States take on some common cultural characteristics, many groups strive to retain a unique identity. In fact, identification based on race or country of origin in the United States persists and even grows, particularly among African Americans and immigrants from Asia, Mexico, and Latin America (Totti 1987).

A more appropriate metaphor for American society than the assimilationist melting pot might be the culturally diverse salad bowl, in which all the ingredients, though mixed together, retain their original flavor and integrity, thereby contributing to the richness of the salad as a whole. This viewpoint, termed **multiculturalism**, calls for respecting cultural diversity and promoting equality of different cultures (Anzaldua 1990).

Young people have their own subcultures in many modern industrial nations. Youth subcultures typically revolve around musical preferences and distinctive styles of dress, language (especially slang), and behavior. Like all subcultures, however, they still accept most of the norms and values of the dominant culture.

Consider the patchwork that is hip-hop. Although it emerged as a subculture in the Bronx, New York, in the mid-1970s, hip-hop owes much of its identity to Jamaica. The first important hip-hop DJ, Kool Herc, was a Jamaican immigrant, and rapping derives from the Jamaican DJ tradition of "toasting": chanting stories into microphones over records. The story of hip-hop is a lesson in the fluidity of contemporary cultural identity. The music is built around beats from other records, but in "sampling" from recordings hip-hop artists often do something more significant: They sample identities, taking on the characteristics of subcultures that can be considerably foreign to them.

Hip-hop's reach has widened over time. Rappers from Queens and Long Island—like Run-D.M.C., LL Cool J, and Public Enemy—recorded some of the first great hip-hop albums. By the end of the 1980s, the music had a national presence in the United States, as Los Angeles artists like N.W.A. and Ice-T developed gangsta rap, which soon had outposts in Oakland, New Orleans, Houston, and elsewhere. White rappers like Kid Rock and Eminem, belatedly following in the footsteps of the Beastie Boys, pioneered a rap-rock synthesis, and a Filipino American crew known as the Invisible Skratch Piklz revolutionized turntable techniques. Hip-hop soon became a global form, with British trip-hop artists like Tricky, French rappers like MC Solaar, and record spinners like Japan's DJ Krush.

The sampled beats of hip-hop can contain nearly anything. The secret is transformation: A portion of an earlier song, recast to fit a new context, can take on an entirely different meaning while still retaining enough of its former essence to create a complicated and richly meaningful finished product. In many ways, hip-hop is a music of echoes: rappers revisiting the funk music and "blaxploitation" films of the 1970s (black action movies, often criticized for glorifying violence and presenting blacks in negative stereotypes); suburban fans romanticizing inner-city street styles. Hip-hop is the soundtrack to an emerging global culture that treats the looks, sounds, and byways of particular subcultures, or particular moments in time, as raw material for the creation of new styles.

The origins of hip-hop culture can be traced back to DJ Kool Herc, who brought the Jamaican disc jockey tradition of "toasting" to New York in the mid-1970s.

Eminem represents one aspect of the widening appeal of hip-hop across cultural lines, arguably for better and for worse.

What does hip-hop tell us about cultural diversity? On the one hand, its history of incorporating an ever-wider circle of influences and participants demonstrates that what is "normal" in one community can quickly be adopted in another community far away, through dissemination via records and other media. On the other hand, the controversies that hip-hop has generated suggest that such cultural crossings also bring uncertainty, misperception, and fear. Finally, hip-hop's evolution suggests that even in a global culture, subcultural distinctions retain an important aura of authenticity. Even today, hip-hop retains aspects of social realities that most Americans would prefer not to contemplate.

Subcultures also develop around types of work associated with unique cultural features. Long-distance truckers, coal miners, Wall Street stockbrokers, computer programmers, professional athletes, corporate lawyers, and artists, for example, form subcultures that value (respectively) physical strength, bravery, shrewdness, speed, knowledge, material wealth, and creativity. However, they seldom stray far from the dominant culture. Even professional thieves share most of the values of U.S. society: They marry and raise children; like most Americans, they want to accumulate wealth, power, and prestige; they eat with knives and forks, drive on the right side of the road, and try to avoid trouble as much as possible (Chambliss 1988).

CULTURAL IDENTITY AND ETHNOCENTRISM

Every culture displays unique patterns of behavior. If you have traveled abroad, you know that aspects of daily life taken for granted in your own culture may not be part of everyday life elsewhere. Even in countries that share the same language, you might find customs to be quite different. The expression *culture shock* is an apt one! Often people feel disoriented when immersed in a new culture because they have lost familiar cultural reference points and have not yet learned how to navigate in the new culture.

As an example of the uniqueness of cultural patterns of behavior, consider the Nacirema, a group described by Horace Miner. He concentrated on their body rituals:

The fundamental belief underlying the whole system appears to be that the human body is ugly and that its natural tendency is to debility and disease. Incarcerated in such a body, man's only hope is to avert these characteristics through the use of the powerful influences of ritual and ceremony. Every household has one or more shrines devoted to this purpose.... The focal point of the shrine is a box or chest which is built into the wall. In the chest are kept the many charms and magical potions without which no native believes he could live. These preparations are secured from a variety of specialized practitioners. The most powerful of these are the medicine men, whose assistance must be rewarded with substantial gifts. However, the medicine men do not provide the curative potions for their clients, but decide what the ingredients should be and then write them down in an ancient and secret language. This writing is understood only by the medicine man and by the herbalists who, for another gift, provide the required charm....

The Nacirema have an almost pathological horror of and fascination with the mouth, the condition of which is believed to have a supernatural influence on all social relationships. Were it not for the rituals of the mouth, they believe that their teeth would fall out, their gums bleed, their jaws shrink, their friends desert them, and their lovers reject them. They also believe that a strong relationship exists between oral and moral characteristics. For example, there is a ritual ablution of the mouth for children which is supposed to improve their moral fibre.

The daily body ritual performed by everyone includes a mouth-rite. Despite the fact that these people are so punctilious about care of the mouth, this rite involves a practice which strikes the uninitiated stranger as

Reggae Music

When those knowledgeable about popular music listen to a song, they can often pick out the stylistic influences that helped shape it. Each musical style, after all, represents a unique way of combining rhythm, melody, harmony, and lyrics. And though it doesn't take a genius to notice the differences among grunge, hard rock, techno, and hip-hop, musicians often combine a

number of styles in composing songs. Identifying the components of these combinations can be difficult. But for sociologists of culture, the effort is often rewarding. Different musical styles tend to emerge from different social groups, and studying how styles combine and fuse is a good way to chart the cultural contacts between groups.

Some sociologists of culture have turned their attention to reggae music because it exemplifies the process whereby contacts between social groups result in the creation of new musical forms. Reggae's roots can be traced to West Africa. In the seventeenth century, large numbers of West Africans were enslaved by the British and brought by ship to work in the sugarcane fields of the West Indies. Although the British attempted to prevent slaves from playing traditional African music, for fear it would serve as a rallying cry to revolt, the slaves managed to keep alive the tradition of African drumming, sometimes by integrating it with the European musical styles imposed by the slave owners. In Jamaica, the drumming of one group of slaves, the Burru, was openly tolerated by slaveholders because it helped meter the pace of work. Slavery

revolting. . . . [T]he ritual consists of inserting a small bundle of hog hairs into the mouth, along with certain magical powders, and then moving the bundle in a highly formalized series of gestures. (Miner 1956)

Who are the Nacirema, and where do they live? You can answer these questions by spelling *Nacirema* backward. The Nacirema are Americans (and other Westerners), and the ritual described is the brushing of teeth. Almost any familiar activity will seem strange if described out of context. Western cleanliness rituals are no more or less bizarre than the customs of some Pacific groups who knock out their front teeth to beautify themselves or of certain South American tribal groups who place discs inside their lips to make them protrude, believing that this enhances their attractiveness.

We cannot understand these practices and beliefs separately from the wider cultures of which they are a part. A culture must be studied in terms of its own meanings and values—a key presupposition of sociology. Sociologists endeavor to avoid **ethnocentrism**, which is the judging of other cultures in terms of the standards of one's own. We must remove our own cultural blinders to see the ways of life of different peoples in an unbiased light. The practice of judging a society by its own standards is called **cultural relativism**.

Applying cultural relativism can be fraught with uncertainty and challenge. Not only is it hard to see things from a completely different point of view, but sometimes troubling questions arise. Does cultural relativism mean that all customs and behaviors are equally legitimate? Are there any universal standards to which all humans should adhere? Consider the ritual acts of what opponents have called "genital mutilation" in some societies. Numerous young girls in certain African, Asian, and Middle Eastern cultures undergo clitoridectomies, a painful cultural ritual in which the clitoris and sometimes all or part of the vaginal labia are removed with a knife or a sharpened stone and the two sides of the vulva are partly sewn

"Rastafarians." The Rastafarian cult soon merged with the Burru, and Rastafarian music came to combine Burru styles of drumming with biblical themes of oppression and liberation. In the 1950s, West Indian musicians began mixing Rastafarian rhythms and lyrics with elements of American jazz and black rhythm and blues. These combinations eventually developed into ska music and then, in the late 1960s, into reggae, with its relatively slow beat, its emphasis on the bass, and its stories of urban deprivation and of the power of collective social consciousness. Many reggae artists, such as Bob Marley, became commercial successes, and by the 1970s, people the world over were listening to reggae music. In the 1980s, reggae was first fused with hip-hop (or rap) to produce new sounds, as can be heard today in the dance hall music of the Jamaican rapper Sean Paul.

The history of reggae is thus the history of contact among different social groups and of the meanings—political, spiritual, and personal—that those groups expressed through their music. Globalization has intensified these contacts. It is now possible for a young musician in Scandinavia, for example, to grow up listening to music produced by men and women in the ghettos of Los Angeles and to be deeply influenced as well by, say, a mariachi performance broadcast live via satellite from Mexico City. If the number of contacts among groups is an important determinant of the pace of musical evolution, we can predict that a veritable profusion of new styles will flourish in the coming years as the process of globalization continues to unfold.

was finally abolished in Jamaica in 1834, but the tradition of Burru drumming continued, even as many Burru men migrated from rural areas to the slums of Kingston.

In these slums, a new religious cult began to emerge—one that would prove crucial for the development of reggae. In 1930, a man who took the title Haile Selassie ("Power of the Trinity") was crowned emperor of the African country of Ethiopia. While opponents of European colonialism throughout the world cheered his accession to the throne, a number of people in the West Indies came to believe that Haile Selassie was a god, sent to earth to lead the oppressed of Africa to freedom. Haile Selassie's original name was Ras Tafari Makonnen, and the West Indians who worshiped him called themselves

together as a means of controlling sexual activity and increasing the sexual pleasure of the man.

In cultures where clitoridectomies have been practiced for generations, they are regarded as normal. A study of two thousand men and women in two Nigerian communities found that nine out of ten women interviewed had undergone clitoridectomies in childhood and that the large majority favored the procedure for their own daughters, primarily for cultural reasons. Yet a significant minority believed that the practice should be stopped (Ebomoyi 1987). Clitoridectomies are regarded with abhorrence by most people from other cultures and by a growing number of women in the cultures where they are practiced (El Dareer 1982; Johnson-Odim 1991; Lightfoot-Klein 1989). These differences in views can result in a clash of cultural values, especially when people from cultures where clitoridectomies are common migrate to countries where the practice is illegal.

France is an example. France has a large North African immigrant population, in which many African mothers arrange for traditional clitoridectomies to be performed on their daughters. Some have been tried and convicted under French law for mutilating their daughters. These African mothers have argued that they were engaging in the same cultural practice that their own mothers had performed on them, that their grandmothers had performed on their mothers, and so on. They complain that the French are ethnocentric, judging traditional African rituals by French customs. Feminists from Africa and the Middle East, while themselves strongly opposed to clitoridectomies, have criticized Europeans and Americans who sensationalize the practice by calling it "backward" or "primitive" without seeking any understanding of the underlying cultural and economic circumstances (Accad 1991; Johnson-Odim 1991; Mohanty 1991). In this instance, globalization has led to a clash of cultural norms and values that has forced members of both cultures to confront some of their most deeply held beliefs. The role of the sociologist is to avoid knee-jerk responses and to examine complex questions carefully from as many angles as possible.

Cultural Universals

When common features of human behavior are found in virtually all societies, they are called **cultural universals**. For example, there is no known culture without a grammatically complex **language**. Also, all cultures possess some recognizable form of family system, in which there are values and norms associated with the care of children. The institution of **marriage** is a cultural universal, as are religious rituals and property rights. All cultures also practice some form of incest prohibition—the banning of sexual relations between close relatives. Other cultural universals include art, dancing, bodily adornment, games, gift giving, joking, and rules of hygiene.

Yet there are variations within each category. Consider the prohibition against incest. Most often, incest is regarded as sexual relations between members of the immediate family; but among some peoples it includes cousins, and in some instances all people bearing the same family name. There have also been societies in which a small proportion of the population engages in incestuous practices. This was the case within the ruling class of ancient Egypt, when brothers and sisters were permitted to have sex with each other.

Among the cultural characteristics shared by all societies, two stand out in particular. All cultures incorporate ways of expressing meaning and communication, and all depend on material means of production. In all cultures, *language* is the primary vehicle of meaning and communication. It is not the only such vehicle, however. Material culture itself carries meanings, as we shall show.

LANGUAGE

Language demonstrates both the unity and the diversity of human culture, because there are no cultures without language yet there are thousands of languages spoken in the world. Although languages with similar origins have words in common with one another—for example, German and English—most major language groups have no words in common at all.

Language is involved in virtually all of our activities. In the form of ordinary talk or speech, it is the means by which we organize most of what we do. (We will discuss the importance of talk and conversation in social life in Chapter 5.) However, language is involved not just in mundane activities but also in ceremony, religion, poetry, and many other spheres. One of its most distinctive features is that it allows us to extend the scope of our thought and experience. Using language, we can convey information about events remote in time or space and can

discuss things we have never seen. We can develop abstract concepts, tell stories, and make jokes.

In the 1930s, the anthropological linguist Edward Sapir and his student Benjamin Lee Whorf advanced the **linguistic relativity hypothesis**, which argues that language influences our perceptions of the world. That is because we are more likely to be aware of things if we have words for them (Haugen 1977; Malotki 1983; Witkowski and Brown 1982). Expert skiers or snowboarders, for example, use terms such as *black ice, corn, powder,* and *packed powder* to describe different snow and ice conditions to more readily perceive potentially life-threatening situations that would escape the notice of a novice. In a sense, then, experienced winter athletes have a different perception of the world—or, at least, a different perception of the alpine slopes—than do novices.

Language also helps give permanence to a culture and identity to a people. Language outlives any particular speaker or writer, affording a sense of history and cultural continuity. In the beginning of this chapter, we argued that the English language is becoming increasingly global, as a primary language of both business and the Internet. Yet local attachments to language persist, often out of cultural pride. For example, the French-speaking residents of the Canadian province of Quebec are so passionate about their linguistic heritage that they often refuse to speak English, the dominant language of Canada, and periodically seek political independence from the rest of Canada. Minority languages are sometimes even outlawed by the majority government: Turkey restricts the use of the Kurdish language, and the "English-only" movement in the United States seeks to restrict the language of education and government to English, even though numerous other languages are spoken throughout the country.

Protesting against the English-only initiative in Colorado, parents and students voice their opposition to Amendment 31, which would have changed the state constitution in 2002 to require schools to replace bilingual education with intensive English-immersion programs. Voters did not ratify the bill.

Regensburg Cathedral, built in the Middle Ages, stands at the center of Regensburg, Germany, and towers over the city, symbolizing the central role Christianity played in medieval European life.

Before the terrorist attacks of September 11, 2001, the World Trade Center dominated the New York City skyline. Today, the buildings of lower Manhattan's financial district still stand significantly taller than those in other areas of the city. Commerce and business occupy the symbolic center of contemporary American culture.

Languages—indeed, all symbols—are representations of reality. Symbols may signify things we imagine, such as mathematical formulas or fictitious creatures, or they may represent (that is, "re-present," or make present again in our minds) things initially experienced through our senses. Human behavior is oriented toward the symbols we use to represent "reality," rather than toward the reality itself—and these symbols are determined within a particular culture. When you see a four-footed furry animal, for example, you must determine which cultural symbol to attach to it. Do you decide to call it a dog, a wolf, or something else? If you determine it is a dog, what cultural meaning does that convey? In American culture, dogs are typically regarded as household pets and lavished with affection. In Guatemalan Indian culture, however, dogs are more often seen as watchdogs or scavengers and treated with an indifference that might seem cruel to Americans. Among the Akha of northern Thailand, dogs are seen as food and treated accordingly. The diversity of cultural meanings attached to the word *dog* thus requires an act of interpretation. In this way, human beings are freed, in a sense, from being directly tied to the physical world.

SPEECH AND WRITING

All societies use speech as a vehicle of language. However, there are other ways of expressing language—most notably, writing. The invention of writing marked a major transition in human history. Writing first began as the drawing up of lists: Marks made on wood, clay, or stone served to keep records about significant events, objects, or people. For example, a mark, or sometimes a picture, might represent each tract of land possessed by a particular family or set of families (Gelb 1952). Writing began as a means of storing information and as such was closely linked to the administrative needs of the early civilizations. A society that possesses writing can locate itself in time and space. Documents can be accumulated that record the past, and information can be gathered about present-day events and activities.

Written documents or *texts* have qualities distinct from the spoken word. The effect of speech is limited to the contexts in which words are uttered. Ideas and experiences can be passed down through generations in cultures without writing, but only by word of mouth. Texts, on the other hand, can endure for thousands of years, and through them those from past ages can address us directly. This is why documentary research is so important to historians.

SEMIOTICS AND MATERIAL CULTURE

The symbols expressed in speech and writing are the chief ways in which cultural meanings are formed and expressed. But they are not the only ways. Both material objects and aspects of behavior can generate meanings. A **signifier** is any vehicle of meaning—any set of elements used to communicate. The sounds made in speech are signifiers, as are the marks made on paper or other materials in writing. Other signifiers include dress, pictures or visual signs, modes of eating, forms of building or architecture, and many other material features of culture (Hawkes 1977). Styles of dress, for example, normally signify differences between the sexes. Until relatively recently, women in our culture wore skirts and men pants. In other cultures, this is reversed: Women wear pants and men skirts (Leach 1976).

Semiotics—the analysis of nonverbal cultural meanings—opens up a fascinating field for both sociology and anthropology because it allows us to contrast the ways in which different cultures are structured. For example, the buildings in cities are not simply places where people live and work; they often have a symbolic character. In traditional cities, the main temple or church usually sat on high ground in or near the city center to symbolize the all-powerful influence of religion. In modern societies, by contrast, the skyscrapers of big business often occupy that symbolic position.

Of course, material culture is not simply symbolic but is also vital for catering to physical needs—in the tools or technology used to acquire food, make weaponry, construct dwellings, and so forth. We have to study both the practical and the symbolic aspects of material culture to understand it completely.

Culture and Social Development

Cultural traits are closely related to overall patterns in the development of society. The level of material culture reached in a given society influences other aspects of its cultural development. Consider level of technology. Many aspects of modern culture—cars, telephones, computers, running water, electric light—depend on technological innovations that have occurred very recently in human history.

The same is true of earlier phases of social development. Before the invention of the smelting of metal, for example, goods had to be made of organic or naturally occurring materials like wood or stone—a limitation on the artifacts that could be constructed. Variations in material culture primarily distinguish different forms of human society, but other factors are also influential. Writing is an example. The development of writing altered the scope of human cultural potentialities, making possible different forms of social organization.

We now turn to analyzing the main types of society that existed in the past and that are still found in the world today. Whereas we are accustomed to societies that contain millions of people, many of them crowded together in urban areas, for most of human history the earth was much less densely populated. To understand the forms of society that existed before modern industrialism, we call on the historical dimension of the sociological imagination.

☑ CONCEPT CHECKS

1. Explain the nature/nurture debate.
2. Why do sociologists disagree with the claim that biology is destiny?
3. Give examples of subcultures that are typical of American society.

4. What is the difference between cultural ethnocentrism and cultural relativism?
5. Why is language considered to be a cultural universal?
6. What is the linguistic relativity hypothesis?

Premodern Societies

The explorers, traders, and missionaries sent out during Europe's great age of discovery met many different peoples. As the anthropologist Marvin Harris wrote in his work *Cannibals and Kings* (1978):

> In some regions—Australia, the Arctic, the southern tips of South America and Africa—they found groups still living much like Europe's own long-forgotten stone age ancestors: bands of twenty or thirty people, sprinkled across vast territories, constantly on the move, living entirely by hunting animals and collecting wild plants. These hunter-collectors appeared to be members of a rare and endangered species. In other regions—the forests of eastern North America, the jungles of South America, and East Asia—they found denser populations, inhabiting more or less permanent villages, based on farming and consisting of perhaps one or two large communal structures, but here too the weapons and tools were relics of prehistory....
>
> Elsewhere, of course, the explorers encountered fully developed states and empires, headed by despots and ruling classes, and defended by standing armies. ...There was China—the greatest empire in the world, a vast, sophisticated realm whose leaders scorned the "red-faced barbarians," supplicants from puny kingdoms beyond the pale of the civilised world. And there was India—a land where cows were venerated and the unequal burdens of life were apportioned according to what each soul had merited in its previous incarnation. And then there were the native American states and empires, worlds unto themselves, each with its distinctive arts and religions: the Incas, with their great stone fortresses, suspension bridges, over-worked granaries, and state-controlled economy; and the Aztecs, with their bloodthirsty gods fed from human hearts and their incessant search for fresh sacrifices.

This seemingly unlimited variety of premodern societies encompasses three main categories: hunters and gatherers (Harris's "hunter-collectors"), larger agrarian or pastoral societies (involving agriculture or the tending of domesticated

TABLE 3.1

Types of Human Society

TYPE	PERIOD OF EXISTENCE	CHARACTERISTICS
Hunting and gathering societies	50,000 B.C.E. to the present. Now on the verge of complete disappearance.	Consist of small numbers of people gaining their livelihood from hunting, fishing, and the gathering of edible plants. Few inequalities. Differences of rank limited by age and gender.
Agrarian societies	12,000 B.C.E. to the present. Most are now part of larger political entities and are losing their distinct identity.	Based on small rural communities, without towns or cities. Livelihood gained through agriculture, often supplemented by hunting and gathering. Stronger inequalities than among hunters and gatherers. Ruled by chiefs.
Pastoral societies	12,000 B.C.E. to the present. Today mostly part of larger states; their traditional ways of life are being undermined.	Size ranges from a few hundred people to many thousands. Depend on the tending of domesticated animals for their subsistence. Marked by distinct inequalities. Ruled by chiefs or warrior kings.
Traditional societies or civilizations	6000 B.C.E. to the nineteenth century. All traditional states have disappeared.	Very large in size, some numbering millions of people (though small compared with larger industrialized societies). Some cities exist, in which trade and manufacture are concentrated. Based largely on agriculture. Major inequalities exist among different classes. Distinct apparatus of government headed by a king or emperor.

animals), and nonindustrial civilizations or traditional states. We shall look at the main characteristics of these societies in turn (Table 3.1).

The Earliest Societies: Hunters and Gatherers

For all but a tiny part of our existence on this planet, human beings have lived in small **hunting and gathering societies**, often numbering no more than thirty or forty people. Hunters and gatherers gain their livelihood from hunting, fishing, and gathering wild edible plants. Such cultures still exist in some parts of the world, such as in a few arid parts of Africa and the jungles of Brazil and New Guinea. Most such cultures, however, have been destroyed or absorbed by the spread of Western culture. Currently, less than a quarter of a million people in the world support themselves through hunting and gathering—only 0.001 percent of the world's population (Global Map 3.1).

Compared with larger societies—particularly modern societies, such as the United States—there was little inequality in most hunting and gathering groups. Because necessary material goods were limited to weapons for hunting, tools for digging and building, traps, and cooking utensils, there was little difference among members of the society in the number or kinds of material possessions—there were no divisions of rich and poor. Differences of position or rank were based on age and gender; men were almost always the hunters, while

The Decline of Hunting and Gathering Societies

World population: 10 million
Hunters and gatherers: 100%

10,000 B.C.E.

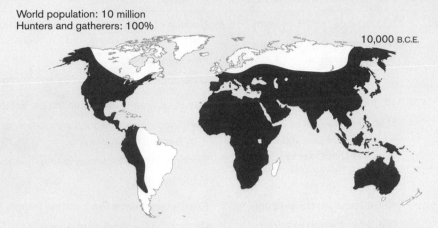

World population: 350 million
Hunters and gatherers: 1.0%

1500 C.E.

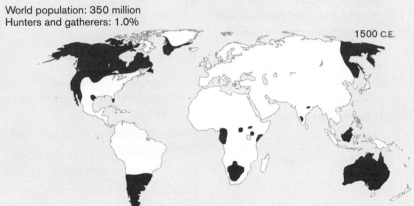

World population: 6 billion
Hunters and gatherers: 0.001%

2000 C.E.

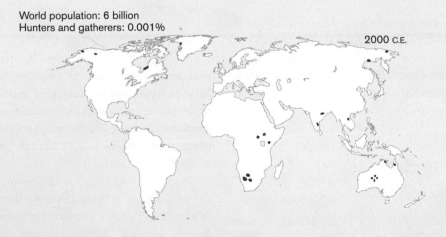

SOURCE: Richard B. Lee and Irven De Vore, eds., *Man the Hunter* (Chicago: Aldine Press, 1968), updated by authors.

women gathered wild crops, cooked, and brought up the children.

The oldest and most experienced men usually had an important say in major decisions affecting the group, but differences of power were much less distinct than in larger types of society. Hunting and gathering societies were usually participatory rather than competitive: All adult male members assembled in the face of important decisions or crises.

Hunters and gatherers moved about a good deal within fixed territories, around which they migrated from year to year. Because they lacked animal or mechanical means of transport, they could take very few goods or possessions with them. Many hunting and gathering communities did not have a stable membership; people often moved between camps, or groups split up and joined others within the same territory.

Hunters and gatherers had little interest in developing material wealth; their main concerns were with religious values and ritual activities. Members participated regularly in elaborate ceremonials and often spent time preparing the dress, masks, paintings, or other sacred objects used in such rituals.

Hunters and gatherers are not merely primitive peoples whose ways of life no longer hold interest for us. Studying their cultures demonstrates that some of our institutions are far from natural features of human life. We shouldn't idealize the circumstances in which hunters and gatherers lived, but the lack of inequalities of wealth and power and the emphasis on cooperation are reminders that the world of modern industrial civilization cannot necessarily be equated with progress.

Pastoral and Agrarian Societies

About fifteen thousand years ago, some hunting and gathering groups started raising domesticated animals and cultivating fixed plots of land as their means of livelihood. **Pastoral societies** relied mainly on domesticated livestock, whereas **agrarian societies** grew crops (practiced agriculture). Some societies had mixed pastoral and agrarian economies.

Depending on the environment, pastoralists reared cattle, sheep, goats, camels, or horses. Some pastoral societies exist in the modern world, especially in areas of Africa, the Middle East, and Central Asia. They are usually found in regions of dense grasslands or in deserts or mountains. Such regions are not amenable to agriculture but may support livestock.

At some point, hunting and gathering groups began to sow their own crops rather than simply to collect those growing in the wild. This practice developed as *horticulture,* in which small gardens were cultivated by the use of simple hoes or digging instruments. Like pastoralism, horticulture provided

TABLE 3.2

Some Agrarian Societies Still Remain

COUNTRY	PERCENT OF WORKFORCE IN AGRICULTURE
Nepal	92.9
Rwanda	90.2
Ethiopia	82.0
Uganda	79.6
China	66.0
Bangladesh	54.7
INDUSTRIALIZED SOCIETIES DIFFER	
Japan	3.8
Australia	4.5
Germany	2.4
Canada	2.3
United States	2.0
United Kingdom	1.8

SOURCE: Earth Trends 2003.

a more reliable food supply than hunting and gathering and therefore could support larger communities. Because they were not on the move, people who practiced horticulture could develop larger stocks of material possessions than people in either hunting and gathering or pastoral communities. Some peoples still rely primarily on horticulture for their livelihood (Table 3.2).

Traditional Societies or Civilizations

From about 6000 B.C.E. onward, we find evidence of societies larger than and different from any that existed before. These societies were based on the development of cities, led

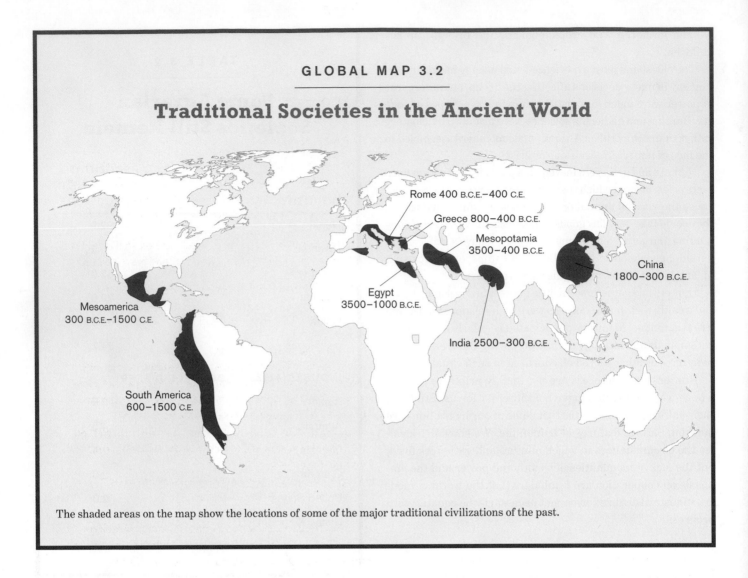

Traditional Societies in the Ancient World

Rome 400 B.C.E.–400 C.E.

Greece 800–400 B.C.E.

Mesopotamia
3500–400 B.C.E.

China
1800–300 B.C.E.

Egypt
3500–1000 B.C.E.

India 2500–300 B.C.E.

Mesoamerica
300 B.C.E.–1500 C.E.

South America
600–1500 C.E.

The shaded areas on the map show the locations of some of the major traditional civilizations of the past.

to pronounced inequalities of wealth and power, and were ruled by kings or emperors. Because writing was present and science and art flourished, these societies are often called *civilizations*.

The earliest civilizations developed in the Middle East, usually in fertile river areas (Global Map 3.2). The Chinese Empire originated in about 1800 B.C.E., at which time powerful states also existed in what are now India and Pakistan. By the fifteenth century, large civilizations also existed in Mexico and Latin America, such as the Aztecs of the Mexican peninsula and the Incas of Peru.

Most traditional (premodern) civilizations were also empires: They conquered and incorporated other peoples (Kautsky 1982). This was true, for instance, of traditional Rome and China. At its height in the first century C.E., the Roman Empire stretched from Britain in northwest Europe to beyond the Middle East. The Chinese Empire covered most of the massive region of eastern Asia now occupied by modern China.

☑ CONCEPT CHECKS

1. Compare the three main types of premodern societies.
2. What transformations led to the development of civilizations?

Societies in the Modern World

What happened to destroy the forms of society that dominated the whole of history up to two centuries ago? The answer, in a word, is **industrialization**—the emergence of machine production based on the use of inanimate power resources (such as steam or electricity). The industrialized, or modern, societies differ in several key respects from any previous type of social

TABLE 3.3

Societies in the Modern World

TYPE	PERIOD OF EXISTENCE	CHARACTERISTICS
Industrialized "First World" societies	Eighteenth century to the present.	Based on industrial production and generally free enterprise. Majority of the population lives in towns and cities; a few live in rural areas and engage in agricultural pursuits. Major class inequalities, though less pronounced than in traditional states. Distinct political communities or nation-states, including the nations of the West, Japan, Australia, and New Zealand.
Communist "Second World" societies	Early twentieth century (following the Russian Revolution of 1917) to early 1990s.	Based on industry, but the economic system is centrally planned. Minority of the population works in agriculture; most live in the towns and cities. Major class inequalities persist. Distinct political communities or nation-states—until 1989, included the Soviet Union and Eastern Europe; but social and political changes began to transform their planned economies in free-enterprise economic systems.
Developing "Third World" societies	Eighteenth century (mostly as colonized areas) to the present.	Based on agricultural production, some of which is sold on world markets; some have free-enterprise systems, others are centrally planned. Majority of the population works in agriculture, using traditional methods of production. Most people live in poverty. Distinct political communities or nation-states, including China, India, and most African and South American nations.
Newly industrializing economies	1970s to the present.	Former developing societies now based on industrial production and generally free enterprise. Majority of the population lives in towns and cities; a few pursue agricultural production for their livelihood. Some have major class inequalities, more pronounced than in industrialized societies. Average per capita income considerably less than in industrialized societies, with the exception of Singapore; includes Hong Kong, South Korea, Singapore, Taiwan, Brazil, and Mexico.

order, and their development has had consequences stretching far beyond their European origins (Table 3.3).

The Industrialized Societies

Industrialization originated in eighteenth-century Britain as a result of the Industrial Revolution, a complex set of technological changes that affected people's means of gaining a livelihood. These changes included the invention of new machines (such as the spinning jenny for creating yarn), the harnessing of power resources (especially water and steam) for production, and the use of science to improve production methods. Because discoveries and inventions in one field lead to more in others, the pace of technological innovation in **industrialized societies** is extremely rapid compared with that of traditional social systems.

In even the most advanced of traditional civilizations, most people worked on the land. By contrast, in industrialized societies today the majority of the employed population works in factories, offices, or shops. And over 90 percent of people live and work in towns and cities. The largest cities are vastly larger than the urban settlements of traditional civilizations. In the cities, social life becomes impersonal and anonymous, and many encounters are with strangers. Large-scale organizations, such as business corporations or government agencies, influence the lives of virtually everyone.

The political systems of modern societies are more developed than forms of government in traditional states; there, monarchs and emperors had little influence on the customs of most of their subjects, who lived in self-contained villages. With industrialization, transportation and communications became much more rapid, promoting a more integrated "national" community.

The industrialized societies were the first **nation-states**: political communities with clearly delimited borders, rather than vague frontier areas that separated traditional states. Nation-state governments have extensive powers over many aspects of citizens' lives, framing laws that apply to all those living within their borders. The United States is a nation-state, as are virtually all other societies in the world today.

The application of industrial technology not only has served peaceful processes of economic development but also has altered ways of waging war, creating weaponry and modes of military organization much more advanced than those of nonindustrial cultures. Together, superior economic strength, political cohesion, and military superiority account for the worldwide spread of Western culture over the past two centuries.

Global Development

From the seventeenth to the early twentieth century, Western countries established colonies in numerous areas previously occupied by traditional societies. Although all these colonies have by now attained independence, the process of **colonialism** helped shape the social map of the globe as we know it today. In some regions, such as North America, Australia, and New Zealand, which were only thinly populated by hunting and gathering or pastoral communities, Europeans became the majority population. In other areas, including much of Asia, Africa, and South America, the local populations remained in the majority.

Societies of the first category, including the United States, have become industrialized. Those in the second category have experienced a much lower level of industrial development and are often referred to as less developed societies, or the **developing world**. Such societies include China, India, most of the African countries (such as Nigeria, Ghana, and Algeria), and countries in South America (such as Brazil, Peru, and Venezuela).

You may hear developing countries referred to as part of the third world. The term **third world** was originally part of a contrast drawn among three main types of society in the early twentieth century. **First world** countries were (and are) the industrialized states of Europe, the United States, Canada, Australasia (Australia, New Zealand, and Melanesia), South Africa, and Japan. Nearly all first world societies have multiparty, parliamentary systems of government. **Second world** societies meant the communist countries of the former Soviet Union (USSR) and Eastern Europe. These countries' centrally planned economies allowed little role for private property or competitive economic enterprise. They were also one-party states, with the Communist party dominating both the political and the economic systems. For some seventy-five years, world history was affected by a global rivalry between the Soviet Union and Eastern European countries on the one hand and the capitalistic societies of the West and Japan on the other. Today that rivalry is over. With the ending of the cold war and the disintegration of communism in the former USSR and Eastern Europe, the second world has disappeared.

Even though the three worlds distinction is still mentioned in sociology textbooks, it has become less relevant to today's world. For one thing, the second world of socialist and communist countries no longer exists, and even exceptions such as China are adopting capitalist economies. More important, the ranking of first, second, and third worlds reflects a value judgment in which "first" means "best" and "third" means "worst," and it is therefore best avoided.

The Developing World

The majority of less developed societies are in areas that underwent colonial rule in Asia, Africa, and South America. A few colonized areas gained independence early, such as Haiti, which became the first autonomous black republic in 1804. The Spanish colonies in South America acquired their freedom in 1810, while Brazil broke away from Portuguese rule in 1822.

Some countries that were never ruled from Europe were nonetheless strongly influenced by colonial relationships. China, for example, was compelled from the seventeenth century on to enter into trading agreements with European powers, which assumed government over certain areas, including major seaports. Hong Kong was the last of these. Most nations in the developing world have become independent states only since World War II—often following bloody anticolonial struggles. Examples include India, which shortly after achieving self-rule split into India and Pakistan; a range of other Asian countries (like Myanmar, Malaysia, and Singapore); and countries in Africa (such as Kenya, Nigeria, the Democratic Republic of Congo, Tanzania, and Algeria).

Although they may include peoples living in traditional fashion, developing countries differ from earlier forms of traditional society. Their political systems, following Western models, make them nation-states. Although most of the population still live in rural areas, a rapid process of city development is occurring. Although agriculture remains the main economic activity, many crops are produced for sale in world markets. Developing countries are not merely societies that have "lagged behind" the more industrialized areas; they have been created by contact with Western industrialism, which has undermined the more traditional systems.

Conditions in the more impoverished societies have deteriorated over the past few years. There are nearly 1.1 billion people living on less than $1 per day and an additional 1.5 billion people living on less than $2 per day (United Nations Development Programme [UNDP] 2005). Some third of the world's poor live in South Asia, in countries such as India, Myanmar, and Cambodia. China, however, has made great strides, reducing by half the number of people living in poverty since 1990. About half of the world's poor (44 percent) are in Africa, where the impoverished population has grown by 100 million people since 1990 (UNDP 2005). However, a substantial proportion lives on the doorstep of the United States—in Central and South America (Global Map 3.3).

Once more, global poverty shouldn't be seen as remote from the concerns of Americans. Whereas in previous generations the bulk of immigrants to the United States came from European countries, most now come from poor, developing societies (Figure 3.1). Recent years have seen waves of Hispanic immigrants, nearly all from Latin America. Some U.S. cities

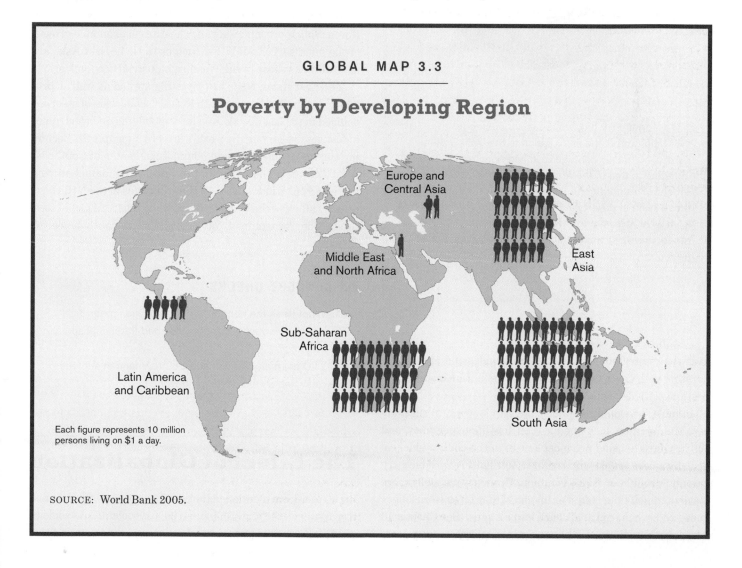

GLOBAL MAP 3.3

Poverty by Developing Region

Each figure represents 10 million persons living on $1 a day.

SOURCE: World Bank 2005.

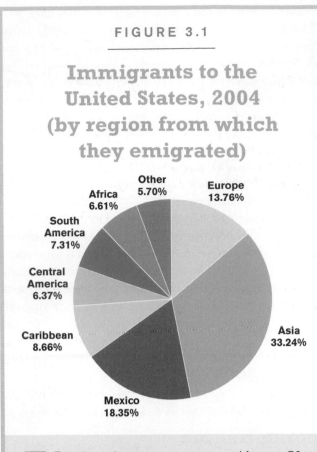

FIGURE 3.1

Immigrants to the United States, 2004 (by region from which they emigrated)

- Other 5.70%
- Africa 6.61%
- Europe 13.76%
- South America 7.31%
- Central America 6.37%
- Caribbean 8.66%
- Asia 33.24%
- Mexico 18.35%

Together, what two areas accounted for over 50 percent of the immigration to the United States? How does the percentage of immigrants from Mexico compare to that of the rest of Central and South America? According to the reading, almost half of those living in poverty in the United States immigrated from what region of the world? How does the most recent wave of immigration to the United States differ from previous generations?

SOURCE: Department of Homeland Security 2004.

The poor in developing countries live in conditions almost unimaginable to Americans. Many have no permanent dwellings apart from shelters made of cartons or loose pieces of wood. Most have no running water, sewer systems, or electricity. Nonetheless, millions of poor people also live in the United States, and there are connections between poverty in America and global poverty. Almost half of the impoverished people in the United States immigrated from developing countries. This is true of the descendants of the black slaves brought over by force centuries ago, and it is true of more recent, and willing, immigrants who have arrived from Latin America, Asia, and elsewhere.

The Newly Industrializing Economies

Some developing countries have successfully embarked on a process of industrialization. Referred to as **newly industrializing economies (NIEs)**, they include Brazil, Mexico, South Korea, Singapore, and Taiwan. The rates of economic growth of the most successful NIEs, such as those in East Asia, are several times those of the Western industrial economies.

The East Asian NIEs are investing abroad as well as promoting growth at home. South Korea's production of steel has doubled in the last decade, and its shipbuilding and electronics industries are among the world's leaders. Singapore is becoming the major financial and commercial center of Southeast Asia. Taiwan is an important presence in the manufacturing and electronics industries. All these changes in the NIEs have directly affected the United States, whose share of global steel production, for example, has dropped significantly since the 1970s.

☑ CONCEPT CHECKS

1. What does the concept *industrialization* mean?
2. How has industrialization weakened traditional social systems?
3. Why are many African and South American societies classified as the developing world?

near their entry points, such as Los Angeles and Miami, are bursting with new immigrants and also maintain trading connections with developing countries.

In most developing societies, poverty is worst in rural areas. Malnutrition, lack of education, low life expectancy, and substandard housing are most severe in the countryside, especially where arable land is scarce, agricultural productivity low, and drought or floods common. Women are usually more disadvantaged than men. For instance, they often work longer hours and, when paid at all, earn lower wages. (See Chapter 10 for a lengthier discussion of gender inequality.)

The Effect of Globalization

In Chapter 1, we mentioned that the focus of sociology has historically been the study of industrialized societies. As sociologists, can we thus ignore the developing world, leaving this as the domain of anthropology? We certainly cannot. The industrialized and the developing societies overlapped in their development and are today more closely related than ever before. Those of us living in industrialized societies depend on many raw materials and manufactured products coming from developing countries. Conversely, the economies of most developing states depend on trading networks with the industrialized countries. We can fully understand the industrialized order only against the backdrop of societies in the developing world—where most of the world's population live.

As the world rapidly moves toward a single, unified economy, businesses and people move about the globe in increasing numbers in search of new markets and economic opportunities. As a result, the cultural map of the world changes: Networks of peoples span national borders and continents, providing cultural connections between their birthplaces and their adoptive countries (Appadurai 1986). A handful of languages dominate, and in some cases replace, the thousands of languages that were once spoken on the planet.

It is increasingly impossible for cultures to exist as islands. Few, if any, places on earth can escape radio, television, air travel—and its throngs of tourists—or the computer. A generation ago, some tribes' ways of life were untouched by the rest of the world. Today these peoples use tools made in the United States or Japan, wear clothing manufactured in the Dominican Republic or Guatemala, and take medicine manufactured in Germany or Switzerland to combat diseases contracted through contact with outsiders. Within a generation or two, all the world's once-isolated cultures will be touched by global culture, despite their efforts to preserve their age-old ways of life.

Two African American children play near their home and an open sewer. This poverty-stricken area of Tunica, Mississippi, is sometimes referred to as "Sugarditch."

The forces that produce a global culture are discussed throughout this book. These include

- Television, which brings U.S. culture into homes throughout the world daily and which adapts other cultural products for the U.S. audience
- The emergence of a unified global economy, with businesses whose factories, management structures, and markets span continents and countries
- "Global citizens," such as managers of large corporations, who may spend so much time crisscrossing the globe that they identify with a global, cosmopolitan culture rather than with their own nation's culture
- A host of international organizations—including UN agencies, regional trade and mutual defense associations,

Due to extreme poverty and the lack of land in El Salvador, many Salvadorans are forced to make their homes in public cemeteries.

Two Masai natives in Africa proudly display T-shirts bearing the logos of American football teams. There is almost no place on earth untouched by the globalization of culture.

multinational banks and other global financial institutions, international labor and health organizations, and global tariff and trade agreements—that are creating a global political, legal, and military framework

- Electronic communications (telephone, fax, e-mail, the Internet, and the World Wide Web), which make instantaneous communication with almost any part of the planet an integral part of daily life in the business world

Does the Internet Promote a Global Culture?

Many believe that the rapid worldwide growth of the Internet will hasten the spread of a global culture resembling the cultures of Europe and North America (Global Map 3.4). Belief in such values as equality between men and women, the right to speak freely, democratic participation in government, and the pursuit of pleasure through consumption are diffused throughout the world over the Internet. Moreover, Internet technology itself seems to foster such values: Global communication, seemingly unlimited (and uncensored) information, and instant gratification all characterize the new technology.

Yet it may be premature to conclude that the Internet will sweep aside traditional cultures. Evidence shows that it is in many ways compatible with traditional cultural values, perhaps even a means of strengthening them.

Consider the Middle Eastern country of Kuwait, a traditional Islamic culture that has recently experienced strong American and European influences. Kuwait, an oil-rich country on the Persian Gulf, has one of the highest average per-person incomes in the world. The government provides free public education through the university level, resulting in high rates of literacy and education for both men and women.

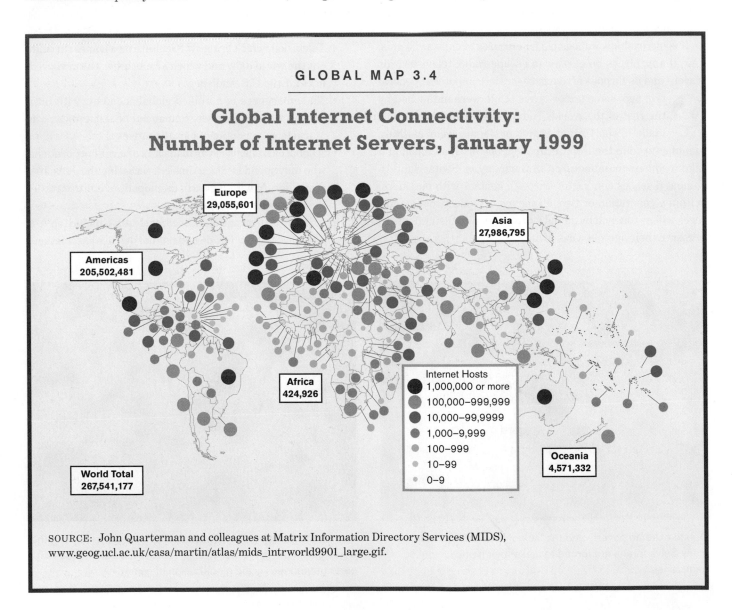

GLOBAL MAP 3.4

Global Internet Connectivity: Number of Internet Servers, January 1999

Europe
29,055,601

Asia
27,986,795

Americas
205,502,481

Africa
424,926

Internet Hosts
- 1,000,000 or more
- 100,000–999,999
- 10,000–99,9999
- 1,000–9,999
- 100–999
- 10–99
- 0–9

Oceania
4,571,332

World Total
267,541,177

SOURCE: John Quarterman and colleagues at Matrix Information Directory Services (MIDS), www.geog.ucl.ac.uk/casa/martin/atlas/mids_intrworld9901_large.gif.

Kuwaiti television frequently carries National Football League games and other U.S. programming, although broadcasts are regularly interrupted for the traditional Muslim calls to prayer. Half of Kuwait's approximately two million people are under twenty-five years old; like their youthful counterparts in Europe and North America, many surf the Internet for new ideas, information, and consumer products.

Although Kuwait is in many respects a modern country, Kuwaiti law treats men and women differently. Legally, women have equal access to education and employment, yet they are barred from voting or running for political office. Cultural norms treating men and women differently are almost as strong: Women are expected to wear traditional clothing that leaves only the face and hands visible, and they are forbidden to leave home at night or be seen in public at any time with a man who is not a spouse or relative.

Deborah Wheeler (1998) spent a year studying the effect of the Internet on Kuwaiti culture. She reports that Kuwaiti teenagers are flocking to Internet cafés, where they spend time in chat rooms or visiting pornographic sites—two activities frowned on by traditional Islamic culture. According to Wheeler (1998),

> Many young people told me of encounters they were having with the opposite sex in cyberspace. There are even keyboard symbols for kisses (*), kisses on the lips (:*), and embarrassed giggles (LOL)—all those interactions and reactions that make courtship exciting and, in this case, safe.

The new communications technologies are clearly enabling men and women to talk with each other in a society that restricts such communications outside marriage. Wheeler also notes that ironically men and women are segregated in the Internet cafés. Furthermore, she finds that Kuwaitis are reluctant to voice strong opinions or political views online. With the exception of discussing conservative Islamic religious beliefs, which are freely disseminated over the Internet, Kuwaitis are remarkably inhibited online. Wheeler (1998) attributes this to the cultural belief that giving out too much information about oneself is dangerous:

> In Kuwait, information is more of a potential threat than a means for individual empowerment. It is a weapon to use against your enemies, a tool for keeping conformity, or a reinforcement of regulations of daily life. . . . Kuwait's transition to the information age is influenced by these attitudes and the desire to keep one's reputation protected.

Wheeler concludes that Kuwaiti culture, which is hundreds of years old, will not likely be transformed by simple exposure to different beliefs and values on the Internet. The fact that young people participate in global chat rooms does not mean that Kuwaiti culture is adopting American sexual attitudes or even Western-type relations between men and women. The culture that emerges as a result of the new technologies will not be the same as American culture; it will be uniquely Kuwaiti.

Globalization and Local Cultures

The world has become a single *social system* as a result of growing ties of interdependence, both social and economic, that affect everyone. But it would be a mistake to think of increasing globalization simply as the growth of world unity. Rather, it is primarily the reordering of *time and distance* in social life as our lives are increasingly influenced by events far removed from our everyday activities.

Globalizing processes have brought many benefits to Americans, such as a much greater variety of goods and foodstuffs. At the same time, those processes have helped create some of the most serious problems American society faces, such as the threat of terrorism.

The growing global culture has provoked numerous reactions at the local level. Many local cultures remain strong or are experiencing rejuvenation, partly out of the concern that a global culture, dominated by North American and European cultural values, will corrupt the local culture. For example, the Islamic Taliban movement in Afghanistan sought to impose traditional, tribal values

Using the Internet to connect with the world around them is common among young people across cultures. Here, an Iranian girl at a Tehran Internet café reads the latest news on the Iraq crisis.

throughout the country by banning music, closing movie theaters, abolishing the use of alcohol, requiring men to gro w full beards, and forbidding women to work outside their homes or be seen in public with men who were not their spouses or relatives. Violations of these rules were severely punished, sometimes by death. The rise of the Taliban can be understood partly as a rejection of the spread of Western culture.

The resurgence of local cultures is evident in the rise of **nationalism**, a sense of identification with one's people expressed through a common set of strongly held beliefs. Nationalism can be highly political, involving attempts to assert the power of a nation based on a shared ethnic or racial identity over people of a different ethnicity or race. The strife in the former Yugoslavia, as well as parts of Africa and the former Soviet Union, bear tragic witness to the power of nationalism. The world of the twenty-first century may well witness responses to globalization that celebrate ethnocentric nationalist beliefs, promoting intolerance and hatred rather than acceptance of diversity.

New nationalisms, cultural identities, and religious prac tices are constantly being forged throughout the world. When you socialize with students from the same cultural background or celebrate traditional holidays with friends and family, you are sustaining your culture. The very technology that helps foster globalization also supports local cultures: The Internet enables you to communicate with others who share your cultural identity, even when they are dispersed around the world. A casual search of the Web reveals thousands of pages devoted to different cultures and subcultures.

Although sociologists do not fully understand these processes, they often conclude that despite the powerful forces of globalization, local cultures remain strong. But it is too soon to tell whether and how globalization will result in the homogenization of the world's cultures, the flourishing of many individual cultures, or both.

☑ CONCEPT CHECKS

1. How does global culture influence local cultures?
2. How is the Internet transforming local cultures?

Study Outline

www.wwnorton.com/studyspace

The Sociological Study of Culture

- Culture consists of the values held by a given group, the norms they follow, and the material goods they create.
- The sociology of culture has attracted renewed interest, a phenomenon known as the cultural turn. Attention focuses on culture as a set of scripts that shape our beliefs, values, and actions and on the many meanings of cultural symbols.

The Development of Human Culture

- Human cultures, which evolved over thousands of years, reflect both human biology and the physical environment in which the cultures emerged. A defining feature of humankind is its inventiveness in creating new forms of culture.
- Most sociologists acknowledge that biology helps shape human behavior, especially through the interaction between biology and culture. Sociologists' main concern, however, is with how behavior is learned from the individual's interaction with society.
- Forms of behavior found in virtually all cultures are called cultural universals. Language, the prohibition against incest, institutions of marriage, the family, religion, and property are the main types of cultural universals—but within these categories are many variations in values and behaviors among societies.
- We live in a world of symbols, or representations, and one of the most important forms of symbolization is language. The linguistic relativity hypothesis argues that language influences perception. Language is also an important source of cultural continuity, and the members of a culture are often passionate about their linguistic heritage.
- Cultural diversity is a chief aspect of modern culture; in the United States it is evident in the large number of subcultures as well as in countercultures. Although some people advocate assimilating subcultures into one mainstream culture, others favor multiculturalism.
- Sociologists avoid ethnocentrism and instead adopt a stance of cultural relativism, attempting to understand a society relative to its own cultural norms and values.

Premodern Societies

- There are several types of premodern society. In hunting and gathering societies, people gain their livelihood from gathering plants and hunting animals. In pastoral societies, people raise domesticated animals as their major source of subsistence. Agrarian societies depend on the cultivation of fixed plots of land. Larger, more developed, urban societies form traditional states or civilizations.

Societies in the Modern World

- The development of industrialized societies and the expansion of the West led to the conquest of many parts of the world through colonialism, which radically changed long-established social systems and cultures.
- In industrialized societies, industrial production (whose techniques are also used in the production of food) is the basis of the economy. Industrialized countries include the nations of the West, plus Japan, Australia, and New Zealand. They now include industrialized societies ruled by communist governments. The developing world, where most of the world's population live, is almost all formerly colonized areas. The majority of the population works in agricultural production, some of which supplies world markets.

The Effect of Globalization

- Increased global communications and economic interdependence represent more than the growth of world unity. Time and distance are being reorganized in ways that bring us all closer together; but even as globalization threatens to make all cultures seem alike, local cultural identifications are resurging. This is evident in the rise of nationalism, which can result in ethnic conflict as well as ethnic pride.

Key Concepts

agrarian societies (p. 73)
assimilation (p. 64)
colonialism (p. 76)
cultural relativism (p. 66)
cultural turn (p. 57)
cultural universals (p. 68)
culture (p. 54)
developing world (p. 76)
ethnocentrism (p. 66)
first world (p. 76)
hunting and gathering societies (p. 71)
industrialization (p. 74)
industrialized societies (p. 75)
instincts (p. 61)
language (p. 68)
linguistic relativity hypothesis (p. 68)
marriage (p. 68)
material goods (p. 54)
multiculturalism (p. 64)
nationalism (p. 82)
nation-states (p. 76)
newly industrializing economies (NIEs) (p. 78)
norms (p. 54)

pastoral societies (p. 73)
second world (p. 76)
semiotics (p. 70)
signifier (p. 69)
society (p. 56)
sociobiology (p. 59)
subcultures (p. 63)
third world (p. 76)
values (p. 54)

Review Questions

1. What are the main elements of a culture? Give an example of each element from your own cultural group.
2. How does culture instill a willingness to conform among its members?
3. How do sociologists address the nature/nurture debate?
4. Describe three ways subcultures develop. Discuss them in relation to a subcultural group of which you are a part.
5. Compare and contrast assimilationist and multicultural models of cultural integration.
6. Compare and contrast ethnocentrism and cultural relativism. Which stance do sociologists strive to adopt and what are the difficulties associated with that position?
7. What are the three main categories of premodern societies? List some of the characteristics of each.
8. Describe some of the changes brought about by industrialization.
9. What forces produce global culture?
10. What challenges and opportunities does globalization pose for cultural diversity?

Thinking Sociologically Exercises

1. Mention at least two cultural traits that you would claim are universals; mention two others you would claim are culturally specific traits. Use case study materials from different societies to show the differences between universal and specific cultural traits. Are the cultural universals you have discussed derivatives of human instincts? Explain your answer.
2. What does it mean to be ethnocentric? How is ethnocentrism dangerous in conducting social research? How is ethnocentrism problematic among nonresearchers in their everyday lives?

Learning Objectives

Culture, Society, and Child Socialization

Learn about socialization (including gender socialization) and the most important agents of socialization.

Socialization through the Life Course

Learn the stages of the life course and see the similarities and differences among cultures.

CHAPTER FOUR

SOCIALIZATION AND THE LIFE CYCLE

t the start of J. K. Rowling's first Harry Potter adventure, *Harry Potter and the Sorcerer's Stone*, the wizard Albus Dumbledore leaves Harry, an orphaned infant, at the doorstep of Harry's nonmagician (or "Muggle") uncle and aunt's house. Harry has already shown unique powers, but Dumbledore is concerned that if left in the wizarding world, Harry won't mature healthily. "It would be enough to turn any boy's head," he says. "Famous before he can walk and talk! Famous for something he won't even remember. Can't you see how much better off he'll be, growing up away from all that until he's ready to take it?" (Rowling 1998).

The Harry Potter novels are based on the premise that there is no adventure greater than that of growing up. Although Harry attends the Hogwarts School of Witchcraft and Wizardry, it's still a school, because everyone, even a young wizard with limitless power, needs help developing a set of values. We all pass through important life stages: from childhood to adolescence and then to adulthood. So, for example, as the Harry Potter series progresses, Harry feels the onset of sexual urges, to which he responds with a common awkwardness. Because sports help children learn about camaraderie and ambition, Harry plays the wizard sport Quidditch. Rowling uses the paranormal to help us see the enchanting complexities behind the fundamentals of everyday life. In her universe, owls deliver letters; is this really any stranger than the postal system or e-mail? The function of all classic children's stories is to make the process of growing up more understandable, whether they're set in a fairy-tale universe, our own world, or—as with the Harry Potter series—both.

Socialization is the process whereby the helpless infant gradually becomes a self-aware, knowledgeable person, skilled in the ways of his or her culture. Socialization among the young contributes to **social reproduction**—the process whereby societies have structural continuity over time. During socialization, especially in the early years, children learn the ways of their elders, thereby perpetuating their values, norms, and social practices. All societies have characteristics that endure over time, even though their members change as individuals are born and die. American society, for example, has many distinctive social and cultural characteristics that have persisted for generations—such as the fact that English is the main language spoken.

Socialization connects different generations to one another (Turnbull 1983). The birth of a child alters the lives of those who are responsible for its upbringing—who themselves therefore undergo new learning experiences. Older people still remain parents when they become grandparents, of course, thus forging another set of relationships connecting the generations. Although cultural learning is much more intense in infancy and early childhood than later, learning and adjustment go on through the whole life cycle.

In the sections to follow, we continue the theme of nature interacting with nurture, introduced in the previous chapter. We first analyze human development from infancy to early childhood, identifying the main stages of change. Different writers have offered a number of theoretical interpretations about how and why children develop as they do, and we describe and compare these, including theories that explain how people develop gender identities. Finally, we discuss the main groups and social contexts that influence socialization during the various phases of life.

Culture, Society, and Child Socialization

"Unsocialized" Children

What would children be like if they were raised without the influence of adults? Obviously no humane person could bring up a child away from social influence. There are, however, a number of much-discussed cases of children who spent their early years without normal human contact.

On January 9, 1800, a strange creature emerged from the woods near the village of Saint-Serin in southern France. In spite of walking erect, he looked more animal than human, although he was soon identified as a boy of about eleven or twelve. He spoke in shrill, strange-sounding cries. The boy had no sense of personal hygiene and relieved himself where and when he chose. He was taken to a nearby orphanage. In the beginning he tried constantly to escape and was only recaptured with difficulty. He refused to wear clothes, tearing them off as soon as they were put on him. No parents ever came forward to claim him.

A thorough medical examination of the child showed no major physical abnormalities. On being shown a mirror, he seemingly saw an image but did not recognize himself. On one occasion, he tried to reach through the mirror to seize a potato he saw in it. (The potato was being held behind his head.) After several attempts, without turning his head, he took the potato by reaching back over his shoulder. A priest who was observing the boy daily and who described this incident wrote: "All these little details, and many others we could add prove that this child is not totally without intelligence, reflection, and reasoning power. However, we are obliged to say that, in every case not concerned with his natural needs or satisfying his appetite, one can perceive in him only animal behavior. If he has sensations, they give birth to no idea. He cannot even compare them with one another. One would think that there is no connection between his soul or mind and his body" (quoted in Shattuck 1980; see also Lane 1976).

Later the boy was moved to Paris and an attempt was made to change him "from beast to human." The endeavor was only partly successful. He was toilet trained, accepted clothes, and learned to dress himself. Yet he was uninterested in toys or games and never learned or spoke more than a few words. So far as anyone could tell, on the basis of detailed descriptions of his behavior and reactions, he was not mentally retarded. He seemed either unwilling or unable to master human speech fully. He made little further progress and died in 1828.

No one knows how long the wild boy of Aveyron lived on his own in the woods or whether he had a congenital defect that prevented him from developing like a normal human being. However, more recent examples reinforce some of the observations made about his behavior. Consider Genie, a California girl who was locked in a room when she was about one and a half until she was over thirteen. Genie's father kept his wife, who was going blind, confined to the house. The

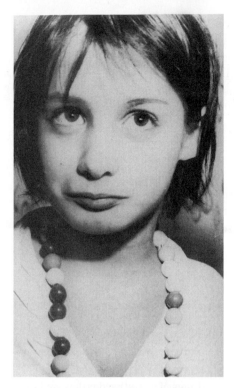

This is the only photograph of Genie to appear in the press on her discovery in 1970. Having been deprived of almost all human contact for the first thirteen years of her life, Genie provided some sense of what an unsocialized child would be like.

main connection between the family and the outside world was through a teenage son, who attended school and did the shopping.

Genie had a hip defect from birth that prevented her from walking properly. Her father frequently beat her. When Genie was twenty months old, her father apparently decided she was retarded and put her away in a closed room with the curtains drawn and the door shut. She stayed there for the next eleven years, seeing other family members only when they came to feed her. Genie had not been toilet trained and spent part of her time harnessed, naked, to a toddler's potty chair. Sometimes at night she was put into another restraining garment, a sleeping bag within which her arms were imprisoned. Tied up in this way, she was also enclosed in an infant's crib with wire-mesh sides and a mesh cover. She had almost no opportunity to overhear any conversation between others in the house. If she attempted to make a noise or to attract attention, her father would beat her. He never spoke to her, but instead made barking sounds if she did anything to annoy him. She had no toys or other objects to occupy her time.

In 1970, the mother escaped from the house, taking Genie with her. The girl's condition came to the notice of a social worker, and she was placed in the rehabilitation ward

of a children's hospital. When first admitted, she could not stand erect; could not run, jump, or climb; and walked only in a shuffling, clumsy fashion. A psychiatrist described her as "unsocialized, primitive, hardly human." Once in a rehabilitation ward, however, Genie learned to eat normally, was toilet trained, and tolerated being dressed like other children. Yet she was silent almost all of the time, except when she gave a high-pitched and unreal laugh. She masturbated constantly in public. Later she lived as a foster child in the home of one of the doctors from the hospital. She gradually developed a fairly wide vocabulary and could make a number of basic utterances, but her mastery of language never progressed beyond that of a three- or four-year-old.

Genie was studied intensively and was tested over seven years. The tests indicated that she was not retarded, nor did she have other congenital defects. What seems to have happened to Genie, as to the wild boy of Aveyron, is that by the time she came into close human contact, she had grown beyond the age at which children readily learn language and other human skills. The wild boy and Genie provide some sense of what an unsocialized child would be like. Each retained many "nonhuman" responses. Yet, in spite of their deprivations, neither displayed any lasting viciousness. They responded quickly to others who treated them sympathetically and were able to acquire a minimum level of ordinary human capabilities.

Of course, we have to be cautious about interpreting cases of this sort. In each example, it is possible that there was an undiagnosed mental abnormality. Alternatively, the children's experiences may have inflicted psychological damage that prevented them from gaining the skills most children acquire at a much earlier age. Yet there is sufficient similarity between these two case histories, and others that have been recorded, to suggest how limited our faculties would be without an extended period of early socialization.

Theories of Child Development

One of the most distinctive features of human beings, compared with other animals, is that humans are *self-aware*. How should we understand the emergence of a sense of self—the awareness that the individual has a distinct identity separate from others? During the first months of life, the infant possesses little or no understanding of differences between human beings and material objects and has no awareness of self. Children do not grasp concepts such as *I, me,* and *you* until the age of two or after. Only gradually do they understand that others have distinct identities, consciousness, and needs separate from their own.

The problem of the emergence of self is much debated among contrasting theoretical perspectives. To some extent, this is because the most prominent theories about child development emphasize different aspects of socialization. The American philosopher and sociologist George Herbert Mead mainly considered how children learn to use the concepts of *I* and *me*. Jean Piaget, the Swiss student of child behavior, studied many aspects of child development, but his best-known writings concern **cognition**—the ways in which children learn to *think* about themselves and their environment.

G. H. MEAD AND THE DEVELOPMENT OF SELF

Because Mead's ideas underlie a general tradition of theoretical thinking, *symbolic interactionism,* they have had a broad impact in sociology. Symbolic interactionism emphasizes that interaction between human beings occurs through symbols and the interpretation of meanings (see Chapter 1). But Mead's work also describes the main phases of child development, concentrating on the emergence of a sense of self.

According to Mead, infants and young children develop as social beings by imitating the actions of those around them. Play is one way in which this occurs. A small child will make mud pies, having seen an adult cooking, or dig with a spoon, having observed someone gardening. Children's play evolves from simple imitation to more complicated games in which a child of four or five years old will act out an adult role. Mead called this "taking the role of the other." It is only at this stage that children acquire a developed sense of self. Children achieve an understanding of themselves as separate agents—as a "me"—by seeing themselves through the eyes of others.

Using their toy wheelbarrows to help their father with the gardening, these boys are, according to Mead, "taking on the role of the other" and achieving an understanding of themselves as separate social agents.

We achieve self-awareness, according to Mead, when we learn to distinguish the *me* from the *I*. The *I* is the unsocialized infant, a bundle of spontaneous wants and desires. The *me* is the **social self**. Individuals develop **self-consciousness**, Mead argued, by coming to see themselves as others see them. A further stage of child development occurs when the child is eight or nine years old, the age at which children take part in organized games rather than unsystematic play. At this period children begin to understand the *values* and *morality* that govern social life. To learn organized games, children must understand the rules of play and notions of fairness and equal participation. Children at this stage learn to grasp what Mead termed the **generalized other**—the general values and moral rules of the culture in which they are developing.

JEAN PIAGET AND THE STAGES OF COGNITIVE DEVELOPMENT

Piaget emphasized the child's active capability to make sense of the world. Children do not passively soak up information, but instead select and interpret what they see, hear, and feel. Piaget described distinct stages of cognitive development during which children learn to think about themselves and their environment. Each stage involves the acquisition of new skills and depends on the successful completion of the preceding one.

Piaget called the first stage, from birth up to about age two, the **sensorimotor stage**, because infants learn mainly by touching objects, manipulating them, and physically exploring their environment. Until age four months or so, infants cannot differentiate themselves from their environment. For example, a child will not realize that her own movements cause the sides of her crib to rattle. Objects are not differentiated from persons, and the infant is unaware that anything exists outside her range of vision. Infants gradually learn to distinguish people from objects, realizing that both have an existence independent of their immediate perceptions. The main accomplishment of this stage is children's understanding that their environment has distinct and stable properties.

The next phase, the **preoperational stage**, is the one to which Piaget devoted the bulk of his research. During this stage, which lasts from age two to seven, children master language and use words to represent objects and images in a symbolic fashion. A four-year-old might use a sweeping hand, for example, to represent the concept *airplane*. Piaget termed the stage "preoperational" because children are not yet able to use their developing mental capabilities systematically. Children in this stage are **egocentric** in the sense that they interpret the world exclusively in terms of their own position. The child does not understand, for instance, that others see objects from a different perspective. Holding a book upright, the child may ask about a picture in it, not realizing that the person sitting opposite can see only the back of the book.

Children at the preoperational stage are not able to hold connected conversations with another. In egocentric speech, what each child says is more or less unrelated to what the other speaker said. Children talk together, but not *to* one another in the same sense as adults. During this stage, children have no general understanding of categories of thought that adults take for granted: concepts such as causality, speed, weight, or number. Even if the child sees water poured from a tall, thin container into a shorter, wider one, she will not understand that the volume of water remains the same—and she will conclude that there is less water because the water level is lower.

A third period, the **concrete operational stage**, lasts from age seven to eleven. During this phase, children master abstract, logical notions such as causality. A child at this stage of development will recognize the false reasoning involved in the idea that the wide container holds less water than the thin, narrow one, even though the water levels are different. The child becomes capable of carrying out the mathematical operations of multiplying, dividing, and subtracting. Children by this stage are much less egocentric. In the preoperational stage, if a girl is asked, "How many sisters do you have?" she may correctly answer, "One." But if asked, "How many sisters does your sister have?" she will probably answer, "None," because she cannot see herself from the point of view of her sister. The concrete operational child can easily answer such a question.

The years from eleven to fifteen cover the **formal operational stage**. During adolescence, the developing child becomes able to grasp highly abstract and hypothetical ideas. When faced with a problem, children at this stage are able to review all the possible ways of solving it and go through them theoretically to reach a solution. The young person at the formal operational stage can understand why some questions are trick ones. To the question, "What creatures are both poodles and dogs?" the individual might not be able to give the correct reply but will understand why the answer "poodles" is right and appreciate the humor in it.

According to Piaget, the first three stages of development are universal; but not all adults reach the formal operational stage. The development of formal operational thought depends in part on processes of schooling. Adults of limited educational attainment tend to continue to think in more concrete terms and retain large traces of egocentrism.

Agents of Socialization

Sociologists often speak of socialization as occurring in two broad phases, involving numerous **agents of socialization**— that is, groups or social contexts in which significant processes of socialization occur. Primary socialization, which occurs in infancy and childhood, is the most intense period of cultural learning. It is the time when children learn language and basic behavioral patterns that form the foundation for later learning. The family is the main agent of socialization during this phase. Secondary socialization occurs later in childhood and in maturity. In this phase, other agents of socialization such as schools, peer groups, organizations, the media, and the workplace become socializing forces. Social interactions in these contexts help people learn the values, norms, and beliefs of their culture.

THE FAMILY

Because family systems vary widely, the infant's range of family contacts is not standard across cultures. The mother everywhere is normally the most important individual in the child's early life, but the nature of relationships between mothers and their children is influenced by the form and regularity of their contact. This is, in turn, conditioned by the character of family institutions and their relation to other groups in society.

In modern societies, most early socialization occurs within a small-scale family context. Most American children grow up within a domestic unit containing mother, father, and perhaps one or two other children. In many other cultures, by contrast, aunts, uncles, and grandparents are part of a single household and serve as caretakers even for very young infants. Yet even within American society there are variations in family contexts. Some children grow up in single-parent households; some have two mothering and fathering agents (divorced parents and stepparents). Many women with families are employed outside the home and return to their paid work soon after the births of their children. In spite of these variations, the family normally remains the major agent of socialization from infancy to adolescence and beyond—in a sequence of development connecting the generations.

Families have varying "locations" within the overall institutions of a society. In most traditional societies, the family into which a person was born determined the individual's lifelong social position. In modern societies, social position is not inherited at birth, yet the region and social class of the family affects patterns of socialization distinctly. Children pick up ways of behavior characteristic of their parents or others in their neighborhood or community.

Varying patterns of child rearing and discipline, together with contrasting values and expectations, are found in different sectors of large-scale societies. It is easy to understand the differing influence of family background if we imagine the life of, say, a child growing up in a poor black family living in a rundown city neighborhood compared to one born into an affluent white family living in an all-white suburb (Kohn 1977).

"Does Day Care Make Kids Behave Badly? Study Says Yes"

Working parents couldn't help but feel a tinge of guilt and self-doubt after picking up the daily newspaper in March 2007. Nearly every major newspaper, television network, and news Web site blazed headlines like "Child Care Tied to Behavior Problems" (Zwillich 2007) or "The Trouble with Day Care" (Lang 2007). These news stories cautioned nervous parents that children who spent considerable time in day care would go on to have more serious behavior problems—like getting into fights, arguing, and being disobedient—by the time they reached sixth grade.

Many parents wrestled with the tough question, Should I pull my child out of day care? while conservative pundits used the headlines to bolster their arguments that mothers should remain in the home rather than work for pay. Yet many social scientists

responded to the headlines by urging parents and policy makers to look beyond the sound byte that "child care hurts" and to instead ask themselves what the study *really* found. The study was based on data from the National Institute of Child Health and Human Development (NICHD) Study of Early Child Care and Youth Development, the nation's longest-running study of child care in the United States. The researchers, led by Dr. Jay Belsky of Birkbeck University of London, tracked more than 1,300 children from birth through sixth grade. They collected detailed data on how the children were cared for and what proportion of their lives they had spent in a variety of different care settings. The study's authors were particularly interested in comparing children who were cared for by relatives, by nonrelatives, and by paid child care providers. They also measured the "quality" of the care received, based on periodic observations of the child care centers. They examined whether the site, duration, and quality of care were associated with a variety of child outcomes, including performance on vocabulary tests, social skills, work habits, emotional adjustment, behavior problems, and relationships with their school teachers.

Of course, few children unquestioningly adopt their parents' outlook. This is especially true in the modern world, in which change is pervasive. Moreover, the very existence of a range of socializing agents in modern societies leads to divergences among the outlooks of children, adolescents, and parents.

SCHOOLS

Another important socializing agent is the school. Schooling is a formal process: Students pursue a definite curriculum of subjects. Yet schools are agents of socialization in more subtle respects. Children must be quiet in class, be punctual at lessons, and observe rules of discipline. They must accept the authority of the teaching staff. Reactions of teachers also affect the expectations children have of themselves, which in turn become linked to their job experience when they leave school. Peer groups are often formed at school, and the system of age-based classes reinforces their influence.

PEER RELATIONSHIPS

The **peer group** consists of individuals of a similar age. In some cultures, particularly small traditional societies, peer groups are formalized as **age-grades** (normally confined to males), with ceremonies or rites that mark the transition from one age-grade to another. Those within a particular age-grade

Belsky and his colleagues did indeed find that children who spent more time in child-care centers had more behavior problems in elementary school, even after the researchers "held constant" or statistically controlled for other possible risk factors for problematic behaviors, such as parents' socioeconomic resources and mental health. However, the researchers did not jump to the conclusion that child care "caused" behavior problems. Rather, they honestly noted that the effect sizes were very modest; that is, the differences in behavior problems between those children in child care versus family care were quite small.

Moreover, the scientists believed that several of their other findings were much more important. First, they found that children who were in high-quality child-care settings went on to have higher vocabulary scores than other children. Second, they found that the quality of parenting mattered much more than where a child was cared for. The authors wrote that *"parenting quality* significantly predicted all the developmental outcomes and much more strongly than did any of the *child care predictors."* One reason why parents matter more than child-care arrangement is that they are an enduring presence in the children's lives, while day care is often just a short-term experience.

As Belsky and his coauthors noted, "most children…experienced multiple different classrooms and after-school arrangements subsequent to school entry. In comparison, family experiences and parenting were relatively stable."

If the study author himself admitted that child care had only a modest effect, and it was the quality of parenting that mattered for children's well-being, then why did so many TV news anchors caution parents that child care was bad? Many sociologists believe that Belsky's research findings may not have appeared very exciting, so media outlets chose to highlight the more contentious, though less powerful, findings of the study. The media's selective presentation of Belsky's research offers important lessons to sociology students, and highlights questions that every student should ask when the results of a "pathbreaking" new study pop up on Internet news sites each day. This case reveals the important questions that students should ask when they read about a new social science study in the media.

Questions

- According to the researchers, what is their study's most important finding or "strongest" effect?

- What finding did most journalists focus on?
- What do you think accounts for the difference between the journalists' and researchers' portrayals of the study findings?
- What criteria do you think reporters should use when selecting research findings to present in their news articles?

FOR FURTHER EXPLORATION

Belsky, Jay, Deborah Lowe Vandell, Margaret Burchinal, K. Alison Clarke-Stewart, Kathleen McCartney, Margaret Tresch Owen, NICHD Early Child Care Research Network. 2007. "Are There Long-Term Effects of Early Child Care?" *Child Development* 78(2): 681–701.

Lang, Heide. 2007. "The Trouble with Day Care: Are Researchers Telling Parents the Whole Truth about Day Care? The Verdict Isn't Good and Parents Won't Like It." *Psychology Today* (May).

Zwillich, Todd. 2007. "Child Care Tied to Behavior Problems, but Vocabulary Benefits Seen from High-Quality Care, Say Researchers." www.webmd.com/parenting/news/20070327/child-care-tied-to-behavior-problems (accessed June 20, 2007).

generally maintain close connections throughout their lives. A typical set of age-grades consists of childhood, junior warriorhood, senior warriorhood, junior elderhood, and senior elderhood. Men move through these grades not as individuals, but as whole groups.

Although the family's importance in socialization is obvious, it is less apparent, especially in Western societies, how significant peer groups are. Yet even without formal age-grades, children over the age of four or five usually spend a great deal of time in the company of friends the same age. Given the high proportion of women now in the workforce whose children play together in day-care centers, peer relations are even more important today than before (Corsaro 1997; Harris 1998).

In her book *Gender Play* (1993), the sociologist Barrie Thorne explored how children learn what it means to be male and female (you will learn three classic theories of gender socialization later in this chapter). Rather than seeing children as passively learning the meaning of gender from their parents and teachers, she examined how children actively create and re-create the meaning of gender in their interactions with each other. The social activities that schoolchildren do together can be as important as other agents for their socialization.

Thorne spent two years observing fourth and fifth graders at two schools in Michigan and California, sitting in the classroom with them and observing their activities outside the classroom. She watched games—such as "chase and kiss," "cooties," and "goin' with"—and teasing to learn how children construct and experience gender meanings in the classroom and on the playground.

Thorne found that peer groups greatly influence gender socialization, particularly as children talk about their changing bodies. The social context determined whether a child's bodily change was experienced with embarrassment or worn with pride. As Thorne (1993) observed, "If the most popular women started menstruating or wearing bras (even if they didn't need to), then other girls wanted these changes too. But if the popular didn't wear bras and hadn't . . . gotten their periods, then these developments were viewed as less desirable."

Thorne's research is a powerful reminder that children are social actors who help create their social world and influence their own socialization. Still, the effect of societal and cultural influences is tremendous because children's activities and values are determined by influences such as their families and the media.

Peer relations have a significant effect beyond childhood and adolescence. Informal groups of people of similar ages, at work and in other situations, are usually of enduring importance in shaping individuals' attitudes and behavior.

THE MASS MEDIA

Newspapers, periodicals, and journals flourished in the West from the early 1800s onward, but they had a limited readership. It was not until a century later that such printed materials became part of the daily experience of millions of people, influencing their attitudes and opinions. The spread of **mass media** soon included electronic communication—radio, television, audio recordings, and videos. American children now spend the equivalent of almost a hundred schooldays per year watching television.

Much research has assessed the effects of television programs on audiences, particularly children. Perhaps the most commonly researched topic is the effect of television on propensities to crime and violence.

The most extensive studies are those by George Gerbner and his collaborators, who have analyzed samples of primetime and weekend daytime TV for all the major American networks each year since 1967. The number and frequency of violent acts and episodes are charted for a range of programs. Violence is defined as physical force directed against the self or others, in which physical harm or death occurs. Television drama emerges as highly violent. On average, 80 percent of programs contain violence, with a rate of 7.5 violent episodes per hour. Children's programs show even higher levels of violence, although killing is less common. Cartoons depict the highest number of violent acts and episodes of any type of television program (Gerbner et al. 1985).

Research on the effects of television has tended to treat children as passive and undiscriminating. However, Robert Hodge and David Tripp (1986) emphasize that children's responses to TV involve interpreting, or reading, what they see, not just registering content. Hodge and Tripp suggest that most research has not considered the complexity of children's mental processes. TV watching, even of trivial programs, is not an inherently low-level intellectual activity; children read programs by relating them to other systems of meaning in their lives. According to Hodge and Tripp, it is not the violence alone that affects behavior but rather the general framework of attitudes within which it is both presented and read.

As home video games have become widespread, social codes have developed based on the games and their characters. In his book *Video Kids* (1991), Eugene Provenzo analyzes the effect of Nintendo. In 2006, over 201 million video game units amounting to almost $6.5 billion were sold in the United States alone. Over 28 percent of game players (video and computer games) are under the age of eighteen (Entertainment Software Association 2007). The games are often linked to the characters or stories in films and TV programs; in turn, television programming has been based on Nintendo games. Video games, Provenzo concludes, have become a key part of the culture and experience of childhood today.

But is this effect a negative one? It is doubtful that a child's involvement with Nintendo harms her achievement at school. However, when strong pressures from other influences deflect students' interest in schoolwork, absorption with TV or video pursuits will reinforce these attitudes. Video games and TV then can become a refuge from a disliked school environment.

Video games have become a key part of the culture and experience of childhood today. Studies have indicated that playing video games might have a positive effect on children's social and intellectual development.

However, video games may also hone skills that might be relevant both to formal education and to wider participation in a society that depends on electronic communication. The sound and look of video games have significantly influenced the development of rave music, rockers like Trent Reznor of Nine Inch Nails, and even films like *The Matrix, Lara Croft: Tomb Raider,* and *Final Fantasy.* According to media scholar Marsha Kinder (1991), her son's adeptness at Nintendo transferred fruitfully to other spheres. For example, the better he became at video games, the more interested and skillful he was at drawing cartoons. Patricia Greenfield (1993) has argued that "video games are the first example of a computer technology that is having a socializing effect on the next generation on a mass scale, and even on a world-wide basis."

The mass media are an important influence on socialization in all forms of society. Few societies in current times, even among more traditional cultures, remain untouched by the media. Electronic communication is accessible even to those who cannot read and write; and in the most impoverished parts of the world, it is common to find people owning radios and television sets.

WORK

Work is, in all cultures, an important agent of socialization, although only in industrial societies do large numbers of people go to places of work separate from the home. In traditional communities where people farmed nearby land or had workshops in their dwellings, work was not as distinct from other activities as it is for members of the workforce in the modern West. In industrialized countries the work environment often poses unfamiliar demands, perhaps calling for major adjustments in the person's outlook or behavior.

Social Roles

Through socialization, individuals learn about **social roles**—socially defined expectations for a person in a given social position. The social role of doctor, for example, encompasses a set of behaviors that all doctors should enact, regardless of their personal opinions or outlooks. Because all doctors share this role, we can speak in general terms about the professional role behavior of doctors.

Some sociologists, particularly those associated with the functionalist school, regard social roles as unchanging parts of a society's culture. They are social facts. According to this view, individuals learn the expectations for social positions in their culture and perform those roles largely as they have been defined. Social roles do not involve negotiation or creativity. Rather, they direct an individual's behavior. Through

socialization, individuals internalize social roles and learn how to carry them out.

This view, however, is mistaken. It suggests that individuals simply take on roles rather than creating or negotiating them. In fact, socialization is a process in which humans can exercise agency; they are not passive subjects waiting to be instructed or programmed. Individuals come to understand and assume social roles through an ongoing process of social interaction.

Identity

The cultural settings in which we grow up influence our behavior, but that does not mean that humans lack individuality or free will. The fact that from birth to death we are involved in interaction with others certainly conditions our personalities, values, and behavior; yet socialization is also at the origin of our individuality and freedom. In the course of socialization, each of us develops a sense of identity and the capacity for independent thought and action.

The concept of *identity* in sociology is multifaceted. Broadly speaking, **identity** relates to people's understandings about who they are and what is meaningful to them. These understandings are formed in relation to certain attributes that take priority over other sources of meaning. Some of the main sources of identity are gender, sexual orientation, nationality or ethnicity, and social class. Sociologists often speak of two types of identity: social identity and self-identity (or personal identity). These types are analytically distinct but closely related to one another. **Social identity** refers to the characteristics that other people attribute to an individual—markers that indicate who, in a basic sense, that individual is. At the same time, they place that individual in relation to others who share the same attributes. Examples of social identities are student, mother, lawyer, Catholic, homeless, Asian, dyslexic, and married. Many individuals have social identities comprising more than one attribute, reflecting the many dimensions of their lives. A person could simultaneously be a mother, an engineer, a Muslim, and a city council member. Although this plurality of social identities can be a potential source of conflict, most individuals organize meaning and experience in their lives around a primary identity that is continuous across time and place.

Social identities therefore involve a collective dimension. They mark ways that individuals are the same as others. Shared identities—predicated on common goals, values, or experiences—can form an important base for social movements. Feminists, environmentalists, labor unionists, and supporters of religious fundamentalist and/or nationalist movements are examples of cases in which a shared social identity serves as a powerful source of personal meaning or self-worth.

If social identities mark ways in which individuals are the same as others, **self-identity** (or personal identity) sets us apart as distinct individuals. Self-identity refers to the process of self-development through which we formulate a unique sense of ourselves and our relationship to the world. The notion of self-identity draws heavily on the work of symbolic interactionists. It is the individual's constant negotiation with the outside world that shapes his or her sense of self, linking the individual's personal and public worlds. Though the cultural and social environment is a factor in shaping self-identity, individual agency and choice are key.

Tracing the changes in self-identity from traditional to modern societies, we can see a shift away from the fixed, inherited factors that previously guided identity formation, such as membership in social groups bound by class or nationality. People's identities are now more multifaceted and less stable owing to urban growth, industrialization, and the breakdown of earlier social formations. Individuals have become more socially and geographically mobile. Freed from the homogeneous communities of the past, people now find that other sources of personal meaning, such as gender and sexual orientation, play a greater role in their sense of identity.

Today we have unprecedented opportunities to create our own identities. We are our own best resources in defining who we are, where we have come from, and where we are going. Now that the traditional signposts of identity have become less essential, the social world confronts us with a dizzying array of choices about who to be, how to live, and what to do, without offering much guidance about which selections to make. The decisions we make in our everyday lives—about what to wear, how to behave, and how to spend our time—help make us who we are. Through our capacity as self-conscious, self-aware human beings, we constantly create and re-create our identities.

Gender Socialization

Let's now turn to the study of **gender socialization**, the learning of **gender roles** through social factors such as the family and the media.

REACTIONS OF PARENTS AND ADULTS

Many studies have examined the degree to which gender differences are the result of social influences. Studies of mother-infant interaction show differences in the treatment of boys and girls even when parents believe their reactions to both are the same. Adults asked to assess the personality of a baby give different answers according to whether they believe the child is a girl or a boy. In one experiment, five young mothers were observed interacting with a six-month-old called Beth. They smiled at her often and offered her dolls to play with. She was seen as "sweet," having a "soft cry." The reaction of a second group of mothers to a child the same age, named Adam, was noticeably different. They offered him a train or other "male" toys to play with. Beth and Adam were actually the same child, dressed in different clothes (Will et al. 1976).

GENDER LEARNING

Gender learning by infants is almost certainly unconscious. Before a child can label itself as either a boy or a girl, it receives preverbal cues. For instance, male and female adults usually handle infants differently. Women's cosmetics contain scents different from those the baby might associate with males. Systematic differences in dress, hairstyle, and so on provide visual cues for the infant in the learning process. By age two, children have a partial understanding of what gender is. They know whether they are boys or girls, and they can usually categorize others accurately. Not until age five or six, however, does a child know that a person's sex does not change, that everyone has gender, and that sex differences between girls and boys are anatomically based.

Children's toys, picture books, and television programs all tend to emphasize male and female attributes. Toy stores and mail-order catalogs usually categorize their products by gender. Even some toys that seem gender neutral are not so in practice. For example, toy kittens and rabbits are recommended for girls, whereas lions and tigers are seen as more appropriate for boys.

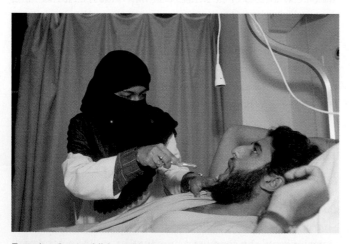

People often exhibit multiple social identities simultaneously, sometimes seemingly conflicting ones. Focusing on her primary identity as a medical professional in this context, a male patient at King Fahd Military Medical Complex in Saudi Arabia allows a doctor who is also a Muslim woman to examine him.

Toys play a major role in children's gender learning, as they often emphasize the difference between male and female attributes.

Vanda Lucia Zammuner (1986) studied the toy preferences of children between seven and ten years of age in Italy and Holland; stereotypically masculine and feminine toys as well as toys presumed not to be gender typed were included. The children and their parents were asked which toys were suitable for boys and which for girls. There was close agreement between the adults and the children. On average, the Italian children chose gender-differentiated toys more often than the Dutch children—a finding that conformed to expectations because Italian culture holds a more traditional view of gender divisions than does Dutch society. As in other studies, girls from both societies chose gender-neutral or boys' toys far more than boys chose girls' toys.

STORYBOOKS AND TELEVISION

In the 1970s, Lenore Weitzman and her colleagues (1972) analyzed gender roles in some of the most widely used preschool children's books and found several clear differences in gender roles. Males played a much larger part in the stories and pictures than females, outnumbering females by a ratio of 11 to 1. When animals with gender identities were included, the ratio was 95 to 1. The activities of males and females also differed. The males engaged in adventurous pursuits and outdoor activities demanding independence and strength. When girls did appear, they were portrayed as passive and confined mostly to indoor activities. Girls cooked and cleaned for the males or awaited their return. Much the same was true of the adult characters. Women who were not wives and mothers were imaginary creatures like witches or fairy godmothers. There was not a single woman in all the books analyzed who held an occupation outside the home. By contrast, the men were depicted as fighters, policemen, judges, kings, and so forth.

More recent research suggests a slight change but notes that the bulk of children's literature remains the same (Davies 1991). Fairy tales, for example, embody traditional attitudes toward gender and expectations for boys' and girls' ambitions. In versions of fairy tales from several centuries ago, the idea that "someday my prince will come" usually implied that a girl from a poor family might dream of wealth and fortune. Today that notion is tied to the ideals of romantic love. Some feminists have tried to rewrite some of the most celebrated fairy tales, reversing their usual emphases: "He's not nearly as attractive as he seemed the other night. So I think I'll just pretend that this glass slipper feels too tight" (Viorst 1986). Like this version of "Cinderella," however, these rewrites are mainly directed to adult audiences and have hardly affected the tales told in innumerable children's books.

Although there are exceptions, analyses of children's television programs conform to the findings about children's books. In the most popular cartoons, most leading figures are male and males dominate the active pursuits. Similar images appear in the commercials that air throughout the programs.

THE DIFFICULTY OF NONSEXIST CHILD REARING

June Statham (1986) studied a group of parents committed to nonsexist child rearing. Thirty adults in eighteen families were involved in the research, which included children ages six months to twelve years. The parents were middle class, mostly teachers or professors. Most of the parents did not simply try to modify traditional gender roles by seeking to make girls more like boys, but wanted to foster new combinations of the feminine and masculine. They wished boys to be more sensitive to others' feelings and capable of expressing warmth, while they encouraged girls to seek opportunities for learning and self-advancement. All the parents found existing patterns of gender learning difficult to combat. They were reasonably successful at persuading the children to play with gender-neutral toys, but even this proved more difficult than they had expected. One mother commented:

> If you walk into a toy shop, it's full of war toys for boys and domestic toys for girls, and it sums up society the way it is. This is the way children are being socialized: it's all right for boys to be taught to kill and hurt.... I try not to go into toy shops, I feel so angry. (Statham 1986)

Practically all the children in fact possessed, and played with, gender-typed toys, given to them by relatives.

There are now some storybooks available with strong independent girls as the main characters, but few depict boys in nontraditional roles. The mother of a five-year-old boy told of

In her "Pink & Blue" project, photographer JeongMee Yoon records girls' obsession with the color pink. What are the implications of the gender-typed packaging and color-coding that we see in children's toys and clothing?

her son's reaction when she reversed the sexes of the characters in a story she read to him:

> In fact he was a bit upset when I went through a book which has a boy and a girl in very traditional roles, and changed all the he's to she's and she's to he's. When I first started doing that, he was inclined to say "you don't like boys, you only like girls." I had to explain that that wasn't true at all, it's just that there's not enough written about girls. (Statham 1986)

Clearly, gender socialization is very powerful, and challenges to it can be upsetting. Once a gender is "assigned," society expects individuals to act like females and males. It is in the practices of everyday life that these expectations are fulfilled and reproduced (Bourdieu 1990; Lorber 1994).

The Debate about Gender Socialization

FREUD'S THEORY

Perhaps the most influential—and controversial—theory of the emergence of gender identity is that of Sigmund Freud. According to Freud, the learning of gender differences in infants

and young children centers on the possession or absence of the penis. "I have a penis" is equivalent to "I am a boy," while "I am a girl" is equivalent to "I lack a penis." Freud is careful to say that it is not just the anatomical distinctions that matter; the possession and absence of the penis are symbolic of masculinity and femininity.

At around age four or five, the theory goes, a boy feels threatened by the discipline and autonomy his father demands of him, fantasizing that the father wishes to remove his penis. Partly consciously, but mostly unconsciously, the boy recognizes the father as a rival for the affections of his mother. In repressing erotic feelings toward the mother and accepting the father as a superior being, the boy identifies with the father and becomes aware of his male identity. The boy gives up his love for his mother out of an unconscious fear of castration by his father. Girls, on the other hand, supposedly suffer from "penis envy" because they do not possess the visible organ that distinguishes boys. The mother becomes devalued in the little girl's eyes, because she also lacks a penis and is unable to provide one. When the girl identifies with the mother, she takes over the submissive attitude involved in the recognition of being "second best."

Once this phase is over, the child has learned to repress his erotic feelings. The period from about five years of age to puberty, according to Freud, is one of latency—sexual activities are suspended until the biological changes of puberty reactivate erotic desires. The latency period, covering the early and middle years of school, is the time at which same-sex peer groups are most important in the child's life.

Major objections have been raised against Freud's views, particularly by feminists but also by many other authors (Coward 1984; Mitchell 1975). First, Freud seems to identify gender identity too closely with genital awareness; other, more subtle factors are surely involved. Second, the theory seems to depend on the notion that the penis is superior to the vagina, which is thought of as just a lack of the male organ. Yet why shouldn't the female genitals be considered superior to those of the male? Third, Freud treats the father as the primary disciplining agent, whereas in many cultures the mother is more significant in imposing discipline. Fourth, Freud believes that gender learning is concentrated at age four or five. Later authors have emphasized the importance of earlier learning, beginning in infancy.

CHODOROW'S THEORY

Although many writers have used Freud's approach in studying gender development, they have modified it in major respects. An important example is the sociologist Nancy Chodorow (1978, 1988), who argues that learning to feel male or female derives from the infant's attachment to the parents from an early age. She emphasizes much more than Freud the importance of the mother rather than the father. Children become emotionally involved with the mother because she is the most dominant influence in their early lives. At some point this attachment has to be broken for the child to achieve a separate sense of self—to become less closely dependent.

Chodorow argues that the breaking process occurs in a different way for boys and girls. Girls remain closer to the mother—able, for example, to go on hugging and kissing her and imitating what she does. Because there is no sharp break from the mother, the girl, and later the adult woman, develops a sense of self that is more continuous with other people. Her identity is more likely to be merged with or depend on another's: first her mother's, later a man's. In Chodorow's view, this fosters sensitivity and emotional compassion in women.

Boys gain a sense of self via a more radical rejection of their original closeness to the mother, forging their understanding of masculinity from what is not feminine. They learn not to be sissies or mama's boys. As a result, boys are relatively unskilled in relating closely to others; they develop more analytical ways of looking at the world. They take a more active view of their lives, emphasizing achievement, but they have repressed their ability to understand their own feelings and those of others.

To some extent, Chodorow reverses Freud's emphasis. Masculinity, rather than femininity, is defined by a loss, the forfeiting of continued close attachment to the mother. Male identity is formed through separation; thus men later in life unconsciously feel that their identity is endangered if they become involved in close emotional relationships with others. Women,

Nancy Chodorow argues that boys are socialized to be less attached to or dependent on their parents at an earlier age than girls. Girls are able to remain close to their mother, which in Chodorow's view encourages characteristics like sensitivity and compassion. In contrast, boys define their masculinity by rejecting behaviors they consider "feminine" and are less skilled in relating closely to others.

on the other hand, feel that the absence of a close relation to another person threatens their self-esteem. These patterns are passed on from generation to generation, because of women's primary role in the early socialization of children. Women express and define themselves mainly in terms of relationships. Men have repressed these needs and adopt a more manipulative stance toward the world.

Chodorow's work has met with various criticisms. Janet Sayers (1986), for example, has suggested that Chodorow does not explain the struggle of women, particularly in current times, to become autonomous, independent beings. Women (and men), Sayers points out, are more contradictory in their psychological makeup than Chodorow's theory suggests. Femininity may conceal feelings of aggressiveness or assertiveness, which are revealed only obliquely or in certain contexts (Brennan 1988). Chodorow has also been criticized for her narrow conception of the family based on a white, middle-class model. What happens, for example, in one-parent households or, as in many Chicano communities, in families where children are cared for by more than one adult (Segura and Pierce 1993)?

These criticisms don't undermine Chodorow's ideas, which remain important. They teach us a good deal about the nature of femininity, and they help us understand the origins of "male inexpressiveness"—the difficulty men have in revealing their feelings to others (Balswick 1983).

GILLIGAN'S THEORY

Carol Gilligan (1982) further developed Chodorow's analysis, concentrating on the images adult women and men have of themselves and their attainments. Women, she agrees with Chodorow, define themselves in terms of personal relationships and judge their achievements in terms of their ability to care for others. Women's place in the lives of men is traditionally that of caretaker and helpmate. But the qualities developed in these tasks are devalued by men, who see their own emphasis on individual achievement as the only form of success. Concern with relationships on the part of women appears to men as a weakness rather than as the strength that in fact it is.

Gilligan carried out intensive interviews with about two hundred American women and men of varying ages and social backgrounds. She asked a range of questions concerning their moral outlook and conceptions of self. Consistent differences emerged between the men's and women's views. When asked, What does it mean to say something is morally right or wrong? the men mentioned abstract ideals of duty, justice, and individual freedom, whereas the women raised the theme of helping others.

The women were more tentative in their moral judgments than the men, seeing possible contradictions between following a strict moral code and avoiding harming others. Gilligan

Japanese and American Teenagers

Studies comparing socialization in a variety of cultural settings show some interesting contrasts. For example, the idea of the teen years as an extended period of transition between childhood and adulthood emerged in America before it did in Japan. In fact, the Japanese term *cheenayja* is an adaptation of the American *teenager*. In premodern Japan, the movement from childhood to adulthood occurred in an instant, because it happened as part of an age-grade system (one that included girls). A child would become an adult when he or she participated in a special rite. Japanese boys became adults at some point between the ages of eleven and sixteen, depending on their social rank. The parallel ceremony at which girls were recognized as women was the *kami* age, the age at which they began to wear their hair up rather than down.

Just as in most other nonmodern societies, including those of medieval Europe, young people in Japan knew who they would be and what they would be doing when they became adults. The teenage years weren't a time to experiment. Japanese children were schooled to follow closely the ways of their parents, to whom they owed strict obedience; family norms emphasizing the duties of children toward their parents were very strong.

Such norms have endured to the present day, but they have also come under strain with the high pace of industrial

development in contemporary Japan. So are Japanese teenagers now just like American ones? Merry White, a sociologist at Boston University, attempted to answer this question. White (1993) interviewed one hundred teens in each culture over a period of three years, trying to gain an in-depth view of their attitudes toward sexuality, school, friendship, and parents. She found big differences between the Japanese and the American teenagers but also came up with unexpected conclusions about both. In neither culture are most teenagers the rebels she expected to find. Instead, she found a fairly high degree of

suggests that this outlook reflects the traditional situation of women, anchored in caring relationships, rather than the outward-looking attitudes of men. Women's views of themselves are based on successfully fulfilling the needs of others, rather than on pride in individual achievement (Gilligan 1982).

☑ CONCEPT CHECKS

1. What is social reproduction? What are some specific ways that the four main agents of socialization contribute to social reproduction?
2. According to Mead, how does a child develop a social self?
3. What are the four stages of cognitive development, according to Piaget?
4. Compare and contrast social roles and social identities.
5. How do the media contribute to gender role socialization?

Socialization through the Life Course

The transitions through which individuals pass during their lives seem to be biologically fixed—from childhood to adulthood and eventually to death. But the stages of the human **life course** are social as well as biological. They are influenced by conformity to wider cultural ideas and an expressed respect for parents in both countries.

What the adults say of their teenage offspring in Japan and the United States is much the same: "Why don't you listen more to what I say?" "When I was your age..." The Japanese and American teens also echo each other in some ways: "Do you like me?" "What should I aim for in my life?" "We're cool, but they aren't." Pop music, films, and videos figure large in the experience of both—as does at least a surface sexual knowledgeability, because from an early age in both cultures sexual information, including warnings about sexual disease, is widespread.

The Japanese teenagers, however, come out well ahead of the Americans in terms of school achievements: 95 percent of Japanese teenagers reach a level in academic tests met by only the top 5 percent of young Americans. And although both express respect for parents, the Japanese teenagers remain much closer to theirs than do most of the American teenagers.

The Japanese teenagers are certainly interested in sex but place it at the bottom of a list of priorities White presented them with; the Americans put it at the top. Teenagers in Japan are nonetheless very sexually active, probably even more so than their American counterparts. Two thirds of Japanese girls by age fifteen are sexually active. White reports that they are, by Western standards, amazingly forthcoming about their sexual fantasies and practices; nearly 90 percent of the Japanese girls reported that they masturbate twice or more a week.

The Japanese clearly separate three areas of sexuality that are more mixed up for the American teenagers: physical passion, socially approved pairing or marriage, and romantic fantasies. *Love marriages,* in which two people establish a

relationship on the basis of emotional and sexual attraction, are now common in Japan. However, they are often the result of an initial introduction of suitable partners arranged by parents, followed by falling in love before marriage. Even the most sexually experienced young person in Japan may continue to prefer to have a mature adult arrange an appropriate marriage.

Japanese teenagers often stress that love should grow in marriage rather than being the basis of choosing a partner in the first place. The sexual activity of young girls tends to involve several older boys and not be bound up with dating. White quotes as typical of young, unmarried Japanese women a respondent who was in her early twenties when interviewed. She first had sexual intercourse at fifteen—like three quarters of her friends—and since had accumulated many "sex friends." These were not *boifurends* (boyfriends), a relationship that implies emotional attachment. She said, "I do it [have sex] because it is fun. However, marriage is a totally different story, you know. Marriage should be more realistic and practical" (White 1993).

cultural differences and material circumstances in various types of society. For example, in the modern West, death is usually thought of in relation to old age, because most people enjoy a life span of seventy years or more. In traditional societies of the past, however, more people died in younger age groups than survived to old age.

Childhood

In modern societies, childhood is considered a distinct stage of life between infancy and the teen years. Yet the concept of childhood has developed only over the past two or three centuries. In earlier societies, the young moved directly from a lengthy infancy into working roles within the community.

The French historian Philippe Ariès (1965) has argued that *childhood* did not exist in medieval times. In the paintings of medieval Europe, children are portrayed as little adults, with mature faces and the same style of dress as their elders. Children took part in the same work and play activities as adults, rather than in the childhood games we now take for granted.

Right up to the twentieth century, in the United States and most other Western countries, children were put to work at what now seems a very early age. There are countries in the world today, in fact, where young children do full-time work, sometimes in physically demanding circumstances (for example, in coal mines). The ideas that children have rights and that child labor is morally repugnant are recent developments.

Because of the long period of childhood that we recognize today, societies now are in some respects more child centered

Duccio da Buoninsegna's *Madonna and Child,* painted in the thirteenth century, depicts the infant Jesus with a mature face. Until recently, children in Western society were viewed as little adults.

Before the twentieth century, young children in many Western countries were put to work at an early age. Some, like the coal-mining boys above, were made to do dangerous or physically demanding work.

than traditional ones. But a child-centered society, it must be emphasized, is not one in which all children experience love and care from parents or other adults. The physical and sexual abuse of children is a commonplace feature of family life in present-day society, although the extent of such abuse has only recently come to light. Child abuse has clear connections with what seems to us today like the frequent mistreatment of children in premodern Europe.

It is possible that as a result of changes in modern societies the separate character of childhood is again diminishing. Some observers have suggested that children now grow up so fast that this is in fact the case. They point out that even small children may watch the same television programs as adults, thereby becoming much more familiar early on with the adult world than did preceding generations.

The Teenager

The idea of the teenager also didn't exist until recently. The biological changes involved in puberty (the point at which a person becomes capable of adult sexual activity and reproduction) are universal. Yet in many cultures, these do not produce

the turmoil and uncertainty often found among young people in modern societies. In cultures that foster age-grades, for example, with ceremonies that signal a person's transition to adulthood, the process of psychosexual development seems easier to negotiate. Adolescents in such societies have less to "unlearn" because the pace of change is slower. There is a time when children in Western societies are required to put away their toys and break with childish pursuits. In traditional cultures, in which children are already working alongside adults, this process of unlearning is much less jarring.

In Western societies, teenagers are betwixt and between: They often try to follow adult ways, but they are treated in law as children. They may wish to go to work, but they are constrained to stay in school. Teenagers in the West live in between childhood and adulthood, growing up in a society subject to continuous change.

Young Adulthood

Young adulthood seems increasingly to be a stage in personal and sexual development in modern societies (Goldscheider and Waite 1991). Particularly among affluent groups, people in their early twenties are taking the time to travel and explore sexual, political, and religious affiliations. The importance of this postponement of the responsibilities of full adulthood is likely to grow, given the extended period of education many people now undergo.

Mature Adulthood

Most young adults in the West today can expect to live well into old age. In premodern times, few could anticipate such a future. Death through sickness or injury was much more frequent among all age groups than it is today, and women faced a high rate of mortality in childbirth.

However, some of the strains we experience now were less pronounced in previous times. People usually maintained a closer connection with their parents and other kin than in today's mobile populations, and their work routines were the same as those of their forebears. In current times, major uncertainties must be resolved in marriage, family life, and other social contexts. We have to make our own lives more than people did in the past. The creation of sexual and marital ties, for instance, now depends on individual initiative and selection rather than being fixed by parents. This represents greater freedom for the individual, but the responsibility can also impose difficulties.

Keeping a forward-looking perspective in middle age has become particularly important in modern societies. Most people do not expect to be doing the same thing all their lives, as in traditional cultures. Individuals who have spent their lives in one career may find the level they have reached in middle age unsatisfying and further opportunities blocked. Women who have spent their early adulthood raising a family and whose children have left home may feel they lack social value. The midlife crisis is very real for many middle-aged people. A person may feel that she has thrown away the opportunities that life had to offer or that she will never attain goals cherished since childhood. Yet growing older need not lead to

resignation or despair; a release from childhood dreams can be liberating.

Old Age

In traditional societies, older people were accorded great respect. Among cultures that included age-grades, the elders usually had a major—often the final—say over matters of importance to the community. Within families, the authority of both men and women increased with age. In industrialized societies, by contrast, older people tend to lack authority within both the family and the social community. Having retired from the labor force, they may be poorer than ever before in their lives. At the same time, there has been a great increase in the proportion of the population over age sixty-five. In 1900, only one in thirty people in the United States was over age sixty-five; the proportion today is one in eight and will likely rise to one in five by the year 2030 (U.S. Bureau of the Census 1996a). The same trend is found in all the industrially advanced countries.

Transition to the age-grade of elder in a traditional culture often marked the pinnacle of an individual's status. In modern societies, retirement brings the opposite. No longer living with their children and often having retired from paid work, older people may find it difficult to make the final period of their life rewarding. People used to think that those who successfully

In traditional societies, older people are given a great deal of respect and play a major role in the community. The Tatas of Togo delegate an elder to greet a new chief.

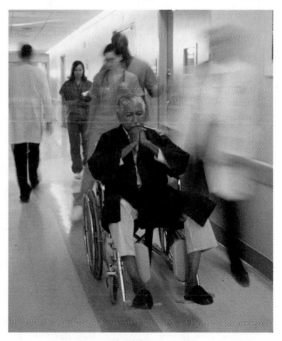

In modern industrial societies, many elderly people face social isolation.

Dorm Rooms and Socialization

The rooms we occupy are more than just containers for doing things and storing stuff. They are the places where we usually feel most secure and comfortable. How we arrange and decorate them mark them as ours, which not only makes us feel "at home" but also announces who we are to visitors. This is particularly true of the college dorm room. A dorm room represents a transition zone separating childhood from maturity and the objects displayed therein straddle this divide awkwardly. How do these photographs and drawings capture the "betwixt and between" quality of college life? For example, kitty-corner across from the *Clockwork Orange* and *Psycho* posters in the diagram below is *Willie Wonka* and a poster of Audrey

> Over the last century photographs and drawings of dorm rooms at Wheaton College in Norton, Massachusetts show both consistency and change. For example, a student today would easily recognize that the desk in the left hand corner of this photo from 1889, upon which a student has set a bookcase, is a place for her collection of photographs. They would also notice that music was an important form of personal expression for students and that the posters on the wall of fashionably dressed women were models of what students at the time found attractive or evocative.

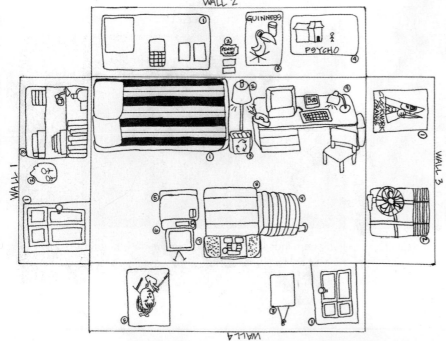

> Wheaton College admitted men for the first time in 1988. Both men and women adorn their rooms in a similar fashion with photographs, posters, and personal memorabilia, but the contents of these objects vary, as do the colors schemes in the room. Women's memorabilia tend to be tokens of relationships, something that reminds them of a person or an experience. By contrast, men's mementos mark personal transitions and claims on status: empty liquor bottles, objects that remind them that they traveled, rather than what they saw or who they met. Men also tend to favor conversation starters that provide them with an opportunity to expound on what interests them, like the *Willie Wonka and the Chocolate Factory* cardboard cutout labeled number 2 on wall 1.

Created by John Grady.

Hepburn. Of course, it may have always been so. The photograph on page 102 has posters of knowing Gibson Girls on the wall, but also features a china-face doll hanging from a peg on the screen at the right side of the image.

While there has been marked continuity in dorm life over the last century, there are also noticeable changes. Students appear to have more stuff in their rooms after 1970. This is especially true with electronic equipment where computers, CD and DVD players, and television sets have replaced record players and typewriters with added levels of functionality. A student has more information within the confines of a machine not much larger than a book than was available in the entire college library just twenty years ago. It is also true that students are permitted to display cultural messages on the walls of their rooms that would have had them expelled less than a half century ago. Nevertheless, one of the most important functions of the dorm room, and how it is furnished and decorated as a staging area that prepares the self for life's challenges, appears unchanged. How do young people who don't go to college, or students who live at home, manage their living space? Are they less involved in their space than students in a residential liberal arts college? How might their living arrangements affect their transition to adulthood?

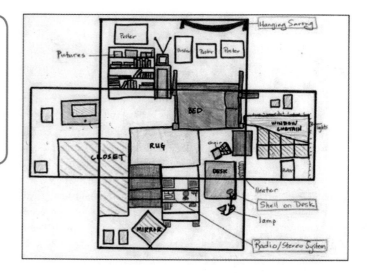

➡ In addition, students in 2000 report that when they are alone or going to sleep they like to look at, and think about, those personal objects which they cherish. For example, the female student who drew this floor and wall plan of her room explains why she put one of her favorite objects, a sarong she bought during her junior year in New Zealand, on the ceiling above her head:

This way, I can lie on my bed and look up at it. Many people comment on it, as soon as they enter my room, because it is very prominent. I love looking at it, because it reminds me of all the wonderful things I saw and did while abroad.

⬆➡ Dorm rooms are also centers for socializing with small groups of friends. Whether studying together, or gossiping and chatting idly, students often share their beds with friends. The photo on the right from 1970 shows students using one of the beds in their room as a resting place while they engage in various activities. Almost any of the collection of photographs in the Wheaton College Archives that include people in them will have one or more with students socializing on their beds, including 1898. No photos were taken with students in them during the early twentieth century but the photo above shows a bed that is clearly used for lounging.

cope with old age rely on their inner resources, becoming less interested in the material rewards of social life. Although this may be true, it seems likely that in a society in which many are physically healthy in old age, an outward-looking view will become more prevalent. Those in retirement might find renewal in the "third age," in which a new phase of education begins (see also Chapter 12 on lifelong learning).

✓ **CONCEPT CHECKS**

1. What are the five stages of the life course, and what are some of the defining features of each stage?
2. Describe how the life course stage of childhood has changed since medieval times.

Study Outline

www.wwnorton.com/studyspace

Culture, Society, and Child Socialization

- Socialization is the process whereby, through contact with other human beings, the helpless infant gradually becomes a self-aware, knowledgeable human being, skilled in the ways of the given culture.
- According to G. H. Mead, the child comes to understand being a separate agent by seeing how others behave toward him or her in social contexts. At a later stage, entering into organized games and learning the rules of play, the child comes to understand "the generalized other"—general values and cultural rules.
- Jean Piaget distinguishes several stages in the child's capability to make sense of the world. Each stage involves acquiring new cognitive skills and depends on the successful completion of the preceding one. According to Piaget, these stages of cognitive development are universal features of socialization.

Socialization through the Life Course

- Agents of socialization are structured groups or contexts within which significant processes of socialization occur. In all cultures, the family is the principal socializing agent during infancy. Other influences include peer groups, schools, and the mass media.
- Through the process of socialization and interaction with others, individuals learn about social roles—socially defined expectations for a person in a given social position. One result of this process is the development of a social identity, the characteristics that other people attribute to an individual. If social identities mark ways in which individuals are the same as others, self-identity sets us apart as distinct individuals. The concept of self-identity, which draws on symbolic interactionism, refers to the process of self-development through which we formulate a unique sense of ourselves and our relationship to the world.

- The development of mass communications has enlarged the range of socializing agents. The spread of mass printed media was later accompanied by the use of electronic communication. TV exerts a particularly powerful influence, reaching people of all ages every day.
- Gender socialization begins as soon as an infant is born. Even parents who believe they treat children equally tend to produce different responses to boys and girls. These differences are reinforced by many other cultural influences.
- Socialization continues throughout the life cycle. At each phase of life there are transitions to be made or crises to be overcome.

Key Concepts

age-grades (p. 90)
agents of socialization (p. 89)
cognition (p. 88)
concrete operational stage (p. 89)
egocentric (p. 88)
formal operational stage (p. 89)
gender roles (p. 94)
gender socialization (p. 94)
generalized other (p. 88)
identity (p. 93)
life course (p. 98)
mass media (p. 92)
peer group (p. 90)
preoperational stage (p. 88)
self-consciousness (p. 88)
self-identity (p. 94)
sensorimotor stage (p. 88)
social identity (p. 93)
socialization (p. 86)
social reproduction (p. 86)
social roles (p. 93)
social self (p. 88)

Review Questions

1. Define *socialization* and describe how it contributes to social reproduction.
2. The authors explain that what differentiates humans from other species is self awareness. Briefly discuss Mead's theory of childhood development.
3. The authors explain that what differentiates humans from other species is self awareness. Briefly discuss Piaget's theory of childhood development.
4. What are the agents of socialization? In your opinion, what is the most important or influential agent of socialization and why?
5. Define *social roles* and give an example of a social role that pertains to your own life.
6. What is the difference between personal and social identity? List some of the sources of both personal and social identity.
7. Describe how people learn gender roles and elaborate on the roles of the family and the media in this learning process.
8. What are the difficulties of non-sexist child rearing? Do you think this is an important goal? Why or why not?
9. Compare and contrast Freud and Chodorow's theories of development of gender identity.
10. What are the stages of the life course? Describe how they vary culturally and historically.

Thinking Sociologically Exercises

1. Concisely review how an individual becomes a social person according to the three leading theorists discussed in this chapter: G. H. Mead, Jean Piaget, and Sigmund Freud. Which theory seems most appropriate and correct to you? Explain why.
2. Consuming alcoholic beverages is one of many things we do as a result of socialization. Suggest how the family, peers, schools, and mass media help establish the desire to consume alcoholic drinks. Of these influences, which force is the most persuasive? Explain.

Learning Objectives

The Study of Daily Life in the Internet Age

Familiarize yourself with the study of everyday life.

Nonverbal Communication

Know the various forms of nonverbal communication.

The World as a Stage

Understand the core concepts of the "impression management" perspective. See how we use impression management techniques in everyday life.

Social Context and Shared Understandings

Learn about the ethnomethodology approach to studying human interaction.

Social Rules and Talk

Learn the research process of ethnomethodology, the study of our conversations, and how we make sense of each other.

Interaction in Time and Space

Understand that interaction is situated, that it occurs in a particular place and for a particular length of time. See that the way we organize our social actions is not unique by learning how other cultures organize their social lives.

Linking Microsociology and Macrosociology

See how face-to-face interactions and broader features of society are closely related.

CHAPTER FIVE

SOCIAL INTERACTION AND EVERYDAY LIFE IN THE AGE OF THE INTERNET

matt Kehoe is a waiter at the Spotted Pig, an upscale bar in New York City where he has worked for the past five years. He comes to work every day from Brooklyn on the subway. In his subway car, he is in the presence of hundreds of people who are almost always strangers. After he walks a few blocks from the subway exit to the Spotted Pig, Matt enters a place where he knows dozens of people at any time. Most of them are patrons who come to eat and drink, while others are current and former employees who hang out at the bar when they are not working.

The movement from a social context where most of the people around him are strangers to one where they are known implies a different kind of interaction in each place, yet there are commonalities. In both the bar and the subway car personal space is limited. For example, in the subway car, bodies touch as commuters hold on to metal bars or squeeze into seats next to others. In the bar, tables, chairs, and stools are all located closely together with little room in between. As on the train, bodies constantly crisscross as they negotiate a space.

It is almost impossible for Matt, elbow to elbow with people from the time he gets on the subway in the morning until the times he gets home from work, to move anywhere in these physical spaces without making eye contact—on the train with a stranger, in the bar with someone he has at least met. But like many urbanites, Matt makes an effort to maintain his sense of personal space by creating some semblance of solitude. On the subway, he wears an iPod and

Walking along a crowded city street, one engages in civil inattention. Though the people in this photo can hear the phone conversations these men are having, they make no indication of their awareness.

reads his text messages, which makes it possible for him to go into "his own zone" and "extend his personal space" (Goffman 1971), generally ignoring the people around him. At times when he does inadvertently make eye contact with strangers, he quickly shifts his gaze—an action which sociologists call a norm of everyday life.

In the bar, it would be socially inappropriate for Matt to continue wearing the iPod, because he is expected to be present in the scene in a different way. Yet, even here there is an appropriate balance between eye contact and looking away. He will greet certain patrons and fellow workers the first time he sees them, but afterward it is usually understood that they will go about their own business without acknowledging one another in the way they did earlier.

When passersby—either strangers or intimates—quickly glance at each other and then look away again, they demonstrate what Erving Goffman (1967, 1971) calls the **civil inattention** we require of each other in many situations. Civil inattention is not the same as merely ignoring another person. Each individual indicates recognition of the other person's presence but avoids any gesture that might be taken as too intrusive. Can you think of examples of civil inattention in your own life? Perhaps when you are walking down the hall of a dormitory or trying to decide where to sit in the cafeteria or simply walking across campus? Civil inattention to others is something we engage in more or less unconsciously, but it is of fundamental importance to the existence of social life, which must proceed efficiently and, sometimes among total strangers, without fear. When civil inattention occurs among passing

strangers, an individual implies to another person that she has no reason to suspect his intentions, be hostile to him, or in any other way specifically avoid him.

The best way to see the importance of this is by thinking of examples for which it doesn't apply. When a person stares fixedly at another, allowing her face openly to express a particular emotion, it is frequently with a lover, family member, or close friend. Strangers or chance acquaintances, whether encountered on the street, at work, or at a party, virtually never hold the gaze of another in this way. To do so may be taken as an indication of hostile intent. It is only where two groups are strongly antagonistic to one another that strangers might indulge in such a practice—for example, when whites in the United States have been known in the past to give a "hate stare" to blacks walking past.

Even friends in close conversation need to be careful about how they look at one another. Each individual demonstrates attention and involvement in the conversation by regularly looking at the eyes of the other but not staring into them. To look too intently might be taken as a sign of mistrust about, or at least failure to understand, what the other is saying. Yet if each party does not engage the eyes of the other at all, each is likely to be thought evasive, shifty, or otherwise odd.

The Study of Daily Life in the Internet Age

Erving Goffman, the first to develop the concept of civil inattention, was a sociologist who created a new field of study called *microsociology* or **social interaction**. Goffman believed that sociologists needed to concern themselves with seemingly trivial aspects of social behavior. Passing someone on the street or exchanging a few words with a friend seem minor and uninteresting activities, things we do countless times a day without giving them any thought. Goffman argued that the study of such apparently insignificant forms of social interaction is of major importance in sociology and, far from being uninteresting, is one of the most absorbing of all areas of sociological investigation. There are three reasons for this.

First, our day-to-day routines, with their almost constant interactions with others, give structure and form to what we do; we can learn a great deal about ourselves as social beings, and about social life itself, from studying them. Our lives are organized around the repetition of similar patterns of behavior from day to day, week to week, month to month, and year to year. Think of what you did yesterday, for example, and the day before that. If they were both weekdays, in all probability you got up at about the same time each day (an important routine in itself). You may have gone off to class fairly early in the morning, making a journey from home to school or college that you make virtually every weekday. You perhaps met some friends for lunch, returning to classes or private study in the afternoon. Later, you retraced your steps back home, possibly going out later in the evening with other friends.

Of course, the routines we follow from day to day are not identical, and our patterns of activity on weekends usually contrast with those on weekdays. If we make a major change in our life, like leaving college to take a job, alterations in our daily routines are usually necessary, but then we establish a new and fairly regular set of habits again.

Second, the study of everyday life reveals to us how humans can act creatively to shape reality. Although social behavior is guided to some extent by forces such as roles, norms, and shared expectations, individuals perceive reality differently according to their backgrounds, interests, and motivations. Because individuals are capable of creative action, they continuously shape reality through the decisions and actions they take. In other words, reality is not fixed or static—it is created through human interactions.

Third, studying social interaction in everyday life sheds light on larger social systems and institutions. All large-scale social systems, in fact, depend on the patterns of social interaction we engage in daily. This is easy to demonstrate. Consider the case of two strangers passing on the street. Such an event may seem to have little direct relevance to large-scale, more permanent forms of social organization. But when we take into account many such interactions, they are no longer irrelevant. In modern societies, most people live in towns and cities and constantly interact with others whom they do not know personally. Civil inattention is one among other mechanisms that give public life, with its bustling crowds and fleeting, impersonal contacts, the character it has.

When we published the first edition of this book, the study of face-to-face communication was a well-settled territory. There is reason to think that social interaction over the past decade or so has undergone a major transformation, however, because of the Internet. In this chapter, we will review the traditional findings of the field, but we will also ask how these findings must be modified in the light of the rise of e-mail, Internet chatting, and social networking sites like Facebook. We will first learn about the nonverbal cues (facial expressions and bodily gestures) all of us use when interacting with each other. We then move on to analyze everyday speech—how we use language to communicate to others the meanings we wish to convey. Finally, we focus on the ways in which our lives are structured by daily routines, paying particular attention to how we coordinate our actions across space and time.

☑ CONCEPT CHECKS

1. What is microsociology?
2. What are three reasons it is important to study daily social interaction?

Nonverbal Communication

Social interaction requires numerous forms of **nonverbal communication**—the exchange of information and meaning through facial expressions, gestures, and movements of the body. Nonverbal communication is sometimes referred to as "body language," but this is misleading, because we characteristically use such nonverbal cues to eliminate or expand on what is said with words.

Face, Gestures, and Emotion

One major aspect of communication is the facial expression of emotion. Paul Ekman and his colleagues have developed what they call the Facial Action Coding System (FACS) for describing movements of the facial muscles that give rise to particular expressions (Ekman and Friesen 1978). By this means, they have tried to inject some precision into an area notoriously open to inconsistent or contradictory interpretations—for there is little agreement about how emotions are to be identified and classified. Charles Darwin, one of the originators of evolutionary theory, claimed that basic modes of emotional expression are the same in all human beings. Although some have disputed the claim, Ekman's research among people from widely different cultural backgrounds seems to confirm Darwin's view. Ekman and W. V. Friesen carried out a study of an isolated community in New Guinea, whose members had previously had virtually no contact with outsiders. When they were shown pictures of facial expressions conveying six emotions (happiness, sadness, anger, disgust, fear, surprise), the New Guineans were able to identify these emotions.

According to Ekman, the results of his own and similar studies of different peoples support the view that the facial expression of emotion and its interpretation are innate in human beings. He acknowledges that his evidence does not conclusively demonstrate this, and it may be that widely shared cultural learning experiences are involved; however, his conclusions are supported by other types of research. I. Eibl-Eibesfeldt (1972) studied six children born deaf and blind to see how far their

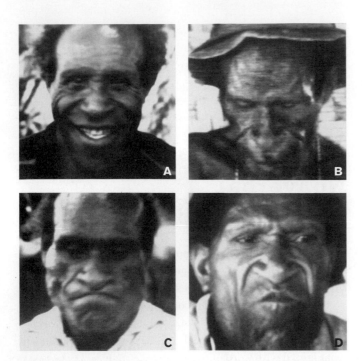

Paul Ekman's photographs of facial expressions from a tribesman in an isolated community in New Guinea helped test the idea that basic modes of emotional expression are the same among all people. Here the instructions were to show how your face would look if you were a person in a story and (A) your friend had come and you were happy, (B) your child had died, (C) you were angry and about to fight, and (D) you saw a dead pig that had been lying there a long time.

facial expressions were the same as those of sighted and hearing individuals in particular emotional situations. He found that the children smiled when engaged in obviously pleasurable activities, raised their eyebrows in surprise when sniffing at an object with an unaccustomed smell, and frowned when repeatedly offered a disliked object. Because the children could not have seen other people behaving in these ways, it seems that these responses must be innately determined.

Using the FACS, Ekman and Friesen identified a number of the discrete facial muscle actions in newborn infants that are also found in adult expressions of emotion. Infants seem, for example, to produce facial expressions similar to the adult expression of disgust (pursing the lips and frowning) in response to sour tastes. But although the facial expression of emotion seems to be partly innate, individual and cultural factors influence what exact form facial movements take and the contexts in which they are deemed appropriate. How people smile, for example, the precise movement of the lips and other facial muscles, and how fleeting the smile is all vary among cultures.

There are no gestures or bodily postures that have been shown to characterize all, or even most, cultures. In some societies, for instance, people nod when they mean no, the opposite of Anglo-American practice. Gestures Americans tend to use a great deal, such as pointing, seem not to exist among certain peoples (Bull 1983). Similarly, a straightened forefinger placed in the center of the cheek and rotated is used in parts of Italy as a gesture of praise but appears to be unknown elsewhere.

Like facial expressions, gestures and bodily posture are continually used to fill out utterances as well as to convey meanings when nothing is actually said. All three can be used to joke, show irony, or show skepticism. The nonverbal impressions that we convey inadvertently often indicate that what we say is not quite what we really mean. Blushing is perhaps the most obvious example, but innumerable other subtle indicators can be picked up by other people. Genuine facial expressions tend to evaporate after four or five seconds. A smile that lasts longer could indicate deceit. An expression of surprise that lasts too long may indicate deliberate sarcasm—to show that the individual is not in fact surprised after all.

On the Internet, it is very difficult to capture dimensions of emotion that are present only with facial expression. At first, the need that Internet users felt to approximate facial gestures resulted in at least two common faces:

:) or :-)

As time passed, a need for greater subtlety resulted in other widely understood variations, such as this winking smiley face:

;-)

which means that a comment is meant to be taken with a grain of salt.

Electronic mail may have once been devoid of facial expression, but today the average e-mail user expects to insert different emotions into a message. The strong need human beings feel to communicate with their faces has also led to other innovations, like the Web Camera, which has become a relatively inexpensive and widely used technology. But in general, people who communicate over the Internet or even the telephone lack the benefit of seeing the faces of their conversational partners as they speak.

How might this matter? On the telephone, an individual person will frequently talk longer for a stretch of time than they would in face-to-face conversation. Unable to see the face of a conversational partner, they can't as readily adjust what they say in response to a sense that someone already "gets it" or thinks he or she is going down an unproductive (or silly) path. Yet, the telephone maintains at least some immediacy of feedback that e-mail lacks. This is why in e-mail disputes people who are unable to make mutual adjustments in response to verbal or facial cues will end up saying much

How are technologies like webcams, email, and mobile phones transforming the ways that we interact with each other?

more—communicated in the form of long messages—than they would say in conversation.

Which is better? Would you prefer to make your point in e-mail or in person? Using sociological insights like these might make you prefer electronic communication at some times and face-to-face communication at others. For example, if you are dealing with a powerful person and want to get your thoughts across, you may want to avoid a situation where the person can signal with facial gestures that your idea is silly and thus intimidates you from making all your points. The power to signal with facial gestures is one of the things that people do to control the flow of a conversation. On the other hand, face-to-face communication gives you an opportunity to try out an idea on someone more powerful than yourself without going too far down the road if the person is actually unreceptive.

☑ CONCEPT CHECKS

1. What is nonverbal communication?
2. Describe several ways that individuals communicate their emotions to one another.
3. How do e-mail and in-person communication differ?

The World as a Stage

Impression Management ("Striking a Pose")

Goffman and other writers on social interaction often use notions from drama and theater in their analyses. The concept of *social role,* for example, originated in a theatrical setting.

Broadly speaking, **roles** are socially defined expectations that a person in a given **status** (or **social position**) follows. To be a teacher is to hold a specific position; the teacher's role consists of acting in specified ways toward her pupils. Goffman sees social life as though played out by actors on a stage—or on many stages because how we act depends on the roles we are playing at a particular time. People are sensitive to how they are seen by others and use many forms of **impression management** to compel others to react to them in the ways they wish. Although we may sometimes do this in a calculated way, usually it is among the things we do without conscious attention. When someone attends a business meeting, he wears a suit and is on his best behavior; that evening, when going to a club, he may first work out and then wear "sexy" garments. This is impression management, or more colloquially, "striking a pose."

A central insight of sociology since Goffman has been that a crucial aspect of social interaction is that every human being possesses a self that is fragile and vulnerable to embarrassment or even humiliation at every turn. People are intensely attuned to what others think of them and how they are being viewed. Seeking approval and respect, they want to "save face" at every turn. In social interactions, human beings tend to collaborate with others to make sure that the interaction ends without embarrassment for anyone. As a stage, social life has many players and they must collaborate to make each scene work.

Think of examples from your own life when people will not collaborate with you. If you go to a club and someone whom you don't want to meet approaches you, you will likely try to

New York Governor Elliot Spitzer and his wife hold a press conference announcing his resignation on March 12, 2008. In his public life, Spitzer was known as a crusader against corruption and organized crime. In private, Spitzer was apparently a frequent customer of high-priced prostitutes. How are Spitzer's actions examples of front stage and back stage?

end the interaction in a way that is least embarrassing to the other person. If you were to simply tell the person "Get lost!" rather than help them save face, that would be highly unusual. This is because there is a norm of collaboration by which human beings try to move through life without embarrassing or humiliating others. When this collaboration does not occur, the interaction is notable for participants.

The pose that we adopt depends highly on our social role, but no particular role implies any particular presentation of self. A person's demeanor can be different depending on the social context. For instance, as a student you have a certain status and are expected to act a certain way when you are around your professors. Some pupils will enact the self-presentation of the dutiful student, while others will enact an uncaring or apathetic pose. For example, in many poor minority schools, students afraid of being accused of "acting white" will adopt a more oppositional stance. Yet, even the appearance may not give an accurate sense of what is going on inside. A student who takes on the demeanor of the "street" may be studying just as hard as someone who appears to act in accordance with old-fashioned propriety.

ADOPTING ROLES—INTIMATE EXAMINATIONS

For an example of collaboration in impression management that also borrows from the theater, let's look at one particular study in some detail. James Henslin and Mae Biggs (1971, 1997) studied a specific, highly delicate type of encounter: a woman's visit to a gynecologist. At the time of the study, most pelvic examinations were carried out by male doctors, and hence the experience was (and sometimes still is) fraught with potential ambiguities and embarrassment for both parties. Men and women in the West are socialized to think of the genitals as the most private part of the body, and seeing, and particularly touching, the genitals of another person is ordinarily associated with intimate sexual encounters. Some women feel so worried by the prospect of a pelvic examination that they refuse to visit the doctor, male or female, even when they suspect there is a strong medical reason to do so.

Henslin and Biggs analyzed material collected by Biggs, a trained nurse, from a large number of gynecological examinations. They interpreted what they found as having several typical stages. Adopting a dramaturgical metaphor, they suggested that each phase can be treated as a distinct scene, in which the parts the actors play alter as the episode unfolds. In the prologue, the woman enters the waiting room preparing to assume the role of patient and temporarily discarding her outside identity. Called into the consulting room, she adopts the "patient" role, and the first scene opens. The doctor assumes a businesslike, professional manner and treats the patient as a proper and competent person, maintaining eye contact and listening politely to what she has to say. If he decides an examination is called for, he tells her so and leaves the room; scene one is over.

As he leaves, the nurse comes in. She is an important stagehand in the main scene shortly to begin. She soothes any worries that the patient might have, acting as both a confidante—knowing some of the "things women have to put up with"—and a collaborator in what is to follow. Crucial to the next scene, the nurse helps alter the patient from a person to a "nonperson" for the vital scene—which features a body, part of which is to be scrutinized, rather than a complete human being. In Henslin and Biggs's study, the nurse not only supervises the patient's undressing but also takes over aspects that normally the patient would control. Thus she takes the patient's clothes and folds them. Most women wish their underwear to be out of sight when the doctor returns, and the nurse makes sure that this is so. She guides the patient to the examining table and covers most of the patient's body with a sheet before the physician returns.

The central scene now opens, with the nurse as well as the doctor taking part. The presence of the nurse helps ensure that the interaction between the doctor and the patient is free of sexual overtones and provides a legal witness should the physician be charged with unprofessional conduct. The examination proceeds as though the personality of the patient were absent; the sheet across her separates the genital area from the rest of her body, and her position does not allow her to watch the examination itself. Save for any specific medical queries, the doctor ignores her, sitting on a low stool, out of her line of vision. The patient collaborates in becoming a temporary nonperson, not initiating conversation and keeping any movements to a minimum.

In the interval between this and the final scene, the nurse again plays the role of stagehand, helping the patient become a full person once more. After the doctor has left the room, the two may again engage in conversation, the patient expressing relief that the examination is over. Having dressed and regroomed herself, the patient is ready to face the concluding scene. The doctor reenters and, in discussing the results of the examination, again treats the patient as a complete and responsible person. Resuming his polite, professional manner, he conveys that his reactions to her are in no way altered by the intimate contact with her body. The epilogue is played out when the patient leaves the physician's office, taking up again her identity in the outside world. The patient and the doctor have thus collaborated in such a way as to manage the interaction and the impression each participant forms of the other.

Focused and Unfocused Interaction

In many social situations, we engage in what Goffman calls **unfocused interaction** with others. Unfocused interaction takes place whenever individuals exhibit mutual awareness of one another's presence. This is usually the case anywhere large numbers of people are assembled, as on a busy street, in a theater crowd, or at a party. When people are in the presence of others, even if they do not directly talk to them, they continually communicate nonverbally through their posture and facial and physical gestures.

Focused interaction occurs when individuals directly attend to what others say or do. Except when someone is standing alone, say, at a party, all interaction involves both focused and unfocused exchanges. Goffman calls an instance of focused interaction an **encounter**, and much of our day-to-day life consists of encounters with other people—family, friends, colleagues—frequently occurring against the background of unfocused interaction with others present. Small talk, seminar discussions, games, and routine face-to-face contacts (with ticket clerks, waiters, shop assistants, and so forth) are all examples of encounters.

Encounters always need "openings," which indicate that civil inattention is being discarded. When strangers meet and begin to talk at a party, the moment of ceasing civil inattention is always risky because misunderstandings can easily occur about the nature of the encounter being established (Goffman 1971). Hence making eye contact may first be ambiguous and tentative. A person can then act as though she had made no direct move if the overture is not accepted. In focused interaction, each person communicates as much by facial expression and gesture as by the words actually exchanged.

Goffman distinguishes between the expressions individuals give and those they give off. The first are the words and facial expressions people use to produce certain impressions on others. The second are the clues that others may spot to check their sincerity or truthfulness. For instance, a restaurant owner listens with a polite smile to the statements of customers about how much they enjoyed their meals. At the same time, he is noting how pleased they seemed to be while eating the food, whether a lot was left over, and the tone of voice they use to express their satisfaction.

Think about how Goffman's concepts of focused and unfocused interaction, developed mainly to explain face-to-face social encounters, would apply to our current age. Can you think of a way in which unfocused interaction occurs in G-mail chatting, Facebook, or Web sites that have a chat forum? In some of these small online communities, everyone can have a mutual awareness of who else is on line, without being in direct contact with them. In some of these programs, people are constantly broadcasting elements of what they are doing or their current situation through status messages.

These status messages make it possible for people in unfocused interaction to have even more control over how they are perceived than people who are merely in one another's presence. Instead of revealing their facial expressions or posture, which they may be unconscious of, people can consciously choose what message they wish to broadcast.

Audience Segregation

Although people cooperate to help one another "save face," they also endeavor individually to preserve their own dignity, autonomy, and respect. One of the ways that people do this is

Identify examples of focused and unfocused interaction in this photograph by Jeff Wall. What are some of the messages these individuals give off?

by arranging for "audience segregation" in their lives. In each of their roles they act somewhat differently, and they endeavor to keep what they do in each role distinct from each of the others. This means that they can have multiple selves. Frequently these selves are consistent, but sometimes they are not. People find it very stressful when boundaries break down or when they cannot reconcile their role in one part of life with their role in another. For example, some people have two friends who do not like one another. Rather than choose between them, they spend time with both friends but never mention to either friend that they are close with the other. Or, some people live very different lives at home and at work. For example, due to discrimination against gays and lesbians, some people will appear "straight" at work and gay at home. Like all people who engage in "audience segregation," they show a different face to different people, "striking a (different) pose" in each context (Brekhus 2003).

Goffman saw social life as a precarious balancing act, but he also studied those instances in which audience segregation could not be maintained. Thus, in the book *Asylums,* he conducted an ethnographic study of St. Elizabeth's mental hospital in Washington, D.C. This was a place where the barriers between different spheres of life (sleep, play, and work) break down. In such an environment, which Goffman called a "total institution," human beings need to adapt to the fact that their private spheres are so limited. Other examples of "total institutions," in which all aspects of life are conducted in the same place, would include prisons, monasteries, and army boot camps.

"MY WORST E-MAIL DISASTER": IMPRESSION MANAGEMENT IN THE INTERNET AGE

The concept of "audience segregation" helps us understand some of the dilemmas of electronic communication. Many people are very sensitive about having things sent to their business e-mail address which they don't want their co-workers or supervisors to know about. Thus, they maintain different addresses for home (**"back region"**) and office (**"front region"**), a practice which is increasingly important because many companies have policies against sending personal e-mails from a company's computer. In 2007, employees of New Jersey's PNC Bank discovered the hard way how important it is to maintain such boundaries. Heidi Arace was fired in 2007 after forwarding a picture of a bare-breasted woman attached to Hillary Clinton's face.

Or consider the social situation of a copied message. You write a message to a friend asking him whether he prefers to go to the early show or the late show. You also tell your friend that you have a new boyfriend whom you hope he will like. He replies and copies the other people who are thinking of going to the movie, many of whom you never intended to tell about the new romance. Suddenly, the audience segregation you had imagined has broken down.

In recent years, undergraduate students have posted pictures of themselves drinking at parties, or even naked, only to discover that future employers have found these and other postings available before making a hiring decision. Some of these items remain on the Internet long after anyone would normally remember the situation that gave rise to them.

Disasters like this, and ones far worse, occur frequently in the age of e-mail. One of the most troublesome of breakdowns occurs due to "Autofill," the tool on e-mail that fills in the rest of an address. Here is one common story:

My worst e-mail disaster was not too long ago when I composed an e-mail using my work e-mail (MS Outlook) asking my friend Krista for a link to a porn site. My e-mail was something like "Yo Krista! where's the link to that porn site? I need to forward it to Jenny!"

Anyone who uses MS Outlook knows that it has this autofill feature for the "To:" field, and instead of selecting "Krista," I selected "Kirsten," who's a co-worker!

Stacy Snyder was an aspiring teacher who was about to graduate from Millersville University's School of Education in 2006 when a campus official discovered a photograph on her MySpace page that showed Snyder sipping from a plastic cup and wearing a pirate hat. The photo's caption read "Drunken Pirate." Although Snyder was of legal drinking age, school administrators labeled her conduct unprofessional and refused to give her a teaching certificate. How is this refusal an example of impression management?

I had no idea I sent it to the wrong person until Kirsten e-mailed me back, asking if the e-mail I just sent her was meant for her or "someone else"!

I still can't look Kirsten in the eye. And I never send personal e-mail using my work e-mail account. EVER.

☑ CONCEPT CHECKS

1. What is impression management?
2. Compare and contrast focused and unfocused interaction.
3. Why do we segregate our audiences in daily life?

Social Context and Shared Understandings

We can make sense of what is said in conversation only if we know the social context, which does not appear in the words themselves. Take the following conversation (Heritage 1985):

A: *I have a fourteen-year-old son.*

B: *Well, that's all right.*

A: *I also have a dog.*

B: *Oh, I'm sorry.*

What do you think is happening here? What is the relation between the speakers? What if you were told that this is a conversation between a prospective tenant and a landlord? The conversation then becomes sensible: Some landlords accept children but don't permit their tenants to keep pets. Yet if we don't know the social context, the responses of individual B seem to bear no relation to the statements of A. Part of the sense is in the words, and part is in the way in which the meaning emerges from the social context.

Shared Understandings

The most inconsequential forms of daily talk presume complicated, shared knowledge brought into play by those speaking. In fact, our small talk is so complex that it has so far proved impossible to program even the most sophisticated computers to converse with human beings. The words used in ordinary talk do not always have precise meanings, and we "fix" what we want to say through the unstated assumptions that back it up. If Maria asks Tom, "What did you do yesterday?" the words in the question themselves suggest no obvious answer. A day is a long time, and it would be logical for Tom to answer, "Well, at seven sixteen, I woke up. At seven eighteen, I got out of bed, went to the bathroom and started to brush my teeth. At seven nineteen, I turned on the shower. . . ." We understand the type of response the question calls for by knowing Maria, what sort of activities she and Tom consider relevant, and what Tom usually does on a particular day of the week, among other things.

Ethnomethodology

Ethnomethodology is the study of the "ethnomethods"—the folk, or lay, methods—people use to make sense of what others do and particularly of what they say. We all apply these methods, normally without having to give any conscious attention to them. This field was created by Harold Garfinkel, who was the second most important figure in the study of micro interaction.

Garfinkel argued that in order to understand the way people use context to make sense of the world, sociologists need to study the "background expectancies" with which we organize ordinary conversations. He highlighted these in some experiments he undertook with student volunteers (1963). The students were asked to engage a friend or relative in conversation and to insist that casual remarks or general comments be actively pursued to make their meaning precise. If someone said, "Have a nice day," the student was to respond, "Nice in what sense, exactly?" "Which part of the day do you mean?" and so forth. One of the exchanges that resulted ran as follows. S is the friend; E, the student volunteer (Garfinkel 1963):

S: *How are you?*

E: *How am I in regard to what? My health, my finances, my school work, my peace of mind, my . . .*

S: *(red in the face and suddenly out of control): Look! I was just trying to be polite. Frankly, I don't give a damn how you are.*

Why do people get so upset when apparently minor conventions of talk are not followed? The answer is that the stability and meaningfulness of our daily social lives depend on the sharing of unstated cultural assumptions about what is said and why. If we weren't able to take these for granted, meaningful communication would be impossible. Any question or contribution to a conversation would have to be followed by a massive "search procedure" of the sort Garfinkel's subjects were told to initiate, and interaction would simply break down. What seem at first sight to be unimportant conventions of talk,

How do background expectancies influence our conversations? Try Garfinkel's experiment yourself and see how your friends and relatives react.

therefore, turn out to be fundamental to the very fabric of social life, which is why their breach is so serious.

Note that in everyday life, people on occasion deliberately feign ignorance of unstated knowledge. This may be done to rebuff the others, poke fun at them, cause embarrassment, or call attention to a double meaning in what was said. Consider, for example, this classic exchange between parent and teenager:

P: *Where are you going?*

T: *Out.*

P: *What are you going to do?*

T: *Nothing.*

The responses of the teenager are effectively the opposite of those of the volunteers in Garfinkel's experiments. Rather than pursuing inquiries where this is not normally done, the teenager declines to provide appropriate answers at all—essentially saying, "Mind your own business!"

The first question might elicit a different response from another person in another context:

A: *Where are you going?*

B: *I'm going quietly round the bend.*

B deliberately misreads A's question to ironically convey worry or frustration. Comedy and joking thrive on such deliberate misunderstandings of the unstated assumptions involved in talk. There is nothing threatening about this so long as the parties concerned recognize that the intent is to provoke laughter.

☑ CONCEPT CHECKS

1. Why do we make small talk?
2. What do ethnomethodologists do?

Social Rules and Talk

Although we routinely use nonverbal cues in our own behavior and in making sense of the behavior of others, much of our interaction is done through talk—casual verbal exchange—carried on in informal conversations with others. Sociologists have always accepted that language is fundamental to social life. However, an approach has been developed that is specifically concerned with how people use language in the ordinary contexts of everyday life.

"Interactional Vandalism"

We have already seen that conversations are one of the main ways in which our daily lives are maintained in a stable and coherent manner. We feel most comfortable when the tacit conventions of small talk are adhered to; when they are breached, we can feel threatened, confused, and insecure. In most everyday talk, conversants are carefully attuned to the cues they get from others—such as changes in intonation, slight pauses, or gestures—to facilitate conversation smoothly. By being mutually aware, conversants "cooperate" in opening and closing interactions and in taking turns to speak. Interactions in which one party is conversationally "uncooperative," however, can give rise to tensions.

Garfinkel's students created tense situations by intentionally undermining conversational rules as part of a sociological experiment. But what about situations in the real world in which people make trouble through their conversational practices? One study investigated verbal interchanges between pedestrians and street people in New York City to understand why such interactions are often seen as problematic by passersby. The researchers used a technique called **conversation analysis** to compare a selection of street interchanges with samples of everyday talk. Conversation analysis is a methodology that examines all facets of a conversation for meaning—from the smallest filler words (such as "um" and "ah") to the precise timing of interchanges (including pauses, interruptions, and overlaps).

The study looked at interactions between black men—many of whom were homeless, alcoholic, or drug addicted—and white women who passed by them on the street. The men would often try to initiate conversations with passing women by calling out to them, paying them compliments, or asking them questions. But something "goes wrong" in these conversations, because the women rarely respond as they would in a normal interaction. Even though the men's comments are rarely hostile in tone, the women tend to quicken their step and stare fixedly ahead. The following shows attempts by Mudrick, a black man in his late fifties, to engage women in conversation (Duneier and Molotch 1999):

[Mudrick] begins this interaction when a white woman who looks about twenty-five approaches at a steady pace:

1. **Mudrick:** *I love you baby.*
She crosses her arms and quickens her walk, ignoring the comment.

Mudrick, pictured above, approaches a woman on the sidewalk in New York City.

2. **Mudrick:** *Marry me.*
Next, it is two white women, also probably in their mid-twenties:

3. **Mudrick:** *Hi girls, you all look very nice today. You have some money? Buy some books.*
They ignore him. Next, it is a young black woman.

4. **Mudrick:** *Hey pretty. Hey pretty.*
She keeps walking without acknowledging him.

5. **Mudrick:** *'Scuse me. 'Scuse me. I know you hear me.*
Then he addresses a white woman in her thirties.

6. **Mudrick:** *I'm watching you. You look nice, you know.*
She ignores him.

Negotiating smooth "openings" and "closings" to conversations is a fundamental requirement for urban civility. These crucial aspects of conversation were highly problematic between the men and the women. Where the women resisted the men's attempts at opening conversations, the men ignored the women's resistance and persisted. Similarly, if the men succeeded in opening a conversation, they often refused to respond to cues from the women to close the conversation once it had gotten under way (Duneier and Molotch 1999):

1. **Mudrick:** *Hey pretty.*
2. **Woman:** *Hi how you doin.'*
3. **Mudrick:** *You alright?*
4. **Mudrick:** *You look very nice you know. I like how you have your hair pinned.*
5. **Mudrick:** *You married?*
6. **Woman:** *Yeah.*
7. **Mudrick:** *Huh?*
8. **Woman:** *Yeah.*
9. **Mudrick:** *Where the rings at?*
10. **Woman:** *I have it home.*
11. **Mudrick:** *Y' have it home?*
12. **Woman:** *Yeah.*
13. **Mudrick:** *Can I get your name?*
14. **Mudrick:** *My name is Mudrick, what's yours?*
She does not answer and walks on.

In this instance, Mudrick made nine out of the fourteen utterances in the interaction to initiate the conversation and to elicit further responses from the woman. From the transcript alone, it is quite evident that the woman is not interested in talking, but when conversation analysis is applied to the tape recording, her reluctance becomes even clearer. The woman delays all of her responses, even when she does give them, while Mudrick replies immediately, his comments sometimes overlapping hers. Timing in conversations is a very precise indicator; delaying a response by even a fraction of a second is

Keith, who works on the same block as Mudrick, starts a conversation with a woman passing by. How do the two men take advantage of social conventions and politeness to interact with women?

adequate in most everyday interactions to signal the desire to change the course of a conversation. By betraying these tacit rules of sociability, Mudrick was practicing conversation in a way that was "technically" rude. The woman, in return, was also technically rude in ignoring Mudrick's repeated attempts to engage her in talk. It is the technically rude nature of these street interchanges that make them problematic for passersby to handle. When standard cues for opening and closing conversations are not adhered to, individuals feel a sense of profound and inexplicable insecurity.

The term **interactional vandalism** describes cases like these in which a subordinate person breaks the tacit rules of everyday interaction that are of value to the more powerful. The men on the street often do conform to everyday forms of speech in their interactions with one another, local shopkeepers, the police, relatives, and acquaintances. But when they choose to, they subvert the tacit conventions for everyday talk in a way that leaves passersby disoriented. Even more than physical assaults or vulgar verbal abuse, interactional vandalism leaves victims unable to articulate what has happened.

This study of interactional vandalism provides another example of the two-way links between micro-level interactions and forces that operate on the macro level. To the men on the street, the white women who ignore their attempts at conversation appear distant, cold, and bereft of sympathy—legitimate "targets" for such interactions. The women, meanwhile, may often take the men's behavior as proof that they are indeed dangerous and best avoided. Interactional vandalism is closely tied up with overarching class, gender, and racial structures. The fear and anxiety generated in such mundane interactions help constitute the outside statuses and forces that, in turn,

influence the interactions themselves. Interactional vandalism is part of a self-reinforcing system of mutual suspicion and incivility.

How would issues of this kind play themselves out on the Internet? Timing is a far less precise indicator in electronic communications. In the case of Mudrick and the woman above, her long pauses signaled that she wanted to end the exchange. On a chat service, pauses are very hard to interpret. They may be commonplace as one partner is called temporarily away from the computer or even only to another computer window. On the other hand, the very possibility can make intentional pauses seem like a gentler way to prevent conversation than nonresponsiveness in physical space.

And what about "interactional vandalism"? Can we think of ways in which less powerful people engaged in electronic communications undermine the taken-for-granted rules of interaction that are of value to the more powerful? The very existence of the Internet creates spaces in which less powerful people can make their superiors accountable in ways they never were before. Think of all the blogs in which workers talk anonymously about their bosses, or the common situations in which workers forward rude messages from their boss to other employees. Because of the Internet, powerful people are less able to segregate their audiences—treating some people poorly behind the scenes and treating others very nicely in public.

Response Cries

Some kinds of utterances are not talk but consist of muttered exclamations, or what Goffman (1981) has called **response cries**. Consider Lucy, who exclaims, "Oops!" after knocking over a glass of water. "Oops!" seems to be merely an uninteresting reflex response to a mishap, rather like blinking your eye when a person moves a hand sharply toward your face. It is not a reflex, however, as shown by the fact that people do not usually make the exclamation when alone. "Oops!" is normally directed toward others present. The exclamation demonstrates to witnesses that the lapse is only minor and momentary, not something that should cast doubt on Lucy's command of her actions.

"Oops!" is used only in situations of minor failure, rather than in major accidents or calamities—which also demonstrates that the exclamation is part of our controlled management of the details of social life. Moreover, the word may be used by someone observing Lucy, rather than by Lucy herself, or it may be used to sound a warning to another. "Oops!" is normally a curt sound, but the "oo" may be prolonged in some situations. Thus someone might extend the sound to cover a critical moment in performing a task. For instance, a parent may utter an extended "Oops!" or "Oopsadaisy!" when playfully tossing a child in the air. The sound covers the brief phase when the child may feel a loss of control, reassuring him and probably at the same time developing his understanding of response cries.

This may all sound very contrived and exaggerated. Why bother to analyze such an inconsequential utterance in this detail? Surely we don't pay as much attention to what we say as this example suggests? Of course we don't—on a conscious level. The crucial point, however, is that we take for granted an immensely complicated, continuous control of our appearance and actions. In situations of interaction, we are never expected just to be present. Others expect, as we expect of them, that we will display what Goffman calls *controlled alertness*. A fundamental part of being human is continually demonstrating to others our competence in the routines of daily life.

Personal Space

There are cultural differences in the definition of **personal space**. In Western culture, people usually maintain a distance of at least three feet when engaged in focused interaction with others; when standing side by side, they may stand closer together. In the Middle East, people often stand closer to each other than is thought acceptable in the West. Westerners visiting that part of the world are likely to find themselves disconcerted by this unexpected physical proximity.

Edward T. Hall (1969, 1973), who has worked extensively on nonverbal communication, distinguishes four zones of personal space. Intimate distance, of up to one and a half feet, is

Cultural norms frequently determine the acceptable boundaries of personal space. In the Middle East, for example, people frequently stand closer to each other than is common in the West.

reserved for very few social contacts. Only those involved in relationships in which regular bodily touching is permitted, such as lovers or parents and children, operate within this zone of private space. Personal distance, from one and a half to four feet, is the normal spacing for encounters with friends and close acquaintances. Some intimacy of contact is permitted, but this tends to be strictly limited. Social distance, from four to twelve feet, is the zone usually maintained in formal settings such as interviews. The fourth zone is that of public distance, beyond twelve feet, preserved by those who are performing to an audience.

In ordinary interaction, the most fraught zones are those of intimate and personal distance. If these zones are invaded, people try to recapture their space. We may stare at the intruder as if to say, "Move away!" or elbow her aside. When people are forced into proximity closer than they deem desirable, they might create a kind of physical boundary: A reader at a crowded library desk might physically demarcate a private space by stacking books around its edges (Hall 1969, 1973).

☑ CONCEPT CHECKS

1. What is the purpose of conversation analysis?
2. Describe the purpose of interactional vandalism.
3. How and why do we try to protect our "personal space"?

Interaction in Time and Space

Understanding how activities are distributed in time and space is fundamental to analyzing encounters and to understanding social life in general. All interaction is situated—it occurs in a particular place and has a specific duration in time. Our actions over the course of a day tend to be "zoned" in time as well as in space. Thus, for example, most people spend a zone—say, from 9:00 A.M. to 5:00 P.M.—of their daily time working. Their weekly time is also zoned: They are likely to work on weekdays and spend weekends at home, altering the pattern of their activities on the weekend days. As we move through the temporal zones of the day, we are also often moving across space as well: To get to work, we may take a bus from one area of a city to another or perhaps commute in from the suburbs. When we analyze the contexts of social interaction, therefore, it is often useful to look at people's movements across **time–space**.

The concept of **regionalization** will help us understand how social life is zoned in time–space. Take the example of

Does the Use of an iPod Affect Public Social Conduct?

Christine Miranda, a junior at Princeton University, wanted to know whether the use of iPods had an impact on users' receptivity to strangers. Comparing the behavior of iPod users and nonusers, she embarked on a study in New York's subway system.

Armed with a notepad and a pen, she began to document interactions with iPod users (and nonusers) on the 6 train on the East Side of Manhattan. She chose the 6 train because it is a north-south train that runs from the financial district of downtown Manhattan through Chinatown, Soho, Greenwich Village, Grand Central Terminal, the Upper East Side, and East Harlem, all the way to the Bronx, encompassing a vast range of socioeconomic diversity.

Miranda's methods included observation, interviews, and experiments. Boarding a subway car, she would take note of whether people possessed iPods, their positioning in relation to herself, and their race, sex, and approximate age. In addition to denoting users' and nonusers' responses to interactions, Miranda took note of cues such as body language and facial gestures. She systematically recorded exchanges between users and nonusers, as well as interactions involving auditory interruptions, invasions of physical space, and sexual offenses.

Sometimes, Miranda would simply watch naturally occurring interactions—for example, the responses of users and nonusers when a panhandler petitioned for donations. At other times, she would act as the "confederate," or intruder, interrupting an iPod user to ask about the train's last stop. She asked similar questions of nonusers as well, seeking to determine whether iPod users would be less eager or less willing to respond.

What Miranda found was that iPod users seemed just as open to providing useful information as nonusers. Among the iPod users, no one she asked seemed to mind removing headphones long enough to provide an answer; indeed, the users she asked seemed more courteous than the nonusers. Having offered the information that was requested, however, iPod users promptly went back to listening to their music. (Likewise, nonusers who were reading when she asked them went back to their newspapers and books, and those engaged in conversation went back to talking.)

One interesting result was that her interviews suggested that iPod users tended to be *perceived* as less approachable. So while most users seemed happy to offer information that was requested of them, they were less likely than nonusers to be asked in the first place. "The personal stereo presents an opportunity to block off the outside environment and to reduce the likelihood of being approached, but when social conduct does occur, the user's behavior is not much different from the nonuser's."

Miranda concluded that while the personal stereo presents the illusion of separation, making a user appear less approachable, "this wall can be easily broken when we simply disrupt a person's personal space with words or actions." It may initially take a bit more effort to get the attention of an iPod user, for their senses may be somewhat dulled compared to a more alert nonuser. When a true attempt to get an iPod user to interact is made (for example, asking a pointed question), the iPod user seems as open to interruption as the nonuser.

a private house. A modern house is regionalized into rooms, hallways, and floors (if there is more than one story). These spaces are not just physically separate areas but are zoned in time as well. The living rooms and kitchen are used most in the daylight hours, the bedrooms at night. The interaction that occurs in these regions is bound by both spatial and temporal divisions. Some areas of the house form back regions, with "performances" taking place in the others. At times, the whole house can become a back region. Once again, this idea is beautifully captured by Goffman (1973):

> On a Sunday morning, a whole household can use the wall around its domestic establishment to conceal a relaxing slovenliness in dress and civil endeavor, extending to all rooms the informality that is usually restricted to kitchen and bedrooms. So, too, in American middle-class neighborhoods, on afternoons the line between children's playground and home may be defined as backstage by mothers, who pass along it wearing jeans, loafers, and a minimum of make-up. . . .

Clock Time

In modern societies, the zoning of our activities is strongly influenced by **clock time**. Without clocks and the precise timing of activities, and thereby their coordination across space, industrialized societies could not exist (Mumford 1973). The measuring of time by clocks is today standardized across the globe, making possible the complex international transport systems and communications we now depend on. World standard time was first introduced in 1884 at a conference of nations held in Washington, D.C. The globe was then partitioned into twenty-four time zones, each one hour apart, and an exact beginning of the universal day was fixed.

Fourteenth-century monasteries were the first organizations to try to schedule the activities of their inmates precisely across the day and week. Today, there is virtually no group or organization that does not do so—the greater the number of people and resources involved, the more precise the scheduling must be. Eviatar Zerubavel (1979, 1982) demonstrated this in his study of the temporal structure of a large modern hospital. A hospital must operate on a twenty-four-hour basis, and coordinating the staff and resources is a highly complex matter. For instance, the nurses work for one time period in ward A, another time period in ward B, and so on, and are called on to alternate between day- and night-shift work. Nurses, doctors, and other staff, plus the resources they need, must be integrated both in time and in space.

Social Life and the Ordering of Space and Time

The Internet is another example of how closely forms of social life are bound up with our control of space and time. The Internet makes it possible for us to interact with people we never see or meet, in any corner of the world. Such technological change rearranges space—we can interact with anyone without moving from our chair. It also alters our experience of time, because communication on the electronic highway is almost immediate. Until about fifty years ago, most communication across space required a duration of time. If you sent a letter to someone abroad, there was a time gap while the letter was carried, by ship, train, truck, or plane, to the person to whom it was written.

People still write letters by hand today, of course, but instantaneous communication has become basic to our social world. Our lives would be almost unimaginable without it. We are so used to being able to switch on the TV and watch the news or make a phone call or send an e-mail message to a friend in another state that it is hard for us to imagine what life would be like otherwise.

The Compulsion of Proximity

In modern societies, in complete contrast to the !Kung—as explored in the chapters that follow—we are constantly interacting with others whom we may never see or meet. Almost all of our everyday transactions, such as buying groceries or making a bank deposit, bring us into contact—but indirect

The November 2007 Middle East peace talks in Annapolis, Maryland, are an example of what Molotch and Boden call the *compulsion of proximity*. Individuals prefer face-to-face interaction because these situations provide richer information about how other people think or feel.

Communication and Cell Phones

People have chatted with each other since the beginning of time, or at least since humans began to use language. Talking is how we communicate our desires and needs, respond to others, and—whether huddled around a campfire or shoulder to shoulder in a tavern—organize our lives, try to realize our dreams, and reassure ourselves that we are not alone. But are modern ways of living changing this? Is our contact with others being replaced by silent soliloquies that we carry on with television shows, computers, and piles of other electronic and digital gadgets? Are we losing our ability to communicate with each other?

We are in the middle of a revolution in personal communication that began at the turn of the last century and has only intensified during the last generation. Will it be used to keep people—even those close to us—at a distance, or will it instead be used to create new ways in which we share experience with others? What do you think?

> What are the monks doing in this photo? Where are they? Whom are they talking to, and what are they talking about? How often do they use these phones? Do they use them in their daily lives or only on special occasions? Are they worried that cell phones will change their ancient monastic life, or do they care?

> Whom is the woman in New York talking to? Is she just chatting, or has something serious happened? She seems oblivious to her surroundings. Preoccupied? But is she any less connected to the world than those passing her by? How do her social ties today differ from those of her parents and grandparents when they were her age?

Created by John Grady.

Cellphone subscribers per 100 people, 1994–2006

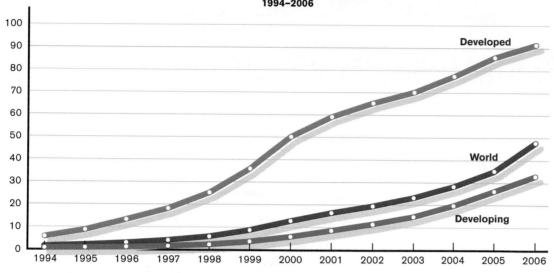

Developed

World

Developing

As of 2008, over three billion people, more than half of the world's population, had access to a mobile phone. In recent years, cell phone use has spread most rapidly in the poorest continent in the world, Africa. Have cell phones changed how people communicate around the globe? What do people in societies that have no land line phones, and with state controlled media, talk about? Does having a cell phone create new economic opportunities or political and social networks? Will their use foster social cooperation or conflict?

How often do young adults (between 22 and 40 years old) keep in touch with people other than co-workers and family? We know that they watch less television than young adults did twenty years ago and that, if anything, they report increased contact with their relatives and circle of friends. But what about talking to their most trusted friends who are neither co-workers nor family?

Hours of TV watched by 22–40 year olds (1972–2006)

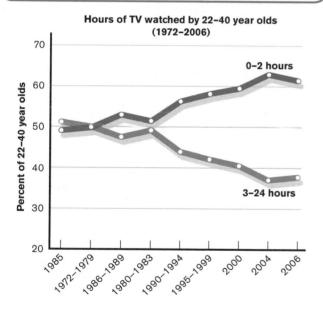

0–2 hours

3–24 hours

(a) Contact with trusted friend 1985

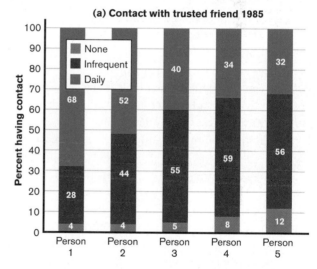

(b) Contact with trusted friend 2004

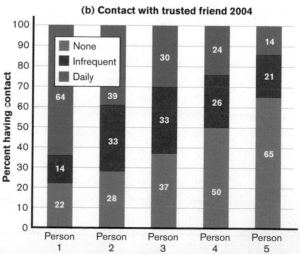

This chart reveals what appears to be a very disturbing trend. On the one hand, in 1985 and 2004 about two out of every three young adults reported having talked on almost a daily basis to the first person they had identified as a trusted friend. On the other hand, daily contact with the four other people they might have mentioned drops precipitously, so that by 2004, only about a third report having any contact at all with a fifth confidant. Are young adults living in a world with a narrowing circle of people whom they feel they can talk to and less contact with those who remain?

Online Interaction in China

Almost 16 percent of China's population uses the Internet (Internet World Stats, 2008b). These estimated 210 million Internet users make China a very close second only to the United States in terms of sheer number of users. But Chinese Internet users are expected to outnumber the online population of the United States within a few years. Even still, there are big differences in who is going online in each country. Currently only 20 percent of people living in Chinese cities use the Internet, most of whom are men under the age of thirty. In contrast, in the United States over 70 percent of urban dwellers use the Internet, men and women use the Internet in about equal numbers, and only about one third are younger than thirty years old (Fallows 2005).

As more and more Chinese people start to use the Internet, big changes are expected. The Internet offers opportunities for communication between people who speak different languages. Because the Internet offers a common written system, it is possible for speakers of the multitude of Chinese dialects to communicate with each other. Tools that translate the text on Web pages from one language to another can facilitate cross-cultural communication. Such tools make global cyberspace available to Chinese Internet users, while English speakers can gain access to the quickly developing Chinese cyberspace. The rapid growth of Chinese Internet users, however, may reshape all of cyberspace. While the dominant language of the Internet is currently English, as more and more Chinese come online, English speakers will have to share cyberspace with Chinese speakers as more and more Web pages will be written in Chinese.

The experience of being online in China may be similar to how Internet users interact online in other parts of the world. For instance, Chinese college students, just like their U.S. counterparts, have been drawn to social networking sites. Sites like Xiaonei.com are the Chinese equivalent of Facebook.com and have a similar look and features, such as personal profile pages, blogs, adding friends, photo hosting, groups, event sharing, and others. Xiaonei.com was recently purchased by a competing social networking site, 5Q.com, in a deal financed in part by a former executive at Amazon.com. The combined social network has over a million participants (Chen 2006). Considering that students make up about a third of China's Internet users, social networking sites are playing an important role in bringing together China's online community. The Internet also is a highly sought-after venue for advertising to the next generation of highly educated Chinese who are poised to take the lead in China's continued transformation into a market economy.

---

contact—with people who may live thousands of miles away. The banking system, for example, is international. Any money you deposit is a small part of the financial investments the bank makes worldwide.

Some people are concerned that the rapid advances in communications technology such as e-mail, the Internet, and e-commerce will only increase this tendency toward indirect interactions. Our society is becoming "devoiced," some claim, as the capabilities of technology grow ever greater. According to this view, as the pace of life accelerates, people are increasingly isolating themselves; we now interact more with our televisions and computers than with our neighbors or members of the community.

Now that e-mail, instant messages, electronic discussion groups, and chat rooms have become facts of life for many people in industrialized countries, what is the nature of these interactions and what new complexities are emerging from them? One study conducted at Stanford University found that about 20 percent of Internet users use the medium to communicate with people whom they do not know (Nie et al. 2004). At the same time, the study found that Internet use reduces face-to-face socializing, TV watching, and sleep. In another study of office workers conducted by Raymond Friedman and Steven Currall in 1997, almost half of the respondents said that the Internet had replaced the need for face-to-face communication. A third of them admitted to using e-mail deliberately to avoid the need for direct communication. Others reported that the use of abusive or offensive e-mails within the workplace had resulted in the complete breakdown of some office relations. The substitution of e-mail for face-to-face communication in

China's rapid economic growth is also taking place in cyberspace, a new frontier for generating profit. Multiplayer online games, such as World of Warcraft and Lineage II, have generated large markets for buying and selling—with real money—virtual currency and other commodities that provide advantages while playing the game. In China, "factories," often called "gold farms," have emerged that hire young people to play massively multiplayer games, exploiting aspects of the game to "farm" valuable items, such as currency, magic spells, equipment, and even whole characters, which are then sold online to players in other parts of the world.

Ge Jin, graduate student researcher at the University of California, San Diego, has found that "China is currently the world factory of virtual commodities" (Jin 2006). Large gold farms are far from virtual: They include dormitories and actual meals, along with alternating twelve-hour shifts at the same computer in "mining operations" that run around the clock. Gold farmers receive modest pay, but some farmers are willing to work for free as long as they have a place to live and can play games for free. Gold farms are sometimes referred to as "sweatshops." Jin noted that "gold farms reflect China's current role in the global economy, which is mainly a source of cheap labor. The gold farmers are being exploited by farm owners and international brokers. . . . Sitting in front of a computer and killing monsters for 10 hours a day can be detrimental to their health" (Jin 2006).

Still, many gold farmers, who are mostly men in their early twenties, do not have better alternatives, facing unemployment or far worse jobs if they were to leave. At the same time, some of these young men enjoy their work, which they may have played as a hobby before becoming a "professional." Jin concluded that "the game world can be a space of empowerment and compensation for them. In contrast to their impoverished real lives, their virtual lives give them access to power, status and wealth which they can hardly imagine in real life. . . . This is a paradox that the term 'sweatshop' cannot convey: in the gold farms exploitation is entangled with empowerment and productivity is entangled with pleasure" (Jin 2006).

View a short documentary on gold farming by Jin at youtube.com/watch?v=ho5Yxe6UVv4.

the office has led to a weakening of social ties and a disruption of techniques used in personal dialogue for avoiding conflict. As a result, online communication seems to allow more room for misinterpretation, confusion, and abuse than more traditional forms of communication (Friedman and Currall 2003). An MSN survey in 2001 reported that for the age group under twenty-five, e-mail was fast replacing face-to-face contact. For instance, 44 percent of the respondents felt that e-mail was an acceptable medium for sending thank you notes, some 27 percent had sent an electronic card for a seasonal or a birthday greeting, and about 10 percent of the women surveyed said that they had used e-mail to end a relationship.

The problem lies in the nature of human communication. We think of it as a product of the mind, but it's done by bodies: faces move, voices intone, bodies sway, hands gesture. . . . On the Internet, the mind is present but the body is gone. Recipients get few clues to the personality and mood of the person, can only guess why messages are sent, what they mean, what responses to make. Trust is virtually out the window. It's a risky business. (Locke and Pascoe 2000)

Many Internet enthusiasts disagree. They argue that, far from being impersonal, online communication has many inherent advantages that cannot be claimed by more traditional forms of interaction such as the telephone and face-to-face meetings. The human voice, for example, may be far superior in terms of expressing emotion and subtleties of meaning, but it can also convey information about the speaker's age, gender,

"It's Official: Men Talk More Than Women"

Common wisdom tells us that women talk more than men. Television comedies often show images of vivacious women chatting away, while their silent husbands quietly nod and mutter, "Yes, Dear." It came as a great surprise to many Americans, then, when the November 2007 news headlines told us "Chatty Cathy? More Like Gabby Gary" (Dube 2007) and "It's Official: Men Talk More than Women" (Keim 2007).

The media were reporting on a recent study that found men talk slightly more than women. However, a close inspection of the study revealed that this difference was very small and that the gender gap in talkativeness varied widely across social situations. The study authors, Campbell Leaper and Melanie M. Ayres, psychologists at University of California–Santa Cruz, acknowledged that "on average, men are slightly more talkative than women. In reality, though, as with most

gender differences, the differences are very small."

The psychologists' findings were based on a *meta-analysis*. Meta-analysis is a systematic review and synthesis of prior published research. Researchers

Do men talk more than women in your workplace? How does men's speech differ from that of women?

calculate a statistical summary of the findings of prior studies—all of which are exploring a similar research question. The authors reviewed studies on gender differences in communication that were

published between 1960 and 2005. They focused on sixty-three studies exploring gender differences in amount of talking, forty-seven studies on the use of affiliative speech, and thirty-nine studies on the use of assertive speech.

The researchers said that their most important finding was the gender gap in *how* men and women speak, rather than *how much* they speak. For instance, they found that men tend to use more "assertive speech," such as giving directions, sharing their opinions, and disagreeing with others. Women, by contrast, are more likely to engage in "affiliative" speech, such as giving emotional support, acknowledging others, and agreeing with others. The authors also emphasized the important ways that social context affects social interaction. Men and women would alter both what they said and how much they spoke, depending on who was in their conversation group. Women were more talkative when

ethnicity, or social position—information that could be used to the speaker's disadvantage. Electronic communication, it is noted, masks all these identifying markers and ensures that attention focuses strictly on the content of the message. This can be a great advantage for women or other traditionally disadvantaged groups whose opinions are sometimes devalued in other settings (Lock and Pascoe 2000). Electronic interaction is often presented as liberating and empowering because people can create their own online identities and speak more freely than they would elsewhere.

Who is right in this debate? How far can electronic communication substitute for face-to-face interaction? There is little question that new media forms are revolutionizing the way people communicate, but even when it is more expedient to

interact indirectly, humans still value direct contact—possibly even more highly than before. People in business, for instance, continue to attend meetings, sometimes flying halfway around the world to do so, when it would seem much simpler and more effective to transact business through a conference call or video link. Family members could arrange virtual reunions or holiday gatherings using electronic real-time communications, but we all recognize that they would lack the warmth and intimacy of face-to-face celebrations.

An explanation for this phenomenon comes from Deidre Boden and Harvey Molotch (1994), who have studied what they call the **compulsion of proximity**: the need of individuals to meet with one another in situations of *copresence,* or face-to-face interaction. People put themselves out to attend conversing with children and their college classmates, while men were chattier when talking to their spouses and strangers. When talking to strangers, men often tried to influence the listener, whereas women tried to form a connection with the person. Men also spoke more than women when they were in mixed-gender settings.

The study also reveals the importance of social changes in gender role expectations over time. The psychologists found that the gender gap in how men and women communicate has narrowed over time, as more and more men engage in "affiliative" speech. They noted, "It's becoming more acceptable for men to be expressive."

Around the same time that the Leaper and Ayres study hit the news, another study reported in *Science* found that college-age women speak slightly more than 16,000 words per day, while their male peers speak slightly less than 16,000 words per day—a difference that is not statistically significant. The study, conducted by University of Arizona psychologist Matthias Mehl and colleagues, focused on a sample of 400 college-age students over the time period of 1984 to 2004 (Mehl et al. 2007). The students were outfitted with an electronically activated recorder (EAR), a device that automatically recorded their speech for 30-second periods, every 12.5 minutes, over a 10-day span. Students did not know when the device was recording. The device recorded roughly 4 percent of all the words that each student uttered in a day. Mehl believes that his findings are important because they help to chip away at stereotypes such as "female chatterbox and silent male" and instead highlight the ways that small gender differences are often overblown in the media: "We use our gender magnifying glass and overgeneralize from that" (Knox 2008).

Overall, the authors of both studies emphasized the important role that social science can play in erasing stereotypes about gender and language. Leaper said, "These findings compellingly debunk simplistic stereotypes about gender differences in language use.... Gender differences appear and disappear, depending on the interaction context" (Leaper and Ayres 2007).

Questions

- According to the study authors, which gender talks more? Is this gender difference statistically significant?
- What is a meta-analysis?
- In which specific ways do men's and women's speech patterns differ?

- Do you believe the "female chatterbox" and "silent male" stereotypes persist today? Why or why not?

FOR FURTHER EXPLORATION

Dube, Rebecca. 2007. "Chatty Cathy? More Like Gabby Gary." *Globe and Mail,* November 22, 2007. www.theglobeandmail.com/servlet/story/RTGAM.20071122.wlchatty22/BNStory/GlobeSportsOther/ (accessed January 11, 2008).

Keim, Brandon. 2007. "It's Official: Men Talk More Than Women." *Wired,* November 9, 2007. http://blog.wired.com/wiredscience/2007/11/its-official-me.html (accessed January 11, 2008).

Knox, Richard. 2008. "Study: Men Talk Just as Much as Women." National Public Radio, July 5, 2007. www.npr.org/templates/story/story.php?storyId=11762186 (accessed January 11, 2008).

Leaper, Campbell, and Melanie Ayres. 2007. "A Meta-Analytic Review of Gender Variations in Adults' Language Use: Talkativeness, Affiliative Speech, and Assertive Speech." *Personality and Social Psychology Review* 11: 328–363.

Mehl, Matthias, Simine Vazire, Nairan Ramirez-Esparza, Richard B. Slatcher, and James W. Pennebaker. 2007. "Are Women Really More Talkative Than Men?" *Science* 317 (July 6, 2007): 317.

meetings, Boden and Molotch suggest, because situations of copresence, for reasons documented by Goffman in his studies of interaction, supply much richer information about how other people think and feel and about their sincerity than any form of electronic communication.

Only by actually being in the presence of people who make decisions affecting us in important ways do we feel able to learn what is going on and feel confident that we can impress them with our own views and our own sincerity. "Copresence," Boden and Molotch (1994) say, "affects access to the body part that 'never lies,' the eyes—the 'windows on the soul.' Eye contact itself signals a degree of intimacy and trust; copresent interactants continuously monitor the subtle movements of this most subtle body part."

One reminder of the need for proximity is those many situations in which people who meet through e-mail or a listserv feel to be together physically. One listserv for fans of the television show *My So-Called Life,* which ran for one season in 1994–1995, has resulted in eleven couples. Several of the couples had one or both partners move to a different country to live with the other. The seven children these couples have already produced are perhaps the best possible evidence for the compulsion of proximity!

☑ CONCEPT CHECKS

1. How does time structure human life?
2. Is face-to-face interaction, or copresence, an important aspect of human action? Why or why not?

"A Message from Bill Cosby"

Elijah Anderson, a professor at the University of Pennsylvania, has spent two decades studying inner-city Philadelphia and his insightful and provocative representations of ghetto life have extended far into the public realm. Anderson uses an ethnographic approach in his work, which means that he writes about the black community from firsthand experience. His findings are based on participant observation, interviewing, and socializing with residents of low-income communities. Through his work, he has developed as deep an understanding of these neighborhoods as any sociologist working today.

While vacationing with his family a few years ago, Anderson received a phone call from comedian Bill Cosby, who asked the professor if they could meet at a church in Newark, New Jersey, where Cosby had been invited to speak at a town hall meeting. Cosby had recently ignited an intense public debate by claiming that poor African Americans needed to take responsibility for their own problems. Blaming the problems of blacks on the street culture of the ghetto, Cosby implored African Americans to "hold up their end of the deal" (CNN 2004b). Many Americans believed that Cosby had hit the nail on the head, but Anderson, who had written a great deal about ghetto culture in the 1990s, held a different view.

Ever since the beginning of research on the American ghetto, scholars have observed that residents' basic values are the source of significant conflicts in ghetto neighborhoods. Such conflicts arise because people from many economic classes have been forced to live together due to racial discrimination. As a result, people who would not normally choose to be neighbors are thrown together in the same neighborhoods.

Anderson has worked in the tradition of trying to

Elijah Anderson

understand these conflicts over basic values, and has noted that poor black communities are often divided between people who define themselves as "decent" and people who define themselves as "street."

Anderson's reference to "street" people and "decent" people is an attempt to show how the residents of these communities view themselves. This is very different from labeling some groups as "street" and others as "decent" and adopting those categories himself. The labels and categories are not his own, yet some people who read his work believe that Anderson himself supports the "decent" people. This may be the way Cosby had interpreted Anderson's work when he invited him to the church. Anderson knew that his subtle analysis of these

Linking Microsociology and Macrosociology

As we saw in Chapter 1, microsociology, the study of everyday behavior in situations of face-to-face interaction, and *macrosociology*, the study of the broader features of society like race, class, or gender hierarchies, are closely connected. We now

examine social encounters on a crowded city sidewalk to illustrate this point.

Gender and Nonverbal Communication

Is there a gender dimension to everyday social interaction? There are reasons to believe there is. Because interactions are problems could become a basis for blaming the "street" for its own conditions, but rather than back away from a potentially difficult situation, he decided to embrace the opportunity to engage in a dialogue and accepted Cosby's invitation.

A recent spike in gang violence in Newark had resulted in the death of a local teenager, and caused both outrage and concern in the community. The mayor's office had responded by planning the town hall meeting at which Cosby would speak in addition to a panel of prominent local ministers, educators, physicians, political leaders, and Anderson.

Part of Anderson's work has focused on the ways that tense social interactions—the type that can quickly lead to violence—are the result of a complicated set of rules that govern how people on the street should act and react to one another. Anderson's *Code of the Street* (1999), explains that the issue of respect is critical for young people growing up in tough environments. "Hard won but easily lost," respect forms the foundation for the code of the street and must be constantly guarded. Anderson finds that gang members in particular are sensitive to advances and slights, which often serve as warnings of an impending confrontation. In places where the police provide only a limited form of personal protection, the code of the street dictates the rules for developing a reputation that can maintains an individual's personal safety. Small variations in hand gestures, eye contact, and conversational tone can make the difference between a handshake and a homicide. Even for kids growing up in so-called "decent" families, the code of the street must be learned to avoid conflict. What may appear as aggressive behavior to an outsider may actually be a set of facial, physical, and verbal expressions geared toward *avoiding* conflict. "To grow up in the streets you have to learn how to walk, how to talk, [and] how to deal with threats," Anderson says. Many people in the audience at the town meeting understood this from experience.

Sitting in the choir section of New Hope Baptist Church that night were members of the Crips and the Bloods, two Newark gangs that had recently come together to broker a cease-fire. The gang members listened with their heads down as the speakers, including Bill Cosby, told them they "should be ashamed" of themselves, and that instead of pulling the trigger, they should "get back in school" and try to live moral lives. Many people, including the majority of those in attendance that evening, believe that Cosby's earlier remarks were correct, that individuals need to make better choices and should be blamed for their actions when things go wrong. But Anderson believes it is also important to consider the conditions under which people make their choices. For those who grow up according to the code of the street, violating that code may actually be a dangerous move. For these kids, as with all kids, "choices" involve a balancing act between what we make of ourselves and what society makes of us.

When Anderson rose to speak that night, he recalled his working-class background and the feeling of stability that came along with his father's job at the Studebaker plant in South Bend, Ind., during the 1950s, '60s, and '70s. Starting about thirty years ago, however, such jobs began to disappear from inner-city neighborhoods as the economy changed. Employment became harder to find as industries left cities like Pittsburgh, Chicago, Cleveland, New York, Philadelphia, and Newark. Stable, well-paying jobs are scarce now, even for kids from "decent" families who have not succumbed to the temptations of street life. Middle-class families with the means to escape have moved out of these cities, leaving behind an isolated group of jobless and troubled residents. Increases in gang violence were directly associated with these changes.

Anderson believes that rather than casting blame, we need to "encourage young people to develop a positive sense of the future," since so much of the violence is really "a reflection of not feeling secure, [of] having short fuses and little patience." In his speech that night, Anderson took pains to explain that although conditions like job loss and family disruption do not excuse criminality, including drug dealing and violence, they may help us better understand why members of the Bloods and Crips may have joined gangs in the first place: to preserve a sense of community in the midst of communities that were falling apart.

shaped by the larger social context, it is not surprising that both verbal and nonverbal communication may be perceived and expressed differently by men and women. Understandings of gender and gender roles are greatly influenced by social factors and are related broadly to issues of power and status in society. These dynamics are evident even in standard interactions in daily life. Take as an example one of the most common nonverbal expressions—eye contact. Individuals use eye contact in a wide variety of ways, often to catch someone's attention or to begin a social interaction. In societies where men on the whole dominate women in both public and private life, men may feel freer than women to make eye contact with strangers.

A particular form of eye contact—staring—illustrates the contrasts in meaning between men and women of identical forms of nonverbal communication. A man who stares at a woman can be seen as acting in a "natural" or "innocent" way; if the woman is uncomfortable, she can evade the gaze by looking away or choosing not to sustain the interaction. On the other hand, a woman who stares at a man is often regarded as behaving in a suggestive or sexually leading manner. Taken individually, such cases may seem inconsequential; when viewed collectively, they help reinforce patterns of gender inequality.

There are other gender differences in nonverbal communication as well. Studies have shown that men tend to sit in a more relaxed manner than do women. Men tend to lean back with their legs open, whereas women tend to have a more closed body position, sitting upright, with their hands in their lap and their legs crossed. Women also tend to stand closer to the person they are talking to than do men. Men also make physical contact with women during conversation far more often than the other way around (and women are expected to view this as normal). Studies have also shown that women tend to show their emotions more obviously (through facial expressions) and that they seek and break eye contact more often than men. Sociologists have argued that these seemingly small-scale micro-level interactions reinforce the wider macro-level inequality in our society. Men control more space when standing and sitting than do women because they tend to stand farther away from the person they are talking to and because they tend to sprawl when sitting; they demonstrate control through more frequent physical contact of women. Women, it has been argued, seek approval through eye contact and facial

expression, and when men make eye contact a woman is more likely to look away than is another man. Thus, it is argued, micro-level studies of nonverbal forms of communication provide subtle cues that demonstrate men's power over women in wider society (Young 1990).

Women and Men in Public

Take, for example, a situation that may seem micro on its face: A woman walking down the street is verbally harassed by a group of men. In a study published as *Passing By: Gender and Public Harassment,* Carol Brooks Gardner (1995) found that in various settings, most famously the edges of construction sites, these types of unwanted interaction occur as something women frequently experience as abusive.

Although the harassment of a single woman might be analyzed in microsociological terms by looking at a single interaction, it is not fruitful to view it that simply. Such harassment is typical of street talk involving men and women who are strangers (Gardner 1995). These kinds of interactions cannot be understood without also looking at the larger background of gender hierarchy in the United States. In this way we can see how microanalysis and macroanalysis are connected. For example, Gardner linked the harassment of women by men to the larger system of gender inequality, represented by male privilege in public spaces, women's physical vulnerability, and the omnipresent threat of rape.

Without making this link between microsociology and macrosociology, we can have only a limited understanding of these interactions. It might seem as though these types of interactions were isolated instances or that they could be eliminated by teaching people good manners. Understanding the link between micro and macro helps us see that to attack the problem at its root cause, one would need to focus on eliminating the forms of gender inequality that give rise to such interactions.

Immediate assumptions based on race, gender, economic status, and style of dress, among other signs and behavioral cues, affect the way strangers behave toward each other. Elijah Anderson's study of social interaction between strangers on urban streets showed a strong connection between such micro-level interactions and the creation of social order.

Blacks and Whites in Public

Have you ever crossed to the other side of the street when you felt threatened by someone behind you or someone coming toward you? One sociologist who tried to understand simple interactions of this kind is Elijah Anderson.

Anderson began by describing social interaction on the streets of two adjacent urban neighborhoods. In his book *Streetwise: Race, Class, and Change in an Urban Community* (1990), Anderson notes that studying everyday life sheds light on how social order is created by the individual building blocks of infinite micro-level interactions. He was particularly interested in understanding interactions when at least one party was viewed as threatening. Anderson showed that the ways many blacks and whites interact on the streets of a northern city had a great deal to do with the structure of racial stereotypes, which is itself linked to the economic structure of society. In this way, he showed the link between micro interactions and the larger macro structures of society.

Anderson began by recalling Erving Goffman's description of how social roles and statuses come into existence in particular contexts or locations: "When an individual enters the presence of others, they commonly seek to acquire information about him or bring into play information already possessed. . . . Information about the individual helps to define the situation, enabling others to know in advance what he will expect of them and they may expect of him" (Anderson 1990).

Following Goffman's lead, Anderson asked, what types of behavioral cues and signs make up the vocabulary of public interaction? He concluded that

skin color, gender, age, companions, clothing, jewelry, and the objects people carry help identify them, so that assumptions are formed and communication can occur. Movements (quick or slow, false or sincere, comprehensible or incomprehensible) further refine this public communication. Factors like time of day or an activity that "explains" a person's presence can also affect in what way and how quickly the image of "stranger" is neutralized. If a stranger cannot pass inspection and be assessed as "safe," the image of predator may arise,

and fellow pedestrians may try to maintain a distance consistent with that image. (Anderson 1990)

Anderson showed that the people most likely to pass inspection are those who do not fall into commonly accepted stereotypes of dangerous persons: "children readily pass inspection, while women and white men do so more slowly, black women, black men, and black male teenagers most slowly of all." In showing that interactional tensions derive from outside statuses such as race, class, and gender, Anderson shows that we cannot develop a full understanding of the situation by looking at the micro interactions themselves. This is how he makes the link between micro interactions and macro processes.

Anderson argues that people are streetwise when they develop skills such as "the art of avoidance" to deal with their felt vulnerability toward violence and crime. According to Anderson, whites who are not streetwise do not recognize the difference between different kinds of black men (e.g., middle-class youths vs. gang members). They may also not know how to alter the number of paces to walk behind a suspicious person or how to bypass bad blocks at various times of day.

☑ CONCEPT CHECKS

1. Describe three ways that men and women differ in their nonverbal communication.
2. How would you explain the street harassment that women often experience?

 Study Outline

www.wwnorton.com/studyspace

The Study of Daily Life in the Internet Age

- *Microsociology* is the study of individual and group interaction. Erving Goffman, who pioneered this field of research, argued that studying *social interaction* was important for three reasons. First, our social lives are based on personal interactions and we tend to engage in these interaction in routine ways. Studying them can tell us a lot about how our society is organized. In addition, people tend to innovate and improvise in their daily lives, breaking their routines in creative ways. Studying microsocial behavior can tell us a lot about agency and the creative ability of people to shape reality. Finally, micro-level interactions can tell us a lot about large social processes and institutions. These institutions, like class or gender hierarchies, are reliant upon daily, micro-level social processes.

Nonverbal Communication

- The exchange of information and meaning through facial expressions, gestures and movements of the body are forms of *nonverbal communication*. The context and content of nonverbal communication are generated by the combination of innate reflexes and culture. E-mail and other forms of electronic communication seriously limit the context of nonverbal communication. For instance, conversing through e-mail requires a lot more words than face-to-face conversation, and disputes are more likely to occur over e-mail than in person.

The World as a Stage

- Each of us uses *impression management* to prepare the presentation of our *social roles*. Roles are the socially defined expectations that a person in a given *status* (or social position) follows. Status is the prestige or social honor accorded to members of a particular group by society. People tend to want to avoid embarrassment, so they collaborate with others in daily activities to "save face."

- *Unfocused interaction* is the mutual awareness of individuals have of one another in large gatherings when not directly in conversation together. *Focused interaction,* which can be divided up into distinct encounters, or episodes of interaction, is when two or more individuals are directly attending to what the other or others are saying and doing.
- Social interaction can often be illuminatingly studied by applying the *dramaturgical model*—studying social interaction as if those involved were actors on a stage, having a set and props. As in the theater, in the various contexts of social life there tend to be clear distinctions between *front regions* (the stage itself) and *back regions,* where the actors prepare themselves for the performance and relax afterward.

Social Contexts and Shared Understandings

- The most inconsequential forms of daily talk presume complicated shared knowledge brought into play by those speaking. *Ethnomethodology,* the study of ordinary talk and conversation, was first coined by Harold Garfinkel. Ethnomethodology is the analysis of the ways in which we actively—although usually in a taken-for-granted way—make sense of what others mean by what they say and do.

Social Rules and Talk

- Much of our interaction is done through *talk*—casual verbal exchange—carried on in informal conversations with others. Conversation analysis examines all facets of a conversation for meaning. Studying talk can give powerful insights into class, gender, and racial structures. For instance, the rules of conversation can be deliberately subverted through *interactional vandalism.* Conversation analysts also study *response cries,* which are the seemingly involuntary exclamations individuals make when they are taken by surprise, expressing pleasure, or in pain. Conversation analysts also study *personal space*—the physical space individuals maintain between themselves and others. Norms around personal space depend on cultures and social roles.

Interaction in Time and Space

- All social interaction is situated in time and space. We can analyze how our daily lives are "zoned" in time and space by looking at how activities occur during definite durations and at the same time involve spatial movement.
- Modern societies are characterized largely by indirect impersonal transactions (such as making bank deposits), which lack any *copresence.* This leads to what has been called the *compulsion of proximity,* the tendency to want to meet in person whenever possible, perhaps because this makes it easier to gather information

about how others think and feel, and to accomplish impression management.

Linking Microsociology and Macrosociology

- *Nonverbal communication* links gender to status and can be discerned as behaving differently in different cultures. Gardner linked the harassment of women by men in public spaces to the larger system of *gender inequality,* represented by male privilege in public spaces, women's physical vulnerability, and the omnipresent threat of rape. Racial (mis)understandings at the macro level also structure interaction between racial groups at the micro level. For instance, Anderson found that studying everyday life sheds light on how social order is created by the individual building blocks of micro-level interactions.

Key Concepts

back region (p. 114)
civil inattention (p. 108)
clock time (p. 121)
compulsion of proximity (p. 126)
conversation analysis (p. 116)
encounter (p. 113)
ethnomethodology (p. 115)
focused interaction (p. 113)
front region (p. 114)
impression management (p. 111)
interactional vandalism (p. 118)
nonverbal communication (p. 109)
personal space (p. 119)
regionalization (p. 119)
response cries (p. 118)
roles (p. 111)
social interaction (p. 108)
social position (p. 111)
status (p. 111)
time–space (p. 119)
unfocused interaction (p. 113)

Review Questions

1. Why is it important to study microsociology?
2. According to Goffman, why do people cooperate in impression management?

3. Briefly define "social role" and provide an example from your own life that illustrates how social roles change in different contexts.

4. What is a "total institution"?

5. How can the desire for audience segregation be frustrated by e-mail communication?

6. Why are shared meanings a central concern of ethnomethodology?

7. What is conversation analysis?

8. How is the Internet re-shaping our "compulsion of proximity"?

9. What does it mean to say that social life is "zoned in time–space" and how is that changing because of the Internet?

10. Why is it important to link microsociological analysis to macrosociological analysis? Give an example.

Thinking Sociologically Exercises

1. Identify the important elements to the dramaturgical perspective. This chapter shows how the theory might be applied in the ministrations of the nurse to his or her patient. Apply the theory similarly to account for a plumber's visit to a client's home. Are there any similarities? Explain.

2. Smoking cigarettes is a pervasive habit found in many parts of the world and a habit that could be explained by both microsociological and macrosociological forces. Give an example of each that would be relevant to explain the proliferation of smoking. How might your suggested micro- and macro-level analyses be linked?

Learning Objectives

Social Groups

Learn the variety and characteristics of groups as well as the effect groups have on individual behavior.

Networks

Understand the importance of social networks and the advantages they give some people.

Organizations

Know how to define an organization and understand how organizations developed over the last two centuries.

Theories of Organizations

Learn Max Weber's theory of organizations and view of bureaucracy. Understand the importance of the physical setting of organizations and Michel Foucault's theory of surveillance.

Beyond Bureaucracy?

Become familiar with alternatives to bureaucracy that have developed in other societies or in recent times. Think about the influence of technology on organizations.

Organizations That Span the World

See how organizations have become truly global in scale.

How Do Groups and Organizations Affect Your Life?

Learn how social capital helps people accomplish their goals and increase their influence.

CHAPTER SIX

GROUPS, NETWORKS, AND ORGANIZATIONS

the U.S. Military Academy—West Point—is very hard to get into. Over fifty thousand high school students open files at the academy, of whom perhaps twelve thousand are qualified to apply. Another four thousand are nominated by a congressional representative, a senator, or the White House. Yet out of all these, barely two thousand pass the physical fitness test, and only twelve hundred are admitted. From "Reception Day" (R-Day) on, the academy emphasizes conformity to group norms.

On R-Day you surrender your old self in stages. You've already left behind family and control over your environment. In the fluorescent Thayer hallways, you hand over your belongings, then file to the treasurers' office to give up your cash; any sum greater than forty dollars gets banked.... "No talking," cadre announce. "Do not move, do not smile. Hands will remain cupped at all times. You need to look at anything, look at my wall." Unless you had an unlucky home life, this is the first time anybody has spoken to you this way. The candidates are just blank eyes now, mouths so tight the lips appear to be hiding. ... Now the army demands your clothing. In their dressing room, male candidates tuck on black gym shorts and white T-shirts with a speed that suggests graded events. "You *must* put on a jockstrap," a TAC-NCO commands. "Let's go—move with a purpose." ... Then the academy takes custody of your actual skin. "If you have," the sergeant booms, "any tattoo, brand, or body piercing, regardless of whether it is visible while wearing a uniform, you must declare it at this time to the registration desk at my rear...." Then the army takes your hair.... Every few minutes the guy working the push broom sweeps away what looks like a whole discarded wig. The barbers place bets on R-Day's yield.... Now you're shorn of everything. You look, act, dress like everyone beside you, maybe for the first time in your life. In five hours, West Point has reduced you to just the meat your parents made, topped by its frenetic, calculating brain.... The cadre introduces [you] to the basics of body language: how to stand, how to listen, how to respond with the grammar of obedience. (Lipsky 2003a)

David Lipsky, a writer for *Rolling Stone,* specialized in stories about youth culture—young people in colleges and universities, the media, TV actors, and movie stars. Then he was asked to write an article on the West Point class of 2002. Lipsky, who had been raised in a liberal family and held a dim view of the military, initially resisted, but after the academy gave him unrestricted access to the cadets, he wound up staying the full four years. He wanted "to find out what kind of men and women would subject themselves to the intense discipline of West Point" (Lipsky 2003a).

What he discovered was "a place where everyone tried their hardest. A place where everybody—or at least most people—looked out for each other.... Of all the young people I'd met, the West Point cadets—although they are grand, epic complainers—were the happiest" (Lipsky 2003a). Part of the reason, Lipsky concluded, was the military value system, which emphasizes self-sacrifice, discipline, honor, respect, and loyalty: "One of the efficient by-products of plebe-year stress is what's called *unit cohesion,* the bonds that cadets form. In battle, what often drives soldiers isn't simply courage but a complicated version of crisis loyalty, the desire not to let down their friends."

Military discipline depends on group loyalty and conformity. After all, some day a soldier's life may depend on such values. The strict training regimen of military academies such as West Point is designed to foster these values—to create uniform ways of thinking and acting among young people raised in a culture that often emphasizes the very opposite. "We are a culture that stresses individually pleasing yourself. What surprised me, getting to know the officers and getting to know the cadets who love the army, is that often the best way to please yourself individually is to live that other way. We're group animals. There's a part of us that really responds to meeting challenges together" (Lipsky 2003b).

In this chapter, we will examine the ways in which all of us—not just West Point cadets—are group animals. We will learn about different kinds of groups and their role in shaping our experiences. How does group size affect behavior in groups and how does it influence the nature of leadership? Special attention is given to sociological research into individual conformity to group norms, helping us understand how an institution such as West Point can take a cross-section of American teenagers and produce tightly disciplined officers who place the highest value on group loyalty. We will also examine the role of organizations in American society, the major theories of modern organizations, and the ways in which organizations are changing in the modern world. The effect of technology on organizations and the prominence of the Internet in group life are also explored. The chapter concludes by discussing the debate over declines in social capital and social engagement in the United States today.

Social Groups

Nearly everything of importance in life occurs through some type of social group. You and your roommate make up a social group, as do the members of your sociology class. A **social group** is a collection of people who have a common identity and regularly interact with one another on the basis of shared expectations concerning behavior. People who belong to the same social group identify with each other, expect each other to conform to certain ways of thinking and acting, and recognize the boundaries that separate them from other groups or people. In our need to congregate and belong, we have created a rich and varied group life that gives us our norms, practices, and values—our whole way of life.

Groups: Variety and Characteristics

We sometimes feel alone, yet we are seldom far from one kind of group or another. Every day nearly all of us move through various social situations. We hang out with friends, study with classmates, play team sports, and go online to find new friends or people who share our interests.

But just because people find themselves in each other's company does not make them a social group. People milling around in crowds, waiting for a bus, or strolling on a beach make up what is called a **social aggregate**: a collection of people who happen to be together in a particular place but do not significantly interact or identify with each other. People waiting together at a bus station, for example, may be aware

What makes the people on the left a social aggregate and the people on the right a social group?

of each other, but they are unlikely to think of themselves as a "we"—the group waiting for the next bus to Poughkeepsie or Des Moines. By the same token, people may make up a **social category**, people sharing a common characteristic, such as gender or occupation, without necessarily interacting or identifying with one another.

IN-GROUPS AND OUT-GROUPS

The "sense of belonging" that characterizes social groups is sometimes strengthened by scorning other groups (Sartre 1965; orig. 1948). This is especially true of racist groups, which promote their identity as superior by hating "inferior" groups. In the United States, Jews, Catholics, African Americans and other people of color, immigrants, and gay people are often the targets of such hatred. This sense of group identity created through scorn is dramatically illustrated by the Web site rantings of a racist skinhead group called Combat 18 (1998): "We are the last of our warrior race, and it is our duty to fight for our people. The Jew will do everything to discredit us, but we hold that burning flame in our hearts that drove our ancestors to conquer whole continents."

Such proud, disdainful language illustrates the sociological distinction between in-groups and out-groups. **In-groups** are groups toward which one feels loyalty and respect—the groups that "we" belong to. **Out-groups** are groups toward which one feels antagonism and contempt—"*those* people." At one time or other, many of us have used in-group–out-group imagery to trumpet what we believe to be our group's strengths vis-à-vis another group's presumed weaknesses. For example, fraternity or sorority members may bolster their feelings of superiority—in academics, sports, or campus image—by ridiculing the members of a different house. Similarly, an ethnic group may prefer its sons and daughters to marry only within the group, a religion often holds up its truths as the only ones, and immigrants are sometimes accused of ruining the country for "real" Americans.

PRIMARY AND SECONDARY GROUPS

Group life differs greatly in how intensely members experience it. Beginning with the family—the first group to which most of us belong—many of the groups that shape our personalities and lives are those in which we experience strong emotional ties. This is common not only for families but also for groups of friends, including gangs and other peer groups, all of which are known as primary groups. **Primary groups** are usually small groups characterized by face-to-face interaction, intimacy, and a strong sense of commitment. Members of primary groups often experience unity, a merging of the self with the group into one personal "we." The sociologist Charles Horton Cooley (1864–1929) termed such groups "primary" because he believed that they were the basic form of association, exerting a long-lasting influence on the development of our social selves (Cooley 1964; orig. 1902).

In contrast, **secondary groups** are large and impersonal and seldom involve intense emotional ties, enduring relationships, powerful commitments to the group itself, or experiences of unity. Examples of secondary groups include businesses, schools, work groups, athletic clubs, and governmental bodies. We rarely feel we can be ourselves in a secondary group; rather, we are often playing a role, such as employee or student. Cooley argued that people belong to primary groups mainly because it is fulfilling, but people join secondary groups to achieve a specific goal: to earn a living, get a college degree, or compete on a sports team. Secondary groups may of course become primary groups. For example, when students taking a course together socialize after class, they create bonds of friendship that constitute a primary group.

For most of human history, nearly all interactions took place within primary groups. This began to change with the emergence of larger, agrarian societies, which included such secondary groups as those based on governmental roles or occupation. Today most of our waking hours are spent within secondary groups, although primary groups remain a basic part of our lives.

Some early sociologists, such as Cooley, worried about a loss of intimacy as more and more interactions revolved around large impersonal organizations. However, what Cooley saw as the growing impersonality and anonymity of modern life may also offer an increasing tolerance of individual differences. Primary groups often enforce strict conformity to group standards (Durkheim 1964; orig. 1893; Simmel 1955). Secondary groups are more likely to be concerned with accomplishing a task than with enforcing conformity.

REFERENCE GROUPS

We often judge ourselves by how we think we appear to others, which Cooley termed the "looking-glass self." Groups as well as individuals provide the standards by which we make self-evaluations. Robert K. Merton (1968; orig. 1938) elaborated on Cooley's work by introducing the concept of the **reference group**: a group that provides a standard for judging one's attitudes or behaviors (see also Hyman and Singer 1968). The family is typically one of the crucial reference groups in our lives, as are peer groups and co-workers. However, you don't have to belong to a group for it to be a reference group. Regardless of his or her station in life, a person may identify with the wealth and power of Fortune 500 corporate executives, admire the contribution of Nobel Prize–winning scientists, or be captivated by the glitter of Hollywood stars. Although few of us interact socially with such reference groups as these, we may take pride in identifying with them, glorify their accomplishments, and even imitate the behavior of their members. This is why it is critical for children—minority children in particular, whose groups are often represented with negative stereotypes in the media—to be exposed to reference groups that will provide positive standards of behavior.

Reference groups may be primary, such as the family, or secondary, such as a group of soldiers. They may even be fictional. One of the chief functions of advertising is to create a set of imaginary reference groups that will influence consumers' buying habits. For example, when cosmetic ads feature thin models with flawless complexions, the message is simple: "If you want to look as though you are part of an in-group of highly attractive, eternally youthful women, buy this product."

Advertising creates a set of imaginary reference groups meant to influence consumers' buying habits by presenting unlikely—often impossible—ideals to which consumers aspire.

In reality, the models seldom have the unblemished features depicted; instead, the ideal features are constructed through artful lighting, photographic techniques, and computer enhancement. Similarly, the happy-go-lucky, physically perfect young men and women seen sailing or playing volleyball or hang gliding in beer commercials have little to do with the reality of most of our lives—or, indeed, with the lives of the actors in those commercials. The message, however, is otherwise: "Drink this beer, and you will be a member of the carefree in-group in this ad."

The Effects of Size

Size is also an important characteristic of groups. Sociological interest in group size can be traced to Georg Simmel (1858–1918), a German sociologist who studied the effect of small groups on people's behavior. Since Simmel's time, small-group researchers have examined the effects of size on both the quality of interaction in the group and the effectiveness of the group in accomplishing certain tasks (Bales 1953, 1970; Homans 1950; Mills 1967).

DYADS

The simplest group, which Simmel (1955) called a **dyad**, consists of two people. Simmel reasoned that dyads, which involve both intimacy and conflict, are likely to be simultaneously intense and unstable. To survive, they require the full attention and cooperation of both parties. If one person withdraws from the dyad, it vanishes. Dyads are typically the source of our most elementary social bonds, often constituting the group in which we are likely to share our deepest secrets. But dyads can be fragile. That is why, Simmel believed, numerous cultural and legal supports for marriage are found in societies in which marriage is an important source of social stability.

TRIADS

Adding a third person changes the group relationship. Simmel used the term **triad** to describe a group of three people. Triads tend to be more stable than dyads because the presence of a third person relieves some of the pressure on the other two members to always get along and energize the relationship. In a triad, one person can temporarily withdraw attention from the relationship without necessarily threatening it. In addition, if two of the members have a disagreement, the third can play the role of mediator, as when you try to patch up a falling-out between two of your friends.

On the other hand, alliances (sometimes termed *coalitions*) may form between two members of a triad, enabling them to gang up on the third and thereby destabilize the group. Alliances are most likely to form when no one member is clearly dominant and when all three members are competing for the same thing—for example, when three friends are given a pair of tickets to a concert and have to decide which two will go. The TV series *Survivor* provides many examples of alliance formation, as the program's characters forge special relationships with each other to avoid being eliminated in the weekly group vote. In forming an alliance, a member of a triad is most likely to choose the weaker of the two other members as a partner, if there is one. In what have been termed *revolutionary coalitions,* the two weaker members form an alliance to overthrow the stronger one (Caplow 1956, 1959, 1969).

LARGER GROUPS

Going from a dyad to a triad illustrates an important sociological principle first identified by Simmel: In most cases, as groups grow in size, their intensity decreases and their stability increases. Increasing a group's size tends to decrease its intensity of interaction, simply because more potential smaller group relationships exist as outlets for individuals who are not getting along with other members of the group. In a dyad, only one relationship is possible; in a triad, three two-person relationships can occur. Adding a fourth person leads to six possible two-person relationships, and this does not count the potential subgroups of more than three. In a ten-person group, the number of possible two-person relationships explodes to forty-five! When one relationship doesn't work out, you can easily move to another, as you probably often do at large parties.

At the same time, larger groups tend to be more stable than smaller ones because they can survive the withdrawal of some members. A marriage or love relationship falls apart if one person leaves, whereas an athletic team or drama club routinely

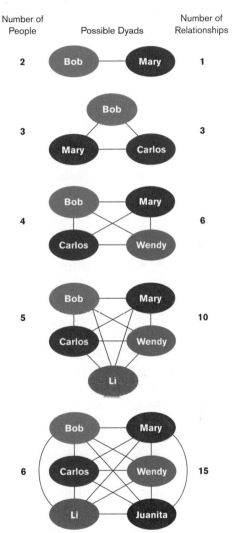

FIGURE 6.1

Dyads

The larger the number of people, the greater the possible number of relationships. Note that this figure illustrates only dyads; if triads and more complex coalitions were to be included, the numbers would be still greater (four people yield ten possibilities). Even a ten-person group can produce forty-five possible dyads!

Number of People	Possible Dyads	Number of Relationships
2	Bob — Mary	1
3	Bob, Mary, Carlos	3
4	Bob, Mary, Carlos, Wendy	6
5	Bob, Mary, Carlos, Wendy, Li	10
6	Bob, Mary, Carlos, Wendy, Li, Juanita	15

Going from just three people to four increases the number of potential relationships by how many? Doubling the size of a group from three to six increases the number of potential relationships by how many? According to the reading, which types of groups are more stable, large or small? Why? Do large or small groups tend to be more exclusive? Why?

survives—though it may temporarily suffer from—the loss of its graduating seniors.

Larger groups also tend to be more exclusive because it is easier for members to limit social relationships to the group itself and avoid relationships with nonmembers. This sense of being part of an in-group or clique is sometimes found in fraternities, sororities, and other campus organizations. Cliquishness is especially likely to occur when a group's members are similar in such social characteristics as age, gender, class, race, or ethnicity. People from rich families, for example, may be reluctant to fraternize with working-class groups, men may prefer to go to the basketball court with other men, and students who belong to a particular ethnic group (for example, African Americans, Latinos, or Asian Americans) may seek out each other in the dorm or cafeteria. Even so, groups do not always restrict relationships with outsiders. A group with a socially diverse membership is likely to foster a high degree of interaction with people outside the group (Blau 1977). For example, if your social group or club has members from different social classes or ethnic groups, it is more likely that you will come to appreciate such social differences from firsthand experience and seek them out in other aspects of your life.

Beyond a certain size, perhaps a dozen people, groups tend to develop a formal structure. Formal leadership roles may arise, such as president or secretary, and official rules may be developed to govern what the group does. We will discuss formal organizations later in this chapter.

Types of Leadership

A **leader** is a person who is able to influence the behavior of other members of a group. All groups tend to have leaders, even if that person is not formally recognized as such. Some leaders are especially effective in motivating the members of their groups or organizations, inspiring them to unusual achievements. Such **transformational leaders** go beyond the routine, instilling in their group a sense of mission or higher purpose and thereby changing the nature of the group itself (Burns 1978; Kanter 1983). These are the leaders who leave their stamp on their organizations. They can be a vital inspiration for social change. For example, Nelson Mandela, the South African leader who spent twenty-seven years in prison after having been convicted of treason against the white-dominated South African society, nonetheless managed to build his African National Congress (ANC) political party into a multiracial force for change. Mandela's transformational leadership was so strong that despite his long imprisonment, as soon as he was freed he assumed leadership of the ANC. After Mandela led

Would you define Nelson Mandela as a transformational leader? Why?

the ANC in overthrowing South Africa's system of apartheid, or racial segregation, he was elected president—leader—of the entire country.

Most leaders are not as visionary as Mandela. Leaders who simply get the job done are termed **transactional leaders**. These are leaders concerned with accomplishing the group's tasks, getting members to do their jobs, and making certain that the group achieves its goals. Transactional leadership is routine leadership. For example, the teacher who simply gets through the lesson plan each day—rather than making the classroom a place where students explore new ways of thinking and behaving—is exercising transactional leadership.

Conformity

Not so long ago, the only part of the body that American teenage girls were likely to pierce was the ears—one hole per ear, enough to hold a single pair of earrings. For the vast majority of boys piercing was not an option at all. Today, earrings are common for males. From teenage boys to male professional athletes to college students, a growing number of males now sport multiple earrings, navel rings, and even studs in their tongues. Pressures to conform to the latest styles are especially strong among teenagers and young adults, among whom the need for group acceptance is often acute.

While wearing navel rings or the latest style of jeans—or rigidly conforming to the military code of West Point—may seem relatively harmless, conformity to group pressure can lead to destructive behavior, such as drug abuse or even murder. For this reason, sociologists and social psychologists have long sought to understand why most people tend to go along with others and under what circumstances they do not.

GOING ALONG WITH THE GROUP: ASCH'S RESEARCH

Some of the earliest studies of conformity to group pressures were conducted by psychologist Solomon Asch (1952). In a classic experiment, Asch asked subjects to decide which of three lines of different length most closely matched the length of a fourth line. The differences were obvious; subjects had no difficulty making the correct match. Asch then arranged a version of the experiment in which the subjects were asked to make the matches in a group setting, with each person calling out the answer one at a time. In this version, all but one of the subjects were actually Asch's accomplices. Each accomplice picked as matches two lines that were clearly unequal in length. The unwitting subject, one of the last to answer, felt enormous group pressure to make the same match. Amazingly, one third of the subjects gave the same answer as the others in the group at least half the time, even though that answer was clearly wrong. They sometimes stammered and fidgeted when doing so, but they nonetheless yielded to the unspoken pressure to conform to the group's decision. Asch's experiments clearly showed that many people are willing to discount their own perceptions rather than buck a group consensus.

OBEDIENCE TO AUTHORITY: MILGRAM'S RESEARCH

Another classic study of conformity was Stanley Milgram's (1963) research. Milgram's work was intended to shed some light on what had happened in Nazi Germany during World War II. How could ordinary German citizens have gone along with—even participated in—the mass extermination of millions of Jews, Romanies (Gypsies), homosexuals, intellectuals, and others who were judged to be inferior or undesirable by the Nazis?

Obedience is a kind of conformity. Milgram sought to find its limits. He wanted to see how far a person would go when ordered by a scientist to give another person increasingly powerful electric shocks. He set up an experiment that he told the subjects was about memorizing pairs of words. In reality, it was about obedience to authority. Milgram's study would not be permitted today because its deception of subjects and

FIGURE 6.2

The Asch Task

In the Asch task, participants were shown a standard line (left) and then three comparison lines. Their task was simply to say which of the three lines matched the standard. When confederates gave false answers first, one third of participants conformed by giving the wrong answer.

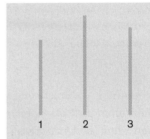

What would cause someone to agree that the line on the left is actually the same length as line number 1? In the research, what portion of people were convinced by the group that two lines that were clearly different lengths were actually the same length? What can we conclude from Asch's experiment?

potential for doing psychological harm would violate current university ethics standards.

The subjects who volunteered for the study were supposedly randomly divided into "teachers" and "learners." In fact, the learners were Milgram's assistants. The teacher was told to read pairs of words from a list that the learner was to memorize. Whenever the learner made a mistake, the teacher was to give him an electric shock by flipping a switch on a fake but real-looking machine. The control board indicated shock levels ranging from "15 volts—slight shock" to "450 volts—danger, severe shock." For each mistake, the voltage was to be increased, until it reached the highest level. In reality, the learner, who was usually concealed from the teacher by a screen, received no shocks.

As the experiment progressed, the learner began to scream out in pain for the teacher to stop delivering shocks. (The screams, increasingly louder as the voltage rose, had actually been prerecorded.) However, the Milgram assistant who was administering the experiment exercised his authority as a scientist and, if the teacher tried to quit, ordered the teacher

(A) The Milgram experiment required participants to "shock" the confederate learner (seated). The research participant (left) helped apply the electrodes that would be used to shock the learner. (B) An obedient participant shocks the learner in the "touch" condition. More than half obeyed the experimenter in this condition. (C) After the experiment, all of the participants were introduced to the confederate learner so they could see he was not actually harmed.

to continue administering shocks. The assistant would say such things as "the experiment requires that you continue," even when the learner was tearfully protesting—even when he shrieked about his "bad heart."

The teacher was confronted with a major moral decision: Should he obey the scientist and go along with the experiment, even if it meant injuring another human being? Much to Milgram's surprise, over half the subjects administered the shocks until the maximum voltage was reached and the learner's screams had subsided into an eerie silence as he presumably died of a heart attack. How could ordinary people so easily obey orders that would turn them into possible accomplices to murder?

The answer, Milgram found, was deceptively simple. Although it is obvious that soldiers in training, such as first-year plebes at West Point, will obey orders given by someone in a position of power or authority, ordinary citizens will often do the same—even if those orders have horrible consequences. From this, we can learn something about Nazi atrocities during World War II, which were Milgram's original concern. Many of the ordinary Germans who participated in the mass executions in concentration camps did so on the grounds that they were just following orders. Milgram's research has sobering implications for anyone who thinks that only "others" will always knuckle under to authority but "not me" (Zimbardo et al. 1977).

GROUPTHINK AND GROUP PRESSURES TO CONFORM: JANIS'S RESEARCH

Common sense tells us that "two heads are better than one." But sociological research has found that pressures to "go along with the crowd" sometimes result in poor decisions rather than

creative solutions. You have probably been in a group struggling with a difficult decision and felt uneasy about voicing your opposition to an emerging consensus. Irving L. Janis (1972, 1989; Janis and Mann 1977) called this phenomenon **groupthink**, a process by which the members of a group ignore ways of thinking and plans of action that go against the group consensus. Not only does groupthink frequently embarrass potential dissenters into conforming, but it can also lead to alternatives being ruled out before they are seriously considered. Groupthink may facilitate reaching a quick consensus, but the consensus may be ill chosen. It may even be downright stupid.

Janis engaged in historical research to see if groupthink had ever influenced U.S. foreign policy. He examined several critical decisions, including that behind the infamous Bay of Pigs invasion of Cuba in 1961. John F. Kennedy, the newly elected president, inherited a plan from the Eisenhower administration to liberate Cuba from the Communist government of Fidel Castro. The plan called for U.S. supplies and air cover to assist an invasion by an ill-prepared army of Cuban exiles at Cuba's Bay of Pigs. Although a number of Kennedy's advisers were certain that the plan was fatally flawed, they refrained from bucking the emerging consensus to carry it out. As it happened, the invasion was a disaster. The army of exiles, after parachuting into a swamp nowhere near their intended drop zone, was immediately defeated, and Kennedy suffered enormous public embarrassment.

Kennedy's advisers were people of strong will and independent judgment who had been educated at elite universities. Why didn't they voice their concerns about the proposed invasion? Janis identified a number of possible reasons. For one, the advisers were hesitant to disagree with the president lest they lose his favor. They also did not want to diminish group harmony in a crisis situation where teamwork was all-important.

In addition, given the intense time pressure, they had little opportunity to consult outside experts who might have offered radically different perspectives, including some that confirmed the advisers' own doubts. All these circumstances contributed to a single-minded pursuit of the president's initial ideas rather than an effort either to look at them objectively or to generate alternatives.

Although groupthink does not always shape decision making, it sometimes plays a major role. To avoid groupthink, a group must ensure the full and open expression of all opinions, even strong dissent.

☑ CONCEPT CHECKS

1. What is the difference between social aggregates and social groups? Give examples that illustrate this difference.
2. Describe the main characteristics of primary and secondary groups.
3. When groups become large, why does their intensity decrease but their stability increase?
4. What is groupthink? How can it be used to explain why some decisions made by a group can lead to negative consequences?

Networks

"Who you know is often as important as what you know." This adage expresses the value of having "good connections." Sociologists refer to such connections as **networks**—all the direct and indirect connections that link a person or a group with other people or groups. Your personal networks thus include people you know directly (such as your friends) as well as people you know indirectly (such as your friends' friends). Personal networks often include people of similar race, class, ethnicity, and other types of social background, although there are exceptions. For example, if you subscribe to an online mailing list, you are part of a network that consists of all the people on the list, who may be of different racial or ethnic backgrounds. Because groups and organizations, such as sororities or religious groups, can also be networked—for example, all the chapters of Gamma Phi Beta or Hillel that the national organization comprises—belonging to such groups can greatly extend your reach and influence.

Social groups are an important source for acquiring networks, but not all networks are social groups. Many networks lack the shared expectations and sense of common identity that are the hallmark of social groups. For example, you are not likely to share a sense of identity with the subscribers to an online mailing list, nor will you probably even know the neighbors of most of your co-workers at the office, even though they do form part of your social network.

Networks serve us in many ways. Sociologist Mark Granovetter (1973) demonstrated that there can be enormous strength in weak ties, particularly among higher socioeconomic groups. Granovetter showed that upper-level professional and managerial employees are likely to hear about new jobs through connections such as distant relatives or remote acquaintances. Such weak ties can be beneficial because relatives or acquaintances tend to have very different sets of connections than one's close friends, whose social contacts are likely to be similar to one's own. Among lower socioeconomic groups, Granovetter argued, weak ties are not necessarily bridges to other networks and so do not really increase opportunities (see also Knoke 1990; Marsden and Lin 1982; Wellman et al. 1988). After graduation, you may rely on good grades and a strong résumé to find a job. But it also may help that your second cousin went to school with a top person in the organization in which you are seeking work.

Most people depend on personal networks to gain advantages, but not everyone has equal access to powerful networks. Some sociologists argue that women's business and political networks are weaker than men's, so that women's power in these spheres is reduced (Brass 1985). The Bohemian Grove is a case in point. This is an annual political gathering that has been held on the Russian River, north of San Francisco, each summer since 1879. Its all-male membership includes Republican leaders, the heads of major corporations, businessmen, and entertainers. The highly exclusive weekend includes horseback riding, meetings, entertainment, "lakeside talks," informal discussion groups—and some serious deal making. In 1999, the

Breakfast at Owls Nest Camp, Bohemian Grove, California July 23, 1967. Members of the elite campground and club, which includes executives and U.S. presidents, discuss politics over a Gin Fizz breakfast.

"The Lonely American"

Most college students find it hard to go a day without checking out what their friends are doing on Facebook.com. Many were surprised, then, to read news reports in June 2006 that "Social Isolation [Is] Growing in U.S." (Vedantam 2006) and "The Lonely American Just Got a Bit Lonelier" (Fountain 2006). How can Americans be "lonely" when their e-mail in-boxes are overflowing and they get more Facebook "pokes" than they can keep up with? According to a recent study by sociologists at Duke University and the University of Arizona, Americans have fewer confidants than in the past, and a growing number can't name a single person with whom they share "important matters" (McPherson, Smith-Lovin, and Brashears 2006).

How did the researchers evaluate whether friendships were declining over time? What accounts for these declines? The study was based on face-to-face interviews with a nationally representative sample of nearly 1,500 American adults. All had participated in the long-running General Social Survey, and they were asked questions about their social networks. Specifically, they were asked to identify people with whom they had dis-

Do you think Americans are more socially isolated than they used to be? Why?

cussed "matters [that are] important to you" in the past six months. On average, they named 2.08 people in 2004, compared with 2.94 persons in 1985. The proportion who reported that there was no one with whom they discussed important matters jumped from 10 percent in 1985 to 25 percent in 2004.

The researchers attribute these patterns to increases in the number of people living and working in isolated suburbs and reliance on "technological means" of keeping in touch with friends. E-mail and social networking Web sites are not a meaningful substitute for heart-to-heart talks, according to the study authors. Duke sociologist and study coauthor Lynn Smith-Lovin explained, "The kinds of connections we studied are the kinds of people you call on for support, for real concrete help when you need it.... E-mailing somebody far away is not the same as them going to pick up your child at daycare or bringing you chicken soup" (Fountain 2006).

Although the raw number of confidants among Americans has decreased, the study also found evidence that some relationships are growing stronger. For example, the proportion saying that they could confide in their spouse

---

Bohemians included former president George H. W. Bush, then Texas governor (and later president) George W. Bush, former secretary of state Henry Kissinger, retired general Colin Powell (later secretary of state), and former Speaker of the House Newt Gingrich (Bohan 1999; Domhoff 1974).

In general, sociologists have found that women's job market networks comprise fewer ties than do men's, meaning that women know fewer people in fewer occupations (Marsden 1987; Moore 1990). Meager networks tend to channel women into female-typical jobs, which usually offer lower pay and fewer opportunities for advancement (Drentea 1998; Ross and Reskin 1992). Still, as more and more women move into higher-level positions, the resulting networks can foster further

advancement. One study found that women are more likely to be hired or promoted into job levels that already have a high proportion of women (Cohen et al. 1998).

Networks confer more than economic advantage. You are likely to rely on your networks for a broad range of contacts, from obtaining access to your congressperson to finding a date for Saturday night. Similarly, when you visit another country to study a foreign language or see the Olympics, your friends, school, or religious organization may steer you to their overseas connections, who can then help you find your way around in the unfamiliar environment. When you graduate, your alumni group can further extend your network of social support.

increased. Smith-Lovin said this pattern likely reflects "the fact that men's and women's lives are more structurally similar now than in the past." Compared to earlier generations, women are more likely to work for pay, and men are more likely to help around the house. As a result, "spouses literally have more to talk about," said Smith-Lovin (Fountain 2006). Yet the increasing closeness among spouses might have occurred at the expense of friendships. A full 80 percent of persons in 2004 reported that they talked only to family members about important personal matters, compared with just 57 percent in 1985.

Some social scientists are not convinced that these findings support the claim that Americans are isolated or lonely. Rather, some argue that "weak" social ties, such as those with acquaintances, may be perfectly acceptable and rewarding for some people. Others, still, prefer to have many casual acquaintances rather than a handful of deep friendships. For example, University of Toronto sociologist Barry Wellman believes that the study offers important findings about "intimate ties" but questions whether these findings should be taken as evidence that Americans are lonely and isolated. Rather, he notes that people's overall ties are actually increasing compared to previous decades, due

in part to the Internet. He estimates that the average person today has about 250 ties with friends and relatives, although some of these ties are admittedly weaker than others. He also proposes that people rely on different relationships for different things: "We are getting a division of labor in relationships. Some people give emotional aid, some give financial aid."

Smith-Lovin acknowledges the importance of such weak ties but maintains that they do not provide the same level of integration as the confidant relationship: "We're not saying people are completely isolated. They may have 600 friends on Facebook.com and email 25 people a day, but they are not discussing matters that are personally important" (Vedantam 2006). Both researchers agree that the debate is not resolved and that the very nature of personal relationships will continue to shift as Internet social interaction Web sites proliferate.

Questions

- How many confidants did the average American have in 2004 versus 1985? What proportion say they have no confidant?
- How was "confidant" measured in the McPherson, Smith-Lovin, and Brashears study?

- Do you believe the researchers' data support the claim that Americans are "lonely" and "socially isolated"? Why or why not?

FOR FURTHER EXPLORATION

Allen, Scott. 2006. "It's Lonely Out There: Connections Frayed in Wired America, Study Finds." *Boston Globe* (June 23, 2006). www.boston.com/news/nation/articles/2006/06/23/its_lonely_out_there/ (accessed January 11, 2008).

Fountain, Henry. 2006. "The Lonely American Just Got a Bit Lonelier." *New York Times* (July 2, 2006). www.nytimes.com/2006/07/02/weekinreview/02fountain.html?pagewanted=print (accessed January 11, 2008).

McPherson, Miller, Lynn Smith-Lovin, and Matthew E. Brashears. 2006. "Social Isolation in America: Changes in Core Discussion Networks over Two Decades." *American Sociological Review* 71: 353–375.

Radhakrishnan, Bharathi. 2006. "Americans Have Fewer Friends, Researchers Say." *ABC News* (June 23, 2006). http://abcnews.go.com/print?id=2107907 (accessed January 11, 2008).

Vedantam, Shankar. 2006. "Social Isolation Growing in U.S., Study Says." *Washington Post* (June 23, 2006), A3. www.washingtonpost.com/wp-dyn/content/article/2006/06/22/AR2006062201763_pf.html (accessed January 11, 2008).

The Internet as Social Network

The advantages and potential reach of networks are evident in an increasingly productive means of networking all but unknown ten years ago: the Internet. Internet use has exploded in recent years. Until the early 1990s, when the World Wide Web was developed, there were few Internet users outside university and scientific communities. But by 2008, an estimated 220.1 million Americans used the Internet (Internet World Stats 2008a), and on any given day in the United States, 147 million people are online (Pew 2007). With such rapid communication and global reach, it is now possible to radically extend one's personal networks. The Internet is especially useful for

networking with like-minded people in areas such as politics, business, hobbies, and romance (Southwick 1996; Wellman et al. 1996). It also enables people who might lack face-to-face contact with others to become part of global networks. For example, shut-ins can join chat rooms, and people in rural communities can take distance-learning through courses on the Web.

The Internet fosters the creation of relationships, often without the emotional and social baggage or constraints that are part of face-to-face encounters. Although this might lead to fleeting, impersonal relationships, it also creates opportunities for the expression of intimate feelings or discussion of topics that might be suppressed in face-to-face encounters.

FIGURE 6.3

Differences in Rates of Internet Access: Effects of Age, Education, Gender, Race, Ethnicity, and Income

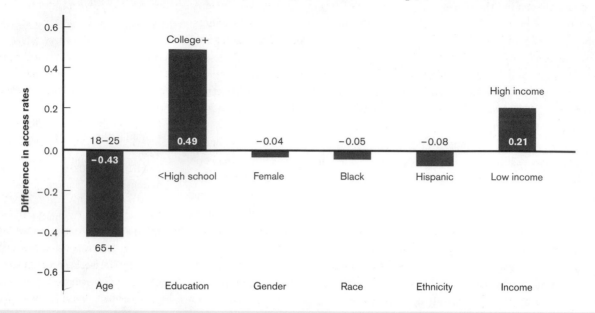

These bars reveal the difference in Internet usage rates between subgroups of Americans. For instance, there is a 20 percentage point difference in the number of high- versus low-income persons who use the Internet. What are the biggest factors affecting Internet usage? Who is more likely to have access to the Internet, an eighteen-year-old or a senior citizen? Do race, ethnicity, or gender differences affect who accesses the Internet? How does access to the Internet help people build networks?

SOURCE: Nie and Ebring 2000.

For example, chat rooms offer support for lesbians and gay men who can't find acceptance in their local communities. Some Web sites for teenagers provide answers to important questions on health and sexuality that teens may be shy about asking their parents. Internet communication also helps us to strengthen the bonds between friends and acquaintances who would otherwise seldom see each other (Wellman et al. 1996).

Without the usual physical and social cues, such as skin color and home address, people can meet electronically on the basis of shared interests. Such factors as social position, wealth, race, ethnicity, gender, and physical disability are less likely to cloud social interaction (Coate 1994; Jones 1995; Kollock and Smith 1996). The Internet thus enables people to communicate first and then decide if the relationship is

worth continuing in person. As a consequence, Internet-based social networks may be socially broader than other networks (Wellman 1994). Whether this strengthens social diversity—or downgrades its importance—is a matter of ongoing debate.

The Internet can also help people join organizations they otherwise might not have access to. In particular, it has become instrumental in politics (Townsend 2002), as demonstrated by MoveOn.org's fund-raising for the 2004 presidential election and by the mobilization of protests against the war in Iraq that drew eight million marchers into the streets of cities around the world on February 15, 2003 (Ali 2003). Of course, there is a downside to these opportunities, too, as in the case of hate groups that use the Internet to recruit members. Some evidence indicates that hate groups concentrate on

Launched in 2004, Facebook.com has over eighty million registered accounts and is one of the most popular tools for building online social networks.

the Internet, where potential members and lone wolves who are attracted to racist notions but not fully committed to the movement can participate without exposing their identities (Intelligence Report 2001).

Another issue is that not everyone has equal access to the Internet. Though gender, racial, and class differences affect who is using the Internet and what they use it for, the most pronounced differences affecting Internet use are age and education (Nie and Ebring 2000). Still, within the span of a few years, Internet use has become much more widespread among all groups (Nielsen Media Research 2001; Pew Internet 2005). In the words of one recent study that tracked Internet use among different socioeconomic groups, "The Internet was, at first, an elitist country club reserved only for individuals with select financial abilities and technical skills. . . . Now, nearly every socioeconomic group is aggressively adopting the Web" (Nielsen Media Research 2001).

The United States has one of the highest rates of Internet use in the world. Americans are by far the largest Internet users in the world. Alongside North America, Internet use is highest in the wealthy countries of Europe and East Asia. Some sociologists think that the Internet's inevitable strengthening of global ties may come at the expense of local ones. Being able to connect with anyone in the world who has similar interests may mean that one's own community becomes less important. If this happens, will the ties that have bound people to locality throughout human history slowly disappear?

✅ CONCEPT CHECKS

1. According to Granovetter, what are the benefits of weak ties? Why?

Organizations

People frequently band together to pursue activities that they cannot do by themselves. A principal means for accomplishing such cooperative actions is the **organization**, a group with an identifiable membership that engages in concerted collective actions to achieve a common purpose (Aldrich and Marsden 1988). An organization can be a small primary group, but it is more likely a larger, secondary one: Universities, religious bodies, and business corporations are all examples of organizations. Such organizations are a central feature of all societies, and their study is a core concern of sociology today.

Organizations tend to be highly formal in modern industrial and postindustrial societies. A **formal organization** is designed to achieve its objectives, often by means of explicit rules, regulations, and procedures. The modern bureaucratic organization, discussed later in this chapter, is a prime example of a formal organization. As Max Weber (1979; orig. 1921) recognized almost a century ago, there has been a long-term trend in Europe and North America toward formal organizations, in part because formality is often a requirement for legal standing. For a college or university to be accredited, for example, it must satisfy explicit written standards governing everything from grading policy to faculty performance to fire safety. Today, formal organizations are the dominant form of organization throughout the world.

Social systems in the traditional world developed as a result of custom and habit. Modern organizations are designed with definite aims and housed in buildings or physical settings constructed to help realize those aims. Organizations play a more important part in our everyday lives than ever before. Besides delivering us into this world (hospital), they also mark our progress through it (school) and see us out of it when we die (hospital, funeral home). Even before we are born, our mothers, and often our fathers, are involved in birthing classes, pregnancy checkups, and so forth, all carried out within hospitals and other medical organizations. Today every child born is registered by government organizations, which collect information on all of us from birth to death. Most people today die in a hospital—not at home, as was once the case—and each death must be formally registered with the government.

It is easy to see why organizations are so important today. In the premodern world, families, relatives, and neighbors provided for most needs—food, the instruction of children, work, and leisure-time activities. In modern times, many of our requirements are met by people we never meet and who might live and work thousands of miles away. Substantial coordination of activities and resources—which organizations provide—is needed in such circumstances.

But the tremendous influence organizations have on our lives cannot be seen as wholly beneficial. Organizations often take things out of our own hands and put them under the control of officials or experts over whom we have little influence. For instance, we are required to do certain things the government tells us to do—pay taxes, obey laws, fight wars—or face punishment. As sources of social power, organizations can subject people to dictates they may be powerless to resist.

☑ CONCEPT CHECKS

1. What role do organizations play in contemporary society?

Theories of Organizations

Max Weber developed the first systematic interpretation of modern organizations. Organizations, he argued, are ways of coordinating the activities of human beings, or the goods they produce, in a stable way across space and time. Weber emphasized that the development of organizations depends on the control of information, and he stressed the central importance of writing in this process: An organization needs written rules to function and files in which its "memory" is stored. Weber saw organizations as strongly hierarchical, with power tending to concentrate at the top. Was Weber right? It matters a great deal. For Weber detected a clash as well as a connection between modern organizations and democracy that he believed had far-reaching consequences for social life.

Bureaucracy

All large-scale organizations, according to Weber, tend to be bureaucratic. The word *bureaucracy* was coined by Monsieur de Gournay in 1745, who added the word *bureau,* meaning both an office and a writing table, to *cracy,* a term derived from the Greek verb meaning "to rule." **Bureaucracy** is thus the rule of officials. The term was first applied only to government officials, but it gradually came to refer to large organizations in general.

From the beginning, the concept was used disparagingly. De Gournay spoke of the developing power of officials as "an illness called bureaumania." The nineteenth-century French novelist Honoré de Balzac saw bureaucracy as "the giant power wielded by pygmies." This view persists today. Bureaucracy is frequently associated with red tape, inefficiency, and

wastefulness. Others, however, have seen bureaucracy as a model of carefulness, precision, and effective administration. Bureaucracy, they argue, is the most efficient form of human organization, because in bureaucracies all tasks are regulated by strict procedures.

Weber's account of bureaucracy steers a way between these two extremes. A limited number of bureaucratic organizations, he pointed out, existed in the traditional civilizations. For example, a bureaucratic officialdom in imperial China was responsible for the overall affairs of government. But it is only in modern times that bureaucracies have developed fully.

According to Weber, the expansion of bureaucracy is inevitable in modern societies; bureaucratic authority is the only way of coping with the administrative requirements of large-scale social systems. However, as we will see, Weber also believed bureaucracy exhibits a number of major failings that have important implications for modern social life.

To study the origins and nature of bureaucratic organizations, Weber constructed an **ideal type** of bureaucracy. (*Ideal* here refers not to what is most desirable but to a *pure* form of bureaucratic organization, one that accentuates certain features of real cases so as to pinpoint essential characteristics.) Weber (1979, orig. 1921) listed several characteristics of the ideal type of bureaucracy:

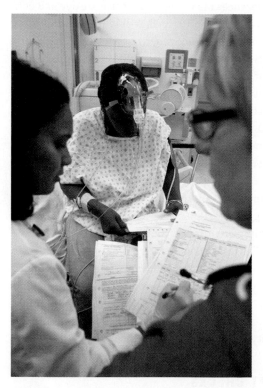

A woman suffering from severe asthma fills out paperwork in an emergency room at San Francisco General Hospital. Modern hospitals are complex organizations with impersonal structures and procedures—but they are designed for a personal outcome.

1. **There is a clear-cut hierarchy of authority.** Tasks in the organization are distributed as "official duties." A bureaucracy looks like a pyramid, with the positions of highest authority at the top. There is a chain of command stretching from top to bottom, thus making coordinated decision making possible. Each higher office controls and supervises the one below it in the hierarchy.

2. **Written rules govern the conduct of officials at all levels of the organization.** This does not mean that bureaucratic duties are just a matter of routine. The higher the office, the more the rules tend to encompass a wide variety of cases and demand flexibility in their interpretation.

3. **Officials are full time and salaried.** Each job in the hierarchy has a definite and fixed salary attached to it. Individuals are expected to make a career within the organization. Promotion is possible on the basis of capability, seniority, or a combination of the two.

4. **There is a separation between the tasks of an official within the organization and his life outside.** The home life of the official is distinct from his activities in the workplace and is also physically separated from it.

5. **No members of the organization own the material resources with which they operate.** The development of bureaucracy, according to Weber, separates workers from the control of their means of production. In traditional communities, farmers and craft workers usually had control over their processes of production and owned the tools they used. In bureaucracies, officials do not own the offices they work in, the desks they sit at, or the office machinery they use.

Weber believed that the more an organization approaches the ideal type of bureaucracy, the more effective it will be in reaching its goals. He likened bureaucracies to sophisticated machines operating according to rational principles (see Chapter 1). Yet he recognized that bureaucracy could be inefficient and that many bureaucratic jobs are dull, offering little opportunity for creativity. Although Weber feared that the rationalization of society could have negative consequences, he concluded that bureaucratic routine and the authority of officialdom are the prices we pay for the technical effectiveness of bureaucratic organizations. Since Weber's time, the rationalization of society has become more widespread. Critics of this development who share Weber's initial concerns have questioned whether the efficiency of rational organizations comes at a cost greater than Weber could have imagined. The most prominent of these costs is known as "the McDonaldization of society" and will be discussed later in this chapter.

FORMAL AND INFORMAL RELATIONS WITHIN BUREAUCRACIES

Weber's analysis of bureaucracy gave prime place to **formal relations** within organizations, relations as stated in the rules of the organization. Weber had little to say about the informal connections and small-group relations that exist in all organizations. But in bureaucracies, informal ways of doing things often allow for a flexibility that couldn't otherwise be achieved.

In a classic study, Peter Blau (1963) looked at **informal relations** in a government agency that investigated possible income-tax violations. Agents who came across difficult cases were supposed to discuss them with their immediate supervisor; the rules of procedure stated that they should not consult colleagues at the same level as themselves. Most agents were wary about approaching their supervisors, however, because they felt it might suggest a lack of competence on their part and reduce their chances for promotion. Hence they usually consulted one another, violating the official rules. This breaking of the rules not only helped provide concrete advice but also reduced the anxieties involved in working alone. A cohesive set of loyalties of a primary group kind developed among those working at the same level. The problems these workers faced, Blau concludes, were probably addressed more effectively as a result. The group was able to develop informal procedures that allowed for more initiative and responsibility than were provided for by the formal rules of the organization.

Informal networks tend to develop at all levels of organizations. At the top, personal ties and connections may be more important than the formal situations in which decisions are supposed to be made. For example, meetings of boards of directors and shareholders supposedly determine the policies of business corporations. In practice, a few members of the board often run the corporation, making their decisions informally and expecting the rest of the board to approve them. Informal networks of this sort can also stretch across different corporations. Business leaders from different firms frequently consult one another in an informal way and may belong to the same clubs and leisure-time associations.

John Meyer and Brian Rowan (1977) argue that formal rules and procedures are usually quite distant from the practices actually adopted by an organization's members. Formal rules, in their view, are often "myths" that people profess to follow but that have little substance in reality. The rules serve to legitimate—to justify—ways in which tasks are carried out, even while these ways may diverge greatly from how things are "supposed to be done." Formal procedures, Meyer and Rowan point out, often have a ceremonial or ritual character. People make a show of conforming to them but get on with their real work using other, more informal procedures. For example, rules governing ward procedure in a hospital help justify how nurses act toward patients. Thus a nurse will faithfully fill in the chart at the end of a patient's bed but will actually check progress by means of other, informal criteria—how the patient looks and whether the patient seems alert and lively. Rigorously keeping up the charts impresses the patients and keeps the doctors happy but is not always essential to the nurse's assessments.

Deciding how much informal procedures help or hinder the effectiveness of organizations is not simple. Systems that resemble Weber's ideal type tend to give rise to a multitude of unofficial ways of doing things. This is partly because the flexibility that is lacking ends up being achieved by unofficial tinkering with formal rules. For those in dull jobs, informal procedures often create a more satisfying work environment. Informal connections among officials in higher positions may be effective in ways that aid the organization as a whole.

THE DYSFUNCTIONS OF BUREAUCRACY

Robert Merton (1957), a functionalist scholar, examined Weber's bureaucratic ideal type and concluded that several elements inherent in bureaucracy could undermine the smooth functioning of the bureaucracy itself. He referred to these as "dysfunctions of bureaucracy." First, Merton noted that bureaucrats are trained to rely on written rules and procedures. They are not encouraged to be flexible, to use their own judgment in making decisions, or to seek creative solutions; bureaucracy is about managing cases according to a set of objective criteria. Merton feared that this rigidity could lead to *bureaucratic ritualism,* a situation in which the rules are upheld at any cost, even when another solution might be better for the organization as a whole.

A second concern of Merton's was that adherence to bureaucratic rules could eventually take precedence over the underlying organizational goals. Because so much emphasis is placed on correct procedures, it is possible to lose sight of the big picture. A bureaucrat responsible for processing insurance claims, for example, might refuse to compensate a policyholder for legitimate damages, citing the absence of a form or a form's being completed incorrectly. In other words, processing the claim correctly comes to be more important than the needs of the client who has suffered a loss.

Merton foresaw the possibility of tension between the public and bureaucracy in such cases. His concern was not entirely misplaced. Most of us regularly interact with large bureaucracies—from insurance companies to local government to the Internal Revenue Service (IRS). Not infrequently we encounter situations in which public servants and bureaucrats seem unconcerned with our needs. One of the major

How was the federal government's handling of the Hurricane Katrina disaster an example of a dysfunctional bureaucracy?

weaknesses of bureaucracy is the difficulty it has in addressing cases that need special treatment and consideration.

Organizations as Mechanistic and Organic Systems

Can bureaucratic procedures be applied effectively to all types of work? Some scholars have suggested that bureaucracy makes sense for routine tasks but can be problematic when work demands change unpredictably. In their research on innovation and change in electronics companies, Tom Burns and G. M. Stalker (1994) found that bureaucracies are of limited effectiveness in industries in which being flexible and on the cutting edge are prime concerns.

Burns and Stalker identified two types of organizations: *mechanistic* and *organic.* Mechanistic organizations are bureaucratic systems in which there is a hierarchical chain of command, with communication flowing vertically through clear channels. Each employee is responsible for a discrete task; once the task is completed, responsibility passes onto the next employee. Work within such a system is anonymous, with people at the top and those at the bottom rarely communicating with one another.

Organic organizations, by contrast, are characterized by a looser structure in which the overall goals of the organization take precedence over narrowly defined responsibilities. Communication flows and directives are more diffuse, moving along many trajectories, not simply vertical ones. Everyone in the organization is seen as possessing legitimate knowledge that can be drawn on in solving problems; decisions are not the exclusive domain of people at the top.

According to Burns and Stalker, organic organizations are better equipped to handle the changing demands of an innovative market, such as telecommunications, computer software, or biotechnology. The more fluid internal structure means that they can respond more quickly and appropriately to shifts in the market and can come up with solutions more creatively and rapidly. Mechanistic organizations are better suited to more traditional forms of production that are less susceptible to swings in the marketplace. Although first published in the 1960s, their study is highly relevant to present-day discussions of organizational change. Burns and Stalker anticipated many of the issues in recent debates over globalization, flexible specialization, and debureaucratization.

The Physical Setting of Organizations

Most modern organizations function in specially designed physical settings. A building that houses a particular organization possesses specific features relevant to the organization's activities, but it also shares important architectural characteristics with buildings of other organizations. The architecture of a hospital, for instance, differs in some respects from that of a business firm or a school. The hospital's separate wards, consulting rooms, operating rooms, and offices give the overall building a definite layout, whereas a school may consist of classrooms, laboratories, and a gymnasium. Yet there is a general resemblance: Both are likely to contain hallways off of which are multiple rooms and to use standard decoration and furnishings throughout. Apart from the differing dress of the people moving through the corridors, the buildings in which modern organizations are usually housed can have a definite sameness. They often look similar from the outside as well. It would not be unusual, on driving past a school, to initially identify it as a hospital, and vice versa.

FOUCAULT'S THEORY OF ORGANIZATIONS: THE CONTROL OF TIME AND SPACE

Michel Foucault (1971, 1979) showed that the architecture of an organization is directly involved with its social makeup and

system of authority. By studying the physical characteristics of organizations, we can shed new light on the problems Weber analyzed. The offices Weber discussed abstractly are also architectural settings—rooms, separated by corridors. The buildings of large firms are sometimes actually constructed as a hierarchy, in which the more elevated one's position, the nearer to the top of the building one's office is; not for nothing does "the top floor" refer to those who hold ultimate power in an organization.

In many other ways, the geography of an organization affects its functioning, especially when systems rely heavily on informal relationships. Physical proximity makes forming primary groups easier, whereas physical distance can polarize groups, resulting in a "them" and "us" attitude between departments.

SURVEILLANCE IN ORGANIZATIONS

The arrangement of rooms, hallways, and open spaces in an organization's buildings provides basic clues to how the organization's system of authority operates. In some organizations, people work collectively in open settings. Because of the dull, repetitive nature of certain kinds of industrial work, such as assembly-line production, regular supervision is needed

Workers on an assembly line build the circuit board and other computer devices that will become an electronic gambling machine for a Las Vegas casino. This arrangement allows for a high level of what Foucault calls *surveillance*.

The *Columbia* Shuttle Disaster: A Sociological Perspective

The tragic disintegration of the Space Shuttle *Columbia* on February 1, 2003 set me on an unexpected and remarkable eight-month journey in public sociology. In the hours after the accident, I was deluged with calls from the press. I had studied the causes of the 1986 *Challenger* disaster and written the book, *The Challenger Launch Decision: Risky Technology, Culture, and Deviance at NASA* (1996). I was defined as an expert the press could consult to give them bearings on this latest accident. Viewing this as both a teaching opportunity and professional responsibility, I tried to respond to everyone.

What I was teaching were the theoretical explanation and key concepts of the book, linking them to data about *Challenger* and *Columbia* as the changing press questions dictated. Because the investigation went on for months, these conversations became an ongoing exchange where the press brought me new information and I gave a sociological interpretation. I noticed that the concepts of the book—the normalization of deviance, institutional failure, organization culture, structure, missed signals—began appearing in print early in the investigation and continued, whether I was quoted or not.

The book also led to my association with the *Columbia* Accident Investigation Board. Two weeks after the accident, the publicity director at Chicago sent a copy of *The Challenger Launch Decision* to retired Admiral Harold Gehman, who headed the Board's investigation. ***

Diane Vaughan

The new centrality of sociological ideas and the connection with the *Challenger* accident were not lost on the media. In press conferences, Admiral Gehman stressed the importance of the social causes and used the book's central concepts. When he announced that I would testify before the Board in Houston, the field's leading journal, *Aviation Week and Space Technology,* headlined "*Columbia* Board Probes the Shuttle

to ensure that workers sustain the pace of labor. The same is often true of routine work carried out by telephone operators who respond to calls for information and who sit together where their activities are visible to their supervisors. Foucault laid great emphasis on how visibility, or lack of it, in the architectural settings of modern organizations influences and expresses patterns of authority. The level of visibility determines how easily subordinates can be subject to what Foucault calls **surveillance**, the supervision of activities in organizations. In modern organizations, everyone, even those in relatively high positions of authority, is subject to surveillance; but the

lowlier a person is, the more his or her behavior tends to be scrutinized.

Surveillance takes two forms. One is the direct supervision of the work of subordinates by superiors. Consider the example of a school classroom. Pupils sit at tables or desks, usually arranged in rows, all in view of the teacher. Children are supposed to look alert or be absorbed in their work. Of course, how far this actually happens depends on the abilities of the teacher and the inclinations of the children to do what is expected of them.

The second type of surveillance is more subtle but equally

Program's Sociology," while the *New York Times* ran "Echoes of *Challenger.*" Unaware of the extent of the book's influence on the Board's thinking, however, I arrived in Houston in late April anxious about the public grilling to come.

But subsequent events showed me the Board was receptive to sociological analysis. I met separately with the Group 2 investigators assigned the decision making and organization chapters to discuss their data and analysis, then gave the Board a pre-testimony briefing, which turned into a three-hour conversation. My testimony covered the social causes of the *Challenger* accident, compared it to the *Columbia* incident, and identified systemic institutional failures common to both. The book's theory and concepts traveled farther as my testimony—like that of other witnesses—was shown live on NASA TV and videostreamed into television, radio, and press centers and the Internet.

***

So the Board's report gave equal weight to social causes of the accident—not only because the Admiral believed in the potential of sociology, but also because I, a sociologist, became part of this large team of Board and staff, working under deadline. Information and ideas flew fast and freely between people and chapters. Their extraordinary investigative effort, data, analysis, and insights were integrated into my chapter; sociological connections and concepts became integrated into theirs. *****

The Admiral kept the press informed of report changes, so prior to report publication, the *New York Times* announced the equal weight the report would give to technical and social causes, identifying me as the source of the Board's approach and author of Chapter 8. Upon the August 26 [2003] release, the language of sociology became commonplace in the press. The theory of the book traveled one more place that week. An

[Associated Press] wire story, "NASA Finally Looks to Sociologist," revealed that NASA had invited me to headquarters to talk with top officials, who had shifted from denial to acknowledge that the systemic institutional failures that led to *Challenger* also caused *Columbia.*

Never did I foresee the extent of my involvement or the impact that I ultimately had. ***** The theory and concepts that explained *Challenger* were an analogical fit with the *Columbia* data and made sense of what happened for journalists and the Board. Analogy was the mechanism that enabled the theory and concepts of the book to travel. My book and university affiliation gave me the opportunity to engage in ongoing dialogic teaching—akin to daily grassroots activism—but with two tribunals of power with authoritative voice. Together, the press and the Board were a "polished machinery of dissemination," as Burawoy calls powerful advocacy groups, translating the ideas of the book into grist for critical public dialogue.

SOURCE: Diane Vaughan, "How Theory Travels: A Most Public Public Sociology," *Public Sociology in Action,* ASA Footnotes, Nov/Dec. 2003. www.asanet.org/footnotes/nov03/fn7.html (last accessed April 24, 2006).

important. It consists of keeping files, records, and case histories about people's work lives. Weber realized the importance of written records (nowadays usually computerized) in modern organizations but did not fully explore how they can be used to regulate behavior. Employee records usually provide complete work histories, including personal details and often giving character evaluations. Such records are used to monitor employees' behavior and assess recommendations for promotion. In many businesses, individuals at each level in the organization prepare annual reports on the performances of those in the level just below them. School records and college

transcripts are also used to monitor individuals' performance as they move through the organization. Records are kept on file for academic staff, too.

Organizations cannot operate effectively if employees' work is haphazard. In business firms, as Weber pointed out, people are expected to work regular hours. Activities must be consistently coordinated in time and space, something promoted both by the physical settings of organizations and by the precise scheduling of detailed timetables. **Timetables** regularize activities across time and space—in Foucault's words, they "efficiently distribute bodies" around the organization. Timetables are a condition of organizational discipline, because they slot the activities of large numbers of people together. If a university did not observe a lecture timetable, for example, it would soon collapse into complete chaos.

UNDER SURVEILLANCE! THE PRISON

Foucault paid a great deal of attention to organizations, like prisons, in which people are incarcerated—kept hidden away—from the external social environment. A prison clearly illustrates the nature of surveillance because it seeks to maximize control over inmates' behavior. According to Foucault, the modern prison has its origins in the Panopticon, a structure planned by the philosopher and social thinker Jeremy Bentham in the eighteenth century. "Panopticon" was the name Bentham gave to an ideal prison that he designed and tried to sell to the British government. The design was never fully implemented, but some of its principles were incorporated into prisons built in the nineteenth century in the United States, Britain, and Europe. The Panopticon was circular, with the cells built around the outside edge. In the center was an inspection tower. Each cell had two windows, one facing the inspection tower and the other facing outside.

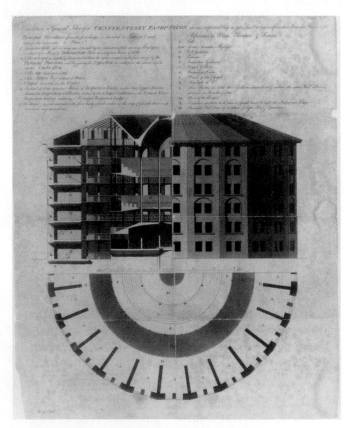

Elevation, cross section, and plan of Jeremy Bentham's Panopticon, drawn in 1790.

The aim of the design was to make prisoners visible to guards at all times. The windows in the tower itself were equipped with venetian blinds, so that while the staff could constantly observe the prisoners, they themselves could be unobserved if necessary.

THE LIMITS OF SURVEILLANCE

Even today, most prisons look remarkably like the Panopticon. Foucault was right about the central role of surveillance in modern societies, an issue that has increased in importance because of the growing effect of information and communications technologies. We live in what some have called the **surveillance society** (Lyon 1994)—a society in which information about our lives is gathered by all types of organizations.

But Weber's and Foucault's argument that the most effective way to run an organization is to maximize surveillance—to have clear and consistent divisions of authority—is wrong, at least if we apply it to businesses, which don't (unlike prisons) exert total control over people's lives in closed settings. Prisons are not a good model for organizations as a whole. Direct supervision may be necessary when the people involved, as in prisons, are hostile to those in authority and do not want to be where they are. But in organizations in which managers desire others to cooperate with them in reaching common goals, the situation is different. Too much direct supervision actually alienates employees, rather than making them work more effectively (Grint 1991; Sabel 1982).

This is one of the main reasons that organizations founded on the principles formulated by Weber and Foucault, such as large factories with assembly-line production and rigid authority hierarchies, eventually ran into trouble. Workers weren't inclined to devote themselves to their work in such settings. Continuous supervision was in fact *required* to get them to work reasonably hard at all, but it promoted resentment and antagonism (for further discussion, see Chapter 14).

People are also likely to resist high levels of surveillance in the second sense mentioned by Foucault, the collection of information about them. Such collection of information was a principal cause of the breakdown of Soviet-style communist societies. In those societies, people were spied on regularly either by the secret police or by others in the pay of the secret police—even relatives and neighbors. The government kept detailed information on its citizenry to clamp down on possible opposition. The result was a society that was politically authoritarian and, toward the end, economically inefficient. The whole society did indeed come almost to resemble a gigantic prison, with all the discontents, conflicts, and modes of opposition prisons generate—and from which, in the end, the population broke free.

Bureaucracy and Democracy

Even in democracies like the United States, government organizations hold enormous amounts of information about us, from records of our birth dates, schools attended, and jobs held to data on income used for tax collecting and information for issuing drivers' licenses and allocating Social Security numbers. Because we don't have access to the files of most government agencies, such surveillance activities can infringe on the principle of democracy.

The diminishing of democracy with the advance of modern forms of organization worried Weber a great deal (see also Chapter 13). What especially disturbed him was the prospect of rule by faceless bureaucrats. How can democracy be anything other than meaningless in the face of the increasing power of bureaucratic organizations? After all, Weber reasoned, bureaucracies are necessarily specialized and hierarchical. Those near the bottom of the organization inevitably carry out mundane tasks and have no power over what they do; power resides with those at the top. Weber's student Robert Michels (1967; orig. 1911) invented a phrase, which has since become famous, to refer to this loss of power: In large-scale organizations, and more generally in a society dominated by organizations, he argued, there is an **iron law of oligarchy**. **Oligarchy** means rule by the few. According to Michels, the flow of power toward the top is an inevitable part of an increasingly bureaucratized world—hence the term "iron law."

Was Michels right? It surely is true that large-scale organizations involve the centralizing of power. Yet there is reason to believe that the iron law of oligarchy is not quite as hard and fast as Michels claimed. The connections between oligarchy and bureaucratic centralization are more ambiguous than he supposed.

First, unequal power is not just a function of size. Marked differences of power exist even in modest-sized groups. In a small business, for instance, in which the activities of employees are directly visible to the directors, much tighter control might be exerted than in larger organizations. As organizations expand in size, power relationships often become looser. Those at the middle and lower levels may have little influence over policies forged at the top. On the other hand, because of the specialization and expertise involved in bureaucracy, people at the top may lose control over many of the administrative decisions made by those lower down.

In many modern organizations, power is often delegated downward from superiors to subordinates. The heads of huge corporations are so busy coordinating different departments, coping with crises, and analyzing budget and forecast figures that they have little time for original thinking. Consequently, they delegate consideration of policy issues to others, whose task is to develop proposals. Many corporate leaders admit that for the most part they simply accept the conclusions given to them.

Gender and Organizations

Until the late twentieth century, organizational studies paid little attention to gender. Weber's theory of bureaucracy and many of the influential responses to it were written by men and presumed an organizational model with men squarely at the center. The rise of feminist scholarship in the 1970s, however, led to the examination of gender relations in all institutions in society, including organizations and bureaucracies. Feminist sociologists not only focused on the imbalance of gender roles within organizations but also explored the ways in which modern organizations had developed in a specifically gendered way.

Feminists have argued that the emergence of the modern organization and the bureaucratic career depended on a particular gender configuration. They point to two main ways in which gender is embedded in the structure of modern organizations. First, bureaucracies are characterized by occupational gender segregation. As women began to enter the labor market in greater numbers, they tended to be segregated into categories of occupations that were low paying and involved routine work. These positions were subordinate to those occupied by men and did not provide opportunities for promotion. Women were used as a source of cheap, reliable labor but were not granted the same opportunities as men to build careers.

Second, the idea of a bureaucratic career was in fact of a male career in which women played a supporting role. In the workplace, women performed the routine tasks—as clerks, secretaries, and office managers—thereby freeing up men to advance their careers. Men could concentrate on landing big accounts and building up new business because the female support staff handled much of the busywork. In the domestic sphere, women also supported the male career by caring for the home, the children, and the man's day-to-day well-being. Women serviced the needs of the male bureaucrat by allowing him to work long hours, travel, and focus solely on his work without concern for personal or domestic issues.

As a result of these two tendencies, early feminist writers argued, modern organizations have developed as male-dominated preserves in which women are excluded from power, denied opportunities for advancement, and victimized on the basis of their gender through sexual harassment and discrimination.

Although most early feminist analysis focused on a common set of concerns—unequal pay, discrimination, and the male hold on power—there was no consensus about the best way to work for women's equality. Two of the leading feminist works on women and organizations exemplified the split between liberal and radical feminist perspectives.

One was Rosabeth Moss Kanter's *Men and Women of the Corporation* (1977), an early examination of women in bureaucratic settings. Kanter investigated the position of women in corporations and analyzed how they were excluded from power. She focused on "male homosociability"—the way in which men kept power within a closed circle and allowed access only to those who were part of their in-group. Women and ethnic minorities were shut out of the social networks and personal relationships that were crucial for promotions.

Although Kanter was critical of these gender imbalances within modern corporations, she was not entirely pessimistic about the future. In her eyes, the problem was one of *power,* not gender. Women were in a disadvantaged position not because they were women per se, but because they did not wield sufficient power within organizations. As greater numbers of women assumed powerful roles, according to Kanter, the imbalances would be swept away. Her analysis can be described as a liberal feminist approach because she is primarily concerned with equality of opportunity and ensuring that women are able to attain positions comparable with those of men.

The radical feminist approach, presented by Kathy Ferguson in *The Feminist Case against Bureaucracy* (1984), differs greatly from Kanter's. Ferguson did not see the gender imbalance within organizations as something that could be resolved with the promotion of more women to positions of power. In Ferguson's view, modern organizations were fundamentally tainted by male values and patterns of domination. Women would always be relegated to subordinate roles within such structures, she argued. The only solution was for women to build their own organizations on principles very different from those used by men. Women, she argued, have the capacity to organize in a way that is more democratic, participatory, and cooperative than men, who are prone to authoritarian tactics, inflexible procedures, and an insensitive management style.

WOMEN IN MANAGEMENT

As more and more women have entered professional occupations in recent decades, the debate over gender and organizations has taken new turns. Many scholars now see an opportunity to assess the effect of women leaders and managers on organizations. Was Kanter correct when she predicted that gender imbalances would diminish as more women entered powerful positions? One of the most contested questions today is whether women managers are making a difference

Brenda Barnes, CEO of Sara Lee, at the company's headquarters in Chicago. Sara Lee is the largest U.S. corporation headed by a woman. As women climb the corporate ladder, will they change the methods as well as the face of management?

by introducing a "female" style of management into contexts that have long been dominated by male culture, values, and behavior.

Organizations of all types need to become more flexible, efficient, and competitive in today's global economy. In recent years, leadership qualities commonly associated with women have been held up as assets for organizations attempting to become more flexible. Rather than relying on top-down, rigid management styles, organizations are encouraged to adopt policies that ensure employee commitment, enthusiasm for organizational goals, shared responsibility, and a focus on people. Communication, consensus, and teamwork are cited by management theorists as key approaches that will distinguish successful organizations in the global age. These so-called soft management skills are ones traditionally associated with women.

Some claim that this shift toward a more "female" management style can already be felt. Women are exerting unprecedented influence at the top levels of power, they argue, and are doing so according to their own rules (Rosener 1997). As the success of women's leadership is felt throughout the organizational world, some predict that men will adopt many of the techniques long favored by women, such as delegating responsibility, sharing information and resources, and setting collective goals.

Others do not believe that women are successfully exercising distinctly female management. In *Managing Like a Man*

(1998), Judy Wajcman argues that the number of women who actually make it to the top is small. Yes, she says, women are making substantial progress in middle management, but they are still largely absent at the highest levels. One out of thirteen senior executives (executive vice president or higher) is a woman. This is a dramatic increase from one in forty in 1995 (Epstein 2003). Even though women have increasingly made their way into the highest levels of management, this comes with costs, such as delaying or forgoing altogether having children or marital relationships (Figure 6.4). However, many of these positions held by women are "staff" positions or are otherwise removed from direct influence on profit margins. In Fortune 500 companies, 90 percent of executive positions with direct influence on profit and loss were held by men (Epstein 2003). Men continue to receive higher pay for equivalent work and are employed in a broader spectrum of roles than are women, who tend to cluster in fields such as human resources and marketing.

When women do reach top management positions, they tend to manage like men. Although advances have been made since the 1980s in the areas of equal employment, sexual harassment policies, and overall consciousness about gender issues, Wajcman argues that organizational culture and management style remain overwhelmingly male. In her study of 324 senior-level managers in multinational corporations, she found that management techniques are dominated more by the overall organizational culture than by the gender or personal style of individual managers. For women to gain access to power and maintain their influence, they must adapt to the prevailing managerial style, which emphasizes aggressive leadership, tough tactics, and top-down decision making.

Wajcman argues forcefully that organizations are thoroughly gendered, in ways both obvious and subtle. The day-to-day organizational culture—including the way in which people talk to each other—is dominated by quick, competitive interactions. Despite a drop in overt sexual harassment—no longer tolerated in most organizations—more subtle sexualized relations persist in the workplace, usually to the disadvantage of women. Social networks and informal ties are the crucial elements behind job promotions and advancement, but these continue to be run in the style of an old-boys network. Many women find this realm alienating or uncomfortable, as one of Wajcman's (1998) respondents explained:

> You've got to be one of the boys. . . . I don't mind going down to the pub with the boys. . . . I don't get offended by the jokes. . . . [T]hat's how you get to the top . . . you start to see the breaks or where something's not going quite right and you make use of it. . . . I personally don't like playing that game. It's not worth the hassle.

FIGURE 6.4

Balancing Act?

More women are breaking into the upper reaches of corporate America . . .

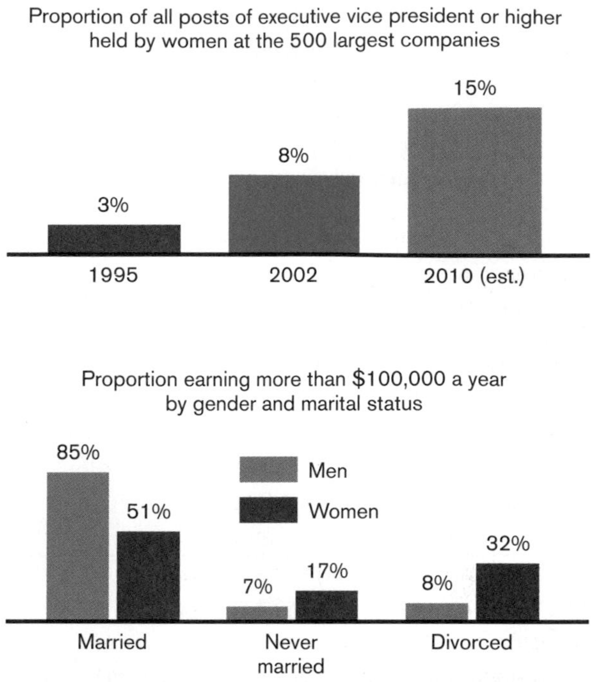

Proportion of all posts of executive vice president or higher held by women at the 500 largest companies

Proportion earning more than $100,000 a year by gender and marital status

What is the percentage increase in the number of women serving as executive vice president or higher between 1995 and 2002? How many women does the U.S. Bureau of Labor Statistics estimate will serve as executives in 2010? Why is it difficult for women to move into the highest ranks of organizations? Do women's earnings vary based on their marital status?

SOURCE: Epstein 2003.

There is also reason to believe that it is difficult for women to take advantage of traditional mentoring patterns. The model of mentoring has long been the older man who takes on a protégé in whom he sees traces of himself at a younger age. The mentor works behind the scenes to advance the young employee's interests and to facilitate his career moves. This dynamic is less easy to replicate between older male bosses and younger female employees, and there are not enough women in senior positions to serve as mentors to younger women.

Among Wajcman's respondents, women were more likely than men to cite a lack of career guidance as a major barrier in their advancement.

Wajcman is skeptical about claims that a new age of flexible, decentralized organizations is upon us. Her findings reveal that traditional forms of authoritarian management are still firmly present. In her view, certain surface attributes of organizations may have been transformed, but the gendered nature of organizations—and the overwhelmingly dominant power of men within them—has not been challenged.

☑ CONCEPT CHECKS

1. What does the term *bureaucracy* mean?
2. Describe five characteristics of an ideal type of bureaucracy.
3. According to Merton, what are some of the drawbacks of bureaucracies?
4. Explain how modern organizations have developed in a gendered way.

Beyond Bureaucracy?

For quite a long while in Western societies, Weber's model, closely mirrored by that of Foucault, held good. In government, hospital administration, universities, and business organizations, bureaucracy was dominant. Even though, as Peter Blau showed, informal social groups always develop in bureaucratic settings and are in fact effective, it seemed as though the future might be what Weber had anticipated: constantly increasing bureaucratization.

Bureaucracies still exist in the West, but Weber's idea that a clear hierarchy of authority, with power and knowledge concentrated at the top, is the only way to run a large organization is starting to look archaic. Numerous organizations are overhauling themselves to become less, rather than more, hierarchical.

In the 1960s, Burns and Stalker concluded that traditional bureaucratic structures can stifle innovation and creativity in cutting-edge industries; in today's electronic economy, few would dispute these findings. Departing from rigid vertical command structures, many organizations are turning to "horizontal," collaborative models to become more responsive to fluctuating markets. In this section we examine some of the forces behind these shifts, including globalization and information technology, and consider some of the ways in which late modern organizations are reinventing themselves.

Organizational Change: The Japanese Model

Many of the changes now seen in organizations around the world were pioneered in Japanese companies several decades ago. Although the Japanese economy has suffered in recent years, it was phenomenally successful during the 1980s. This success was often attributed to the distinctive characteristics of large Japanese corporations—which differed substantially from most business firms in the West (Vogel 1979). Japanese companies, especially in the 1980s and 1990s, diverged from the characteristics that Weber associated with bureaucracy in several ways:

1. **Bottom-up decision making.** Big Japanese corporations do not form a pyramid of authority as Weber portrayed it, with each level responsible only to the one above. Rather, workers low down in the organization are consulted about policies being considered by management, and the top executives regularly meet with them.

2. **Less specialization.** In Japanese organizations, employees specialize less than their counterparts in the West. Take the case of Sugao, as described by William Ouchi (1982). Sugao is a university graduate who has joined the Mitsubeni Bank in Tokyo. He will enter the firm in a management-training position, spending his first year learning how the various departments of the bank operate. He will then work in a local branch as a teller and will subsequently be brought back to headquarters to learn commercial banking. Then he will move out to yet another branch dealing with loans. From there he is likely to return to headquarters to work in the personnel department. Ten years will have elapsed by this time, and Sugao will have reached the position of section chief.

   By the time Sugao reaches the peak of his career, some thirty years after beginning as a trainee, he will have mastered all the important tasks. In contrast, a typical American bank-management trainee of the same age will almost certainly specialize in one area of banking early on and stay in that specialty for her entire working life.

3. **Job security.** Large Japanese corporations are committed to the long-term employment of those they hire; the employee is guaranteed a job. Pay and responsibility are geared to seniority—how many years a worker has been with the firm—rather than to a competitive struggle for promotion. This remains a value, although it has weakened in recent years.

4. **Group orientation.** At all levels of the corporation, people are involved in small cooperative teams, or work

groups. The groups, rather than individuals, are evaluated in terms of their performance. Unlike their Western counterparts, the *organization charts* of Japanese companies show only groups, not individual positions.

5. **Merging of work and private lives.** In Weber's bureaucracy, there is a clear division between people's work within the organization and their activities outside. This is true of most Western corporations, in which the relation between firm and employee is an economic one. Japanese corporations, by contrast, provide for many of their employees' needs, expecting in return a high level of loyalty to the firm. Japanese employees, from workers on the shop floor to top executives, often wear company uniforms. They may sing the company song each morning, and they regularly take part in weekend leisure activities organized by the corporation. (A few Western corporations, like IBM and Apple, now have company songs.) Workers receive material benefits from the company over and above their salaries. The electrical firm Hitachi, for example, studied by Ronald Dore (1980), provided housing for all unmarried workers and nearly half of its married male employees. Company loans were available for education and to help with weddings and funerals.

Studies of Japanese-run plants in the United States and Britain indicate that bottom-up decision making does work outside Japan. Workers seem to respond positively to the greater level of involvement these plants provide (White and Trevor 1983). It is reasonable to conclude, therefore, that the Japanese model does have some lessons for the Weberian conception of bureaucracy. Organizations that closely resemble Weber's ideal type are probably much less effective than they appear on paper, because they do not permit lower-level employees to develop a sense of control over, and involvement in, their work.

Although it is impossible to ignore production-level practices developed by the Japanese, a large part of the Japanese approach focuses on management–worker relations and ensures that employees at all levels feel a personal attachment to the company. The emphasis on teamwork, consensus building, and broad-based employee participation contrast starkly with traditional Western forms of management, which are more hierarchical and authoritarian.

The Transformation of Management

In the 1980s, many Western organizations introduced management techniques to boost productivity and competitiveness.

The increasing popularity of two branches of management theory—*human resource management* and the *corporate culture* approach—indicated that the Japanese model had not gone unnoticed in the West. **Human resource management** regards a company's workforce as vital to its competitiveness: If the employees are not dedicated to the firm and its product, the firm will not be a leader in its field. To generate employee enthusiasm and commitment, organizational culture must be retooled so that workers have an investment in the workplace and in the work process. According to human resource management theory, human resource issues should be a top priority for all members of company management.

The second management trend—the **corporate culture** approach—is closely related to human resources management. To promote loyalty to the company and pride in its work, management works with employees to develop rituals, events, and traditions unique to the company. These activities are designed to draw together all members of the firm—from senior managers to the most junior employees—so that they make common cause with each other and strengthen group solidarity. Company picnics, casual Fridays (days on which employees can dress down), and company-sponsored community service projects are examples of techniques for building a corporate culture.

In recent years a number of Western companies have been founded according to the management principles described above. Rather than constructing themselves according to a traditional bureaucratic model, companies like the car manufacturer Saturn have organized themselves along these new managerial lines. At Saturn, employees at all levels can spend time in other areas of the company to gain a better sense of the operation as a whole. Shop-floor workers spend time with the marketing team, sharing insights into the way the vehicles are made. Sales staff rotate through the servicing department

Workers at a Saturn plant rotate through different positions so they can learn how the company operates.

to become aware of maintenance problems that might concern prospective buyers. Representatives from sales and the shop floor work with product design teams to discuss shortcomings in earlier models that management may not have been aware of. A corporate culture focused on friendly and knowledgeable customer service unifies company employees and enhances company pride.

Technology and Modern Organizations

The development of **information technology**—computers and electronic communication media such as the Internet—is another factor currently influencing organizational structures (Attaran 2004; Bresnahan et al. 2002; Castells 2000, 2001; Kanter 1991; Kobrin 1997; Zuboff 1988). Anyone who draws money from a bank or buys an airline ticket depends on a computer-based communications system. Because data can be processed instantaneously in any part of the world linked to such a system, there is no need for physical proximity between those involved. As a result, new technology has allowed many companies to "reengineer" their organizational structure. Such changes, while good for efficiency, can have positive and negative consequences for the individuals within the organization.

For example, one company found the sales of some of its products falling and needed to reduce costs. The traditional route would be to lay off staff. Instead, the firm set up as independent consultants those who would have been laid off and established a computerized support network called Xanadu to provide basic office services to each of them working out of their homes. The company then bought back a substantial proportion of the former employees' working time for a number of years but also left them free to work for other clients. The idea was that the new arrangement would provide the corporation with access to the skills of its former employees but at a cheaper rate because it no longer provided office space or company benefits (pension, health insurance, and so on). The former employees, in turn, had the opportunity to build up their own businesses. Initially, at least, the arrangement has worked well for both parties. In such a scheme, though, the burden is on the former employees because they have to compensate for the loss of benefits with new business.

This is just one example of how large organizations have become more decentralized and flexible (Burris 1998). Another example is the rise of telecommuting. A good deal of office work can be carried out by telecommuters using the Internet and other mobile technologies, such as cell phones, to work at home or somewhere other than their employer's primary office. Worldwide there are an estimated 137 million workers who telework (Telework Coalition 2004). According to the Telework Coalition, 44.4 million Americans telecommuted in 2004, which is approximately one fifth of the population of adult workers in the United States (Davis and Polonko 2001; Telework Coalition 2004). Of these, 21 percent worked at home, while the rest are about equally divided between working at special telework centers, working at satellite offices, or working while traveling (International Telework Association Council [ITAC] 2004). Telecommuters in the United States are typically males from the Northeast and West who have college degrees and work in professional or managerial positions (Davis and Polonko 2001). To reduce costs and increase productivity, large firms may have set up information networks connecting employees who work from home with the main office. In 2001 AT&T reported saving $65 million annually in increased productivity

Barbara Magnoni telecommutes from her Manhattan apartment. She finds that working from home requires stern self-discipline and an ability to tune out her spouse, children, and pets. For the more sociable or emotionally needy, it can feel like house arrest, especially if the phone hasn't rung in a while.

and $25 million annually in real estate costs (ITAC 2004). With the advent of high-speed Internet access, telecommuting has become even more efficient: ITAC estimated that employers could save $5000 per year per teleworking employee by providing its teleworkers with broadband access (Pratt 2003). In 2004, over eight million teleworkers working at home did so over broadband (Telework Coalition 2004).

One reason that telecommuting increases productivity is that it eliminates commuting time, thereby permitting greater concentration of energy on work. Hartig et al. (2003) found that telecommuters actually spend more time on paid work when working at home than their counterparts do when working in the office. Employers view these longer hours as a primary benefit of telecommuting (ITAC 2004). However, these new work arrangements are not perfect. First, the employees lose the human side of work; computer terminals are no substitute for face-to-face interaction with colleagues and friends at work. Second, telecommuters experience isolation, distraction, and conflicting demands of work and home responsibilities (Ammons and Markham 2004). In addition, female telecommuters face more stress from increased housework and child-care responsibilities (Ammons and Markham 2004; Olson 1989; Olson and Primps 1984). On the plus side for telecommuters, management cannot easily monitor employees working offsite (Dimitrova 2003; Kling 1996). While this may create problems for employers, it allows employees greater flexibility in managing their nonwork roles, thus contributing to increased worker satisfaction (Davis and Polonko 2001). According to surveys by *Computer World* (2002) magazine, in the information technology field, the possibility of telecommuting is significant in determining the desirability of a job. Telecommuting also creates new possibilities for older and disabled workers to remain independent, productive, and socially connected (Bricourt 2004). Finally, telecommuting is contributing to new trends in housing—space for home offices is a priority—and residential development. With people able to work at a distance from city centers, residential development no longer need be tied to commuting practices.

Although computerization has resulted in increased flexibility and a reduction in hierarchy, it has created a two-tiered occupational structure composed of technical "experts" and less-skilled production or clerical workers. In these restructured organizations, jobs have been redefined more in terms of technical skill than rank or position. For "expert" professionals, traditional bureaucratic constraints are relaxed to allow for creativity and flexibility (Burris 1993). Although professionals benefit from this expanded autonomy, computerization makes production and service workers more visible and vulnerable to supervision (Wellman et al. 1996; Zuboff 1988). For instance, organizations can now monitor work patterns to the point at which they can count the number of seconds per phone call or keystrokes per minute, which in turn can lead to higher levels of stress for employees.

Granted, workplace computerization does have some positive effects. It has made some of the mundane tasks of clerical jobs more interesting. It can also promote social networking (Wellman et al. 1996). Office computers can be used for recreation; private exchanges with co-workers, friends, or family; and work-related interaction. But in most workplaces, computerization benefits the professionals who possess the knowledge and expertise about how to gain from it. It has not brought commensurate improvements in the career opportunities or salaries of the average worker (Kling 1996).

Organizations as Networks

Traditionally, identifying the boundaries of organizations has been fairly straightforward. Organizations were generally located in defined physical spaces, such as an office building; a suite of rooms; or, in the case of a hospital or university, a campus. In addition, the mission or tasks of an organization were usually clear cut. A central feature of bureaucracies, for example, was adherence to a defined set of responsibilities and procedures for carrying them out. Weber's bureaucracy was a self-contained unit that intersected with outside entities at limited and designated points.

We have already seen how the physical boundaries of organizations are being broken down by the capacity of information technology to transcend countries and time zones. The same process is affecting the work that organizations do and the way in which it is coordinated. Many organizations no longer operate as independent units. A growing number are finding that they run more effectively when they are part of a web of complex relationships with other organizations and companies. No longer is there a clear dividing line between the organization and outside groups. Globalization, information technology, and trends in occupational patterns mean that organizational boundaries are more open and fluid than they once were.

In *The Rise of the Network Society* (1996), Manuel Castells argues that the "network enterprise" is the organizational form best suited to a global, informational economy. By this he means that it is increasingly impossible for organizations—large corporations or small businesses—to survive if they are not part of a network. What enables networking to occur is the growth of information technology, whereby organizations around the world are able to enter into contact and coordinate joint activities through an electronic medium. Castells cites several examples of organizational networking that originated in diverse cultural and institutional contexts. According to Castells, however, they all represent "different dimensions of

Social Networks and Music Taste

Are our music choices a matter of personal taste or an example of conforming behavior? We tend to think of the music that we listen to as an intensely personal choice made independently of the people around us and that reflects our individual personalities and preferences. How much, however, do our social networks shape our most personal of decisions like our aesthetic tastes?

Social scientists Matthew Salganik, Peter Dodds, and Duncan Watts (2006) conducted research to test the effects of the influence of social networks on musical choices. To do so, they created an artificial cultural market on a Web site named Music Lab. Over fourteen thousand participants registered with the site and were asked to listen to music by bands that they were unfamiliar with and then rate how much they liked the songs. If they liked the music, they could download songs. The researchers first divided their sample into two groups. The control group was unable to use the Web site to see what other participants were listening to. The experimental or "treatment" group, the "social influence" group, was able to see what other participants on the Web site were listening to as well as downloading. The social influence group was further divided into eight "worlds," and participants could see only the rankings and number of downloads of people in their world.

The researchers found that in the social influence groups, the most popular songs were more popular than those in the control group—that is, when participants knew what songs were favored by others, they were more likely to favor those songs themselves. The most popular song in each world was also different, providing further evidence of the importance of group influence. This suggests that the determinants of popularity in music were based on the listener's social "world." That

a fundamental process"—the disintegration of the traditional, rational bureaucracy.

An example of organizations as networks is the powerful alliances formed between top companies. Increasingly, the large corporation is less and less a big business and more an "enterprise web"—a central organization that links smaller firms together. IBM, for example, used to be a highly self-sufficient corporation, wary of partnerships with others. Yet in the 1980s and early 1990s, IBM joined with dozens of U.S.-based companies and more than eighty foreign-based firms to share strategic planning and cope with production problems.

Recent high-profile mergers among media and telecommunications companies have shown that even large and profitable corporations feel pressure to keep ahead of the rapidly changing market. The intentions of AOL, the online provider, and Time Warner, the television and print media giant, in their merger were to produce the world's largest corporation and link the Internet and traditional media products. At a time when technological innovation is essential to remain competitive, it is difficult for even leading firms to remain on top without drawing on the skills and resources of others. And as the financial difficulties of the AOL–Time Warner merger show, technological innovation by itself does not guarantee success.

Decentralization is another process that contributes to organizations functioning as networks. When change becomes more profound and more rapid, highly centralized Weberian-style bureaucracies are too cumbersome and too entrenched in their ways to cope. Stanley Davis (1988) argues that as business firms, as well as other organizations, come to be networks, they go through a process of decentralization by which power and responsibility are devolved downward throughout the organization, rather than remaining concentrated at the top.

Networked organizations offer at least two advantages over more bureaucratic ones: They can foster the flow of information, and they can enhance creativity. As we've seen, bureaucratic hierarchy can impede the flow of information: One must go through the proper channels, fill out the right forms, and avoid displeasing people in higher positions. These processes not only hinder the sharing of information but also stifle creative problem solving. In networked organizations, when a problem arises, instead of writing a memo to your boss and waiting for a reply, you can simply pick up the phone or dash off an e-mail to the person responsible for working out a solution. As a result, members of networked organizations learn more easily from one another than do bureaucrats. It is therefore easier to solve routine dilemmas and to develop

MUSIC LAB — COLUMBIA UNIVERSITY

CLICK HERE TO START

FREE MUSIC DOWNLOADS

is, the "intrinsic" quality of the music mattered less than the number of people in each world who were listening to the song, giving it high ratings, and downloading it. The authors of the study described the effect of social networks as a "cumulative advantage" where "if one object happens to be slightly more popular than another at just the right point, it will tend to become more popular still. As a result, even tiny, random fluctuations can blow up, generating potentially enormous long-run

differences among even indistinguishable competitors—a phenomenon that is similar in some ways to the famous 'butterfly effect' from chaos theory" (Watts 2007). The butterfly effect proposes that small variations may produce large variations in the long term behavior of a system or organism. Their study revealed the impact of our social networks, which are now increasingly virtual networks, on our music decisions.

Studying how consumers make decisions is a part of a much deeper sociological tradition that is concerned with conformity, propaganda, and the question of how leaders have persuaded whole populations to take part in horrific deeds. The Holocaust, which claimed the lives of more than six million Jews and others, left many social scientists searching to understand how, why, and under what conditions ordinary people will conform to authority. Many students who have seen or read about Stanley Milgram's laboratory experiments or the Stanford Prison experiments (both discussed in this chapter) tend to think that they would not conform to the demands of an authority figure like the study participants did.

Yet, the music market study reveals how social environments affect our behavior and how we all, at times, conform to the movements of larger social groups even in something as personal as the music that we like. How do you think social influence affects your own, presumably personal, decisions?

innovative solutions to all types of problems (Hamel 1991; Powell and Brantley 1992; Powell et al. 1996).

The "McDonaldization" of Society?

Not everyone agrees that society and its organizations are moving away from rigid Weberian bureaucracies. Some point out that a few high-profile examples of less bureaucratic companies—such as the Saturn car corporation or Benetton—are seized on by the media and commentators, who in turn pronounce the birth of a trend that does not in fact exist.

As part of the debate over debureaucratization, George Ritzer (1993) used a vivid metaphor to express his view of the transformations in industrialized societies. He argues that although tendencies toward debureaucratization have indeed emerged, on the whole what we are witnessing is the "McDonaldization" of society: the process by which the principles of the fast-food restaurants are coming to dominate more and more sectors of American society as well as the rest of the world. Ritzer uses the four guiding principles of McDonald's

restaurants—efficiency, calculability, uniformity, and control through automation—to show that our society is becoming ever more rationalized.

If you have visited McDonald's in two different countries, you will have noticed that there are few differences between them. The interior decoration may vary slightly and the language will most likely differ, but the layout, the menu, the procedure for ordering, the uniforms, the tables, the packaging, and the "service with a smile" are virtually identical. The McDonald's experience is designed to be the same whether you are in Bogota or Beijing. No matter where they are, McDonald's customers can expect quick service with a minimum of fuss and a standardized product that is reassuringly consistent. The McDonald's system is constructed to maximize efficiency and minimize human responsibility and involvement in the process. Except for certain key tasks such as taking orders and pushing the start and stop buttons on cooking equipment, the restaurants' functions are highly automated and largely run themselves.

Ritzer argues that society as a whole is moving toward this highly standardized and regulated model. Many aspects of our daily lives, for example, now involve automated systems and computers instead of human beings. E-mail and voice mail are replacing letters and phone calls, e-commerce is threatening to

What is McDonaldization? What are the consequences of highly standardized experiences?

overtake trips to the stores, bank machines outnumber bank tellers, and prepackaged meals provide a quicker option than cooking. And if you have recently tried to call a large organization, such as an airline, you know that it is almost impossible to speak to a human being. Automated touch-tone information services are designed to answer your requests; only in certain cases will you be connected to a live employee. Ritzer, like Weber before him, is fearful of the harmful effects of rationalization on the human spirit and creativity. He argues that McDonaldization is making social life more homogeneous, more rigid, and less personal.

☑ CONCEPT CHECKS

1. What are the differences between the Japanese model of organizations and the Weberian approach to bureaucracy?
2. How has the Japanese model influenced the Western approach to management?
3. Explain how the development of information technology has changed the ways people live and work.
4. According to George Ritzer, what are the four guiding principles used in McDonald's restaurants?

Organizations That Span the World

For the first time in history, organizations have become truly global. Information technologies have rendered national borders less meaningful because they can no longer contain key economic, cultural, and environmental activities. As a

consequence, international organizations are expected to grow in number and importance, providing a measure of predictability and stability in a world where nations are no longer the all-powerful actors (Union of International Associations 2005). Sociologists study international organizations to understand how it is possible to create institutions that span national borders and what the effects of such institutions will be. Some even argue that global organizations will push the world's countries to become more and more alike (McNeely 1995; Scott and Meyer 1994; Thomas et al. 1987).

International organizations are not new. For example, organizations concerned with managing trade across borders have existed for centuries. The Hanseatic League, an alliance among German merchants and cities, dominated trade in the North and Baltic seas from the mid-thirteenth to the mid-seventeenth century. But it was not until the creation of the short-lived League of Nations in 1919 that a truly global organization, with an elaborate bureaucracy and member nations around the world, was formed. The United Nations, created in 1945, is perhaps the most prominent modern example of a global organization.

Sociologists divide international organizations into two principal types: *international governmental organizations* and *international nongovernmental organizations*. We will consider each of these separately.

International Governmental Organizations

An **international governmental organizations (IGO)** is established by treaties among governments for purposes of conducting business among the member nations. Such organizations emerge for reasons of national security (both the League of

EU president Jose Manuel Barroso, French president Nicolas Sarkozy, British prime minister Gordon Brown, German chancellor Angela Merkel, and Italian prime minister Romano Prodi address the media during a press conference for the January 2008 European Union Summit at the Foreign Office in London, England.

Nations and the United Nations were created after highly destructive world wars), the regulation of trade (for example, the World Trade Organization), social welfare or human rights, or, increasingly, environmental protection. At the beginning of the twentieth century, there were only about three dozen IGOs. Today it is estimated that there are as many as 7,350 international governmental organizations (Union of International Organizations 2005).

Some of the most powerful IGOs were created to unify national economies into large and powerful trading blocks. One of the most advanced IGOs is the European Union (EU), whose rules now govern twenty-seven countries, mostly in Western Europe. The EU was formed to create a single European economy in which businesses could operate freely across borders and workers could search for jobs without having to go through customs or show passports. EU members have common economic policies; thirteen of them even share a single currency (the euro). Thirteen additional countries, mostly Eastern European and representing 168 million people, have applied for membership, ten of which joined in 2004 (Europa.eu 2004). Not all Europeans welcome this development, however, because member countries must surrender most of their economic decision making to the EU as a whole.

IGOs can also wield considerable military power, provided their member nations are willing to do so. The North Atlantic Treaty Organization (NATO) and the United Nations (UN), for example, used the full weight of their members' combined military might against Iraq during the Gulf War in 1991 and again in Kosovo, in the former Yugoslavia, in 1999. Yet because nations ultimately control their own use of military force, there are limits to the authority of even the most powerful military IGOs. In the face of violent civil strife in Bosnia and the African countries of Somalia and Rwanda, for example, UN peacekeeping efforts have proved largely ineffective.

IGOs often reflect inequalities in power among their member nations. For example, the UN Security Council, with fifteen member countries, is responsible for maintaining international peace and security and is therefore the most powerful organization within the United Nations. Its five permanent members are Britain, the United States, China, France, and Russia, giving these countries significant control over the council's actions. The remaining ten countries are elected by the UN General Assembly for two-year terms and thus have less ongoing power than the permanent members.

International Nongovernmental Organizations

The second type of global organization is the **international nongovernmental organization (INGO)**. INGOs are established by agreements among individuals or private organizations. Examples include the International Planned Parenthood Federation, the International Sociological Association, the International Council of Women, Amnesty International, and Greenpeace. As with IGOs, the number of INGOs has exploded in recent years—from fewer than 200 in the early twentieth century to about 44,000 international nongovernmental organizations today (Union of International Organizations 2005).

In general, INGOs promote the global interests of their members, largely through influencing individual governments and IGOs. They also engage in research and education and spread information through international conferences, meetings, and journals. One prominent example of an INGO is the International Campaign to Ban Landmines (ICBL). The ICBL is affiliated with over a thousand other INGOs in some sixty countries. Together they have focused public attention on the dangers of the more than one hundred million antipersonnel mines that are a deadly legacy of wars fought in Europe, Asia, and Africa. Unlike other weapons, these mines can remain active for decades after hostilities have ended, terrorizing whole populations. In Cambodia, for example, where acres of fertile croplands still contain mines, farmers not willing to risk a misstep that could reduce them or their families to a shower of scraps face the possibility of starvation. The campaign, along with its founder, Jody Williams, was awarded the Nobel Peace Prize in 1997 for its success in getting a majority of the world's countries to sign a treaty banning the use of land mines. The treaty became international law in March 1999 and has been ratified by 155 countries. Thirty-eight additional countries have not signed the treaty but have made a political commitment to joining, and they have a legal obligation not to take actions that would violate the treaty, while two other countries have signed but not yet ratified the treaty (ICBL 2007).

Although they are more numerous than IGOs and have achieved some major successes, INGOs have far less influence

Jody Williams, founder of the International Campaign to Ban Landmines, was awarded the Nobel Peace Prize in 1997 for her work and its eventual success in effecting the end of landmine use by a majority of the world's countries.

because legal power (including enforcement) ultimately lies with governments. In the effort to ban land mines, for instance, although most major powers signed the treaty, the United States, citing security concerns in Korea, refused, as did Russia.

☑ CONCEPT CHECKS

1. Compare and contrast international governmental organizations (IGOs) with international nongovernmental organizations (INGOs).
2. Give an example of an INGO, including its main goal and strategy for achieving that goal.

How Do Groups and Organizations Affect Your Life?

One of the principal reasons people join organizations is to gain connections and increase influence. The time and energy invested in an organization can bring welcome returns. Parents who belong to the Parent-Teacher Association (PTA), for example, are more likely to influence school policy than those who do not belong. PTA members know whom to call, what to say, and how to exert pressure on school officials.

Sociologists call the fruits of organizational membership **social capital** (Coleman 1988, 1990; Loury 1987; Putnam 1993, 1995, 2000). Social capital includes useful social networks; a sense of mutual obligation and trustworthiness; an understanding of the norms that govern effective behavior; and other social resources that enable people to act effectively. College students often become active in the student government or the campus newspaper partly because they hope to learn skills and make connections that will pay off when they graduate. They may get to interact with professors and administrators, who then will go to bat for them when they are looking for a job or applying to graduate school.

Differences in social capital mirror larger social inequalities. In general, men have more social capital than do women, whites more than nonwhites, the wealthy more than the poor. The Bohemian Grove you read about earlier, an important source of social capital for those who belong, is limited to wealthy, mainly white males. Attendance gives these men access to powerful social, political, and business resources, helping extend their wealth and influence. Differences in social capital can also be found among countries. According to the World Bank (2001), countries with high levels of social capital, where businesspeople can develop the "networks of trust" that foster healthy economies, are more likely to experience economic growth. An example is the rapid growth of many East Asian economies in the 1980s, a growth some sociologists have argued was fueled by strong business networks.

Robert Putnam (2000), an American political scientist, distinguishes two types of social capital: *bridging social capital*, which is outward looking and inclusive, and *bonding social capital*, which is inward looking and exclusive. Bridging social capital unifies people across social cleavages. The capacity to unify people can be seen in such examples as the civil rights movement, which brought blacks and whites together in the struggle for racial equality, and interfaith religious organizations. Bonding social capital reinforces exclusive identities and homogeneous groups; it can be found in ethnic fraternal organizations, church-based women's reading groups, and fashionable country clubs.

People who belong to organizations are more likely to feel connected; they feel engaged, able to make a difference. From the standpoint of the larger society, social capital, the bridging form in particular, provides people with a feeling that they are part of a wider community, one that includes people who are different from themselves. Democracy flourishes when social capital is strong. Indeed, cross-national surveys suggest that levels of civic engagement in the United States are among the highest in the world (Putnam 1993, 2000). But there is equally strong evidence that during the past quarter century, political involvement, club membership, and other forms of social and civic engagement significantly eroded in America. Could democracy be eroding as a result?

Such declines in organizational membership, neighborliness, and trust in general have been paralleled by a decline in political participation. Voter turnout has dropped by 25 percent since the 1960s. In recent presidential elections, for example, the winning candidate (George H. W. Bush in 1988, Bill Clinton in 1992 and 1996, and George W. Bush in 2000 and 2004) received roughly a quarter of the votes of all those who were eligible to cast a ballot. About half the eligible voters did not go to the polls. Even the 2004 and 2008 presidential elections, which drew record numbers of voters, represented just over 60 percent of those eligible to vote. Similarly, attendance at public meetings concerning education or civic affairs has dropped sharply since the 1970s, and three out of four Americans today tell pollsters that they either "never" trust the government or do so only "sometimes" (Putnam 1995). Yet, after the terrorist attacks of September 11, 2001, researchers witnessed a resurgence of trust in government, with those saying that they trust the government "some of the time" doubling to nearly 60 percent (Pew 2003). Since then, trust has declined to 46 percent, but this is still significantly higher than in previous decades. This trend has remained relatively stable, as recent Gallup polls reveal. About 51 percent of Americans say they have a "great deal" or "fair amount" of trust in the federal government to handle international problems (Gallup 2007).

Even the recent increase in membership in organizations such as the Sierra Club, the National Organization for Women (NOW), and the AARP (with thirty-nine million members) is deceiving: The majority of these organizations' members simply pay their annual dues and receive a newsletter. Very few actively participate; most members fail to develop the social capital Putnam regards as an important underpinning of democracy. Many of the most popular organizations today, such as twelve-step programs or weight-loss groups, emphasize personal growth and health rather than collective goals to benefit society as a whole.

There are undoubtedly many reasons for these declines. For one, women, who were traditionally active in voluntary organizations, are now more likely to hold jobs. For another, people are increasingly disillusioned with government and less likely to think that their vote counts. Furthermore, the flight to the suburbs and exurbs increases commutes, using up time and energy that might have been available for civic activities. But the principal source of declining civic participation, according to Putnam, is simple: television. The many hours Americans spend at home watching TV have replaced social engagement in the community.

☑ CONCEPT CHECKS

1. What is social capital?
2. Describe the difference between bridging social capital and bonding social capital.

Conclusion

You now know better how the groups and organizations you belong to influence your life. They help determine whom you know and, in many ways, who you are. The primary groups of your earliest years were crucial in shaping your sense of self—a sense that changes very slowly thereafter. Throughout life, groups are a wellspring of norms and values.

Although groups remain central in our lives, group affiliation in the United States is changing. As you have seen, conventional groups appear to be losing ground. For example, today's college students are less likely to join civic groups and organizations—or even vote—than were their parents, a decline that may well signal a lower commitment to their communities. Some sociologists worry that this signals a weakening of society itself, which could bring about social instability.

As you have also seen, the global economy and information technology are redefining group life in many ways. For instance, your parents are likely to spend much of their careers in a few long lasting, bureaucratic organizations; you are more likely to be part of a larger number of networked, "flexible" ones. Many of your group affiliations will be created through the Internet or through other, even newer forms of communication. It will become increasingly easy to connect with like-minded people anywhere, creating geographically dispersed groups that span the planet—and whose members may never meet face to face.

How will these trends affect your social relationships? For nearly all of human history, most people interacted exclusively with those who were close at hand. The Industrial Revolution, which facilitated the rise of large, impersonal bureaucracies where people knew one another little if at all, changed social interaction. Today, the information revolution is once again changing human interaction. Tomorrow's groups and organizations could provide renewed communication and social intimacy—or they could spell further isolation and social distance.

Study Outline

www.wwnorton.com/studyspace

Social Groups

- *Social groups,* collections of people who share a sense of common identity and regularly interact with one another on the basis of shared expectations, shape nearly every experience in our lives. Among the types of social groups are *in-groups* and *out-groups, primary groups* and *secondary groups.*
- *Reference groups* provide standards by which we judge ourselves in terms of how we think we appear to others, what sociologist Charles Horton Cooley termed the "looking-glass self."
- Size is an important factor in group dynamics. Larger groups tend to be more stable than smaller groups of two (*dyads*) or three (*triads*). Groups of more than a dozen or so people usually develop a formal structure.
- *Leaders* influence the behavior of the other members of a group. The most common form of leadership is *transactional*—that is, routine leadership concerned with getting the job done. Less common is *transformational leadership,* which is concerned with changing the very nature of the group itself.
- Research indicates that people are highly susceptible to group pressure. Many will do what others tell them to do, even when the consequences could involve injury to others, as demonstrated by Stanley Milgram.

Networks

- *Networks* constitute a broad source of relationships, direct and indirect, including connections that may be important in business and politics. Women, people of color, and lower-income people typically have less access to the most influential economic and political networks than do white males in American society.

Organizations

- All modern organizations are to some degree bureaucratic. Bureaucracy is characterized by a clearly defined hierarchy of authority, written rules governing the conduct of officials (who work full-time for a salary), and a separation between tasks within the organization and life outside it. Members of the organization do not own the material resources with which they operate. Max Weber argued that modern bureaucracy is a highly effective means of organizing large numbers of people.
- Informal networks tend to develop at all levels within and between organizations. These informal ties are as important as the more formal characteristics on which Weber concentrated.
- The physical settings of organizations strongly influence their social features. The architecture of modern organizations is closely connected to surveillance as a means of securing obedience to those in authority. *Surveillance* refers to the supervision of people's activities as well as to the keeping of files and records about them.

Theories of Organizations

- The work of Weber and Michels identifies a tension between bureaucracy and democracy. On the one hand, the centralization of decision making is associated with the development of modern societies. On the other, one of the main features of the past two centuries has been expanding pressures toward democracy. The trends conflict, with neither one in a position of dominance.
- Modern organizations have evolved as gendered institutions. Women have traditionally been segregated into occupational categories that support the ability of men to advance their careers. In recent years, women have been entering professional and managerial positions in greater numbers, but some believe that women have to adopt a traditionally male management style to succeed at top levels.

Beyond Bureaucracy?

- Large organizations have started to become less bureaucratic and more flexible. Many Western firms have adopted aspects of Japanese management systems: more consultation of lower-level workers by managerial executives; pay and responsibility linked to seniority; and groups, rather than individuals, evaluated for their performance.
- New information technology is changing the way organizations work. Many tasks can now be completed electronically, a fact that allows organizations to transcend time and space. Many organizations now work as loose networks, rather than as self-contained independent units.

Organizations That Span the World

- Two important forms of global organization are *international governmental organizations (IGOs)* and *international nongovernmental organizations (INGOs).* Both play important roles in the world today, and IGOs—particularly the United Nations—may become key organizational actors as the pace of globalization increases.

How Do Groups and Organizations Affect Your Life?

- *Social capital* refers to the knowledge and connections that enable people to cooperate with one another for mutual benefit and extend their influence. Some social scientists have argued that social capital has declined in the United States during the last quarter century, a decline that may indicate a lessening of Americans' commitment to civic engagement.

Key Concepts

bureaucracy (p. 148)
corporate culture (p. 159)
dyad (p. 138)
formal organization (p. 147)
formal relations (p. 149)
groupthink (p. 142)
human resource management (p. 159)
ideal type (p. 148)
informal relations (p. 149)
information technology (p. 160)
in-groups (p. 137)
international governmental organization (IGO) (p. 164)
international nongovernmental organization (INGO) (p. 165)
iron law of oligarchy (p. 155)
leader (p. 140)
networks (p. 143)
oligarchy (p. 155)
organization (p. 147)
out-groups (p. 137)
primary groups (p. 137)
reference group (p. 138)
secondary groups (p. 137)
social aggregate (p. 136)
social capital (p. 166)
social category (p. 137)
social group (p. 136)
surveillance (p. 152)
surveillance society (p. 154)
timetables (p. 153)
transactional leaders (p. 140)
transformational leaders (p. 140)
triad (p. 139)

Review Questions

1. What is a social group? How is it different from a social aggregate or social category?
2. Discuss how membership in different types of groups contributes to feelings of belonging in a social group.
3. Briefly explain Stanley Milgram's experiment and the importance of his findings.
4. What are weak ties? What is the strength of weak ties according to Mark Granovetter?
5. How has the Internet changed social networks? What are some of the advantages and disadvantages of the Internet in facilitating access to social networks?
6. What is an organization? Why, according to Max Weber, are formal organizations so pervasive in modern society?
7. How does Weber define an ideal-type bureaucracy?
8. What can the physical characteristics of an organization tell us about its structure of authority?
9. What does Ritzer mean by the "McDonaldization of society"?
10. Why is organizational membership considered a form of social capital? What is the relationship between social capital and inequality?

Thinking Sociologically Exercises

1. According to George Simmel, what are the primary differences between dyads and triads? Explain, according to his theory, how the addition of a child would alter the relationship between a husband and wife. Does the theory fit this situation?
2. The advent of computers and the computerization of the workplace may change our organizations and relationships with co-workers. Explain how you see modern organizations changing with the adaptation of newer information technologies.

Learning Objectives

The Study of Deviant Behavior

Learn how we define deviance and how it is related to social power and social class. See the ways in which conformity is encouraged. Understand traditional explanations for deviance and their limitations as theories.

Society and Crime: Sociological Theories

Know the leading sociological theories of crime and how each is useful in understanding deviance.

Crime and Crime Statistics

Recognize the helpfulness and limitations of crime statistics. Learn important differences between men and women related to crime. Familiarize yourself with some of the varieties of crime. Think about the best solutions to reduce crime.

Victims and Perpetrators of Crime

Understand that some individuals or groups are more likely than others to commit or be the victims of crime.

Crime-Reduction Strategies

Consider the ways in which individuals and governments can address crime.

CHAPTER SEVEN

CONFORMITY, DEVIANCE, AND CRIME

Willie was a street vendor who lived and worked on a street in New York City during the early 1990s. He earned money by taking magazines out of recycled trash and reselling them to passersby. Willie lived on a corner for about six years after serving a prison sentence for robbery. Like Willie, approximately six hundred thousand people are released from prison every year—about sixteen hundred per day (Mauer 2004).

In 2006, the number of prisoners in federal, state, and county facilities exceeded 2.2 million. One and a half million Americans were detained for drug offenses, a threefold increase since 1980 (U.S. Bureau of Justice Statistics 2007a). The extreme focus on drug offenses has made the United States the world leader in incarceration rates, surpassing Russia. The U.S. rate of incarceration is five to eight times higher than that of Canada and the countries of western Europe (Garland 2002).

This dramatic increase in incarceration has significantly affected the African American and Latino populations in particular. According to Marc Mauer (2004), "In 1997, the state-wide population of Maryland, Illinois, North Carolina, South Carolina, and Louisiana was two thirds or more white, but prison growth since 1985 was 80% non-white. . . . In New York, where the state's adult minority population is less than 31.7%, nine out of ten new prisoners are from an ethnic or racial minority."

FIGURE 7.1

Incarceration Rates in Selected Industrialized Nations

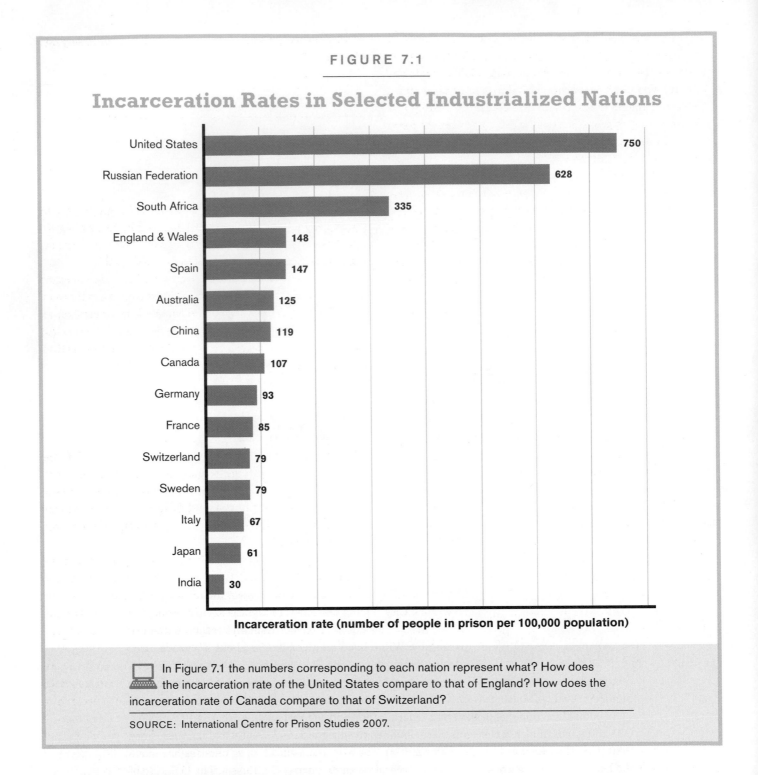

Incarceration rate (number of people in prison per 100,000 population)

In Figure 7.1 the numbers corresponding to each nation represent what? How does the incarceration rate of the United States compare to that of England? How does the incarceration rate of Canada compare to that of Switzerland?

SOURCE: International Centre for Prison Studies 2007.

The effect of the criminal justice system is clear in the lives of people like Willie. While in prison they are not part of the labor force, and thus significant joblessness is not reflected in the unemployment rates reported by the government. At the same time, incarceration increases the long-term likelihood of unemployment for men like Willie after their release (Western and Beckett 1999).

Although the United States has imprisoned over two million people over recent years, it has failed to make adequate preparations for their release (Gonnerman 2004). From prison, Willie went directly to the streets. He had nowhere to work and nowhere else to go. Former prisoners were already living on a particular corner, and he heard he could find them there.

Many people would define Willie as a deviant—someone who refuses to live by the rules that the majority of us follow. Sometimes they're violent criminals, drug addicts, or down-and-outs, who don't fit normal standards of acceptability. These are the cases that seem easy to identify. Yet things are not quite as they appear—a lesson sociology teaches us, for it encourages us to look beyond the obvious. The notion of the deviant is actually not easy to define.

We have learned in previous chapters that social life is governed by norms that define some kinds of behavior as appropriate in particular contexts and others as inappropriate. **Norms** are principles or rules people are expected to observe; they represent the dos and don'ts of society. Orderly behavior on the highway, for example, would be impossible if U.S. drivers didn't observe the rule of driving on the right. No deviants here, you might think, except for drunken or reckless drivers. If you did think this, you would be incorrect. When we drive, most of us are not merely deviants but criminals, for most of us regularly exceed the legal speed limits—assuming there isn't a police car in sight. In such cases, breaking the law is normal behavior!

We are all rule breakers as well as conformists. We are all also rule creators. Most American drivers may break the law on the freeways, but in fact they've evolved informal rules superimposed on the legal rules. When the legal speed limit is 65 mph, most drivers don't go above 75 mph or so, and they drive more slowly through urban areas.

When we study deviant behavior, we must consider which rules people are observing and which ones they are breaking. Nobody breaks *all* rules, just as no one conforms to all rules. Even someone who doesn't seem to be part of respectable society, such as Willie, is likely following many rules of the groups he belongs to.

For example, when Willie had enough money for a meal, he would go to a small Chinese restaurant and eat egg rolls, chow mein, and egg drop soup with the same manners as other diners. In this restaurant, he hardly appeared as a deviant. Out on the street, though, he followed the rules of the people who subsist on the street. In the world of street vendors, he was usually a conformist. Indeed, some "deviant" groups such as the homeless have informal but strict codes of social behavior. Those who deviate from these codes may be expelled from the group (Duneier 1999).

Willie's life illustrates what happens to many people with drug convictions who spend time in the American criminal justice system. Because prisons and jails make little accommodation for people after release, many former prisoners cannot find homes or jobs. Working on the street is hardly a long-term solution for men like Willie, and after six years of "staying clean" on Sixth Avenue he was rearrested for another drug offense. This is very common: Almost two thirds of all released prisoners are rearrested within three years (Mauer 2004).

The Study of Deviant Behavior

The study of deviant behavior reveals that none of us is as normal as we think. It also shows that people whose behavior appears incomprehensible or alien can be seen as rational beings when we understand why they act as they do.

The study of deviance directs our attention to social *power* as well as the influence of social class—the divisions between rich and poor. When we look at deviance from or conformity to social rules or norms, we always have to ask, Whose rules? As we shall see, social norms are strongly influenced by divisions of power and class.

What Is Deviance?

Deviance may be defined as nonconformity to a set of norms that are accepted by a significant number of people in a community or society. No society can be simply divided between those who deviate from norms and those who conform to them, because most people sometimes transgress generally accepted rules of behavior.

The scope of the concept of deviance is very broad, as some examples will illustrate. Consider Kevin Mitnick, described as the "world's most celebrated computer hacker." In fact, the thirty-six-year-old Californian is probably revered and despised in equal measure. To the world's estimated hundred thousand computer hackers, Mitnick is a pioneering genius whose five-year imprisonment in a U.S. penitentiary was unjust and unwarranted—proof of how misunderstood computer hacking has become. To U.S. authorities and high-tech corporations, Mitnick is one of the world's most dangerous men. A survey by the U.S. Secret Service and Carnegie-Mellon University found that hackers are responsible for 26 percent of computer crime (E-Crime Watch 2007). Mitnick was captured by the FBI in 1995 and convicted of downloading source codes and stealing software allegedly worth millions of dollars. As a condition of his release from prison in January 2000, Mitnick was forbidden to use computers or to speak publicly about technology issues.

Over the past decade or so, hackers have gone from being a little-noticed population of computer enthusiasts to a much-maligned group of deviants who allegedly threaten the stability

"Self-Mutilation Rampant"

The life of college students today isn't easy. The pressures of earning good grades, paying for school, and preparing for an uncertain future can be overwhelming. A large and growing number of college students reportedly are engaging in a drastic and deviant behavior when they're under pressure—they're purposely injuring themselves. That's the finding of a study that captured national headlines in the summer of 2006. The media reported ominous messages, like "Self-Injury Epidemic" (Capriccioso 2006), "Self-Mutilation Rampant at 2 Ivy League Schools" (MSNBC 2006), and "Dangerous Relief: Teens Increasingly Turn to Self-Abuse to Cope with Stress" (Leonard 2006).

The media reported that "self-abuse is on the rise," citing results from a recently published study in the journal *Pediatrics* (Whitlock, Eckenrode, and Silverman 2006). The study, conducted by a team of researchers at Cornell and Princeton universities, investigated the self-injuring behaviors (SIB) of college students. The

researchers found that 17 percent of the students in their sample reported that they had ever had an SIB incident. Women were more likely than men to report such behaviors (20 percent versus

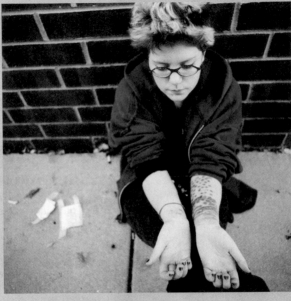

A woman shows the scars on her arms from burning herself with cigarette butts.

14 percent). Three quarters of those who had ever self-injured also said that they had done so more than once. One third said that no one knew that they had been hurting themselves. The study also found

that self-abusers were far more likely than noninjurers to have thought about or attempted suicide, to have a history of emotional abuse, to have high levels of psychological distress, and to have an eating disorder.

It's not surprising that these statistics captured the media's attention and raised serious worries among parents and college administrators. But do these data suggest that an "epidemic of self-injury" is occurring (Brumberg 2006)? Is this evidence that rates of self-injury are "increasing" (Leonard 2006)? To really understand how widespread SIBs are requires an in-depth look at the study details. The researchers drew a random sample of 8,300 undergraduate and graduate students at Cornell and Princeton. This random sample included one third of all students enrolled at the two universities. They sent an invitation to the randomly selected students to participate in their study and provided a link to the Web-based survey. Just 35 percent (or 2,875) of those students contacted went on to complete the survey.

of the information age. The distributed denial of service (DDoS) attacks on prominent e-commerce Web sites in February 2000 provoked "hacker hysteria" in the media, in the corporate world, and among international law-enforcement bodies. Some of the Internet's most heavily trafficked sites—such as Yahoo!, eBay, and Amazon.com—came to a standstill as their servers received millions of phony requests for information from computers around the world. Before anyone was apprehended, fingers were pointed at computer hackers—portrayed

as socially maladjusted young people (mostly male) who avoid contact with others by creating alternative lives behind anonymous online user names.

Yet, according to Mitnick and other hackers, such pathological depictions could not be further from the truth. "*Hacker* is a term of honor and respect," claimed Mitnick (2000) in an article written after his release from prison. "It is a term that describes a skill, not an activity, in the same way that *doctor* describes a skill. It was used for decades to describe talented

Study participants were asked to check off any of the sixteen different SIBs they had engaged in. The most commonly reported behaviors were the more mild forms of SIB. Of the 17 percent who engaged in any SIBs, half had "severely scratched or pinched" themselves, and nearly 40 percent had "banged or punched objects to the point of bruising or bleeding." Serious forms of self-mutilation such as "carving words or symbols into skin" and "burning" were reported far less frequently (15 and 13 percent, respectively).

These statistics are cause for concern, because any form of SIB is a sign of trouble and distress. However, the study did not show that rates were "increasing." Rather, the researchers obtained data from students at just one point in time and thus have no data on change over time. Further, the *sampling frame*—or universe of all persons eligible for the study—was students at two prestigious Ivy League universities and thus not "representative" of all young Americans. Most important, the study had a very low *response rate*—just one in three contacted for the study ultimately completed the online survey. Most social scientists believe that it is important to question why a study had a low response rate before taking the findings as valid. Perhaps those students who completed the study are more likely than nonrespondents to have engaged in SIBs or to have thought about such issues. As a result, the sample may be *nonrepresentative,* meaning it would be overrepresentative of self-harmers and underrepresentative of young people who avoid such behaviors. Finally, the proportion of students who reported engaging in extreme behaviors, like carving or burning, was relatively low—although the news headlines touted that "self-mutilation" was rampant.

Skeptics also have raised questions about the use of an Internet survey. Young people fill out these questionnaires in private, without the presence of a live interviewer. As a result, they may underreport behaviors that others would deem "deviant." However, defenders of such methods counter that Web-based surveys may be a particularly good way to explore "hidden" or "deviant" behaviors, in that young people will feel less embarrassed than they would have been sitting face-to-face with an interviewer.

Although self-abuse probably does not constitute an "epidemic," the *Pediatrics* study casts light on a serious problem afflicting a minority of young people. As study coauthor Daniel Silverman cautioned, "unless we start talking about [self-abuse] and making it more acceptable for people to come forward, it will remain hidden" (MSNBC 2006).

Questions

- What proportion of students in the study reported that they had engaged in self-injurious behaviors?
- What was the sampling frame? What was the study response rate?
- Which behaviors were the most commonly mentioned self-injurious behaviors?
- Do you believe that Whitlock and colleagues found evidence of an "epidemic of self-injury"? Why or why not?

FOR FURTHER EXPLORATION

Brumberg, Joan. 2006. "Are We Facing an Epidemic of Self-Injury." *Chronicle of Higher Education* (December 6, 2006).

Capriccioso, Rob. 2006. "Self-Injury Epidemic." *Inside Higher Education* (June 5, 2006). www.insidehighered.com/news/2006/06/05/injury (accessed January 12, 2008).

Leonard, Shana. 2006. "Dangerous Relief: Teens Increasingly Turning to Self-Abuse to Cope with Stress." *MTV News* (June 13, 2006). www.mtv.com/news/articles/1534223/20060613/index.jhtml?headlines=true# (accessed January 12, 2008).

Science Daily. 2006. "Self-Injury Is Prevalent among College Students, Survey Shows." *Science Daily* (June 5, 2006). www.sciencedaily.com/releases/2006/06/060605155351.htm (accessed January 12, 2008).

MSNBC. 2006. "Self-Mutilation Rampant at 2 Ivy League Schools." MSNBC.com (June 5, 2006). www.msnbc.msn.com/id/13141254/ (accessed January 12, 2008).

Whitlock, Janis, John Eckenrode, and Daniel Silverman. 2006. "Self-Injurious Behaviors in a College Population." *Pediatrics* 117: 1939–1948.

computer enthusiasts, people whose skill at using computers to solve technical problems and puzzles was—and is—respected and admired by others possessing similar technical skills." Hackers are quick to point out that most of their activities are not criminal. Rather, they are primarily interested in exploring the edges of computer technology, trying to uncover loopholes and to discover how far they can penetrate into other computer systems. Once flaws have been discovered, the "hacker ethic" demands sharing the information publicly. Many hackers have even served as consultants for large corporations and government agencies, helping defend their systems against outside intrusion.

As another example, consider the career of Ted Bundy. His way of life seemed to conform to the norms of behavior of a good citizen. In the 1970s he led what seemed not only a normal life but a most worthy one. For example, he played an active role in The Samaritans, an association that organizes a twenty-four-hour phone-in service for people who are

Defining Deviance: The Sociological Debate

Many people assume that a well-structured society is designed to prevent deviant behavior. But Émile Durkheim argued otherwise. He believed that deviance is important in a well-ordered society, because by defining what is deviant we become aware of the standards we share as members of a society. Thus we should aim not to completely eliminate deviance but to keep it within acceptable limits.

Seventy years after Durkheim's work appeared, the sociologist Kai Erikson published *Wayward Puritans,* a study of deviance in seventeenth-century New England. Erikson (1966) sought "to test [Durkheim's] notion that the number of deviant offenders a community can afford to recognize is likely to remain stable over time." His research led him to conclude that a community's capacity for handling deviance, let us say, can be roughly estimated by counting its prison cells and hospital beds, its policemen and psychiatrists, its courts and clinics.... The agencies of control often seem to define their job as that of keeping deviance within bounds rather than obliterating it altogether."

Erikson hypothesized that societies need their quotas of deviance and that they function in such a way as to keep them intact.

What does a society do when the amount of deviant behavior gets out of hand? In a controversial 1993 article, "Defining Deviance Down," the former New York senator Daniel Patrick Moynihan argued that the levels of deviance in American society have increased so much that we have been "redefining deviance so as to exempt much conduct previously stigmatized" and raising the "normal" level to include some behavior considered abnormal by an earlier standard. Moynihan cites

Computer hacker Kevin Mitnick was arrested in 1995 and later convicted of stealing millions of dollars worth of software from a number of technology companies. His release in 2000 was conditioned on the understanding that he would refrain from using computers or speaking publicly about technology issues.

distressed or suicidal. Yet Bundy also carried out a series of horrific murders. Before sentencing him to death, the judge at his trial praised Bundy for his abilities (he had prepared his own defense) but noted what a waste he had made of his life. Bundy's career shows that a person can seem entirely normal while secretly engaging in acts of extreme deviance.

Deviance can also apply to the activities of groups. Consider the religious Heaven's Gate cult, which was established in the early 1970s when Marshall Herff Applewhite preached his beliefs throughout the U.S. West and Midwest, ultimately advertising on the Internet his belief that civilization was doomed and that the only way people could be saved was to kill themselves so their souls could be rescued by a UFO. In 1997, thirty-nine members of the cult followed his advice in a mass suicide at a wealthy estate in Rancho Santa Fe, California.

The Heaven's Gate cult was a **deviant subculture** whose members functioned easily within the wider society, supporting themselves by running a Web site business and recruiting new members via e-mail. They had plenty of money and lived together in an expensive home in a wealthy California suburb. Their position clearly diverges from the deviant subculture of the homeless, discussed earlier.

Homeless people sleep in the parking lot of the Day Resource Center in Dallas, Texas. Most of the center's clients are mentally ill and rely on the center for basic social services.

the deinstitutionalization movement within the mental health profession that began in the 1950s. Instead of being forced into institutions, the mentally ill were treated with tranquilizers and released. As a result, the number of psychiatric patients in New York dropped from ninety-three thousand in 1955 to eleven thousand by 1992.

What happened to all those psychiatric patients? Many of them are the homeless who today are sleeping in doorways. In "defining deviance down," people sleeping on the street are defined not as insane but as lacking affordable housing. At the same time, the normal acceptable level of crime has risen. Moynihan points out that whereas in 1929 the nation was outraged at the murder of seven gangsters in one day, today violent gang murders are so common that there is hardly any public reaction. Moynihan also sees the underreporting of crime as another form of normalizing it. He concludes, "We are getting used to a lot of behavior that is not good for us."

Norms and Sanctions

We follow social norms because, as a result of socialization, we are used to doing so. Individuals become committed to social norms through interactions with people who obey the law. Through these interactions, we learn self-control. The more numerous these interactions, the fewer opportunities there are to deviate from conventional norms. Over time, the longer that we interact in conventional ways, the more we have at stake in continuing to act in that way (Gottfredson and Hirschi 1990).

All social norms carry sanctions that promote conformity and protect against nonconformity. A **sanction** is any reaction from others that is meant to ensure that a person or group complies with a given norm. Sanctions may be positive (the offering of rewards for conformity) or negative (punishment for behavior that does not conform). They can also be formal or informal. Formal sanctions are applied by a specific group or agency to ensure that a particular set of norms is followed. Informal sanctions are less organized and more spontaneous reactions to nonconformity, such as when a student's friends teasingly accuse him of working too hard or being a "nerd" if he spends an evening studying rather than going to a party.

Courts and prisons represent the main types of formal sanctions in modern societies. The police are charged with bringing offenders to trial and possibly to imprisonment. **Laws** are norms defined by governments as principles that their citizens must follow; sanctions are used against people who do not conform to them. Where there are laws, there are also **crimes**, because crime constitutes any type of behavior that breaks a law.

It is important to recognize, however, that the law is only a guide to a society's norms. Often, subcultures invent their own dos and don'ts. For example, the street people that Willie lived among had their own norms for determining where each of them could set up their magazines to sell on the sidewalk. Other homeless vendors didn't set up in Willie's spot because that would have shown "disrespect." This example further illustrates that even members of so-called deviant groups usually follow some norms. They are deviant because some of their norms are at odds with those of mainstream society.

We now turn to the main sociological theories that interpret and analyze deviance. After looking at biological and psychological explanations, we discuss the four approaches that have been influential within the sociology of deviance: *functionalist theories, interactionist theories, conflict theories,* and *control theories.*

The Biological View of Deviance

Some of the first attempts to explain crime were biological. The Italian criminologist Cesare Lombroso, working in the 1870s, believed that criminal types could be identified by the shape of the skull. He accepted that social learning could influence the development of criminal behavior, but he regarded most criminals as biologically degenerate or defective. Lombroso's ideas became thoroughly discredited, but similar views have repeatedly been suggested. Another popular method of

Picture of criminals, according to Cesar Lombroso.

relating heredity to criminal tendencies involved the study of family trees. But this demonstrates virtually nothing about the influence of heredity, because it is impossible to disentangle inherited and environmental influences.

A later theory distinguished three types of human physique and associated one type directly with delinquency. Muscular, active types (mesomorphs), the theory went, are more likely to become delinquent than those of thin physique (ectomorphs) or more fleshy people (endomorphs) (Glueck and Glueck 1956; Sheldon et al. 1949). This research has also been widely criticized. Even if there were a relationship between body type and delinquency, this would show nothing about the influence of heredity. Muscular people may be drawn toward criminal activities because they offer opportunities to display athleticism. Moreover, nearly all studies in this field have treated delinquents in reform schools, and it may be that the athletic-looking delinquents are sent to such schools more often than fragile-looking ones. Although older studies on the biological explanations of crime have been dismissed, recent research has sought to rekindle the argument. In a study of New Zealand children, researchers tried to link children's propensity to aggression with biological factors present at birth (Moffitt 1996).

However, such studies only show that some individuals might be inclined toward irritability and aggressiveness, which could be reflected in crimes of physical assault. There is no decisive evidence that any personality traits are inherited in this way; even if they were, their connection to criminality would be distant. In fact, the New Zealand study did not propose a biological cause to crime. Rather, it claimed that biological factors, when combined with certain social factors such as the home environment, could lead to social situations involving crime.

The Psychological View of Deviance

Like biological interpretations, psychological theories of crime associate criminality with particular types of personality. Some have suggested that in a minority of individuals, an amoral, or psychopathic, personality develops. **Psychopaths** are withdrawn, emotionless characters who delight in violence for its own sake.

Individuals with psychopathic traits do sometimes commit violent crimes, but there are major problems with the concept of the psychopath. It isn't at all clear that psychopathic traits are inevitably criminal. Nearly all studies of people said to possess these characteristics have been of convicted prisoners, and their personalities tend to be presented negatively. If we describe the same traits positively, the personality type sounds quite different, and there seems no reason why such people should be inherently criminal. If we were looking for psychopathic individuals for a research study, we might place the following ad:

ARE YOU ADVENTUROUS?

Researcher wishes to contact adventurous, carefree people who've led exciting, impulsive lives. If you're the kind of person who'd do almost anything for a dare, call 337-XXXX anytime. (Widom and Newman 1985)

Such people might be explorers, spies, gamblers, or just college students bored with the routines of daily life. They *might* be prepared to contemplate criminal adventures but might just as likely seek challenges in socially respectable ways.

Psychological theories of criminality can explain only some aspects of crime. Although certain criminals may possess distinctly abnormal personality characteristics, it is highly improbable that the majority of criminals do. There are all kinds of crimes, and it is implausible to suppose that the perpetrators share specific psychological characteristics. Even if we consider just one category, such as crimes of violence, different circumstances are involved. Some violent crimes are carried out by lone individuals, others by organized groups. It is unlikely that the psychological makeup of loners has much in common with gang members. Even if we could link consistent differences to forms of criminality, we still couldn't be sure which way the line of causality would run. Perhaps becoming involved with criminal groups influences people's outlooks, rather than the outlooks actually producing criminal behavior.

Both biological and psychological approaches to criminality presume that deviance is a sign of something "wrong" with the individual and that factors outside an individual's control, embedded in either the body or the mind, cause the crime. Therefore, if scientific criminology could identify the causes of crime, it would be possible to treat those causes. In this respect, both biological and psychological theories of crime are *positivist*. As we learned in Chapter 1, positivism is the belief that applying scientific methods to the study of the social world can reveal its basic truths. In the case of positivist criminology, this led to the belief that empirical research could pinpoint the causes of crime and make recommendations for eradicating it.

☑ CONCEPT CHECKS

1. How do sociologists define deviance?
2. What are the main similarities and differences between biological and psychological views of deviance?

Society and Crime: Sociological Theories

Later generations of scholars argued that any satisfactory account of the nature of crime must be sociological, for what crime is depends on the social institutions of a society. Sociological thinking about crime especially emphasizes the interconnections between conformity and deviance in different social contexts. Modern societies contain many subcultures, and behavior that conforms to the norms of one subculture may be regarded as deviant outside it; for instance, there may be strong pressure on a member of a boys' gang to prove himself by stealing a car. Moreover, wide divergences of wealth and power in society greatly influence criminal opportunities for different groups. Theft and burglary are carried out mainly by people from the poorer segments of the population; embezzling and tax evasion are limited to persons in positions of affluence.

Functionalist Theories

Functionalist theories see crime and deviance resulting from structural tensions and a lack of moral regulation within society. If the aspirations held by individuals and groups do not coincide with available rewards, the disparity between desires and fulfillment will be felt in the deviant motivations of some of the society's members.

CRIME AND ANOMIE: DURKHEIM AND MERTON

The notion of **anomie** was introduced by Émile Durkheim, who suggested that in modern societies traditional norms and standards become undermined without being replaced by new ones. Anomie exists when there are no clear standards to guide behavior in a given area of social life. Under such circumstances, Durkheim believed, people feel disoriented and anxious; anomie therefore influences dispositions to suicide.

Durkheim saw crime and deviance as inevitable and necessary elements in modern societies. According to Durkheim, people in the modern age are less constrained than they were in traditional societies. Because there is more room for individual choice in the modern world, inevitably there will be some nonconformity. Durkheim recognized that no society would ever be in complete consensus about the norms and values that govern it.

Deviance is also necessary for society, according to Durkheim. First, deviance has an *adaptive* function: By introducing new ideas and social challenges, deviance brings about change. Second, deviance promotes *boundary maintenance* between "good" and "bad" behaviors. A criminal event can provoke a collective response that heightens group solidarity and clarifies social norms. For example, residents of a neighborhood facing a problem with drug dealers might join together in the aftermath of a drug-related shooting and commit themselves to maintaining the area as a drug-free zone.

Durkheim's ideas on crime and deviance helped shift attention from individual explanations to social forces. His notion of anomie was applied by the American sociologist Robert K. Merton (1957), who located the source of crime within the very structure of American society.

Merton modified the concept of anomie to refer to the strain put on individuals' behavior when accepted norms conflict with social reality. In American society—and to some degree in other industrial societies—values emphasize material success through self-discipline and hard work. Accordingly, it is believed that people who work hard can succeed no matter what their starting point in life. This idea is not in fact valid, because most disadvantaged people have limited conventional opportunities for advancement or none at all. Yet those who do not "succeed" are condemned for their apparent inability to make material progress. Thus there is pressure to get ahead by any means, legitimate or illegitimate. According to Merton, then, deviance is a by-product of economic inequalities.

Merton identifies five possible reactions to the tensions between socially endorsed values and the limited means of achieving them. *Conformists* accept generally held values and

According to Durkheim, deviance has two important functions—it brings about change and it provokes a collective response that solidifies norms. For instance, these Pittsburgh neighbors joined together to form a neigborhood watch group to patrol the streets after an escalation in drug-related violence.

the conventional means of realizing them, whether or not they meet with success. Most of the population falls into this category. *Innovators* accept socially approved values but use illegitimate or illegal means to follow them. Criminals who acquire wealth through illegal activities exemplify this type.

Ritualists conform to socially accepted standards although they have lost sight of the underlying values. They compulsively follow rules for their own sake. A ritualist might dedicate herself to a boring job, even though it has no career prospects and provides few rewards. *Retreatists* have abandoned the competitive outlook, rejecting both the dominant values and the approved means of achieving them. An example would be the members of a self-supporting commune. Finally, *rebels* reject both the existing values and the means but work to substitute new ones and reconstruct the social system. The members of radical political groups fall into this category.

Merton's writings addressed one of the main puzzles in the study of criminology: At a time when society is becoming more affluent, why do crime rates continue to rise? By emphasizing the contrast between rising aspirations and persistent inequalities, Merton identifies a sense of relative deprivation as an important element in deviant behavior.

SUBCULTURAL EXPLANATIONS

Later researchers examined subcultural groups who adopt norms that encourage or reward criminal behavior. Like Merton, Albert Cohen saw the contradictions within American society as the main cause of crime. But while Merton emphasized individual deviant responses, Cohen saw the responses occurring collectively through subcultures. In *Delinquent Boys* (1955), Cohen argued that frustrated boys in the lower working class often join delinquent *subcultures,* such as gangs. These subcultures replace middle-class values with norms that celebrate nonconformity and defiance, such as delinquency.

Richard A. Cloward and Lloyd E. Ohlin (1960) agree with Cohen that most delinquent youths emerge from the lower working class. But they argued that such gangs arise in subcultural communities where the chances of achieving success legitimately are slim, such as among deprived ethnic minorities. Cloward and Ohlin's work emphasized connections between conformity and deviance: Lack of opportunity for success in the terms of the wider society is the differentiating factor between those who engage in criminal behavior and those who do not.

Research by sociologists has examined the validity of claims that immediate material deprivation can lead people to commit crimes. A survey of homeless youth in Canada, for instance, shows a strong correlation between hunger, lack of shelter, and unemployment on the one hand, and theft, prostitution, and violent crime on the other (Hagan and McCarthy 1992).

Functionalist theories rightly emphasize connections between conformity and deviance in different social contexts. We should be cautious, however, about the idea that people in poorer communities, like Willie, aspire to the same level of success as more affluent people. Most adjust their aspirations to the reality of their situation. Merton, Cohen, and Cloward and Ohlin can all be criticized for presuming that middle-class values are accepted throughout society. It would also be wrong to suppose that only the less privileged experience a mismatch of aspirations and opportunities. There are pressures toward criminal activity among other groups too, as indicated by the white-collar crimes of embezzlement, fraud, and tax evasion, which we will study later.

Members of a Los Angeles gang show off scars and tattoos. Are these men, like those in Cohen's *Delinquent Boys* (1955), replacing the values of the middle class with norms that express pride in defiance and nonconformity—in this case bullet and knife wounds?

Interactionist Theories

Sociologists studying crime and deviance in the interactionist tradition focus on deviance as a socially constructed phenomenon. Rejecting the idea that some types of conduct are inherently "deviant," they ask how behaviors get defined as deviant and why only certain groups get labeled as deviant.

LEARNED DEVIANCE: DIFFERENTIAL ASSOCIATION

In 1949, Edwin H. Sutherland advanced a notion that influenced much interactionist work: He linked crime to what he called **differential association**. In a society with a variety of subcultures, some social environments encourage illegal activities, whereas others do not. Individuals become delinquent through associating with people who follow criminal norms. According to Sutherland, criminal behavior is learned within primary groups, particularly peer groups. This theory contrasts with the view that psychological differences separate criminals from other people; it sees criminal activities as learned in the same way as law-abiding ones and as serving the same needs and values. Thieves try to make money just like other people; they just do so illegally.

Differential association applies to Willie's life. Before going to prison, he lived with a group of homeless men from whom he learned how to target and rob restaurant delivery boys, who were unlikely to report the crime because many of them were illegal immigrants from Mexico and China. Willie would not have known these facts unless he had learned them from associating with others who were already the carriers of criminal norms.

LABELING THEORY

One of the most important interactionist approaches to understanding criminality is **labeling theory**. It was originally associated with Howard S. Becker's (1963) studies of marijuana smokers. In the early 1960s, marijuana use was a marginal activity of subcultures rather than the mainstream lifestyle choice that it is today (Hathaway 1997). Becker found that becoming a marijuana smoker depended on one's acceptance by and close association with experienced users and on one's attitudes toward nonusers. Because labeling theorists like Becker interpret deviance as a *process* of interaction between deviants and nondeviants, it is not the act of marijuana smoking that makes one a deviant but the way others react to it. Thus labeling theorists seek to discover why some people become labeled "deviant" in order to understand the nature of deviance itself.

People who represent law and order or who impose definitions of morality on others do most of the labeling. Thus the

How is Howard Becker's research on marijuana smokers an example of labeling theory?

rules in terms of which deviance is defined express the power structure of society; such rules are framed by the wealthy for the poor, by men for women, by older people for younger people, and by ethnic majorities for minority groups. For example, many children wander into other people's gardens, steal fruit, or play truant. In an affluent neighborhood, parents, teachers, and police might regard such activities as relatively innocent. In poor areas, they might consider them acts of juvenile delinquency.

Once a child is labeled a delinquent, teachers and prospective employers may consider him to be untrustworthy. The child then relapses into further criminal behavior, widening the gulf with orthodox social conventions. Edwin Lemert (1972) called the initial act of transgression **primary deviation**. **Secondary deviation** occurs when the individual accepts the label and sees himself as deviant. One study examining self-appraisals of a random national sample of young men showed that such appraisals are strongly tied to levels of criminality (Matsueda 1992).

Consider Luke, who smashes a shop window while out on the town with friends. The act may be called the accidental result of overboisterous behavior, an excusable characteristic of young men. Luke might escape with a reprimand and a small fine—a likely result if he is from a respectable background and is seen as being of good character. The window smashing stays at the level of primary deviance. If, however, the police and courts hand out a suspended sentence and make Luke report to a social worker, the incident could become the first step on the road to secondary deviance. The process of "learning to be deviant" tends to be reinforced by the very organizations set up to correct deviant behavior—prisons and social agencies.

Labeling theory assumes that no act is intrinsically criminal but may become so through the formulation of laws and their interpretation by police, courts, and correctional institutions. Although some critics of labeling theory argue that certain acts—such as murder, rape, and robbery—are prohibited across all cultures, this view is surely incorrect; even within our own culture, killing is not always regarded as murder. In times of war, killing the enemy is approved, and until recently, the laws in most U.S. states did not recognize sexual intercourse forced on a woman by her husband as rape.

We can criticize labeling theory on more convincing grounds, though. First, labeling theorists neglect the processes that lead to acts being defined as deviant. Indeed, labeling certain activities as deviant is not arbitrary; differences in socialization, attitudes, and opportunities influence how far people engage in behavior likely to be labeled deviant. For instance, many children from deprived backgrounds are more likely to steal from shops than are richer children. It is not the labeling that leads them to steal so much as their background.

Second, it is not clear whether labeling actually has the effect of increasing deviant conduct. Delinquent behavior tends to increase after a conviction, but is this the result of the labeling itself? Other factors, such as increased interaction with other delinquents or learning about new criminal opportunities, may be involved.

Conflict Theory

Conflict theory draws on elements of Marxist thought to argue that deviance is deliberate and often political. Conflict theorists deny that deviance is "determined" by factors such as biology, personality, anomie, social disorganization, and labels. Rather, they argue, individuals choose to engage in deviant behavior in response to the inequalities of the capitalist system. Thus members of countercultural groups regarded as deviant—such as supporters of the black power movement or gay liberation movement—are engaging in political acts that challenge the social order. Theorists of the **new criminology** analyze crime and deviance in terms of the social structure and the preservation of power among the ruling class.

For example, they argue that laws serve the powerful to maintain their privileged positions. These theorists reject the idea that laws are applied evenly across the population. Instead, as inequalities increase between the ruling class and the working class, law becomes the key instrument for the powerful to maintain order. This dynamic is evident in the criminal justice system, which has become increasingly oppressive toward working-class offenders, or in tax legislation that disproportionately favors the wealthy. This power imbalance is not restricted to the creation of laws, however. The powerful also break laws, scholars argue, but are rarely caught. These crimes are much more significant than the everyday crime and delinquency that attract the most attention. But fearful of the implications of pursuing white-collar criminals, law enforcement instead targets less powerful members of society, such as prostitutes, drug users, and petty thieves (Chambliss 1988; Pearce 1976).

These studies and others widened the debate about crime and deviance to include questions of social justice, power, and politics. They emphasized that crime occurs in the context of inequalities and competing interests among social groups.

Control Theory

Control theory posits that crime results from an imbalance between impulses toward criminal activity and the social or physical controls that deter it. Control theory assumes that people act rationally and that, given the opportunity, everyone would engage in deviant acts. One of the best-known control theorists, Travis Hirschi, argues that humans are fundamentally selfish beings who make calculated decisions about whether to engage in criminal activity by weighing the benefits and risks. In *Causes of Delinquency* (1969), Hirschi identifies four types of bonds that link people to society and law-abiding behavior, thus maintaining social control and conformity: attachment, commitment, involvement, and belief. If these bonds are weak, delinquency and deviance may result. Hirschi's approach suggests that delinquents have low levels of self-control that result from inadequate socialization at home or at school (Gottfredson and Hirschi 1990).

Some control theorists see the growth of crime as an outcome of the increasing opportunities and targets for crime in modern society. As the population grows more affluent and

How are gated communities an example of target hardening? What are the social consequences of sequestering certain communities behind guards and gates?

consumerism becomes more central, more people own goods such as televisions, video equipment, computers, cars, and designer clothing—favorite targets for thieves. Residential homes are increasingly empty during the daytime as more women work outside the home. Motivated offenders can select from a broad range of suitable targets.

Many official approaches to crime prevention in recent years have focused on limiting the opportunities for crime via *target hardening*—making it more difficult for crimes to occur by intervening in potential crime situations. Control theorists argue that rather than changing the criminal, the best policy is to take practical measures to control the criminal's ability to commit crime.

Target-hardening techniques and zero-tolerance policing have been successful in some contexts in curtailing crime, but these measures do not address the underlying causes of crime. The growing popularity of private security services, car alarms, house alarms, guard dogs, and gated communities suggests that segments of the population feel compelled to defend themselves against others. This tendency is occurring not only in the United States but also in countries such as South Africa, Brazil, and those of the former Soviet Union, where a fortress mentality has emerged among the privileged.

There is another unintended consequence of such policies: As popular crime targets are hardened, patterns of crime may simply shift from one domain to another. Target-hardening and zero-tolerance approaches may simply displace criminal offenses from better-protected areas into more vulnerable ones.

THE THEORY OF BROKEN WINDOWS

Target hardening and zero-tolerance policing are based on a theory known as *broken windows* (Wilson and Kelling 1982), which arose from a study by the social psychologist Philip Zimbardo (1969). Zimbardo abandoned cars without license plates and with their hoods up in two social settings: the wealthy community of Palo Alto, California, and a poor neighborhood in the Bronx, New York. In both places, both cars were vandalized once passersby, regardless of class or race, sensed that the cars were abandoned. Extrapolating from this study, Wilson and Kelling argued that any sign of social disorder in a community, even the appearance of a broken window, encourages more serious crime. One unrepaired broken window is a sign that no one cares, so breaking more windows—that is, committing more serious crimes—is a rational response by criminals to this situation of social disorder. Thus minor acts of deviance lead to a spiral of crime and social decay.

In the late 1980s and 1990s, the broken windows theory underpinned policing strategies that aggressively focused on

In the early 1990s, New York City mayor Rudy Giuliani and police commissioner William Bratton applied the broken windows theory to New York's petty crime problem. They started producing "graffiti-proof" subway cars and the city's police force cracked down on vandals, public drinking, and jumping subway turnstiles. During the 1990s the crime rate in the city dropped to pre-1970s levels.

minor crimes such as traffic violations and drinking or using drugs in public. Studies have shown that proactive policing directed at maintaining public order can reduce more serious crimes such as robbery (Sampson and Cohen 1988). However, one flaw of the broken windows theory is that it lacks a systematic definition of disorder and thus the police can see almost anything as a sign of disorder and anyone as a threat. In fact, as crime rates fell throughout the 1990s, the number of complaints of police abuse and harassment went up, particularly by young, urban, black men who fit the "profile" of a potential criminal.

Linking Microsociology and Macrosociology: Saints and Roughnecks

The connections between deviant behavior and the larger class structure were noted by William Chambliss in a famous study, "The Saints and the Roughnecks" (1973). Chambliss studied two groups of delinquents in an American high school, one from upper-middle-class families ("the Saints") and the other from poor families ("the Roughnecks"). Although the Saints were constantly involved in petty crimes, none of their members was ever arrested. The Roughnecks were involved in similar criminal activities, yet they were constantly in trouble with the police. After Chambliss concluded that neither group was more delinquent than the other, he sought other factors to explain the different reaction of the police and the broader community to these two groups.

Chambliss found, for example, that the upper-class gang members had cars and thus could remove themselves from the eyes of the community, but the lower-class boys had to congregate in a public area. Chambliss concluded that differences like this reflected the class structure of American society, which gave wealthier groups advantages in terms of deviant labeling. For instance, the Saints' parents saw their sons' crimes as harmless pranks, whereas the Roughnecks' parents acquiesced to the police labeling of their sons' behavior as criminal. The community also seemed to agree with these labels.

These boys went on to have lives consistent with the labeling; the Saints lived conventional middle-class lives and the Roughnecks had continual problems with the law. As we saw earlier in the chapter, this outcome is linked to what Lemert called secondary deviance, resulting from a person's inability to carry on as "normal" once that person has been labeled as a deviant.

Chambliss's study is widely cited by sociologists for showing the connection between macrosociological factors such as social class and microsociological phenomena such as how people become labeled as deviant. The study illustrates how difficult it is to isolate micro- and macro-level factors in the social construction of deviance.

Theoretical Conclusions

The contributions of the sociological theories of crime are two-fold. First, these theories emphasize the continuities between criminal and respectable behavior. The contexts in which particular activities are seen as criminal and punishable by law vary widely. Second, all agree that context is important. Whether someone engages in a criminal act or comes to be regarded as a criminal is influenced by social learning and social surroundings.

In spite of its deficiencies, labeling theory is perhaps the most widely used approach to understanding crime and deviant behavior. It explains how some activities become defined as punishable in law and the power relations that form such definitions, as well as the circumstances in which particular individuals fall afoul of the law.

The way in which crime is understood affects the policies developed to combat it. For example, if crime is seen as the product of deprivation or social disorganization, policies might be aimed at reducing poverty and strengthening social services. If criminality is seen as freely chosen, attempts to counter it will take a different form.

☑ CONCEPT CHECKS

1. How do Merton's and Durkheim's definitions of anomie differ?
2. According to subcultural explanations, how does criminal behavior get transmitted from one group to another?
3. What is the core idea behind differential association theory?
4. What are two criticisms of labeling theory?
5. What are the root causes of crime, according to conflict theorists?
6. How does the theory of broken windows exemplify the core ideas of control theory?

Crime and Crime Statistics

How dangerous *are* our streets? Is American society more violent than other societies? You should be able to use the sociological skills you have developed already to answer these questions.

In Chapter 2, for example, we learned about interpreting statistics. Most TV and newspaper reporting is based on official crime statistics collected by the police and published by the government. But many crimes—possibly half of all serious crimes, such as robbery with violence—are never reported to the police. The proportion of less serious crimes, especially small thefts, that go unreported is even higher. Since 1973, the U.S. Bureau of the Census has been interviewing households across the country in its National Crime Victimization Survey, which confirms that the overall rate of crime is higher than the reported crime index. For instance, in 2004, only 50 percent of violent crime was reported, including just 36 percent of rapes, 61 percent of robberies, 45 percent of simple assaults, and 53 percent of burglaries. Auto theft is the crime most frequently reported to the police (85 percent) (Catalano 2005).

Public concern in the United States focuses on crimes of violence—murder, assault, and rape—even though only 12.4 percent of all crimes are violent (Figure 7.2). In the United States, the most common victims of murder and other violent crimes (with the exception of rape) are young, poor, African American men in the larger cities (Figure 7.3). The rate of murder among black male teenagers is over five times the rate for their white counterparts, although this disparity has declined in recent years. In general, whether indexed by police statistics or by the National Crime Victimization Survey, violent crime, burglary, and car theft are more common in cities than in

FIGURE 7.2

Crime Rates in the United States, 1985–2006

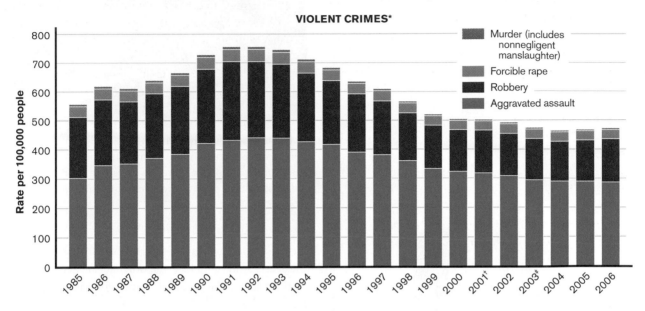

VIOLENT CRIMES*

Legend:
- Murder (includes nonnegligent manslaughter)
- Forcible rape
- Robbery
- Aggravated assault

y-axis: Rate per 100,000 people

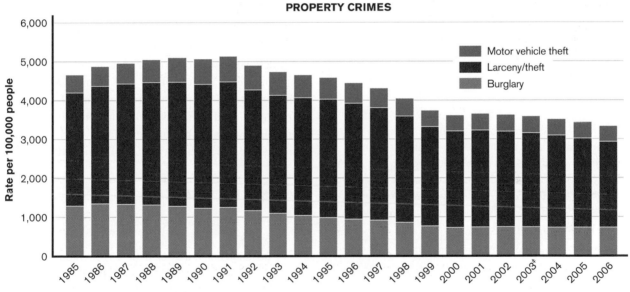

PROPERTY CRIMES

Legend:
- Motor vehicle theft
- Larceny/theft
- Burglary

y-axis: Rate per 100,000 people

During what year were property crimes the highest? What is the general trend of violent crime rates between 1985 and 2006? From 1985 through 2006, which is greater: the rate of reported violent crimes or the rate of reported property crimes? What percentage of all crimes are violent crimes? Why might the figures above not represent an accurate account of the number of violent and property crimes reported in the United States?

*Although arson data are included, sufficient data are not available to estimate totals for this offense.
†The murder and nonnegligent homicides that occurred as a result of the events of September 11, 2001, are not included in this table.
‡The 2003 crime figures have been adjusted.
SOURCE: Federal Bureau of Investigation 2007a.

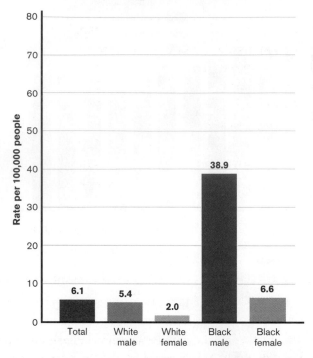

FIGURE 7.3

Murder Victims: Homicide Rates per 100,000 Population, 2003

Rate per 100,000 people

Total	6.1
White male	5.4
White female	2.0
Black male	38.9
Black female	6.6

In 2003, who was most likely to be a victim of homicide? Was a white male or a black female a more likely victim? Based on the figure above, in a U.S. city with a population of one million people, how many white females might we guess would have been murdered in 2003? According to the reading, what is the most common context for murder?

SOURCE: U.S. Bureau of the Census 2007a.

At this traveling gun show in West Palm Beach, the public can purchase weapons ranging from assault rifles to handguns with flash suppressors (silencers). Is there a relationship between the availability of guns and violent crime rates in the United States?

efforts by local police to stop the use of guns contributed to the decrease in homicides, but other social factors were also at work, including the declining market for crack cocaine and the stigmatization of crack among young urban dwellers. Another factor was the booming economy of the 1990s, which provided job opportunities for those who may have otherwise worked in the drug trade (Butterfield 1998).

A notable feature of most crimes of violence is their mundane character. Most assaults and homicides bear little resemblance to the murderous, random acts of gunmen or the carefully planned homicides highlighted in the media. Murders generally happen in the context of family and other interpersonal relationships; the victim usually knows the murderer.

☑ CONCEPT CHECKS

1. What are the main sources of crime data in the United States?
2. Describe crime trends in the 1970s through today.
3. How would sociologists explain the high rate of violent crime in the United States?

suburbs, and more common in suburbs than in smaller towns. The most likely explanation for the overall high level of violent crime in the United States is a combination of the availability of firearms, the general influence of the frontier tradition, and the subcultures of violence in the large cities.

In the 1990s, the overall U.S. crime rate dropped to its lowest levels since 1973, when the victimization survey was first used. Rates of violent crime dropped substantially: murders by 31 percent and robberies by 32 percent. There is no prevailing explanation among sociologists for this decline. Aggressive

Victims and Perpetrators of Crime

Are some individuals or groups more likely to commit crimes or to become the victims of crime? Criminologists say yes—research and crime statistics show that crime and victimization are not randomly distributed among the population. Men are more likely than women, for example, to commit crimes; the young are more often involved than older people.

The likelihood of someone becoming a victim of crime is linked to the area where he or she lives. Inner-city residents run a much greater risk of becoming victims than do residents of affluent suburban areas. The fact that ethnic minorities are concentrated in inner-city regions appears to be a significant factor in their higher rates of victimization.

Gender and Crime

Like other areas of sociology, criminological studies have traditionally ignored half the population: Women are largely invisible in both theoretical considerations and empirical studies. Since the 1970s, important feminist works have noted the way in which criminal transgressions by women occur in different contexts from those by men and how women's experiences with the criminal justice system are influenced by gendered assumptions about appropriate male and female roles. Feminists have also highlighted the prevalence of violence against women, both at home and in public.

MALE AND FEMALE CRIME RATES

The statistics on gender and crime are startling. For example, of all crimes reported in 2006, an overwhelming 76.2 percent of arrestees were men (Table 7.1). There is also an enormous imbalance in the ratio of men to women in prison, not only in the United States but in all the industrialized countries. Women made up only 7.1 percent of the prison population in 2004. There are also contrasts between the types of crimes men and women commit. Women's offenses rarely involve violence and are almost all small scale. Petty thefts like shoplifting and public order offenses such as public drunkenness and prostitution are typical female crimes.

Perhaps the real gender difference in crime rates is smaller than the official statistics show. In the 1950s, Otto Pollak suggested that certain crimes perpetrated by women go unreported, because women's domestic role enables them to commit crimes at home and in the private sphere. Pollak regarded women as naturally deceitful and highly skilled at covering up their crimes. He claimed this was grounded in biology, as women had learned to hide the pain and discomfort of menstruation from men and were able to fake interest in sexual intercourse in a way that men could not! Pollak (1950) also argued that female offenders are treated more leniently because male police officers adopt a "chivalrous" attitude toward them.

TABLE 7.1

Percentage of Crimes Committed by Men, 2006

CRIME	PERCENT MALE*
Total	**76.2**
Murder and nonnegligent manslaughter	89.1
Forcible rape	98.7
Robbery	88.7
Aggravated assault	79.3
Burglary	85.5
Larceny–theft	62.3
Motor vehicle theft	82.3
Arson	83.0

* Data represent arrests (not charges), estimated by the FBI.

SOURCE: Federal Bureau of Investigation 2007c.

Pollak's portrayal of women as conniving and deceptive is based in groundless stereotypes, yet the suggestion that the criminal justice system treats them more leniently has prompted much debate. The *chivalry thesis* has been applied in two ways. First, police and other officials may indeed regard female offenders as less dangerous than men and excuse activities for which males would be arrested. Second, in sentencing for criminal offenses, women get sent to prison much less than men. A number of empirical studies have tested the chivalry thesis, but the results remain inconclusive. One difficulty is assessing the relative influence of gender compared to other factors such as age, class, and race. For example, older women offenders tend to be treated less aggressively than their male counterparts. Other studies have shown that black women receive worse treatment than white women at the hands of the police.

Another perspective, which feminists have adopted, examines how social understandings about femininity affect women's experiences in the criminal justice system. One argument is that women receive harsher treatment when they have allegedly deviated from the norms of female sexuality. For example, young girls who are perceived to be sexually promiscuous are more often taken into custody than boys. Such young women are seen as doubly deviant—not only breaking the law but also flouting appropriate female behavior. In such cases, they are judged less on the nature of the offense and more on their deviant lifestyle. Thus the criminal justice system operates under a double standard, considering male aggression and violence as natural but female offenses as reflecting psychological imbalances (Heidensohn 1985).

To make female crime more visible, feminists have conducted detailed investigations on female criminals—from girl gangs to female terrorists to women in prison. Such studies have shown that violence is not exclusively a characteristic of male criminality. Women are much less likely than men to participate in violent crime but are not always inhibited from doing so. Why, then, are female rates of criminality so much lower than those of men?

Some evidence shows that female lawbreakers often avoid coming before the courts because they persuade the police or other authorities to see their actions in a particular light. They invoke the *gender contract*—the implicit contract between men and women whereby to be a woman is to be erratic and impulsive on the one hand and in need of protection on the other (Worrall 1990).

Yet differential treatment cannot account for the vast difference between male and female rates of crime. The reasons are probably the same as those that explain gender differences in other spheres: Male crimes remain "male" because of differences in socialization and because men's activities are still more nondomestic than those of most women.

Ever since the late nineteenth century, criminologists have predicted that gender equality would reduce or eliminate the differences in criminality between men and women; but as yet, crime remains a gendered phenomenon.

CRIMES AGAINST WOMEN

In certain categories of crime—domestic violence, sexual harassment, sexual assault, and rape—men are overwhelmingly the aggressors and women the victims. Although each of these has been practiced by women against men, they remain almost exclusively crimes against women. It is estimated that one quarter of women are victims of violence at some point, but all women face the threat of such crimes either directly or indirectly.

For many years, these offenses were ignored by the criminal justice system; victims had to persevere tirelessly to gain legal recourse. Even today, the prosecution of crimes against women is hardly straightforward. Yet feminist criminology raised awareness of crimes against women and integrated such offenses into mainstream debates on crime. In this section we examine the crime of rape, leaving discussions of domestic violence and sexual harassment to other chapters (see Chapters 10 and 15).

The extent of rape is very difficult to assess accurately. Only a small proportion of rapes come to the attention of the police and are recorded in the statistics. In 2005, 127,430 cases of rape or attempted rape and 61,530 cases of sexual assault were reported. However, from surveys of victims, we know that only about 38 percent of rapes are reported to the police (U.S. Bureau of Justice Statistics 2005a).

During the 1990s, there were an increased number of reported incidents in which the attacker knew the victim: 62 percent of sexual assaults were committed by relatives, friends, former partners, or recent acquaintances—so-called date or acquaintance rapes. By 2005, this rate had risen to 65.5 percent (U.S. Bureau of Justice Statistics 2005b). It is estimated that half of all acquaintance rapes involve someone whom the victim has known for less than twenty-four hours. While the number of acquaintance rapes has risen, the number of reported rapes involving strangers has dropped, accounting for 24.2 percent of all attacks in 2005 (U.S. Bureau of Justice Statistics 2005b).

There are many reasons that a woman might not report sexual violence. The majority of rape victims either wish to put the incident out of their minds or are unwilling to participate in the humiliating process of medical examination, police interrogation, and courtroom cross-examination. The legal process takes a long time and can be intimidating. Courtroom procedure is public, and the victim must face the accused. Proof of penetration, the identity of the rapist, and the fact that the act occurred without the woman's consent all have to be forthcoming. A woman may feel that *she* is the one on trial, particularly if her own sexual history is examined publicly, as is often the case.

Recently, women's groups have sought change in both legal and public thinking about rape, stressing that rape should not be seen as a sexual offense but as a violent crime. It is not just a physical attack but an assault on an individual's integrity and dignity. Rape is clearly related to the association of masculinity with power, dominance, and toughness. It is not primarily the result of overwhelming sexual desire but of the ties between sexuality and feelings of power and superiority. The sexual act itself is less significant than the debasement of the woman (Estrich 1987). The campaign has managed to change legislation, and rape is today generally recognized in law as a type of criminal violence.

In a sense, all women are victims of rape. Women who have never been raped may be afraid to go out alone at night, even on crowded streets, and may be almost equally fearful of being alone in a house or apartment. Susan Brownmiller (1975) has argued that rape is part of a system of male intimidation that keeps all women in fear. Those who are not raped are affected by the anxieties thus provoked and by the need to be more cautious in everyday aspects of life than men have to be.

Crimes against Gays and Lesbians

Feminists claim that understandings of violence are highly gendered and are influenced by perceptions about risk and responsibility. Because women are considered less able to defend themselves, common sense holds that they should modify *their* behavior to reduce the risk of victimhood. For example, not only should women avoid walking in unsafe neighborhoods alone and at night but they also should not dress provocatively or behave in a manner that could be misinterpreted. Women who fail to do so can be accused of "asking for trouble." In a court setting, their behavior can be a mitigating factor in considering the perpetrator's act of violence (Dobash and Dobash 1992; Richardson and May 1999).

It has been suggested that a similar logic applies in violent acts against gay men and lesbians. Victimization studies reveal that homosexuals experience a high incidence of violent crime and harassment. A national survey of over four thousand gay men and women found that in the previous five years, one third of gay men and one quarter of lesbians had been the victim of at least one violent attack. One third had experienced some form of harassment, including threats or vandalism. Fully 75 percent had been verbally abused in public.

Because sexual minorities remain stigmatized and marginalized in many societies, they are more often treated as deserving of crime rather than as innocent victims. Homosexual relationships are still seen as belonging to the private realm, whereas heterosexuality is the norm in public spaces. Lesbians and gay men who display their homosexual identities in public are often blamed for making themselves vulnerable to crime, in a sense even provoking it.

This notion forms the basis of the "homosexual panic" legal defense that can be used to reduce a charge of murder to that of manslaughter. The accused murderer can claim that an unwanted homosexual advance caused him or her to lose control and to attack the victim. Such a defense was used unsuccessfully by a young man in Wyoming in the 1999 murder trial of university student Matthew Shepard. The accused and two other men severely beat Shepard outside a bar before leaving him tied to a fence in the woods, in near-freezing temperatures. After eighteen hours he was found, and he died several days later. In cases like the Matthew Shepard murder, some homophobic observers may view this type of violence as a justifiable response to a behavior or life choice they view as immoral. Yet such reactions to hate-related attacks ultimately

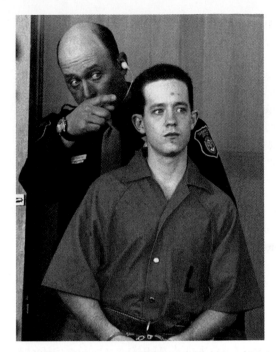

Aaron McKinney, one of the men who killed Matthew Shepard, attempted to use the "homosexual panic" defense to reduce his sentence from murder to manslaughter, but the court disallowed it and he was convicted of first-degree felony murder.

denies both the essential personhood and right to life of the victim. Such crimes have led many social groups to call for hate crime legislation to protect the human rights of groups who remain stigmatized.

Youth and Crime

Popular fear about crime centers on offenses such as theft, burglary, assault, and rape—seen as the domain of young working-class males. Media coverage of rising crime rates often focuses on moral breakdown among young people and highlights vandalism, school truancy, and drug use to illustrate society's increasing permissiveness. This equation of youth with criminal activity is not new, according to some sociologists. Young people are often taken as an indicator of the health and welfare of society.

Official crime statistics do reveal high rates of offense among young people. About 34 percent of all offenders arrested for criminal offenses in 2006 were under the age of twenty-one (Federal Bureau of Investigation 2007b). For both males and females, arrests peak around age eighteen or nineteen and decline thereafter (Federal Bureau of Investigation 2005a). Yet moral panics about youth criminality may not reflect social reality. An isolated event can be transformed symbolically into a full-blown crisis of childhood, demanding tough law-and-order responses. The mass murder at Columbine High School is an example of how moral outrage can deflect attention from larger issues. Columbine was a watershed event in media portrayals of youth crime, possibly leading to copycat killings in high schools in other states. Even though the number of murders in schools has been declining, media attention has led many to think that all young children are potentially violent. Although the Columbine perpetrators were labeled "monsters" and "animals," less attention was paid to how easily they obtained the murder weapons.

Similar caution should apply to the popular view of drug use by teenagers. Every year, the Department of Health and Human Services conducts the National Survey of Drug Use and Health in teens. In 2006, nearly 51 percent of noninstitutionalized respondents between the ages of twelve and seventeen reported being current drinkers of alcohol and participating in binge drinking at least once in the 30 days prior to the survey. About 10.4 percent had smoked a cigarette, while 8.3 percent had used an illicit drug in the last month (U.S. Department of Health and Human Services 2006a). Trends in drug use have shifted away from hard drugs such as heroin and toward combinations of substances such as amphetamines, prescription drugs like OxyContin, alcohol, and the drug ecstasy. The war on drugs, some have argued, criminalizes large segments of the youth population who are generally law abiding (Muncie 1999).

What makes one drug a psychological tool and another a national menace? Consider ecstasy, the chemical compound methylenedioxymethamphetamine (MDMA), which gives users a sustained feeling of pleasure by sending waves of the neurotransmitters serotonin and dopamine into the brain. In this regard, it is not dissimilar to antidepressants such as Prozac, which also influences serotonin levels. The use of ecstasy and antidepressants by college students has risen dramatically in recent years, yet one is illegal and the other is routinely prescribed. Admittedly, the amphetamine-like and mildly hallucinogenic effects of ecstasy are considerably more dramatic and short-lived than the effects of Prozac, and long-term ecstasy use may cause brain damage. Nonetheless, MDMA was legal in the United States until 1985; because it can overcome emotional inhibitions, some therapists used it on their patients in therapy sessions. More recently, MDMA has been prescribed for rape victims in Spain, sufferers from post-traumatic stress disorder in Switzerland, and end-stage cancer patients in the United States.

The divergent views toward ecstasy and Prozac illustrate how deviant behavior is socially defined. From the perspective of lawmakers, MDMA became a dangerous drug once it was associated with youth culture, parties, and hedonism rather than medicine. Media coverage of ecstasy has also been monolithic. When teen-oriented television shows such as *One Tree Hill* present the obligatory ecstasy episode, invariably the protagonist taking ecstasy for the first time has a bad reaction and gets rushed to the hospital. This is easier to portray than the more common experience: Early experiences with the drug may be blissful, with problems occurring over time as the brain's receptivity to the drug diminishes.

Taking illegal drugs is often defined in racial, class, and cultural terms; different drugs become associated with different groups and behaviors. When crack cocaine appeared in the 1980s, the media defined it as the drug of choice for black, inner-city kids who listened to hip-hop. Perhaps as a result, jail sentences for crack possession were set at higher levels than sentences for possession of cocaine, which was associated more with white and suburban users. Ecstasy has, until recently, had similar white and middle- or upper-class associations.

Crimes of the Powerful

Although there are connections between crime and poverty, it would be a mistake to suppose that crime is concentrated among the poor. Crimes by people in positions of power and wealth can have farther-reaching consequences than the often petty crimes of the poor.

The term **white-collar crime**, introduced by Edwin Sutherland (1949), refers to crime by affluent people. This category of criminal activity includes tax fraud, antitrust violations, illegal sales practices, securities and land fraud, embezzlement, the manufacture or sale of dangerous products, and illegal environmental pollution as well as straightforward theft. The distribution of white-collar crimes is even harder to measure than that of other types of crime; most do not appear in the official statistics at all.

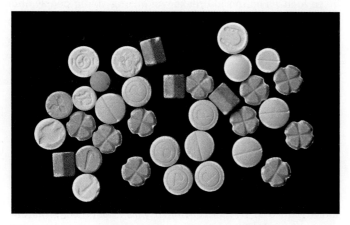

What drives the popularity of drugs such as MDMA?

Efforts to detect white-collar crime are limited, and rarely do those who are caught go to jail. Although the authorities regard white-collar crime more tolerantly than crimes of the less privileged, the amount of money involved in white-collar crime in the United States is forty times greater than the amount involved in crimes against property, such as robberies, burglaries, larceny, forgeries, and car thefts (President's Commission on Organized Crime 1986). Some forms of white-collar crime, moreover, affect more people than lower-class criminality does. An embezzler might rob thousands—or today, via computer fraud, millions—of people.

CORPORATE CRIME

Corporate crime describes the offenses committed by large corporations. Pollution, product mislabeling, and violations of health and safety regulations affect much larger numbers of people than does petty criminality. The increasing power and influence of large corporations and their global reach mean that they touch our lives in many ways—from producing the cars we drive and the food we eat to affecting the natural environment and financial markets.

Quantitative and qualitative studies of corporate crime have concluded that many corporations do not adhere to legal regulations (Slapper and Tombs 1999). Corporate crime is pervasive and widespread. Studies have revealed six types of violations: *administrative* (paperwork or noncompliance), *environmental* (pollution, permit violations), *financial* (tax violations, illegal payments), *labor* (working conditions, hiring practices), *manufacturing* (product safety, labeling), and *unfair trade practices* (anticompetition, false advertising).

Sometimes there are obvious victims, as in environmental disasters such as the 1984 spill at the Bhopal chemical plant in India and the health dangers posed to women by silicone breast implants. The most famous recent case of white-collar crime with obvious victims was the Enron scandal, in which the company and its accountants lied about its profits and concealed its debts. The victims included pension holders, employees, and investors. Recently those injured in car crashes or relatives of those who were killed have called for the executives of car manufacturers to be brought to trial when the companies have shown negligence. But very often victims of corporate crime do not see themselves as such. Distances in time and space mean that victims may not realize they have been victimized or may not know how to seek redress.

The effects of corporate crime are often experienced unevenly within society. Those who are disadvantaged by other socioeconomic inequalities suffer disproportionately. For example, safety and health risks in the workplace tend to occur in low-paying occupations. Many of the risks from health-care

In May 2006, Enron founder and former chief executive Kenneth Lay was convicted of conspiracy and fraud. Lay died of heart disease in July 2006 before he could be sentenced.

products and pharmaceuticals have affected women more than men, as with contraceptives and fertility treatments with harmful side effects (Slapper and Tombs 1999).

Violent aspects of corporate crime are less visible, but they are just as real—and may have much more serious consequences. For example, the flouting of regulations in the preparation of new drugs, safety in the workplace, or pollution may cause physical harm or death to large numbers of people. Deaths from hazards at work far outnumber murders, although precise statistics about job accidents are difficult to obtain. Of course, we cannot assume that all, or even the majority, of these deaths and injuries are the result of employer negligence in relation to safety factors for which the employers are legally liable. Nevertheless, there is some basis for supposing that many involve the neglect of legally binding safety regulations by employers or managers.

Organized Crime

Organized crime embraces illegal gambling, drug dealing, prostitution, large-scale theft, and protection rackets, among other activities. In *End of Millennium* (1998), Manuel Castells argues that organized crime groups are becoming

Drug Trafficking

How easy would it have been for you to purchase marijuana in high school? How easy would it be to do so today? Lamentable as it may seem to some, most young people in the United States have relatively easy access to illegal drugs. According to the National Survey on Drug Use and Health, nearly 11 percent of individuals between twelve and seventeen years old have used illegal drugs in the last month but less than 1 percent have tried heroin. Almost 53 percent of those between eighteen and twenty-five have tried marijuana at least once and nearly 2 percent have tried heroin (U.S. Department of Health and Human Services 2005a).

What factors determine the availability of illegal drugs in your community? The level of police enforcement is important, of course, as is the extent of local demand. But no less important is the existence of networks of traffickers able to transport the drugs from the countries in which they are grown to your hometown. These networks have been able to flourish in part because of globalization.

While the cultivation of marijuana in the United States represents a major illicit industry, almost all of the world's

coca plants and opium poppies are grown in the developing world. The U.S. government spends billions of dollars each year to assist developing nations with eradication efforts and devotes significant resources to stopping the flow of drugs past U.S. borders. In 1995, the federal government spent more than $8.2 billion on the war on drugs, and between 1981 and

increasingly international, with the coordination of criminal activities across borders—facilitated by new information technologies—becoming a central feature of the global economy. Involved in activities ranging from the narcotics trade to counterfeiting to smuggling immigrants and human organs, organized crime groups operate in flexible international networks rather than within their own territories.

According to Castells, criminal groups set up strategic alliances with each other. The international narcotics trade, weapons trafficking, the sale of nuclear material, and money laundering have all become linked across borders and crime groups. Criminal organizations are based in "low-risk" countries where there are few threats to their activities. In recent years, the former Soviet Union has been one of the main points of convergence for international organized crime. The flexible nature of networked crime makes it relatively easy to evade law-enforcement initiatives: If one criminal safe haven becomes risky, the organizational geometry can shift to form a new pattern.

The international nature of crime has become evident in the United States, where the newest arrivals include criminals from the former Soviet Union. Russian criminal networks are deeply involved in money laundering, linking activities with Russia's largely unregulated banks. Some think the Russian groups may become the world's largest criminal networks, based in a mafia-riddled Russian state. The most worrying possibility is that Russia's new mobsters are smuggling nuclear materials (taken from the old Soviet nuclear arsenal) on an international scale.

The narcotics trade is one of the most rapidly expanding international criminal industries. The United Nations Office on Drugs and Crime (2005) estimated that in 2004 the global trade in illegal drugs was worth more than the global trade in coffee, grains, or meat. Heroin networks stretch across the Far East, particularly South Asia, and are also located in North Africa, the Middle East, and Latin America. Supply lines also pass through Vancouver and other parts of Canada; from there, drugs travel to the United States.

1996, it spent $65 billion (Bertram et al. 1996). By 2007, the federal budget for the war on drugs had climbed to $12.7 billion, but this figure excludes the costs of incarceration and military involvement (Office of National Drug Control Policy 2005). It also excludes funds spent to wage the war on drugs by state governments, which is estimated to be an additional $30 billion (DrugWarFacts.org 2005). Despite this massive expenditure, there is little evidence that eradication or interdiction efforts have significantly decreased the supply of illegal drugs in the United States. Why have these efforts failed?

One answer is that the profit is simply too great. Farmers struggling to scratch out a living for themselves in Bolivia or Peru, members of the Colombian drug cartels, and low-level street dealers in the United States all receive substantial monetary rewards for their illegal activities. These rewards create a strong incentive to devise ways around antidrug efforts and to run the risk of getting caught.

Another answer—one discussed at a summit attended by leaders of the eight major industrial powers—is that drug traffickers have been able to take advantage of globalization. First, in their attempts to evade the authorities, traffickers make use of all the communications technologies that are available in a global age. As one commentator put it, drug traffickers "now use sophisticated technology, such as signal interceptors, to plot radar and avoid monitoring . . . [and] they can use faxes, computers and cellular phones to coordinate their activities and make their business run smoothly" (Chepesiuk 1998).

Second, the globalization of the financial sector has helped create an infrastructure in which large sums of money can be moved around the world electronically in a matter of seconds, making it relatively easy to "launder" drug money (i.e., to make it appear as if it came from a legitimate business venture). Third, recent changes in government policy designed to allow the freer flow of persons and legitimate goods across international borders have increased the opportunities for smuggling.

At the same time, globalization may create new opportunities for governments to work together to combat drug trafficking. Indeed, world leaders have called for greater international cooperation in narcotics enforcement, stressing the need for information sharing and coordinated enforcement efforts.

Cybercrime

It seems certain that the information and telecommunications revolution will change the face of crime. In 2007, a survey of computer security practitioners conducted by the FBI found that nearly 46 percent of companies experienced a security incident related to their computer systems and that cybercrime cost almost $67 million to American businesses (Computer Security Institute 2007). Yet only 29 percent of security violations were reported to the police out of fears that negative publicity would damage the company's stock price or that competitors would steal valuable information. A similar survey in the United Kingdom reported that 89 percent of respondents had experienced unauthorized access to their firm's computer networks and that computer crime cost those businesses over £2.4 billion in 2004 (National Hi Tech Crime Unit 2005).

Cybercrime is already on the decline. Internet-based fraud was the fastest-growing category of crime in the United States in the late 1990s. From 1999 to 2000, losses from Internet fraud and forgery rose from $12 million to $117 million over the course of one year, yet declined to $52.5 million in 2006 (Gordon, Loeb, Lucyshyn, and Richardson 2007).

The global reach of telecommunications crime poses challenges for law enforcement in terms of detecting and prosecuting crimes. Police from the countries involved must determine the jurisdiction in which the act occurred and agree on extraditing the offenders and providing evidence for prosecution. Although police cooperation across national borders may improve with the growth of cybercrime, at present cybercriminals have a great deal of room to maneuver.

At a time when financial, commercial, and production systems in countries worldwide are being integrated electronically, rising levels of Internet fraud and unauthorized electronic intrusions are potent warnings of the vulnerability of computer security systems. From the FBI to the Japanese government's antihacker police force, governments are scrambling to contend with new and elusive forms of cross-national computer activity.

1. Contrast the following two explanations for the gender gap in crime: behavioral differences and biases in reporting.
2. How does the study of teenage drug use illustrate the social construction of deviance?
3. What are some consequences of white-collar crime?

Crime-Reduction Strategies

Despite the misleading picture presented by official statistics, when they are considered along with data from victimization surveys it becomes clear that criminal offenses play a prominent role in society today. Moreover, citizens perceive themselves to be at greater risk of victimization than previously—especially residents of inner-city areas.

In the face of so many changes and uncertainties, we are all engaged in a constant process of risk management. Yet it is not only individuals that face risk management: Governments now manage societies that seem more dangerous and uncertain than ever before. One of the central tasks of social policy in modern states has been controlling crime and delinquency. But if at one time government sought to guarantee security, policies now are increasingly aimed at managing insecurity.

Are Prisons the Answer?

Although as measured by police statistics (problematic, as we have seen) rates of violent crime have declined since 1990, many people in the United States view crime as their most serious social concern—more so than unemployment or the state of the economy (Lacayo 1994). Americans also favor tougher prison sentences for all but relatively minor crimes. The price of imprisonment, however, is enormous: It costs an average of $25,327 to keep a prisoner in the federal prison system for one year (US Department of Justice 2003). Moreover, even if the prison system were expanded, it wouldn't significantly reduce the level of serious crime. Only about a fifth of all serious crimes known to the police result in arrest, and no more than half of those arrests result in conviction. Even so, America's prisons are so overcrowded (Figure 7.4) that the average convict serves only a third of his or her sentence. The United

States already locks up more people (nearly all men) per capita than any other country.

The United States has by far the most punitive justice system in the world. More than 2.2 million people are presently incarcerated in American prisons, with another 4.5 million falling under the jurisdiction of the penal system (McDonough 2005; Slevin 2005). Although the United States makes up only 4.5 percent of the world's overall population, it accounts for 23 percent of the world's prisoners (International Centre for Prison Studies 2005).

The American prison system employs more than 750,000 people (Slevin 2005) and costs nearly $200 billion annually to maintain (U.S. Bureau of Justice Statistics 2005c). It has also become partially privatized, with private companies building and administering prisons to accommodate the growing inmate population. Critics charge that a "prison-industrial complex" has emerged: Large numbers of people—including bureaucrats, politicians, and prison employees—have vested interests in the existence and further expansion of the prison system.

Support for *capital punishment* (the death penalty) is high in the United States. In 2006, approximately 65 percent of adults surveyed said that they believed in capital punishment; 32 percent opposed it (ABC News/Washington Post Poll 2006). This represents a significant shift from 1965, when 38 percent of those surveyed supported the death penalty and 47 percent were opposed. However, given the choice between the death penalty and life imprisonment, the share of those supporting the death penalty falls to 50 percent (ABC News/Washington Post Poll 2006). The number of individuals awaiting execution has climbed steadily since 1977, when the Supreme Court upheld state capital punishment laws. Since that time there have been 1,099 executions in the United States (Death Penalty Information Center 2007a). Two thirds of these executions have taken place in five states: Texas (405), Virginia (98), Oklahoma (86), Missouri (66), and Florida (64). At the end of 2006, a total of 3,300 prisoners were held on death row (Death Penalty Information Center 2007a). The group was 98 percent men, 45 percent white, and 42 percent black. In 2007 (until September), a total of 42 prisoners were executed in ten states and all were men. Of these, 20 were white, 14 were black, and 6 were Latino (Death Penalty Information Center 2007b).

More than one quarter of African American men are either in prison or under the control of the penal system. More than half (55 percent) of individuals in U.S. federal prisons are serving sentences for nonviolent drug-related crimes, while only 23 percent are serving time for a violent offense (The Sentencing Project 2004).

There is little evidence to support the view that imprisoning large numbers of people or stiffening sentences deters individuals from committing crimes. In fact, sociological studies

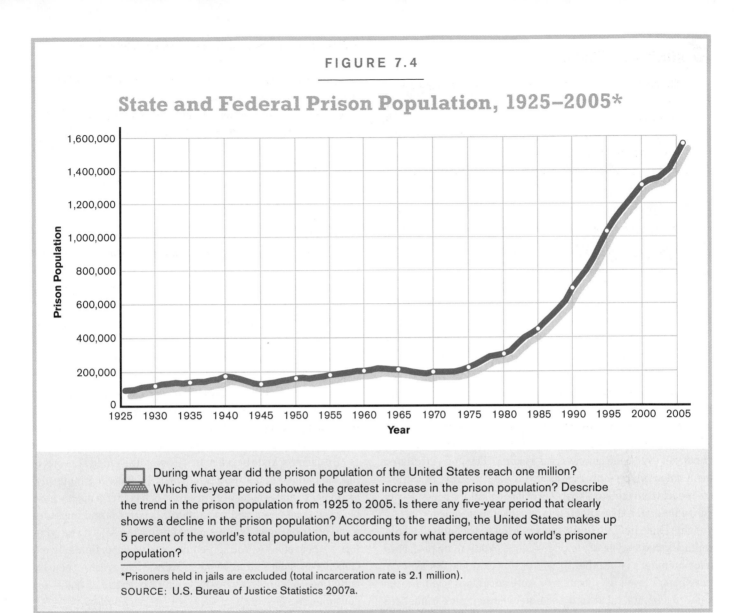

FIGURE 7.4

State and Federal Prison Population, 1925–2005*

During what year did the prison population of the United States reach one million? Which five-year period showed the greatest increase in the prison population? Describe the trend in the prison population from 1925 to 2005. Is there any five-year period that clearly shows a decline in the prison population? According to the reading, the United States makes up 5 percent of the world's total population, but accounts for what percentage of world's prisoner population?

*Prisoners held in jails are excluded (total incarceration rate is 2.1 million).
SOURCE: U.S. Bureau of Justice Statistics 2007a.

have demonstrated that prisons often make offenders more hardened criminals. The more harsh and oppressive prison conditions are, the more likely inmates are to be brutalized by the experience. Yet if prisons were attractive and pleasant places to live, would they have a deterrent effect?

Although prisons do keep some dangerous men (and a tiny minority of dangerous women) off the streets, evidence suggests a need for other means to deter crime. Robert Gangi, director of the Correctional Association of New York, says that "building more prisons to address crime is like building more graveyards to address a fatal disease" (quoted in Smolowe 1994). A sociological interpretation of crime makes clear that there are no quick fixes. The causes of crime, especially crimes of violence, are bound up with structural conditions of American society, including widespread poverty, the condition of the inner cities, and the deteriorating life circumstances of many young men.

The Mark of a Criminal Record

An experiment by sociologist Devah Pager (2003) showed the long-term consequences of prison on felons. Pager had pairs of young black and white men apply for real entry-level job openings throughout the city of Milwaukee. The applicant pairs were matched by appearance, interpersonal style, and—most important—all job-related characteristics such as educational level and prior work experience. In addition to varying the

How do factors such as race or a criminal record affect an individual's ability to get a job? Elton Luckey looks at a list of potential employers at a job fair for ex-convicts in Dallas, Texas. Police said more than 5,000 people attended the event, which was co-sponsored by churches and advocacy groups for former inmates.

race of the applicant pairs, Pager had applicants alternate presenting themselves to employers as having criminal records. One member of each pair would answer yes to the question, Have you ever been convicted of a crime? The pair alternated each week which young man would play the role of the ex-offender, to make sure that it was the criminal record—not the individual—that affected employment outcomes.

This experimental design controls for all the individual differences that may lead members of one group to be preferred over members of another. If whites, for example, on average have higher levels of education or more steady work experience than blacks, it's hard to determine whether race influences their employment opportunities or whether these other skill differences do. The same problem applies to how individuals with criminal records fare in the job market. Some would argue that a criminal record doesn't hold people back; instead, it's the fact that people with criminal records don't work as hard as nonoffenders or aren't as qualified. The experiment allowed Pager to test whether employers respond differently to otherwise equal candidates on the basis of race or criminal record alone.

Pager's study revealed some striking findings. Whites were much preferred over blacks, and nonoffenders were much preferred over ex-offenders. Whites with a felony conviction were half as likely to be considered by employers as equally qualified nonoffenders. For blacks, the effects were even larger. Black ex-offenders were only one third as likely to receive a callback compared to nonoffenders. Most surprising was the comparison of these two effects: Blacks with *no criminal history* fared no

better than did whites with a felony conviction. These results suggest that being a black male in America today is about the same as being a convicted criminal, at least in the eyes of Milwaukee employers. For those who believe that race no longer represents a major barrier to opportunity, these results represent a powerful challenge. Being a black felon is a particularly tough obstacle to overcome.

Situational Crime Prevention

"Situational" crime prevention—such as target hardening and surveillance systems—has been a popular approach. Policy makers often favor such techniques because they are relatively simple to introduce alongside existing policing techniques, and they reassure citizens by giving the impression of decisive action against crime. Yet because such techniques do not address underlying causes of crime, they mainly just protect certain segments of the population and displace delinquency into other realms.

This dynamic is evident in the physical exclusion of certain categories of people from common spaces—such as libraries, parks, and street corners—in an attempt to reduce crime and its perceived risk. Practices such as police monitoring, private security teams, and surveillance systems are aimed at protecting the public against potential risks. In shopping malls, for example, security measures are part of a contractual bargain between businesses and consumers: To attract and maintain a customer base, businesses must ensure the safety and comfort of their clients. Young people are disproportionately excluded from such spaces, being perceived as a greater security threat because malls typically create "locations of trust" for consumers.

Police forces have also expanded in response to growing crime and public clamor for more protection. Governments eager to appear decisive on crime favor increasing the number and resources of the police. But it is not clear that a greater police presence translates into lower crime rates. In the United States, official statistics on the violent crime rate and number of police cast doubt on the link (Figure 7.5). This raises puzzling questions: If increased policing does not prevent violent crime, why does the public demand a visible police presence? What role does policing play in our society?

Policing

Some sociologists and criminologists have suggested that visible policing techniques, such as patrolling the streets, are reassuring for the public. Such activities support the perception that the

FIGURE 7.5

Justice Employment and Crime Rates

Although the number of police steadily increased between 1982 and 2004, the crime rate dropped, increased, and dropped again during this period. Therefore, no causal link can be made between the number of police and the crime rate.

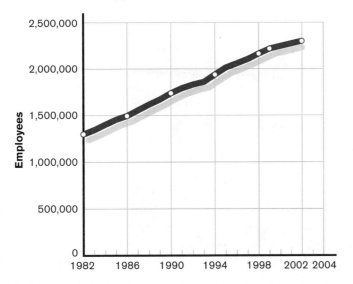

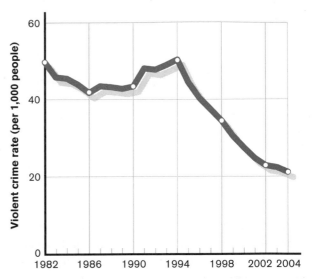

From 1982 to 1994 did the justice employment rate increase or decrease? During that same period, did the crime rate generally increase or decrease? Between 1982 and 1994, approximately how many additional justice employees (police, etc.) were added? What are the approximate crime rates in 1982 and 1994? According to the reading, the informational demands of what industry now directly shape the way in which police work?

SOURCE: U.S. Bureau of Justice Statistics 2002c, 2004d.

police actively control crime, investigate offenses, and support the criminal justice system. But sociologists also see a need to reassess the role of policing in the late modern age. Policing, they argue, is now less about controlling crime and more about detecting and managing risks. Mostly it involves communicating knowledge about risk to other institutions in society that demand that information (Ericson and Haggerty 1997).

According to this view, police are primarily "knowledge workers," spending time processing information, drafting reports, or communicating data. Consider the "simple" case of an automobile accident in Ontario, Canada. A police officer is called to the scene of an automobile accident involving two vehicles, with minor injuries and one drunk driver. The investigation takes one hour; the drunk driver is criminally charged with the impaired operation of a motor vehicle causing bodily harm

and with operating a motor vehicle with excess alcohol. The driver's license is automatically suspended for twelve hours.

Following this routine investigation, the officer spends three hours writing up sixteen reports. Here the role of police as brokers of information becomes clear:

- The *provincial motor registry* requires information about the location of the accident and the vehicles and people involved. This is used for risk profiling in accident prevention initiatives, traffic management, and resource allocation.
- The *automobile industry* needs to know about the vehicles involved to improve safety standards, to report to regulatory agencies, and to provide safety information to consumer groups.

When a Dissertation Makes a Difference

For Devah Pager, a young sociologist from Honolulu, "kulia i ka nu'u"—"to strive for the summit"—means to do research that can influence policy, a realistic quest for her if the last few years are any indication.

As a graduate student at the University of Wisconsin, she studied the difficulties of former prisoners trying to find work and, in the process, came up with a disturbing finding: It is easier for a white person with a felony conviction to get a job than for a black person whose record is clean.

Ms. Pager's study won the American Sociological Association's award for the best dissertation of the year in August (2003), prompting a *Wall Street Journal* columnist to write about it. Howard Dean repeated her main finding in stump speeches and interviews throughout his glory days as the front-runner in the presidential race.

Then, addressing the overall problem convicted felons have reentering the job market, President Bush announced in the State of the Union message a $300 million program to provide mentoring and help them get work. Jim Towey, the director of the White House Office of Faith-Based and Community Initiatives, said that Ms. Pager's study was one of the many sources of information that helped shape the administration's four-year plan.

Ms. Pager, 32, is thrilled to see the issue receive national attention. More than half a million inmates will leave penal institutions this year, and "the Administration is finally recognizing

Devah Pager

that the problems created by our incarceration policies can no longer be ignored," she said. Even if the promised amount is trivial, she said, the gesture is important symbolically.

Conversation with Ms. Pager flows easily. Over a plate of pancakes, she brushes aside a crush of thick loose auburn curls to punctuate less serious points with flashes of the wide, arresting smile her colleagues say is emblematic. She is known for her good nature and charismatic style, but it is her research that has made her one of the most promising young sociologists around.

- The *insurance companies* involved need information to determine responsibility and to make awards in the case. They also require police information to develop statistical profiles of risk to set premiums and compensation levels for clients.
- The *public health system* requires details on the injuries. This knowledge is used for statistical profiles and to plan emergency service provision.
- The *criminal courts* require police information as material for the prosecution and as proof that the scene was properly investigated and evidence collected.

- The *police administration* itself requires reports on the incident for both internal records and national computer databases.

This example reveals how police work is increasingly about "mapping" and predicting risk within the population.

The informational demands of other institutions, such as the insurance industry, now require that police gather and report information in a way that is compatible with the needs of outside agencies. Computerized systems and forms define the way in which police report information. Rather than writing

Initially Ms. Pager's interest was race, stirred by her move from Hawaii to Los Angeles to attend the University of California. "I was struck by the level of separation between racial groups on campus, throughout the city," she said. "Race seemed to define space. Hawaii, by contrast, has the highest rate of intermarriage in the country. Growing up, every other person, it seemed, was hapa, or half, the term used to describe someone multiracial or mixed." She added, "When you grow up with that being normal, everything else seems strange—and wrong."

She completed a master's degree at Stanford University and a second master's at the University of Cape Town in South Africa ***.

***

The interest in released prisoners arose while she was studying for her doctorate in Madison, Wisconsin. She *** volunteered for an organization that provides services and shelter to homeless men. There she met many black men with prison records. "It was a nice break to get out and do some direct service," she said. She spent time with the men *** and made herself available "as a resource, to allow them to unload." Those who had served jail time often talked about how it complicated the job search. "That was one of the first things that clued me into what an immutable barrier it was standing in their way," she said.

At about this time Human Rights Watch and the Sentencing Project reported that in seven states felony convictions had permanently disenfranchised one in four African American men. An innovative but difficult research plan began to take shape.

Both of her main advisers, Robert M. Hauser and Erik Olin Wright, tried to dissuade her, gently suggesting how hard it is for graduate students to obtain financial support, manage complicated field work and end up with meaningful results.

"She was undaunted," Mr. Wright said. "Her pluckiness is part of what makes her successful. She knew she could do it."

To isolate the effect of a criminal record on the job search, Ms. Pager sent pairs of young, well-groomed, well-spoken college men with identical resumes to apply for 350 advertised entry-level jobs in Milwaukee. The only difference was that one said he had served an 18-month prison sentence for cocaine possession. Two teams were black, two white.

*** For her black testers, the callback rate was 5 percent if they had a criminal record and 14 percent if they did not. For whites, it was 17 percent with a criminal record and 34 percent without.

"I expected there to be an effect of race, but I did not expect it to swamp the results as it did," Ms. Pager said. "It really was a surprise."

Jeff Manza, a colleague at Northwestern University, where she teaches, said, "Devah's work demonstrates in a new and convincing way the extent to which the 'second chance' that Bush talks about runs headlong into the realities of race and the fear of crime and criminals."

Similarly, Reginald Wilkinson, Ohio's top corrections official and the president of the Association of State Correctional Administrators, was impressed by her findings and methodology. "In my estimation, we can't eliminate the race question when we're talking about re-entry," he said. "I think what Professor Pager has done is raise consciousness about this."

***

Ms. Pager is replicating her research on a grander scale with one of the field's leading experts, Bruce Western of Princeton University ***.

The new study is another chance to further document the effects of race and imprisonment, another chance at "kulia i ka nu'u."

SOURCE: Brooke Kroeger, "When a Dissertation Makes a Difference," *New York Times*, March 20, 2004.

narrative accounts, police input the facts of a case into standardized forms by checking off boxes and choosing among available options. The information is used to categorize people and events as part of creating risk profiles. But such closed-ended reporting formats influence what police observe and investigate, how they understand and interpret an incident, and the approach they take to resolving a problem. This emphasis on information collection and processing can alienate and frustrate many police officers, who see a distinction between real police work—such as investigating crimes—and the bureaucratic "donkey work" of reports and paper trails.

Crime and Community

Preventing crime and reducing fear of crime are both closely related to rebuilding strong communities. As we saw in our earlier discussion of the broken windows theory, one of the most significant discoveries in criminology in recent years has been that the decay of day-to-day civility relates directly to criminality. For a long while attention was focused almost exclusively on serious crime—robbery, assault, and other violent crime. More minor crimes and forms of public disorder, however, tend to have a cumulative effect. When asked to describe their problems, residents of troubled neighborhoods mention abandoned cars, graffiti, prostitution, youth gangs, and similar phenomena.

People act on their anxieties about these issues: They leave the areas in question if they can, or they buy heavy locks for their doors and bars for their windows and abandon public places. Fearful citizens stay off the streets, avoid certain neighborhoods, and curtail their normal activities and associations. As they withdraw physically, they also withdraw from roles of mutual support with fellow citizens, thereby relinquishing the social controls that formerly helped maintain civility within the community.

COMMUNITY POLICING

One popular idea to combat this development is that police should work closely with citizens to improve local community standards and civil behavior, using education, persuasion, and counseling instead of incarceration.

Community policing implies not only involving citizens but also changing the outlook of police forces. A renewed emphasis on crime prevention rather than law enforcement can support the reintegration of policing with the community and reduce the siege mentality that develops when police have little regular contact with ordinary citizens.

To be successful, partnerships among government agencies, the criminal justice system, local associations, and community organizations have to include all economic and ethnic groups (Kelling and Coles 1997). Government and business can act together to repair urban decay. One model is the creation of business improvement districts providing tax breaks for corporations that participate in strategic planning and offer investment in designated areas. Such schemes demand a long-term commitment to social objectives.

Emphasizing these strategies does not mean denying the links among unemployment, poverty, and crime. Rather, when coordinated with community-based approaches to crime prevention, these approaches can contribute directly and indirectly to furthering social justice. Where social order has decayed along with public services, other opportunities, such as new jobs, decline also. Improving the quality of life in a neighborhood by providing job opportunities and public services can lead to a revival of such areas.

SHAMING AS PUNISHMENT

The current emphasis on imprisonment as a means of deterring crime can cripple the social ties within certain communities. In recent years, **shaming**, a form of punishment that maintains the ties of the offender to the community, has grown in popularity as an alternative to incarceration. Some criminologists see the fear of being shamed within one's community as an important deterrent to crime. As a result, the public's formal disapproval could deter crime as effectively as incarceration, without the high costs of building and maintaining prisons.

Criminologist John Braithwaite (1996) has suggested that shaming practices can take two forms: reintegrative shaming and stigmatizing shaming. Stigmatizing shaming is related to labeling theory, discussed earlier, by which a criminal is labeled as a threat to society and is treated as an outcast. The labeling process and society's efforts to marginalize the individual reinforce that person's criminal conduct, perhaps leading to future criminal behavior and higher crime rates. The much different practice of reintegrative shaming works as follows. People central to the criminal's immediate community—such as family members, employers and co-workers, and friends—are brought into court to state their condemnation of the offender's behavior. At the same time, these people must accept responsibility for reintegrating the offender back into the community. The goal is to rebuild the social bonds of the individual to the community as a means of deterring future criminal conduct.

Japan, with one of the lowest crime rates in the world, has successfully implemented this approach. The process is based on a voluntary network of over five hundred thousand local crime prevention associations dedicated to facilitating reintegration into the community and on a criminal justice system that attempts to be lenient for this purpose. As a result, in Japan only 5 percent of convicted individuals serve time in prison, compared to 30 percent in the United States. Reintegrative shaming is already a familiar practice in American social institutions such as the family. When a child misbehaves, the parent may express disapproval and try to make the child feel ashamed of her conduct but at the same time reassure her that she is a loved member of the family.

Could reintegrative shaming succeed in the U.S. criminal justice system? In spite of the beliefs that these tactics are "soft" on crime, that Americans are too individualistic to participate in community-based policing, and that high-crime areas are less community oriented, community networks have successfully worked with the police in preventing crime. These social bonds could also be fostered to increase the power of shame and to reintegrate offenders into local networks of community involvement.

☑ CONCEPT CHECKS

1. How does imprisonment affect the life chances of ex-cons?
2. Why has the U.S. prison population increased steeply over the past three decades?
3. What are the primary tasks that police officers do each day?
4. What are two specific ways that community members can combat local crime?

The Study of Deviant Behavior

- Deviant behavior involves actions that transgress commonly held norms. What is regarded as deviant can shift from time to time and place to place; normal behavior in one cultural setting may be labeled deviant in another.
- *Sanctions,* formal or informal, are applied by society to reinforce social norms. Laws are norms defined and enforced by governments; *crimes* are acts that are not permitted by those laws.
- Biological and psychological theories have claimed that crime and other forms of deviance are genetically determined, but these have been largely discredited. Sociologists argue that conformity and deviance intertwine in different social contexts. Divergences of wealth and power strongly influence opportunities open to different groups of individuals and determine what kinds of activities are regarded as criminal. Criminal activities are learned in the same way as law-abiding ones and in general serve the same needs and values.

Society and Crime: Sociological Theories

- Functionalist theories see crime and deviance as produced by structural tensions and a lack of moral regulation within society. Durkheim's term *anomie* refers to a feeling of anxiety and disorientation that accompanies the breakdown of traditional life in modern society. Robert Merton extended the concept to include the strain felt by individuals whenever norms conflict with social reality. Subcultural explanations draw attention to groups, such as gangs, that reject mainstream values and instead adopt norms celebrating defiance, delinquency, or nonconformity.
- *Interactionist theories* focus on deviance as a socially constructed phenomenon. Sutherland linked crime to *differential association,* the concept that individuals become delinquent through associating with people who are carriers of criminal norms. *Labeling theory,* a strain of interactionist theory that assumes that labeling someone as deviant will reinforce their deviant behavior, starts from the assumption that no act is intrinsically criminal (or normal). Labeling theorists are interested in how some behaviors become defined as deviant and why certain groups, but not others, are labeled as deviant.
- *Conflict theories* analyze crime and deviance in terms of the structure of society, competing interests between social groups, and the preservation of power among elites.
- *Control theories* posit that crime occurs when there are inadequate social or physical controls to deter it. The growth of crime is linked to the increasing opportunities and targets for crime in modern societies. The theory of broken windows suggests a direct connection between the appearance of disorder and actual crime.

Crime and Crime Statistics

- Victimization surveys, like the National Crime Victimization Survey, are one of the main ways that sociologists track crime trends. Crime rates have declined since their peak in the early 1990s, due in part to a strong economy and a declining market for crack cocaine in the mid- and late 1990s.

Victims and Perpetrators of Crime

- Rates of criminality are much lower for women than for men, probably because of socialization differences between men and women, and the greater involvement of men in nondomestic spheres. Unemployment and the crisis of masculinity have been linked to male crime rates. In some types of crimes, women are overwhelmingly the victims. Rape is almost certainly much more common than the official statistics reveal. In a sense all women are victims of rape, since they have to take special precautions for their protection and live in fear of rape. Homosexual men and women experience high levels of criminal victimization and harassment, yet they are often seen as "deserving" of crime rather than as innocent victims because of their marginalized position in society.
- Popular fear about crime often focuses on street crimes that are largely the domain of young, working-class males. Official statistics reveal high rates of offense among young people, yet we should be wary of moral panics about youth crime. Much deviant behavior among youth, such as antisocial behavior and nonconformity, is not criminal.
- *White-collar crime* and *corporate crime* occur in the more affluent sectors of society. The consequences of such crime can be farther-reaching than the petty crimes of the poor, but law enforcement pays less attention to them. *Organized crime* involves institutionalized forms of criminal activity, in which many of the characteristics of orthodox organizations appear but the activities are illegal. *Cybercrime* describes criminal activity carried out with the help of information technology, such as electronic money laundering and Internet fraud.

Crime-Reduction Strategies

- Prisons have developed partly to protect society and partly to reform the criminal. But they do not seem to deter crime, and the degree to which they rehabilitate prisoners to face the outside world without relapsing into criminality is dubious. Alternatives to prison include community-based punishment.

Key Concepts

anomie (p. 179)
community policing (p. 200)

4. Discuss Merton's five possible reactions to tensions produced by anomie. Why is he considered a functionalist?

5. Compare and contrast interactionist and conflict theories of deviance. What theory is most convincing to you?

6. What is broken windows theory and its policy trajectory? What are some critiques of this theory?

7. What are the main sources of data on crime in the United States? What are some methodological issues about the measurement of crime? How are these issues illustrated in the rates of rape in the United States?

8. Compare theories that are used to explain the difference in crime rates among men and women.

9. How do crimes committed by powerful groups complicate theories of crime that link it to impoverished social conditions?

10. What are some current methods of reducing crime? Are they effective? If you were a policy maker in the criminal justice system, what strategies would you employ?

Review Questions

1. How does deviance lead to increased levels of social solidarity according to Èmile Durkheim and Kai Erikson? Give a contemporary example that illustrates these theories.

2. What are sanctions and what are the various forms that they take? Give an example of each type of sanction.

3. How do sociological theories differ from biological and psychological explanations of deviance?

Thinking Sociologically Exercises

1. Summarize several leading theories explaining crime and deviance presented in this chapter: differential association, anomie, labeling, conflict, and control theories. Which theory appeals to you the most? Explain why.

2. Explain how differences in power and social influence can play a significant role in defining and sanctioning deviant behavior.

PART THREE

STRUCTURES OF POWER

Power is an ever-present phenomenon in social life. In all human groups, some individuals have more authority or influence than others, and groups themselves have varying degrees of power. Power and inequality are closely linked. The powerful are able to accumulate valued resources, such as property and wealth; possession of such resources in turn generates more power.

In this part, we explore some of the main systems of power and inequality. Chapter 8 discusses stratification and class structure—the ways in which inequalities are distributed within societies. Chapter 9, on global inequality, examines the ways in which inequalities are distributed across societies. Chapter 10 analyzes the differences and inequalities between men and women and how these inequalities relate to others based on class and race. Chapter 11, on ethnicity and race, examines the tensions between people who are physically or culturally different from one another. Chapter 12 discusses the experience of growing old and analyzes related social problems. Chapter 13 examines the state, political power, and social movements. Governments are specialists in power; they are the source of the directives that influence many of our daily activities. However, they are also the focus of resistance and rebellion, political action that can lead to political and social change.

Learning Objectives

Systems of Stratification

Learn about social stratification and the importance of social background in an individual's chances for material success.

Classes in Western Societies Today

Know the class differences in U.S. society, what influences them, and how they are defined and determined.

Inequality in the United States: A Growing Gap between Rich and Poor

Recognize the ways in which the gap between rich and poor has grown larger.

Social Mobility

Understand the dynamics of social mobility and think about your own mobility chances.

Poverty in the United States

Learn about the conditions of poverty in the United States today, competing explanations for why it exists, and means for combating it.

Social Exclusion

Learn the processes by which people become marginalized in a society and the forms that marginalization takes.

Theories of Stratification in Modern Societies

Know the most influential theories of stratification—including those of Karl Marx, Max Weber, and Erik Olin Wright.

Growing Inequality in the United States

Learn how changes in the American economy have led to growing inequalities since the 1970s.

CHAPTER EIGHT

STRATIFICATION, CLASS, AND INEQUALITY

Kate and Ellen were joking with Robert about having found him a date for the dance. I did not catch the name of the girl they were making fun of, but they told him he could go with that 'big, fat, blond girl.' This inspired Robert to start making jokes about the trouble he would have wrapping his arms around the girl and to laugh about how she would roll over him (Milner 2004)." This high school conversation was recorded as part of a study of teenage behavior by sociologist Murray Milner. He wanted to find out why American teenagers are so status conscious—why it is so important to look good and be popular that high school students spend large amounts of money on clothing and other goods while ruthlessly putting down anyone who in their view doesn't make the grade.

Milner's book—*Freaks, Geeks, and Cool Kids*—is based on interviews with hundreds of college students about their high school experiences as well as observations of a single high school over a three-year period. It addresses questions about behavior that have troubled American teenagers for over half a century:

Why are many teenagers obsessed with who sits with them at lunch, the brand of clothes they wear, what parties they are invited to, the privacy of their bedrooms, who is dating or hooking up with whom, what is the latest popular music? Why have alcohol, drug use, and casual sex become so widespread? . . . Why are teenagers frequently mean and even cruel to one another? Why do girls see one another as more petty and catty than the boys? (Milner 2004)

The answers, Milner argues, have to do with teenage power, or rather the lack of it. Teenagers have little economic or political power. Stuck between childhood and adulthood, they spend most of their days in class, where they have little influence. After school, their parents have the last say (or think they should). Teenagers respond by creating social worlds in which their ability to evaluate one another—usually by standards unlike their parents' or teachers'—gives them a sense of power.

Milner calls such power "status power." Sociologists define **status** as the prestige that goes along with one's social position. Status power derives from the ability to increase one's own prestige, often at the expense of others; it depends largely on one's social location—in this case, in the high school pecking order. Whom you date matters, because the people you hang out with influence your social status. Putting others down keeps the in-crowd a small, exclusive club. Dressing like the in-crowd, or having the latest model cell phone, iPod, or other consumer gadget, is another marker of status. In fact, consumerism in general is a key source of status power. As Milner (2004) notes, "consumerism in high schools is not only about clothes, but also a broader array of expensive items, such as the limousine to go to the prom or the hotel suite that is rented for the all-night party afterward, or where you will fly to for spring break."

Corporations target the high school market with a vengeance. Milner argues that although many high schools fail to fully achieve their educational goals, they certainly teach a "desire to consume"—not through the curriculum, "but through the status concerns and peer groups that intensify during adolescence." This is a key feature of American consumer capitalism: producing lifelong consumers.

Sociologists speak of **social stratification** to describe inequalities among individuals and groups. Stratification relates not only to assets or property, but also to attributes such as gender, age, religious affiliation, and military rank. The three key aspects of social stratification are class, status, and power (Weber 1947). They frequently overlap, but not always. The "rich and famous" often enjoy high status; their wealth may provide them with political influence and direct access to political power. Yet there are exceptions. Drug lords, for example, may be wealthy and powerful, but they usually have low status. In contrast, Mahatma Gandhi chose to live in poverty but enjoyed the highest status and power in India, having led his country to independence from Britain through nonviolent civil disobedience. In this chapter, we focus on stratification in terms of inequalities based on wealth and income, status, and power. In later chapters, we will consider how gender (Chapter 10), race and ethnicity (Chapter 11), and age (Chapter 12) contribute to stratification.

Individuals and groups enjoy unequal access to rewards depending on their position within the stratification scheme. Thus stratification can be defined as **structured inequalities** among different groups of people. Sociologists see these inequalities as built into the system, rather than resulting from individual differences or chance occurrences, such as winning a lottery. We can think of stratification like the geological layering of rock in the earth's surface: Societies consist of "strata" in a hierarchy, with the more favored at the top and the less privileged nearer the bottom.

How do students derive status power from the products they buy and the clothes they wear? Do you know students who increase their prestige at the expense of others?

Systems of Stratification

All socially stratified systems share three characteristics:

1. **The rankings apply to social categories of people who share a common characteristic without necessarily interacting or identifying with each other.** Women may be ranked differently from men, wealthy people differently from the poor. This does not mean that individuals cannot change their rank; however, the category continues to exist even if individuals move out of it and into another category.

2. **People's life experiences and opportunities depend on the ranking of their social category.** Being male or female, black or white, upper class or working class

makes a difference in terms of your life chances—often as big a difference as personal effort or good fortune.

3. **The ranks of different social categories change very slowly over time.** In U.S. society, for example, only in the last quarter century have women begun to achieve equality with men (see Chapter 10) and have significant numbers of African Americans begun to obtain economic and political equality with whites—even though discrimination was outlawed in the 1950s and 1960s (see Chapter 11).

As you saw in Chapter 3, stratified societies have changed throughout history. The earliest human societies, based on hunting and gathering, had very little social stratification—mainly because there wasn't much wealth or other resources to divide up. The development of agriculture produced more wealth and, thus, an increase in stratification. Social stratification in agricultural societies came to resemble a pyramid, with many people at the bottom and a successively smaller number of people toward the top. Today, stratification within advanced industrial societies resembles a teardrop, with many people in the middle and lower-middle ranks (the middle class), a slightly smaller number of people at the bottom, and very few people toward the top.

Before turning to stratification in modern societies, let's review the three basic systems of stratification: slavery, caste, and class.

Slavery

Slavery is an extreme form of inequality in which certain people own other people as property. The legal conditions of slave ownership have varied among societies. Sometimes slaves were deprived of almost all rights, as in the pre–Civil War southern United States; sometimes they were more like servants, as in the ancient Greek city-state of Athens, where they may have occupied positions of great responsibility. Although excluded from political positions and from the military, Athenian slaves were accepted in most other occupations. Some were literate and worked as government administrators; many were trained in craft skills. Even so, not all slaves had such a good fate. The less fortunate slaves spent their days in hard labor.

Because slaves have often resisted their subjection, systems of slave labor have tended to be unstable. High productivity required constant supervision and brutal punishment. Slave-labor systems eventually broke down, partly because of the struggles they provoked and partly because people work more efficiently under positive incentives than under compulsion. Moreover, starting around the eighteenth century, many

A slave family picking cotton in the 1860s near Savannah, Georgia.

people in Europe and America began to see slavery as morally wrong. Today, slavery is illegal in every country, but it still exists in some places and remains a significant human rights violation. People are still taken by force and held against their will—from enslaved brick makers in Pakistan to sex slaves in Thailand and domestic slaves in France (Bales 1999). It is estimated that in 2001 one million women and girls were forced or lured into prostitution and sold in the international sex trafficking business, which is valued at an estimated $7 billion a year (Hughes 2001).

Caste Systems

In a **caste system**, social status is bestowed for life. Everyone's social status is based on personal characteristics—such as perceived race or ethnicity (often based on such physical characteristics as skin color), parental religion, or parental caste—that are considered unchangeable. **Caste societies** are a special type of class society—in which class position is ascribed at birth, rather than achieved through personal accomplishment. They typically occur in agricultural societies that have not developed industrial capitalist economies, such as South Africa before the end of white rule in 1992 or rural India.

Before modern times, caste systems existed throughout the world. In Europe, for example, Jews were frequently forced to live in restricted neighborhoods and barred from intermarrying (and in some instances even interacting) with non-Jews. The term *ghetto* may derive from the Venetian word for "foundry," the site of one of Europe's first official Jewish ghettos, established by the government of Venice in 1516. The term eventually applied to sections of European towns where Jews were legally compelled to live, long before it applied to minority neighborhoods in U.S. cities with their caste-like qualities of racial and ethnic segregation.

In caste systems, intimate contact with members of other castes is strongly discouraged. "Purity" of a caste is maintained by rules of marriage within one's social group as required by custom or law.

CASTE IN INDIA AND SOUTH AFRICA

The few remaining caste systems are being seriously challenged by globalization. Consider the Indian caste system, which reflects Hindu religious beliefs and is more than two thousand years old. Its four major castes are associated with broad occupational groupings: *Brahmins* (scholars and spiritual leaders) on top, followed by *Ksyatriyas* (soldiers and rulers), *Vaisyas* (farmers and merchants), and *Shudras* (laborers and artisans). Beneath the four castes are the "untouchables," or *Dalits* ("oppressed people"), who are to be avoided at all costs. They perform the worst jobs in society such as removing human waste, and they often beg and search in garbage for their food. In traditional areas of

Women from the Dalit caste (formally known as untouchables) earn a living as sewage scavengers in the slums of Ranchi. They are paid between 30 and 100 rupees ($0.65 and $2.20) per house per month for retrieving human waste from residential dry latrines and emptying the buckets into nearby gutters and streams.

India, some members of higher castes still regard physical contact with untouchables to be so contaminating that mere touching requires cleansing rituals. India made it illegal to discriminate on the basis of caste in 1949, but aspects of the caste system remain today, particularly in rural areas.

As India's modern capitalist economy brings people of different castes together, whether in workplaces, airplanes, or restaurants, it is increasingly difficult to maintain the barriers of the caste system. As more of India becomes affected by globalization, its caste system will likely weaken further.

Before its abolition in 1992, the South African caste system, termed *apartheid* (pronounced "a-PART-ide"; Afrikaans for "separateness"), rigidly separated black Africans, Indians, "colored" (people of mixed races), and Asians from whites. In this case, caste was based entirely on race. A small minority of whites controlled all of the country's wealth, owned most of the usable land, ran the principal businesses and industries, and had a monopoly on political power because blacks lacked the right to vote. Blacks—who made up three quarters of the population—were segregated into impoverished *bantustans* ("homelands") and were allowed out only to work for the white minority.

Apartheid, widespread discrimination, and oppression created intense conflict between the white minority and the black, mixed-race, and Asian majority. Decades of struggle against apartheid finally proved successful in the 1990s. The most powerful black organization, the African National Congress (ANC), mobilized a devastating global boycott of South African businesses, forcing South Africa's white leaders to dismantle apartheid, which was abolished by popular vote among South African whites in 1992. In 1994, in the country's first ever multiracial elections, the black majority won control of the government, and Nelson Mandela—the black leader of the ANC, who had spent twenty-seven years imprisoned by the white government—was elected president.

CASTE IN THE UNITED STATES

In the South in the United States before the Civil War, African Americans were members of a lower caste based on race. Most were born as slaves and died as slaves, forbidden to marry across racial lines, and legally treated as the property of their white owners. Although slavery officially ended in 1865, legal segregation of schools, restaurants, and public facilities maintained aspects of the caste system in many southern states for another century. The U.S. Supreme Court, in the *Brown v. Board of Education* decision in 1954, ended legal segregation in public schools, and the Civil Rights Act of 1964 abolished racial discrimination. Yet the unequal treatment of African Americans continues in the form of discrimination and prejudice—for example, not until 2000 did Alabama voters delete a part of the state's constitution that prohibited interracial marriages. Studies show that when equally qualified black and white individuals apply for the same job, whites are much more likely than blacks to be hired (Bendick et al. 1993). Blacks are also more likely than whites to be denied bank loans for mortgages, automobile insurance, or small businesses (*Business Journal* 2000; Hamilton 2000).

Milner's study of high school status systems reveals its caste-like qualities. High school cliques are closed groups based on informal dress codes, dating patterns, and intense peer pressure. Like the Indian caste system, students in the in-group avoid associating with lower-status students—except for purely practical purposes: "the beautiful cheerleader can work with a bright nerd on a class project, [just as] the Brahmin can supervise Untouchables working in the field ... but when work is done, they go their separate ways" (Milner 2004). Group membership often reflects the accidents of birth: High schools are frequently stratified by race and ethnicity as well as by social class. The wealthiest students hang out together, their status being marked by patterns of consumption that other students can only envy: fancy cars, large homes, expensive vacations.

Class

The concept of **class** is important for analyzing stratification in industrialized societies like the United States. A social class is a large group of people who occupy a similar economic position in the wider society. The concept of life chances, introduced by Max Weber, is the best way to understand what class means. Your **life chances** are the opportunities you have for achieving economic prosperity. A person from a humble background, for example, has less chance of ending up wealthy than someone from a more prosperous one. And the best chance an individual has of being wealthy is to start off as wealthy in the first place.

America supposedly is the land of opportunity. Indeed, many people have risen from lowly circumstances to great wealth and power. Yet there are more cases of people who have not, especially women and members of minority groups. The idea of life chances emphasizes that although class is an important influence, it is not completely determining. Class divisions do affect which neighborhoods we live in, what lifestyles we follow, and which sexual or marriage partners we choose (Mare 1991; Massey 1996), yet they don't constrain people for life. A person born into a caste position has no opportunity of escaping from it; the same is not true of class.

Class systems differ from slavery and castes in four main respects:

1. **Class systems are fluid.** Because they are not established by legal or religious provisions, the boundaries between classes are never clear cut. There are no formal restrictions on intermarriage between classes.

2. **Class positions are in some part achieved.** An individual's class is not irrevocably assigned at birth. Social mobility—movement upward and downward in the class structure—is more common than in the other types of stratification systems.

3. **Class is economically based.** Classes depend on inequalities in the possession of material resources. In the other types of stratification systems, noneconomic factors (such as race in the former South African caste system) are most important.

4. **Class systems are large scale and impersonal.** In the other types of stratification systems, inequalities are expressed in personal relationships of duty or obligation—between slave and master, or between lower- and higher-caste individuals. Class systems, by contrast, operate mainly through large-scale, impersonal associations—for instance, through inequalities of pay and working conditions.

WILL CASTE GIVE WAY TO CLASS?

There is some evidence that globalization will hasten the end of legally sanctioned caste systems throughout the world. Most official caste systems have already given way to class-based ones in industrial capitalist societies; South Africa is the most prominent recent example. Modern industrial production requires that people move about freely, work at whatever jobs they are suited or able to do, and change jobs according to economic conditions. The rigid restrictions of caste systems interfere with this freedom. Furthermore, as the world becomes a single economic unit, caste-like relationships become more vulnerable to economic pressures. Nonetheless, elements of caste persist even in advanced industrial societies. For example, some Indian immigrants to the United States seek to arrange traditional marriages for their children along caste lines, and the small number of intermarriages between blacks and whites in the United States suggests the strength of caste barriers.

Contrary to popular belief, moving up in the American class structure is difficult: As we will see later in this chapter, the social class into which one is born has a large effect on where one winds up later. To the extent that inequality and poverty continue to increase, the prospects of improving one's class position will likely diminish even further.

IS INEQUALITY DECLINING IN CLASS-BASED SOCIETIES?

Until recently, the class systems in mature capitalist societies became increasingly open to movement between classes, thereby reducing the level of inequality. In 1955, the Nobel Prize–winning economist Simon Kuznets proposed a hypothesis that has since been called the **Kuznets curve**: a formula showing that inequality increases during the early stages of capitalist development, then declines, and eventually stabilizes at a relatively low level (Figure 8.1). Studies of European countries, the United States, and Canada suggest that inequality peaked in these places before World War II, declined through the 1950s, and remained roughly the same through the 1970s

---

FIGURE 8.1

The Kuznets Curve

The Kuznets curve, named for the Nobel Prize–winning economist who first advanced the idea in 1955, argues that inequality increases during early industrialization, then decreases during later industrialization, eventually stabilizing at low levels. There is some evidence that inequality may increase once again during the transition to postindustrial society.

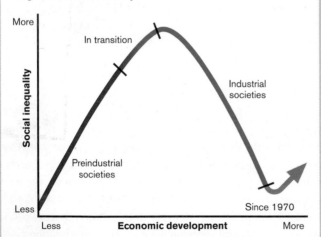

According to the reading, why does the Kuznets curve predict that social inequality will go down as nations transition from preindustrial societies to industrial societies? What actions can individual governments in industrial societies take that would lower the level of social inequality?

SOURCE: Nielsen 1994.

(Berger 1986; Nielsen 1994). Lowered postwar inequality was due in part to economic expansion in industrial societies, which created opportunities for people at the bottom to move up, and in part to government health insurance, welfare, and other programs aimed at reducing inequality. However, Kuznets's prediction may apply only to a particular phase of economic growth in industrial societies. As you will see later in this chapter, as well as in Chapter 14, during the past quarter century or so inequality has actually been increasing in the United States.

☑ CONCEPT CHECKS

1. What are the three shared characteristics of socially stratified systems?
2. What are two examples of caste systems in the world today?
3. How is the concept of class different from that of caste?

Classes in Western Societies Today

Let's begin our exploration of class differences in modern societies by looking at basic divisions of income, wealth, educational attainment, and occupational status within the population as a whole.

Income

Income refers to wages and salaries earned from paid occupations, plus unearned money from investments. One of the most significant changes over the past century has been the rising real income of the majority of the working population. (Real income is income excluding rises owing to inflation, to provide a fixed standard of comparison from year to year.) Blue-collar workers in Western societies now earn three to four times as much in real income as their counterparts in the early 1900s, even if their real income has dropped over the past twenty years. Gains for white-collar, managerial, and professional workers have been higher still. In terms of earnings per person (per capita) and the range of goods and services that can be purchased, the majority of the population today are vastly more affluent than any peoples have previously been in human history. One of the most important reasons for this is increasing productivity—output per worker—through technological development in industry.

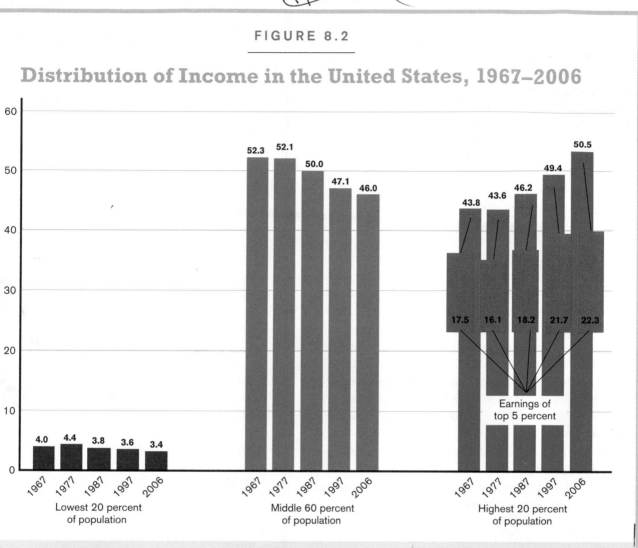

FIGURE 8.2

Distribution of Income in the United States, 1967–2006

Percentage of total U.S. income earned

Lowest 20 percent of population
1967: 4.0
1977: 4.4
1987: 3.8
1997: 3.6
2006: 3.4

Middle 60 percent of population
1967: 52.3
1977: 52.1
1987: 50.0
1997: 47.1
2006: 46.0

Highest 20 percent of population
1967: 43.8
1977: 43.6
1987: 46.2
1997: 49.4
2006: 50.5

Earnings of top 5 percent
1967: 17.5
1977: 16.1
1987: 18.2
1997: 21.7
2006: 22.3

In 2006, the lowest 20 percent of the population earned what percentage of the total U.S. income? Did the percentage of income earned by the middle 60 percent of the population generally increase or decrease from 1967 to 2006? Did the percentage of income earned by the top 5 percent of the income earners increase or decrease from 1967 to 2006? According to the reading, during what year since the government began keeping records did the net worth of Americans as a whole decline? Briefly describe the trend in percentage of total income earned for each category of the population between 1987 and 1997.

SOURCE: U.S. Bureau of the Census 2007b.

Nevertheless, income distribution is unequal. In 2006, the top 5 percent of households in the United States received 22.3 percent of total income; the highest 20 percent obtained 50.5 percent; and the bottom 20 percent received only 3.4 percent (Figure 8.2). Between 1977 and 2006, income inequality increased dramatically. The average household earnings (calculated at 2006 dollars) of the bottom 20 percent of people in the United States rose by almost 15 percent

(U.S. Bureau of the Census 2007b). During the same period, the richest fifth saw their incomes grow by 60 percent, while for the richest 5 percent of the population income rose by more than 85 percent. Despite the growth of the economy and millions of new jobs, these trends continued throughout the 1990s and into the new century, leading some observers to deem the United States a "two-tiered society" (Freeman 1999).

Wealth

Wealth refers to all assets individuals own: cash, savings and checking accounts, investments in stocks, bonds, real estate properties, and so on. Although most people make money from work, the wealthy often derive the bulk of theirs from investments, some of them inherited. Some scholars argue that wealth—not income—is the real indicator of social class.

The best source of information about wealth comes from the national Survey of Consumer Finances, conducted every three years by the Governors of the Federal Reserve Bank. These data show that wealth is highly concentrated in the United States, with enormous differences according to income, age, and education. The wealthiest 10 percent of families in 2004, for example, had a median net worth of $924,100—123 times as much as the poorest 20 percent of families, whose median net worth was only $7,500 (Table 8.1). Also, the median net worth of college graduates is more than eleven times greater than that of high school dropouts. Owning a home makes a great difference, because homes are the principal asset for most families: Homeowners' median net worth is $184,400, compared with only $4,000 for renters. Age matters also: Net worth, like income, increases with age, although it peaks by age sixty-five, after which savings are generally used as income and thus depleted.

Excluding the ownership of cars and homes—which are not really sources of wealth that can be used to pay the bills or to get richer—the difference in wealth between high-income families and everyone else is even more pronounced. Net financial assets are far lower for minority groups than for whites (Oliver and Shapiro 1995). Between 1983 and 2000, the median net financial assets of white Americans nearly tripled, from $19,900 to $67,000 (Table 8.2). Most African Americans began to accumulate net financial assets only in the 1990s; by 2000, the median net worth was $6,166. For Hispanic households, median financial net worth grew from effectively $0 in 1998 to $6,766 in 2000, surpassing that of African American households.

What are some of the reasons for the racial disparity in wealth? Is it simply that blacks have less money to purchase assets? To some degree, the answer is yes. The old adage "It takes money to make money" is a fact of life for those who start with little or no wealth. Because whites historically have enjoyed higher incomes and levels of wealth than blacks, whites can accrue even more wealth, which they pass on to their children (Conley 1999). But family advantages are not the only factors. Melvin Oliver and Thomas Shapiro (1995) argue that it is easier for whites to obtain assets, even when they have fewer resources than blacks, because discrimination affects the racial gap in home ownership. Blacks are rejected for mortgages 60 percent more often than whites, even with the same

qualifications and creditworthiness. When blacks do receive mortgages, they are more likely to take "subprime" mortgage loans that charge more in interest. In 2006, 30.3 percent of blacks took out subprime home loans, compared to 24 percent of Hispanics and 17.7 percent of whites. Research shows that

---

TABLE 8.1

Median Family Net Worth, by Percentile of Family Income, Age, and Housing Tenure, 2004

POPULATION	MEDIAN NET WORTH ($)
All Families	93,100
Percentile of Income	
Less than 20	7,500
20–39.9	34,300
40–59.9	71,600
60–79.9	160,000
80–89.9	311,100
90–100	924,100
Education of Household Head	
No high school diploma	20,600
High school diploma	68,700
Some college	69,300
College degree	226,100
Age of Head (years)	
Less than 35	14,200
35–44	69,400
45–54	144,700
55–64	248,700
65–74	190,100
75 or older	163,100
Housing Status	
Owner	184,400
Renter or other	4,000
Percentile of Net Worth	
Less than 25	1,700
25–49.9	43,600
50–74.9	170,700
75–89.9	506,800
90–100	1,430,100

SOURCE: FRB Survey of Consumer Finances 2006.

[handwritten annotations: "major difference" pointing to income percentile rows; "By Class"]

TABLE 8.2

Median Financial Net Worth ($), 1983–2000: Whites, African Americans, and Latinos

By race (handwritten)

RACE/ETHNICITY	1983	1989	1992	1995	1998	2000
White	19,900	26,900	21,900	19,300	37,600	67,000
African American	0	0	200	200	1,200	6,166
Latino	0	0	0	0	0	6,766

11 times lower (handwritten)

SOURCE: C. Hartman 2000; U.S. Bureau of the Census 2003a; Wolff 2000.

subprime loans are offered by only a few lenders, but those lenders focus on minority communities, whereas the prime lenders are unable or unwilling to lend in those communities (Avery and Canner 2005). These issues are particularly important because home ownership constitutes American families' primary means for accumulating wealth.

In 1998, the bottom 60 percent of Americans accounted for less than 5 percent of the country's total net worth (Wolff 2000). For this group, accumulating stocks or bonds in hopes of cashing them in to pay for their children's college educations is not even a fantasy. In fact, it is more likely that people in this group owe far more than they own. In recent years, as credit has become more available, many Americans have gone increasingly into debt, using credit cards and refinancing their mortgages to pay for their lifestyles rather than relying on their earnings. In 2000, there were 984 million bank-issued Visa and MasterCard credit card and debit card accounts in the United States. Total U.S. consumer debt (which includes installment debt but not mortgage debt) reached $2.46 trillion in June 2007, up from $2.398 trillion at the end of 2006 (creditcards.com). The median amount owed on credit cards was $2,200. Increased debt means less net worth, which for Americans as a whole declined in 2000 for the first time since the government began recording such figures in 1945 (Leonhardt 2001).

College students often live on credit; in 2004, the typical student owed nearly $2,200 on a credit card (Nellie Mae 2005). Seniors have also fallen increasingly into debt; among sixty-five- to sixty-nine-year-olds, for example, credit card debt more than tripled between 1992 and 2001, to an average of nearly $6,000 (SeniorJournal.com 2004).

Wealth is highly unequal globally as well. The world's richest 500 individuals have a combined income greater than that of the poorest 416 million. The poorest 40 percent of the world's population—those living on less than $2 per day—account for only 5 percent of global income, but the richest 10 percent, who all live in high-income countries, account for 54 percent of global income (United Nations 2005). But even the poorest 10 percent of Americans are better off than two thirds of the world population (*The Guardian* 2002). We'll come back to this in Chapter 20.

Differences in wealth often take the form of differences in privilege, which affect life chances as much as income does. Members of Congress, high-level military officers at the Pentagon, and White House staff members do not have gargantuan salaries like the chief executive officers of corporations. What they do have, however, are privileges that translate into wealth. Members of Congress and White House staff members enjoy access to limousines and military aircraft, not to mention expense accounts that pay for many of their meals and hotel bills when they travel.

Education

Education is an important dimension of social stratification. The value of a college education has increased significantly in recent years as a result of the increased demand for and wages paid to educated workers in the computer- and information-based economy (Danziger and Gottschalk 1995). In fact, education is one of the strongest predictors of occupation, income, and wealth later in life. As we will see later in this chapter, how much education one receives is often influenced by the social class of one's parents.

Racial differences in levels of education persist, which partly explains why racial differences in income and wealth also

Income Inequality in the Global Economy

Although many economists, politicians, and businesspeople have sung the praises of globalization, there is reason to approach such claims cautiously. Globalization may well be increasing economic inequality in the world's advanced industrial societies. Even though the U.S. economy has been consistently growing since the end of the recession of 1982–1983, the gap between the wages of high-skilled and low-skilled workers has also been increasing. In 1979, college graduates taking entry-level positions earned on average 37 percent more than those without college degrees. By 2005, the differential had grown to 104 percent (U.S. Bureau of the Census 2007c). Although this growing "wage premium" has encouraged more Americans to go to college—such that nearly 29 percent of the American workforce had college degrees in 2005, compared with 18 percent in 1979 (*Business Week* 1997; U.S. Bureau of the Census 2005c)—it has also helped widen the gap between the wealthiest and the poorest workers.

As an analyst for the U.S. Department of Labor (1997) put it, "it is by now almost a platitude . . . that wage inequality has

persist. In 2006, of those age eighteen and older, 89.7 percent of whites and 87.1 percent of Asian Americans had completed high school, whereas only 80 percent of African Americans had a high school degree (U.S. Bureau of the Census 2007d).

Occupation

Status refers to the prestige of one's social position. In the United States and other industrialized societies, occupation is an important indicator of social standing. In studies in which people rate jobs in terms of how "prestigious" they are, those requiring the most education are ranked most highly (Treiman 1977). Research shows that physicians, college professors, lawyers, and dentists are at the top of the scale, whereas garbage collectors and gas station attendants are at the bottom. At the middle are jobs such as registered nurse, computer programmer, and insurance sales representative. Similar rankings

occur regardless of who does the ranking and in what country (Table 8.3).

Class and Lifestyle

In analyzing class location, sociologists have relied on conventional indicators such as market position, relations to the means of production, and occupation. Some recent authors, however, seek to include cultural factors such as lifestyle and consumption patterns as well. According to this approach, symbols and markers related to *consumption* are playing an ever-greater role in daily life. Individual identities are structured more around *lifestyle choices*—such as how to dress, what to eat, how to care for one's body, and where to relax—and less around traditional class indicators such as employment.

The French sociologist Pierre Bourdieu (1984) sees class groups as identifiable according to their levels of *cultural and* increased quite sharply since the late 1970s, for both men and women."

Although few studies have directly implicated globalization as a cause of this growing inequality, there is reason to view it as an indirect causal factor. It is true that, whereas countries such as the United States, Canada, and the United Kingdom have witnessed a growth in earnings inequality since the late 1970s, countries like Germany, Japan, and France—which have, presumably, been equally affected by the forces of globalization—have seen either a decline or little change in inequality. At the same time, many of the factors that sociologists see as causes of inequality are clearly linked to globalization. First, in some cases, U.S. companies that manufacture in the United States lowered wages to compete with other U.S. firms that manufacture their products overseas, especially in the developing world. Second, globalization has encouraged immigration to the United States. Immigrants—many of whom are relegated to low-wage work—increase the competition for jobs among those in the low-wage labor pool, lowering wages somewhat in this segment of the labor market. Third, globalization has undermined the strength of U.S. labor unions. A number of studies have shown that when firms that used to do the bulk of their manufacturing in one region begin to spread their manufacturing base out across countries and continents, it becomes increasingly difficult for unions to organize workers

and negotiate with management. But strong unions decrease earnings inequality through their commitment to raising wages.

Of course, globalization is not the only cause of inequality. Many researchers, for example, blame increasing inequality on the spectacular growth of high-tech industries, which employ mostly well-paid, white-collar workers and offer little in the way of traditional blue-collar employment. Still, it seems safe to conclude that globalization is not without its role in the growing stratification of American society.

economic capital. Increasingly, individuals distinguish themselves not according to economic or occupational factors but on the basis of cultural tastes and leisure pursuits. Consider the proliferation of "need merchants," people who present and represent goods and services—either symbolic or actual—for consumption. Advertisers, marketers, fashion designers, style consultants, interior designers, personal trainers, therapists, and Web page designers, to name but a few, are all involved in influencing cultural tastes and promoting lifestyle choices.

It would be difficult to dispute that stratification within classes, as well as between classes, now depends not only on occupational differences but also on differences in consumption and lifestyle. The rapid expansion of the service economy and the entertainment and leisure industry, for example, reflects an increasing emphasis on consumption within industrialized countries. Modern societies have become consumer societies, and in some respects a consumer society is a "mass society" where class differences are overridden; thus people

from different class backgrounds may all watch similar television programs or shop for clothing in the same mall stores. Yet class differences can also become *intensified* through variations in lifestyle and "taste" (Bourdieu 1984).

However, we must not ignore the critical role of economic factors in the reproduction of social inequalities. For the most part, individuals experiencing extreme social and material deprivations are not doing so as part of a lifestyle choice. Rather, their circumstances are constrained by factors relating to the economic and occupational structure (Crompton 1998).

A Picture of the U.S. Class Structure

Although money cannot buy everything, one's class position can make an enormous difference in terms of lifestyle. Most

TABLE 8.3

Occupational Prestige in the United States and around the World

OCCUPATION	UNITED STATES	AVERAGE OF 55 COUNTRIES	OCCUPATION	UNITED STATES	AVERAGE OF 55 COUNTRIES
Supreme Court judge	85	82	Professional athlete	51	48
College president	82	86	Social worker	50	56
Physician	82	78	Electrician	49	44
College professor	78	78	Secretary	46	53
Lawyer	75	73	Real estate agent	44	49
Dentist	74	70	Farmer	44	47
Architect	71	72	Carpenter	43	37
Psychologist	71	66	Plumber	41	34
Airline pilot	70	66	Mail carrier	40	33
Electrical engineer	69	65	Jazz musician	37	38
Biologist	68	69	Bricklayer	36	34
Clergy	67	60	Barber	36	30
Sociologist	65	67	Truck driver	31	33
Accountant	65	55	Factory worker	29	29
Banker	63	67	Store sales clerk	27	34
High school teacher	63	64	Bartender	25	23
Registered nurse	62	54	Lives on public aid	25	16
Pharmacist	61	64	Cab driver	22	28
Veterinarian	60	61	Gas station attendant	22	25
Classical musician	59	56	Janitor	22	21
Police officer	59	40	Waiter or waitress	20	23
Actor or actress	55	52	Garbage collector	13	13
Athletic coach	53	50	Street sweeper	11	13
Journalist	52	55	Shoe shiner	9	12

SOURCE: Treiman 1977.

sociologists identify social classes in terms of wealth and income, noting how social class affects consumption, education, health, and access to political power. The following discussion describes broad class differences in the United States. Bear in mind that there are no sharply defined boundaries between the classes.

THE UPPER CLASS

The **upper class** consists of the very wealthiest Americans—those households earning more than $297,405, or approximately 5 percent of all American households (U.S. Bureau of the Census 2007c). Most Americans in the upper class are wealthy but not superrich; only a relatively small proportion are extraordinarily wealthy. They likely own a large suburban home as well as a town house or a vacation home, drive expensive automobiles, fly first class to vacations abroad, educate their children in private schools and colleges, and have a staff of servants. Their wealth stems largely from investments in stocks and bonds and real estate. They are politically influential at the national, state, and local levels. The upper class includes the superwealthy as well—the heads of major corporations, people who have made large amounts of money through investments or real estate, those who inherited great wealth, a few highly successful celebrities and professional athletes, and a handful of others.

At the very top of this group are the superrich, people whose vast fortunes permit them to enjoy a lifestyle unimaginable to most Americans. The superrich are highly self-conscious of their privileged social class position; some give generously to the fine arts, hospitals, and charities. Their common class identity is strengthened by such things as being listed in the social register or having attended the same exclusive private secondary schools (to which they also send their children). They sit on the same corporate boards of directors and belong to the same private clubs. They contribute large sums of money to their favorite politicians and are likely on a first-name basis with members of Congress and perhaps even with the president (Domhoff 1998).

The turn of the twenty-first century saw extraordinary opportunities for the accumulation of such wealth. Globalization is one reason. Entrepreneurs who invest globally often prosper by selling products to foreign consumers and by making profits through low-wage labor in developing countries. The information revolution is another reason for the accumulation of wealth. Before the dot-com bubble burst in 2001, young entrepreneurs with startup high-tech companies such as Yahoo! or eBay made legendary fortunes. As a consequence, the number of superrich Americans has exploded in recent years. In 2006, there were 9.3 *million* millionaire households in the United States (TNS 2007), along with 946 *billionaires* (*Forbes* 2007a). The 400 richest Americans are worth more than $1.25 *trillion*—equal to almost one tenth the gross domestic product of the United States and only slightly less than the gross domestic product of Mexico (*Forbes* 2007a; Sklar 1999). There are billionaires outside the United States as well. The collective net worth of the world's 946 billionaires was $3.5 trillion in 2006 (*Forbes* 2007a), approximately 80 percent of the gross domestic product of India.

Unlike "old-money" families such as the Rockefellers or the Vanderbilts, who accumulated their wealth in earlier generations, the "new wealth" often consists of upstart entrepreneurs such as Microsoft's Bill Gates, whose net worth—estimated by Forbes (2007a) at $56 billion—makes him the wealthiest individual in the world for the thirteenth year in a row.

THE MIDDLE CLASS

The large majority of Americans claim to be middle class, partly because of the cultural belief that the United States is relatively free of class distinctions. Few people want to be considered too rich or too poor. Many blue-collar workers, for example, think of themselves as middle class rather than as

Jerry Yang, co-founder of Yahoo!, was part of the explosion of wealth associated with the dot-com information revolution.

working class (although sociologists classify them as working class). Because people rarely interact with others outside their social class, they regard themselves as like "most other people," whom they consider "middle class" (Kelley and Evans 1995).

The **middle class** is a catchall for a diverse group of occupations, lifestyles, and people who earn stable incomes at primarily white-collar jobs. The middle class grew during most of the twentieth century, then shrank in the last quarter century. During the late 1990s, however, economic growth halted this decline. Currently, the middle class includes slightly more than half of all American households. Although once largely white, today it is racially and culturally diverse, including African Americans, Asian Americans, and Latinos.

The Upper Middle Class The *upper middle class* consists of relatively high-income professionals (for example, doctors, lawyers, engineers, and professors), mid-level corporate managers, people who own or manage small businesses and retail shops, and some large-farm owners. Household incomes range from about $168,170 to perhaps $297,405. The upper middle class includes approximately 20 percent of all American households (U.S. Bureau of the Census 2007e). Its members are likely to be college educated (as are their children) with advanced degrees. Their jobs are secure and provide retirement and health benefits. They own comfortable homes, drive expensive late-model cars, have some savings and investments, and are often active in local politics and civic organizations. However, they tend not to enjoy the same high-end luxuries, social connections, or extravagancies as members of the upper class.

"Number of Millionaires Hits Record"

Many Americans are striving for the elusive goal of becoming a millionaire—at least that's the impression that nightly television would give us. Optimistic contestants flock to game shows like *Who Wants to Be a Millionaire* and *Deal or No Deal* with the hopes of winning a million dollars. In the early 2000s, young women competed to snare wealthy husbands in reality shows like *Joe Millionaire* and *Who Wants to Marry a Multi-Millionaire?* Legitimate news sources also tell us that more Americans than ever before are millionaires: Recent headlines report that "Number of Millionaires Hits New Record" (Brewster 2006) and "Millionaire Households at Record" (Sahadi 2007). Although a small and growing number of Americans have assets that would classify them as "millionaires," the proportion of Americans who are at risk of losing their most valuable asset— their home—is increasing even more rapidly.

Recent studies conducted by private research firms like TNS Financial Services, Spectrem Group, and Merrill Lynch have counted the number of U.S. households that report a net worth of at least a million dollars. Net worth refers to the total value of one's assets, including savings and investments, minus one's liabilities, or what one owes. These calculations do not include one's primary home (that is, where one lives) but do include second homes and investment properties.

Economists agree that the number of millionaire households is higher than ever before, yet they disagree on exactly what the count is. Organizations like TNS use household survey data, and they estimate that there are now 9.3 million millionaire households in the United States. By contrast, Merrill Lynch uses a more complex

Most millionaires do not look like the wealthy couple from *Gilligan's Island*. Who is the typical millionaire today?

economic analysis that considers the total wealth of a county as well as county size and other population characteristics. According to Merrill Lynch estimates, roughly two million households are part of the "millionaire's club."

The survey-based measures tend to be more widely accepted. According to those estimates, the number of millionaire households in the United States reached an all-time high of 9.3 million in 2007, representing a 5 percent increase over the prior year. The average net worth of millionaire households was $2.5 million in 2007. The recent increase in the number of millionaires is a continuation of a trend dating back to 2002. The number of millionaire households has increased every year since then, with the biggest increase occurring in 2004, when the number of high net worth households jumped by 33 percent over 2003. In prior years, however, the number of millionaires dropped from 7.1 million in 1999 to just 5.5 million in 2002, reflecting the Internet bubble burst and the economic fallout after September 11, 2001.

New Jersey now boasts the greatest number of millionaires, although Hawaii was ranked number one in prior years. In 2007, 7.1 percent of New Jersey's 3.2 million households boasted more than $1 million in net worth (Johnson 2008). Although the word *millionaire* conjures up images of young celebutantes with lavish homes, designer wardrobes, and dinners at ritzy restaurants, a glimpse into the characteristics of millionaires offers a less glamorous portrait. Most millionaire householders are older persons. The median age of millionaire householders was fifty-nine. Almost one half were already retired, and another 16 percent were semiretired. Roughly 15 percent had owned their own businesses.

Although the increasing number of millionaire households may lead to the conclusion that more Americans than ever before are rich in assets, the focus on millionaires may draw attention away from the fact that record numbers of Americans are losing their homes because they can't afford the high monthly mortgage payments. According to the Mortgage Bankers Association, more than 2.1 million American home owners had missed at least one mortgage payment in 2007, and the rate of new home foreclosures reached a record high (Nutting 2007). More than 42,000 homes were repossessed in August 2007 alone. Experts say that many working- and middle-class Americans got caught up in the housing boom of the early 2000s, and many were forced to turn to subprime loans to achieve their dream of home ownership (Reuters 2007).

Subprime lending refers to the practice of making loans to borrowers who do not qualify for market interest rates because they have a troubled credit history or because they do not have a high enough income to support the monthly payment on the loan for which they are applying. Anxious home buyers were attracted to subprime loans by their initially low interest rates, but then the interest rate promptly increased drastically—forcing new home owners to pay monthly mortgages that were far higher than they had anticipated. Some social scientists say that the same real estate boom that increased the value of wealthy persons' real estate investments also put homes beyond the comfortable reach of middle-

Over the last two decades Tony Barbagallo has collected around $3.6 million in stock options from companies he has worked for. Despite his good fortune, he is surprised that, like most other Americans, he worries about matters as varied as the soaring cost of health care, the high price of college, and the pressure to save more money for retirement.

class and poorer Americans, with now dire consequences. Blacks, Hispanics, and women are particularly likely to have taken out subprime mortgages, leading some analysts to wonder whether the recent foreclosure crisis will further compromise the economic well-being of these groups in the longer term (Leland 2008)—and permanently thwart their hopes of someday joining the millionaire ranks.

Questions

- Define *net worth*.
- What proportion of American households are considered "millionaire" households today? How is "millionaire household" defined?
- Describe the typical American millionaire.
- What evidence can be used to support the claim that many Americans are at risk of losing their main asset today, their home?

FOR FURTHER EXPLORATION

Brewster, Deborah. 2006. "Number of Millionaires Hits New Records." *Financial Times* (April 19, 2006). www.msnbc.msn.com/id/12393877/ (accessed January 20, 2008).

Christie, Lee. 2005. "Number of Millionaires Hits Record." CNN (May 25, 2005). http://money.cnn.com/2005/05/25/pf/record_millionaires/ (accessed January 20, 2008).

Johnson, Linda. 2008. "NJ Tops U.S. in Number of Millionaires." Associated Press. http://news.yahoo.com/s/ap/20080111/ap_on_re_us/ap_most_millionaires&printer=1;_ylt=At20YW9uHSDRyuFhrCSd40VH2ocA (accessed January 20, 2008).

Leland, John. 2008. "Baltimore Finds Subprime Crisis Snags Women." *New York Times* (January 15, 2008). www.nytimes.com/2008/01/15/us/15mortgage.html?pagewanted=print (accessed January 20, 2008).

Nutting, Rex. 2007. "Foreclosures More than Double in Past Year." *MarketWatch* (September 18, 2007), www.marketwatch.com/news/story/realtytrac-data-show-more-doubling/story.aspx?guid=%7b0181631D-A2E4-4EFD-9372-BAB7A60D1E37%7d&print=true&dist=printTop (accessed January 20, 2008).

Reuters. 2007. "Rate of Home Foreclosures Hits Record." *New York Times* (September 7, 2007). www.nytimes.com/2007/09/07/business/07mortgage.html?sq=record%20foreclosures&scp=4&pagewanted=print (accessed January 20, 2008).

Sahadi, Jeanne. 2007. "Millionaire Households at Record." CNN (April 30, 2007). http://money.cnn.com/2007/04/30/pf/millionaire_counties/index.htm (accessed January 20, 2008).

The Lower Middle Class The *lower middle class* consists of trained office workers (for example, secretaries and bookkeepers), elementary and high school teachers, nurses, salespeople, police officers, firefighters, and others who provide skilled services. Often members of this group enjoy fairly high status; it is their relatively low income that determines their class position. Household incomes in this group, which includes about 40 percent of American households, range from about $48,223 to $76,329 (U.S. Bureau of the Census 2007e). They may own a modest house, although many live in rental units. Their automobiles may be late models, but not the more expensive ones. Almost all have a high school education, and some have college degrees. They want their children to attend college, although this usually requires work-study programs and student loans. They are rarely politically active beyond exercising their right to vote.

THE WORKING CLASS

The **working class**, about 20 percent of all American households, includes primarily blue-collar and pink-collar laborers (for example, factory workers, mechanics, clerical aids, sales clerks, and restaurant and hotel workers). Household incomes range from perhaps $28,777 to $48,223 (U.S. Bureau of the Census 2007e), and at least two household members work to make ends meet. Family income just covers basic living expenses and perhaps a summer vacation. Many blue- and pink-collar jobs are threatened by economic globalization, so members of the working class generally feel insecure about their future.

The working class is racially and ethnically diverse. While older members of the working class may own a home, younger members are likely to rent. The home or apartment is likely in a lower-income suburb or a city neighborhood. The household car, a lower-priced model, is rarely new. Children who graduate from high school are unlikely to go to college and immediately seek work instead. Most members of the working class are not politically active even in their own community, although they may vote.

THE LOWER CLASS

The **lower class**, roughly 15 percent of American households, includes those who work part time or not at all; household income is typically lower than $28,777 (U.S. Bureau of the Census 2007e). Most lower-class individuals live in cities, sometimes working in semiskilled or unskilled manufacturing or service jobs (for example, making clothing in sweatshops or cleaning houses). Their jobs are unlikely to lead to promotion or substantially higher income, and their work does not

provide medical insurance, disability, or Social Security. Even if they find a full-time job, it may not last. Many people in the lower class live in poverty, either renting or being homeless. If they own a car, it is likely to be a used car. A high percentage of the lower class is nonwhite, more so than other social classes. Its members do not participate in politics, and they seldom vote.

THE "UNDERCLASS"

Some sociologists have recently identified a group that is "beneath" the class system in that its members lack access to the world of work and mainstream patterns of behavior. Located in the highest-poverty neighborhoods of the inner city, the **underclass** is sometimes called the "new urban poor."

The underclass includes many African Americans, who have been trapped for more than one generation in a cycle of poverty from which there is little possibility of escape (Wacquant 1993, 1996; Wacquant and Wilson 1993; Wilson 1996). Their numbers grew rapidly over the past quarter century and today include unskilled and unemployed men, young single mothers and their children on welfare, teenagers from welfare-dependent families, and many of the homeless. They live in poor neighborhoods troubled by drugs, teenage gangs, drive-by shootings, and high levels of violence. They are truly disadvantaged people with little hope of ever making it out of poverty.

The emergence of the new urban poor has been attributed to social forces that have converged during the past quarter century (Sawhill 1989; Wacquant 1993, 1996; Wilson 1996). First, economic globalization has led to unemployment among workers lacking education and skills, since many unskilled and semiskilled jobs have moved to low-wage countries. This has led to depressed wages in the remaining unskilled jobs. Because African Americans and recent immigrants from Latin America and parts of Africa and the Caribbean (and to some extent Asia) provide much of the unskilled labor in the United States, they are particularly disadvantaged in today's labor market. Furthermore, racial discrimination has made it difficult for minority groups to compete for the dwindling supply of unskilled jobs.

Second, government assistance programs were cut back sharply during the 1980s under the Reagan and elder Bush administrations, leaving the poor with few resources to get ahead. During the Clinton administration, welfare reforms severely restricted the length of time people could remain on welfare. This approach reduced the number of people on welfare, and the growing economy of the 1990s provided low-wage jobs for many welfare recipients. A sustained economic slowdown, however, could leave a growing number of people both jobless and without welfare benefits.

Some sociologists argue that members of the underclass perpetuate their own inequality because the difficult conditions they face have made them "ill suited to the requirements of the formally rational sector of the economy" (Wacquant 2002). Although these scholars trace such behavior to the social structure, they believe the culture of the underclass has taken on a life of its own, serving as both cause and effect. Such claims have generated considerable controversy. Opponents argue that the urban poor are not simply a "defeated" and disconnected class. Earlier studies of fast-food workers and homeless street vendors have argued that the separations between the urban poor and the rest of society are not as great as scholars of the underclass believe (Duneier 1999; Newman 2000).

✓ CONCEPT CHECKS

1. What are the four components of social class? How do blacks and whites differ along these four components?
2. What are the five major social class groups in the United States today? Describe at least two ways (other than their income) that these five groups differ from one another.
3. What factors have contributed to the growth of the "underclass" over the past quarter century?

Inequality in the United States: A Growing Gap between Rich and Poor

The United States prides itself on being a nation of equals. Indeed, except for the Great Depression of the 1930s, inequality declined throughout much of the twentieth century. But during the past quarter century the rich have gotten much richer, middle-class incomes have stagnated, and the poor have grown in number and are poorer than they have been since the 1960s. The gap between rich and poor is the largest since the Census Bureau started measuring it in 1947 (U.S. Bureau of the Census 2000a) and the largest in the industrial world (Figure 8.3). One statistical analysis found that the United States had the most unequal distribution of household income among all twenty-one industrial countries studied (Sweden had the most equal) (Smeeding 2000).

In 2006, the richest 20 percent of all U.S. households accounted for slightly more than half of all income generated in the United States (Figure 8.2, p. 211). Moreover, their share has steadily increased. Table 8.4 compares the average after-tax income of five groups in 2006 with the income each group would have had if its share of total income had remained the same as in 1974—that is, if inequality had not increased during

---

TABLE 8.4

How Has an Increase in Income Inequality Affected American Households during the Last Thirty-Two Years?

INCOME CATEGORY	ACTUAL 2006 MEAN INCOME ($)[a]	2006 INCOME IF INEQUALITY HAD NOT CHANGED FROM 1974 ($)[b]	DIFFERENCE: HOW MUCH POORER OR RICHER ($)
Lowest fifth	11,352	12,052	−700
Second fifth	28,777	29,954	−1,177
Middle fifth	48,223	48,272	−49
Fourth fifth	76,329	69,717	+6,612
Highest fifth	168,170	123,519	+44,651
Top 5 percent	297,405	187,749	+109,656

SOURCE: (a) U.S. Bureau of the Census 2007e; (b) calculations based on historical inflation rate change of 333.05 percent between January 1974 and December 2006, inflationdata.com/inflation/Inflation_Rate/InflationCalculator.asp (accessed fall 2007).

FIGURE 8.3

Income Inequality in Selected Industrialized Countries: Ratio of Richest 20 Percent to Poorest 20 Percent for 2008

In the 1990s, the richest fifth of all Americans were on average nine times richer than the poorest fifth, one of the highest ratios in the industrialized world. In Japan, at the other extreme, the ratio was about 3.4 to 1.

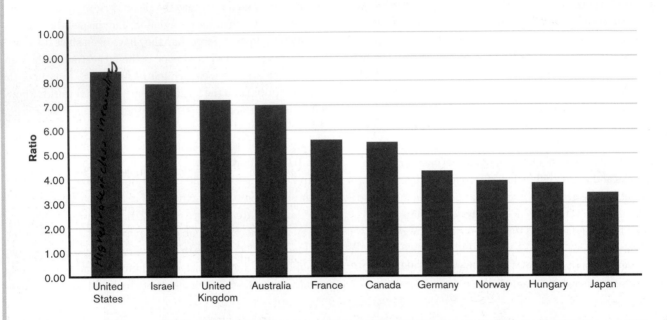

What is the ratio in this figure measuring? In Canada, how many times richer were the richest fifth of the population compared to the poorest fifth of the population? In Japan, the world's second largest economy, how did the ratio of income inequality compare to that of the United States? How much did the average CEO's pay grow between 1990 and 2004 compared to the increase in pay for a production worker? How did the Reagan, Bush, and Clinton administrations exacerbate the problems of the poor?

SOURCE: United Nations 2007a.

---

the twenty-five-year period. Three of the groups were worse off in 2006 than they would have been had inequality not increased. The top 20 percent, on the other hand, was $44,651 richer; the top 5 percent, $109,656 richer.

Corporate Executives versus Their Workers

The earnings gap between top corporate officials and average working Americans has ballooned. According to *Forbes* magazine (2007b), the average pay of the twenty-five best-paid chief executive officers (CEOs) in the United States was $125.14 million in 2007 (calculated from the top twenty-five CEO compensation list published by *Forbes* in 2007). The CEOs of the largest five hundred American corporations earned $7.5 billion in 2007, up 38 percent from 2006.

The average American blue-collar worker made $16.77 an hour in 2006, earning $34,892 for the entire year (U.S. Bureau of Labor Statistics 2007b). William Domhoff (2005) estimates that between 1990 and 2004, CEO pay increased by 300 percent while production worker pay increased by only 4.5

percent. Yet when inflation is taken into account, the purchasing power of the federal minimum wage actually declined by 6 percent in the same period.

The difference between executive and worker compensation is even more pronounced if one considers that U.S. firms rely increasingly on workers in low-income countries. For example, in 2007 H. Lee Scott Jr., the president and CEO of Wal-Mart, took home some $29.7 million in compensation—$1.3 million in salary and $28.4 million in bonuses (including long-term compensation for that financial year) and was awarded stock options worth approximately $2.5 million (*Forbes* 2007c). All of the thousands of factories that make Wal-Mart products are in low-wage countries such as China, where top workers earn $3 a day. The wage gap between Scott's compensation and a Chinese factory worker is in the range of 6,500 to 1 (if stock options are included, the gap widens to 29,304 to 1!).

Minorities versus White Americans

There are substantial differences in income based on race and ethnicity because minorities in the United States generally hold the lowest-paying jobs. Black and Latino household income, for example, averages between two thirds and three quarters that of whites (Figure 8.4). For blacks, this is a slight improvement over previous years, as more blacks have gone to college and found middle-class occupations. For Latinos, however, the situation has worsened, as recent immigrants from rural Mexico and Central America work at low-wage jobs (U.S. Bureau of the Census 2001).

Oliver and Shapiro (1995) found that the "wealth gap" between blacks and whites is even greater than the income gap. While blacks on average earned two thirds that of whites, their net worth was only one tenth as much. More recent data show that the wealth gap has decreased only slightly: In 2004, whites had a median net worth of $140,700, compared with $24,800 for nonwhites or Hispanics (U.S. Bureau of the Census 2007e). Oliver and Shapiro also found that when blacks attained educational or occupational levels comparable to whites, the wealth gap still did not disappear.

Oliver and Shapiro (1995) argue that blacks have encountered barriers to acquiring wealth throughout American history. After the Civil War ended slavery in 1865, legal discrimination (such as mandatory segregation in the South) tied the vast majority of blacks to the lowest rungs of the economic ladder. Even though the Civil Rights Act of 1964 made racial discrimination illegal, it has continued. Although some blacks moved into middle-class occupations, many remained poor or in low-wage jobs with no opportunities for accumulating wealth. Many of those who successfully started businesses found racial barriers to breaking into the more profitable white markets. In effect, many blacks have suffered from a vicious circle: Less wealth means less social and cultural capital (fewer dollars to invest in schooling for one's children, a business, or the stock market)—investments that would create greater wealth for future investments.

Single-Parent Families versus Married-Couple Families

Single-parent families are especially likely to have low incomes. Those headed by men earned only 67.5 percent as much as all married families in 2006, whereas those headed by women earned only 48 percent as much as all married families. Race and ethnicity also play a significant role: Black married-couple families earned 79 percent as much as white married-couple families, while Latino married-couple families earned only 65 percent as much. Finally, nonwhite families headed by single women are the worst off: Black female-headed families earned only about 35.5 percent as much as white married-couple families, while Latino female-headed families earned 39 percent as much as white married-couple families (U.S. Bureau of the Census 2007f).

☑ **CONCEPT CHECKS**

1. What are two pieces of statistical evidence used to support the claim that the gap between the rich and the poor is growing in the United States?
2. How would you explain the wealth gap between blacks and whites in the United States today?

Social Mobility

There are two ways of studying **social mobility**, which refers to the movement of individuals and groups between different class positions as a result of changes in occupation, wealth, or income. First, we can look at people's careers—how far they move up or down the socioeconomic scale during their working lives. This is called **intragenerational mobility**. Second, we can analyze where children are on the scale compared with their parents or grandparents. Mobility across the generations is called **intergenerational mobility**. Sociologists have long studied both types of mobility, but with the exception of

FIGURE 8.4

Black and Latino Household Income Compared to Whites'

Since the mid-1980s, the gap between black and white household income has narrowed, although blacks still earn, on average, only two thirds as much as whites earn. In 1972, the average black income was 57 percent of white income; by 2006, the gap had dropped slightly to 65 percent (the average household income in 2006 was $42,454 for blacks and $68,603 for whites). Latino households are today roughly the same relative to white households as they were in 1972: In that year Latino household income averaged 74 percent, whereas in 2006 they averaged 70 percent (the average household income in 2006 for Latinos was $50,574). While black households experienced steady gains over the period, Latino households experienced a worsening condition relative to white households until the 1990s. The economic growth at that time improved the relative situation of both blacks and Latinos, although some of these gains have been lost since 2000.

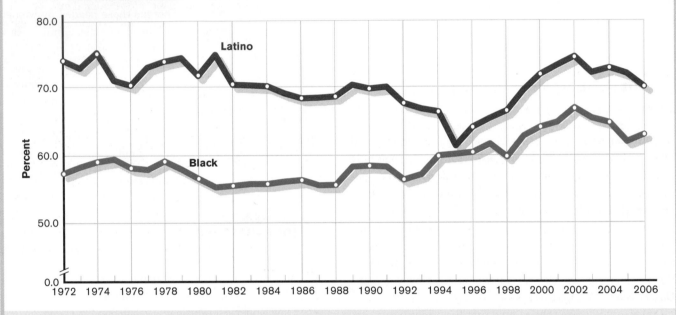

The figure above measures the income of Latinos and blacks compared to what? Between 1972 and 2006, approximately what gain in percentage did blacks achieve toward earning an equal income to that of whites? In 2000, how did the median net worth of whites compare to that of blacks and Latinos? From 1995 to 2006, how did the Latino change in income compare to that of blacks? During what year did blacks' income clearly rise above 60 percent of whites' income?

SOURCE: U.S. Bureau of the Census 2007e.

some recent studies, much of this research has addressed male mobility—particularly that of white males. We shall look at some of this research in the sections to follow.

Another important distinction is between structural mobility and exchange mobility. In a hypothetical society with complete equality of opportunity—in which each person has the same chance of success as everyone else—there would be a great deal of downward as well as upward mobility. This is **exchange mobility**: an exchange of positions, such that more talented people in each generation move up the economic hierarchy, while the less talented move down.

In practice, no society approaches full equality of opportunity. Most mobility, whether intragenerational or intergenerational, is **structural mobility**—upward mobility made possible by an expansion of better-paid occupations at the expense of poorly paid ones. Most mobility in the United States since World War II has depended on continually increasing prosperity. Levels of downward mobility, therefore, have been historically low.

Intergenerational Mobility

Much of the research on intergenerational mobility has been motivated by the **industrialism hypothesis**, which says that societies become more open to movement between classes as they become more technologically advanced (Kerr et al. 1960). As societies become more industrial, workers increasingly get jobs because of *achievement* or skill rather than because of **ascription**, which refers to placement in a particular social status based on characteristics such as family, race, and gender.

Some evidence supports the industrialism hypothesis. A review of mobility patterns in thirty-five countries finds a gradual increase in openness over time within all of the countries (Ganzeboom et al. 1989). However, much research contradicts the industrialism hypothesis. The earliest study of comparative mobility, by Pitirim Sorokin (1927), analyzed a range of societies, from traditional Rome and China to the United States. Sorokin concluded that opportunities for rapid ascent in the United States were more limited than American folklore suggested. The techniques he used to gather his data, however, were relatively primitive. Another classical study of social mobility, carried out by Seymour Lipset and Reinhard Bendix (1959), drew on data from Britain, France, West Germany, Sweden, Switzerland, Japan, Denmark, Italy, and the United States to examine the mobility of men from blue-collar to white-collar work. They also found no evidence that the United States was more open to social mobility than the European societies. They concluded that all of the countries were experiencing an expansion of white-collar jobs, which led to an "upward surge of mobility." More recently, Robert Erikson and John Goldthorpe (1992) compared twelve European and three non-European industrialized nations. They found that most countries had similar patterns of intergenerational mobility. However, they also discovered significant variations: Sweden, for example, was considerably more open to social mobility than the other Western countries. In contrast to the industrialism hypothesis, societies did not become more open to movement between classes over time.

There are also big differences within societies—for example, differences in mobility between racial and ethnic groups (Featherman and Hauser 1978). The obvious comparison in the United States is between African Americans and whites. The black middle class is much smaller than the white middle class relative to the proportions of blacks and whites in the population as a whole. Someone born in a black inner-city ghetto has only a fraction of the chance of a person from a white background of obtaining a white-collar or professional job.

Most research on intergenerational mobility has found that children of parents in low-status or high-status occupations are likely to work at occupations with similar status. Children of parents with middle-status occupations, such as crafts or service, are relatively more mobile (Featherman and Hauser 1978; Grusky and Hauser 1984).

Intragenerational Mobility

Less research has focused on intragenerational mobility. The work finds that earnings, status, and satisfaction increase most dramatically when workers are in their twenties, with more subtle increases later on (Spilerman 1977). Workers tend to be promoted twice: first by the time they are thirty-four and then again between their mid-thirties and early fifties (DiPrete and Soule 1988; Lashbrook 1996; Rosenbaum 1979).

Women are more likely to continue changing jobs after the early part of their careers than are men (DiPrete and Nonnemaker 1997). In addition, women workers have been affected by a decline in occupational gender segregation and increased labor force participation. This means that women are more likely now than they were in the 1950s to hold the same jobs as men (Goldin 1990). And many more women are working today than in the 1950s (Quinn and Burkhauser 1994; Siegel 1993).

Former president George W. Bush shares a joke with his brother Jeb, former governor of Florida, and his father, former president George H. W. Bush. How would Bourdieu explain the vertical mobility of the Bush family?

Bridging the Gap: Sociology and the *New York Times*

On Sunday morning of Labor Day weekend 2005, nearly two million copies of the *New York Times* were delivered to doorsteps around the country. Hurricane Katrina had on August 31 inflicted catastrophic damage on the central Gulf Coast, most notably by causing extensive flooding in New Orleans, Louisiana, and reporters like Jason DeParle (2005) were just beginning to make sense of the tragedy:

> What a shocked world saw exposed in New Orleans last week wasn't just a broken levee. It was a cleavage of race and class, at once familiar and startlingly new, laid bare in a setting where they suddenly amounted to matters of life and death. Hydrology joined sociology throughout the story line, from the settling of the flood-prone city, where well-to-do white people lived on the high ground, to its frantic abandonment. No one was immune, of course. With 80 percent of the city under water, tragedy swallowed the privilege [*sic*] and poor, and traveled spread [*sic*] across racial lines. But the divides in the city were evident in things as simple as access to a car. The 35 percent of black households that didn't have one, compared with just 15 percent among whites [*sic*].

On the same day, reporters were also grappling with inequality closer to home. With race and class debates already

Andrew Beveridge

stirred into a frenzy by the hurricane, Sam Roberts (2005) broke news of rising inequality in Manhattan, home to the *New York Times* headquarters and over 1.6 million of the richest and poorest residents in America living side by side:

> Trump Tower on Fifth Avenue is only about 60 blocks from the Wagner Houses in East Harlem, but they might as well be light years apart. They epitomize the highest- and lowest-earning census tracts in Manhattan, where the disparity between rich and poor is now greater than

Opportunities for Mobility: Who Gets Ahead?

Many people in modern societies believe anyone can reach the top through hard work and persistence. Why should it be difficult to do so? Sociologists have sought to understand which social factors are most influential in determining an individual's status in society.

In a classic study of social mobility in the United States, the sociologists Peter Blau and Otis Dudley Duncan (1967) surveyed over twenty thousand men in order to assess intergenerational mobility. Blau and Duncan concluded that most

vertical mobility, or movement along the socioeconomic scale, was between occupational positions close to one another. Long-range mobility—that is, from working class to upper-middle class—was rare. Why? By assessing the effect of social background in determining ultimate social status, Blau and Duncan concluded that the key factor behind status was educational attainment. But a child's education is influenced by the family's social status; this, in turn, affects the child's social position later in life. The sociologists William Sewell and Robert Hauser (1980) later confirmed Blau and Duncan's conclusions. They added that the connection between family background and educational attainment occurs because parents, teachers, in any other county in the country. That finding, in an analysis conducted for the *New York Times,* dovetails with other new regional economic research.... The top fifth of earners in Manhattan now make 52 times what the lowest fifth make—$365,826 compared with $7,047—which is roughly comparable to the income disparity in Namibia.... Put another way, for every dollar made by households in the top fifth of Manhattan earners, households in the bottom fifth made about 2 cents.

Much of what we read in newspapers consists of statistics—that 35 percent of black households in New Orleans didn't have a car compared to just 15 percent of white households, that the top 20 percent of incomes in New York City average $365,826 compared to only $7,047 for the bottom fifth. These statistics reveal important patterns about race and class in America and help us understand how power is concentrated in our society. But where do these statistics come from? Is there somewhere that reporters like DeParle and Roberts can go to find reliable statistics about class and inequality in America?

For the past thirteen years, they have gone to Andrew Beveridge, a professor of sociology at Queens College in New York City. Beveridge has a formal partnership with the *New York Times* to answer these questions and back them up with data. This partnership is a unique example of how a sociologist can help provide information to the public while framing that information in a sociological way. For example, in the days before and after Katrina hit the Gulf Coast, millions of viewers around the country watched local residents pack the roadways in an effort to escape the storm. Many suspected that those trapped behind lacked access to a car, but who knew for sure? Reporters and news anchors were scrambling to find out the real story. For the answer, they contacted Beveridge. On very short notice, he conducted and delivered a demographic analysis of the New Orleans area using U.S. census data on car ownership.

Within hours he had produced the first solid statistics on the issue and helped work with reporters to craft stories that explained to general readers how class inequality may have been what drove some to escape and others to drown.

Harlem lies 1,315 miles northeast of New Orleans on the island of Manhattan and houses many of New York's poorest residents living within walking distance of mansions (such as the Duke-Semans townhouse) which sell for up to $50 million. Manhattan is known to attract some of the most talented and driven professionals from around the world, so it is not surprising that levels of inequality exist in New York City. What is surprising is that those levels have increased dramatically over the past few decades. When Beveridge brought this to the attention of editors at the *Times,* they assigned reporters to the story immediately. Again using census data for his analysis, Beveridge showed that as of 2000, the top fifth of earners made fifty-two times what the lowest fifth make in Manhattan. Ten years earlier, in 1990, the number for the top fifth was thirty-two times greater than the bottom fifth. In 1980, the difference was a factor of only twenty-one. Since the 1980s, "the gains are all going to the top," Beveridge said. "It's a massive class disparity" (Roberts 2005).

Beveridge uses his role as a public sociologist to help the general public understand tough issues like class in America. Americans can (and often do) change their class positions over time, which makes class a difficult thing to understand. For example, although we know that money matters in America, it's hard to draw lines that separate one class from another. This has led many academics to conclude that class distinctions do not exist in the United States like they do in other places. Beveridge has no patience for these dismissals. "People can talk about class all they want, but it's not until you see Katrina and these Manhattan statistics that you start to really understand what it's like to be left behind in America." Far from diminishing, "class has actually become more and more important" over the past three decades.

and friends influence the educational and career aspirations of the child and that these aspirations influence the status attainment process throughout the child's life. Sewell and Hauser sought to prove that social status was influenced by a pattern of related social influences going back to one's birth: Family background affects the child's aspirations, which affect the child's educational attainment, which affects the adult's later occupational prestige, and so on.

The French sociologist Pierre Bourdieu (1984, 1988) has emphasized the cultural advantages that parents can provide to their children. He argues that most important is the transmission of cultural capital. Just as those who own economic

capital often pass much of it on to their children, the same is true of the cultural advantages of coming from a "good home." These advantages stem partly from having greater economic capital, which succeeding generations inherit, thus perpetuating inequalities. As we have seen, wealthier families send their children to better schools, an economic advantage that benefits the children's social status as adults. In addition to this material advantage, most parents from the upper and middle classes are highly educated themselves and are more involved in their children's education—reading to them, helping with homework, purchasing books and learning materials, and encouraging their progress. Bourdieu notes that working-class parents are concerned about their children's education but lack the economic and cultural capital to make a difference. Bourdieu's study found that a majority of office professionals with high levels of educational attainment and income were from families of the "dominant class" in France. Likewise, office clerical workers often originated from the working classes.

The socioeconomic order in the United States is similar. The wealthy and powerful have many chances to pass along their advantages to their offspring. Studies of people who have become wealthy show that the majority did so on the basis of inheriting or being given at least a modest amount initially—which they then used to make more. In American society, it's better to start at the top than at the bottom (Duncan et al. 1998; Jaher 1973; Rubinstein 1986).

Your Own Mobility Chances

Sometime in the next four years, you will graduate from college and face the prospect of starting a new career. Do you have any idea what you will do? If you are like most of your classmates, you have no idea. Perhaps you will start your own business, or perhaps you will work your way up the hierarchy of an organization in a formal career. What implications can you draw from mobility studies? Managerial and professional jobs may continue to expand relative to lower-level positions. Those who have earned a college degree are most likely to fill these openings and make a high income. Indeed, 60 percent of Americans in the top fifth of income earners graduated from college, whereas in the bottom fifth, just 6 percent hold a college degree (Cox and Alm 1999). Educational attainment seems to be the key variable for upward mobility in the United States (Hout 1988).

Research indicates, however, that the effect of education on mobility chances has decreased somewhat (Hout 1988; Hout and Lucas 1996). Because you are a college student, chances are that one or both of your parents are college educated and middle class or above. Even if you earn a good income, you might not enjoy upward mobility. In addition, as a result of global economic competition, not nearly enough well-paid positions are open for all who wish to enter them. Even if a higher proportion of jobs are created at managerial and professional levels, the overall number of jobs available in the future may not keep pace with the number of people with college degrees seeking work. Reasons include the growing number of women entering the workforce and the increasing use of information technology in production processes. Because computerized machinery can now handle tasks—even highly complicated ones—that only humans could do before, many jobs may be eliminated.

If you are a woman, although your chances of entering a good career are improving, you face certain obstacles. Male managers and employers still discriminate against female applicants, partly because they believe that women are not really interested in careers and are likely to leave the workforce to begin families. The latter factor substantially affects opportunities for women, who often must choose between a career and having children because men are rarely willing to share equal responsibility for domestic work and child care.

Downward Mobility

Although downward mobility is less common than upward mobility, about 20 percent of men in the United States are downwardly mobile intergenerationally. Most of this movement is short range, involving movement from one job to another that is similar—for example, from a routine office job to semiskilled blue-collar work. Downward intragenerational mobility is often associated with psychological problems and anxieties, as some people cannot sustain the lifestyle into which they were born. Another source of downward mobility involves company mergers or takeovers. During the late 1980s and 1990s, many middle-aged male executives in corporate America lost their jobs and either could not find new ones or found only lower-paying jobs.

Many of the intragenerational downwardly mobile are women, who often abandon promising careers to raise children. Such women often return to the paid workforce at a level lower than when they left—for instance, in poorly paid, part-time work. (This situation is changing, although not as fast as might be hoped.)

Unemployed executives and management personnel meet at the Pikes Peak Workforce Center in Colorado Springs, Colorado. According to sociologists, who is most susceptible to downward mobility?

Downward mobility is particularly common among divorced or separated women with children. Consider the life of Sandra Bolton, described by John Schwarz and Thomas Volgy in *The Forgotten Americans* (1992). Sandra's fate belies the idea that people who work hard and follow the rules will prosper. Her husband regularly assaulted her during the six years of their marriage, and child welfare officials considered him a threat to their two children. She divorced her husband after the Child Protective Services told her that the state would take her children if she didn't leave him.

Sandra receives no maintenance from her ex-husband, who, two weeks before the divorce was finalized, piled their furniture and valuables into a truck and drove away, not to be seen again. Whereas while married she sustained a moderately comfortable, middle-class way of life, Sandra now lives a hand-to-mouth existence. She tried to remain in college, supporting herself and her children by doing menial jobs, but was unable to earn enough money to keep up.

A neighbor looked after her children while she took a full-time job as a secretary. Taking courses at night and during the summers, she eventually completed a college degree. Although she applied at many places, she couldn't find a position paying more than her secretarial job. She took on a second job, as a checkout person in a supermarket, in the evenings just to make ends meet. "You try to do the responsible thing," she said, "and you're penalized, because the system we have right now doesn't provide you with a way to make it" (Schwarz and Volgy 1992). As a result of her divorce, Sandra sank from a life of some comfort to living in poverty. She is not alone.

Gender and Social Mobility

Although much research into social mobility has focused on men, more attention is now focusing on women. At a time when girls are outperforming boys in school and females are outnumbering males in higher education, it is tempting to conclude that long-standing gender inequalities in society may be relaxing their hold. Has the occupational structure become more open to women, or are their mobility chances still guided by family and social background?

One study traced the lives of nine thousand people born during the same week in 1970 (Bynner et al. 1997). The most recent survey of the respondents, at age twenty-six, found that for both men and women family background and class of origin remain powerful influences. The study concluded that those who were coping best with the transition to adulthood had obtained a better education, postponed children and marriage, and had fathers in professional occupations. Individuals from disadvantaged backgrounds were more likely to remain there.

The study found that, on the whole, women today have much greater opportunity than did their counterparts in the previous generation. Middle-class women have benefited the most, being just as likely as their male peers to attend college and to find well-paid jobs. This trend was also reflected in women's heightened confidence and sense of self-esteem, compared with a similar cohort of women born just twelve years earlier.

☑ CONCEPT CHECKS

1. Contrast intragenerational and intergenerational mobility.
2. According to classic studies of mobility in the United States, how does family background affect one's social class in adulthood?
3. According to Pierre Bourdieu, how does the family contribute to the transmission of social class from generation to generation?
4. Describe at least three reasons for downward mobility.

Poverty in the United States

At the bottom of the class system in the United States are the millions of impoverished people. Many do not maintain a proper diet and live in miserable conditions; their average life expectancy is lower than that of the majority of the population. In addition, the number of homeless has greatly increased over the past twenty years.

Definitions of poverty distinguish between absolute and relative poverty. **Absolute poverty** means that a person or family can't get enough to eat; they are undernourished and, in situations of famine, may actually starve to death. Absolute poverty is common in the poorer developing countries.

In the industrial countries, **relative poverty** is a measure of inequality. It means being poor compared with the standards of living of the majority. It is reasonable to call a person poor in the United States if he or she lacks the resources to maintain a decent standard of housing and healthy living conditions.

Measuring Poverty

When President Lyndon B. Johnson began his War on Poverty in 1964, around thirty-six million Americans lived in poverty. Within a decade, the number had dropped to around twenty-three million (Figure 8.5 shows changes in poverty rates since

FIGURE 8.5

Percentage of Americans Living in Poverty, 1959–2004

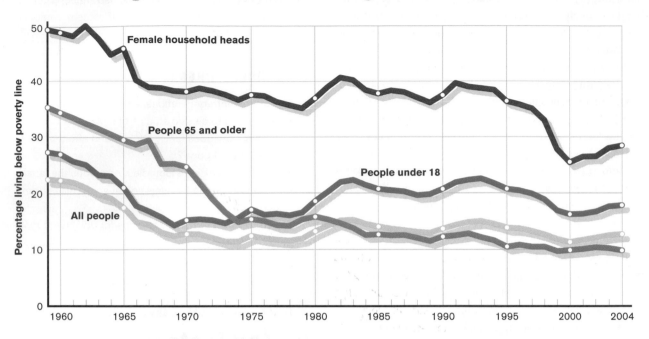

What is the percentage of female household heads living below the poverty line in 1960? Which ten-year period saw the most drastic decrease in poverty for people sixty-five and older? During the 1980s, what was the overall trend for the percentage of children living in poverty? How does the percentage of all people living below the poverty line in the United States in 2004 compare to the percentage in 1970? According to the reading, how does the U.S. government calculate the poverty line?

SOURCE: DeNavas-Walt et al. 2005; U.S. Bureau of the Census 2005e.

1959). But beginning in the early 1970s, poverty again began to climb, peaking in 1993 at thirty-nine million people. Since that time, the number of poor has dropped but is on the increase again. In 2003, the number of people living in poverty stood at thirty-seven million, roughly 12.7 percent of the population (DeNavas-Walt et al. 2005). Yet even this level of poverty greatly exceeds that of most other advanced industrial nations. In the mid-1990s, for example, when the U.S. poverty rate was around 14 percent, France's was 10 percent; Canada's and Germany's, 7 percent (Smeeding et al. 2000).

What does it mean to be poor in the world's richest nation? The U.S. government calculates the **poverty line** as an income equal to three times the cost of a nutritionally adequate diet—a no-frills budget that assumes a nutritionally adequate diet could be purchased in 1999 for only $3.86 per day for each member, along with about $7.72 on all other items (including rent and utilities, clothing, medical expenses, and transportation). For a family of four in 2007, that works out to an annual cash income of $20,650 (*Federal Register* 2007).

How realistic is this formula? Some critics believe it overestimates the amount of poverty, claiming that it overlooks noncash forms of income such as food stamps, Medicare, Medicaid, and public housing subsidies as well as cash obtained from work at odd jobs that is concealed from the government. For example, one study on the poorest tenth of all families with children compared government survey data on their reported income with comparable data on their reported expenditures (as cited in Whitman 1994). These families actually spent twice as much, on average, as the income they reported to the government.

Other critics argue that the government's formula greatly underestimates the amount of poverty. They argue that to label a three-person family as "nonpoor" in 2007 because it earned more than $17,170 ($47 a day) is simply unrealistic. Some scholars point out that such figures are based on an assumption from a half century ago that an "average" family spends a third of its income on food, even though more recent studies show that the actual figure is closer to one sixth, and that as much as three quarters of a poor family's income may go to rent alone (Dolbeare 1995; Joint Center for Housing Studies 1994; Schwarz and Volgy 1992; Stone 1993). By this reasoning, food expenditures should be multiplied by at least 6, rather than 3, to yield the poverty level. Patricia Ruggles (1990, 1992), an adviser to the University of Wisconsin's Institute for Research on Poverty, estimates that this formula would double the official number of Americans living in poverty.

The official U.S. poverty rate is the highest among the major advanced industrial nations, more than three times that of Sweden or Norway (Smeeding et al. 2000). The largest concentrations of poverty in the United States are in the South and the Southwest, in central cities, and in rural areas. Among the poor, 15.6 million Americans (or 5.4 percent of the country) live in extreme poverty: Their incomes are only *half* of the official poverty level, meaning that they live at near-starvation levels (DeNavas-Walt et al. 2005).

Who Are the Poor?

Most Americans of all social classes think of the poor as people who are unemployed or on welfare. Americans also express more negative attitudes toward welfare provisions and benefits than people in other Western countries do. Surveys repeatedly show that most Americans regard the poor as being responsible for their own poverty and do not support "government handouts." For example, a Gallup poll found that 55 percent of the public believed that lack of effort by the poor was the principal reason for poverty. Nearly two thirds believed that government assistance programs reduced incentives to work. A survey by National Public Radio in 2001 found similar results but discovered that attitudes blaming the poor for lack of motivation were even stronger among respondents who lived just above the poverty line. These views, however, are out of line with the realities of poverty: The poor are as diverse as other groups.

WORKING POOR

The **working poor** are those whose earnings are not high enough to lift them above poverty. The federal minimum wage, the legal floor for wages in the United States, was first set in 1938 at $0.25 an hour. Individual states can set higher minimum wages than the federal standard, and fifteen have done so. Although the federal minimum wage has increased over the years, since 1965 it has failed to keep up with inflation (Figure 8.6). As a result, as of 2008, the U.S. minimum wage of $5.85

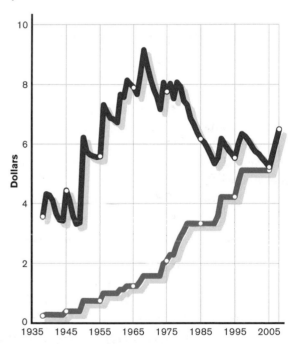

FIGURE 8.6

Changes in the Federal Minimum Wage, 1938–2008

The red line shows the federal minimum wage in each year, in "current" dollars—that is, dollars that are unadjusted for inflation. The blue line shows the same wage in "constant" 2007 dollars, thereby controlling for inflation.

What is the difference between the blue line and the red line? When did the minimum wage have the most value (based on its value adjusted for inflation)? Has the value of the minimum wage increased or decreased since the 1990s? Can a family earning minimum wage live above the poverty level? Why or why not?

SOURCE: U.S. Department of Labor 2007.

What does Katherine Newman's research reveal about the working poor? What obstacles do they have to overcome to make ends meet?

an hour resulted in a yearly income of only $11,700 for full-time workers—barely three quarters of poverty-level income ($17,170) for a single parent supporting two children (*Federal Register* 2007). About one third of those officially living in poverty are actually working. Most poor people don't receive welfare payments, because they earn too much to qualify. Only 5 percent of all low-income families with a full-time, full-year worker receive welfare benefits, and over half rely on public health insurance rather than employer-sponsored insurance. The working poor are disproportionately nonwhite and immigrant (Urban Institute 2005).

Katherine Newman (2000) spent two years documenting the lives of three hundred low-wage workers and job seekers at fast-food restaurants in Harlem, a predominantly African American section of New York City. The people she interviewed were hard workers who valued their jobs despite the low status associated with "slinging burgers." Moreover, Newman found that the working poor had to overcome enormous obstacles simply to survive: They lacked adequate educations, and some attended school while working; they had no health insurance; and many were supporting families on poverty-level wages.

POVERTY, RACE, AND ETHNICITY

The nation's official poverty rate declined for the first time this decade, from 12.6 percent in 2005 to 12.3 percent in 2006 (U.S. Census Bureau News 2007). However, poverty rates are much higher among most minority groups, even though more than two thirds of the poor are white. As Table 8.5 shows, blacks and Latinos earn around two thirds of what whites earn in the United States while experiencing three times the poverty rate of whites. This is because they often work at the lowest-paying jobs and because of racial discrimination. Asian Americans have the highest income of any group, but their poverty rate is almost one and a half times that of whites, reflecting the recent influx of relatively poor immigrant groups.

Latinos have somewhat higher incomes than blacks, although their poverty rate is comparable. Nonetheless, the number of blacks living in poverty has declined in recent years. In 1959, 55.1 percent of blacks were living in poverty; by 2006, that figure had dropped to 24.3 percent. A similar pattern holds for Latinos: Poverty grew steadily between 1972 and 1994, peaking at 30.7 percent of the Latino population. By 2006, however, the poverty rate for Latinos had fallen to 20.6 percent (U.S. Census Bureau News 2007).

TABLE 8.5

Median Income and Poverty Rates for Households in 2006, by Race and Ethnicity

	WHITE	ASIAN AMERICAN	LATINO	BLACK	TOTAL U.S.
Median income ($)[a]	52,423	64,238	37,781	31,969	48,201
Percentage of median income of whites	100.0	122.5	72.1	61.0	91.9
Poverty rate (%)[b]	8.0	10.3	20.6	24.3	12.3

SOURCE: (a) U.S. Bureau of the Census 2007g; (b) DeNavas-Walt et al. 2005.

Much of the growth in poverty reflects an increase in the proportion of the poor who are female. Growing rates of divorce, separation, and single-parent families have placed women at a particular disadvantage because it is extremely difficult for unskilled or semiskilled, low-income, poorly educated women to raise children by themselves while also holding down a job that could lift them out of poverty. As a result, in 2007, 28.3 percent of all single-parent families headed by women were poor, compared to only 4.9 percent of married couples with children (U.S. Bureau of the Census 2007g).

The **feminization of poverty** is particularly acute among families headed by Latino women (Table 8.6). Although the rate declined by almost 30 percent since its peak in the mid-1980s (64 percent in 1985), 42.5 percent of all female-headed Latino families lived in poverty in 2006. An almost identical percentage (43.6 percent) of female-headed African American families also lived in poverty; both percentages are considerably higher than those for either white (30.2 percent) or Asian (24.1 percent) female-headed households (U.S. Bureau of the Census 2007g).

A single woman raising children alone faces a vicious circle of hardship and poverty. If she finds a job, someone must take care of her children because she cannot afford a baby-sitter or day care. She will actually take in more money if she accepts welfare and seeks illegal part-time jobs that pay cash rather than a regular full-time job paying minimum wage. Even though welfare will not get her out of poverty, with a regular job she would lose her welfare altogether. As a result, she and her family may even be worse off economically.

CHILDREN IN POVERTY

Children are the principal victims of poverty in the United States, where child poverty rates (defined as poverty among people under eighteen) are the highest in the industrial world. The child poverty rate declines when the economy expands or the government increases spending on antipoverty programs, and it rises when the economy slows and government antipoverty spending falls. The child poverty rate declined from 27.3 percent of all children in 1959 to 14.4 percent in 1973—a period of economic growth and the War on Poverty declared by the Johnson administration (1963–1969). During the late 1970s and 1980s, as economic growth slowed and cutbacks occurred in government antipoverty programs, child poverty grew. The economic expansion of the 1990s saw a drop in child poverty, and in 2002 the rate had fallen to 16.3 percent (U.S. Bureau of the Census 2003d). Yet, today child poverty rates are again increasing, reaching 17.8 percent in 2004 (DeNavas-Walt et

TABLE 8.6

Families with Children: Percentage in Poverty, by Race and Ethnicity, Marital Status, and Sex of Head of Household, 2006

	MARRIED COUPLE	MALE HEAD	FEMALE HEAD
White	3.7	13.6	30.2
Black	9.2	26.0	43.6
Latino	15.6	22.8	42.5
Asian	7.2	15.4[a]	24.1

[a]Figure from 2005.

SOURCE: U.S. Bureau of the Census 2007h.

al. 2005) and falling only slightly to 17.4 percent by 2006 (U.S. Bureau of the Census 2007g).

The statistics are significantly higher for racial minorities and children of single mothers. Of children under age eighteen living in poverty in 2004, 10.5 percent were white, 33.6 percent were black, 10 percent were Asian, and 28.9 percent were Hispanic; furthermore, 28.4 percent lived with single mothers (DeNavas-Walt et al 2005).

As the statistics show, child poverty is most severe among children living with single mothers. During the past forty years, the number of single-parent families headed by women more than doubled, contributing to the increase in child poverty.

Explaining Poverty: The Sociological Debate

Some theories see poor individuals as responsible for their own poverty, and other theories view poverty as produced and reproduced by structural forces in society. These approaches are sometimes described as "blame the victim" and "blame the system" theories, respectively. We shall briefly examine each.

How Tough Is It in the Bottom Fifth?

According to data from the U.S. Census the gap between rich and poor has widened since 1967. But how true is this picture? Some—mostly conservative—commentators have claimed that the data on income distribution in America from the U.S. Bureau of the Census is incomplete, because they don't use a more comprehensive definition of what constitutes income. They argue that it should include:

both cash assistance (Social Security, unemployment insurance, etc.) and the value of various subsidies and programs, such as housing subsidies, food stamps, school lunch programs, and health programs (Medicare/Medicaid). This definition…include[s] both market income and government assistance as well as adjusting for most taxes. (Bernstein, Michel, and Brocht 2000)

By factoring in this "disposable income," Conservatives argue that there has been very little, if any, growth of income inequality over the past 30 years.

> ⬇ Owning a house is the most widespread form of wealth in the United States and provides many people with a tangible sense of security. This graph shows that members of the lowest income class (46%) are only half as likely as those in the top group (89%) to own their homes. In addition, the poorer group's homes must not be particularly expensive, as no one in the bottom fifth reports more than $250,000 in personal wealth compared to just over three out of every four in the top group (76%).

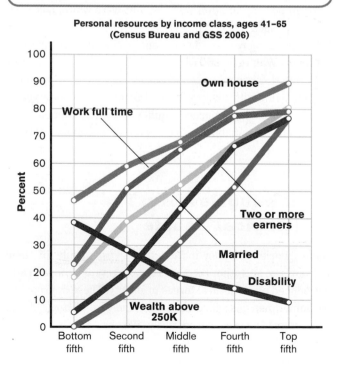

Personal resources by income class, ages 41–65 (Census Bureau and GSS 2006)

Own house · Work full time · Two or more earners · Married · Disability · Wealth above 250K

Any contact with named friend by income class, ages 41–65 (GSS 2004)

Legend: Friend 1, Friend 2, Friend 3, Friend 4, Friend 5

	Bottom fifth	Second fifth	Middle fifth	Fourth fifth	Top fifth
Friend 1	63	71	77	74	85
Friend 2	55	62	74	66	82
Friend 3	41	52	67	58	76
Friend 4	25	35	46	50	61
Friend 5	10	25	31	37	49

> ⬆ Every one of us needs friends to turn to when times get tough. In 2004, the GSS asked Americans to name those people with whom they had discussed important matters over the prior six months. This graph shows that people in the lowest quintile were far less likely to have those networks, while those at the top appear to have a larger circle of good friends.

Created by John Grady.

Furthermore, they claim the Census Bureau does not account for the fact that household size has been steadily decreasing during this period and that lower income classes have smaller households. Because the same amount of money goes further with a smaller household, conservatives contend that, in general, people are doing better than they were forty years ago and the widening gap between rich and poor is an illusion.

If we consider household size, however, we have gone beyond just making economic adjustments to income. Rather, we are introducing an explicitly social factor into the mix. What other social factors should we consider? The Census Bureau makes the most of what it can glean from the various surveys it conducts, but the questions it asks are limited and it never interviews people about what they believe, or feel, about their life situations. Fortunately, the General Social Survey (GSS) has a variable, REALINC, which can be recoded into income classes, as well as many other questions that might help us depict just how life for those at the bottom of the income scale might differ from life for those at the top. In what follows, the GSS data will be restricted to respondents in their peak earning years, from forty-one to sixty-five years old. While the economic definitions of poverty are contested by different groups, the differences between the poorest and the richest groups are dramatic on just about any issue that addresses whether people have the material, social, and emotional resources to overcome adversity. It's simply a lot tougher being poor, and these data suggest that it might be getting worse.

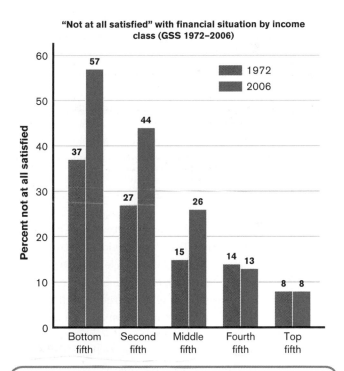

"Not at all satisfied" with financial situation by income class (GSS 1972–2006)

This figure tells us how many people are dissatisfied with their financial situation. The lowest income class has always been much more likely to report dissatisfaction than the top group. But note that by 2006 this dissatisfaction has increased to well over one half of the group (57%) and close to one half of the second income class (44%). Only the top two groups remain unchanged.

This figure concerns health issues and demonstrates that members of the lowest income group report that their health is only "fair or poor" far more often (54%) than members of the top fifth (7%) do, and that those in the poorest group are four times more likely to say that "pain interferes with their normal work" (41%) than are those in the highest income class (9%).

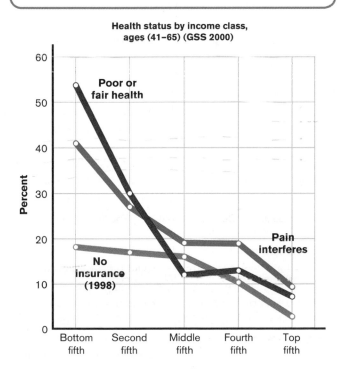

Health status by income class, ages (41–65) (GSS 2000)

There is a long history of attitudes holding the poor responsible for their own disadvantaged positions. For example, the poorhouses of the nineteenth century were grounded in a belief that the poor were unable—due to lack of skills, moral or physical weakness, absence of motivation, or below-average ability—to succeed in society. Social standing was seen to reflect a person's talent and effort; those who deserved to succeed did so, while others less capable were doomed to fail.

Such outlooks reemerged in the 1970s and 1980s as the political emphasis on entrepreneurship and ambition rewarded those who "succeeded" and held those who did not succeed responsible for their unfortunate circumstances. Often, explanations for poverty targeted the lifestyles and attitudes of poor people. Oscar Lewis (1968) proposed one of the most influential theories, arguing that poverty results from a larger social and cultural atmosphere into which poor children are socialized. The **culture of poverty** is transmitted across generations because young people see little point in aspiring to something more. Instead, they resign themselves to a life of impoverishment.

The culture of poverty thesis was taken further by Charles Murray (1984), who placed individuals who are poor through "no fault of their own"—such as widows or widowers, orphans, or the disabled—into a different category from those who are part of the **dependency culture**. This term refers to poor people who rely on welfare rather than entering the labor market. Murray argued that the growth of the welfare state undermines personal ambition and the capacity for self-help: Welfare erodes people's incentive to work.

Such theories seem to resonate among the U.S. population. Surveys have shown that the majority of Americans regard the poor as responsible for their own poverty and are suspicious of those who live "for free" on "government handouts." Many believe that people on welfare could find work if they were determined to do so. Yet, as we have seen, these views are out of line with the realities of poverty.

A second approach to explaining poverty emphasizes larger social processes that are difficult for individuals to overcome. In this view, structural forces within society—class, gender, ethnicity, occupational position, educational attainment, and so forth—shape the way in which resources are distributed (Wilson 1996). Advocates of this approach argue that the lack of ambition among the poor is a consequence of their constrained situations, not a cause of it. Reducing poverty thus requires policy measures aimed at distributing income and resources more equally throughout society, such as child-care subsidies, a minimum hourly wage, and guaranteed income levels for families.

Both theories play a role in public debates about poverty. Critics of the culture of poverty accuse its advocates of blaming the poor for circumstances beyond their control. They see the poor as victims, not as freeloaders. Yet we cannot accept uncritically the view that poverty originates exclusively in the structure of society. Such an approach implies that the poor passively accept their difficult situations.

Combating Poverty: Welfare Systems

Well-developed and systematically administered welfare programs, in conjunction with government policies that help bring down unemployment, can reduce poverty levels. But such an approach requires high levels of taxation, and the government bureaucracies that administer the complex welfare system acquire considerable power, even though they are not democratically elected.

Being poor does not necessarily mean being *mired* in poverty. Many poor people either have enjoyed better conditions previously or can be expected to escape poverty in the future.

Critics of welfare institutions in the United States point to "welfare dependency," meaning that people become materially and psychologically dependent on the very programs that are supposed to enable them to become independent. Others deny that such dependency is widespread. "Being on welfare" is a source of shame, they say, and most people in such a position probably strive to escape from it.

However widespread welfare dependency may be, tackling it has become a target of reform. Among the most significant reforms have been welfare-to-work programs, whose goal is to move recipients from public assistance into paid jobs. Daniel Friedlander and Gary Burtless (1994) studied four such government-initiated programs, which provided financial benefits for welfare recipients who actively searched for jobs as well as guidance in job-hunting techniques and opportunities for education and training. Friedlander and Burtless found that the people involved in such programs were able either to enter employment or to start working sooner than others who didn't participate. In all four programs, the earnings produced were several times greater than the net cost of the program. The programs were least effective, however, in helping those who needed them the most—the long-term unemployed.

In 1996, President Bill Clinton signed into law the Temporary Assistance for Needy Families (TANF) program, which required that welfare recipients begin work after receiving benefits for two years. Families would be cut off entirely after a cumulative five years of assistance. Before this reform, there were no time limits or work requirements imposed by the federal government for welfare recipients, many of whom are single mothers.

Although welfare-to-work programs reduced welfare claims from 5.1 million families to 2.7 million families in their first

FIGURE 8.7

Percentage of the U.S. Population on Welfare since 1960

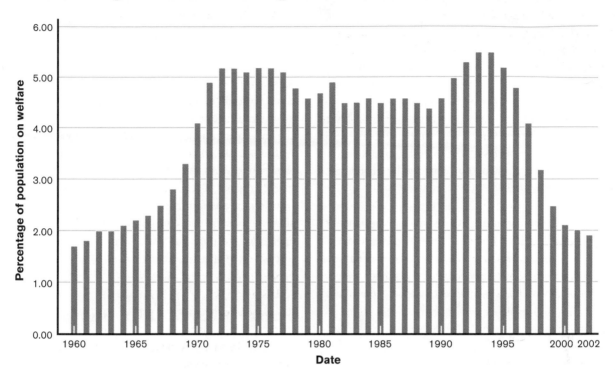

In the past forty years, what is the greatest percentage of the U.S. population to be on welfare? In 2002, the percentage of the population on welfare reached its lowest point since what year? In which three-year period did the percentage of the population on welfare increase the most? According to the reading, the welfare-to-work programs have succeeded for many people, but not for which population? TRUE or FALSE: The vast majority of those who left welfare to go to work found jobs that paid at least as much as they had received while on welfare and provided health insurance.

SOURCE: U.S. Department of Health and Human Services 2004.

three years (Figure 8.7), some statistics suggest that the short-term outcomes are not entirely positive. Among those who left welfare for work, only 61 percent found jobs, 20 percent relied on help from family members or private charities, and about 19 percent had no work or source of independent income. Among those working, the average wage was $6.61 an hour. For about half of this group, this was less than what they had received from welfare. Only 23 percent had health insurance through their employer (Loprest 1999).

Kathryn Edin and Laura Lein (1997) have shown that for low-income mothers, the costs of leaving welfare for work can outweigh the advantages. These mothers face expenses for food, rent, and other necessities that often exceed their income. Mothers who work must often pay for child care, so that their expenses surpass those of unemployed mothers. In addition, their jobs tend to be less stable and to pay less than welfare.

Because their expenses exceed their income, both working and welfare mothers must find other sources of money. Many mothers on welfare rely on aid from charitable agencies or side work, which is likely unreported. (Reporting additional income can reduce or end welfare benefits.) Low-income working mothers also rely on support from their social networks, such as family members or boyfriends, to help pay the costs of living. Thus critics argue that the apparent success of welfare-to-work

LuAnne St. Clair and her children, Tyrone, Kelley, and Keith, pose at their home. Residents of the White Earth Reservation in Mahnomen, Minnesota, the family relies on welfare.

initiatives conceals troublesome patterns in the experiences of those who lose their welfare benefits. Moreover, even the most hopeful studies were conducted during a period of economic expansion. When growth slows—or declines—it becomes difficult, if not impossible, for welfare recipients to find any jobs at all.

☑ CONCEPT CHECKS

1. What is the poverty line, and how does the U.S. government calculate this statistic?
2. Describe the demographic characteristics of the poor in the United States.
3. Why are women and children at a high risk of becoming impoverished in the United States today?
4. Contrast the culture of poverty argument and structural explanations for poverty.
5. What are welfare-to-work programs? Assess how effective they have been in fighting poverty in the United States today.

Social Exclusion

The idea of **social exclusion** refers to ways in which individuals may become cut off from the wider society. A broader concept than that of the underclass, it emphasizes *processes*—mechanisms of exclusion. For instance, people who live in a dilapidated housing project, with poor schools and few employment opportunities, may lack opportunities for self-betterment that most other people have. The concept is also different from poverty, because it focuses on a range of factors that eliminate opportunities enjoyed by the majority of the population. An important example of social exclusion is Milner's (2004) study of high school status systems: One way that teenagers mark themselves as "superior" is by excluding others whom they perceive as "inferior." In fact, exclusion and inclusion may be seen in economic, political, and social terms.

The concept of social exclusion raises the question of agency—someone or something being shut out by another. In some instances, individuals are excluded through decisions outside their control. Banks might refuse to grant a current account or credit cards to individuals living in a certain ZIP code area. Insurance companies might reject a policy application on the basis of an applicant's personal history and background.

But social exclusion can also result from people excluding themselves from aspects of mainstream society. Individuals might drop out of school, turn down a job opportunity and quit working, or abstain from voting. In considering social exclusion, we must be conscious of the interaction between human agency and responsibility on the one hand and the role of social forces on the other hand.

Forms of Social Exclusion

Sociologists have explored the ways in which individuals and communities experience exclusion, focusing on topics as diverse as housing, education, the labor market, crime, young people, and the elderly. We will discuss several examples of exclusion in industrialized societies.

HOUSING AND NEIGHBORHOODS

While many people in industrialized societies live in comfortable, spacious housing, others reside in dwellings that are overcrowded, inadequately heated, or structurally unsound. Individuals secure housing on the basis of their existing and projected resources; thus a dual-income childless couple is likely to obtain a mortgage for a home in an attractive area, whereas a household whose adults are unemployed or in low-paying jobs face less desirable options in the rental or public-housing sector.

Stratification occurs at both the household and the community levels. Just as disadvantaged individuals are excluded from desirable housing options, whole communities can be excluded from opportunities and activities that are norms for the rest of society. Exclusion can be spatial: Neighborhoods vary in terms of safety, environmental conditions, and services and public facilities. For example, low-demand neighborhoods have fewer banks, grocery stores, and post offices than more desirable areas. Community spaces such as parks, playing fields, and libraries may also be limited. Yet the residents often depend on what few facilities are available. Unlike residents of more affluent areas, they may not have access to transportation (or funds) that would allow them to shop and use services elsewhere.

In deprived communities, it can be difficult for people to take steps to engage more fully in society. Weak social networks limit the circulation of information about jobs, political activities, and community events. High unemployment and low income levels place strains on family life; crime and juvenile delinquency undermine the quality of life. Low-demand housing areas often experience high household turnover rates as some residents move on to more desirable housing while new, disadvantaged residents continue to arrive. Finally, because most public schools are financed with property taxes, poor neighborhoods are likely to have underfunded schools, implying a lower quality of education.

RURAL AREAS

Some social workers and caregivers believe that exclusion in the countryside is as great as, if not greater than, that in cities. In small villages and sparsely populated areas, access to goods, services, and facilities is not as extensive as in more settled areas. In most industrial societies, proximity to basic services such as doctors, post offices, schools, houses of worship, libraries, and government services is a necessity for an active, full, and healthy life. But rural residents often have limited access to such services and depend on the facilities available within their local community.

Access to transportation is one of the biggest factors affecting rural exclusion. If a household owns or has access to a car, for example, family members can consider jobs in other

Social exclusion can be particularly bad for those living in rural areas. What are the main factors that can isolate rural residents?

towns, shopping trips to areas with a larger selection of shops, and visits to friends or family in other areas. Young people can be fetched home from parties. People without access to a car, however, depend on public transportation, and in rural areas such services are limited.

SOCIAL EXCLUSION AT THE TOP

In recent years, new dynamics of "social exclusion at the top" have been emerging. This means that a minority of individuals at the very top of society can opt out of participation in mainstream institutions by merit of their affluence, influence, and connections.

Exclusion at the top can take a number of forms. The wealthy might retreat from public education and health-care services, preferring to pay for private services. Affluent residential communities—gated communities located behind tall walls and security checkpoints—are increasingly popular. Tax payments and financial obligations can be drastically reduced through the help of private financial planners. Particularly in the United States, active political participation among the elite is often replaced by large donations to political candidates who represent their interests. Just as social exclusion at the bottom undermines social solidarity and cohesion, exclusion at the top is similarly detrimental to an integrated society.

Crime and Social Exclusion

Some sociologists see strong links between crime and social exclusion in industrialized societies such as the United States. There is a trend, they argue, away from inclusive goals (based on citizenship rights) and toward arrangements that accept and promote the exclusion of some citizens (Young 1998, 1999). Crime rates may reflect the fact that a growing number of people do not feel valued by—or do not feel they have an investment in—the societies in which they live.

Elliott Currie (1998) argues that American society is a "natural laboratory" demonstrating the "ominous underside" of market-driven social policy: rising poverty and homelessness, drug abuse, and violent crime. He notes that young people increasingly grow up without guidance and support from the adult population. While facing the seductive lure of consumer goods, young people also confront diminishing job opportunities to sustain a livelihood. This can cause a profound sense of relative deprivation and a willingness to turn to illegitimate means of sustaining a desired lifestyle.

Currie sees several links between crime and social exclusion. First, shifts in the labor market and government taxation and minimum wage policies have led to enormous growth in both relative and absolute poverty. Second, this rise in social exclusion occurs in local communities, which suffer from a loss of stable livelihoods, transient populations, increasingly expensive housing, and weakened social cohesion. Third, economic deprivation and community fragmentation strain family life. Adults in many poor families work at multiple jobs—a situation that produces perpetual stress, anxiety, and absence from home. Thus the socialization and nurturing of children is weakened; the "social impoverishment" of the community offers little opportunity for parents to turn to other families or relatives for support. Fourth, the state has rolled back many programs and public services that could reincorporate the socially excluded, such as early childhood intervention, child care, and mental health care.

Finally, the socially excluded population cannot, through legitimate means, meet the standards of economic status and consumption that are promoted within society. Thus, according to Currie (1998), legitimate channels are bypassed in favor of illegal ones: Crime is favored over alternative means, such as the political system or community organization.

With a sign for assistance strapped to his back, Rick Cathy, his wife, and their five-year-old daughter make their way to Sacramento. The family, originally from Buffalo, New York, was on the road continuously for more than eighteen months after losing their home.

THE HOMELESS

The growing problem of homelessness is one of the most distressing signs of changes in the American stratification system. Traditionally a common sight in nearly every U.S. city and town, the **homeless** are increasingly found in rural areas as well. Two generations ago, the homeless were mainly elderly, alcoholic men living on the skid rows of the largest metropolitan areas. Today, the homeless are primarily young, single men, often of working age. The fastest-growing group of homeless, however, consists of families with children (National Law Center on Homelessness and Poverty [NLCHP] 2004). Approximately 42 percent of those children are under the age of five. In 2004, the National Law Center on Homelessness and Poverty estimated that 41 percent of the homeless are single males and 14 percent are single females. Equal shares of the homeless population are black and white (40 percent), 11 percent are Hispanic, and 8 percent are Native American. Very few homeless are Latino or Asian American immigrants, possibly because of these groups' close-knit family and community ties (Waxman and Hinderliter 1996). The National Coalition of Homeless Veterans estimates that there are nearly 200,000 homeless veterans on the streets on any given day (NCVH 2007).

Because it is extremely difficult to count people who do not have a stable residence (Appelbaum 1990), estimates of the number of homeless vary widely. The most recent estimate is that there are 754,000 persons living in emergency shelters, transitional housing, and on the streets on any given night while 155,623 are chronically homeless in the United

States (U.S. Department of Housing and Urban Development 2007).

There are many reasons why people become homeless, including problems with alcohol, drugs, and mental health (NLCHP 2004). The number of beds in state mental hospitals has declined by as many as half a million since the early 1960s, leaving many mentally ill people with no institutional alternative to a life on the streets or in homeless shelters. Such problems are compounded by the fact that many homeless people lack family, relatives, or other social networks to provide support.

The rising cost of housing is another factor, particularly in light of the increased poverty noted elsewhere in this chapter. Declining incomes at the bottom and rising rents create an affordability gap between the cost of housing and what poor people can pay in rents (Dreier and Appelbaum 1992). The burden of paying rent is extreme for low-income families whose heads work for minimum wage or slightly higher; those families are barely a paycheck away from a missed rental payment and eventual eviction (National Low Income Housing Coalition [NLIHC] 2000). The housing affordability gap has been worsened by the loss of government programs providing low-cost housing during the 1980s, which removed a crucial safety net just as poverty was increasing in the United States.

During a time when American firms are moving their lowest-paying, least-skilled work overseas, unskilled workers are especially vulnerable to job loss and homelessness. This is not to say that only poor, unskilled people run the risk of becoming homeless: If you have ever volunteered at a homeless shelter, you may have encountered formerly middle-class families who "ran out of luck." But the people overwhelmingly at risk of becoming homeless are those who face a combination of low-paying jobs, poverty, and high housing costs along with a tangle of personal problems such as alcoholism, depression, or family problems (Burt 1992).

☑ CONCEPT CHECKS

1. Describe the concept of social exclusion.
2. According to Elliott Currie, how are crime and social exclusion in the United States related?
3. Describe the demographic characteristics of the homeless population in the United States today.
4. What are the main reasons that people become homeless?

Theories of Stratification in Modern Societies

In this section, we look at some broad theories regarding stratification. The most influential approaches were developed by Karl Marx and Max Weber. Most subsequent theories of stratification are heavily indebted to their ideas.

Marx: Means of Production and the Analysis of Class

For Marx, the term *class* refers to people who have a common relationship to the **means of production**—the means by which they gain a livelihood. In modern societies, the two main classes are those who own the means of production—industrialists, or **capitalists**—and those who earn their living by selling their labor to them—the working class. The relationship between classes, according to Marx, is exploitative. During the working day, workers produce more than employers actually need to repay the cost of hiring them. This **surplus value** is the source of profit, which capitalists put to their own use.

Marx (1977; orig. 1864) believed that the maturing of industrial capitalism would cause an increasing gap between the wealth of the minority and the poverty of the mass of the population. In his view, the wages of the working class could never rise far above subsistence level, while wealth would pile up in the hands of those owning capital. In addition, laborers would daily face work that is physically wearing and mentally tedious, as in many factories. At the lowest levels of society, particularly among those frequently or permanently unemployed, there would develop an "accumulation of misery, agony of labor, slavery, ignorance, brutality, moral degradation."

Marx was right about the persistence of poverty in industrialized countries and in anticipating continued inequalities of wealth and income. He was wrong in supposing that the income of most of the population would remain extremely low. Most people in Western countries today are much better off materially than were comparable groups in Marx's day.

Weber: Class and Status

There are two main differences between Weber's theory and that of Marx. First, according to Weber, class divisions derive not only from control or lack of control of the means of production but also from economic differences that have nothing to do with property. Such resources include people's skills and credentials. Those in managerial or professional occupations earn more and enjoy more favorable conditions at work, for example, than people in blue-collar jobs. Their qualifications, such as degrees, diplomas, and skills they have acquired, make them more "marketable" than others without such qualifications. At a lower level, among blue-collar workers, skilled craft workers secure higher wages than the semiskilled or unskilled.

Second, Weber distinguished another aspect of stratification, which he called "status." *Status* refers to differences between groups in the social honor, or prestige, others accord them. Status distinctions can vary independently of class divisions. Social honor may be either positive or negative. For instance, doctors and lawyers have high prestige in American society. **Pariah groups**, on the other hand, are negatively privileged status groups, subject to discrimination that prevents them from taking advantage of opportunities open to others. The Jews were a pariah group in medieval Europe, banned from participating in certain occupations and from holding official positions.

Possession of wealth normally confers high status, but there are exceptions. In Britain, for instance, individuals from aristocratic families enjoy social esteem even after their fortunes have been lost, but individuals with "new money" are often scorned by the well-established wealthy.

Whereas class is an objective measure, status depends on people's subjective evaluations of social differences. Classes derive from the economic factors associated with property and earnings; status is governed by the varying lifestyles that groups follow.

Weber's writings on stratification show that other dimensions besides class strongly influence people's lives. Most sociologists hold that Weber's scheme offers a more flexible and sophisticated basis for analyzing stratification than Marx's.

Davis and Moore: The Functions of Stratification

Kingsley Davis and Wilbert E. Moore (1945) provided a functionalist explanation of stratification, arguing that it has beneficial consequences for society. They claimed that certain positions in society are functionally more important than others, such as brain surgeons, and these positions require special skills. However, only a few individuals have the talents or experience appropriate to these positions. To attract the most qualified people, rewards need to be offered, such as money, power, and prestige. Davis and Moore determined that because the benefits of different positions in any society must be unequal, all societies must be stratified. They concluded that social stratification and social inequality are functional because they ensure that the most qualified people, attracted by the rewards bestowed by society, fill the roles that are most important to a smoothly functioning society.

Davis and Moore's theory suggests that a person's social position is based solely on innate talents and efforts. It is not surprising that their theory has been criticized by other sociologists. For example, Melvin Tumin (1953) argued that the functional importance of a particular role is difficult to measure and that the social rewards bestowed on those in "important" roles do not reflect their actual importance. For instance, who is more important, a lawyer or a schoolteacher? If, on average, a lawyer earns four or five times the amount that a schoolteacher earns, does that accurately reflect their relative importance to society? Tumin also argued that Davis and Moore overlooked the ways in which stratification limits the discovery of talent in a society. As we have seen, the United States is not entirely a meritocratic society. Those at the top have special access to economic and cultural resources, such as the highest quality education, that help transmit their privileged status from one generation to the next. For those without access to these resources, even those with superior talents, social inequality is a barrier to reaching their full potential.

Erik Olin Wright: Contradictory Class Locations

The American sociologist Erik Olin Wright (1978, 1985, 1997) developed a theoretical position that owes much to Marx but also incorporates ideas from Weber. According to Wright, there are three dimensions of control over economic resources in modern capitalist production, and these allow us to identify the major classes:

1. Control over investments or money capital

2. Control over the physical means of production (land or factories and offices)

3. Control over labor power

Members of the capitalist class have control over each of these dimensions of the production system. Members of the working class have control over none of them. Between these two main classes, however, are the groups whose position is more ambiguous—managers and white-collar workers. These people are in what Wright calls **contradictory class locations**, because they can influence some aspects of production but lack control over others. White-collar and professional employees, for example, have to contract their labor power to employers to make a living, in the same way as manual workers do. Yet they have a greater degree of control over the work setting than do most people in blue-collar jobs. Wright terms the class position of such workers "contradictory," because they are neither capitalists nor manual workers, yet they share certain common features with each.

A large segment of the population—85 to 90 percent, according to Wright (1997)—falls into the category of those who must sell their labor because they do not control the means of production. Yet within this population is a great deal of diversity, ranging from the traditional manual working class to white-collar workers. To differentiate class locations within this large population, Wright considers two factors: the relationship to authority and the possession of skills or expertise. First, many middle-class workers, such as managers and supervisors, enjoy *relationships to authority* that are more privileged than those of the working class. Such individuals assist capitalists in controlling the working class—for example, by monitoring an employee's work or by conducting personnel reviews and evaluations—and are rewarded by earning higher wages and receiving regular promotions. Yet these individuals remain under the control of the capitalist owners. In other words, they are both exploiters and exploited.

The second factor that differentiates class locations within the middle classes is the *possession of skills and expertise.* According to Wright, middle-class employees possessing skills that are in demand in the labor market have a specific form of power in the capitalist system: They can earn a higher wage. The lucrative positions available to information technology specialists in the knowledge economy illustrate this point.

Moreover, Wright argues, because employees with knowledge and skills are more difficult to monitor and control, employers secure their loyalty and cooperation by rewarding them accordingly.

Frank Parkin and Social Closure

Frank Parkin (1971, 1979), a British author, has proposed an approach drawing more heavily on Weber than on Marx. Parkin agrees with Marx, as Weber did, that ownership of property—the means of production—is the foundation of class structure. Property, however, according to Parkin, is only one form of social closure that can be used as a basis of power by one group over others. **Social closure** can be any process whereby groups try to maintain exclusive control over resources, limiting access to them. Besides property or wealth, most of the characteristics Weber associated with status differences, such as ethnic origin, language, or religion, may be used to create social closure.

Two types of processes are involved in social closure. The first type, *exclusion,* involves strategies that groups adopt to separate outsiders from themselves, denying them access to valued resources. An emphasis on credentials is one major way by which groups exclude others in order to hold on to their own power and privilege. In most U.S. public school systems, for example, only those with a secondary-school teaching certification in their subject, awarded by a school of education, are allowed to teach.

The second type of process involved in social closure, *usurpation,* involves attempts by the less privileged to acquire resources previously monopolized by others—as when blacks struggle to achieve the rights of union membership.

The strategies of exclusion and usurpation may serve simultaneously in some circumstances. Labor unions, for instance, might engage in usurpatory activities against employers (going on strike to obtain a greater share of the resources or a position on the board of directors of a firm) but at the same time exclude ethnic minorities from membership. Parkin calls this dual closure, which concerns much the same processes as Wright's concept of contradictory class locations. Both notions indicate that those in the middle of the stratification system cast their eyes toward the top yet also distinguish themselves from others lower down.

☑ CONCEPT CHECKS

1. According to Karl Marx, what are the two main classes and how do they relate to one another?
2. What are the two main differences between Max Weber's and Karl Marx's theories of social stratification?

3. According to Kingsley Davis and Wilbert E. Moore, how does social stratification contribute to the functioning of society? What is wrong with this argument, according to Melvin Tumin?

Growing Inequality in the United States

Throughout this chapter, we have mentioned the various ways in which changes in the American economy have affected social stratification; we emphasized both globalization and changes in information technology. The global spread of an industrial capitalist economy, driven in part by the information revolution, has helped to break down closed caste systems around the world and replace them with more open class systems. The degree to which this process will bring greater equality in countries undergoing capitalist development is the focus of the next chapter.

What do these changes hold for you? On the one hand, new jobs are opening up, particularly in high-technology fields that require special skills and pay high wages. A flood of new products entering the United States, many made with cheap labor that has lowered their costs, has enabled consumers such as yourselves to buy everything from computers to automobiles, thereby contributing to a rising standard of living.

On the other hand, these benefits carry potentially significant costs. In today's fast-paced world, you may have to compete for jobs with workers in other countries who work for lower wages. This has already been the case for the manufacturing jobs—from automobiles to apparel to electronics—that used to support the working class and segments of the middle class. Will the same hold true for other, more highly skilled jobs—jobs in the information economy itself? The global spread of dot-com companies will bring vastly expanded job opportunities for those with the necessary skills and training, but it will also bring expanded global competition for those jobs.

The global economy has permitted the accumulation of vast fortunes at the same time that it has contributed to declining wages, economic hardship, and poverty in the United States. Homelessness is in part due to these processes, as is the emergence of an underclass of the new urban poor. Although the working class is especially vulnerable, the middle class is not exempt: A growing number of middle-class households experienced downward mobility from the late 1970s through the mid-1990s, until several years of economic growth (now over) benefited all segments of American society. Another spell of economic adversity struck following September 11, 2001. Although global economic integration will likely increase, how it will affect your jobs and careers—and stratification in the United States—is difficult to foresee.

☑ CONCEPT CHECKS

☑ CONCEPT CHECKS

1. How has globalization affected the life chances of young adults in the United States today?

Study Outline
www.wwnorton.com/studyspace

Systems of Stratification

- *Social stratification* involves the division of people socioeconomically into layers, or strata, meaning that they occupy unequal positions in society. In the larger traditional societies and in industrialized countries today there is stratification in terms of *wealth,* property, and access to material goods and cultural products.
- Three major types of stratification systems are *slavery, caste,* and *class.* Whereas the first two depend on legal or religiously sanctioned inequalities, class divisions are not "officially" recognized but stem from economic factors affecting people's material circumstances.

Classes in Western Society Today

- Classes derive from inequalities in possession and control of material resources and access to educational and occupational opportunities. An individual's class position is partly achieved, not simply "given" from birth. Some recent authors have suggested that cultural factors such as lifestyle and consumption patterns influence class position. According to such a view, individual identities are now more structured around lifestyle choices than around traditional class indicators such as occupation.
- Class is of major importance in industrialized societies, although there are many complexities in the class system within such societies. The main class divisions are among people in the *upper, middle,* and *lower working classes* and the *underclass.*

Inequality in the United States: A Growing Gap between Rich and Poor

- Most people in modern societies are more affluent today than several generations ago. Yet the distribution of *wealth* and *income* remains highly unequal. Between the early 1970s and the late 1990s, partly as a result of economic globalization, the gap between rich and poor grew. Incomes at the top increased sharply, while many ordinary workers and families saw their incomes drop as higher-wage manufacturing jobs moved to low-wage countries.

Social Mobility

- In the study of *social mobility,* there is a distinction between *intragenerational* and *intergenerational* mobility. Intragenerational mobility is movement up or down the social scale within an individual's working life. Intergenerational mobility is movement across the generations, as when the daughter or son from a blue-collar background becomes a professional. Social mobility is mostly of limited range. Most people remain close to the level of the family from which they came, though the expansion of white-collar jobs has provided the opportunity for considerable short-range upward mobility.

Poverty in the United States

- Poverty remains widespread in the United States. Two methods of assessing poverty exist. *Absolute poverty* is a lack of basic resources needed to maintain a healthy existence. *Relative poverty* involves assessing the gaps between the living conditions of some groups and those enjoyed by the majority of the population.
- Problems of declining income and poverty are pronounced among racial and ethnic minorities, families headed by single women, and persons lacking education. The *feminization of poverty* is especially strong among young, poorly educated women raising children on their own.

Social Exclusion

- Social exclusion refers to processes by which individuals become cut off from full involvement in the wider society. People who are socially excluded, due to poor housing, inferior schools, or limited transportation, may lack the opportunities for self-betterment that most people in society have. Homelessness is one of the most extreme forms of social exclusion, shutting out many everyday activities that most people take for granted.

Theories of Stratification in Modern Societies

- The most influential theories of stratification were developed by Marx and Weber. Marx emphasized class, which he saw as an objectively given characteristic of the economic structure of society. He saw a fundamental split between the owners of capital and the workers, who do not own capital. Weber accepted a similar view but distinguished another aspect of stratification, *status*. Status refers to the esteem, or "social honor," given to individuals or groups.

Growing Inequality in the United States

- Technological advances mean that high-skilled, high-wage jobs are available to young people. At the same time, globalization means that Americans will be competing in a global labor market for those jobs.

Key Concepts

absolute poverty (p. 229)

ascription (p. 225)

capitalists (p. 241)

caste societies (p. 207)

caste system (p. 207)

class (p. 209)

contradictory class locations (p. 242)

culture of poverty (p. 236)

dependency culture (p. 236)

exchange mobility (p. 224)

feminization of poverty (p. 233)

homeless (p. 240)

income (p. 210)

industrialism hypothesis (p. 225)

intergenerational mobility (p. 223)

intragenerational mobility (p. 223)

Kuznets curve (p. 210)

life chances (p. 209)

lower class (p. 220)

means of production (p. 241)

middle class (p. 217)

pariah groups (p. 241)

poverty line (p. 230)

relative poverty (p. 229)

slavery (p. 207)

social closure (p. 243)

social exclusion (p. 238)

social mobility (p. 223)

social stratification (p. 206)

status (p. 206)

structural mobility (p. 224)

structured inequalities (p. 206)

surplus value (p. 241)

underclass (p. 220)

upper class (p. 216)

vertical mobility (p. 226)

wealth (p. 212)

working class (p. 220)

working poor (p. 231)

Review Questions

1. What are the three critical aspects of systems of stratification according to Max Weber? Describe how these may or may not overlap.
2. Describe how systems of stratification shape society and affect the life chances of individuals.
3. What are three types of system of stratification? How does a class system differ from the others?
4. What are some reasons for the persistence of racial disparity in wealth?
5. What is an "underclass"? What are its demographic characteristics in the United States and why has it grown in recent years?
6. How do Oliver and Shapiro explain the persistence of a "wealth gap" between whites and African Americans.
7. Compare the culture of poverty theory to structural explanations of poverty. Which theory better accounts for the working poor?
8. How does the concept of "social exclusion" explain patterns of crime?
9. What was Marx's conception of class and why did he consider class relations exploitative?
10. According to Frank Parkin, how is the concept of social closure related to class?

Thinking Sociologically Exercises

1. If you were doing your own study of status differences in your community, how would you measure people's social class? Base your answer on the textbook's discussion of these matters to explain why you would take the particular measurement approach you've chosen. What would be its value(s) and shortcoming(s) compared with those of alternative measurement procedures?
2. Using occupation and occupational change as your mobility criteria, view the social mobility within your family for three generations. As you discuss the differences in jobs among your grandfather, father, and yourself, apply all these terms correctly: *vertical* and *horizontal mobility, upward* and *downward mobility, intragenerational* and *intergenerational mobility*. Explain why you think people in your family have moved up, moved down, or remained at the same status level.

Learning Objectives

Global Inequality: Differences among Countries

Understand the systematic differences in wealth and power among countries.

Life in Rich and Poor Countries

Recognize the impact of different economic standards of living on people throughout the world.

Can Poor Countries Become Rich?

Analyze the success of newly industrializing economies.

Theories of Global Inequality

Consider various theories explaining why some societies are wealthier than others, as well as how global inequality can be overcome.

Why Global Economic Inequality Matters to You

Learn how globalization might shape global inequality in the future.

CHAPTER NINE

GLOBAL INEQUALITY

the past quarter century has seen the appearance of more global billionaires than ever before. In 2007, there were 946 billionaires worldwide—with 178 newcomers over last year, including 19 Russians, 14 Indians, 13 Chinese, and 10 Spaniards, as well as the first billionaires from Cyprus, Oman, Romania, and Serbia (*Forbes* 2007d). Their combined assets in 2007 were estimated at $3.5 trillion—greater than the total gross national income of all but the top ten economies of the world (calculated from World Bank 2007a). The success of America's high-technology economy, coupled with the financial crisis in Asia in the late 1990s, enabled the United States to lay claim to over half the world's billionaires.

As of 2007, the wealthiest person in the world was Microsoft Corporation's founder Bill Gates, with a net worth of $56 billion in that year—down from $63 billion in 2000, owing to the decline in the stock market. Gates, whose fortune is based largely on ownership of his company's stock, seems the personification of American entrepreneurialism: a computer nerd turned capitalist. During the late 1990s, Gates was the first person in history to have a net worth in excess of $100 billion. Shortly thereafter, the value of Microsoft's stock began to decline, leaving Gates's fortune greatly reduced but still sufficient to rank him number one in wealth in the world for eleven consecutive years.

Gates was followed by the financier Warren Buffett, at $52 billion. Buffett is an investor and CEO of Berkshire Hathaway, Inc., which owns companies such as Geico Direct Auto Insurance, Dairy Queen, and See's Candies. In 2003, Buffett became an adviser to California's governor, Arnold Schwarzenegger.

The third richest person in the world is also Latin America's richest man. Carlos Slim Helu made his way to the top of the list based on his investment in two Mexican telecom companies as well as significant shares of American-based MCI, which has been bought out by Verizon. His net worth is $49 billion, up $19 billion since last year. Fourth on the list is Invar Kamprad, owner of IKEA, whose investments have established his worth at $33 billion (*Forbes* 2007d). Among the twenty-eight richest people, eleven were from the United States, seven were from Europe, four were from India, two were from Hong Kong, one was from Russia, one was from Canada, one was from Saudi Arabia, and one was from Mexico (*Forbes* 2007d). If Bill Gates typifies the American high-tech entrepreneur, Hong Kong's Li Ka-shing—number twenty-two on the list and Asia's richest man—represents a rags-to-riches story characterizing the success of many Asian businessmen. Li started out making plastic flowers; in 2005, his $13 billion in personal wealth derived from a range of real estate and other investments throughout Asia.

Globalization—the increased economic, political, and social interconnectedness of the world—has produced opportunities for unthinkable wealth but also widespread poverty and suffering. Consider Wirat Tasago, a garment worker in Bangkok, Thailand. Tasago—along with more than a million other Thai garment workers, most of whom are women—labors from 8 A.M. until about 11 P.M. six days a week, earning little more than $3 an hour (Dahlburg 1995). Billions of workers such as Tasago are being drawn into the global labor force, many working in oppressive conditions that would be unacceptable, if not unimaginable, under U.S. labor laws. And these are the fortunate ones: Those outside the global economy are frequently even worse off.

In the previous chapter, we noted vast differences among individuals' income, wealth, work, and quality of life. Just as we can speak of rich or poor individuals within a country, so we can talk about rich or poor countries in the world system. A country's position in the global economy affects how its people live, work, and die. In this chapter, we examine the differences in wealth and power among countries in the late twentieth and early twenty-first centuries. We discuss differences in economic standards of living and then turn to the newly industrializing economies to understand which countries are improving their fortunes and why. This leads to a discussion of different theories on the causes of global inequality and what can be done about it. We conclude by speculating on the future of economic inequality in a global world.

Global Inequality: Differences among Countries

Global inequality refers to the systematic differences in wealth and power among countries. These differences exist alongside differences within countries: Even the wealthiest countries have growing numbers of poor people, while less wealthy nations are producing many of the world's superrich. Sociology's challenge is not merely to identify such differences but to explain why they occur—and how they might be overcome.

One way to classify countries in terms of global inequality is to compare the wealth produced by each country for its average citizen. The *per-person gross national income (GNI)* is a measure of a country's yearly output of goods and services per person. The World Bank (2007b), an international lending organization that provides loans for development projects in poorer countries, uses this measure to classify countries as high income (an annual 2007 per person GNI of $11,456 or more, in 2007 dollars), upper middle income ($3,706–$11,455), lower middle income ($936–$3,705), or low income (under $935). This system of classification will help show why there are such vast differences in living standards among countries.

Figure 9.1 shows how the World Bank (2007c) divides 208 countries' economies into the three economic classes. Although nearly 40 percent of the world's population live in low-income countries, less than 16 percent live in high-income countries. Because this classification is based on *average* income for each country, it masks income inequality *within* each country. Such differences can be significant, although we do not focus on them in this chapter. For example, the World Bank classifies India as a low-income country, yet despite widespread poverty India also boasts a large and growing middle class. China, in contrast, was reclassified in 1999 from low to middle income on the basis of its per capita GNI, yet it has hundreds of millions of people living in poverty.

Comparing countries on the basis of economic output alone may be misleading, because GNI includes only goods and services produced for cash sale. Many people in low-income countries produce only for their own families or for barter, involving noncash transactions. The value of their crops and animals is not reflected in the statistics. Furthermore, economic output is not a country's whole story: Poor countries are no less rich in history and culture than their wealthier neighbors, even though the lives of their people are much harsher.

[handwritten margin note: political power of the power of the upper class]

FIGURE 9.1

Population and Per Capita Income in Low-, Middle-, and High-Income Countries, 2004

Like most countries, the world as a whole is highly unequal. Nearly 20 percent (19.4 percent) of the people in the world live in low-income countries, whereas around 16 percent live in high-income countries. The average income of people in high-income countries is 69 times that of people in low-income countries. The remainder of the world's population—about 65 percent—live in middle-income countries. According to the World Bank, the world has become considerably more "middle class" in recent years: In 1999, the World Bank reclassified China from low income to middle income, moving its 1.3 billion people (22 percent of the world's population) into the latter category. Although China's average income has risen to global middle-class standards, the large majority of China's people remain distinctly low income.

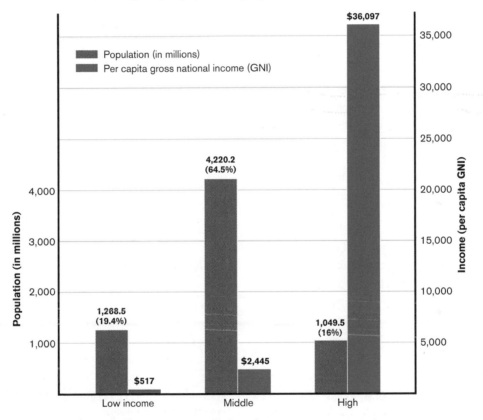

Low-income and middle-income nations comprise what percentage of the world's total population? What is the per capita gross national income in low-income countries? TRUE or FALSE: As demonstrated by the blue bars, most of the people in today's world live in high-income nations, while just a small percentage live in low-income nations. Explain. How many people live in low-income countries? This figure represents data from what year? According to the reading, how is the gross national income measured? The World Bank's decision to move which country from low income to middle income in 1999 greatly changes the percentage of the world they report as middle income?

SOURCE: World Bank 2007e.

High-Income Countries

High-income countries are generally those that industrialized first, a process that began in England some two hundred fifty years ago and then spread to Europe, the United States, and Canada. About thirty years ago, Japan joined their ranks, while Singapore, Hong Kong, and Taiwan did so only within the last decade or so.

High-income countries have 15.5 percent of the world's population, yet they command 75.8 percent of the world's annual output of wealth (derived from World Bank 2007dw). Although high-income countries often have large numbers of poor people, they offer decent housing, adequate food, drinkable water, and other comforts—a standard of living unimaginable by the majority of the world's people.

Middle-Income Countries

The *middle-income countries* are primarily found in East and Southeast Asia and also include the oil-rich countries of the Middle East and North Africa, the Americas (Mexico, Central America, Cuba and other countries in the Caribbean, and South America), and the once-communist republics that formerly made up the Soviet Union and its East European allies (Global Map 9.1). Having begun to industrialize relatively late in the twentieth century, most are not yet as developed (nor as wealthy) as the high-income countries. The countries of the former Soviet Union, however, are highly industrialized, although their living standards have eroded as a result of the collapse of communism and the move to capitalist economies. In Russia, for example, the wages of ordinary people dropped by nearly a third between 1998 and 1999, while retirement pensions dropped by nearly half (Central Intelligence Agency [CIA] 2000). Since then, the Russian economy has recovered somewhat, with foreign investment gradually increasing and the energy market booming.

In 2006, middle-income countries included 46.7 percent of the world's population (3.08 billion people) but accounted for only 20.8 percent of the wealth produced in that year. Although many residents are substantially better off than their neighbors in low-income countries, most do not enjoy anything resembling the standard of living common in high-income countries.

Low-Income Countries

The *low-income countries* include much of eastern, western, and sub-Saharan Africa; Vietnam, Cambodia, Indonesia, and a few other East Asian countries; India, Nepal, Bangladesh, and Pakistan in South Asia; eastern and central European countries such as Georgia and Ukraine; and Haiti and Nicaragua in the Western Hemisphere. They have mostly agricultural economies and are just beginning to industrialize. Scholars debate the reasons for their late industrialization and widespread poverty, as we will see later.

In 2006, the low-income countries included over 36.36 percent of the world's population (2.4 billion people) yet produced only 3.33 percent of the world's yearly output of wealth (World Bank 2007d). Moreover, this inequality is increasing—partly as a result of higher fertility, for large families provide additional farm labor or otherwise contribute to family income. In fact, the populations of low-income

---

TABLE 9.1

Differences in Fertility and Population Growth: Low-, Middle-, and High-Income Countries

	INCOME LEVEL			
	LOW	MIDDLE	HIGH	WORLD
Annual births per woman, 2006	4.3	2.2	1.7	2.5
Average yearly percent population growth, 1990–2006	2.2	1.0	0.7	1.2

SOURCE: World Bank 2007e.

countries (with the principal exception of India) grew 2.6 times as fast as those of high-income countries between 1990 and 2005 (Table 9.1).

In many low-income countries, people struggle with poverty, malnutrition, and starvation. Most people live in rural areas, although recently hundreds of millions of people have been moving to densely populated cities, where they live either in dilapidated housing or on the streets (see Chapter 19).

Growing Global Inequality: The Rich Get Richer, the Poor Get Poorer

During the last forty-some years, the overall standard of living in the world has risen. The average global citizen is better off than ever before (Table 9.2). Illiteracy is down, infant deaths and malnutrition are less common, people are living longer, average income is higher, and poverty is down. However, many of these gains have been in the high- and middle-income countries, while living standards in many of the poorest countries have declined. Overall, the gap between rich and poor countries has widened.

Between 1988 and 2006, average per-person GNI increased by 105.4 percent in high-income countries and 75.7 percent in low-income countries, widening the global gap between rich and poor (Figure 9.2). Most of the growth in low-income per capita income has been since 2000, when it was $380 per person (it was $370 in 1988, declined to a low of $310 in 1993–1994, and then increased back to 1970s levels by 2000). But by 2004, per capita income in low-income countries had jumped to $510. Per capita income in middle-income countries has grown steadily, more than doubling in the twenty-year period between 1994 and 2006.

In 2006, the average person in a typical high-income country earned $36,487 (per capita GNI; Atlas method based on current U.S. dollars), fifty-six times as much as the $650 earned by his or her counterpart in a low-income country (World Bank 2007e). About half of the world's population are estimated to live on less than $2 a day (Global Issues 2006).

☑ CONCEPT CHECKS

1. Explain how the World Bank measures global inequality, and discuss some of the problems associated with measuring global inequality.
2. Compare and contrast high-income, middle-income, and low-income countries.

TABLE 9.2

The Global Quality of Life Has Risen during the Past Forty Years

QUALITY OF LIFE INDICATORS	1967–1970	2002–2004	2006
Percentage illiterate[a, b]	53	22	
Average number of children per woman[a, c]	6	2.6	2.5
Mortality rate for children under five years (per 1,000 population)[c, d]	147	80	72
Infant mortality rate (per 1,000 births)[d, e]	96	54	
Number of people suffering from malnutrition[a, f]	4 out of 10	1 out of 4	
Life expectancy at birth[a, c]	50 years	67 years	68 years
Annual per person income (per capita GNI)[a, c]	$640	$6,280	$7,468
Percent living on less than $1/day[a, b]	~50	~20	

SOURCE: (a) Data for 1968, Salter 1998; (b) data for 2004, World Bank 2005; (c) World Bank 2007e; (d) data for 1970, United Nations 2005; (e) data for 2003, United Nations 2005, (f) data for 2002, United Nations 2005.

Rich and Poor Countries: The World by Income, 2007

Like individuals in a country, the countries of the world as a whole can be seen as economically stratified. In general, those countries that experienced industrialization the earliest are the richest, while those that remain agricultural are the poorest. An enormous—and growing—gulf separates the two groups.

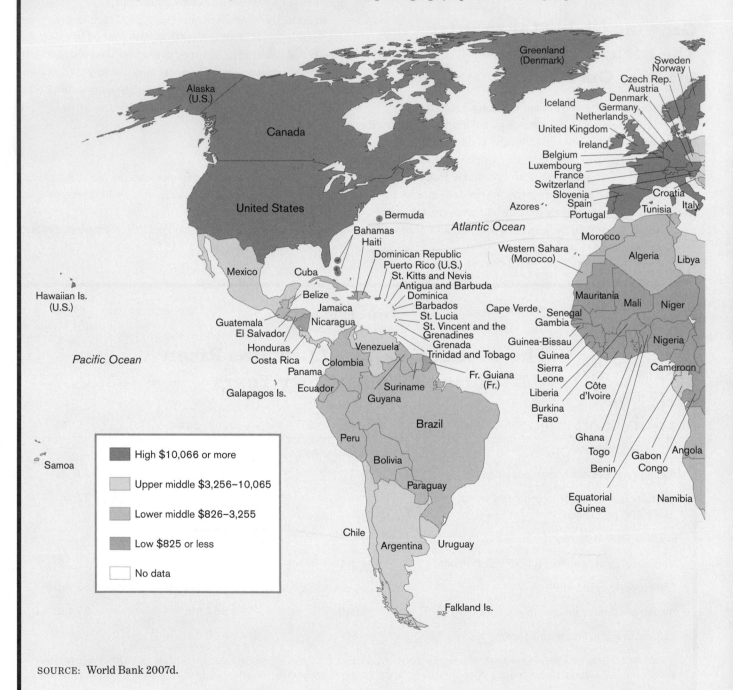

Legend:
- High $10,066 or more
- Upper middle $3,256–10,065
- Lower middle $826–3,255
- Low $825 or less
- No data

SOURCE: World Bank 2007d.

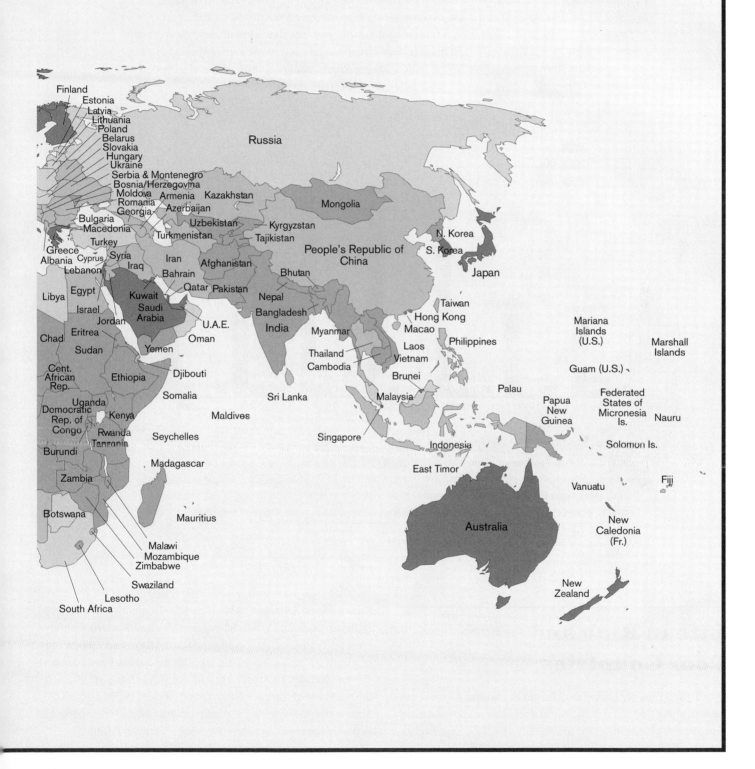

FIGURE 9.2

GNI per Person in Low-, Middle-, and High-Income Countries, 1983–2004

Despite overall growth in the global economy, the gap between rich and poor countries has not declined in recent years. Between 1984 and 2004, per-person GNI in low-income countries increased an average of 2.9 percent a year, far less than in high-income countries (6.5 percent). As a consequence, the average person in a high-income country earned roughly sixty-three times as much as the average person in a low-income country. Average per-person GNI in middle-income countries split the difference and increased by an average 4.3 percent.

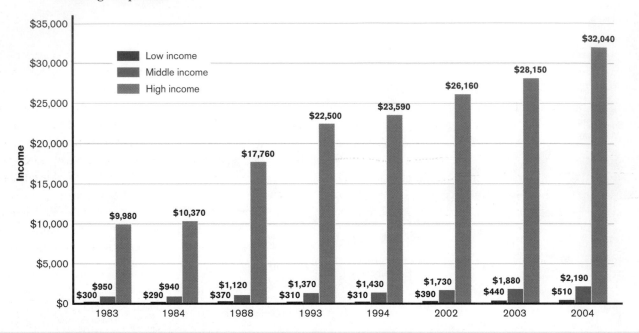

Between 1984 and 2004, what was the increase in GNI per person in low-income countries? Between 1984 and 2004 does GNI per person in high-income countries increase, decrease, or stay the same, and if so by how much? What does the figure indicate about the gap in GNI per capita between rich and poor countries? According to the reading, what is misrepresented by the reporting of global trends that include the average of all nations?

SOURCE: World Bank 2005.

Life in Rich and Poor Countries

Wealth and poverty make life different in a host of ways. For instance, about one third of the world's poor are undernourished, and almost all are illiterate and lack access to even primary-school education. Over half of the world's population now live in urban areas; by 2030, 82 percent (United Nations Conference on Trade and Development 2004). More than 40 percent of all urban residents in developing countries live in slums (United Nations Food and Agriculture Organization [UN FAO] 2004). Many of the poor come from tribes or racial and ethnic groups that differ from the dominant groups, and their poverty is partly the result of discrimination (Narayan 1999).

Health

People in high-income countries are far healthier than their counterparts in low-income countries. Low-income countries generally suffer from inadequate health facilities, and the few hospitals or clinics seldom serve the poorest people. Residents of low-income countries also lack proper sanitation, drink polluted water, and risk contracting infectious diseases. They are more likely to suffer malnourishment, starvation, and famine. All these factors contribute to physical weakness and poor health. There is growing evidence that the high rates of HIV/AIDS infection in many African countries reflect the weakened health of impoverished people (Stillwagon 2001).

Because of poor health conditions, people in low-income countries are more likely to die in infancy and less likely to live to old age than people in high-income countries. Infants are thirteen times more likely to die at birth and—if they survive birth—are likely to live twenty years fewer (Table 9.3). Children often die of illnesses that are readily treated in wealthier countries, such as measles or diarrhea. In some parts of the world, such as sub-Saharan Africa, a child is more likely to die before the age of five than to enter secondary school (World Bank 2005). Still, conditions have improved in low- and middle-income countries: Between 1980 and 2005, for example, the infant mortality rate dropped from 97 (per thousand live births)

to 75.3 in low-income countries and from 60 to 29.6 in middle-income countries (World Bank 2005). AIDS and growing poverty have increased infant mortality in the poorest countries in recent years.

During the past three decades, some improvements have occurred in most of the middle-income countries and in some of the low-income ones: Infant mortality has been cut in half, and average life expectancy has increased by ten years or more because of the wider availability of modern medical technology, improved sanitation, and rising incomes.

Hunger, Malnutrition, and Famine

Hunger, malnutrition, and famine have always been global sources of poor health. What seems to be new is their extent—the fact that so many people today are on the brink of starvation (Global Map 9.2). The United Nations Food and Agriculture Organization (UN FAO 2007) estimates that 854 million people go hungry every day, 96 percent of them in developing countries. The program defines "hunger" as a diet of 1,800 or fewer calories a day—an amount insufficient to provide adults with the nutrients required for active, healthy lives.

According to the United Nations World Food Programme (UN FAO 2007), 146 million of the world's hungry are children under age five, who are underweight because they lack

TABLE 9.3

Differences in Infant Mortality and Life Expectancy: Low-, Middle-, and High-Income Countries, 2004

	INCOME LEVEL			
	LOW	MIDDLE	HIGH	WORLD
Infant mortality rate (per 1,000 live births)	79	30	6	54
Life expectancy at birth (years)	59	70	79	67

SOURCE: World Bank 2007f.

An Afghan shepherd leads his herd in search of water in Kabul. Four years of harsh and successive droughts in many areas of land-locked Afghanistan has caused the water level to drop drastically. Hundreds of people and tens of thousands of animals have died due to drought-related problems in various parts of the country.

Hunger Is a Global Problem

Hunger is a global problem, although it is disproportionately found in the poorest regions of the world. The world's great concentrations of hunger are in central and sub-Saharan Africa, followed by the Indian subcontinent. Although somewhat less widespread, significant amounts of hunger are also found in parts of Asia, Russia, and other republics of the former Soviet Union, South America, Central America, and Mexico. It is estimated that at any given time, 852 million people are hungry, 200 million of whom are children.

Legend:
- <2.5% Extremely low
- 2.5–4% Very low
- 5–19% Moderately low
- 20–34% Moderately high
- >35% Very high
- No data

SOURCE: UN FAO 2007.

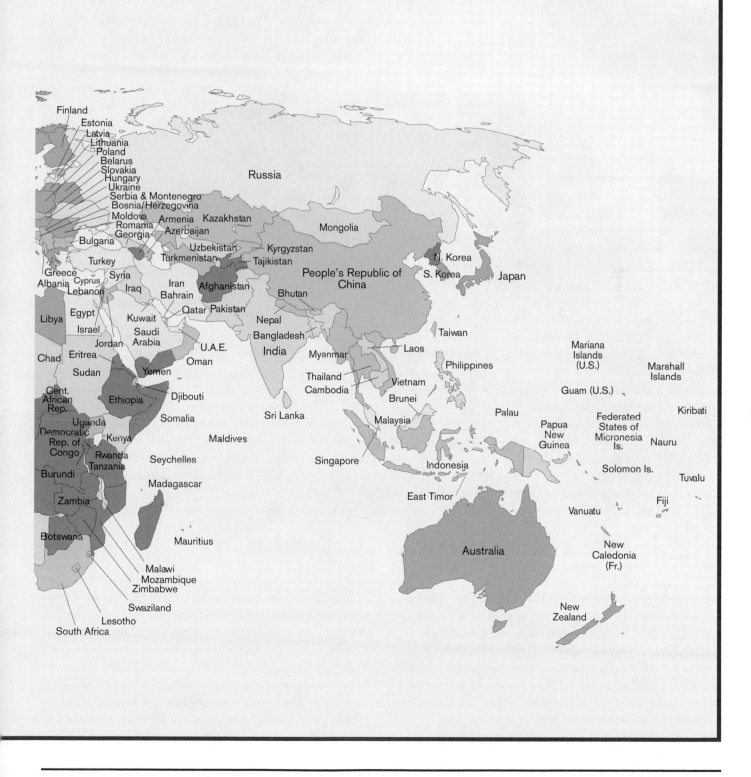

Finland
Estonia
Latvia
Lithuania
Poland
Belarus
Slovakia
Hungary
Ukraine
Serbia & Montenegro
Bosnia/Herzegovina
Moldova
Romania
Georgia
Bulgaria
Greece
Albania
Cyprus
Lebanon
Libya
Egypt
Israel
Jordan
Chad
Eritrea
Sudan
Cent.
African
Rep.
Uganda
Democratic
Rep. of
Congo
Burundi
Zambia
Botswana
Malawi
Mozambique
Zimbabwe
Swaziland
Lesotho
South Africa

Turkey
Syria
Iraq
Kuwait
Saudi
Arabia
Yemen
Ethiopia
Somalia
Kenya
Rwanda
Tanzania
Madagascar
Mauritius
Seychelles

Russia

Armenia
Azerbaijan
Uzbekistan
Turkmenistan
Iran
Bahrain
Qatar
U.A.E.
Oman
Djibouti

Kazakhstan

Kyrgyzstan
Tajikistan
Afghanistan
Pakistan
Nepal
Bangladesh
India
Maldives
Sri Lanka

Mongolia

People's Republic of
China

Bhutan

Myanmar
Thailand
Cambodia
Laos
Vietnam
Malaysia
Singapore
Indonesia
East Timor

N. Korea
S. Korea
Japan

Taiwan

Philippines

Brunei

Palau

Australia

New
Zealand

Mariana
Islands
(U.S.)

Guam (U.S.)

Papua
New
Guinea

Marshall
Islands

Federated
States of
Micronesia
Is.

Solomon Is.

Vanuatu

New
Caledonia
(Fr.)

Kiribati

Nauru

Tuvalu

Fiji

"U.S. Babies Die at Higher Rates"

The United States is one of the wealthiest countries in the world, so it was a surprise to many when news headlines in 2006 told readers that "U.S. Has Second Worst Newborn Death Rate in Modern World" (Green 2006). According to the annual *State of World's Mothers* report, conducted by Save the Children (2007), American newborns are two to three times more likely to die than infants born in Japan, Finland, Iceland, or Norway. Among thirty-three industrialized nations, the United States ranked second to last, trailed only by Latvia. While children's health advocates believe that these numbers are an important call to improve the national health care system, health researchers say that the rates are biased because the nations studied calculated infant mortality in inconsistent ways.

The *State of World's Mothers* report analyzed data from governments, research institutions, and international agencies from 125 high-, middle-, and low-income nations. The data captured ten different aspects of child and mother well-being such as infant mortality rates, maternal mortality rates, and the political status

of women. (Infant mortality rate is the number of babies per 1,000 births in a given year that will die before age one.) The report found that the infant mortality rate in the United States was 5 deaths per 1,000, about the same rate as less wealthy industrialized nations such as Hungary, Poland, and Slovakia. By contrast, the rate was 1.8 per 1,000 in Japan and 2 per 1,000 in most northern European nations, such as Finland and Norway.

These national rankings have been held up to scrutiny by social and medical scientists, however. Bernadine Healy (2006), former director of the National Institutes of Health, has criticized these rankings along several methodological grounds. First, infant mortality rates are calculated slightly differently across countries. An infant mortality rate is defined as the number of all deaths to babies under one year old, divided by the total number of "live births" that year.

The World Health Organization (WHO) defines a "live birth" as a newborn showing any signs of life, such as a heart beat or gasp of breath (Glueck and Cihak 2005). The United States follows the WHO recommendation and counts all live births—including very small or premature babies. By contrast, other nations do not count as "live births" extremely low birth weight infants (Austria and Germany), infants that are less than twelve inches long (Switzerland), and babies that are born at less than twenty-six weeks (Belgium and France). As a result, says Healy, reports like those from Save the Children are comparing apples and oranges. WHO economist John Goodman echoes her sentiments: "taking into account such data-reporting differences," infant mortality rates in the United States are about the same as those in other European nations (Glueck and Cihak 2005).

---

adequate food. Every five seconds a child dies because he or she is hungry (UN FAO 2006). Every year 10.9 million children under the age of five die; 60 percent of those deaths are a result of hunger. Every year another 17 million children are born with low birth weight stemming from inadequate maternal nutrition (UN WFP 2004). Yet more than three quarters of all malnourished children under the age of five live in countries that produce a food surplus (Lappe et al. 1998).

Most famine and hunger today are the result of a combination of natural and social forces. Drought alone affects an estimated 100 million people. In countries such as Sudan, Ethiopia, Eritrea, Indonesia, Afghanistan, Sierra Leone, Guinea, and Tajikistan, the combination of drought and internal warfare has wrecked food production, resulting in starvation and death for millions. The role of conflict and warfare in creating hunger is increasing: Conflict and economic problems were cited as

Healy (2006) also believes that the media's reporting of infant mortality may lead to the erroneous conclusion that neonatal medical care for infants is poor in the United States. She notes that most infants who die in the United States are born critically ill, and 40 percent of all infant deaths take place in the first day of life. The causes of death are prematurity, low birth weight, and congenital malformations—rather than quality of care. Other social factors matter as well. Multiple-birth pregnancies, such as twins or triplets, are more likely to result in infant death. Rates of multiple births are high in the United States, as older women hoping to have children often rely on fertility treatments.

Despite these methodological concerns, most public health experts agree that infant death is still a serious problem in the United States because it is particularly common among babies born to poor women and to African Americans. The U.S. infant mortality rate is 5 per 1,000 overall, but is 9 deaths per 1,000 among African Americans. The relatively high rates among black babies reflect poor prenatal care, which is a serious problem for women who lack health insurance. Other factors include social, economic, and health problems affecting young African American women. For instance, teenage pregnancy and obesity—which disproportionately strike black women— are risk factors for having a low weight or premature birth, and babies who are born at low weight or prematurely are precisely the babies at greatest risk of death.

Some critics worry that attention to the gap between infant mortality rates in the United States versus infant mortality rates in other wealthy nations may draw attention away from another serious social problem—the high infant mortality rates in poor nations in Africa and South Asia. An astounding 99 percent of all infant deaths each year are in developing nations. In Liberia, the country ranked last of the 125 nations in the Save the Children report, infant mortality rates are roughly 65 per 1,000 births. Other countries at the bottom of the list were Afghanistan, Angola, and Iraq, countries where armed conflict may impede newborn survival. The major causes of infant death in nations such as Liberia are very different from the causes in developing nations. While most infants in the United States die from congenital problems, infants in the developing world die from infection, tetanus, and diarrhea. Rankings aside, most global health experts agree that high infant mortality rates can and should be combated with improved vaccination programs, with better nutrition, and by creating safe political and social environments for families (Lallanilla 2005).

Questions

- What is an infant mortality rate?
- What is the infant mortality rate in the United States versus that in several other developed nations?

- What methodological explanations have been offered for the relatively high infant mortality rate in the United States?
- What social explanations have been given for the infant mortality rate in the United States?

FOR FURTHER EXPLORATION

Fox News. 2006. "Infant Mortality Rate High in the U.S." *Fox News* (May 9, 2006).

Glueck, Michael Arnold, and Robert Cihak. 2005. "Infant Mortality Myths." *Ocean County Register* (March 16, 2005).

Green, Jeff. 2006. "U.S. Has Second Worst Newborn Death Rate in Modern World." *CNN* (May 8, 2006). www.cnn.com/2006/HEALTH/parenting/05/08/mothers.index/index.html (accessed January 19, 2006).

Healy, Bernadine. 2006. "Behind the Baby Count." *U.S. News and World Report* (September 24, 2006). http://health.usnews.com/usnews/health/articles/060924/2healy.htm (accessed January 19, 2008).

Lallanilla, Marc. 2005. "U.S. Babies Die at Higher Rate: Infant Mortality Rates Are Rising in U.S. while Rates in Other Countries are Improving." *ABC News* (November 1, 2005). http://abcnews.go.com/print?id=1266515 (accessed January 19, 2008).

Save the Children. 2007. *Saving the Lives of Children under Age 5.* Westport, CT: Save the Children. www.savethechildren.org/publications/mothers/2007/SOWM-2007-final.pdf (accessed January 20, 2008).

---

the main cause of 35 percent of food shortages between 1992 and 2003, compared with 15 percent between 1986 and 1991 (UN FAO 2005). In Latin America and the Caribbean, 53 million people (11 percent of the population) are malnourished—a number that rises to 180 million (33 percent) in sub-Saharan Africa and 525 million (17 percent) in Asia (UN WFP 2001).

The AIDS epidemic has also contributed to food shortages and hunger, killing many working-age adults. One study by the FAO (2001) predicts that HIV/AIDS-caused deaths in the ten African countries most afflicted by the epidemic will reduce the labor force by 26 percent by the year 2020. Of the estimated 33.2 million people worldwide infected with HIV, 68 percent are in sub-Saharan Africa (UNAIDS 2007a). Of the 2.1 million people who died from AIDS in 2007, about 500,000 were children. According to the FAO (2001), the epidemic can be devastating to nutrition, food security, and agricultural production, affecting "the entire society's ability to maintain and reproduce itself."

The countries affected by famine and starvation are too poor to pay for new technologies that would increase food production. Nor can they afford sufficient food imports. At the same time, paradoxically, as world hunger grows, food production continues to increase, often in the very countries experiencing hunger emergencies (UN FAO 2004). This growth, however, is not evenly distributed around the world. In much of Africa, for example, food production per person has declined. Surplus food produced in high-income countries such as the United States is seldom affordable to the countries that need it most.

Education and Literacy

Because education and literacy are important routes to economic development, lower-income countries are disadvantaged because they lack high-quality public education systems. Thus children in high-income countries get more schooling, and adults in those countries are more likely to be literate (Table 9.4). While virtually all high school–age males and females attend secondary school in high-income countries, in 2005 only 78 percent did so in middle-income countries and only 43 percent in low-income countries. In 2004, 28 percent of male adults and half of female adults in low-income countries were unable to read and write. In 2005, the adult literacy rate in low-income countries was only 61 percent. One reason for these differences is that high-income countries spend a much larger percentage of gross domestic product on education than do low-income countries (World Bank 2005).

Education is important for several reasons. First, it contributes to economic growth, because people with advanced schooling provide the skilled workers necessary for high-wage industries. Second, education offers the only hope for escaping the cycle of harsh working conditions and poverty, because poorly educated people are condemned to low-wage, unskilled jobs. Finally, educated people have fewer children, thus slowing the global population explosion that contributes to global poverty (see Chapter 19).

☑ CONCEPT CHECKS

1. Why do people who live in high-income countries have better health than those who live in low-income countries?

TABLE 9.4

Differences in Education and Literacy: Low-, Middle-, and High-Income Countries

	INCOME LEVEL		
	LOW	MIDDLE	HIGH
School enrollment secondary (% gross), 2004	46	75	105
Public spending on education, total (% of GDP), 2005[a]	3	4.5	5.9
Literacy rate, adult male (% of males aged 15 and above), 2004	72	94	No data
Literacy rate, adult female (% of females aged 15 and above), 2004	50	87	No data

[a]GDP, gross domestic product.

SOURCE: World Bank 2005, 2007f.

Can Poor Countries Become Rich?

By the mid-1970s several low-income countries in East Asia were undergoing a process of industrialization that appeared to threaten the global economic dominance of the United States and Europe (Amsden 1989). This process began with Japan in the 1950s but quickly extended to the **newly industrializing economies (NIEs)** in East Asia and Latin America. The East Asian NIEs included Hong Kong in the 1960s and Taiwan, South Korea, and Singapore in the 1970s and 1980s. Other Asian countries followed in the 1980s and the early 1990s, including China, Malaysia, Thailand, and Indonesia. Today, most are middle income, and some—such as Hong Kong, South Korea, Taiwan, and Singapore—have reached the high-income category.

The low- and middle-income economies of the East Asian region averaged 7.7 percent growth per year from 1980 to 1999, a rate that is extraordinary by world standards (World Bank

2000–2001). By 1999, the gross domestic product (GDP) per person in Singapore was the same as that in the United States. China, the world's most populous country, has one of the most rapidly growing economies on the planet. At an average annual growth rate of 10 percent between 1980 and 1999, the Chinese economy more than doubled.

Economic growth in East Asia has had some costs, including the sometimes violent repression of labor and civil rights, terrible factory conditions, the exploitation of an increasingly female workforce, the exploitation of immigrant workers, and widespread environmental degradation. Nonetheless, large numbers of people in these countries are prospering.

How do social scientists account for the rapid economic growth in the East Asian NIEs? The answer may hold some crucial lessons for low-income countries elsewhere that hope to follow in the steps of the NIEs and could even lead to a rethinking of the causes of global inequality. The economic success of the East Asian NIEs can be attributed to a combination of factors. Some of these factors are historical, including those stemming from world political and economic shifts. Some are cultural. Still others involve the ways these countries pursued economic growth.

1. **Historically, Taiwan, South Korea, Hong Kong, and Singapore were part of colonial situations that, while imposing hardships, also paved the way for economic growth.** Taiwan and Korea were tied to the Japanese Empire; Hong Kong and Singapore were former British colonies. Japan eliminated large landowners who opposed industrialization, and Britain and Japan encouraged industrial development, constructed roads and other transportation systems, and built relatively efficient governmental bureaucracies in these colonies. Britain also developed Hong Kong and Singapore as trading centers (Cumings 1987; Gold 1986). Elsewhere in the world—for example, in Latin America and Africa—countries that are today poor did not fare so well in their dealings with richer, more powerful nations.

2. **The East Asian region benefited from a long period of world economic growth.** Between the 1950s and the mid-1970s, the growing economies of Europe and the United States provided a big market for the clothing, footwear, and electronics that were increasingly made in East Asia, creating an opportunity for economic development there. Furthermore, periodic economic slowdowns in the United States and Europe forced businesses to cut their labor costs and spurred the relocation of factories to low-wage East Asian countries (Henderson and Appelbaum 1992).

3. **Economic growth in East Asia took off at the high point of the cold war, when the United States and**

Singapore, along with Taiwan, South Korea, and Hong Kong, was transformed from a low-income country to a relatively prosperous, newly industrialized country.

its allies, in erecting a defense against communist China, provided economic and military aid.** Direct aid and loans fueled investment in transistors, semiconductors, and other electronics, spurring the development of local industries. Military assistance favored strong (often military) governments that used repression to keep labor costs low (Amsden 1989; Castells 1992; Cumings 1987, 1997; Deyo 1987; Evans 1987; Haggard 1990; Henderson 1989; Mirza 1986).

4. **Some sociologists argue that the economic success of Japan and the East Asian NIEs is due in part to their cultural traditions, especially their shared Confucian philosophy.** Over a century ago, Max Weber (1977; orig. 1904) argued that the Protestant belief in thrift, frugality, and hard work partly explained the rise of capitalism in western Europe. Weber's argument has been applied to Asian economic history. Confucianism, it is argued, inculcates respect for elders and superiors, education, hard work, and proven accomplishments as the key to advancement as well as a willingness to sacrifice today for a greater reward tomorrow. These

values make Asian workers and managers highly loyal to their companies, submissive to authority, hardworking, and success oriented. Workers and capitalists alike are said to be frugal and likely to reinvest their wealth in further economic growth (Berger 1986; Berger and Hsiao 1998; Helm 1992; Redding 1990; Wong 1986).

This explanation has some merit, but it overlooks the fact that businesses are not always revered and respected in Asia. Students and workers throughout the East Asian NIEs have opposed unfair business and governmental policies, often at the risk of imprisonment and sometimes death (Deyo 1989; Ho 1990). Furthermore, such Confucian cultural values as thrift may be declining in Japan and the NIEs, as young people increasingly value conspicuous consumption over austerity and investment (Helm 1992).

5. **Many East Asian governments followed strong policies that favored economic growth.** Their governments played active roles in keeping labor costs low, encouraged economic development through tax breaks and other economic policies, and offered free public education.

Whether the growth of these economies will continue is unclear. In 1997–1998, a combination of poor investment decisions, corruption, and world economic conditions abruptly halted their economic expansion. The experience of Hong Kong was typical: After thirty-seven years of continuous growth, the economy stalled and its stock market lost more than half its value. Yet the "Asian meltdown" turned out to be merely a blip in the region's growth. China in particular has been growing at a high rate and is today the world's fourth largest economy.

☑ CONCEPT CHECKS

1. What are the factors that have facilitated the economic success of the newly industrialized East Asian economies?

Theories of Global Inequality

Four kinds of theories have been advanced to explain global inequality: market-oriented, dependency, world-systems, and state-centered theories. Each theory has strengths and weaknesses. One shortcoming of all four is that they underemphasize the role of women in economic development. By putting the theories together, however, we should be able to answer a question facing the 85 percent of the world's population living outside high-income countries: How can they move up in the world economy?

Market-Oriented Theories

Market-oriented theories assume that the best economic consequences will result if individuals are free—from governmental constraint—to make their own economic decisions. Unrestricted capitalism is seen as the avenue to economic growth. Government bureaucracy should not dictate which goods to produce, what prices to charge, or how much to pay workers. According to market-oriented theorists, governmental direction of the economies of low-income countries blocks economic development; thus, local governments should get out of the way of development (Berger 1986; Ranis 1996; Ranis and Mahmood 1992; Rostow 1961; Warren 1980).

Market-oriented theories reflect the belief that "any country can make it if it does it 'our way' "—that is, like the United States and other similar high-income countries. These theories inspired U.S. government foreign-aid programs that provided money, expert advisers, and technology to low-income countries, paving the way for U.S. corporations to make investments there.

One influential proponent of such theories was W. W. Rostow, an economic adviser to former U.S. president John F. Kennedy, whose ideas helped shape U.S. foreign policy toward Latin America during the 1960s. Rostow's explanation, termed **modernization theory**, argues that low-income societies can develop economically only if they adopt modern economic institutions, technologies, and cultural values that emphasize savings and productive investment.

According to Rostow (1961), the traditional cultural values and social institutions of low-income countries impede their economic effectiveness. For example, many people in low-income countries, in Rostow's view, lack a strong work ethic: They would sooner consume today than invest for the future. Large families also contribute to "economic backwardness," since a breadwinner with many mouths to feed can hardly save money for investment purposes.

But to modernization theorists, the problems in low-income countries run even deeper because their cultures support a value system that views hardship and suffering as unavoidable. Acceptance of one's lot in life discourages people from working hard and being thrifty to overcome their fate. In this view, a country's poverty is due largely to the cultural failings of the people themselves, which are reinforced by government policies that set wages and control prices and generally interfere in the operation of the economy. How can low-income countries break out of their poverty? Rostow viewed economic growth as going through several stages, which he likened to the journey of an airplane:

1. **Traditional stage.** This stage is characterized by low rates of savings, the supposed lack of a work ethic, and a fatalistic value system. The airplane is not yet off the ground.

2. **Takeoff to economic growth.** Economic takeoff occurs when poor countries begin to jettison their traditional values and institutions and start to save and invest money for the future. Wealthy countries, such as the United States, can facilitate this growth by financing birth-control programs or providing low-cost loans for electrification, road and airport construction, and new industries.

3. **Drive to technological maturity.** With the help of money and advice from high-income countries, the airplane of economic growth would taxi down the runway, pick up speed, and become airborne. The country would then approach technological maturity and climb to cruising altitude, improving its technology, reinvesting its recently acquired wealth in new industries, and adopting the institutions and values of the high-income countries.

4. **High mass consumption.** Now people can enjoy the fruits of their labor by achieving a high standard of living. The airplane (country) cruises on automatic pilot, having entered the ranks of high-income countries.

Rostow's ideas remain influential. Indeed, the prevailing view among economists today, **neoliberalism**, argues that free-market forces, achieved by minimizing governmental restrictions on business, provide the only route to economic growth. Neoliberalism holds that global free trade will enable all countries to prosper; eliminating governmental regulation is necessary. Neoliberal economists therefore seek an end to restrictions on trade and often challenge minimum wage and other labor laws, as well as environmental restrictions on business.

Sociologists, however, focus on the cultural aspects of Rostow's theory: whether and how certain beliefs and institutions hinder development (So 1990). These include religious values, moral beliefs, belief in magic, and folk traditions and practices, as well as the belief that moral decay and social unrest accompany business and trade.

Dependency Theories

During the 1960s, a number of sociologists and economists from the low-income countries of Latin America and Africa rejected the idea that their countries' economic underdevelopment was due to their own cultural or institutional faults. Instead, they built on the theories of Karl Marx, who argued that world capitalism would create a class of countries manipulated by more powerful countries, just as capitalism within countries leads to the exploitation of workers. Adherents to **dependency theories** argue that the poverty of low-income countries stems from their exploitation by wealthy countries and the multinational corporations based in those wealthy countries. In their view, global capitalism has locked their countries into a downward spiral of exploitation and poverty.

Two British generals are served tea in Bangalore, India. India was part of the British Empire until 1947.

What Can You Do about Child Labor?

Does child labor still exist in the world today? According to a United Nations International Labor Organization (ILO) report with the hopeful title *The End of Child Labor within Reach* (ILO 2006), in 2004 (the most recent year for which the ILO had gathered systematic data) more than 218 million boys and girls between the ages of five and seventeen were working in developing countries, or about one out of every seven children in the world. Among these, more than half (126 million) were laboring under hazardous conditions. Child labor was found throughout the developing world. In the Asia-Pacific region 20 percent of the children ages five through seventeen were working (122 million; in Africa, 26 percent (48 million); in Latin America, 5 percent (6 million). Children are forced to work because of a combination of family poverty, lack of education, and traditional indifference among some people in many countries to the plight of those who are poor or who are ethnic minorities.

Two thirds of working children labor in agriculture, with the rest in manufacturing, wholesale and retail trade, restaurants and hotels, and a variety of services such as working as servants in wealthy households. At best, these children work for long hours with little pay and are therefore unable to go to school and develop the skills that might eventually enable them to escape their lives of poverty. Many, however, work at hazardous and exploitative jobs under slavelike conditions, suffering a variety of illnesses and injuries. The ILO (2000) provides a grisly summary: "wounds, broken or complete loss of body parts, burns and skin diseases, eye and hearing impairment, respiratory and gastro-intestinal illnesses, fever, headaches from excessive heat in the fields or factories."

A United Nations (UNICEF 1997) report provides several examples:

In Malaysia, children may work up to 17-hour days on rubber plantations, exposed to insect and snake bites. In the United Republic of Tanzania, they pick coffee, inhaling pesticides. In Portugal, children as young as 12 are subject to the heavy labor and myriad dangers of the construction industry. In Morocco, they hunch at looms for long hours and little pay, knotting the strands of luxury carpets for export. In the United States, children are exploited in garment industry sweatshops. In

the Philippines, young boys dive in dangerous conditions to help set nets for deep-sea fishing.

Conditions in many factories are horrible:

Dust from the chemical powders and strong vapors in both the storeroom and the boiler room were obvious.... We found 250 children, mostly below 10 years of age, working in a long hall filling in a slotted frame with sticks. Row upon row of children, some barely five years old, were involved in the work. (UNICEF 1997)

One form of child labor that is close to slavery is "bonded labor." In this system, children as young as eight or nine are pledged by their parents to factory owners in exchange for small loans. These children are paid so little that they never manage to reduce the debt, condemning them to a lifetime of bondage. One recent case of bonded labor that attracted international attention was that of Iqbal Masih, a Pakistani child who, at age four, was sold into slavery by his father to borrow six hundred rupees (roughly $16) for the wedding of his firstborn son. For six years, Iqbal spent most of his time chained to a carpet-weaving loom, tying tiny knots for hours on end. After fleeing the factory at age ten, he began speaking to labor organizations and schools about his experience. Iqbal paid a bitter price for his outspokenness: At age thirteen, while riding his bicycle in his hometown, he was gunned down by agents believed to be working for the carpet industry (Free the Children 1998; Bobak 1996).

Abolishing exploitative child labor will require countries around the world to enact strong child-labor laws and be willing to enforce them. International organizations, such as the United Nations ILO, have outlined a set of standards for such laws to follow. In June 1999, the ILO adopted Convention 182, calling for the abolition of the "Worst Forms of Child Labor." These are defined as including

- all forms of slavery or practices similar to slavery, such as the sale and trafficking of children, debt bondage and serfdom, and forced or compulsory labor, including forced or compulsory recruitment of children for use in armed conflict
- the use, procuring, or offering of a child for prostitution, for the production of pornography, or for pornographic performances
- the use, procuring, or offering of a child for illicit activities, in particular for the production and trafficking of drugs as defined in the relevant international treaties; and
- work that, by its nature or the circumstances in which it is carried out, is likely to harm the health, safety, or morals of children.

Countries must also provide free public education and require that children attend school full time (UNICEF 2000). But at least part of the responsibility for solving the problem lies with the global corporations that manufacture goods using child labor—and, ultimately, with the consumers who buy those goods. Here are two things that you can do right now:

1. **Check the label.** Mind what you are buying. Begin by looking at the label. When you purchase clothing, rugs, and other textiles, the label will tell you where it was made, if unionized labor was used, and, in a few cases, whether it is certified to be "sweatshop free." Avoid buying garments made in countries with known human rights abuses, such as Myanmar (Burma). If the product has a label indicating it was made with union labor, it is likely to be free from child labor. "Sweatshop free" labels, although still rare, are likely to become more common in coming years, as labor and consumer groups pressure the U.S. government to more closely monitor imported goods. In one well-publicized campaign that grew out of Iqbal's tragic experience, Indian human rights activists developed the "Rugmark" label, which certifies that the carpet is free of child labor. The U.S. Department of Labor is also working toward a way to certify goods that are sold in the United

States to be sweatshop free, although at this time there is no way to do so reliably: The millions of factories around the world involved in making consumer goods are too vast and dispersed to monitor.

2. **Join up.** Join (or start) an antisweatshop campaign at your own college or university. There is a national campaign, organized by United Students Against Sweatshops, to require schools to engage in "responsible purchasing" when they buy or sell clothing, athletic equipment, and other goods that carry the school logo. Schools are urged to sign agreements with all their vendors that require full disclosure of the names and locations of the factories where the goods are made, certifying that the goods are free from child labor and other forms of exploitation. School sales are a multibillion-dollar business, and if schools set a high standard, manufacturers will be forced to take notice.

The anti child labor campaign is having an effect. The ILO reports that between 2000 and 2004, the number of children ages five through seventeen who were working actually declined by 11 percent (28 million), with the steepest declines (33 percent) for children ages five through fourteen engaged in the most hazardous work. Significant improvements were seen throughout the world, with the exception of sub-Saharan Africa. The report attributes these declines to political efforts on the part of workers, nongovernmental organizations, and consumers, along with heightened awareness of the problems on the part of employers and governments. One recent milestone was the ILO's adoption of a convention calling for the elimination of the worst forms of child labor in 1999, which has since been ratified by 165 countries.

In a global economy, you can choose what you buy and influence others to make informed and ethical choices about the products they consume. Be a smart shopper—it can make a difference.

According to dependency theories, the exploitation began with **colonialism**. Powerful nations colonized other countries to procure raw materials (such as petroleum, copper, and iron) for their factories and to control markets for the manufactured products. Although colonialism typically involved European countries establishing colonies in North and South America, Africa, and Asia, some Asian countries (such as Japan) had colonies as well.

Even though colonialism largely ended after World War II, the exploitation did not: Transnational corporations continued to reap enormous profits from their branches in low-income countries. According to dependency theory, these global companies, often with the support of the powerful banks and governments of rich countries, established factories in poor countries, using cheap labor and raw materials to maximize production costs without governmental interference. In turn, the low prices for labor and raw materials prevented poor countries from accumulating the profit necessary to industrialize themselves. Local businesses that might compete with foreign corporations were prevented from doing so. In this view, poor countries are forced to borrow from rich countries, thereby increasing their economic dependency.

Low-income countries are seen not as underdeveloped, but as misdeveloped (Amin 1974; Emmanuel 1972; Frank 1966, 1969a, 1969b, 1979; Prebisch 1967, 1971). Except for a few local politicians and businesspeople serving the interests of the foreign corporations, people fall into poverty. Peasants must choose between starvation and working at near-starvation wages on foreign-controlled plantations and in foreign-controlled mines and factories. Most dependency theorists reject such exploitation and call for revolutionary changes that would push foreign corporations out of their countries altogether (Frank 1966, 1969a, 1969b).

Whereas market-oriented theorists usually ignore political and military power, dependency theorists regard the exercise of power as central to enforcing unequal economic relationships: Whenever local leaders question such unequal arrangements, their voices are suppressed. Unionization is usually outlawed, and labor organizers are jailed or killed. When people elect a government opposing these policies, it is likely to be overthrown by the country's military, often backed by armed forces of the industrialized countries. Dependency theorists cite many examples, such as the role of the CIA in overthrowing the Marxist governments of Guatemala in 1954 and Chile in 1973 and in undermining support for the leftist government in Nicaragua in the 1980s. In the view of dependency theory, global economic inequality is backed up by force: Economic elites in poor countries, backed by their counterparts in wealthy ones, use police and military power to keep the local population under control.

Although Nigeria is the world's eighth largest producer of oil, the overwhelming majority of the profits generated in the energy trade go to oil companies and the military government, providing no benefit to the country's poverty-stricken inhabitants. These women are protesting Royal Dutch Shell's exploitation of Nigeria's oil and natural gas resources.

The Brazilian sociologist Enrique Fernando Cardoso argued that some degree of **dependent development** was nonetheless possible—that under certain circumstances, poor countries can still develop economically, although only in ways shaped by their reliance on wealthier countries (Cardoso and Faletto 1979). In particular, the governments of these countries could help steer a course between dependency and development (Evans 1979). Today, Cardoso has changed his thinking, calling for greater integration of Brazil into the global economy.

World-Systems Theory

Although dependency theories hold that individual countries are economically tied to one another, **world-systems theory** argues that the world capitalist economic system of countries engaging in diplomatic and economic relations with one another must be understood as a single unit. This approach is identified with the work of Immanuel Wallerstein and his colleagues. Wallerstein (1974a, 1974b, 1979, 1990, 1996a, 1996b) showed that capitalism has functioned as a global economic system ever since the extension of markets and trade in Europe in the fifteenth and sixteenth centuries (Hopkins and Wallerstein 1996). The world system comprises four overlapping elements (Chase-Dunn 1989):

- A world market for goods and labor
- The division of the population into different economic classes, particularly capitalists and workers
- An international system of formal and informal political relations among the most powerful countries, whose competition helps shape the world economy
- The division of the world into three unequal economic zones, with the wealthier zones exploiting the poorer ones

World-systems theorists term these zones *core, periphery,* and *semiperiphery*. **Core countries** are the most advanced industrial countries, taking the most profits. These include Japan, the United States, and the countries of western Europe. The **periphery** comprises low-income, largely agricultural countries that are often manipulated by core countries for their own economic advantage. Examples are found throughout Africa and to a lesser extent in Latin America and Asia. Natural resources, such as agricultural products, minerals, and other raw materials, flow from periphery to core—as do the profits. The core, in turn, sells finished goods to the periphery, also at a profit—essentially making itself wealthy while limiting the economic development of peripheral countries. Finally, the **semiperiphery** comprises semi-industrialized, middle-income countries that extract profits from the more peripheral countries and in turn yield profits to the core countries. Examples include Mexico in North America; Brazil, Argentina, and Chile in South America; and the newly industrializing economies of East Asia. The semiperiphery, though to some degree controlled by the core, can exploit the periphery. Moreover, the greater economic success of the semiperiphery holds out to the periphery the promise of similar development.

Although the world system changes very slowly, once-powerful countries eventually lose their economic power to others. For example, some five centuries ago the Italian city-states of Venice and Genoa dominated the world capitalist economy, but eventually they were superseded by the Dutch, then the British, and currently the United States. Today, American dominance may be giving way to a more "multipolar" world where economic power will be shared among the United States, Europe, and Asia (Arrighi 1994).

An important offshoot of the world-systems approach is a concept that emphasizes the global nature of economic activities. **Global commodity chains** are worldwide networks of labor and production processes yielding a finished product. These networks consist of all pivotal production activities that form a tightly interlocked "chain" extending from the raw materials to the final consumer (Appelbaum and Christerson 1997; Gereffi 1995, 1996; Hopkins and Wallerstein 1996).

Female workers make Barbie dolls at a toy factory in the Guangdong province of China.

The commodity-chain approach sees manufacturing as becoming increasingly globalized. Manufactures accounted for approximately three quarters of the world's total economic growth during the period 1990–1998. The sharpest growth was among middle-income countries: Manufactures accounted for only 54 percent of these countries' exports in 1990, compared with 71 percent in 1998. Yet the high rate of increase of manufactures as a share of world exports has since slowed; in 2006, 70.1 percent of world exports were manufactures (World Trade Organization [WTO] 2007). China, which moved from the ranks of low- to middle-income countries in part because of its exports of manufactured goods, partly accounts for this trend. Yet the most profitable activities in the commodity chain—engineering, design, and advertising—usually occur in core countries, whereas the least profitable activities, such as factory production, occur in peripheral countries.

Consider the manufacture of Barbie, the most profitable toy in history. Although she sells mainly in the United States, Europe, and Japan, she can also be found in 140 other countries. She is a truly global citizen (Tempest 1996), not only in sales but also in terms of her birthplace. The first doll was made in Japan in 1959, when that country was recovering from World War II and wages were low. As wages rose in Japan, Barbie moved to other low-wage countries in Asia. Her multiple origins today tell us a great deal about the operation of global commodity chains.

Barbie is designed in the United States, where her marketing and advertising strategies are devised and where most of the profits are made. But the only physical aspect of Barbie that is "made in the U.S.A." is her cardboard packaging, along with some of the paints and oils used to decorate her. Barbie's body and wardrobe span the globe in their origins:

Global Inequality

In his book, *Material World,* Peter Menzel and his staff interview and photograph people whose earnings place them somewhere near the middle of the income distribution in their respective societies. Looking at who constitutes a society's middle class and what they have and comparing their situation to counterparts in poorer and richer societies are particularly illuminating. Society's middle class marks off the standard

Rick Skeen is a cable splicer for a utility company in Pearland, Texas. The money that he and his wife Pattie—who is employed half time as a teacher in a Christian academy—earn puts them right in the center of the American middle class. They have a nice 1,600-square-foot home in a suburb of Houston, two kids, a dog. Certainly, there are many things the Skeen family would dread losing, but it is a safe bet that the array of kitchen appliances sitting on the washer, range, and dryer in the upper right-hand corner of the photograph would not be among them.

Ambrosio and Carmen Castillo Balderas and their four children are the Skeens' Mexican counterparts. Their home in Guadalajara, however, is less than half the size of the Skeens' and accommodates half again as many people. They too have possessions, both functional and prized, but they amount to far fewer things. Ernesto is a distributor of wholesale produce, does freelance welding, and when he has time, continues building his home. Carmen is a homemaker. Their income puts them in the Mexican middle class. Nevertheless, in dollar terms it is less than one seventh of what the Skeens earn.

Created by John Grady.

of living that, by definition, half of a particular society would be happy to have and which the rest would fear losing. The middle class is also the point of comparison that people in poorer societies use to measure their distance from the dream-life in the richer nations that they see portrayed on television.

As you compare the photos of families, you might ask yourself, what sorts of changes will need to take place in how we produce and consume goods and services if people around the world are to ever enjoy their dreams of a steadily improving standard of living? Will we need to alter the priorities in our lives? Can advanced technology that in great part has produced waste products like CO_2 play a role in providing remedies? What if, in the end, our dreams outdistance our capacities to realize them? What happens then?

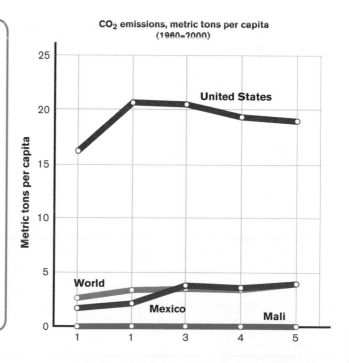

This image is a portrait of the Natomo family. There are eleven people in this extended family, which subsists on an income that amounts to about 12 percent of what the Mexican family earns and only 1 percent of what the Skeens take home. Their cooking utensils make up a sizable portion of what they own. Losing those utensils would leave the Natomo family with virtually nothing.

Economic development is an uneven and volatile process. Measured in terms of the growth of wealth and income, economic development has a great many winners but quite a few losers, and even when the rewards are many, the process is unsettling and can often dislocate people physically, emotionally, and socially. Economic development also makes demands on the environment that we have begun to appreciate as a problem of global proportions only in the last several decades. All of the stuff we possess and consume requires enormous quantities of raw materials, water, and energy to produce, transport, and maintain.

One important indicator of the impact on the environment is emissions of carbon dioxide (CO_2). This greenhouse gas, which contributes to global warming, is produced in great quantity by most industrial processes. This figure charts how many metric tons of CO_2 each of the three societies discussed above has emitted on an annual basis since 1960. This chart also reflects the level of economic development of Mali, Mexico, and the United States and the extent of each society's footprint on the environment. Put simply, a Mexican on average emits eighty times as much CO_2 as a citizen of Mali. Nevertheless, an American is responsible for producing almost five times as much CO_2 as a Mexican and four hundred times what a person in Mali does. This figure also reveals that the worldwide production of CO_2 per person has leveled off and that in the United States it has even started to decline.

CO_2 emissions, metric tons per capita (1960–2000)

United States

World

Mexico

Mali

- Barbie begins her life in Saudi Arabia, where oil is extracted and refined into the ethylene that is used to create her plastic body.
- Taiwan's state-owned oil importer, the Chinese Petroleum Corporation, buys the ethylene and sells it to Taiwan's Formosa Plastic Corporation, the world's largest producer of polyvinyl chloride (PVC) plastics, which are used in toys. Formosa Plastic converts the ethylene into the PVC pellets that will be shaped to make Barbie's body.
- The pellets are shipped to one of the four Asian factories that make Barbie—two in southern China, one in Indonesia, and one in Malaysia. The plastic-mold injection machines that shape her body, which are the most expensive part of Barbie's manufacture, are made in the United States and shipped to the factories.
- Once Barbie's body is molded, she gets her nylon hair from Japan. Her cotton dresses are made in China, with Chinese cotton—the only raw material in Barbie that actually comes from the country where most Barbies are made.
- Hong Kong plays a key role in the manufacturing process of the Chinese Barbies. Nearly all the material used in her manufacture is shipped into Hong Kong and then trucked to the factories in China. The finished Barbies leave by the same route. Some twenty-three thousand trucks make the daily trip between Hong Kong and southern China's toy factories.

So where is Barbie actually from? The cardboard and cellophane box containing the My First Tea Party Barbie is labeled "Made in China," but almost none of the materials that go into making her originate there. For a $20 Barbie, China gets only about 70 cents, mainly in wages paid to the eleven thousand peasant women who assemble her in the two factories. Back in the United States, however, Mattel makes about $2 in profits.

What about the rest of the money that is made when Barbie is sold for $20? Only 65 cents is needed to cover the plastics, cloth, nylon, and other materials used in her manufacture. Most of the money covers machinery and equipment, transoceanic shipping and domestic trucking, advertising and merchandising, retail floor space—and, of course, the profits of Toys "R" Us and other retailers.

Although manufacturing in the global commodity chain typically takes place in peripheral countries, an exception has developed. Low-wage, low-profit factories known as sweatshops are reappearing in core countries, sometimes for the first time in half a century or more. A sweatshop is a small factory that violates numerous wage, health, and safety laws. In New York City and Los Angeles, for example, more than a hundred thousand workers labor in tiny garment factories that

Barbie, the quintessentially American doll, has never actually been produced in the United States. Since she was first made in Japan in 1959, rising wages in Asia have moved Barbie production from one low-wage country to another. The four factories that currently make Barbie are located in southern China, Indonesia, and Malaysia.

make many of the brands of clothing sold in major department stores. Many laborers work for less than minimum wage, in buildings described by government officials as firetraps.

The private experience of these workers is shaped by larger social forces. First, garment workers in New York and Los Angeles are in direct competition with workers in the Caribbean and Mexico, where wages are a tenth as much as in the United States. If workers in New York and Los Angeles want to keep their jobs, they must settle for sweatshop wages and conditions. Otherwise, the work will be moved to another country. Second, most garment workers are illegal immigrants. If they complain about their working conditions, they risk losing their jobs and being deported.

The global economy has not only brought sweatshops back to the United States, but it has also provided the immigrants to work in them.

State-Centered Theories

Differing sharply from market-oriented theories, **state-centered theories** argue that appropriate government policies do not interfere with economic development but, rather, can be key in promoting it. Considerable research now suggests that in some regions, such as East Asia, successful economic development has been state led. Even the World Bank, a strong proponent of free-market theories of development, has changed its thinking about the role of the state. In its 1997 report *The State in a Changing World,* the World Bank concludes that without an effective state, "sustainable development, both economic and social, is impossible."

Strong governments contributed in various ways to economic growth in the East Asian NIEs during the 1980s and 1990s (Amsden et al. 1994; Appelbaum and Henderson 1992; Cumings 1997; Evans 1995; World Bank 1997):

1. **East Asian governments have sometimes aggressively acted to ensure political stability while keeping labor costs low.** They have accomplished this by outlawing trade unions, banning strikes, jailing labor leaders, and, in general, silencing the voices of workers. The governments of Taiwan, South Korea, and Singapore in particular have engaged in such practices.

2. **East Asian governments have frequently sought to steer economic development in desired directions.** For example, state agencies have provided cheap loans and tax breaks to businesses that invest in industries favored by the government. Sometimes this strategy has backfired, resulting in bad loans held by the government (one of the causes of the region's economic problems during the late 1990s). Some governments have prevented businesses from investing their profits in other countries, forcing them to invest in economic growth at home. Sometimes governments have owned and controlled key industries.

3. **East Asian governments have often been heavily involved in social programs such as low-cost housing and universal education.** The world's largest public housing systems (outside of socialist or formerly socialist countries) have been in Hong Kong and Singapore, where government subsidies keep rents extremely low. Because workers don't require high wages to pay for housing, they can compete better with American and European workers in the global labor market. In Singapore, which has an extremely strong central government, well-funded public education and training provide workers with the skills they need to compete in the global labor market. The Singaporean government also requires businesses and individual citizens alike to save a large percentage of their income for investment in future growth.

Evaluating Global Theories of Inequality

Each of the four sets of theories of global inequality has strengths and weaknesses. Together, they enable us to better understand the causes and cures for global inequality.

1. **Market-oriented theories recommend the adoption of modern capitalist institutions to promote economic development.** They further argue that countries can develop economically only if they open their borders to trade, and they cite evidence to support this argument. But market-oriented theories overlook economic ties between poor countries and wealthy ones—ties that can impede economic growth under some conditions and enhance it under others. They blame low-income countries for their poverty rather than acknowledging outside factors, such as the business operations of more powerful nations. Market-oriented theories also ignore the ways government can work with the private sector to spur economic development. Finally, they fail to explain why some countries take off economically while others remain grounded in poverty and underdevelopment.

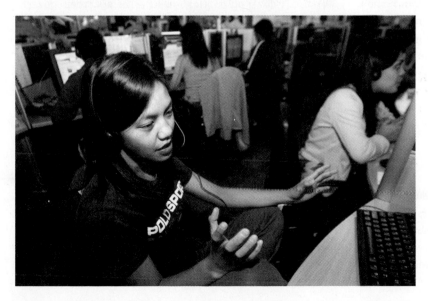

Filipino university graduates work the graveyard shift at ClientLogic's call center in Baguio City, Philippines. The average worker at the call center earns 12,000 pesos ($220) a month.

Sociology in South Africa

Public sociologists must balance a commitment to the university with a desire to work with groups beyond campus walls. When this tension is balanced well, public involvement enriches and sustains good academic research, provides a real-life context that improves teaching, and initiates a dialogue with wider publics about important issues in society. At other times, however, strong commitments to public sociology can have more serious consequences.

On January 8, 1978, Richard Turner, a lecturer at the University of Natal, South Africa, was killed by an assassin's bullet. Beginning in the 1960s, Turner had combined academic teachings with social activism designed to rally whites in South Africa to unite in opposition to the repressive apartheid government, a regime based on the strict separation of the races. Because for years he had successfully translated black social and political unrest into a language embraced by progressive whites, Turner was viewed as a threat to the stability of the South African government. In addition to encouraging white students to get involved in black labor organizations and helping create the race-blind National Union of South African Students, Turner was a moving force behind the Institute for Industrial Education and the Durban strikes of 1973. In the years immediately before his assassination, Turner helped recruit and train labor organizers who would fight vigorously to dismantle the apartheid regime and establish a comprehensive bill of rights for black workers.

Turner lived with his family in a modest suburban home outside the city of Durban. Shortly after midnight on January 8, a bullet entered the home through a downstairs window and struck Turner in the chest. His thirteen-year-old daughter, Jann, was awakened by the shooting and ran to her father's side. Minutes later, Turner died in his daughter's arms. After a

Richard Turner

brief police investigation turned up no clues, Professor Richard Turner's case was promptly closed.

Professor David Webster was a contemporary of Turner's in the anti-apartheid struggle. Webster's dissertation on migrant workers exposed him to the methods used by business and government to exploit black workers. While living alongside his research subjects, Webster developed what would become a lifelong commitment to racial justice through political activism. As a professor at the University of Witwatersrand in Johannesburg, he frequently agitated government authorities by hosting "tea parties" at his home. Tea may have been served, but the purpose of each gathering was to mobilize support for the release of individuals who had been detained by the state.

To crack down on political dissent, the apartheid government had begun to secretly imprison and detain those considered to be threats to state stability. Month after month, individuals would disappear from their homes. Frantic relatives had few places to turn for answers. Webster responded by organizing the Detainees' Parents' Support Committee

2. **Dependency theories emphasize how wealthy nations have exploited poor ones.** However, although these theories account for much of the economic backwardness in Latin America and Africa, they cannot explain the occasional success stories such as Brazil, Argentina, and Mexico or the rapidly expanding economies of East Asia. In fact, some formerly low-income countries have risen economically despite the presence of multinational corporations. Even some former colonies, such as Hong Kong and Singapore, are among the success stories.

(DPSC), a support group for relatives of a rapidly growing list of detainees and banished people. While maintaining his academic responsibilities at the university, Webster helped relatives track down the whereabouts of loved ones who had disappeared.

"He wrote letters and documents chronicling and protesting against the conditions of repression. He did not keep quiet and was always there for detainees and their families. In this concrete sense he was a thorn in the flesh of the state—an obstacle to the success of their emergency strategy of removing activists from their society" (*Grassroots* 1989).

During the late 1980s, Webster began research in a remote part of KwaZulu-Natal province called Kosi Bay. He was especially interested in the psychological trauma experienced by detainees during interrogations by the state, and he had started conducting extensive anthropology fieldwork to explore the issue. Kosi Bay happened to be close to the Tembe Elephant Park, which doubled as a secret training ground for government assassins during apartheid. Eugene De Kock, the leader of the infamous "Vlakplaas" assassins' brigade, was rumored to have trained his soldiers at Tembe. Although evidence remains unclear, some suspect that during his research Webster learned the truth behind the Tembe Elephant Park and became too curious.

On May 1, 1989, a man named Ferdi Barnard approached Webster outside his home in the city Johannesburg, just miles from the university where he taught. Barnard was an employee of a covert apartheid police force called the Civil Co-Operation Bureau that specialized in assassinations. After aiming his shotgun, Barnard fired at point blank range. Webster died immediately.

As after Turner's death, the public outcry was emotional and sustained. Friends, family, and students of both professors demanded answers from government officials who for decades had systematically buried evidence of atrocities committed under their watch. No answers were forthcoming. An editorial published in the wake of Webster's death courageously stated that "the South African police have always denied allegations that they have been involved in political assassinations. Despite their denials, many serious questions remain unanswered. The most obvious is why have none of the killings been solved?" (*Grassroots* 1989).

It was not until 1998, four years after the rise of President Nelson Mandela and the establishment of democratic rule in South Africa, that Ferdi Barnard was convicted of Webster's murder. Barnard, who had received a bonus of 40,000 rand (approximately $8,000) for the killing, was sentenced to two life terms plus sixty-three years for atrocities committed under the apartheid regime. As of 2006, the case of Richard Turner remains unsolved.

Jann Turner, Richard's daughter, is now forty-one years old, and she has spent her life trying to identify her father's killer. She recently paid a visit to Eugene De Kock, the former commander of the Vlakplaas who would likely have ordered her father's death. If he recalled the circumstances, he did not reveal them to Jann during their meeting. As she looked into his eyes and asked him questions, as she listened to his stories about nightmares and he listened to her own, Jann realized that her search was about something more. "I've spent years looking for my father's killer, for the killer," she writes in a journal she now keeps on the Web (www.jannturner.co.za). "Instead I found a killer—and for me this is about understanding"— a fitting reminder of the true purpose of public sociology: to connect public issues and private troubles in a way that leads, sometimes painfully, sometimes tragically, toward greater collective enlightenment.

David Webster

3. **World-systems theory analyzes the world economy as a whole, looking at the complex global web of political and economic relationships that influence development and inequality in poor and rich nations alike.** The concept of *global commodity chains* focuses on global businesses and their activities rather than relationships between countries. World-systems theory is thus well suited to understanding the global economy at a time when businesses are increasingly free to set up operations anywhere, acquiring an economic importance rivaling that

of many countries. Yet this is also a weakness of the commodity chains approach: It emphasizes the importance of business decisions over other factors, such as the roles of workers and governments in shaping a country's economy (Amsden 1989; Cumings 1997; Deyo 1989; Evans 1995).

4. **State-centered theories stress the government's role in fostering economic growth.** They thus offer a useful alternative to both the prevailing market-oriented theories, with their emphasis on states as economic hindrances, and dependency theories, which view states as allies of global business elites in exploiting poor countries. When combined with the other theories—particularly world-systems theory—state-centered theories can explain the radical changes now transforming the world economy.

 CONCEPT CHECKS

1. Describe the main assumptions of market-oriented theories of global inequality.
2. Why are dependency theories of global inequalities often criticized?
3. Compare and contrast core, peripheral, and semiperipheral nations.
4. How have strong governments of some East Asian nations contributed to the economic development of that region?

Why Global Economic Inequality Matters to You

Today, the social and economic forces leading to a single global capitalist economy seem irresistible. The principal challenge to this outcome—socialism—came to an end with the collapse of the Soviet Union in 1991. The largest remaining socialist country, the People's Republic of China, is rapidly adopting many capitalist economic institutions and is the fastest-growing economy in the world. It is too soon to tell whether the future leaders of China will eventually adopt a complete market-oriented economy or some combination of state controls and capitalist institutions. Yet most China experts agree that as China, with its 1.3 billion people, becomes a central participant in the world capitalist system, it will continue to have a major worldwide effect. China's enormous workforce, much of which is well trained and educated and now receives very low wages,

will be extremely competitive in a global economy and will force wages down from London to Los Angeles.

What does rapid globalization mean for the future of global inequality? Many scenarios are possible. In one, our world might be dominated by large, global corporations, with falling wages for many people in high-income countries and rising wages for a few in low-income countries. Average income worldwide might level out, although at a level much lower than that currently enjoyed in the United States and other industrialized nations. In this scenario, the polarization between the haves and the have-nots within countries would grow, as the whole world would be divided into those who benefit from the global economy and those who do not. Such polarization could fuel conflict between ethnic groups and even nations, as those suffering from economic globalization would blame others for their plight (Hirst and Thompson 1992; Wagar 1992).

In another scenario, a global economy could mean greater opportunity for everyone, as the benefits of modern technology stimulate worldwide economic growth. Indeed, the more successful East Asian NIEs, such as Hong Kong, Taiwan, South Korea, and Singapore, might be a sign of things to come. Other NIEs such as Malaysia and Thailand will soon follow, along with China, Indonesia, Vietnam, and other Asian countries. India, the world's second most populous country, already boasted a middle class of around 300 million people in 2007, about a third of its total population (David 2007). A countervailing trend, however, is the widening technology gap between rich and poor countries. The gap is a result of the disparity in wealth among nations, but it also reinforces those disparities. Poor countries cannot easily afford modern technology—yet, in the absence of modern technology, they face major barriers to overcoming poverty. They are caught in a vicious downward spiral.

Jeffrey Sachs (2000), director of the Center for International Development and professor of international trade at Harvard University, and an adviser to many eastern European and developing countries, claims that the world is divided into three classes: technology innovators, technology adopters, and the technologically disconnected.

Technology innovators are regions that provide most of the world's technological inventions; they represent around 15 percent of the world's population. *Technology adopters* are regions that adopt technologies invented elsewhere, applying them to production and consumption; they account for 50 percent of the world's population. Finally, the *technologically disconnected* are regions that neither innovate nor adopt technologies developed elsewhere; they account for 35 percent of the world's population. Note that Sachs speaks of regions rather than countries: In today's increasingly borderless world, technology use (or exclusion) does not always respect national frontiers. For example, Sachs (2000) notes that technologically disconnected regions include "southern Mexico and pockets of tropical Central America; the Andean countries; most of tropical Brazil; tropical sub-Saharan Africa; most of the former Soviet Union aside from the areas nearest to European and Asian markets; landlocked parts of Asia such as the Ganges valley states of India; landlocked Laos and Cambodia; and the deep-interior states of China." These impoverished regions lack access to markets or major ocean trading routes. They are caught in what Sachs (2000) terms a "poverty trap," plagued by "tropical infectious disease, low agricultural productivity and environmental degradation—all requiring technological solutions beyond their means."

Innovation requires a critical mass of ideas and technology to become self-sustaining. That is why technological innovation in the United States is concentrated in regions rich in universities and high-tech firms: for example, California's Silicon Valley. Poor countries are ill equipped to develop such high-tech regions; most lack even a science adviser to their government. Moreover, these countries are too poor to import computers, cell phones, fax machines, computerized factory machinery, or other kinds of high technology. Nor can they afford to license technology from the foreign companies that hold the patents.

What can be done to overcome the technological abyss that divides rich and poor countries? Sachs calls on wealthy, high-technology countries to provide much greater financial and technical assistance to poor countries than they now do. For example, lethal infectious diseases such as malaria, measles, and diarrhea claim millions of lives each year in poor countries. The modern medical technology necessary to eradicate these illnesses would cost only $10 billion a year—less than $15 from every person who lives in a high-income country, if the cost were shared equally.

Sachs urges the governments of wealthy countries, along with international lending institutions, to provide loans and grants for scientific and technological development. Very little money is currently available to support research and development in poor countries. The World Bank, a major source of funding, spends only $60 million a year supporting tropical, agricultural, or health research and development in poor countries. In comparison, Pfizer—the world's largest pharmaceutical corporation in terms of market share—spends 141 times that much ($8.5 billion [converted from €5.8 billion] in 2007) for research and development for its own products (FierceBiotech 2007). Moreover, universities in wealthy nations could establish overseas research and training institutes that would foster collaborative research projects. From computers and the Internet to biotechnology, the wealth of nations increasingly depends on modern information technology. As long as major regions of the world remain technologically disconnected, it seems unlikely that global poverty will be eradicated.

In the most optimistic view, the republics of the former Soviet Union, as well as the formerly socialist countries of Eastern Europe, will eventually become high-income countries. Economic growth will spread to Latin America, Africa, and the rest of the world. Because capitalism requires that workers be mobile, the remaining caste societies will be replaced by class-based societies, which will experience enhanced opportunities for upward mobility.

What is the future of global inequality? It is difficult to be entirely optimistic. Global economic growth has slowed, and many of the once promising economies of Asia now seem to be in trouble. The Russian economy, in its move from socialism to capitalism, has encountered many pitfalls, leaving many Russians poorer than ever. It remains to be seen whether countries will learn from one another and work together to create better lives for their peoples. What is certain is that the past quarter century has witnessed a global economic transformation of unprecedented magnitude. The effects of this transformation in the next quarter century will leave few lives on the planet untouched.

☑ CONCEPT CHECKS

1. What is the role of technology in deepening existing global inequalities?

Study Outline

www.wwnorton.com/studyspace

Global Inequality: Differences among Countries

- Countries can be stratified according to their per-person gross national product. Forty percent of the world's population live in low-income countries, compared with only 16 percent in high-income countries.
- An estimated 1.3 billion people, or nearly one in four people, live in poverty today, an increase since the early 1980s. Many are the victims of discrimination based on race, ethnicity, or tribal affiliation.

Life in Rich and Poor Countries

- In general, people in high-income countries enjoy a far higher standard of living than their counterparts in low-income countries. They are likely to have more food to eat, less likely to starve or suffer from malnutrition, and likely to live longer. They are far more likely to be literate and educated and therefore have higher-skilled, higher-paying jobs. They are less likely to have large families, and their children are much less likely to die of malnutrition or childhood diseases.

Can Poor Countries Become Rich?

- Such newly industrializing economies as Hong Kong, Singapore, Taiwan, and South Korea have experienced explosive economic growth since the mid-1970s. This growth is due partly to historical circumstances; to a lesser degree to cultural characteristics; and most important, to the central role of their governments. Whether this growth will continue is in question, given the economic difficulties some of these countries currently face.

Theories of Global Inequality

- Market-oriented theories, such as modernization theory, claim that cultural and institutional barriers to development explain the poverty of low-income societies. In this view, to eliminate poverty, fatalistic attitudes must be overcome, government meddling in economic affairs ended, and a high rate of savings and investment encouraged.
- Dependency theories claim that global poverty is the result of the exploitation of poor countries by wealthy ones. Dependent development theory argues that even though the economic fate of poor countries is ultimately determined by wealthy ones, some development is possible within dependent capitalistic relations.

- World-systems theory focuses on the relationships among core, peripheral, and semiperipheral countries in the global economy; long-term trends in the global economy; and global commodity chains that erase national borders.
- State-centered theories emphasize the role of governments in fostering economic development. These theories draw on the experience of the rapidly growing East Asian newly industrializing economies.

Why Global Inequality Matters to You

- No one can say whether global inequality will increase or decrease in the future. It is possible that some leveling out of wages will occur worldwide, as wages decline in wealthy countries and rise in poor countries. It is also possible that all countries will someday prosper as the result of a unified global economy.

Key Concepts

colonialism (p. 267)
core countries (p. 267)
dependency theories (p. 263)
dependent development (p. 266)
global commodity chains (p. 267)
global inequality (p. 248)
market-oriented theories (p. 262)
modernization theory (p. 262)
neoliberalism (p. 263)
newly industrializing economies (NIEs) (p. 260)
periphery (p. 267)
semiperiphery (p. 267)
state-centered theories (p. 270)
world-systems theory (p. 266)

Review Questions

1. How does the World Bank measure inequality between countries? Why might their approach be misleading?
2. In the last half of the twentieth century, the average overall standard of living improved. At the same time, the gap between rich and poor countries increased. What explains this situation?
3. Describe the social factors that contribute to famine and hunger.

4. Economic growth in East Asia can be attributed to a number of factors. Discuss three of these factors and some of the costs associated with rapid economic development.

5. What does modernization theory say countries need to do to get out of poverty?

6. How does dependency theory explain inequality and what, according to this view, is the solution?

7. What are the zones of the modern world system? How are they related?

8. What is a commodity chain and how does it help explain global inequality?

9. What do state-centered theories of development say the role of the state should be in fostering economic development? How does this compare to the ideas of modernization theory?

10. How does the use of technology relate to poverty on a global scale?

Thinking Sociologically Exercises

1. Summarize the four theories that explain why there are gaps between nations' economic development and resulting global inequality: market-oriented theory, dependency theory, world-systems theory, and state-centered theories. Briefly discuss the distinctive characteristics of each theory and how each differs from the others. Which theory do you feel best explains economic developmental gaps?

2. This chapter states that global economic inequality has personal relevance and importance to people in advanced, affluent economies. Briefly review this argument. Explain whether you were persuaded by it or not.

Learning Objectives

Gender Differences: Nature versus Nurture

Consider whether differences between women and men are the result of biological differences or of social and cultural influences.

Forms of Gender Inequality

Recognize that gender differences are part of our social structure and create inequalities between women and men. Learn the forms these inequalities take, particularly in the workplace, the family, the educational system, and the political system and as violence against women.

Gender Inequality in Global Perspective

Understand the ways in which women worldwide experience economic and political inequality.

Analyzing Gender Inequality

Think about various explanations for gender inequality and apply them to a real-life example. Learn some feminist theories about achieving gender equality.

Why Gender Inequality Matters

Learn how globalization has transformed ideas about women's rights.

CHAPTER TEN

GENDER INEQUALITY

round midnight one cold night in December, right before the end of the second shift, Andrea Ellington is standing in the workers' lounge, cleaning out her pocketbook. She empties its contents, which include a gold plastic makeup bag, a wallet, and some monthly bills. "I gotta go wake my five-year-old daughter up at my mother's house," she says as she opens the makeup bag. "Then I go to the other baby-sitter and get my baby twins. Then I take them home and they've gotta go back to sleep, try to go back to sleep. By the time my daughter gets back to sleep, it's time for her to get back up again" (interview by the authors).

An African American woman of twenty-three, Andrea Ellington supports her three children on a low-rung clerical salary of $20,000 per year. She has been working at a Chicago law firm for four years, believing that with hard work eventually she might advance enough to move out of public housing, her foremost goal.

Most of the five hundred or so employees in the law office where she works are not attorneys but "support staff," who work in one of many departments at the center of the floors, surrounded by plush attorneys' offices on the perimeter. The Network Center where she types is a night-time word-processing department, with shifts from 4 P.M. to midnight and midnight to 8 A.M. The people who work here are all women, sitting at computer terminals in one of four clusters separated by gray partitions. Almost all of these women are also rearing children during the day. Most live far from the law firm's gleaming downtown building.

Balancing the commitments of work and family is a challenge in terms of not only time but also money. Andrea lives from paycheck to paycheck, seeking out extra work to help cover living expenses. As she says, working "overtime has helped me pay bills on time, buy clothes for my children, and buy food that I normally have had to wait until each paycheck to get." As a result of Andrea's persistence, her supervisor assigned her an extra eight hours of overtime per week, on Sundays. Andrea worked the first two Sundays and then began missing her weekend assignments because she couldn't find a baby-sitter. When her supervisor learned of the absences, she canceled the overtime.

Many people who encounter someone like Andrea might make certain assumptions—for example, that a disproportionate number of women become typists and word processors because women are naturally suited to certain kinds of occupations, including secretarial jobs. They might also assume that mothers should be responsible for taking care of children. Finally, they might assume that Andrea's poverty and low social position are a result of her natural abilities. It is the job of sociology to analyze these assumptions and take a wider view of our society and people like Andrea—to understand why women are likely to have low-paying clerical jobs, spend more time on child care, and be less powerful in society than men.

This chapter explores a sociological approach to gender differences and gender inequality. According to the social concept of gender, men and women have different identities and social roles and, thus, are expected to think and act in different ways. Because in almost all societies men's roles are valued more than women's, gender also serves as a social status denoting unequal power, prestige, and wealth. Despite advances by many women in the United States and other Western societies, this remains true today. Sociologists explore not only how society differentiates between women and men but also how these differences underlie social inequalities (Chafetz 1990). Some sociologists also consider ways in which women can achieve positions of equality with men.

In this chapter, we examine the origins of gender differences, assessing the debate over biological versus social influences on gender roles. We then review forms of gender inequality in American society, focusing on the workplace, the family, the educational system, and the political system. We also examine how women are the targets of sexual violence and how economic and political inequality affects women worldwide. After reviewing various forms of feminism and prospects for future change toward a gender-equal society, we analyze some theories of gender inequality and apply them to the circumstances of Andrea's life. We conclude by considering the role of women worldwide in the early twenty-first century.

Gender Differences: Nature versus Nurture

As we explore the origins of the differences between boys and girls, men and women, the nature–nurture debate, noted in Chapter 3, comes into play. Scholars disagree about the degree to which biological characteristics affect gender identities as "feminine" or "masculine" and the social roles based on those identities. The debate is really about how much learning there is; some scholars assign more prominence than others to social influences.

Before reviewing the competing theories, we need to make an important distinction between sex and gender. While **sex** refers to physical differences of the body, **gender** concerns the psychological, social, and cultural differences between males and females. The distinction between sex and gender is fundamental, because many differences between males and females are not biological.

The Role of Biology

How much are differences in the behavior of women and men the result of sex—that is, biological differences—rather than gender? Some researchers hold that innate behavioral differences between women and men appear in some form in all cultures and that the findings of sociobiology strongly support this. For example, the fact that in almost all cultures men rather than women take part in hunting and warfare indicates that men possess biologically based tendencies toward aggression that women lack. In the present-day case of women who work as word processors, they might point out that typing is a more passive occupation than being a bicycle messenger (an equivalent job category), which requires more physical strength and aggressiveness in traffic.

Most sociologists are unconvinced by these arguments. Men's aggressiveness, they say, varies widely among cultures, and women are expected to be more passive or gentle in some cultures than in others (Elshtain 1981). Theories of "natural difference" are often grounded in data on animal behavior, critics say, rather than in anthropological or historical evidence about human behavior, which reveals variation over time and place. In the majority of cultures, most women spend a significant part of their lives caring for children and therefore cannot readily participate in hunting or war.

Although the hypothesis that biological factors determine behavior patterns cannot be dismissed out of hand, nearly a century of research to identify the physiological origins of this influence finds no evidence of mechanisms linking such biological forces with the complex social behaviors of human men and women (Connell 1987). Theories based on an innate predisposition neglect the vital role of social interaction in shaping human behavior.

What does the evidence show? One possible source of information is the differences in hormonal makeup. Some have claimed that the male sex hormone, testosterone, is associated with the propensity to violence (Rutter and Giller 1984). Research has indicated, for instance, that male monkeys castrated at birth become less aggressive than noncastrated monkeys; conversely, female monkeys given testosterone become more aggressive than normal females. However, it has also been found that providing monkeys with opportunities to dominate others actually increases testosterone level. Aggressive behavior may thus affect production of the hormone, rather than the hormone causing increased aggression.

Another possible source of evidence is direct observations of animal behavior. Writers who connect male aggression with biological influences often stress male aggressiveness among the higher animals. Among chimpanzees, they say, males are invariably more aggressive than females. Yet there are large differences between types of animals. Gibbons, for instance, show few differences in aggression between the sexes. Moreover, many female apes or monkeys are highly aggressive in some situations, such as when their young are threatened.

Another source of information comes from the experience of identical twins, who derive from a single egg and have *exactly the same* genetic makeup. In one case, one identical male twin was seriously injured while being circumcised, and the decision was made to reconstruct his genitals as a female. He was thereafter raised as a girl. The twins at age six demonstrated typical male and female traits as found in Western culture. The little girl enjoyed playing with other girls, helped with the housework, and wanted to get married when she grew up. The boy preferred the company of other boys, his favorite

Many children's toys may promote gender stereotyping.

toys were cars and trucks, and he wanted to become a firefighter or police officer.

For some time, this case was treated as a conclusive demonstration of the overriding influence of social learning on gender differences. However, when the girl was a teenager she was interviewed during a television program and revealed some unease about her gender identity, even wondering if perhaps she was "really" a boy after all. She had by then learned of her unusual background, and this knowledge may have led to an altered perception of herself (Ryan 1985).

Gender Socialization

Gender socialization involves the learning of gender roles through social agents such as the family and the media (see also Chapter 4). This approach distinguishes between biological sex and social gender—an infant is born with the first and develops the second. Through contact with primary and secondary agents of socialization, children internalize the social norms and expectations that correspond with their sex. Gender differences are not biologically determined; they are culturally produced.

Functionalists support theories of gender socialization, seeing boys and girls as learning "sex roles" and the masculinity and femininity that accompany them. Children are guided in this process by positive and negative sanctions, that is, socially applied forces that reward or restrain behavior. For example, a small boy could be positively sanctioned ("What a brave boy you are!") or negatively ("Boys don't play with dolls"). If an individual develops gender practices that do not correspond with his or her biological sex—that is, if he or she is deviant—the explanation is inadequate or irregular socialization. According to this functionalist view, socializing agents help maintain the social order by overseeing the smooth gender socialization of new generations.

This rigid interpretation of sex roles and socialization has been criticized on a number of fronts. Many writers argue that gender socialization is not an inherently smooth process; different agents such as the family, schools, and peer groups may be at odds with one another. Moreover, socialization theories ignore individuals' ability to reject or modify the social expectations surrounding sex roles.

Indeed, humans are not passive objects or unquestioning recipients of gender programming, as some sociologists have suggested. People actively create and modify roles for themselves. Although any wholesale adoption of the sex roles approach may be inadvisable, many studies have shown that to some degree gender identities *are* a result of social influences.

Consider the following two scenes. Two newborns a few hours old lie in the nursery of a hospital maternity ward. One, a male, is wrapped in a blue blanket; the other, a female, is in a pink blanket. Their grandparents are seeing them for the first time. The conversation between one pair of grandparents runs along these lines:

Grandma A: *There he is—our first grandchild, and a boy.*

Grandpa A: *Hey, isn't he a hefty little fellow? Look at that fist he's making. He's going to be a regular little fighter, that guy is. (Grandpa A smiles and throws out a boxing jab to his grandson.) At-a-boy!*

Grandma A: *I think he looks like you. He has your strong chin. Oh, look, he's starting to cry.*

Grandpa A: *Yeah—just listen to that set of lungs. He's going to be some boy.*

Grandma A: *Poor thing—he's still crying.*

Grandpa A: *It's okay. It's good for him. He's exercising and it will develop his lungs.*

Grandma A: *Let's go and congratulate the parents. I know they're thrilled about little Fred. They wanted a boy first.*

Grandpa A: *Yeah, and they were sure it would be a boy too, what with all that kicking and thumping going on even before he got here.*

When they depart to congratulate the parents, the grandparents of the other child arrive. The dialogue between them goes like this:

Grandma B: *There she is . . . the only one with a pink bow taped to her head. Isn't she darling.*

Grandpa B: *Yeah—isn't she little. Look at how tiny her fingers are. Oh, look—she's trying to make a fist.*

Grandma B: *Isn't she sweet. . . . You know, I think she looks a little like me.*

Grandpa B: *Yeah, she sorta does. She has your chin.*

Grandma B: *Oh, look, she's starting to cry.*

Grandpa B: *Maybe we better call the nurse to pick her up or change her or something.*

Grandma B: *Yes, let's. Poor little girl. (To the baby) There, there, we'll try to help you.*

Grandpa B: *Let's find the nurse. I don't like to see her cry . . .*

Grandma B: *Hmm. I wonder when they will have their next one. I know Fred would like a son, but little Fredericka is well and healthy. After all, that's what really matters.*

Grandpa B: *They're young yet. They have time for more kids. I'm thankful too that she's healthy.*

Grandma B: *I don't think they were surprised when it was a girl anyway . . . she was carrying so low.* (Walum 1977)

The contrast between the two conversations sounds so exaggerated that it's tempting to think they were made up. In fact, they are composed of transcripts of actual dialogue recorded in a maternity ward. The first question usually asked of a new parent—in Western culture, at least—is, "Is it a boy or a girl?" Once the child is marked as male or female, everyone who interacts with the child will treat it in accordance with its gender. They do so on the basis of the society's assumptions, which lead people to treat women and men differently, even as opposites (Renzetti and Curran 1995).

Clearly, gender socialization is very powerful, and challenges to it can be upsetting. Once a gender is "assigned," society expects individuals to act like "females" and "males." These expectations are fulfilled and reproduced in the practices of everyday life (Bourdieu 1990; Lorber 1994).

The Social Construction of Gender

Recently, socialization and gender role theories have been criticized by a growing number of sociologists. Rather than seeing sex as biologically determined and gender as culturally learned, they argue that both sex and gender are socially constructed products. Not only is gender a purely social creation that lacks a fixed essence, but the human body itself is subject to social forces that shape and alter it in various ways.

Writers who focus on gender roles and role learning accept a biological basis to gender differences. In the socialization approach, a biological distinction between the sexes provides a framework that becomes culturally elaborated in society itself. In contrast, theorists who believe in the **social construction of gender** reject all biological bases for gender differences. Gender identities emerge, they argue, in relation to perceived sex differences in society and in turn help shape those differences. For example, a society in which ideas of masculinity are characterized by physical strength and tough attitudes will encourage men to cultivate a specific body image and set of mannerisms. In other words, gender identities and sex differences are inextricably linked within individual human bodies (Butler 1989; Connell 1987; Scott and Morgan 1993).

Gender Identity in Everyday Life

Gender is more than learning to act like a girl or boy; we all, as some sociologists put it, "do gender" in our daily interactions with others (West and Zimmerman 1987). For instance, Jan Morris, a celebrated travel writer, used to be a man. As James Morris, she was a member of the British expedition, led by Sir Edmund Hillary, that successfully climbed Mount Everest. She was a very "manly" man—a race car driver and an athlete. Yet she had always felt herself to be a woman in a male body. So she underwent a sex-change operation and lived the rest of her life as a woman.

Jan Morris had to learn how to do gender when she discovered how differently she was expected to behave as a woman, rather than as a man. As she says, there is "no aspect of existence" that is not gendered.

The top photo, dated November 30, 1952, shows George Jorgensen before his sex change. After he was discharged from the U.S. Army he traveled to Copenhagen, Denmark, where he had a sex-change operation. After the operation he changed his name to Christine. The bottom photo shows Christine Jorgensen, returning from a nightclub engagement in Cuba in 1953.

> It amuses me to consider, for instance, when I am taken out to lunch by one of my more urbane men friends, that not so many years ago th[e] waiter would have treated *me* as he is now treating *him*. Then he would have greeted me with respectful seriousness. Now he unfolds my napkin with a playful flourish, as if to humor me. Then he would have taken my order with grave concern, now he expects me to say something frivolous (and I do). (Morris 1974)

The subtle ways in which we do gender are so much a part of our lives that we don't notice them until they are missing or radically altered.

This differentiation not only occurs in face-to-face interaction but also is part of society's institutions, such as the economy, the political system, the educational system, religions, and family forms. Because gender is so pervasive in structuring social life, gender statuses must be clearly differentiated if society is to function in an orderly manner. However, gender differentiation can also be the basis for inequalities between men and women (Lorber 1994; West and Fenstermaker 1995).

Findings from Other Cultures

If gender differences were mostly the result of biology, then we could expect that gender roles would not vary much from culture to culture. However, one set of findings that helps show gender roles are in fact socially constructed comes from anthropologists, who have studied gender in other times and cultures.

NEW GUINEA

In her classic New Guinea study, *Sex and Temperament in Three Primitive Societies,* Margaret Mead (1963) observed such variability among gender role prescriptions—and such marked differences from those in the United States—that any claims to the universality of gender roles had to be rejected. Mead studied three tribes in New Guinea. In Arapesh society, both males and females had characteristics and behaviors that

Gender Norms

In *Gender Advertisements,* written in 1976, Erving Goffman argues that there were explicit gender norms regulating how men and women should be displayed in advertisements, especially when they are depicted together. Put simply, men should be shown in control of the situation, alert to their surroundings, ready to act and protective of women and children. In contrast, women should be represented as vulnerable, distracted by their thoughts, more to be acted upon than to act, and subservient to men. In his book, Goffman focuses on women and identifies a number of distinct aesthetic conventions in their display catalogues numerous other aspects of body language, like the head tilt in the photos below, that make it easy for the viewer to distinguish that which is feminine from that which is masculine.

Advertisements, and posed images generally, are idealized versions of how people *think* they should be

⬇ ➡ Goffman included these two photos in *Gender Advertisements* (1976). How would you characterize the body language of the men and women?

⬇ No formal studies have been done to see how often Goffman's gender norms are being violated, but it is increasingly possible to find credible gender bending in advertisements. Contrast the woman in the ad below with the women in Goffman's *Gender Advertisements.* How is her body language different?

GIORGIO ARMANI
178, Sloane Street, London

Created by John Grady.

seen and depicted, which are, in turn, based on how people actually *wish* they could appear in real life. How many people when told to pose for a picture, for example, immediately assume the proper position for their gender identity without a second thought? Would a close look at our photo albums show us all smiling and looking at the camera but also show us doing many masculine and feminine things that we might notice only if the men were acting like women and vice versa?

While Goffman implies that some of these norms are very old and might be rooted in our primate heritage, he explicitly acknowledges that his is a picture of middle-class America in the late 1970s. Is there any reason to believe that this picture might be changing? Three trends that measure women's role in the economy suggest that a basis is being set for growing independence. In 1975, exactly half (50%) of women were in the civilian labor force. By 2005 women's participation had leveled off at 60 percent. Just over a quarter of family income (26%) was contributed by wives in 1975. By 2000, their share had risen to well over one third (35%). Perhaps more telling is the fact that in 1975 less than one out of six (16%) wives earned more than their husbands in dual-earner families, whereas by 2005 over a quarter did (26%). If women are becoming more independent and their families are relying on this increasingly important role in the paid labor force, shouldn't this be reflected in how they are depicted? Have we become more comfortable viewing females displayed in traditional male poses? How about males depicted in more female postures?

➡ **Is this woman any less a woman for not being displayed with a "feminine touch" and for exercising authority and direction over men?**

WANTED:
LEADERSHIP THAT INSPIRES
MARINES UNDER YOUR COMMAND,
AND AMERICANS EVERYWHERE.

THERE ARE NO FEMALE MARINES. ONLY MARINES.

MARINES
THE FEW. THE PROUD.

ETERNITY

love, sweet love

Calvin Klein
fragrances for men and women

⬅⬆ **These photos from print and television advertisements depict women and men together in two different settings: at home and in the work place. How gendered are these encounters? How have they changed since the scenes dramatized in the photos from 1976? Have we changed as well? How about our parents' generation? Does it matter to you? Should it matter?**

would typically be associated with the Western female role: Both sexes were passive, gentle, unaggressive, and emotionally responsive to the needs of others. In contrast, in the Mundugumor, both males and females were aggressive, suspicious, and, from a Western observer's perspective, excessively cruel, especially toward children. In both cultures, however, men and women were expected to behave very similarly.

Mead then studied the Tchambuli, for whom gender roles were almost exactly reversed from those in Western society. Mead (1972) reported in her autobiography that "among the Tchambuli the expected relations between men and women reversed those that are characteristic of our own culture. For it was Tchambuli women who were brisk and hearty, who managed the business affairs of life, and worked comfortably in large cooperative groups."

The children also exhibited these characteristics. Girls were considered the brightest and most competent and displayed "the most curiosity and the freest expression of intelligence." The Tchambuli boys "were already caught up in the rivalrous, catty, and individually competitive life of the men" (Mead 1972). Mead also reported that while the women managed the affairs of the family, the men were engaged differently: "Down by the lake shore in ceremonial houses the men carved and painted, gossiped and had temper tantrums, and played out their rivalries."

THE !KUNG

 Among the !Kung of the Kalahari Desert, although "men hunt and women gather," a majority of their food comes from the gathering activities of women (Draper 1975). In addition, women return from their gathering expeditions armed not only with food for the community but also with valuable information for hunters. Draper (1975) noted that "women are skilled in reading the signs of the bush, and they take careful note of animal tracks, their age, and the direction of movement. . . . In general, the men take advantage of women's reconnaissance and query them routinely on the evidence of game movements, the location of water and the like."

Due to the nonconfrontational parenting practices of the !Kung, who oppose violent conflict and physical punishment, children learn that aggressive behavior will not be tolerated by either men or women. The !Kung do have specific sex roles, but both men and women engage in child care. Whereas in the United States it is still common for boys and girls to have distinct upbringings, this is not true in the !Kung society (Draper 1975).

SUDHEST ISLAND

The anthropologist Maria Lepowsky did ethnographic research with the people of Sudhest Island, two hundred miles south of Papua, New Guinea, in the South Pacific. After living with them for two years, she concluded that the Vanatinai society "offers any adult, regardless of sex or kin group, the opportunity of excelling at prestigious activities" (Lepowsky 1990). Men even participate in child care. However, Lepowsky did not find absolute equality: Women sweep up pig excrement whereas men hunt wild boar.

MULTIPLE GENDERS

The understanding that only two genders exist is not true among all societies. The Spaniards who came to North and South America in the seventeenth century noticed men in the native tribes who had taken on the mannerisms of women, as well as women who occupied male roles. Indeed, many U.S. citizens who are intolerant of same-sex marriage are surprised to learn that Native Americans have a long tradition in which men enact female roles and women enact male roles and that allows same-sex marriage. This practice has been documented in over 155 Native American tribes.

A person occupying an opposite gender role is called a *berdache*. But many scholars are unhappy with this term because its derivation does not come from Native American cultures (it derives from Persia), and some believe it has a negative connotation. Others argue that it is a substitute for lover or boyfriend (Roscoe 2000). In any event, some anthropologists have tried to replace *berdache* with "two-spirit." In fact, "two-spirit" has become a contemporary label used by Native Americans who are gay, lesbian, bisexual, or transgendered.

Berdaches are not the counterpart of transsexuals or transvestites in the United States, however. Roscoe (1991) studied Zuni berdaches and noted that their cross-dressing is routine, public, and without erotic motives. Moreover,

A !Kung woman picking berries in the Kalahari Desert, Botswana.

A *we'wha* (or *berdache*) of the Zuni people of New Mexico.

berdaches are not necessarily homosexual; some are heterosexual, some homosexual, and others sexually oriented toward other berdaches.

In one society, Roscoe found that both males and females have characteristics associated with the female role in the West. In another group, both males and females are aggressive. In both cultures, men and women are expected to behave similarly. These findings demonstrate that culture—not biology   underlies gender differences.

At one time in the development of feminist approaches, gender roles and gender socialization were the dominant concepts in explaining why women cluster in particular occupations. More recently, however, sociologists have noted that while society teaches "masculine" and "feminine" gender roles, such an approach does not explain where these gender roles come from or how they can be changed. For this, we need to see how gender is built into social institutions (Lorber 1994).

☑ CONCEPT CHECKS

1. What is the difference between sex and gender?
2. How do both biology and gender socialization contribute to differences between men and women?
3. How can studies of gender in other cultures contribute to the argument that gender is socially constructed?

no natural order of things

Forms of Gender Inequality

Anthropologists and historians have found that most groups, collectives, and societies throughout history differentiate between women's and men's societal roles. Although there are considerable variations across cultures, rarely are women more powerful than men. Women everywhere are primarily concerned with child rearing and maintaining the home, while political and military activities are resoundingly men's concerns. Nowhere do men have primary responsibility for the rearing of children. Conversely, there are few if any cultures in which women have the main responsibility for herding large animals, hunting large game, deep-sea fishing, or plow agriculture (Brown 1977).

Just because women and men perform different tasks or have different responsibilities does not mean that women are unequal to men. However, if the work and activities of women and men are valued differently, then the division of labor can become the basis for unequal gender relations. In modern societies, the division of labor has become less clear cut than in premodern cultures, but men still outnumber women in all spheres of power and influence.

Male dominance in a society is **patriarchy**. Although men are favored in almost all societies, the degree of patriarchy varies. In the United States, women have made tremendous progress, but several forms of gender inequality persist.

Sociologists define **gender inequality** as the difference in the status, power, and prestige women and men have in groups, collectives, and societies. In thinking about gender inequality, we can ask the following questions: Do women and men have equal access to valued societal resources—for example, food, money, power, and time? Do women and men have similar life options? Are women's and men's roles and activities valued similarly? Keep these questions in mind as we now examine gender inequality in the workplace, in the home, in educational systems, and in politics, as well as in the violence practiced on women.

Women and the Workplace

Rates of employment of women outside the home, for all classes, were quite low until well into the twentieth century. Even as late as 1910 in the United States, more than a third of gainfully employed women were maids or house servants. The female labor force consisted mainly of young, single women and children. When women or girls worked

The Political Work of Drag

Although many sociologists tend to focus on abstract concepts or faraway places, some scholars write about the issues and places that are part of their everyday lives—their own communities. Verta Taylor and Leila Rupp are two of the United States' leading scholars of gender and social movements. Their 2003 book *Drag Queens of the 801 Cabaret* is an example of how

sociological research can be used to illuminate the aspects of everyday community life that are usually taken for granted.

Taylor is chair of the department of sociology at the University of California, Santa Barbara (UCSB), and Rupp is chair of the Women's Studies Program; but when they are not occupied in Santa Barbara they live in Key West, Florida, where they have a second home. Key West is a small island city with diverse communities—Cuban, Bahamian, gay, hippie—and is a destination for many gay and lesbian tourists. Taylor and Rupp have been going there for over twenty years and know the town intimately.

One night they walked into the 801 Cabaret to see a new drag show, and they were utterly entranced with what was going on. They had seen men impersonating women in other drag shows, but these performers made no effort to pass as women. They spoke in their male voices, talked about tucking away their male genitals, and mimed sexual acts with various audience members. Through their performance, the drag queens were remolding and simultaneously creating new gender and sexual possibilities. Knowing that drag has a long history building gay communities and educating straight audiences about gay life and alternative gender forms, Taylor and Rupp saw this as a perfect research project.

To depict the social world of the 801 Cabaret, Taylor and Rupp used ethnographic methods. They spent three years attending the shows and hanging out behind the scenes. In the process, they developed a special rapport with the drag queens and got them to open up about all aspects of their lives. They also conducted focus groups with audience members to find out why all sorts of people—gay and straight, men and women, tourists and locals—come to the show and what they take away. The book is naturalistic ethnography because it shows the way people live in their natural setting. It teaches readers about the people behind a stereotype and humanizes them in the best traditions in careful ethnography.

in factories or offices, employers often sent their wages to their parents. When they married, they withdrew from the labor force.

Since then, women's participation in the paid labor force

has risen more or less continuously, especially since the 1950s (Figure 10.1). In 2006, 59.4 percent of women age sixteen and older were in the labor force, in contrast to 38 percent in 1960. An even greater change has occurred among married mothers

next day in the student paper, *The Nexus:* "When I first came to this school, I was under the impression that many of the students here were pretty closed minded. So I was nervous for the drag queens...when I heard they would be doing a special performance for the 800 or so Sociology 1 students. ...My assumption was wrong....The ladies put on an incredible show filled with entertainment as well as subtle political messages. The packed crowd ate it up. From the moment the three queens came out on the stage doing their rendition of En Vogue's 'Free Your Mind,' guys and girls alike were waving dollar bills in the air."

The UCSB student went on to write: "Here at UCSB, we are used to seeing tan, buff men and gorgeous blondes walking around campus. This time, we got both in one. It takes balls—pun definitely intended—to bare it all in front of a group of 18 to 22 year olds. I expected some people to walk out. No one did. ...I just wanted to thank the drag queens for coming all the way from Key West and opening our hearts and minds. They are an inspiration to all to be confident in who you are....I also want to thank Verta Taylor for believing we could handle such an event. I myself am thankful that my stereotypical impression of the students here has been challenged. And to the girls at the 801 Cabaret, you made my day."

In addition, Taylor and Rupp make an important argument about what the drag queens are doing. Not only are they dancing and entertaining but something more serious is taking place. The performers are doing political work because their shows solidify community among gay, lesbian, bisexual, and transgender audience members at the same time that they impart messages about the blurred boundaries between masculine and feminine and gay and straight to curious tourists who wander into the show.

How is work like this public sociology? Because it stimulates discussion about what it means to be a man or a woman and what it means to be gay or straight in a number of different venues. People in Key West read the book, debating what was going on at the cabaret in the local papers. Across the country, scholars, journalists, and activists respond to the notion that drag performances can serve as an important tactic for gay and lesbian social movements.

After the book appeared, the two professors invited the drag queens to visit their classes at UCSB. Three of the girls performed in Taylor's introduction to sociology class, and for the last number, one of them stripped, leaving on only the wig and makeup. Karen Sikola, a student in the class, wrote the

The drag queens at the 801 Cabaret dressed Verta Taylor and Leila Rupp in drag so that they would understand how the audience objectifies their bodies.

of young children. In 1978, only 14 percent of married women with preschool-age children worked full-time year round, yet this figure increased to 63 percent by 2006 (U.S. Bureau of Labor Statistics 2007c).

One force behind women's increased entry into the labor force was the increasing demand, since 1940, for clerical and service workers like Andrea Ellington, as the U.S. economy expanded and changed (Oppenheimer 1970). From 1940 until

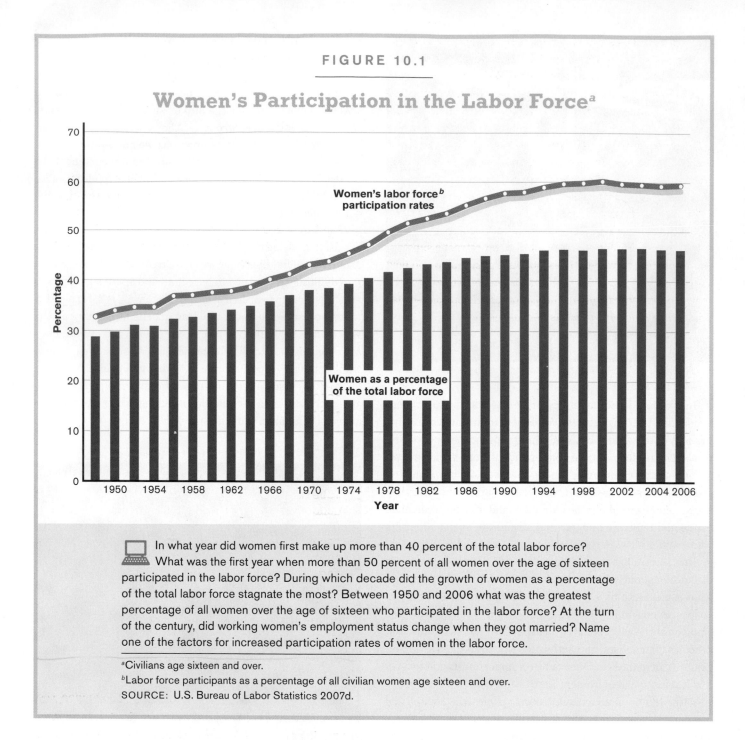

FIGURE 10.1

Women's Participation in the Labor Force[a]

In what year did women first make up more than 40 percent of the total labor force? What was the first year when more than 50 percent of all women over the age of sixteen participated in the labor force? During which decade did the growth of women as a percentage of the total labor force stagnate the most? Between 1950 and 2006 what was the greatest percentage of all women over the age of sixteen who participated in the labor force? At the turn of the century, did working women's employment status change when they got married? Name one of the factors for increased participation rates of women in the labor force.

[a]Civilians age sixteen and over.
[b]Labor force participants as a percentage of all civilian women age sixteen and over.
SOURCE: U.S. Bureau of Labor Statistics 2007d.

the late 1960s, labor force activity increased among women who were past their prime child-rearing years. During the 1970s and 1980s, as the marriage age rose, fertility declined, and women's educational attainment increased, the growth in labor force participation spread to younger women. Many women now postpone family formation to complete their education and establish themselves in the labor force. Despite family obligations, today a majority of women of all educational levels work outside the home during their child-rearing years (Spain and Bianchi 1996).

Inequalities at Work

Until recently, women were overwhelmingly concentrated in routine, poorly paid occupations. The clerk (office worker) provides a good illustration. In 1850 in the United States, clerks held responsible positions requiring accountancy skills and carrying managerial responsibilities; fewer than 1 percent were women. The twentieth century saw a general mechanization of office work (starting with the introduction of the typewriter in the late nineteenth century), accompanied by a downgrading of the clerk's status—together with a related occupation, secretary—into a routine, low-paid occupation. Women filled these occupations as the jobs' pay and prestige declined. Today, most secretaries and clerks are women.

Studies of certain occupations reveal how **gender typing** occurs in the workplace. Expanding areas of lower-level work, such as secretarial positions or retail sales, attract a substantial proportion of women. These jobs are poorly paid and hold few career prospects. Men with good educational qualifications aspire to something higher, whereas others choose blue-collar work. Once an occupation has become gender typed, inertia sets in. Job hierarchies are

> built around the assumption that men will occupy superior positions, while a stream of women will flow through subordinate jobs. Employers are guided in future hiring decisions by gender labels. And the very conditions of most female jobs lead to adaptive responses on the part of women—low job commitment, few career ambitions, high turnover, seeking alternative rewards in social relations—which fortify the image of women as suitable for only lower-level jobs. (Lowe 1987)

These social conditions reinforce outlooks produced by early gender socialization, as women may grow up believing that they should put their husband's career before their own. (Men also are frequently brought up to believe the same thing.)

Women have recently made inroads into occupations once defined as "men's jobs" (Figure 10.2). By the 1990s, women dominated previously male-dominated professions such as accounting, journalism, psychology, public service, and bartending. In fields such as law, medicine, and engineering, women's proportion has risen substantially since 1970. In 2006, a woman was more likely to be in a managerial or professional job than in a clerical or service position.

Another important economic trend since the 1970s has been the narrowing of the gender gap in earnings. Between 1970 and 2006, the ratio of women's to men's earnings among full-time, year-round workers increased from 62 to 80.8 percent (Table 10.1). Moreover, this ratio increased among all races and ethnic groups. During the 1980s, women's hourly wages as a percentage of men's increased from 64 to 71 percent; weekly earnings rose from 63 to 75 percent, and the ratio of annual earnings among all workers (not just those working full time)

TABLE 10.1

Women's Earnings Compared with Men's

Although the earnings gap between women and men is narrowing, it remains substantial. It is also significant that since the early 1990s, the gap has remained fairly constant. Analysts wonder whether this is temporary or permanent. The table shows what women earned for each dollar earned by men.

YEAR	EARNINGS RATIO
1970	.62
1980	.64
1990	.71
1991	.74
1992	.75
1993	.76
1994	.76
1995	.75
1996	.75
1997	.74
1998	.76
1999	.76
2000	.76
2001	.76
2002	.78
2003	.80
2004	.80
2005	.81
2006	.81

SOURCE: U.S. Bureau of Labor Statistics 2007e.

---

increased from 46 to 61 percent (Spain and Bianchi 1996; U.S. Bureau of Labor Statistics 2007e). Despite the decreasing gender gap in pay, men still earn substantially more than women (Figure 10.3). Several competing theories have been offered to explain this gap.

The Gender Pay Gap: The Sociological Debate

The "gender gap" in pay is widely recognized. Even as recently as 2006, women who worked full-time year round earned

FIGURE 10.2

Women at Work

Of all jobs in a given occupation, the following shows the proportion held by women for each year (percentage).

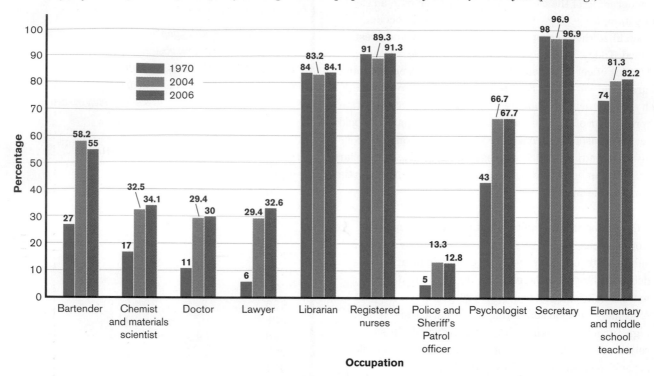

From 1970 to 2006, what is the general trend for the percentage of women holding the jobs shown in this figure? What are the top three jobs in which women occupy the highest proportion of the total? In 2006, what percentage of doctors were women? From 1970 to 2006, what was the percentage change of public officials who are women? In what occupations did women move from the minority in 1970 to the majority in 2006?

SOURCE: Roberts 1995; U.S. Bureau of Labor Statistics 2005a, 2007f.

only 80.7 percent as much as men. What accounts for this discrepancy?

Many sociologists view sex segregation, or gender typing, as a cause of the gender gap in earnings. Sex segregation refers to the fact that men and women are concentrated in different occupations. For instance, in 1989, jobs that were over 80 percent female included secretary, child-care worker, hairdresser, cashier, bookkeeper, telephone operator, receptionist, typist, elementary school teacher, librarian, and nurse. Jobs that were over 80 percent male included doctor, lawyer, dentist, taxi driver, plumber, electrician, carpenter, firefighter, auto mechanic, machinist, and truck driver (Reskin and Padavic 1994).

Sex segregation is problematic because the gender composition of a job is associated with the pay received for that job. This finding has emerged in numerous studies. An analysis of 1980 census data (England 1992) showed that both women and men are disadvantaged by employment in an occupation that is predominantly female. Even "after adjusting for cognitive, social, and physical skill demands, amenities, disamenities, demands for effort, and industrial and organization characteristics, jobs pay less if they contain a higher proportion of females" (England 1992).

The Equal Pay Act, established in 1963, requires employers to provide equal pay to workers in the *same job*. But it has

FIGURE 10.3

The Gender Pay Gap

This figure, in which weekly earnings are shown in constant 2000 dollars, illustrates what has been happening to the gender pay gap over time. After narrowing gradually for years, it widened a little after 1993, when men's inflation-adjusted earnings were increasing slightly and women's were not.

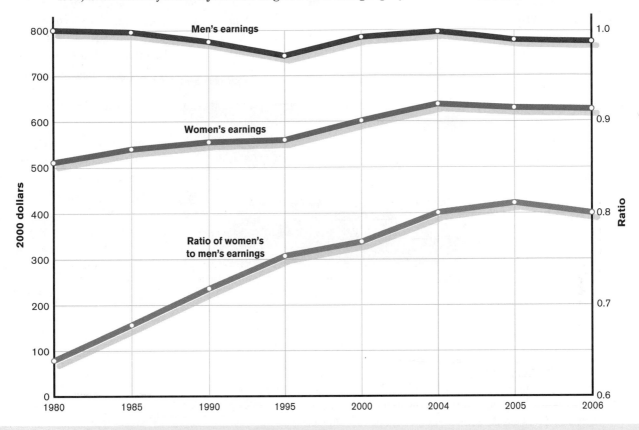

In 1980, what was the ratio of women's median weekly earnings to men's median weekly earnings? As we entered the twenty-first century, what was the dollar amount difference between men's median weekly earnings and women's median weekly earnings? Over the twenty-six-year period from 1980 to 2006, what was the change in the ratio of women's median weekly earning to men's median weekly earnings? What is "human capital"? What is the feminist critique of human capital theory? In what year did the ratio of women's median weekly earnings to men's median weekly earnings stop showing growth?

SOURCE: U.S. Bureau of Labor Statistics 2007g.

done little to eradicate pay differences attributable to gender because men and women rarely work at the same jobs. Thus the best hope for narrowing the pay gap is to establish a pay-equity policy, meaning that pay policies remunerate workers on the basis of the worth of their work and not the sex, race, or other personal characteristics of the majority of workers in

a job (Stryker 1996). Comparable-worth policies would be one such strategy.

However, economists and sociologists differ in explaining *how* occupational segregation leads to a gender gap in pay. Economists focus on women's occupational choices, while sociologists focus on the constraints women face. Many

"Big-City Gals Earn More Than Guys"

If Mary Tyler Moore inspired career-minded young women to flock to Minneapolis in the 1970s, and if Carrie Bradshaw's glamorous lifestyle drew young women to Manhattan in 2000, is it possible that a *New York Times* headline would sizzle enough to lure twenty-something women to major urban areas in 2007? Perhaps. In August 2007, the *New York Times* front page headlines told readers "For Young Earners in a Big City, a Gap in Women's Favor." Other newspapers, Web sites, and television news programs quickly echoed the words that would bring pride to feminists everywhere: "Young Women Earn More Than Men in Big U.S. Cities."

Does that mean that financially savvy, ambitious young women should move to major cities after college graduation—or that young men should instead move to smaller cities or suburbs? Not necessarily. Andrew Beveridge, a sociology professor at Queens College, analyzed data from the U.S. Census Bureau's 2005 American Community Survey. His analysis did indeed show that in 2005, women ages twenty-one to thirty who work full time earned 17 percent more than their male peers in New York and 20 percent more in Dallas. Young women

Melissa Manfro, left, joins her friend Alison Ray for lunch in New York's Rockefeller Center. Young women who live in New York and several other of the nation's largest cities and who work full-time have forged ahead of men in wages, according to an analysis of recent census results.

also earned more than men in Boston, Chicago, Minneapolis, and a few other large cities. By contrast, young women earned 11 percent less than their male peers nationwide (Roberts 2007).

A number of important sociological concepts can help to explain the earnings advantage evidenced by young women in major urban areas. First, the gender gap could be attributable to "social selection" processes. That means that some individuals have personal traits that increase the likelihood that they will engage in a particular behavior (such as moving to an urban area), and that same personal trait also affects their likelihood of experiencing another related outcome (such as high earnings). For example, young women who are hard working, brave, and independent minded might be more likely than other women both to move to a large and potentially daunting city and to seek out (and work hard) at professional opportunities that carry rich financial rewards.

Second, the pattern could reflect "compositional" factors. That means that the demographic composition of the young male and young female populations in major urban areas differ along

economists—as well as employers and public-policy makers—endorse a **human capital theory** explanation. Developed by Gary Becker (1964), the theory argues that individuals make investments in their own "human capital" (such as formal schooling, on-the-job training, and work experience) to increase their productivity and earnings. Those who invest more are considered more productive and consequently are paid higher wages.

Human capital theorists reason that women select occupations that are easy to move in and out of, while still providing moderately good incomes. Central to this argument is the assumption that women's primary allegiance is to home and family; thus they seek undemanding jobs that require little personal investment in training or skills acquisition so that they can better tend to household responsibilities. When women leave the labor force to rear children, their job skills deteriorate and they suffer a wage penalty when they reenter. Moreover, employers may "invest" less in women workers because they believe women will work less continuously than men.

Feminist sociologists critique human capital theory on several grounds. For example, they dispute the claim that women "choose" certain occupations. In fact, the forces blocking women from freely choosing a career may be indirect or direct. For instance, childhood socialization promoting traditional some important traits, such as educational attainment, race, or marital status. It is possible that these compositional differences account for the purported earnings discrepancy rather than simply the gender of the two groups. For example, 53 percent of women in their twenties working in New York in 2005 were college graduates, compared to just 38 percent of men (Roberts 2007). Thus, the average differences in earnings documented between young women and young men in New York could reflect the fact that gender is correlated with education, and a college education is a well-documented correlate of higher earnings.

Similarly, young women in urban areas are more likely than their suburban peers to be single and childless. Both of these factors are associated with remaining in the workforce and climbing the corporate ladder. By contrast, young women who leave the workforce or cut back on their work hours to care for their children experience significant income losses. Beveridge observes that "citified college-women are more likely to be nonmarried and childless, compared with their suburban sisters, so they can and do devote themselves to their careers" (Roberts 2007). Some argue that young women work particularly hard in the early stages of their careers, in anticipation of the fact that they may lose ground in the workplace if they do decide to have children.

Third, the findings could reveal a distinctive life stage effect but say little about gender differences in earnings at other life course stages. Men and women in their twenties tend to be single, yet as they enter into their late twenties and early thirties and start to have children, they alter their work patterns in different ways—based on their gender. Men tend to remain in the workforce after they have children, whereas women are more likely than their husbands to take time out of the workforce to raise their kids. As a result, the earnings advantage detected among women in their twenties fades quickly with age. Beveridge explained: "after age 30, women are no longer ahead" (Roberts 2007).

Although many sociologists are reluctant to say that these recent news headlines are evidence that women's economic disadvantage may be a thing of the past, a handful are optimistic. Some say that women's earnings progress reflects public policies such as affirmative action, where companies are actively trying to recruit, hire, and promote highly qualified women. Others add that women's college graduation rates now surpass men's, so a female earnings advantage will inevitably follow. However, others are pessimistic that urban women's advantage will persist as they marry, especially for those women who abide by a traditional allocation of labor in their homes after they marry.

Questions

- What are the key findings of Andrew Beveridge's study of the earnings of men and women in their twenties?
- Do the results suggest that young women should move to urban areas if they hope to enhance their earnings? Why or why not?
- What are three explanations for the female earnings advantage documented among urban young adults?

FOR FURTHER EXPLORATION

Breitman, Rachel. 2007. "Young Women Earn More Than Men in Big U.S. Cities." Reuters News Service (August 3, 2007). www.reuters.com/article/domesticNews/idUSN0334472920070803 (accessed December 1, 2007).

Hagey, Keach. 2007. "Big-City Gals Earn More Than Guys." CBS News (August 3, 2007). www.cbsnews.com/stories/2007/08/03/the_skinny/printable3130645.shtml (accessed December 1, 2007).

Roberts, Sam. 2007. "For Younger Earners in the City, a Gap in Women's Favor." New York Times: 1A (August 3, 2007). www.nytimes.com/2007/08/03/nyregion/03women.html?n=Top/Reference/Times%20Topics/Subjects/P/Population&pagewanted=print (accessed December 1, 2007).

gender roles may lead young women to choose occupations such as teaching or nursing, which are viewed as compatible with feminine traits such as warmth and nurturance. More direct obstacles include discriminatory bosses, co-workers, and customers. Also, workplace "gatekeepers" prohibit women from entering certain occupations. For example, in 1992 State Farm Insurance was forced to provide back pay to 814 women who were denied jobs as insurance agents because of their sex. Currently a class-action lawsuit against Wal-Mart is in the federal courts; the suit alleges that Wal-Mart discriminated against 1.6 million former and current female employees in making promotions, job assignments, and pay decisions and that it retaliates against women who complain about such practices (Wal-Mart Class 2005).

Sociologists further argue that human capital theory neglects power differentials between men and women in the workplace and society. Numerous studies reveal that even when men and women are in the same job, men are paid more.

Because women's work is devalued by society and by employers, women are rewarded less for their work. Moreover, women's relative powerlessness prevents them from redefining the work they do as "skilled." As long as jobs predominantly filled by women, such as caring for children and the elderly, are viewed as "unskilled," wages in women's jobs will remain low.

In 2004, a federal judge approved a class-action gender discrimination lawsuit against Wal-Mart in what has become one of the largest civil rights cases in U.S. history. From right: Betty Dukes, Patricia Surgenson, Stephanie Odle, and Christine Kwapnoski charge that Wal-Mart, including its Sam's Club division, systematically discriminates against its hourly and salaried female employees by denying them promotions and equal pay.

These competing explanations have very different implications for the future. According to human capital theory, the gender gap in pay could disappear if women and men received equal amounts of education and workplace training and if they took equal responsibility for family commitments, such as child care. If feminist sociologists are correct in arguing that women's work is devalued, a drastic change in gender ideology must occur if men and women are to become equally rewarded for their participation in the workplace.

COMPARABLE WORTH

Comparable worth is a policy that compares pay levels of jobs held disproportionately by women with pay levels of jobs held disproportionately by men and that tries to adjust pay so that the women and men working in female-dominated jobs are not penalized. The policy presumes that jobs can be ranked objectively according to skill, effort, responsibility, and working conditions. After such a ranking, pay is adjusted so that equivalently ranked male- and female-dominated jobs receive equivalent pay (Hartmann et al. 1985).

Only a handful of U.S. states have instituted comparable-worth policies for public sector employees (Blum 1991), partly because such policies raise technical, political, and economic issues. Perhaps most important is the issue of job evaluation, or the identification of common denominators of skill, effort, responsibility, and working conditions so jobs can be compared and ranked independent of the race and gender of job incumbents (Stryker 1996). Effective implementation requires that job evaluations be free from gender bias. However, substantial research shows that it is very difficult to make gender-neutral assessments of jobs and required job skills. Once men and women know which jobs are predominantly male and which are predominantly female, they attribute to them the job content that best fits with gender stereotypes (Steinberg 1990).

Opposition to comparable-worth policies comes from both economists and feminists. Economists worry that comparable worth is inflationary and will cause wage losses and unemployment for some (disproportionately women) because of benefits enacted for others. Feminists counter that comparable worth reinforces gender stereotyping rather than breaking down gender barriers at work (Blum 1991).

Such debates show that the jobs society values are determined not by their market or societal worth but by power relations (Blum 1991).

THE GLASS CEILING AND THE GLASS ESCALATOR

Although women are increasingly entering traditionally male jobs, they may not be seeing increases in pay—and increases in occupational mobility—because of the **glass ceiling**, a promotion barrier that prevents women's upward mobility. The glass ceiling is particularly problematic in male-dominated occupations and the professions. Women's progress is blocked not by virtue of innate inability or lack of basic qualifications but by lack of the sponsorship of powerful senior colleagues to articulate their value to the organization or profession (Alvarez et al. 1996). As a result, women progress into midlevel management positions but do not, in proportionate numbers, move beyond midmanagement ranks.

One explanation for women's blocked mobility is based on gender stereotypes. Research shows that college-educated white males in professional jobs identify potential leaders as people who are like themselves. Women are thus assessed negatively because they deviate from this norm (Cleveland 1996).

Do men who work in female-dominated professions also face subtle obstacles to promotion? On the contrary, the sociologist Christine Williams (1992) has observed that a **glass escalator** pushes these men to the top of their corporate ladders. She found that employers singled out male workers in traditionally female jobs, such as nurse, librarian, elementary school teacher, and social worker, and promoted them to top administrative jobs in disproportionately high numbers. "Often, despite their intentions, they face invisible pressures to move up in their professions. Like being on a moving escalator, they have to work to stay in place," writes Williams (1992). These pressures may take positive forms, such as close mentoring and encouragement from supervisors, or they may be

Sociologist Christine Williams asserts that men in female-dominated professions, such as this elementary school teacher, are routinely promoted to top administrative positions and face constant pressure to advance.

the result of prejudicial attitudes of those outside the profession, such as clients who prefer to work with male rather than female executives. Some of the men in Williams's study faced unwelcome pressure to accept promotions, such as a male children's librarian who received negative evaluations for "not shooting high enough" in his career aspirations.

SEXUAL HARASSMENT IN THE WORKPLACE

Sexual harassment is unwanted or repeated sexual advances, remarks, and behavior that are offensive to the recipient and cause discomfort or interference with job performance. Power imbalances facilitate harassment; even though women can and do sexually harass subordinates, it is more common for men to harass women because men usually hold positions of authority (Reskin and Padavic 1994).

The U.S. courts have identified two types of sexual harassment. One is the quid pro quo, in which a supervisor demands sexual acts from a worker as a job condition or promises work-related benefits in exchange for sexual acts. The other is the "hostile work environment," in which a pattern of sexual language, lewd posters, or sexual advances makes a worker so uncomfortable that it is difficult for her to do her job (Reskin and Padavic 1994).

Recognition of sexual harassment and women's willingness to report it have increased substantially since the testimony of Anita Hill to the Senate Judiciary Committee during the confirmation hearings for Clarence Thomas's 1991 nomination to the U.S. Supreme Court. Hill's recounting of his harassment raised public awareness of the problem and encouraged more women to report incidents (Figure 10.4). In the first six months of 1992 alone, the number of workplace harassment complaints increased by more than 50 percent (Gross 1992).

Despite increased awareness, sociologists have observed that "the great majority of women who are abused by behavior that fits legal definitions of sexual harassment—and who are traumatized by the experience—do not label what has happened to them as sexual harassment" (Paludi and Barickman 1991). Women's reluctance to report may be due to the following factors: (1) many still do not recognize that sexual harassment is an actionable offense; (2) victims may be reluctant to make complaints, fearing that they will not be believed, that their charges will not be taken seriously, or that they will be subject to reprisals; (3) it may be difficult to differentiate between harassment and joking on the job (Giuffre and Williams 1994).

In 1998, the U.S. Supreme Court ruled that the Civil Rights Act outlaws harassment between members of the same sex. The case involved a man who had to quit his job on an offshore oil rig because he had been repeatedly grabbed, ridiculed, and threatened by two male supervisors. The Court ruled that neither "roughhousing" among men, nor "flirtations" between men and women, nor even some types of "verbal or physical harassment" is illegal but that when sexual harassment is so "severely hostile or abusive" that it prevents workers from doing their jobs, it violates the Civil Rights Act—regardless of whether the offender and the harassed person are of the same or the opposite sex (Savage 1998).

The Family and Gender Issues

BALANCING WORK AND CHILD CARE

One key factor affecting women's careers is the male perception that for female employees, work comes second to having children. A study in Britain on the views of managers interviewing female applicants for technical positions in the health services found that the interviewers always asked the women whether they had, or intended to have, children (asking this is now illegal in the United States). They never did so with male applicants. When asked why, the interviewers cited two points: Women with children may require time off for school holidays or if a child falls sick; and child care is the mother's problem, not a parental one. Some managers thought their questions

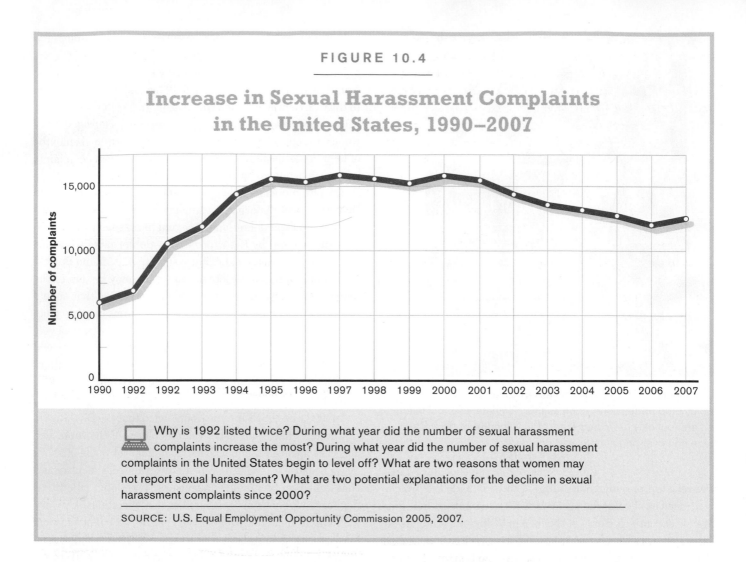

FIGURE 10.4

Increase in Sexual Harassment Complaints in the United States, 1990–2007

Why is 1992 listed twice? During what year did the number of sexual harassment complaints increase the most? During what year did the number of sexual harassment complaints in the United States begin to level off? What are two reasons that women may not report sexual harassment? What are two potential explanations for the decline in sexual harassment complaints since 2000?

SOURCE: U.S. Equal Employment Opportunity Commission 2005, 2007.

indicated an attitude of "caring," but most saw them as assessing a female applicant's reliability (Homans 1987).

Although men cannot bear children, they can be fully involved in and responsible for child care. But this possibility was not considered by any of the managers. Likewise, in terms of promotion, women were seen as likely to interrupt their careers to care for young children, no matter how senior a position they might have reached. The few women in this study who held senior management positions were all without children, and several who planned to have children said they intended to leave their jobs and might retrain for other positions subsequently.

Are women's job opportunities hampered mainly by male prejudices? Some managers commented that women with children should not work but should occupy themselves with child care and the home. Most, however, accepted the principle that women should have the same career opportunities as men. Their bias had less to do with the workplace than with the

domestic responsibilities of parenting. So long as most people assume that parenting cannot be shared equally by women and men, the problems facing women employees will persist.

In her book *Working Women Don't Have Wives* (1994), Terri Apter argues that women want and need economic independence but at the same time want to be mothers to their children. Both goals are reasonable, but while men with wives who take prime responsibility for domestic work can achieve them, women cannot. Greater flexibility in working life is one partial solution. Much more difficult is getting men to alter their attitudes.

HOUSEWORK

Although recent decades have seen revolutionary changes in women's status in the United States, one area of work has lagged far behind: housework. Because of the increase of married women in the workforce and the resulting change in status, it was presumed that men would contribute more to housework. Generally, this has not been the case. Sociologists calculate that working women perform fifteen more hours of housework per week than their husbands, in effect a "second shift" of work (Hochschild and Machung 1989; Shelton 1992). The United Nations (2003) estimates that women in the United States work 6 percent more than men, a majority of which is spent in nonmarket activities. These figures do not include time spent on child care, which if factored in would increase the gap. The United Nations (1995) has estimated that if all of the nonmarket work of women were accounted for, the official estimate of the size of the world economy would be $11 trillion higher. Findings like these have led Arlie Hochschild (1989) to call the state of relations between women and men a "stalled revolution."

Some sociologists see this phenomenon as a result of economic forces: Household work is exchanged for economic support. Because women earn less than men, they generally remain economically dependent on their husbands and thus perform most of the housework. Hochschild suggests that women are thus doubly oppressed by men: once during the first shift, and again during the second shift. But this dependency model breaks down when the wife earns more than her husband. For instance, of the husbands that Hochschild studied who earned less than their wives, none shared in the housework.

Some sociologists apply a symbolic interactionist perspective, asking how the performance or nonperformance of housework relates to gender roles. For example, through interviews and participant observation, Hochschild found that the assignment of household tasks falls along gendered lines. Wives do most of the daily chores, such as cooking and routine cleaning,

U.S. Marine Michael Mink discusses school behavior notes that came home in his sons' backpacks. Mink takes care of his five children while his wife Angela, who is also a Marine, serves in Iraq. Like many families with two working parents, the Minks struggle to balance raising children and working full-time jobs.

How does Arlie Hochschild define the "second shift"? What are sociologists' explanations for the uneven division of housework within families?

while husbands take on more occasional tasks, such as mowing the lawn and doing home repairs. The major difference is the amount of control the individual has over when the work gets done. Women's household jobs bind them to a fixed schedule, whereas men's are more discretionary.

Marjorie Devault (1991) studied how the caring activities within a household are socially constructed as women's work. She argues that women perform housework because the family "incorporates a strong and relatively enduring association of caring activity with the woman's position in the household." Even in households where men contribute, an egalitarian division of household labor breaks down when the couple has children—children require constant attention, and their care schedules are often unpredictable. Mothers overwhelmingly spend more time with child-rearing tasks than do fathers (Shelton 1992).

Sociologists argue that underlying this inequitable distribution of tasks is the implicit understanding that men and women are responsible for different spheres. Men are expected to be providers, women to be caretakers—even if they are breadwinners as well as mothers. By reproducing in everyday life these roles learned during childhood socialization, men and women "do gender" and reinforce it as a means for society to differentiate between men and women.

Education and Unequal Treatment in the Classroom

Schools foster gender differences in outlook and behavior. Although less common today, school regulations compelling girls to wear dresses or skirts served as an obvious means of gender typing. The consequences went beyond mere

appearance. As a result of their clothes, girls lacked the freedom to sit casually, to join in rough-and-tumble games, or to run as fast as they were able. Although strict enforcement of school dress has become rare, differences in informal styles of dress persist, still influencing gender behavior in school. School reading texts also perpetuate gender images. Although this too is changing, storybooks in elementary school often portray boys showing initiative and independence, and girls as more passive and watching their brothers. Stories written especially for girls often have an element of adventure, but usually in a domestic or school setting. Boys' adventure stories are more wide ranging, with heroes who travel to distant places or who in other ways are sturdily independent (Statham 1986).

In general, people interact differently with men and women, and boys and girls (Lorber 1994)—even in elementary schools. Studies document that teachers interact differently, and often inequitably, with male and female students in terms of the frequency and content of teacher–student interactions. Both of the patterns are based on—and perpetuate—traditional assumptions about male and female behavior and traits.

One study shows that regardless of the sex of the teacher, male students interact more with their teachers than female students do. Boys receive more teacher attention and instructional time than girls do. This is partly because boys are more demanding than girls (American Association of University Women [AAUW] 1992). Another study reported that boys are eight times more likely to call out answers in class, thus grabbing their teachers' attention, and that even when boys do not voluntarily participate in class, teachers are more likely to solicit information from them than from girls. However, when girls try to bring attention to themselves by calling out in class without raising their hands, they are reprimanded by comments such as "In this class, we don't shout out answers, we raise our hands" (Sadker and Sadker 1994).

In addition, the content of student–teacher interactions differs depending on the sex of the students. After observing elementary school teachers and students over many years, researchers found that teachers helped boys in working out the correct answers, whereas they simply gave girls the correct answers and did not engage them in the problem-solving process. In addition, teachers posed more academic challenges to boys, encouraging them to think through their answers to find the best possible response (Sadker and Sadker 1994).

Boys were disadvantaged in several ways, however. Because of their rowdy behavior, they were more often scolded and punished than the girls. Moreover, boys outnumber girls in special education programs by startling percentages. Sociologists have argued that school personnel may be mislabeling boys' behavioral problems as learning disabilities.

The differential treatment of boys and girls perpetuates stereotypic gender-role behavior. Girls are trained to be quiet and well behaved and to turn to others for answers, while boys are encouraged to be outspoken, active problem solvers. Female children from ethnic minorities may be doubly disadvantaged. A study of what it was like to be a black female pupil in a white school reported that unlike the boys, the black girls were initially enthusiastic about school but altered their attitudes because of the difficulties they encountered. Even when the girls were young, age seven or eight, teachers would disperse them if they were chatting in a group on the playground—in contrast to the white children, whose similar behavior was tolerated. Once treated as "troublemakers," the black girls rapidly became so (Bryan et al. 1987).

Gender Inequality in Politics

Women play an increasingly important role in U.S. politics, although they are still far from achieving full equality. Before 1993, there were only 2 women in the U.S. Senate (out of 100 Senate members), and 29 in the U.S. House of Representatives (out of 435). As of the November 2008 election, there are 17 women senators but 77 representatives (Women's Policy, Inc. 2008). Women in 2007 held a little more than 23.5 percent of all seats in state legislatures, five times as many as they held in 1971, but only eight governorships (out of fifty) (Center for American Women and Politics [CAWP] 2007b). The U.S. Supreme Court had its first woman justice appointed in 1981, and its second twelve years later. It was not until 1984 that a woman

Senator Hillary Rodham Clinton won eighteen million votes in her bid to become the first female presidential candidate of a major political party. Senator Clinton, House Speaker Nancy Pelosi, and Governors Kathleen Sibelius, Janet Napolitano, and 2008 vice-presidential candidate Sarah Palin are a handful of the growing number of powerful female politicians.

was nominated as the vice presidential candidate of either major party, neither of which has ever nominated a woman for the presidency. Women politicians are overwhelmingly affiliated with the Democratic Party. In the U.S. Congress, 71 percent of women are Democrats and in state legislatures, almost 69 percent of women legislators are Democrats (CAWP 2007a).

The more local the political office, the more likely it is to be occupied by a woman. One reason is that local politics is often part-time work, especially in smaller cities and towns. Local politics can thus be good "women's work," offering low pay, part-time employment, flexible hours, and the absence of a clear career path. The farther from home the political office, the more likely it is to be regarded as "man's work," providing a living wage, full-time employment, and a lifetime career.

Violence against Women

Violence directed against women is found in many societies, including the United States. Studies indicate that between one quarter and one half of all women around the world have been abused in some way by intimate partners (Stop Violence Against Women 2006). One in five worldwide will be a victim of rape or attempted rape in her lifetime (United Nations Population Fund [UNFPA] 2005b). In Japan, three out of five women report having been sexually or physically abused by a partner. In India, an estimated 34,139 women were killed between 2001 and 2005 in dowry-related deaths (NCRB 2006). It has been estimated that more than 130 million girls and women worldwide have been subjected to "genital mutilation" (UNICEF 2005), and about 101 million are "missing," partly as the result of female infanticide in cultures in which boys are more highly valued than girls (Klasen and Wink 2003).

The trafficking of women for forced prostitution, which has been called "the largest slave trade in history," is a growing problem (UNFPA 2005b). The United Nations estimates that each year 800,000 people—80 percent of whom are women and 50 percent of whom are minors—are moved across borders as a part of the worldwide sex trade. Nearly a quarter come from Asia, followed by the former Soviet Union and eastern Europe (UNFPA 2005a). War, displacement, and economic and social inequities between and within countries, as well as the demand for low-wage labor and sex work, drive this illicit trade.

In the United States, many scholars argue that the increased depiction of violence in American popular culture contributes to a climate in which women are victimized. The most common manifestation is rape, although stalking and sexual harassment increasingly constitute a form of psychological (if not physical) violence as well.

Rape can be sociologically defined as the forcing of nonconsensual vaginal, oral, or anal intercourse. Sociologists Pauline Bart and Patricia O'Brien (1985) offer the following classification (see also Brownmiller 1986):

- CONSENSUAL SEX: Intercourse that is desired equally by both partners.
- ALTRUISTIC SEX: One partner (usually female) "goes along" because she feels sorry for or guilty toward her partner.
- COMPLIANT SEX: One partner (usually female) goes along because she feels that the consequences of refusal would be worse than assenting to sex.
- RAPE: One partner (usually female) is forced, often by actual or threatened violence, to have sex against her will.

As one researcher observed, between consensual sex and rape lies "a continuum of pressure, threat, coercion, and force" (Kelly 1987). Common to all forms of rape is the lack of consent: At least in principle, *no* means "no" when it comes to sexual relations in most courts of law in the United States. Virtually all rapes are committed by men against women, although men rape other men in prisons and other all-male institutional environments.

Rape is an act of violence, often carefully planned rather than performed on the spur of the moment to satisfy some uncontrollable sexual desire. Many rapes involve beatings, knifings, and even murder. Even when rape leaves no physical wounds, it is a highly traumatic violation of the victim's person that leaves long-lasting psychological scars.

It is difficult to know how many rapes actually occur because most rapes go unreported. In one comprehensive study of American sexual behavior, 22 percent of the women surveyed reported having been forced into a sexual encounter. Yet the same study found that only 3 percent of the men admitted to having forced a woman into sex, a discrepancy the study's authors attribute to different perceptions between men and women regarding what constitutes forced sex (Laumann et al. 1994). Based on its semiannual survey of nearly 134,000 Americans, the U.S. Department of Justice estimates that in 2005 there were 176,540 sexual assaults on women. The total number of sexual assaults, attempted rapes, and rapes (191,670) was more than 8.7 percent lower than in 2004—part of an overall decrease in violent crimes since 1994 (U.S. Bureau of Justice Statistics 2005b). Most rapes are committed by relatives (fathers or stepfathers, brothers, uncles), partners, or acquaintances. Among college students, most rapes are committed by boyfriends, former boyfriends, or classmates. The National College Women Sexual Victimization (Fisher et al. 2000) study presents a chilling picture of violence against women on campuses across the country (Fisher et al. 2000). The study, conducted during spring semester 1997, asked college women about their experience with rape, attempted rape, coerced sex, unwanted sexual contact, and stalking during the 1996–1997 school year. Overall, since the beginning of the school year, 1.7 percent had been the victim of a completed rape, and 1.1 percent of an attempted rape. Because students were interviewed seven months into the academic year, the authors estimate that over the entire academic year nearly 5 percent of the women in the sample would have fallen victim to a rape or attempted rape. Over the typical five years of a college career, this suggests that between a fifth and a quarter of all women attending college would fall victim to rape or attempted rape—some 2.2 million women.

Moreover, fully a tenth of the female students surveyed had been raped before the study period, and a tenth had been the victims of attempted rape. For both completed and attempted rapes, nine out of ten offenders were known to the victim. About 55 percent of rape victims used physical force in an effort to thwart the rape, as did 69 percent of attempted rape victims.

The incidence of other forms of victimization reported in the study was substantially higher than that of rape. Nearly one out of six female students reported being the target of attempted or completed sexual coercion or unwanted sexual contact during the current academic year, half involving the use or threat of physical force. More than a third reported a threatened, attempted, or completed unwanted sexual assault at some time during their lives. And about one out of every eight reported having been stalked during the current year, almost always by someone they knew—typically a former boyfriend or classmate. Stalking, it was reported, was emotionally traumatizing and in 15 percent of the incidents involved actual or threatened physical harm.

The conclusions of the study are worth quoting at length:

> To summarize, the national-level survey of 4,446 college women suggests that many students will encounter sexist and harassing comments, will likely receive an obscene phone call, and will have a good chance of being stalked or of enduring some form of coerced sexual contact. During any given academic year, 2.8 percent of women will experience a completed and/or attempted rape. . . . Furthermore, the level of rape and other types of victimization found in the survey becomes an increasing concern when the victimization figures are projected over a full year, a full college career, and the full population of women at one college or at colleges across the nation. . . . Although exceptions exist, most sexual victimizations occur when college women are alone with a man they know, at night, and in the privacy of a residence. (Fisher et al. 2000)

WHY ARE WOMEN SO OFTEN THE TARGETS OF SEXUAL VIOLENCE?

Some scholars claim that men are socialized to regard women as sex objects and that this partly explains the high levels of victimization reported to the NCWSV study (Dworkin 1981, 1987; Griffin 1979). Susan Brownmiller (1986), for example, claims that the constant threat of rape contributes to a "rape culture" in which male domination fosters a state of continual fear in women. One aspect of a rape culture is male socialization to a sense of sexual entitlement, which may encourage sexual conquest and promote insensitivity to the difference between consensual and nonconsensual sex (Scully 1990). From seemingly innocent high school locker-room jokes, to television commercials and magazine ads depicting women as sexually inviting, to television and movie images equating masculinity with the conquest of women, many males learn to believe that women exist for their pleasure. Under such circumstances, rape is all too "normal" (Wolf 1992).

The fact that "acquaintance rapes" occur suggests that some men feel entitled to sexual access if they already know the woman. In a survey of nearly 270,000 first-year college students, 55 percent of male students agreed with the following statement: "If two people really like each other, it's all right for them to have sex even if they've known each other only for a very short time." Only 31 percent of female students agreed (American Council on Education [ACE] 2001). Another national study of first-year college students found that one out of five males felt they were entitled to have sex if the women "led them on" (Higher Education Research Institute [HERI] 1990), while yet another national survey reported that 43 percent of all men believed that a woman is partly to blame if she is raped after changing her mind about having sex (Yankelovich 1991). When a man goes out on a date with sexual conquest on his mind, he may force his attentions on an unwilling partner, overcoming her resistance through the use of alcohol, persistence, or both. While such an act may not be legally defined as rape, it would be experienced as such by many women.

Because men are socialized to feel sexual entitlement, rapes are most common when men believe that norms condemning rape do not apply—for example, in times of war. Indeed, war-related rapes are as old as human history. Followers of Rome's legendary founder, Romulus, were reputed to have captured and raped Sabine women to populate Rome. Japanese soldiers raped as many as twenty thousand women when they conquered the city of Nanking in China in 1937 (Chang and Kirby

This sixteenth-century sculpture by Giambologna, titled *The Rape of the Sabines*, depicts the legend in which soldiers following Romulus, the mythical founder of Rome, captured and raped Sabine women to populate Rome.

1997). American soldiers committed rapes during the Civil War and the Vietnam War.

Rape is often a military strategy. During World War II, for example, Japanese soldiers forced as many as two hundred thousand young women and girls to serve as "comfort women" for Japanese troops. These women—mainly Korean but also taken from other Asian countries conquered by the Japanese—were forced to work as sex slaves in military brothels throughout the Pacific. Many died in captivity, often of despair. A large number committed suicide (Stetz and Oh 2001). Rape was widely used as a Serbian strategy in the recent wars in Kosovo and Bosnia. By systematically raping and impregnating

Muslim women, the Serbian forces hoped to humiliate the Muslim population into fleeing their homelands (Allen 1996).

☑ CONCEPT CHECKS

1. Describe at least three examples of how gender inequalities emerge in the workplace. How would a sociologist explain these inequities?
2. How do inequalities in the home, especially with regard to housework and child care, reflect larger gender inequities in society?
3. Do you believe that girls or boys are more disadvantaged in the classroom? Why?
4. What are some important differences between men's and women's political participation?
5. Why are women so often the targets of sexual violence?

Gender Inequality in Global Perspective

Women the world over experience economic and political inequality. Although the United States has made strides during the past quarter century toward greater gender inequality, it is by no means the world's leader in this effort.

Economic Inequality

Women constitute over 40 percent of the world's paid workforce in all regions except northern Africa and western Asia (International Labor Organization [ILO] 2007). Women work in the lowest-wage jobs and generally make less than men doing similar work—although the wage gap is slowly decreasing, at least in industrialized countries (ILO 2007). Because women work a "second shift," caring for children and doing household duties, they also work longer hours than men. A recent UN report found that women in the United States worked on average 25 minutes each day more than men—a difference that was considerably smaller than that in Austria (45 minutes) or Italy (103 minutes). A recent UNICEF report shows that the difference is sometimes larger in developing countries such as Benin (145 minutes), Mexico (105 minutes), and India (66 minutes) (UNICEF 2007). Because of persistent discrimination, higher unemployment, and lower wages, women represent 60 percent of the world's 550 million working poor (ILO 2004a).

A worker cleans the floor at Thailand's new Suvarnabhumi Airport. In all countries, women continue to work in the lowest paying service and industrial sector jobs.

Access to knowledge about birth control enables women to exercise greater control over childbearing so that many can work outside the home. Education also encourages women to seek financial independence from men. More women are getting college degrees and professional jobs than ever before. Women make up about half of all college students in the economically developed countries of the industrial world and nearly half in Latin America, although in much of Africa and Asia they are less likely to go to college. Women's ability to achieve specialized education in science, engineering, business, and government has been limited, even with increased access to secondary and advanced education.

Women remain in the poorest-paying industrial and service-sector jobs in all countries, and in the less industrialized nations they are concentrated in the declining agricultural sector. The feminization of the global workforce has brought increased exploitation of young, uneducated, largely rural women, who labor under conditions that are often unsafe and unhealthy, at low pay and with nonexistent job security.

Yet even poor-paying factory jobs may enable some women to achieve a measure of economic independence and power. In China, for example, forty to fifty million young women have left their home villages in search of factory jobs in large cities. Such "working sisters" earn and save more than their brothers, a fact that has raised their economic status in Chinese society. There is some indication that women's changing economic role has changed their self-concept as well. More rural Chinese women are divorcing their husbands now that they can better afford to end unhappy marriages. And in a society where the oppressiveness of life as a woman contributes to one

of the highest female suicide rates in the world, fewer women appear to be taking their own lives (Farley 1998; Rosenthal 1999).

The International Labor Organization (2004a) has found that although the gap between the number of men and women in the labor force has been decreasing worldwide since 1993, this decrease has varied widely. Women in developed economies, the European Union (EU), central and eastern Europe (non-EU), Commonwealth of Independent States (CIS) and East Asia—where the number of women working per 100 men is about 80—have nearly closed the gap; but in other regions of the world, such as sub-Saharan Africa (75 women per 100 men), Latin America and the Caribbean (69 to 100), the Middle East and North Africa (about 37 to 100), and South Asia (42 to 100), the ratio is much lower.

At the other end of the occupational spectrum, a study by the International Labor Organization concludes that women worldwide still encounter a glass ceiling. Globally they still hold only 2 to 3 percent of the top corporate jobs, and those who make it to the top typically earn less than men. In Japan, for example, women are especially likely to face barriers to upper-level positions: When college-educated Japanese women interview for managerial jobs, they are typically assigned to noncareer secretarial work. As many as 40 percent of Japanese companies hire no women college graduates for management-level positions (French 2001a). In contrast, women in Canada and the United States own 47 and 48 percent of all businesses, respectively (Firestone 2007). Female participation in senior management has reached 50 percent in the Philippines, 19 percent in Canada, and 23 percent in the United States but remains low (14 percent) in Italy (Grant Thornton 2007). In

Xerox president Anne Mulcahy is one of the few female executives in the United States. Why do women continue to struggle to break through the glass ceiling at the highest levels of corporate America?

some developing countries, progress has been even greater: In mainland China, for example, 32 percent of senior managers are women; in Brazil, 42 percent.

Women's share of professional jobs in 2002 was highest in eastern Europe and the former Soviet Union. Over 60 percent of professional jobs in Lithuania (70.2 percent), Latvia (67 percent), Estonia (66 percent), Georgia (64.8 percent), Ukraine (63.7 percent), Slovakia (63.1 percent), Poland (60.9 percent), and Moldova (60.3 percent) were held by women. The reason for these countries' high proportion of women in professional jobs is long-standing policies supporting working mothers (ILO 2004b).

Political Inequality

Women play an increasing role in politics throughout the world. In Japan, for example, where women have traditionally faced barriers to achieving equality with men, five women were appointed to cabinet-level positions by Junichiro Koizumi, the reform-minded prime minister who took office in spring 2001—one in the key position of foreign minister (French 2001b). Yet of 192 countries that belong to the United Nations, only 20 are headed by women. Since World War II, 38 countries have been headed by women; the United States is not among them. Two countries—Monaco and Saudi Arabia—have never had a woman member of government (Worldwide Guide to Women in Leadership 2008).

As of October 2007, women made up only 17.4 percent of the combined membership of the national legislatures throughout the world. In the Scandinavian countries of Sweden (47.3 percent), Finland (42 percent), Norway (37.9 percent), and Denmark (36.9 percent) women make up a significant part of the parliament; in Saudi Arabia there are no women representatives (Interparlimentary Union 2007). It is interesting that Rwanda, which does not even receive a GEM (gender empowerment measure) rating (but rates very low on the United Nations' Human Development Index), has a higher rank than Sweden with 48.8 percent women in the parliament. The U.S. Congress is 16.3 percent female, placing the United States

---

TABLE 10.2

United Nations Gender Empowerment Rankings: The Top Twelve Countries, 2008

RANK	COUNTRY	SEATS IN LEGISLATURE HELD BY WOMEN (%)	FEMALE ADMINISTRATORS AND MANAGERS[a] (%)	FEMALE PROFESSIONAL AND TECHNICAL WORKERS[b] (%)
1	Norway	37.9	30	50
2	Sweden	47.3	30	51
3	Finland	42.0	30	55
4	Denmark	36.9	25	53
5	Iceland	31.7	27	56
6	Netherlands	36.0	26	50
7	Belgium	35.7	32	49
8	Australia	28.3	37	56
9	Germany	30.6	37	50
10	Canada	24.3	36	56
11	New Zealand	32.2	36	53
12	Spain	30.5	32	48

[a]Data refer to the period 1999–2005.

[b]Data refer to the period 1994–2005.

SOURCE: United Nations 2008.

68th out of 189 countries for which data exist. Women are most likely to hold seats in national legislatures in countries in which women's rights are a strong cultural value—where women have long had the right to vote and are well represented in the professions—and in which strong socialist parties play a role in government (Kenworthy and Malami 1999).

The United Nations ranks countries according to a measure of "gender empowerment," which is based on such factors as seats in the national legislature held by women, female administrators and managers (as a percentage of total administrators and managers), female professional and technical workers (as a percentage of total professional and technical workers), and the ratio of women's to men's earned income. By this measure, the United States ranks twelfth—behind the Scandinavian and other northern European countries and Canada and New Zealand (Table 10.2).

☑ CONCEPT CHECKS

1. What are signs of declining economic inequality between men and women from a global perspective?
2. What are some signs of progress in terms of women's political equality from a global perspective?

Analyzing Gender Inequality

Sociologists have tried to explain why gender inequalities exist. One plausible explanation is relatively simple. Women give birth to and care for children. The helplessness of the human infant requires intensive and prolonged care—hence the centrality of "mothering" to women's experience (as emphasized by Chodorow; see Chapter 4). Because of their role as mothers, women are absorbed in domestic activities, becoming what the French novelist and social critic Simone de Beauvoir (1974; orig. 1949) called "the second sex" because of their exclusion from the more public activities that men are free to engage in. Men are not dominant over women as a result of superior physical strength or special intellectual powers but because before the development of birth control, women were at the mercy of their biological constitution. Constant childbirth and continuous caring for infants made them dependent on males for material provision (Firestone 1971; Mitchell 1975).

Many theoretical perspectives have been advanced to explain men's enduring dominance over women—in the realm of economics, politics, the family, and elsewhere. In this section,

we review the main theoretical approaches to explaining gender inequality at the level of society.

Functionalist Approaches

The functionalist approach sees society as a system of interlinked parts that, when in balance, operate smoothly to produce social solidarity. Thus functionalist and functionalist-inspired perspectives on gender hold that gender differences contribute to social stability and integration. Though formerly popular, these perspectives have been heavily criticized for neglecting social tensions at the expense of consensus and for promulgating a conservative view of the social world.

Writers who support the concept of natural differences argue that women and men perform those tasks for which they are biologically best suited. Thus the anthropologist George Murdock (1949) saw it as practical and convenient that women should concentrate on domestic and family responsibilities while men work outside the home. On the basis of a cross-cultural study of more than two hundred societies, Murdock concluded that the sexual division of labor is present in all cultures and that, although not the result of biological programming, it is the most logical basis for the organization of society.

Talcott Parsons studied the role of the family in industrial societies (Parsons and Bales 1955). He was particularly interested in the socialization of children and believed that stable, supportive families are the key to successful socialization. He saw the family as operating most efficiently with a clear-cut sexual division of labor in which women act in expressive roles, providing care and security to children and offering them emotional support, and men perform *instrumental* roles—namely, being the breadwinner. Because of the stressful nature of men's role, women's expressive and nurturing tendencies should also be used to stabilize and comfort men. This complementary division of labor, springing from a biological distinction between the sexes, would ensure the solidarity of the family, according to Parsons.

Another functionalist perspective was advanced by John Bowlby (1953), who argued that the mother is crucial to the primary socialization of children. If the mother is absent or if a child is separated from the mother at a young age, the child may be inadequately socialized. This can lead to serious social and psychological difficulties later in life, including antisocial and psychopathic tendencies. Bowlby argued that a child's well-being and mental health require a close, personal, and continuous relationship with the mother or a female mother substitute. Bowlby's *maternal deprivation* thesis has been used by some to argue that working mothers are neglectful of their children.

Why would a functionalist agree that the division of labor between the homemaking wife and breadwinning husband in this Japanese household is ideal?

Feminists have sharply criticized claims of a biological basis to the sexual division of labor. They argue that women are not prevented from pursuing occupations on the basis of any biological features; rather, humans are socialized into roles that are culturally expected.

A steady stream of evidence suggests that the maternal deprivation thesis is questionable—studies have shown that children's educational performance and personal development are in fact enhanced when both parents work at least part of the time outside the home. Parsons's view on the "expressive" female has similarly been attacked as condoning the subordination of women in the home. There is no basis to the belief that the "expressive" female is necessary for the smooth operation of the family—rather, the role is promoted largely for the convenience of men.

In addition, cross-cultural studies show that societies vary greatly in terms of the degree to which they differentiate and assign tasks as exclusively men's or women's (Coltrane 1992). The extent to which certain tasks can be shared, and even how open groups and societies are to women performing men's activities and roles, differs across cultures and across time. Finally, cultures differ in the degree to which men are seen as "naturally" dominant over women. Thus gender inequalities do not seem to be fixed or static.

Biological determinists see differences based on gender and gender inequalities as inevitable and unchangeable because they are consequences of biological necessities, not of social processes. Social constructionists disagree with biological determinists over the sources of gender inequality and whether there is a potential for change: Sociological approaches look at society rather than at nature. Many sociologists target a society's gendered division of labor and the value that society assigns to men's and women's roles (Baxter and Kane 1995; Chafetz 1997; Collins et al. 1993; Coltrane 1992; Dunn et al.

1993). Furthermore, it is important to recognize that gender inequality is also tied to issues of race and class (Collins 1990).

Feminist Approaches

A large body of **feminist theory** addresses gender inequalities and sets forth an agenda for overcoming them. Feminist writers are all concerned with women's unequal position in society, but their explanations for it vary substantially. Competing schools cite a variety of deeply embedded social processes, such as sexism, patriarchy, capitalism, and racism. The following sections look at the arguments behind four main feminist perspectives—liberal, radical, black, and postmodern feminism.

LIBERAL FEMINISM

Liberal feminism seeks explanations of gender inequalities in social and cultural attitudes. Unlike radical feminists, liberal feminists do not see women's subordination as part of a larger system or structure. Instead, they identify many separate factors that contribute to inequalities—for example, sexism and discrimination in the workplace, educational institutions, and the media. They focus on establishing and protecting equal opportunities for women through legislation and other democratic means. Liberal feminists actively supported legal advances such as the Equal Pay Act and the Sex Discrimination Act, arguing that enshrining equality in law is important to eliminating discrimination against women. Because liberal feminists seek to work through the existing system to bring about reforms in a gradual way, they are more moderate in their aims and methods than radical feminists, who call for an overthrow of the existing system.

Critics charge that liberal feminists are unsuccessful in dealing with the root cause of gender inequality and do not acknowledge the systemic nature of women's oppression in society. They say that by focusing on independent deprivations—sexism, discrimination, the glass ceiling, unequal pay—liberal feminists draw only a partial picture of gender inequality. Radical feminists accuse liberal feminists of encouraging women to accept an unequal society and its competitive character.

RADICAL FEMINISM

At the heart of **radical feminism** is the belief that men are responsible for and benefit from the exploitation of women. The analysis of patriarchy—the systematic domination of females by males—is of central concern, being viewed as a universal phenomenon that has existed across time and cultures. Radical feminists identify the family as one of the primary sources of

How might a feminist theorist critique a site such as this Hooters Casino in Las Vegas?

women's oppression. They argue that men exploit women by relying on their free domestic labor in the home and that, as a group, men also deny women access to positions of power and influence in society.

Radical feminists differ in their interpretations of the basis of patriarchy, but most agree that it involves some form of appropriation of women's bodies and sexuality. Shulamith Firestone (1971) argues that because men control women's roles in reproduction and child rearing, women become dependent materially on men for protection and livelihood. This "biological inequality" is socially organized in the nuclear family. Firestone argues that women can be emancipated only through the abolition of the family and the power relations that characterize it.

Other radical feminists point to male violence against women as central to male supremacy. In this view, domestic violence, rape, and sexual harassment are all part of the systematic oppression of women, rather than isolated cases with their own psychological or criminal roots. Even interactions in daily life—such as nonverbal communication, patterns of listening and interrupting, and women's sense of comfort in public—contribute to gender inequality. Moreover, popular conceptions of beauty and sexuality are imposed by men on women to produce a certain type of femininity. For example, social and cultural norms emphasizing a slim body and a caring, nurturing attitude toward men perpetuate women's subordination. The objectification of women through the media, fashion, and advertising turns women into sexual objects whose main role is to please and entertain men.

Radical feminists do not believe that women can be liberated from sexual oppression through reforms or gradual change. Because patriarchy is a systemic phenomenon, they argue, gender equality can be attained only by overthrowing the patriarchal order.

In asserting that "the personal is political," radical feminists have drawn attention to the many linked dimensions of women's oppression. Their emphasis on male violence and the objectification of women has brought these issues into the heart of mainstream debates about women's subordination.

Many objections can be raised, however, to radical feminist views. A key objection is that the concept of patriarchy is inadequate as a general explanation for women's oppression. Critics argue that the conception of patriarchy as a universal phenomenon does not leave room for historical or cultural variations. It also ignores the influence of race, class, and ethnicity on the nature of women's subordination. In fact, seeing patriarchy as a universal phenomenon risks *biological reductionism*—attributing all the complexities of gender inequality to a simple distinction between men and women.

BLACK FEMINISM

Do the versions of feminism just described apply equally to the experiences of both white and nonwhite women? Many black feminists and feminists from developing countries claim they do not. They argue that the main feminist schools of thought address the dilemmas of white, predominantly middle-class women living in industrialized societies and that it is not valid to generalize theories about women's subordination from the experience of a specific group. Moreover, the very idea of a unified form of gender oppression experienced equally by all women is problematic.

Dissatisfaction with existing forms of feminism has led to the emergence of a **black feminism**, which concentrates on the problems facing black women. In the foreword to her personal memoirs, the African American feminist bell hooks (1996) argues:

Many feminist thinkers writing and talking about girlhood right now like to suggest that black girls have better self-esteem than their white counterparts. The measurement of this difference is often that black girls are more assertive, speak more, appear more confident. Yet in traditional southern-based black life, it was and is expected of girls to be articulate, to hold ourselves with dignity. Our parents and teachers were always urging us to stand up right and speak clearly. These traits were meant to uplift the race. They were not necessarily traits associated with building female self-esteem. An outspoken girl might still feel that she was worthless because her skin was not light enough or her hair wasn't the right texture. These are the variables that white researchers often do not consider when they measure the self-esteem of black females with a yardstick that was designed based on values emerging from white experience.

Surrounded by minority women at the Houston Civic Center, Coretta Scott King speaks about the resolution on minority women's rights that won the support of the National Women's Conference in 1977. The minority resolution, proposed by representatives of many races, declared that minority women suffered discrimination based on both race and sex.

Black feminist writings emphasize aspects of the past that inform current gender inequalities in the black community: the powerful legacy of slavery, segregation, and the civil rights movement. They point out that early black suffragettes supported the campaign for women's rights but realized that the question of race could not be ignored, because black women were discriminated against on the basis of race *and* gender. In recent years, black women have not been central to the women's liberation movement in part because "womanhood" dominated their identities much less than concepts of race did.

It has been argued by hooks that explanatory frameworks favored by white feminists—for example, the view of the family as a mainstay of patriarchy—may not apply in black communities, where the family represents solidarity against racism. In other words, the oppression of black women may be found in different locations from that of white women.

Black feminists contend that any theory of gender equality that does not take racism into account cannot adequately explain black women's oppression. Likewise, class dimensions cannot be neglected. Some black feminists hold that the strength of black feminist theory is its focus on the interplay among race, class, and gender concerns. When these three factors interact, they reinforce and intensify each other (Brewer 1993).

POSTMODERN FEMINISM

Like black feminism, **postmodern feminism** challenges the idea that all women share a unitary basis of identity and experience. (Postmodern approaches in sociology were introduced in Chapter 1, and it may be helpful to review that section.) This strand of feminism draws on the cultural phenomenon of postmodernism in the arts, architecture, philosophy, and economics. Postmodern feminists reject the claim that there is a grand theory that can explain the position of women in society or that there is any universal category of "woman." Consequently, these feminists reject the accounts given by others to explain gender inequality—such as patriarchy, race, or class—as "essentialist" (Beasley 1999).

Instead, postmodernism encourages the acceptance of many different standpoints as equally valid, all of which represent very different experiences (heterosexuals, lesbians, black women, working-class women, and so on). The "otherness" of different groups and individuals is celebrated in all its diverse forms. Emphasis on the positive side of otherness is a major theme in postmodern feminism and symbolizes plurality, diversity, difference, and openness: There are many truths, roles, and constructions of reality. Hence the recognition of difference (of sexuality, age, and race, for example) is central.

As well as recognizing differences among groups and individuals, postmodern feminists have sought to deconstruct male language and a masculine view of the world. In its place, they have attempted to create fluid, open terms and language that more closely reflect women's experiences. For many postmodern feminists, men see the world in terms of pairs or binary distinctions (good versus bad, right versus wrong, beautiful versus ugly). Men, they argue, have cast the male as normal and the female as a deviation from it. The founder of modern psychiatry, Sigmund Freud, for example, saw women as men who lacked a penis and argued that they envied males for possessing one. In this masculine worldview, the female is cast in the role as the "other." Deconstruction involves attacking binary concepts and recasting their opposites in a new and positive manner.

Postmodern feminism is said to have the most difficult relationship with the strands of feminism discussed earlier (Carrington 1994, 1998). This is largely because of its belief that many feminists may be misconceived in assuming that it is possible to provide overarching explanations for women's oppression and to find steps toward its resolution.

Using Sociology to Understand Andrea's Life

We have reviewed how sociologists analyze gender inequality, but let's think about how these approaches illuminate the life of Andrea Ellington, whom we met at the beginning of the chapter. Andrea, a young black woman working the night shift as a word processor at an elite law firm, grew up in a poor neighborhood in Chicago and today is raising three children on her own.

The International Women's Movement

Every year countless American college students are inspired by feminism and enlist in the fight for such causes as reproductive rights, equal pay, or the preservation of welfare benefits for poor women. In today's increasingly globalized world, there is a good chance that those who become active in the U.S. women's movement will come into contact with women pursuing other feminist struggles overseas.

The women's movement, of course, is not simply an American or western European phenomenon. In China, for example, women are working to secure "equal rights, employment, women's role in production, and women's participation in politics" (Zhang and Xu 1995). In South Africa, women played a pivotal role in the battle against apartheid and are fighting in the postapartheid era to improve "the material conditions of the oppressed majority; those who have been denied access to education, decent homes, health facilities, and jobs" (Kemp et al. 1995). In Peru, activists have been working for decades to give women a greater "opportunity to participate in public life" (Blondet 1995), while "in Russia, women's protest was responsible for blocking the passage of legislation that the Russian parliament considered in 1992 that encouraged women to stay home and perform 'socially necessary labor'" (Basu 1995).

Although participants in women's movements have, for many years, cultivated ties to activists in other countries, the number and importance of such contacts has increased

In considering Andrea and women in similar life circumstances, we can employ one of the key insights of contemporary feminist theory in sociology: the intersection of gender, race, and class.

ANDREA'S JOB

The forms of gender inequality in the workplace, as discussed earlier, show that Andrea's experience as a clerical worker in a law firm is typical for women. Today, word processing and secretarial work are predominantly women's occupations, with lower pay, a high degree of sex segregation, and few possibilities for promotion. Typical of jobs created since the 1970s, Andrea's has nonstandard working hours—she works the night shift.

Although biological differences between the sexes do not lead more women than men to work as word processors,

societal forces do. For example, many business colleges in Chicago advertise their secretarial programs with photographs of women, and many firms prefer to hire women for secretarial and word processing positions. Moreover, such positions have traditionally served the clerical needs of the upper class of workers, many of whom are men. An analysis of gender inequality would examine the way that people learn roles associated with gender—both the women who work as word processors and the people who do the hiring. It would also examine how those perceptions of difference become part of the structure of the organization, thereby reinforcing even more inequality.

Andrea's problems as a low-wage worker are not unique, as women are usually found at the lower end of the job ladder. Andrea's position on the lower end of the pay scale may also be due to her age and her lower level of experience in the job, which would be equivalent to that of a poor, similarly as globalization has spread. A prime forum for the establishment of cross-national contacts has been the United Nations Conference on Women, held four times since 1975. Approximately thirty-five thousand people—of whom more than two thirds were women—attended the most recent conference, held in Beijing, China, in 1995. Delegates from 180 nations were in attendance, along with representatives from thousands of nongovernmental organizations (*UN Chronicle* 1995). Seeking ways to "ensure women's equal access to economic resources including land, credit, science and technology, vocational training, information, communication and markets," conference participants spent ten days listening to presentations on the state of women worldwide, debating ways to improve their condition, and building professional and personal ties to one another. Mallika Dutt (1996), one of the attendees, wrote in the journal *Feminist Studies* that "for most women from the United States, Beijing was an eye-opening, humbling, and transformative experience. U.S. women were startled by the sophisticated analysis and well-organized and powerful voices of women from other parts of the world." At the same time, according to Dutt, many of the conference participants left Beijing with a "sense of global solidarity, pride, and affirmation."

The Platform for Action finally agreed to by the conference participants called on the countries of the world to address such issues as

- The persistent and increasing burden of poverty on women
- Violence against women

- The effects of armed or other kinds of conflict on women
- Inequality between men and women in the sharing of power and decision making
- Stereotyping of women
- Gender inequalities in the management of natural resources
- Persistent discrimination against and violation of the rights of the girl child

Must women's movements have an international orientation to be effective? Are women's interests essentially the same throughout the world? What might feminism mean to women in the developing world? These and many other questions are being hotly debated as globalization continues apace.

undereducated white woman her age. However, another barrier is her race. In fact, even within occupations dominated by women there can be hierarchies according to class and/ or race (Brewer 1993; Collins 1990). Thus someone studying gender inequality might look at the intersection of race, class, and gender to ask whether white women working as support staff at many law firms have better-paying secretarial jobs, while black women have word-processing positions with lower pay—quite plausible given the circumstances at the firm where Andrea works.

Finally, one would need to examine the kinds of jobs women can get in the present economy, which is influenced by globalization and economic restructuring. Thus the mere integration of women into the labor market does not necessarily mean more gender equality. Differences based on class and race among women have increased because of certain economic processes (Brewer 1993).

Andrea Ellington at her job at a Chicago law firm.

ANDREA'S FAMILY

Political debates on welfare in the United States have stressed marriage as the solution to the financial problems women like Andrea face: If black single mothers would get married, they wouldn't be poor and wouldn't need public assistance in the form of housing and health care. It is further argued that women like Andrea bear personal responsibility for having children out of wedlock.

A sociological analysis could begin by accepting that Andrea bears some responsibility for having children out of wedlock, while also acknowledging the societal conditions leading many poor women to make that choice. Here, again, there is a link among race, class, and gender. Studies of urban labor markets (Wilson 1987) have demonstrated that the loss of jobs for poor black men in the inner city has made marriage less attractive to many black women. Why should they marry men who don't have jobs? This attitude increases women's independence from men so that they do not necessarily have to marry the fathers of their children (Huber 1992).

In addition, social norms influence women like Andrea. With many other women facing the same structural barriers

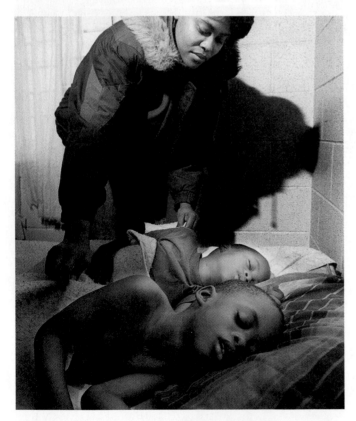

Checking on two of her kids, Cubie and Corey, Andrea Ellington struggles to balance work and family as a single mother. She tries to work overtime to earn extra money, but the lack of reliable child care makes it difficult to keep her weekend shifts.

to meeting men with jobs, it seems logical to have children on their own. The loss of jobs that might facilitate self-support for black men also makes it more difficult for them to provide child support. One reason Andrea does not have enough money to pay her bills and to move out of the housing project is that she has not received enough money from the father of her children.

ANDREA'S CHALLENGES IN COMBINING WORK AND FAMILY

Andrea's negotiations with her employer about overtime are the most prominent example of gender inequalities in the workplace intersecting with inequalities arising from women's roles as mothers.

Because Andrea doesn't earn enough from her low-paying job, she asked if she could work extra hours. When her boss scheduled these extra projects on a Sunday, Andrea couldn't find reliable child care. Because she missed work on several occasions, her boss canceled the extra projects, assumed that Andrea wasn't able to work overtime, and refused to offer her more extra projects. This affected Andrea's attitude about her job, a process that lowers occupational aspirations (Huber 1990).

It is understandable that a reasonable employer would draw such a conclusion about Andrea. Yet a sociological approach would ask whether the incidents reflect a problem with Andrea or with the system of child care. If the system were different, would women like Andrea seem more responsible? A sociological approach might consider how the gender division of labor in our society places the burden of child raising on mothers. In the United States, child care is neither a public responsibility nor the employer's.

The ways in which societies organize the care of children, elderly, and disabled people profoundly shape gender relations. Moreover, in societies that view child care primarily as the task of women yet attach little value to it, mothers in the workplace are disadvantaged. In contrast, if society were to value child care as an important contribution for future generations, women like Andrea might get financial support for taking care of her children herself. Alternatively, if employers and government were to support child care, women like Andrea might find a good-quality child-care center open on a Sunday.

The fact that Andrea's mother usually takes care of Andrea's daughter illustrates how child care can be informally organized across generations of women. Research on African American communities demonstrates that black women used to have kinship and neighborhood networks to share child-raising responsibilities, but these structures of shared motherhood have been crumbling (Brewer 1993; Collins 1990; Glenn 1994).

1. Contrast functionalist and feminist approaches to understanding gender inequality.
2. What are the key ideas of liberal feminism? What are critiques of this perspective?
3. What are the key ideas of radical feminism? What are critiques of this perspective?
4. Do you think that postmodern feminism is incompatible with liberal, radical, and black feminist perspectives? Why or why not?

Why Gender Inequality Matters

A Chinese saying holds that "women hold up half the sky." In fact, women hold up far more than half: In the twenty-first century, women have become a central part of the world's paid workforce while, at the same time, maintaining their traditional responsibilities for home and family.

China was the site of the 1995 United Nations Fourth World Conference on Women, where some thirty-five thousand people, representing 180 governments and seven thousand women's organizations, discussed the problems of women worldwide. The conference grappled with a central problem: What happens when a country's traditional cultural beliefs conflict with modern notions of women's rights? Globalization not only has brought factories and television to nearly every place on the planet but also has exposed people to ideas about equality and democracy. The modern women's movement has become a global champion of universal rights for women.

The conference's action platform was clear: When cultural traditions conflict with women's rights, women's rights should take precedence. The platform called for women's right to control their own reproduction and sexuality as well as to inherit wealth and property—two rights that women are denied in many countries. It concluded that no society can truly hope to better the lives of its citizens until it fosters gender equality:

Empowerment of women and equality between women and men are prerequisites for achieving political, social, economic, cultural and environmental security among all peoples. (Beijing Women's Conference 1995)

Five years after the conference, a special session of the United Nations General Assembly reaffirmed these principles, challenging the world's governments to realize the conference's goals. Noting that women occupied only 13 percent of parliament seats worldwide, the United Nations called for a global increase in women's political power. The Women's Environment and Development Organization, a New York–based women's advocacy group, pushed for equal representation of women in cabinet ministries and legislative bodies by 2005. In the view of the organization's executive director, increased women's representation would help shift a country's policies to real-life concerns, as in Scandinavia, where women are well represented in all levels of government: "Their commitment to the social safety net, to [an] expansive childcare system, to helping women and men balance work and family needs, I think, reflects women's experiences" (Hogan 2000). That goal has not been met. Had it been, the UN Human Development Report (2005) notes, there would be "14 million more girls in primary school today, 6 million of them in India and Pakistan and another 4 million in Sub-Saharan Africa. Trend projections are not encouraging. By 2015 the shortfall from the gender parity target will be equivalent to 6 million girls out of school, the majority of them in Sub-Saharan Africa."

The feminization of labor has altered the world economy. Will the feminization of politics do the same for global governance? The shift to a greater role for women in economics and politics may well signal a shift to greater equality for all people the world over.

☑ CONCEPT CHECKS

1. The message emerging from the Beijing Women's Conference was when cultural traditions conflict with women's rights, women's rights should take precedence. Do you agree with this? Why or why not?

Study Outline

www.wwnorton.com/studyspace

Gender Differences: Nature versus Nurture

- *Sex* in the sense of physical difference is distinct from *gender* (masculine and feminine), which concerns cultural and psychological differences. It is not easy to determine which observable differences are due to biology (sex) and which are socially constructed (gender). Arguments from animal behavior are usually ambiguous. Some researchers claim, for instance, that hormones explain such differences as greater male aggressiveness, but it may be that aggressive behavior causes changes in hormone levels. Studies of gender differences from a variety of human societies have shown no conclusive evidence that gender is biologically determined; rather, biological differences seem to provide a means of differentiating social roles.

- Studies of parent–infant interactions reveal that boys and girls are treated differently from birth; the same features and behaviors are interpreted as either masculine or feminine, depending on the parents' expectations.

Forms of Gender Inequality

- *Patriarchy* refers to male dominance over women. There are few known societies that are not patriarchal, although the degree and character of inequalities between the sexes varies across cultures. In the United States, women have made considerable progress yet are still unequal in many ways.

- Women's participation in the paid labor force has risen steadily, especially that of married women and especially in expanding areas of the economy. Many women, however, are poorly paid and have dim career prospects. Even women who are successful in the corporate world face discrimination in the form of cultural expectations about the proper role of women in society.

- The increasing number of women in the labor force has affected family responsibilities such as child care and housework. Though men contribute more to these responsibilities now than in the past, women still shoulder the bulk of the work. For working women, these household obligations constitute a "second shift."

- The ways schools are organized and classes are taught sustain *gender inequalities.* Rules specifying appropriate dress for girls and boys encourage sex typing, as do texts containing established gender images. There is evidence that teachers treat girls and boys differently, and there is a long history of specialized subjects for separate sexes.

- Violence by men against women occurs in many societies—in the form of spousal abuse, rape, and sexual harassment, for example. Most common is *rape,* the forcing of nonconsensual intercourse. Some scholars argue that women are often the targets of sexual violence because men are socialized to see women as sex objects and to feel a sense of sexual entitlement to women.

Gender Inequality in Global Perspective

- Women worldwide work in the lowest-wage jobs and make less than men doing similar work—although there is some evidence that the wage gap is decreasing slowly, at least in industrialized countries. In developing countries, women experience exploitative job conditions. Yet their enhanced economic role has sometimes brought increased economic independence and greater social status.

- Women do not share the same political power as men, although thirty-eight countries have been headed by a woman since World War II. The United States is about average among countries in terms of women's representation in the national legislature but has never had a woman president.

- *Gender* is one of the most important dimensions of inequality, although it was neglected in the study of stratification for a long time. Although there are few societies in which women have more wealth and status than men, there are significant variations in how women's and men's roles are valued. Sociologists have argued that gender inequalities are not fixed. They have also drawn attention to the links among gender inequality, race, and class.

Analyzing Gender Inequality

- Functionalists emphasize that gender differences and the sexual division of labor contribute to social stability and integration. Feminist approaches reject the idea that gender inequality is natural. Liberal feminists explain gender inequality in terms of social and cultural attitudes, such as sexism and discrimination. Radical feminists argue that men are responsible for the exploitation of women through patriarchy—the systematic domination of females by males. Black feminists identify factors such as class and ethnicity, in addition to gender, as essential for understanding the oppression experienced by nonwhite women.

Why Gender Inequality Matters

- The main message emerging from the Beijing Women's Conference was that when cultural traditions conflict with women's rights, women's rights should take precedence. The United Nations General Assembly reaffirmed these principles.

- Globalization is expected to enhance women's roles in economics and politics, resulting in greater shift toward gender equality worldwide.

Key Concepts

black feminism (p. 308)
comparable worth (p. 296)

6. According to the authors, what explains the gender gap in pay? Compare and contrast economic and sociological explanations of this gender gap.

7. The authors show an increase of women in the workforce since the beginning of the twentieth century. Has this led to an equal distribution of domestic work?

8. The authors cite statistics that indicate high incidences of sexual violence on college campuses. How do sociologists explain the high incidence of sexual violence against women? Do these explanations make sense in the context of sexual violence on your campus?

9. What does gender equity look like in politics in the United States? What does this picture look like in comparison to other countries of the world and what can this tell us about global gender inequality?

10. Compare and contrast main feminist theoretical approaches to gender inequality.

Review Questions

1. What have some theorists argued is the difference between sex and gender? What have been the critiques of these definitions?

2. What sort of evidence is brought to bear to explain differences between men and women based on biology? What are the sociological critiques of these theories?

3. What is the functionalist perspective on gender socialization? What are the critiques of this perspective?

4. What does it mean when sociologists say that we "do gender"? Describe some of the ways that you do gender in your daily life.

5. What do anthropological studies of gender and research on multiple genders tell us about the social construction of gender?

Thinking Sociologically Exercises

1. What does cross-cultural evidence from tribal societies in New Guinea, Africa, and North America suggest about the differences in gender roles? Explain.

2. Why are minority women likely to think very differently about gender inequality than white women? Explain.

Sharon Dawkins (far right) is pictured with her daughters Aisha, Tanika, Rhea, and Imani (on her lap). She has been married to their father, a Jamaican-British man, for more than twenty years. She has participated in a longitudinal ethnography conducted by France Winddance Twine. Photograph by Michael Smyth.

Learning Objectives

Race and Ethnicity: Key Concepts

Learn the cultural bases of race and ethnicity and how racial and ethnic differences create sharp divisions. Learn the leading psychological theories and sociological interpretations of prejudice and discrimination.

Ethnic Relations

Recognize the importance of the historical roots of ethnic conflict, particularly in the expansion of Western colonialism. Understand the different models for a multiethnic society.

Global Migration

Understand global migration patterns and their effects.

Ethnic Relations in the United States

Familiarize yourself with the history and social dimensions of ethnic relations in America.

Racial and Ethnic Inequality

Learn the forms of inequality experienced by racial and ethnic groups in the United States. See that the history of prejudice and discrimination against ethnic minorities has created hardship for many but that some have succeeded despite societal barriers.

CHAPTER ELEVEN

ETHNICITY AND RACE

maureen, a forty-five-year-old black woman who was born in the Caribbean, came to England at age twelve with her family. She is the social services manager for Home Care in Leicester, a city located ninety miles north of London. She has three brothers and ten nieces and nephews. All her brothers have established families with white English women. She describes six of her nieces and nephews as "dual heritage." Yet she also believes that these racially mixed children will be classified as "black" by those outside the family. Here she sums up her view of one of her white sisters-in-law whom she respects: "She very much wants the child to have a black identity. So, every Sunday she would bring [my niece] up to my mum's house so that she knows her black family. If you say 'Do this for her hair,' she'd be religiously doing it. And she's asked for advice about her hair. And you'd see her plaiting it. And her hair is always so pretty." Maureen and her other black Caribbean family members consider her niece to be "racially" black although she has a white birth mother. They recognize that in spite of having a white mother, this girl will be classified as black because of her physical appearance, and thus she should learn to identify herself as a black. The labor required of Maureen's white sister-in-law demonstrates how "race," like ethnicity, is learned. Race and ethnicity are "socially constructed."

In 2001, according to the U.K. census almost 50 percent of U.K.-born men who described their ethnic group as "other Black" and almost 30 percent of "Black Caribbean" men were married to women outside their black ethnic group, in most cases white women (U.K. Statistics Authority 2001). Sociologist France Winddance Twine found in her research among multiracial families in the United States and the United Kingdom that some parents train their children to develop what she terms **racial literacy** skills to help them cope with racial hierarchies and to integrate multiple ethnic identities. Twine (2003) defines one dimension of racial literacy as antiracist training that helps children recognize the forms of racism they might encounter. Twine identifies gaps among how parents viewed their children racially, their children's own racial self-identification, and how they were socially classified outside the home. For example, there were shifts and intense struggles among parents, extended family members, and teachers over a child's racial and ethnic classification (Twine 1991, 1997, 2004). Such research illustrates the difficulty of defining the conditions of racial and ethnic group membership for some multiracial individuals. In recent decades, a number of sociologists have addressed this problem of multiracial identity and racial classification schemes, arguing that a "static measure of race" is not useful for multiracial individuals who assert different identities in different social contexts (Goldstein and Morning 2000; Harris 2003; Harris and Sim 2000).

Race and Ethnicity: Key Concepts

You have no doubt used the terms *race* and *ethnicity* many times, but do you know what they mean? Defining these terms is very difficult, and the first step is to dispense with what you think you know. Do not think of race and ethnicity as two different phenomena.

Ethnicity refers to cultural practices and outlooks of a given community that have emerged historically and set people apart. Members of ethnic groups see themselves as culturally distinct from other groups and are seen as distinct by those other groups. Different characteristics may distinguish ethnic groups from one another, but the most common are some combination of language, history, religious faith, and ancestry—real or imagined—and styles of dress or adornment. Examples of ethnic groups in the United States are Irish Americans, Jewish Americans, Italian Americans, Cuban Americans, and Japanese Americans. Ethnic differences are learned.

The difference between race and ethnicity is not as clear-cut as some people think. In fact, everything that has been said here about ethnicity would apply to Maureen's mixed-race nieces discussed earlier. Their black relatives and white mothers are teaching them many cultural practices that people associate with being black—from how to braid their hair to how to respond to racism. So does this mean that race is a kind of ethnicity?

In a way it is, but race has certain characteristics that make it different from ethnicity. First, at certain historical moments some ethnic differences become the basis of stigmas that cannot be removed by conversion or assimilation. Second, these stigmas become the basis of extreme hierarchy.

The mixed-race children with white mothers and black fathers in the United Kingdom look black to many people. Some aspects of their blackness, such as braiding their hair, are cultural practices akin to ethnicity. Yet what makes their blackness reflect race is the fact that in the United Kingdom dark skin color has historically been stigmatized, as in the United States. This stigma has laid the foundation for extreme hierarchy in England, as in the United States.

Race, then, can be understood as a classification system that assigns individuals and groups to categories that are ranked or hierarchical. But there are no clear-cut "races," only a range of physical variations among human beings. Differences in physical type arise from population inbreeding, which varies according to the degree of contact among different social or cultural groups. Human population groups are a continuum, and the genetic diversity *within* populations that share visible physical traits is as great as the diversity *among* them. Racial distinctions do more than describe human differences—they also affect the reproduction of patterns of power and inequality within society.

The process by which people use understandings of race to classify individuals or groups is **racialization**. Historically, certain groups of people were seen to constitute distinct biological groups on the basis of innate physical features. From the fifteenth century onward, as Europeans had increased contact with different regions of the world, they attempted to systematize their expanding knowledge by categorizing and explaining both natural and social phenomena. Non-European populations were "racialized" in opposition to the European "white race." In some instances this racialization took codified institutional forms, as in the case of slavery in the former British, French, and Spanish colonies in the Americas; slavery in the United States; and the establishment of apartheid in South Africa after World War II. More commonly, everyday political, educational, legal, and other institutions become racialized through legislation. In the United States after the civil rights movement, de facto racial segregation and racial hierarchies persisted even after state-sanctioned segregation was dismantled. Within a racialized system, an individual's social life and overall life chances—including education, employment, incarceration, housing, health care, and legal representation—are all shaped by the racial assignments and racial hierarchies in that system.

Sociologists who study ethnicity in the United States have observed a decline in certain forces leading to ethnic-group collective consciousness. For example, people who are Jewish or Irish no longer face the housing discrimination that led them to cluster in particular neighborhoods before World War II. In addition, intermarriage between members of different religious groups and European and Asian groups has increased substantially. As a result, sociologists have noted that ethnic identity, at least in the United States, has less of an effect on the members of these social groups, unless they choose an ethnic label. In fact, ethnicity is now a choice of whether to be ethnic at all and, if so, which ethnicity to be (Gans 1979; Waters 1990). Because of this phenomenon, sociologists refer to *situational ethnicity* and *symbolic ethnicity*.

Situational ethnicity illustrates how ethnic and racial identification is socially constructed. Some multiracial people may choose either to assert or not to assert a salient aspect of their identity or heritage in particular situations, such as when applying for a job in which certain racial groups predominate. They may not report an identity when it could lead to discrimination. This shows that larger political forces, such as the categories devised by governments, affect the identity people choose to display.

Symbolic ethnicity occurs when members of an ethnic group assimilate into the larger culture, perhaps moving from the old neighborhood to the more ethnically diverse suburbs. Such people might participate in ethnic customs only on symbolic occasions such as Saint Patrick's Day, when they wear green, or at Passover, when they attend a seder. During the rest of the year, their ethnic identity might not be salient at all.

Whereas ethnicity is primarily a symbolic option for white Americans and is sometimes a choice for people of "mixed race" with ambiguous racial characteristics, for members of many racial groups it is not a choice at all. One sociologist wrote: "The social and political consequences of being Asian or, Hispanic or black are not symbolic for the most part, or voluntary. They are real and often hurtful" (Waters 1990). Minority group status can have many negative consequences, such as segregation (discussed later in this chapter).

Despite the increasing number of people in the United States who self-identify as multiracial, many North Americans believe, mistakenly, that human beings can be separated into biologically distinct "races." This is a legacy of European colonialism and scientific racism. Racial classification schemes were invented during a period when Europeans were conquering unfamiliar territories. The Swedish botanist Carolus Linnaeus, the founder of scientific taxonomy, in 1735 published what is considered the first version of a modern classification scheme of human populations. Linnaeus included humans in a larger classification scheme with relations to apes and monkeys. He grouped human beings into four basic varieties—Europaeus, Americanus, Asiaticus, and Africanus. At this time it was believed that human beings descended from a common original ancestor. Physical features, behaviors, and psychological traits were correlated. Linnaeus assumed that each species had innate and unalterable qualities of behavior or temperament. He acquired much of his data from the writings, descriptions, commentaries, and beliefs of plantation owners,

Celebrating the Chinese New Year with performances and decorations is not just a picturesque event every year in Soho, but an important symbol of cultural continuity for London's Chinese community.

missionaries, slave traders, explorers, and travelers. Thus his scientific data were shaped by the prejudices and power that Europeans had over the people whom they conquered (Smedley 1993).

Racial Categories

Census categories have changed over time, reflecting political constituencies and power relations. For example, in 1970 the Hispanic category was added, and other racial categories have been removed—such as "mulatto," which last appeared on the 1920 census. The fact that some racial and ethnic groups appear and disappear from the census challenges the notion that racial groups are based on simple biological differences.

After a three-year study and intense lobbying from a coalition of individuals of multiracial heritage and advocacy groups, a governmental task force proposed that the Office of Management and Budget add a multiracial category to the 2000 U.S. census. For the first time the census allowed individuals to check more than one racial category if they desired.

Four schoolboys represent the "racial scale" in South Africa: black, Indian, half-caste, and white.

The debate surrounding the possible addition of a multiracial category reveals the degree to which Americans continue to believe that racial groups are "natural." Racial and ethnic groups in the United States, as in other nations, are stratified. The census distinguishes four races (American Indian/Alaska Native, Asian and Pacific Islander, black, and white), but the many exceptions and inconsistencies found in the classifications make them largely unworkable.

Racism and Antiracism

Both *racism* and *antiracism* are fairly new terms. *Racism* did not come into use until the 1930s; *antiracism* did not appear in regular usage until the 1960s. Both terms can be defined in many ways because there are different definitions of what constitutes racism in different national contexts.

RACISM

Some people see **racism** as a system of domination operating in social processes and social institutions; others see it as operating in the individual consciousness. *Racism* can refer to explicit beliefs in racial supremacy—such as the systems established in Nazi Germany, before the civil rights movement in the United States, and in South Africa under apartheid.

Yet many have argued that racism is more than the ideas held by bigoted individuals. Rather, it is embedded in the structure and operation of society. The idea of institutional racism suggests that institutions such as the police, the health-care industry, and the educational system all promote policies that favor certain groups while discriminating against others.

The idea of **institutional racism** was developed in the United States in the late 1960s by black power activists (Stokeley Carmichael and Charles Hamilton) and was taken up by civil rights campaigners who believed that white supremacy structured all social relations. In subsequent years, the existence of institutional racism became widely accepted and openly acknowledged. A 1990s investigation into the practices of the Los Angeles Police Department, in light of the beating of a black man named Rodney King, found that institutional racism is pervasive within the police force and the criminal justice system. A similar case occurred in 1999 in New York City, when police officers shot and killed an unarmed African man from Guinea, Amadou Diallo. Similarly, in 2006, plainclothes New York City police detectives shot and killed another unarmed man, twenty-three-year-old Sean Bell, on the day Bell was to be married. In culture and the arts, institutional racism has been found in Hollywood films, television broadcasting (via negative or limited portrayals of racial and ethnic minorities in programming), and the international modeling industry (via industrywide bias against fashion models who appear to be of non-European ancestry and/or mixed race).

Just as the concept of biological race has been discredited, "biological" racism based on differences in physical traits is rarely expressed today. The end of state-sanctioned segregation in the United States in 1954 and the collapse of apartheid in South Africa in 1994 were important turning points in the rejection of biological racism. But racist attitudes have not disappeared from modern societies. Rather, some scholars argue, they have been replaced by a more sophisticated "new racism" (or cultural racism), which excludes certain groups on the basis of cultural differences (Barker 1981).

According to this view, hierarchies of superiority and inferiority are constructed according to the values of the majority culture. Groups that stand apart from the majority can be marginalized or vilified for their refusal to assimilate. It is alleged that new racism has a clear political dimension. The fact that racism is increasingly based on cultural grounds has led some scholars to suggest that we live in an age of "multiple racisms," where discrimination is experienced differently across various segments of the population (Modood et al. 1997).

ANTIRACISM

Antiracism is a concept that began to appear in regular usage in the 1960s. Alistair Bonnett (2000) defines it as

> forms of thought and/or practice that seek to confront, eradicate and/or ameliorate racism. Antiracism implies the ability to identify a phenomenon—racism—and to do something about it. Different forms of antiracism exist because there are different definitions of what constitutes racism in different national contexts.

Some governments embrace opposition to racism as a way to protect their political interests. Affirmative-action programs, which are a form of antiracism, vary tremendously across national contexts. In India and Malaysia, antiracism has served as a component of national identity and a symbol of national allegiance (Bonnett 2000). For example, in the aftermath of race riots in Kuala Lumpur between Malays and Chinese in 1969, the Malaysian government implemented affirmative-action programs. These programs established a quota in which 40 percent of jobs in most industries were reserved for Malays and a target of 30 percent was established for Malay ownership of commercial and industrial enterprises. Another measure empowered the government to require universities

Malay and Indian women share a light moment as they leave the office after work in Putrajaya, Malaysia. Forty years ago, Malaysia instituted extensive affirmative action programs to address ethnic conflicts between its three main ethnic groups.

to lower their qualification entrance requirements for Malay students (Nesiah 1997). Antiracism measures in India provide constitutional safeguards for what are known as the scheduled castes and tribes. Articles 330 and 332 of the Indian Constitution reserve a percentage of the legislative seats in the Lower Parliament for members of these groups. These quotas constitute a stronger form of affirmative action than programs in the United States.

Sociologists have only recently begun to study antiracism, particularly white antiracism. Becky Thompson (2001) interviewed white antiracists all over the United States to understand their political trajectories and how they formed an antiracist constituency and community after World War II. Many students of sociology consider themselves antiracists, although sociologists advise that the science of society should be kept separate from personal politics.

Psychological Interpretations of Prejudice and Discrimination

Psychological theories can illuminate the nature of prejudiced and racist attitudes, as well as why ethnic differences matter so much to people.

PREJUDICE, DISCRIMINATION, AND RACISM

Prejudice refers to opinions or attitudes held by members of one group toward another. These preconceived views are often based on hearsay and are resistant to change even in the

White Racial Images and Attitudes

The advertisement for the Pennsylvania Railroad (below, left) appeared in *LIFE* magazine just following the end of World War II in Europe. It captures the exhilaration and anticipation that all Americans experienced as their loved ones began to return home, often after having been away for many years. But there is another story in this image. Near the center of the advertisement is a lone black figure. His uniform is that of a baggage handler, or "redcap," and he is stooping to pick up the bags of the white passengers. The image of a black man attending to the needs of whites was a familiar image at the time. This was the role he was expected to play in the American Dream.

In the early 1940s when white Americans were asked to tell survey researchers what they felt about their black countrymen, this is what they said. Less than half of whites polled believed that blacks had as much ability as whites (40%) or were entitled to equal jobs (45%). An equivalent number of whites (46%) disapproved of segregated public transportation. Moreover, only about one out of three whites believed that blacks were entitled to attend the same schools as whites (32%) and few (38%) said that they would stay in their neighborhood if a black family moved in. In other words, a significant majority of whites were against the integration of blacks with whites, and they

> ⬇ Over 90 percent of the images in *LIFE* from the 1940s that included blacks were images of men. A great many of these images showed them as porters, baggage handlers, waiters, and the like. They are usually depicted in a bent-over deferential posture and, if they are directly interacting with a white person, smiling in an ingratiating fashion.

> ➡ Does the fact that this image appeared in magazines mean that blacks had finally been accepted as full partners in the American Dream? Does the fact that there are over ten times as many advertisements with black people in them in *LIFE* at the turn of the twenty-first century than there were in the early 1940s—12 percent compared to 1 percent—mean that acceptance had arrived?

TREACLE TART: Calm, sensual personality looking for partner to spend time in the bedroom.

BROOKLYN NIGHTS: Cool, calm individual, great in the bedroom, living room, bathroom...

RICH
FRESH
WARM
CALM

At Dulux we know that Treacle Tart and Brooklyn Nights go together because they come from the same mood group in our new Colour Co-ordination System. This system groups colours into four separate moods: rich, fresh, warm and calm, so when you pick colours from the same mood you can be confident that they'll go together. Come and find the new system in-store, at the Dulux paint mixing area and do some match making of your own.

www.dulux.co.uk

Dulux
We know the colours that go.

Created by John Grady.

held these views as their nation was at war with fascist regimes that celebrated racism.

Fast forward to over a half century later and consider the advertisement for Delux paint on page 322. It depicts another moment of reunion and anticipation. This time it is an interracial couple embracing. During the earlier period, this scene never would have been allowed to appear in an advertisement, and in real life such an encounter might have led to a lynching in some parts of America.

By 2000, blacks in advertising images were depicted with a wide range of skin shades and women were shown as often as men. Black achievements were noted, and we see them enjoying themselves with whites in the workplace and in a wide array of public settings. Does this mean that blacks had finally entered into the white imagination as equals? Or does the fact that pictures of interracial couples are still rare in American advertising at the turn of the century—and that few blacks are shown enjoying themselves with whites in their homes—only mean that whites were just beginning to come to terms with what moral equality between blacks and whites might entail? How much can advertising tell us about white people's attitudes and patterns of behavior? What other types of information could help us paint a fuller picture?

What do attitude surveys reveal about changing white attitudes concerning blacks? Generally speaking, much of the news on this front is positive and suggests that whites are increasingly committed to black civil rights. The General Social Survey (GSS) has been administered only since 1972, but it allows us to see what different groups of people feel about their lives and national issues since then. The figure on the right shows that about two out of every three white young adults (ages twenty-two through forty) in 1972 believed that whites did not have a right to keep blacks out of their neighborhood. By 1996 that figure had climbed so high (92%) that the GSS discontinued asking the question.

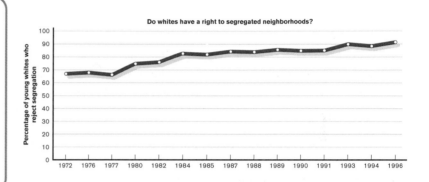

Do attitudes about intermarriage between blacks and whites remain taboo? Here the picture is clearly mixed. On the one hand, This figure shows that when young whites were asked in 1972 whether they were for or against intermarriage laws 70 percent reported being against them. By 2002 nine out of ten young whites were opposed to laws outlawing intermarriage. On the other hand, when young whites were asked in 1990 whether they were in favor of a close relative marrying a black person, less than one out of every sixteen (6%) said yes. By 2000, this figure had increased five-fold, but still fewer than 30 percent favored intermarriage within their family, and this figure hasn't changed much since.

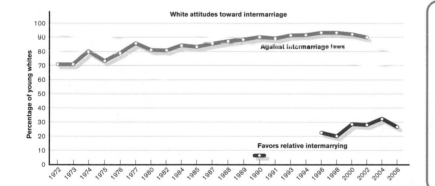

Are these changing attitudes telling us that whites and blacks are getting closer to each other? In 1973 the GSS asked people whether a black person had come to their home for dinner during the past year. The figure to the right shows that less than a quarter (23%) of young whites said yes. By 2006 the number of young whites welcoming blacks into their home for dinner had doubled to just under half (47%).

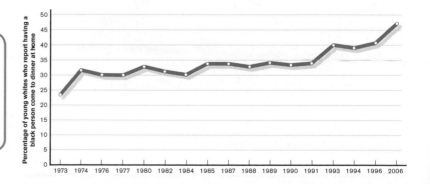

face of direct evidence or new information. People may harbor favorable prejudices toward groups with which they identify and negative prejudices against others.

Discrimination refers to *actual behavior* toward another group. Evident in activities that distribute rewards and benefits unequally based on membership in the dominant ethnic groups, discrimination involves excluding or restricting members of some racial or ethnic groups from opportunities that are available to other groups. For example, blacks have been excluded from and remain underrepresented in entire job categories despite the emergence of an educated black middle class. Discrimination does not necessarily derive directly from prejudice. For example, white homebuyers might avoid properties in predominantly black neighborhoods, not because of hostility toward African Americans but because of worries about declining property values. Prejudiced attitudes in this case influence discrimination, but indirectly.

STEREOTYPES AND SCAPEGOATS

Prejudice operates mainly through **stereotyping**, which means thinking in terms of inflexible categories. Stereotyping is linked to the psychological mechanism of **displacement**, in which feelings of hostility or anger are directed against objects that are not the origin of those feelings. People blame **scapegoats** for problems that are not their fault. Scapegoating is common when two deprived ethnic groups compete with one another for economic rewards. People who direct racial attacks against African Americans, for example, are often in a similar economic position to them. They blame blacks for grievances whose real causes lie elsewhere.

Scapegoating is normally directed against groups that are relatively powerless, because they make an easy target. Protestants, Catholics, Jews, Italians, racial minorities, and

Why is scapegoating directed at relatively powerless groups? Why might attitudes about immigrants and undocumented workers be an example of scapegoating?

others have played the unwilling role of scapegoat at various times throughout Western history. Scapegoating frequently involves *projection,* the unconscious attribution to others of one's own desires or characteristics. For example, research has consistently demonstrated that when the members of a dominant group practice violence against a minority and exploit it sexually, they likely believe that the minority group itself displays these traits of sexual violence. For instance, in the United States before the civil rights movement, some white men's ideas about the lustful nature of African American men probably originated in their own frustrations, since sexual access to white women was limited by the formal nature of courtship. Similarly, in apartheid South Africa, black males were thought to be sexually dangerous to white women—but in fact, virtually all criminal sexual contact was initiated by white men against black women (Simpson and Yinger 1986).

MINORITY GROUPS

The term **minority group** can be confusing because it refers to political power and is not simply a numerical distinction. There are many minorities in a numerical or statistical sense, such as people having red hair or weighing more than 250 pounds, but these are not minorities according to the sociological concept. In sociology, members of a minority group are disadvantaged as compared with the dominant group (a group possessing more wealth, power, and prestige) and have some sense of group solidarity. Being subjected to prejudice and discrimination usually heightens feelings of common loyalty and interests.

Members of minority groups, such as Spanish speakers in the United States, often see themselves as distinct from the majority. Minority groups are sometimes, but not always, physically and socially isolated from the larger community. Although they tend to live in certain neighborhoods, cities, or regions of a country, their children often intermarry with members of the dominant group. People who belong to minority groups sometimes promote endogamy (marriage within the group) to keep alive their cultural distinctiveness.

The idea of a minority group is more confusing today than ever before. Some groups that were once clearly identified as minorities, such as Asians and Jews, now have more resources, intermarry at greater rates, and experience less discrimination. This highlights the fact that the concept of a minority group is really about disadvantage in terms of power, rather than a numerical distinction.

☑ CONCEPT CHECKS

1. Explain the difference between ethnicity and race.
2. What does the term *racialization* refer to?

3. How does prejudice operate in society?

4. Why are Hispanics and African Americans considered to be minority groups in American society?

Ethnic Relations

In today's age of globalization and rapid social change, the rich benefits and complex challenges of ethnic diversity are confronting a growing number of states. As international migration accelerates along with the global economy, the mixing of populations will intensify. Meanwhile, ethnic tensions and conflicts continue, threatening the existence of some multiethnic states and hinting at protracted violence in others. How can ethnic diversity be accommodated and ethnic conflict be averted? Within multiethnic societies, what should be the relation between ethnic minority groups and the majority population? Four primary models of ethnic integration address these challenges: assimilation, the "melting pot," pluralism, and multiculturalism. These will be discussed shortly.

To fully analyze ethnic relations, we must start with a historical and comparative perspective. It is impossible to understand ethnic divisions today without considering the effect of Western colonialism on the rest of the world (Global Map 11.1), as global migratory movements resulting from colonialism helped create ethnic divisions by placing different peoples in close proximity.

Ethnic Antagonism: A Historical Perspective

From the fifteenth century onward, Europeans ventured into previously uncharted seas and unexplored land masses, pursuing exploration and trade but also conquering native peoples and settling in the new areas. Via the slave trade, Europeans also occasioned a large-scale movement of people from Africa to the Americas. The following extraordinary shifts in population have occurred over the past 350 years or so:

1. **Europe to North America.** From the seventeenth century to the present, some 45 million people have emigrated from Europe to what are now the United States and Canada. About 200 million people in North America today trace their ancestry to this migration.

2. **Europe to Central and South America.** About 20 million people, mostly from Spain, Portugal, and Italy, migrated to Central and South America. Some 50 million people in these areas today are of European ancestry.

3. **Europe to Africa and Australasia.** Approximately 17 million people in Africa and Australasia are of European ancestry. In Africa, the majority of emigrants went to the state of South Africa, which was colonized mainly by the British and the Dutch.

4. **Africa to the Americas.** Starting in the sixteenth century, about 10 million blacks were unwillingly transported to the North and South American continents. Fewer than 1 million arrived in the sixteenth century; some 1.3 million, in the seventeenth century; 6 million, in the eighteenth century; and 2 million, in the nineteenth century. Black Africans were brought to the Americas in chains to serve as slaves; families and whole communities were destroyed in the process.

GLOBAL MAP 11.1

Colonization and Ethnicity

This map shows the massive movement of peoples from Europe who colonized the Americas, South Africa, Australia, and New Zealand, resulting in the ethnic composition of populations there today. People from Africa were brought to the Americas to be slaves.

45 Million

20 Million

15 Million

17 Million

To Australia and New Zealand

This is one of eight Indian paintings from the 1531 Huexotzinco Codex. It depicts Mexicans providing products and services as taxes to the Spanish conquistador Hernán Cortes. The banner of the Virgin Mary and baby Jesus reflects the early spread of Christianity.

These population flows underlie the current ethnic composition of the United States, Canada, the countries of Central and South America, South Africa, Australia, and New Zealand. In all these societies, the indigenous populations were decimated by disease, war, and genocide and subjected to European rule. They are now impoverished ethnic minorities. Because the Europeans themselves had diverse national and ethnic origins, they transplanted ethnic hierarchies and divisions to their new homelands. At the height of the colonial era, Europeans also ruled over native populations in South Asia, East Asia, the South Pacific, and the Middle East.

Throughout European expansion, ethnocentric attitudes caused many colonists to believe that, as Christians, they were on a civilizing mission to the rest of the world. Europeans of all political persuasions believed themselves superior to the peoples they colonized and conquered. The fact that many of those peoples possessed technologies, agricultural skills, and knowledge that the Europeans embraced and incorporated (for example, the civil service system in India) seemed irrelevant because the Europeans possessed the power to institutionalize their interpretation. The early period of colonization coincided with the rise of scientific racism, and ever since then the legacy of colonization has generated ethnic divisions that have affected regional and global conflicts. In particular, racist views distinguishing the descendants of Europeans from those of Africans became central to European racist attitudes.

The Rise of Racism

Why has racism flourished? There are several reasons. The first reason lies in the exploitative relations that Europeans established with the peoples they conquered. The slave trade could not have been carried on had Europeans not constructed a belief system that allowed them to justify their actions by claiming that Africans belonged to an inferior race. Racism helped justify colonial rule over nonwhites and denied them the rights of political participation being won by whites in the colonists' European homelands. The relations between whites and nonwhites varied according to different patterns of colonial settlement—and were influenced by cultural differences among Europeans themselves.

Second, an opposition between the colors white and black as cultural symbols was deeply rooted in European culture. White had long been associated with purity, and black with evil (there is nothing natural about this symbolism; in some other cultures, it is reversed). The symbol of blackness held negative meanings *before* the West came into extensive contact with black peoples. These symbolic meanings infused the Europeans' reactions to blacks when they first encountered them on African shores. The sense that there was a radical difference between black and white peoples, combined with the "heathenism" of the Africans, led many Europeans to regard blacks with disdain and fear.

A young girl joins members of the Ku Klux Klan at a demonstration against the Martin Luther King Day holiday in Pulaski, Tennessee, in 1990.

A third factor was the invention and diffusion of the concept of race itself. Racist attitudes have existed for hundreds of years. In China of 300 B.C.E., for example, we find descriptions of barbarian peoples "who greatly resemble monkeys from whom they are descended." But the notion of race as a cluster of inherited characteristics comes from European thought. Count Joseph Arthur de Gobineau (1816–1882), sometimes called the father of modern racism, proposed that three races exist: white, black, and yellow. The white race possesses superior intelligence, morality, and will power, and these inherited qualities underlie the spread of Western influence across the world. The blacks are the least capable, marked by an animal nature, a lack of morality, and emotional instability.

The ideas of de Gobineau and other similar views were presented as supposedly scientific theories. Although completely without value factually, the notion of the superiority of the white race remains a key element of white racism—for example, in the ideology of the Ku Klux Klan—and it was the basis of **apartheid** in South Africa.

Ethnic Conflict

The most extreme and devastating form of group relations involves **genocide**, the systematic destruction of a racial, political, or cultural group. The most horrific recent instance of brutal

destructiveness against such a group was the massacre of six million Jews in the German concentration camps during World War II. Other examples of mass genocide in the twentieth century span the globe. Between 1915 and 1923, over a million Armenians were killed by the Ottoman Turkish government. In the late 1970s, two million Cambodians died under the Khmer Rouge. During the 1990s, in the African country of Rwanda, hundreds of thousands of the minority Tutsis were massacred by the dominant Hutu group. In the former Yugoslavia, Bosnian and Kosovar Muslims were executed by the Serb majority. And in the Darfur region of the Sudan, the conflict between the Arabic-speaking, nomadic *Janjawid* and the non-Arab Sudanese who speak African languages has escalated to genocide, with hundreds of thousands of people being killed and approximately two million being forced to flee their homes.

The conflicts in the former Yugoslavia have involved **ethnic cleansing**, the creation of ethnically homogeneous areas through the mass expulsion of other ethnic populations via targeted violence, harassment, threats, and campaigns of terror. Croatia, for example, has become a "mono-ethnic" state after a costly war in which thousands of Serbs were expelled from the country. The war—which broke out in Bosnia in 1992 among Serbs, Croats, and Muslims—involved the ethnic cleansing of the Bosnian Muslim population at the hands of the Serbs. Thousands of Muslim men were forced into internment camps, and Muslim women were systematically raped. The war in Kosovo in 1999 was prompted by charges that Serbian forces were ethnically cleansing the Kosovar Albanian (Muslim) population from the province.

In Bosnia and Kosovo, ethnic conflict became internationalized. Hundreds of thousands of refugees fled to neighboring areas, further destabilizing the region. Western states intervened diplomatically and militarily to protect the human rights of targeted ethnic groups. In the short term, such interventions succeeded, yet they have had unintended consequences as well. The fragile peace in Bosnia persists only through the presence of peacekeeping troops and the partitioning of the country into separate ethnic enclaves. In Kosovo, reverse ethnic cleansing ensued after the North Atlantic Treaty Organization (NATO) bombing campaign. Ethnic Albanian Kosovars began to drive the local Serb population out of Kosovo; the presence of NATO-led Kosovo Force troops has been inadequate to prevent ethnic tensions from reigniting.

Violent conflicts worldwide are increasingly civil wars with ethnic dimensions. In a world of increasing interdependence and competition, international factors become even more important in shaping ethnic relations, while the effects of internal ethnic conflicts are felt well outside national borders—sometimes provoking military intervention, sometimes requiring international war crimes tribunals. Responding to and preventing ethnic conflict have become key challenges facing individual states and international political structures.

In some areas of the world, the concept of group closure has been institutionalized in the form of **segregation**—a practice whereby racial and ethnic groups are kept physically separate by law, thereby maintaining the superior position of the dominant group. For instance, in apartheid-era South Africa, laws forced blacks to live separately from whites and forbade sexual relations among races. In the United States, African Americans experienced numerous legal forms of segregation including, until 1967, interracial marriage, which had been criminalized for more than 270 years in every state except Alaska and Hawaii. Even today, segregated residential areas still exist in many cities, leading some to claim that an American system of apartheid has developed (Massey and Denton 1993).

Conflict and Economic Power

Many commentators have argued that the best way to reduce ethnic conflicts is to establish democracy and a free market; this would promote peace by giving everyone a say in running the country and by giving all people access to the prosperity that comes from trade. In *World on Fire: How Exporting Free Market Democracy Breeds Ethnic Hatred and Global Instability* (2003), Amy Chua, a professor at Yale University, contests this view.

Chua's starting point is that in many developing countries a small ethnic minority enjoys disproportionate economic power. One example is the white minority that exploited nonwhite ethnic groups in apartheid South Africa. Chua argues that the massacre of Tutsis by Hutus in Rwanda in 1994 and the hatred felt by Serbs toward Croats in the former Yugoslavia were partly related to the economic advantage enjoyed by the Tutsis and the Croats in their respective countries.

Chua often mentions the Chinese ethnic minority in Indonesia, where the free-market policies of the former dictator General Suharto enriched the country's tiny Chinese minority. In turn, Chinese-Indonesians supported the Suharto dictatorship. By 1998, the year that mass prodemocracy demonstrations forced Suharto to resign, Chinese Indonesians controlled 70 percent of Indonesia's private economy but made up just 3 percent of its population. (The prodemocracy demonstrations in Indonesia are discussed in more detail in Chapter 23.) The end of Suharto's regime was accompanied by violent attacks against the Chinese minority. Chua (2003) writes: "The prevailing view among the pribumi [ethnic] majority was that it was 'worthwhile to lose 10 years of growth to get rid of the Chinese problem once and for all.'"

As Suharto's dictatorship collapsed, the United States and other Western countries called for the introduction of democratic elections. Yet Chua argues that introducing democracy to countries with what she calls "market dominant minorities," such as the Chinese in Indonesia, is not likely to bring peace but, instead, a backlash from the country's ethnic majority. Political leaders will emerge who scapegoat the resented minority and encourage the ethnic majority to reclaim the country's wealth for the "true" owners of the nation, as the pribumi majority in Indonesia did against the Chinese minority.

Chua's account illustrates that although democracy and the market economy are in principle beneficent forces, they must be grounded in an effective system of law and civil society. Where they are not, new and acute ethnic conflicts can emerge.

Models of Ethnic Integration

For many years, the two most common positive models of political ethnic harmony in the United States were those of assimilation and the melting pot (Figure 11.1). **Assimilation** meant that new immigrant groups would assume the attitudes and language of the dominant white community. The idea of the **melting pot** involved merging different cultures and outlooks by stirring them all together. A newer model of ethnic relations is **pluralism**, in which ethnic cultures exist separately yet participate in the larger society's economic and political life. A recent outgrowth of pluralism is **multiculturalism**, in which ethnic groups exist separately and *equally*. It seems possible to create a society in which ethnic groups are separate and equal, as in Switzerland, where French, German, and Italian groups coexist in the same society. But this situation is unusual, and it is unlikely that the United States could mirror this achievement in the near future.

☑ CONCEPT CHECKS

1. What are the three reasons racism has flourished in the United States?
2. Compare and contrast three forms of ethnic conflicts.
3. What is the difference between assimilation and melting pot strategies of ethnic integration?

Global Migration

 Floods of refugees and emigrants move restlessly across different regions of the globe, either escaping conflicts or fleeing poverty in search of a better life. Often they reach a new country only to face resentment from

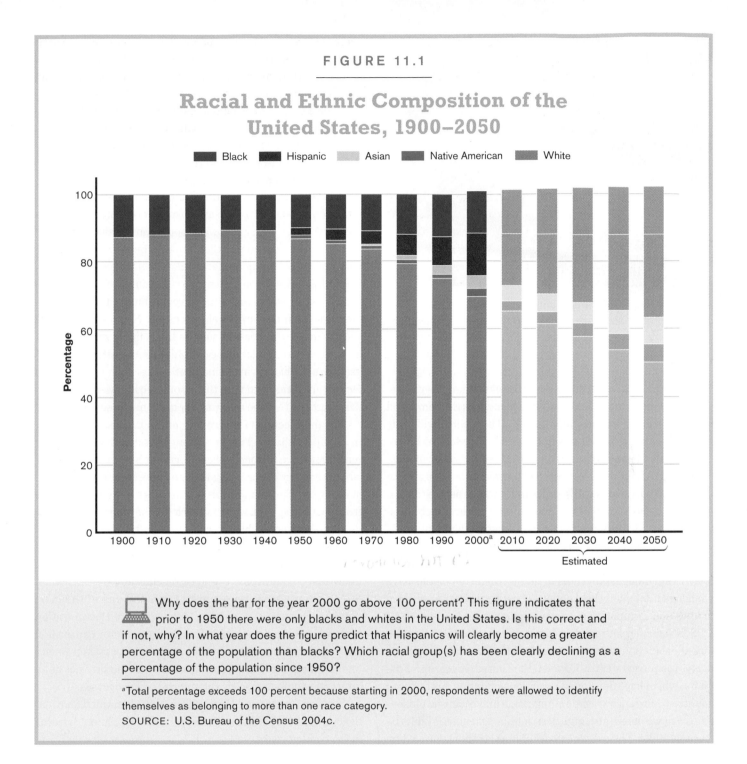

FIGURE 11.1

Racial and Ethnic Composition of the United States, 1900–2050

■ Black ■ Hispanic ■ Asian ■ Native American ■ White

Percentage

(y-axis: 0, 20, 40, 60, 80, 100)

(x-axis: 1900 1910 1920 1930 1940 1950 1960 1970 1980 1990 2000ᵃ 2010 2020 2030 2040 2050)

Estimated

Why does the bar for the year 2000 go above 100 percent? This figure indicates that prior to 1950 there were only blacks and whites in the United States. Is this correct and if not, why? In what year does the figure predict that Hispanics will clearly become a greater percentage of the population than blacks? Which racial group(s) has been clearly declining as a percentage of the population since 1950?

ᵃTotal percentage exceeds 100 percent because starting in 2000, respondents were allowed to identify themselves as belonging to more than one race category.
SOURCE: U.S. Bureau of the Census 2004c.

people whose forebears were immigrants themselves. Sometimes there are reversals, as in some areas of the United States along the Mexican border. Much of what is now California was once part of Mexico. Today, some Mexican Americans might say the new waves of Mexican immigrants are reclaiming what used to be their heritage—except that most of the existing groups in California don't quite see things this way.

Migratory Movements

Migration is accelerating as part of the process of global integration. Worldwide migration patterns reflect the rapidly changing economic, political, and cultural ties among countries. It has been estimated that the world's migrant population in 1990 was more than eighty million people, twenty million of

Aborigines from all over Pitjabjantjaira Country (Australia) gather to protest and protect their land from mining/mineral development.

whom were refugees. In 2006, the number of migrants was estimated at one hundred and ninety-one million (Economic and Social Research Council [ESRC] 2008). The number will likely increase in the twenty-first century, prompting some scholars to label this the "age of migration" (Castles and Miller 1993).

Immigration, the movement of people into a country to settle, and **emigration**, the process by which people leave a country to settle in another, combine to produce global migration patterns linking countries of origin and countries of destination. Migratory movements add to ethnic and cultural diversity and affect demographic, economic, and social dynamics. Rising immigration rates in many Western societies have challenged commonly held notions of national identity and have forced a reexamination of concepts of citizenship.

Scholars offer four models of migration to describe the main global population movements since 1945. The *classic model* applies to countries such as Canada, the United States, and Australia, which have developed as nations of immigrants. These countries have encouraged immigration and promised citizenship to newcomers, although restrictions and quotas limit the annual intake. The *colonial model* of immigration, pursued by countries such as France and the United Kingdom, favors immigrants from former colonies.

Countries such as Germany, Switzerland, and Belgium have followed the *guest workers model:* Immigrants are admitted on a temporary basis, often to fulfill demands within the labor market, but do not receive citizenship rights even after long periods of settlement. Finally, *illegal models* of immigration are increasingly common because of tightening immigration laws in many industrialized countries. Immigrants who gain entry into a country either secretly or under a nonimmigration pretense often live illegally outside the realm of official society. Examples include Mexican illegal aliens in many southern U.S. states and the growing international business of smuggling refugees across national borders.

What are the forces behind global migration, and how are they changing as a result of globalization? Many early theories focused on push and pull factors. *Push factors* were dynamics within a country of origin that forced people to emigrate, such as war, famine, political oppression, and population pressures. *Pull factors* were features of destination countries that attracted immigrants, such as prosperous labor markets, better living conditions, and lower population density.

Recently, push and pull theories have been criticized for offering overly simplistic explanations of a multifaceted process. Instead, scholars of migration are regarding global migration patterns as systems produced through interactions between macro-level and micro-level processes. Macro-level factors refer to overarching issues such as the political situation in an area, laws and regulations controlling immigration and emigration, and changes in the international economy. Micro-level factors are concerned with the resources, knowledge, and understandings that the migrant populations possess.

The intersection of macro and micro processes is evident in Germany's large Turkish immigrant community. On the macro level are factors such as Germany's economic need for labor, its policy of accepting foreign "guest workers," and the state of the Turkish economy, which prevents many Turks from earning at a satisfactory level. On the micro level are the informal networks and channels of mutual support within the Turkish community in Germany and the strong links to family and friends in Turkey. Among potential Turkish migrants, knowledge about Germany and its "social capital"—its human or community resources—make Germany one of the most popular destination countries. Supporters of the migration systems approach emphasize that no single factor can explain the process of migration. Rather, each migratory movement, like that between Turkey and Germany, is the product of an interaction among macro- and micro-level processes.

Stephen Castles and Mark Miller (1993) identified four tendencies that they claim will characterize migration patterns in the coming years:

- **Acceleration.** Migration across borders is occurring in greater numbers than ever before.
- **Diversification.** Most countries now receive immigrants of many different types, in contrast with earlier times when particular forms of immigration, such as labor immigration or refugees, were predominant.
- **Globalization.** Migration has become more global, involving a greater number of countries as both senders and recipients (Global Maps 11.2 and 11.3).

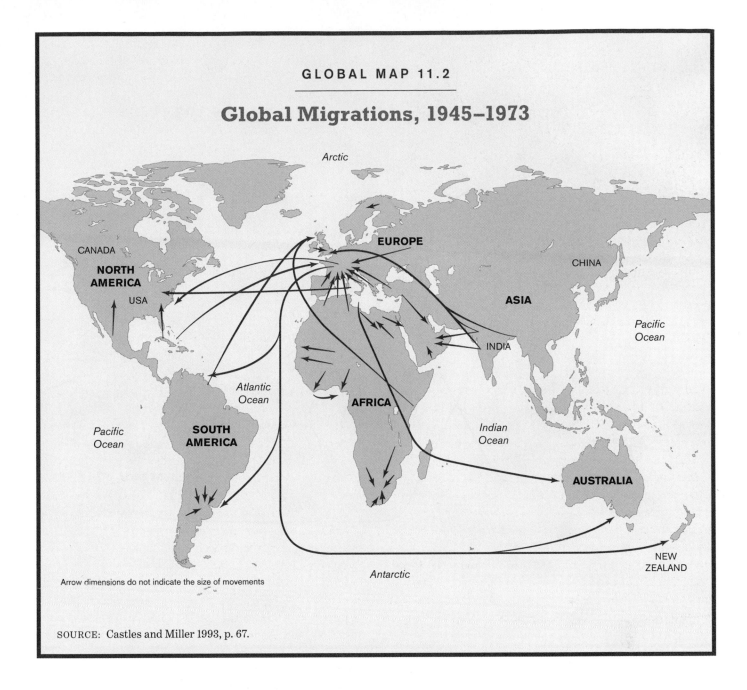

GLOBAL MAP 11.2

Global Migrations, 1945–1973

Arctic

CANADA

NORTH AMERICA

USA

EUROPE

CHINA

ASIA

Pacific Ocean

INDIA

Atlantic Ocean

Pacific Ocean

SOUTH AMERICA

AFRICA

Indian Ocean

AUSTRALIA

NEW ZEALAND

Antarctic

Arrow dimensions do not indicate the size of movements

SOURCE: Castles and Miller 1993, p. 67.

- **Feminization.** A growing number of migrants are women, making contemporary migration much less male dominated than previously. The increase reflects changes in the global labor market, including the growing demand for domestic workers, the expansion of sex tourism, and "trafficking" in women and the "mail-order brides" phenomenon.

Global Diasporas

The term **diaspora** refers to the dispersal of an ethnic population from a homeland into foreign areas, often in a forced manner or under traumatic circumstances. Although members of a diaspora are scattered geographically, they are held together by factors such as a shared history, a collective memory of the homeland, or a common ethnic identity that is nurtured and preserved.

Robin Cohen has argued that diasporas occur in various forms, although the most commonly cited examples are those that result from persecution and violence. In *Global Diasporas* (1997), Cohen adopts a historical approach and identifies five categories of diasporas: *victim* (e.g., African, Jewish, and Armenian), *imperial* (British), *labor* (Indian), *trade* (Chinese), and *cultural* (Caribbean). In certain cases, such as that of the Chinese, large-scale population movements occurred on a voluntary basis.

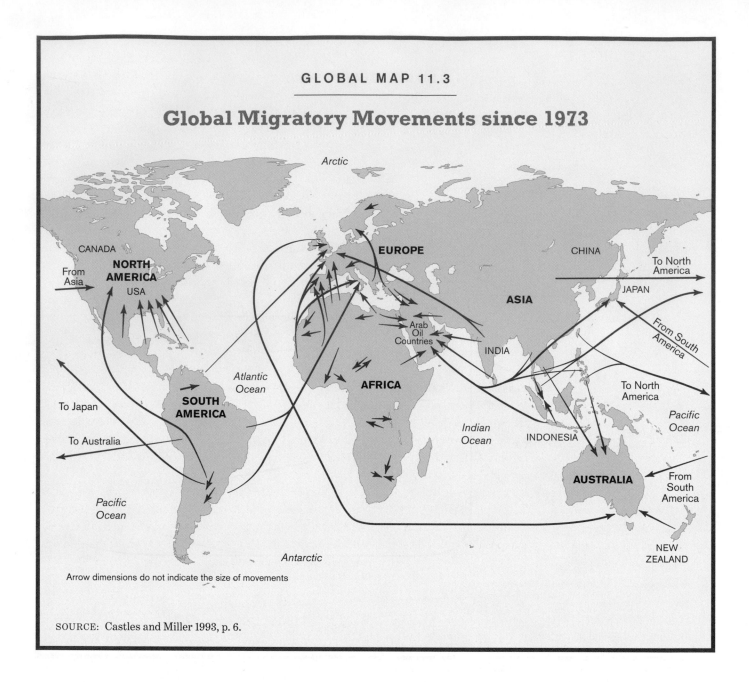

GLOBAL MAP 11.3

Global Migratory Movements since 1973

Arrow dimensions do not indicate the size of movements

SOURCE: Castles and Miller 1993, p. 6.

Despite the diversity of forms, all diasporas share certain key features (R. Cohen 1997):

- A forced or voluntary movement from a homeland to a new region or regions
- A shared memory about the homeland, a commitment to its preservation, and a belief in the possibility of eventual return
- A strong ethnic identity sustained over time and distance
- A sense of solidarity with members of the same ethnic group also living in areas of the diaspora
- A degree of tension in relation to the host societies
- The potential for valuable and creative contributions to pluralistic host societies

Some scholars have accused Cohen of simplifying complex and distinctive migration experiences into a narrow typology, by associating categories of diasporas with particular ethnic groups. Others argue that his conceptualization of diaspora is not sufficiently precise. Yet Cohen's study is valuable for demonstrating that diasporas are nonstatic, ongoing processes of maintaining collective identity and preserving ethnic culture in a rapidly globalizing world.

☑ **CONCEPT CHECKS**

1. According to Castles and Miller, which four trends are likely to characterize migration in the near future?
2. What is diaspora? Explain the role diasporas play in preserving ethnic culture in contemporary societies.

Ethnic Relations in the United States

We concentrate now on the origins and nature of ethnic diversity in the United States (Table 11.1) and its often highly contentious consequences. More than most other societies, this country is peopled almost entirely by immigrants. Less than 1 percent of the population today comprises Native Americans.

Before the American Revolution, the British, French, and Dutch settlers established colonies in what is now the United States. Millions of slaves were brought over from Africa. Huge waves of European, Russian, Asian, and Latin American immigrants have entered the country since then. In this section we address the divisions that have separated whites and nonwhite minority groups, such as African Americans and Hispanic Americans. The emphasis is on *struggle*. Members of these groups have made repeated efforts to defend the integrity of their cultures and advance their social position in the face of prejudice and discrimination.

Early Colonization

At the time of the Declaration of Independence, the majority of the colonial population was of British descent, and almost everyone was Protestant. Settlers from outside the British Isles were at first admitted only with reluctance, but the desire for economic expansion meant having to attract immigrants from other areas. Most came from countries in northwestern Europe, such as Holland, Germany, and Sweden, starting around 1820. In the century following, about thirty-three million immigrants entered the United States. No migrant movement on such a scale has ever been documented before or since.

The early immigrants left Europe to escape economic hardship and religious and political oppression, as well as to acquire land as the drive westward gained momentum. As a result of successive potato famines, 1.5 million people migrated from Ireland and settled primarily in coastal areas, in contrast to most other immigrants from rural backgrounds. Accustomed to hardship and despair, most of the Irish settled in urban industrial areas, where they sought work.

A new influx of immigrants arrived in the 1880s and 1890s, mainly from southern and eastern Europe—the Austro-Hungarian Empire, Russia, and Italy. Each successive group encountered considerable discrimination from people previously established in the country. Negative views of the Irish, for example, emphasized their supposedly low level of intelligence and drunken behavior. Job vacancies often stated, "No Irish need apply." But as they were concentrated within the cities, the Irish Americans organized to protect their interests and gained a strong influence over political life. The Italians and Polish, when they reached America, in turn faced discrimination by the Irish.

Asian immigrants first arrived in large numbers in the late nineteenth century, encouraged by employers who needed cheap labor in the developing industries of the West. Some two hundred thousand Chinese men came with the idea of saving money to send back to their families in China, anticipating that they themselves would later return. Bitter conflicts broke out between white workers and the Chinese when employment opportunities diminished. The Chinese Exclusion Act, passed in 1882, reduced further immigration to a trickle until after World War II.

Japanese immigrants, who arrived not long after the ending of Chinese immigration, also encountered great hostility from whites. Opposition to Japanese immigration intensified in the early twentieth century, leading to strict limits, or quotas, on the numbers of Japanese allowed into the United States.

In the late nineteenth century, thousands of Chinese immigrants in California were employed by the railroads to do the toughest work.

TABLE 11.1

Racial and Ethnic Populations in the United States, 2006

RACE OR ETHNICITY	POPULATION	SHARE OF TOTAL POPULATION[a]
Total U.S. Population	299,398,485	100.00
One race		
White	221,331,507	73.93
Black or African American	37,051,483	12.38
American Indian and Alaska Native	2,369,431	0.79
Asian	13,100,095	4.38
Asian Indian	2,482,141	0.83
Chinese (except Taiwanese)	2,998,518	1.00
Filipino	2,328,097	0.78
Japanese	829,767	0.28
Korean	1,335,075	0.45
Vietnamese	1,475,798	0.49
Other Asian	292,461	0.10
Native Hawaiian and Other Pacific Islander	426,194	0.14
Native Hawaiian	148,598	0.05
Samoan	73,385	0.02
Guamanian or Chamorro	85,628	0.03
Other Pacific Islander	5,990	0.00
Hispanic or Latino	44,252,278	14.78
Mexican	28,339,354	9.47
Puerto Rican	3,987,947	1.33
Cuban	1,520,276	0.51
Other Hispanic or Latino	2,252,414	0.75
Some other race alone	19,007,129	6.35
Two or more races	6,112,646	2.04

[a]Percentages do not total 100 percent because Hispanics or Latinos can be of any race.

SOURCE: U.S. Census Bureau 2006h.

Most immigrant groups in the early twentieth century settled in urban areas and engaged in the developing industrial economy. They also clustered in ethnic neighborhoods, with Chinatowns, Little Italys, and other clearly defined areas becoming features of most large cities. The very size of the influx provoked backlash from the Anglo-Saxon sections of the population. During the 1920s, immigration quotas discriminated against new arrivals from southern and eastern Europe. Many immigrants found the conditions of their new life little better and sometimes worse than those they had left behind.

The immigrants may have gained greater religious and political freedom in their new home, but they faced prejudice and discrimination if their ways of life differed from those of the dominant Anglo-Saxon community. Moreover, competition for jobs allowed employers to impose very long working days, low pay, and unhealthy working conditions. Because new immigrants were commonly hired to replace striking workers, conflicts between them and established groups were frequent. In spite of these conditions, the economy was rapidly growing, and many immigrant workers managed to improve their standards of living.

Immigration to the United States: The Sociological Debate

The cultural and social landscape of the United States is viewed as an amalgam of diverse cultures, largely because of our nation's history as a refuge for immigrants. Today, however, policy makers and social scientists disagree over the social and economic costs of immigration. Do new immigrants help or hinder the nation's economy?

Before discussing this debate, it is important to understand the current state of immigration to the United States. There are over 37.5 million foreign-born individuals in the United States (Migration Policy Institute 2007a). During the 1990s, more than 977,100 legal immigrants arrived each year, and an additional 300,000 entered and stayed in the country illegally (U.S. Bureau of the Census 2006a). From 2002 to 2006, an average of 1,021,884 legal immigrants were admitted each year and another 500,000 illegal immigrants entered the country (Migration Policy Institute 2007b). Unlike the major wave of immigration of the 1880s and 1890s, fewer than 10 percent of immigrants admitted into the United States in the 1980s and 1990s were of European origin. In fact, between 1989 and 1993, more than half came from Mexico, the Philippines, Vietnam, and El Salvador. This change is attributed to two government acts: the 1965 Immigration and Nationality Act Amendments, which abolished preference for northern and western European immigrants and gave preference to "family reunification"—rather than occupational skills—as a reason for accepting immigrants; and the 1986 Immigration Reform and Control Act, which provided amnesty for many illegal immigrants.

Consequently, much of the debate focuses on new immigrants' ability to secure employment and achieve economic self-sufficiency. In his 1994 essay "The Economics of Immigration," economist George Borjas argued that since the 1980s, the United States has attracted "lower-quality" immigrants with less education and few marketable job skills. Moreover, they are less skilled than both natives (i.e., people born in the United States) and earlier migrants; thus they are more reliant on government assistance. Borjas's estimates show that 21 percent of immigrant households participate in social assistance programs such as Medicaid and food stamps, as compared with 14 percent of native households. Because recent immigrants often cannot find gainful employment in the short term, economic assimilation is slow; Borjas estimated that recent immigrants will likely earn 20 percent less than native-born Americans for most of their working lives.

In terms of the effect of immigrants on natives' economic prospects, Borjas argued that large-scale migration of less-skilled workers harms the economic opportunities of less-skilled natives—particularly African Americans. This occurs because immigrants increase the number of workers in the economy; as they create additional competition in the labor market, wages of the least skilled workers fall.

Other economists and policy analysts claim that recent immigration has either a positive effect or no influence on the U.S. economy. Economist Julian Simon (1981, 1989) has argued that immigrants benefit the U.S. economy by joining the labor force and paying into the federal revenue system for their whole lives. By the time they retire and collect government benefits such as Social Security and Medicare, their children will be covering these costs by working and paying into the tax system themselves. Simon's arguments, however, assume that immigrants earn the same wages and are as employable as natives—an assumption refuted by Borjas's research.

This nineteenth-century cartoon, *Where the Blame Lies,* offers an unflattering portrait of new immigrants and characterizes the discrimination that many new immigrants faced after arriving in the United States.

"Uneducated Immigrants Hurt Country"

Among the many hotly debated issues in the 2008 presidential primaries was immigration, with candidates proposing initiatives ranging from permanent amnesty and government-provided health care for undocumented immigrants to building a wall on the U.S.-Mexico border. At the core of the debate over immigration policy is a question that social scientists have wrestled with for decades: Do immigrants ultimately help or hurt our country? Concerned citizens hoping to answer this question did not find answers easily as they consulted their daily newspapers in November 2007. While some headlines told us "Uneducated Immigrants Hurt Country" (Bazar 2007) and "Immigrants, Illegals Use Welfare More Often" (Dinan 2007), others informed us that "Immigrants Pull Weight in Economy" (McGeehan 2007). How could the newspapers offer such different messages, given that they were all reporting on the same social issue? The immigration puzzle highlights an important issue facing social scientists: Statistical data can be interpreted in a variety of ways, depending on the political and philosophical views of the interpreter.

Most news articles that cast immigration in a negative light were reporting the results of a study by Steven Camarota, director of research for the Washington, D.C.-based, nonpartisan Center for Immigration Studies (CIS). CIS, an organization that promotes limits on immigration, estimates that 37.9 million immigrants now reside in the United States, 11.3 million of whom are undocumented.

(Opponents of immigration often refer to "undocumented immigrants" using the more pejorative term "illegal aliens.")

Some statisticians question the 11.3 million figure because counting undocumented immigrants is an inexact science. Although immigrants do respond to government surveys like the census, they are not asked about their legal resi-

Thousands protest at an anti-immigration rally in Los Angeles, California.

dent status. Consequently, research organizations like the Census Bureau and Department of Homeland Security must estimate the number of undocumented persons using sophisticated statistical methods. A widely used method involves using census data counts on the number of immigrants residing in the United States and comparing these numbers with reports from organizations such

as the State Department and Office of Refugee Resettlement, which count the number of persons leaving other nations for the United States. The difference between these two counts is considered an estimate of the number of undocumented persons. Although this method is considered among the most effective ways to count undocumented immigrants, even demographers who use these methods admit that they can be imprecise (Passel 2002).

The CIS study also offers a largely negative portrayal of the characteristics of immigrants and their contributions to U.S. society. For instance, CIS reports that 59 percent of undocumented immigrants and their children (who may be U.S.-born citizens) are living in or near poverty. This rate is considerably higher than for legal immigrants and their children. Slightly more than half of undocumented immigrants and their children lack health insurance, compared to 10 percent of native-born Americans and their children. The study also finds higher rates in the use of public assistance programs by households headed by undocumented immigrants, who are ineligible for almost all benefits but whose spouse or children might qualify for programs if they are U.S.-born citizens or legal immigrants (Dinan 2007).

Critics of the CIS report argue that the study findings are potentially misleading because they offer a snapshot of a single point in time. Angela Kelley, director of the Immigration Policy Center at the advocacy organization American Immigrant Law Foundation, emphasizes the importance of considering the long-term implications of immigration rather than looking at single point in time. Over time, she argues, most assimilate. "Immigrants come to this country, they work hard. If they can get legal status, that improves their chances. They buy homes, they learn English, they intermarry. If given the chance, they naturalize.... That is a story as old as America" (Bazar 2007).

Other critics raise questions about the interpretation of the CIS data. Randy Capps, an immigration researcher at the Washington, D.C.–based nonpartisan Urban Institute, questions whether it's right to broadly conclude that undocumented immigrants "use welfare more" when in fact most use only a handful of specific programs, namely, subsidized school lunches and Medicaid. Capps estimates that illegal immigrant families are less likely than native-born families to rely on welfare (or cash-assistance) programs. Similarly, low-income children of immigrants are less likely than low-income children of native-born parents to rely on social services. Capps explained, "many [immigrant] parents are afraid of being reported to immigration services, or they may not even be aware of the program, so they don't enroll their children" (Aizenman 2007).

The CIS report is considered quite sound on methodological grounds, yet some immigration advocates argue that by focusing on only negative aspects of immigration, and illegal immigration in particular, the CIS is offering an incomplete portrait of immigrants in the United States. Other studies, by contrast, offer a much more positive characterization. A recent report by the New York–based Fiscal Policy Institute (FPI) found that the 4.1 million immigrants in New York State contribute nearly one fourth of the state's economic output and that immigrants are overrepresented in high-skilled professions such as higher education and health care (McGeehan 2007). Although the media often portray immigrants as poorly educated and low skilled, the FPI study found that in some New York counties, immigrants made up roughly one quarter to one third of all doctors and one fifth of all professors. Immigrants make up a large majority of taxi drivers, home health aides, and housekeepers in New York City, yet they also account for 25 percent of CEOs.

David Kallick, a senior fellow at FPI and author of their report *Working for Better Life* (Fiscal Policy Institute 2007), believes that his study yields important findings that the media overlook. As Kallick explained, "there was such a deep misunderstanding about who immigrants were that the political discourse often got far afield from any factual basis of what's really going on" (McGeehan 2007). Kallick underscores an important observation. For social science research to be useful and to inform public policy effectively, the data must be interpreted fairly and accurately, and researchers should be honest about the personal or political agendas that drive their work.

Questions

- According to the Center for Immigration Studies, how many undocumented immigrants currently reside in the United States?
- How are undocumented immigrants counted?
- What are three critiques of the Center for Immigration Studies report?
- Would you characterize immigrants' contributions to the United States as largely positive or negative? Why?

FOR FURTHER EXPLORATION

Aizenman, N. C. 2007. "Illegal Immigrants in MD and VA Out-Earn U.S. Peers, Study Says." *Washington Post* (November

29, 2007). www.washingtonpost.com/wp-dyn/content/story/2007/11/29/ST2007112900161.html (accessed January 21, 2008).

Bazar, Emily 2007. "Study: Uneducated Immigrants Hurt Country." *USA Today* (November 28, 2007). www.usatoday.com/news/nation/2007-11-28-immigrants_N.htm (accessed January 21, 2008).

Camarota, Steven A. 2007. *Immigrants in the United States, 2007: A Profile of America's Foreign Born Population*. Washington, DC: Center for Immigration Studies. www.cis.org/articles/2007/back1007.pdf (accessed January 21, 2008).

Corsi, Jerome. 2007. "'Family Values' Won't Get Help from Immigration." *WorldNet Daily* (April 24, 2007). www.worldnetdaily.com/news/printer-friendly.asp?ARTICLE_ID=55328 (accessed January 21, 2008).

Dinan, Stephen. 2007. "Immigrants, Illegals Use Welfare More Often." *Washington Times* (November 29, 2007). www.washingtontimes.com/apps/pbcs.dll/article?AID=/20071129/NATION/111290083/1001 (accessed January 21, 2008).

Fiscal Policy Institute. 2007. *Working for a Better Life: A Profile of Immigrants in the New York State Economy*. New York: Fiscal Policy Institute. www.fiscalpolicy.org/publications2007/FPI_ImmReport_WorkingforaBetterLife.pdf (accessed January 21, 2008).

McGeehan, Patrick. 2007. "Immigrants Pull Weight in Economy, Study Finds." *New York Times* (November 26, 2007). www.nytimes.com/2007/11/26/nyregion/26report.html?r=1&scp=1&sq=study+immigrants&oref=slogin (accessed January 21, 2008).

Passel, Jeffrey. 2002. *New Estimates of the Undocumented Population in the United States*. Washington, DC: Migration Policy Institute. www.migrationinformation.org/feature/display.cfm?ID=19 (accessed January 21, 2008).

Immigrant America

If globalization is understood as the emergence of new patterns of interconnection among the world's peoples and cultures, then surely one of the most significant aspects of globalization is the changing racial and ethnic composition of Western societies. In the United States, shifting patterns of immigration since the end of World War II have altered the demographic structure of many regions, affecting social and cultural life in ways that can hardly be overstated. Although the United States has always been a nation of immigrants (with the obvious exception of Native Americans), most of those who arrived here before the early 1960s were European. Throughout the nineteenth and early twentieth centuries, vast numbers of people from Ireland, Italy, Germany, Russia, and other European countries flocked to America in search of a new life, giving a distinctive European bent to American culture. (Of course, until 1808, another significant group of immigrants—Africans—came not because America was a land of opportunity but because they had been enslaved.) In part because of changes in immigration policy, however, most of those admitted since 1965 have been Asian or Hispanic.

In the years 2000–2003, for example, of the approximately 4.5 million immigrants who were legally admitted to the United States, almost 1.2 million came from Asia and nearly 2.6 million were from Latin America (U.S. Bureau of the Census 2003i). There are also an estimated 7 to 11 million illegal immigrants living in the United States, about 70 percent of whom

are Mexican (CNN 2003; National Immigration Forum 2006). As a result, as of 2003, over 53 percent of U.S. residents who were foreign born were from Latin America, while 25 percent were from Asia (U.S. Bureau of the Census 2003b). In contrast, in 1900 almost 85 percent of the foreign born were European (Duignan and Gann 1998).

Simon also holds that immigrants are a cultural asset to the United States. In fact, he claims that "the notion of wanting to keep out immigrants to keep our institutions and our values pure is prejudice" (quoted in Brimelow 1995). Moreover, he argues, because human beings have the intelligence to adapt to their surroundings, the more immigrants that come to the United States, the larger the pool of potential innovators and problem solvers our nation will have.

Studies conducted by Simon and the Urban Institute, a non-profit research organization, acknowledge that although some recent immigrants may benefit from federally funded programs such as welfare, these costs are often quite short term.

Immigrant children who benefit from the U.S. educational system go on to become productive, taxpaying workers.

The National Immigration Forum has estimated that immigrant workers contribute significantly to the national economy. Even though most immigrants work in low-wage and hard-labor jobs, without them the gross domestic product of the United States would be $1 trillion less (Rodriguez 2004). Assessing the fiscal costs of immigration proves difficult, however. Although much of the public debate focuses on the costs of providing services to illegal immigrants, actual statistics documenting the number of illegal immigrants are difficult to obtain and verify. Moreover, few policy analysts can predict

Most of these new immigrants have settled in six "port-of-entry" states: California, New York, Texas, Illinois, New Jersey, and Massachusetts. These states are attractive to new immigrants not necessarily because of the job opportunities they afford, but because they house large immigrant communities into which newcomers are welcomed (Frey and Liaw 1998). As the flow of Asian and Hispanic immigration continues, and as some nonimmigrants respond by moving to regions of the country with smaller immigrant populations, the percentage of residents of port-of-entry states who are white will continue to drop. California was approximately 52 percent white in 1996; in 2006, this number dropped to 42.8 percent, and by 2010, it is expected to fall to 40 percent (Maharidge 1996; U.S. Bureau of the Census 2006b). "Other states will follow," Dale Maharidge writes in the book *The Coming White Minority* (1996), "Texas sometime around 2015, and in later years Arizona, New York, Nevada, New Jersey, and Maryland. By 2050 the nation will be almost half nonwhite."

The effect of these demographic changes on everyday social life has been profound. Take California as an example. In California's urban centers, residents fully expect street scenes to be multiethnic in character and would be shocked to visit a state like Wisconsin, where the vast majority of public interactions take place among whites. In some California communities, store and street signs are printed in Spanish or Chinese or Vietnamese, as well as in English. Interracial marriages are on the rise, ethnic restaurants have proliferated, and the schools are filled with nonwhite children. In fact, nonwhites make up two thirds of the undergraduate population at the University of California, Berkeley, where Asian students are on the verge of predominating.

Unfortunately, these changes have exacerbated social tensions. Many white Californians have retreated into prosperous suburban enclaves and have grown resentful of

immigrants and nonwhites. Because rates of voter turnout are higher for whites than for other racial groups in the state and because whites control a significant share of the state's wealth, they have managed to pass a number of laws that seek to preserve opportunities for the coming white minority. Proposition 187, for example, passed in 1994, denied vital public services to illegal immigrants. More recently, the regents of the University of California, in a highly controversial move, decided to abolish affirmative action for the entire nine-campus state university system. Were these decisions based on solid economic and philosophical rationales—the perception that California taxpayers were shouldering too much of the economic burden of illegal immigration or the sense that affirmative action constitutes "reverse discrimination" against whites—or were they motivated principally by xenophobia, the fear of those different from oneself? Whatever the answer, there can be little doubt but that immigration—an important aspect of globalization—is changing the face of American society.

whether U.S. immigration policy—or the characteristics of immigrants themselves—will change drastically in the future.

African Americans in the United States

By 1780, there were nearly four million slaves in the American South. Since there was little incentive for them to work, physical punishment was common. Slaves who ran away were hunted with dogs and on their capture were manacled, sometimes branded with their master's mark, and occasionally castrated. Slaves had no rights in law whatsoever. But they did not passively accept the conditions their masters imposed on them. The struggles of slaves sometimes took the form of direct opposition or disobedience to orders, and occasionally rebellion (although collective slave revolts were more common in the Caribbean than in the United States). On a more subtle level, their response involved a cultural creativity—a mixing of aspects of African cultures, Christian ideals, and cultural threads from their new environments. Some of the art forms they developed—for example, jazz—were genuinely new.

Hostility toward blacks on the part of whites was in some respects stronger in states where slavery had never been known than in the South itself. The French political observer Alexis de Tocqueville (1969; orig. 1835) noted in 1835, "The prejudice of race appears to be stronger in the states that have abolished slavery than in those where it still exists; and nowhere is it so intolerant as in those states where servitude has never been known." Moral rejection of slavery was confined to a few more educated groups. The main factors underlying the Civil War were political and economic; most northern leaders were more interested in sustaining the Union than in abolishing slavery, although the abolition of slavery was an eventual outcome of the conflict. The formal abolition of slavery barely changed the real conditions of life for African Americans in the South. The "black codes"—laws limiting the rights of blacks—restricted the behavior of the former slaves and punished their transgressions in much the same way as under slavery. Acts legalizing segregation of blacks from whites in public places were passed. One kind of slavery was thus replaced by another: that of social, political, and economic discrimination.

INTERNAL MIGRATION FROM SOUTH TO NORTH

Industrial development in the North combined with the mechanization of agriculture in the South produced a progressive movement of African Americans northward. In 1900, more than 90 percent of African Americans lived in the South, mostly in rural areas. Today, three quarters of the black population live in northern urban areas. African Americans used to be farm laborers and domestic servants, but over little more than two generations they have become mainly urban, industrial, and service-economy workers. But African Americans have not assimilated into the wider society in the way white immigrants did. They still face conditions of neighborhood segregation and poverty that other immigrants faced only on arrival. Together with those of Anglo-Saxon origin, African Americans have lived in the United States far longer than most other immigrant groups. What was a transitional experience for most of the later, white immigrants has become a seemingly permanent experience for blacks.

THE CIVIL RIGHTS MOVEMENT

In contrast to other racial and ethnic minorities, blacks and Native Americans have largely been denied opportunities for self-advancement. The National Association for the Advancement of Colored People (NAACP) and the National Urban League were founded in 1909 and 1910, respectively, to promote black civil rights. However, they did not have a significant effect until after World War II, when the NAACP instituted a campaign against segregated public education. This struggle came to a head when the organization sued five school boards, challenging the concept of separate but equal schooling. In 1954, in *Brown v. Board of Education of Topeka, Kansas,* the U.S. Supreme Court unanimously ruled that "separate educational facilities are inherently unequal."

This decision underpinned struggles for civil rights from the 1950s to the 1970s. The strength of the resistance from many whites persuaded black leaders that mass militancy was necessary. In 1955, a black woman, Rosa Parks, was arrested in Montgomery, Alabama, for declining to give up her seat on a bus to a white man. As a result, almost the entire African American population of the city, led by a Baptist minister, Martin Luther King Jr., boycotted the transportation system for 381 days. Eventually the city was forced to abolish segregation in public transportation.

Further boycotts and sit-ins followed, with the object of desegregating other public facilities. The marches and demonstrations began to achieve a mass following from blacks and white sympathizers. In 1963, a quarter of a million civil rights supporters staged a march on Washington and cheered as King announced, "We will not be satisfied until justice rolls down like the waters and righteousness like a mighty stream." In 1964, the Civil Rights Act was passed by Congress and signed into law by President Lyndon B. Johnson, banning discrimination in public facilities, education, employment, and any agency receiving government funds. Subsequent bills outlawed discrimination in housing and ensured that African Americans became fully registered voters.

Martin Luther King Jr. addresses a large crowd at a civil rights march on Washington in 1963. Born in 1929, King was a Baptist minister, civil rights leader, and winner of the 1964 Nobel Peace Prize. He was assassinated by James Earl Ray in 1968.

Although civil rights marchers were beaten up and some lost their lives, and in spite of some barriers to full realization of the Civil Rights Act's provisions, the law was fundamentally important. Its principles applied not just to African Americans but also to anyone subject to discrimination, including other ethnic groups and women. It spurred a range of movements asserting the rights of oppressed groups.

How successful has the civil rights movement been? On one hand, a substantial black middle class has emerged. Many African Americans—such as the writer Toni Morrison, the literary scholar Henry Louis Gates, Secretary of State Condoleezza Rice, media mogul Oprah Winfrey, basketball player Michael Jordan, and President Barack Obama—have achieved positions of power and influence. On the other hand, a significant African American underclass remains trapped in the ghettos. Scholars have debated whether this underclass has resulted primarily from economic disadvantage or from dependency on the welfare system. Later in this chapter we will examine the forms of inequality still experienced by African Americans and other minority groups.

Latinos in the United States

The wars of conquest that created the boundaries of the contemporary United States were directed not only against the Native American population but also against Mexico. The territory that later became California, Nevada, Arizona, New Mexico, and Utah—along with a quarter of a million Mexicans—was taken by the United States in 1848 as a result of the American war with Mexico. The terms *Mexican American* and *Chicano* refer to the descendants of these people, together with subsequent immigrants from Mexico. The term *Latino* refers to anyone from Spanish-speaking regions living in the United States.

The three main groups of Latinos in the United States are Mexican Americans (around 28.3 million), Puerto Ricans (4 million), and Cubans (1.5 million). A further 12 million Spanish-speaking residents are from countries in Central and South America and other Hispanic or Latino regions (U.S. Bureau of the Census 2006c). The Latino population increased by 53 percent between 1980 and 1990, by 58 percent between 1990 and 2000, and by 9.4 percent from 2002 to 2006—mainly via immigration from Mexico (U.S. Bureau of the Census 2006c). Latino residents now slightly outnumber African Americans.

MEXICAN AMERICANS

Mexican Americans reside mainly in California, Texas, and other southwestern states, although there are substantial groups in the Midwest and in northern cities as well. The majority work at low-paying jobs. In the post–World War II period

Dancers celebrate Cinco de Mayo in Pasadena, California. Mexican Americans represent the largest group of Latinos in the United States.

up to the early 1960s, Mexican workers were admitted without much restriction. This was succeeded by a phase of quotas on legal immigrants and deportations of illegal immigrants. Today, illegal immigrants continue to cross the border. Large numbers are intercepted and sent back each year, but most simply try again, and four times as many escape officials as are stopped.

Since Mexico is a relatively poor neighbor of the wealthy United States, this flow of people northward is unlikely to diminish. Illegal immigrants can be employed more cheaply than indigenous workers, and they perform jobs that most of the rest of the population would not accept. Legislation passed by Congress in 1986 has enabled illegal immigrants living in the United States for at least five years to claim legal residence.

Many Mexican Americans resist assimilation into the dominant English-speaking culture and increasingly display pride in their own cultural identity within the United States.

PUERTO RICANS AND CUBANS

Puerto Rico was acquired by the United States through war, and Puerto Ricans have been American citizens since 1917. The island is poor, and many of its inhabitants have migrated to the mainland United States to seek a better life. Puerto Ricans originally settled in New York City, but since the 1960s they have moved elsewhere. A reverse migration of Puerto Ricans began in the 1970s; more have left the mainland than have arrived since that date. One of the most important issues facing Puerto Rican activists is the political destiny of their homeland. Puerto Rico is a commonwealth, not a full state. For years, Puerto Ricans have been divided about whether the island should retain its present status, opt for independence, or attempt to become the fifty-first state of the Union.

Closed Doors: Immigration, Politics, and Public Sociology

In the spring of 2004, Professor Douglas Massey received a troubling e-mail. Massey had recently been invited to author a chapter for the United Nations on international migration, a topic he has studied in depth for over two decades. As co-director of the Mexican Migration Project since 1982 (with Jorge Durand of the University of Guadalajara), Massey has visited countries throughout Central and South America over seventy times to learn about the causes and consequences of U.S. immigration policy at the grassroots level. His findings have been widely published in academic journals, books, and the popular press, and he is considered one of the foremost experts on immigration worldwide. When his name was vetted, however, Bush administration officials informed the United Nations that his participation was unacceptable. No explanation was provided. Massey had been blackballed by his own government (Massey 2006a).

"What Bush's people objected to," Massey (2006a) learned through back channels, "was not my science, but a series of critical articles I had published on U.S. immigration policy" during the Clinton administration. In these articles, Massey argued that closed-door policies, advocating tighter border security, actually increase the problem of undocumented immigration to the United States by forcing migrants to cross in more remote areas and making it more difficult for them to return home. The result of tighter security, according to Massey (2006a), has been an unintended increase in the size of

Douglas Massey

the undocumented immigrant population in the United States "at great financial and human cost."

These conclusions are not simply Massey's personal opinions. They are derived from extensive data on international migration collected over twenty years in Mexico and other Latin American nations. The Mexican Migration Project collects data on documented and undocumented migrants originating in both urban and rural communities throughout Mexico. As a

A third Latino group, the Cubans, differs from the others in key respects. Half a million Cubans fled communism after the rise of Fidel Castro in 1959, and the majority settled in Florida. Unlike other Latino immigrants, most were educated people from white-collar and professional backgrounds. They have thrived within the United States, many finding positions comparable to those they abandoned in Cuba. As a group, Cubans have the highest family income of all Latinos.

A further wave of Cuban immigrants, from less affluent

origins, arrived in 1980 and live in circumstances closer to the rest of the Latino communities in the United States. Both sets of Cuban immigrants are mainly political refugees rather than economic migrants. The later immigrants have become the "working class" for the earlier immigrants. They are paid low wages, but Cuban employers hire them in preference to other ethnic groups. In Miami, nearly one third of all businesses are owned by Cubans, and 75 percent of the labor force in construction is Cuban.

sociologist, Massey is dedicated to the collection of facts about how immigration works, how people make decisions, and why they choose to leave their home countries for opportunities elsewhere. Letting the facts speak for themselves, Massey's data reveal that some common assumptions about immigration are actually false: Immigration from Mexico is not a one-way street—many migrants return home (and come back again) through a process of "circular migration." Migrants are not cut off financially from their families back home—they send money, called *remittances,* to family members on a regular basis. Immigrants are not socially isolated—they form social networks in the United States and in Mexico that yield social capital and increase the likelihood that migratory flows will continue into the future.

Massey believes that sociologists can make a difference only when acting as "objective scientists in possession of important facts about the social world" rather than as citizens with emotionally charged opinions. He is not naive enough to believe that facts automatically make a difference in the real world. "Policy is always about politics and politics is never straightforward," Massey admits. But during the 1990s, when the political climate was more receptive to scientific findings, Massey was able to successfully bridge the gap between science and policy. By looking closely at the U.S. Census, Massey documented that two decades after the Fair Housing Act (1968), blacks in the United States remained more segregated from whites than any other racial or ethnic group. Racial segregation and poverty were interconnected, making the social, economic, and political isolation of urban African Americans more severe as jobs disappeared from inner-city neighborhoods. The nation's slow progress toward racial integration in housing, as revealed by Massey and his colleagues, became front-page news in the *New York Times,* the *Los Angeles Times,* the *Philadelphia Inquirer, USA Today,* and the *Washington Post.*

That was just the beginning. Massey and his colleagues continued their research over the following five years,

producing a body of evidence suggesting that residential segregation not only separates people geographically but "represents a primary cause of racial inequality in the United States" (Massey and Denton 1993). By applying sociological thinking to real-life data, Massey demonstrated how segregation increases the severity of poverty and "perpetuates black disadvantage over time and across the generations" (Massey 2006b). The only other place on earth with comparable patterns of racial segregation was South Africa under apartheid, an official policy that promoted the separate development of racial groups.

Massey and Denton's award-winning book, *American Apartheid* (1993), produced further opportunities for public engagement. Throughout the 1990s, Massey was invited to address a variety of civic groups, fair housing organizations, governmental commissions, and academic audiences. Henry Cisneros, the secretary of Housing and Urban Development (HUD) in the Clinton administration, assigned the book to be read by staff members at HUD and invited Massey to Washington to educate politicians on issues relating to segregation and fair housing enforcement. Translating scientific findings for an audience of national policy makers, Massey helped pass the most important development in housing discrimination law since the late 1960s. The policy recommendations instituted by HUD further strengthened fair housing law and resulted in record settlements in discrimination cases (Massey 2006b).

Whether testifying before Congress, authoring articles, serving on government commissions, or lecturing before a classroom of students, Massey provides an excellent model of a public sociologist at work. For almost three decades and across multiple research topics, Massey has used his sociological understanding to suggest workable and humane solutions based on facts, not on slogans. His ability to translate those facts into more effective public policies, however, depends on political factors that remain largely outside his control.

The Asian Connection

About 4.4 percent of the population of the United States is of Asian origin—13.1 million people (U.S. Bureau of the Census 2006d). Chinese, Japanese, and Filipinos form the largest groups; but now there are also significant numbers of Asian Indians, Pakistanis, Koreans, and Vietnamese. As a result of the war in Vietnam, some 350,000 refugees from that country entered the United States in the 1970s.

Most of the early Chinese immigrants settled in California and worked in heavy industries, such as mining and railroad construction. The retreat of the Chinese into distinct Chinatowns was a response to the hostility they faced. Since Chinese immigration was legally banned in 1882, the Chinese remained isolated from the wider society, at least until recently.

The early Japanese immigrants also settled in California and the other Pacific states. During World War II, after the attack on Pearl Harbor by Japan, all Japanese Americans in

In this 1942 photo, young Japanese Americans wait for baggage inspection upon arrival at a World War II Assembly Center in Turlock, California. From here they were transported to one of several internment camps for Japanese Americans.

the United States were taken to remote "relocation centers" surrounded by barbed wire and gun turrets. Even though most were American citizens, they were compelled to live in the hastily established camps for the duration of the war. Paradoxically, this situation promoted their greater integration within the wider society because, after the war, Japanese Americans did not return to their previously separate neighborhoods. They have attained high levels of education and income, marginally outstripping whites. The rate of intermarriage of Japanese Americans with whites is now nearly 50 percent.

After passage of a new immigration act in 1965, large-scale immigration of Asians again took place. Foreign-born Chinese Americans today outnumber those brought up in the United States. The newly arrived Chinese have avoided the Chinatowns in which the long-established Chinese remain.

☑ CONCEPT CHECKS

1. According to Table 11.1, which ethnic minority group is the largest in American society?
2. How did the civil rights movement help minority groups achieve equal rights and opportunities?

Racial and Ethnic Inequality

Since the civil rights movement of the 1960s, has real progress been made? On the one hand, an increasing number of blacks joined the middle class by acquiring college degrees, professional jobs, and new homes. On the other hand, blacks are far more likely than whites to live in poverty and be socially isolated from good schools and economic opportunity. Also, many immigrants came to the United States throughout the 1980s and 1990s to find new economic opportunity. Yet some of these groups, particularly Mexicans, have among the lowest levels of educational achievement and live in dire poverty. Most sociologists agree on the facts about racial and ethnic inequality but disagree on how to interpret them. Are improving economic conditions for minority groups part of a long-term process, or were they temporary reflections of the booming 1990s economy? Is racial and ethnic inequality primarily the result of a person's racial or ethnic background, or does it reflect a person's class position? In this section, we examine how racial and ethnic inequality is reflected in educational and occupational attainment, income, health, residential segregation, and political power. We then consider divergent social statuses within the largest racial and ethnic groups. We conclude by examining how sociologists try to explain racial inequality.

Educational Attainment

Differences between blacks and whites in levels of educational attainment have decreased, but these seem more the result of long-established trends rather than the direct outcome of the struggles of the 1960s. Young African Americans are for the first time close to whites in terms of finishing high school. The number of blacks over the age of twenty-five with high school degrees increased from about 20 percent in 1960 to 80.7 percent in 2006. By contrast, about 86.1 percent of whites have completed high school (Figure 11.2). However, while more blacks are attending college now than in the 1960s, a much higher proportion of whites than blacks graduate from college. In today's global economy and job market, which value college degrees, the result is a wide disparity in incomes between whites and blacks (see the next section).

Another trend is the large gap in educational attainment between Hispanics and both whites and blacks. Hispanics have by far the highest high school dropout rate of any group in the United States. While rates of college attendance and graduation have improved for other groups, the rate for Hispanics has

FIGURE 11.2

Educational Attainment (People 25 Years Old and Older)

Completed 4 Years of High School or More[a]

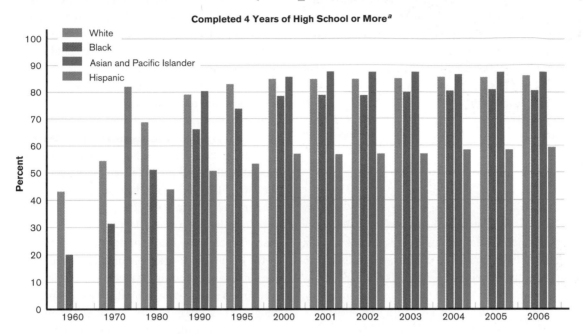

Completed 4 Years of College or More[b]

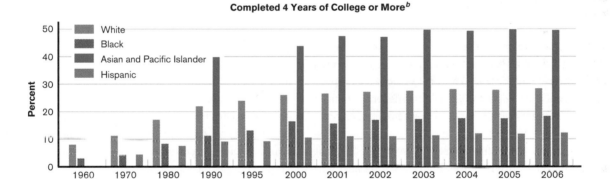

From 1980 to 2006, how did the percentage of blacks who graduated from college change compared to the change in the percentage of Hispanics who graduated from college? During which year did the percentage of whites who graduated from college match the percentage of Hispanics who graduated from college in 2004? What happens to the gap between the percentage of whites and the percentage of blacks who graduated from high school from 1960 to 2000? What happens to the gap between the percentage of whites and the percentage of blacks who graduated from college from 1960 to 2004? From 1980 to 2004, the percentage of blacks who completed four years of high school or more increased and came much closer to the percentage of whites who did so. How does this compare to the percentage of Hispanics during that same time period?

[a] High school graduates or more.
[b] B.A. degree or more.
SOURCE: U.S. Census Bureau 2008a.

held relatively steady since the mid-1980s. Only about 12.4 percent hold a college degree (U.S. Bureau of the Census 2008a). It is possible that these poor results reflect the large number of poorly educated immigrants from Latin America since the 1980s, many of whom have limited English-language skills and whose children encounter difficulties in schools. One study found, however, that even among Mexican Americans whose families have lived in the United States for three generations or more, there has been a decline in educational attainment (Bean et al. 1994). For Hispanics with low levels of education and poor language skills, living in the United States has been "the American nightmare, not the American dream" (Holmes 1997).

Employment and Income

As a result of increased educational attainment, blacks now hold slightly more managerial and professional jobs than in 1960, though still not in proportion to their overall numbers. In 2006, out of 50.4 million managerial or professional positions in the United States, whites held 39.8 million (78.9 percent); African Americans, 4.2 million (8.4 percent); and Hispanics, just under 3.3 million (6.6 percent) (U.S. Bureau of the Census 2008b).

The unemployment rate of black and Hispanic men outstrips that of whites by the same degree today as in the early 1960s. The total unemployment rate for blacks and Hispanics is higher than that for whites (in 2006, 3.2 percent for whites versus about 6.8 percent for blacks and 4.2 percent for Hispanics, U.S. Bureau of the Census 2008c). This difference reduces considerably, however, with education (the unemployment rate with B.A. degree or more is 2.0, 2.8, and 2.2 for whites, blacks, and Hispanics, respectively). There has also been debate about whether employment opportunities for minorities have improved or worsened. Statistics on unemployment don't adequately measure economic opportunity because they reflect only those known to be looking for work. A higher proportion of disillusioned blacks and Hispanics have simply opted out of the occupational system, neither working nor looking for work. Unemployment figures also do not reflect the increasing numbers of young minority men in prison (see also Chapter 7). Finally, although many new jobs were created during the economic boom of the 1990s, most of them available to those without a college degree were in lower-paying service occupations. As we just saw, blacks and Hispanics are underrepresented among college graduates.

Nevertheless, the disparities between the earnings of blacks and whites are gradually diminishing. As measured in terms of median weekly income, black men now earn 70.4 percent of the level of pay of whites (U.S. Bureau of the Census 2008d).

In 1959, the proportion was only 49 percent. In terms of household family income (adjusted for inflation), blacks are the only social group to have seen an improvement during the 1990s. By 2000, poverty rates for African Americans had fallen to their lowest rates since the government started tracking the figure in 1955. These signs of improvement for African Americans have been occurring across the country. Some scholars have warned, however, that the gains could be reversed as the economy falters. They also point out that large gaps between African Americans and whites still exist in terms of college degrees, infant mortality, poverty rates, and household income (Figure 11.3).

Finally, prospects for Hispanics stagnated or worsened over the same period. Between 2000 and 2005, Hispanic household incomes (adjusted for inflation) decreased significantly. Yet the rate of Hispanic household poverty remained very similar to that of blacks (in 2003–2005 the weighted average poverty rate for Hispanics was 20.3 percent versus 22.4 percent for blacks). The large influx of poor immigrants explains some of the decline in average income, but even among Hispanics born in the United States, income levels declined. As one Latino group leader commented, "Most Hispanic residents are caught in jobs like gardener, nanny, and restaurant worker that will never pay well and from which they will never advance" (quoted in Goldberg 1997).

Health

Jake Najman (1993) surveyed the evidence linking health to racial and economic inequalities. He also considered strategies for improving the health of the poorer groups in society. After studying data for a number of countries, including the United States, he concluded that for people in the poorest 20 percent, as measured in terms of income, the death rates were 1.5–2.5 times those of the highest 20 percent of income earners. In the United States, the rate of infant mortality for the poorest 20 percent was four times higher than for the wealthiest 20 percent. When differences were measured between whites and African Americans in the United States, rather than only in terms of income, the contrast in infant mortality rates was even higher—five times higher for blacks than for whites. The contrast between races is also seen in life expectancy. In 2007, whites on average could expect to live 5.3 years longer than African Americans (Arias 2007; orig. April 19, 2006).

How might the influence of poverty and race on health be countered? Extensive programs of health education and disease prevention are one possibility. But such programs work better among prosperous, well-educated groups and usually produce only small changes in behavior. Increased accessibility

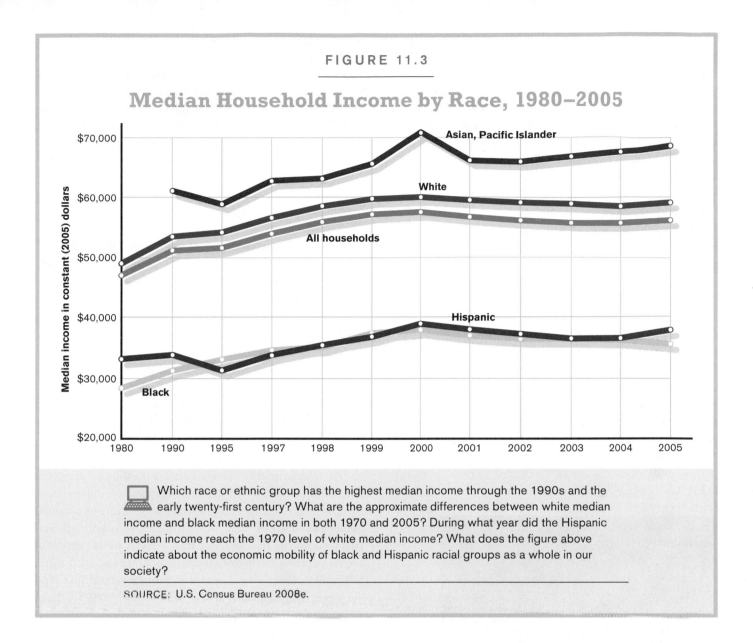

FIGURE 11.3

Median Household Income by Race, 1980–2005

Median income in constant (2005) dollars

Asian, Pacific Islander

White

All households

Hispanic

Black

$70,000

$60,000

$50,000

$40,000

$30,000

$20,000

1980 1990 1995 1997 1998 1999 2000 2001 2002 2003 2004 2005

Which race or ethnic group has the highest median income through the 1990s and the early twenty-first century? What are the approximate differences between white median income and black median income in both 1970 and 2005? During what year did the Hispanic median income reach the 1970 level of white median income? What does the figure above indicate about the economic mobility of black and Hispanic racial groups as a whole in our society?

SOURCE: U.S. Census Bureau 2008e.

to health services would help, but probably to a limited degree. The only really effective policy option, it is argued, would be to attack poverty itself, so as to reduce the income gap between rich and poor (Najman 1993).

Residential Segregation

Neighborhood segregation seems to have declined little over the past quarter century. Studies show that discriminatory practices between black and white clients in the housing market continue (Lake 1981). Black and white children now attend the same schools in most rural areas of the South and in many smaller and medium-size cities throughout the country. Most black college students now also attend the same colleges and

universities as whites, instead of all-black institutions (Bullock 1984). Yet in the larger cities, a high level of educational segregation persists as a result of the continuing movement of whites to suburbs or rural areas.

In *American Apartheid* (1993), Douglas Massey and Nancy A. Denton argue that the history of racial segregation and its urban form, the black ghetto, are responsible for the perpetuation of black poverty and the continued polarization of black and white. Even many middle-class blacks still find themselves segregated from the white society. For them, as for poor blacks, this becomes a self-perpetuating cycle. Affluent blacks who could afford to live in predominantly white neighborhoods may choose not to because of the struggle for acceptance they would face. The black ghetto, the authors conclude, was constructed through a series of well-defined institutional practices of racial discrimination—private behavior and public policies by which whites sought to contain growing urban black populations. Until policy makers, social scientists, and private citizens recognize the crucial role of such institutional discrimination in perpetuating urban poverty and racial injustice, the United States will remain a deeply divided and troubled society.

Political Power

Blacks have made gains in holding local elective offices; the number of black public officials has increased from forty in 1960 to 9,101 as of January 2001, the most recent year for which data are available (Bositis 2001). Blacks have been voted into every major political office. Most notably, in 2008, Barack Obama became the first African American to be elected president. He won by a large margin, including areas where whites predominate. In spite of high profile victories like Obama's, most of these individuals hold relatively minor local positions, although they do include quite a few mayors and judges. The share of representation that Latinos and African Americans have in Congress is not proportionate to their percentage of the population. In 2007, there were forty-two black members of the U.S. House of Representatives. But after the defeat of

Barack Obama became the first African American president of the United States in the historic election of 2008.

Senator Carol Moseley-Braun in 1998, the U.S. Senate had no black members until Barack Obama was elected to represent Illinois in 2004. In addition, three Latinos—Ken Salazar from Colorado, Bob Menendez from New Jersey, and Mel Martinez from Florida—serve in the U.S. Senate. These were the first in three decades. Martinez is the first Cuban American to be elected to the Senate in its history (National Association of Latino Elected Officials 2004).

Gender and Race

The status of minority women in the United States is especially plagued by inequalities (Figure 11.4). Gender and race discrimination combined make it particularly difficult for minority women to escape poverty. Until about twenty-five years ago, most minority women took low-paying occupations such as household work or low-wage manufacturing jobs. Changes in the law and gains in education have enabled more minority women to enter white-collar professions, and their economic and occupational status has improved. Between 1979 and 2006, inflation-adjusted earnings of black women grew by 19 percent, but this increase lagged behind that of white women, who experienced a 29 percent increase in earnings during the same period (U.S. Bureau of Labor Statistics 2007h). Although women made strides in earnings in the past three decades, stark race and gender earnings disparities persist. In 2006, among full-time workers, white women earned about 80 percent as much as their male counterparts, and black and Hispanic women had earnings that were about 88 percent of the earnings of their male counterparts. In actual dollars, full-time workers who were black women earned just $519 per week, compared to $609 for white women, $591 for black men, and $761 for white men in 2006 (U.S. Bureau of Labor Statistics 2007h).

Despite their unequal status and pay, minority women play a critical role in their communities. They are often the major or sole wage earners in their families, yet their incomes are not always sufficient to maintain a family. About half of all families headed by African American or Latino women live at poverty levels.

Divergent Fortunes

Our survey of the development and current position of the major ethnic groups in America indicates that they have achieved varying levels of success. Whereas successive waves of European immigrants have overcome considerable prejudice and discrimination and become assimilated into the wider society, other groups have not. The latter groups include two

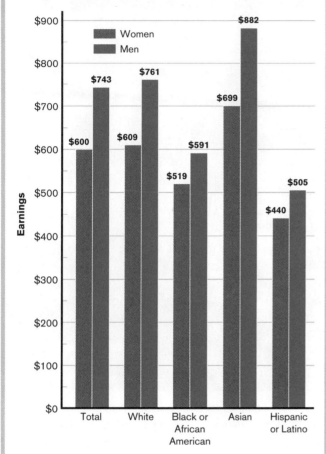

FIGURE 11.4

Median Weekly Income by Gender and Race, 2006

Earnings

Group	Women	Men
Total	$600	$743
White	$609	$761
Black or African American	$519	$591
Asian	$699	$882
Hispanic or Latino	$440	$505

According to the figure above, is the median weekly income of women from any of the three ethnic/racial groups reported to be more than their male counterparts? In 2006, what was the median weekly income of white males? Hispanic females? Which race/ethnic group has the greatest real discrepancy in median weekly income between its men and women? How much below the total male median weekly income is the median weekly income of black males? Think about what that would translate into for a year (fifty-two weeks). What two types of discrimination are illustrated in this figure?

SOURCE: U.S. Bureau of Labor Statistics 2007h.

minorities that have lived in North America for centuries, Native Americans and African Americans, as well as Mexicans, Puerto Ricans, and to some extent Chinese.

THE ECONOMIC DIVIDE WITHIN THE AFRICAN AMERICAN COMMUNITY

After more than two centuries of continuous presence in North America, blacks are in the worst situation, with the sole exception of Native Americans, of any ethnic group in the United States. The reasons lie in the historical backdrop of slavery and its residue in the long years of struggle against open prejudice and discrimination.

It seems probable that a division has arisen between the minority of blacks in white-collar, managerial, or professional jobs—who form a small black middle class—and the majority whose living conditions have not improved. In 1960, most of the nonmanual-labor jobs open to blacks were those serving the black community—as teachers, social workers, or less often, lawyers or doctors. No more than 13 percent of blacks held white-collar jobs, contrasted to 44 percent of whites. However, between 1960 and 1970 the percentage of blacks in white-collar occupations doubled—although this level of growth slowed markedly in the 1980s. The increase was greater than that for the half century previous to 1960. In 2006, African Americans were still underrepresented in white-collar jobs. Although blacks account for roughly 13 percent of the U.S. population, they held 8.4 percent of all managerial, professional, or related occupations and 11.2 percent of all sales and office occupations (U.S. Bureau of Labor Statistics 2007f).

Bart Landry (1988) studied the growing black middle class by surveying white-collar blacks and whites in twenty-one metropolitan areas across the country and analyzing government statistics from the early 1980s. He found that middle-class blacks were much better off, and much more numerous, than their predecessors twenty years before (see also Jacoby 1998). Opportunities opened up partly through changes in legislation resulting from the civil rights movement. However, the population of blacks in middle-class jobs remains well below that of whites, and their average incomes are less.

THE ASIAN SUCCESS STORY

Unlike African Americans, other minority groups have outlasted the open prejudice and discrimination they once faced. Intense hostility toward the Irish, for instance, is now mostly a distant memory. Although prejudice and antagonism still exist between people of Irish and Italian backgrounds in Boston and New York, and from both groups toward Jews, such feelings are much less pronounced than in former times and are not widely expressed in practices of discrimination.

The changing fate of Asians in the United States is especially remarkable. Until about half a century ago, the level of prejudice and discrimination experienced by the Chinese and Japanese in North America was greater than for any other group of nonblack immigrants. Since that time, Asian Americans have achieved a steadily increasing prosperity and decreasing antagonism from the white community. The median income of Asian Americans is now actually higher than that of whites.

Nevertheless, there remain discrepancies between and within different Asian groups; many Asian Americans, including those whose families have resided in the United States for generations, still live in poverty. However, the turnaround in the fortunes of Asian Americans, on the whole, is so impressive that some have referred to their success as a prime example of what minorities can achieve in the United States.

LATINOS: A TALE OF TWO CITIES

Miami and Los Angeles both have large Latino populations. In Los Angeles, the large majority of Latinos hold little privilege and power. But although both cities experience ethnic tensions, in Miami, Latinos have achieved a position of economic and political prominence not found elsewhere.

In *City on the Edge* (1993), Alejandro Portes and Alex Stepik describe the ethnic transformation of Miami. In 1980, whites were already a minority in the city, at 48 percent of the population. African Americans made up 17 percent, and those of Spanish origin, 35 percent. In that year, "the city abandoned, once and for all, the image of a sunny tourist destination and faced that of an uncertain bridge between two worlds." The reason was a large influx of Cuban immigrants. Struggles developed among the new immigrants, whites, and blacks; black leaders accused the Cubans of taking their jobs.

These struggles continue today. In Miami, those of Cuban origin generally wield considerable influence. Some Cubans have become very successful in business and are wealthier than the "old" white families that once ran the city. Because the Cubans have maintained their own customs, institutions, and language, Miami is now a place of "parallel structures" existing alongside one another, each including powerful and wealthy people not integrated into one unified group. There is much tension, but some Anglo and Cuban politicians now speak of Miami as the capital of the Caribbean—a city that is not only part of the United States but also linked to the other societies, mostly developing countries, surrounding it.

Los Angeles points to the Pacific Rim—what some analysts see as the future center of economic power, linking the West Coast of North America with Japan and the newly industrializing countries of Hong Kong, Taiwan, South Korea, and perhaps China. Immigrants from all these countries have arrived in Los Angeles, even as millions of Latinos have settled there.

Los Angeles has been called "the capital of the third world" because of its large Latino and Asian populations. The city

Hundreds of thousands of people marched in Los Angeles on May 1, 2006, to demand basic rights for immigrants.

already contained the largest group of Mexicans in the United States in the 1920s. Then, as now, Mexicans performed most of the menial jobs. Then, as now, most Anglos "were at once aware that this was the case," and "yet they would act as if these people, once they had finished working, went home not to the Old Plaza or, as now, to East L.A., but to another planet" (Rieff 1991).

Some optimistic observers have suggested that Los Angeles in the twenty-first century will combine Asian family loyalty, Hispanic industriousness, and Anglo-Saxon respect for individual liberty. Is such a vision possible? It would take profound social changes even to come close. Los Angeles is an ethnic mosaic that symbolizes the increasing diversity of American society as a whole. Will the Hispanic population there be able to achieve economic success similar to the Cubans in Miami? Will there be separate but equal Hispanic communities in Los Angeles as well as in other U.S. cities in the future? How will such successes, if they happen, affect the black urban poor? These are open questions to which no one can give certain answers.

Understanding Racial Inequality

What distinguishes less fortunate groups such as African Americans and Mexican Americans is not just that they are nonwhite, but that they were present in America as *colonized peoples* rather than as willing immigrants. In a classic analysis, Robert Blauner (1972) drew a sharp distinction between groups who journeyed voluntarily to settle in the new land and those who were incorporated into the society through force or violence. Native Americans are part of American society as a result of military conquest; African Americans were transported in the slave trade; Puerto Rico was colonized as a result of war; and Mexicans were incorporated as a result of the conquest of the Southwest by the United States in the nineteenth century. These groups have consistently been the targets of racism, which both reflects and perpetuates their separation from other ethnic communities.

But, given that this has been the case for most of American history, what explains the growth of the black middle class? William Julius Wilson (1978; see also Wilson et al. 1987) argues that race is of diminishing importance and that these inequalities are now based on class rather than skin color. The old racist barriers are crumbling. What remain are inequalities similar to those affecting all lower-class groups.

Wilson's work has proved controversial. His book won a prize by the American Sociological Association, but the Association of Black Sociologists passed a resolution stating that the book "omits significant data regarding the continuing discrimination against blacks at all class levels" (quoted in Pinkney 1984). The resolution criticized the view that blacks' circumstances have substantially improved or that racism has declined significantly. Most of the changes, it argued, have been relatively minor, and racism has become less evident only since the 1964 Civil Rights Act, rather than diminishing in any substantial sense.

Yet Wilson's book made it clear that the living conditions of poor blacks were deteriorating. In his view, critics have largely ignored this aspect of his work. He has since extended his analysis of the most deprived sectors of the black population. Most middle-class blacks today no longer live in ghetto neighborhoods. Their exodus has caused an even higher concentration of the disadvantaged in these areas. Wilson recognizes that racism plays a part in this situation but holds that other class-related and economic factors are equally important—in particular, the very high rate of unemployment and welfare dependency in the poorest neighborhoods. Wilson's argument is not so much that racism as such has declined but that it has declined in its significance for blacks. Other forms of discrimination based more on economic and class-based disadvantages are as important.

Are racial inequalities to be explained primarily in terms of class? It is true that racial divisions provide a means of social closure whereby privileged class groups can monopolize economic resources. But the argument that racial inequality primarily reflects class domination has never been a satisfactory one. Ethnic discrimination, particularly of a racial kind, is partly independent of class differences; the one cannot be separated from the other. This still seems true in the United States today.

For instance, opinion surveys show a general decline in hostile attitudes toward blacks among white Americans (Bobo and Kluegel 1991; Schuman et al. 1985). The overall level of prejudice seems to be diminishing markedly. David Wellman (1987) argues, however, that the concept of prejudice captures only the more open and individual forms of hostile attitudes toward ethnic minorities. Racism can also be expressed in more subtle ways—in terms of beliefs that defend the position of privileged groups. Many sociologists, according to Wellman, have underestimated the true incidence of racism because they have only examined its more obvious manifestations. Most studies have used surveys, but these do not identify the less obvious, complex aspects of people's views about such emotionally charged topics as ethnicity and race.

Wellman sought to illuminate these complex aspects of racism by means of in-depth interviews with 105 white Americans of various backgrounds. Most interviewees said that they believed everyone is equal and that they held no hostility toward blacks. Their beliefs and attitudes did not show the rigidities characteristic of prejudice and stereotypical thinking. Yet their views about contexts of social life (such as education, housing, or jobs) in which black rights threatened their own position were effectively antiblack. Their opposition to change came out in ways that did not directly express racial antagonism. People would say, for instance, "I'm not opposed to blacks; but if they come into the neighborhood house prices will be affected"—or, as one individual put it, "I favor anything that doesn't affect me personally" (Wellman 1987).

These attitudes can still underlie rigid institutional patterns of discrimination. Ethnic inequalities are structured into existing social institutions, and patterns of behavior having no immediate connection to ethnicity can reinforce them. Rights and opportunities are not the same thing. Even if every member of the population were to agree that members of all ethnic groups have the same civil rights, major inequalities would persist. Many examples demonstrate this. Consider a black person who applies for a bank loan to make home improvements but who gets turned down. The bank might use purely "objective" measures in reaching its decision, based on this type of borrower's statistical likelihood of successfully making loan repayments. Nevertheless, the effect of this institutional racism is the perpetuation of discrimination (Massey and Denton 1993).

In sum, although both individual racism and institutional racism seem to be declining in the United States, the differences between white and nonwhite ethnic groups endure (Conley 1999; Ringer 1985). Moreover, the relative success of white ethnics has been purchased partly at the expense of nonwhites. A combination of continued white immigration and white racism, up to at least the World War II period, kept nonwhites out of the better-paid occupations, forcing them into the least-skilled, most marginal sectors of the economy. With the slowing down of white immigration, this situation is changing, although some newly arrived groups, like the Cubans in Miami, seem to be repeating the process.

☑ CONCEPT CHECKS

1. What are some of the main reasons there is a large gap in educational attainment between Hispanics and blacks in the United States?
2. How do Massey and Denton explain the persistence of residential segregation?
3. Some sociologists argue that racial inequalities should be explained in terms of class rather than race. What are some problems associated with social class–based explanations of racial inequalities?

Study Outline
www.wwnorton.com/studyspace

Race and Ethnicity: Key Concepts

- Ethnic groups have common cultural characteristics that separate them from others within a given population. Ethnic differences are wholly learned, although they are sometimes depicted as "natural."
- *Race* refers to physical characteristics, such as skin color, that are treated by members of a community or society as signaling distinct cultural characteristics. Many popular beliefs about race are untrue. There are no distinct characteristics by which human beings can be allocated to different races.
- *Racism* is prejudice based on socially significant physical distinctions. A racist is a person who believes that some individuals are superior, or inferior, to others as a result of racial differences.
- *Displacement* and *scapegoating* are psychological mechanisms associated with *prejudice* and *discrimination*. In displacement, feelings of hostility become directed against objects that are not the real origin of these anxieties. People project their anxieties and insecurities onto scapegoats. Prejudice involves holding preconceived views about an individual or group; discrimination refers to behavior that prevents members of a group from having opportunities that are open to others. Prejudice usually involves *stereotypical thinking*—that is, thinking in terms of inflexible categories.

Ethnic Relations

- There are four models of possible developments in race and ethnic relations—the first stressing Anglo-conformity, or *assimilation;* the second, the *melting pot;* the third, *pluralism;* and the fourth, *multiculturalism.* Recent years have seen an emphasis on the fourth model, whereby different ethnic identities are accepted as equal and separate within the overall national culture.

Global Migration

- Beginning in the fifteenth century, global migratory movements resulting from exploration, colonialism, and slavery created multiethnic populations in various regions, contributing to ethnic and racial antagonism. Today, migration is increasing as part of the process of globalization.

Ethnic Relations in the United States

- A remarkable diversity of ethnic minorities exists in the United States today, with each group having distinctive cultural characteristics. Some of the most important minority communities numerically, after blacks, are Native Americans, Mexican Americans, Puerto Ricans, Cubans, Chinese, and Japanese.

Racial and Ethnic Inequality

- There is an important distinction between minorities that came to America as willing immigrants and the colonized peoples who either were here already (Native Americans, Mexican Americans) or were brought by force (African Americans) and incorporated by violence. Racism targeted at the latter groups has been most persistent and most destructive. Gender discrimination compounds the difficulties facing women of color; about half of African American and Latino families that depend on women's incomes live in poverty.

Key Concepts

Review Questions

1. What are the similarities and differences between the concepts of ethnicity and race? Give an example to illustrate the complexity of these definitions.

2. Describe two examples of racial classification systems discussed in Chapter 11. What do these examples tell us about the socially constructed nature of race?

3. How do the concepts of "symbolic ethnicity," "situational ethnicity," and "multiraciality" demonstrate the socially constructed nature of race and ethnicity?

4. Discuss the types of racism identified in the text. What are some examples and implications of each?

5. Compare and contrast the definitions of prejudice, discrimination, and racism. Give examples of each.

6. What is the relationship between colonialism and contemporary ethnic conflict? How does globalization intensify ethnic conflict?

7. What are some proposals to reduce ethnic conflict around the globe? What are their weaknesses? What would you propose?

8. Compare and contrast four models of migration. What are the push and pull factors?

9. What are the key characteristics of a diaspora? Give an example of a diasporic community and show how this fits the characteristics described in the text.

10. Describe three theories that sociologists use to explain racial inequality. What explanation do you find most convincing and why?

Thinking Sociologically Exercises

1. Review the discussion of the assimilation of different American minorities. Then write a short essay comparing the assimilation experiences of Asians and Latinos. In your essay, identify the criteria for assimilation and discuss which group has assimilated most readily. Then explain the sociological reasons for the difference in assimilation between the two groups.

2. Does affirmative action still have a future in the United States? On the one hand, increasing numbers of African Americans have joined the middle class by acquiring college degrees, professional jobs, and new homes. On the other hand, blacks are still far more likely than whites to live in poverty, to attend poor schools, and to lack economic opportunity. Given these differences and other contrasts mentioned in the text, do we still need affirmative action?

Learning Objectives

The Graying of U.S. Society

Learn some basic facts about the increase in the proportion of the U.S. population that is becoming elderly.

How Do People Age?

Understand that aging is a combination of biological, psychological, and sociological processes.

Growing Old: Competing Sociological Explanations

Consider the various theories of aging, particularly those that focus on how society shapes the social roles of the elderly and emphasize aspects of age stratification.

Aging in the United States

Evaluate the experience of growing old in the United States.

The Politics of Aging

Understand and analyze the politics of generational equity.

Globalization: The Graying of the World Population

Assess the social issues of graying on a global level.

CHAPTER TWELVE

AGING

When Fenya Crown decided to run her first marathon, the Los Angeles Marathon, she was seventy years old. That was more than twenty-five years ago. Since that time, she has completed eight of the 26.2-mile races, most recently the Rome, Italy, marathon in March 2001. The ninety-six-year-old great-grandmother, who has recovered from three bouts of breast cancer during the past decade, has completed marathons from New York to Shanghai. Born in Ukraine in 1913, Crown emigrated to the United States, where she worked for many years as a dress designer in New York City's garment district.

Like Crown, Rose Freedman also worked as a young woman in the New York City garment industry. Although she never ran a marathon, she nonetheless possessed the endurance to work twelve- to fourteen-hour days as a seamstress in the city's garment factories. In 1911, at age eighteen, Freedman was working in the Triangle Shirtwaist Factory when fire swept through the building. She survived by racing up several floors to the factory's roof and then leaping to the safety of another building. Most of her co-workers—young female Jewish and Italian immigrants—were not so lucky: within thirty minutes, 500 were injured and 146 dead. The Triangle fire spurred the unionization of the garment industry and left Freedman with indelible memories of the disaster. She continued to speak out against abuses in the garment industry until her death in February 2001—at age 107.

John Glenn, born in 1921, was seventy-seven years old when he completed a ten-day research mission in orbit aboard the space shuttle *Discovery* in the fall of 1998. This was not Glenn's first venture into space. Thirty-two years earlier, the longtime Democratic U.S. senator from Ohio was the first American astronaut in space, when he completed three orbits around the earth as part of America's fledgling space program. The purpose of Glenn's most recent trip was to study the effects of aging in the weightless environment of space. Glenn, who exercises daily and lifts weights, is in excellent shape. As expressed by National Aeronautics and Space Administration (NASA) administrator Daniel Goldin, Glenn was "poised to show the world that senior citizens have the right stuff."

More and more Americans are leading longer, healthier, and more productive lives than ever before. In 2005, nearly thirty-seven million Americans were age sixty-five or older, including some five million over eighty-five years old (U.S. Bureau of the Census 2007j). Growing old can be a fulfilling and rewarding experience, as it is with the people just described. Or it can be filled with physical impairment, psychological distress, and social isolation. For most older Americans, the experience of aging lies somewhere in between.

In this chapter, we examine the nature of aging in U.S. society, exploring what it means to grow old in a world that is rapidly changing. We begin with a brief snapshot of how the U.S. population is growing older, before examining biological, psychological, and social aspects of aging. We then look at the ways in which people adapt to growing old, at least in the eyes of sociologists. This will lead us to a discussion of aging in the United States, focusing on some of the special challenges and problems that elderly persons face. We also discuss political issues surrounding the aging of the American population, issues that assume increasing importance given the growing numbers of elderly people. We conclude with a discussion of the graying of the world population and what it can mean for you.

The Graying of U.S. Society

The world's population is getting older. About two thousand years ago, the average newborn baby in Rome could expect to live to the ripe old age of twenty-two. In fact, for most of human history the average life expectancy at birth was less than twenty years, with most people failing to survive the first few years of life. The average baby born into the world today can expect to live to be sixty-seven, although there is enormous variation, depending on where the baby is born—from an average life expectancy of eighty-five for women in Japan to one of thirty-two in Swaziland for both men and women (Weiss 1997; World Bank 2005). These changes are due to many factors. Modern agriculture, sanitation systems, epidemic control, and medicine have all contributed to a decline in mortality throughout the world. In most societies today, fewer children die in infancy, and more adults survive to become elderly.

The U.S. population, like other industrial societies, is aging even faster than the preindustrial societies of the world. Thanks to better nutrition and health care, people are living longer. They are also having fewer children. As a result, the median age of the population is rising. In 1850, half the population were younger than nineteen, and half were older. Today, half are over thirty-five; by the middle of the century, half will be over forty (Figure 12.1).

As a result, the United States and other industrial societies are said to be **graying**—that is, experiencing an increase in the proportion of the population becoming elderly. Graying is the result of two long-term trends in industrial societies: the tendency of families to have fewer children (discussed in Chapter 15) and the fact that people are living longer. The average life expectancy at birth for all Americans increased from forty-seven years for someone born in 1900 to seventy-eight years for someone born today (Figure 12.2). The average U.S. male born today can expect to live to about seventy-five; for females, the figure is over eighty. Most of these gains occurred in the first half of the twentieth century and were largely because of the improved chances for survival among the young. Although relatively few people made it to age sixty-five in the year 1900, most of those who did could expect to live to age seventy-seven—almost as long as most of those people who make it to sixty-five today, who can expect to live to eighty-three (National Center for Health Statistics 2008a). Those persons who were healthy and robust enough to survive through infancy, childhood, early adulthood, and mid-adulthood had protective resources that enabled them to live many years in later life.

Because of the graying of the American population, there are today roughly thirty-seven million Americans older than sixty-five, a figure forecast to top seventy million people by the year 2030 (Treas 1995; U.S. Bureau of the Census 2004a). According to U.S. Bureau of the Census estimates, 25 percent of all people reaching age sixty-five today will live to be ninety. By the middle of this century, that figure is expected to rise to 42 percent. According to some projections, by that time there may be as many as two million living Americans who have celebrated their one-hundredth birthday (Healthful Life Project 2003; Weiss 1997).

These trends have enormous importance for the future of American society. In a culture that often worships eternal youth, what will happen when a quarter of the population is over sixty-five?

FIGURE 12.1

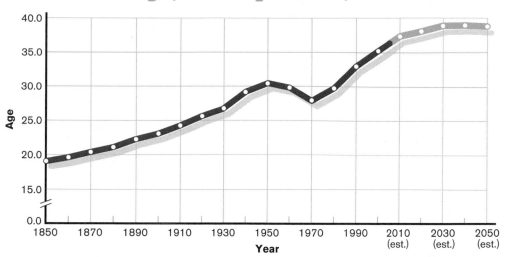

Median Age, U.S. Population, 1850–2050

How much did the median age of the U.S. population rise from 1910 to the estimate in 2010? Did the median age ever decline? If so, in what years and what could be the historical reason for this? How does the increase in median age in the forty years from 1910 to 1950 compare to the forty-year increase from 1970 to the estimate for 2010? What is the predicted trend for the median age of the population from 2030 to 2050? What are two long-term trends in the United States and other industrialized countries that account for the "graying" of these nations?

SOURCE: U.S. Bureau of the Census 2002.

✓ CONCEPT CHECKS

1. What is the graying of the United States population?
2. What two long-term trends have contributed to this graying?
3. By how much will the U.S. elderly population increase over the next five decades?

How Do People Age?

In examining the nature of aging, we will draw on studies of **social gerontology**, a discipline concerned with the study of the social aspects of aging. Studying aging is a bit like examining a moving target: As people grow older, society itself changes at the same time, and so does the very meaning of being "old" (Riley et al. 1988). For Americans born in the first quarter of the twentieth century, a high school education was regarded as more than sufficient for most available jobs, and most people did not expect to live much past their sixties—and then only at the cost of suffering a variety of disabilities. Today those very same people find themselves in their seventies and eighties; many are relatively healthy, unwilling to disengage from work and social life, and in need of more schooling than they ever dreamed would be necessary.

What does it mean to age? **Aging** can be sociologically defined as the combination of biological, psychological, and social processes that affect people as they grow older (Abeles and Riley 1987; Atchley 2000; Riley et al. 1988). These three processes suggest the metaphor of three different, although interrelated, developmental clocks: (1) a biological one, which refers to the physical body; (2) a psychological one, which refers to the mind and mental capabilities; and (3) a social one, which refers to cultural norms, values, and role expectations having to do with age. There is an enormous range of variation in all three of these processes, as we discuss next.

FIGURE 12.2

Average Life Expectancy at Birth for Males and Females, 1900–2007 in the United States

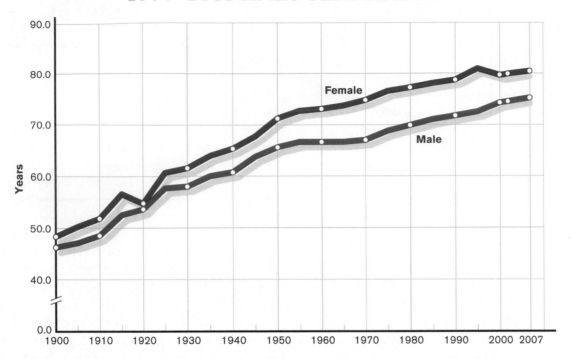

During which years in the last century was male life expectancy at birth greater than that of females? What is the difference in life expectancy at birth (in years) between men and women in 1900? In 1990? During the last century, which decade showed the smallest increase in male life expectancy? During what years did women's life expectancy at birth show a decline? How can age be socially constructed?

SOURCE: U.S. Department at Health and Human Services 2007.

Our notions about the meaning of age are rapidly changing, both because recent research is dispelling many myths about aging and because advances in nutrition and health have enabled many people to live longer, healthier lives than ever before.

Biological Aging

The biological effects of aging are well established, although the exact chronological age at which they occur varies greatly from individual to individual, depending on genetics, lifestyle, and luck. In general, for men and women alike, biological aging typically means:

- Declining vision, as the eye lens loses its elasticity (small print is the bane of most people over fifty)
- Hearing loss, first of higher-pitched tones, then of lower-pitched ones
- Wrinkles, as the skin's underlying structure becomes more and more brittle (billions of dollars invested in skin lotion and increasingly common surgical face lifts only delay the inevitable)
- A decline of muscle mass and an accompanying accumulation of fat, especially around the middle (eating habits that were offset by exercise when you were twenty-five come back to haunt you when you are fifty)
- A drop in cardiovascular efficiency, as less oxygen can be inhaled and used during exercise (lifelong runners who

ran six-minute miles at age thirty are happy to break eight-minute miles once they turn sixty)

The normal processes of aging are inevitable, but they can be partly compensated for and offset by good health, proper diet and nutrition, and a reasonable amount of exercise (John 1988). Lifestyle can make a significant health difference for people of all ages. For many people, the physical changes of aging do not significantly prevent them from leading active, independent lives well into their eighties. Some scientists have even argued that with a proper lifestyle and advances in medical technology, more and more people will be able to live relatively illness-free lives until they reach their biological maximum, experiencing only a brief period of sickness just before death (Fries 1980). Eventually, of course, the biological clock runs out for everyone. About ninety to one hundred years seems to be the upper end of the genetically determined age distribution for most human beings, although some have argued that it may be as high as 120 (Atchley 2000; Fries 1980; Rusting 1992; Treas 1995).

Even though the majority of older Americans suffer no significant physical impairment and remain physically active, unfortunate stereotypes about the "weak and frail elderly" continue to exist (Heise 1987). These stereotypes have more to do with the social than with the biological meaning of aging in U.S. culture, which is preoccupied with youthfulness and fears of growing old and dying.

Psychological Aging

The psychological effects of aging are much less well established than the physical effects. Even though memory, intelligence, skills, and both the capacity and motivation to learn are widely assumed to decline with age, research into the psychology of aging suggests a much more complicated process (Birren and Cunningham 1985; Schaie 1984). Memory and learning ability, for example, do not decline significantly until very late in life for most people, although the speed with which one recalls or analyzes information may slow somewhat, giving the false impression of mental impairment. For most elderly people whose lives are stimulating and rich, such mental abilities as motivation to learn, clarity of thought, and problem-solving capacity do not decline significantly until the late eighties (Abeles and Riley 1987; Atchley 2000; Baltes and Schaie 1977; Cutler and Grams 1988; Schaie 1979; Schooler 1987).

Even **Alzheimer's disease**, the progressive deterioration of brain cells that is the primary cause of dementia in old age, is relatively rare in noninstitutionalized persons under seventy-five, although it may afflict as many as half of all people over eighty-five. Former president Ronald Reagan is perhaps the most famous example of someone who suffered from Alzheimer's (Treas 1995).

Social Aging

Social age consists of the norms, values, and roles that are culturally associated with a particular chronological age. Ideas about social age differ from one society to another and, at least in modern industrial societies, change over historical time. Societies such as Japan and China have traditionally revered elderly people, regarding them as a source of historical memory and wisdom. Societies such as the United States are more likely to dismiss them as nonproductive, dependent people who are out of step with the times—both because they are less likely to have the high-tech skills so valued by young people and because of American culture's obsession with youthfulness. In a country where the approximately seventy-five million once youthful baby boomers born in the decade after World War II are now turning sixty at the rate of one every seven seconds, a fortune is being spent on prescription drugs, plastic surgery, and home remedies that promise eternal youth. These include such things as tummy tucks and face lifts, antibaldness pills and lotions, and pills that claim to increase memory and concentration. In the United States today, doctors prescribe impotence drugs about seventeen million times a year, to roughly five million men. However, this is considerably lower than the nearly forty million prescriptions for osteoporosis medications and one hundred million for antidepressants prescribed each year—underscoring the importance of social, biological, and psychological influences on the aging process (Berenson 2005).

As baby boomers age, the demand for products to make them look and feel younger grows. A recent trend is Botox parties such as the one pictured above, where doctors inject the drug into participants to remove wrinkles.

"Positive Thinking 'Extends' Life"

Can positive thinking bring good health and long life to older adults? In the early 2000s, a flurry of uplifting news headlines informed older adults that "Positive Thinking Extends Life" (BBC News 2002) and "Power of Positive Thinking Extends, It Seems, to Aging" (Duenwald 2002). While no one would argue against positive thinking, social scientists disagree as to whether, how, and by how much optimistic thoughts can improve older adults' health and extend their life span. They also question whether it's in the best interest for older adults to believe that simply *thinking* positive is enough to guarantee a long and healthy life.

Yale University researcher Becca Levy and colleagues have found persuasive evidence that keeping your chin up can help to fend off death (Levy, Slade, Kunkel, and Kasl 2002). Their study focused on a sample of 660 volunteer subjects who were

age fifty and older when the study began in 1975. At that time, the subjects were asked questions about their attitudes toward aging. They reported their level of agreement or disagreement with statements such as "Things keep getting worse as I get older," "As you get older, you are less useful," "I am as happy now as I was when I was younger," and "I have as much pep as I did last year." The researchers followed up the study participants, and

found that by the ten-year follow-up interview, 87 percent of those with positive attitudes yet just 66 percent of those with negative attitudes were still alive. The pattern was even more pronounced at the twenty-two-year follow-up, when 50 percent of those with positive attitudes yet just 27 percent of those with negative attitudes were still alive.

The researchers also found that persons who viewed aging as a positive experience lived 7.5 years longer, on average, than those who had a bleaker outlook. The life-extending effect of having a positive attitude was larger than the effect of positive physiological indicators, such as lowering blood pressure and cholesterol levels—each of which added just four years to life. Health behaviors like exercising, not smoking, and maintaining a healthy weight each added just one to three years to the older adults' life spans.

Role expectations are extremely important sources of one's personal identity. Some of the roles associated with aging in American society are positive: Supreme Court justice, senior adviser, doting grandparent, religious elder, wise spiritual teacher. Other roles may be damaging, leading to lowered self-esteem and isolation. Highly stigmatizing stereotypical roles for older people in American culture include grumpy old man (or woman), old-fashioned senior citizen, spinster, and mentally confused doddering old man. In fact, like all people, older adults do not simply passively play out assigned social roles; they actively shape and redefine them (Riley et al. 1988).

☑ CONCEPT CHECKS

1. What are the three types of aging processes?

2. Compare and contrast biological, psychological, and social aging processes.

Growing Old: Competing Sociological Explanations

Social gerontologists have offered a number of theories regarding the nature of aging in U.S. society. Some of the earliest theories emphasized individual adaptation to changing social roles as a person grows older. Later theories focused on how society shapes the social roles of the elderly, often in inequitable ways,

Levy and collaborators are quick to point out that healthy behaviors are very important and that older adults shouldn't try to replace healthy practices with positive thoughts. They also believe that the protective effects of positive attitudes on life span are probably *indirect effects*. That means that positive attitudes lead to some other trait or behavior which, in turn, adds years to life. Specifically, they hypothesized that those with positive aging attitudes would have a greater will to live, and this greater will to live, in turn, would extend the life span. They conducted statistical analyses and found that the will to live only partly explained the link between positive thinking and long life. The scientists reasoned further that older people who endorse negative attitudes toward aging may respond poorly to stress and thus have more health conditions which shorten their life span.

Some skeptics argue that the relationship between positive aging attitudes and long life span may be *spurious* rather than *causal*, meaning that a third factor—such as a conscientious personality, emotional stability, high-quality interpersonal relationships, or active participation in work, family, or volunteering activities—might be associated with *both* having a positive outlook and having a long life. Levy and her colleagues considered a long list of possible "third factors," such as socioeconomic resources, health, and morale, and found that even after they "controlled" for these possible influences, the life-extending effects of positive thinking were still statistically significant.

Social and medical scientists worry that simplistic messages like "think positive" might have unintended negative consequences for older adults, however. Dr. Morton Lieberman, a psychologist at the University of California at San Francisco, has argued that "it's a bad idea to tell people to cheer up and you'll live longer. We should be beyond the point where we think it's just mind over body" (Duenwald 2002). Other scientists believe that positive attitudes may provide emotional benefits but that people should not expect physical health benefits. University of Pennsylvania researcher James Coyne observes that optimism and positive thinking may "have lots of emotional and social benefits" but that older adults should not have the "expectation that they are extending their lives."

Questions

- Do you find the research by Levy and colleagues to be convincing evidence that positive thoughts can extend older adults' life spans? Why or why not?
- What is a spurious relationship? What is an indirect effect?
- What practical advice for older adults might be drawn from scientific research on positive attitudes and life expectancy?

FOR FURTHER EXPLORATION

BBC News. 2002. "Positive Thinking 'Extends Life.'" BBC News, July 29, 2002. http://news.bbc.co.uk/1/hi/health/2158336.stm (accessed January 11, 2008).

Duenwald, Mary. 2002. "Power of Positive Thinking Extends, It Seems, to Aging." *New York Times,* November 19, 2002. http://query.nytimes.com/gst/fullpage.html?res=9B03E2DA1130F93AA25752C1A9649C8B63 (accessed January 11, 2008).

Hawkes, Nigel. 2007. "Enjoy the Power of Positive Thinking, but It Won't Help You Beat Cancer." *The Times,* October 22, 2007. www.timesonline.co.uk/tol/news/uk/health/article2710130.ece (accessed January 11, 2008).

Levy, Becca, Martin D. Slade, Suzanne R. Kunkel, and Stanislav V. Kasl. 2002. "Longevity Increased by Positive Self-Perceptions of Aging." *Journal of Personality and Social Psychology* 83(2): 261–270.

and emphasized various aspects of age stratification. The most recent theories have been more multifaceted, focusing on the ways in which the elderly actively create their lives within specific institutional contexts (Hendricks 1992).

The First Generation of Theories: Functionalism

The earliest theories of aging reflected the functionalist approach that was dominant in sociology during the 1950s and 1960s. They emphasized how individuals adjusted to changing social roles as they aged and how those roles were useful to society. The earliest theories often assumed that aging brings with it physical and psychological decline and that changing social roles have to take this decline into account (Hendricks 1992).

Talcott Parsons (1960), one of the most influential functionalist theorists of the 1950s, argued that U.S. society needs to find roles for the elderly consistent with advanced age. He expressed concern that the United States, with its emphasis on youth and its avoidance of death, had failed to provide roles that adequately drew on the potential wisdom and maturity of its older citizens. Moreover, given the graying of U.S. society that was evident even in Parsons's time, he argued that this failure could well lead to older people's becoming discouraged and alienated from society. To achieve a "healthy maturity," Parsons (1960) argued, elderly persons need to adjust psychologically to their changed circumstances, while society needs

Some societies have traditionally revered the elderly. Here the young respect the old with an offering of tea, a traditional Chinese custom.

to redefine the social roles of the elderly. Formerly held social roles (such as work) have to be abandoned, while new forms of productive activity (such as volunteer service) need to be identified.

Parsons's ideas set the stage for the development of **disengagement theory**, the notion that it is functional for society to remove people from their traditional roles when they become elderly, thereby freeing up those roles for others (Cumming and Henry 1961; Estes et al. 1992). According to this perspective, given the increasing frailty, illness, and dependency of elderly people, it becomes increasingly dysfunctional for them to occupy traditional social roles they are no longer capable of adequately fulfilling. The elderly therefore should retire from their jobs, pull back from civic life, and eventually withdraw from other activities as well. Disengagement is assumed to be functional for the larger society because it opens up roles formerly filled by the elderly for younger people, who presumably will carry them out with fresh energy and new skills. Disengagement is also assumed to be functional for the elderly person, because it enables them to take on less taxing roles consistent with their advancing age and declining health. A number of studies of older adults indeed report that the large majority feel good about retiring, which they claim has improved their

morale and increased their happiness (Atchley 2000; Crowley 1985; Howard et al. 1986; Palmore et al. 1985).

Although there is some empirical support and ample anecdotal evidence for disengagement theory, the idea that elderly people should completely disengage from the larger society takes for granted the prevailing stereotype that old age necessarily involves frailty and dependence. As a result, no sooner did the theory appear than these very assumptions were challenged, often by some of the theory's original proponents (Cumming 1963, 1975; Hendricks 1992; Henry 1965; Hochschild 1975; Maddox 1965, 1970). These challenges gave rise to another functionalist theory of aging, which drew conclusions quite opposite to those of disengagement theory: *activity theory*.

According to **activity theory**, elderly people who are busy and engaged, leading fulfilling and productive lives, can be functional for society. Activity theory regards aging as a normal part of human development and argues that elderly people can best serve society, as well as themselves, by remaining active as long as possible. Although there may come a time in most people's lives when disengagement will best serve their interests as well as society's, activity theory argues that an active individual is much more likely to remain healthy, alert, and socially useful. In this view, people should remain engaged in their work and other social roles as long as they are capable of doing so. If a time comes when a particular role becomes too difficult or taxing, then other roles can be sought—for example, volunteer work in the community.

Activity theory finds support in research showing that continued activity well into old age is associated with enhanced mental and physical health (Birren and Bengston 1988; Rowe and Kahn 1987; Schaie 1983). For example, there is some evidence that continued part- or full-time employment is associated with higher morale and happiness, possibly because of the expanded friendship networks that result from continued work (Bosse et al. 1987; Conner et al. 1985; Mor-Barak et al. 1992; Riddick 1985; Soumerai and Avorn 1983).

Critics of functionalist theories of aging argue that these theories emphasize the need for the elderly to adapt to existing conditions, either by disengaging from socially useful roles or by actively pursuing them, but that they do not question whether the circumstances faced by the elderly are just. In response to this critique, another group of theorists arose—those growing out of the social conflict tradition (Hendricks 1992).

The Second Generation of Theories: Social Conflict

Unlike their predecessors, who emphasized the ways that elderly persons could be integrated into the larger society, the second generation of theorists focused on sources of social conflict between the elderly and society (Hendricks 1992). Much like other theorists who were studying social conflict in U.S. society during the 1970s and early 1980s, these theorists stressed the ways in which the larger social structure helped shape the opportunities available to the elderly; unequal opportunities were seen as creating the potential for conflict.

According to this view, many of the problems of aging—such as poverty, inadequate health care, or lack of decent nursing homes—are systematically produced by the routine operation of social institutions. A capitalist society, the reasoning goes, favors those who are most economically powerful. While there are certainly some elderly people who have "made it" and are set for life, many have not—and these people must fight to get even a meager share of society's scarce resources.

Conflict theories of aging flourished during the 1980s, when a shrinking job base and cutbacks in federal spending threatened to pit different social groups against each other in the competition for scarce resources. Older persons were seen as competing with the young for increasingly scarce jobs and dwindling federal dollars. Conflict theorists further pointed out that even among the elderly, those who fared worst were women, low-income people, and minorities, in a cumulating spiral of social conflict (Atchley 2000; Estes 1986, 1991; Estes et al. 1982, 1984; Hendricks 1992; Hendricks and Hendricks 1986; McKinlay 1975).

Older people are informed by experience and possess knowledge and skills that can be beneficial to young people. In turn, keeping active and maintaining close contact with young people can be vital in shaping a positive self-concept among the elderly.

The Third Generation of Theories: Self-Concept and Aging

The most recent theories reject what they regard as the one-sided emphases of both functionalism and conflict theory. They view elderly persons as playing an active role in determining their own physical and mental well-being, rather than as merely adapting to the larger society (functionalism) or as victims of the stratification system (social conflict). Circumstances such as family, work, and living situation are important sources of one's self-concept, which in turn affects one's life satisfaction. The elderly are seen as playing a significant role in shaping those circumstances (Dannefer 1989; Hendricks 1992; Schaie and Hendricks 2000).

One research project, for example, involved a partnership between the Margaret Warner School of Education and Human Development at the University of Rochester (New York) and two local nursing homes. The project was set up to study how changes in the organizational culture of the homes—as seen in such things as architecture, physical layout, and programming—can affect resident satisfaction and well-being. The objective was to increase social interaction among

residents, involving them in satisfying and useful activities. In the words of social gerontologist Dale Dannefer, who headed the project, "If we expect people in nursing homes to improve their health and thrive, to remain socially engaged and make contributions to the lives of others, it should show up in measurable gains in their health and functional status" (quoted in Dickman 1999). These recent theories also emphasize the increasing diversity among the elderly, showing how people age differently, depending on their circumstances (Nelson and Dannefer 1992). Many provide detailed ethnographic accounts of what it means to grow old in U.S. society, with concrete illustrations from elderly people's lives (Gubrium 1986, 1991, 1993; Gubrium and Sankar 1994).

☑ CONCEPT CHECKS

1. Summarize the three theoretical frameworks used to describe the nature of aging in U.S. society.
2. What are the main critiques of functionalism and conflict theory?

Aging in the United States

The elderly make up a highly diverse category about whom few broad generalizations can be made. For one thing, elderly persons reflect the diversity of U.S. society that we've noted elsewhere in this textbook: They are rich, poor, and in between; they belong to all racial and ethnic groups; they live alone and in families of various sorts; they vary in their political values and preferences; and they are gay and lesbian as well as heterosexual. Furthermore, like other Americans, they are diverse with respect to health: Although some suffer from mental and physical disabilities, most lead active, independent lives.

There are significant racial differences among the elderly. Whites, on average, live five years longer than African Americans, largely because blacks have much higher rates of poverty and therefore are more likely to suffer from inadequate health care and poor health behaviors. As a result, a much higher percentage of whites are elderly than other racial groups (Table 12.1). The combined effect of race and sex is substantial— white women live, on average, twelve years longer than black men. Hispanics are graying the least, partly because this category includes many young immigrant workers with large families.

Currently, 3.8 million of the elderly population in the United States are foreign born (U.S. Bureau of the Census 2008f). In California, New York, Hawaii, and other states that receive large numbers of immigrants, as much as one fifth of the elderly population were born outside the United States (Treas 1995). Most elderly immigrants either do not speak English well or do not speak it at all. Integrating elderly immigrants into U.S. society poses special challenges: Some are highly educated, but most are not. Many require special education and training programs. Most lack a retirement income, so that they depend on their families or public assistance for support. Among those who arrived in the United States during the 1990s, 22 percent of individuals sixty-five years and over were living in poverty in 1999, over twice the rate of elderly people born in this country (U.S. Bureau of the Census 2000b). In 2005, approximately 632,000 (16.2 percent) foreign-born elders were living below the poverty level in the United States (Pew Hispanic Center 2006).

Finally, as people live to increasingly older ages, the elderly are becoming diverse in terms of age itself. It is useful to distinguish between different age categories of the elderly, such as the **young old** (ages sixty-five to seventy-four), the **old old** (ages seventy-five to eighty-four), and the **oldest old** (ages eighty-five and older) (Figure 12.3). The "young old" are most likely to be economically independent, healthy, active, and engaged; the oldest old—the fastest-growing segment of the elderly population—are most likely to encounter difficulties such as poor health, financial insecurity, isolation, and loneliness. These differences are not necessarily due only to the effects of aging; they may also reflect one's birth cohort. The young old came of age during the post–World War II period of strong economic growth and benefited as a result: They are more likely to be educated; to have acquired wealth in the form of a home, savings, or investments; and to have had many years of stable employment. These advantages are much less likely to be enjoyed by the oldest old, partly because their education and careers began at an earlier time, when economic conditions were not so favorable (Treas 1995).

What is the experience of growing old in the United States? Although the elderly do face some special challenges, most older people lead relatively healthy, satisfying lives. Still, one national survey found a substantial discrepancy between what most Americans under sixty-five thought life would be like

---

TABLE 12.1

Percentage of Population over Sixty-Five and over Seventy-Five, in Different Racial Groups, 2007

Whites make up a higher percentage of the elderly than any other group. This is the result of lower fertility (whites have fewer children on average) and greater longevity (whites tend to live longer than most other racial and ethnic groups).

RACIAL GROUP	OVER AGE 65	OVER AGE 75
White	14.4	7.2
Black	8.5	3.7
Asian	9.4	3.9
American Indian	7.6	3.0
Native Hawaiian/ Other Pacific Islander	6.1	2.2
Hispanic (any race)	5.5	2.3
TOTAL	12.5	6.1

SOURCE: U.S. Bureau of the Census 2008f.

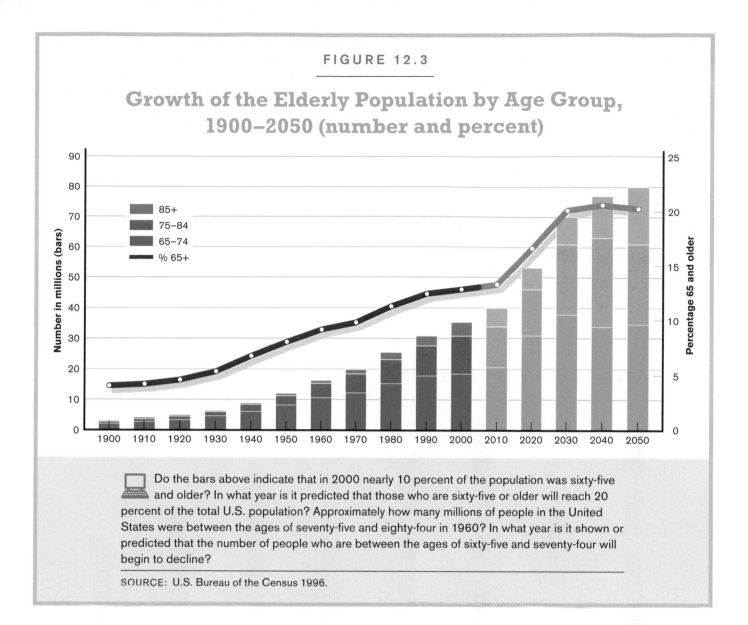

FIGURE 12.3

Growth of the Elderly Population by Age Group, 1900–2050 (number and percent)

Legend:
- 85+
- 75–84
- 65–74
- % 65+

Y-axis (left): Number in millions (bars) — 0, 10, 20, 30, 40, 50, 60, 70, 80, 90

Y-axis (right): Percentage 65 and older — 0, 5, 10, 15, 20, 25

X-axis: 1900, 1910, 1920, 1930, 1940, 1950, 1960, 1970, 1980, 1990, 2000, 2010, 2020, 2030, 2040, 2050

Do the bars above indicate that in 2000 nearly 10 percent of the population was sixty-five and older? In what year is it predicted that those who are sixty-five or older will reach 20 percent of the total U.S. population? Approximately how many millions of people in the United States were between the ages of seventy-five and eighty-four in 1960? In what year is it shown or predicted that the number of people who are between the ages of sixty-five and seventy-four will begin to decline?

SOURCE: U.S. Bureau of the Census 1996.

when they passed that milestone and the actual experiences of those who had (Figure 12.4). In this section, we examine differences among the elderly in the United States, along with some of the common problems that they confront; in the next section, we look at their growing political ability to do something about these problems.

Poverty

Relatively few elderly people live in poverty, although some of the very poorest people are elderly, particularly among minorities. Because older people have for the most part retired from work, their income is based primarily on **Social Security** and private retirement programs. Social Security and **Medicare** have been especially important in lifting many elderly people out of poverty. Yet people who depend solely on these two programs for income and health-care coverage are likely to live modestly at best. Social Security accounts for only about 40 percent of the income of the typical retiree; most of the remainder comes from investments and private pension funds and sometimes earnings. Low-income households in particular are likely to rely heavily on Social Security. According to the Economic Policy Institute (EPI), 65 percent of seniors over the age of sixty-five rely on Social Security for over half their income (Ettlinger and Chapman 2005). Yet even the combination of Social Security and private pensions results in modest retirement incomes for most people (Krueger 1995). Although almost all elderly are covered by Medicare, just over 60 percent of people over age sixty-five are covered by private health insurance as well (DeNavas-Walt et al. 2005).

The economic conditions of the elderly have improved steadily since the 1970s. As Figure 12.5 shows, in 1959, 35 percent of all people over sixty-five lived in poverty. That figure began to drop during President Lyndon B. Johnson's War on Poverty in the mid-1960s, when Medicare was enacted and Social Security benefits increased. By the early 1970s, poverty rates among the elderly had dropped to below 15 percent, and today they hover around 10 percent (9.4 percent in 2006). This is half the rate of poverty among children under eighteen years, 17.4 percent of

whom were poor in 2006 (DeNavas-Walt et al. 2007). Race appears to be much more important than age in explaining poverty among the elderly (Figure 12.6). Among whites, only 4.5 percent of the elderly reported poverty-level incomes in 2006, compared with 14.9 percent of blacks, 9.2 percent of Asians, and 12.8 percent of Hispanics (U.S. Census Bureau 2007k).

Social Isolation

One of the common stereotypes about the elderly is that they are isolated from human contact. This is not true of the

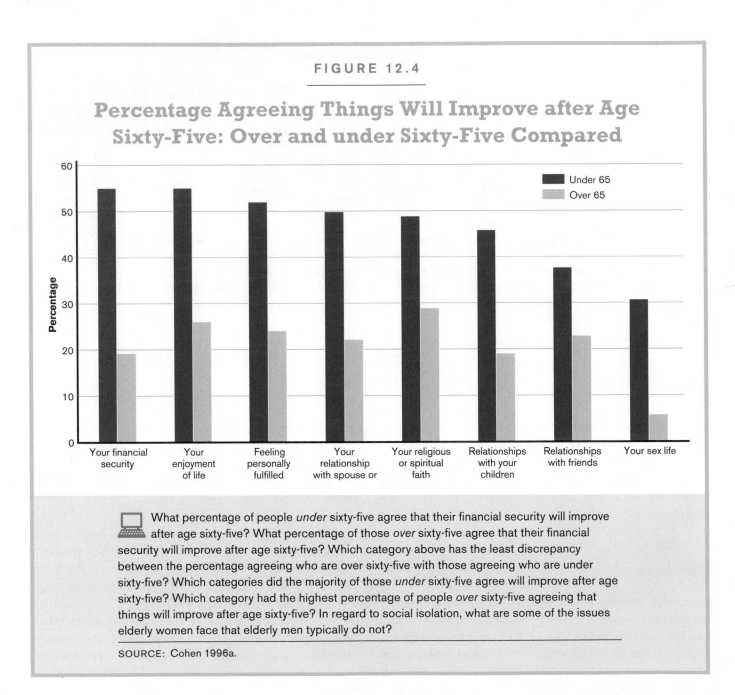

FIGURE 12.4

Percentage Agreeing Things Will Improve after Age Sixty-Five: Over and under Sixty-Five Compared

What percentage of people *under* sixty-five agree that their financial security will improve after age sixty-five? What percentage of those *over* sixty-five agree that their financial security will improve after age sixty-five? Which category above has the least discrepancy between the percentage agreeing who are over sixty-five with those agreeing who are under sixty-five? Which categories did the majority of those *under* sixty-five agree will improve after age sixty-five? Which category had the highest percentage of people *over* sixty-five agreeing that things will improve after age sixty-five? In regard to social isolation, what are some of the issues elderly women face that elderly men typically do not?

SOURCE: Cohen 1996a.

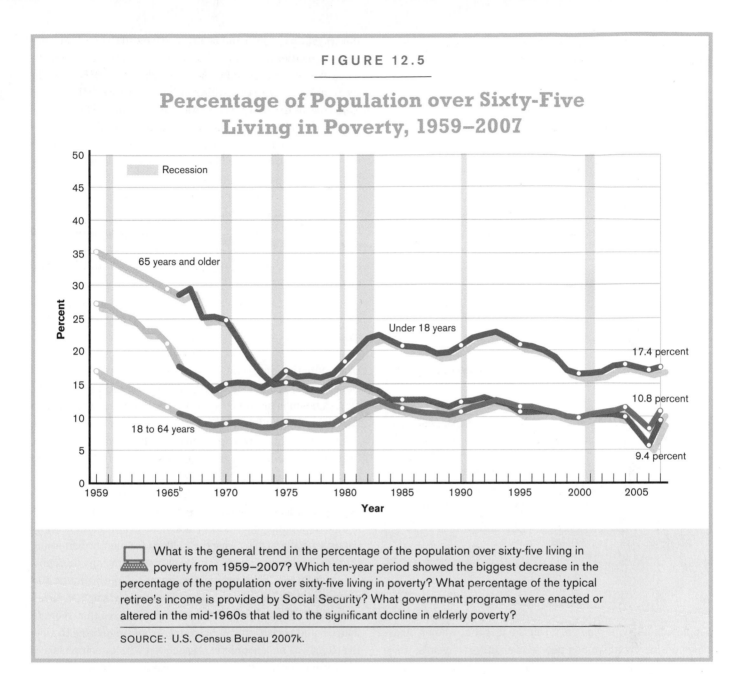

FIGURE 12.5

Percentage of Population over Sixty-Five Living in Poverty, 1959–2007

Recession

65 years and older

Under 18 years

17.4 percent

10.8 percent

18 to 64 years

9.4 percent

Percent

1959   1965[b]   1970   1975   1980   1985   1990   1995   2000   2005

Year

What is the general trend in the percentage of the population over sixty-five living in poverty from 1959–2007? Which ten-year period showed the biggest decrease in the percentage of the population over sixty-five living in poverty? What percentage of the typical retiree's income is provided by Social Security? What government programs were enacted or altered in the mid-1960s that led to the significant decline in elderly poverty?

SOURCE: U.S. Census Bureau 2007k.

majority of older people, however. Four out of five older people have living children, and the vast majority of them can rely on their children for support if necessary (American Association of Retired Persons [AARP] 1997). More than nine out of ten adult children say that maintaining parental contact is important to them, including the provision of financial support if it is needed (Finley et al. 1988). The reverse is also true: Many studies have found that elderly parents continue to provide support for their adult children, particularly during times of difficulty, such as divorce. Most elderly parents and adult children report feeling that the amount of support they receive from the other is fair. In 2006, the U.S. Bureau of the Census

(2007l) reported that there are over 15.4 million households with one or more persons sixty-five years or older. Being geographically distant from family members does not seem to be a problem either, since 85 percent of elderly people with children live close to at least one of them (Bankoff 1983; Bengston et al. 1990; Greenberg and Becker 1988; Moss et al. 1985; Peterson and Peterson 1988).

Future generations may suffer more from social isolation than do elderly people today. Changing patterns of gender relations, including increases in divorce and a decline in remarriage, may mean that an increasing proportion of elderly people will live alone (Goldscheider 1990). A majority of such

FIGURE 12.6

Percentage Poor: White, Black, and Hispanic Elderly, 2007

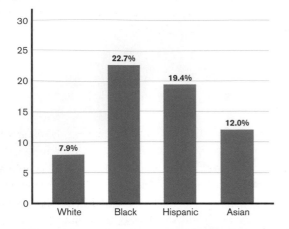

TRUE or FALSE: The figure indicates that whites made up about 8 percent of *all* the elderly poor in 2007. According to the figure, how many times more likely to be poor were elderly blacks than elderly whites in 2007? What could you say about the decline in the percentage of the elderly population living in poverty if you used both Figure 12.5 and Figure 12.6?

SOURCE: U.S. Census Bureau 2007k.

people will likely be women, given the fact that women on average outlive men. Among people over fifty-five years, there are only eighty-one men for every one hundred women; for those eighty-five or older, the number of men per one hundred women drops to forty-six. Partly because of the dearth of older men, only 56.6 percent of all women age sixty-five to seventy-four are married, compared with almost 80 percent of men in that age range. Among those age seventy-five to eighty-four, only 36.4 percent of all women are married; the rate for men is 72.4 percent (Agingstats.gov 2007). Women are also more likely than men to be widowed. In 2006, 28 percent of women and only 7.5 percent of men age sixty-five to seventy-four were widowed (Agingstats.gov 2007).

The fact that women outlive men means that elderly women are more likely to experience problems of isolation and loneliness. These problems are compounded by cultural values that make growing old gracefully easier for men than for women.

In U.S. culture, youth and beauty are viewed as especially desirable qualities for women. Older men, on the other hand, are more likely to be valued for their material success: Graying at the temples is a sign of distinction for a man, rather than a call for a visit to the hairdresser. As a result, elderly divorced or widowed men are much more likely to find a mate than elderly women who are living alone, because the pool of eligible mates for elderly men is more likely to include potential partners who are many years younger. One study of fifty-nine elderly women who had lost their husbands found that some eventually managed to overcome their grief, while others never fully recovered from their husband's death (Hunter 1990). The widows who overcame their grief tended to be much more satisfied with their social support networks than those who did not.

Prejudice

Discrimination on the basis of age is now against federal law. Nonetheless, prejudices based on false stereotypes are common. **Ageism** is prejudice and/or discrimination based on age and, like all prejudices, is fueled in part by stereotypes. The elderly are frequently seen as perpetually lonely, sad, infirm, forgetful, dependent, senile, old-fashioned, inflexible, and embittered.

There are a number of reasons for such prejudice. The previously mentioned American obsession with youthfulness, reflected in popular entertainment and advertising, leads many younger people to disparage their elders, frequently dismissing them as irrelevant. The new information technology undoubtedly reinforces these prejudices, because youthfulness and computer abilities seem to go hand in hand. In the fast-paced world of MTV, the Web, and dot-com businesses that seem to flourish and perish overnight, young people may come to view the elderly as anachronistic. Associated with the emphasis of youthfulness is a fear-filled avoidance of reminders of death and dying. Such fear carries over into negative attitudes toward the elderly, who serve as a constant reminder of one's mortality (Fry 1980).

In one study (Levin 1988), college students were shown a photograph of the same man at ages twenty-five, fifty-two, and seventy-three and were asked to rate him in terms of a variety of personality characteristics. The ratings were significantly more negative for the man depicted at age seventy-three. When he looked old in his photograph, the students were more likely to perceive him negatively, even though they knew absolutely nothing about him. The mere fact of his being elderly was sufficient to trigger a negative cultural stereotype. Widely shared cultural stereotypes of grumpy old men can lead to private opinions that are hurtful to older people.

Physical Abuse

The National Center on Elder Abuse (1999) defines seven types of elder abuse:

- Physical abuse—use of physical force that may result in bodily injury, physical pain, or impairment
- Sexual abuse—nonconsensual sexual contact of any kind with an elderly person
- Emotional abuse—infliction of anguish, pain, or distress through verbal or nonverbal acts
- Financial/material exploitation—illegal or improper use of an elder's funds, property, or assets
- Neglect—refusal, or failure, to fulfill any part of a person's obligations or duties to an elderly person
- Abandonment—desertion of an elderly person by an individual who has physical custody of the elder or by a person who has assumed responsibility for providing care to the elder
- Self-neglect—behaviors of an elderly person that threaten the elder's health or safety

Cases of elderly abuse certainly exist, but most research suggests that it is not as widespread as is commonly believed. Worldwide, it is estimated that between 4 and 6 percent of the elderly experience some form of abuse at home (Hood 2002). Nationwide it is estimated that between one and two million Americans over age sixty-five have been injured, exploited, or otherwise mistreated. Yet, particularly in cases of financial abuse, it is estimated that only one in twenty-five cases are reported, suggesting that there may be five million financial abuse victims every year (National Center on Elder Abuse 2005). One random survey among two thousand noninstitutionalized elderly people in the Boston area found that only about 2 percent had experienced physical violence, although these figures may be somewhat low because abuse rates may be higher among those who are unable to respond to surveys. Older adults who are embarrassed or ashamed of their mistreatment also may be reluctant to report such experiences. Fewer than 1 percent reported being seriously neglected in terms of their daily needs, while about 1 percent claimed they were subject to chronic verbal aggression. These figures represent a small percentage of the elderly population. Still, they do represent eight to nine thousand cases in the Boston area alone. Although elderly men reported higher rates of abuse than did elderly women, 57 percent of the abused women (compared with 6 percent of the men) reported suffering injuries (Pillemer and Finkelhor 1988).

It is widely believed that abuse results from the anger and resentment that adult children feel when confronted with the need to care for their infirm parents (King 1984; Steinmetz 1983). Most studies, however, have found this to be a false stereotype. More than half of the abuse reported in the Boston study was perpetrated by a spouse; only a quarter of the cases occurred at the hands of an adult child (Pillemer and Finkelhor 1988). Furthermore, in cases when a child abused an elderly parent, it was found that he or she was more likely to be financially dependent on the parent, rather than the reverse. The child may feel resentment about being dependent, and the parent may be unwilling to terminate the abusive relationship because he or she feels obligated to help the child (Pillemer 1985).

Health Problems

The prevalence of chronic disabilities among the elderly has declined in recent years (Manton et al. 1993), and most elderly people rate their health as reasonably good and free of major disabilities. Still, older people obviously suffer from more health problems than most younger people, and the number and intrusiveness of health difficulties often increase with advancing age. In 2003, the elderly accounted for about one quarter of all U.S. health-care expenditures (Kaiser Family Foundation 2005). In 2004, over half of all noninstitutionalized persons over sixty-five reported having at least some problems with hypertension, whereas about a third reported suffering from such ailments as arthritis, heart disease, and hearing loss. One out of five elderly have had incidences of some type of cancer (Federal Interagency Forum on Aging-Related Statistics [FIFARS] 2004). In America, 10 to 15 percent of all reported new HIV infections occur among people over the age of fifty. This amounted to 78,000 people in 2005. Age-related chronic health conditions, such as osteoporosis, create complications for the treatment of the elderly living with AIDS and accelerate the progression from HIV to AIDS (UNAIDS 2002).

In 2004, nearly three quarters of noninstitutionalized people over age sixty-five considered their health to be "good" or "good to excellent," and more than two out of three people age eighty-five or older reported the same (Agingstats.gov 2007). It is not surprising that the percentage of people needing help with daily activities increases with age: Whereas only about one in ten people between the ages of sixty-five and seventy-five report needing daily assistance, the figure rises to one in five for people between seventy-five and seventy-nine and to one in three for people between eighty and eighty-four. Half of all people over age eighty-five require assistance (U.S. Bureau of the Census 1996).

Paradoxically, there is some evidence that the fastest-growing group of elderly, the oldest old (those eighty-five and older), tend to enjoy relative robustness, which partially accounts for their having reached their advanced age. This is possibly one of the reasons that health-care costs for a person who dies at ninety are about a third of those for a person who dies at seventy (Angier 1995). Unlike many other Americans, the elderly are fortunate in having access to public health insurance (Medicare) and therefore medical services. The United States, however, stands virtually alone among the industrialized nations in failing to provide adequately for the complete health care of its most senior citizens (Hendricks and Hatch 1993).

Although nearly forty-seven million Americans lacked health insurance in 2005 (about 16 percent of the population) (National Coalition on Health Care 2008), less than 1 percent of the elderly lacked coverage in 2004 (DeNavas-Walt et al. 2005). About 95 percent of the elderly are covered to some extent by Medicare. But because this program covers about half of the total health-care expenses of the elderly, nearly two out of three people supplement Medicare with their own private insurance (DeNavas-Walt et al. 2005; FIFARS 2004). The rising costs of private insurance, unfortunately, have made this option impossible for a growing number of the elderly. Since 1977, the percentage of elderly with out-of-pocket health-care expenses increased from 83 percent to over 95 percent. Despite Medicare, today the elderly still spend on average over one fifth of their income on health care (FIFARS 2004). At present, the rising costs of Medicare have made it a candidate for federal budget cuts.

When the elderly become physically unable to care for themselves, they may end up in nursing homes or assisted living facilities. Only about one out of every twenty people over age sixty-five is in a nursing home, a figure that rises to about one out of every five among people over age eighty-five (Atchley 2000). Medicaid, the government program that provides health insurance for the poor, covers long-term supervision and nursing costs, although only when most of one's assets (except for one's home) have been used up. About 7 percent of elderly people in nursing homes receive assistance from Medicaid (FIFARS 2004). Because the average cost of a nursing home is now over $74,445 a year (New York Life 2006), which perhaps explains the decline in the percentage of elders living in nursing homes (from 10.2 percent in 1990 of elders seventy-five years and older to 7.4 percent in 2006), the non-poor elderly who require such institutionalization may find that their lifetime savings will be quickly depleted (a process dubbed "spending down."). Nursing homes have long had a reputation for austerity and loneliness. In fact, however, the quality of most has improved in recent years because federal programs such as Medicaid help cover the cost of care and because of federal quality regulations. Further, long-term care offers a diverse range of options to older adults, ranging from apartments with partial nursing care and meals to units that

TABLE 12.2

What Is Your Biggest Fear about Growing Old?

When it comes to growing old, most Americans fear losing their health and independence far more than being alone or living in a nursing home.

Losing your health	73%
Losing ability to care for yourself	70%
Losing mental abilities	69%
Running out of money	60%
Not being able to drive/travel on own	59%
Being a burden on your family	54%
Winding up in a nursing home	52%
Not being able to work or volunteer	49%
Being alone	39%
Losing your looks	22%

SOURCE: Cohen and Langer 2005.

provide round-the-clock medical assistance. Many also offer a wide array of cultural, social, and recreational programs for their residents.

Still, living for many years in a nursing home was cited as a concern about growing old by over half of respondents, according to a recent national survey (Table 12.2). Perhaps that is why the average length of stay in nursing homes dropped from 1,026 days in 1985 to 876 days in 2003, as more elderly people seek home care (*Chicago Tribune* 2003; Dey 1997). This trend also reflects technological developments; unhealthy older adults often may remain in their own homes longer today because their loved ones can provide them with modest levels of in-home medical care.

Lifelong Learning

As more and more people live well beyond the age of retirement, they enter a new stage of life for which there are few socially prescribed roles (Laslett 1991; Moen 1995). Many people can look forward to ten or twenty years of relatively healthy living, free from the obligations of paid work and raising a family. Furthermore, the elderly population will be increasingly well educated, because young people today are much more likely to have gone to college than their parents—or grandparents. This process of educational expansion has important implications for the well-being of older adults. Better-educated people tend to be economically comfortable in later life. They also tend to be healthier: They are better informed on health-related issues, more likely to choose a healthy lifestyle, and more likely to seek medical treatment when they require it (Treas 1995).

These trends suggest that the elderly are much more likely to remain a part of mainstream society, rather than to become isolated. As U.S. society continues to age, it will increasingly be forced to confront a growing elderly population that is unwilling to slip quietly into years of retirement and inactivity. It is important for elderly people to maintain a readiness to learn, stimulated by participation in a wide variety of learning activities. As noted earlier, this can contribute to mental alertness, a positive psychological attitude, and even improved physical health (Dychtwald 1990; Plett 1990; Plett and Lester 1991).

Some scholars have even argued that "adult education" will soon become as important as "youth education" (Brookfield 1986). Educators have coined the terms **andragogy** to refer to adult learning (literally, the "leading of adults") and **geragogy** (the "leading of the old") to refer to older-adult learning (John 1988). In contrast to conventional notions of teaching, adult learning methods emphasize building on the extensive life experience of older people rather than providing them with information in a standard undergraduate-classroom format. Adult learning tends to be informal, combining the learners' concrete experience with more theoretical sorts of knowledge. It draws on the interests and concerns of adult learners, who may be unwilling to spend time studying things that seem unrelated to their central cares (John 1988; Plett 1990).

What are the benefits of lifelong learning?

☑ **CONCEPT CHECKS**

1. Contrast the young old, old old, and oldest old.
2. Describe four common problems that older Americans often confront.
3. What characteristics differentiate those older adults who are emotionally and physically well from those who face great distress in later life?

The Politics of Aging

Because of their growing numbers, older adults are a potentially potent voice in Washington. **AARP** (formerly the American Association of Retired People) is a highly effective advocate for the elderly. It is a nonprofit organization that boasts a membership of over thirty-nine million Americans over the age of fifty and which is reportedly the largest member-based organization in the world next to the Roman Catholic Church and over ten times larger than the National Rifle Association (Birnbaum 2005a). Because of their high voter turnout rates—nearly 70 percent of those sixty-five and older voted in the 2004 election—the elderly account for as much as one fifth of all voters (Atchley 2000; Treas 1995; U.S. Bureau of the Census 2005b). This is not to suggest that the elderly all hold the same political views; on the contrary, they are as politically heterogeneous as the other groups in our society. But on issues they perceive as affecting their interests—such as retirement pensions and health-care benefits—they are likely to have strong opinions. Moreover, because cuts in programs for the elderly would shift the burden of supporting them to their families, opposition to significant reductions in these programs is likely to be widespread.

The two principal governmental programs that provide financial support for the elderly are Medicare, which was instituted in 1965, and Social Security, whose benefits were increased at about the same time (the program itself was begun in 1935). The full benefits of Medicare and Social Security are available at age sixty-five, although partial benefits are available to some people a few years earlier.

Social Security and Medicare are financed by workers' payroll deductions, employer contributions, and taxes on those who are self-employed. Working Americans pay into these programs today so they can be eligible for benefits when they are no longer able to earn a living. By providing a degree of economic support for the elderly, such programs also make it economically possible to retire; in the absence of the economic security such programs provide, elderly people would be under

Redefining Retirement

Professor Phyllis Moen has testified before congressional and state legislative committees, appeared on television programs such as *60 Minutes,* and served on review panels for the National Academy of Sciences and the National Institutes of Health. She has given luncheon talks to Senate staffers in Washington, D.C.; provided interviews for national radio broadcasts; and advised nonprofit organizations. But for Moen, these public engagements are only part of her broader ambition as a sociologist: to help reframe the ways Americans—and especially American institutions—define and delimit life chances and life quality around age and gender.

Take the idea of a *career.* Conventional wisdom (left over from the 1950s) holds that life moves in a series of age-graded locksteps: After high school, you go to college, get a job, get married, get promoted, have kids, save money, and retire around age sixty-five. But for most Americans, this storyline is a myth, what Moen (2005) has called the "career mystique." "Lock-step arrangements around education, work, family, and retirement no longer fit the realities and risks of contemporary living," she explains. "Corporate restructuring, chronic job insecurity, and double demands at work and at home" are

Phyllis Moen

drastically changing the paths that men and women take as they grow older. Focusing attention on how private troubles are actually public issues helps foster greater career and

greater economic pressure to continue working as long as they are physically capable.

Medicare, which pays for acute medical costs for the elderly, reached almost forty-five million older adults in 2008, and the estimated budget for 2008 is $454 billion, or about one eighth of the federal budget (Moffit 2007). Medicare is the nation's largest health insurer, processing, in 2004, over one billion medical claims (U.S. Department of Health and Human Services 2005). Because it reaches so many people, Medicare has made an enormous difference in the elderly population's access to adequate health care—although at a high cost. Controversial revisions to the Medicare program in 2003 provide government subsidies for the purchase of medicines by the elderly and provide special assistance to low-income elderly. AARP played an influential role in lobbying Congress during the debate over these changes.

Social Security provides retirement pay for all elderly persons who have worked a certain number of years during their lives and have contributed a portion of their paycheck (typically matched by their employer) into a government fund. The program estimates disbursements of $608 billion, to fifty million individuals in 2008 (Social Security Administration 2008). In 2007, thirty-four million retired people received $36 billion. Most of these were retirees over sixty-five, but some younger retirees and dependents of deceased workers received benefits as well. The amount of the monthly benefit one receives under Social Security depends in part on earnings before retirement. The average monthly benefit in June 2008 was $1,084 for retired workers, $1,005 for disabled workers, and $1,040 for nondisabled widows and widowers (Social Security Administration 2008). Because retired women are less likely than men to have had continuous paid employment throughout retirement flexibilities, such that there are possibilities for second acts and personal renewal at every age and every life stage.

This process of life-course reinvention will likely be driven by the seventy-eight million individuals who make up the baby boom generation, born between 1946 and 1964 in the years after World War II. Starting in the year 2006, baby boomers turn sixty at the rate of one every seven seconds, a pace that will continue for the next two decades. These aging Americans will constitute the nation's largest group of retirement-age men and women, and their collective energy, good health, and productive activity will likely redefine what it means to be old or retired in America. For example, 82 percent of boomers plan to work beyond traditional retirement age (currently set at age sixty-two). Half plan to work their entire lives (Sturdevant 2006).

The concept of retirement is therefore one of those commonsense ideas in need of a twenty-first-century makeover. "We have these categories which become real—old, young, retirement age—and they're changing before our eyes," says Moen. "Let's think of these categories as socially *constructed* by rules and regulations. If they are constructed, then we can also *reconstruct* them." Baby boomers have already started to do so. Moen's research reveals that many individuals in their fifties and sixties prefer to scale back work commitments or start second careers that are part-time or part-year instead of retiring all together. "It is a mistake for policy makers to simply delay the official retirement age," she says. As Americans live longer and lead more productive lives, "people will agree to work longer, but on their own terms. Flexibility is key, as is the desire to do something meaningful, something worthwhile. These talented and experienced boomers constitute a potential windfall, a workforce for community building, a mentoring force for the next generation. But packaging matters; people will demand options that will change the way work is organized." Moen believes that we're on the cusp of rewriting what she calls "retirement scripts," the set of social expectations that guide perceptions of what's possible during the decades after middle age.

Those possibilities, however, will depend heavily on factors beyond the control of any single individual. If the current Social Security system remains unchanged, budgetary pressures will put at risk the government assistance millions of Americans currently depend on to survive. "Worries about the adequacy of personal income are already looming for boomers—and seem bound to get worse. A lot of moderate-income people who do not consider themselves poor today are going to find out that they are poor when they get old. This isn't on their radar screen at all" (Sturdevant 2006). Health care is another pressing issue for older Americans. More and more people work past the normal retirement age not because they are enthusiastic about their jobs but because paid employment provides the only affordable way to secure health-care coverage. Add long-term care, increased life expectancy, pension liability, and housing shortages and a potential crisis seems to await seventy-eight million Americans for whom current public policies are not prepared.

their lives, their average retirement income is correspondingly lower. As these figures suggest, Social Security provides an extremely minimal level of support for the elderly—by itself, barely enough to keep recipients out of poverty (Belgrave 1988; Treas 1995; Social Security Administration 1997).

The elderly population is likely to be at the center of one of the major political debates of this century: the extent to which the government should continue funding programs that virtually eliminated poverty among the elderly since the 1970s. Programs such as Social Security and Medicare will become increasingly costly as more and more Americans retire. As people live longer, the first baby boomers retire, and the birth rate remains low, the share of the population funding Social Security shrinks. As a result, the worker-to-beneficiary ratio has fallen from 16.5:1 in 1950 to 3.3:1 today. Within forty years it will be 2:1. At that point, there will not be enough workers to pay for the benefits required by retired persons (Social Security Administration 2005b). There is particular concern over whether the Social Security system will remain financially sound as retiring baby boomers collect their pensions. It is currently expected to have sufficient assets to pay full benefits until at least 2029, although if it is to avoid running out of money in the long run, changes will have to be made in the way the system is run (Social Security Administration 2005a). A variety of solutions have been proposed, including "means-testing," or allocating benefits based on an older person's financial means and needs. In the past decade, there also have been calls to privatize at least part of Social Security—that is, to enable workers to invest part of their Social Security withholdings in the stock market, rather than simply paying it all into a government fund. The effectiveness of this approach depends, of course, on how well the stock market performs in the

Protestors at rally in Olympia, Washington. The demonstrators were asking lawmakers to not cut the budgets for long-term health care facilities such as nursing homes and assisted living facilities.

future. Although it looked promising in the 1990s when stocks were soaring, today it does not look nearly so hopeful. In his February 2005 State of the Union Address, President George W. Bush argued for the privatization of Social Security. As of early 2008, however, proposals to privatize Social Security seemed unlikely to be adopted by Congress.

Do the Elderly Get an Unfair Amount of Government Support?

The costs of providing for the elderly come largely out of taxes paid by working people. In the United States, for example, the growing ratio of the elderly to the working-age population has alarmed policy makers. They point out that for every one hundred people of working age (eighteen to sixty-four years old) in 1990, there were twenty people over sixty-five. By the year 2030, there will be thirty-six elderly people for every one hundred working-age people. A rapidly aging population will pose serious challenges to public policy throughout this century.

Do government programs adequately promote **generational equity**, the striking of a balance between the needs and interests of members of different generations? The issue of generational equity was first raised by an organization called Americans for Generational Equity (AGE), created in 1984 by Dave Durenberger, a U.S. senator from Minnesota, to challenge the notion that elderly people are entitled to Social Security benefits (Quadagno 1989). AGE's chief criticisms were of the program's method of funding, which requires working people

to contribute a portion of their earnings to a government-managed trust fund to pay for their retirement.

AGE argued that as the U.S. population grays, those who are working will bear an increasing burden for those who are not. AGE also argued that Social Security unfairly favors retirees over other needy groups in society. For example, AGE pointed out that retirees are sometimes wealthier than the working people whose taxes fund Social Security and that there are nearly four times as many impoverished children under eighteen than impoverished people over sixty-five: 13 million versus 3.5 million (DeNavas-Walt et al. 2005). In the early 1990s, roughly a third of the total budget for Medicaid, the federal health insurance program for the poor, was used to provide long-term health care for the elderly. The elderly, blind, and disabled made up only a fifth of all Medicaid beneficiaries, yet required 70 percent of all Medicaid spending (Hudson 1995; Quadagno 1989).

The difficulty arises from the fact that there are fewer and fewer working-age people to shoulder the tax burden necessary to support more and more retirees. There may come a time when a predominantly white elderly retired population is supported by taxes paid by a predominantly nonwhite working population.

☑ CONCEPT CHECKS

1. Describe the two main government programs that provide financial support for the elderly in the United States.
2. Describe the debate surrounding the future of Social Security programs in the United States.
3. What is "generational equity"?

Globalization: The Graying of the World Population

An "elder explosion" is sweeping the world today. In 2002, the United Nations (2003) estimated that there were 629 million people over age sixty in the world. Globally, the population of older persons is growing by 2 percent each year, considerably faster than the population as a whole (United Nations 2005). A 1998 report of the UN Population Fund (UNFPA) notes that the sixty-five and older population worldwide grew by about 9 million in 1998. By 2010, the elderly population will grow by 14.5 million; by 2050, 21 million. In 2050, the number of people over age sixty is expected to be 2 billion. The most rapid growth of the sixty-five and older group will take place in the industrialized nations of the world, where families have fewer children and people live longer than in poorer countries. By region, over half of the world's elderly live in Asia and a quarter live in Europe. In the industrialized countries, the percentage of the population that is elderly grew from 8 percent in 1950 to 15 percent in 2003, and it is projected to reach 25 percent by 2050 (FIFARS 2004). After the middle of the century, developing nations will follow suit as they experience their own elder explosion, though only in the United States and other developed nations will the elderly continue to outnumber the population under fifteen (U.S. Bureau of the Census 1998).

The populations of most of the world's societies are aging as the result of a decline in both birth and death rates, although the populations of the poorer countries continue to have shorter life spans because of poverty, malnutrition, and disease (see Chapter 19). According to UN estimates (UNFPA 1998), the world's average life expectancy grew from forty-six in 1950 to fifty in 1985 and will reach seventy-one by 2025. At that time, some eight hundred million people will be over sixty-five, nearly a threefold increase in numbers from 1990. Among the very old (those over eighty-five), whose medical and service needs are the greatest, the number will increase by half in North America, while it will double in China and grow nearly one and a half times in West Africa (Sokolovsky 1990). This growth will place major demands on the resources of many countries that are already too poor to support their populations adequately.

This explosion has enormous implications for social policy. More than 150 nations currently provide public assistance for people who are elderly or disabled or for their survivors when they die. Elderly people are especially likely to require costly health-care services. Their rapid growth in numbers threatens to strain the medical systems in many industrial nations, where the cost of providing health care to the elderly threatens to overwhelm government budgets.

Countries vary widely in what they are doing to cope with their growing numbers of older people. As we have seen already, the United States relies primarily on Social Security and Medicare to serve the financial and health needs of the elderly. Other industrial nations provide a much broader array of services. In Japan, for example, men and women remain

Fukashi Kanematsu, age eighty-four, lives in Okinawa, Japan. He eats only fish and vegetables and doesn't drink or smoke; in his spare time he makes Japanese symbolic items, like three rice bag ornaments. He is constantly busy and physically active.

Aging in Global Perspective

According to the World Health Organization (WHO), there were 600 million people aged sixty and over in the year 2000. By 2025, there are expected to be 1.2 billion people in this age group, and this number will reach 2 billion by 2050. The "graying" of society is most pronounced in advanced industrial nations, because of their low birthrates and conditions that promote good health over the life course. As the charts below show, countries such as Japan, Italy, and Germany have the highest percentages of population who are over sixty, while countries such as Uganda, Niger, and Mali have the highest percentage of young people (*The Economist* 2007). Currently, two thirds of all older people live in advanced industrial nations. This is estimated to increase to 75 percent by 2050. The fastest growing population group in advanced industrial nations is comprised of people aged eighty and over (World Health Organization 2007). These statistics paint a picture of global age demographics—graying advanced industrial nations and a much younger developing world.

What are the political, economic, and social implications of these shifts in age demographics? Around the globe, older persons play crucial social roles. They often provide unpaid care work for family members, they volunteer valuable social services, and they are an important source of social knowledge, traditions, and wisdom. They also require health services and, in some cases, assistance in carrying out everyday life tasks.

International organizations have begun to raise awareness about these shifts in global age demographics. In 2007, the WHO declared October 1, 2007 International Day of Older Persons and recently released a report that surveyed older adults and their caregivers from around the world and offered proposals to accommodate cities to the needs of older adults. Despite these

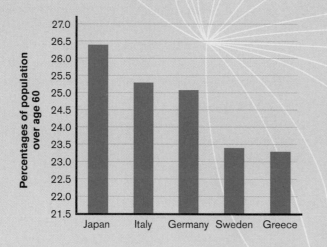

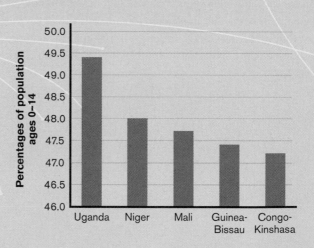

active well into old age because the Japanese culture encourages this activity and because business policies often support postretirement work with the same company one worked for before retirement. A number of national laws in Japan support the employment and training of older workers, and private businesses also support retraining.

Societies that have large extended families and practice ancestor worship are more likely to treasure their elders,

honoring them at public events and seeking their counsel in political matters. In countries such as Thailand, China, and Japan, reverence for ancestors remains strong (Cowgill 1968; Falk et al. 1981; Glascock and Feinman 1981; Seefeldt and Keawkungwal 1985). Yet globalization has begun to change the treatment of the elderly throughout the world (Cowgill 1986; Foner 1984; Fry 1980; Holmes 1983). As more and more people live to old age, respect for them has tended to decline.

efforts, many questions remain about the care of large populations of elderly people in advanced industrial countries. What sort of policies will be needed to manage the care of an increasingly older population? Who will provide care for them?

ELDERCARE: FOCUS ON ITALY

Sociologist Francesca DeGiuli's research on eldercare in Italy demonstrates the ways in which globalization is changing how advanced industrial societies manage growing populations of elderly persons. Italy is an important site in which to study how families respond to the financial, health, and emotional needs of their elder relatives. The country has one of the largest proportions of elderly people in the world, due in part to the nation's very low birth rate (with a total fertility rate of just 1.3 today). Over recent decades there has been a marked decrease in government-sponsored or affordable social services for them. Interviewing both eldercare workers and the families who employed them, DeGiuli found that many families relied on migrant women—often without legal immigration status—to care for their aging relatives. Relatively affordable eldercare allowed Italian women, who historically provided care for aging relatives, to have careers outside the home. In her work, DeGiuli described a typical twenty-four-hour day of a home eldercare worker which entailed cooking, cleaning, administering medications, and cleansing wounds. She also detailed the emotional labor involved in these jobs, including providing companionship for the elders and dealing with family members who are often distressed by the care needs of their aging relatives. The women DeGiuli spoke with reported many exploitative aspects of their jobs: long hours, low pay, lack of health services despite extremely demanding physical work, and little recourse to seek redress for these working conditions because of their vulnerable status as immigrants. At the same time, DeGiuli's interviewees described the intimacy of the relationships that developed among immigrant workers, elders, and their families (DeGiuli 2007).

The implications of DeGiuli's research reach beyond Italy and are pertinent to many other countries. How will advanced

Seniors protest pension reform in Rome, Italy.

industrial countries handle their aging populations? Eldercare not only is economically difficult but also can be a source of emotional strain for older adults and their families. The reliance on immigrant, often undocumented, women from the developing world for the care of the elderly is prevalent in most advanced industrial countries. These jobs are invisible to many and often go unregulated, which may result in many problems for elders and especially the women who care for them. How governments provide care for elderly citizens and regulate eldercare jobs is a global policy issue that will need to be addressed as the populations of advanced industrial nations continue to get older.

References

DeGiuli, Francesca. 2007. "Laboring Lives: A Look at Transnational Work Practices: The Case of Eldercare Work in Italy." Dissertation Thesis, Sociology, University of California, Santa Barbara.

The Economist. 2007. Pocket World in Figures 2008 Edition.

World Health Organization. 2007. "Ageing and the Life Course." http://www.who.int/ageing/en/ (accessed December 23, 2007).

The reason is partly that their growing numbers result in a greater economic burden on their families. Additionally, as previously agrarian societies become a part of the emerging global economy, traditional ways of thinking and behaving are likely to change. When extended families are uprooted from farms and move into cities in search of factory work, their ability to support nonworking members is likely to decline. In those societies that are highly family oriented, the responsibility for supporting elderly parents and working for outside income often falls on young women. Research conducted in Taiwan, for example, has found that young girls often work a full day in a nearby factory, returning home during lunch and after work to care for infirm parents or grandparents (Cheng and Hsiung 1992).

The combination of graying and globalization will shape the lives of elderly people throughout the world well into this century. Traditional patterns of family care will be challenged, as family-based economies continue to give way to labor on the farms and in the offices and factories of global businesses. Like the industrial nations earlier in the twentieth century, all societies will be challenged to find roles for their aging citizens. This challenge will include identifying new means of economic support, often financed by government programs. It will also entail identifying ways to incorporate rather than isolate the elderly, by drawing on their considerable reserves of experience and talents.

 **CONCEPT CHECKS**

1. What is the graying of the world's population?
2. What two long-term processes have contributed to this graying?
3. By how much will the global elderly population increase over the next five decades?
4. What are the implications of the graying world population for social policy?

 # Study Outline
www.wwnorton.com/studyspace

The Graying of U.S. Society

- Because of low mortality and fertility rates, American society is rapidly graying, or aging. There are today some thirty-six million Americans older than sixty-five, a figure forecast to reach seventy million by the year 2030. The elderly are a large and rapidly growing category that is extremely diverse economically, socially, and politically.

How Do People Age?

- Biological, psychological, and social aging are not the same and may vary considerably within and across cultures. It is important not to confuse a person's social age with his or her chronological age.
- Physical aging is inevitable, but for most people, proper nutrition, diet, and exercise can preserve a high level of health well into old age.

Growing Old: Competing Sociological Explanations

- Functionalist theories of aging originally argued that the disengagement of the elderly from society was desirable. *Disengagement theory* held that the elderly should pull back from their traditional social roles as younger people move into them. *Activity theory,* on the other hand, soon came to emphasize the importance of being engaged and busy as a source of vitality.
- Conflict theorists of aging have focused on how the routine operation of social institutions produces various forms of inequality among the elderly.
- The most recent theories regard the elderly as capable of taking control over their own lives and playing an active role in politics and the economy.

Aging in the United States

- Most of the elderly in U.S. society manage to lead independent lives that they report to be largely satisfying and fulfilling. Still, some suffer from poverty, social isolation, and costly medical problems, as well as from *ageism,* prejudice, and discrimination based on age.
- By providing the elderly with retirement income and critical health-care insurance, Social Security and Medicare have helped raise a significant number of elderly people out of poverty. There is some debate over whether these programs are overly generous to the elderly and therefore threaten *generational equity.* In fact, however, the levels of support they offer are modest. Considerable debate nonetheless exists over whether their future funding is likely to be sound.

The Politics of Aging

- The elderly are as politically and socially diverse as any group in society. But on issues that affect their interest, they are capable of exerting a great deal of uniform political pressure. Their political influence is likely to increase as their numbers grow.
- The elderly are capable of lifelong learning, and it seems likely that as their numbers increase, so will efforts to provide *andragogy* (adult-centered education) and *geragogy* (older-adult learning) for those who want it.

Globalization: The Graying of the World Population

- Globalization threatens the traditional roles of the elderly in many societies. The role of the elderly throughout the world is in a rapid state of transition.

Key Concepts

AARP (p. 371)
activity theory (p. 362)

6. How diverse is the older population in the United States? What are the effects of race, gender, and class on the standards of living among older people?

7. Describe the different age categories of older adults. Why is it important to distinguish between these categories?

8. What are some of the problems that older adults confront? What can they do about these problems?

9. Describe two major government programs for older adults in the United States. What are the debates around these programs?

10. How has globalization affected treatment of older adults around the world?

Review Questions

1. What does the term *graying of society* mean? What is this caused by?

2. How do sociologists define aging? Discuss each of the processes that sociologists include when they study aging.

3. Compare and contrast disengagement and activity theories of aging.

4. Discuss conflict theories of aging. What are some of the critiques of this theoretical perspective?

5. Discuss theories of self-concept and aging. Give an example of this theoretical perspective.

Thinking Sociologically Exercises

1. Briefly discuss the competing theories about growing old that are presented in this chapter. How do these theories compare with each other? Which theory do you feel is most appropriate to explain aging, and why do you feel this way about that theory?

2. What do you think the United States could do socially and politically to alleviate the problems of aging for its elder citizens? How likely is it that your suggestions for alleviating the problems of age could be adopted into the American political process, and why?

Learning Objectives

The Concept of the State

Understand basic concepts underlying modern nation-states.

Democracy

Learn about different types of democracy, how this form of government has spread around the world, some theories about power in a democracy, and some of the problems associated with modern-day democracy.

Political and Social Change

Learn some theories about social movements and apply them to the feminist movement in the United States. Assess the effect of globalization and technology on social movements today. Learn about nationalism and the importance of nationalist movements.

The Nation-State, National Identity, and Globalization

Evaluate whether or not globalization is weakening national identity.

Terrorism

Learn how social scientists define terrorism and the ways that new-style terrorism differs from the old.

CHAPTER THIRTEEN

GOVERNMENT, POLITICAL POWER, AND SOCIAL MOVEMENTS

O n March 20, 2003, the United States launched its "shock and awe" air campaign in Iraq. Intense bombing of strategic targets in the capital, Baghdad, and other Iraqi cities preceded the invasion by 130,000 combat troops, mainly from the United States with some from Britain and a few other countries. Iraq's cities and oil fields were secured quickly; by the end of April, Iraq appeared to be in American hands. On May 2, President George W. Bush, dressed in a flight suit, celebrated the seeming victory aboard an aircraft carrier surrounded by sailors and a banner proclaiming "Mission Accomplished." It was a made-for-television moment. It also turned out to be badly mistaken.

Although the military objectives had been accomplished in record time, winning the war turned out not to be the same as winning on the battlefield. During the next four years, as Iraqis struggled to build a democracy under the tutelage (and military protection) of the United States, long-suppressed conflicts claimed the lives of about 4,000 American soldiers. Estimates of deaths to Iraqi civilians are harder to quantify, with reports ranging anywhere from 45,000 to 223,000 deaths (Altman and Oppel 2008). Three years after President Bush's "mission accomplished" speech, nearly 140,000 U.S. soldiers (and another 15,000 British soldiers) remained in Iraq, training Iraqi security forces while fighting a growing insurgency. The reasons for the invasion of Iraq—and the causes of its bloody aftermath—reveal a great deal about the issues we discuss in this chapter.

One feature of modern politics is that in today's highly globalized world, even a country as powerful as the United States is under pressure to follow established international procedures before engaging in war. In the case of the Iraq War, one of the justifications for the invasion was Iraq's alleged possession of weapons of mass destruction (WMDs)—chemical, biological, and nuclear materials—that it might use against the West and sell to terrorist organizations. The United States accordingly made its case to the United Nations (UN) Security Council, providing its best evidence that Iraq was violating disarmament obligations worked out after its 1991 defeat in the Persian Gulf War. At that time, Iraq had agreed to end production of WMDs and allow monitoring by UN inspectors. Saddam Hussein had stopped cooperating with the United Nations in 1998, and the inspections were ended.

In response to the U.S. presentation, the UN Security Council passed Resolution 1441, requiring Iraq to resume inspections and fully disclose its WMD program and threatening "serious consequences" if these conditions were not met. Although Iraq resumed inspections and issued an extensive declaration of its weapons program, the United States claimed that Iraq was still hiding its WMDs and then justified its invasion on the basis of the UN resolution. In modern times, for war to be legitimate, it requires some form of international authorization—in this case, that of the United Nations.

The buildup to the war illustrates another feature of modern politics: the importance of media, including the Internet. The Bush administration took its case to the American public, with frequent television appearances by the president and administration officials emphasizing what they viewed as the threat posed by Iraq's WMDs, Saddam's possible connections to Osama bin Laden and al Qaeda, and the potentially dire consequences of inaction. Opponents of the U.S.-led invasion also used the media, challenging claims that Iraq had WMDs or posed an immediate threat to the United States and identifying flaws in the U.S. intelligence reports on which the allegations were based. They also argued that contrary to the Bush administration's claims, Saddam Hussein, who had long persecuted religious nationalists such as al Qaeda, was highly unlikely to cooperate with his former enemies. Critics' claims, which circulated widely on the Internet, were supported by government leaks, former intelligence officials, and UN inspectors—and turned out to be correct: Neither WMDs nor Iraqi connections with Osama bin Laden were ever found. From activist blogs to Internet-based smart mobs (mobilizers) such as MoveOn.org, such information circulated around the globe. The largest antiwar demonstrations in history were held on a weekend in February 2003, involving simultaneous protests by ten million people in eighty countries

and eight hundred cities. Such well-coordinated global demonstrations resulted from an international network of nongovernmental organizations, which are an increasing force in global governance.

The violence that followed Saddam Hussein's defeat illustrates another aspect of modern politics: the challenges of building a democracy. One of the reasons for the invasion, apart from ending the threat of WMDs, was the need to foster democracy in the Middle East, a region largely ruled by princes, military leaders, and corrupt government officials. Bush administration officials argued that toppling Saddam Hussein not only would remove a brutal dictator, ending a major source of instability in the Middle East, but also would show others in the region that democracy was possible. A parallel was made with eastern Europe, where, beginning in 1989, social movements had peacefully toppled communist dictatorships, leading to democratically elected governments in East Germany, Poland, Hungary, Czechoslovakia, Romania, Bulgaria, Albania, and other countries.

Unlike eastern Europe, however—where democracy was generated by grassroots social movements—in Iraq, democracy came from above: an invasion by the U.S.-led coalition, followed by an occupying force charged with creating democratic institutions, enforcing elections, and keeping the peace. Such an assignment proved fraught with difficulties. As we will see, a modern nation-state requires that citizens see themselves as one people under a single government. Previously ruled by Ottomans and the British, the "state of Iraq" comprises many tribal, ethnic, and religious groups, principal among which are the Sunni Kurds in the northern region; Sunni Arab Muslims in the central region (which includes Baghdad); and Shiite Arab Muslims, the large majority, in the southern region. When the British governed the region, they had supported the Sunni Arab leadership; after the British were ousted, Sunni Arabs continued to rule with a vengeance under Saddam Hussein, a Sunni military leader who assumed power in 1979. Under Saddam's rule, Kurds and Shiite Muslims were often persecuted.

Many experts on the region predicted that the overthrow of Saddam Hussein might lead to a civil war in which Sunnis, Shiites, and Kurds would fight bitterly over power and resources while settling old scores. Sunni Arabs, constituting less than 15 percent of the population, had enjoyed a disproportionate share of Iraqi wealth under Saddam, wealth that was largely generated by oil fields in the Kurdish north and the Shiite south. Moreover, the politics of creating democracy were complicated by the presence of Islamists—religious nationalists, influenced (and perhaps supported) by Osama bin Laden, who sought to create a fundamentalist religious state and were willing to engage in suicide bombing to achieve their goals. Furthermore, many Iraqis, whatever their ethnic identity or religious beliefs, resented the invasion, the occupying forces, and the escalating violence associated with the occupation.

Although democratization is a major political force in the world, how best to achieve it is not clear-cut. Like other aspects of contemporary societies, the realm of government and politics is undergoing major changes. **Government** refers to the regular enactment of policies, decisions, and matters of state by officials within a political apparatus; as Iraq shows, creating a stable and successful government can be a challenge in the modern world. **Politics** involves the use of power to affect the scope and content of governmental activities. The sphere of the *political* may extend beyond that of government itself. As Iraq shows, television and the Internet are among the means of exerting political influence; violence is another. In this chapter, we study the main factors affecting political life today. Although many people find politics remote and uninteresting, all of our lives are touched by the political sphere. Governments influence quite personal activities and, in wartime, can even order us to give our lives for their aims. The sphere of government is the sphere of political power. All political life is about power: who holds it, how they achieve it, and what they do with it.

Power and Authority

Power is the ability of individuals or groups to make their own interests or concerns count, even when others resist. It sometimes involves the use of force, such as when the U.S.-led coalition invaded Iraq to overthrow Saddam Hussein. Power is present in almost all social relationships, such as that between employer and employee. This chapter focuses on governmental power, which is almost always accompanied by ideologies to justify the actions of the powerful. For example, the U.S. government justified its invasion of Iraq partly on the basis of fostering democracy; perpetrators of the escalating violence there justify their own actions in terms of Iraqi nationalism in the face of a foreign occupation and religious conviction.

Authority is a government's legitimate use of power; those subject to a government's authority consent to it. Power is thus different from authority. In Iraq, although power is increasingly in the hands of new political institutions, the authority of those institutions remains in doubt. Contrary to what many believe, democracy is not the only type of legitimate government. Dictatorships can have legitimacy as well, as can states governed by religious leaders. But as we shall see later, democracy is presently the most widespread form of government considered legitimate.

The Concept of the State

A **state** exists where a political apparatus of government (institutions like a parliament or congress, plus civil service officials) rules over a territory; its authority is backed by a legal system and by the capacity to use military force to implement its policies. All modern states claim specific territories, have formalized codes of law, and are backed by the control of military force. **Nation-states** have developed at various times in different parts of the world (e.g., the United States in 1776 and the Czech Republic in 1993). Their main characteristics, however, contrast with those of states in traditional civilizations.

Characteristics of the State

SOVEREIGNTY

The territories ruled by traditional states were poorly defined because the central government's level of control was quite weak. The notion of **sovereignty**—that a government possesses authority over an area with clear-cut borders, within which it is the supreme power—had little relevance. All nation-states, by contrast, are sovereign states.

CITIZENSHIP

In traditional states, most of the population were unaware of or uninterested in those who governed them, and they had no political rights or influence. Normally only the dominant classes or affluent groups felt a sense of belonging to a political community. In modern societies, by contrast, most people living within the borders of the political system are **citizens**, having common rights and duties and knowing they are members of a national community (Brubaker 1992). Although some people are political refugees or are "stateless," almost everyone in the world today is a member of a national political order.

NATIONALISM

Nation-states are associated with the rise of **nationalism**, which can be defined as a set of symbols and beliefs providing the sense of membership in a single political community—such as being American, Canadian, or Russian. Although people may have always identified with their family, village, or religious community, nationalism appeared only with the development of the modern state. It is the main expression of identity with a distinct sovereign community.

Freedom in Global Perspective

The level of freedom is based on the political rights and civil liberties individuals have in each country. And in Africa, a number of previously undemocratic nations—including Benin, Ghana, Mozambique, and South Africa—have come to embrace democratic ideals, while some others have experienced fallbacks— Congo has moved from partly free to not free. Freedom House estimates that 47 percent of the world population lives in free countries, 30 percent in partly free and the remaining 23 percent in countries that are designated as not free (Freedom House 2007a).

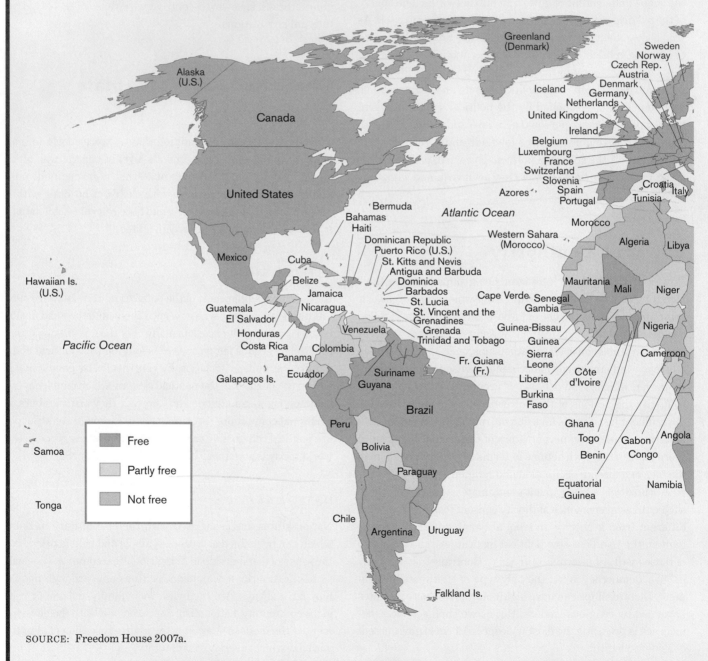

SOURCE: Freedom House 2007a.

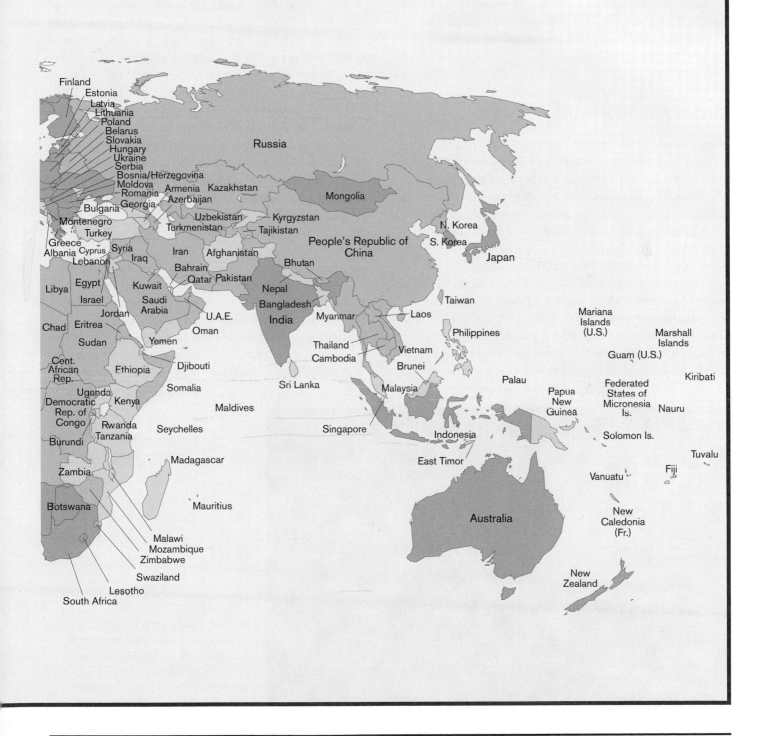

Nationalistic loyalties do not always fit the physical borders marking nations' territories. Because all nation-states comprise communities of diverse backgrounds, **local nationalisms** frequently arise in opposition to those fostered by the states—such as nationalist feelings among the French-speaking population in Quebec, Canada. Yet, while the relation between the nation-state and nationalism is complicated, the two are part of the same process. (We will return to nationalism when we explore its effect on international politics.)

Essentially, a nation-state possesses a government with recognized sovereign rights within a territorial area and can back its claims to sovereignty by the control of military power. Furthermore, many of its citizens have positive feelings of commitment to its national identity.

Citizenship Rights

Most nation-states became centralized political systems through the activities of monarchs who concentrated power in their own hands. Citizenship did not originally carry rights of political participation. Such rights came largely through struggles either limiting the power of monarchs, as in Britain, or overthrowing them—sometimes by revolution, as in the United States and France, followed by a period of negotiation between the new ruling elites and their subjects (Tilly 1996).

Three types of rights are associated with citizenship (Marshall 1973). First, **civil rights** are rights of the individual in law, including privileges that took a long while to achieve (and are not fully recognized in all countries). Examples are the freedom of individuals to live where they choose, freedom of speech and religion, the right to own property, and the right to

equal justice before the law. These rights were not fully established in most European countries until the early nineteenth century (Global Map 13.1), and not all groups were allowed the same privileges. Although the U.S. Constitution granted such rights to Americans well before most European states had them, African Americans were excluded. Even after the Civil War, when blacks legally obtained these rights, they were unable to exercise them.

The second type of citizenship rights consists of **political rights**, especially the right to participate in elections and to run for public office. Again, these were not won easily or quickly. Except in the United States, the achievement of full voting rights even for all men is relatively recent and occurred only after a struggle. In most European countries, the vote was at first limited to male citizens owning a certain amount of property—in other words, an affluent minority. In most Western countries, the vote for women was achieved partly through the efforts of women's movements and partly as a consequence of women entering the formal economy during World War I.

The third type is **social rights**, the right of every individual to enjoy a minimum standard of economic welfare and security. Social rights include sickness benefits, unemployment benefits, and a guaranteed minimum wage—in other words, welfare provisions. In most societies, social rights have developed last because the establishment of civil and political rights has underpinned the fight for social rights. Social rights have been won largely through poorer groups' political strength expressed after obtaining the vote.

A **welfare state** exists when government organizations provide material benefits for those who cannot support themselves adequately through paid employment—the unemployed, the sick, the disabled, and the elderly. All Western countries today

Inmates wear orange jumpsuits in a holding center for illegal immigrants in Brownsville, Texas. The men are all OTMs (Other Than Mexicans) who have entered the United States through Mexico.

provide welfare benefits. In many poorer countries, these benefits are nonexistent.

Although an extensive welfare state was considered the ideal expression of citizenship rights, welfare states have come under pressure from increasing global economic competition and the movement of people from poor, underdeveloped societies to richer, developed countries. As a result, the United States and some European countries have sought to reduce benefits to noncitizens and to prevent additional immigration. For example, in 1994 voters in California passed Proposition 187, which denied social benefits to all illegal immigrants living there. At the national level, the welfare reform act of 1996 denied numerous benefits to *legal* immigrants. And for many years, the U.S. government has patrolled and fenced its border with Mexico to keep out illegal immigrants. Similar patterns of exclusion have occurred in Europe, particularly in Germany and Britain. In these ways, citizenship has been a powerful instrument of social closure, whereby prosperous nation-states have attempted to exclude the migrant poor from the status and benefits that citizenship confers (Brubaker 1992).

☑ CONCEPT CHECKS

1. Describe three main characteristics of the state.
2. What is a welfare state? Can the United States be classified as a welfare state? Why or why not?

Democracy

The word *democracy* has its roots in the Greek term *demokratia*, from *demos* (people) and *kratos* (rule); its basic meaning is a political system in which the people, not monarchs or aristocracies, rule. What does it mean to be ruled by the people? David Held (1987) has identified questions about each part of that phrase.

Regarding "the people":

1. Who are the people?
2. What kind of participation are they allowed?
3. What conditions are assumed to be conducive to participation?

Regarding "rule":

1. How broad or narrow should the scope of rule be? Should it be confined to the sphere of government, or can democracy operate in other spheres, such as the economy?

2. Can rule cover the daily administrative decisions of governments, or should it refer only to major policy decisions?

Regarding "rule by":

1. Must the rule of the people be obeyed? What is the place of obligation and dissent?
2. Should some of the people act outside the law if they believe existing laws are unjust?
3. Under what circumstances, if any, should democratic governments use coercion against those who disagree with their policies?

Answers to these questions have varied over time and in different societies. For example, "the people" have been variously understood as owners of property, white men, educated men, men, and adult men and women. In some societies, **democracy** is limited to the political sphere; in others, it extends to other areas of social life.

Participatory Democracy

Participatory democracy (or **direct democracy**), in which decisions are made communally by those affected by them, was the original type of democracy practiced in ancient Athens. The citizens, constituting a small minority of Athenian society, regularly assembled to consider policies and make major decisions. Participatory democracy has limited importance in modern societies, where the mass of the population have political rights and it would be impossible for everyone to participate in making all the decisions that affect them.

Yet some facets of participatory democracy remain vital. Consider the referendum, whereby the majority of citizens vote on a controversial issue. Direct consultation of large numbers of people occurs via one or two questions on the issue. Referenda regularly occur at the national level in some European countries and frequently on the state level in the United States. Another element of participatory democracy, a meeting of the whole community, occurs at the local level—for example, in annual New England "town meetings."

Monarchies and Liberal Democracies

Very few modern states (e.g., Britain and Belgium) still have monarchs, but their real power is usually limited or nonexistent. In a handful of countries (e.g., Saudi Arabia and Jordan), monarchs still have some control over government, but in most cases they are primarily symbols of national identity. The queen of England, the king of Sweden, and the emperor of Japan are all **constitutional monarchs**: Their real power is severely restricted by their countries' constitutions, which vest authority in the elected representatives of the people. The vast majority of modern states are republican—there is no king or queen, and almost every one, including constitutional monarchies, professes adherence to democracy.

Countries in which voters can choose between two or more parties and in which the mass of the adult population has the right to vote are **liberal democracies**. The United States, the western European countries, Japan, Australia, and New Zealand fall into this category. Some developing countries, such as India, also have liberal democratic systems.

The Spread of Liberal Democracy

For much of the twentieth century, political systems worldwide were divided primarily between liberal democracy and communism, which existed in the former Soviet Union and still exists in China, Cuba, and North Korea. **Communism** is a system of one-party rule in which voters choose not between different parties but between different candidates of the same party—the Communist Party; sometimes only one candidate runs. The Communist Party was the dominant power in Soviet-style societies: It controlled not just the political system but the economy as well.

Since 1989, when the hold of the Soviet Union over Eastern Europe was broken, processes of democratization have swept across the world. The number of democratic nations almost doubled between 1989 and 2005 from 66 to 123 (Freedom House 2007b). Countries such as Nicaragua in Central America and Zambia and South Africa in Africa have established liberal democratic governments. In China, which holds about a fifth of the world's population, the communist government is facing strong pressures toward democratization. During the 1990s, thousands of people remained in prison in China for nonviolently expressing their desire for democracy. But some groups, resisted by the Communist government, are still seeking a transition to a democratic system.

The trend toward democracy is not irreversible. Since 2004, Russia has returned to authoritarianism, according to some observers (Freedom House 2005). Moreover, electoral democracy does not ensure that voters will choose liberal democratic governments; in recent elections in Palestine, Turkey, Morocco, and Iraq, voters chose Islamist parties over more secular, democratic ones.

Why has democracy become so popular? The reasons have to do with the social and economic changes discussed throughout this book. First, democracy is associated with competitive capitalism, and capitalism has been superior to communism as a wealth-generating system. Second, the more social activity becomes globalized and people's lives become influenced by distant events, the more they seek information about how they are ruled—and, therefore, the more they seek greater democracy (Huntington 1991). Third is the influence of mass communication, particularly television, which makes visible most events in the world today. Particularly with the spread of satellite and cable television technologies, governments cannot control what their citizens see.

THE INTERNET AND DEMOCRATIZATION

The Internet is another powerful democratizing force. It transcends national and cultural borders, facilitates the spread of ideas globally, and allows like-minded people to find one another in cyberspace. More and more people worldwide access the Internet regularly and consider it important to their lifestyles.

With the click of a mouse (and the miracle of Google), it is now possible to obtain, instantly and effortlessly, information on any topic. During the 2003 Iraq War, those who tired of news reports by NBC or CNN or Fox could choose among dozens of other news sources from around the world, from the official U.S. site military.com to the Web site of the Arab news service Al Jazeera. Concerned citizens can e-mail their opinions to their elected representatives while putting up a Web site to share their thoughts with anyone and everyone.

Whether Americans use this technology to become better informed and more involved is another matter. While 72.5 percent of Americans report using the Internet, those most likely to have access to it are well-to-do whites with college degrees living in urban or suburban areas. It is not surprising that the young are much more likely to go online than the elderly (Lenhart et al. 2003; Internet World Stats 2008a).

One survey (Rainie et al. 2003) of sixteen hundred adults in the United States, conducted about a week after the war in Iraq began, reported that among the country's 116 million adult Internet users, more than three quarters used the Internet to get information about the war, through e-mail and Web sites. Of these, nearly a quarter sought images that were too gruesome for newspaper or television (Fallows and Rainie 2004). Still, only 17 percent of Internet users reported that the Internet was their main source of war news; nine out of ten relied primarily on television (roughly the same percentage as non-Internet users). In fact, the principal Internet use was to search U.S. television network, newspaper, and government Web sites. Only 6 percent reported viewing sites of groups that opposed the war, which may be why the survey found that

Critical Mass organizes bicycle rides to draw attention to alternative transportation and environmental and urban issues. The group uses the Internet, cell phones, and text messaging to coordinate its rallies.

support for the war was higher among Internet users than among nonusers (Rainie et al. 2003).

One prominent example of the political role of the Internet is MoveOn.org, a liberal organization originally created to electronically mobilize opposition to the impeachment of then-president Bill Clinton. MoveOn.org played a central role in the antiwar protest on February 15, 2003, when millions of people peacefully demonstrated in cities worldwide to express opposition to U.S. plans for military intervention in Iraq. The Web-based organization, with a paid staff of only four people, found out about the protest only a month before it was scheduled to occur. It used its Web site to spread the word, enlist volunteers, and coordinate organization in numerous cities. The day after the demonstrations, MoveOn.org held a "virtual march on Washington" in which a million Americans e-mailed, faxed, and telephoned antiwar messages to their representatives. The ability to engage in such "smart mobbing"—gathering large masses of people electronically, often in only a few hours—has been heralded as a new form of "Internet democracy" (Packer 2003).

Today MoveOn.org claims over 3.3 million members. It has organized smart mobs around other issues—for example, playing a key role in convincing Congress to defeat the proposed Terrorism Awareness Information Program, which would have enabled the government to collect extensive electronic information on private citizens. In December 2003, it organized some twenty-two hundred simultaneous "house parties" throughout the United States, at which tens of thousands of people viewed a documentary opposing the Iraq War. The organization collects millions of dollars through its Web site in

support of liberal causes and has attracted some big-money contributors as well: Billionaires George Soros and Peter Lewis together gave the fledgling organization $5 million in late 2003 (Avins 2003; Brownstein 2003; Menn 2003; Neuman 2003).

In 2008, political organizations and presidential candidates applied the lessons learned from the Moveon.org 2003 campaign. Barack Obama mobilized grassroots support via the Internet and raised contributions totaling a record-breaking $639 million. His campaign also used his Web site to organize volunteers for phone banks and get-out-the-vote efforts.

Obama's Internet campaign is notable because it turned conventional wisdom on its head. Social scientists and politicians believed political indifference and voter apathy would limit the success of campaigns for other contributions.

In the wake of Obama's presidential victory, how might future grassroots efforts use Internet democracy to affect political outcomes?

CENSORSHIP AND SURVEILLANCE ON THE INTERNET

Some governments—especially authoritarian ones—perceive the spread of the Internet as a threat because of the potential of online activity to subvert state authority. Although the Internet has existed more or less freely in most countries, some governments are curbing its use.

China, for example, saw the number of Internet users quadruple from 2.1 million to 8.9 million in 1999—and then explode to 253 million by 2008 (Internet World Stats 2008a). In June

Globalization, Democracy, and Governance

Since the early 1980s, a number of countries in Latin America, such as Chile, Bolivia, and Argentina, have undergone the transition from authoritarian military rule to democracy. Similarly, with the collapse of the Communist bloc in 1989, many Eastern European states—Poland and the former Czechoslovakia, for example—have become democratic, adopting written constitutions, working to ensure that disputes will be resolved according to the rule of law, and, most important, holding popular elections. The resignation of the Indonesian dictator Suharto in 1998 following weeks of massive popular protest marked a turning point in which democratic forces have come to prevail in that country. In Africa, a number of previously undemocratic nations—including Benin, Ghana, Mozambique, and South Africa—have embraced democratic ideals. Other nations have experienced fallbacks—such as Thailand and Congo, which have changed from partly free to not free. Freedom House estimates that 47 percent of the world's population live in "free" countries, 30 percent live in "partly free" countries, and the remaining 23 percent live in countries that are designated as "not free" (Freedom House 2007a).

These classifications reflect efforts by the *Freedom House*, a non-partisan political watchdog organization, to measure the degree of *democracy* and *political freedom* in every nation. Nations are rated on a scale from 1 (most free) to 7 (least free), using criteria such as level of political rights and civil liberties. According to one recent estimate, 64 percent of the world's nations now rely on electoral processes to select their leaders (Freedom House 2007b; Puddington 2007). Yet, the move toward democracy has stalled recently. In 2007, Thailand experienced a military coup, transforming a free democratic country into military dictatorship. Kenya, an African country that had previously held democratic elections, found itself convulsed with protests when its presidential election in late 2007 was widely believed to be rigged in favor of the incumbent. China, the world's most populous country, has made little move toward democracy.

Setbacks aside, it would appear as though the principles of democracy have made significant strides over the last few decades, inaugurating a new era of global political freedom.

The growing number of cross-national cultural contacts that globalization has brought with it has invigorated democratic movements in many countries. Globalized media, along with advances in communications technology, have exposed inhabitants of many nondemocratic nations to democratic ideals, increasing internal pressure on political elites to hold elections. Of course, such pressure does not automatically result from the gradual global spread of the notion of democracy. More important is that with globalization, news of democratic revolutions and accounts of the mobilizing processes that lead to them are quickly spread on a regional level. News of the revolution in Poland in 1989, for example, took little time to travel to Hungary, providing prodemocracy activists there with a useful, regionally appropriate model around which to orient their work.

But at the same time, globalization has brought to the fore new, powerful countertrends that weaken or challenge democratic governance. The interconnection of the global economy constrains the ability of democratic governments to set policy. As management guru Kenichi Ohmae has claimed, "Nation states have become increasingly vulnerable to the discipline imposed by economic choices made elsewhere by people and institutions over which they have no practical control" (1990: p. 11). For instance, the World Trade Organization (WTO) prohibits certain trade policies, such as raising tariffs in order to protect a vulnerable industry. Such prohibitions on certain trade and industrial policies tie the hands of developing countries, limiting the means by which they can promote domestic economic development. Similarly, financial markets impose discipline on nation-states. For instance, when in 2002 Lula da Silva, a socialist leader of the Brazilian Workers' Party, successfully campaigned for president by condemning the negative effect of globalization, bond rating companies downgraded Brazilian bonds, signaling to the global investors that Brazil was no longer a safe place to invest their money (*Los Angeles Times* 2002). In the view of global financial markets, the election of a socialist in Brazil would be detrimental to foreign investment in Brazil—and they made it clear to Brazilians that electing a socialist would be punished by global financial markets.

Additionally, transnational corporations (TNCs) are able to seek out those places in the world where products can be made the cheapest, where returns on investments will be the highest, and where taxes on profits are the lowest. TNCs are highly flexible, and they use this flexibility to leverage concessions from national and local governments. Sometimes corporations will leave the country of their origin and set up operations in a country where wages are lower. Sometimes they threaten to do so just to seek concessions from the governments regulating their business activities.

These examples demonstrate how the interconnections of the global economy limit the policy options of governments and weaken their ability to respond to democratic processes. While it has become common sense that governments should work to improve the economic and social conditions of their citizens, this is difficult when governments are vulnerable to coercion from global economic actors. When the economy is global, when the rules for economic activity are no longer defined by domestic political actors, and when businesses can relocate to more profitable countries, how can governments regulate the activities that take place in their boundaries?

Further still, greater global interconnection has produced social backlashes. Increasing nationalism, including the religious nationalism that fueled the terrorist attacks of September 11, 2001, can be understood as a response to pressures created by globalization. Globalization has brought Western modernism to all parts of the globe, but it is not equally

Thai police face off against demonstrators during a rally in Bangkok. The demonstrators, mostly supporters of ousted Thai prime minister Thaksin Shinawatra, called for the return to democracy in Thailand. Thaksin was forced from power in a bloodless coup in September 2006.

welcome, as local groups seek to retain their unique identities and social relationships. Some people reject the values of the global market and instead seek to resist it, producing new kinds of social movements, radical and conservative alike. Combined with weak states, subnational groups have become powerful actors, playing their struggles out on a global stage. These countertrends, in their most violent forms, also pose significant challenges to the ability of democratic governments to govern. How can democratic governments balance the rights to privacy against the need for security? Can demands for self-rule be accommodated in a democratic framework? What does it mean to be "democratic" in this age of globalization?

References

Freedom House. 2007. "Freedom in the World 2007." www.freedomhouse.org/template.cfm?page=351&ana_page=334&year=2007 (accessed December 24, 2007).

Los Angeles Times. 2002. "Toss a Life Buoy to Brazil." Op-ed. *Los Angeles Times,* July 6.

Ohmae, Kenichi. 1996. *The End of the Nation State: The Rise of Regional Economies.* New York: HarperCollins.

Puddington, Arch. 2007. "Freedom in the World 2007: Freedom Stagnation amid Pushback Against Democracy." Freedom House. www.freedomhouse.org/template.cfm?page=130&year=2007 (accessed December 24, 2007).

2007, there were nearly 1.31 million Web sites in China, but the number is estimated to be doubling every six months (China Internet Network Information Center 2007; White 2003). In response, the Chinese government has banned the publication of "state secrets" on the Internet, has blocked direct and indirect links between domestic Chinese and foreign Web sites, and has initiated a system of Web censors to monitor the context of news and information exchanged on the Internet.

The Chinese Communist leadership sees the Internet as threatening state security by enabling political opposition groups to coordinate their activities. In April 1999, for example, thousands of supporters of Falun Gong—a spiritual movement whose members believe that breathing exercises prolong life—mobilized over the Internet and gathered in Beijing for a silent protest. Moreover, sensitive information on China's military and technological capacities has supposedly been published on Chinese Web sites. Such events confirm to the government that the Internet is a powerful medium of communication that must be controlled. The government requires Internet service providers (ISPs) to report detailed information on users and Internet activities, censoring all "subversive" content—which includes information on HIV/AIDS, as well as stories about democracy and Tibet. Much of the filtering is facilitated by U.S. companies that provide the software. Following a deadly fire in an Internet café in 2002, the Chinese government closed down thousands of such cafés, citing safety concerns (Reporters without Borders [RWB] 2003).

Other authoritarian governments have also concluded that the Internet threatens their power. The Burmese government has banned the dissemination of information "detrimental to government" through the Internet or e-mail. Malaysian authorities have demanded that cyber cafés keep lists of all

Students use an Internet cafe in Yangon, Myanmar's biggest city. Myanmar has some of the world's toughest Internet controls.

individuals who use their computers. In Russia, local ISPs must join an electronic monitoring scheme overseen by the federal security service. Reporters without Borders (2003) reports that (as of December 2003) fifty-three "cyberdissidents" are being held around the world for their Internet activities, mainly in China, and firms such as Google, which hope to establish themselves in the lucrative Chinese Internet market, have agreed to some degree of government censorship. Moreover, the disclosure that the U.S. government has conducted secret monitoring of telephone conversations, e-mail, and Internet communication between U.S. citizens and suspected foreign terrorists has raised the question of whether such spying—without a warrant—violates U.S. laws and even the Constitution (Risen and Lichtblau 2005).

The U.S. government expanded its surveillance activities after the attacks of September 11, 2001. The FBI immediately requested all major ISPs to install Carnivore software, which would allow it to record, filter, and store e-mails on the basis of specific words. Internet surveillance was further strengthened by the USA Patriot Act, enacted in October 2001, which expanded the types of Internet activity that could be obtained without the consent of a judge. The Pentagon's Information Awareness Office is developing software to track Internet use, including credit-card and airline-ticket purchases, while the FBI is reportedly working on "magic lantern" software that can secretly record the keystrokes of an Internet user, enabling the agency to overcome surveillance barriers posed by encryption software (Hentoff 2002).

Democracy in the United States

POLITICAL PARTIES

A political party is an organization of individuals with broadly similar political aims, oriented toward achieving legitimate control of government through an electoral process. Two parties dominate the political system where elections are based on the principle of winner take all, as in the United States. The candidate who gains the most votes wins the election, no matter what proportion of the overall vote he or she gains (Duverger 1954). Exceptions to this general rule in the United States involve presidential elections, which are decided by the electoral college. At three times in American history, one candidate won the majority of votes from citizens but still lost the electoral college vote. This occurred most recently in 2000, when Al Gore outpolled George W. Bush by about 500,000 votes but still lost the electoral vote by 271 to 267. Where elections are based on different principles, as in proportional representation (in which seats in a representative

An overflow crowd waits to vote in Honolulu, Hawaii. Why does the United States have a historically low voter turnout rate?

assembly are allocated according to the proportions of the vote attained), five or six or more parties may be represented in the assembly. When they lack a majority, some of the parties have to form a coalition—an alliance with each other to form a government.

In the United States, the political system has become a two-party one between Republicans and Democrats, although there is no formal restriction on the number of political parties. Two-party systems lead to a concentration on the middle ground, where most votes are found. Often cultivating a moderate image, the two parties may resemble one another so closely that the choice they offer is relatively slight—even though each party supposedly represents a plurality of interests. Multiparty systems allow more direct expression of divergent interests and provide scope for the representation of radical alternatives. Green party representatives or representatives of far right parties, found in some European parliaments, are cases in point. However, no one party can achieve an overall majority, and the resulting government by coalition may lead to either a stalemate (if compromises can't be made) or a rapid succession of elections and new governments, none remaining in power for long.

Some writers have studied the connection between voting patterns and class differences. Liberal and leftist parties gain most votes from lower-class groups, whereas conservative or rightist parties gain the affluent groups' votes (Lipset 1981). The party system in the United States is unique among Western societies because there is no large leftist party. Although the Democratic Party has tended to appeal more to lower-class groups, and the Republicans have drawn support from the more affluent sectors, the connections are not absolute. Each party has a conservative and a liberal wing; conservative and liberal members of one party commonly align themselves with those holding similar opinions in the other party on certain issues.

POLITICS AND VOTING

The founders of the American governmental system did not foresee a role for parties in the political order. George Washington recognized that interest groups would develop, but he warned against "the harmful effects of the spirit of party." Thomas Jefferson echoed these sentiments but in fact became the leader of one of the earliest party organizations. The early parties endorsed candidates for Congress, and the subsequent national division of parties spread to the state legislatures. Soon the parties developed into state organizations representing specific interests and points of view. A two-party system was well established by the 1830s, and its fundamental nature has not altered greatly to this day.

Building mass support for a party in the United States is difficult, because the country is so large and includes so many regional, cultural, and ethnic groups. The parties have all cultivated electoral strength by forging broad regional bases of support and by campaigning for very general political ideals.

As measured by levels of membership, party identification, and voting support, each of the major American parties is in decline (Wattenberg 1996). One study showed that the numbers declaring themselves to be "independent" of either party grew from 22 percent in 1952 to over 38 percent in 2004 (Pew Research Center 2004). This proportion has remained stable, with 37 percent of Americans identifying as "independent" voters in 2007 (Saad 2007b).

Although Democrats held an edge in party identification during the Clinton years, by the end of 2003 roughly the same number of Americans (30–31 percent) identified with both parties. By July 2007, Democrats had regained a slight edge in voter identification, with 32 percent of Americans saying that they were Democrats versus 29 percent Republicans (Saad 2007). Moreover, Democrats and Republicans have become increasingly polarized. For example, Republicans are more likely to favor an assertive national security strategy, whereas Democrats are increasingly critical of business and favor stronger government support for the poor (Pew Research Center 2003; Wattenberg 1996).

Since the early 1960s, voter turnout in the United States has steadily decreased, and today only slightly more than half the electorate vote in presidential elections. The turnout for congressional elections is around 40 percent (National Election Studies [NES] 2003). Furthermore, there are significant differences by race and ethnicity, age, educational attainment, and income. Turnout is highest among whites and lowest among Hispanics, with blacks and Asian Americans in

"Dewey Defeats Truman"?
"Gore Defeats Bush"?

In the history of journalism, two headlines still bring shame to political reporters everywhere. On the morning after the 1948 U.S. presidential election, the *Chicago Daily Tribune* front-page headline blazed, "Dewey Defeats Truman." Roughly fifty years later, at 7:49 P.M. on election night November 7, 2000, senior NBC newsmen Tom Brokaw and Tim Russert were the first of the TV news networks to proclaim that Al Gore had won Florida and that he was almost assuredly the forty-third President of the United States. As everyone now knows, Harry S. Truman and George W. Bush ultimately took office. What happened? The Truman/Dewey debacle revealed longstanding methodological problems that have vexed political pollsters, while the Bush/Gore embarrassment highlights the limitations of using exit poll data to predict an election outcome (Carr 2005).

Experts still don't agree fully on why Dewey was named victor in 1948, but most say that the incident triggered improvements in modern polling techniques. First, pollsters learned that they had to keep polling up until the last minute, because personal preferences could

change—especially in the final days leading up to the election. Second, they moved away from "quota sampling" to "random sampling." Quota sampling involves interviewing a set number of people from different ethnic and racial groups, whereas random sampling means every person in a given population has an equal

chance of being chosen. Third, pollsters recognized that it's not only opinions that count, but also whether or not the person with that opinion actually gets out and votes. Pollsters have developed sophisticated measures of who is likely to vote, and now they typically include only "registered voters" or "likely voters" in their samples. This sampling consideration is

important because "likely voters" tend to include fewer ethnic minorities, fewer union members, and more members of wealthy households, and thus tend to lean Republican more so than broad samples of "American adults."

While important sampling issues have been resolved since 1948, a new set of challenges has arisen for political researchers. First, response rates (or the proportion of people who agree to answer a pollster's questions) are lower than ever before, hovering around 30 percent (and even lower in metropolitan areas). In an era of overzealous telemarketers, voice mail, and caller ID, potential interviewees are often too busy (or too skeptical) to pick up their phone and answer a pollster's question. Some people have more than one chance of being contacted: wealthier people often have two (or more) phones, which increases their chances of getting picked. Poorer people and those without phones, by contrast, are less likely to be contacted by pollsters. Young people who move often, or who rely on cell phones rather than landlines, also are less likely to be contacted by pollsters.

between. Generally, turnout increases with age: Only a little more than a third of all voters age eighteen to twenty-four voted for president in 2000, compared with nearly three quarters of voters in their sixties. However, in the 2008 presidential election, the number of young voters (under age thirty) swelled to about twenty-four million because of an effective voter mobilization campaign. Education also influences voting

behavior: Fewer than two in five persons who lack a high school diploma voted in 2000, compared with four out of five with college degrees. Turnout was only about a third among individuals earning under $5,000, rising to three quarters among those earning over $75,000.

People give many reasons for not voting. In one study of the 2000 presidential election, two out of five nonvoters felt that

Two other methodological issues are cited as the key reasons behind the incorrect declaration of Al Gore as winner in 2000. First, news agencies extrapolated the results of initial election returns to the overall population—even when only a small fraction of returns were in. That means that they assumed that the precincts that reported their results early in the evening were representative of a state's overall political leanings. Second, the TV networks relied on exit polling data supplied to them by Voter News Service (VNS), a consortium funded by the networks and the Associated Press. VNS has accurately predicted many elections in the past; however, exit poll data are problematic when it comes to projecting a winner. These data are obtained by asking people face-to-face, as they exit their polling place, whom they voted for. For exit polls to work, pollsters must rely on adequate and representative samples, and this matters all the more in a close election (such as in 2000 when Bush and Gore grabbed 47.9 percent and 48.4 percent of the popular vote, respectively).

Exit polls do have several strengths. They reveal the ways that specific demographic groups voted and the reasons behind their votes. They also help to pinpoint voter turnout in demographic groups; this is an important piece of information for voter registration drives and public awareness campaigns. However, exit polls are at their worst when used as a tool for projecting a winner in a close race.

Sociologists believe that the proliferation of political polls also creates serious problems for prediction, by creating a self-fulfilling prophecy. Last-minute poll results can generate a possible "bandwagon" effect, where people want to be on what they are told is the "winning" side. On the other hand, an opposite "underdog" effect is possible; people feel sorry for and ultimately support a candidate because he or she is said to have little chance of winning. Other voters, still, want to feel that they are independent minded and vote for the person lagging in the polls. Some observers attribute Hillary Clinton's surprise victory in the 2008 New Hampshire primary to the fact that she was lagging behind Barack Obama in the polls—and this "underdog" effect was exacerbated by the appearance that her opponents were "ganging up" on her in debates (Steinberg and Elder 2008). Polling results also can help (or hurt) the candidate as he or she works to secure campaign contributions.

Despite their many possible limitations, however, well-designed polls remain the single best way to measure the pulse of voters' political sentiments. Before believing the media's reports of these poll data, however, readers should carefully scrutinize the method of poll taking used.

Questions

- What explanation have pollsters given for why the *Chicago Tribune* erroneously named Thomas E. Dewey as the victor in the 1948 presidential election?
- What explanation have pollsters given for why the major television news networks erroneously named Al Gore as the victor in the 2000 presidential election?
- What are two strengths and weaknesses of exit polls?
- How might political poll data affect voters' behavior?

FOR FURTHER EXPLORATION

Carr, Deborah. 2005. "Political Polls: A Primer" and "20 Questions a Sociologist Should Ask about Poll Results." *Contexts* 4(1): 32–33.

Chicago Daily Tribune. 1948. "Dewey Defeats Truman." *Chicago Daily Tribune,* November 3, 1948.

Steinberg, Jacques, and Janet Elder. 2008. "Analyzing the New Hampshire Surprise." *New York Times,* January 10, 2008. www.nytimes.com/2008/01/10/us/politics/10media .html?_r=1&scp=1&sq=hillary+clinton+ victory+new+hampshire&oref=slogin (accessed January 20, 2008).

voting was not worth the effort: 21 percent reported they were "too busy," while another 20 percent stated they either didn't like the candidates or simply weren't interested. Many of the remaining nonvoters cited an illness or other emergency, lack of transportation or some other inconvenience, bad weather, being out of town, or forgetfulness. Only 7 percent cited problems in registering to vote, although this is likely a greater difficulty for lower-income voters (NES 2003). Clearly, voting is not a high priority among many Americans.

Voter turnout in the United States is among the world's lowest. Many studies have found that countries with high rates of literacy, high average incomes, and well-established political freedoms and civil liberties have high voter turnouts. Even though the United States ranks high on all these measures, it fails to motivate people to vote. Sweden's International Institute for Democracy and Electoral Assistance tracked voter turnout in all countries holding national elections during the period 1945–2002. Voter turnout in the United States averaged only 48 percent overall, earning it 138th place (out of 169 countries). In comparison, voter turnout in Europe averaged 74 percent; Asia, 70 percent; South America, 62 percent; Mexico, Central America, and the Caribbean, 60 percent; and Africa, 55 percent (Pintor and Gratschew 2002).

Why is voter turnout so low in the United States? Whereas throughout Europe compulsory registration is common and registration is easy, in the United States voters must register well in advance of elections; many fail to do so and are thus disqualified from voting. Thirty-three countries now practice compulsory voting. Even where enforcement is weak or nonexistent, voter turnout is higher where voting is mandated by law (Pintor and Gratschew 2002).

Another reason may be that because winner-take-all-type elections discourage the formation of third parties, voters may feel a lack of viable choices. A staunch environmentalist may see no point in voting if the Green Party candidate has no chance of winning a seat in Congress; an antigovernment voter may draw the same conclusion in regard to the Libertarian Party's chances. In many countries (including most European countries), some system of proportional representation is practiced, under which parties receive seats in proportion to the vote they get in electoral districts. Thus, for example, if a district has ten seats in Parliament, and the Conservative Party gets 30 percent of the vote, that district would send three representatives to Parliament. Under this system, even small parties can often muster sufficient support to elect one or two representatives. When voters have a wider range of choices, they are more likely to vote.

Finally, the range of elections for offices at all levels—including sheriffs, judges, city treasurers, and many other posts—is much more extensive in the United States than in other Western societies. Americans are entitled to do about three or four times as much electing as citizens elsewhere. Low voter turnout thus must be balanced against the wider extent of voter choice.

INTEREST GROUPS

An **interest group** is any organization that attempts to persuade elected officials to consider its aims when deciding on legislation. The American Medical Association, the National Organization for Women, and the National Rifle Association are examples. Some interest groups are national; others are statewide. Some are permanently organized; others are short lived. *Lobbying* is the act of persuading influential officials to

Former Vice President Dick Cheney (*center*) accepts a rifle from the president (Kayne Robinson, *right*) and vice president (Wayne R. LaPierre, *left*) of the National Rifle Association after concluding his keynote address at the association's 2004 annual convention.

vote in favor of a cause or otherwise lend support to the aims of an interest group.

The U.S. Lobbying Disclosure Act of 1995 requires all organizations employing lobbyists to register with Congress and to disclose whom they represent, whom they lobby, what they are lobbying for, and how much they are paid. As of December 2005, nearly thirty-five thousand lobbyists were registered (Birnbaum 2005b; Center for Public Integrity 2003; Political Money Line 2003). To run as a candidate is enormously expensive, and interest groups provide much of the funding at all levels of political office. In the 2000 presidential election, for example, the Republican ticket (Bush-Cheney) raised nearly $200 million; the Democrats (Gore-Lieberman) nearly $135 million (Center for Responsive Politics [CRP] 2003). The Republican candidate for the November 2008 presidential election, John McCain, raised over $360 million and the Democratic candidate, Barack Obama, raised over $639 million (CRP 2008). Even to run for the House or Senate costs a small fortune. As of January 2008, it cost over three hundred thousand dollars to run for the House of Representatives and over three times as much to run for Senate.

In the 2004 congressional election, 399 out of 407 incumbents running for reelection to the House of Representatives beat their challengers—a 98 percent success rate. Incumbents have an enormous advantage in soliciting money. In the 2004 race for the House, for example, they raised about six times as much money as their challengers (CRP 2005). In the 2008 election, incumbents in the House of Representatives raised more than $539 million compared to only $193 million by their challengers. Incumbents are favored as fund-raisers partly because they can curry favor with special interests and other contributors, since they are in a position to ensure favorable votes and obtain spending on their contributors' pet issues. Incumbency also provides familiarity—a formidable obstacle for most challengers to overcome. The cost of beating an incumbent has increased significantly in the last quarter century (Figure 13.1), which is perhaps why 43 percent of all newly elected congressional representatives in 2002 were millionaires. (At least 40 percent of all senators are also millionaires.)

Corporations, which have a strong stake in getting favorable legislation and government contracts, are the largest contributors to campaigns, accounting for nearly three quarters of the total in the 2002 election cycle (Figure 13.2). About three fifths of all corporate contributions go to Republican candidates. Labor unions overwhelmingly favor Democrats.

About a third of the funding in congressional elections comes from political action committees (PACs), which are set up by interest groups to raise and distribute campaign funds. PACs raised a total of $17.9 million, representing 22 percent of the receipts during the first six months of 2007. In 2007–2008, Operating Engineers Union made the largest contribution, totaling $1.4 million. Close behind is International Brotherhood of Electric Workers ($1.1 million). Labor unions also weigh in heavily, accounting for nearly half of the largest contributors. Since 1989, the American Federation of State, County, and Municipal Employees has been the largest overall donor, giving nearly $37 million over fifteen years to various candidates for office (CRP 2008).

Interest groups and PACs not only help elect candidates, they also influence the outcome of votes in Congress. The Medicare Reform Act of 2003, which created a $400 billion program to extend prescription drug benefits to the elderly, was heavily pushed by the pharmaceutical industry, which since 1996 has spent more than a half a billion dollars to lobby

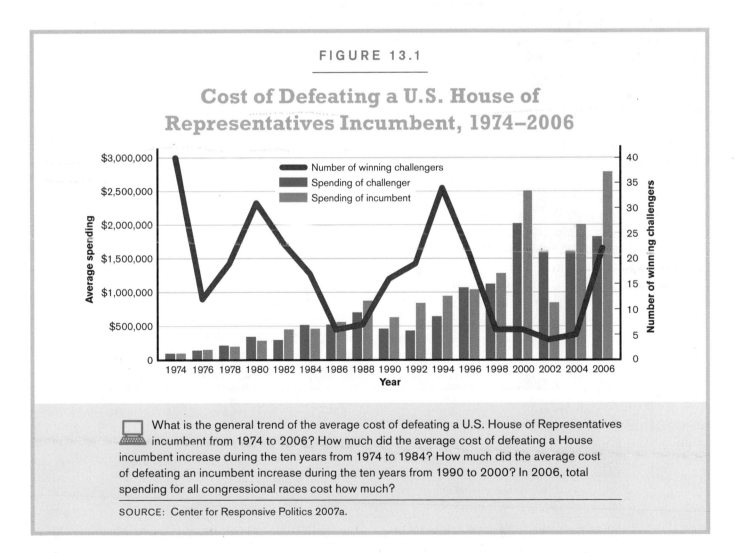

FIGURE 13.1

Cost of Defeating a U.S. House of Representatives Incumbent, 1974–2006

What is the general trend of the average cost of defeating a U.S. House of Representatives incumbent from 1974 to 2006? How much did the average cost of defeating a House incumbent increase during the ten years from 1974 to 1984? How much did the average cost of defeating an incumbent increase during the ten years from 1990 to 2000? In 2006, total spending for all congressional races cost how much?

SOURCE: Center for Responsive Politics 2007a.

FIGURE 13.2

Business-Labor-Ideology Split in PAC and Individual Donations to Candidates and Parties, 2006 Election Cycle

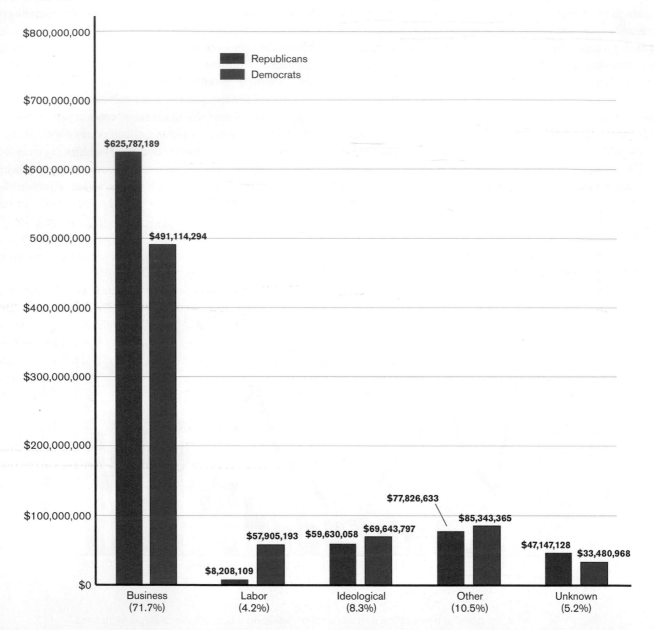

Which groups supported the Republican candidates and party in the 2006 election cycle more than the Democrats? "Business" donated what percentage of the total donations to both political parties and candidates during the 2006 election cycle? Which group most clearly favored one political party over the other with their donations, and which party do they favor?

SOURCE: Center for Responsive Politics 2007b.

Congress, the White House, and federal regulators as well as to launch advertising campaigns aimed at the general public (Common Cause 2003). Although members of Congress hotly debated the long-run benefit to the elderly, there is no question that drug companies reap considerable benefit.

In 2002, Congress passed the McCain-Feingold campaign finance reform law, which severely restricted unlimited campaign contributions. Under federal laws, corporations and labor unions are prohibited from contributing to federal campaigns. Legal loopholes, however, permit unlimited "soft-money" contributions to the political parties' "nonfederal accounts," supposedly destined for party-building activities unrelated to federal campaigns. In fact, almost all the money finds its way back into presidential and congressional elections (Common Cause 2002). The McCain-Feingold law closes the loophole. Candidates for federal elections are once again restricted to raising money from individuals—$2,000 per candidate, $25,000 to political parties. However, campaigns have already found a new loophole: 527 organizations. These groups are political organizations that campaign and lobby for candidates and are funded by unlimited soft-money donations. They cannot coordinate their actions with any of the candidates, but they typically support one party or the other. In the 2004 presidential campaign, 527s like MoveOn.org and the Swift Vets and POWs for Truth spent a total of nearly $400 million.

The Political Participation of Women

The early women's movements saw the vote as the symbol of political freedom and as the means of achieving greater economic and social equality. In the United States, women's leaders underwent considerable hardships to reach this end. Even today, in many countries, women do not have the same voting rights as men.

Women's obtaining the vote has not greatly altered the nature of politics. Women's voting patterns, like those of men, are shaped by party preferences, policy options, and the choice of candidates. Many political observers attribute Hillary Clinton's victory in the January 2008 New Hampshire Democratic primary to the outpouring of women voters who came to show their support for Clinton. The influence of women on politics cannot be assessed solely through voting patterns, however. Feminist groups have impacted political life independently of the franchise, particularly in recent decades. Since the early 1960s, the National Organization for Women (NOW) and other women's groups in the United States have been instrumental in the passing of equal opportunity acts and in getting a range of issues directly affecting women on the political agenda. Such issues include equal rights at work, the availability of abortion, changes in family and divorce laws, and lesbian rights. In 1973, women achieved a legal victory when the Supreme Court ruled in *Roe v. Wade* that women had a legal right to abortion. The 1989 Court ruling in *Webster v. Reproductive Health Services,* which placed restrictions on that right, caused a resurgence of involvement in the women's movement.

Most European countries lack comparable national women's organizations, but a "second wave" of feminism has brought the same issues to the center of the political stage. Although some matters—such as whether abortion should be freely available—have proved highly controversial among women as well as men, it seems clear that many concerns affecting women, which previously had seemed outside politics, are now central to political debates.

Yet, in general, women are poorly represented among political elites. As of the November 2008 elections in the United States, there were seventy-seven female members in the House

Senator Hillary Clinton signs autographs during her 2008 presidential campaign.

of Representatives, making up just over 16 percent of the total membership. This number has almost tripled since the early 1970s, but it is still not representative of the number of female citizens in the population. In 2008, there were only seventeen women in the Senate, representing 17 percent of the upper chamber's membership.

Most surprising about the figures on women's involvement at higher levels of political organizations is the slowness of change. In the business sector, men still monopolize the top positions, but women are making more inroads than previously. This does not seem to be happening in the political sphere—even though nearly all political parties today are nominally committed to securing equal opportunities for women and men. Since 1990, female candidates for political office have been successful *when they have run for office*. The critical factor seems to be that political parties (which are largely run by men) have not recruited as many women to run for office.

The factors that impede women's advancement in the economy also operate in the realm of politics. Rising within a political organization requires considerable effort and time, which women shouldering major domestic burdens can rarely generate. But there may be an additional influence in political life, where a high level of power is concentrated: Perhaps men are especially reluctant to abandon their dominance in such a sphere.

Who Rules? Theories of Democracy

DEMOCRATIC ELITISM

One of the most influential views of the nature and limits of modern democracy was set out by Max Weber and, in modified form, by economist Joseph Schumpeter (1983; orig. 1942). Their ideas are called the theory of **democratic elitism**.

Weber held that direct democracy is impossible as a means of regular government in large-scale societies—not only for the logistical reason that millions of people cannot meet to make political decisions, but also because running a complex society demands *expertise*. Participatory democracy, Weber believed, can succeed only in small organizations where the work is straightforward. When complicated decisions or policies are involved, even in modest-size groups—such as a small business firm—specialized knowledge and skills are necessary. Because experts carry out their jobs on a continuous basis, positions requiring expertise cannot be subject to regular election by people with vague knowledge of the necessary skills and information. Although higher officials, responsible for overall policy decisions, are elected, there must be a large substratum of full-time bureaucratic officials who play a large part in running a country (Weber 1979; orig. 1921).

In Weber's view, the development of mass citizenship, which is closely connected with the idea of general democratic participation, greatly expands the need for bureaucratic officialdom. For example, provision for welfare, health, and education requires permanent, large-scale administrative systems.

Representative multiparty democracy, according to Weber, helps defend against both arbitrary decision making on the part of political leaders (because they are subject to popular elections) and power being completely usurped by bureaucrats (because elected officials set overall policy). But under these circumstances, the contribution of democratic institutions falls short of achieving pure democracy. "Rule by the people" is possible in only a very limited sense. To achieve power, political parties must become organized in a systematic way—must become bureaucratized. "Party machines" then develop that threaten the autonomy of parliaments or congresses in discussing and formulating policies. If a party with a majority representation can dictate policy, and if that party is run by officials who are permanently in control, then the level of democracy is slim.

For democratic systems to be effective, Weber argued, two conditions must be met. First, there must be parties that represent different interests and have different outlooks. If the policies of competing parties are basically the same, voters lack any effective choice. Weber held that one-party systems cannot be democratic in any meaningful way. Second, there must be political leaders with imagination and courage to escape the inertia of bureaucracy. Weber emphasized the importance of *leadership* in democracy, which is why his view is known as democratic elitism: Rule by elites is inevitable; ideally they will represent our interests in an innovative and insightful fashion. Parliaments and congresses give rise to political leaders who can counter the influence of bureaucracy and command mass support. Weber valued multiparty democracy more for the quality of leadership it generates than for the mass participation in politics it makes possible.

Joseph Schumpeter (1983) agreed with Weber about the limits of mass political participation and about democracy being important as a method of generating effective and responsible government. Democracy, Schumpeter (1983) stated, is the rule of *the politician,* not *the people.* To achieve voting support, however, politicians must be minimally responsive to the demands and interests of the electorate. Only if there is competition to secure votes can arbitrary rule be avoided.

PLURALIST THEORIES

Pluralists accept that individual citizens can have little or no *direct* influence on political decision making. But they argue that the presence of interest groups can limit the centralization of power in the hands of government officials. Competing interest groups or factions are vital to democracy because they divide up power, reducing the exclusive influence of any one group or class (Truman 1981).

In the pluralist view, government policies in a democracy are influenced by bargaining among interest groups—business organizations, trade unions, ethnic groups, environmental organizations, religious groups, and so forth. A democratic political order involves a balance among competing interests, all having some effect on policy but none dominating the mechanisms of government. Elections are also influenced by this situation, for to achieve a majority of votes the parties must be responsive to diverse interest groups. The United States is considered the most pluralistic of industrialized societies and, therefore, the most democratic. Competition among interest groups occurs not only at the national level but also within the states and in local communities.

THE POWER ELITE

C. Wright Mills's celebrated work *The Power Elite* (1956) is different from pluralist theories. According to Mills, early in its history American society did show flexibility and diversity at all levels; however, this has since changed.

Mills argues that during the twentieth century a process of institutional centralization occurred in the political order, the economy, and the military. On the political side, individual state governments used to be very powerful and were loosely coordinated by the federal government. But political power today, Mills argues, is tightly coordinated at the federal level. Similarly, the economy once comprised many small units, businesses, banks, and farms but now is dominated by a cluster of very large corporations. Finally, since World War II, the military, once restricted in size, has grown to a giant establishment at the heart of the country's institutions.

Not only has each sphere become more centralized, according to Mills, but they have increasingly merged into a unified system of power. Those holding the highest positions in all three institutional areas have similar social backgrounds, have parallel interests, and often know one another personally. They have become a **power elite** that runs the country and, given the international position of the United States, influences much of the rest of the world.

The power elite mainly comprises white Anglo-Saxon Protestants (WASPs) who are from wealthy families, have attended the same prestigious universities, belong to the same clubs, and sit on government committees with one another. They have closely connected concerns. Business and political leaders work together, and both have close relationships with the military through weapons contracting and the supply of

goods for the armed forces. There is considerable movement among top positions in the three spheres. Politicians have business interests; business leaders often run for public office; higher military personnel sit on the boards of the large companies.

In opposition to pluralist interpretations, Mills sees three distinct levels of power in the United States. The power elite occupies the highest level, formally and informally making key decisions affecting both domestic and foreign policy. Interest groups operate at the middle levels of power, together with local government agencies. Their influence over major policy decisions is limited. At the bottom is the mass of the population, who have virtually no influence on policy decisions because these are made within closed settings by the power elite. Because the power elite spans the top of both party organizations, the choices open to voters in presidential and congressional elections are so small as to be of little consequence.

Since Mills published his study, other researchers have analyzed the social background and interconnections of leading figures in American society (Dye 1986). All studies find that the social backgrounds of those in leading positions are highly unrepresentative of the population as a whole (Domhoff 1971, 1979, 1983, 1998).

The main argument among sociologists about the distribution of power in the United States now focuses on the relative power of government officials and of the business leaders who run large corporations. Some scholars argue that true power lies with politicians in government and that business leaders are much less powerful (Amenta 1998; Orloff 1993; Skocpol 1992). Other scholars hold that corporate business executives and families of great wealth form a capitalist class that greatly influences government officials and experts through lobbying, campaign contributions, the sponsorship of think tanks, and the appointment of top corporate leaders to important government positions (Domhoff 1998). Both sides agree, however, that it is not inevitable for business leaders or government officials to always be dominant. Although an elite class—whether elected, expert, or corporate—rules America, the power of groups can change over time, leaving open the possibility that those who are now powerless could be dominant in the future.

THE ROLE OF THE MILITARY

Mills's argument that the military plays a central role in the power elite was buttressed by a well-known warning from a former military hero and U.S. president, Dwight David Eisenhower. In his farewell presidential speech in 1961, Eisenhower warned of the dangers of the "military-industrial complex": "In the councils of government, we must guard against the acquisition of unwarranted influence, whether sought or unsought,

TABLE 13.1

World's Fifteen Largest Military Budgets, 2008

RANK	COUNTRY	AMOUNT (BILLIONS)	PERCENT WORLD SHARE
1	United States	$711.0	48.00%
2	China	122.0	8.00
3	Russia	70.0	5.00
4	United Kingdom	55.4	4.75
5	France	54.0	3.76
6	Japan	41.1	2.79
7	Germany	37.8	2.57
8	Italy	30.6	2.08
9	Saudi Arabia	29.5	2.00
10	South Korea	24.6	1.67
11	India	22.4	1.52
12	Australia	17.2	1.17
13	Brazil	16.2	1.10
14	Canada	15.0	1.02
15	Spain	14.4	0.98
Subtotal (top 15)		1,261.2	86.41
World		1,472.7	100.00

Notes: Figures are for latest year available, 2006. Expenditures are used in a few cases where official budgets are significantly lower than actual spending.

SOURCE: Shah 2008.

by the military-industrial complex. The potential for the disastrous rise of misplaced power exists and will persist" (Eisenhower Institute 1961).

With the collapse of the Soviet Union in 1991, the United States became the world's unrivaled military superpower, accounting for nearly half of total military spending—more than that of the next fifteen countries combined (Table 13.1). In 1989, at the end of the cold war, U.S. defense spending—which had reached $300 billion in that year—began to decline slightly. But the decline was short lived. There turned out to be no "peace dividend" to spend on improving schools, repairing highways, or other domestic needs. By 2001 military spending once again topped $300 billion. It reached $400 billion in 2004, and $696 billion by 2008, an increase of almost 10 percent from 2007 (Shah 2008).

The global war on terrorism, discussed later in this chapter, has instead triggered another cycle of military spending. Eisenhower's dire warning seems no less true today than when he uttered it almost fifty years ago.

Democracy in Trouble?

Democracy almost everywhere is in some difficulty. This is not only because it is hard to set up a stable democratic order in places such as Russia and other erstwhile communist societies. Democracy is in trouble even in its countries of origin—such as the United States. For example, voter turnout in presidential and other elections has been declining. In surveys, many people say they don't trust politicians.

In 1964, confidence in government was fairly high: Nearly four out of five people answered *Most of the time* or *Just about always* when asked, "How much of the time do you trust the government in Washington to do the right thing?" This level of confidence dropped steadily for the following twenty years, then rose somewhat in the 1980s, then dropped to a low of one in five in 1994. Following the terrorist attacks of September 11, 2001, a solid majority (55 percent) of Americans reported that they trust the government "most of the time" or "just about always." Recently, however, trust in the government has declined as scandals surrounding wiretapping, the war in Iraq, and indicted lobbyists have filled the news. In 2007, just 24 percent of Americans said the government in Washington could be trusted to do what was right just about always or most of the time (Connelly 2007).

Of those expressing trust in government, most vote in presidential elections; of those who lack trust, most do not vote. Younger people have less interest in electoral politics than older generations have, although the young have a greater interest than their elders in issues such as the environment (Nye 1997). Some scholars have argued that such trends indicate an increasing skepticism toward traditional forms of authority, along with a shift from "scarcity values" to "postmaterialist values" (Inglehart 1997). This means that after reaching a certain level of economic prosperity, voters become concerned less with economic issues than with the quality of their individual (as opposed to collective) lifestyles, such as having meaningful work. As a result, voters are less interested in national politics, except for areas involving personal liberty.

The last few decades have also seen, in several Western countries, the welfare state coming under attack. Rights and benefits have been contested and cut back. Rightist parties have attempted to reduce levels of welfare expenditure in their countries. Even in states led by socialist governments, such as Spain, government provision of public resources has been restricted. One reason is the declining revenues available to governments as a result of the world recession that began in the early 1970s. Yet there is also increasing skepticism, not only by some governments but also by many citizens, about relying on the state for essential goods and services. This skepticism is based on the belief that the welfare state is bureaucratic, alienating, and inefficient and that welfare benefits can create perverse consequences that undermine what they were designed to achieve (Giddens 1998).

Among the major industrial democracies, the United States spends the lowest portion of its total economy on government at the federal, state, and local levels: roughly one third of its gross domestic product (GDP). In comparison, Sweden devotes more than half of its GDP to government spending; the European Union, 44 percent; and all industrial countries combined, 38 percent. Americans have lower taxes than other industrial democracies, but they also receive lower levels of support for health care, housing, education, unemployment compensation, and social services in general. This may be another reason for low levels of confidence in government and poor voter turnout: Americans expect less, and get less, from their government.

Why are so many people dissatisfied with the very political system that seems to be sweeping across the world? The answers are bound up with the very factors that help spread democracy—the effect of capitalism and the globalizing of social life. For instance, while capitalist economies generate more wealth than any other type of economic system, the wealth is unevenly distributed (see Chapter 8). And economic inequalities influence who votes, joins parties, and gets elected. Wealthy individuals and corporations back interest groups that lobby elected officials to support their aims when deciding on legislation. Not being subject to election, interest groups are not accountable to the majority of the electorate.

Economic inequalities also create an underclass of people living in poverty—about 20 percent of the population of liberal democracies. Most Western liberal democracies establish policies to reduce poverty levels, but they vary in spending to achieve that aim. Societies that implement a complex welfare system require a higher level of taxation and a larger non-elected government bureaucracy. The question arises, How much of an economic and political price is a society willing to pay to reduce poverty, and what is the effect of this cost?

Two theories have been put forward to account for this changing political situation. One is the theory of **state overload** (Britain 1975; Nordhaus 1975). In this view, governments in the twentieth century acquired more responsibilities than they could fund and manage, from establishing public ownership of industries, utilities, and transportation to creating extensive welfare programs. One reason is that political parties tried to woo voters by promising too many benefits and services. Governments were unable to deliver because state expenditures rose beyond the resources provided by tax revenues: State responsibilities were overloaded (Etzioni-Halévy 1985). Consequently, voters have become skeptical about claims made by governments and political parties. For example, the Democratic Party in the United States and leftist parties elsewhere have lost some of their traditional support from lower-class groups, who need the promised (but undelivered) services. The rise of new right politics reflects an attempt to cope with this situation by trimming back the state and encouraging private enterprise.

A rival theory, developed by Jürgen Habermas (1975), is that of **legitimation crisis** (Offe 1984, 1985). In this theory, modern governments lack the legitimacy to carry out tasks they are required to undertake, such as providing highways, public housing, and health care. People who feel that they pay most for these services through higher taxes—the more affluent—may believe that they gain least from them. On the one hand, governments must take more responsibility for providing health care for those who cannot afford it; on the other, taxpayers either resist increases in taxation or want taxes reduced. Governments cannot cope with the contradictory demands of lower taxes and more responsibilities, leading to decreased public support and general disillusionment about government's capabilities. According to Habermas, legitimation crises could probably be overcome if the electorate were persuaded to accept high taxation in return for a wide range of government services.

As sociologist Daniel Bell (1976) has observed, national government is too small to address the big questions, such as the influence of global economic competition or the destruction of the world's environment, but it has become too big to address the small questions, such as issues affecting cities or regions. Governments have little power, for instance, over giant business corporations, the main actors within the global economy. A U.S. corporation may shut down its production plants in America and set up a new factory in Mexico instead, to lower costs and compete with other corporations. The result is that thousands of American workers lose their jobs and expect the government to do something, but national governments cannot control processes bound up with the world economy. All a government can do is soften the blow—for example, by providing unemployment benefits or job retraining.

At the same time that governments have shrunk in relation to global issues, they have become more remote from the lives of most citizens. Many Americans resent that "power brokers" in Washington—party officials, interest groups, lobbyists, and bureaucratic officials—make decisions affecting their lives. They also believe that government is unable to address important local issues, such as crime and homelessness. Thus Americans' faith in government has dropped substantially, which affects their willingness to participate in the political process.

☑ CONCEPT CHECKS

1. Why is it problematic for contemporary states to have participatory democracy?
2. What are the differences between democracy and communism?
3. Describe the role interest groups play in American politics.
4. Compare and contrast pluralist theories of modern democracy and the power elite model.

Political and Social Change

Political life is by no means carried on only within the framework of political parties, voting, and representation in legislative and governmental bodies. When groups' objectives or ideals cannot be achieved within, or are blocked by, this framework (as under authoritarian regimes), political and social change may require unorthodox forms of political action.

The most dramatic example of unorthodox political action is **revolution**—the overthrow of an existing political order by means of a mass movement, using violence. Yet for all their high drama, revolutions occur relatively infrequently. The most common type of unorthodox political activity occurs through **social movements**, which are collective attempts to further a common interest or secure a common goal through action outside the sphere of established institutions. Social movements are as evident in the contemporary world as are the formal, bureaucratic organizations they often oppose. Many contemporary social movements are international and utilize information technology in linking local campaigners to global issues.

Why Do Social Movements Occur?

Because mass social movements have been so important in world history over the past two centuries, many theories try to account for them. Some theories were formulated early in the history of the social sciences; the most important was that of

Karl Marx. He intended his views not just to analyze the conditions of revolutionary change but to actually promote such change. Indeed, Marx's ideas had an immense practical effect on twentieth-century social change.

We examine four frameworks for the study of social movements, many of which were developed in the context of revolution: economic deprivation, resource mobilization, structural strain, and fields of action.

ECONOMIC DEPRIVATION

Marx's view of social movements arises from his interpretation of human history (see Chapter 1). According to Marx, the development of societies involves periodic class conflicts that lead to revolutionary change. Class struggles derive from the *contradictions*—unresolvable tensions—in societies. In any stable society, there is a balance among the economic structure, social relationships, and the political system. As the forces of production change, contradiction intensifies, leading to open clashes between classes—and ultimately to revolution.

Marx applied this model to the past development of feudalism and to the future evolution of industrial capitalism. The feudal societies of Europe were based on peasant (serf) production under a class of wealthy lords. Economic changes gave rise to towns and cities, where trade and manufacture developed. This new economic system, created *within* feudal society, threatened its very basis. Rather than being founded on the traditional lord–serf relationship, the emerging economic order encouraged industrialists to produce goods for sale in open markets. The contradictions between the old feudal economy and the emerging capitalist one eventually took the form of violent conflicts between the rising capitalist class and the feudal landowners. Revolution was the outcome, the most important example being the French Revolution of 1789. Through such revolutions and revolutionary changes occurring in other European societies, Marx argued, the capitalist class achieved dominance.

But industrial capitalism, according to Marx, sets up new contradictions, which will lead to revolutions prompted by ideals of socialism or communism. Industrial capitalism, an economic order based on the private pursuit of profit and on competition between firms to sell their products, creates a gulf between a rich minority who control the industrial resources and an impoverished majority of wage workers. Labor movements and political parties representing the working population eventually challenge the rule of the capitalist class and overthrow the existing political system. When a dominant class is particularly entrenched, Marx believed, violence is necessary to achieve the required transition. In other circumstances, this process might happen peacefully through

Deprivation of the peasantry compared to the elite in France led to the overthrow of the monarchy.

parliamentary action; a revolution (in the sense defined above) would not be necessary.

Contrary to Marx's expectations, revolutions failed to occur in the advanced industrialized societies of the West. Why? Sociologist James Davies (1962), a critic of Marx, identified periods of history when people lived in dire poverty but did not rise up in protest. Constant poverty or deprivation does not make people into revolutionaries; rather, they usually endure with resignation or mute despair. Social protest, and ultimately revolution, is more likely when people's living conditions *improve*. Then people's expectations also go up. If improvement in actual conditions subsequently slows down, propensities to revolt develop because rising expectations are frustrated.

Thus it is not absolute deprivation that leads to protest but **relative deprivation**—the discrepancy between people's actual lives and what they think could realistically be achieved. Davies's theory illuminates the connections between revolution and modern social and economic development. The ideals of progress, together with expectations of economic growth, induce rising hopes, which, if frustrated, spark protest. Such protest gains strength from the ideas of equality and democratic political participation, which were key not only in the American Revolution of 1776 and the Russian Revolution of 1917 but also in the revolutions of 1989 in Europe.

As Charles Tilly (1978) has pointed out, however, Davies's theory does not explain how and why different groups mobilize to seek revolutionary change. Protest might often occur against a backdrop of rising expectations; to understand how it becomes a mass social movement, we need to identify how groups collectively organize to make effective political challenges.

RESOURCE MOBILIZATION

In *From Mobilization to Revolution* (1978), Tilly analyzed processes of revolutionary change in the context of broader forms of protest and violence. He distinguished four main components of **collective action** taken to contest or overthrow an existing social order:

1. The *organization* of the group or groups involved. Protest movements are organized in many ways, varying from the spontaneous formation of crowds to tightly disciplined revolutionary groups. The Russian Revolution, for example, began as a small group of activists.
2. *Mobilization,* the ways in which a group acquires resources to make collective action possible. Such resources may include material goods, political support, and weaponry. Lenin acquired material and moral support from a sympathetic peasantry, together with many townspeople.
3. The *common interests* of those engaging in collective action, what they see as the gains and losses resulting from their policies. Common goals always underlie mobilization to collective action. Lenin built a broad coalition of support because many people had a common interest in removing the existing government.

Possibilities for Change in American Communities

Teaching and learning sociology often involves finding ways to bring the outside world into the classroom. To more meaningfully connect students to the contexts within which social change efforts occur, I have developed the "Possibilities for Change in American Communities" program at Brandeis University. The yearlong program combines two semesters of in-class work with a month of bus travel around the eastern United States. In the classroom, our goal is to present theories of social change and introduce particular movements that we will experience firsthand during our travels. We then board a bus that serves as our home on wheels for a month, carrying us to a wide range of communities where we apply and test recently acquired ideas about social movements and social change.

The point of our travel is to connect students with activists and social movement organizations and to the local communities in which these movements operate. Our route is designed to expose the group to a broad set of communities, consistent with our overall strategy of comparatively examining the contexts in which change occurs. Frequently, our students—typically raised in urban or suburban areas around Boston, New York, Chicago, or Los Angeles—learn enduring lessons in areas that diverge most sharply from their own backgrounds. Following a meeting with a local advocacy organization in rural North Carolina, for instance, the group's leader invited us to dinner at his truck-stop restaurant on the outskirts of town. We gladly accepted, and were treated not only to a delicious meal, but also to back-room political negotiations when our host and several of his colleagues held an impromptu meeting

David Cunningham

over barbeque with the local mayor and town planner. While readings and class discussions may focus on the tight-knit, highly interdependent nature of rural and small-town social relations, such lessons have a lasting impact when we see these connections in action.

Our time spent on the road also provides an opportunity for students to engage in a range of community-based work. Our aim is not to passively study communities and organizations, but to integrate ourselves into their perspectives and activities. The groups we select are purposely wide-ranging, and include direct service, advocacy, and community organizing ventures. Over the course of a single month, we cooked and distributed meals with Food Not Bombs in Chapel Hill, North Carolina; spoke out for gun control legislation on CNN's *Talk Back Live* in Atlanta, Georgia; stuffed envelopes to support

4. *Opportunity.* Chance events may provide opportunities to pursue revolutionary aims. Numerous forms of collective action, including revolution, are influenced by such incidental events. Lenin's success depended on contingent factors, including success in battle. If Lenin had been killed, would there have been a revolution?

Collective action can be defined as people acting together in pursuit of shared interests—for example, gathering to demonstrate in support of their cause. Some of the people may be intensely involved; others may lend more passive or irregular support. Effective collective action, such as action that culminates in revolution, usually moves through stages 1 to 4.

Sister Helen Prejean's Moratorium Campaign in New Orleans; helped restore a house with Habitat for Humanity in Baton Rouge, Louisiana; lobbied our congressional representatives in Washington, D.C.; and helped recruit participants in the Kensington Welfare Rights Union's battle for affordable housing and health care in Philadelphia. Alongside this work, we also met with participants in past and current activist efforts, spoke with several noted social movement scholars, and visited a number of historically important sites.

To many of the people we encounter along the way, our mode of travel seems at least as interesting as our educational mission. A sleeper bus is something used mostly by bands or touring theater groups—they stand out due to their large size, lack of windows, and airbrushed artwork. Considering the space constraints, the interior is really quite comfortable, providing living and sleeping space for fifteen. Importantly, the tight living arrangement provides plenty of opportunity for us to forge our own functioning community. And combining our accommodations with our mode of transportation is exceedingly efficient, as it allows us to travel at night while we sleep. We thus spend the vast majority of our waking hours at our destinations rather than in transit.

Quite literally, the bus provides a vehicle to understand the longer-term impacts of social movement activity, linking causes to effects and the past to the present. In Jackson, Mississippi, for instance, we visited with Bob Moses and Dave Dennis, both veterans of civil rights work with the Student Non-Violent Coordinating Committee during the 1960s. For the past twenty years, both have worked to develop the Algebra Project, a math literacy program that they view as key to students' future economic access in the same way that sharecroppers' ability to vote had determined their political access a generation earlier.

Just two days before our visit to Jackson, we spent time in Selma, Alabama, the site of the 1965 "Bloody Sunday" march in which several hundred civil rights marchers were brutally beaten by police officers seeking to prevent them from crossing the Edmund Pettus Bridge to begin their fifty-mile trek to the state capitol in Montgomery. In Selma, we were able

to follow the aborted march route over the Pettus Bridge and hear firsthand accounts by local participants at the nearby National Voting Rights Museum and Institute. We also canvassed Selma neighborhoods to interview longtime residents about their lives since the 1960s, and met with current Mayor James Perkins, the first African American resident elected to that post in Selma.

By connecting to movement activists and directly experiencing the sites of social movement activity, we are able to explore more fully the long-term impact of specific events like the Selma-to-Montgomery march, and the larger civil rights movement. We also forge links to ongoing movements, gaining an on-the-ground understanding of their strategies, tactics, and day-to-day operations. These links are first put into action following our return, when students work on ambitious projects tied to our travels. From creating campus partnerships with community organizations to further their ongoing campaigns, to analyzing interview and archival data to formulate strategic plans to improve citizens' access to community resources, students continue to apply their experience and knowledge actively. Such activities provide a means to understand the dynamics of social movement activity, while creating long-term benefits both for our students and for the communities that they will be part of in the future.

Social movements, in Tilly's view, develop as a way of mobilizing group resources either when people have no institutionalized means of voicing their concerns or when the state authorities repress their needs. Although collective action at some point involves open confrontation with the political authorities, it is not likely to affect established patterns of power unless groups who are systematically organized support it.

Modes of collective action and protest vary with historical and cultural circumstances. In the United States today, for example, most people are familiar with mass marches, large assemblies, and street riots. Other types of collective protest, however, have become less common or have disappeared (such as fights between villages, machine breaking, or lynching). Protesters can also build on examples taken from

In 2007, Buddhist monks protested against the military government of Myanmar. Soldiers brutally put an end to the demonstration, killing around 200 marchers.

other places; for instance, guerrilla movements proliferated in various parts of the world once disaffected groups learned how successful guerrilla actions could be against regular armies. And, as discussed earlier, a new form of collective action may be emerging—smart-mobbing and other forms of social protest accomplished through the Internet.

When and why does collective action become violent? After studying many incidents in western Europe since 1800, Tilly concluded that most collective violence develops from action that is not initially violent. Whether violence occurs depends not so much on the nature of the activity as on other factors—in particular, how the authorities respond. Consider the street demonstration; the vast majority of such demonstrations occur without damage to people or property. A few lead to violence and are then labeled as riots. Sometimes the authorities step in when violence has already occurred; more often, the historical record shows, they are the originators of violence and, in fact, are responsible for the most deaths and injuries. This is not surprising given their special access to arms and military discipline. The groups they attempt to control, conversely, do greater damage to objects and property.

Revolutionary movements, according to Tilly, are a type of collective action that occurs in situations of **multiple sovereignty**—when a government lacks full control over the areas it is supposed to administer. Multiple sovereignty can arise as a result of external war, internal political clashes, or both. Whether a revolutionary takeover of power succeeds depends on how far the ruling authorities maintain control over the armed forces, the extent of conflicts within ruling groups, and the level of organization of the protest movements trying to seize power.

Tilly's concepts have wide application, and his use of them is sensitive to the variabilities of historical time and place. How social movements are organized, the resources they mobilize, the common interests of groups contending for power, and chance opportunities are all important facets of social transformation.

Tilly says little, however, about the circumstances underlying multiple sovereignty—a serious omission. According to Theda Skocpol (1979), Tilly assumes that social movements are guided by the deliberate pursuit of interests and that successful revolutionary change occurs when people realize these interests. Skocpol, in contrast, sees social movements as more ambiguous and indecisive in their objectives. Revolutions, she emphasizes, largely emerge as unintended consequences of more partial aims:

> In fact, in historical revolutions, differently situated and motivated groups have become participants in complex unfoldings of multiple conflicts. These conflicts have been powerfully shaped and limited by existing social, economic and international conditions. And they have proceeded in different ways depending upon how each revolutionary situation emerged in the first place. (Skocpol 1979)

Skocpol's argument seems correct when we analyze the revolutionary changes that occurred in Eastern European societies in 1989, compared with earlier revolutionary episodes.

STRUCTURAL STRAIN

Neil Smelser (1963) distinguished six conditions underlying the origins of collective action in general and social movements in particular: structural conduciveness, structural strain in society, generalized beliefs, precipitating factors, effective leadership, and the nature of social control directed against the social movement.

1. *Structural conduciveness* refers to the social conditions promoting or inhibiting the formation of social movements. For example, in Smelser's view, the

sociopolitical system of the United States leaves open certain avenues of mobilization for protest because there is little or no state regulation in those areas. For example, there is no state-sponsored religion. People are free to exercise their religious beliefs. This creates a conducive environment in which religious movements might compete for individuals, so long as they do not transgress criminal or civil law.

2. Conducive conditions are not enough to bring a social movement into being. There must be **structural strain**—tensions (in Marx's terminology, contradictions) that produce conflicting interests. Uncertainties, anxieties, ambiguities, and direct clashes of goals are expressions of such strains. Sources of strain may be general or specific. Thus sustained inequalities among ethnic groups create overall tensions; these may become focused in specific conflicts when, say, blacks begin to move into a previously all-white area.

3. Social movements do not develop simply as responses to vaguely felt anxieties or hostilities. They are shaped by the influence of *generalized beliefs*—definite ideologies—that crystallize grievances and suggest courses of action to remedy them. Revolutionary movements, for instance, are based on ideas about why injustice occurs and how it can be alleviated by political struggle.

4. *Precipitating factors* are events that trigger direct action by those involved in the movement. In 1955, when a black woman named Rosa Parks refused to give up her seat to a white man on a bus in Montgomery, Alabama, her action helped spark the civil rights movement (see Chapter 11).

5. The first four conditions combined might occasionally lead to street disturbances or outbreaks of violence, but such incidents do not promote the development of social movements unless a coordinated group mobilizes for action. *Leadership* and some means of *regular communication* among participants, together with funding and material resources, are necessary for a social movement to exist.

6. Finally, the manner in which a social movement develops is influenced by the *operation of social control*. The governing authorities may respond initially by intervening in the conditions of conduciveness that gave rise to the movement. For instance, steps might be taken to reduce ethnic inequality that generates resentment and conflict. Other important aspects of social control concern the responses of the police or armed forces. A harsh response might spark further protest and help solidify the movement. Also, doubt and divisions within the police and military can be

Rosa Parks's refusal to give up her seat to a white man on a bus sparked the civil rights movement and is an example of a precipitating factor.

crucial in deciding the outcome of confrontations with revolutionary movements.

Smelser's model is useful for analyzing the sequences in the development of social movements and collective action in general. Each stage "adds value" to the overall outcome; also, each stage is a necessary condition for the next one. But Smelser's theory bears some criticism as well. For example, some social movements become strong without precipitating incidents. Conversely, a series of incidents might highlight the need to establish a movement to change the circumstances that gave rise to them. Also, a movement itself might create strains, rather than develop in response to them. For example, the women's movement has sought to identify and combat gender inequalities where previously those had gone unquestioned. Smelser's theory treats social movements as responses to situations, rather than acknowledging that members might spontaneously organize to achieve desired social changes. In this respect, his ideas contrast with the approach developed by Alain Touraine.

FIELDS OF ACTION

Alain Touraine (1977, 1981) developed his analysis of social movements on the basis of four main ideas. The first, which he called **historicity**, explains why there are many more social movements in the modern world than in earlier times. In modern societies, individuals and groups know that social activism can achieve social goals and reshape society.

Second, Touraine focused on the *rational objectives* of social movements. Such movements are not irrational responses to social divisions or injustices; rather, they develop from specific views and rational strategies for overcoming injustices.

Third, Touraine saw a process of *interaction* in the shaping of social movements. Movements develop in deliberate antagonism with established organizations and sometimes with rival social movements. According to Touraine, other theories of social movements have not adequately considered how the objectives of a social movement are shaped by encounters with others holding divergent positions as well as by the ways in which they themselves influence their opponents' outlooks and action. For instance, the objectives and outlook of the women's movement were shaped in opposition to the male-dominated institutions that it seeks to alter. The movement's goals and outlook have shifted in relation to its successes and failures and have influenced men's perspectives. These changed perspectives in turn stimulated a reorientation in the women's movement.

Fourth, social movements and change occur in the context of "fields of action." A **field of action** comprises the connections between a social movement and the forces or influences against it. Mutual negotiation among antagonists in a field of action may produce the social changes sought by the movement as well as changes in the movement itself and in its antagonists. In either circumstance, the movement may evaporate or become institutionalized as a permanent organization. For example, labor-union movements became formal organizations when they achieved the right to strike and to engage in types of bargaining acceptable to both workers and employers. These changes were forged out of earlier processes involving widespread violent confrontation on both sides. Where there are continuing sources of conflict (as in the relation between unions and employers), new movements still tend to reemerge.

Touraine's analysis can also be applied to movements concerned with individual change. For instance, Alcoholics Anonymous is a movement based on medical findings about the harmful effects of alcohol on people's health and social activities. The movement has been shaped by its own opposition to advertising that encourages alcoholic drinking and by its attempt to confront the pressures faced by alcoholics in a society that readily tolerates drinking.

Feminist Movements

As we just saw, theories of revolution overlap with those of social movements. Charles Tilly's emphasis on resource mobilization, for example, has been applied to social movements such as the feminist movement.

The first organized groups promoting women's rights appeared immediately following the American and French Revolutions (Evans 1977). In the 1790s, inspired by the revolutionaries' ideals of freedom and equality, several women's clubs were formed in Paris and major provincial cities. The clubs provided meeting places for women and petitioned for equal rights in education, employment, and government. Marie Gouze, a leader of one of the clubs, drew up a statement titled "Declaration of the Rights of Women," based on the Declaration of the Rights of Man and the Citizen, the main constitutional document of the French Revolution. How could true equality be achieved, she argued, when half the population was excluded from the privileges that men share?

The response from the male revolutionary leaders was less than sympathetic—Gouze was executed in 1793, charged with "having forgotten the virtues which belong to her sex." The women's clubs were subsequently dissolved by government decree. Feminist groups and women's movements have formed repeatedly in Western countries since that date, almost always encountering hostility and sometimes provoking violence from established authorities.

In the nineteenth century, feminism became more advanced in the United States than elsewhere, and most women's movements in other countries took the struggles of American women as a model. In the 1840s and 1850s, American feminists were involved with groups devoted to the abolition of slavery. Yet, having no formal political rights (the Constitution did not give women the right to vote), women were excluded from political lobbying and from attending a world antislavery convention held in London in 1840. This fact led the women's groups to directly consider gender inequalities. In 1848, women leaders in the United States met to approve the "Declaration of Sentiments and Resolutions," modeled on the Declaration of Independence. "We hold these truths to be self-evident," it began, "that all men and women are created equal." The declaration set out a long list of the injustices to which women were subject (Hartman and Banner 1974). However, few real gains were made during this period. When slavery ended, Congress ruled that only freed male slaves should be given the vote.

Some African American women joined the early women's movement in the United States, although they often encountered hostility and racism from their white sisters. One, Sojourner Truth, spoke out against both slavery and the disenfranchisement of women. Although Truth played a prominent part in women's struggles of the period (hooks 1981), other black women who tried to participate became disillusioned with the prejudice they encountered. African American feminists as a result were few.

Militant campaigner for female suffrage Emmeline Pankhurst and one of her daughters are welcomed to a meeting of fellow suffragettes with banners and flowers.

One of the most important events in the early development of feminist movements in Europe was the presentation of a petition to the British Parliament in 1866, demanding that electoral reforms include full voting rights for women. The petition was ignored; in response, its organizers set up the National Society for Women's Suffrage. Known as suffragettes, the members continued to petition Parliament to extend voting rights to women. By the early twentieth century, the world influence of British feminism rivaled that of feminists in the United States. During this period, women's movements mushroomed in all the major European countries, together with Australia and New Zealand.

Emmeline Pankhurst, a leading suffragette, participated in several speaking tours of the United States, recounting the British struggles to large audiences. Two Americans who had become involved in the campaigns in Britain, Alice Paine and Harriet Stanton Blatch, organized massive marches and parades through New York and other eastern cities from 1910 onward.

By 1920, women had attained the right to vote in several Western countries (Table 13.2). Thereafter, though, most feminist movements fell into decline. Radical women were absorbed into other movements, such as those combating fascism, a political doctrine of the extreme right gaining ground in Germany, Italy, and elsewhere in the 1930s. Little was left of feminism as a movement against male-dominated institutions. The achievement of equal political rights did little to extend equality to other spheres of women's lives.

THE RESURGENCE OF FEMINISM

In the late 1960s, women's movements again gained prominence (Chafe 1974, 1977). Since then, feminism has become a major influence worldwide, even in the developing world. The resurgence began in the United States, influenced by the civil rights movement and by the student activism of the period. Women involved in these causes often were relegated by male activists to subordinate roles, and civil rights leaders were resistant to including women's rights in their manifestos of equality. Hence women's groups established independent organizations concerned primarily with feminist issues.

The women's movement today involves a variety of interest groups and organizations. Among the most prominent in the United States is the National Organization for Women (NOW), with more than half a million members (men as well as women, although the large majority are women). Another group is the National Women's Political Caucus (NWPC). Some organizations are concerned with single issues such as abortion, education, or pension rights. Other groups consist of women in various occupations, like the American Association of University Women (AAUW).

FEMINIST MOVEMENTS: AN INTERPRETATION

The rise of women's movements over the past century can be interpreted in terms of Tilly's concepts. Social movements arise, Tilly argues, when people cannot make themselves heard or lack outlets for their aspirations. In the first phase of development of feminist movements, in the nineteenth and early twentieth centuries, feminist leaders sought a *voice* for women in the political process via the right to vote. In the second phase, women's movements sought economic as well as political equality.

In both phases, the leaders of women's movements *mobilized collective resources* to pressure the governing authorities. During the early period, women activists' chief resource was mass marches and demonstrations. Later on, organizations (such as NOW) fought for women's rights in a more consistent and organized way. The *common interests* to which women's group leaders have appealed include the concern that women should have a role in political decision making, be able to engage in paid work, and have equal rights in divorce proceedings.

Finally, the *opportunity* of feminist activists to influence social change has been affected by numerous factors. The outbreak of World War I, for example, helped secure the vote: Governments fighting the war needed the support and active involvement of women in the war effort. In the second phase of the development of feminism, the civil rights movement was the spark that ignited a new wave of activism.

Social movements not only provide subject matter for study but also help shift the ways in which sociologists examine certain areas of behavior. The women's movement, for instance, is relevant to sociology not just because it provides material for research. It also has identified weaknesses in frameworks

TABLE 13.2

The Year in Which Women Achieved the Right to Vote on an Equal Basis with Men, by Country

1893	New Zealand	1945	France, Hungary, Italy, Japan, Vietnam, Yugoslavia, Bolivia
1902	Australia	1946	Albania, Romania, Panama
1906	Finland	1947	Argentina, Venezuela
1913	Norway	1948	Israel, Korea
1915	Denmark, Iceland	1949	China, Chile
1917	Soviet Union	1950	El Salvador, Ghana, India
1918	Canada	1951	Nepal
1919	Austria, Germany, the Netherlands, Poland, Sweden, Luxembourg, Czechoslovakia	1952	Greece
		1953	Mexico
1920	**United States**	1954	Colombia
1922	Ireland	1955	Nicaragua
1928	Great Britain	1956	Egypt, Pakistan, Senegal
1929	Ecuador	1957	Lebanon
1930	South Africa	1959	Morocco
1931	Spain, Sri Lanka, Portugal	1962	Algeria
1932	Thailand	1963	Iran, Kenya, Libya
1934	Brazil, Cuba	1964	Sudan, Zambia
1936	Costa Rica	1965	Afghanistan, Guatemala
1937	Philippines	1971	Switzerland
1941	Indonesia	1977	Nigeria
1942	Dominican Republic, Uruguay	1979	Peru, Zimbabwe

SOURCE: Tuttle 1986.

of sociological thought and developed concepts (such as that of patriarchy) that illuminate issues of gender and power. There is a continuing dialogue not only between social movements and the organizations that they confront (such as government) but also between social movements and sociology itself.

Globalization and Social Movements

Social movements vary widely. Some have only a few dozen members; others include thousands or millions of people. Although some social movements operate within the laws, others are illegal or underground groups. Protest movements operate near the margins of what is legally permissible.

Social movements often seek change on a public issue, such as expanding civil rights for a segment of the population. In response, countermovements sometimes arise in defense of the status quo. The campaign for women's right to abortion, for example, has been challenged by antiabortion ("prolife") activists, who believe that abortion should be illegal.

Often, laws or policies are altered as a result of the action of social movements. These changes can have far-ranging effects. For example, it used to be illegal for workers' groups to call their members out on strike, and striking was punished with various degrees of severity in different countries. Eventually, however, the laws were amended, making the strike a permissible tactic of industrial conflict.

NEW SOCIAL MOVEMENTS

The last few decades have seen an explosion of social movements around the globe. These movements—ranging from the civil rights and feminist movements of the 1960s and 1970s, to the antinuclear and ecological movements of the 1980s, to the gay rights campaign of the 1990s—are called **new social movements**. They are often concerned with the quality of private life as much as with political and economic issues, calling for changes in the way people think and act.

What makes new social movements "new" is that, unlike conventional social movements, they are not based on single-issue objectives related to the distribution of economic resources or power. Rather, they seek collective identities based around entire lifestyles, often calling for sweeping cultural changes. New social movements have emerged around issues such as ecology, peace, gender and sexual identity, gay and lesbian rights, women's rights, alternative medicine, and opposition to globalization.

Because new social movements involve new collective identities, they can provide a strong incentive for action. Participation is viewed as a moral obligation (and even a pleasure) rather than a calculated effort to achieve some specific goal. Moreover, the forms of protest chosen by new social movements constitute an "expressive logic" whereby participants make a statement about who they are: Protest is an end in itself, a way of affirming one's identity as well as a means to achieving concrete objectives (Polletta and Jasper 2001).

The rise of new social movements is a reflection of the changing risks facing human societies. Traditional political institutions are increasingly unable to cope with the challenges before them, such as threats to the natural environment, the potential dangers of nuclear energy and genetically modified organisms, and the powerful effects of information technology. Because existing democratic political institutions cannot fix these problems, they go ignored or avoided until a full-blown crisis occurs.

As a cumulative effect of these new challenges and risks, people feel less secure and more isolated—a combination that leads to a sense of powerlessness. By contrast, corporations, governments, and the media appear to be dominating more aspects of people's lives, heightening the sensation of a runaway world. There is a growing sense that globalization presents ever-greater risks to citizens' lives.

Although faith in traditional politics seems to be waning, the growth of new social movements is evidence that citizens in late modern societies are not apathetic or uninterested in politics. Rather, there is a belief that direct action and participation are more useful than reliance on politicians and political systems. More than ever before, people are supporting social movements as a way of putting complex moral issues at the center of social life. In this respect, new social movements are helping revitalize civic culture and **civil society**—the sphere between the state and the marketplace occupied by family, community associations, and other noneconomic institutions.

Technology and Social Movements

Recently, two of the most influential forces in late modern societies—information technology and social movements—have come together with astonishing results. Social movements worldwide can now join in huge regional and international

How is this environmental group demonstrating at the UN Climate Change Conference an example of a new social movement?

networks including nongovernmental organizations, religious and humanitarian groups, human rights associations, consumer protection advocates, environmental activists, and others campaigning in the public interest. These electronic networks can respond immediately to events as they occur, gain access to and share sources of information, and put pressure on corporations, governments, and international bodies as part of their campaigning strategies. The enormous protests against the World Trade Organization (WTO) that took place in Seattle, Prague, and Genoa, for example, were organized in large part through Internet-based networks. Web-based organizations such as MoveOn.org have been influential in the anti–Iraq War movement. The Internet has been at the forefront of these changes, although mobile phones, fax machines, and satellite broadcasting have also hastened their evolution.

The ability to electronically coordinate international political campaigns is worrisome for governments and inspiring to participants in social movements. Indeed, the number of international social movements has grown steadily with the spread of the Internet. From global protests in favor of canceling third world debt to the international campaign to ban land mines (which culminated in a Nobel Peace Prize), the Internet has united campaigners across national and cultural borders. Some observers argue that the information age is witnessing a migration of power away from nation-states into new nongovernmental alliances and coalitions.

Manuel Castells (1997) examines social movements that, although dissimilar, have all attracted international attention to their cause through the effective use of information technology. The Mexican Zapatista rebels, the American militia movement, the Japanese Aum Shinrikyo cult, and al Qaeda have all used media skills to spread their message of opposition to the effects of globalization and to express their anger at losing control over their own destinies.

According to Castells, each of these movements relies on information technologies as its organizational infrastructure. Without the Internet, for example, the Zapatista rebels would remain an isolated guerrilla movement in southern Mexico. Instead, within hours of their armed uprising in January 1994, local, national, and international support groups had emerged online to promote the rebels' cause and to condemn the Mexican government's brutal repression of the rebellion. The Zapatistas used telecommunications, videos, and media interviews to voice their objections to trade policies, such as the North American Free Trade Agreement (NAFTA), that further exclude impoverished Indians of the Oaxaca and Chiapas areas from the benefits of globalization. With their cause highlighted in the online networks of social campaigners, the Zapatistas managed to force negotiations with the Mexican government and draw international intention to the harmful effects of free trade on indigenous populations.

Nationalist Movements

Some of the most important social movements today are nationalist movements. Although the world has become more interdependent, especially since the 1970s, this interdependence has not spelled the end of nationalism. It may even have helped intensify it. Recent thinkers have contrasting ideas about why this is so. There are also disagreements about the stage of history at which nationalism, the nation, and the nation-state came into being.

NATIONALISM AND MODERN SOCIETY

Perhaps the leading theorist of nationalism is Ernest Gellner (1925–1995). Gellner (1983) argues that nationalism, the nation, and the nation-state are all products of modern civilization, whose origins lie in the industrial revolution of the late eighteenth century. He claims that nationalism and the feelings associated with it do not have deep roots in human nature; instead, they are the products of the large-scale society that industrialism creates.

First, a modern industrial society features rapid economic development and a complex division of labor. Thus, Gellner holds, modern industrialism creates the need for a more effective system of state and government than existed before. Second, in the modern state, individuals constantly interact with strangers, since the basis of society is no longer the local village or town. Mass education, based on an official language taught in the schools, enables a large-scale society to be organized and unified.

Gellner's theory has been criticized in more than one respect. It is a functionalist theory, critics say, that argues that education produces social unity. As with the functionalist approach more generally, this view underestimates the role of education in producing conflict and division. Gellner's theory does not really explain the passions that nationalism can arouse. The power of nationalism is probably related not just to education but also to its capacity to create an *identity* for people—something that individuals cannot live without.

The need for identity is not just born with the emergence of modern industrial society. Critics therefore argue that Gellner is wrong to separate nationalism and the nation so strongly from premodern times. Nationalism is in some ways quite modern, but it also draws on sentiments and forms of symbolism that extend further into the past. According to one of the best-known current scholars of nationalism, Anthony Smith (1988), nations have direct lines of continuity with earlier ethnic communities, or "ethnies." An **ethnie** is a group that shares ideas of common ancestry, a common cultural identity, and a link with a specific homeland.

Many nations, Smith points out, do have premodern continuities, and in earlier times there have been ethnic communities

Activists of the ultra Hindu nationalist party, Shiv Sena, kick and burn an effigy of Pakistan's leader, Pervez Musharraf, in New Delhi to protest killings in the contested territory of Kashmir.

resembling nations. The Jews, for example, have formed a distinct ethnie for more than two thousand years. At certain periods, Jews clustered in communities that had some of the characteristics of nations. But only after World War II were all these elements brought together in the nation-state of Israel. Like most other nation-states, Israel was not formed from a single ethnie. The Palestinian minority in Israel traces its origins to a different ethnic background and claims that the creation of the Israeli state has displaced the Palestinians from their ancient homelands—hence their persistent tensions with Jews in Israel, the tensions between Israel and most surrounding Arab states, and the violence between Palestinians and Israelis that has escalated in the twenty-first century.

Different nations have followed divergent patterns of development in relation to ethnies. In some, including most of the nations of western Europe, a single ethnie expanded and pushed out earlier rivals. Thus, in France in the seventeenth century, several other languages were spoken and different ethnic histories were linked to them. As French became the dominant language, most of these rivals disappeared. Yet remnants persist in a few areas. One is in the Basque country overlapping the French and Spanish frontiers. The Basque language is different from either French or Spanish, and the Basques claim a separate cultural history. Some Basques want their own nation-state. Although there has been nothing like the level of violence seen in other areas—such as East Timor, or Chechnya in southern Russia—separatist groups in the Basque country have sporadically used bombing campaigns to further their goal of independence.

NATIONS WITHOUT STATES

The persistence of well-defined ethnies within established nations leads to the phenomenon of **nations without states**.

These situations reflect many essential characteristics of a nation, but those who make up the nation lack an independent political community. Separatist movements are driven by the desire to establish an autonomous, self-governing state.

Several types of nations without states can be recognized, depending on the relationship between the ethnie and the nation-state in which it exists (Guibernau 1999):

1. In some situations, a nation-state may accept the cultural differences among its minority or minorities and allow them a certain amount of active development. Thus in Great Britain, Scotland and Wales are recognized as having histories and cultural features partly divergent from the rest of the United Kingdom, and to some extent they have their own institutions. The majority of Scots, for instance, are Presbyterians, and Scotland has long had a separate educational system from that of England and Wales. Scotland and Wales achieved further autonomy within the United Kingdom with the creation of a Scottish Parliament and a Welsh Assembly in 1999.

2. Some nations without states have a higher degree of autonomy. In Quebec (the French-speaking province of Canada) and Flanders (the Dutch-speaking area in the southwestern Netherlands), regional political bodies have the power to make major decisions without being fully independent. They also contain nationalist movements agitating for complete independence.

3. Some nations completely lack recognition from the state that contains them. In such cases, the larger nation-state uses force to deny recognition to the minority. The Palestinians are an example (although some would argue that their acts of terrorism and violence against Israelis have encouraged the Israeli army's show of force). Others include the Tibetans in China and the Kurds, whose homeland overlaps parts of Turkey, Syria, Iran, and Iraq.

NATIONS AND NATIONALISM IN DEVELOPING COUNTRIES

In most of the developing world, the course followed by nationalism, the nation, and the nation-state has been different from that of industrial societies. Most less-developed countries were once colonized by Europeans and achieved independence in the second half of the twentieth century. In many of these countries, boundaries between colonial administrations that were set arbitrarily in Europe ignored economic, cultural, or ethnic divisions among the population being colonized. As a consequence, most colonized areas contained a mosaic of ethnies and other groups.

Given this background, when former colonies achieved independence it was hard to create a sense of nationhood. Although nationalism played a great part in securing the independence of colonized areas, it was confined to small groups of activists and did not reflect the majority of the population. Even today, many postcolonial states are continually threatened by internal rivalries and competing claims to political authority.

The continent that was most completely colonized was Africa. Nationalist movements promoting independence in Africa following World War II sought to free the colonized areas from European domination. Once this had been achieved, the new leaders faced enormous problems in trying to create national unity. Many of the leaders in the 1950s and 1960s had been educated in Europe or the United States, and there was a vast gulf between them and their citizens, most of whom were illiterate, poor, and unfamiliar with the rights and obligations of democracy. Under colonialism, some ethnic groups had prospered more than others; these groups had different interests and goals and legitimately saw each other as enemies.

Civil wars broke out in several postcolonial states in Africa, such as Sudan, Zaire, and Nigeria, while ethnic rivalries and antagonisms characterized many others in both Africa and Asia. In Sudan, about 40 percent of the population spoke Arabic and claimed Arabic ethnic origins. Elsewhere in the country, particularly in the south, Arabic was barely spoken at all. Once the nationalists took power, they set up a program for national integration with Arabic as the national language. The attempt was only partly successful, and the stresses it produced are still visible. The severe problems faced by much of the African continent are a result of difficulties like these.

The ongoing civil war in Sudan has displaced more than four million people. Some fled to southern cities, such as Juba; others trekked as far north as Khartoum and even into Ethiopia, Kenya, Uganda, Egypt, and other neighboring countries. These refugees were unable to grow food or earn money to feed themselves, and malnutrition and starvation became widespread. Lack of investment also created what international humanitarian organizations call a "lost generation," who lack educational opportunities and access to basic health-care services and who have few prospects for employment in the small and weak economies of the south and the north.

In summary, most states in the developing world underwent different processes of nation formation from those in the industrialized world. States were imposed externally on areas that often had no prior cultural or ethnic unity, leading to problems that are very difficult to overcome. Modern nations have arisen most effectively either in areas that were never fully colonized or where there was already much cultural unity—such as Japan, Korea, and Thailand.

The Nation-State, National Identity, and Globalization

In some parts of Africa, nations and nation-states are not yet fully formed. Yet in other areas of the world, some writers are speaking of the "end of the nation-state" in the face of globalization. According to Japanese writer Kenichi Ohmae (1995), we live in a borderless world in which national identity is weakening.

How valid is this point of view? All states are certainly affected by globalizing processes. The very rise of "nations without 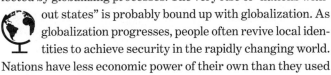 out states" is probably bound up with globalization. As globalization progresses, people often revive local identities to achieve security in the rapidly changing world. Nations have less economic power of their own than they used to have, as a result of the spreading global marketplace.

Yet it wouldn't be accurate to say that we are witnessing the end of the nation-state. In some ways the opposite is the case. Today the nation-state has become a universal political form. Until quite recently it still had rivals; after all, for most of the twentieth century colonized areas and empires existed alongside nation-states. It is arguable that the last empire disappeared only in 1990 with the collapse of Soviet communism. The satellite states constituting the Soviet Union's former empire in Eastern Europe now have become independent nation-states, as have many areas inside the former Soviet Union itself. There are far more sovereign nations today than there were twenty-five years ago.

Terrorism

The same forces that led to nationalist movements in the nineteenth and twentieth centuries also led to a new form of violence—terrorism. Social scientists disagree whether the term **terrorism** can be used in a reasonably objective way, and terrorism is a notoriously difficult issue to define (Laqueur 2003). One issue concerns the shifting moral assessments people make of terrorism and terrorists. It's often said that "one person's terrorist is another person's freedom fighter." Also, former terrorists can later condemn terror just as violently as they once practiced it. Only a few decades ago, the former South African leader Nelson Mandela was reviled as a potential terrorist, but he is now one of the most revered political figures of recent times. For *terrorism* to be a useful term, it must be freed from moral valuation that shifts across time or the perspective of the observer.

It is sensible to restrict the notion of terrorism to groups and organizations working outside the state. Otherwise the concept becomes too close to that of war. We can neutrally define terrorism as "any action [by a nonstate organization] . . . that is intended to cause death or serious bodily harm to civilians or non-combatants, when the purpose of such an act . . . is to intimidate a population, or to compel a Government or an international organization to do or to abstain from doing any act" (Panyarachun et al. 2004). In other words, terrorism concerns attacks on civilians designed to persuade a government to alter its policies or to damage its standing in the world.

Old- and New-Style Terrorism

Terrorism is a modern phenomenon that can be distinguished from acts of violence designed to terrorize in previous periods, such as the ancient razing of cities. As described earlier, terrorism is connected to changes in communications technology. To terrorize populations on a wide spectrum, information about the violence has to reach the affected populations quickly. The rise of modern communications in the late nineteenth century made this possible. Before the telegraph, information could take days or months to spread.

There is a distinction between old- and new-style terrorism. **Old-style terrorism**, dominant for most of the twentieth century and still occurring today, is associated with the rise of nationalism and the establishment of nations as sovereign, territorially bonded entities. A patchwork of nations mapped out by colonial administrators or founded by force has led in various cases to nations that do not have their own state—that is, nations claiming a common cultural identity but lacking the territorial and state apparatus that normally belongs to a

An example of an old-style terrorist movement, these Basque Nationalists are mostly concerned with territorial control and the formation of states.

nation. Most forms of old-style terrorism are linked to nations without states.

The point of old-style terrorism is to establish states in areas where nations do not have control of the territory's state apparatus. This is true, for example, of Irish nationalists and the Basque nationalists in Spain. The main issues are territorial integrity and identity in the formation of a state. In such cases, terrorists are prepared to use violence to achieve their ends. This type of terrorism is fundamentally local because its ambitions are local. It wants to establish a state in a specific national area.

NEW-STYLE TERRORISM

New-style terrorism is another matter (Tan and Ramakrishna 2002). Facilitated by the changes in communications technology that are driving globalization, it has a global spread. This type of terrorism is most famously associated with the Islamic fundamentalism of al Qaeda, although it is not limited to it. New-style terrorism differs from old-style terrorism in several ways. The first involves the scope of their claims. One distinguishing feature of al Qaeda, for example, is that it has global geopolitical aims. Parts of the al Qaeda leadership want to reconstruct an Islamic society stretching from the Indian subcontinent into Europe by establishing Islamic governments throughout the Middle East and recapturing northern Africa. Al Qaeda's supporters argue that over the last millennium the West has expelled Islamic groups from areas to which it has legitimate claim. Such areas include the Balkans and parts of Spain that were previously ruled by the Moors (Muslims from North Africa who controlled much of Spain between the eighth and fifteenth centuries). Al Qaeda aims to reestablish the global role of Islam in these areas and thereby reverse the tide of world power (Gray 2003).

Second, the two types of terrorism have different organizational structures. Although careful not to take this parallel too far, sociologist Mary Kaldor identifies several similarities between the infrastructure of new terrorist groups, notably al Qaeda, and international nongovernmental organizations (NGOs) such as Oxfam and Friends of the Earth. (NGOs are discussed in more detail in Chapter 6.) New-style terrorist organizations and NGOs both are driven by a sense of mission and commitment, which allows a fairly loose global organization to flourish (Glasius et al. 2002).

Both NGOs and new terrorist organizations are based on highly decentralized networks. There is a lot of autonomy in individual cells, which can reproduce without strong direction from the center. Furthermore, terrorist organizations and NGOs both have supporters in many countries. Experts on terrorism disagree over the extent to which al Qaeda survived the American-led attack on Afghanistan in 2001, but it has been estimated that al Qaeda cells persist in around sixty countries, drawing on approximately twenty thousand people who are willing to die violently for the cause; most of these cells exist semiautonomously from the center.

Also, new terrorist groups and NGOs both work with states. No NGO could flourish completely as a nonstate organization. NGOs all have some contacts and support from states, and this is true, Kaldor argues, of new-style terrorist organizations as well. The Libyan government's involvement in the bombing of a passenger plane that exploded over the Scottish village of Lockerbie in 1988 is an example.

Of course, the analogy between new terrorist organizations and NGOs may seem inappropriate, given their very different missions; but in their organizational structures and shared sense of mission, al Qaeda could be seen as a malign kind of NGO.

Third, the two styles differ in terms of means. Old-style terrorism has relatively limited objectives, so the violence is normally limited. New-style terrorism seems much more ruthless in the means it is prepared to use. Al Qaeda Web sites, for example, talk in extremely destructive language about killing as many people as possible. There are some cases in which the two styles of terrorism overlap, as in Chechnya in the former Soviet Union, which turned from a separatist struggle to a recruiting ground for newer forms of terrorism.

Terrorism and War

How should we respond to the threat of new-style terrorism? Terrorism of the kind seen on September 11 raises difficult questions for political sociologists. Can terrorism be fought like an enemy in conventional wars? Despite some successes against new-style terrorism through conventional warfare, in many cases the levels of violence, aims, and organizational structure of new-style terrorist groups differentiate them from conventional enemies, such as hostile nation-states. The debate raises further difficult questions regarding the relationship between terrorism and the nation-states, like Afghanistan, that have supported it. In turn, this leads to questions about global governance. In a global age, what international support and proof are needed to respond to and prevent a perceived threat? And what are the best institutions to deal with a global terrorist threat?

☑ CONCEPT CHECKS

1. According to sociologists, is "terrorism" a useful concept? Why or why not?
2. Compare and contrast old- and new-style terrorism.

 ## Study Outline
www.wwnorton.com/studyspace

The Concept of the State

- The term *government* refers to a political apparatus in which officials enact policies and make decisions. *Politics* refers to the use of power to affect government actions.
- *Power* is the capacity to achieve one's aims even against the resistance of others, and it often involves the use of force. A government has *authority* when its use of power is legitimate, deriving from the consent of those being governed. The most common form of

legitimate government is democratic, but other legitimate forms are also possible.
- A *state* comprises a political apparatus (government institutions), including civil service officials, ruling over a geographically defined territory; its authority is backed by a legal system, and it has the capacity to use force to implement policies.
- All modern states have additional features: *sovereignty,* the idea that government has authority over a given area; *citizenship,* the idea that people have common rights and duties and are aware of their part in the state; and *nationalism,* the sense of being part of a broader political community.
- Most nation-states became centralized through the activities of monarchs who concentrated social power. Citizens initially had few

(or no) rights of political participation; such rights were achieved only through a long process of struggle. *Civil rights* are freedoms and privileges guaranteed to individuals by law. *Political rights* ensure that citizens may participate in politics (by voting, for example). *Social rights* guarantee every individual a minimum standard of living. Social rights are the basis for the *welfare state,* which supports citizens who cannot support themselves.

Democracy

- The term *democracy* literally means rule by the people, but this phrase can be interpreted in various ways. For instance, "the people" has often meant "adult male property owners," whereas "rule" might refer to government policies, administrative decisions, or both.
- Different forms of democracy exist, including *participatory democracy* (also called *direct democracy*), which occurs when everyone is involved in all decision making, although this can be cumbersome for larger groups; *liberal democracy,* a system in which citizens have a choice to vote between at least two political parties for representatives who will be entrusted with decision making; and *constitutional monarchy,* which includes a royal family whose powers are severely restricted by a constitution putting authority in the hands of democratically elected representatives.
- A *political party* is an organization oriented toward achieving legitimate control of government through an electoral process. There is usually some connection between voting patterns and class differences. Many Western countries have recently seen a decline in allegiance to traditional parties and a growing disenchantment with the party system in general.
- Women achieved the right to vote much later than men in all countries and continue to be poorly represented among political elites. They have been influential on social and civil rights issues, and most Western countries have by now passed equal rights legislation.
- According to Weber and Schumpeter, the level of democratic participation that can be achieved in a modern, large-scale society is limited. The rule of *power elites* is inevitable, but multiparty systems provide the possibility of choosing *who* exercises power. *Pluralist theorists* add the claim that the competition of *interest groups* limits the degree to which ruling elites can concentrate power in a few hands.
- The number of countries with democratic governments has increased in recent years, due largely to the effects of globalization and mass communication and to the spread of competitive capitalism. But democracy also has problems; people everywhere have begun to lose faith in the capacity of politicians and governments to solve problems and to manage economies, and many people no longer vote.

Political and Social Change

- *Revolution* is the overthrow of an existing political order by a mass movement, using violence. *Social movements,* by contrast, involve a collective attempt to further common interests through collaborative action outside the sphere of established institutions. *New social movements* have arisen in Western countries since the 1960s in response to the changing risks facing human societies. Unlike earlier social movements, new social movements are single-issue campaigns with nonmaterial goals, and they draw support from across class lines. Information technology has become a powerful organizing tool for many new social movements.
- Theories of social movements and revolutions overlap. Marx argued that class struggles deriving from the *contradictions,* or unresolvable tensions, within society lead to revolutionary changes. Davies argues that social movements occur from *relative deprivation,* a discrepancy between people's lives and what people believe to be possible. Tilly analyzes revolutionary change from a broader context of *collective action,* which refers to action that contests or overthrows an existing social order. Collective action culminating in social movements progresses from organization to mobilization, the perception of common interests, and the opportunity to act. For Tilly, social movements occur in circumstances of *multiple sovereignty,* in which the government lacks full control.
- Smelser's theory treats social movements as responses to situations that undergo a series of stages. Touraine argues that social movements rest on *historicity,* the idea that people know that social activism can shape history and affect society. Social movements occur in *fields of action,* which refers to the connection between a movement and the forces acting against it.
- Social movements not only provide subject matter for sociologists but also challenge the established frameworks of thought of sociology (e.g., the effect of the women's movement on the study of gender).

The Nation State, National Identity, and Globalization

- *Nationalism* refers to symbols and beliefs that provide the sense of being part of a single political community. It emerged alongside the development of the modern state. *Nations without states* refers to cases in which a national group lacks political sovereignty over the area it claims as its own.

Terrorism

- *Terrorism* can be defined as tactics aimed at harming or killing civilians or noncombatants to compel a government or a population to act or stop acting in a particular way. Old-style terrorism is used by nations to establish a state where no state previously existed. In contrast, new-style terrorism has much broader goals, such as reshaping global society, and has a decentralized organizational structure that relies on networks. The new-style terrorist groups frequently have contact with and get support from states, and they are willing to be more ruthless in the means of violence they use.

Key Concepts

authority (p. 383)

citizens (p. 383)

civil rights (p. 386)

civil society (p. 413)

collective action (p. 405)

communism (p. 388)

constitutional monarchs (p. 388)

democracy (p. 387)

democratic elitism (p. 400)

direct democracy (p. 387)

ethnie (p. 414)

field of action (p. 410)

government (p. 383)

historicity (p. 410)

interest group (p. 396)

legitimation crisis (p. 403)

liberal democracies (p. 388)

local nationalisms (p. 386)

multiple sovereignty (p. 408)

nationalism (p. 383)

nation-states (p. 383)

nations without states (p. 415)

new social movements (p. 413)

new-style terrorism (p. 417)

old-style terrorism (p. 417)

participatory democracy (p. 387)

political rights (p. 386)

politics (p. 383)

power (p. 383)

power elite (p. 401)

relative deprivation (p. 405)

revolution (p. 404)

social movements (p. 404)

social rights (p. 386)

sovereignty (p. 383)

state (p. 383)

state overload (p. 403)

structural strain (p. 409)

terrorism (p. 417)

welfare state (p. 386)

Review Questions

1. What is the difference between power and authority?
2. What are the three types of rights associated with citizenship? What does it mean to say that citizenship has been a "powerful instrument of social closure"?
3. In what ways is the Internet a democratizing force? What are its limitations in promoting democracy?
4. Compare and contrast winner-take-all and proportional representation systems of democracy. In your opinion, which system is superior for democratic governance?
5. What are some explanations for why voter turnout is so low in the United States compared to other wealthy, literate, and democratic countries?
6. Why, according to Max Weber, is participatory democracy impossible on a large scale? What did he propose instead?
7. Describe C. Wright Mills's theory of the Power Elite. How does it differ from pluralist theories?
8. What is the relationship between social movements and sociology?
9. What is a new social movement? Give an example and explain why it fits this understanding of the meaning of a social movement.
10. How is new-style terrorism different from old-style terrorism? Why has new-style terrorism arisen?

Thinking Sociologically Exercises

1. Discuss the differences between the pluralistic and the power elite theories of democratic political processes. Which theory do you find most appropriate to describe U.S. politics in recent years?
2. Your textbook offers a variety of explanations on the formation of social movements. Briefly review the predisposing conditions for social movements, and then discuss their relevance in the development of the feminist social movement in the United States.

PART FOUR

SOCIAL INSTITUTIONS

Social institutions are the cement of social life. They are the basic living arrangements that human beings work out with one another, by means of which continuity is achieved across the generations.

We begin in Chapter 14 with work and economic life. Although the nature of work varies widely both within and across societies, work is one of the most pervasively important of all human pursuits.

In Chapter 15, we look at the institutions of kinship, marriage, and the family. Although the social obligations associated with kinship vary among different types of societies, the family is everywhere the context within which the young are provided with care and protection. Marriage is more or less universally connected to the family because it is a means of establishing new kin connections and forming a household in which children are brought up. In traditional cultures, much of the direct learning a child receives occurs within the family context. In modern societies, children spend many years of their lives in special places of instruction outside the family—schools and colleges. They also are constantly fed images and information from the mass media. Chapter 16 looks at the ways in which formal education is organized, concentrating particularly on how the educational system relates to the mass media.

The subject of Chapter 17 is religion. Although religious beliefs and practices are found in all cultures, the changes affecting religion in modern societies have been particularly acute. We analyze the nature of these changes, considering in what ways traditional types of religion still maintain their influence.

Learning Objectives

The Social Significance of Work

Assess the sociological ramifications of paid and unpaid work.

The Social Organization of Work

Understand that modern economies are based on the division of labor and economic interdependence. Learn Marx's theory of alienation. Familiarize yourself with modern systems of economic production.

The Modern Economy

See the importance of the rise of large corporations; consider particularly the global effect of transnational corporations.

The Changing Nature of Work

Learn about the effect of global economic competition on employment. Consider how work will change over the coming years.

CHAPTER FOURTEEN

WORK AND ECONOMIC LIFE

Chastity Ferguson kept watch over a sleepy three-year-old late one Friday as she flipped a pack of corn dogs into a cart at her new favorite grocery store: Wal-Mart. At this Las Vegas Supercenter, pink stucco on the outside, a wide-aisled, well-lighted emporium within, a full-scale supermarket is combined with a discount mega-store to offer shoppers everything they might need in their daily lives. For Ferguson, a harried, 26-year-old mother, the draw is obvious. "You can't beat the prices," said the hotel cashier, who makes $400 a week. "I come here because it's cheap."

Across town, another mother also is familiar with the Supercenter's low prices. Kelly Gray, the chief breadwinner for five children, lost her job as a Raley's grocery clerk late in 2002 after Wal-Mart expanded into the supermarket business in Las Vegas. California-based Raley's closed all 18 of its southern Nevada stores, laying off 1,400 workers. Gray earned $14.98 an hour with a pension and family health insurance. Wal-Mart grocery workers typically make less than $10 an hour, with inferior benefits. "It's like somebody came and broke into your home and took something huge and important away from you," said the 36-year-old. "I was scared. I cried. I shook."

Halfway around the world, 20-year-old Li Xiao Hong labors in a Guangzhou factory that turns out millions of the Mattel toys that Wal-Mart sells across America. She is part

423

of an army of 40 million newly proletarianized peasants who are turning South China into the workshop of the world. The plant's work areas are so poorly lighted that they seem permanently shrouded in grey. A smell of solvent wafts across the facility as rows of workers hunch over pedal-operated sewing machines and gluepots. Li is the fastest worker on a long, U-shaped assembly line of about 130 women. They put together animated, Disney-themed dolls that can be activated by the nudge of a small child. Li's hands move with lightning speed, gluing the pink bottom, screwing it into place, getting the rest of the casing to adhere, tamping it down with a special hammer, pulling the battery cover through its slats, soldering where she glued, then sending it down the line. The entire process takes 21 seconds. Li generally works five and one half days a week, up to 10 hours at a time. Her monthly wage—about $65—is typical for this part of China, enough for Li to send money back home to her rural family. But Li pays a heavy price. Her hands ache terribly, and she is always exhausted, but she seems resigned more than angry.

—*From Nelson Lichtenstein, "Wal-Mart: A Template for Twenty-First Century Capitalism." (Lichtenstein 2006: 5–6)*

The stories of these women illustrate two interrelated trends in the changing nature of work and economic life in the twenty-first century: The rise of transnational corporations, particularly giant retailers such as Wal-Mart that are reshaping the global economy, and the rapid growth of manufacturing in low-wage developing countries such as China.

Nelson Lichtenstein, a labor historian who spent many years studying Wal-Mart, believes that the world's largest corporation symbolizes the future of global capitalism. Wal-Mart, he points out, provides us with a steady stream of low-cost products, making it possible for millions of Americans, including Chastity Ferguson and others like her of limited means, to feed and clothe their families. Wal-Mart permits many Americans to enjoy a lifestyle of consumption that would otherwise not be possible. Wal-Mart also provides jobs, although most are not nearly as well-paying as the millions of manufacturing jobs that have been lost in recent years. Wal-Mart's jobs do not even provide the pay or benefits of Kelly Gray's job at the rival supermarket chain, many of whose stores went out of business when Wal-Mart opened its doors. The one place where jobs have been gained, and in large numbers, is the developing world. Manufacturing has boomed in China, where as many as a hundred million new workers such as Li Xiao Hong now labor under harsh conditions, in millions of factories that turn out everything from running shoes to flat panel TVs to iPods. China's factories provide the goods that are sold in Wal-Mart's thousands of U.S. stores, linking the economies of both countries tightly together. Wal-Mart's global supply chains, along with those of all corporations that design, make, and sell products today, link the world in a web of production networks that now reach every place on the planet. For better or for worse, the lives and work of all of us—indeed, of all people everywhere—are increasingly intertwined.

Work may be defined as carrying out tasks that require the expenditure of mental and physical effort, which has as its objective the production of goods and services that cater to human needs. An **occupation**, or job, is work that is done in exchange for a regular wage, or salary. In all cultures, work is the basis of the economic system, or **economy**. The economy consists of institutions that provide for the production and distribution of goods and services.

Most adults spend the better part of their waking hours at work. The job they do determines their economic prospects, shapes their lifestyle, and provides them with friends and acquaintances. Yet the nature of work is often determined by forces far beyond our control, and sometimes even beyond our understanding. In this chapter, we analyze the nature of work in modern societies and look at the major changes affecting economic life today. We investigate the changing nature of industrial production, the ownership structure of large business corporations, and the changing nature of work itself. Modern industry, as has been stressed in other parts of this book, differs in a fundamental way from premodern systems of production, which were based above all on agriculture. In modern societies, in contrast, most people no longer work on farms or in fields. Nor do large numbers work in factories, as was the case for much of the twentieth century. Rather, today's jobs involve providing services to others—services that range from high-paying professional jobs, such as managers of giant corporations, to low-paying labor requiring limited skills and training such as sales clerks in Wal-Mart.

The study of economic institutions is of major importance in sociology, because the economy influences all segments of society and, therefore, social life in general. And economic institutions are themselves always changing. One reason for such changes is **technology**—the harnessing of science to machinery in order to produce an ever-increasing variety of goods more cheaply. Another reason is globalization, which creates global competition not only among firms but also among workers: Whether you are an auto worker in a Detroit factory, an engineer in Silicon Valley, or a graphic designer in New York

City, there is likely to be someone a half a world away with the skill, talent, and drive to challenge you for your job.

The Social Significance of Work

To tackle these issues, we need to relate work to the broad contours of our society and to industrial organization as a whole. We often associate the notion of work with drudgery—with a set of tasks that we want to minimize and, if possible, escape from altogether. You may have this very thought in mind as you set out to read this chapter! Is this most people's attitude toward their work, and if so, why? We will try to find out in the following pages.

Work has more going for it than drudgery, or people would not feel so lost and disoriented when they become unemployed. How would you feel if you thought you would never get a job? In modern societies, having a job is important for maintaining self-esteem. Even where work conditions are relatively unpleasant, and the tasks involved dull, work tends to be a structuring element in people's psychological makeup and the cycle of their daily activities. Several characteristics of work are relevant here.

- *Money.* A wage or salary is the main resource many people depend on to meet their needs. Without such an income, anxieties about coping with day-to-day life tend to multiply.
- *Activity level.* Work often provides a basis for the acquisition and exercise of skills and capacities. Even where work is routine, it offers a structured environment in which a person's energies may be absorbed. Without it, the opportunity to exercise such skills and capacities may be reduced.
- *Variety.* Work provides access to contexts that contrast with domestic surroundings. In the working environment, even when the tasks are relatively dull, individuals may enjoy doing something different from home chores.
- *Structuring one's time.* For people in regular employment, the day is usually organized around the rhythm of work. Although work may sometimes be oppressive, it provides a sense of direction in daily activities. Those who are out of work frequently find boredom a major problem and develop a sense of apathy about time. As one unemployed man remarked, "Time doesn't matter now as much as it used to.... There's so much of it" (Fryer and McKenna 1987).
- *Social contacts.* The work environment often provides friendships and opportunities to participate in shared activities with others. Separated from the work setting, a person's circle of possible friends and acquaintances is likely to dwindle.
- *Personal identity.* Work is usually valued for the sense of stable social identity it offers. For men in particular, self-esteem is often bound up with the economic contribution

Gabriela Chavez (*left*) a hair dresser at a beauty salon in New York City, talks with a customer while washing the hair of another. Her work as a stylist puts her into contact with hundreds of friends and acquaintances in her community.

Stock traders work the phones and watch their monitors. How has technology transformed work?

they make to the maintenance of the household. In addition, job conditions, such as the opportunity to work in jobs that are challenging, not routinized, and not subject to close supervision, are known to affect a person's sense of self-worth (Kohn 1977).

Against the backdrop of this formidable list, it is not difficult to see why being without work may undermine individuals' confidence in their social value.

Unpaid Work

We often tend to think of work, as the notion of being "out of work" implies, as equivalent to having a paid job, but in fact this is an oversimplified view. Nonpaid labor (such as repairing one's own car or doing one's own housework) looms large in many people's lives. Many types of work do not conform to orthodox categories of paid employment. Much of the work done in the informal economy, for example, is not recorded in any direct way in the official employment statistics. The term **informal economy** refers to transactions outside the sphere of regular employment, sometimes involving the exchange of cash for services provided, but also often involving the direct exchange of goods or services.

Someone who comes to fix the television may be paid in cash, "off the books," without any receipt being given or details of the job recorded. People may exchange pilfered or stolen goods with friends or associates in return for other favors. The informal economy includes not only "hidden" cash transactions, but many forms of *self-provisioning* that people carry on inside and outside the home. Do-it-yourself activities and household appliances and tools, for instance, provide goods and services that would otherwise have to be purchased (Gershuny and Miles 1983).

Housework, which has traditionally mostly been carried out by women, is usually unpaid. But it is work, often very hard and exhausting work, nevertheless. Volunteer work, for charities or other organizations, has an important social role. Having a paid job is important for all the reasons listed earlier—but the category of "work" stretches more widely.

☑ CONCEPT CHECKS

1. Describe six characteristics that shape one's everyday experiences at work.
2. Define and provide an example of an informal economy.

The Social Organization of Work

One of the most distinctive characteristics of the economic system of modern societies is the existence of a highly complex **division of labor**: Work has become divided into an enormous number of different occupations in which people specialize. In traditional societies, nonagricultural work entailed the mastery of a craft. Craft skills were learned through a lengthy period of apprenticeship, and the worker normally carried out all aspects of the production process from beginning to end. For example, a metalworker making a plow would forge the iron, shape it, and assemble the implement itself. With the rise of modern industrial production, most traditional crafts have disappeared altogether, replaced by skills that form part of more large-scale production processes. An electrician working in an industrial setting today, for instance, may inspect and repair only a few parts of one type of machine; different people will deal with the other parts and other machines.

The contrast in the division of labor between traditional and modern societies is truly extraordinary. Even in the largest traditional societies, there usually existed no more than twenty or thirty major craft trades, together with such specialized pursuits as merchant, soldier, and priest. In a modern industrial system, there are literally thousands of distinct occupations. The U.S. Bureau of the Census lists some twenty thousand distinct jobs in the American economy. In traditional communities, most of the population worked on farms and were economically self-sufficient. They produced their own food, clothes, and other necessities of life. One of the main features of modern societies, by contrast, is an enormous expansion of **economic interdependence**. We all depend on an immense number of other workers—today stretching right across the world—for the products and services that sustain our lives. With few exceptions, the vast majority of people in modern societies do not produce the food they eat, the houses in which they live, or the material goods they consume.

Taylorism and Fordism

Writing some two centuries ago, Adam Smith, one of the founders of modern economics, identified advantages that the division of labor provides in terms of increasing productivity. His most famous work, *The Wealth of Nations* (1776), opens with a description of the division of labor in a pin factory. A person working alone could perhaps make twenty pins per day. By breaking down that worker's task into a number of simple operations, however, ten workers carrying out specialized jobs in collaboration with one another could collectively produce forty-eight thousand pins per day. The rate of production per worker, in other words, is increased from twenty to forty-eight hundred pins, each specialist operator producing 240 times more than when working alone.

More than a century later, these ideas reached their most developed expression in the writings of Frederick Winslow Taylor, an American management consultant. Taylor's approach to what he called "scientific management" involved the detailed study of industrial processes to break them down into simple operations that could be precisely timed and organized. **Taylorism**, as scientific management came to be called, was not merely an academic study. It was a system of production designed to maximize industrial output, and it had a widespread effect not only on the organization of industrial production and technology but on workplace politics as well. In particular, Taylor's time and motion studies wrested control over knowledge of the production process from the worker and placed such knowledge firmly in the hands of management, eroding the basis on which craft workers maintained autonomy from their employers (Braverman 1974). As such, Taylorism has been widely associated with the deskilling and degradation of labor.

The principles of Taylorism were appropriated by the industrialist Henry Ford. In 1908, Ford designed his first auto plant at Highland Park, Michigan, to manufacture only one product—the Model T Ford—thereby allowing the introduction of specialized tools and machinery designed for speed, precision, and simplicity of operation. One of Ford's most significant innovations was the introduction of the assembly line, said to have been inspired by Chicago slaughterhouses, in which animals were disassembled section by section on a moving conveyor belt. Each worker on Ford's assembly line was assigned a specialized task, such as fitting the left-side door handles as the car bodies moved along the line. By 1929, when production of the Model T ceased, more than fifteen million cars had been assembled.

Ford was among the first to realize that mass production requires mass markets. Ford reasoned that if standardized commodities such as the automobile were to be produced on an ever-greater scale, the presence of consumers who were able to buy those commodities must also be ensured. In 1914, Ford took the unprecedented step of unilaterally raising wages at his Dearborn, Michigan, plant to $5 for an eight-hour day—a very generous wage at the time and one that ensured a working-class lifestyle that included owning such an automobile. As Harvey (1989) remarks, "The purpose of the five dollar, eight hour day was only in part to secure worker compliance with the discipline required to work the highly productive assembly-line system. It was coincidentally meant to provide workers with sufficient income to consume the mass-produced products the corporations were about to turn out in ever vaster quantities." Ford also enlisted the services of a small army of social workers who were sent into the homes of workers to educate them in the proper habits of consumption.

Fordism is the name given to designate the system of mass production tied to the cultivation of mass markets. In certain contexts, the term has a more specific meaning, referring to a historical period in the development of post–World War II capitalism in which mass production was associated with stability in labor relations and a high degree of unionization. Under Fordism, firms made long-term commitments to workers, and wages were tightly linked to productivity growth. As such, collective bargaining agreements—formal agreements negotiated between firms and unions that specified working conditions

One of Henry Ford's most significant innovations was the introduction of the assembly line, which allowed for mass production of the Model T.

such as wages, seniority rights, benefits, and so on—created a virtuous circle that ensured worker consent to automated systems of production, as well as sufficient demand for mass-produced commodities. The system is generally understood to have broken down in the 1970s, giving rise to greater flexibility and insecurity in working conditions.

The reasons for the demise of Fordism are complex and intensely debated. As firms in a variety of industries adopted Fordist production methods, the system encountered certain limitations. Fordism was not suitable for all industries; it could be applied successfully only to industries that produced standardized commodities for large markets. At one time, it looked as though Fordism represented the likely future of industrial production as a whole. This has not proved to be the case. Setting up mechanized production lines is enormously expensive, and once a Fordist system is established, it is quite rigid; to alter a product, for example, substantial reinvestment is needed. Fordist production is easy to copy if sufficient funding is available to set up the plant. But firms in countries in which labor power is expensive find it difficult to compete with those where wages are cheaper. This was one of the factors originally leading to the rise of the Japanese car industry (although Japanese wage levels today are no longer low), followed by South Korea, and most recently China.

Work and Alienation

Karl Marx was one of the first writers to grasp that the development of modern industry would reduce many people's work to dull, uninteresting tasks. According to Marx, the division of labor alienates human beings from their work. For Marx, **alienation** refers to feelings of estrangement and even hostility—initially to one's job and eventually to the overall framework of capitalist industrial production. In Marx's view, workers in capitalist society lack ownership of the products they make, which they often cannot even afford to buy; they are dehumanized by tedious and demeaning labor processes over which they have no control; and they find themselves in competition with their fellow workers for scarce jobs. Marx saw this as counter to human nature, which he believed involved creativity, control over one's activities, and cooperation with others (Marx 2000; orig. 1844).

In traditional societies, he pointed out, work was often exhausting—peasant farmers sometimes had to toil from dawn to dusk. Yet peasants held a real measure of control over their work, which required much knowledge and skill. Many industrial workers, by contrast, have little control over their jobs, contribute only a fraction to the creation of the overall product, and have no influence over how or to whom it is eventually sold. Work thus appears as something alien, a task that the worker must carry out to earn an income but that is in itself unsatisfying.

Low-Trust and High-Trust Systems

Fordism and Taylorism are what some industrial sociologists call **low-trust systems**. Jobs are set by management and are geared to machines. Those who carry out the work tasks are closely supervised and are allowed little autonomy of action. Where there are many low-trust positions, the level of worker dissatisfaction and absenteeism is high, and industrial conflict is common. A **high-trust system** is one in which workers are permitted to control the pace and even the content of their work, within overall guidelines. Such systems are usually concentrated at the higher levels of industrial organizations.

Industrial Conflict

There have long been conflicts between workers and those in economic and political authority over them. Riots against conscription and high taxes and food riots at periods of harvest failure were common in urban areas of Europe in the eighteenth century. These "premodern" forms of labor conflict continued up to not much more than a century ago in some countries. For example, there were food riots in several large Italian towns in 1868 (Geary 1981). Such traditional forms of confrontation were not just sporadic, irrational outbursts of violence: The threat or use of violence had the effect of lowering the price of grain and other essential foodstuffs (Booth 1977; Rudé 1964; Thompson 1971).

Industrial conflict between workers and employers at first tended to follow these older patterns. In situations of confrontation, workers would quite often leave their places of employment and form crowds in the streets; they would make their grievances known through their unruly behavior or by engaging in acts of violence against the authorities. Workers in some parts of France in the late nineteenth century would threaten disliked employers with hanging (Holton 1978). Use of the strike as a weapon, today commonly associated with organized bargaining between workers and management, developed only slowly and sporadically.

STRIKES

We can define a **strike** as a temporary stoppage of work by a group of employees to express a grievance or enforce a demand (Hyman 1984). All the components of this definition are important in separating strikes from other forms of opposition and conflict. A strike is *temporary* because workers intend to

Writers Guild of America members picket outside Paramount Studios in Los Angeles during their 2008 strike.

return to the same job with the same employer; when workers quit altogether, the term *strike* is not appropriate. As a *stoppage of work,* a strike is distinguishable from an overtime ban or "slowdown." A *group* of workers has to be involved, because a strike is a collective action, not the response of one individual worker. That those involved are *employees* serves to separate strikes from protests such as may be conducted by tenants or students. Finally, a strike involves seeking to make known a grievance or press a demand; workers who miss work to go to a ball game could not be said to be on strike (Figure 14.1).

Strikes represent only one aspect or type of conflict in which workers and management may become involved. Other closely related expressions of organized conflict are lockouts (in which the employers rather than the workers bring about a stoppage of work), output restrictions, and clashes in contract negotiations. "Work to rule" is a form of organized labor action in which workers do the minimum work that is legally required of them, carefully following health, safety, and other regulations. Work to rule usually results in costly slowdowns for the firm because workers routinely exceed the requirements of their contracts and often may even violate health, safety, and wage and hour regulations in order to get the job done. Work to rule is typically done in situations where strikes may be illegal, such as among school teachers, whose contracts often forbid strikes. Less-organized expressions of conflict may include high labor turnover, absenteeism, and interference with production machinery.

Workers choose to go on strike for many specific reasons. For much of the twentieth century, U.S. workers typically went on strike to secure higher wages, better hours, safer working conditions, and security of employment, as well as to occasionally protest against technological changes that would make their work duller or lead to layoffs. In all these circumstances the strike is essentially a mechanism of power: a weapon of people who are relatively powerless in the workplace and whose working lives are affected by managerial decisions over which they have little or no control. It is usually a weapon of last resort, to be used when other negotiations have failed, because workers on strike either receive no income or depend on union funds, which might be limited.

Throughout much of the latter half of the twentieth century, at least in the automobile, steel, and other industries where labor unions were strong, strikes were usually successful. An expanding economy, coupled with well-organized labor militancy, assured that workers would share in economic growth. During the past quarter century, however, globalization has eroded many of these gains. Competition with low-wage labor elsewhere in the world has resulted in factory closures and layoffs, undermining the effectiveness of strikes and other militant forms of labor action. As Figure 14.1 shows, the number of strikes plummeted beginning in the mid-1970s, and today strikes are increasingly rare. Workers in many industries have instead accepted pay cuts in hopes of keeping their jobs, and, as we will discuss in the next section, labor union membership has declined significantly.

Labor Unions

Although their levels of membership and the extent of their power vary widely, union organizations exist in all Western countries, which also all legally recognize the right of workers to strike in pursuit of economic objectives. Why have unions become a basic feature of Western societies? Why does union-management conflict seem to be a more or less ever-present possibility in industrial settings?

In the early development of modern industry, workers in most countries had no political rights and little influence over the conditions of work in which they found themselves. Unions developed as a means of redressing the imbalance of power between workers and employers. Whereas workers had virtually no power as individuals, through collective organization their influence was considerably increased. An employer can do without the labor of any particular worker but not without that of all or most of the workers in a factory or plant. Unions originally were mainly "defensive" organizations, providing the means whereby workers could counter the overwhelming power that employers wielded over their lives.

Workers today have voting rights in the political sphere, and there are established forms of negotiation with employers, by means of which economic benefits can be pressed for and grievances expressed. However, union influence, both at the level of the local plant and nationally, still remains primarily

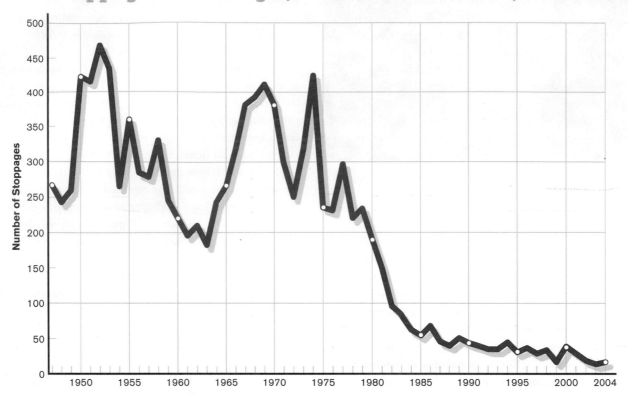

FIGURE 14.1

Work Stoppages Involving 1,000 Workers or More, 1947–2004

During what year since the end of World War II did the greatest number of work stoppages involving 1,000 workers or more occur? Is it accurate to say that the number of work stoppages involving 1,000 workers or more has consistently declined since 1950? During what year did the decline in work stoppages involving 1,000 workers or more begin and fail to recover to any significant levels of the past? During which of the last twenty years has the number of work stoppages involving 1,000 workers or more come close to reaching the levels of the 1950s? What are some specific reasons that workers may go on strike? Name two causes of union decline that are consistent with the decline in union density within and among industries.

SOURCE: U.S. Bureau of the Census 2006a.

veto power. In other words, using the resources at their disposal, including the right to strike, unions can only block employers' policies or initiatives, not help formulate them in the first place. There are exceptions to this, for instance when unions and employers negotiate periodic contracts covering conditions of work.

The post–World War II period witnessed a dramatic reversal in the positions of unions in advanced industrial societies. In most developed countries, the period from 1950 to 1980 was a time of steady growth in **union density**, a statistic that represents the number of union members as a percentage of the number of people who could potentially be union members. Union density across the Western economies was highly variable, however. In the United States, for example, union density peaked in the late 1950s, much earlier than in Europe. Countries that reached the highest levels of union density— Belgium, Denmark, Finland, and Sweden, with more than 80 percent of all workers belonging to labor unions in 1985— shared three features in common (Western 1997). First, strong working-class political parties created favorable conditions for labor organizing. Second, bargaining between firms and labor unions was coordinated at the national level rather than occurring separately in different industries, or at the local level. Third, unions rather than the state directly administered unemployment insurance, ensuring that workers who lost their jobs did not leave the labor movement. Countries in which some combination but not all three of these factors were present had lower rates of union density, ranging between two fifths and two thirds of the working population.

After 1980, unions suffered declines across the advanced industrial countries. In the United States, the decline began even earlier, with unionization peaking at more than a third of the workforce during the 1950s and declining steadily since that time, to only 12.1 percent in 2007 (Dickens and Leonard 1985; U.S. Bureau of Labor Statistics 2008a). There is, however, considerable variation in union membership by occupation and industry (U.S. Bureau of Labor Statistics 2008a). For example, while only about 7.5 percent of all private-sector wage and salary workers were unionized in 2007, the rate was nearly three times as higher transportation and utilities (22.1 percent), and twice as high in construction (13.9 percent), but much lower in agriculture and related industries (1.5 percent), and financial services (2 percent). The highest rates of unionization were among public-sector workers, nearly five times higher on average than the private sector: more than a third (35.9 percent) of all government employees belonged to unions, reaching 41.8 percent for local government.

Earnings tend to be higher in those industries that are more heavily unionized. For example, unionized construction workers had median weekly earnings of $1000 in 2007; manufacturing workers, $783. In wholesale and retail trade, median weekly earnings for unionized workers were only $639; among leisure and hospitality workers, $580. Government workers, where unionization rates are the highest, have seen a steady increase in earnings since 2000 (Figure 14.2), with median weekly earnings reaching $901 by 2007 (U.S. Bureau of Labor Statistics 2008a).

There are several possible explanations for the difficulties confronted by unions since 1980. Perhaps the most common is the decline of the older manufacturing industries and the rise of the service sector. The United States, for example, has lost many manufacturing jobs during recent years, and manufacturing has traditionally been a stronghold for organized labor, whereas jobs in such services as wholesale and retail trade, education, health services, or leisure and hospitality have historically been more resistant to unionization. Yet it is precisely these sorts of service sector jobs that have grown most rapidly (U.S. Bureau of the Census 2008b). Some of the largest employers of the growing number of service workers have been highly effective at stifling all efforts of their workforce to unionize. Wal-Mart, the world's largest corporation, is

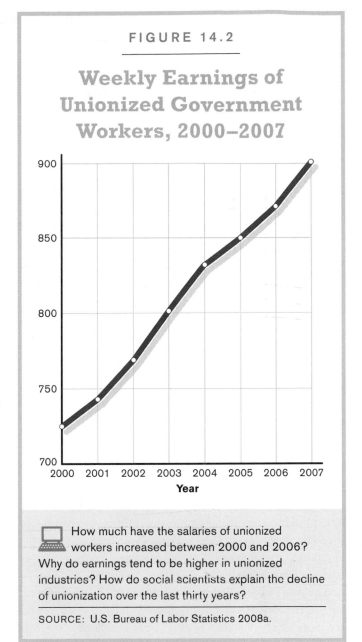

FIGURE 14.2

Weekly Earnings of Unionized Government Workers, 2000–2007

How much have the salaries of unionized workers increased between 2000 and 2006? Why do earnings tend to be higher in unionized industries? How do social scientists explain the decline of unionization over the last thirty years?

SOURCE: U.S. Bureau of Labor Statistics 2008a.

one example: its nearly two million employees worldwide, with few exceptions, have not been allowed to form unions. (Under pressure from the Chinese government, Wal-Mart recently allowed its growing number of stores in China to be unionized, although by the official governmental union rather than more independent ones.)

Attributing the decline of unionization to the rise of service sector employment, however, has a number of weaknesses. Sociologist Bruce Western (1997) argues that this factor alone cannot account for the experience of the 1970s in many advanced industrial economies (the United States was an exception), which was generally a good period for unions and yet was

Dukes v. Wal-Mart Stores, Inc.

After six years of hard work and excellent performance reviews, Betty Dukes was finally promoted to management in 2000. Working at the customer-complaint desk at Wal-Mart, Dukes was given a raise to $6.45 an hour. In San Francisco, where she continues to work, that's below the poverty line.

In 2001, Dukes filed a lawsuit against Wal-Mart claiming that she had been systematically denied training and the opportunity for advancement. Dukes were frustrated, and she wasn't the only one. As more and more female employees came forward to tell their stories, the picture became clear: At stores across the country, women were being paid less and offered fewer promotions than men. Stephanie Odle, an assistant store manager in Riverside, California, was shocked to learn that a male assistant manager working at the same Wal-Mart store was making $60,000 a year, $23,000 more than she was earning. She said, "When I went to the district manager, he first goes, 'Stephanie, that assistant manager has a family and two children to support.' I told him, 'I'm a single mother and I have a 6-month-old child to support' " (Greenhouse and Hays 2004). Gina Espinoza, a Wal-Mart employee in northern California, recalled being sexually and even racially harassed by her boss on more than one occasion. "He used to call me the little Mexican princess," she said. Espinoza was fired from her job shortly after filing a sexual harassment complaint (Greenhouse and Hays 2004).

The suit *Dukes v. Wal-Mart Stores, Inc.,* was eventually expanded to represent 1.6 million current and former employees across the United States, making Dukes the lead plaintiff in the largest civil rights class-action lawsuit in history. The suit charged Wal-Mart with violating Title VII of the 1964 Civil Rights Act, which protects workers from sex discrimination in the workplace. Wal-Mart denied the allegations, claiming that women in the company have as many opportunities for advancement as men. And while anecdotes from individual

William Bielby

employees like Stephanie Odle and Gina Espinoza may provide powerful storylines, evaluating the legal claim that women as a group—as a class of people—have endured discrimination takes sociological thinking.

Professor William Bielby, a sociologist at the University of Pennsylvania, has spent nearly twenty years studying inequality in the workplace. His reputation for communicating complicated ideas to audiences not familiar with terms like *centralized coordination* and *personnel policy* qualified him to serve as an expert witness in the *Dukes* trial. In the trial, Bielby's main task was to look at Wal-Mart's policies and practices and compare them to scientific theories of how gender bias happens in organizations. At the heart of the case was whether Wal-Mart has a workplace culture that discriminates against women and whether those women as a group could force Wal-Mart to change the way it treats its female employees, both in the past (by providing backpay to women like Dukes) and in the future

also characterized by a shift from manufacturing to services. Moreover, at least some of the growth in service sector employment in the United States has been in areas that have been successfully unionized in recent years. The fastest-growing U.S. labor union is the Service Employees International Union (SEIU), which has nearly two million members (1.9 million members and 50,000 retirees) in such diverse areas as health care, janitorial work, security, state and local government, public school employees, bus drivers, and child care (SEIU 2008).

(by increasing the opportunities available to all employees regardless of their gender).

In his role as expert witness, Bielby reviewed hundreds of organizational charts, memos, reports, and presentations. He studied Wal-Mart's policies relating to personnel, diversity, and equal employment opportunity as well as documents describing the culture and history of the company. What evidence, if any, did Bielby find? He started by explaining that men and women making different amounts of money does not necessarily mean that the company is discriminating. How can that be?

It all comes down to the issue of qualifications. "There are many reasons why men and women can have different career trajectories," Bielby (2005) states in his report. "For example, jobs may have job-related skill and experience requirements that differ, on average, between men and women. Gender disparities arising from such factors would not be considered discriminatory, so long as the employer is not responsible for differences in men's and women's qualifications (e.g., by not providing equal access to training)."

Discrimination comes into play once people start making decisions about training, compensation, and promotion based on beliefs about a person's gender instead of on his or her qualifications or experience. Bielby says, "Employers also create gender barriers when they ignore (or encourage) an organizational climate that is hostile towards women and inhibits them from performing to their full potential." Bielby explained to the court that

> gender stereotypes are beliefs about traits and behaviors that differ between men and women. For example, men are believed to be competitive, aggressive, assertive, strong, and independent, while women are believed to be nurturing, cooperative, supportive, and understanding. Men are assumed to place a high priority on their careers, whereas women are assumed to be more strongly oriented towards family, even though research demonstrates that the commitments of men and women with similar job opportunities and family situations are virtually identical. These kinds of stereotypes are relevant to how men and women advance in careers with Wal-Mart. For example, if women are believed to be committed to

and constrained by family circumstances, and men are not, women will not be given the same consideration as men for management positions that are believed to interfere with family obligations.

In other testimony reviewed by Bielby, a male-centered, traditional culture was reinforced by those who made biblical references or noted the "long hours" to discourage female employees from pursuing promotions. Some women who had achieved senior management positions said that they were forced to go to strip bars and Hooters restaurants for office outings and that senior management fostered a climate in which sexually demeaning comments and attitudes were the norm (Porter 2004).

Bielby supplemented his analysis of gender stereotypes with statistical evidence on job placements that was highly suggestive of gender discrimination. At Wal-Mart, women make up 89.5 percent of cashiers, 79 percent of department heads, 37.6 percent of assistant store managers, and 15.5 percent of store managers, compared to other discount stores like Target, Costco, and Home Depot, where women hold 57 percent of management positions (Bielby 2005). Bielby played an important role in bringing potential discrimination to light. In a 2003 ruling allowing the civil suit to proceed, Judge Jenkins, after reviewing Bielby's testimony, found that "women working at Wal-Mart stores are paid less than men in every region, that pay disparities exist in most job categories, that the salary gap widens over time, that women take longer to enter management positions, and that the higher one looks in the organization the lower the percentage of women" that can be found (Ackman 2004).

Dukes still works at Wal-Mart. Since she filed the discrimination suit in 2001, she has received multiple raises and now makes over $12.00 an hour as a greeter at the same San Francisco store where she was originally hired. But she didn't file suit only for personal gain. As lead plaintiff, she believes that entrenched gender inequality within the nation's largest company is a violation of civil rights. For Bielby, who decided to become a professor in the 1960s to help "address issues that have to do with social change and social justice," the *Dukes* case provided him a rare opportunity to make a difference in the public realm (Dubilet 2005).

The rapid fall in union membership in the United States is due to a combination of factors, chief among which is the loss of once-unionized manufacturing jobs to low-wage countries around the world, particularly in East Asia, and most notably China—a country where independent labor unions are illegal.

Such job loss—real or threatened—has greatly weakened the bargaining power of unions in the manufacturing sector, and as a result lowered their appeal to workers. Why join a union and pay union dues if it cannot deliver wage increases or job security? Unionization efforts in the United States have also been hampered in recent years by decisions of the National Labor Relations Board (NLRB), the government agency responsible for protecting the right of workers to form unions and engage in collective bargaining. The NLRB has proven ineffective in protecting efforts to unionize workplaces, failing to take aggressive action when businesses harass or fire union organizers (Estlund 2006; Clawson and Clawson 1999).

It is significant that the service jobs that have been successfully unionized by such unions as SEIU are precisely those that cannot be exported to other countries: janitors, nurses, and state and local government employees. These are all jobs that are tied to a specific location, where well-organized workers can still achieve some measure of job security and wage gains without fear that their place of employment will close shop and move to a low-wage country. Labor unions traditionally tied to manufacturing have recognized this and now are actively seeking new members in those service sectors where the jobs cannot be exported. The United Auto Workers (UAW), for example, has branched out to organize technical, office, and professional workers, including graduate students at the University of California and some twenty other colleges and universities. United Steelworkers members now include workers in offices, nursing homes, hospitals, hotels, restaurants, and colleges and universities—in fact, as their Web site boasts, "in just about every job imaginable" (United Steel Workers 2007).

In the United States, unions clearly face a crisis of even greater dimensions than their counterparts in most European countries. Union-protected working conditions and wages have eroded in major industries over the past twenty-five years. Workers in the trucking, steel, and car industries have all accepted lower wages than those previously negotiated. The unions came out second best in several major strikes, beginning with the crushing of the air traffic controllers' union in the early 1980s. In recent years the UAW has been forced to reach agreements with Ford, Chrysler, and General Motors that conceded wage cuts, in exchange for a freeze on outsourcing jobs, along with promises of employer support for retired workers' health care.

One consequence of the erosion of workers' power has been a revolt within the labor movement itself. A number of unions have challenged the dominance of the once-powerful American Federation of Labor and Congress of Industrial Organizations (AFL-CIO), a confederation of fifty six unions representing 10.5 million workers (AFL-CIO, 2008). Frustrated with the AFL-CIO's inability to organize more workers or achieve significant gains, in 2005 seven leading unions broke off to form "Change to Win," a more militant federation that is composed in large part of six million women and minority service-sector workers. The unions that make up this new organization represent more than a third of the original membership of the AFL-CIO. The revolt was led by SEIU and its charismatic leader Andy

Stern and includes the SEIU, Teamsters, and five other unions. Change to Win is currently concentrating its organizing in areas where the jobs cannot be sent overseas, for example, Wal-Mart employees, hotel workers, and truckers who move goods from U.S. container ports. Among their demands is the passage of the Employee Free Choice Act, which would require employers to recognize a union if the majority of its workers sign cards saying they are in favor. This "card check" approach to union membership would bypass elections, as currently required by law. Proponents claim that elections are seldom democratic, because companies often harass or fire union organizers, threaten workers who support the union, and coerce workers into voting against union formation.

Whether Change to Win will succeed in revitalizing the U.S. labor movement remains to be seen, but it is perhaps significant that in 2007 *Fortune* magazine listed SEIU head Andy Stern as one of four "scary power people business hates to see coming" (another was sociologist William Bielby, whose expert testimony in job discrimination lawsuits against Wal-Mart and other large corporations is profiled in the "Public Sociology" box in this chapter; Tkaczyk 2008).

What Do Workers Want?

An individual's quality of life depends on his or her position in the labor market. Arguably this is more true in the United States than in any other comparably developed economy. Americans spend more time at work than do citizens of other advanced industrial countries. U.S. living standards also reflect income and employment-related benefits more directly than do living standards in other comparably developed countries where governments universally guarantee paid vacation, job training, and health insurance. There is also more variability in terms of pay and work conditions in the U.S. labor market than elsewhere. Yet, in spite of the overwhelming importance of the labor market for the life conditions of working Americans, there has been relatively little investigation of how workers view the framework through which the U.S. labor market is governed. For this reason, Richard Freeman of Harvard University and Joel Rogers of the University of Wisconsin set out to find out what workers want in regard to the conditions under which they labor. Freeman and Rogers (1999) designed the Worker Representation and Participation Survey (WRPS) to canvass workers systematically in a wide variety of professions for their opinions about their employment and how their workplaces could be improved.

Freeman and Rogers's findings are based on a national telephone survey of 2,400 workers in private-sector establishments that employ twenty-five or more people. They excluded top managers, the self-employed, owners of firms or

Members of the Service Employees International Union picketing outside city hall in Los Angeles. The county workers—who include nurses and medical staff; library workers; and staff workers at the civic center, beaches, and harbors—are demanding raises, improved job security, and better benefits.

their relatives, public-sector workers, and employees in small firms. Overall, the population from which survey respondents were selected covers approximately 75 percent of all private-sector workers. Freeman and Rogers's findings range across a wide variety of aspects of people's work lives, including causes of worker dissatisfaction, attitudes toward unionization, views of management, and worker knowledge of protective labor legislation. In-depth follow-up interviews were conducted with 801 workers, who were asked about their views of alternative institutional designs for American workplaces.

The overwhelming finding of Freeman and Rogers's study is that what workers want is more influence at work. American workers believe that if they had more say over how production is carried out, not only would they enjoy work more but also their firms would be more competitive and problems would be solved more effectively. Furthermore, influence is associated with a broader range of attitudes about work: Workers satisfied with their degree of influence report that they enjoy going to work, grade employee–management relations as excellent, and trust their employer. In contrast, workers who are dissatisfied with their degree of influence tend to dislike going to work, report poor relations with management, and distrust their employers.

One of the most surprising findings of the WRPS concerns the kind of institutional arrangement that workers consider ideal for achieving greater say. Contrary to what Freeman and Rogers expected, workers prefer an organization run jointly by workers and management to one run by employees alone. Workers were also asked to choose between two hypothetical organizations, "one that management cooperated with in discussing issues, but had no power to make decisions," and "one that had more power but management opposed." Sixty-

three percent of all employees chose the former organization, whereas only 22 percent stated that they would prefer the latter. These results—in which workers effectively indicated that they would prefer weaker to stronger organizations, in spite of the fact that they also reported wanting more say at work—make sense in light of another question on Freeman and Rogers's survey. When asked if they thought an organization could be effective without managerial support, three quarters of all respondents indicated that they believed an employee organization could function only with management cooperation.

☑ CONCEPT CHECKS

1. Using the concept of division of labor, describe the key differences in the nature of work in traditional versus modern societies.
2. What are two key differences between Taylorism and Fordism?
3. What is a labor union? Why have unions in the United States suffered from a decline in membership since the 1980s?
4. According to Freeman and Rogers' research, how can workplaces be changed to better meet the desires of modern workers?

The Modern Economy

Modern societies are, in Marx's term, capitalistic. **Capitalism** is a way of organizing economic life that is distinguished by the following important features: private ownership of the means of production; profit as incentive; free competition for markets to sell goods, acquire cheap materials, and use cheap labor; and restless expansion and investment to accumulate capital. Capitalism, which began to spread with the growth of the Industrial Revolution in the early nineteenth century, is a vastly more dynamic economic system than any other that preceded it in history. Although the system has had many critics, such as Marx, it is now the most widespread form of economic organization in the world.

So far in this chapter, we have been looking at industry mostly from the perspective of occupations and employees. We have studied how patterns of work have changed and the factors influencing the development of labor unions. But we have also to concern ourselves with the nature of the business firms in which the workforce is employed. (It should be recognized that many people today are employees of government organizations, although we will not consider these here.) What is happening to business corporations today, and how are they run?

"Money Really Can't Buy Happiness"

College students who are searching for an academic major or a future profession might be particularly intrigued by a study of job satisfaction that recently captured national headlines. The message? "Money Really Can't Buy Happiness" (Rose 2007) and "Service to Others Not Just a Job" (Herrndobler 2007). Readers were told that the happiest, most satisfied Americans were those who worked in helping professions. Topping the list of satisfied workers were clergy, physical therapists, firefighters, and education administrators. If that's the case, should engineering majors switch to religious studies? Or should aspiring medical researchers instead pursue physical therapy? The answers can be found in a recent University of Chicago study entitled *Job Satisfaction in the United States* (Smith 2007).

This recent study reported on the analysis of data from the General Social Survey (GSS), a survey of more than 27,500 randomly selected Americans. The GSS has collected job satisfaction data dating back to 1988. In their recent analysis, the researchers ranked 198

jobs, based on the proportion in each job who said that they were "very satisfied" with their work. This is the first time that the GSS has broken down job satisfaction at the level of specific occupation. Overall, 47 percent of American workers said that they were "very satisfied," with proportions ranging from a

Those in helping professions, such as nurses and physical therapists, enjoyed their work the most.

high of 87 percent of clergy, compared with just 20 percent among roofers, waiters, and laborers—the three jobs at the bottom of the list. Other highly satisfying jobs included physical therapists and firefighters, three-quarters of whom were "very satisfied" with their

work. Creative professions also brought rewards; roughly 60 percent of painters, sculptors, and authors were very satisfied with their work. Educators also enjoyed their work: educational administrators, teachers, and special education teachers rounded out the top 10 list. According to Smith, "the most satisfying jobs are mostly professions, especially those involving caring for, teaching and protecting others and creative pursuits."

A closer look at the data reveal that not all helping or creative professions carry psychological rewards. Rather, it's those helping professions that are white-collar, relatively high status jobs that pay reasonably well. Smith noted that job satisfaction generally rises with social status and that higher status often goes hand in hand with high pay. One exception he pointed out is physician. Physician is a high-paying profession that usually ranks number one in studies of occupational prestige. Surprisingly, only 58 percent of doctors reported that they were "very satisfied," despite the fact that the average physician earns twice what the average physical therapist earns.

Corporations and Corporate Power

Since the turn of the twentieth century, modern capitalist economies have been more and more influenced by the rise of large business **corporations**. The share of total manufacturing assets held by the two hundred largest *manufacturing* firms in the United States has increased by 0.5 percent each year from 1900 to the present day; these two hundred corporations now

control over half of all manufacturing assets. The two hundred largest *financial* organizations—banks, building societies, and insurance companies—account for more than half of all financial activity. There are numerous connections among large firms. For example, financial institutions hold well over 30 percent of the shares of the largest two hundred manufacturing firms.

Of course, there still exist thousands of smaller firms and enterprises within the American economy. In these companies,

Helping professions that require physical labor, late-night hours, and low levels of educational attainment appeared toward the bottom of the list. For instance, just 26 percent of bartenders said they were "very satisfied," although lending an ear to those in trouble is a frequent job task. Other workers whose main tasks involve meeting the needs of others—including waiters, waitresses, clothing sales persons, hotel maids, welfare service workers, and customer service representatives—also were toward the bottom of the list. One of the more surprising findings, according to Smith, was that just 59 percent of police officers, yet 80 percent of firefighters—both helping professions—reported that they were very satisfied. Smith speculated "firefighters get a much more positive response, and they're not dealing with the kinds of problems that police officers deal with—the worst of society" (Paulson 2007).

Skeptics say that some job holders may feel a strong pressure to say that they love their work. For example, J. Pittman McGehee, a former dean of Houston, Texas's Christ Church Cathedral, said that out of respect for ordination, clergy might have felt compelled to tell researchers that they are very satisfied, while other workers might not feel that pressure.

Still, the study provides a glimpse into the important question, what makes

Jobs requiring difficult working conditions and heavy labor such as roofing had the lowest job satisfaction rates.

workers happy? As Smith noted, "one wants certain material benefits" from work, "but the bottom line in a person's life may not be their income—it may be 'Am I happy? Am I getting satisfaction' out of this job?" As the GSS study reveals, happiness and satisfaction come both from having a profession (rather than a manual job) and from performing tasks that allow one to be creative and of service to others.

Questions

- What jobs have the highest levels of satisfaction? Which jobs have the lowest?
- What general characteristics define those occupations with high levels of satisfaction?
- What general characteristics define those occupations with low levels of satisfaction?
- Will these study findings affect your choice of an occupation? Why or why not?

FOR FURTHER EXPLORATION

General Social Survey. 2007. "Looking for Job Satisfaction and Happiness in a Career? Start by Choosing a Job that Helps Others." Chicago: University of Chicago. www-news.uchicago .edu/releases/07/070417.jobs.shtml (accessed January 21, 2008).

Herrndobler, Kristina. 2007. "Service to Others Not Just a Job." *Houston Chronicle,* April 20, 2007. www-news.uchicago.edu/ citations/07/070420.jobsatisfaction-chron .html (accessed January 21, 2008).

Paulson, Amanda. 2007. "In U.S., Workers Who Help Others Report Most Happiness." *Christian Science Monitor,* April 17, 2007. www-news.uchicago.edu/citations/ 07/070417.jobs-csmonitor.html (accessed January 21, 2008).

Rose, Barbara. 2007. "Money Really Can't Buy Happiness, Study Finds." *Chicago Tribune,* April 17, 2007. www-news.uchicago .edu/citations/07/070417.smith-ct.html (accessed January 21, 2008).

Smith, Tom. 2007. *Job Satisfaction in the United States.* Chicago: National Opinion Research Center/University of Chicago. www-news .uchicago.edu/releases/07/pdf/070417.jobs .pdf (accessed January 21, 2008).

the image of the **entrepreneur**—the boss who owns and runs the firm—is by no means obsolete. The large corporations are a different matter. Ever since Adolf Berle and Gardiner Means published their celebrated study *The Modern Corporation and Private Property* (1982; orig. 1932) in the 1930s, it has been accepted that most of the largest firms are not run by those who own them. In theory, the large corporations are the property of their shareholders, who have the right to make all important decisions. But Berle and Means argue that because share ownership is so dispersed, actual control has passed into the hands of the managers who run firms on a day-to-day basis. Ownership of the corporations is thus separated from their control. ownership vs control

Whether they are run by owners or managers, the power of the major corporations is very extensive. When one or a handful of firms dominate in a given industry, they often cooperate in setting prices rather than freely competing with one another. Thus the giant oil companies normally follow one another's lead in the price charged for gasoline. When one firm occupies a commanding position in a given industry, it is said to be in a **monopoly** position. More common is a situation of oligopoly, in which a small group of giant corporations predominate. In situations of **oligopoly**, firms are able more or less to dictate the terms on which they buy goods and services from the smaller firms that are their suppliers.

The emergence of the global economy has contributed to a wave of mergers and acquisitions on an unprecedented scale, which have created oligopolies in industries such as communications and media. In 1998, the German automaker Daimler-Benz purchased Chrysler for $38 billion, and Exxon purchased the oil giant Mobil for $86 billion. In 1999, AT&T acquired the media corporation MediaOne for $5 billion to create what was at the time the world's largest cable company. Also in 1999, CBS purchased Viacom for $35 billion. In 2000, Britian's Vodafone Airtouch took over Germany's Mannesmann for $130 billion in the world's largest hostile takeover. In that same year, Time Warner and the Internet service provider America Online announced the largest merger in history—worth over $166 billion (Public Broadcasting System [PBS] 2003). By 2006, the combined value of global mergers and acquisitions reached an all-time high of $3.8 trillion, a third higher than in the previous year. This included some fifty-five deals greater than $10 billion (ACG 2007).

A number of factors have contributed to this trend, including technological advances, which have lowered global transportation and communications costs; a relaxation of regulation of corporate business activities; and new and efficient ways of financing and pooling the large sums of capital needed to conduct a merger or acquisition. Yet over 70 percent of the mergers and acquisitions have been between businesses competing in the same industry (United Nations Conference on Trade

Shoppers look at food produce at a Wal-Mart store in Beijing. Wal-Mart has become the largest retail chain in China. Transnational corporations such as Wal-Mart generate more revenue than many countries.

and Development [UNCTAD] 2005). This suggests that the primary aim of the recent wave of business consolidations has been to eliminate direct competition and productive overcapacity. Overcapacity is a problem that occurs when businesses produce more goods than the market will consume. Following the logic of supply and demand, this leads to decline in the value of the goods that they produce and to a decline in profits. Consolidation of firms is an attempt to avoid this problem. Yet it doesn't always work. In response to the declining success of AOL, Time Warner dropped AOL from its name and posted a $99 billion loss for 2002 (PBS 2003). In 2007, Daimler-Benz sold Chrysler for the same reason.

Types of Corporate Capitalism

There have been three general stages in the development of business corporations, although each overlaps with the others and all continue to coexist today. The first stage, characteristic of the nineteenth and early twentieth centuries, was dominated by **family capitalism**. Large firms were run either by individual entrepreneurs or by members of the same family and then passed on to their descendants. The famous corporate dynasties, such as the Rockefellers and Fords, belong in this category. These individuals and families did not just own a single large corporation but held a diversity of economic interests and stood at the apex of economic empires.

Most of the big firms founded by entrepreneurial families have since become public companies—that is, shares of their stock are traded on the open market—and have passed into managerial control. But important elements of family capitalism remain, even within some of the largest corporations, such as News Corporation, the world's third largest media conglomerate, owner of Fox Films, Fox Broadcasting, HarperCollins, Dow Jones, the *Wall Street Journal,* and a host of newspapers, cable networks, and satellite broadcasters around the world. News Corporation's Australian-born CEO Rupert Murdoch took over his father's struggling media business in 1953, building it into a global media empire, which he plans to hand over to his son James when he eventually retires (Murdoch was seventy-six in 2007). Among small firms, such as local shops run by their owners, small plumbing and house-painting businesses, and so forth, family capitalism continues to dominate. Some of these firms, such as shops that remain in the hands of the same family for two or more generations, are also dynasties on a minor scale. However, the small business sector is highly unstable, and economic failure is common; the proportion of firms that are owned by members of the same family for extended periods of time is minuscule.

In the large corporate sector, family capitalism was increasingly succeeded by **managerial capitalism.** As managers came to have more and more influence through the growth of very large firms, the entrepreneurial families were displaced. The result has been described as the replacement of the family in the company by the company itself. The corporation emerged as a more defined economic entity. In studying the two hundred largest manufacturing corporations in the United States, Michael Allen (1981) found that in cases in which profit showed a decline, family-controlled enterprises were unlikely to replace their chief executive, but manager-controlled firms did so rapidly.

There is no question that managerial capitalism has left an indelible imprint on modern society. The large corporation drives not only patterns of consumption but also the experience of employment in contemporary society—it is difficult to imagine how the work lives of many Americans would be different in the absence of large factories or corporate bureaucracies. Sociologists have identified another area in which the large corporation has left a mark on modern institutions. **Welfare capitalism** refers to a practice that sought to make the corporation—rather than the state or trade unions—the primary shelter from the uncertainties of the market in modern industrial life. Beginning at the end of the nineteenth century, large firms began to provide certain services to their employees, including child care, recreational facilities, profit-sharing plans, paid vacations, and group life and unemployment insurance. These programs often had a paternalistic bent, such as that sponsoring "home visits" for the "moral education" of employees. Viewed in less benevolent terms, a major objective of welfare capitalism was coercion, as employers deployed all manner of tactics—including violence—to avoid unionization. As such, conventional histories typically suggest that welfare capitalism met its demise in the depression years as labor unions achieved unprecedented levels of influence and as the New Deal administration began to guarantee many of the benefits provided by firms. In contrast to this standard interpretation, others argue that welfare capitalism did not die but instead went underground during the height of the labor movement (Jacoby 1997). In firms that avoided unionization during the period between the 1930s and 1960s—such as Kodak, Sears, and Thompson Products—welfare capitalism was modernized, shedding blatantly paternalistic aspects and routinizing benefit programs. When the union movement began to weaken after 1970, these companies offered a model to many other firms, which were then able to press their advantage against flanking unions, reasserting the role of the firm as "industrial manor" and workers as "industrial serfs."

Despite the overwhelming importance of managerial capitalism in shaping the modern economy, many scholars now see the contours of a third, different phase emerging in the evolution of the corporation. They argue that managerial capitalism has today partly ceded place to **institutional capitalism**. This term refers to the emergence of a consolidated network of business leadership, concerned not only with decision making within single firms but also with the development of corporate power beyond them. Institutional capitalism is based on the practice of corporations holding shares in other firms. In effect, interlocking boards of directors exercise control over much of the corporate landscape. This reverses the process of increasing managerial control because the managers' shareholdings are dwarfed by the large blocks of shares owned by other corporations. One of the main reasons for the spread of institutional capitalism is the shift in patterns of investment that has occurred since the 1970s. Rather than investing directly by buying shares in a business, individuals now invest in money market, trust, insurance, and pension funds that are controlled by large financial organizations, which in turn invest these grouped savings in industrial corporations.

The Transnational Corporations

With the intensifying of globalization, most large corporations now operate in an international economic context. When they establish branches in two or more countries, they are referred to as **transnational** or **multinational corporations**. *Transnational* is the preferred term, indicating that these companies operate across many different national boundaries. The United Nations Committee on Trade and Development estimated that as of 2006 over 78,400 transnational corporations controlled the assets of some 777,650 affiliates outside their home countries (UNCTAD 2007).

The largest transnationals are gigantic; their wealth outstrips that of many countries (Table 14.1). The scope of these companies' operations is staggering. The combined revenues of the world's largest five hundred transnational corporations totaled $20.9 trillion in 2006—a number nearly half as large (43 percent) of the $48.2 trillion in goods and services produced by the entire world (*Fortune* 2008; World Bank 2007g). Wal-Mart, the world's largest corporation, had 2006 revenues of $351.1 billion, placing it twenty-second among the world's economies. While business revenues and national figures for goods and services are not strictly comparable, they do give a sense of the relative magnitude of the world's largest businesses. Of the top 500 transnational corporations in the world, 162 are based in the United States, contributing about 35 percent of the total revenues of all 500. The share of American companies has, however, fallen in recent years, as the number of transnational corporations based in other countries—especially Asian countries such as South Korea and China—has increased. As seen in Table 14.2, between 2005 and 2007, among the world's largest 500 transnational corporations, the U.S. share declined

TABLE 14.1

Corporate Globalization: The World's Fifty Largest Economies Are Not All Countries[a] (in billions of dollars)

1	United States	$13,201.8		26	**Royal Dutch Shell Group**	**$318.8**
2	Japan	4,340.1		27	Norway	311.0
3	Germany	2,906.7		•	Saudi Arabia	309.8
4	China (including Hong Kong)	2,857.9		•	Denmark	275.2
5	United Kingdom	2,345.0		30	**BP (British Petroleum)**	**274.3**
6	France	2,230.7		31	South Africa	255.0
7	Italy	1,844.7		32	Greece	245.0
8	Canada	1,251.5		33	Iran	222.9
9	Spain	1,224.0		•	Ireland	222.7
10	Brazil	1,068.0		•	Argentina	214.1
11	Russian Federation	986.9		•	Finland	209.4
12	India	906.3		37	**General Motors**	**207.3**
13	Korea, Rep.	888.0		38	Thailand	206.2
14	Mexico	839.2		39	**Toyota Motor**	**204.7**
15	Australia	768.2		40	**Chevron Texaco**	**200.6**
16	Netherlands	657.6		41	Portugal	192.6
17	Turkey	402.7		•	Venezuela	181.9
18	Belgium	392.2		43	**ConocoPhillips**	**172.5**
19	Sweden	384.9		•	**Total (Petrol refining)**	**168.4**
20	Switzerland	379.8		•	**General Electric**	**168.3**
21	Indonesia	364.5		•	**ING Group (Dutch, insurance)**	**158.2**
22	**Wal-Mart Stores**	**351.1**		•	Malaysia	148.9
23	**Exxon-Mobil**	**347.3**		48	**Citigroup**	**146.8**
24	Poland	338.7		49	Chile	145.8
25	Austria	322.4		50	Czech Republic	141.8

[a] 2007 data.

SOURCE: *Fortune* 2008.

---

from 176 to 162, while Japan's share declined from 81 to 67. During the same period, China saw its share increase from 16 to 24 and South Korea from 11 to 14. (The European Union has remained roughly the same, with 163 in 2007.) While U.S.- and European-based transnational corporations continue to dominate the global economy by a wide margin, China has begun to have a significant presence and may well emerge as the equal of Japan within the next decade or so.

Contrary to common belief, three quarters of all foreign direct investment occurs among the industrialized countries. Of the five hundred largest transnational corporations, four are from Russia and one each is from Mexico, Saudi Arabia, Poland, and Turkey. The rest are all from North America, Europe, and Asia; none are from Latin America or Africa.

Nevertheless, the involvements of transnationals in developing-world countries are extensive, with Brazil, Mexico, and India showing the highest levels of foreign investment. The most rapid rate of increase in corporate investment by far has been in the Asian newly industrializing economies (NIEs) of China, Singapore, Taiwan, Hong Kong, South Korea, and Malaysia.

Transnational corporations have assumed an increasingly important place in the world economy over the course of this century. They are of key importance in the **international division of labor**—the specialization in producing goods for the world market that divides regions into zones of industrial or agricultural production or high- or low-skilled labor (Fröbel et al. 1979; McMichael 1996). Just as national economies have become increasingly concentrated—dominated by a limited

TABLE 14.2

The World's 500 Largest Transnational Corporations— Number by Leading Economies

	2005	2006	2007	2008
European Union	161	163	163	184
United States	176	170	162	153
Japan	81	70	67	64
China	16	20	24	29
Korea	11	12	14	15

SOURCE: *Fortune* 2008.

number of very large companies—so has the world economy. In the case of the United States and several of the other leading industrialized countries, the firms that dominate nationally also have a wide-ranging international presence. Many sectors of world production (such as agribusiness) are oligopolies. Over the past two or three decades, international oligopolies have developed in the automobile, microprocessor, and electronics industries and in the production of some other goods marketed worldwide.

The reach of the transnationals since the mid-1970s would not have been possible without advances in transport and communications. Air travel now allows people to move around the world at a speed that would have seemed inconceivable even sixty years ago. Technological innovations, referred to together as "containerization," have permitted the rapid movement and distribution of bulk goods around the world. The best example of containerization is the development of extremely large ocean-going vessels (superfreighters) that carry tractor trailers full of goods. These trailers can be easily loaded and sealed at the point of manufacture, loaded onto ships and moved across an ocean, then transferred onto a train or truck and delivered to a store, where the trailers are finally opened and unloaded.

Telecommunications technologies now permit more or less instantaneous communication from one part of the world to another. Satellites have been used for commercial telecommunications since 1965, when the first satellite could carry 240 telephone conversations at once. Current satellites can carry 12,000 simultaneous conversations! The larger transnationals

now have their own satellite-based communications systems. The Mitsubishi Corporation, for instance, has a massive network across which five million words are transmitted to and from its headquarters in Tokyo each day.

Container ships are cargo ships that carry all of their load in truck-size containers. As this technique greatly accelerates the speed by which goods can be transported to and from ports, these ships now carry the majority of the world's dry cargo.

Transnational Corporations Plan on a World Scale

The global corporations have become the first organizations able to plan on a truly world scale. Coca-Cola ads reach billions. A few companies with developed global networks are able to shape the commercial activities of diverse nations. There are four webs of interconnecting commercial activity in the new world economy. These are what Richard Barnet and John Cavanagh (1994) call the Global Cultural Bazaar, the Global Shopping Mall, the Global Workplace, and the Global Financial Network.

The Global Cultural Bazaar is the newest of the four but already the most extensive. Global images and global dreams are diffused through movies, TV programs, music, videos, games, toys, and T-shirts, sold on a worldwide basis. All over the earth, even in the poorest developing countries, people use the same electronic devices to see or listen to the same commercially produced songs and shows.

The Global Shopping Mall is a "planetary supermarket with a dazzling spread of things to eat, drink, wear and enjoy," according to Barnet and Cavanagh. It is more exclusive than the Cultural Bazaar because the poor do not have the resources to participate—they have only the status of window shoppers. Of the 6.6 billion people who make up the world's population, nearly three out of five lack the cash or credit to purchase any consumer goods.

The third global web, the Global Workplace, is the increasingly complex global division of labor that affects all of us. It consists of the massive array of offices, factories, restaurants, and millions of other places where goods are produced and consumed or information is exchanged. This web is closely bound up with the Global Financial Network, which it fuels and is financed by. The Global Financial Network consists of billions of bits of information stored in computers and portrayed on computer screens. It entails almost endless currency exchanges, credit card transactions, insurance plans, and buying and selling of stocks and shares.

The Twenty-First-Century Corporation: Different from Its Twentieth-Century Counterpart

There are big differences between the large corporation of the early twenty-first century and its mid-twentieth-century counterpart. Many of the names are the same—General Motors, Ford, IBM, AT&T—but these have been joined by other giant firms, largely unknown in the 1950s, such as Wal-Mart, Microsoft, and Intel. They all wield great power, and their top executives still inhabit the large buildings that dominate so many city centers.

But below the surface similarities between today and half a century ago, some profound transformations have taken place. The origin of these transformations lies in that process we have encountered often in this book: globalization. Since the 1950s, the giant corporations have become more and more caught up in global competition; as a result, their internal composition, and in a way their very nature, has altered.

The former U.S. Labor Secretary Robert Reich (1991) writes:

> Underneath, all is changing. America's core corporation no longer plans and implements the production of a large volume of goods and services; it no longer invests in a vast array of factories, machinery, laboratories, inventories, and other tangible assets; it no longer employs armies of production workers and middle-level managers. . . . In fact, the core corporation is no longer even American. It is, increasingly, a facade, behind which teems an array of decentralized groups and subgroups continuously contracting with similarly diffuse working units all over the world.

The large corporation is less and less a big business than an "enterprise web"—a central organization that links smaller firms together. IBM, for example, which used to be one of the most jealously self-sufficient of all large corporations, in the 1980s and early 1990s joined with dozens of U.S.-based companies and more than eighty foreign-based firms to share strategic planning and cope with production problems. Nelson Lichtenstein has characterized this shift as a shift from General Motors to Wal-Mart, which he describes as "a template for twenty-first century capitalism":

> GM workers were often life-time employees so factory turnover was exceedingly low: these were the best jobs around, and they were jobs that rewarded longevity. . . . At Wal-Mart, in contrast, employee turnover approaches 50 percent a year, which means it must be even higher for those hired at an entry level wage. . . . The hours of labor, the very definition of a full work day, constitutes the other great contrast dividing America's old industrial economy from that of its retail future . . . at Wal-Mart a 32 hour work week is considered "full time" employment. This gives managers great flexibility and power, enabling them to parcel out the extra hours to fill in the schedule, reward favored employees, and gear up for the holiday rush. But the social consequences of this policy are profound: Unlike General Motors, Wal-

Mart is not afraid to hire thousands of new workers each year, but employee attachment to their new job is low, and millions of Americans find it necessary, and possible, to moonlight with two part time jobs. (Lichtenstein 2006: 27–28)

 Some corporations remain strongly bureaucratic and centered in the United States. However, most are no longer so clearly located anywhere. The old transnational corporation used to work mainly from its American headquarters, from where its overseas production plants

FIGURE 14.3

Where Does Your Car Come From?

Automobile parts are produced in several countries and then sent to a central plant for final production of the car.

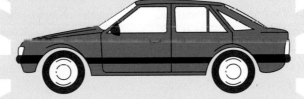

France

Alternator, cylinder head, master cylinder, brakes, underbody coating, weather strips, clutch release bearings, steering shaft and joints, seat pads and frames, transmission cases, clutch cases, tires, suspension bushing, ventilation units, heater, hose clamps, sealers, hardware

Britain

Carburetor, rocker arm, clutch, ignition, exhaust, oil pump, distributor, cylinder bolt, cylinder head, flywheel ring gear, heater, speedometer, battery, rear wheel spindle, intake manifold, fuel tank, switches, lamps, front disc, steering wheel, steering column, glass, weather strips, locks

Germany

Locks, pistons, exhaust, ignition, switches, front disc, distributor, weather strips, rocker arm, speedometer, fuel tank, cylinder bolt, cylinder head gasket, front wheel knuckles, rear wheel spindle, transmission cases, clutch cases, clutch, steering column, battery, glass

The Netherlands

Tires, paints, hardware

Denmark

Fan belt

Canada

Glass, radio

Sweden

Hose clamps, cylinder bolt, exhaust pipes, hardware

Belgium

Tires, tubes, seat pads, brakes, trim

United States

EGR valves, wheel nuts, hydraulic tappet, glass

Austria

Tires, radiator and heater hoses

Spain

Wiring harness, radiator and heater hoses, fork clutch release, air filter, battery, mirrors

Italy

Cylinder head, carburetor, glass, lamps, defroster, grills

Switzerland

Underbody coating, speedometer, gears

Japan

Starter, alternator, cone and roller bearings, windshield-washer pump

Norway

Exhaust flanges, tires

The figure above demonstrates the globalization of manufacturing and corporations. Based on your reading, explain why we could call the Japanese Honda Accord an American automobile. What does the term "enterprise web" mean? Give an example other than a car.

and subsidiaries were controlled. Now, with the transformation of space and time noted earlier (Chapter 5), groups situated in any region of the world are able, via telecommunications and computer, to work with others. Nations still try to influence flows of information, resources, and money across their borders. But modern communications technologies make this more and more difficult, if not impossible. Knowledge and finances can be transferred across the world as electronic blips moving at the speed of light.

Even the production of the technology that makes the global activities of transnational corporations possible is spread out over the globe. The California-based computer-chip manufacturer Intel in 2006 had 94,100 employees; thirteen production sites; eleven assembly sites spread over seven countries; and 20,000 research and development employees in thirty countries, including China, India, and the Russian Federation. One third of its workforce is located outside the United States. Intel is especially interested in China, where it has been operating laboratories, manufacturing facilities, and testing facilities for twenty years. Its new $2.5 billion chip fabrication plant in Dalian, China, is the first such plant the company has located in a developing country. The reason China was selected? Not low labor costs (chip fabrication depends on expensive equipment rather than cheap labor), but rather China's growing supply of talented engineers, along with generous financial incentives provided by the Chinese government (UNCTAD 2005; Kanellos 2007).

The products of the transnational companies similarly have an international character. When is something "made in America," and when not? There is no longer any clear answer. What could be more American than a Ford? Today, the answer may be a Toyota or Honda. Automobiles contain over twenty thousand different parts, and the production and the manufacture of vehicles have become a truly globalized system (Figure 14.3). In 2007, Toyota employed over thirty-six thousand people in North America and spent over $28 billion on American parts and accessories (Toyota 2008). The Toyota Avalon, for example, built at a production facility in Kentucky, is made up of 70 percent U.S. or Canadian parts. This is a higher percentage than the Chrysler-built PT Cruiser. And GM's use of a Honda-made engine in its Saturn cars actually increased the percentage of its parts and accessories made in the United States (*Charleston Business Journal* 2003). In fact, all of the Honda Accords sold in the United States contain almost entirely domestic parts and accessories and are assembled at one of Honda's several North American production facilities (Fukui 2004).

☑ CONCEPT CHECKS

1. What are the main features of capitalism?
2. Compare and contrast four types of corporate capitalism.
3. What are three defining characteristics of transnational corporations?

The Changing Nature of Work

The globalizing of economic production, together with the spread of information technology, is altering the nature of the jobs most people do. As discussed in Chapter 8, the proportion of people working in blue-collar jobs in industrial countries has progressively fallen. Fewer people work in factories than before. New jobs have been created in offices and in service centers such as supermarkets and airports. Many of these new jobs are filled by women.

Work and Technology

The relationship between technology and work has long been of interest to sociologists. How is our experience of work affected by the type of technology that is involved? As industrialization has progressed, technology has assumed an ever-greater role at the workplace—from factory automation to the computerization of office work. The current information technology revolution has attracted renewed interest in this question. Technology can lead to greater efficiency and productivity, but how does it affect the way work is experienced by those who carry it out? For sociologists, one of the main questions is how the move to more complex systems influences the nature of work and the institutions in which it is performed.

AUTOMATION AND THE SKILL DEBATE

The concept of **automation**, or programmable machinery, was introduced in the mid-1800s, when Christopher Spencer, an American, invented the Automat, a programmable lathe that made screws, nuts, and gears. Automation has thus far affected relatively few industries, but with advances in the design of industrial robots, its effect is certain to become greater. A robot is an automatic device that can perform functions ordinarily done by human workers. The term *robot* comes from the Czech word *robota,* or serf, popularized about fifty years ago by the playwright Karel Čapek.

The majority of the robots used in industry worldwide are to be found in automobile manufacture. Although one of the

Robots weld car frames at the Hyundai factory in Beijing.

Taylorism — &deskill labor make management control everything

first industrial robots was used in a General Motors plant, the Japanese automobile industry pioneered their extensive use. Most recently—and perhaps significantly—China has begun to mass produce its Chery automobile for the global market, convincing one of the world's leading automation firms, ABB Robotics, to relocate its corporate headquarters from Detroit to Shanghai. While it may seem likely that automated production will spread rapidly in coming years, as robots decline in cost while becoming increasingly sophisticated, their usage may well have peaked, at least for the time being: Robots have proven costly to maintain, leading many automobile manufacturers to emphasize more efficient management practices over the latest high-tech automation (Bradsher 2000).

The spread of automation provoked a heated debate among sociologists and experts in industrial relations over the effect of the new technology on workers, their skills, and their level of commitment to their work. In his now-classic *Alienation and Freedom* (1964), Robert Blauner examined the experience of workers in four different industries with varying levels of technology. Using the ideas of Durkheim and Marx, Blauner measured the extent to which workers in each industry experienced alienation in the form of powerlessness, meaninglessness, isolation, and self-estrangement. He concluded that workers on assembly lines were the most alienated of all but that levels of alienation were somewhat lower at workplaces using automation. In other words, Blauner argued that the introduction of automation to factories was responsible for reversing the otherwise steady trend toward increased worker alienation. Automation helped integrate the workforce and gave workers a sense of control over their work that had been lacking with other forms of technology.

A very different thesis was set forth by Harry Braverman in his highly influential *Labor and Monopoly Capital* (1974). In Braverman's eyes, automation was part of the overall "deskilling" of the industrial labor force. By imposing Taylorist organizational techniques and breaking up the labor process into specialized tasks, managers were able to exert control over the workforce. In both industrial settings and modern offices, the introduction of technology contributed to this overall degradation of work by limiting the need for creative human input. Instead, all that was required was an unthinking, unreflective body capable of endlessly carrying out the same unskilled task.

A newer study sheds some more light on this debate. Sociologist Richard Sennett (1998) studied the people who worked in a bakery that had been bought by a large food conglomerate and automated with the introduction of high-tech machinery. Computerized baking radically altered the way that bread was made. Instead of using their hands to mix the ingredients and knead the dough and their noses and eyes to judge when the bread was done baking, the bakery's workers had no physical contact with the materials or the loaves of bread. In fact, the entire process was controlled and monitored via computer screen. Computers decided the temperature and baking time of the ovens. Although at times the machines produced excellent-quality bread, at other times the results were burned, blackened loaves. The workers at this bakery (it would be erroneous to call them bakers) were hired because they were skilled with computers, not because they knew how to bake bread. Ironically, these workers used very few of their computer skills. The production process involved little more than pushing buttons on a computer. In fact, one time when the computerized machinery broke down, the entire production process was halted because none of the bakery's "skilled" workers were trained or empowered to repair the problem. The workers that Sennett (1998) observed wanted to be helpful, to make things work again, but they could not, because automation had diminished their freedom to make decisions. The introduction of computerized technology in the workplace has led to a general increase in all workers' skills, but it has also led to a split workforce composed of a small group of highly skilled professionals with high degrees of flexibility and freedom in their jobs and a larger group of clerical, service, and production workers who lack such autonomy.

The skill debate is very difficult to resolve, however. Both the conceptualization and measurement of skill are problematic. As feminist researchers have argued, what constitutes "skill" is socially constructed (Steinberg 1990). As such, conventional understandings of "skilled" work tend to reflect the social status of the typical incumbent of the job rather than the difficulty of the task in an objective sense. The history of occupations is rife with examples of jobs in which the very same task was assigned a different skill level (and even renamed!) once women entered the field (Reskin and Roos 1990). To take but one example, the occupation of "private secretary" was once a prestigious male occupation. Once a growing number of women moved into secretarial positions in the twentieth century, however, the job became reclassified as merely a clerical position, its tasks were downgraded, and it ceased to be a step on the ladder for management positions (Davies 1983). The same, of course, holds for other low-status workers, such as racial minorities. Even where gender and racial biases are not in operation, skill has multiple dimensions; the same job may be downgraded on one dimension while simultaneously upgraded on another (Block 1990). Thus opinions as to whether automation has deskilled work depend on which dimension of skill is examined. In his comprehensive review of the skill debate, Spenner (1983) notes that studies examining skill in terms of the actual complexity of tasks have tended to support the "upskilling" position, whereas those that have examined skill in terms of the autonomy and/or control exercised by the worker have tended to find that work has in fact been "deskilled" through automation (Vallas and Beck 1996; Zuboff 1988).

INFORMATION TECHNOLOGY

Blauner's and Braverman's opposing perspectives on the effects of automation are echoed today in debates over the effect of information technology (IT) in the workplace. Certainly there is little question that the Internet, e-mail, teleconferencing, and e-commerce are changing the way in which companies do business. But they are also affecting the way in which employees work on a daily basis. Those who take an optimistic approach, as Blauner did, argue that IT will revolutionize the world of work by allowing new, more flexible ways of working to emerge. These opportunities will permit us to move beyond the

Employees at a call center in the northeastern Indian city of Siliguri provide service support to customers throughout the world.

routine and alienating aspects of industrial work into a more liberating informational age giving workers greater control over and input into the work process. Enthusiastic advocates of technological advances are sometimes referred to as "technological determinists," because they believe in the power of technology to determine the nature and shape of work itself.

Others are not convinced that IT will bring about an entirely positive transformation of work. As Shoshana Zuboff (1988) concluded in her research into the use of IT in firms, management can choose to use IT toward very different ends. When embraced as a creative, decentralizing force, IT can help break down rigid hierarchies, engage more employees in decision making, and involve workers more closely in the day-to-day affairs of the company. On the other hand, it can just as easily be used to strengthen hierarchies and surveillance practices. The adoption of IT in the workplace can cut down on face-to-face interactions, block channels of accountability, and transform an office into a network of self-contained and isolated modules. According to this approach, the effect of IT is influenced by how the technology is used and how those using the technology understand its role.

The spread of IT will certainly produce exciting and heightened opportunities for some segments of the labor force. In the fields of media, advertising, and design, for example, IT enhances creativity in the professional realm and introduces flexibility into personal work styles. The vision of wired workers and telecommuting comes closest to being realized for highly skilled professionals. Yet at the other end of the spectrum are thousands of low-paid, unskilled individuals working in call centers and data-entry companies, many of them in India, where English is the official language and wages are a fraction of those in the United States. These positions, which are largely a product of the telecommunications explosion in recent years, are characterized by degrees of isolation and alienation that rival those of Braverman's deskilled workers.

Employees at call centers are part of a burgeoning industry known as "business processing outsourcing" that includes travel bookings, technical support, accounting, and other financial transactions. They work according to strictly standardized formats with little or no room for employee discretion or creative input. Employees are closely monitored, and their interactions with customers are tape recorded for "quality assurance." The information revolution seems to have produced a large number of routine, unskilled jobs on a par with those of the industrial economy.

Post-Fordism

Since the 1970s, flexible practices have been introduced in a number of spheres, including product development, production techniques, management style, the working environment, employee involvement, and marketing. Group production, problem-solving teams, multitasking, and niche marketing are just some of the strategies that have been adopted by companies attempting to restructure themselves under shifting conditions. Some commentators have suggested that, taken collectively, these changes represent a radical departure from the principles of Fordism; they contend that we are now operating in a period that can best be understood as **post-Fordism** (Table 14.3). Post-Fordism, a phrase initially popularized by Michael Piore and Charles Sabel in *The Second Industrial Divide* (1984), describes a new era of capitalist economic production in which flexibility and innovation are maximized to meet market demands for diverse, customized products—albeit often with adverse impacts on the workforce.

Post-Fordism - customizable products!

TABLE 14.3

Fordist versus Post-Fordist Production Systems

FORDISM	POST-FORDISM
Bureaucratic/vertical	Flexible/horizontal
Mass production	Mass customization
Most work in-house (local)	Most work outsourced (global)
Job security (high wage, long-term, full-time, high career advancement)	Job insecurity (low wage, short-term, part-time, low career advancement)

The idea of post-Fordism is somewhat problematic, however. The term is used to refer to a set of overlapping changes that are occurring not only in the realm of work and economic life but throughout society as a whole. Some writers argue that the tendency toward post-Fordism can be seen in spheres as diverse as party politics, welfare programs, and consumer and lifestyle choices. While observers of late modern societies often point to many of the same changes, there is no consensus about the precise meaning of post-Fordism or, indeed, if this is even the best way of understanding the phenomenon we are witnessing.

Despite the confusion surrounding the term *post-Fordism*, several distinctive trends within the world of work have emerged in recent decades that seem to represent a clear departure from earlier Fordist practices. These include the replacement of highly bureaucratic, vertically organized business structures with more flexible, horizontally organized networked approaches; the transition from mass production to mass customization; a shift from in-house production to **global outsourcing**; and the resulting severe erosion in job security for employees. We now consider each of these in turn.

FLEXIBLE BUSINESS STRUCTURES

One of the most important changes in worldwide production processes over the past few years has been an increase in the organizational flexibility of many large firms. For much of the twentieth century, the most important business organizations were large manufacturing firms that controlled both the making of goods and their final sales. Giant automobile companies such as Ford and General Motors typified this approach. Such companies employed tens of thousands of factory workers making everything from components to the final cars, which were then sold in the manufacturers' showrooms. Such manufacture-dominated production processes were organized as large bureaucracies, often controlled by a single firm.

If General Motors represented the prototypical corporation of the twentieth century, Wal-Mart may well prove to be symbolic of the twenty-first. Sociologist Gary Hamilton has described a world in which "big buyers"—global retailers—are becoming increasingly dominant in the global economy, not only reshaping business structures but also driving economic development in those regions (such as East Asia) that supply their products (Petrovic and Hamilton 2006). While both General Motors and Wal-Mart are giant transnational corporations, GM was organized vertically: most of its production was done under its own roof, controlled by its own management structure in a highly bureaucratized fashion. GM designed, marketed, and produced the cars that it sold. Control, in other words, was highly centralized. Wal-Mart, by way of contrast, designs very little of what it sells and produces

Employees build Sony LCD televisions in Nitra, Slovakia. How has technology and the ability to produce and ship products at the last minute transformed the global supply chain?

next to nothing. Wal-Mart sells products designed by others—the thousands of brands and labels that are available in its stores. Those brands and labels, in turn, seldom actually make the products they design: that task falls to factories around the world. Like GM, Wal-Mart exerts control over its suppliers—but in this case, the suppliers are outside the firm rather than a part of it.

The resulting network of retailers, brands, and factories enables each to respond quickly to changes in market conditions, in a way that the more vertically organized GM never could hope to do. If an economic slowdown or changing buyer tastes, caused a drop in sales for GM, the corporation still had to cover the cost of expensive plant and equipment, as well as meet the payroll of hundreds of thousands of employees, from management to the factory floor. While Wal-Mart has plenty of stores to maintain (some 6,800 worldwide), its situation is markedly different from GM's: If Sony flat panel TVs are not moving, Wal-Mart can simply tell Sony it is reducing its orders and shift to Panasonic. Sony, in turn, can respond by canceling orders in some of the contract factories that are its suppliers. Those factories then either switch to other labels (perhaps Panasonic) or else lay off workers.

Wal-Mart controls its suppliers through the IT that has revolutionized the field of supply chain management. In today's world of flexible production, there are complex networks of buyers and suppliers: A clothing company such as The Gap may have thousands of independently owned factories supplying its stores, while each of those factories may in turn be making clothing for many competing brands. Coordinating these activities requires sophisticated computer technology—electronic data interchange

(EDI) software systems that enable firms to share relevant data, beginning with the information on the bar code attached to each product that is scanned at the time of purchase. The most advanced systems, such as those pioneered by Wal-Mart, enable firms to order just the right number of products to meet demand, to shift their orders among different suppliers, and to respond "nimbly"—a favored term of business—to changing market conditions. Today, even large automobile manufacturers such as GM have moved down the post-Fordist path, outsourcing as much work as possible and using advanced information systems to manage their supply chains.

MASS CUSTOMIZATION

Controlling such far-flung networks of suppliers is only part of the challenge faced by modern businesses. They must also cater to the changing demands of their customers—demands that are shaped, in turn, by a constant flow of advertising in magazines, newspapers, television, radio, and films such as *Spider-Man 3,* which was accompanied by a deluge of toys based on the movie. Although Taylorism and Fordism successfully produced mass products (that were all the same) for mass markets, they were completely unable to produce small orders of goods, let alone goods specifically made for an individual customer. GM or Ford changed the overall design of its cars every couple of years, and the changes were often largely cosmetic: Large tail fins adorned cars in the 1950s, marketed as providing "greater stability on the nation's highways."

Mass customization has changed all this (Pine 1999). It combines the large-volume production associated with Fordism with the flexibility required to tailor products to consumers' needs. Computer-aided designs, coupled to other types of computer-based technology such as EDI, now permit factories to alter their assembly lines for small-batch production, serving (and creating) particular market niches. Information can be solicited about individual consumers and analyzed to determine the key types of consumer preferences for particular products, which are then manufactured to those specifications.

In a modern car factory, several different models can even be built on the same assembly line. Dell Computer was one of the first computer companies to carry mass customization to a high level: It is now commonplace for consumers to custom-design their computer on-line, charge the purchase to their credit card, and within a week receive their custom-made computer at their door. Dell is often thought of as a computer manufacturing company, but in fact the company does not make any significant computer components: Instead, it assembles components produced by others, controlling its supply chains through EDI. In effect, Dell has turned traditional ways of doing business upside down. Firms used to build a product first, then worry about selling it. Now, mass customizers like

Dell Computer has discovered a unique way to reconcile giving customers exactly what they want while maintaining a low production cost. By using the Internet to process orders, avoiding the expense of keeping a retail space, and producing only what is ordered and no more, Dell has succeeded in creating a system to rapidly produce custom-made products at an affordable price.

Dell sell first and build second. Such a shift has important consequences for industry. The need to hold stocks of parts on hand—a major cost for manufacturers—has been dramatically reduced. In addition, an increasing share of production is outsourced. Thus, the rapid transfer of information between manufacturers and suppliers is essential to the successful implementation of mass customization.

GLOBAL OUTSOURCING

Changes in industrial production include not only how products are manufactured but also where products are manufactured, as we saw earlier with the example of an "American-made" car. In **flexible production** systems, there is truly a global assembly line: The companies that design and sell products seldom make them in their own factories, instead outsourcing production to factories around the world. As Figure 14.3 shows, the components of an automobile typically originate in many countries. Or to take another example, the 30-gigabite Apple iPod, discussed in the "Globalization and Everyday Life" box in this chapter, is made by dozens of companies in half a dozen countries. Of the approximately $300 retail price, less than half goes to pay for the 451 component parts whose manufacture is outsourced; the bulk is for retailing, marketing, distribution, and Apple's revenues (Linden, Kraemer, and Dedrick 2007).

Few if any industries are as globalized as the industry that makes the clothing and footwear that fill your closet. Almost no major U.S. companies today make their own apparel or footwear; rather, they outsource to independently owned factories that do the work for them. These factories are found in more than a hundred different countries and range from tiny sweatshops to giant plants owned by transnational corporations. Sociologists Edna Bonacich and Richard Appelbaum (2000), for example, show that most so-called garment manufacturers actually employ no garment workers at all. Instead, they rely on thousands of factories around the world to make their apparel, which they then sell in department stores and other retail outlets. Clothing manufacturers do not own any of these factories and are therefore free to use them or not, depending on their needs. While this provides the manufacturers with the flexibility previously discussed, it creates great uncertainty for the factories, which must compete with one another for orders, and the workers in those factories, who may lose their jobs if their factory loses business.

One interesting trend in globalized production is the emergence of giant transnational corporations, owned by businessmen from Hong Kong, Taiwan, South Korea, and China, that operate apparel, electronic assembly, and other consumer goods factories around the world. For example, when you buy a pair of jeans, whatever its brand might be, it might well have been made in Mexico, Nicaragua, or the African country of Lesotho, in a factory owned by the Nien Hsing Corporation—a Taiwanese textile firm that makes clothing for such well-known brands as Calvin Klein, DKNY, Tommy Hilfiger, Nautica, Mudd Jeans, GAP, Levis, JC Penney, Wal-Mart, Target, Lee, Wrangler, Sears, and No Excuses (Nien Hsing 2007). Or to take another example, you probably have never heard of Yue Yuen, the Hong Kong subsidiary of a Taiwanese firm that specializes in footwear—but if you have ever owned an athletic shoe designed by Nike, adidas, Reebok, Asics, New Balance, Timberland, or Rockport, the chances are good that it was made by some of Yue Yuen's 280,000 Chinese, Vietnamese, or Indonesian production workers. Yue Yuen makes one out of every branded six athletic shoes in the world today. Its sprawling factory in Dongguan, in southern China, employs 110,000 workers to produce nearly a million pairs of athletic shoes a month for Nike, adidas, and other major brands (Appelbaum and Lichtenstein 2006; Yue Yuen 2007).

JOB INSECURITY

Flexible production has produced some benefits for consumers and the economy as a whole, but the effect on workers has not been wholly positive. Though some workers undoubtedly do learn new skills and have less monotonous jobs, the majority find their work lives less secure than before. For many workers inside the United States, the long-term employment, rising wages, career advancement, and health and retirement

The iPod: The Global Production of Value

In 2007, Apple reported that it had sold the one hundred millionth iPod (Apple, Inc. 2007a). Apple's iPod and its online music store have transformed how young people in the United States buy and listen to music. Yet the Cupertino, California–based company does not actually manufacture the iPod. Instead, it contracts the entire production process to other firms located in a variety of places outside the United States. In the first fiscal quarter of 2008, Apple generated $9.6 billion in revenue, more than a forty percent of which came from the sale of over 22 million iPods (Apple, Inc. 2008). So where is the iPod made and how does Apple profit?

Researchers at the University of California–Irvine, sponsored by the Alfred P. Sloan Foundation, studied the way in which the iPod accrues value as it is assembled (Linden et al. 2007). They show how innovation in the electronics industry spreads wealth beyond the firm whose brand appears on the product and who was the primary actor conceiving, coordinating, and marketing the new item. The mechanism by which wealth gets distributed in the process of manufacturing is called a value chain. In a value chain, each producer purchases inputs to make a component and in the process of making it adds value to it. The difference between the cost of raw materials at each stage and the value of the product at the next stage is called the "value added." This added value then becomes part of the cost of the next stage of production. The sum of the value added by everyone in the chain plus the cost of materials equals the final wholesale product price, once it has been assembled and delivered to a store for sale.

The iPod is composed of 451 component parts. Some of these are quite complicated, such as the visual display, and are made up of numerous subcomponents. The retail value of the 30-gigabyte video iPod was $299 when the researchers examined it. They estimated that the cost of all of the components required to make the iPod was about $144. The bulk of that cost was made up by the 10 most complicated and expensive parts. These included the hard drive, which was manufactured by Toshiba and cost about $73. Other expensive parts included the visual display (about $20), the processor chip ($8), and the controller chip ($5). These components are the most likely to incorporate innovative and proprietary knowledge, and they account for the largest share of the cost of assembling the iPod. The rest of the 440 or so parts, plus assembly in China, contributed about $10 to the wholesale cost of the iPod.

The hard drive, provided by the Japanese company Toshiba, was estimated to require about $54 in parts and labor to make. But Toshiba contracts the manufacture of its hard drives to companies located in China and the Philippines. Therefore, some portion of the $54—the cost of parts and labor provided by firms in those two countries—is value created and retained by them. The remainder of the $73 is attributed to Japan's economy.

At the other end of the value chain, the difference between the retail price ($299) and the wholesale price ($144) can be divided into retail, distributor, and Apple's profit. For each iPod,

benefits once associated with a job at a General Motors or Ford plant have become a thing of the past. To keep their jobs, as previously noted, U.S. workers have had to accept pay cuts and reduced benefits packages. And, of course, many have lost their jobs to overseas competition.

For workers in low-wage countries, the downside of flexible production can be onerous. Given the far-flung nature of global supply chains, it is virtually impossible to know where all of the components that go into a product are made.

Bonacich and Appelbaum (2000) argue that such flexible production, driven by global competition, has resulted in a global "race to the bottom," in which retailers and manufacturers will go anyplace on earth where they can find the lowest wages, least environmental restrictions, and most lax governmental regulations. This is a system that invites abuses—as evidenced by the well-publicized cases of toxic toys, made in Chinese factories under contract to leading U.S. brands such as Mattel.

How many parts go into making an Apple iPod?

The iPod is typical of the new global organization of production. In the past, consumer electronics were designed and developed by large companies, which often also produced all components required to make them. In this way, companies created and captured a large share of the value of their products. Because the value was created in-house, it stayed in the home country of the company. But today, value chains have global dimensions, which spread the creation of wealth across several countries. In the case of the iPod, the researchers estimated that there was value created in at least six countries, but that number could be much higher if the value chains of components are taken into consideration, because so much of the production of components and subcomponents is outsourced. At the same time, most of the wealth accrues to Apple and other American firms, even though Apple itself does not make the product. Apple profits because it conceptualizes, designs, and markets the iPod, while coordinating the global production process. These are the most profitable parts of the value chain, which demonstrates how profitability is linked to innovation—most profit accrues to those who design and organize rather than those who actually manufacture and assemble.

Apple makes about $80, which is greater than the cost of any single component required to make it. About half of the retail value of the iPod was retained by American firms, with the rest distributed over several countries contributing components to make the iPod. Even though final assembly of the product in China contributed less than 1 percent of the value, based on the way trade statistics are calculated, each iPod shipped from there to stores in the United States is said to have contributed about $150 to the U.S. trade deficit with China—but adds much less to China's trade surplus. This is because China ships a $150 iPod to the United States, but to do so, the country imports a substantial part of the components that go into the iPod from other places in Asia.

References

Apple, Inc. 2007a. "100 Million iPods Sold." Press release. www.apple.com/pr/library/2007/04/09ipod.html (accessed December 23, 2007).

Apple, Inc. 2007b. "Unaudited Second Quarter 2007 Summary Data." http://images.apple.com/pr/pdf/q207data_sum.pdf (accessed December 23, 2007).

Linden, Greg, Kenneth L. Kramer, and Jason Dedrick. 2007. "Who Captures Value in a Global Innovation System? The Case of Apple's iPod." Personal Computing Industry Center. http://pcic.merage.uci.edu/papers/2007/AppleiPod.pdf (accessed December 24, 2007).

Trends in the Occupational Structure

The occupational structure in all industrialized countries has changed substantially since the beginning of the twentieth century (Figure 14.4). In 1900, about three quarters of the employed population were in manual work, either farming or blue-collar work such as manufacturing. White-collar professional and service jobs were much fewer in number. By 1960, however, more people worked in white-collar professional and service jobs than in manual labor. By 1993, the occupational system had basically reversed its structure from 1900. Today, almost three quarters of the employed population work in white-collar professional and service jobs, while the rest work in blue-collar and farming jobs.

During the period 2000–2006, the United States lost one out of every six manufacturing jobs, 3.3 million jobs in all. During the same period, the largest growth occurred in the

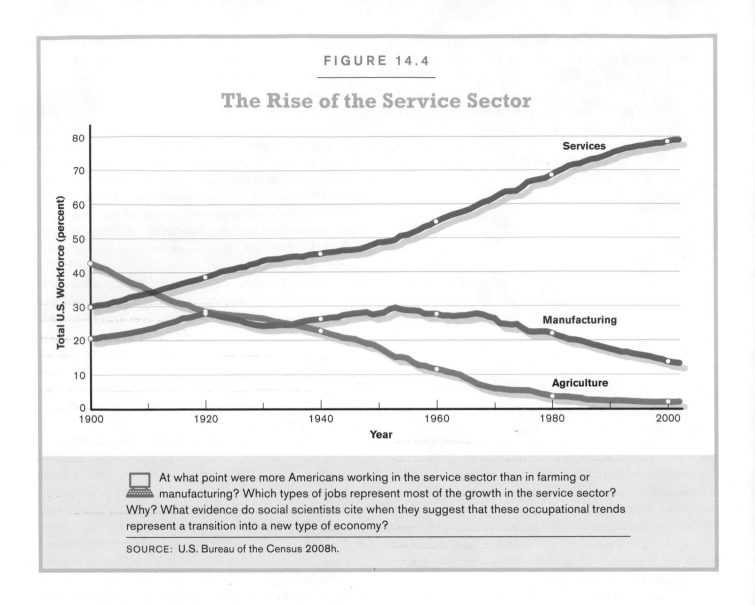

FIGURE 14.4

The Rise of the Service Sector

Y-axis: Total U.S. Workforce (percent); X-axis: Year

Services
Manufacturing
Agriculture

At what point were more Americans working in the service sector than in farming or manufacturing? Which types of jobs represent most of the growth in the service sector? Why? What evidence do social scientists cite when they suggest that these occupational trends represent a transition into a new type of economy?

SOURCE: U.S. Bureau of the Census 2008h.

service sector. Employment in professional and business services, which pay relatively high wages, grew by 1.2 million. But most service sector growth occurred in areas that typically pay lower wages than the manufacturing jobs that were lost. For example, wholesale and retail trade, education, leisure and hospitality, and health care and social assistance together gained 6.1 million jobs, accounting for four fifths of the employment increase during the six-year period (U.S. Bureau of the Census 2008g).

By 2014, blue-collar work will have declined even further, with most of the increase in new jobs occurring in lower-wage service industries. Of the fifteen occupations predicted to grow the most between 2004 and 2014, just one will require a two-year college degree (registered nurses), while only four will require a college degree or higher (elementary school teachers, accountants and auditors, managers, and college teachers).

Together, these five relatively high-paying occupations are predicted to add slightly more than two million new jobs. The rest—adding twice as many jobs and paying low wages—will require for the most part only on-the-job training. The largest increase, 736,000 jobs, is predicted for retail salespersons, such as workers for Wal-Mart (U.S. Bureau of the Census 2008h).

There are several reasons for the transformation of the occupational structure. One is the continuous introduction of labor-saving machinery, culminating in the spread of IT and computerization in industry in recent decades. Another is the rise of the manufacturing industry in other parts of the world, primarily Asia. The older industries in Western societies have experienced major job cutbacks because of their inability to compete with the more efficient Asian producers, whose labor costs are lower. As we have seen, this global economic transformation has forced American companies to adopt new forms of production, which in turn forced some employees to learn new skills for new occupations as manufacturing-related jobs moved to other countries. In many cases, however, the transition to new jobs has meant forgoing higher-paid, unionized jobs in manufacturing for lower-paid, non-unionized work in services. Related to this is one final important trend: the decline of full-time paid employment with the same employer over a long period of time. Not only has the transformation of the global economy affected the nature of day-to-day work but it has also changed the career patterns of many workers.

THE KNOWLEDGE ECONOMY

Taking these trends into account, some observers suggest that what is occurring today is a transition to a new type of society no longer based primarily on industrialism. We are entering, they claim, a phase of development beyond the industrial era altogether. A variety of terms have been coined to describe this new social order, such as the *postindustrial society,* the *information age,* and the *"new" economy.* The term that has come into most common usage, however, is the **knowledge economy**.

A precise definition of the knowledge economy is difficult to formulate, but in general terms, it refers to an economy in which ideas, information, and forms of knowledge underpin innovation and economic growth. In a knowledge economy, much of the workforce is involved not in the physical production or distribution of material goods, but in their design, development, technology, marketing, sale, and servicing. These employees can be termed "knowledge workers." The knowledge economy is dominated by the constant flow of information and opinions and by the powerful potentials of science and technology.

How widespread is the knowledge economy at the start of the twenty-first century? A study by the Organisation for Economic Cooperation and Development (OECD) (1999) attempted to gauge the extent of the knowledge economy among developed nations by measuring the percentage of each country's overall business output that can be attributed to knowledge-based industries (Figure 14.5). Knowledge-based industries are understood broadly to include high technology, education and training, research and development, and the financial and investment sector. Among OECD countries as a whole, knowledge-based industries accounted for more than half of all business output in the mid-1990s. Germany had a high figure of 59 percent, and the United States, Japan, Britain, Sweden, and France were all at or over 50 percent.

Investments into the knowledge economy—in the form of public education, spending on software development, and research and development—now make up a significant part of many countries' budgets. Sweden, for example, invested nearly

11 percent of its overall gross domestic product in the knowledge economy in 1995. France was a close second because of its extensive spending on public education.

THE PORTFOLIO WORKER

In light of the effect of the knowledge economy and the demand for a flexible labor force, some sociologists and economists have argued that more and more people in the future will become "portfolio workers." They will have a skill portfolio—a number of different job skills and credentials—that they will use to move between several jobs during the course of their working lives. Only a relatively small proportion of workers will have continuous careers in the current sense.

Some see this move to the **portfolio worker** in a positive light: Workers will not be stuck in the same job for years on end and will be able to plan their work lives in a creative way (Handy 1994). Others hold that flexibility in practice means that organizations can hire and fire more or less at will, undermining any sense of security their workers might have. Employers will have only a short-term commitment to their workforces and will be able to minimize the paying of extra benefits or pension rights.

A study of Silicon Valley, California, claims that the economic success of the area is already founded on the portfolio skills of its workforce. The failure rate of firms in Silicon Valley is very high: About three hundred new companies are established every year, but an equivalent number also go bust. The workforce, which has a high proportion of professional and technical workers, has learned to adjust to this. The result, the authors say, is that talents and skills migrate rapidly from one firm to another, becoming more adaptable on the way. Technical specialists become consultants, consultants become

Google "knowledge workers" relax in the game room of their New York office.

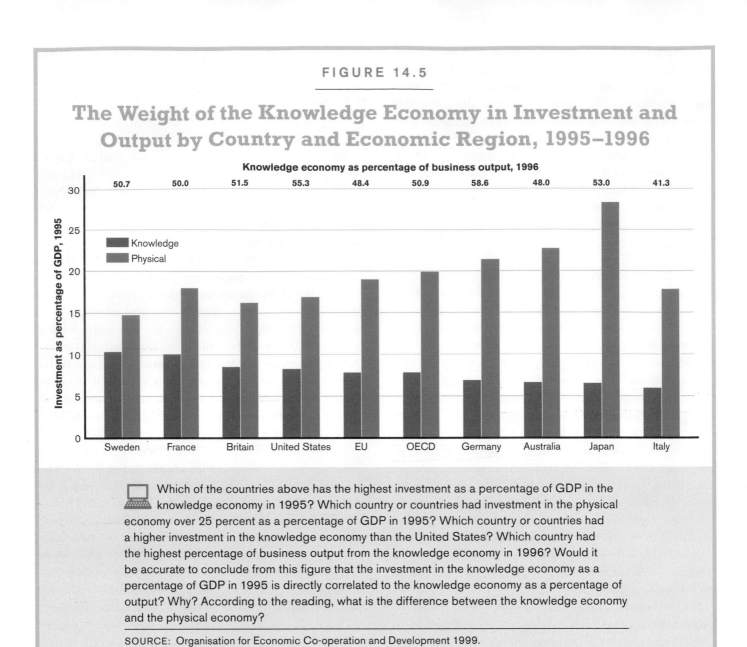

FIGURE 14.5

The Weight of the Knowledge Economy in Investment and Output by Country and Economic Region, 1995–1996

Knowledge economy as percentage of business output, 1996

| | 50.7 | 50.0 | 51.5 | 55.3 | 48.4 | 50.9 | 58.6 | 48.0 | 53.0 | 41.3 |

(Chart: Investment as percentage of GDP, 1995)

Legend: Knowledge, Physical

Countries (left to right): Sweden, France, Britain, United States, EU, OECD, Germany, Australia, Japan, Italy

Which of the countries above has the highest investment as a percentage of GDP in the knowledge economy in 1995? Which country or countries had investment in the physical economy over 25 percent as a percentage of GDP in 1995? Which country or countries had a higher investment in the knowledge economy than the United States? Which country had the highest percentage of business output from the knowledge economy in 1996? Would it be accurate to conclude from this figure that the investment in the knowledge economy as a percentage of GDP in 1995 is directly correlated to the knowledge economy as a percentage of output? Why? According to the reading, what is the difference between the knowledge economy and the physical economy?

SOURCE: Organisation for Economic Co-operation and Development 1999.

managers, employees become venture capitalists—and back again (Bahrami and Evans 1995).

THE CONTINGENT WORKFORCE

Another important employment trend of the past decade has been the replacement of full-time workers by part-time workers who are hired and fired on a contingency basis. Most temporary workers are hired for the least-skilled, lowest-paying jobs. But many of the portfolio workers whom we just discussed take jobs on a part-time basis as well. As a general rule, part-time jobs do not include the benefits associated with full-time

work, such as medical insurance, paid vacation time, or retirement benefits. Because employers can save on the costs of wages and benefits, the use of part-time workers has become increasingly common. Researchers estimate that contingency workers make up approximately 4 percent of the American workforce, or about 5.7 million people (U.S. Bureau of Labor Statistics 2005b).

The temporary employment agency Manpower, Inc., founded in Milwaukee, Wisconsin, in 1948, has become a global leader in the provision of temporary workers. This company employed 5.0 million temps (which Manpower refers to as "Associates") in eighty countries in 2007 and was the 120th largest corporation in the United States and 408th on the Fortune list of the Global 500 (Manpower, Inc. 2008). Manpower provides labor on a flexible basis to virtually all Fortune 500 companies. Clearly, temporary labor has become a critical component of the worldwide organization of work and occupations.

There has been some debate over the psychological effects of part-time work on the workforce. Many temporary workers fulfill their assignments promptly and satisfactorily, but others rebel against their tenuous positions by shirking their responsibilities or sabotaging their results. Some temporary workers have been observed trying to "look busy" or to work longer than necessary on rather simple tasks. Finally, contingency workers have tried to avoid emotionally intensive work that would require them to become psychologically committed to their employer.

However, some recent surveys of work indicate that part-time workers register higher levels of job satisfaction than those in full-time employment. Some individuals seem to find reward precisely in the fact that they are able to balance paid work with other activities and enjoy a more varied life. Others might choose to "peak" their lives, giving full commitment to paid work from their youth to their middle years, then perhaps changing to a second career, which would open up new interests.

Unemployment

The idea of work is actually a complex one. All of us work in many ways besides in paid employment. Cleaning the house, planting a garden, and going shopping are plainly all work. But for two centuries or more, Western society has been built around the central importance of paid work. The experience of unemployment—being unable to find a job when one wants it—is still a largely negative one. And unemployment does bring with it unfortunate effects including, sometimes, falling into poverty. Yet as we shall see, some today are arguing that we should think about the relation between being "in work" and "out of work" in a completely different way from the way we did in the recent past.

Rates of unemployment fluctuated considerably over the course of the twentieth century. In Western countries, unemployment reached a peak in the early 1930s, when some 20 percent of the workforce was out of work in the United States. Economist John Maynard Keynes, who strongly influenced public policy in Europe and the United States during the post–World War II period, believed that unemployment results from consumers' lacking sufficient resources to buy goods. Governments can intervene to increase the level of demand in an economy, leading to the creation of new jobs, and the newly employed then have the income with which to buy more goods,

deficit spending

A former Ford Motor Company employee attends a job fair hosted by the United Auto Workers Union.

thus creating yet more jobs for people who produce them. State management of economic life, most people came to believe, meant that high rates of unemployment belonged to the past. Commitment to full employment became part of government policy in virtually all Western societies. Until the 1970s, these policies seemed successful, and economic growth was more or less continuous. *then conservatives*

During the 1970s and 1980s, however, Keynesianism was largely abandoned. In the face of economic globalization, governments lost the capability to control economic life as they once did. At the same time, there was a growing belief, particularly among economists, that the "free market" by itself—rather than the government—was best equipped to assure economic prosperity. These ideas were especially appealing to conservative politicians, initially in the United States and Britain in the 1980s, and to a lesser extent in other Western industrialized economies. During the same period, unemployment rates shot up in many countries.

Several factors probably explain the increase in unemployment levels in Western countries at that time. One was the rise of international competition in industries on which Western prosperity used to be founded. In 1947, 60 percent of steel production in the world was carried out in the United States. Today, the figure is only about 7.9 percent, whereas steel production has risen by 300 percent in Japan, Singapore, Taiwan, and Hong Kong (Worldsteel.org 2008). A second factor was the worldwide economic recession of the late 1980s. A third reason was the increasing use of microelectronics in industry, the net effect of which has been to reduce the need for labor power. Finally, beginning in the 1970s more women sought paid employment, meaning that more people were chasing a limited number of available jobs.

During this time, rates of unemployment tended to be lower in the United States, for example, than in some European nations. This is perhaps because the sheer economic strength of the country gives it more power in world markets than smaller, more fragile economies. Alternatively, it may be that the exceptionally large service sector in the United States provides a greater source of new jobs than in countries where more of the population has traditionally been employed in manufacturing. As we have noted, many of these jobs provide low pay and limited job security. A final explanation, based on research by Chris Kollmeyer (2003), is that most European countries provide much longer-term unemployment compensation than the United States, along with universal health insurance and other forms of social protection. As a result, European workers are under less economic pressure to find work when they are laid off and so are able to wait until a relatively good job comes along. In the United States, Kollmeyer finds, workers are more likely to take any job that comes along in order to maintain some income. The trade-off, he concludes, is that European countries are willing to accept higher levels of longer-term unemployment for the benefit of having access to higher-quality jobs. In the United States, on the other hand, the choice is for

lower levels of shorter-term unemployment but at the cost of moving into lower-quality jobs.

Within countries, unemployment is not equally distributed. It varies by race or ethnic background, by age, and by industry and geographic region (Figure 14.6). Ethnic minorities living in central cities in the United States have much higher rates of long-term unemployment than the rest of the population. A substantial proportion of young people are among the long-term unemployed, again especially among minority groups.

The Future of Work

Since the mid-1980s, in all the industrialized countries except the United States, the average length of the working week has become shorter. Workers still undertake long stretches of overtime, but some governments are beginning to introduce new limits on permissible working hours. In France, for example, annual overtime is restricted to a maximum of 130 hours a year. In most countries, there is a general tendency toward shortening

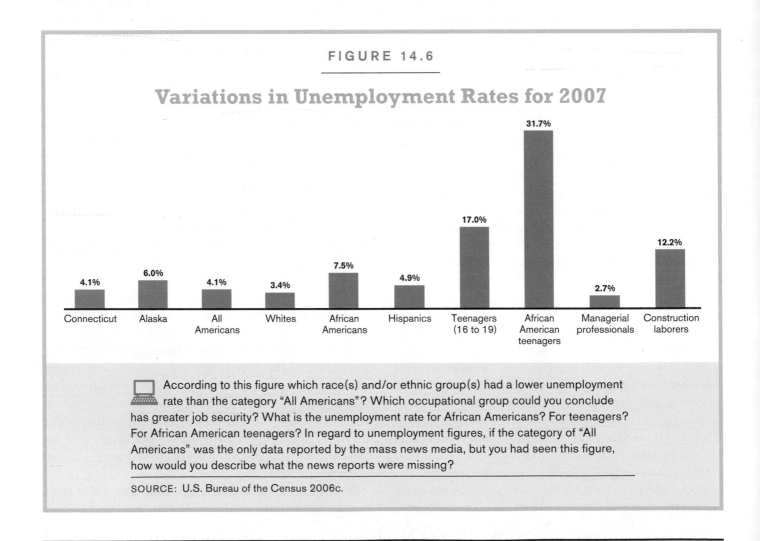

FIGURE 14.6

Variations in Unemployment Rates for 2007

Connecticut 4.1% · Alaska 6.0% · All Americans 4.1% · Whites 3.4% · African Americans 7.5% · Hispanics 4.9% · Teenagers (16 to 19) 17.0% · African American teenagers 31.7% · Managerial professionals 2.7% · Construction laborers 12.2%

According to this figure which race(s) and/or ethnic group(s) had a lower unemployment rate than the category "All Americans"? Which occupational group could you conclude has greater job security? What is the unemployment rate for African Americans? For teenagers? For African American teenagers? In regard to unemployment figures, if the category of "All Americans" was the only data reported by the mass news media, but you had seen this figure, how would you describe what the news reports were missing?

SOURCE: U.S. Bureau of the Census 2006c.

the average working career. More people would probably quit the labor force at sixty or earlier if they could afford to do so.

If the amount of time given over to paid employment continues to shrink, and the need to have a job becomes less central, the nature of working careers might become substantially reorganized. Job sharing or flexible working hours, which arose primarily as a result of the increasing numbers of working parents trying to balance the commitments of workplace and family, for example, might become more common. Some work analysts have suggested that sabbaticals of the university type should be extended to workers in other spheres: People would be entitled to take a year off to study or pursue some form of self-improvement. Perhaps more individuals will engage in life planning, in which they arrange to work in different ways (paid, unpaid, full or part time, etc.) at different stages in their lives. Thus some people might choose to enter the labor force in their late thirties, having followed a period of formal education in their early twenties with time devoted to pursuits such as travel. People might opt to work part time throughout their lives rather than being forced to because of a lack of full-time employment opportunities.

The Future of Work Program, funded by the Russell Sage and Rockefeller Foundations, studied nearly 500 businesses in 25 industries, surveying some 10,000 workers and conducting interviews with more than 1,700 managers and workers. The research offers a complex picture of the changing workplace, particularly for lower-wage workers. In some cases, they are being displaced by advanced technologies (think about the last time you made a phone call and spoke to an electronic voice rather than an actual person—or ordered something on-line rather than speaking with a salesperson). In other cases, businesses have partnered with their employees to develop creative ways to combine new technologies with upgraded (and higher-paying) work. The study found that even the temporary work industry does not always lead to dead-end jobs: About half of all temp jobs lead eventually to permanent ones (Applebaum, Bernhardt, and Murnane 2003).

Sociologist Joyce Rothschild (2000), who has studied workplace trends for many years, offers a hopeful picture of the possibility for greater worker participation in the workplace. She argues that the move toward more networked forms of business organization could result in a democratization of the workplace. She identifies a number of trends in support of this possibility. These include a drive toward flatter, more team-based forms of organization, sometimes called quality circles or total quality management; workplaces in which the workers help to shape the use of technology; the inclusion of women and minorities on teams; and even worker-based management of firms.

The nature of the work most people do and the role of work in our lives, like so many other aspects of the societies in which we live, are undergoing major changes. The chief reasons are global economic competition, the widespread introduction of IT and computerization, and the large-scale entry of women into the workforce.

How will work change in the future? It appears very likely that people will take a more active look at their lives than in the past, moving in and out of paid work at different points. These are only positive options, however, when they are deliberately chosen. The reality for most is that regular paid work remains the key to day-to-day survival and that unemployment is experienced as a hardship rather than an opportunity.

☑ CONCEPT CHECKS

1. Why does automation lead to worker alienation?
2. What are some of the changes that occurred in the occupational structure in the twentieth century? How can they be explained?
3. How did Keynes explain unemployment? What was his solution to high unemployment rates?
4. In your opinion, how will globalization change the nature of work?

Study Outline
www.wwnorton.com/studyspace

The Social Significance of Work

- *Work* is the carrying out of tasks that involve the expenditure of mental and physical effort and has as its objective the production of goods and services catering to human needs. An *occupation* is work that is done in exchange for a regular wage. In all cultures work is the basis of the *economy*.

The Social Organization of Work

- A distinctive characteristic of the economic system of modern societies is the development of a highly complex and diverse *division of labor*. The division of labor means that work is divided into different occupations requiring specialization. One result is *economic interdependence:* We are all dependent on each other to maintain our livelihoods.

- One manifestation of this division is *Taylorism,* or scientific management. Taylorism divides work into simple tasks that can be timed and organized. *Fordism* extended the principles of scientific management to mass production tied to mass markets. Fordism and Taylorism can be seen as *low-trust systems* that maximize worker alienation. A *high-trust system* allows workers control over the pace and even content of their work.

- Union organizations, together with recognition of the right to *strike,* are characteristic features of economic life in all Western countries. Unions emerged as defensive organizations, concerned to provide a measure of control for workers over their conditions of labor. Today, union leaders quite often play an important role in formulating national economic policies.

The Modern Economy

- The modern economy is dominated by large *corporations.* When one firm has a commanding influence in a given industry, it is in a *monopoly* position. When a cluster of firms wields such influence, a situation of *oligopoly* exists. Through their influence on government policy and on the consumption of goods, the giant corporations have a profound effect on people's lives.

- Corporations have undergone profound transformations in recent years because of increasing world interdependence, or globalization. The modern corporation is increasingly an enterprise web of many smaller firms linked together, rather than a single big business.

- *Multinational* or *transnational corporations* operate across different national boundaries. The largest of them exercise tremendous economic power. Half of the one hundred largest economic units are not countries, but privately owned companies.

The Changing Nature of Work

- In recent years, computer-aided design and planning tools have provided the capability to develop *flexible production* systems. *Automation* involves the use of robots in the production process. Group production, often used with automation, establishes collaborative work groups such as the quality circle, in which workers actively participate in the design and implementation of production methods.

- Major changes have occurred in the occupational system during the course of the century. Particularly important has been the relative increase in nonmanual occupations at the expense of manual ones. The interpretation of these changes, however, is disputed. Some speak of the arrival of the *portfolio worker*—the worker who has a portfolio of different skills and will be able to move readily from job to job. Such workers do exist, but for many people in the workforce flexibility is more likely to be associated with poorly paid jobs with few career prospects.

- Unemployment was a recurrent problem in the industrialized countries in the twentieth century. As work is a structuring element in a person's psychological makeup, the experience of unemployment is often disorienting. The effect of new technology seems likely to further increase unemployment rates.

- Major changes are currently occurring in the nature and organization of work. It seems certain that changes such as a move toward globalization, and the rise of large corporations will become even more important in the future. Nonetheless, work remains for many people the key basis of generating resources necessary to sustain a varied life.

Key Concepts

alienation (p. 428)
automation (p. 444)
capitalism (p. 435)
corporations (p. 436)
division of labor (p. 426)
economic interdependence (p. 426)
economy (p. 424)
entrepreneur (p. 437)
family capitalism (p. 438)
flexible production (p. 449)
Fordism (p. 427)
global outsourcing (p. 447)
high-trust system (p. 428)
informal economy (p. 426)
institutional capitalism (p. 439)
international division of labor (p. 440)
knowledge economy (p. 453)
low-trust systems (p. 428)
managerial capitalism (p. 438)
monopoly (p. 438)
multinational corporations (p. 439)
occupation (p. 424)
oligopoly (p. 438)
portfolio worker (p. 453)
post-Fordism (p. 447)
strike (p. 428)
Taylorism (p. 427)
technology (p. 424)
transnational corporations (p. 439)
union density (p. 430)
welfare capitalism (p. 439)
work (p. 424)

Review Questions

1. What are two global trends shaping the nature of work today as described by the text? Give an example of their impact.

2. What is the social significance of work? Why is being without work so detrimental to a person's well-being?

3. What is the "division of labor"? How has it changed between traditional and modern societies?

4. How did Henry Ford adopt the ideas of Taylorism? What is meant by *Fordism?*

5. Why has union membership been declining in the United States?

6. How do the findings of Freeman and Rogers's study of worker's opinions relate to Marx's ideas about worker alienation?

7. Why are transnational corporations important for the international division of labor?

8. How are ideas of "skill" shaped by social constructions of gender and race? Give an example.

9. What are the reasons for the transformation of the occupational structure in industrialized countries?

10. Why does the United States tend to have lower unemployment levels than Europe?

Thinking Sociologically Exercises

1. Explain the meaning of globalization of the modern economy. Explain how this textbook sees globalization affecting workers in third world countries and in advanced industrial societies.

2. Discuss some of the important ways that the nature of work will change for the contemporary worker as companies apply more automation and larger-scale production processes and as oligopolies become more pervasive. Explain each of these trends and how they affect workers, both now and in the future.

Learning Objectives

Theoretical Perspectives on the Family

Review the development of sociological thinking about the family and family life.

The Family in History

Learn how the family has changed over the last five hundred years.

Changes in Family Patterns Worldwide

See that although there are diverse family forms in different societies, changes are occurring that relate to globalization.

Marriage and the Family in the United States

Learn about patterns of marriage, childbearing, and divorce. Analyze how these patterns today differ from those of other periods.

The Dark Side of the Family

Learn about sexual abuse and violence within families.

Alternative Forms of Marriage and the Family

Recognize alternatives to traditional marriage and family patterns.

CHAPTER FIFTEEN

FAMILIES AND INTIMATE RELATIONSHIPS

s the American family in a state of crisis? Or are family arrangements simply changing along with economic, technological, and social changes in the United States?
Sociologists David Popenoe and Judith Stacey offer differing perspectives. Popenoe
(1993, 1996) argues that the family has changed for the worse since 1960. Since then,
divorce, nonmarital births, and cohabitation rates have increased, while marriage
and marital fertility rates have decreased. He claims these trends underlie social ills such as
child poverty, adolescent pregnancy, substance abuse, and juvenile crime. Increasing rates of
divorce and nonmarital births have created millions of female-headed households and have removed men from the child-rearing process. Popenoe argues that this is harmful for children.

Stacey (1990, 1993, 1996) counters that the traditional American family of the 1950s—praised
by Popenoe and conservative politicians as the panacea for all social problems—is a dated and
oppressive institution. According to Stacey, the "modern family" with "breadwinner-father and
child-rearing-mother" perpetuated the "segregation of the sexes by extracting men from, and
consigning white married women to, an increasingly privatized domestic domain." The modern
family has been replaced by the "postmodern family"—single mothers, blended families, cohabiting couples, lesbian and gay partners, communes, and two-worker families. The postmodern
family is well suited to meet the challenges of the current economy and is an appropriate setting
for raising children, who need capable, loving caretakers—regardless of their gender, marital
status, or sexual orientation, argues Stacey.

Popenoe agrees that children need capable, loving care-takers, yet he maintains that "two parents—a father and a mother—are better for a child than one parent." He claims that biological fathers make "distinctive, irreplaceable contributions" to their children's welfare. Fathers offer a strong male role model to sons, act as disciplinarian for trouble-prone children, provide daughters with a male perspective on heterosexual relationships, and, through their unique play styles, teach their children about teamwork, competition, independence, self-fulfillment, self-control, and regulation of emotions. Mothers, alternatively, teach their children about communion, the feeling of being connected to others. Both needs can be met only through the gender-differentiated parenting of a mother and father, argues Popenoe.

Stacey retorts that the postmodern family is better suited to the postmodern economy, in which employment has shifted from unionized heavy industries to nonunionized clerical, service, and new industrial sectors. The loss of union-protected jobs means that men no longer earn enough to support a wife and children. At the same time, demand for clerical and service labor, escalating consumption standards, increases in women's educational attainment, and continuing high divorce rates have led women to seek employment outside the home.

Stacey also disagrees with media rhetoric and claims by conservatives, such as Popenoe, who elevate the married, two-parent family as the ideal family form. Their condemnation of other family forms is particularly harmful to the millions of children who live with gay or lesbian parents. Rather than condemning nontraditional family forms, Stacey reasons, family sociologists and policy makers should develop strategies to mitigate the harmful effects of divorce and single parenthood on children. She suggests restructuring work schedules and benefit policies to accommodate familial responsibilities; redistributing work opportunities to reduce unemployment rates; enacting comparable-worth standards of pay equity to enable women as well as men to earn a family wage; providing universal health, prenatal, and child care, and sex education; and rectifying the economic inequities of divorce.

Claiming that "marriage must be reestablished as a strong social institution," Popenoe argues that employers should stop relocating married couples with children and should provide more generous parental leave. He also supports a two-tiered system of divorce law. Marriages without minor children would be relatively easy to dissolve, but marriages with young children would be dissolvable only by mutual agreement or on grounds involving a wrong by one party against the other. The proposal has encountered skepticism among feminist scholars who address the costs for children and adults alike of reinstating grounds of fault for divorce.

Changes affecting the personal and emotional spheres are widespread, differing only in degree and cultural context. In 2001, for example, China made divorce more difficult to obtain and increased the penalties for domestic abuse, bigamy, infidelity, and extramarital cohabitation. At the same time, China's new laws better protect the privacy rights of couples wishing to divorce by no longer requiring their employers' approval (China.org.cn 2001). In the late 1960s, liberal marriage laws established marriage as a working contract that can be dissolved "when husband and wife both desire it" or, if one partner objects, when "mutual affection" has gone from the marriage. Only a two-week wait is required. The Chinese divorce rate is still low compared with that in Western countries, but it is rising rapidly, as in the other developing Asian societies. Despite the reforms, between 2004 and 2005 the number of divorces in China rose by over 12 percent to 1.12 million (Weihua 2006). In Chinese cities, both divorce and cohabitation are becoming more frequent. In the vast Chinese countryside, by contrast, marriage and the family are much more traditional—in spite of the official policy of limiting childbirth through incentives and punishment. Marriage is an arrangement between two families, fixed by the parents. Interestingly, many of those currently divorcing in the urban centers were married in the traditional manner in the countryside.

In China as well as many Western countries, there is debate over protecting the "traditional family." Defenders argue that the emphasis on relationships weakens the family as a basic social institution. After all, they claim, the family is the meeting point of trends affecting society as a whole—increasing equality between the sexes, the widespread entry of women into the labor force, changes in sexual behavior and expectations, the changing relationship between home and work.

Basic Concepts

A **family** is a group of people directly linked by kin connections, the adult members of which take care of the children. **Kinship** ties are connections among individuals, established either through marriage or through the lines of descent that connect blood relatives (mothers, fathers, offspring, grandparents, etc.). **Marriage** can be defined as a socially acknowledged and approved sexual union between two adult individuals. When two people marry, they become kin to one another; however, the marriage bond also connects a wider range of kinspeople. Parents, brothers, sisters, and other blood relatives become relatives of the partner through marriage.

Family relationships are always recognized within wider kinship groups. All societies contain what sociologists and anthropologists call the **nuclear family**, two adults living together in a household with their own or adopted children. In most traditional societies, the nuclear family was part of a larger kinship network. When close relatives in addition to a

An extended Kazak family in Mongolia. Kazaks usually live in extended families and collectively herd their livestock. The youngest son will inherit the father's house, and the elder sons will build their own houses close by when they get married.

Parents wait for the train with their daughter. How is a nuclear family different from an extended family?

married couple and children live either in the same household or in a close and continuous relationship with one another, we speak of an **extended family**. An extended family may include grandparents, brothers and their wives, sisters and their husbands, aunts, and nephews.

Whether nuclear or extended, families can be divided into **families of orientation** and **families of procreation**. The first is the family into which a person is born; the second is the family into which one enters as an adult and within which a new generation of children is brought up. A further distinction concerns place of residence. In the United States, when two people marry, they usually set up their own household in the same area where the bride's or groom's parents live, or in a different town or city. In some other societies, however, married couples live close to or within the same dwelling as the parents of the bride or groom. When the couple live near or with the bride's parents, the arrangement is **matrilocal**. In a **patrilocal** pattern, the couple live near or with the groom's parents.

In Western societies, marriage, and therefore the family, is associated with **monogamy**. It is illegal for a man or woman to be married to more than one individual at any time. But monogamy is not the most common type of marriage worldwide. In a comparison of several hundred twentieth-century societies, George Murdock (1949) found that **polygamy**, a marriage that allows a husband or wife to have more than one spouse, was permitted in over 80 percent. There are two types of polygamy: **polygyny**, in which a man may have two or more wives at the same time, and **polyandry**, much less common, in which a woman may have two or more husbands simultaneously.

Theoretical Perspectives on the Family

The study of the family and family life encompasses contrasting approaches. Many perspectives adopted even a few decades ago now seem less convincing in the light of recent research and changes in the social world. Nevertheless, it is valuable to trace the evolution of sociological thinking before discussing contemporary approaches to the study of the family.

Functionalism

In the functionalist perspective, the family performs important tasks that contribute to society's basic needs and help perpetuate social order. Sociologists in the functionalist tradition regard the nuclear family as fulfilling specialized roles in modern societies. With the advent of industrialization, the family became less important as a unit of economic production and more focused on reproduction, child rearing, and socialization.

According to American sociologist Talcott Parsons, the family's two main functions are **primary socialization** and **personality stabilization** (Parsons and Bales 1955). Primary socialization is the process by which children learn their society's cultural norms. Because this happens during early childhood, the family is the most important area for the development of the human personality. Personality stabilization refers to the role of the family in assisting adult family members emotionally. Marriage between adult men and women is the arrangement through which adult personalities are supported and kept healthy. In industrial society, the role of the family in stabilizing adult personalities becomes critical because the nuclear family is often distanced from its extended kin and cannot draw on larger kinship ties.

Parsons regarded the nuclear family as best equipped to handle the demands of industrial society. In the "conventional" family, one adult can work outside the home while the second adult cares for the home and children. In practical terms, this specialization of roles involves the husband adopting the "instrumental" role as breadwinner and the wife assuming the "affective," emotional role in domestic settings.

Today, Parsons's view of the family seems inadequate and outdated. Yet viewed in historical context, his theories are more understandable. The immediate post–World War II years (when Parsons proposed his theories) saw women returning to their traditional domestic roles and men reassuming positions as sole breadwinners. We can criticize functionalist views of the family on other grounds, however. In emphasizing the importance of the family, such theories neglect the role of other social institutions—such as government, media, and schools—in socializing children. The theories also neglect family forms that do not reflect the nuclear family. Families that did not conform to the white, suburban, middle-class ideal were considered deviant.

Feminist Approaches

For many people, the family provides solace and comfort, love and companionship. Yet it can also be a locus for exploitation, loneliness, and profound inequality. In this regard, feminism has challenged the vision of the family as harmonious and egalitarian. In 1965, the American feminist Betty Friedan wrote of "the problem with no name"—the isolation and boredom of many suburban American housewives trapped in an endless cycle of child care and housework. Others followed, exploring the phenomenon of the "captive wife" (Gavron 1966) and the damaging effects of "suffocating" family settings on interpersonal relationships (Laing 1971).

During the 1970s and 1980s, feminist perspectives dominated debates and research on the family. Where previously the sociology of the family had focused on family structures, the historical development of the nuclear and extended family, and the importance of kinship ties, feminism directed attention inside families to examine women's experiences in the domestic sphere. Many feminist writers questioned the vision of the family as a cooperative unit based on common interests and mutual support, arguing instead that unequal power relationships within the family mean that certain family members benefit more than others.

Among a broad spectrum of topics, three main feminist themes are particularly important. One is the *domestic division of labor*—the way in which tasks are allocated among household members. Feminists disagree about the historical emergence of this division. While some see it as an outcome of industrial capitalism, others link it to patriarchy and thus see it as predating industrialization. Although a domestic division of labor probably did exist before industrialization, capitalist production caused a sharper distinction between the domestic and work realms. This process resulted in the crystallization of "male spheres" and "female spheres" and power relationships that persist today. Until recently, the male breadwinner model has been widespread in most industrialized societies.

Feminist sociologists have studied the way men and women share domestic tasks, such as child care and housework. They have investigated the validity of claims such as that of the "symmetrical family" (Young and Willmott 1973)—the belief that, over time, family roles and responsibilities are becoming more egalitarian. Findings have shown that women still bear the main responsibility for domestic tasks and enjoy less leisure time than men, even though more women are working in paid employment outside the home than before (Gershuny et al. 1994; Hochschild and Machung 1989; Sullivan 1997). Some sociologists have examined the contrasting realms of paid and unpaid work, focusing on the contribution of women's unpaid domestic labor to the overall economy (Oakley 1974). Others have investigated the distribution of resources among family members and the patterns of access to and control over household finances (Pahl 1989).

A second theme is the *unequal power relationships* within many families, especially the phenomenon of domestic violence. Wife battering, marital rape, incest, and the sexual

What conclusions have feminist sociologists made about the division of household work within families?

abuse of children have all received more public attention as a result of feminists' claims that the violent and abusive sides of family life have long been ignored in both academic contexts and legal and policy circles. Feminist sociologists consider how the family serves as an arena for gender oppression and physical abuse.

Caring activities constitute a third theme that feminists address. This broad realm encompasses a variety of processes, from attending to a family member who is ill to looking after an elderly relative over a long period. Sometimes caring means simply being attuned to someone else's psychological well-being. Not only do women shoulder concrete tasks such as cleaning and child care, but they also invest significant emotional labor in maintaining personal relationships (Duncombe and Marsden 1993). While caring activities are grounded in love and deep emotion, they also require an ability to listen, perceive, negotiate, and act creatively.

New Perspectives in the Sociology of the Family

Recent theoretical and empirical studies conducted from a feminist perspective have generated increased interest in the family among both academics and the general population. Terms such as the *second shift*—referring to women's dual roles at work and at home—have entered our vocabulary. But because feminist studies often focused on issues within the domestic realm, they did not always address trends and influences outside the home.

Since the 1990s, an important body of sociological literature on the family has emerged that draws on feminist perspectives but is not strictly informed by them. Of primary concern are the larger transformations in family forms—the formation and dissolution of families and households, and the evolving expectations within personal relationships. The rise in divorce and single parenting, the emergence of "reconstituted families" and gay families, and the popularity of cohabitation are all subjects of concern. Yet these transformations cannot be understood apart from larger changes occurring at the societal, and even global, level.

☑ CONCEPT CHECKS

1. According to the functionalist perspective, what are the two main functions of the family?
2. According to feminist perspectives, what three aspects of family life are sources of concern? Why are these three aspects troubling to feminists?

The Family in History

Sociologists once thought that before the modern period, the predominant form of family in western Europe was of the extended type. Research has disproved this view: The nuclear family seems long to have been preeminent. Premodern household size was indeed larger than it is today, but not by much. In the United States, for example, throughout the seventeenth, eighteenth, and nineteenth centuries the average household size was 4.75 persons. The current average is 2.57 (U.S. Bureau of the Census 2007l). Because the earlier figure includes domestic servants, the difference in family size is small.

Children in the premodern United States and Europe often worked—helping their parents on the farm—from seven or eight years of age. Most who did not remain in the family enterprise left the parental household at an early age to do domestic work for others or to follow apprenticeships. Children who went away to work rarely saw their parents again.

Other factors made family groups then even more impermanent than they are now. Rates of mortality (numbers of deaths per thousand of the population in any one year) for people of all ages were much higher. A quarter or more of all infants in early modern Europe did not survive beyond the first year of life, and women frequently died in childbirth. The death of children or of one or both spouses often shattered family relations.

The Development of Family Life

Historical sociologist Lawrence Stone (1980) distinguishes three phases in the development of the family from the 1500s to the 1800s. Early in this period, from the 1500s to the early seventeenth century, the main form was a type of nuclear family that lived in fairly small households but maintained deeply embedded relationships within the community, including with other kin. This family structure was not clearly separated from the community. According to Stone (although some historians have challenged this), the family was not a major focus of emotional attachment or dependence for its members, as we associate with family life today. Sex within marriage was not regarded as a source of pleasure but as a necessity to produce children.

Individual freedom of choice in marriage and other matters of family life were subordinated to the interests of parents, other kin, or the community. Outside aristocratic circles, where it was sometimes actively encouraged, erotic or romantic love was regarded by moralists and theologians as a sickness. As Stone (1980) puts it, the family during this period "was an open-ended, low-keyed, unemotional, authoritarian institution. . . . It was also very short-lived, being frequently dissolved

Balancing Family and Work

How many hours each week did your parents spend doing paid work when you were growing up? Did their commitment to work affect the way you or your siblings were raised? One of the ways globalization has affected family life in the United States is by increasing the amount of time that people spend each week at work. While there is some disagreement among researchers as to whether Americans, on average, are putting in more hours at work now than they did in the past, many sociologists give credence to the findings of economist Juliet Schor, author of the 1992 book *The Overworked American*. Schor argues that workers today spend on average 164 more hours each year at work than they did in the 1970s. Workers are also taking less vacation time than they did previously. Perhaps more significant, the percentage of mothers who are working full-time has increased dramatically since the end of World War II. In fact, in a comprehensive study of the multiple roles that modern women occupy, Daphne Spain and Suzanne Bianchi (1996) found that the group of women seeing the most dramatic increase in labor force participation in the United States was married women with young children. Taken together, these facts suggest that parents today have less time available to spend with their children than was the case in decades past.

by the death of the husband or wife or the death or very early departure from the home of the children."

Next came a transitional form of family that lasted from the early seventeenth century to the beginning of the eighteenth. Although largely a feature of the upper reaches of society, this form was very important because from it spread attitudes that have since become almost universal. The nuclear family became a more separate entity, distinct from other kin and the local community. There was a growing stress on marital and parental love, although the authoritarian power of fathers also increased.

The third phase, which emerged in the mid-eighteenth century and persisted through the mid-twentieth century, gave rise to the type of family system widespread in the West today. This family is a group tied by close emotional bonds, domestic privacy, and child rearing. It is marked by **affective individualism**, marriage ties based on personal selection, and sexual attraction or romantic love. Sexual aspects of love became glorified within marriage instead of in extramarital relationships. The family became geared to consumption rather than production, as a result of workplaces being separate from the home. Women became associated with domesticity and men with being the breadwinners. Originating among affluent groups, this family type became fairly universal in Western countries with the spread of industrialization.

In premodern Europe marriage usually began as a property arrangement, was in its middle mostly about raising children, and only in the end was about love. Few couples married for love, but many grew to love each other as they jointly managed their household, reared their offspring, and shared life's experiences. By contrast, in most of the modern West, marriage *begins* with love; in its middle, it is still mostly about raising children (if there are children); and in the end, it is—often—about property, by which point love is absent or a distant memory (Boswell 1995).

As a result, there has been a significant increase in the percentage of children enrolled in day-care programs—and, some would argue, a palpable increase in tension and stress within families as more of the day-to-day parental role is offloaded onto child-care providers.

In her book *The Time Bind* (1997), sociologist Arlie Hochschild suggests that these developments may be related to globalization. Globalization, of course, is not responsible for the gains women have made in securing positions in the paid labor force. Nevertheless, some corporations, according to Hochschild, have responded to the pressures of global competition by encouraging their salaried employees to put in longer hours at work, thus increasing levels of productivity. Why would employees willingly agree to spend so much time at their jobs—often considerably more than forty hours each week—when they are not paid to do so, when they know that such a commitment disrupts their family life, and in an age when computerization has greatly improved workplace efficiency? Shouldn't technological progress enable workers to spend more time with their families rather than less? Hochschild's answer to this question is that some corporations rely on the power of workplace norms to elicit a greater time commitment from their workers. New employees are socialized into a corporate culture in which working long hours is seen as a badge of dedication and professionalism. Employees, seeking status and the approval of their peers and supervisors, become motivated to put as much time into work as possible and to make sure that those around them know precisely how much time they spend working. In some cases, such a corporate culture has arisen unintentionally, as workers respond to the threat of

corporate downsizing by redoubling their commitment to the organization. In other cases—as with the corporation Hochschild studied—executives have consciously sought to shape the culture of the organization, reminding employees through handbooks, speeches, and newsletters that working more than forty hours a week is the mark of a "good" worker.

Although globalization has touched all the nations of the world, its effects on work time varies by country. In France and Germany, for example, workers—sometimes acting through unions, sometimes making their power known at the voting booth—have rejected corporate calls for a longer workweek and are instead pressuring employers to reduce the workweek and to grant longer vacations. Do Europeans simply value family and leisure time more than Americans? Or would American workers be making the same demands if unions were stronger in this country?

Myths of the Traditional Family

Many people today feel that family life is being undermined. They contrast the apparent decline of the family with more traditional forms of family life. Was the family of the past as harmonious as many people recall it, or is this an idealized fiction? As Stephanie Coontz (1992) points out, the rosy light shed on the "traditional family" dissolves when we study previous times.

Many admire the colonial family as disciplined and stable, but it suffered from the same disintegrative forces as its counterparts in Europe. Especially high death rates meant that the average marriage lasted less than twelve years, and more than half of all children saw the death of at least one parent by the time they were twenty-one. The much-admired discipline of the colonial family was rooted in the strict authority of parents over their children, which would seem exceedingly harsh by today's standards.

The Victorian family of the 1850s was also less than ideal. In this period, wives were more or less forcibly confined to the home. Women were supposed to be strictly virtuous, while men were sexually licentious. In fact, wives and husbands often had little to do with one another, communicating only through their children. Moreover, domesticity wasn't even an option for poorer groups. African American slaves in the South lived and worked in appalling conditions. In the factories and workshops of the North, white families worked long hours with little time for home life. Child labor was widespread.

Many people regard the 1950s as the time of the ideal American family, when women worked only in the home and men earned the family wage. Yet many women felt miserable and trapped in their domestic role. They had held paid jobs during

Kids in Cartoons

Adults often don't know what kids are up to. This includes petty larceny, lies, gratuitous cruelty, lots of mischief, and plenty of innocent fun. In the past most adults assumed that children, if left to their own devices, would get into trouble. Parents, however, were so busy that they had little time to oversee much of what their kids were doing. They relied on strict moral codes, the evidence of unfinished chores, observant neighbors, and delegating responsibility for the care of younger children to their older siblings. By the 1930s, however, these traditional means of social control had been weakened by a lowered birth rate and dramatic changes in how communities, families, and work were organized. Relaxed moral codes and new living arrangements diminished the community's ability to police its children. In addition, parents were increasingly preoccupied with figuring out how to succeed in new and changing status hierarchies that were emerging in the community and at work. It took adults decades to realize that a momentous consequence of the combined effect of all these changes had altered some previously unexamined assumptions about what relationships between parents and children should be like.

"What other bad words do you know?"

This cartoon from 1931, captures a comfortable middle class scene where children were able to create a separate sphere within the confines of an adult world.

In this 1930s cartoon mocking the rich, a mother arrives, like a store manager taking inventory, to inspect her children. Her kids and their nanny are astonished as she muses about how many children she might have.

Created by John Grady.

"But I thought I had another, an older one."

The *New Yorker* began publication in 1925 and quickly became America's premier literary magazine, and it is famous for its cartoons. The 1930s *New Yorker* cartoons reveal a world of well-off children whose material needs are more than cared for but who have been shunted aside by indulgent, yet negligent, parents. These images include children ordering servants to satisfy their whims, pre-adolescents flirting with each other and trying to communicate with adults who seem very much into their own concerns and out of touch with what is going on around them. The children are often bewildered and confused by an adult world that seems to have no place for them. In all of these cartoons children are very much on their own.

It is a different picture when we reach the present. Adults and children are now very much involved in each other's lives. In many ways these recent cartoons are the inverse image of those in the 1930s. In the earlier period, kids were depicted in one of two ways: either happily enjoying their own company and pursuits or apprehensively reminding adults that they were being neglected. By the turn of the century, a new order has been established. Kids are no longer neglected, and they live completely under the shadow of adult concern, which has had the ironic effect of requiring adults to reorganize their own lives in an endless quest to fulfill their children's undisciplined and boundless desires.

In this recent *New Yorker* cartoon, a child reassures his friend that he can expect to be comfortable in his home because his own parents are so child-centered. Adult authority in this new era is exercised uneasily lest it displease children. Kids aren't told what to do but have to be persuaded that what an adult has contrived is something that children will most likely enjoy.

"Now you're probably all asking yourselves, 'Why must I learn to read and write?'"

This 1994 cartoon offers another contemporary example of how relationships between children and adults have changed. In it, an anxious elementary school teacher feels compelled to justify the basis of formal education to her young charges before she starts class.

"You'll like my parents. They're very child-centered."

This 1999 cartoon is one of many that suggest that adults find these expectations annoying and children's behavior even worse. How might the relationships between adults and children change when the products of a child-centered age become parents?

"Your daughter is a pain in the ass."

World War II as part of the war effort but lost those jobs when men returned from the war. Moreover, men were still emotionally removed from their wives and often observed a sexual double standard, seeking sexual adventures for themselves but setting strict codes for their spouses.

Betty Friedan's best-selling book *The Feminine Mystique* appeared in 1963, but its research referred to the 1950s. Friedan struck a chord in the hearts of thousands of women when she spoke of the oppressive domestic life bound up with child care, domestic drudgery, and a husband who was rarely home and who allowed little emotional communication. Even more severe were the alcoholism and violence suffered within many families during a time when society was unprepared to confront these issues.

Let's now examine the changes affecting personal life, marriage, and the family today. No doubt some of these changes are profound and far-reaching. But interpreting their likely implications, particularly in the United States, means acknowledging just how unrealistic it is to contrast present conditions with a mythical view of the traditional family.

☑ CONCEPT CHECKS

1. Briefly describe changes in family size over the past three centuries.
2. Stephanie Coontz has dispelled the myth of the peaceful and harmonious family believed to exist in past decades. Give two examples of problems facing the family in past centuries.

Changes in Family Patterns Worldwide

Many family forms exist today. In some areas, such as remote regions in Asia, Africa, and the Pacific Rim, traditional family systems are essentially unchanged. In most developing countries, however, changes are occurring. Among the complex origins of these changes, one is the spread of Western ideals of romantic love. Another factor is the development of centralized government in areas previously comprising autonomous smaller societies. People's lives become influenced by their involvement in a national political system; moreover, governments attempt to alter traditional ways of behavior. Because of rapid population growth, states frequently introduce programs advocating smaller families, the use of contraception, and so forth.

Another influence is large-scale migration from rural to urban areas. Often men go to work in towns or cities, leaving family members in the home village. Alternatively, a nuclear-family group moves to the city. In both cases, traditional family forms and kinship systems may weaken. Finally, and perhaps most important, employment opportunities away from the land and in organizations such as government bureaucracies, mines, plantations, and industrial firms disrupt family systems previously centered on landed production in the local community.

These changes are creating a worldwide movement toward the predominance of the nuclear family, breaking down extended-family systems and other types of kinship groups. This was first documented by William J. Goode in his book *World Revolution in Family Patterns* (1963) and has been borne out by subsequent research.

Directions of Change

The most important changes occurring worldwide are the following:

1. Clans and other kin groups are declining in influence.
2. There is a general trend toward the free choice of a spouse.
3. The rights of women are more widely recognized, in respect to both initiating marriage and making decisions within the family.
4. Kin marriages are less common.
5. Higher levels of sexual freedom are developing in societies that were formerly very restrictive.
6. There is a general trend toward extending children's rights.

There are differences in the speed at which change is occurring, as well as reversals and countertrends. A study in the Philippines, for example, found a higher proportion of extended families in urban areas than in rural regions. Leaving the rural areas, cousins, nephews, and nieces go to live with their relatives in the cities to take advantage of employment opportunities there. Parallel examples have also been noted elsewhere (Stinner 1979), including some industrialized nations. Certain regions of Poland, for instance, show a rejuvenation of the extended family. Many industrial workers in Poland have farms that they tend part time. In the cities, grandparents move in with their children's family, run the household, and bring up the grandchildren, while the younger generation takes outside employment (Turowski 1977).

Given the ethnically diverse character of the United States, there are considerable variations in family and marriage within the country. Some of the most striking include differences between white and African American family patterns. After considering these differences, we will examine divorce, remarriage, and stepparenting in relation to contemporary patterns of family life.

☑ CONCEPT CHECKS

1. What are four conditions that have contributed to changing family forms throughout the world?
2. How has migration from rural to urban areas affected the family?
3. What are the six most important changes occurring in the family worldwide?

Marriage and the Family in the United States

The United States has long had high marriage rates; over 90 percent of adults in their early fifties today are or have previously been married (U.S. Bureau of the Census 2006). The age at which first marriages occur has risen, however, over the past twenty years. There are several explanations for this trend. Some researchers contend that increases in cohabitation among younger people account for the decreases (or delays) in marriage among this group. Others argue that increases in postsecondary school enrollment, especially among women, are partially responsible. Similarly, women's increased participation in the labor force means many women establish careers before marrying and starting a family (Oppenheimer 1988). Labor force participation also increases economic independence among women, as well as leading to a relative deterioration of men's economic position that makes them less attractive as mates and less ready to marry. Some researchers cite this "marriageable men hypothesis" to explain the especially low marriage rates among blacks, because black men have suffered the worst economic conditions in recent decades. Finally, some researchers believe that modernization and a secular change in attitudes promote individualism and downplay the importance of marriage. Although the true reason for the decline in marriage is likely a combination of all these factors, we must be careful in making comparisons. Whereas some have argued that the trend since 1970 toward later marriage is a break from tradition, it actually is close to the age of first marriage for the period 1890–1940. To say that people today are postponing marriage is true only if we compare ourselves with the 1950s generation. It might be more accurate to say that the 1950s generation married at an unusually young age.

In 1960, the average age of first marriages was 22.8 for men and 20.3 for women. Comparable ages in 2005 were 27 for men and 26 for women (Popenoe 2007). If we examine the proportions of people who remain unmarried before a certain age (Figure 15.1), we find that in 1960 just 28 percent of women under 24 years of age had never married. In 2006, that proportion was more than 75 percent. The U.S. census now incorporates a category of "unmarried couples sharing the same household." As the practice of cohabitation is new, it is not easy to make direct comparisons with preceding years. Nonetheless, we can estimate that the number of younger-age couples who have ever lived together without being married has risen steeply (Figure 15.2) from half a million couples around 1970 to almost three million in 1990. By 2006, over five million couples were cohabiting in the United States (National Marriage Project 2007). By age 30, about 50 percent of women will have cohabited outside marriage (Bramlett and Mosher 2002). The U.S. Bureau of the Census (2007i) estimated that in 2006 there were roughly 5.2 million heterosexual unmarried couples, or about 4.7 percent, cohabiting, which is low by European standards; for example, in Sweden, about 28 percent of unmarried couples are cohabiting (Popenoe 2005).

No one knows how the trend toward cohabitation will develop in the future, but we can get useful information from other industrial countries. In France, cohabiting relationships are more widespread than in the United States and last longer. A survey in that country published in the late 1980s found that over half of cohabiting couples "did not think about marriage." For most people, cohabitation is a phase of life in which partners want to leave their options open (Cherlin 1992; Sassler 2004). We return to the topic of cohabitation as an alternative to marriage later in this chapter.

An extraordinary increase in the proportion of people living alone in the United States has also occurred recently—a phenomenon that partly reflects the high levels of marital separation and divorce. More than one in every four households (27 percent) now consists of one person, a rise of 44 percent since 1960 (U.S. Bureau of the Census 2007i). There has been a particularly sharp rise for individuals living alone in the 24- to-44 age bracket.

Some people still think the average American family consists of a husband who works in paid employment and a wife who looks after the home, living together with their two children. However, only about 25 percent of children live in households that fit this picture. One reason is the rising divorce rate: A substantial proportion of the population live either

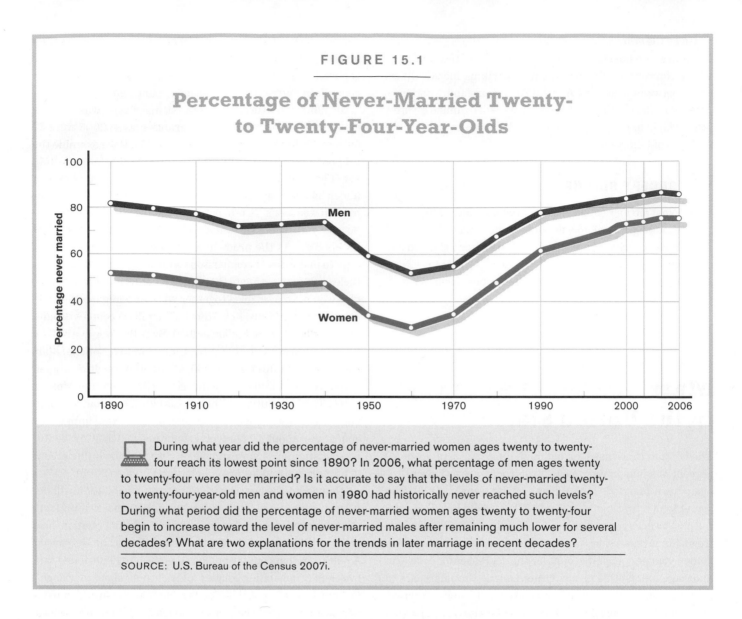

FIGURE 15.1

Percentage of Never-Married Twenty- to Twenty-Four-Year-Olds

Percentage never married

Men

Women

1890 1910 1930 1950 1970 1990 2000 2006

During what year did the percentage of never-married women ages twenty to twenty-four reach its lowest point since 1890? In 2006, what percentage of men ages twenty to twenty-four were never married? Is it accurate to say that the levels of never-married twenty- to twenty-four-year-old men and women in 1980 had historically never reached such levels? During what period did the percentage of never-married women ages twenty to twenty-four begin to increase toward the level of never-married males after remaining much lower for several decades? What are two explanations for the trends in later marriage in recent decades?

SOURCE: U.S. Bureau of the Census 2007i.

in single-parent households or in stepfamilies, or both. Another is the high proportion of women who work. Dual-career marriages and single-parent families are now the norm (Figure 15.3). The majority of married women working outside the home also care for one or more children. Although many working women have poor or nonexistent promotion prospects, the standard of living of many American couples depends on the wife's income, as well as her unpaid work in the home (see also Chapter 14).

There are also significant differences in patterns of childbearing between parents in the 1950s and later generations. The birthrate rose sharply just after World War II and again during the 1950s. Women in the 1950s had their first child earlier than later generations did, and subsequent children were born closer together. Since the late 1960s, the average age at which women have their first child has risen. And women are leaving larger gaps between children. In 1976, only 20 percent

of births were to women over age thirty. By 2005, this proportion had grown to 37.3 percent even though the proportion of women in the population aged thirty to thirty-four years declined between 2000 to 2005. The number of births to women thirty-five to thirty-nine years old has increased even more dramatically—by over 52 percent since 1990 (Centers for Disease Control and Prevention [CDC] 2007c).

Race, Ethnicity, and the American Family

ASIAN AMERICAN FAMILIES

The Asian American family is characterized by dependence on the extended family. In many Asian cultures, family concerns take priority over individual concerns. Family interdependence

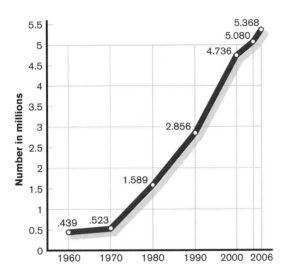
also helps Asian Americans prosper financially. In fact, family and friend networks often pool money to help their members start a business or buy a house; this help is reciprocated through contributions to the others. The result is a median family income for Asian Americans higher than that for non-Hispanic whites.

Although there is less research on differences among Asian American subgroups than among Hispanic subgroups, some fertility differences have been established. Chinese American and Japanese American women have much lower fertility rates than do any other racial or ethnic group. Chinese, Japanese, and Filipino families have lower levels of nonmarital fertility than all other racial or ethnic groups, including non-Hispanic whites. Low levels of nonmarital fertility combined with low levels of divorce for most Asian American groups demonstrate

the emphasis on marriage as the appropriate forum for family formation and maintenance.

NATIVE AMERICAN FAMILIES

Kinship ties are very important in Native American families. As Cherlin (1999) notes, "kinship networks constitute tribal organization; kinship ties confer identity" for Native Americans. However, for those who live in cities or away from reservations, kinship ties may be less prominent. Furthermore, Native Americans have higher rates of intermarriage than any other racial or ethnic group. In fact, in 1990, fewer than half of all married Native Americans were married to other Native Americans (Sandefur and Liebler 1997).

The Native American fertility experience is similar to that of African Americans. Native American women have a high fertility rate and a high percentage of nonmarital fertility. Over 63 percent of all Native American women giving birth in 2005 were not married (CDC 2007c). Sandefur and Liebler (1997) also report a high divorce rate for Native Americans.

LATINO FAMILIES

Hispanics are heterogeneous when it comes to family patterns. Mexicans, Puerto Ricans, and Cubans are the three largest Hispanic subgroups. In the U.S. census American Community Survey of 2006, Mexicans constituted 64 percent of the whole Hispanic population. Puerto Ricans constituted 9 percent, down from 12 percent in 1990, and Cubans were just 3.4 percent; the rest of the Hispanic population was made up of much smaller groups from many Latin American nations (U.S. Bureau of the Census 2007j).

Mexican American families primarily live in multigenerational households and have a high birthrate. Economically, Mexican American families are more successful than Puerto Rican families but less so than Cuban families. Defying cultural stereotypes of a Mexican American home with a male breadwinner and female homemaker, more than half of all Mexican American women are in the labor force (Ortiz 1995). However, this is because of necessity rather than desire. Many Mexican American families would prefer the breadwinner–homemaker model but are constrained by finances (Hurtado 1995).

Although Puerto Rico is a U.S. commonwealth, Puerto Ricans are still considered part of the umbrella category of Hispanics. However, because of their status as U.S. citizens, Puerto Ricans move freely between Puerto Rico and the mainland without the difficulties encountered by immigrants. When barriers to immigration are high, only the most able (physically, financially, and so on) members of a society can move to another country; but because Puerto Ricans face fewer barriers, even the least able can manage the migration process.

FIGURE 15.3

The Changing Structure of American Families with Children

Percentage of American children seventeen and younger living in each of four types of families, 1790–1990.

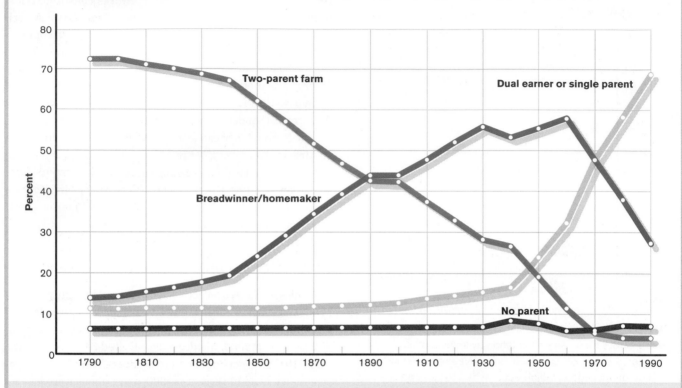

During what year did the percentage of children age seventeen and younger living in breadwinner-homemaker family structures reach more than 50 percent? What percentage decline did the number of children living on two-parent farms experience from 1790 to 1990? Which is the only type of family structure to increase since 1940? In 1990, what percentage of American children under the age of seventeen lived in breadwinner-homemaker structured homes?

SOURCE: Hernandez 1993.

Thus they are the most economically disadvantaged of all the major Hispanic groups. Puerto Rican families have a higher percentage of children born to unmarried mothers than any other Hispanic group—61.7 percent in 2005 (CDC 2007c). Only African Americans (69.9 percent) and Native Americans (64 percent) had higher rates of births to unmarried women (CDC 2007c). However, consensual unions—cohabiting relationships in which couples consider themselves married but are not legally married—are often the context for births to unmarried mothers. Nancy Landale and Kelly Fennelly (1992) studied the marital experiences of Puerto Rican women and found that many lived in consensual unions. They suggest that Puerto Ricans respond to tough economic times by forming consensual unions as the next best option to a more expensive legal marriage.

Cuban American families are the most prosperous of all the Hispanic groups but less prosperous than whites. Most Cuban Americans have settled in the Miami area, forming enclaves in which they rely on other Cubans for their business and social needs (such as banking, schools, and shopping). The relative wealth of Cuban Americans is driven largely by family business ownership. In terms of childbearing, Cuban Americans have lower levels of fertility than non-Hispanic whites and equally low levels of nonmarital fertility.

AFRICAN AMERICAN FAMILIES

There are important differences in white and black family patterns. Blacks have higher rates of childbearing outside of marriage, are less likely to ever marry, and are less likely to marry after having a nonmarital birth. These differences are of particular interest to sociologists because single parenthood is associated with high rates of poverty in the United States (Harknett and McLanahan 2004).

More than forty years ago, Senator Daniel Patrick Moynihan (1965) described black families as "disorganized" and caught up in a "tangle of pathology." Moynihan, among others, sought reasons for this in the history of the black family. For one thing, the circumstances of slavery prevented blacks from maintaining the cultural customs of their societies of origin; for example, members of similar tribal groups were dispersed to different plantations. Also, although some owners treated their slaves considerately and fostered their family life, others regarded them as little better than livestock and inherently promiscuous and, therefore, unworthy of marriage.

After emancipation, new cultural experiences and structural factors wreaked havoc on black families. Among these were new forms of discrimination against African Americans, changes in the economy such as the development of sharecropping in the South after the Civil War, and the migration of black families to northern cities early in the twentieth century (Jones 1986).

The divergence between black and white family patterns has become greater since the 1960s, when Moynihan's study was published, and we look mainly to present-day influences to explain them. In 2006, 55.3 percent of white families included a married couple, compared to 30.5 percent of black families (U.S. Bureau of the Census 2007l). In 1960, women headed 21 percent of African American families; among white families, the proportion was 8 percent. By 2006, the proportion (including married but spouse absent, divorced, separated, never married, and widowed categories) for black families had risen to more than 39.9 percent, while that for white families was 23.9 percent (U.S. Bureau of the Census 2007l) (Figure 15.4). Female-headed families are more prominently represented among poorer blacks. One social condition that has exacerbated this situation is a shortage of black men. Marriage opportunities for women are constrained if there are not enough men employed in the formal labor market. Recent

FIGURE 15.4

Family Arrangements for Black and White Children, 2006

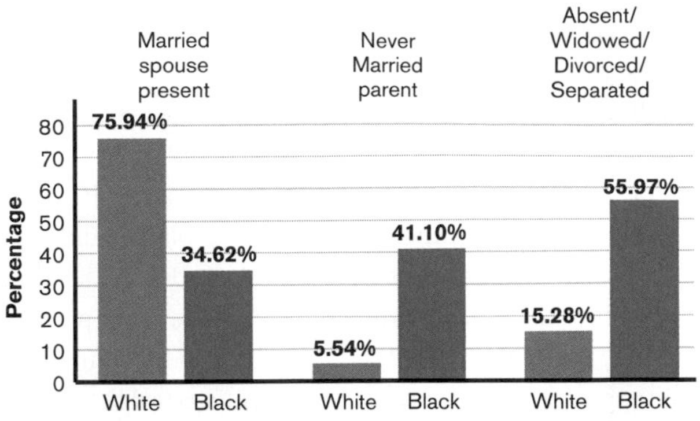

What is the combined percentage of black children who live with a separated or divorced parent or a never-married parent? What percentage of white children live in some form of two-parent household? In which category of family arrangement structure do black and white children share the most similar percentage? According to the text, what promotes stability within families headed by African American females who are more impoverished?

SOURCE: U.S. Bureau of the Census 2007l.

research confirms that one of the best predictors of whether parents marry after a nonmarital birth is the availability of eligible partners in a geographic area (Harknett and McLanahan 2004), demonstrating the continued importance of marriage markets even after the birth of a child.

But the situation of African American families is not entirely negative. White anthropologist Carol Stack (1997) lived in a black ghetto community in Illinois to study the support systems that poor black families form. Getting to know the kinship system from the inside, she demonstrated that families adapted to poverty by forming large, complex support networks. Thus a mother heading a one-parent family is likely to have a close and supportive network of relatives to depend on. A far higher proportion of female-headed families among African Americans have other relatives living with them than do white families headed by females. This contradicts the idea that black single parents and their children form unstable families.

Class and the American Family

While Stack's arguments addressed racial differences in the organization of the extended family, contemporary researchers have concluded that "the differences between black and white extended family relationships are mainly due to contemporary differences in social and economic class positions of group members. Cultural differences are less significant" (Sarkisian and Gerstel 2004).

This leads to an interesting question: Are racial differences in family formation primarily due to economic or to cultural factors? Consider an example of four individuals, all women, who are the heads of their households: (1) a black doctor, (2) a white doctor, (3) a black nurse's aide, and (4) a white nurse's aide. The cultural argument suggests that blacks and whites are different, which means that the black doctor and black nurse's aide should have family lives that are more similar to each other than they are to the family lives of the white doctor or white nurse's aide. The class argument argues the opposite, that the two nurse's aides and the two doctors will be more similar to each other than they will be to people of the same race but from a different class position.

One of the problems with the culture–class debate is that there is little research on middle-class black families or low-income white families. Despite the fact that there are no good empirical answers to this question, it does suggest the importance of considering how class differences could affect family life in America.

Nonmarital Childbearing

Researchers have been moving away from exclusively using race categories in analyzing family life. For example, the number of children born out of wedlock is six times higher now than in the 1950s and is increasing among the poor of all races. This suggests that examining the family by race alone while ignoring class is too narrow.

Katherine Edin and Maria Kefalas (2005) ask why low-income women continue to have children out of wedlock when they can hardly afford to do so. Following in the tradition of scholars such as Stack and Anderson, Edin and Kefalas lived with their subjects—among poor blacks, whites, and Puerto Ricans in Philadelphia and in Camden, New Jersey. Their interviews with 165 low-income single mothers in black and white neighborhoods led them to argue that marriage has not lost its meaning in such communities and that we must seek reasons for this trend. Women of all ethnicities whom they interviewed highly valued marriage but believed that marriage commitments at that time would make things worse, either committing them to terrible relationships or leading to divorce. As one

The number of children born out of wedlock is six times higher now than it was fifty years ago, and such births are increasingly occurring among the poor of all races. Often unable to afford other housing, many poor families pay rent by the month to live in motels like this one in downtown Las Vegas.

woman told Edin and Kefalas, "I'd rather say I had a child out of wedlock than that I married this idiot." Or, as others said, a failed marriage would be worse than having children on their own. In an environment in which more men than ever were going to prison or were unemployed, these women needed to be able to fend for themselves.

Two thirds of the pregnancies in the study were neither planned nor actively avoided. In these poor communities, women stop using contraception when the relationship becomes serious, even if the woman and man have not planned to have children together. But why do women have children out of wedlock in the first place? For one thing, the researchers find that young people in poor communities feel very confident about their ability to raise children, more so than most middle-class people do. This is because most of the pregnant mothers came from social environments in which young people help raise the other children in a family or in a building.

Second, the poor place an extraordinarily high value on children, perhaps even higher than that of middle-class families. Whereas middle-class people have more things to make their lives meaningful, the poor have fewer. For them, one of the worst things is to be childless. Finally, many women in the study reported that having a child actually saved their lives, bringing order to an otherwise chaotic life.

A third reason to "retreat from marriage" has to do with the changing meaning of marriage in low-income communities. Although low-income women do value marriage, what qualifies a man as a potential marital partner has changed over the last fifty years. Edin and Kefalas comment that "in the 1950s all but the most marginally employed men found women who were willing to marry them. Now, however, even men who are stably employed at relatively good jobs at the time of the

Anne Stevenson poses for a portrait with her son Reece in front of her off-campus housing when, as a single parent, she attended Tufts University. She graduated and still heads a group fighting for single parents' rights. Single parents attending college often have trouble finding affordable places to live since most schools do not offer family housing or daycare.

child's birth ... aren't automatically deemed marriageable." This suggests that women have become pickier. When women who value motherhood highly also set the bar higher for marriage, higher rates of nonmarital fertility follow.

Through Edin and Kefalas's (2005) work, we can understand the worldviews of black, white, and Puerto Rican young people who are having children out of wedlock. While it was beyond the scope of the researchers' project to study the outcome of these family formations for the children who are born into them, American sociology must continue to address the fact that nonmarital childbearing leads to deleterious outcomes for children, including lower-than-average rates of high school graduation, higher rates of incarceration, and continued poverty. This is a topic we revisit in our consideration of single-parent families.

CLASS-BASED CULTURAL PRACTICES

The relationship between social class and family life in the contemporary United States is central to another recent work of field-based sociology. Annette Lareau (2003) closely observed twelve families—six white, five black, and one interracial—and found that middle-class and working-class people have different cultural practices for raising children.

Middle-class parents engage in "concerted cultivation," working hard to cultivate their children's talents through many non–school-based activities as well as continuous linguistic interaction. Working-class and poor parents adopt a different style of child rearing, the "accomplishment of natural growth": Talk is brief and instrumental, children learn to be more compliant with adult directives, and they have few organized activities outside of school. They learn to occupy themselves, often playing with neighborhood friends.

As a result of these child-rearing strategies, Lareau claims, middle-class children develop a sense of entitlement and value an individualized sense of self. They become comfortable questioning authority and making demands on adults and institutions. In contrast, the working-class child-rearing strategy promotes a sense of constraint in children, who become more cautious in dealing with adults, bureaucratic institutions, and authority. Like Stack, Lareau also finds that working-class and low-income parents stress close ties to kin; thus these children develop closer relationships with their siblings, cousins, and other relatives.

Lareau argues that there are important signs of hidden advantages and disadvantages "being sown at early ages"; but because her research subjects were young, it was not possible to make claims about the way these child-rearing strategies affect adult outcomes. Further research would benefit from testing some of Lareau's hypotheses in large samples of children.

Like Edin and Kefalas, Lareau recognizes that social class is crucial to understanding family life in the contemporary

According to Annette Lareau, middle-class parents tend to work especially hard to cultivate their children's talents through immersion in many non–school-based organized activities, while working-class children tend to have few organized activities and learn to occupy themselves, often by playing with neighborhood friends.

"Are Women Giving Up on Marriage?"

Wedding singers and nuptial planners might have questioned their career choice if they had picked up the newspaper or turned on the television in January 2007. Headlines posed questions like "Are Women Giving Up on Marriage?" (Jacoby 2007), and readers were told that "51% of Women Are Now Living without Spouse" (Roberts 2007). Instantly, bloggers, call-in radio programs, and television talk-shows debated whether women "need" men and whether marriage is an outdated and irrelevant institution. What does the "51%" statistic mean? Does it suggest that women are "giving up on marriage"? Or is there another plausible explanation?

Wedding planners should rest assured that they are not out of a job. The statistic that "51% of women are now living without a spouse" does not necessarily mean that the majority of adult American women are spending their whole lives

without a husband. Rather, this statistic raises important questions about definitions of "singlehood" and raises questions about who is the appropriate target population when studying marriage. Demog-

Michelle Huneven, a writer and single woman, pictured at home with her dog Piper. Why are there more people living alone in modern Western societies?

raphers were quick to point out that the statistic of 51 percent was calculated by the U.S. Census Bureau, and it characterized the population of women *ages fifteen and older*. Some critics argue that young women ages fifteen to eighteen or even

fifteen to twenty-one are not "at risk" of marriage, meaning that they not likely to marry at such a young age and thus should not be included in the population being studied. As a result, the statistic of 51 percent is misleading because it includes women who are too young to even consider marriage, in most cases.

The news headlines also suggested that unmarried women were "giving up on marriage." In reality, the large population of "unmarried women" in the United States includes women who were once married, including those who are divorced, separated, and widowed. The latter group is particularly large and growing, as the number of Americans who are ages 65 and older increases. Because men die younger than women, older women are more likely to outlive their husbands and spend the final years of their lives as widows. The fact that older widows often live many years alone also partly

United States. Her work sets a new standard in showing how these differences emerge and operate as well as their potential implications. She emphasizes that the differences between working-class and middle-class culture do not reflect radically different values and priorities but, instead, vastly different levels of income and wealth. Her evidence suggests that if poor and working-class people had more money, their child-rearing strategies would change.

Divorce and Separation

Recent decades have seen major increases in divorce rates and more relaxed attitudes toward divorce. Whereas for centuries

in the West marriage was regarded as indissoluble, today most countries are making divorce more easily available.

Divorce rates (based on the number of divorces per thousand married men or women per year) have fluctuated in the United States in different periods (Figure 15.5). They rose, for example, after World War II, then dropped off before increasing steeply from the 1960s to 1980 (thereafter declining somewhat). It used to be common for divorced women to move back to their parents' homes; today most set up their own households.

Divorce exerts an enormous impact on children. Since 1970, more than one million American children per year have been affected by divorce. In one calculation, about one half of children born in 1980 became members of a one-parent family.

explains why women are more likely than men to be unmarried; married men typically die before their wives. Widowed and divorced men are also more likely to remarry, whereas their female counterparts are more likely to remain single after their marriages end.

Another explanation for the apparent increase in the number of women living without a husband is that a small—yet recently increasing—number of married women are living apart from their spouses, either because they have jobs in different cities or because their husbands are in the military or institutionalized. Of the sixty-three million women ages fifteen and older who are married, two million live apart from their husbands.

Despite these caveats, demographers clearly agree that the proportion of all women who are currently unmarried or living alone without a husband in their home is higher than at most other points in history. But that doesn't mean that women have turned their backs on marriage. Women are delaying marriage until after they have completed their schooling and established careers, so the number who are still unmarried in their late twenties and thirties is higher than ever before. Other women are choosing to live with their boyfriend rather than marrying them and will delay marriage

until both they and their partners feel ready to wed. For example, between 1950 and 2000, the proportion of women ages twenty-five to thirty-four who were married plummeted from 82 percent to 58 percent. However, the vast majority of unmarried women ages twenty-five to thirty-four will go on to marry someday.

The take-home message of the "husbandless majority" debate is not that marriage is dead or that heterosexual women prefer to live their lives without men. Rather, it reveals the importance of several sociological concepts. First, it shows that social scientists should clearly define who their "population at risk" is if they are going to document the proportion of a population who experiences a particular event such as marriage. Second, it reveals the importance of considering the vast diversity within social categories such as "unmarried women," which comprises cohabiting, never married, divorced, and widowed women. Finally, it emphasizes the importance of life course issues; just because a twenty-five-year-old woman is single today doesn't mean that she won't be married at thirty-four; that is, she's not permanently single or "turning her back" on marriage. Marriage is clearly here to stay.

Questions

- What proportion of American women are currently married? Which American women are included in this statistic?
- Can this statistic be taken as evidence that women are "giving up on marriage"? Why or why not?
- Describe three important methodological issues revealed by debate over the media's coverage of the "51%" statistic.

FOR FURTHER EXPLORATION

Jacoby, Jeff. 2007. "Are Women Giving Up on Marriage?" *Boston Globe,* January 21, 2007. www.boston.com/news/globe/editorial_opinion/oped/articles/2007/01/21/are_women_giving_up_on_marriage/ (accessed January 10, 2008).

Roberts, Sam. 2007. "51% of Women Are Now Living Without Spouse." *New York Times,* January 16, 2007. www.nytimes.com/2007/01/16/us/16census.html (accessed January 10, 2008).

Zernike, Kate. "Why Are There So Many Single Americans." *New York Times,* January 21, 2007. www.nytimes.com/2007/01/16/us/16census.html (accessed January 10, 2008).

Since two thirds of women and three fourths of men who are divorced eventually remarry, most of these children nonetheless grew up in a family environment. Only just over 4.6 percent of children under eighteen in the United States today are not living with either parent (U.S. Census 2007l). The remarriage figures are substantially lower for African Americans. Only 32 percent of black women and 55 percent of black men who divorce remarry within ten years. Black children are half as likely as white children to live with both parents or one parent and a stepparent (Cherlin 1992).

Lenore Weitzman (1985) has argued that no-fault divorce laws have helped recast the psychological context of divorce positively (reducing some of the hostility it once generated) but that they have negatively affected the economic position

of women. Laws designed to be gender neutral have had the unintended consequence of depriving divorced women of the financial protections provided under the old laws. Women are expected to be as capable as men of supporting themselves after divorce. Yet because most women's careers are still secondary to their work as homemakers, they may lack the qualifications and earning power of men. The living standards of divorced women and their children fell by 27 percent in the first year following the divorce settlement. The average standard of living of divorced men, by contrast, rose by 10 percent. Most court judgments left the former husband with a high proportion of his income intact; therefore, he had more to spend on his own needs than while he was married (Peterson 1996).

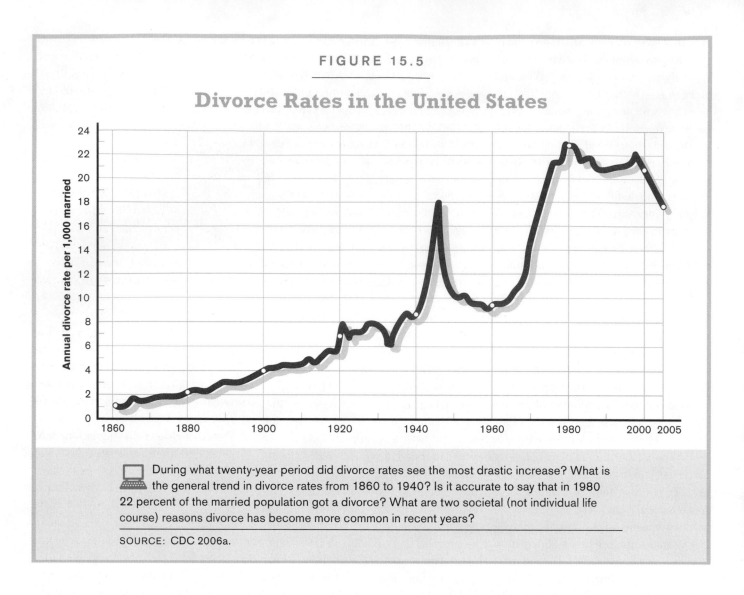

FIGURE 15.5

Divorce Rates in the United States

Annual divorce rate per 1,000 married (y-axis: 0 to 24)
(x-axis: 1860 to 2005)

During what twenty-year period did divorce rates see the most drastic increase? What is the general trend in divorce rates from 1860 to 1940? Is it accurate to say that in 1980 22 percent of the married population got a divorce? What are two societal (not individual life course) reasons divorce has become more common in recent years?

SOURCE: CDC 2006a.

REASONS FOR DIVORCE

Divorce rates are not a direct index of marital unhappiness. For example, they do not include separated people who are not legally divorced. Moreover, unhappily married people may stay together because they believe in the sanctity of marriage, worry about the consequences of breaking up, or decide to remain together for the sake of the children.

Why has divorce become more common? There are several reasons, which involve the wider changes in modern societies and social institutions. First, changes in the law have made divorce easier. Second, except for a few wealthy people, marriage no longer reflects the desire to perpetuate property and status across generations. As women become more economically independent, it is easier for them to establish a separate household (Lee 1982). The fact that little stigma now attaches to divorce is partly the result of these developments but adds momentum to them also. Third,

there is a growing tendency to evaluate marriage in terms of personal satisfaction. Rising divorce rates do not indicate dissatisfaction with marriage as such, but an increased determination to make it a rewarding and satisfying relationship (Cherlin 1990).

Other factors showing a positive correlation to the likelihood of divorce include

- Parental divorce (people whose parents divorce are more likely to divorce)
- Premarital cohabitation (people who cohabit before marriage have a higher divorce rate)
- Premarital childbearing (people who marry after having children are more likely to divorce)
- Marriage at an early age (people who marry as teenagers have a higher divorce rate)
- A childless marriage (couples without children are more likely to divorce)

- Low incomes (divorce is more likely among couples with low incomes) (White 1990)

THE EXPERIENCE OF DIVORCE

It is extremely difficult to draw up a balance sheet of the social advantages and costs of high levels of divorce. More tolerant attitudes toward divorce mean less social ostracism. However, marriage breakup is almost always emotionally stressful and may create financial hardship, especially for women.

Diane Vaughan (1986) interviewed 103 recently separated or divorced people (mainly from middle-class backgrounds) to chart the transition from living together to living apart. Her notion of "uncoupling" refers to the social separation that occurs before the actual physical parting—at least one of the partners developed a new life pattern, following new pursuits and making new friends in contexts apart from the other. This usually meant keeping secrets—especially when a relationship with a lover was involved.

According to Vaughan's research, uncoupling often begins unintentionally. One individual—the "initiator"—becomes more dissatisfied with the relationship than the other and creates an independent "territory" of activities. Before this, the initiator may have tried unsuccessfully to change the partner, foster shared interests, and so forth. Ultimately feeling that this attempt has failed and that the relationship is fundamentally flawed, the initiator becomes preoccupied with the ways in which the relationship or the partner is defective. Vaughan suggests that this is the opposite of the process of falling in love.

DIVORCE AND CHILDREN

The effects of divorce on children are difficult to gauge. How contentious the relationship is between the parents before

separation; the ages of the children; whether there are siblings, grandparents, and other relatives; the children's relationship with their individual parents; and how frequently the children continue to see both parents—all affect the adjustment process. Because children whose parents are unhappy but stay together may also be affected, assessing the consequences of divorce for children is doubly problematic.

Research indicates that children often suffer marked emotional anxiety right after their parents' separation. Judith Wallerstein and Joan Kelly (1980) studied 131 children of sixty families in Marin County, California, after the separation of the parents. They contacted the children at the time of the divorce, a year and a half after, and five years after. Almost all the children experienced intense emotional disturbance at the time of the divorce. Preschool-age children were confused and frightened, blaming themselves for the separation. Older children better understood their parents' motives but worried about its effects on their future and expressed anger. At the end of the five-year period, however, two thirds were coping reasonably well with their home lives and their commitments outside. A third remained dissatisfied, were subject to depression, and expressed feelings of loneliness, even when the parent they were living with had remarried.

Wallerstein continued studying 116 of the original 131 subjects at the end of ten-year and fifteen-year periods. She found that these children brought memories and feelings of their parents' divorce into their own romantic relationships. Almost all felt they had suffered from their parents' mistakes. Most of them shared a hope for something their parents had failed to achieve—a good, committed marriage based on love and faithfulness. Nearly half entered adulthood as "worried, underachieving, self-deprecating, and sometimes angry young men and women." Although many of them got married, the legacy of their parents' divorce lived with them. Those who appeared

Tomeryl Collier and her mother, Cheryl Ellis, sit on Tomeryl's bed. Cheryl and her husband planned on getting a divorce but stayed together for several years for Tomeryl. They are now divorced.

to manage the best had supportive relationships with one or both parents.

The parents and children studied all came from an affluent white area and might or might not be representative of the wider population. Moreover, the families were self-selected: They had approached counselors. Those who actively seek counseling might be less (or more) able to cope with separation than those who do not.

A more recent study found that the majority of people with divorced parents did not have serious mental health problems. The researchers did find small differences in mental health between those whose parents divorced and those whose parents stayed together (favoring those whose parents stayed together), but much of the difference had been identified in the children at age seven, before the families experienced divorce (Cherlin et al. 1998). The most prominent sociologist of the family in the United States, Andrew Cherlin (1999), has argued that the general effects of divorce on children are

- Almost all children experience an initial period of intense emotional upset after their parents separate.
- Most resume normal development without serious problems within two years after the separation.
- A minority of children experience some long-term problems as a result of the breakup that may persist into adulthood.

Remarriage and Stepparenting

Before 1900, almost all marriages in the United States were first marriages. Most remarriages involved at least one widowed person. With the progressive rise in the divorce rate, the level of remarriage also began to climb, and in an increasing proportion of remarriages at least one person was divorced.

Today, around one third of marriages involve at least one previously married person. Up to age thirty-five, the majority of remarriages are between divorced people. After that age, the proportion of remarriages with widows or widowers rises. By age fifty-five, the proportion of such remarriages is larger than those following divorce.

People who have been married and divorced are more likely to marry again than single people in similar age groups are to marry for the first time. At all age levels, divorced men are more likely to remarry than divorced women. Many divorced individuals choose to cohabit instead of remarry. In statistical terms, at least, remarriages are less successful than first marriages: Divorce rates are higher.

This does not mean that second marriages are doomed to fail. Divorced people may have higher expectations of

Thirty-five out of every one hundred marriages involve at least one previously married person. While most families don't look like the Bradys, they find their own ways to adjust to the relatively new circumstances in which they find themselves.

marriage than those who remain with their first spouses; hence they may be more ready to dissolve new marriages. The second marriages that endure are usually more satisfying than the first.

A **stepfamily** may be defined as a family in which at least one of the adults is a stepparent. Many who remarry become stepparents of children who regularly visit rather than live in the same household. By this definition, the number of stepfamilies is much greater than official statistics indicate, because these usually refer only to families with whom stepchildren live. Stepfamilies give rise to kin ties resembling those of some traditional societies in non-Western countries. Children may now have two "mothers" and two "fathers"—their natural parents and their stepparents. Some stepfamilies regard all the children and close relatives (including grandparents) from previous marriages as part of the family.

Certain difficulties arise in stepfamilies. First, there is usually a biological parent living elsewhere whose influence over the child or children remains powerful. Cooperative relations between divorced individuals often become strained when one or both remarry. Consider a woman with two children who marries a man with two children, all six living together. If the "outside" parents demand the same times of visitation as previously, the tensions on the newly established family will likely be intense. It may prove impossible to have the new family all together on weekends.

Second, since most stepchildren belong to two households, the possibilities of clashes of habits and outlooks are considerable. There are few established norms defining the relationship between stepparent and stepchild. Should a child call a new stepparent by name, or is "Dad" or "Mom" more appropriate? Should the stepparent play the same part in disciplining the children as the natural parent? How should a stepparent treat the new spouse of his or her previous partner when picking up the children?

Research on family-structure effects on children shows that girls experience more detrimental outcomes from stepfamily living, whereas boys demonstrate more negative outcomes from single-parent family living. The more negative effects for boys may be because single-parent family living generally means living with a mother only, without the male role model. Girls are more likely to bond with their mothers in this type of family. A remarriage that introduces a stepfather may cause girls to feel that their close relationship with their mother is threatened. This may be why girls living in stepfamilies experience more negative outcomes.

Single-Parent Households

As a result of increasing divorce rates and births before marriage, about one half of all children spend some time in a single-parent family (Furstenberg and Cherlin 1991). In 2006, about 20.6 million children under the age of eighteen lived with one parent, 17.1 million with their mother and 3.5 million with their father (U.S. Bureau of the Census 2007l). The vast majority of such families are headed by women, because the mother usually obtains custody of the children after a divorce (in a few single-parent households, the individual, again almost always a woman, has never been married). There were 12.9 million single-parent households in the United States in 2006, 10.4 million single-mother and 2.5 million single-father families (Figure 15.6), constituting 30.3 percent of all families with dependent children (U.S. Bureau of the Census 2007l). They

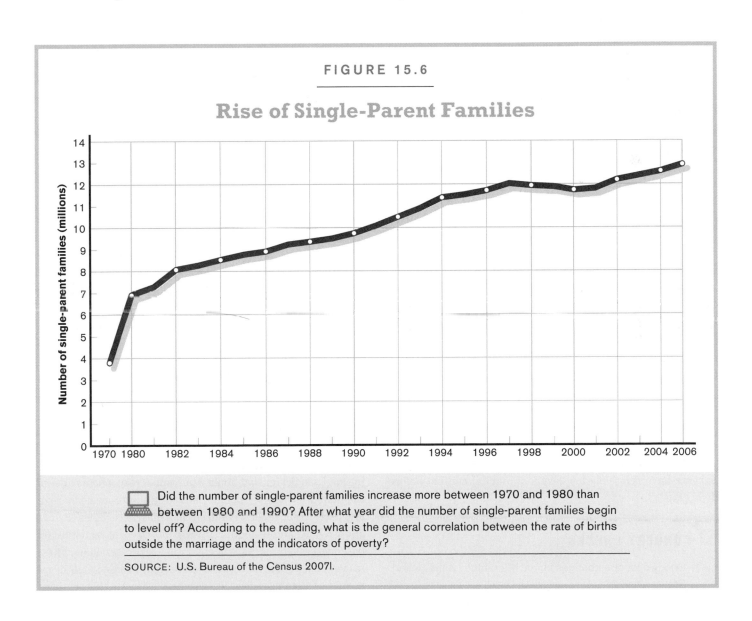

FIGURE 15.6

Rise of Single-Parent Families

Did the number of single-parent families increase more between 1970 and 1980 than between 1980 and 1990? After what year did the number of single-parent families begin to level off? According to the reading, what is the general correlation between the rate of births outside the marriage and the indicators of poverty?

SOURCE: U.S. Bureau of the Census 2007l.

are among the poorest groups in contemporary society. Many single parents, whether previously married or not, still face social disapproval as well as economic insecurity.

The category of single-parent household is internally diverse. For instance, more than half of widowed mothers are homeowners, but the majority of never-married single mothers live in rented accommodations. Single parenthood tends to be a changing state. For a person who is widowed, the break is clear cut—although he or she might have been living alone for some while if the partner was hospitalized before death. About 60 percent of single-parent households today, however, are the result of separation or divorce. In such cases, individuals may live together sporadically over a quite lengthy period.

Most people do not wish to be single parents, but a growing minority choose to have a child or children without the support of a spouse or partner. "Single mothers by choice" aptly describes some parents who possess sufficient resources to manage as a single-parent household. For the majority of unmarried or never-married mothers, however, the reality is different: There is a high correlation between the rate of births outside marriage and indicators of poverty and social deprivation. These are key influences underlying the high proportion of single-parent households among families of African American background in the United States.

Sociologists debate the effect on children of growing up with a single parent. Empirical research by Sara McLanahan and Gary Sandefur (1994) rejects the claim that children raised by only one parent do just as well as children raised by both parents. A large part of the reason is economic—the sudden drop in income associated with divorce. Other reasons include inadequate parental attention and lack of social ties. Separation or divorce weakens the connection between child and father, as well as the link between the child and the father's network of friends and acquaintances. The authors conclude it is a myth that strong support networks or extended family ties are usually available to single mothers. Others have also pointed out that although most children growing up in single-parent homes are disadvantaged, it is better for children's mental health if parents in extremely high-conflict marriages divorce rather than stay together (Amato et al. 1995). Divorce may benefit children growing up in high-conflict households while harming children whose parents have relatively low levels of marital conflict before divorcing.

☑ CONCEPT CHECKS

1. Briefly describe changes in family structure in the United States since 1960.

2. Contrast both general and nonmarital fertility rates among whites, blacks, Hispanics, Asians, and Native Americans in the United States.
3. According to Edin and Kefalas, why do many low-income women have babies out of wedlock?
4. What are the main reasons divorce rates increased rapidly during the latter half of the twentieth century?
5. How does divorce affect the well-being of children?

The Dark Side of the Family

Family life encompasses the whole range of emotional experience. Family relationships—between wife and husband, parents and children, brothers and sisters, or more distant relatives—can be warm and fulfilling. But they can equally be extremely tense, driving people to despair or imbuing them with anxiety and guilt. The dark side of family life belies the rosy images of family harmony frequently depicted in TV commercials and programs. It can take many forms. Among the most devastating are the incestuous abuse of children and domestic violence.

Family Violence

Violence within families is primarily a male domain. The two broad categories of family violence are child abuse and spousal abuse. Because of the sensitive and private nature of violence within families, it is difficult to obtain national data on levels of domestic violence. Data on child abuse are particularly sparse because of the cognitive development and ethical issues involved in studying child subjects.

CHILD ABUSE

The most common definition of child abuse is serious physical harm (trauma, sexual abuse with injury, or willful malnutrition) with intent to injure. One national study of married or cohabiting adults indicates that about 3 percent of respondents abused their children in 1993, though cohabiting adults are no more or less likely to abuse their children than married couples (Brown 2004; Sedlak and Broadhurst 1996). More recent statistics are based on national surveys of child welfare professionals. These surveys miss children who are not seen by professionals or reported to state agencies. Researchers estimate that as many as 50 to 60 percent of child deaths from abuse or neglect are not recorded (U.S. Department of Health and Human Services [DHHS] 2006b). In the 1993 National Incidence Study (NIS) of Child Abuse and Neglect, almost half of all substantiated cases of child abuse and neglect fell into the neglect category (47 percent). Physical abuse was the next most common violation (25 percent), followed by sexual abuse (15 percent) (Sedlak and Broadhurst 1996). The most recent statistics based on the National Child Abuse and Neglect Reporting System indicate that in 2005 there were more than 899,000 reported child victims of abuse or neglect. Of these, 62.8 percent suffered neglect, 16.6 percent suffered physical abuse, 7.1 percent suffered from emotional maltreatment, and 9.3 percent were sexually abused (DHHS 2006b). Almost 80 (79.4) percent of child abuse or neglect is perpetrated by the child's parents, and 6.8 percent were other relatives of the victim. Almost half (49.7 percent) of all victims of child abuse or neglect are white and just under a quarter (23.1 percent) are black (DHHS 2006b). The number of reported cases of child abuse has stayed about the same since 1990, when there were 860,000 victims of child abuse or neglect. The number of victims rose to just over one million in 1994 before declining to 899,000 in 2005.

SPOUSAL ABUSE

A 1985 study by Straus and his colleagues found that spousal violence had occurred at least once in the past year in 16 percent of all marriages and at some point in the marriage in 28 percent of all marriages. This does not, however, distinguish between severe acts, such as beating up and threatening with or using a gun or knife, and less severe acts, such as slapping, pushing, grabbing, or shoving. When the authors disaggregated this number, they found that approximately 3 percent of all husbands admitted perpetrating at least one act of severe violence on their spouse in the previous year, and this is likely an underestimate.

The national survey by Straus and his colleagues also uncovered a somewhat surprising finding: Women reported perpetrating about the same amount of violent acts as men. This contrasts with much of the literature based on crime statistics, hospital records, and shelter administrative records, which all indicate that spousal violence is almost exclusively man-on-woman violence.

Michael Johnson (1995) untangled these inconsistencies, recognizing that the data generating such conflicting findings came from two very different samples. In the shelter samples, respondents are generally women who were severely beaten by their husbands or partners. The severity of their situation drew them to a shelter. In contrast, those responding to a national survey are generally living at home and have the time,

energy, or wherewithal to complete a survey. It is unlikely that individuals experiencing extreme violence in the home would respond to a national survey. Furthermore, it is unlikely that those experiencing less severe violence (e.g., slapping) would end up in a shelter. Therefore, the two groups of people are very different.

Johnson argued that the spousal abuse in the two samples was also different in character. The extreme abuse experienced by many in the shelter samples was "patriarchal terrorism," perpetuated by feelings of power and control. The violence reported in national surveys is "common couple violence," which generally relates to a specific incident and is not rooted in power or control.

Social Class Although no social class is immune to spousal abuse, several studies indicate that the abuse is more common among low-income couples (Cherlin 1999). More than three decades ago, William Goode (1971) suggested that low-income men may be more prone to violence because they have few other means to control their wives, such as through higher levels of income or education. In addition, the stress induced by poverty and unemployment may lead to more violence. In support of these assertions, Gelles and Cornell (1990) found that unemployed men are nearly twice as likely as employed men to assault their wives.

☑ CONCEPT CHECKS

1. How do social scientists measure and track patterns of child abuse?
2. Describe gender differences in patterns of spousal abuse.

Alternative Forms of Marriage and the Family

Cohabitation

Cohabitation—in which a couple lives together in a sexual relationship without being married—has become increasingly widespread in most Western societies. Until a few decades ago, cohabitation was regarded as somewhat scandalous; but during the 1980s, the number of unmarried men and women sharing a household went up sharply. Cohabitation has become widespread among college and university students, although they did not initiate this trend. Bumpass and co-workers (1991)

Improving Child-Care Safety

As professor of sociology at the Graduate Center, City University of New York, Julia Wrigley researched relationships between parents and their children's child-care providers. Caregivers often said they had more trouble dealing with parents—their employers—than with the children in their charge. Caregivers usually seemed to manage their relationships with children, but there were tragic exceptions. Wrigley heard about several cases in which nannies had injured or even killed the children in their care. One case involved a nine-month-old boy, Kieran Dunne, who pulled on his caregiver's long hair. The caregiver, Ann Franklin, violently threw him to the floor. He died six days later of a skull fracture. Another case dominated the national media for months. Nineteen-year-old British au pair Louise Woodward was convicted of second-degree murder after she shook eight-month-old Matthew Eappen and slammed his head into a table on February 5, 1997.

Wrigley wanted to know more about such rare but devastating occasions. Did many children suffer harm in child care? Were the caregivers who harmed them mentally unstable, or were they ordinary people who snapped? The cases in the media usually involved caregivers in private homes. What about child-care centers? Were they safer or less safe?

Wrigley looked for data to answer these questions. She found none. No agency collected information on injuries or fatalities in child care. This was surprising, because child care has become part of families' daily lives. The percentage of mothers working full-time has increased dramatically since World War II, causing an increase in the percentage of children enrolled in day-care programs nationwide. As more and more parents rely on child-care providers to successfully balance work and family responsibilities, new tensions have surfaced

Julia Wrigley

about child rearing in the twenty-first century. Although many workers depend on child care, every parent who entrusts his or her child to outside care worries about safety.

Unsatisfied with reading about isolated cases, Wrigley decided to look for concrete answers. To gather information, Wrigley and her colleague and student Joanna Dreby analyzed reports of 1,362 fatalities from 1985 to 2003 by investigating media reports, legal cases, and state records. More than eight million children are in paid child care every day in America, but until recently little was known about their safety. The results caught Wrigley and Dreby by surprise. Deaths from violence in child-care centers were almost nonexistent. Almost every fatality took place in a private home, whether that care was offered in the child's home by a nanny or in an arrangement called family day care, by which a provider looks after neighborhood children in her own home.

How could this be? Mothers and fathers across the country often believe that private care is a safer, more intimate, and educationally rich way for their child to spend the day. But Wrigley and Dreby (2005) conclude that centers, not private homes, are the safest form of child care, largely because centers afford children multiple forms of protection. Staff members at centers do not work alone; they cooperate with each other to maintain an environment of emotional control and are, therefore, less likely to experience unbearable frustration. In addition, center workers dedicate time and energy to professional training and watch for outsiders who may pose risks to children.

In other words, child-care centers have fundamentally different organizational environments than private homes. "The striking success of centers at controlling fatal violence against children—indeed, almost eliminating it—and their relative safety in terms of protection against accidents suggests the power of social organization in reducing risks" (Wrigley and Dreby 2005). When single *individuals* provide care without the protective influences of co-workers and constant supervision, children are at greater risk of violent abuse. "Not a single shaken baby fatality was found in a child care center, while 203 were reported in arrangements in private homes. The stress of infant crying, in particular, can drive caregivers to impulsive acts of violence. With little professional training, without supervisors or coworkers, and often paid very little for long hours of work, even some experienced caregivers can lose emotional control" (Wrigley and Dreby 2005). Although the tragic deaths caused by Ann Franklin and Louise Woodward may have been isolated incidents, they fit a general pattern. Both fatalities occurred in private homes at the hands of unsupervised individuals who lashed out in frustration. Although extremely rare, Wrigley and Dreby believe those deaths are preventable.

As a public sociologist, Wrigley helped spark a dialogue about how public policy might improve child welfare in organizational settings. "Child care is quite safe overall, but it could be made safer," says Wrigley. "We need to recognize what a stressful and demanding job it is to look after young children. Improved safety will only come with more resources and closer regulation of care." Wrigley notes that there are three main care options available: child-care centers, family day care, and nannies working in the children's homes, each of which she believes would benefit from closer public attention. A major expansion of center care would be expensive, requiring a substantial social investment in the form of a federal or state subsidy, but research has consistently shown that centers can have a positive effect on child development (in terms of safety and intellectual stimulation). If this option is politically unfeasible, states could try to improve the safety of family day care by strengthening licensing requirements. Although many fatalities are unexpected, some deaths are attributable to child-care providers with long records of abuse. In addition to helping better identify facilities with poor records, increased regulation would also enable states to invest in improved training and certification of child-care workers, especially those who care for children alone.

Wrigley's overall goal is to help develop public policies that keep kids safe. In a recent op/ed piece for *Newsday,* Wrigley (2006) argues on the basis of her child-care findings that better regulation of day-care providers is necessary to ensure child safety. In New York and other states, many individuals who receive public money to provide informal child care remain unregulated by the state. No background checks are necessary. In New York, individuals are asked to voluntarily report to parents whether they have been convicted of a felony or have a history of child abuse. They also attest to the safety of the premises without inspection. In an act of almost willful blindness, "the state accepts these statements at face value." The result: "Very young children are being cared for by wholly unregulated providers who do not even have to undergo the most basic tests of fitness" (Wrigley 2006).

Many American families have luxuries of choice that are unavailable to other families. Some choose to raise children at home. Others choose services that provide a stimulating and healthy environment for children. But for families with little or no choice in child care, Wrigley believes that part of government responsibility is to ensure that all children be provided their most basic rights of protection and all parents be spared the frantic phone call from a caregiver telling them that their baby is not breathing.

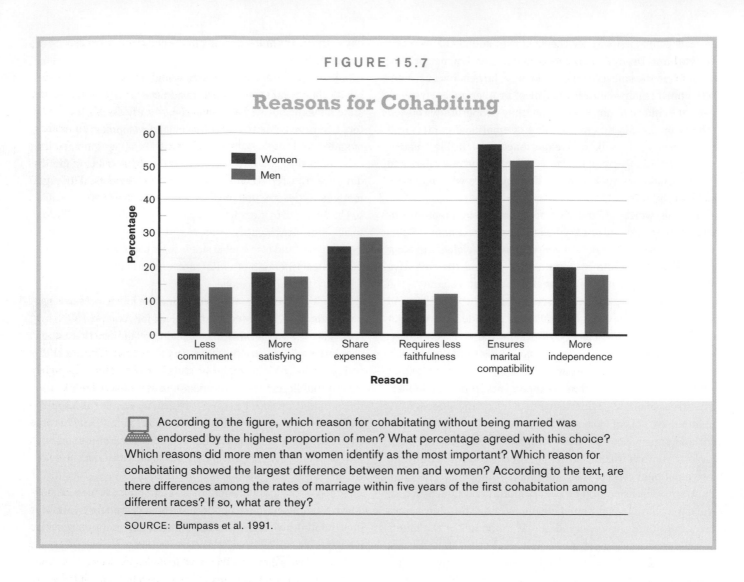

FIGURE 15.7

Reasons for Cohabiting

According to the figure, which reason for cohabitating without being married was endorsed by the highest proportion of men? What percentage agreed with this choice? Which reasons did more men than women identify as the most important? Which reason for cohabitating showed the largest difference between men and women? According to the text, are there differences among the rates of marriage within five years of the first cohabitation among different races? If so, what are they?

SOURCE: Bumpass et al. 1991.

found that the cohabitation phenomenon started with lower-educated groups in the 1950s—probably as a substitute for marriage, which may involve economic constraints.

While for some cohabitation today may be a substitute for marriage, for many it is a stage in the process of relationship building that precedes marriage. Young people usually come to live together by drifting into it, rather than through calculated planning. A couple having a sexual relationship spend increasing time together, eventually giving up one of their individual homes. Figure 15.7 shows that the most important reason for cohabiting for both women and men is so that "couples can be sure they are compatible before marriage."

Most cohabiting couples either marry or stop living together, although the chances of a cohabiting union transitioning to a first marriage is related to several socioeconomic factors. For instance, the probability that the first cohabitation will become a marriage within five years is 75 percent for white women but only 61 percent for Hispanic women and 48 percent for black women. Similarly, the likelihood of a first marriage resulting from cohabitation is positively associated with higher education, the absence of children during cohabitation, and higher family income. It is also more likely in communities with low male unemployment rates (Bramlett and Mosher 2002). For many people, it does not end in marriage. Only about 35 percent of cohabitors married their partners within three years of starting to live together. Increasingly, evidence shows that rather than being a "stage in the process" between dating and marriage, cohabitation may be an end in itself.

Judith Seltzer (2000) finds that an increasing proportion of cohabiting unions are not leading to marriage. Also, the rate of childbearing within cohabiting unions has increased by 25 percent (Seltzer 2000). At the same time, the percentage of all children born to unmarried parents has increased from about 18 percent in 1980 to just under 37 percent in 2005 (CDC 2007c). Cohabiting couples are the source of much of this increase. In the early 1980s, 29 percent of all nonmarital births were to those in cohabiting unions. A recent Pew survey finds that about half of all nonmarital births are to cohabiting couples (Taylor et al. 2007). The latest information available indicates that in 2002, among first births to Hispanic women, one in five occurred within cohabiting unions, compared with one in ten of first births to white women and one in seven first births to black women (CDC 2006b). Finally, in the past, couples who got pregnant before they were married often married before the birth of the baby. Currently, only 11 percent of single women who have a pregnancy that results in a live birth are married by the time the child is born. Although the percentage of those who marry before the birth of a child that was conceived while the couple was single has declined, there has been an increase in the rate at which unmarried women begin cohabiting with their partner once they find out they are pregnant. Currently, 11 percent of single women who have a pregnancy that results in a live birth begin cohabiting by the time the baby is born. Thus equal percentages of couples now marry and begin cohabiting to "legitimate" a pregnancy.

Recent research, however, has shown that cohabitation is less stable than marriage. Whereas the likelihood of a first marriage ending in separation or divorce within five years is 20 percent, there is a 49 percent chance that a premarital cohabitation will break up within five years. Similarly, after ten years, the probability of a first marriage ending is 33 percent, compared with 62 percent for cohabitations (Bramlett and Mosher 2002).

The United States is not alone in the increasing prevalence of cohabitation. Many European countries are experiencing similar, if not greater, proportions of unions beginning with cohabitation. Denmark, Sweden, Finland, and France show particularly high rates of cohabitation. However, unions in Spain, Greece, Italy, Ireland, and Portugal still largely begin with marriage.

As cohabitation becomes increasingly common, children are spending more time in cohabiting unions. Larry Bumpass and Hsien-Hen Lu (2000) find that about two fifths of all children spend some time living with their mother and a cohabiting partner and that approximately one third of the time children spend with unmarried mothers is actually spent in cohabitation. The effects of this alternative family form on children will become apparent only as these children grow older.

DOES LIVING TOGETHER HELP REDUCE THE CHANCES FOR DIVORCE?

Since the countercultural revolution of the 1960s, scholars such as anthropologist Margaret Mead (1966) predicted that living together would allow people to make better decisions about marriage. To some extent this might be true: The act of living together is a kind of trial marriage that can help poorly matched couples avoid a failed marriage (Elwert 2005).

Yet many people would be surprised to learn that individuals who live with their partner before marrying them are more likely to divorce than are individuals who do not cohabit with their partner before marrying them. How could this be so?

The Selection Explanation One compelling explanation suggests that there is nothing about living together that promotes cohabitation. This explanation cites the fact that people who live together would be more likely to divorce whether or not they had lived together first. This might sound odd until we recognize that the condition of living together may not be the

Does living together reduce the chances of divorce? Apparently not. People who live with their partner before marriage are more likely to divorce than those who do not cohabit before marriage. However, this relationship reflects social selection rather than causation.

cause of more divorce. Instead, perhaps the very people who choose to cohabit differ from those who don't. For example, people who cohabit are less religious, and people who refuse to cohabit are more religious (Dush et al. 2003). People who are less religious would be less likely to stay married in any event, whereas people who are more religious would be more likely to stay married. So people who elect to cohabit are the ones who are less religious and more likely to get divorced anyway.

The Experience of Living Together Explanation This explanation suggests that living together is the kind of experience that erodes beliefs in the experience of marriage. Particularly as people go through their twenties living with various partners, they see that relationships can be started and ended more easily and that they have many options for intimate relations outside of marriage (Teachman 2003).

Which explanation is right? The best evidence seems to indicate that while cohabitation may slightly increase the probability of divorce, the majority of divorces among those who cohabit are due to the fact that people who choose to live together before marrying have characteristics (such as low levels of religiosity) that would make divorce more likely for them anyway.

One other interesting fact bears on this discussion. People who cohabit only with the person they marry have as low a divorce rate as people who never cohabit. Perhaps this is because such people don't live together with enough partners to get a sense that relationships can be started and ended at will. Or perhaps it is because the very kinds of people who would live with only one partner have characteristics, such as higher religiosity, that keep divorce down.

Gay-Parent Families

Many homosexual men and women now live in stable relationships as couples, and there is a swiftly developing movement afoot to legally recognize these unions as marriages. Recent decisions in the United States, Canada, Mexico, and several European nations demonstrate the current pulse of this movement.

In 1998, voters in Hawaii approved a state constitutional amendment limiting legal marriages to one man and one woman. Before the issue was put to the electorate, the Hawaii Supreme Court was close to legalizing gay marriage. In fact, in 1993 the state's supreme court ruled that restricting marriage to heterosexual couples was sex discrimination, and the court asked the state of Hawaii to show a compelling reason for the restriction. Many legal observers believe the court would have ruled for gay marriage if not for the vote on the constitutional amendment.

In 1999, the Supreme Court of Canada ruled that same-sex couples are entitled to equal legal treatment (i.e., the same benefits) as married couples. The case was initiated when a lesbian filed for spousal support from her former partner. Initially, Ontario's Family Law Act had permitted only partners of the opposite sex to make a claim for spousal support after a breakup. The court therefore decided to first resolve the constitutional issue of whether same-sex couples have a right to seek spousal support. The Supreme Court's decision was that the Family Law Act's restriction to opposite-sex partners was unconstitutional.

Another decision on the issue of same-sex couples came in July 2000, when the Vermont legislature voted to allow same-sex partners to register their "civil unions" with town clerks, thereby gaining access to all the state-granted rights, privileges, and responsibilities of marriage. Though this was a big victory for gay and lesbian marriage advocates, the measure fell short of calling the partnerships "marriage" and instead opted for "civil unions." Civil unions are generally not recognized outside of the state of Vermont, although there is voluntary recognition in several jurisdictions. California's domestic partnership laws recognize Vermont civil unions, and New York City's Domestic Partnership Law recognizes civil unions

Maria Castillo (*left*) and Georjina Graciano hold their marriage license at City Hall in San Francisco, California, on February 16, 2004. The mayor of San Francisco, Gavin Newsom, ignited a passionate nationwide debate by allowing 4,037 same-sex couples to wed over a four-week period before the California high court annulled the marriages.

formalized in other jurisdictions. In 2003, the Massachusetts Supreme Court ruled that the state constitution does not forbid gay men and lesbians to marry and gave the Massachusetts State Legislature six months to rewrite the state's marriage laws to permit gay marriages. On May 17, 2004, the nation's first legal same-sex marriage was performed in Massachusetts. Just three months earlier, the mayor of San Francisco, Gavin Newsom, started issuing marriage licenses to gay and lesbian couples. Mayor Newsom argued that the state referendum passed in 2000, which defined marriage as between a man and a woman, violates the state constitution, which prevents discrimination against any social group. This prompted a response from California's governor to order the state attorney general to halt the action and for President George W. Bush to publicly endorse a constitutional amendment "defining and protecting marriage as a union of a man and woman as husband and wife" (CNN 2004a). (The president did not call for a ban on civil unions between homosexuals, which would be left up to the states to determine.)

Since 2005, more jurisdictions have shown support for gay unions. In 2007, Oregon and Washington legalized domestic partnerships, and New Hampshire governor John Lynch signed into law a bill allowing same-sex civil unions. That same year, Coahuila became the second state in Mexico to legalize civil unions. Between 2005 and 2008, the Czech Republic, Slovenia, Switzerland, and the United Kingdom were among the countries passing laws enabling civil unions.

Although the ultimate outcome—whether state law will respect these marriages—is yet to be determined, these events demonstrate the growing social movement toward legalizing gay marriages.

Meanwhile, same-sex couples are forming families with children. Less-intolerant attitudes toward homosexuality have been accompanied by a growing tendency for courts to allocate custody of children to mothers living in lesbian relationships. Techniques of artificial insemination mean that lesbians may have children and become same-sex families without any heterosexual contact. Moreover, only one of the fifty U.S. states—Florida—has laws explicitly preventing lesbians and gay men from adopting children.

Staying Single

Several factors have combined to increase the numbers of people living alone in modern Western societies. One is a trend toward later marriages; another is the rising rate of divorce; another is the growing number of old people whose partners have died. Being single means different things at different periods of the life cycle. A larger proportion of people in their twenties are unmarried than used to be the case. By their mid-thirties, however, very few men and women have never been married. The majority of single people age thirty to fifty are divorced and "in between" marriages. Most single people over age fifty are widowed.

More than ever, young people are leaving home simply to start an independent life rather than to get married. Hence "staying single" or living on one's own may be part of the societal trend toward valuing independence at the expense of family life. Still, a large majority of these people (over 90 percent) will eventually marry (Goldscheider and Goldscheider 1999).

☑ CONCEPT CHECKS

1. Describe cohabitation patterns in the United States over the past four decades.
2. Why has cohabitation become so common in the United States and worldwide?
3. Does cohabitation lead to divorce? Why or why not?
4. Briefly describe two legal turning points in the gay marriage movement.

Study Outline
www.wwnorton.com/studyspace

Theoretical Perspectives on the Family

- *Kinship, family,* and *marriage* are closely related terms of key significance for sociology and anthropology. Kinship comprises either genetic ties or ties initiated by marriage. A family is a group of kin having responsibility for the upbringing of children. Marriage is a union of two persons living together in a socially approved sexual relationship.
- A *nuclear family* is a household in which a married couple or single parent lives with their own or adopted children. Where kin in addition to parents and children live in the same household or have close and continuous relationships, we speak of an *extended family.*
- In Western societies, marriage, and therefore the family, is associated with *monogamy* (a culturally approved sexual relationship between one man and one woman). Many other cultures tolerate or encourage *polygamy,* in which an individual may have two or more

spouses at the same time. *Polygyny,* in which a man may marry more than one wife, is far more common than *polyandry,* in which a woman may have more than one husband.

The Family in History

- The modern Western family, which features close emotional bonds, domestic privacy, and a preoccupation with child rearing, is characterized by *affective individualism,* meaning that marriage partners are chosen on the basis of romantic love. This was not always the norm. In premodern Europe, parents, extended family members, or landlords decided on marriage partners, basing their choices largely on social or economic considerations.

Changes in Family Patterns Worldwide

- There are many types of families, but there is a trend toward the Western norm of the nuclear family. Some reasons for this trend include the Western ideal of romantic love, the growth of urbanization and of centralized governments, and employment in organizations outside traditional family influence.

Marriage and Family in the United States

- There have been major changes in patterns of family life in the United States during the post–World War II period: A high percentage of women are in the paid labor force, there are rising divorce rates, and substantial proportions of the population either live in single-parent households or live with stepfamilies. *Cohabitation* (in which a couple lives together in a sexual relationship outside of marriage) is increasingly common in many industrial countries.

The Dark Side of the Family

- Family life is not always harmonious and happy. The "dark side" of the family comprises patterns of abuse and family violence. Although no social class is immune to spousal abuse, it is more common among low-income couples.

Alternative Forms of Marriage and the Family

- Cohabitation and homosexuality have become more common recently. Although alternative forms of social and sexual relationships will surely flourish further, marriage and the family remain firmly established institutions.

Key Concepts

affective individualism (p. 466)
cohabitation (p. 485)
extended family (p. 463)
family (p. 462)
families of orientation (p. 463)
families of procreation (p. 463)
kinship (p. 462)
marriage (p. 462)
matrilocal (p. 463)
monogamy (p. 463)
nuclear family (p. 462)
patrilocal (p. 463)
personality stabilization (p. 463)
polyandry (p. 463)
polygamy (p. 463)
polygyny (p. 463)
primary socialization (p. 463)
stepfamily (p. 482)

Review Questions

1. What are the debates about traditional and postmodern families? What are the policies proposed by each side of the debate?
2. What are the two main functions of the family according to Talcott Parsons? What are critiques of the functionalist perspective?
3. Discuss three main themes studied by feminist theorists of the family.
4. What are the three phases of the development of the family from the 1500s to the 1800s? What does this historical study tell us about current conceptions of the "traditional family"?
5. What are some of the social processes that are changing family structures around the world?
6. Why should racial and class background be considered in research on families? Give an example.
7. What are some of the factors that explain the rise in divorce rates in the United States in the past thirty years?
8. What are the various types of single-parent households? What are some of the potential effects on children from single-parent homes?
9. What are some of the negative aspects of family life? What are some of the social factors involved?
10. Describe alternate forms of the family.

Thinking Sociologically Exercises

1. Compare the structures and lifestyles among contemporary white non-Hispanic, Asian American, Hispanic, and African American families using the text's presentation.

2. Increases in cohabitation and single-parent households suggest that marriage may be losing ground in contemporary society. However, this chapter claims that marriage and the family remain firmly established social institutions. Explain the rising patterns of cohabitation and single-parent households, and show how these seemingly paradoxical trends can be reconciled with the claims offered by this textbook.

Learning Objectives

Sociological Theories of Education

Understand the social functions of schooling. Learn three major sociological perspectives on the role of schooling in society.

Education, Inequality, and American Schools Today

Become familiar with the most important research on whether education reduces or perpetuates inequality. Learn the social and cultural influences on educational achievement.

Academic Achievement and Differential Outcomes

Learn sociologists' explanations for achievement gaps between different groups of students.

Education and Literacy in the Developing World

Know some basic facts about the education system and literacy rates of developing countries.

Communication and the Mass Media

Recognize the important effect of the mass media on society and learn some important theories about that effect.

Technological Change, Media, and Education

See the ways in which technological change is transforming the mass media and education.

CHAPTER SIXTEEN

EDUCATION AND THE MASS MEDIA

Christine is an eighteen-year-old Puerto Rican who lives in the Bronx, New York. She is bright young woman who for many years has dreamed of becoming a doctor. When she graduated from eighth grade, she was assigned to a notoriously dangerous, low-performing public high school called UPHS about two miles away from her home. UPHS, like many urban schools around the country, was in the process of being dismantled and made into several small, theme-based schools. Small schools had become the latest trend in urban school restructuring. Often, a group of public school educators will team up with a community-based organization or a private company to create a school for students interested in a particular profession. Many of these small schools have good reputations, and there is a perception among students and parents that the small schools have better resources, such as state-of-the-art computers, than the traditional large public high schools. When Christine arrived at UPHS, she was pleased to learn that a new small school partnered with a local hospital had opened up. The school was designed for students with an interest in the medical professions. Christine applied and was informed by her counselor that all slots for the new school had already been filled. The counselor explained to Christine that he would put her on the list for another small school about to open up for students interested in careers in law enforcement.

Christine's father had passed away when she was nine and her mother suffered chronic and serious medical problems, so Christine had no one to advocate for her. For two years, she attended classes and waited for the new small school to be established. Christine enjoyed some of her classes but felt ambivalent about others. Some classes were overcrowded, and there was immense pressure on teachers to prepare students for state-mandated standardized tests. To make matters worse, there were a number of students who were underprepared for high school–level work in her classes, and misbehavior was common. Not all teachers had the patience or the ability to deal with the difficult situation effectively. Christine also had to contend with the general disorder and violence in the school and the heavy police presence that had been added to the school in an effort to restore order. It wasn't uncommon for Christine to hear of a disconcerting incident in which a classmate or friend was seriously injured in a fight. But it was becoming an even more common occurrence to hear that a friend or her boyfriend had gotten into a confrontation with the police in the school hallways and ended up getting arrested. Like many of the students at UPHS, Christine came to view the heavy policing of students as another reason school was becoming less and less welcoming and enjoyable.

Several times during that period, Christine's mother was hospitalized, and Christine had to go into foster care. At one point during her mother's extended hospitalization, Christine moved in with a foster mother who lived several miles from the school. She began having trouble making it to school on time or at all. She would meet with her counselor at school regularly to express her interest in a transfer. She believed she would do better in a school closer to where she was living and one that offered a more flexible or accelerated program, as she was beginning to fall behind with her course credits and wanted very much to graduate on time.

At the beginning of her third year of high school, Christine finally transferred to a new school and was back living with her mother. Things were going well for a while, but she began feeling pressured to make some money, as her mother was living on a fixed income and had no spare money for Christine. Christine worked at a supermarket for a while, and then at a restaurant. But the competing demands of school and paid work proved to be a tough challenge. Eventually, she was unable to keep the difficult pace. She took a leave of absence from school and finally decided that she would enter a GED program to get her general equivalency degree.

Like many young people in her position looking for a way to secure a future, Christine was then recruited by a proprietary (or for-profit) school that offered training and a credential in medical billing. College seemed to be a long way off, so Christine viewed this as an opportunity to enter into the medical profession while her dream of becoming a doctor was deferred. She knew she would need to work hard to make it happen, especially since the proprietary school was expensive and tuition would use up the financial aid she would have otherwise used

for college. If the program didn't work out for her, her options without any financial aid would be severely limited.

Today, Christine works full-time in a supermarket and attends the proprietary school. She is getting good grades but has missed classes on occasion because of her grueling schedule. She still needs to pass her GED exam. Christine, like so many other young working-class people today, is struggling without much help or options to gain some financial security.

Christine's story touches on many of the issues of interest to sociologists of education today.

Sociological Theories of Education

When we think of education, we tend to see it from an individual perspective. We may think of our own or Christine's purpose in attending school, to cultivate our intelligence or to prepare for a career. We also tend to think of education in terms of our own goals and think of it as a means to upward mobility. But sociologists tend to go beyond this common-sense way of thinking and look beyond the individual student and his or her goals to connect these to the larger social functions of schools. What follows is an explanation of three major sociological theories of the role schooling plays in the larger society: schooling as a process of assimilation or acculturation, schooling as a credentialing mechanism, and schooling as a process of social, or cultural, reproduction.

The first perspective, schooling as a process of assimilation, focuses on what might be called the official curriculum and looks at questions such as how learning a common language and the facts of a common history and geography creates a sense of "affinity" among members of society, which is something less than full consensus (Shils 1972). The official

What is the role of schooling in the assimilation process?

curriculum promotes feelings of nationalism and is instrumental in the development of national societies, constituted of citizens from different regions who would know the same history and speak a common language (Ramirez and Boli 1987; Shils 1972). In this approach, the content of education is particularly important in creating a common culture. Christine, for example, whose mother came from Puerto Rico, learned much about American culture through her experiences in school. But even children whose parents are part of the country's dominant culture depend upon the official curriculum to develop an image of themselves as Americans with a common history.

A second influential perspective is credentialism. Adherents to this way of thinking place less emphasis on the content of an official curriculum. They argue that the content of education is much less relevant than the diploma. The primary social function of mass education derives from the need for degrees to determine one's credentials for a job, even if the work involved has nothing to do with the education one has received (Collins 1979). Over time, the practice of credentialism results in demands for higher credentials, which require higher levels of educational attainment. Jobs, such as that of a sales representative, that thirty years ago would have required a high school diploma now require a college degree. Since educational attainment is closely related to class position, credentialism reinforces the class structure within a society.

A third perspective, known as "critical" or Marxist, places the emphasis on social reproduction. In the context of education, *social reproduction* refers to the ways in which schools help perpetuate social and economic inequalities across the generations. A number of sociologists have argued that the **hidden curriculum** is the mechanism through which social reproduction occurs. The hidden curriculum refers to the idea that students from different social class backgrounds are provided different types of education, both in terms of curricular materials and the kinds of interactions in which they are engaged by their teachers. More specifically, the notion of the hidden curriculum suggests that the expansion of education was brought about by employers' needs for certain personality characteristics in their workers—self-discipline, dependability, punctuality, obedience, and the like—which are all taught in schools.

In their seminal study of social reproduction, Samuel Bowles and Herbert Gintis (1976) provide an example of how the hidden curriculum works. They argue that modern education is a response to the economic needs of industrial capitalism. Schools help provide the technical and social skills required by industrial enterprise, and they instill discipline and respect for authority into the labor force. Schools also socialize children to get along with each other. "Playing well with others" is, after all, an important characteristic for being a good worker.

Authority relations in school, which are hierarchical and place strong emphasis on obedience, directly parallel those dominating the workplace. The rewards and punishments held out in school also replicate those found in the world of work. Schools help motivate some individuals toward "achievement" and "success," while discouraging others, who find their way into low-paying jobs.

A cruder way of putting this is that schools facilitate the ruling class's need to exploit a docile or cooperative work force. Here the emphasis is on the fact that much of what is learned in school has nothing directly to do with the formal content of lessons. Schools, by the nature of the discipline and regimentation they entail, tend to teach students an uncritical acceptance of the existing social order. These lessons are not consciously taught; they are implicit in school procedures and organization. Thus, the hidden curriculum teaches children like Christine that their role in life is "to know their place and to sit still with it" (Illich 1983). Children spend long hours in school, and they learn a great deal more in the school context than is contained in the lessons they are actually taught. Children get an early taste of what the world of work will be like, learning that they are expected to be punctual and apply themselves diligently to the tasks that those in authority set for them. From this perspective, even if Christine learned very little in her classes, the basic training she received in arriving on time for class would end up serving her well as a worker at the checkout counter in the supermarket. Such an analysis can be quite depressing, but it may be a realistic way of understanding the place of education in the lives of such people.

Adherents to this perspective don't completely dismiss the content of the official curriculum. They accept that the development of mass education has had many beneficial consequences. Illiteracy rates are low compared with premodern times, and schooling provides access to learning experiences that are intrinsically self-fulfilling. Yet because education has expanded mainly as a response to economic needs, the school system falls far short of what enlightened reformers had hoped

Two students at a vocational high school in Florida learn how to wire a light switch. Career academies like this one encourage students to work toward national industry certifications.

from it. That is, according to this perspective, schooling has not become the "great equalizer"; rather, within the current economic and political system, schooling reproduces social class stratification.

Another seminal figure who wrote about education and reproduction is the French sociologist Pierre Bourdieu, who argued that schools reproduce social class inequality by rewarding certain cultural norms over others (1984, 1988). Bourdieu's focus on the role of culture in the process of reproduction distinguished his theory from a strict Marxist analysis that focused on how schools mirrored and reproduced economic class structures. For this reason he uses the term *cultural reproduction.* In relation to his theory of cultural reproduction, Bourdieu argued that there were many kinds of capital that people could possess other than financial capital. Specifically, he was concerned with the existence of what he called **cultural capital.** That is, his theory of cultural reproduction proposes that middle- and upper-class children come to schools with a certain kind of cultural capital—speech patterns, demeanors, tastes, and so on—that is valued, and thus rewarded, by the school. Bourdieu argues that children from low-income or working-class homes, however, do not possess these same cultural characteristics valued by the school and thus are placed at a disadvantage in schools. Another important concept Bourdieu offers is the notion of habitus. *Habitus* refers to a class-based set of dispositions, such as tastes, language use, and demeanors. For Bourdieu, these dispositions are internalized unconsciously through social practices within one's social group. Put simply, poor and working-class children are socialized into a particular habitus—one that is not valued within the school system. In arguing that working-class individuals are unconsciously socialized into a working-class culture (and therefore are not likely to obtain the dispositions required for school success), Bourdieu, like Bowles and Gintis, ultimately proposes a theory of reproduction in which the cycle of domination seems unbreakable.

These kinds of theories have been challenged by the notion of schools as contested spaces (Aronowitz and Giroux 1991; Willis 1977). In other words, it has been proposed that social reproduction does not happen without struggle or opposition from oppressed groups. Written over twenty-five years ago, but still important today, Willis's seminal ethnographic study of working-class British youth known as "the lads" shows how working-class students exhibit an implicit understanding that schooling is not structured to benefit their group (industrial factory workers) as a whole. The lads express their understanding that schooling is not designed to better their own conditions as members of the working class by embracing a working-class culture that valorizes manual labor and a counter-school culture. In doing so, they participate in the reproduction of their own class subordination. Willis suggests that these insights demonstrate that working-class youth are not passive dupes in the process of reproduction. Willis also suggests that the emphasis on the lads' being in control of their destiny points to possibilities for organized resistance. A number of subsequent studies of resistance in schooling in the U.S. context (Foley 1990; McLaren 1985; McLeod 1995; Solomon 1992; Valenzuela 1999) have expanded our understanding of schools as contested spaces.

Let's return for a moment to Christine's story. What sociological theories might be relevant to her experience of schooling? Christine was very likely assimilated into a common American culture to some extent through her schooling experiences. She also has attempted to gain credentials through the proprietary school in order to enter a particular profession. But perhaps a theory of reproduction is most relevant to Christine's experience. What do you think Christine's future will hold? How have school curriculum, interactions with school personnel, and her own choices impacted that future? One thing is for sure: One's educational path is often quite complicated and shaped by myriad influences. It is also important to recognize that, whatever we are left thinking after examining these theories, Christine's future is not written in stone. She is resourceful and intelligent. And recent sociological research offers us some reason to believe that Christine will one day find herself in a satisfying job in the medical profession.

We are now acquainted with four of the dominant perspectives that come out of sociology for understanding modern education. These ideas are not necessarily alternatives to one another. It is not necessary to choose between them because each can open our minds to different aspects of the educational system.

☑ **CONCEPT CHECKS**

1. Describe the assimilation versus acculturation perspectives on schooling.
2. Contrast the credentialism and social reproduction perspectives.
3. What is cultural capital?
4. According to Willis, how do working-class boys view the formal educational system?

Education, Inequality, and American Schools Today

In the previous section, we learned that the purpose and function of schooling have been viewed from a variety of perspectives. On the one hand, education has consistently been seen as a means of equalization. Access to universal education, it has been argued, could help reduce disparities of wealth and power. On the other hand, some theorists have argued that schools serve to perpetuate, or reproduce, inequalities. Are educational opportunities equal for everyone? Has education in fact proved to be a great equalizer? There is a vast amount of research that examines these questions. Below, we outline some of the important research and major theoretical concepts related to educational equality and differential outcomes (when one group consistently does better than another group in terms of educational achievement). The concepts offered here help to frame recent debates in education in the United States.

"Savage Inequalities"

Between 1988 and 1990, the journalist Jonathan Kozol studied schools in about thirty neighborhoods around the United States. There was no special logic to the way he chose the schools, except that he went where he happened to know teachers, principals, or ministers. What startled him most was the segregation within these schools and the inequalities among them. Kozol brought these terrible conditions to the attention of the American people in his book *Savage Inequalities* (1991), which became a best-seller.

In his passionate opening chapter, he first took readers to East St. Louis, Illinois, a city that is 98 percent black, had no regular trash collection, and had few jobs. Three quarters of its residents were living on welfare at the time. City residents were forced to use their backyards as garbage dumps, which attracted a plague of flies and rats during the hot summer months. One resident told Kozol about "rats as big as puppies" that lived in his mother's yard. City residents also contended with pollution fumes from two major chemical plants in the city. Another public health problem resulted from raw sewage, which regularly backed up into people's homes. East St. Louis also had some of the sickest children in the United States, with extremely high rates of infant death, asthma, and poor nutrition and extremely low rates of immunization. Only 55 percent of the children had been fully immunized for polio, diphtheria, measles, and whooping cough. Among the city's other social problems were crime, dilapidated housing, poor health care, and lack of education.

Kozol showed how the problems of the city often spilled over into the schools, in this case literally. Over the course of two weeks, raw sewage backed up into the school on three occasions, each time requiring the evacuation of students and the cancellation of classes. Kozol documented other problems as well, which he argued stemmed from inadequate and disparate funding. Teachers often had to hold classes without chalk or paper. One teacher commented on the school's poor conditions

The problem of schools falling into disrepair is a chronic one in poverty-stricken areas all over the country. Dilapidated schools like this one in the South Bronx lack funding for even the most basic necessities and, once they have fallen into a state of ruin, there is no money to undertake necessary repairs.

by saying, "Our problems are severe. I don't even know where to begin. I have no materials with the exception of a single textbook given to each child. If I bring in anything else—books or tapes or magazines—I bring it in myself. The high school has no VCRs. They are such a crucial tool. So many good things run on public television. I can't make use of anything I see unless I unhook my VCR and bring it into school. The AV equipment in the school is so old that we are pressured not to use it." Comments from students reflected the same concerns. "I don't go to physics class, because my lab has no equipment," said one student. Another added, "The typewriters in my typing class don't work." A third said, "I wanted to study Latin but we don't have Latin in this school." Only 55 percent of the students in this high school ultimately graduate, about one third of whom go on to college.

Kozol also wrote about the other end of the inequality spectrum, taking readers into a wealthy suburban school in Westchester County outside of New York City. This school had

96 computers for the 546 students. Most studied a foreign language (including Latin) for four or five years. Two thirds of the senior class were enrolled in an advanced placement (AP) class. Kozol visited an AP class to ask students about their perceptions of inequalities within the educational system. Students at this school were well aware of the economic advantages that they enjoyed at both home and school. In regard to their views about students less well off than themselves, the general consensus was that equal spending among schools was a worthy goal but it would probably make little difference because poor students lack motivation and would fail because of other problems. These students also realized that equalizing spending could have adverse affects on their school. As one student said, "If you equalize the money, someone's got to be shortchanged. I don't doubt that [poor] children are getting a bad deal. But do we want everyone to get a mediocre education?"

It is impossible to read these descriptions of life in East St. Louis and Westchester County without believing that the extremes of wealth and poverty in the public schools are being exposed. Indeed, Kozol's poignant journalistic account of educational inequality has become part of our nation's conventional wisdom on the subject of educational inequality. But many sociologists have argued that although Kozol's book is a moving portrait, it provides an inaccurate and incomplete view of educational inequality. Why would Kozol's research not be compelling? There are several reasons, including the unsystematic way that he chose the schools that he studied. But it is most important that sociologists have proposed a variety of theories and have identified myriad factors contributing to inequality and differential outcomes.

Coleman's Study of Between-School Effects in American Education

The study of between-school effects has been the focus of sociological research on the educational system for the past several decades. One of the classic investigations of educational inequality was undertaken in the United States in the 1960s. The Civil Rights Act of 1964 required the commissioner of education to prepare a report on educational inequalities resulting from differences of ethnic background, religion, and national origin. James Coleman, a sociologist, was appointed director of the research program. The outcome was a study based on one of the most extensive research projects ever carried out in sociology (Coleman et al. 1966).

Information was collected on more than half a million pupils who were given a range of achievement tests assessing verbal and nonverbal abilities, reading levels, and mathematical skills. Sixty thousand teachers also completed forms providing data for about four thousand schools. The report found that a large majority of children went to schools that effectively segregated black from white. Almost 80 percent of schools attended by white students contained only 10 percent or fewer African American students. White and Asian American students scored higher on achievement tests than did blacks and other ethnic minority students. Coleman had supposed his results would also show mainly African American schools to have worse facilities, larger classes, and more inferior buildings than schools that were predominantly white. But it was surprising that the results showed far fewer differences of this type than had been anticipated.

Coleman, therefore, concluded that the material resources provided in schools made little difference to educational performance; the decisive influence was the children's backgrounds. The report stated, "Inequalities imposed on children by their home, neighborhood, and peer environment are carried along to become the inequalities with which they confront adult life at the end of school" (Coleman et al. 1966). There was, however, some evidence that students from deprived backgrounds who formed close friendships with those from more favorable circumstances were likely to be more successful educationally.

Not long after Coleman's study, Christopher Jencks and co-workers (1972) produced an equally celebrated work that reviewed empirical evidence accumulated on education and inequality up to the end of the 1960s. Jencks reaffirmed two of the earlier study's conclusions: (1) that educational and occupational attainment are governed mainly by family background and nonschool factors, and (2) that on their own, educational reforms can produce only minor effects on existing inequalities. Jencks's work has been criticized on methodological grounds, but the study's overall conclusions remain persuasive. Subsequent research has tended to confirm them.

Inequality as an Issue of Access

TRACKING AND WITHIN-SCHOOL EFFECTS

The practice of **tracking**—dividing students into groups that receive different instruction on the basis of assumed similarities in ability or attainment—is common in American schools. In some schools, students are tracked only for certain subjects; in others, for all subjects. Sociologists have long believed that tracking is entirely negative in its effects. The conventional wisdom has been that tracking partly explains why schooling seems to have little effect on existing social inequalities, since being placed in a particular track labels a student as either able or otherwise. As we have seen in the case of labeling and deviance, once attached, such labels are hard to break away from. Children from more privileged backgrounds, in which academic work is encouraged, are likely to find themselves in the higher tracks early on—and by and large stay there (Figure 16.1).

Jeannie Oakes (1985) studied tracking in twenty-five junior and senior high schools, both large and small and in both urban and rural areas. But she concentrated on differences *within* schools rather than between them. She found that although several schools claimed they did not track students, virtually all of them had mechanisms for sorting students into groups that seemed to be alike in ability and achievement, to make teaching easier. In other words, they employed tracking but did not choose to use the term *tracking* itself. Even where tracking existed only in this informal fashion, she found strong labels developing—high ability, low achieving, slow, average, and so on. Individual students in these groups came to be defined by teachers, other students, and themselves in terms of such labels. A student in a high-achieving group was considered a high-achieving *person*—smart and quick. Pupils in a low-achieving group came to be seen as slow, below average—or, in more forthright terms, as dummies, sweathogs, or yahoos. What is the effect of tracking on students in the low group? A subsequent study by Oakes (1990) found that these students received a poorer education in terms of the quality of courses, teachers, and textbooks made available to them. Moreover, the negative effect of tracking affected mostly African American, Latino, and poor students.

The usual reason given for tracking is that bright children learn more quickly and effectively in a group of others who are equally able and that clever students are held back if placed in mixed groups. Surveying the evidence, Oakes attempted to show that these assumptions are wrong. The results of later research investigations are not wholly consistent, but a path-breaking study by sociologist Adam Gamoran and his colleagues (1995) concluded that Oakes was partially correct in her arguments. They agreed with Oakes's conclusions that tracking reinforces previously existing inequalities for average or poor students but countered her argument by asserting that tracking does have positive benefits for "advanced" students. The debate about the effects of tracking is sure to continue as scholars continue to analyze more data.

☑ CONCEPT CHECKS

1. According to Kozol, has education become an equalizer in American society? Why or why not?

FIGURE 16.1

Educational Attainment for Different Racial and Ethnic Groups, 2007

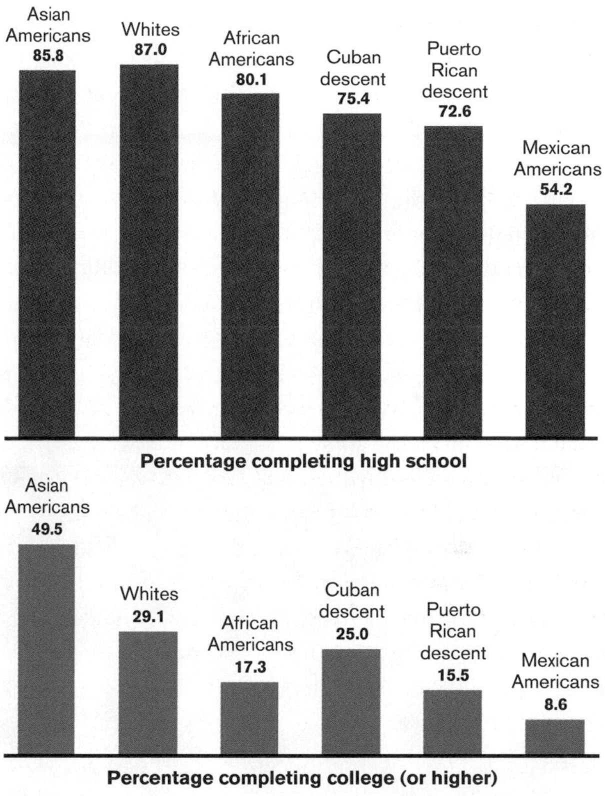

Percentage completing high school

Asian Americans 85.8
Whites 87.0
African Americans 80.1
Cuban descent 75.4
Puerto Rican descent 72.6
Mexican Americans 54.2

Percentage completing college (or higher)

Asian Americans 49.5
Whites 29.1
African Americans 17.3
Cuban descent 25.0
Puerto Rican descent 15.5
Mexican Americans 8.6

How does the relationship between those who completed high school and those who completed college vary among Asian Americans and whites? How does the relationship between those who completed high school and those who completed college vary among African Americans and people of Cuban descent?

SOURCE: U.S. Bureau of the Census 2008f.

2. How do Coleman's findings differ from the results of Kozol's research? Whose theory, in your opinion, can better explain the racial gap in educational achievement?

3. What effect does tracking have on academic achievement?

The Internationalization of Education

How many foreign students are enrolled in your sociology course? How many foreign students are there at your university? In 1943, approximately 8,000 foreign students were enrolled in American colleges and universities. By 2006, this number had skyrocketed to more than 564,766 (Institute of International Education [IIE] 2007a). Early IIE reports indicate that numbers for 2007 were higher at 582,984.Although the American university system as a whole grew considerably during this period, such that 564,766 students represented only 3.9 percent of total 2006 student enrollment, it is

clear that foreign students are flocking to the United States in record numbers. Most foreign students today come from Asia—China, Japan, Taiwan, India, and South Korea all send sizeable contingents of students abroad. The United States takes in more foreign students than any other country, and there are six times as many foreign students in the United States as there are American students overseas. What do foreign students in the United States study? At the undergraduate level, more than 18 percent focus on business and management, 16 percent study engineering, and 9 percent concentrate on physical and life sciences IIE 2006). More than 20 percent of foreign graduate students study engineering, and of those receiving a doctorate in engineering, 60 percent were foreign students (Lambert 1995; National Center for Education Statistics 2005).

Some scholars regard the exchange of international students as a vital component of globalization. Foreign students, in addition to serving as global "carriers" of specialized technical and scientific knowledge, play an important cultural role in the globalizing process. Cross-national understandings are enhanced, and xenophobic and isolationist attitudes are minimized as native students in host countries develop social ties to their foreign classmates and as foreign students return to their countries of origin with an appreciation for the cultural mores of the nation in which they have studied.

Academic Achievement and Differential Outcomes

Historically, inequality in education has produced an **achievement gap** in educational outcomes between different groups of students. What this means is that certain groups, such as African Americans and other minorities and girls, have achieved lower scores on standardized tests and other measures of academic success (such as graduation and entrance into college)

in comparison to their white, male counterparts. Sociologists have sought to explain the existence of achievement gaps in a variety of ways.

Intelligence

Suppose differences in educational attainment, and in subsequent occupations and incomes, directly reflected differential intelligence. In such circumstances, it might be argued, there is in fact equality of opportunity in the school system, for people find a level equivalent to their innate potential.

Yet there is considerable debate in the United States about what is sometimes called the "internationalization of education." On most college and university campuses, it is not hard to find disgruntled students who complain that the influx of foreign students deprives deserving Americans of educational opportunities—especially given the increasingly competitive nature of the U.S. higher education system,. Moreover, although more than two thirds of foreign students receive nothing in the way of scholarships, some top-notch foreign students *are* given financial inducements to attend American schools. The outcry against this practice has been loudest at public universities, which receive support from tax revenues. Critics charge that U.S. taxpayers should not shoulder the financial burden for educating foreign students whose families have not paid U.S. taxes and who are likely to return home after earning their degrees.

Supporters of international education find such arguments unconvincing. Some Americans may lose out to foreign students in the competition for slots at prestigious universities, but this is a small price to pay for the economic, political, and cultural benefits the United States receives from having educated millions of foreign business executives, policy makers, scientists, and professionals over the years—many of whom became sympathetically disposed to the United States as a result of their experiences here. And although some foreign students receive scholarships from American universities, most are supported by their parents. In fact, it is estimated that foreign students pump hundreds of millions of dollars each year into the U.S. economy—over $14.5 billion in 2007 (IIE 2007a). Rather than curtail the number of foreign students admitted to American universities, supporters of international education suggest that even more should be done to encourage the exchange of students. On the one hand, greater effort should be made to recruit foreign students, to help them select the university and program that will best meet their needs, and to provide them with a positive social and educational experience while they are in the United States. On the other hand, more Americans should be encouraged to study abroad. American students are notorious for having poor or no foreign-language skills and for knowing little about global geography, much less about the cultures of other nations. This cultural and linguistic ignorance puts the United States at a disadvantage relative to other countries as the world becomes increasingly globalized; encouraging Americans to study overseas may be the best way to inculcate a global worldview.

Should there be a greater focus on international education in American colleges and universities? Should the international exchange of students be expanded? These are among the issues that educational institutions are forced to confront in the context of globalization. Still, more and more U.S. students are studying abroad—223,534 in 2006–2007, an 8.5 percent increase over the year before (IIE 2007b).

WHAT IS INTELLIGENCE?

For years, psychologists, geneticists, statisticians, and others have debated whether there exists a single human capability that can be called **intelligence** and, if so, whether it rests on innately determined differences. Intelligence is difficult to define because, as the term is usually employed, it covers qualities that may be unrelated to one another. We might suppose, for example, that the "purest" form of intelligence is the ability to solve abstract mathematical puzzles. However, people who are very good at such puzzles sometimes show low capabilities in other areas, such as history or art. Because the concept has proved so resistant to accepted definition, some psychologists have proposed (and many educators have by default accepted) that intelligence should simply be regarded as "what **IQ (intelligence quotient)** tests measure." Most IQ tests consist of a mixture of conceptual and computational problems. The tests are constructed so that the average score is 100 points: Anyone scoring below is thus labeled "below-average intelligence," and anyone scoring above is "above-average intelligence." In spite of the fundamental difficulty in measuring intelligence, IQ tests are widely used in research studies, as well as in schools and businesses.

IQ AND GENETIC FACTORS: THE SOCIOLOGICAL DEBATE

Scores on IQ tests do in fact correlate highly with academic performance (which is not surprising, because IQ tests were originally developed to predict success at school). They therefore also correlate closely with social, economic, and ethnic differences, because these are associated with variations in levels of educational attainment. White students score better, on average, than African Americans or members of other disadvantaged minorities. An article published by Arthur Jensen in 1967 caused a furor by attributing IQ differences between blacks and whites in part to genetic variations (see also Jensen 1979).

More recently, the psychologist Richard J. Herrnstein and the sociologist Charles Murray have reopened the debate about IQ and education in a controversial way. They argue in their book *The Bell Curve* (1994) that the accumulated evidence linking IQ to genetic inheritance has now become overwhelming. The significant differences in intelligence among various racial and ethnic groups, they say, must in part be explained in terms of heredity. According to Herrnstein and Murray, the available evidence strongly indicates that some ethnic groups on average have higher IQs than other groups. Asian Americans, particularly Japanese Americans and Chinese Americans, on average possess higher IQs than whites, although the difference is not large. The average IQs of Asians and whites, however, are substantially higher than those of blacks. Summarizing the findings of 156 studies, Herrnstein and Murray find an average difference of 16 IQ points between these two racial groups. The authors argue that such differences in inherited intelligence contribute in an important way to social divisions in American society. The smarter an individual is, the greater the chance that he or she will rise in the social scale. Those at the top are there partly because they are smarter than the rest of the population—from which it follows that those at the bottom remain there because, on average, they are not as smart.

Herrnstein and Murray's claim created a great deal of controversy and raised the ire and indignation of countless liberals, social scientists, and members of the African American community. Although Herrnstein and Murray's claims may be seen as racist and reprehensible, is this sufficient reason to attack their work? Or are their conclusions based on faulty social research? The answer to both questions is a resounding yes. A team of sociologists at the University of California at Berkeley have reanalyzed much of the data that Herrnstein and Murray based their conclusions on and came up with quite different findings.

In the original analysis, Herrnstein and Murray analyzed data from the National Longitudinal Study of Youth (NLSY), a survey of more than ten thousand young Americans who were interviewed multiple times over more than a decade. As part of this study, subjects were given the Armed Forces Qualifying Test (AFQT), a short test that assesses IQ. Herrnstein and Murray then conducted statistical analyses, which used the AFQT score to predict a variety of outcomes. They concluded that having a high IQ was the best predictor of later economic success and that low IQ was the best predictor of poverty later in life.

The Berkeley sociologists, in their 1996 book *Inequality by Design* (Fischer et al. 1996), countered that the AFQT does not necessarily measure intelligence, but only how much a person has learned in school. Moreover, they found that intelligence is only one factor among several that predict how well people do in life. Social factors including education, gender, community conditions, marital status, current economic conditions, and—perhaps most important—parents' socioeconomic status better predict one's occupational and economic success. In the original analysis, Herrnstein and Murray measured parents' socioeconomic status by taking an average of mother's education, father's education, father's occupation, and family income.

The Berkeley sociologists recognized that each of these four factors matters differently in predicting a child's occupational outcomes and thus weighted the four components differently. Their analysis showed that the effects of socioeconomic background on a young adult's risk of later poverty were substantially greater than Herrnstein and Murray had originally found. The Berkeley sociologists also recognized that IQ is closely associated with one's level of education. They reanalyzed the NLSY data, taking into consideration the individuals' level of education, and found that Herrnstein and Murray drastically overestimated the effects of IQ on a person's later achievements.

The relationship between race and intelligence is also best explained by social rather than biological causes, according to the Berkeley sociologists. All societies have oppressed ethnic groups. Low status, often coupled with discrimination and mistreatment, leads to socioeconomic deprivation, group segregation, and a stigma of inferiority. The combination of these forces often prevents racial minorities from obtaining education, and consequently, their scores on standardized intelligence tests are lower.

The average lower IQ score of African Americans in the United States is remarkably similar to that of deprived ethnic minorities in other countries—such as the "untouchables" in India (who are at the very bottom of the caste system), the Maori in New Zealand, and the *burakumin* of Japan. Children in these groups score an average of 10 to 15 IQ points below children belonging to the ethnic majority. The burakumin—descendants of people who in the eighteenth century, as a result of local wars, were dispossessed from their land and became outcasts and vagrants—are a particularly interesting example. They are not in any way physically distinct from other Japanese, although they have suffered from prejudice and discrimination for centuries. In this case, the difference in average IQ results cannot derive from genetic variations because there are no genetic differences between them and the majority population; yet the IQ difference is as thoroughly fixed as that between blacks and whites. Burakumin children in America, where they are treated like other Japanese, do as well on IQ tests as other Japanese.

Such observations strongly suggest that the IQ variations between African Americans and whites in the United States result from social and cultural differences. This conclusion receives further support from a comparative study of fourteen nations (including the United States) showing that average IQ scores have risen substantially over the past half century for the population as a whole (Coleman 1987). IQ tests are regularly updated. When old and new versions of the tests are given to the same group of people, they score significantly higher on the old tests. Present-day children taking IQ tests from the 1930s outscored 1930s groups by an average of 15 points—just the kind of average difference that currently separates blacks and whites. Children today are not innately superior in intelligence to their parents or grandparents; the shift presumably derives from increasing prosperity and social advantages. The average social and economic gap between whites and African Americans is at least as great as that between the different generations and is sufficient to explain the variation in IQ scores. Although there may be genetic variations between individuals that influence scores on IQ tests, these have no overall connection to racial differences.

Cultural and Social-Psychological Explanations

Current scholarship on achievement in education, by and large, has rejected genetic explanations for the differential outcomes that exist between students from minority groups and white (male) students. Many researchers in the field of sociology examine possible cultural and social-psychological explanations for the achievement gap that exists between white, male students and minority and female students.

Race and the "Acting White" Thesis

In attempting to explain the racial achievement gap in education, anthropologists John Ogbu and Signithia Fordham (1986) proposed the **"acting white" thesis.** Based on ethnographic research of the educational experiences of black students, Ogbu and Fordham concluded that the achievement gap can be partially explained through black students' reluctance to embrace school norms, which the black students associate with white culture. In subsequent years, however, the "acting white thesis" has been challenged by a number of researchers. For example, Roslyn Mickelson's research (1990) on the achievement attitudes of African American students revealed that students held both **abstract and concrete attitudes** toward schooling. Their abstract attitudes were consistent with mainstream attitudes that place a high value on education and the attainment of academic credentials for future success. However, these students also held concrete antiachievement attitudes that were based on their experiences in school and their perception that there were few options for them in terms of entrance into higher education or lucrative careers even if they were to obtain a high school diploma.

More recently, sociologist Prudence Carter's study (2005) of the experiences of high school students in New York City revealed that black and Latino students overwhelmingly believe in the importance of school and the need for educational credentials. Carter notes that black and Latino students' academic and social experiences are heterogeneous, and the most successful students are not necessarily the ones who assimilate to white, mainstream speech patterns, styles, and tastes. Instead, students whom she calls **cultural navigators**—those who draw from resources from their home cultures and the mainstream culture—tend to be highly successful in school. Ultimately, Carter argues that schools must promote intercultural communication and understanding with communities, parents, and students to mitigate unequal academic outcomes.

Gender and Achievement

For many years, girls on average did better than boys in terms of school results until they reached the middle years of secondary education. They then fell behind: boys did better than girls, particularly in math and science. However, in recent years the trend has dramatically turned around. That is, today's **gender gap** places girls ahead of boys. Sociologists have attempted to explain the reversal in the gender gap in a variety of ways. Some have argued that girls are doing better in schools today because of changes in the economy that have created more opportunities for women in the new service economy while factory jobs, traditionally a male terrain, have decreased in numbers because of new technologies and the relocation of manufacturing industries to developing countries. Other studies focus on the achievements made within the women's movement and its effect on women's self-esteem and expectations. Another important impact of the women's movement is that

What If We Ended Social Promotion?

[In 1998], I chaired a study of appropriate uses of testing for the National Research Council. The NRC panel was a diverse group of fifteen scholars from all over the country. We wrote our report, "High Stakes: Testing for Tracking, Promotion and Graduation," in response to a congressional mandate. The study was prompted by the Clinton administration's proposal, in 1997, for voluntary national tests of fourth grade reading and eighth grade math. The panel took no position about the value of voluntary national testing for its stated purposes—to tell American students, parents, and teachers how well they are doing relative to high national standards—but we recommended strongly against such tests' use for any high-stakes purpose. The report, published [in 1999], has a lot of useful information about proper test use, and I commend it to readers. One of the strongest recommendations is that "accountability for educational outcomes should be a shared responsibility of states, school districts, public officials, educators, parents, and students. High standards cannot be established and maintained merely by imposing them on students."

Early in its work, the NRC panel decided to consider whether good tests could serve bad purposes. Thus, we evaluated the consequences of high-stakes educational decisions that may be based, at least in part, on test scores. In particular, we found—as American schools presently operate—that decisions to place students in typical lower-level tracks and decisions to hold students back to repeat the same grade are not educationally sound. Those decisions hurt students, and good tests will not improve them. This is not to say that all forms of tracking are bad for students, or that all grade retention is necessarily bad for students. Our findings were based on the actual and typical, not the ideal. But research evidence based on actual experience should inform new policies.

Robert M. Hauser

***

We should know that a new policy works before we try it out on a large scale. In its plan to end social promotion, the administration appears to have mixed a number of fine and credible proposals for educational reform with an enforcement provision—flunking kids by the carload lot—about which the great mass of evidence is strongly negative. And this policy [would] hurt poor and minority children most of all.

***

Students who have been held back typically do not catch up; in fact, low-performing students learn more if they are promoted—even without remedial help—than if they are held

teachers have become more aware of gender discrimination in the classroom and have taken steps to avoid gender stereotyping. Many teachers now incorporate learning materials that are free of gender bias, and they encourage girls to explore traditionally "male" subjects.

Some sociologists today are wary of all the attention directed at underachieving boys. They contend that, although girls have forged ahead, they are still less likely than boys to choose subjects in school leading to careers in technology, science, and engineering. Boys pull away from girls by about age eleven in science and continue to outperform girls through college. And women continue to be disadvantaged in the job market despite the fact that they are entering college at higher rates than young men.

back. One reason for this is that the elementary and secondary school curriculum does not change radically from one grade to the next; there is a lot of review and overlap. Another is that it is simply boring to repeat exactly the same material.

Students who have been held back are much more likely to drop out before completing high school. That effect often occurs many years after a student is held back in grade and thus is invisible—without careful longitudinal study—to those who make the retention decision. The teachers and administrators who make decisions to hold children back do not have to live with the long-term consequences of their decisions.

***

There is one more critical point on which the National Research Council report provides strong evidence: We do not practice social promotion in the United States now, and we have not practiced it for many years. Our statistics are not very good; neither the federal government nor most states collect the right data, but we do know a few things.

Age at entry to first grade has increased since 1970. At that time, almost all six-year-olds were in the first grade (about 4 percent of six-year-old boys and 8 percent of six-year-old girls were enrolled below the first grade). In 1996, 18 percent of six-year-olds were enrolled below the first grade. Part of that change is due to holding children back in kindergarten.

Many students are held back during elementary and secondary school. Nationally, among children who entered school in the late 1980s, 21 percent were enrolled below the usual grade at ages six to eight; 28 percent were below the usual grade at ages nine to eleven; 31 percent at ages twelve to fourteen; and this rose to 36 percent at ages fifteen to seventeen. Not counting kindergarten and the later grades of high school, this means that at least 15 percent of children—and probably 20 percent—have been held back at some time in their childhood.

Worse yet, minorities and poor children are the most likely to be held back. Black, Hispanic, and white children enter first grade at just about the same ages, but between entry and adolescence, about 10 percent of white girls fall behind in grade, while 25 percent to 30 percent of minority children fall behind.

By ages fifteen to seventeen, 45 percent to 50 percent of black and Hispanic youths are below the expected grade levels for their ages.

Holding students back—flunking them—has a much greater impact on minority and poor youths than on majority, middle-class children. It decreases educational opportunity, and it makes opportunities less equal among groups. For thirty-five years, American education has aimed to reduce social inequality. While much remains to be done, we have made major gains—narrowing differences in test scores in the 1970s and 1980s and reducing the dropout difference between majority and minority children. If we start holding back ever larger numbers of children, we are likely to reverse the progress of the past four decades.

SOURCE: Robert M. Hauser, "What If We Ended Social Promotion?" *Education Week,* April 7, 1999.

ROBERT M. HAUSER is the Vilas research professor of sociology in the Center for Demography at the University of Wisconsin–Madison. He is the editor, with Jay P. Heubert, of the National Research Council's report "High Stakes: Testing for Tracking, Promotion, and Graduation" (National Academy Press 1999).

Stereotype Threat

Differential outcomes between white students and minority students and between girls and boys have also been explained in social psychological terms. Claude Steele's influential work (1995, 2004) on **stereotype threat** suggests that when African American students (or female students) believe they are being judged not as individuals but as members of a negatively stereotyped social group, they will do worse on tests.

School Discipline

We have pointed out that schooling is often viewed as a process of socialization. As such, academic achievement has not been the only interest of sociologists of education. In recent years, for example, there has been a growing scholarly interest in school discipline and its relationship to issues of equality. Some sociologists have noted that there has been a shift in school discipline toward more punitive policies that mirror current trends in our nation's criminal justice system. One of the major changes in school discipline came in 1994 when the Gun-Free School Act was first passed. This act and subsequent federal mandates established a "zero tolerance" policy for weapons and drugs in schools. Zero tolerance was initially meant to address school violence by mandating suspension or expulsion for possession of drugs or weapons in school. However, as it was implemented nationwide, it expanded to include a broad range of misbehavior. Critics of the policy argue that it has led to unnecessary police intervention in schools and has increased racial bias. Activists and educators opposed to zero tolerance have coined the term *school-to-prison-pipeline* as a way of emphasizing the negative impact of the policies.

Disciplinary practices in schools, it has been argued, also appear to be influenced by media representations and negative images of black and Latino youth. Ann Arnett Ferguson's ethnographic study of middle school children (2000), for example, shows how institutional discourses (such as the use of prison metaphors), the subjective views of teachers, and the treatment black boys receive in school influence the ways in which black boys see themselves, that is, as criminally oriented.

Other researchers have noted that punitive school discipline policies appear to be, in part, a response to low performance in inner-city schools populated by low-income, minority students. Based on ethnographic research in an urban school, Nolan and Anyon (2004) theorize that, within our current economy, criminalizing school discipline policies are a means to manage an economically and educationally marginalized group. They also contend that when students embrace an oppositional culture, they may no longer be participating in the reproduction of their status as manual laborers, as Willis argued. Instead, as misbehavior comes to be managed by the police in schools, students may be participating in the reproduction of themselves as "criminalized subjects," or as individuals who will spend a lifetime entangled in one way or another (incarceration, parole, probation) with the criminal justice system.

Educational Reform in the United States

Research done by sociologists has played a big role in reforming the educational system. The object of James Coleman's research, commissioned as part of the 1964 Civil Rights Act, was not solely academic; it was undertaken to influence policy. And influence policy it certainly did. On the basis of the act,

In 1970 a U.S. judge in North Carolina ordered that black students be bused to white schools and that white students be bused to black schools. It was hoped that this crosstown school busing would end the de facto segregation of public schools caused by white students living in predominantly white neighborhoods and black students living in predominantly black neighborhoods.

it was decided in the courts that segregated schools violated the rights of minority pupils. But rather than attacking the origins of educational inequalities directly, as Christopher Jencks's later work suggested was necessary, the courts decided that the schools in each district should achieve a similar racial balance. Thus began the practice of busing students to other schools.

Busing provoked a great deal of opposition, particularly from parents and children in white areas, and led to episodes of violence at the gates of schools where the children were bused in from other neighborhoods. White children paraded with placards reading: "We don't want them!" Busing in fact met with a good deal of success, reducing levels of school segregation quite steeply, particularly in the South. But busing has also produced a number of unintended consequences. Some white parents reacted to busing by either putting their children into private schools or moving to mainly white suburbs where busing wasn't practiced. As a result, in the cities, some schools are virtually as segregated as the old schools were in the past. Busing, however, was only one factor prompting the white flight to the suburbs. Whites also left as a reaction to urban decay: to escape city crowding, housing problems, and rising rates of crime.

While busing is less prominent today as an issue, another problem regarding the American educational system has become an important focus of research: functional illiteracy. Most of the population can read and write at a very basic level, but one in every five adults is functionally illiterate—when they leave school, they can't read or write at the fourth-grade level (U.S. Department of Education 1993). Of course, the United States is a country of immigrants, who when they arrive may not be able to read and write and who may also have trouble with English. But this doesn't explain why America lags behind most other industrial countries in terms of its level of functional illiteracy, because many people affected are not recent immigrants at all.

What is to be done? Some educationists have argued that the most important change that needs to be made is to improve the quality of teaching, either by increasing teachers' pay or by introducing performance-related pay scales, with higher salaries going to the teachers who are most effective in the classroom. Others have proposed giving schools more control over their budgets (a reform that has been carried out in Britain). The idea is that more responsibility for and control over budgeting decisions will create a greater drive to improve the school. Further proposals include the refunding of federal programs such as Head Start to ensure healthy early child development and thus save millions of dollars in later costs. Another proposal that has gained numerous supporters in recent years is that public education should be privatized.

Education Policy Today

The most significant piece of federal legislation influencing education today is the 2001 No Child Left Behind (NCLB) Act enacted by President George W. Bush. NCLB reauthorized the 1965 Elementary and Secondary Education Act but also expands it by implementing a host of policies meant to improve academic outcomes for all children and close the achievement gap. Indeed, NCLB is the most expansive and comprehensive piece of legislation passed since 1965 addressing virtually every aspect of education—including, for example, testing, school choice, teacher quality, the education of English-language learners, military recruitment in schools, and school discipline. At the top of its agenda is instituting standardized testing as a means of measuring students' academic performance. The act also provides a strong push for school choice; that is, in the spirit of competition, parents are to be given choices as to where they send their children to school. Low-performing schools, at risk of losing students, thus jeopardize their funding and become subject to being closed. Another significant implication of NCLB is that for the first time since 1968, states are not required to offer non–English-speaking students bilingual

education. Instead, the act emphasizes learning English over using students' native language to support learning objectives and favors English-only program models. NCLB also provides support for a "zero tolerance" approach to school discipline that was first mandated in the 1994 Gun-Free School Act.

PRIVATIZATION

Widespread concern about the crisis in education has opened the door for *public–private partnerships* aimed at injecting private-sector know-how into failing public schools. In 1994, then President Bill Clinton signed into law the Goals 2000: Educate America Act, which authorized states to use federal funds for experiments with school privatization. Local school districts can choose to contract out specific educational services—or the entire school administration—to private companies without losing federal funding. In the past decade, a number of U.S. school districts—including large urban systems such as those in Hartford, Baltimore, and Minneapolis—have invited for-profit educational companies to run their school systems.

Supporters of school privatization argue that state and federal education authorities have shown that they are unable to improve the nation's schools. The educational system, they argue, is wasteful and bureaucratic; it spends a disproportionate amount of its funding on noninstructional administrative costs. Because of their top-heavy nature, it is nearly impossible for school systems to be flexible and innovative. Incompetent teachers are difficult to remove because of the strength of teacher unions.

What backers of school privatization claim can solve these problems is a strong dose of private-sector ideology: competition, experimentation, and incentive. For-profit companies can run school systems more efficiently and produce better outcomes by applying private-sector logic. Good teachers would be attracted to teaching—and retained—by performance-based pay schemes, while underperforming teachers could be removed more easily. Competition within and between schools would lead to higher levels of innovation; privatized schools would have more liberty to institutionalize the results of successful experiments.

One of the leading players in the U.S. market for privatized education is the Edison Project, an educational company that manages a chain of eighty public schools in sixteen different states. The verdict on whether the Edison Project is improving educational outcomes in its schools is mixed, and the company itself has been heavily criticized on a number of fronts, including for poor financial management. Critics have been quick to point out that the Edison Project's vision for schools is little more than a slick repackaging of well-known practices from public education, such as cooperative learning and pupil-centered teaching (Molnar 1996). The company requires that all students in Edison schools have a computer at home—and

"U.S. Teens Trail Peers around World on Math-Science Test"

News reports regularly tell American teens and young adults that they're lagging behind their peers in Asia and Europe when it comes to math and science. A recent *Wall Street Journal* headline gave the gloomy assessment: "Economic Time Bomb: U.S. Teens Are among the Worst at Math" (Kronholz 2004). But a glimpse behind the headlines tells us that things are not so simple. While one recent study shows that American students fared miserably on a standardized math and science exam (OECD 2007), another study (Lowell and Salzman 2007) shows that American students have made tremendous strides in math and science over the past two decades—and the job market may not be able to employ this large pool of qualified mathematicians and scientists. How do we make sense of these competing findings? An in-depth look at the two studies gives us an answer.

An analysis of data from the 2006 Program for International Student Assessment (PISA) showed that the average science score of fifteen-year-olds in the United States lagged behind the scores of students in sixteen of thirty countries in the Organisation for Economic Cooperation and Development (OECD), a group that represents the world's richest nations. American students fared even worse in science, ranking twenty-third out of the thirty countries. The PISA test measures high school students' perfor-

What are the implications of a test-score gap between students from the United States and other countries?

mance on math and science questions. Rather than testing specific knowledge, it assesses "real life" and applied knowledge. Most of the American teenagers who take the exam are in ninth and tenth grade. About 400,000 students worldwide, including 5,600 in the United States, completed the exam in 2006. Of the thirty nations ranked, students in Finland ranked first and Mexico ranked thirtieth on both math and science scores. Canada, Japan, and Korea were among the many nations that outperformed the United States.

These headlines have raised alarm among policy makers, education specialists, and employers. "How are our children going to be able to compete with the children of the world? The answer is not well," posed Roy Romer, chair of Strong American Schools, a nonpartisan group aiming to make education a key issue in the 2008 presidential election (Glod 2007). The PISA test results suggest that too few U.S. students are prepared to become engineers, physicians, and scientists—leaving some to worry that such prestigious jobs will be filled largely by foreigners in coming years.

Around the same time that the PISA findings shed negative light on the U.S. educational system, the Urban Institute issued a study saying that American students were doing just fine. Countering the "science education myth" (Wadhwa

assists those families that cannot afford them—but it is less clear how this enthusiasm for technology is linked into the curriculum in a meaningful way.

Opponents of school privatization argue that companies such as the Edison Project are less serious about reforming education and reducing inequalities than about promoting education reform as a lucrative market for wealthy investors.

Additionally, they argue that privatization schemes divert resources from traditional public schools still serving the majority of America's children and create new ways of tracking students along class and racial lines. This occurs when educated middle-class parents, based on their cultural and social capital and resources, are better able than working-class and poor parents to take advantage of the best public–private

2007), study authors Harold Salzman of the Urban Institute and B. Lindsay Lowell of Georgetown University found that "math, science and reading test scores at the primary and secondary level have increased steadily" over the past twenty-five years, and U.S. students are now close to the top of the international rankings." Further, the report cautioned that the U.S. education system was producing more qualified science and engineering graduates than could find jobs.

What accounts for these two very different portrayals of science and math education? Salzman and Lowell believe that social scientists have incorrectly interpreted the findings from the PISA and other international studies. For example, they noted that different countries administer the test to different populations—some give the test to a random sample of all fifteen-year-olds, while others give the exam only to the most elite young people, thus biasing results. For example, Germany excludes special needs students from its sample. Moreover, the PISA test is given to students on the basis of age rather than school grade; fifteen-year-olds may have had different levels of training thus far, across the different national settings. It is most important, though, that the PISA tests *general skills,* rather than *specific knowledge,* so test scores do not necessarily reflect national education quality, but rather the general resources (or disadvantages) that children have for the first fifteen years of life.

The policy implications of the "science test gap" or "science education myth" vary widely based on which results policy makers find to be more persuasive. While the PISA data might suggest that math and science education in the United States needs to be improved, the Urban Institute study suggests that the United States is training young scientists well—so well, in fact, that there may not be jobs for all these newly minted scientists and mathematicians. Harvard Law School fellow Vivek Wadhwa observes that between 1985 and 2000, about 435,000 Americans earned degrees in science and education each year. By contrast, just 150,000 new jobs were added to the science and engineering workforce during that same time period.

Wadhwa concluded that "a well-educated workforce . . . will help the U.S. keep its global edge. But emphasizing math and science education over humanities and social sciences may not be the best prescription. . . . We need our children to receive a balanced and broad education" (Wadhwa 2007). The OECD, which administers the PISA exam, concurs with Wadhwa's assessment and concludes that math and science education is not necessarily the fix-all. Rather, the OECD notes that "PISA is not an assessment of what young people learned during their previous year at school, or even during their secondary school years. It is an indicator of the learning development that has occurred since birth. . . . For some countries, this may mean taking measures to safeguard the health development of young children . . . for others, it may mean socioeconomic reforms that enable families to provide better care for their children" (2003: 195).

Questions

- What are the key findings of the OECD study?
- What are the key findings of the Urban Institute study?
- What are three possible explanations for the conflicting findings?
- Which study do you find more persuasive? What kind of policies would you recommend, based on your assessment of the two studies?

FOR FURTHER EXPLORATION

Glod, Maria. 2007. "U.S. Teens Trail Peers around World on Math-Science Test." *Washington Post* (December 5, 2007), A07. www.washingtonpost.com/wp-dyn/content/article/2007/12/04/AR2007120400730.html?hpid=sec-education (accessed January 15, 2008).

Kronholz, June. 2004. "Economic Time Bomb: U.S. Teens Are among the Worst at Math." *Wall Street Journal* (December 7, 2004), B1. www.mathnasium.com/press/wsj1204.pdf (accessed January 15, 2008).

Lowell, B. Lindsay, and Harold Salzman. 2007. *In the Eye of the Storm: Assessing the Evidence on Science and Engineering Education, Quality, and Workforce Demand.* Washington, D.C.: The Urban Institute. www.urban.org/UploadedPDF/411562_Salzman_Science.pdf (accessed January 15, 2008).

OECD. 2003. PISA 2003 Technical Report. Geneva: OECD.

OECD. 2007. *Programme for International Student Association (PISA) 2006: Science Competencies for Tomorrow's World.* Geneva: OECD. www.pisa.oecd.org/dataoecd/30/17/39703267.pdf (accessed January 15, 2008).

school partnerships. Finally, as public–private school partnerships expand, their success has been called into question. For example, in 2006, the Federal Education Department conducted a study that suggests children in charter schools—one of the most common types of private–public partnerships—have performed lower on standardized tests than their traditional public school counterparts.

The crisis in American schools won't be solved in the short term, and it won't be solved by educational reforms alone, no matter how thoroughgoing. The lesson of sociological research is that inequalities and barriers in educational opportunity reflect wider social divisions and tensions. While the United States remains wracked by racial tensions and the polarization between decaying cities and affluent suburbs persists, the

Demonstrators protest the privatization of public schools by Edison Schools, Inc.

A 2006 study by the U.S. Department of Education found that schools identified for improvement were disproportionately urban, high poverty schools, and that "school poverty and district size better predicted existing improvement status than the improvement strategies undertaken by the schools" (p.xii). Further, schools have narrowed their course offerings to focus much more heavily on tested subject areas while cutting time in science, social studies, music, art, and physical education (CEP 2007).

☑ CONCEPT CHECKS

1. How do schools perpetuate inequalities across generations?
2. Explain the relationship between race and intelligence. Do you find the evidence compelling?
3. What are three possible explanations for the racial gap in educational performance?
4. Name two factors that have contributed to the closing and reversal of the traditional "gender gap" in education.
5. What are the goals of the No Child Left Behind Policy? What are criticisms of this policy?

crisis in the school system is likely to prove difficult to turn around. Anyon's (2006) analysis of how political and economic forces influence schooling helps to clarify these challenges. She argues that not until educational reform is linked to economic reform, such as job creation and training programs and corporate tax reform, will schools improve.

Education and Politics

Education has long been a political battleground. In the 1960s, some politicians, educators, and community activists pushed for greater equality and universal access to education through such initiatives as busing programs to mitigate racial segregation, bilingual education programs, multicultural education, open admissions to college, the establishment of ethnic studies programs on campuses, and more equitable funding schemes. Such initiatives were seen as supporting civil rights and equality. Today's proponents of NCLB similarly purport that its provisions are meant to provide quality education for all children and close the achievement gap. But NCLB has sparked heated debates within the educational arena and the political arena.

Some of the major critiques of NCLB are that it is a punitive model of school reform (i.e., teachers and principals at under-performing schools risk job loss), that achievement gaps have not changed, and that the policy neglects the important fact that the broader socioeconomic context affects school functioning.

Education and Literacy in the Developing World

Literacy is the "baseline" of education. Without it, schooling cannot proceed. We take it for granted in the West that the majority of people are *literate,* but as has been mentioned, this is only a recent development in Western history, and in previous times no more than a tiny proportion of the population had any literacy skills.

Today, over 23 percent of the population of developing countries is still illiterate (Global Map 16.1). The Indian government has estimated the number of illiterate people in that country alone to be over 268 million (39 percent of the population), a number that almost equals the total population of the United States. The last census of India shows that only 64.8 percent of the population is literate with regional and gender based differences. Whereas 75.3 percent of men are literate, only 53.7 percent of women are. Urban literacy rates are much higher at almost 80 percent, whereas rural rates are lower at roughly 59 percent (Census of India 2007a). Even if the provision of primary education increased to match the level of population growth, illiteracy would not be markedly reduced for years, because a high proportion of those who cannot read or write are adults. The absolute number of illiterate people is actually rising (Coombs 1985). According to the United Nations Educational, Scientific, and Cultural Organization (UNESCO 2003) estimates, the total grew from 569 million in 1970 to 625 million in 1980 to 826 million in 2003. The absolute number of illiterate people seems to have peaked in the 1990s. According to UNESCO (2006) estimates, the total grew from 569 million in 1970 to 625 million in 1980 to 871 million in 1990 and fell to 771 million in 2004. The number of illiterate people has decreased by 100 million since 1990. In large part, that reduction in global illiteracy figures was due to efforts made in China, where there are 94 million fewer illiterate people today than in 1990. Currently UNESCO estimates that one in five adults is illiterate, of which two thirds are women.

Although countries have instituted literacy programs, these have made only a small contribution to a problem of large-scale dimensions. Television, radio, and the other electronic media can be used, where they are available, to skip the stage of learning literacy skills and convey educational programs directly to adults. But educational programs are usually less popular than commercialized entertainment.

During the period of colonialism, colonial governments regarded education with some trepidation. Until the twentieth century, most believed indigenous populations to be too primitive to be worth educating. Later, education was seen as a way of making local elites responsive to European interests and ways of life. But to some extent, the result was to foment discontent and rebellion, because the majority of those who led anticolonial and nationalist movements were from educated elites who had attended schools or colleges in Europe. They were able to compare firsthand the democratic institutions of the European countries with the absence of democracy in their lands of origin.

The education that the colonizers introduced usually pertained to Europe, not the colonial areas themselves. Educated Africans in the British colonies knew about the kings and queens of England and read Shakespeare, Milton, and the English poets, but they knew next to nothing about their own countries' histories or past cultural achievements. Policies of educational reform since the end of colonialism have not completely altered the situation even today.

Partly as a result of the legacy of colonial education, which was not directed toward the majority of the population, the educational system in many developing countries is top-heavy: Higher education is disproportionately developed relative to primary and secondary education. The result is a correspondingly overqualified group who, having attended colleges and universities, cannot find white-collar or professional jobs. Given the low level of industrial development, most of the better-paid positions are in government, and there are not enough of those to go around.

In recent years, some developing countries, recognizing the shortcomings of the curricula inherited from colonialism, have tried to redirect their educational programs toward the rural poor. They have had limited success, because usually there is insufficient funding to pay for the scale of the necessary innovations. As a result, countries such as India have begun programs of self-help education. Communities draw on existing resources without creating demands for high levels of finance. Those who can read and write and who perhaps possess job skills are encouraged to take others on as apprentices, whom they coach in their spare time.

☑ CONCEPT CHECKS

1. What are some of the reasons there are many illiterate people in the developing world?
2. Name at least one strategy developed to help reduce illiteracy in developing nations.

Communication and the Mass Media

The modern world depends on the continuous communication or interaction between people widely separated from one another. If we were not so dependent on "communication across distance," schooling would be less necessary. In traditional cultures, most knowledge was what anthropologist Clifford Geertz (1983) has called **local knowledge**. Traditions were passed on through the local community, and although general cultural ideas gradually spread across large areas, processes of cultural diffusion were long, drawn out, slow, and inconsistent. Today, we live in "the whole world" in a way that would have been quite inconceivable to anyone living in cultures of the past.

We learn a great deal about the world from formal schooling. But we also learn much from the various communication media, which operate outside the context of schools. All of us are aware of situations and events that happen thousands of miles away—electronic communication makes such awareness almost instantaneous. Changes in the spread of information, and in information technologies, are as much a part of the development of modern societies as any aspect of industrial production (Kern 1983). During the twentieth century, rapid transportation and electronic communication such as the Internet greatly intensified the global diffusion of information.

The **mass media**—newspapers, magazines, movies, compact discs, digital video discs, TV, and the Internet—are often

Adult Literacy Rates Worldwide
(15 years and older)

Greenland
(Denmark)

Sweden
Norway
Czech Rep.
Austria
Iceland
Denmark
Germany
Netherlands
United Kingdom
Ireland
Belgium
Luxembourg
France
Switzerland
Slovenia
Croatia
Azores
Spain
Italy
Portugal
Tunisia

Alaska
(U.S.)

Canada

United States

Bermuda
Bahamas
Haiti
Dominican Republic
Puerto Rico (U.S.)
St. Kitts and Nevis
Antigua and Barbuda
Dominica
Barbados
St. Lucia
St. Vincent and the
Grenadines
Grenada
Trinidad and Tobago

Atlantic Ocean

Morocco
Western Sahara
(Morocco)
Algeria
Libya

Mexico
Cuba
Belize

Hawaiian Is.
(U.S.)

Cape Verde
Senegal
Gambia
Mauritania
Mali
Niger

Jamaica
Nicaragua
Guatemala
El Salvador
Honduras
Costa Rica
Panama

Venezuela
Colombia

Guinea-Bissau
Guinea
Sierra
Leone
Liberia
Nigeria
Cameroon
Côte
d'Ivoire

Pacific Ocean

Fr. Guiana
(Fr.)

Burkina
Faso

Galapagos Is.
Ecuador
Suriname
Guyana

Peru
Brazil

Ghana
Togo
Benin
Gabon
Congo
Angola

Samoa

Bolivia

Equatorial
Guinea
Namibia

Paraguay

Chile

Argentina
Uruguay

Falkland Is.

Percentage literate

Rates above 95%
Rates between 80% and 95%
Rates between 60% and 79%
Rates between 40% and 59%
Rates below 40%
No data

SOURCE: UNESCO 2006.

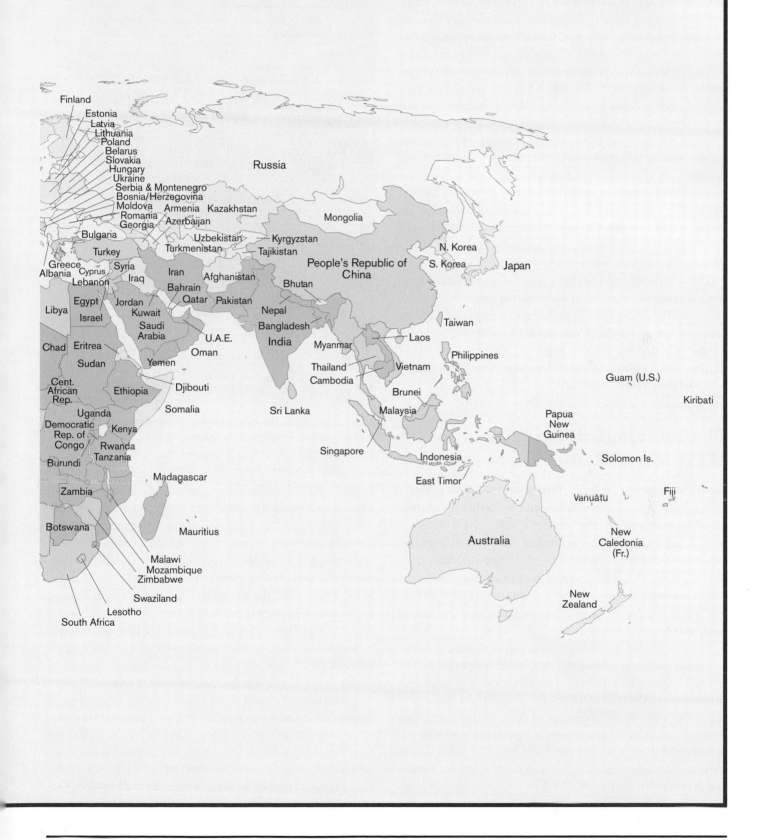

associated with entertainment and therefore are seen as rather marginal to most people's lives. Such a view is quite misleading. Mass communications enter our social activities at many different points. For instance, a bank account is no longer a pile of money kept in a safe; it is a series of digits printed on an account sheet and stored in a computer, and monetary transactions are now mainly performed through the exchange of information between computers. Anyone who uses a credit card is connected with a very complex system of electronically stored and transmitted information, which has now become the very basis of modern financial accounting. Today, many people use the Internet to buy CDs and books.

Even "recreational" media such as newspapers or TV have a wide-ranging influence over our experience. This is not just because they affect our attitudes in specific ways but because they are the *means of access* to the knowledge on which many social activities depend. Voting in national elections, for example, would be quite different if information about current political events, candidates, and parties were not generally available. Even those who are largely uninterested in politics and have little knowledge of the personalities involved have some awareness of national and international events, such as former President Bill Clinton's impeachment trial. Only a complete hermit would be entirely detached from the "news events" that impinge to some degree on the consciousness of all of us—and we could suspect that a modern hermit might very well own a transistor radio!

The Sociological Study of the Mass Media

How do we go about studying the influence of the mass media on our lives? A basic concept needed here is that of **communication**, which means the transfer of information from one person, context, or group to another. We saw in Chapter 6 that the communication and storage of information have been fundamental to the development of modern societies. Sociologically speaking, therefore, we need to put the rise of the mass media and popular culture in the context of the basic trends analyzed earlier.

There are close connections between the rise of the media and the development of modern systems of mass education. The two can be properly understood sociologically only in relation to one another. German social thinker Jürgen Habermas (1989; orig. 1962) offers a useful concept to describe this connection when he speaks of the emergence of a **public sphere** with the early development of the industrial societies. The public sphere is a sphere of communication, in which public opinion is formed and attitudes shaped. In earlier forms of society, most communication was local and simply carried through speech, the

New technologies like moveable type and the printing press led to the creation of the first newspapers in the 1700s. As literacy expanded, mass circulation of printed texts grew.

ordinary daily talk of neighbors and friends in village communities. A rudimentary public sphere developed in early civilizations, well before the emergence of industrial societies. But it was very restricted, because only small groups were literate—could read and write. Moreover, written documents had to be laboriously prepared by hand, so there weren't many in circulation. From about the sixteenth century onward in Europe, as the new technology of printing spread and levels of literacy grew, the public sphere began to expand. The first local newspapers appeared in the mid-1700s. Mass-circulation newspapers followed about a century later, to be joined in our century by the electronic media of radio, TV, and other forms.

Learning to read and write and mastering other forms of knowledge are necessary for us to play a part in this developing wider society of communication. In the industrialized countries today, most people can read and write, but in historical terms, this is a recent development, dating back no more than a hundred years. The sorts of outlooks and knowledge acquired in school allow us to participate in the public sphere—to be able to read newspapers and magazines, for example. But the mass media might often also crosscut the goals of formal schooling. For instance, perhaps literacy and other educational skills are beginning to slump now that television and other forms of electronic media play such a large part in our lives. It isn't obvious, after all, that being able to do well at Nintendo games helps much with school achievement. The increasing influence of television is probably the single most important development in the media over the past forty years. Television is as important as books, magazines, and newspapers in the expansion of indirect forms of communication characteristic of modern societies. It frames the ways in which we interpret and respond to the social world by helping to order our experience of it. Assumptions built into the overall character of TV production and distribution may perhaps be more significant than whatever particular programs are shown. If current trends continue, by age eighteen, the average child born today will have spent more time watching TV than doing any other activity save sleeping. Virtually every industrialized household now possesses a television set. In the United States, the average set is switched on between five and six hours a day, and much the same is true in the European countries (Goodhardt et al. 1987).

Theories of the Mass Media's Influence on Society

THE GLOBAL VILLAGE

One influential early theorist of the mass media was the Canadian author Marshall McLuhan. According to McLuhan (1964), "the medium is the message." That is to say, the nature of the media found in a society influences its structure much more than the content, or the messages, that the media convey. Television, for instance, is a very different medium from the printed book. It is electronic, visual, and composed of fluid images. A society in which television plays a basic role is one in which everyday life is experienced differently from one that only has print. Thus the TV news conveys global information instantaneously to millions of people. The electronic media, McLuhan thought, are creating what he called a **global village**—people throughout the world see major news items unfold and hence participate in the same events as one another. Millions of people in different countries, for example, knew about Princess Diana's life, her problems with the British royal family, and her death in an automobile accident in Paris.

Jean Baudrillard, whose ideas we will look at in this section, has been strongly influenced by the ideas of McLuhan. We turn first, however, to the theories of German sociologist and philosopher Jürgen Habermas.

JÜRGEN HABERMAS: THE PUBLIC SPHERE

German philosopher and sociologist Jürgen Habermas is linked to the "Frankfurt School" of social thought. The Frankfurt School was a group of authors inspired by Marx who nevertheless believed that Marx's views needed radical revision to bring them up to date. Among other things, they believed that Marx had not given enough attention to the influence of culture in modern capitalist society.

The Frankfurt School made extensive study of what it called the "culture industry," meaning the entertainment industries of film, TV, popular music, radio, newspapers, and magazines. The Frankfurt School argued that the spread of the culture industry, with its undemanding and standardized products, undermines the capacity of individuals for critical and independent thought. Art disappears, swamped by commercialization—"Mozart's Greatest Hits."

Habermas (1989; orig. 1962) has taken up some of these themes, but he developed them in a different way. He analyzes the development of media from the early eighteenth century up to the present moment, tracing out the emergence—and subsequent decay—of the public sphere.

The public sphere, according to Habermas, developed first in the salons and coffeehouses of London, Paris, and other European cities. People met in such salons to discuss issues of the moment, using as a means for such debate the news sheets and newspapers that had just begun to emerge. Political debate became a matter of particular importance. Although only small numbers of the population were involved, Habermas argues that the salons were vital to the early development of democracy, for they introduced the idea of resolving political problems through public discussion. The public sphere—at least in principle—involves individuals coming together as equals in a forum for public debate.

However, the promise offered by the early development of the public sphere, Habermas concludes, has not been fully realized. Democratic debate in modern societies is stifled by the development of the culture industry. The development of the mass media and mass entertainment causes the public sphere to become largely a sham. Politics is stage managed in government and the media, while commercial interests triumph over those of the public. Public opinion is not formed through open, rational discussion, but through manipulation and control—as, for example, in advertising.

JEAN BAUDRILLARD: THE WORLD OF HYPERREALITY

One of the most influential current theorists of media is French author Jean Baudrillard. Baudrillard (1988) regards the impact of modern mass media as being quite different from and much more profound than that of any other technology. The coming of the mass media, particularly electronic media such as television, has transformed the very nature of our lives. Television does not just "represent" the world to us; it increasingly defines what the world in which we live actually is.

Consider as an example the O. J. Simpson trial, a celebrated court case that unfolded in Los Angeles in 1994–1995. Simpson originally became famous as an American football star but later became known around the world as a result of appearing in several popular films, including the *Naked Gun* series. He was accused of the murder of his wife, Nicole, and after a very long trial was acquitted (although subsequently Simpson was found guilty in a civil suit filed by the families of Nicole Brown Simpson and the man who was murdered with her, Ronald Goldman). The criminal trial was televised live and was watched in many countries, including Britain. In America, six television channels covered the trial on a continuous basis.

The trial did not just happen in the courtroom. It was a televisual event linking millions of viewers and commentators in the media. The trial is an illustration of what Baudrillard calls **hyperreality**. There is no longer a "reality" (the events in the courtroom), which television allows us to see. The "reality" is actually the string of images on the TV screens of the world, which defined the trial as a global event.

During the O. J. Simpson trial six television channels broadcast the court proceedings simultaneously. This excess of exposure, where televised events seem more real than the actual events, is an example of Baudrillard's concept of hyperreality.

Just before the outbreak of hostilities in the Persian Gulf in 1991, Baudrillard wrote a newspaper article titled "The Gulf War Cannot Happen." When war was declared and a bloody conflict took place, it might have seemed obvious that Baudrillard had been wrong. Not a bit of it. After the end of the war, Baudrillard wrote a second article, "The Gulf War Did Not Happen." What did he mean? He meant that the war was not like other wars that have happened in history. It was a war of the media age, a televisual spectacle, in which, along with other viewers throughout the world, George Bush and Saddam Hussein watched the coverage by CNN to see what was actually "happening." Baudrillard argues that in an age where the mass media are everywhere, in effect a new reality—hyperreality—is created, composed of the intermingling of people's behavior and media images.

JOHN THOMPSON: THE MEDIA AND MODERN SOCIETY

Drawing in some part on the writings of Habermas, John Thompson (1990, 1995) has analyzed the relation between the media and the development of industrial societies. From early forms of print through to electronic communication, Thompson argues, the media have played a central role in the development of modern institutions. Thompson believes that the main founders of sociology—including Marx, Weber, and Durkheim—gave too little attention to the role of media in shaping even the early development of modern society.

Thompson's theory of the media depends on a distinction among three types of interactions. Face-to-face interaction, such as people talking at a party, is rich in clues that individuals use to make sense of what others say. **Mediated interaction** involves the use of a media technology—paper, electrical connections, electronic impulses. Characteristic of mediated interaction is that it is stretched out in time and space—it goes well beyond the contexts of ordinary face-to-face interaction. Mediated interaction takes place between individuals in a direct way—for instance, two people talking on the telephone—but there isn't the same variety of clues as when people are face to face.

A third type of interaction is **mediated quasi-interaction**. This refers to the sort of social relations created by the mass media. Such interaction is stretched across time and space, but it doesn't link individuals directly: hence the term *quasi-interaction*. The two previous types are "dialogical": Individuals communicate in a direct way. Mediated quasi-interaction is "monological": A TV program, for example, is a one-way form of communication. People watching the program may discuss it, and perhaps address some remarks to the TV set—but, of course, it doesn't answer back.

Thompson's point is not that the third type comes to dominate the other two—essentially the view taken by

Baudrillard—but rather that all three types intermingle in our lives today. The mass media, Thompson suggests, change the balance between the public and the private in our lives. Contrary to what Habermas says, much more comes into the public domain than before, and this leads quite often to debate and controversy.

An example would be former President Bill Clinton's televised testimony about his affair with Monica Lewinsky. Viewers learned a great deal about the president's private business, perhaps more details than they cared to know. At the time, Clinton's affairs were widely discussed by many Americans. The media's reporting of the affair also sparked debate about the division between the private and public, not only in newspapers and on television, but in homes, bars, offices, and Internet chat rooms across the country.

GLOBALIZATION AND MEDIA IMPERIALISM

If today we all live in "one world," it is in large part a result of the international scope of the communications media. Anyone who switches on the TV set and watches the world news ordinarily gets what the description suggests: a presentation of events that occurred that day or shortly before in many different parts of the world. Television programs are sold to large international markets, and hundreds of millions of people watch them. Like other aspects of the global society, the development of a **world information order**—an international system for the production, distribution, and consumption of information—has been uneven and reflects the divisions between the developed societies and developing countries.

The paramount position of the industrialized countries, above all the United States, in the production and diffusion of media has led many observers to speak of *media imperialism*. A cultural empire, it is argued, has been established. Developing countries are held to be especially vulnerable, because they lack the resources to maintain their own cultural independence.

Via the electronic media, Western cultural products have certainly become widely diffused across the globe. Pico Iyer (1989) speaks of "video nights in Katmandu," of frequenting discos in Bali. American videos are commonplace in the Islamic republic of Iran, as are audiotapes of Western popular music, brought in on the black market (Sreberny-Mohammadi 1992). Not only more popular entertainment forms are at issue, however. Control of the world's news by the major Western agencies, it has been suggested, means the predominance of a first world outlook in the information conveyed. Thus it has been claimed that attention is given to the developing world in news broadcasts mainly in times of disaster, crisis, or military

confrontation and that the daily files of other types of news kept on the industrialized world are not maintained for developing world coverage.

Herbert Schiller (1989, 1991) has claimed that control of global communications by U.S. firms has to be seen in relation to various factors. He argues that American TV and radio networks have fallen increasingly under the influence of the federal government and particularly the Department of Defense. He points out that RCA, which until 1986 owned the NBC television and radio networks, is also a leading defense subcontractor to the Pentagon. American television exports, coupled with advertising, propagate a commercialized culture that corrodes local forms of cultural expression. Even where governments prohibit commercial broadcasting within their borders, radio and television from surrounding countries can often be directly received.

Schiller argues that although Americans were the first to be affected by the "corporate-message cocoon. . . . [W]hat is now happening is the creation and global extension of a new total corporate informational-cultural environment" (Schiller 1989). Because U.S. corporations and culture are globally dominant, they have "overwhelmed a good part of the world," such that "American cultural domination . . . sets the boundaries for national discourse" (Schiller 1991).

☑ CONCEPT CHECKS

1. How is the rise of the mass media related to changes in educational levels in a society?

2. According to Habermas, why has the "public sphere" not lived up to its potential?
3. Do you believe that the United States is a media "imperialist"? Why or why not?

Technological Change, Media, and Education

Although we have concentrated so far on newspapers, television, and other parts of the "culture industry," we should not think of the media of communication only in those terms. Particularly as influenced by the computer, the media are affecting what we do in many other areas as well.

The Internet

By the early 1990s, many experts in the computer and technology industries were conceding that the reign of the personal computer was over. It was becoming increasingly clear to them that the future lay not with the individual computer but with a global system of interconnected computers—the *Internet*. Although many computer users may not have realized it at the time, the PC was quickly to become little more than a point of access to events happening elsewhere—events happening on a network stretching across the planet, a network that is not owned by any individual or company.

ORIGINS OF THE INTERNET

The Internet has come about in a spontaneous way. It is the product of an undivided world—a world after the fall of the Berlin wall. Yet its first origins were in the cold war period that preceded 1989. The Internet had its beginnings in the Pentagon, the headquarters of the American military. It was established in 1969 and was first named the ARPA net, after the Pentagon's Advanced Research Projects Agency. The aim was limited. The ARPA sought to allow scientists working on military contracts in different parts of America to pool their resources and to share the expensive equipment they were using. Its originators thought up a way, almost as an afterthought, of sending messages, too. Thus electronic mail—e-mail—was born.

Until the early 1980s, the Pentagon Internet consisted of five hundred computers, all located in military laboratories and university computer science departments. Other people in universities then started catching on and began using the system for their own purposes. By 1987 the Internet had expanded to include twenty-eight thousand host computers, at many different universities and research labs.

For several years, the Internet remained confined to universities. With the spread of home-based personal computers, however, it began to move outside—and then entered a period of explosive growth. By the year 2003, 61.8 percent of American households owned computers, and in 2007 more than 215 million adult Americans (71.4 percent of the population) actively logged on to the Internet each month, with an average of 70 million using the Internet on any given day (Internet World Stats 2008b; Pew Internet 2005). The spread of commercial Internet service providers (ISPs) that offer dial-up access through modems and faster direct access through phone lines (DSL) and cable has fueled the growing proportion of households with online capabilities. Online services, electronic bulletin boards, chat rooms, and software libraries were uploaded onto the Internet by a bewildering variety of people, no longer situated just in North America, but all over the world. Corporations also got in on the act. In 1994, companies overtook universities as the dominant users of the network.

Access to the Internet is highly uneven. In 1998, 88 percent of the world's Internet users lived in the developed world. North America accounted for more than 50 percent of all users, although it contains only 5 percent of the total world population. By 2007, however, the share of Internet users located in North America had dropped to about 17 percent, indicating the rise of Internet usage worldwide (Internet World Stats 2008b). The United States has the highest level of computer ownership and online access. More than 215 million Americans use the Internet; in Germany there are over 53 million Internet users, and the United Kingdom boasts more than 40 million. In Japan, a country where the Internet craze arrived somewhat late, nearly 68.7 percent of the population (87 million people) used the Internet in 2007 (Internet World Stats 2008b). These numbers are expected to grow rapidly in the coming years.

THE EFFECT OF THE INTERNET

In a world of quite stunning technological change, no one can be sure what the future holds. Many see the Internet as exemplifying the new global order emerging at the close of the twentieth century. Users of the Internet live in "cyberspace." **Cyberspace** means the space of interaction formed by the global network of computers that compose the Internet. In cyberspace, much as Baudrillard might say, we are no longer people but instead are messages on each other's screens. Apart from e-mail, where users usually identify themselves, no one on the Internet can be sure of who anyone else really is, whether they are male or female, or where they are in the world.

How is online communication, such as virtual environments such as Second Life, transforming social interaction?

The spread of the Internet across the globe has raised important questions for sociologists. The Internet is transforming the contours of daily life—blurring the boundaries between the global and the local, presenting new channels for communication and interaction, and allowing more and more everyday tasks to be carried out online. Yet at the same time as it provides exciting new opportunities to explore the social world, the Internet also threatens to undermine human relationships and communities. Although the information age is still in its early stages, many sociologists are already debating the complex implications of the Internet for late modern societies.

Opinions on the effects of the Internet on social interaction fall into two broad categories. On the one hand are those observers who see the online world as fostering new forms of electronic relationships that either enhance or supplement existing face-to-face interactions. While traveling or working abroad, individuals can use the Internet to communicate regularly with friends and relatives at home. Distance and separation become more tolerable. The Internet also allows the formation of new types of relationships: Anonymous online users can meet in chat rooms and discuss topics of mutual interest. These cyber contacts sometimes evolve into fully fledged electronic friendships or even result in face-to-face meetings. Many Internet users become part of lively online communities that are qualitatively different from those they inhabit in the physical world. Scholars who see the Internet as a positive addition to human interaction argue that it expands and enriches people's social networks.

Not everyone takes such an enthusiastic stance, however. As people spend more and more time communicating online and handling their daily tasks in cyberspace, it may be that they spend less time interacting with one another in the physical world. Some sociologists fear that the spread of Internet technology will lead to increased social isolation and atomization. They argue that one effect of increasing Internet access in households is that people are spending less quality time with their families and friends. The Internet is encroaching on domestic life as the lines between work and home are blurred: Many employees continue to work at home after hours—checking e-mail or finishing tasks that they were unable to complete during the day. Human contact is reduced, personal relationships suffer, traditional forms of entertainment such as the theater and books fall by the wayside, and the fabric of social life is weakened.

How are we to evaluate these contrasting positions? Most certainly there are elements of truth on both sides of the debate. The Internet is undoubtedly broadening our horizons and presents unprecedented opportunities for making contact with others. Yet the frenzied pace at which it is expanding also presents challenges and threats to traditional forms of human interaction. Will the Internet radically transform society into a fragmented, impersonal realm where humans rarely venture out of their homes and lose their ability to communicate? It seems unlikely. About fifty years ago very similar fears were expressed as television burst onto the media scene. In *The Lonely Crowd* (1961), an influential sociological analysis of American society in the 1950s, David Riesman and his colleagues expressed concern about the effects of TV on family and community life. Some of their fears were justified, but television and the mass media have also enriched the social world in many ways.

Just like television before it, the Internet has aroused both hopes and fears. Will we lose our identities in cyberspace? Will computerized technology dominate us rather than the reverse? Will human beings retreat into an antisocial online world? The answer to each of these questions, fortunately, almost certainly is no. For example, people don't use video conferencing if they can get together with others in an ordinary way. Business executives have far more forms of electronic communication available to them than ever before. At the same time, the number of face-to-face business conferences has shot up.

Education and New Communications Technology

The spread of information technology looks set to influence education in a number of different ways, some of which may perhaps be quite fundamental. The new technologies are affecting the nature of work, replacing some types of human work by machines. The sheer pace of technological change is creating a much more rapid turnover of jobs than once was the case. Education can no longer be regarded as a stage of preparation before an individual enters work. As technology changes, necessary skills change, and even if education is seen from a purely vocational point of view—as providing skills relevant to

Programs such as One Laptop per Child have brought technology and the Internet to even the most impoverished countries. How does the networked world increasingly blur the boundaries between global and local communities?

work—most observers agree that lifelong exposure to education will be needed in the future.

TECHNOLOGIES OF EDUCATION

The rise of education in its modern sense was connected with a number of other major changes happening in the nineteenth century. One was the development of the school. One might naively think that there was a demand for education and that schools and universities were set up to meet that demand. But that was not how things happened. Schools arose, as Michel Foucault has shown, as part of the administrative apparatus of the modern state. The hidden curriculum was about discipline and about the control of children.

A second influence was the development of printing and the arrival of "book culture." The mass distribution of books, newspapers, and other printed media was as distinctive a feature of the development of industrial society as were machines and factories. Education developed to provide skills of literacy and computation giving access to the world of printed media. Nothing is more characteristic of the school than the schoolbook or textbook.

In the eyes of many, all this is set to change with the growing use of computers and multimedia technologies in education. It has been said that "around 70–80 percent of telecommunications trials conducted in the emerging multimedia technologies around the world involve education or at least have an education component" (quoted in Kenway et al. 1995).

As in many other areas of contemporary social life, markets and information technology are major influences on educational change. The commercializing and marketizing of education also reflect such pressures. Schools are being reengineered in much the same way as business corporations.

Many of those likely to enter the education field will be organizations whose relation to schooling was previously marginal or nonexistent. They include cable companies, software houses, telecommunication groups, filmmakers, and equipment suppliers. Their influence will not be limited to schools or universities. They are already forming part of what has been called "edutainment"—a sort of parallel education industry linked to the software industry in general, to museums, science parks, and heritage areas.

EDUCATION AND THE TECHNOLOGY GAP

Whether the new technologies will have the radical implications for education that some claim is still an open question. Critics have pointed out that, even if they do have major effects, these may act to reinforce educational inequalities. **Information poverty** might be added to the material deprivations that currently have such an effect on schooling. The sheer pace of technological change and the demand of employers for computer-literate workers may mean that those who are technologically competent "leapfrog" over people who have little experience with computers.

Some already fear the emergence of a "computer underclass" within Western societies. Although developed countries have the highest levels of computer and Internet usage in the world, there are stark inequalities in computer use within those societies. Many schools and colleges are suffering from underfunding and long-standing neglect; even if these institutions become beneficiaries of schemes that distribute secondhand computer hardware to schools, they must gain the technical expertise and ability to teach information technology skills to pupils. Because the market for computer specialists is so strong, many schools are struggling to attract and keep information technology teachers, who can earn far greater incomes in the private sector.

Yet the technology gap within Western societies appears minor compared to the digital divide separating Western classrooms from their counterparts in the developing world. As the global economy becomes increasingly knowledge based, there is a real danger that poorer countries will become even more marginalized because of the gap between the information rich and the information poor.

Internet access has become a new line of demarcation between the rich and the poor. South Asia, with 23 percent of the world's total population, has less than 1 percent of world's Internet users. In Africa, there are a mere seven Internet hosts per one million people. Even though 14 percent of the world's population live on the African continent, there are just under twenty-four million Internet users, or 3.6 percent of all Internet users (Internet World Stats 2008b). About 10 percent of these individuals are located in South Africa, by far the most developed and prosperous African nation. In the Middle East, Internet usage has increased dramatically over the last five years—by over 325 percent. Yet the Middle East still represents only 3 percent (41,939,200) of the world's population of Internet users (Internet World Stats 2008b).

Information technology enthusiasts argue that computers need not result in greater national and global inequalities—that their very strength lies in their ability to draw people together and to open up new opportunities. Schools in Asia and Africa that are lacking textbooks and qualified teachers can benefit from the Internet, it is claimed. Distance-learning programs and collaboration with colleagues overseas could be the key to overcoming poverty and disadvantage. When technology is put in the hands of smart, creative people, they argue, the potential is limitless.

Technology can be breathtaking and open important doors, but it has to be recognized that there is no such thing as an easy "techno-fix." Underdeveloped regions struggling with mass illiteracy and lacking telephone lines and electricity need an improved educational infrastructure before they can truly benefit from distance-learning programs. The Internet cannot be substituted for direct contact between teachers and pupils under these conditions.

Lifelong Learning

New technologies and the rise of the knowledge economy are transforming traditional ideas about work and education. The sheer pace of technological change is creating a much more rapid turnover of jobs than once was the case. Training and the attainment of qualifications are now occurring throughout people's lives, rather than just once early in life. Mid-career professionals are choosing to update their skills through continuing education programs and Internet-based learning. Many employers now allow workers to participate in on-the-job training as a way of enhancing loyalty and improving the company skills base.

As our society continues to transform, the traditional beliefs and institutions that underpin it are also undergoing change. The idea of education—implying the structured transmission of knowledge within a formal institution—is giving way to a broader notion of learning that takes place in a diversity of settings. The shift from education to learning is not an inconsequential one. Learners are active, curious social actors who can derive insights from a multiplicity of sources, not just within an institutional setting. Emphasis on learning acknowledges that skills and knowledge can be gained through all types of encounters—with friends and neighbors, at seminars and museums, in conversations at the local Starbucks, through the Internet and other media, and so forth.

The shift in emphasis toward *lifelong learning* can already be seen within schools themselves, where there are a growing number of opportunities for pupils to learn *outside* the confines of the classroom. The boundaries between schools and the outside world are breaking down, not only via cyberspace, but in the physical world as well. "Service learning," for example, has become a mainstay of many American secondary schools. As part of their graduation requirements, pupils devote a certain amount of time to volunteer work in the community. Partnerships with local businesses have also become commonplace in the United States, fostering interaction and mentor relationships between adult professionals and pupils.

Lifelong learning should and must play a role in the move toward a knowledge society. Not only is it essential to a well-trained, motivated workforce, but learning should also be seen in relation to wider human values. Learning is both a means and an end to the development of a well-rounded and autonomous self-education in the service of self-development and self-understanding. There is nothing utopian in this idea; indeed it reflects the humanistic ideals of education developed by educational philosophers. An example already in existence is lifelong learning programs for the elderly, which provide retired people with the opportunity to educate themselves as they choose, developing whatever interests they care to follow.

☑ CONCEPT CHECKS

1. Describe the main uses of the Internet.
2. Researchers have documented a "digital gap." Which populations have low rates of internet usage? Why?
3. What is the purpose of lifelong learning?

Study Outline

Sociological Theories of Education

- Schools play three major roles in the larger society: assimilation or acculturation; credentialism; and social or cultural reproduction.

Education, Inequality, and American Schools Today

- Education in its modern form, involving the instruction of pupils within specially designated school premises, began to emerge with the spread of printed materials and higher levels of literacy. Knowledge could be retained, reproduced, and consumed by more people in more places. With industrialization, work became more specialized, and knowledge was increasingly acquired in more abstract rather than practical ways—the skills of reading, writing, and calculating.
- The expansion of education in the twentieth century has been closely tied to perceived needs for a literate and disciplined workforce. Although reformers have seen education for all as a means of reducing inequalities, its effect in this respect is fairly limited. Education tends to express and reaffirm existing inequalities more than it acts to change them.
- The formal school curriculum is only one part of a more general process of social reproduction influenced by many informal aspects of learning, education, and school settings. The *hidden curriculum* plays a significant role in such reproduction.

Academic Achievement and Differential Outcomes

- Because *intelligence* is difficult to define, there has been a great deal of controversy about the subject. Some argue that genes determine one's *IQ;* others believe that social influences determine it. The weight of the evidence appears to be on the side of those arguing for social and cultural influences. A major controversy about IQ has developed as a result of the book *The Bell Curve.* The book claims that races differ in terms of their average level of inherited intelligence. Critics reject this thesis completely.

Education and Literacy in the Developing World

- Over 23 percent of the population of developing countries is illiterate today. An estimated two-thirds of the illiterate population worldwide are female.

- Illiteracy is a consequence of colonial education systems, which targeted the elite rather than the poor. Some developing countries today have thus redirected educational programs toward the rural poor.

Communication and the Mass Media

- The *mass media* have come to play a fundamental role in modern society. The mass media are media of communication—newspapers, magazines, television, radio, movies, videos, CDs, DVDs, and other forms—that reach mass audiences. The influence of the mass media on our lives is profound. The media not only provide entertainment but also provide and shape much of the information that we utilize in our daily lives.
- A range of different theories of media and popular culture have been developed. McLuhan argued that media influence society more in terms of how they communicate than what they communicate. In McLuhan's words, "the medium is the message": TV, for example, influences people's behavior and attitudes because it is so different in nature from other media, such as newspapers or books.
- Other important theorists include Habermas, Baudrillard, and Thompson. Habermas points to the role of the media in creating a *public sphere*—a sphere of public opinion and public debate. Baudrillard has been strongly influenced by McLuhan. He believes that new media, particularly television, actually change the "reality" we experience. Thompson argues that the mass media have created a new form of social interaction—*mediated quasi-interaction*—that is more limited, narrow, and one-way than everyday social interaction.

Technological Change, Media, and Education

- The sense today of inhabiting one world is in large part a result of the international scope of media of communication. A *world information order*—an international system of the production, distribution, and consumption of informational goods—has come into being. Given the paramount position of the industrial countries in the world information order, many believe that the developing countries are subject to a new form of media imperialism.
- Recent years have seen the emergence of multimedia, linked to the development of the Internet. *Multimedia* refers to the combination on a single medium of what used to be different media needing different technologies, so that a CD-ROM, for example, can carry both visuals and sound and be played on a computer. Many claims have been made about the likely social effects of these developments, but it is still too early to judge how far these will be borne out.

Key Concepts

abstract and concrete attitudes (p. 505)
achievement gap (p. 502)
"acting white" thesis (p. 505)
communication (p. 516)
cultural capital (p. 498)
cultural navigators (p. 505)
cyberspace (p. 520)
gender gap (p. 505)
global village (p. 517)
hidden curriculum (p. 497)
hyperreality (p. 518)
information poverty (p. 522)
intelligence (p. 503)
IQ (intelligence quotient) (p. 503)
local knowledge (p. 513)
mass media (p. 513)
mediated interaction (p. 518)
mediated quasi-interaction (p. 518)
public sphere (p. 516)
stereotype threat (p. 507)
tracking (p. 500)
world information order (p. 519)

Review Questions

1. Discuss the three major sociological theories on education. What are their similarities and differences?
2. Discuss the sociological perspectives on education and inequality.

3. What is school tracking? What are some of the ideas about its impact on education?
4. What is the "achievement gap"? How do sociologists explain its existence?
5. What are recent shifts in school discipline? How do these shifts impact educational inequality?
6. What educational reforms have taken place in the past decades?
7. What is the relationship between colonialism and low rates of literacy in the developing world?
8. Compare and contrast Habermas, Baudrillard, and Thompson's theories of the mass media.
9. How do sociologists explain the rise of media imperialism?
10. What are the effects of the Internet on social relationships? What are some of the inequalities associated with the Internet?

Thinking Sociologically Exercises

1. From your reading of this chapter, describe what might be the principal advantages and disadvantages of having children go to private versus public schools in the United States at this time. Assess whether privatization of our public schools would help improve them.
2. Back in 1964, Marshall McLuhan argued that the developments of radio and television helped to produce a global village. Carefully explain what he meant by the term *global village* and its importance. Explain how the advent of the Internet and cell phones will be likely to extend the concept of the global village further and faster than ever before.

Learning Objectives

The Sociological Study of Religion

Learn the elements that make up a religion.

Theories of Religion

Know the sociological approaches to religion developed by Marx, Durkheim, and Weber; the contemporary debate over secularization; and the religious economy approach.

Types of Religious Organizations

Learn the ways religious communities are organized and how they have become institutionalized.

Gender and Religion

Recognize the changing interrelationships between gender and religion.

World Religions

Know the forms religion takes in traditional and modern societies.

Religion in the United States

Learn about the sociological dimensions of religion in the United States, including the rise of fundamentalism and the electronic church.

Globalization and Religion

Recognize how religious activism in poor countries and the rise of religious nationalist movements reflect the globalization of religion.

CHAPTER SEVENTEEN

RELIGION IN MODERN SOCIETY

O n September 11, 2001, a well-organized group of nineteen men, equipped with box cutters, a rudimentary knowledge of piloting commercial jet aircraft, and fervent religious conviction, forever changed our world.

American Airlines Flight 11 and United Flight 175 were hijacked shortly after takeoff and flown into the twin towers of New York City's World Trade Center. American Airlines Flight 77 was hijacked over Kansas and flown to Washington, D.C., where it plummeted into the Pentagon. A fourth plane, United Airlines Flight 93, crashed into a field in Pennsylvania, most likely because passengers overpowered the hijackers.

The hijacking was organized by al Qaeda, a global network of religious extremists dedicated to restoring their version of traditional Islamic rule. Al Qaeda had previously unleashed violent attacks, including two 1998 car bombings of the U.S. embassies in Kenya and Tanzania and an attack on the U.S. destroyer *Cole* in 2000. The organization had also planned to blow up a dozen trans-Pacific U.S. commercial flights on a single day in 1995, a plot that was thwarted when one of the perpetrators was caught in the Philippines.

What explains the rise of militant, often violent, religious movements in the modern world? Under what conditions does religion unite communities, and under what conditions does it divide them? To study these issues, we ask what religion actually is, consider various forms of religious beliefs and practices, and analyze different types of religious organizations. The emphasis is on social change. Religious concerns today can be understood only in relation to social changes affecting the position of religion in the wider world.

In analyzing religious practices, we must be sensitive to ideals that inspire profound conviction in believers, yet we must also take a balanced view of them. We must confront ideas that seek the eternal while recognizing that religious groups also promote mundane goals, such as acquiring money or followers. We need to recognize the diversity of religious beliefs and modes of conduct but also probe the nature of religion as a general phenomenon.

The Sociological Study of Religion

Religion is one of the oldest human institutions. According to anthropologists, there have probably been about one hundred thousand religions throughout human history (Hadden 1997a). Sociologists define **religion** as a cultural system of commonly shared beliefs and rituals that provides a sense of ultimate meaning and purpose by creating an idea of reality that is sacred, all-encompassing, and supernatural (Berger 1967; Durkheim 1965, orig. 1912; Wuthnow 1988). There are three key elements in this definition:

1. Religion is a form of *culture,* which consists of the shared beliefs, values, norms, and material conditions that create a common identity among a group of people. Religion has all these characteristics.
2. Religion involves beliefs that take the form of ritualized practices—special activities in which believers take part and that identify them as members of the religious community.
3. Religion provides a feeling that life is ultimately meaningful. It does so by explaining coherently and compellingly what transcends or overshadows everyday life, in ways that other aspects of culture (such as an educational system or a belief in democracy) cannot (Geertz 1973; Wuthnow 1988).

What is absent from the sociological definition of religion is just as important as what is included: Nowhere is there mention of god. We often think of **theism**—a belief in one or more supernatural deities—as basic to religion, but this is not necessarily the case. As we shall see, some religions, such as Buddhism, believe in spiritual forces rather than a singular god.

How Sociologists Think about Religion

When sociologists study religion, they do so as unbiased scientists and not as believers (or disbelievers) in any particular faith. This stance has several implications:

1. **Sociologists are not concerned with whether religious beliefs are true or false.** The sociological perspective regards religions as socially constructed by human beings. Thus sociologists put aside their personal beliefs and address the human rather than the divine aspects of religion. Sociologists ask: How is the religion organized? What are its principal beliefs and values? How is it related to the larger society? What explains its success or failure in recruiting and retaining believers? The question of whether a particular belief is "good" or "true" is not something that sociologists can address. (As individuals they may have strong opinions on the matter, but as sociologists they must keep these opinions from biasing their research.)

2. **Sociologists are especially concerned with the social organization of religion.** Not only are religions a primary source of the deepest-seated norms and values, but they are practiced through an enormous variety of social forms. Within Christianity and Judaism, for example, religious practice often occurs in formal organizations, such as churches or synagogues. Yet within Hinduism and Buddhism, religious practices occur in the home as well as in temples or other natural settings. The sociology of religion considers how different religious institutions and organizations actually function. The earliest European religions were often indistinguishable from the larger society, as beliefs and practices were incorporated into daily life. In modern industrial society, however, some religions have become established in separate, often bureaucratic, organizations (Hammond 1992). This institutionalization has led some sociologists to view religions in the United States and Europe as similar to business organizations, competing with each other for members (Warner 1993).

3. **Sociologists often view religions as a major source of social solidarity in that they offer believers a common set of norms and values.** Religious beliefs, rituals, and bonds create a "moral community" in which all members know how to behave (Wuthnow 1988). If a single religion dominates a society, the religion may be an important source of social stability. If a society's members adhere to competing religions, however, religious differences may lead to destabilizing social conflicts. Recent examples of religious conflict within a society include struggles among

Religious differences frequently lead to social conflict. For instance, in 2004 the store of Abid Sheikh and Mohammad Aslam was vandalized with anti-Muslim graffiti and burned down in Everett, Washington.

Sikhs, Hindus, and Muslims in India; clashes between Muslims and Christians in Bosnia and other parts of the former Yugoslavia; and "hate crimes" against Jews, Muslims, and other religious minorities in the United States.

4. **Sociologists explain the appeal of religion in terms of social forces rather than personal, spiritual, or psychological factors.** Sociologists do not question the depth of believers' transcendent feelings and experiences, yet they also do not limit themselves to a purely spiritual explanation of religious commitment. In fact, some researchers argue that people often "get religion" when their fundamental sense of social order is threatened by economic hardship, loneliness, loss or grief, physical suffering, or poor health (Berger 1967; Glock 1976; Schwartz 1970; Stark and Bainbridge 1980). In explaining the appeal of religious movements, sociologists are more likely to focus on problems in the social order than on the individual's psychological response.

What Do Sociologists of Religion Study?

Several types of social forces are of special interest to sociologists of religion. First, sociologists study the ways in which a crisis in prevailing beliefs promotes religious fervor. Such a crisis occurred in the United States during the 1960s as a result of widespread opposition to the Vietnam War, the civil rights movement, social movements among racial and ethnic minorities, and the youth-oriented counterculture. Consequently, large numbers of people were attracted to religious teachers, ranging from Indian gurus to fundamentalist preachers, who offered everything from meditation and yoga to astrology and New Age religions (Wuthnow 1988).

Second, sociologists study how competition among religious organizations leads some to thrive and others to perish. This study has sparked an increased interest in the organizational dynamics of religious groups (Finke and Stark 1988, 1992; Hammond 1992; Roof and McKinney 1990; Stark and Bainbridge 1987).

Third, sociologists address the relationship among religion, ethnic identity, and politics. This is seen in the resurgence of ethnically based religion in pluralist societies such as the United States, as well as in the rise of religious nationalism worldwide (Juergensmeyer 1993; Lawrence 1989; Merkyl and Smart 1983; Sahliyeh 1990; see the discussion below of religious nationalism).

☑ CONCEPT CHECKS

1. What are the three main components of religion as a social institution?
2. How do sociologists differ from other scholars in their approach to studying religion?

Theories of Religion

Sociological approaches to religion are strongly influenced by the ideas of Marx, Durkheim, and Weber. None of the three theorists was religious himself, and each argued that religion was fundamentally an illusion: The very diversity of religions and their obvious connection to different societies and regions made their advocates' claims inherently implausible, according to these early theorists.

Marx: Religion and Inequality

Karl Marx never studied religion in any detail. His thinking on religion was mostly derived from the writings of Ludwig Feuerbach, who believed that through a process he called **alienation**, human beings attribute their own culturally created values and norms to alien, or separate, beings (i.e., divine forces or gods) because they do not understand their own history. Thus the story of the Ten Commandments given to Moses by God is a mythical version of the origins of moral precepts that govern the lives of Jewish and Christian believers.

Marx accepted the view that religion represents human self-alienation. In a famous phrase, he declared that religion

"Living the Question"

As a young boy growing up in rural Kansas, the son of tenant farmers living twelve miles from the nearest town, Bob Wuthnow remembers contemplating questions he was too young to understand. Why had his father dropped out of school after eighth grade? How had the dogs found their way into the chicken coop again? He had particular trouble understanding why one day his friend, Harry Charles Kitchen, did not come home from the hospital, having passed away from something called an appendectomy. "This was the first time someone my own age actually died," Wuthnow remembers. "It hit my own mortality—all sixty-five pounds of it—like a ton of bricks. Suddenly all those sermons I'd heard at the little Baptist church where Harry Charles and I attended Sunday School together took on painful urgency" (Wuthnow 1990).

Although Wuthnow eventually left Kansas behind, he has never stopped wrestling with important questions, such as the role religion plays in our individual and collective lives. Especially in the wake of September 11, 2001, religious institutions, beliefs, trends, and differences have become central concerns to our national life. Increasing our knowledge of how religion functions in modern society is an important task for sociologists, and translating that knowledge for public audiences and policy makers is one of Wuthnow's main strengths as a scholar.

On multiple occasions Wuthnow has been invited to serve as a mediator to those serving on the front lines of religion and politics in the United States, helping clarify trends and navigate solutions. Early in his first term, President George W. Bush created the Office of Faith-Based and Community Initiatives, to help provide social services to those in need, and appointed John Dilulio Jr. director. To promote dialogue among religious leaders, the White House, and the press, Wuthnow invited Dilulio to Princeton to speak and field questions about how new initiatives would work on the ground. On another occasion, Wuthnow joined religious leaders from various denominations throughout the United States for their annual, off-the-record meeting to help them compare notes, build trust, and sort out differences.

Whereas many people are driven by the search for answers, Wuthnow believes in living the questions. "It's not so much whether stories can be verified by science," explains Wuthnow.

Robert Wuthnow

"Faith is a matter of living our stories—living the questions: Why are we here? Where did we come from? Where are we going? What is good? How should we live? . . . We make sense of our lives by telling stories," he says, but quickly points out that "those stories are *real*."

Questions line not only the path to faith. They constitute social inquiry, and social scientists like Wuthnow play an important role in asking and answering such questions. As a society, where did we come from? Where are we going? What directions might we take, and what might be the consequences? Living the questions provides a way for Wuthnow to connect the personal and the professional, to understand public issues in terms of personal experience. In the winter of 2005, Wuthnow delivered a public address at Yale University. His words are evidence of the sociological imagination at work, helping us better understand how religion relates to both individual experience and social change in American society. Sociology is not just a topic we study in school. To Wuthnow (2005),

Sociology is a way of relating to our humanity. I believe we need to understand that and affirm it, whether we are social scientists or theologians. Some sociologists have taken a rather different approach to the relationship between sociology and theology. Believing that theology is primarily about God, they have tried to imagine what a God-centered sociology would look like, and, especially, how it might be different from a humanistic one. They have argued, for instance, that Marxist approaches would not qualify because Marxism has no place for God. They favor theories in which human agency has a larger place than social structure because they believe in free-will. And so on. Their view is that social science cannot adequately speak of faith unless it is explicitly informed by faith and is thus distinctive. My view is rather different. I want a good physicist to respect and try to understand the physical universe. I want a good doctor to understand human physiology and anatomy. I want a good sociologist to understand social interaction and society. If these realities are understood as a created order, if they are understood as reality that is sacred in the broadest sense of that word, then the obligation of the researcher is to be true to them and pay attention to the truth within them. That is the first consideration in bringing responsible voices into the public arena.

In ordinary life, ordinary people experience the depths of their humanity in an extraordinary variety of ways. In the fears of our own mortality and the mortality of our loved ones, to the pain we observe in doing volunteer work or reading the morning newspaper, we experience the frailty of human life, and in laughter of children and the embraces of friends, we experience its joy. We have a remarkable capacity, though, to insulate ourselves from that which we do not want to experience. Especially in middle America, it is easy from day to day to remain oblivious—comfortably watching television that purports to be reality, but is not, and devoting our hours to acquiring what we do not need. Calling attention to that which we would just as soon ignore—engaging in the debunking of everyday assumptions, as Peter Berger once wrote—should be high on the agenda of social research.

***

Conversations with social scientists, though, suggest that the idiosyncrasies of personal backgrounds often guide their research to a great extent. Immigrants study immigrants, single mothers study single mothers, and so on. If we are to understand the public role of social scientists, if we are interested in furthering that project and linking it with faith, we clearly must go behind the scenes, behind the public utterances and into the private realm, into the family, where fundamental convictions are shaped.

In my case, early childhood experiences, I have come to realize, provide the single best explanation for my lifelong interest in trying to understand social change. I grew up on a small farm in the middle of Kansas. I loved the farm, went to church in the community, and loved the community. I expected to grow up and live in that community. But the county in which I grew up was one of the poorest in the state. During the time I lived there, more farms went out of business than had during the Great Depression. My father died when I was eighteen. That summer, as I mourned his death and plowed his fields for the last time, I declared to myself that this was the end of an era, just as the era of horse-drawn farming had ended a generation earlier when my grandfather died. I moved on, struggled through college not knowing which way to turn, got married, gravitated toward the social sciences because it was something I felt I could do, and wound up as a graduate student in Berkeley at the height of the campus unrest. I was not interested in sociology of religion at the time, but took a course in it from Charles Glock. The only thing I remember from the course was a sloping line he drew on the chalkboard one day. I don't remember if it sloped up or down, but it represented social change. Glock was convinced we were living in a time of significant social change. Having recently driven from Kansas to Berkeley, I appreciated his point.

The connection of all this to theology, as I explained to another audience one time, is best expressed in an image Madeleine l'Engle has used. She writes of going out to a quiet place at night and looking up at the stars. When she does this, she sometimes hears music—the music of the universe, the music of God. I go back to Kansas once in a while to see what remains of the life I left behind. I go to the town where the Baptist church I attended as a child once stood. There is a small marker saying the church was torn down in 1978. I stop at the place where our farm buildings once stood—where my father came home from World War II, not in good health, and renovated an old ramshackle house, put a new roof on the barn, and planted a shelter belt of trees. Down in the ditch, under a clump of dead sunflowers, I find a small roll of rusted barbed wire. It is all that remains. I feel like a displaced person, a refugee. Like Madeleine l'Engle, I sometimes imagine the music of the universe. But it is music in a minor key.

was the "opium of the people." Religion defers happiness and rewards to the afterlife, he said, teaching a resigned acceptance of conditions in the earthly life—including inequalities and injustices. Religion contains a strong ideological element: Religious belief can provide justifications for those in power. For example, "The meek shall inherit the earth" suggests humility and nonresistance to oppression.

Durkheim: Religion and Functionalism

In contrast to Marx, Émile Durkheim extensively studied religion, concentrating on totemism as practiced by Australian aboriginal societies. In *The Elementary Forms of the Religious Life* (1965; orig. 1912), Durkheim connected religion not with social inequalities or power but with the overall nature of a society's institutions. His argument was that totemism represents religion in its most "elementary" form.

Durkheim defined religion in terms of a distinction between the sacred and the profane. **Sacred** objects and symbols, he held, are treated as apart from routine aspects of day-to-day existence—the realm of the **profane**. A totem (an animal or plant believed to have symbolic significance), Durkheim argued, is a sacred object, regarded with veneration and surrounded by ritual activities that bind the members of groups together.

Durkheim's theory of religion is a good example of the functionalist tradition. To analyze the function of a social behavior or social institution like religion is to study its contribution to the continuation of a group, community, or society. According to Durkheim, religion promotes a coherent society by ensuring that people meet regularly to affirm common beliefs and values.

Weber: World Religions and Social Change

Whereas Durkheim based his arguments on a restricted range of examples, Max Weber conducted a massive study of religions worldwide. No scholar before or since has undertaken a task of the scope Weber attempted. Weber's writings on religion differ from those of Durkheim because they concentrate on the connection between religion and social change, and they contrast with those of Marx because Weber argued that religion was not necessarily a conservative force; on the contrary, religiously inspired movements have often produced dramatic social transformations. Thus Protestantism, particularly Puritanism, according to Weber, was the source of the capitalist outlook found in the modern West. The early entrepreneurs were mostly Calvinists. Their drive to succeed, which helped initiate Western economic development, was originally prompted by a desire to serve God. Material success was considered a sign of divine favor.

Weber's discussion of the effect of Protestantism on the development of the West was connected to a comprehensive attempt to understand the influence of religion on social and economic life in various cultures. After analyzing the Eastern religions, Weber concluded that they prevented the widespread development of industrial capitalism because they were oriented toward different values, such as escape from the toils of the material world.

In traditional China and India, Weber held, periodic development of commerce, manufacture, and urbanism did not generate the radical patterns of social change that led to industrial capitalism in the West. Religion significantly inhibited such change. Consider Hinduism, which sees material reality as a veil hiding the true spiritual concerns to which humankind should be oriented. Confucianism also directs activity away from economic "progress" because it emphasizes harmony with the world rather than promoting an active mastery of it. Although China was long the most powerful and most culturally developed civilization in the world, its dominant religious values acted as a brake on a stronger commitment to economic development.

Weber regarded Christianity as a *salvation religion*—one in which human beings can be "saved" if they accept the beliefs of the religion and follow its moral tenets. The notions of sin and of being rescued from sinfulness by God's grace generate

Max Weber categorized Eastern religions as "other-worldly" and Christianity as a "salvation religion." Weber believed that Hinduism stressed escaping material existence to locate a higher plane of being, which cultivated an attitude of passivity. In contrast, he argued that Christianity and its emphasis on salvation and constant struggle could stimulate revolt against the existing order.

an emotional dynamism absent from the Eastern religions. Whereas Eastern religions cultivate an attitude of passivity or acceptance, Christianity demands a constant struggle against sin and thereby can stimulate revolt against the existing order. Religious leaders—such as Luther or Calvin—have arisen who reinterpret doctrines in such a way as to challenge the existing power structure.

Critical Assessment of the Classical View

Marx was right to claim that religion often has ideological implications, serving to justify the interests of ruling groups at the expense of others. There are innumerable examples in history. Consider the European missionaries who sought to convert "heathen" peoples to Christian beliefs; their motivations may have been sincere, yet their teachings reinforced the destruction of traditional cultures and the imposition of white domination. Also, almost all Christian denominations tolerated or endorsed slavery in the United States and other parts of the world into the nineteenth century. Doctrines were developed proclaiming slavery to be based on divine law, with disobedient slaves being considered guilty of an offense against God as well as their masters (Stampp 1956).

Weber was correct to emphasize the unsettling and often revolutionary effect of religious ideals on the established social order. In spite of the churches' early support for slavery in the United States, church leaders later played a key role in fighting to abolish the institution. Religious beliefs have at times prompted social movements against unjust systems of authority; for instance, religious sentiments were prominent in the civil rights movements of the 1960s. Religion has also generated social change through wars fought for religious motives.

The divisive influences of religion find little mention in Durkheim's work, which emphasized the role of religion in promoting social cohesion. Yet it is not difficult to redirect his ideas toward explaining religious division, conflict, and change as well as solidarity. After all, much of the strength of feeling generated against other religious groups derives from the commitment to religious values that bind each community of believers.

Durkheim's emphasis on ritual and ceremony is important. All religions hold regular assemblies of believers, at which ritual prescriptions are observed. As Durkheim rightly points out, ritual activities also mark the major transitions of life—birth, entry to adulthood (rituals associated with puberty), marriage, and death (van Gennep 1977).

Marx, Durkheim, and Weber's theories on religion were based on their studies of societies in which a single religion predominated. Thus it seemed reasonable to examine the relationship between a predominant religion and the society as a whole. However, since the 1950s, some U.S. sociologists have challenged this classical view. Living in a society that is highly tolerant of religious diversity, contemporary theorists have focused on religious pluralism rather than on religious domination. In contrast, Marx, Durkheim, and Weber believed religion reflected and reinforced society's values, or at least the values of those who were most powerful; provided solidarity and social stability; and was an engine of social change. According to this view, religion is threatened by **secular thinking**, particularly as seen in the rise of science, technology, and rational thought.

Secularization is typically accompanied by a decrease in religious belief and involvement, and it results in a weakening of the social and political power of religious organizations. Peter Berger (1967) has described religion in premodern societies as a "sacred canopy" that covers all aspects of life and is seldom questioned. In modern society, however, the sacred canopy is more like a quilt, a patchwork of different religious and secular belief systems. When beliefs are compared, it becomes increasingly difficult to sustain the idea that there is any single true faith.

Secularization: The Sociological Debate

The debate over secularization is one of the most complex areas in the sociology of religion. Basically, the disagreement is between supporters of the secularization thesis (who see religion as diminishing in power and importance in the modern world) and opponents (who argue that religion remains a significant force, albeit often in new and unfamiliar forms).

There is little consensus about how secularization should be measured and even how religion should be defined. Some argue that religion is best understood in terms of the traditional church; others seek a much broader view to include dimensions such as personal spirituality and deep commitment to certain values.

We can evaluate secularization according to a number of dimensions. Some are objective, such as the *level of membership* of religious organizations—how many people belong to a church or other religious body and attend services or other ceremonies. With the exception of the United States, the industrialized countries have all experienced considerable secularization according to this index. The pattern of religious decline seen in Britain is found in most of western Europe, including Catholic countries such as France and Italy. More Italians than French attend church regularly and participate in the major rituals (such as Easter Communion), but

The Spread of New Age Religions

If you pick up a local newspaper in any U.S. city and turn to the classified ads section, you are likely to find a number of listings relating to spirituality and the New Age movement. You have probably seen advertisements like these before: "A course in miracles. Personal coaching by the hour." "Soul purpose, past lives, intuitive healing." "Under the guidance of a Living Spiritual Teacher, you can be guided to take the next step in your spiritual unfoldment." These ads appeal to those who feel strong spiritual yearnings, who have a sense that their lives are not going quite the way they should, and who have become disenchanted with more established religions. While some of the advertisements are clearly attempts to profit from the willingness of some to believe anything they are told, most participants in the New Age movement see themselves as being on a sincere spiritual quest for self-enlightenment. Religious studies scholar Paul Heelas, in his 1996 book *The New Age Movement,* describes the New Age movement that has sprung up in response to this spiritual demand as having three essential characteristics: "It explains why life—as conventionally experienced—is not what it should be; it provides an account of what it is to find perfection; and it provides the means for

obtaining salvation." By most estimates, the number of people interested in such concerns is growing. Meditation groups, psychic fairs, spirituality discussion groups, training sessions designed to help participants reach their "true" spiritual potential, tarot card readings, books on spirituality and psychological self-help—all have proliferated since the 1960s.

the overall pattern of declining religious observance is similar in both cases.

A second dimension of secularization concerns how far churches and other religious organizations maintain their *social influence, wealth,* and *prestige.* In earlier times, religious organizations wielded considerable influence over governments and social agencies and commanded high respect in the community. How much is this still the case? Looking just at the twentieth century, we see that religious organizations have lost much of their former social and political influence, particularly in the advanced industrial nations. Church leaders can no longer expect to be influential with the powerful. Although some established churches remain very wealthy and new religious movements may rapidly build up fortunes, the material circumstances of many long-standing religious organizations are insecure. Churches and temples have to be sold off or are in disrepair, and entire dioceses have considered filing for bankruptcy.

A third dimension of secularization concerns beliefs and values—the dimension of *religiosity.* As in the other dimensions, we need an accurate understanding of the past to see how far religiosity has declined today. Supporters of the secularization thesis argue that in the past, religion was far more important to daily life than it is now. The church was at the heart of local affairs and strongly influenced family and personal life. Yet critics argue that just because people attended church more regularly does not prove that they were more religious. In many traditional societies, including medieval Europe, commitment to religious belief was less strong and less important in daily life than might be supposed. Research into English history, for example, shows lukewarm commitment to religious beliefs among the ordinary people. Religious skeptics seem to have existed in most cultures, particularly in the larger traditional societies (Ginzburg 1980).

Yet, doubtless, the hold of religious ideas today is weaker than in the traditional world—particularly if we include the

From the perspective of the sociology of religion, we can ask a number of questions about these developments. To what extent do these diverse phenomena form part of a coherent whole? What sociological factors account for the current popularity of the New Age movement? In what ways does the New Age movement differ from traditional forms of religiosity?

With respect to the last of these questions, one unique feature of the New Age movement is its eclecticism. Religions, of course, have always borrowed from one another. But most religions—no matter how much they adapt to current social and moral conditions—place a heavy emphasis on maintaining religious tradition. The faithful are often required by religious authorities to believe in the essential dogmas held by previous generations of worshipers. New Agers, however, tend to question the value of clinging to well-defined religious traditions. Instead, they believe that individuals should pick and choose those spiritual beliefs and practices that suit them best. Heelas writes: "Much of the New Age would appear to be quite radically detraditionalized (rejecting voices of authority associated with established orders)." Individuals, New Agers believe, should learn to listen to their intuition or "inner voice" to help them select the spiritual practices and make the life choices that are right for them.

The social organization of the New Age movement is entirely consistent with this philosophy. The movement consists of thousands of different groups, varying tremendously in size, with each group oriented around a different eclectic appropriation of the world's spiritual traditions. Many groups borrow heavily from Eastern spirituality—from Tibetan Buddhism, for

example. Others incorporate certain Native American traditions. Still others combine these with elements of Christianity. There is an almost infinite number of permutations.

What does this have to do with globalization? New Agers insist that they should be free to borrow any spiritual practices that are right for them. Why, they ask, should Tibetan Buddhism be reserved for Tibetans, or Native American rituals for Native Americans? Without wishing to rob these groups of their rich cultural heritage, New Agers firmly believe that the geographic borders of nation-states are entirely irrelevant to spirituality. Their eclecticism is truly global, and, primarily through books and travel, they scour the world in search of meaningful forms of spirituality. If the differences between nation-states begin to fade in a globalized world, New Agers may well embody the growing penetration of globalization into the religious realm.

range of the supernatural. Most of us no longer experience our environment as permeated by divine or spiritual entities. Some of the major tensions in the world today—such as those afflicting the Middle East and the Balkans or the violence perpetrated by the al Qaeda terrorist network—derive from religious differences. But the majority of conflicts and wars are now mainly secular, concerned with divergent political goals or material interests.

Contemporary Approaches: Religious Economy

A recent and influential approach to the sociology of religion is tailored to societies such as the United States that encompass many different faiths. Taking their cue from economic theory, sociologists who favor the **religious economy** approach argue that religions can be understood as organizations in competition with one another for followers (Finke and Stark 1988, 1992; Hammond 1992; Moore 1994; Roof and McKinney 1990; Stark and Bainbridge 1987; Warner 1993).

These sociologists argue that competition is preferable to monopoly when it comes to ensuring religious vitality. Whereas the classical theorists Marx, Durkheim, and Weber assumed that religion weakens when challenged by different religious or secular viewpoints, the advocates of the religious economy perspective argue that competition increases the overall level of religious involvement in society. First, the competition makes each religious group try that much harder to win followers. Second, the presence of numerous religions means there is likely something for everyone. In a culturally diverse society, a single religion will probably appeal to a limited range of followers, whereas the presence of, say, Indian gurus and fundamentalist preachers, in addition to mainline churches, will likely encourage a high level of religious participation.

How Secular Are We?

On February 11, 1858, the Blessed Virgin Mary, the Mother of Jesus Christ, appeared to Bernadette Soubirous, a fourteen-year-old peasant girl, in a cave near the town of Lourdes in Southwestern France, close to the Spanish border. It was the first of eighteen such visitations that took place between February and mid-July of that year. At least that is what a great many Roman Catholics, and other Christians, believe. So many, in fact, that presently close to five million visitors a year easily fill the nearly three hundred hotels that have been built near the small town during the century and a half since the apparitions. Most come

as pilgrims, many to be healed—or to bring their loved ones to be healed—of their afflictions and maladies.

For Karl Marx, and a great many other sociologists since, practices and beliefs like those at Lourdes are a kind of painkiller, or, as he put it: "Religion is the sigh of the oppressed creature, the heart of a heartless world, and the soul of soulless conditions. It is the opium of the people." Modern society, by contrast, with its technological power, improved living standards, and individual freedoms, was expected to replace belief in the sacred with something secular. Many sociologists expected that a world enchanted

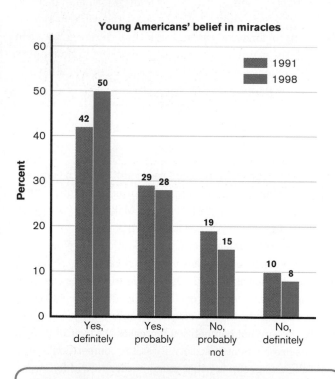

Young Americans' belief in miracles

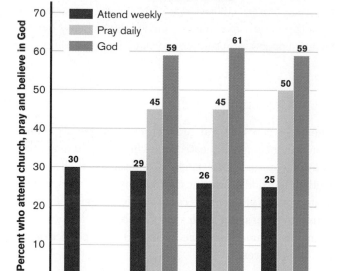

Young Americans' churchgoing, praying and belief in God

⬆ How widespread are beliefs in divine, or supernatural, intervention in the United States? In 1991 and 1998, the General Social Survey (GSS) asked a representative sample of Americans whether they believed in miracles. Around three quarters of people age eighteen to forty stated that they did, with close to half stating that they "definitely believed" in religious miracles.

⬆ As you can see in the figure above, between the early 1980s and 2006, three out of five young Americans reported that "they knew God really exists and had no doubts about it." It, however, also shows a far smaller number attending church weekly, and that number appears to be getting smaller. So, at the beginning of the new millennium, most young people say they believe in God, fewer pray daily, and only one out of four go to church weekly.

Created by John Grady.

by religious faith and miracles would wither away as a more rational, this-worldly, approach to life prevailed. Whether that could happen under capitalism was a matter of some dispute, but most social scientists agreed that belief, and trust, in the supernatural should disappear as newer, more modern, generations took their parents' and grandparents' place. But is it necessarily true that modernity and the supernatural are like oil and water and that an embrace of a scientifically based, technologically driven culture rules out belief in divine intervention and miracles? Does our secular society promise anything more than abundance and freedom? Who, or what, should be our guide in regulating and judging our "heart" or the quality of our relationships with other beings? What can satisfy the yearning of our "soul" for purpose and meaning? Are these some of the reasons why religious belief persists long after it was supposed to have withered away and why kids who have embraced modernity still go on pilgrimages?

⬇ Nearly thirty years ago, Marrie Bot documented Lourdes and other Christian pilgrimage sites in Europe, capturing the pilgrims' expressions of deep faith and penitential devotion. In her photographs, pilgrims implore the Holy Mother to intercede with God on their behalf, pleading for remission of their sins and release from their pain.

⬇ In May 2004, hundreds of pilgrims participate in a trip to Lourdes. Many of the photos show pilgrims walking and being wheeled to the Grotto where the Virgin is believed to have appeared.

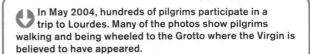

⬅ Pilgrims also enjoyed lighter moments: eating and drinking, enjoying each other's company at night, and, of course, posing for the camera. How similar are these photos to those that we might take of our friends? How alike are the poses they assume to those in our photo collections? Are they really serious pilgrims or just tourists having a good time?

➡ The Lourdes apparitions occurred in the mid-nineteenth century. Nevertheless, a list of more recent claims of apparition-like phenomena have attracted millions of people. For instance, Fred Whan of Ontario attracted wide attention when he discovered this fish stick, which he believes bears the image of Jesus.

Religious economy scholars believe that competition between religions leads to religious vitality. They also argue that successful religious groups have effective representatives spreading their beliefs and rituals. For example, the fall of communism in Mongolia brought religious freedom to this sparsely populated country located between China and Russia. It also brought foreigners eager for converts to Mongolia, like the Mormon missionaries pictured here, Korean Christians, and Catholics.

This analysis is adapted from the business world, in which competition presumably encourages the emergence of specialized products appealing to specific markets. In fact, religious economists borrow the language of business in describing the conditions that lead to the success or failure of a particular religious organization. According to Roger Finke and Rodney Stark (1992), a successful religious group must be well organized for competition, have eloquent preachers who are effective "sales reps" in spreading the word, offer beliefs and rituals that are packaged as an appealing product, and develop effective marketing techniques. Television evangelists have been especially good businesspeople in selling religious products.

Thus religious economy scholars such as Finke and Stark do not see competition as undermining religious beliefs and contributing to secularization. Rather, they argue that modern religion constantly renews itself through active marketing and recruitment. Although a growing body of research supports the notion that competition is good for religion (Finke and Stark 1992; Stark and Bainbridge 1980, 1985), not all research comes to this conclusion (Land et al. 1991).

The religious-economy approach overestimates the extent to which people rationally choose a religion. Among deeply committed believers, even in societies where people can choose among religions, most practice their childhood religion without considering alternatives. Wade Clark Roof's 1993 study of fourteen hundred baby boomers found that a third remained loyal to their childhood faith, while another third continued to profess their childhood beliefs although they no longer belonged to a religious organization. Thus only a third were actively seeking a new religion, making the sorts of choices presumed by the religious economy approach.

☑ CONCEPT CHECKS

1. Why did Karl Marx call religion "the opium of the people"?
2. What are the differences between classical and contemporary approaches to understanding religion?

Types of Religious Organizations

Although the sociology of religion has included non-European religions since its origins in the writings of Durkheim and Weber, there has been a tendency to view all religions through concepts based in the European experience. For example, notions such as *denomination* or *sect* presuppose formally organized religious institutions; they are of questionable utility in studying religions that emphasize spiritual practice as a part of daily life or that pursue the complete integration of religion with civic and political life. Recently, there has been an effort to create a comparative sociology of religion that examines religious traditions from within their own frames of reference (Juergensmeyer 1993; Smart 1989; van der Veer 1994; Wilson 1982).

Early theorists such as Max Weber (1963; orig. 1921), Ernst Troeltsch (1931), and Richard Niebuhr (1929) described religious organizations according to the degree to which they were well established and conventional: Churches are conventional and well established, cults are neither, and sects fall somewhere in the middle. These distinctions were based on the study of European and U.S. religions. There is much debate over how well they apply to the non-Christian world.

Today, sociologists are aware that the terms *sect* and *cult* have negative connotations, so instead they use the phrase *new religious movements* to characterize novel religious organizations lacking the respectability that comes with being well established for a long period (Hadden 1997b; Hexham and Poewe 1997).

Churches and Sects

Churches are large, established religious bodies; one example is the Roman Catholic Church. They normally have a formal, bureaucratic structure with a hierarchy of officials. Churches often represent the conservative face of religion, because they are integrated within the existing institutional order. Most of their adherents are born into and grow up with the church.

Sects are smaller, less organized groups of committed believers, usually set up in protest against an established church, as Calvinism and Methodism were initially. Sects aim at following the "true way" and either try to change the surrounding society or withdraw into communities of their own, a process known as *revival*. The members of sects regard established churches as corrupt. Many sects have few or no officials, and all members are equal participants. For the most part, people are not born into sects but join them to further personal beliefs.

Denominations and Cults

A **denomination** is a sect that has become an institutionalized body rather than an activist protest group. Sects that survive over time become denominations. Calvinism and Methodism were sects during their early period when they generated great fervor among their members, but over the years they have become more established. (Calvinists today are called Presbyterians.) Denominations are recognized as legitimate by churches, often cooperating harmoniously with them.

Cults resemble sects, but their emphases are different. The most loosely knit and transient of all religious organizations, cults comprise individuals who reject the values of the outside society. They are a form of religious innovation rather than revival. Their focus is on individual experience, bringing like-minded people together. Like sects, cults often form around the influence of an inspirational leader.

Cults are often in a high degree of tension with the larger society. A tragic example occurred in 1993 when eighty members of the Branch Davidian religious cult burned to death in their Waco, Texas, compound during an assault by federal officials that ended a lengthy armed standoff. Federal officials maintain that the cult members were prisoners of their charismatic leader, David Koresh, who was allegedly stockpiling illegal weapons, practicing polygyny, and having sex with some of the children. Koresh reportedly preferred mass suicide to surrender (Tabor and Gallagher 1995). In 1997, thirty-nine members of Heaven's Gate, a cult whose members believed that they were destined for a "higher level," took their lives to ascend to a spaceship they believed lurked behind the Hale-Bopp comet.

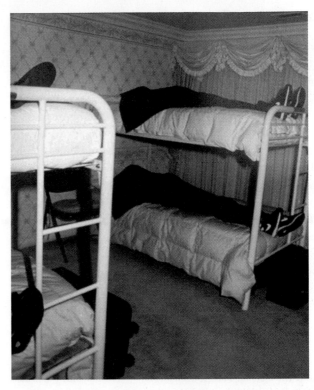

Members of the Heaven's Gate cult, who killed themselves in a mass suicide in 1997.

Like sects, cults flourish when there is a breakdown in well-established societal belief systems. This is happening worldwide today, in places as diverse as Japan, India, and the United States. When such a breakdown occurs, cults may either originate within the society itself or be "imported" from outside. In the United States, examples of homegrown, or indigenous, cults include New Age religions based on spiritualism, astrology, and religious practices adapted from Asian or Native American cultures. Examples of imported cults include the Reverend Sun Myung Moon's Unification Church ("Moonies"), which originated in South Korea, and the transcendental meditation movement, which was promoted by the Maharishi Mahesh Yogi in India.

A cult in one country may be an established religious practice in another. When Indian gurus (religious teachers) practice in the United States, what might be considered an established religion in India is regarded as a cult in the United States. Christianity began as an indigenous cult in ancient Jerusalem, and in many Asian countries today Evangelical Protestantism is regarded as a cult imported from the United States. A leading sociologist of religion, Jeffrey K. Hadden (1997a), points out that all the approximately one hundred thousand religions that humans have devised were once new; most were initially despised cults from the standpoint of respectable religious belief of the times. For example, Jesus was crucified because his ideas threatened the established order of the Roman-dominated religious establishment of ancient Judaea.

Religious Movements

Religious movements represent a subtype of social movement. A religious movement is an association of people who spread a new religion or promote a new interpretation of an existing religion. Religious movements are larger than sects and less exclusive in their membership—although like churches and sects, movements and sects (or cults) are not always clearly distinct from each other. In fact, all sects and cults can be classified as religious movements. Examples of religious movements include the groups that originally founded and spread Christianity in the first century, the Lutheran movement that split Christianity in Europe about fifteen hundred years afterward, and the groups involved in the more recent Islamic revolution (discussed later in the chapter).

Religious movements pass through phases of development. In the first phase, the movement derives life and cohesion from a powerful leader. Max Weber classified such leaders as **charismatic**—that is, having inspirational qualities capable of capturing the imagination and devotion of a mass of followers. (Charismatic leaders in Weber's formulation could include political as well as religious figures—revolutionary China's Mao Zedong, for example, as well as Jesus and Muhammad.) The leaders of religious movements usually criticize the religious establishment and proclaim a new message. In their early years, religious movements are fluid; they do not have an established authority system. Their members are normally in direct contact with the charismatic leader, and together they spread the new teachings.

The second phase occurs following the death of the charismatic leader, when the movement must face what Weber termed the "routinization of charisma." To survive, the movement has to create formalized rules and procedures, because it can no longer depend on the central role of the original leader in organizing the followers. Many movements fade away when their leaders die or lose influence. A movement that takes on a permanent character becomes a church—a formal organization of believers with an established authority system and established symbols and rituals. The church itself might later become the origin of other movements that question its teachings and either set themselves up in opposition or break away.

New Religious Movements

Sociologists use the term **new religious movements** to encompass the broad range of religious and spiritual groups, cults, and sects that have emerged in Western countries, including the United States, alongside mainstream religions. New religious movements comprise an enormous diversity of groups, from spiritual and self-help groups within the New Age movement to exclusive sects such as the Hare Krishnas (International Society for Krishna Consciousness).

Many new religious movements are derived from mainstream religious traditions, such as Hinduism, Christianity, and Buddhism, whereas others have emerged from traditions that were almost unknown in the West until recently. Some new religious movements are creations of the charismatic leaders who head their activities. This is the case with the Unification Church, led by the Reverend Sun Myung Moon, whose members are expected to fraternize only with each other, to donate their property to the cult, and to obey Moon's commands. (This movement was introduced into the United States at the beginning of the 1960s, and it appealed to many who were rejecting traditional religion and looking for insight in Eastern religious teachings.) Membership in new religious movements mostly consists of converts rather than individuals brought up in a particular faith. Members are usually well educated and from middle-class backgrounds.

Various theories explain the popularity of new religious movements. Some observers argue that they reflect liberalization and secularization within society and within traditional churches. People who feel that traditional religions have become ritualistic and devoid of spiritual meaning may find comfort and a greater sense of community in smaller, less impersonal, new religious movements.

Others see new religious movements as an outcome of rapid social change (Wilson 1982). As traditional social norms are disrupted, people search for explanations and reassurance. The rise of groups and sects emphasizing personal spirituality, for example, suggests that many individuals need to reconnect with their own values or beliefs in the face of instability and uncertainty.

Furthermore, new religious movements may appeal to people who feel alienated from mainstream society. The collective, communal approaches of sects and cults, some authors argue, can offer support and a sense of belonging. For example, today's middle-class youth are not marginalized from society in a material sense, but they may feel isolated emotionally and spiritually. Membership in a cult can overcome this alienation (Wallis 1984).

New religious movements fall into three broad categories: *world-affirming, world-rejecting,* and *world-accommodating* movements. Each category is based on the relationship of the group to the larger social world.

WORLD-AFFIRMING MOVEMENTS

World-affirming movements are more like self-help or therapy groups than conventional religious groups. These movements often lack rituals, churches, and formal theologies, focusing

"World-affirming groups," such as the Church of Scientology, focus on members' spiritual well-being and do not reject the outside world's values. Science-fiction writer L. Ron Hubbard established scientology in 1954.

instead on members' spiritual well-being. World-affirming movements do not reject the outside world or its values. Rather, they seek to enhance their followers' abilities to perform and succeed in that world by unlocking human potential.

The Church of Scientology is one such group. Founded by L. Ron Hubbard, it has grown from its original base in California to include a large membership worldwide. Scientologists believe people are all spiritual beings but have neglected their spiritual nature. Through training that makes them aware of their real spiritual capacities, people can recover forgotten supernatural powers, clear their minds, and reveal their full potential.

Many strands of the so-called **New Age movement** are world-affirming movements. The New Age movement emerged from the counterculture of the 1960s and 1970s and encompasses a broad spectrum of beliefs, practices, and ways of life. Pagan teachings (Celtic, Druidic, Native American, and others), shamanism, forms of Asian mysticism, Wiccan rituals, and Zen meditation are among activities that are thought of as New Age.

The mysticism of the New Age movement appears to contrast with the modern societies in which it is favored. Followers of New Age movements develop alternative ways of life to cope with the challenges of modernity. Yet New Age activities should not be interpreted as simply a radical break with the present. They are also part of a larger cultural trajectory exemplifying mainstream culture. In late modern societies,

individuals possess unparalleled degrees of autonomy and freedom to chart their own lives. In this respect, the aims of the New Age movement coincide closely with the modern age: People are encouraged to move beyond traditional values and expectations and to live actively and reflectively.

WORLD-REJECTING MOVEMENTS

World-rejecting movements are highly critical of the outside world and often demand significant lifestyle changes from their followers—such as living ascetically, changing their dress or hairstyle, or following a certain diet. World-rejecting movements are frequently exclusive, in contrast to world-affirming movements, which are inclusive. Some world-rejecting movements display characteristics of **total institutions**; members subsume their individual identities into that of the group, follow strict ethical codes or rules, and withdraw from activity in the outside world.

Most world-rejecting movements demand more of their members, in terms of time and commitment, than older established religions. Some groups use the technique of "love bombing" to gain the individual's total adherence. A potential convert is overwhelmed by attention and constant displays of affection until he or she is drawn emotionally into the group. Some new movements, in fact, have been accused of brainwashing their adherents—robbing them of the capacity for independent decision making.

Many world-rejecting cults and sects have come under the intense scrutiny of state authorities, the media, and the public. Certain extreme cases have attracted much concern. For example, the Japanese group Aum Shinrikyo released deadly sarin gas into the Tokyo subway system in 1995, injuring thousands of commuters. As noted earlier in the chapter, the Branch Davidian cult, based in Waco, Texas, became embroiled in a deadly confrontation with federal authorities in 1993 after accusations of child abuse and weapons stockpiling.

WORLD-ACCOMMODATING MOVEMENTS

World-accommodating movements emphasize the importance of inner religious life over more worldly concerns. Members of such groups seek to reclaim the spiritual purity that they believe has been lost in traditional religious settings. Whereas followers of world-rejecting and world-affirming groups may alter their lifestyles in accordance with their religious activity, many adherents of world-accommodating movements carry on their lives and careers with little visible change. One example is Pentecostalism. Pentecostalists believe that the Holy Spirit can be heard through individuals who are granted the gift of "speaking in tongues."

The enduring popularity of new religious movements presents another challenge to the secularization thesis. Opponents point to the diversity and dynamism of new religious movements and argue that religion and spirituality remain central facets of modern life. As traditional religions lose their hold, they claim, religion is not disappearing but is heading in new directions. Not all scholars agree, however. Proponents of secularization hold that these movements remain peripheral to society, even if they profoundly impact the lives of their followers. New religious movements are fragmented and relatively unorganized; they also suffer from high turnover rates. Compared to a serious religious commitment, proponents argue, participation in a new religious movement appears to be little more than a hobby or lifestyle choice.

☑ CONCEPT CHECKS

1. Describe four types of religious organizations.
2. Compare and contrast religious movements and new religious movements.
3. What are three types of new religious movements?

Gender and Religion

Churches and denominations resemble other social institutions in that women have been mostly excluded from power. The following sections examine some of the interrelations of religion and gender. The issue is important because this is an area in which significant changes are occurring.

Religious Images

In Christianity, although Mary, the mother of Jesus, is sometimes treated as having divine qualities, God is "the Father," a male figure, and Jesus took the human shape of a man. Genesis, the first book of the Bible, teaches that woman was created from a man's rib. These facts have not gone unnoticed by women's movements. Over a hundred years ago, Elizabeth Cady Stanton published a series of commentaries on the Scriptures, titled *The Woman's Bible*. In her view, the deity had created women and men as beings of equal value, and the Bible should fully reflect this fact. The "masculinist" character of the Bible reflected the fact that it was written by men. In 1870, the Church of England established a Revising Committee to revise and update the biblical texts, but the committee contained no women. Stanton asserted that there was no reason to suppose that God is a man, because it was clear in the Scriptures that all human beings were fashioned in the image of God. She subsequently organized the Women's Revising Committee in America, composed of twenty-three women, to advise her in preparing *The Woman's Bible,* which was published in 1895.

In some Buddhist orders, especially Mahayana Buddhism, women are represented in a favorable light. But on the whole, Buddhism is "an overwhelmingly male-created institution dominated by a patriarchal power structure," in which the feminine is mostly "associated with the secular, powerless, profane, and imperfect" (Paul 1985). The contrasting pictures of women that appear in the Buddhist texts no doubt mirror the ambiguous attitudes of men toward women in the secular world: Women are portrayed as wise, maternal, and gentle yet also as mysterious, polluting, and destructive, threatening evil.

The Role of Women in Religious Organizations

In both Buddhism and (later) Christianity, women were allowed to express strong religious convictions by becoming nuns. Although the first orders for women were probably established in the twelfth century, their membership remained small until the 1800s. At that time, many women took religious vows to become teachers and nurses because these occupations were largely controlled by the religious orders. Nonetheless, female religious orders remained subject to a male hierarchy, and elaborate rituals reinforced this subjugation. For example, all nuns were regarded as "brides of Christ." Until some orders made changes in the 1950s and 1960s, "marriage" ceremonies were carried out during which the novice would cut her hair, receive her religious name, and sometimes be given a wedding ring. After several years, a novice would take a vow of perpetual profession, after which she was required to receive dispensation if she chose to leave.

Women's orders today show considerable diversity. In some convents, nuns still dress in traditional habit and live in communities removed from the secular world. In other convents, nuns wear ordinary dress and live in apartments or houses. Traditional restrictions such as not talking to others at certain periods of the day or walking with hands folded and hidden under the habit are rarely evident.

Despite such liberalization, women have filled only lower status positions in religious organizations. This situation is changing, in line with changes affecting women in society generally. In recent years, women's groups have pressed for equal status in religious orders. Increasingly, the Catholic

Women are playing an increasingly important role as religious leaders today. Laura Geller is the senior rabbi at Temple Emanuel in Beverly Hills, one of the country's largest synagogues. When she was ordained in 1976, Geller was only the third female rabbi in the United States; she was the first to become the head rabbi at a major synagogue.

and Episcopalian churches are under strong pressure to allow women an equal voice in their hierarchies. Yet in 1977, the Sacred Congregation for the Doctrine of the Faith in Rome declared that women could not be admitted to the Catholic priesthood; the reason was that Jesus had not called a woman to be one of his disciples. Ten years later, 1987 was officially designated as the "Year of the Madonna," in which women were advised to recall their traditional role as wives and mothers. The barriers to Catholic women in the hierarchy of the church thus remain formidable. In a letter published in May 1994, Pope John Paul II reaffirmed the Roman Catholic Church's ban on the ordination of women.

The Episcopal Church has allowed women into its priesthood since 1976. Altogether, women have been ordained as ministers in about half of the Protestant denominations in the United States, including the Presbyterian Church (U.S.A.), the Evangelical Lutheran Church in America, the African Methodist Episcopal Church, and the United Methodist Church. And except within Orthodox Judaism, women in the United States can become rabbis as well.

Women and Islam

Before the militant Islamic nationalists called the Taliban took over Afghanistan, Shafiqa Habibi's face was known throughout the country: She was Afghanistan's most popular television news anchor. But during the Taliban's rule, she spent her time at home hidden from public view. When she ventured out, her body had to be covered by a tentlike garment with a screen sewn into the fabric over her face to hide her eyes but allow some ability to see (Filkins 1998).

Habibi's experience was shared by all Afghan women. The Taliban's extreme Islamic beliefs forbade women to work outside the home, attend school, or appear in public without covering their bodies from head to toe. Women seen in public with any man who was not their husband or relative were brutally beaten or killed. Since the overthrow of the Taliban in 2001, women have begun to regain their rights in Afghanistan, at least in the capital city of Kabul. But throughout much of the rest of the country, local religious leaders, including the Taliban, have begun to make a comeback, and women are afraid to exercise their legal rights for fear of retribution.

☑ CONCEPT CHECKS

1. Describe three recent turning points for women in U.S. religious denominations.
2. How has the Taliban takeover of Afghanistan affected women?

World Religions

Although there are thousands of religions worldwide, three of them—Christianity, Islam, and Hinduism—are embraced by nearly three quarters of the people on earth (Figure 17.1 and Global Map 17.1).

Christianity

With its estimated 2.1 billion followers—roughly a third of the world's population—Christianity encompasses enormously divergent denominations, sects, and cults. Common to all is the belief that Jesus of Nazareth was the Christ (Messiah, or "anointed one") foretold in the Hebrew Bible. Christianity is a form of **monotheism**—belief in a single all-knowing, all-powerful God—although in most Christian faiths God is also regarded as a trinity embracing a heavenly Father, His Son the Savior, and His sustaining Holy Spirit.

When Christianity emerged in Palestine some two thousand years ago, it was a persecuted sect outside mainstream Jewish and Roman religious practices. Yet within four centuries, Christianity had become the official religion of the Roman Empire. In the eleventh century, Christianity divided into the

Major Religions of the World

Missionaries and military force are two reasons that the majority of people in the world profess only a handful of religions today. Although Christianity (Catholicism and Protestantism) is the most widespread religion, its followers are becoming outnumbered by followers of Islam. Many of the predominantly Catholic countries of Central and South America have strong and, in some cases, growing Protestant minorities.

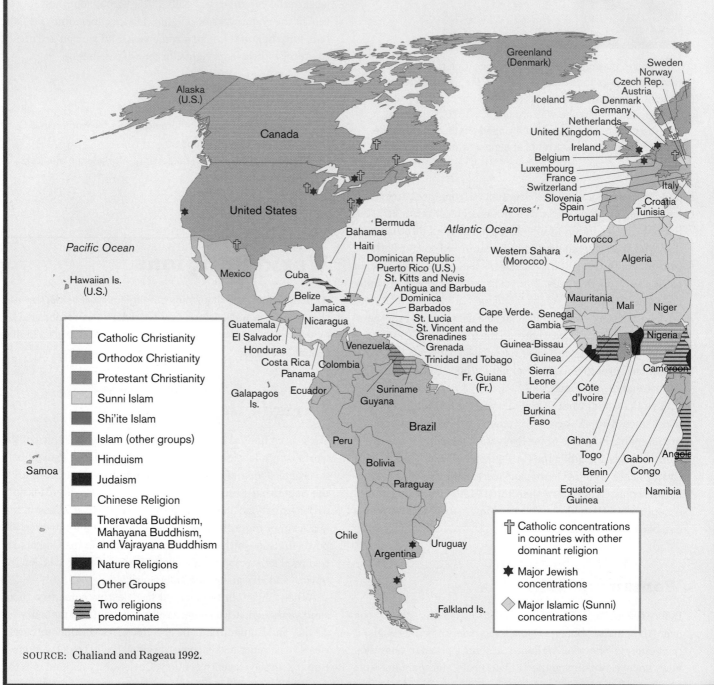

SOURCE: Chaliand and Rageau 1992.

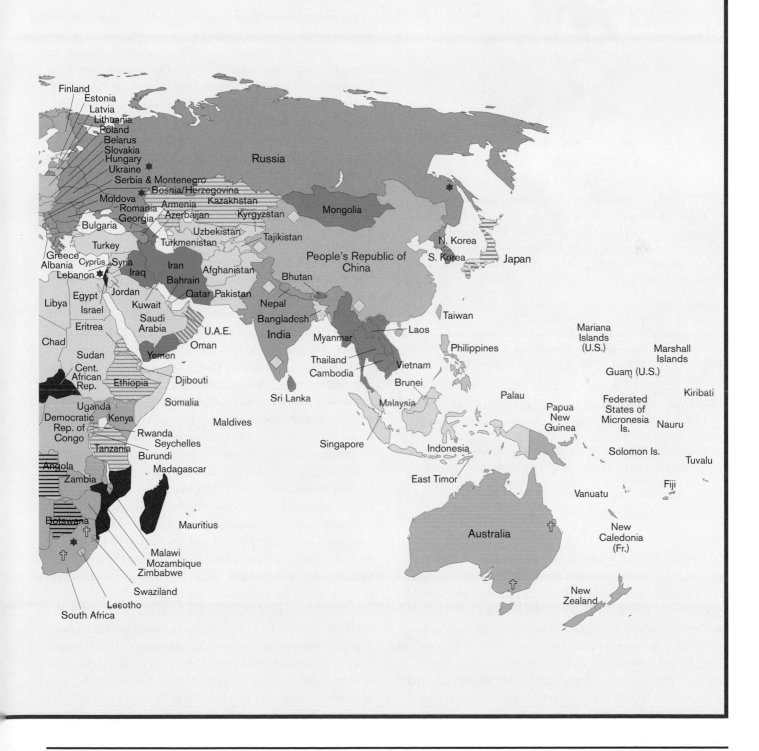

Finland
Estonia
Latvia
Lithuania
Poland
Belarus
Slovakia
Hungary
Ukraine
Serbia & Montenegro
Bosnia/Herzegovina
Moldova
Romania
Armenia
Georgia
Azerbaijan
Bulgaria
Turkey
Greece
Albania
Cyprus
Syria
Lebanon
Egypt
Israel
Jordan
Libya
Iran
Iraq
Bahrain
Qatar
Kuwait
Saudi
Arabia
U.A.E.
Oman
Yemen
Chad
Eritrea
Sudan
Cent.
African
Rep.
Ethiopia
Djibouti
Somalia
Uganda
Democratic
Rep. of
Congo
Kenya
Rwanda
Seychelles
Tanzania
Burundi
Madagascar
Angola
Zambia
Botswana
Mauritius
Malawi
Mozambique
Zimbabwe
Swaziland
Lesotho
South Africa

Russia
Kazakhstan
Turkmenistan
Uzbekistan
Tajikistan
Kyrgyzstan
Afghanistan
Pakistan
Mongolia
People's Republic of
China
N. Korea
S. Korea
Japan
Nepal
Bhutan
Bangladesh
India
Myanmar
Laos
Taiwan
Thailand
Cambodia
Vietnam
Sri Lanka
Philippines
Maldives
Malaysia
Brunei
Singapore
Indonesia
East Timor

Mariana
Islands
(U.S.)
Marshall
Islands
Guam (U.S.)
Kiribati
Palau
Papua
New
Guinea
Federated
States of
Micronesia
Is.
Nauru
Solomon Is.
Tuvalu
Vanuatu
Fiji
Australia
New
Caledonia
(Fr.)
New
Zealand

FIGURE 17.1

Percentages of Religious Adherents Worldwide

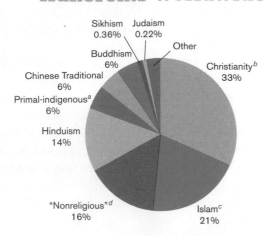

Sikhism 0.36% · Judaism 0.22% · Other · Buddhism 6% · Chinese Traditional 6% · Primal-indigenous[a] 6% · Hinduism 14% · "Nonreligious"[d] 16% · Islam[c] 21% · Christianity[b] 33%

Which three religions are adhered to by almost 75 percent of the Earth's population? According to your chapter, which of the religions above is the fastest growing? Why? What might the effects of globalization be on the number of adherents for the religions above?

[a] Includes African Traditional/Diasporic.
[b] Includes Catholic, Protestant, Eastern Orthodox, Pentecostal, Anglican, Monophysite, African Independent Churches, Latter-Day Saints, Evangelical, Seventh-Day Adventists, Jehovah's Witnesses, Quakers, Assembly of God, nominal, etc.
[c] Shiite, Sunni, etc.
[d] Includes agnostic, atheist, secular humanist, and people answering "none" or no religious preference; half of this group is "theistic" but nonreligious.
Note: Total adds up to more than 100 percent due to rounding and because upper bound estimates were used for each group.
SOURCE: Adherents.com 2007.

Christianity was spread through conquest and missionary work. The European colonization of much of Africa, Asia, and North and South America that began in the fifteenth century brought Christian teachings, churches, and large-scale conversion of native peoples. In some places, converts were people from the impoverished classes, for whom Christianity was a means of social mobility. Only in Asia are Christians a small minority, largely because countries like Japan and China successfully resisted most colonization and the accompanying Christianization.

Recently, Protestant evangelical groups have increased their efforts to convert people throughout the world, making significant inroads in traditionally Catholic countries. In Mexico, for example, the number of Evangelical Protestants grew from nine hundred thousand to four million between 1970 and 1990, owing to the efforts of local (Mexican) missionaries. The growth of evangelical Christianity may prove difficult to sustain. It makes considerable demands on its followers, so it remains to be seen whether the children of new converts will remain true to their parents' faith once they become adults (Bowen 1996).

Islam

Islam is the second largest and fastest growing religion in the world today. There are about 1.8 billion Muslims in the world in 2007 (Muslim is the name for those who practice *al-islam,* an Arabic term meaning submission without reservation to God's will), and the number is increasing by 25 million each year. Islam began as and remains the official faith of Arabs and other peoples of the Middle East and has spread into Africa, Europe, the former Soviet Union, India, Pakistan, China, and Indonesia. Today, more than sixty different ethnic groups of a million or more people practice Islam. In fact, far more non-Arabs than Arabs identify themselves as Muslims.

Muslims believe in absolute, unquestioning, positive devotion to Allah (God). Although modern Islam dates to the Arab Prophet Muhammad (c. 570–632), Muslims trace their religion to the ancient Hebrew prophet Abraham, also regarded as the founder of Judaism. The precepts of Islam are believed to have been revealed to Muhammad and are contained in a sacred book dictated to his followers called the Koran (the common English form of the book's name, which means "recitation"; another is Qur'ān, which is closer to the Arabic pronunciation). Muhammad's ideas were not accepted in his birthplace of Mecca, so in 622 he and his followers moved to Medina (both in what is today Saudi Arabia). This migration, called the *hijra,* marks the beginning of Islam, which soon spread throughout Arabia. Muslims do not worship Muhammad but regard him as a great teacher and prophet, the last in a line that includes Abraham, Noah, Moses, and Jesus.

Eastern Orthodox Church (based in Turkey) and the Catholic Church (based in Rome). A second great split occurred within the Catholic branch in the sixteenth century, when the Protestant Reformation gave rise to numerous Protestant denominations, sects, and cults. Protestants emphasize a direct relationship between the individual and God, with each person being responsible for his or her own salvation. Catholics, in contrast, emphasize the importance of the church hierarchy as the means to salvation, with the pope in Rome being the highest earthly authority.

Every able-bodied Muslim who can afford to is obligated to make the pilgrimage to Mecca, Saudi Arabia, at least once in a lifetime. The pilgrims pictured here surround the *ka'aba,* a small cube-shaped building which houses the Hajar el Aswad (the Black Stone). Muslims believe that this stone fell from the sky during the time of Adam and that it has the power to cleanse worshipers of their sins by absorbing them into itself. The stone is believed to have originally been white, but it is said to have turned black because of the sins it has absorbed over the years.

Islam is an all-encompassing religion. The sacred *sharia* (way) includes prescriptions for worship, daily life, ethics, and government. Although U.S. standards might find Muslim beliefs to be extremely restrictive, Muslims frequently view American life as spiritually undisciplined, corrupt, and immoral (Abdul-Rauf 1975; Arjomand 1988; Esposito 1984; Kedouri 1992; MacEnoin and al-Shahi 1983; Martin 1982).

Just as Christianity comprises different religious groups, so does Islam. The principal division is between Sunnis (about 85 percent of all Muslims) and Shiites (15 percent). Sunni Muslims follow a series of traditions deriving from the Qur'ān that tolerate a diversity of opinion, in contrast to the more rigid views of Shiites. Shiism split from the main body of orthodox Islam early in its history and has remained influential ever since. Iran (once known as Persia) is the only major Islamic country that is overwhelmingly Shiite, although there are Shiite majorities in several other countries, including Iraq. There are large numbers of Shiites in other Middle Eastern countries, as well as in Turkey, Afghanistan, India, and Pakistan.

Shiism has been the official religion of Iran since the sixteenth century and was fundamental to the religiously conservative Iranian Revolution of 1978–1979. The Shiites trace their beginnings to Imam Ali, a seventh-century religious and political leader who showed outstanding virtue and personal devotion to God. Ali's descendants were considered the rightful leaders of Islam, because they were held to belong to the prophet Muhammad's family, unlike the dynasties actually in power. The Shiites believed that the rule of Muhammad's rightful heir would eventually be instituted, doing away with the tyrannies and injustices associated with existing regimes. Muhammad's heir would be a leader directly guided by God, governing in accordance with the Qur'ān.

There is no separation of church and state in a few highly religious Islamic societies, such as Iran. In most Muslim countries, however, religious leaders live in uneasy alliance with secular governments. Egypt, Algeria, Turkey, and Indonesia, for example, are all predominantly Muslim societies in which mosque and state are separate. In Algeria, religious groups that would have created an Islamic state won the popular vote in 1991, only to see the elections overturned by the military government. The result has been escalating violence and bloodshed (Juergensmeyer 1995a).

Judaism

With just under fifteen million followers worldwide, Judaism is by far the smallest of the world's major religions, yet it has exerted an influence greater than its limited numbers would suggest. First, it is the source of the world's two largest religions, Islam and Christianity. Second, in European and U.S. culture, Jews have played a role disproportionate to their numbers in such diverse fields as music, literature, science, education, and business. Third, the existence of Israel as a Jewish state since 1948 has given the Jewish faith international prominence. Israel has existed in nearly constant tension with many of its neighboring Arab countries since its founding and has seldom been out of the news.

Jews have often suffered persecution. From the twelfth century on, European and Russian Jews were often forced to live in special districts termed "ghettos," where they lacked full rights as citizens and were sometimes the target of harassment, attacks, and murders. Partly in reaction to these conditions, and partly because the Torah identifies the city of Jerusalem as the center of the Jewish homeland, some Jews embraced *Zionism,* a movement calling for the return of Jews to Palestine and the creation of a Jewish state. (Zion is a biblical name for the ancient city of Jerusalem.) Although secular Zionists viewed Israel as a country where persecuted Jews could seek refuge, religious Zionists saw it as the one Jewish homeland, returning to which would fulfill biblical prophecies. Zionists established settlements in Palestine early in the twentieth century, living peacefully with their Arab and Palestinian neighbors. However, after World War II and the

Nazi extermination of six million Jews during the Holocaust, the League of Nations and United Nations approved of the creation of the state of Israel as a homeland for the survivors. This action ended the once relatively peaceful relationship between Zionists and their neighbors.

Hinduism

Hinduism, which dates to about 2000 B.C.E. and is one of the world's oldest religions, is the source of Buddhism and Sikhism. It is not based on the teachings of any individual, and its followers do not trace their national origins to a single god. Hinduism is an ethical religion that calls for an ideal way of life. Today there are nearly nine hundred million Hindus worldwide, primarily in India. The census of India estimated that in 2001, 80 percent of its population—amounting to over 827 million people—was Hindu (Census of India 2007b).

As we saw in Chapter 8, India's social structure is characterized by a caste system in which people are believed to be born to a certain status that they occupy for life. Although the caste system was abolished in 1949, it remains powerful. The caste system has its origins in Hindu beliefs, which hold that an ideal life is partly achieved by performing the duties appropriate to one's caste.

Perhaps because Hinduism does not have a central organization or leader, its philosophy and practice are extremely diverse. Religious teachings direct all aspects of life, but in a variety of ways—ranging from promoting the enjoyment of sensual pleasures to advising the renunciation of earthly pursuits. Mahatma Gandhi was a modern example of a man who devoted his life to the Hindu virtues of "honesty, courage, service, faith, self-control, purity, and nonviolence" (Potter 1992).

Despite the teaching that life is *maya,* or illusion, Hindu religious beliefs have an earthly quality. For example, although temples and pilgrimage centers are located on sacred sites, any location may be a place of devotion. Hindus believe in the godlike unity of all things, yet their religion also has aspects of **polytheism**, the belief that different gods represent various categories of natural forces. For example, Hindus worship gods representing aspects of the whole, such as the divine dimension of a spiritual teacher (Basham 1989; Kinsley 1982; Potter 1992; Schmidt 1980).

☑ CONCEPT CHECKS

1. What three religious groups are the largest in the world?
2. What three factors explain the influence of Judaism on the world?
3. Describe the origin of the caste system in India.

Religion in the United States

In comparison with the citizens of other industrial nations, Americans are highly religious. Even though secularization may have weakened the power of religious institutions in the United States, it has not diminished the strength of religious beliefs.

More than half (55 percent) of all Americans surveyed in 1995–1996 claimed to be "strong believers" in God or the sacred (Roof 1999). About 45 percent report having attended religious services in the past week (Barna Group 2006), and 54 percent live in a household where at least one person is a member of a church, mosque, or synagogue (Kosmin et al. 2001). According to public opinion polls, most Americans believe in God and claim they regularly pray, the majority one or more times a day (Barna Group 2006; General Social Survey [GSS] 1997). The 2004 GSS, a random sample survey of American adults, reports that over 90 percent of people who believe now always have believed in God. More than eight out of ten Americans report that they believe in an afterlife, and a substantial majority claim to believe in the devil as well (Roof 1999).

Yet one long-term measure of religiosity, based on indicators such as belief in God, religious membership, and attendance at religious services, found that the index reached its highest levels in the 1950s and has declined ever since—in part because post–World War II baby boomers were less religious, at least in the traditional sense, compared to their predecessors (Roof 1999). As Table 17.1 shows, in one national survey overwhelming majorities of Catholics, liberal Protestants,

TABLE 17.1

Weekly Attendance at Religious Services

GROUP	AGE	
	8–10	EARLY 20s
Roman Catholics	95	28
Liberal Protestants	82	18
Conservative Protestants	91	40

SOURCE: Roof 1999.

and conservative Protestants reported attending church on a weekly basis while they were children, although their attendance had dropped sharply by the time they reached their early twenties. Among the three groups, attendance had declined the most among liberal Protestants and least among conservative Protestants (Roof 1999). However, multiple studies show that rates of religious attendance increase again when adults reach their 30s and 40s, as many want to instill formal religious training and practice in their children (Wilson and Sherkat 1994).

One survey of nearly 114,000 adults in 1990 and over 50,000 adults in 2001 found that religious identification had declined sharply during the eleven-year period. In 1990, 90 percent of all respondents identified with some religious group; in 2001, only 81 percent. The principal decline was among self-identified Christians. This decline was not because more respondents identified with other religions; rather, it was because the number of respondents identifying with no religion whatever had grown from 8 percent to 14 percent of the survey population. Membership in religious institutions showed a parallel decline (Kosmin et al. 2001).

Civil Religion

Although there is a constitutional separation of church and state in the United States, its presidents have all attended church, and some have been deeply and publicly religious. In fact, sociologists have argued that the United States has a **civil religion**, a set of religious beliefs through which a society interprets its own history in light of some conception of ultimate reality (Bellah 1968, 1975). Civil religion usually consists of "god-language used in reference to the nation," including "historical myths about the society's divine origins, beliefs about its sacred historical purpose, and occasionally religious restrictions on societal membership" (Wuthnow 1988).

The importance of civil religion in the United States is seen in the Pledge of Allegiance. By referring to "one nation, under God," the pledge infuses civic life with a religious belief derived from the Judeo-Christian heritage. The phrase "under God" was added by Congress in 1954, during the height of cold war fears about "godless communism." Even though the Bill of Rights of the U.S. Constitution calls for a separation of church and state, the pledge posits a theistic religious belief as central to U.S. citizenship.

Trends in Religious Affiliation

It is difficult to estimate the number of people belonging to religious organizations because the U.S. government does not collect such data. Nonetheless, based on occasional surveys, public-opinion polls, and church records, sociologists of religion have concluded that church membership has grown steadily since the United States was founded. About one in six Americans belonged to a religious organization at the time of the Revolutionary War, one in three at the time of the Civil War, one in two at the turn of the nineteenth century, and two in three in the 1990s (Finke and Stark 1992).

One reason so many Americans are religiously affiliated is that religious organizations are an important source of social ties and friendship networks. Churches, synagogues, and mosques are communities of people with shared beliefs and values who support one another during times of need. Religious communities thus often play a family-like role.

Another reason so many people belong to religious organizations is that the United States has more than fifteen hundred religions that one can belong to (Melton 1989). Yet the vast majority of people belong to a relatively small number of denominations (Figure 17.2). About 53 percent of Americans identify themselves as Protestant, 25 percent as Catholic, 2 percent as Jewish, and 11 percent as "other," a category that includes Eastern Orthodox, Mormon, and Muslim. The remainder (9 percent) have no religious affiliation at all (U.S. Bureau of the Census 2003c).

Roof's (1993) study of baby boomers, *A Generation of Seekers,* found that even though two out of three had dropped out of a church or synagogue in their teens, most still remain. Increasingly, however, religious experience is sought outside established religions, often in a highly personalized fashion.

PROTESTANTISM: THE GROWING STRENGTH OF CONSERVATIVE DENOMINATIONS

A clearer picture of trends in American religion emerges if we break down the Protestant category into major subgroups. According to the American Religious Identification Survey of more than fifty thousand households in 2001, Baptist households account for 31 percent of all Protestants—well over twice the percentage of the second largest group, Methodists (13 percent). There were far fewer Lutherans (9 percent), Presbyterians (5 percent), and Episcopalians (3 percent) (Kosmin et al. 2001). More than half of all Protestants describe themselves as "born again" (*The Economist* 2003).

These figures indicate the growing strength of conservative Protestants, who emphasize a literal interpretation of the Bible, morality in daily life, and conversion through evangelizing. In contrast are the more historically established liberal Protestants, who adopt a more flexible, humanistic approach to religious practice. Somewhere in between are moderate Protestants.

FIGURE 17.2

Religious Affiliation (percentage of U.S. populace)

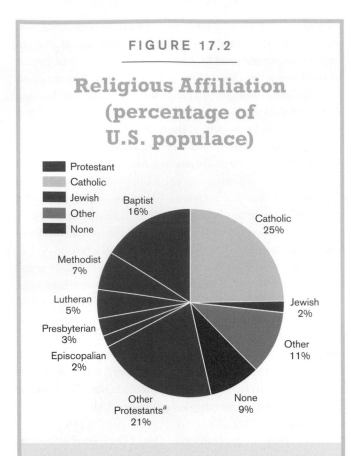

Legend:
- Protestant
- Catholic
- Jewish
- Other
- None

Pie chart labels:
- Baptist 16%
- Catholic 25%
- Methodist 7%
- Jewish 2%
- Lutheran 5%
- Other 11%
- Presbyterian 3%
- Episcopalian 2%
- Other Protestants[a] 21%
- None 9%

Name one religion that may be included in the green pie section labeled "Other." According to the figure, what percentage of the United States reported a religious affiliation that could broadly be labeled Christian? What is the single largest Christian denomination? What percentage of the total population reports some religious affiliation? Name one reason that so many Americans are religiously affiliated other than specific religious beliefs.

[a] Includes other, no denomination given, or a nondenominational church.

SOURCE: Kosmin et al. 2001; U.S. Bureau of the Census 2003c.

Since the 1960s, both liberal and moderate churches have experienced declining membership, whereas the number of conservative Protestants has exploded. The conservative denominations inspire deep loyalty and commitment, and they are highly effective in recruiting new members, particularly young people. Today twice as many people belong to conservative Protestant groups as liberal ones, and conservative Protestants outnumber moderates as well (Green 2004; Roof and McKinney 1990). Liberal Protestantism in particular has suffered. The aging members of the liberal Protestant denominations have not been replaced, commitment is low, and some

current members are switching to other faiths. As Figure 17.3 indicates, from 1965 to 1989 declines were substantial for Evangelical Lutherans, United Methodists, the United Church of Christ, Episcopalians, Presbyterians, and Disciples of Christ. Together these six denominations lost nearly twenty-three million members—almost the same number that was gained by such conservative Protestant denominations as the Southern Baptists, the Church of the Nazarene, the Seventh-Day Adventists, the Assemblies of God, the Church of God, and the Mormon Church. Black Protestant churches also thrive in the United States, as their members move into the middle class and achieve economic and political prominence (Finke and Stark 1992; Roof and McKinney 1990).

Since the 1960s, the fastest-growing religious group has been self-identified evangelicals. Moreover, the more conservative religions experienced a net gain in converts during the 1990s, whereas the more liberal religions experienced a net loss (Kosmin et al. 2001) (Table 17.2).

CATHOLICISM

Although the number of Catholics continues to increase, church attendance has declined over the past few decades,

---

TABLE 17.2

Changes in Religious Self-Identification in the United States, 1970–2005

RELIGIOUS SELF-IDENTIFICATION	NET GAIN OR LOSS
Evangelical/Born Again	12.8%
No religion	4.5
Muslim	1.2
Buddhist	0.8
Atheist	0.4
Hindu	0.3
Catholic	−1.0
Jewish	−1.3
Protestant	−7.5

SOURCE: Encyclopaedia Britannica Online 2006.

FIGURE 17.3

Loss and Gain in Church Membership, 1965–1989, for Selected Moderate/Liberal and Conservative Protestant Churches

During the twenty-four-year period from 1965 to 1989, such mainstream denominations as the United Methodists, the United Church of Christ, the Episcopalians, the Presbyterians, and the Disciples of Christ lost between one fifth and one half of their membership. Conversely, such conservative Protestant churches as the Assemblies of God, the Mormons, and the Church of God more than doubled their membership.

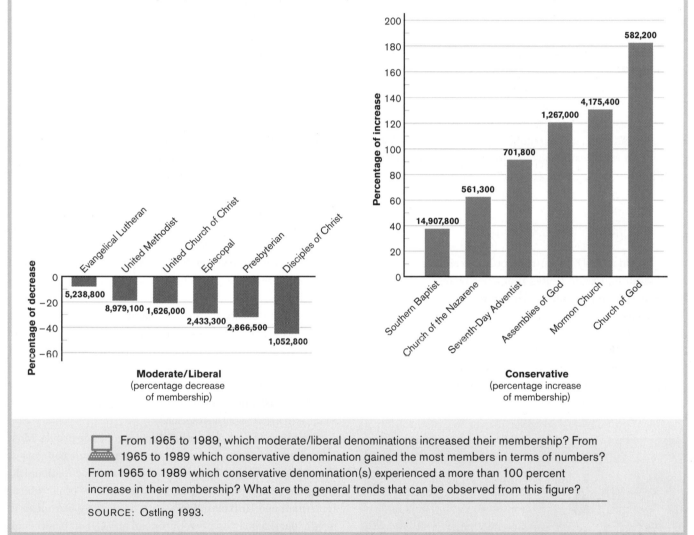

Moderate/Liberal
(percentage decrease
of membership)

Conservative
(percentage increase
of membership)

From 1965 to 1989, which moderate/liberal denominations increased their membership? From 1965 to 1989 which conservative denomination gained the most members in terms of numbers? From 1965 to 1989 which conservative denomination(s) experienced a more than 100 percent increase in their membership? What are the general trends that can be observed from this figure?

SOURCE: Ostling 1993.

beginning in the 1960s and leveling off in the mid-1970s. One of the main reasons was the papal encyclical of 1968 that reaffirmed the ban on the use of contraceptives by Catholics. People whose conscience allowed for the use of contraceptives were faced with disobeying the Church, and many did just that. According to one study conducted by the Centers for Disease Control and Prevention (2005a), 96 percent of all Catholic women who have had sexual relations report having used contraceptives; the General Social Survey (Smith 1998) found that three out of five Catholics say that contraceptives should be available to teens even without parental approval.

The Catholic Church has shown by far the largest increase in membership, partly because of immigration from Mexico and Central and South America. Yet the growth in membership has slowed recently, as some followers have either ceased to identify themselves as Catholics or shifted to Protestantism.

OTHER RELIGIOUS GROUPS

The number of Jews has declined as a result of low birthrates, intermarriage, and assimilation. Yet even assimilated Jews often identify themselves as Jewish, and there has been a resurgence of interest among some younger American Jews in rediscovering orthodox practices (Bamberger 1992; Blech 1991; Danzger 1989; Davidman 1991; Eisen 1983; Goldberg and Rayner 1987).

Among other denominations, growing immigration from Asia and Africa may change the U.S. religious profile. For example, estimates of the number of Muslims in the United States run as high as three million; many come from Asia or are African refugees from countries like Somalia and Ethiopia (Finke and Stark 1992; Haddad 1979; Roof and McKinney 1990).

NEW CULTS

Since World War II, more religious movements have been founded in the United States than ever before in its history. Most have proved short lived, but a few have achieved notable followings.

An example is the Unification Church, founded by the Korean Sun Myung Moon. The cult boasts a membership of fifty thousand in the United States and three million worldwide (Melton 1996). Other new religious movements include

Unification Church leader Reverend Sun Myung Moon and his wife marry 2,075 pairs of his followers at Madison Square Garden on New Year's Day 1982.

Scientology, Wiccan, Eckankar, Druid, Santería, and Rastafarianism. Their beliefs might seem unusual mixtures of traditional and modern religious ideas, but in fact all long-established religions mix elements from diverse cultural sources.

Religious Affiliation and Socioeconomic Status

Substantial socioeconomic and regional differences exist among the principal religious groupings in the United States (see Table 17.3 for differences among Protestants). *Liberal Protestants* are well educated, somewhat upper income, and middle or upper class. They are concentrated in the Northeast and, to a small extent, in the West. Ethnically, they comprise white Anglo-Saxon Protestants (WASPs) of British or German origins. *Moderate Protestants* have a lower level of education, income, and social class. In fact, they are typical of the national average on these measures. They live in the Midwest and, to some extent, in the West. Moderate Protestants are from a variety of European ethnic backgrounds, including British, German, Scandinavian, Irish, and Dutch. Black Protestants are the least educated, poorest, and least middle class of any of the religious groups listed in Table 17.3. *Conservative Protestants* have a similar profile, although they have a slightly higher level on all these measures. They comprise a diverse profile of European ethnicities, although some are African American as well.

Catholics strongly resemble moderate Protestants in terms of their socioeconomic profile. They are largely concentrated in the Northeast, although many live in the West and the Southwest as well. The largest ethnic group is European in origin (primarily German, Italian, Slavic, and Irish, and to a lesser extent English and French), followed by Latinos from Mexico and Central and South America.

Jews have the most successful socioeconomic profile. Most are college graduates in middle- or upper-income categories. One study found that Jewish educational and occupational attainment was significantly higher than that of other whites (Hartman and Hartman 1996). Jews are largely European in origin, particularly Eastern European and German, although some are from northern Africa (Roof and McKinney 1990). Whereas the large majority of Jews once lived in the Northeast, today only half do. One recent study suggests that their high degree of geographical mobility is associated with lowered involvement in Jewish institutions. Jews who move throughout the country are less likely to belong to synagogues or temples, have Jewish friends, or be married to Jewish spouses (Goldstein and Goldstein 1996).

TABLE 17.3

Characteristics of Liberal, Moderate, Conservative, and Black Protestant Denominations

CHARACTERISTICS	LIBERAL	MODERATE	CONSERVATIVE	BLACK
Principal period of appearance	Historic "mainline" churches (pre–Revolutionary War)	Nineteenth century	Twentieth century	Nineteenth and twentieth centuries
Biblical interpretation	Humanistic, flexible	Fairly literal interpretation	Literal interpretation	Fairly literal interpretation, including emphasis on civil rights
Predominant income group	Middle and upper income	Middle income ("middle America")	Lower and middle income	Lower income
Higher education	Many college educated	Some college educated	Few college educated	Few college educated
Predominant region	Northeast, West	Midwest, West	South	South
Examples of denominations	Episcopalian, Presbyterian, United Church of Christ	Methodist, Lutheran, Disciples of Christ, Northern Baptist, Reformed churches	Southern Baptist Convention; Churches of Christ; Church of the Nazarene; Assemblies of God; Seventh-Day Adventist; Fundamentalist, Pentecostal and holiness groups	Black Methodist and Baptist churches

SOURCE: Adapted from Roof and McKinney 1990.

In sum, Jews and liberal Protestants are the most heavily middle and upper class; moderate Protestants and Catholics are somewhat in the middle (although the growing number of poor Catholic Latino immigrants may be changing this position); conservative and black Protestants are overwhelmingly lower class. These groupings correspond roughly to social and political liberalism and conservatism as well. In terms of civil liberties, racial justice, and women's rights, Jews are by far the most tolerant. Liberal Protestants and Catholics are somewhat more tolerant than the average American, while moderate Protestants and black Protestants are somewhat less tolerant. Conservative Protestants are the least tolerant of all religious groupings (Roof and McKinney 1990).

There are political differences across religious groups as well. Jews are the most heavily Democratic; fundamentalist and evangelical Christians, the most Republican. The more moderate Protestant denominations are somewhere in between (Kosmin et al. 2001).

Secularization or Religious Revival in America?

According to Phillip Hammond (1992), there have been three historical periods in the United States when religion has undergone **disestablishment**—that is, the political influence of established religions has been successfully challenged. The first such disestablishment occurred with the 1791 ratification of the Bill of Rights, which calls for separation of church and state. Some sociologists see this separation as characteristic of the industrial societies of Europe and North America, in which different institutions specialize in different functions—from economics to medicine and from education to politics. Religion is no exception (Chaves 1993, 1994; Parsons 1951, 1960). The second disestablishment occurred between the 1890s and 1920s, fed by an influx of about seventeen million immigrants (mainly European), many of whom were Catholic. The long-standing notion of a predominantly Protestant United States

"Religion Is Good for Kids"

Sociologists dating back to Émile Durkheim have written about the personal benefits of religion, such as providing a sense of purpose, meaning, and community. But can religion make young children better behaved and better adjusted socially? That's what the news headlines told us in April 2007. Readers were told that "Religion Is Good for Kids" (Wenner 2007), "Highly Religious Parents Have Better Behaved Kids" (Barrick 2007), and "Children Thrive When Parents Follow Religious Beliefs" (Schultz 2007). Should parents bring their young children to religious services every week, in an effort to have angelic, well-mannered offspring? Not necessarily. The newspapers were reporting on the findings of a study conducted by Mississippi State University sociologist John P. Bartkowski and colleagues, published in *Social Science Research*. The study did provide some evidence that young children from religious homes had better self-control and social skills, but the researchers were cautious about jumping to the sweeping conclusion that "religion is good for kids."

The research team analyzed data from the Early Childhood Longitudinal Study, a study of more than fifteen thousand first graders, their parents, and their school teachers. This study is the first to explore the ways parental religious behaviors and practices shape the psychological development and social adjustment of young

Is there a correlation between religious attendance and the behavior of children?

children. In the study, both parents and teachers rated the six-year-old children on several dimensions of development such as self-control, interpersonal skills, sadness, behavior problems, and approaches to learning. Self-control reflected behaviors like throwing tantrums, controlling one's temper, and respecting

others' property. Interpersonal skills included getting along with people who are different, helping others, and showing sensitivity. Sadness referred to feelings of sadness and loneliness. Behavior problems encompassed arguing, fighting, and being disruptive. Approaches to learning referred to the child's eagerness to learn, persistence, and attentiveness.

The researchers also collected data on the parents' religious behavior, including frequency of attending religious services, talking about religion at home, arguing about religion at home, and an indicator of how similar the parents were in terms of their religious attendance. The study's goal was to examine whether these religious behaviors and practices were associated with the child's developmental outcomes. Other potential influences on child development, such as social class and family size, were controlled. ("Controlling" is a strategy for screening out other possible explanations for a statistical relationship.) The researchers did not explore whether religious denomination affected the children.

was challenged, and the mainstream Protestant churches never regained their influence in politics or in defining national values. The third disestablishment occurred during the 1960s and 1970s, when core religious beliefs and values were eroded by the anti–Vietnam War movement, the fight for racial equality, and experimentation with alternative lifestyles. Fundamental challenges arose in areas such as sexuality, family authority, sexual and lifestyle preferences, women's rights, and birth control (Glock and Bellah 1976; Hammond 1992; Hunter 1987; Roof and McKinney 1990; Wuthnow 1976, 1978).

The third (most recent) disestablishment of religion brought a reduction in the political influence of religion. This does not mean, however, that religion is less important to individuals, or that secular influences are on the rise. On the contrary, the religious beliefs of many Americans appear to be stronger than ever (Roof et al. 1995). In fact, some sociologists argue that the absence of an official state religion has forced religious groups to compete with each other for followers, the result being religious practices tailored to public tastes (Moore 1994). Furthermore, for many people, religious beliefs have

The study found that when a parent, especially both parents, attended religious services frequently and talked to their children about religion, the children had better self-control, interpersonal skills, and approaches to learning than did children with less devout parents. However, the researchers found that religion did not always bring benefits; children whose parents argued frequently about religion were more likely to have behavioral problems. The researchers concluded that "religion can undermine child development when it is a source of conflict among families."

The authors proposed several explanations for their findings. First, they suggested that religious communities may provide social support to parents which could help them develop better parenting skills. Second, they proposed that religion may provide parents a sense of meaning, which they pass down to their children. Third, they noted that values and norms such as self-sacrifice are common in some congregations, and these values may encourage parents to invest much time and effort in raising well-behaved children.

However, the researchers also acknowledged that their findings may be subject to two potential methodological critiques: reporter bias and reverse causation. The study findings revealed that the positive effects of parents' religious behavior on the child's outcomes were larger and more often statistically significant when the parent's (rather than the teacher's) assessment of the child was used as an outcome.

One explanation is that religious parents are effective disciplinarians, and thus their children do not act out at home when their parents are present. Yet an equally plausible explanation is that religious parents feel social pressure to report that their children are very well-behaved and may offer excessively positive evaluations of their children.

The researchers also acknowledge that correlation is not causation, and it's possible that well-behaved children enable their parents to attend religious services more often. Bartkowski noted "there are certain expectations about children's behavior ... particularly within religious worship services." Attending services may be "a less viable option if [parents] feel their kids are really poorly behaved" (Barrick 2007). Further, the researchers recognize that religious participation is just one type of community engagement and that other forms of activities might also benefit children. According to Bartkowski, their study findings "do not negate the effect of Boys and Girls Clubs involvement, extracurricular activities and other things that steer youth toward positive developmental outcomes" (Martin 2007).

Questions

- Which aspects of parental religious behaviors have positive effects on young children's developmental outcomes?
- Which aspects of parental religious behaviors have negative effects on

young children's developmental outcomes?
- Name and describe two methodological concerns that may weaken the persuasiveness of the study findings.
- Do you believe that highly religious parents raise better-behaved children than less religious or nonreligious parents? Why or why not?

FOR FURTHER EXPLORATION

Barrick, Audrey. 2007. "Study: Highly Religious Parents Have Better Behaved Kids." *Christian Post* (April 25, 2007). www.christianpost.com/article/20070425/27087_Study:_Highly_Religious_Parents_Have_Better_Behaved_Kids.htm (accessed January 12, 2008).

Bartkowski, John P., Xiaohe Xu, and Martin L. Levin. In press. "Religion and Child Development: Evidence from the Early Childhood Longitudinal Study." *Social Science Research*.

Martin, Allie. 2007. "Study Finds Religion Has Positive Impact on Children." OneNewsNow.com, www.onenewsnow.com/2007/05/study_finds_religion_has_posit.php (accessed January 12, 2008).

Schultz, Gudrun. 2007. "Children Thrive When Parents Follow Religious Beliefs." LifeSiteNews.com (April 25, 2007). www.lifesite.net/ldn/2007/apr/07042506.html (accessed January 12, 2008).

Wenner, Melissa. 2007. "Study: Religion Is Good for Kids." Fox News (April 27, 2007). www.foxnews.com/printer_friendly_story/0,3566,268081,00.html (accessed January 12, 2008).

become increasingly private as more people seek spiritual experiences outside established religious organizations. Roof (1993) found that religion has become a highly personal (rather than public) experience for many people. Finally, counter to the overall trend toward religious disestablishment in the United States, some evidence indicates that in recent years conservative Protestant religious organizations have increasingly made their voices heard in U.S. politics.

Roger Finke and Rodney Stark (1992) argue that disestablishment is a normal process through which mainstream

groups become self-satisfied, losing followers to more aggressive sects and cults that promise to revitalize religious experience. In fact, Finke and Stark question whether the third disestablishment occurred at all, noting that cult formation in the 1960s was only slightly higher than in the 1950s. Some research (Kosmin 1991; Melton 1989) suggests that relatively minuscule numbers of people belong to groups such as the Unification Church (five thousand members), Krishna Consciousness (three thousand), Scientology (fifty-five thousand), and other New Age groups (twenty thousand) (Kosmin 1991; Melton

1989; U.S. Bureau of the Census 2003c). Most scholars agree that the most liberal, intellectualized, and inclusive religious denominations have lost members but that the most conservative, traditional, and exclusive ones have thrived.

The Resurgence of Evangelicalism

Evangelicalism, a belief in spiritual rebirth (being "born again"), may be a response to growing secularism, religious diversity, and the decline of once-core Protestant values in American life (Wuthnow 1988). Recent years have seen enormous growth in Evangelical denominations, paralleled by a decline in mainstream Protestant religious affiliations. Many Protestants are seeking the more direct, personal, and emotional religious experience promised by Evangelical denominations.

Evangelical organizations are good at mobilizing resources to achieve their religious and political objectives. They have become extremely competitive "spiritual entrepreneurs" in the "religious marketplace" (Hatch 1989). Some Evangelicals use radio and television as marketing technologies to reach a wider audience. Called *televangelists* because they conduct their Evangelical ministries over television, these ministers preach a "gospel of prosperity": the belief that God wants the faithful to be financially prosperous and satisfied rather than to sacrifice and suffer. This approach differs considerably from the austere emphasis on hard work and self-denial associated with traditional conservative Protestant beliefs (Bruce 1990; Hadden and Shupe 1987). Theology and fund-raising are staples of televangelism, which must support not only the television ministries themselves but schools, universities, theme parks, and sometimes the lavish lifestyles of its preachers.

Interior of the Crystal Cathedral in Garden Grove, California.

There is considerable debate over the number of people who watch such religious broadcasting. One of the most reliable studies (Bruce 1990), conducted in 1985 at the height of televangelism's popularity, estimated that the average audience for the top ten programs was about eight million people. During a typical month, about 40 percent of all U.S. households tuned in at least once. Yet even at their peak, it is not clear that television ministries were bringing large numbers of new people "into the fold." Instead, they may have been merely providing an additional type of religious observation to those who were already well established in their local churches (Diekema 1991; Hadden 1990; Hadden and Shupe 1987; Hadden and Swann 1981).

During the late 1980s, several prominent televangelists were involved in sexual and financial scandals. At the same time, the rising cost of television broadcasting made it more difficult to engage profitably in television ministries. Yet with the advent of cable and satellite television, televangelists have found a cost-effective market niche. The current large number of religious television networks includes the American Christian Television System, the Christian Broadcasting Network, the Eternal Word Broadcasting Network, and Family Net. Some scholars argue that these ministries are stronger today than ever before (Hadden 2004).

The electronic preaching of religion has become particularly prevalent in Latin America, where North American programs are shown. As a result, Protestant movements, most of them Pentecostal, have made a dramatic impact on such countries as Chile and Brazil, which are predominantly Catholic (Martin 1990).

Although some Evangelicals combine a modern lifestyle with traditional religious beliefs, others strongly reject many contemporary beliefs and practices. **Fundamentalists** are Evangelicals who are antimodern, calling for strict codes of morality and conduct. These frequently include taboos against drinking, smoking, and other "worldly evils"; a belief in biblical infallibility; and a strong emphasis on Christ's impending return to earth (Balmer 1989).

Beginning with the Reverend Jerry Falwell's Moral Majority in the 1970s, some groups of fundamentalists have become increasingly involved in the New Christian Right in national politics, particularly in the conservative wing of the Republican Party (Kiecolt and Nelson 1991; Simpson 1985; Woodrum 1988). Groups such as the Christian Voice and the Religious Roundtable have advanced a political agenda compatible with fundamentalist beliefs. Antiabortion groups such as the Christian Action Council, Focus on the Family, and Prayers for Life were effective in getting the federal government to greatly restrict abortions between 1989 and 1992, despite public opinion polls showing that a majority of Americans considered abortion an acceptable alternative in some cases.

On the campaign trail in 1999, presidential candidate George W. Bush addresses the Christian Coalition One Nation Under God Road to Victory Conference.

Fundamentalist religious organizations helped shape Republican Party ideology and policies during the Reagan administration, as well as during both Bush administrations. White evangelical Protestants make up an estimated third of all registered voters, and they are overwhelmingly politically conservative. They have become a core constituency of the Republican Party, whose program reflects fundamentalist religious beliefs on such topics as opposition to gay marriage and abortion and a reduced role for government (*The Economist* 2003).

☑ CONCEPT CHECKS

1. What are the reasons so many Americans belong to religious organizations?
2. Describe the main differences between conservative and liberal Protestants.
3. How do sociologists explain the resurgence of evangelicalism in the United States in the late twentieth century?

Globalization and Religion

Religion is one of the most truly global of all social institutions, affecting many aspects of life. The current globalization of religion is reflected in religious activism in poor countries and in the rise of religious nationalist movements in opposition to the modern secular state.

Activist Religion and Social Change

Religion has played a particularly important role in global social changes of recent decades. In Vietnam in the 1960s, Buddhist priests burned themselves alive to protest the policies of the South Vietnamese government. Their sacrifice, seen on television sets worldwide, contributed to growing U.S. opposition to the war. Buddhist monks in Thailand currently protest deforestation and care for victims of AIDS.

An activist form of Catholicism, **liberation theology**, combines Catholic beliefs with a passion for social justice for the poor, particularly in Central and South America and in Africa. Catholic priests and nuns organize farming cooperatives, build health clinics and schools, and challenge government policies that impoverish the peasantry. Islamic socialists in Pakistan and Buddhist socialists in Sri Lanka play a similar role (Berryman 1987; Juergensmeyer 1993; Sigmund 1990). Many religious leaders have paid with their lives for their activism, which government and military leaders often regard as subversive.

In some central and eastern European countries once dominated by the former Soviet Union, long-suppressed religious organizations had a key role in overturning socialist regimes during the early 1990s. In Poland, for example, the Catholic Church was allied with the Solidarity movement, which toppled the socialist government in 1989. Yet religion has also been central in reviving ancient ethnic and tribal hatreds. In Bosnia and elsewhere in the former Yugoslavia, for example, religious differences helped to justify "ethnic cleansing," with Christian Serbs and Croats engaging in the mass murder, rape, and deportation of Muslims from communities and farmlands where they had lived for centuries.

The Global Rise of Religious Nationalism

Religious nationalism involves the linking of deep religious convictions with beliefs about a people's social and political destiny. In numerous countries, religious nationalist movements call for a revival of traditional religious beliefs that are embodied in the nation and its leadership (Beyer 1994). These movements represent a strong reaction against the impact of technological and economic modernization on local religious beliefs. In particular, religious nationalists oppose the destructive aspects of "Western" influence on local culture and religion, ranging from U.S. television to the missionary efforts of foreign evangelicals.

Religious nationalist movements accept many aspects of modern life, including modern technology, politics, and

Nicolas Menchú, the brother of Nobel laureate Rigoberta Menchú, translates a liberation theology sermon during the first Catholic mass held in Chimel, Guatemala, since 1978 when the village was burned by army troops.

economics. For example, Islamic fundamentalists fighting the Russian army in Chechnya have developed Web sites to spread their views. Even Osama bin Laden used video and television to reach millions of Muslims worldwide. However, Islamic fundamentalists also emphasize a strict interpretation of religious values and reject the notion of secularization (Juergensmeyer 1993, 2001). Nationalist movements do not simply revive ancient religious beliefs. Rather, they partly "invent" the past, drawing on different traditions and reinterpreting events to serve their current beliefs and interests. Violent conflicts between religious groups sometimes result from their differing interpretations of the same historical event (Anderson 1991; Juergensmeyer 1993, 2001; van der Veer 1994).

Religious nationalism is rising because in times of rapid social change, unshakable ideas have strong appeal. The collapse of the Soviet Union, the end of the cold war, and today's sweeping global economic and political changes have led many nations to reject the secular solutions offered by the United States and its former socialist enemies and to look instead to their own past and cultures (Juergensmeyer 1995b). In the Middle East, many Palestinian Muslims as well as Israeli Orthodox Jews renounce the notion of a secular democratic state, arguing for a religious nation purged of nonbelievers. In India, Hindus, Muslims, and Sikhs face off against each other.

Islamic nationalism has triumphed in Iran, Sudan, and until 2001, Afghanistan; it has also made significant inroads in Egypt, Algeria, Turkey, Pakistan, Palestine, Malaysia, and elsewhere. Since the 1970s, Islamic nationalism has shaped the contours of both national and international politics. To understand this phenomenon, we must look both to aspects of Islam as a traditional religion and to secular changes affecting countries where its influence is pervasive.

Islamic Nationalism

Islam, like Christianity, has continually stimulated activism. The Qur'ān is full of instructions to believers to "struggle in the way of God" against both unbelievers and those within the Muslim community who introduce corruption. Over the centuries there have been successive generations of Muslim reformers, and Islam has become as internally divided as Christianity.

ISLAM AND THE WEST

During the Middle Ages, there was continuous struggle between Christian Europe and the Muslim states. During the height of Islamic power, the *caliphs* (Islamic rulers) ruled over an area extending from what later became Spain, Greece, the former Yugoslavia, Bulgaria, and Romania to India, Pakistan, and Bangladesh. Europeans eventually reclaimed most of the lands conquered by the Muslims, and many of their possessions in North Africa were colonized in the eighteenth and nineteenth centuries. These reverses were catastrophic for Muslim religion and civilization, which Islamic believers held to be the highest and most advanced possible. In the late nineteenth century, the inability of the Muslim world to resist the spread of Western culture led to reform movements seeking to restore Islam to its original purity and strength. A key idea was that Islam should respond to the Western challenge by affirming the identity of its beliefs and practices.

This idea developed in various ways in the twentieth century and underlay the Islamic revolution in Iran of 1978–1979, which was fueled initially by internal opposition to the shah (the king), Mohammad Reza Pahlavi (1941–1979). When the shah's premier, Mohammad Mossadeq, nationalized the oil industry in 1951, a conflict ensued between the pro-West shah and the supporters of the nationalistic Mossadeq. The shah eventually fled the country but returned in 1953 when a U.S.- and British-led coup overthrew Mossadeq. The shah tried to promote forms of modernization modeled on the West—for example, land reform, extending the vote to women, and developing secular education. He also used the army and secret police to brutally repress those who opposed his regime. The fact that he had been installed by Western powers helped fuel nationalist sentiments that eventually led to the revolution that overthrew him. A dominant figure in the revolution was Ayatollah Ruhollah Khomeini, a religious leader exiled in France during the shah's reign, who provided a radical reinterpretation of Shiite ideas.

Khomeini established a government in strict accordance with traditional Islamic law, fusing religion and the state. It made Islam the basis of all social, political, and economic life in Iran. Men and women were kept rigorously segregated, women had to cover their heads in public, homosexuals could be shot by a firing squad, and women accused of adultery were stoned to death. The strict code reflected a pronounced nationalistic outlook, strongly rejecting Western influences.

The aim of the Islamic Republic in Iran was to organize government and society so that Islamic teachings would dominate all spheres. A Guardian Council of religious leaders determines whether laws, policies, and candidates for Parliament conform to Islamic beliefs, even though Iran has a U.S.-style constitution providing for elected officials and the separation of powers.

Recent years have seen a growing movement to liberalize the country. Mohammed Khatami, the reform-minded president, and his allies recaptured control of Parliament in the 2000 elections. But that victory proved to be short-lived: The Guardian Council disqualified twenty-four hundred liberal candidates (nearly a third of all candidates) during the 2004 elections, and Mahmoud Ahmadinejad, a conservative candidate close to Iran's religious leaders, won the presidency. The reformist movement now controls less than a quarter of the seats in Parliament.

THE SPREAD OF ISLAMIC REVIVALISM

Although the ideas underlying the Iranian revolution were supposed to unite the whole Islamic world against the West, governments of countries where the Shiites are in a minority have not aligned themselves with the Islamic Revolution in Iran. Yet Islamic fundamentalism (often referred to as "Islamism," the complete adherence to Islamic law along with rejection of most non-Islamic influences) has become popular in most of these states, and various forms of Islamic revivalism elsewhere have been stimulated by it.

Although Islamic fundamentalist movements have grown in many countries in North Africa, the Middle East, and

In 1998 Osama bin Laden issued a *fatwa*, saying that any American, whether Muslim or not, should be killed. A *fatwa* is a religious decree or judgment issued by a recognized Islamic legal authority. Upon bin Laden's issuing of the *fatwa*, Mullah Omar (the head of the Taliban in Afghanistan) issued a statement saying that bin Laden was not qualified to give a *fatwa* because he "had not undergone the requisite Islamic schooling."

South Asia, they have won power in only two states: Sudan and Afghanistan. Sudan has been ruled since 1989 by Hassan al-Turabi's National Salvation Front. The fundamentalist Taliban regime consolidated its hold on the fragmented state of Afghanistan in 1996 but was ousted at the end of 2001 by Afghan opposition forces and the U.S. military. In many other states (such as Egypt, Turkey, and Algeria), however, Islamic fundamentalist uprisings have been suppressed by the state or the military.

Islamic opposition is building in states such as Malaysia and Indonesia. Several provinces in Nigeria have implemented *sharia* (strict Islamic law), and the war in Chechnya has attracted Islamic militants who support the establishment of an Islamic state in that region.

Al Qaeda is an example of a loosely knit transnational network of militant religious fundamentalists with a global vision. Founded by Osama bin Laden, al Qaeda seeks to overthrow what it regards as corrupt Muslim governments, drive Western influence from the Middle East, and eventually establish a religiously based government that would encompass a billion Muslims throughout Europe, Africa, and Asia. Islamic rule would be subject to strict religious discipline, as it was during the rule of the Taliban in Afghanistan.

Such Islamic revivalism cannot be understood wholly in religious terms. It largely represents a reaction against what Iranian writer Jalal Al Ahmad (1997; orig. 1962) called "West-struckedness" or "Westoxification"—the seductive (and, in his view, corrupting) power of Western cultural beliefs and practices. In countries where as much as half the population are under age fifteen, where poverty is widespread, and where many well-educated young men and women face a life of marginal employment and uncertainty, such beliefs find fertile ground.

The strong Western presence in the Middle East has provided additional fuel for anti-Western sentiments. In his fatwas (opinions that he claimed to be grounded in Islamic law), bin Laden repeatedly condemned U.S. troop presence in Saudi Arabia (which, as the land of Muhammad, is regarded by Islam as its most sacred place), U.S. support for Israel in its conflict with the Palestinians, the first Gulf War against Iraq, and what bin Laden claimed were a million deaths resulting from the postwar economic sanctions against Iraq. In a videotaped statement that was televised worldwide after the September 11 attacks, bin Laden also stated that "what the United States tastes today is a very small thing compared to what we have tasted for tens of years. Our nation has been tasting this humiliation and contempt for more than 80 years" (BBC News 2001). He was referring to the collapse of the Ottoman Empire after World War I when more than a thousand years of Islamic rule came to a humiliating end.

RELIGIOUS NATIONALISM AND VIOLENCE

To what extent are bin Laden's views shared in the Muslim world? In 2002 and 2003, the Pew Research Center (2003) polled fifty thousand people worldwide. Large majorities, including Muslims, reported that such things as television, the Internet, and cellular phones were making their lives better. (Pakistan, one of the world's largest Islamic countries, was a notable exception.) Most people (including most Muslims) felt that foreign TV, movies, and music were a "good thing" (again, except for Pakistan). At the same time, large majorities of Muslims and others also believed that their traditional ways of life were being lost and needed protection against foreign influence. Although expressing concern that "there are serious threats to Islam today," the vast majority rejected suicide bombings and other forms of violence against civilians as a legitimate means of "defending Islam against its enemies."

Bin Laden's belief that "Westoxification" is a serious problem calling for a violent solution is clearly not widely shared among ordinary Muslims. His appeal appears to be strongest among Muslims whose religious convictions are sufficiently deep that they are willing to die for their beliefs.

How could Islamic religious views—or any religious views—give rise to such a culture of violence? Sociologist Mark Juergensmeyer (2001) has made a startling conclusion: Even though all major religious traditions call for compassion and understanding, violence and religion nonetheless go hand in hand. Juergensmeyer, who has studied religious violence among Muslims, Sikhs, Jews, Hindus, Christians, and Buddhists, argues that under the right conditions ordinary conflicts can become recast as religious "cosmic wars" between good and evil that must be won at all costs. He argues that a violent conflict is most likely to seek religious justification as a cosmic war when (1) the conflict is regarded as decisive for defending one's basic identity and dignity—for example, when one's culture is seen as threatened, and (2) when losing the conflict is unthinkable, although (3) winning the conflict is unlikely.

If any of these conditions is present, Juergensmeyer says, it is more likely that:

> a real-world struggle may be perceived in cosmic terms as a sacred war. The occurrence of all three simultaneously strongly suggests it. A struggle that begins on worldly terms may gradually take on the characteristics of a cosmic war as solutions become unlikely and awareness grows of how devastating it would be to lose.

In such instances, the proponents of cosmic warfare justify the loss of innocent lives as serving God's larger purpose. According to Juergensmeyer, bin Laden and al Qaeda exemplify such cosmic warfare in seeking to defend Islam against an all-engulfing Westernization. He also argues that responding to al Qaeda's violence with still greater violence runs the risk of showing the Islamic world that the conflict is indeed cosmic, particularly if the most powerful nations on earth become embroiled. Based on interviews with proponents of terrorism, Juergensmeyer concludes that this is just what al Qaeda wants—to be elevated from the status of a minor criminal terrorist organization to a worthy opponent in a global war against the West. This will increase the appeal of al Qaeda to a wider group of young Islamic men who blame the West for declining Islamic influence and growing hardships faced by many Muslims worldwide.

☑ CONCEPT CHECKS

1. What is religious nationalism? Why can't it be viewed as a reaction to economic modernization of local religious beliefs and Westernization?
2. What factors are behind the spread of Islamic revivalism?

Conclusion

In the expression of fundamentalism and in the diversity of new groups and sects worldwide, religion remains a vital force in society. It might appear strange, therefore, to suggest that the influence of religion in the modern world is declining.

However, sociologists acknowledge such a decline, at least as a long-term trend.

Until the modern period, churches rivaled and frequently surpassed monarchs and governments in political power and wealth. The priesthood controlled literacy, scholarship, and learning. However, as industrialization took hold, churches and religious organizations in Western countries lost most of their secular power. Governments took over tasks that the churches had previously controlled, including education.

Toward the end of the nineteenth century, German philosopher Friedrich Nietzsche announced, "God is dead." Religions, he argued, used to be a point of reference for our sense of purpose and meaning. Henceforth, we would have to live without this security. Living in a world without God means creating our own values and getting used to what Nietzsche called "the loneliness of being"—understanding that our lives are without purpose and that no superior entities watch over our fate.

Today, modern rationalist thought and religious outlook exist in an uneasy state of tension. A rationalist perspective permeates a good portion of our existence, and its hold will probably not weaken in the foreseeable future. Yet there are bound to be reactions against rationalism, leading to periods of religious revivalism. Meanwhile, science and rationalist thinking remain silent on questions of the meaning and purpose of life, matters that have always been at the core of religion.

Study Outline
www.wwnorton.com/studyspace

The Sociological Study of Religion

- There are no known societies that lack religion, although religious beliefs and practices vary across cultures. All religions involve a set of shared beliefs and rituals practiced by a community of believers.
- The sociology of religion is not concerned with whether a particular religion is true or false, but with how it operates as an organization and its relationship to the larger society. Religions arise from social relationships and provide a sense of social solidarity to followers.

Theories of Religion

- Sociological approaches to religion have been most influenced by the ideas of Marx, Durkheim, and Weber. All three classical thinkers believed that religion is fundamentally an illusion. They held that the "other" world that religion creates is *our* world, distorted through the lens of religious symbolism.
- To Marx, religion contains a strong ideological element: Religion justifies inequalities of wealth and power in society. To Durkheim, religion is important because it serves cohesive functions, especially ensuring that people meet regularly to affirm common beliefs and values. To Weber, religion is important because of its role in social change, particularly the development of Western capitalism.
- According to the classical view, religion in modern society is threatened by a long-term process of *secularization* in which the challenge of scientific thinking, as well as the coexistence of competing religions, leads to the complete demise of religion.
- The *religious economy* approach draws the opposite conclusion: that competition among religious groups and the challenges of secularization force religions to work harder to win followers, thereby strengthening the groups and countering any trend toward secularization.

Types of Religious Organizations

- Several types of religious organization can be distinguished. A *church* is a large, established religious body having a bureaucratic structure. *Sects* are small and aim at restoring the purity of doctrines that have become "corrupted" in the hands of official churches. A *denomination* is a sect that has become institutionalized, having a permanent form. A *cult* is a loosely knit group of people who follow the same leader or pursue similar religious ideals.
- Although traditional churches have seen declining membership, many new religious movements have emerged alongside mainstream religions. New religious movements encompass a range of religious and spiritual groups, cults, and sects. They can be broadly divided into world-affirming movements, which are akin to self-help groups; world-rejecting movements, which withdraw from and criticize the outside world; and world-accommodating movements, which emphasize inner religious life over worldly concerns.

Gender and Religion

- Feminist scholars argue that the deity created men and women as beings of equal value, and the Bible should reflect this fact.
- Despite drastic liberalization in recent years, women continue to hold lower status positions in many religious organizations today.

World Religions

- The three most influential *monotheistic* religions (religions in which there is one God) in world history are Judaism, Christianity, and Islam. *Polytheism* (belief in several or many gods) is common in other religions, such as Hinduism.

Religion in the United States

- The United States is one of the most religious of all industrial nations. Although only about one quarter of all Americans report regularly attending church, the majority claim to believe in God and to engage in regular prayer. Although church and state are legally separated by the U.S. Constitution, religious imagery and rituals pervade politics and civic life.
- Liberal and moderate Protestant religious denominations in the United States have seen declining membership, while more conservative or *evangelical* groups have seen an increase. These groups recently have sought to expand their influence in U.S. politics.

Globalization and Religion

- Religion has always been one of the most global of all social institutions. Fundamentalism has become common among different religious groups worldwide. *Fundamentalists* believe in returning to the fundamentals of their religious doctrines. Islamic fundamentalism has affected many countries in the Middle East since the 1979 Islamic revolution in Iran, which set up a religiously inspired government.
- Adherents to *liberation theology* play an important role in fostering social justice and economic inequality, particularly in Latin America and Africa.
- Religious nationalism is an important force today, existing in a precarious relationship with modern secular states. Religious nationalists often recast ordinary conflicts as religious cosmic wars between good and evil that must be won at all costs. This is especially the case when the conflict is central to one's beliefs, losing it would be unthinkable, and winning it is unlikely.

Key Concepts

alienation (p. 529)
charismatic (p. 540)
churches (p. 539)
civil religion (p. 549)
cults (p. 539)
denomination (p. 539)
disestablishment (p. 553)
evangelicalism (p. 556)
fundamentalists (p. 556)
liberation theology (p. 557)
monotheism (p. 543)
New Age movement (p. 541)
new religious movements (p. 540)
polytheism (p. 548)
profane (p. 532)
religion (p. 528)
religious economy (p. 535)
religious movements (p. 540)

religious nationalism (p. 557)
sacred (p. 532)
sects (p. 539)
secularization (p. 533)
secular thinking (p. 533)
theism (p. 528)
total institutions (p. 541)
world-accommodating movements (p. 541)
world-affirming movements (p. 540)
world-rejecting movements (p. 541)

Review Questions

1. How do sociologists define religion? What is absent from this definition?
2. What types of social forces do sociologists of religion tend to study?
3. How did Durkheim understand religion? Why is this considered an example of functionalist theory?
4. According to the text, how did Weber's approach to the study of religion differ from that of Durkheim?
5. According to the text, what is the central debate over secularization? What are the dimensions of this debate?
6. How did Max Weber characterize the phases of development that religious movements pass through?
7. What are the theories that explain the emergence of new religious movements?
8. How does the growth of new religious movements factor into debates over secularization?
9. What is a civil religion? Give an example.
10. What is *disestablishment?* What has been the effect of periodic disestablishment of religion in the United States?

Thinking Sociologically Exercises

1. Karl Marx, Émile Durkheim, and Max Weber had different viewpoints on the nature of religion and its social significance. Briefly explain the viewpoints of each. Which theorist's views have the most to offer in explaining the rise of national and international fundamentalism today? Why?
2. Drawing on this textbook's discussion, summarize the role of religion for most Americans today and assess whether religion is increasing or decreasing in importance for most people. Explain what it means for people to become more secular or fundamentalist in their religious practices. Are Americans becoming more secular or fundamentalist in their religious observances?

PART FIVE

SOCIAL CHANGE IN THE MODERN WORLD

Throughout human history, the pace of social change was slow; most people followed ways of life similar to those of their forebears. By contrast, today's world is subject to dramatic and continuous transformation. In the remaining chapters, we consider some of the major areas of change.

The growing field known as sociology of the body addresses one of the most far-reaching influences of globalization. Chapter 18 examines how global processes affect our bodies, including diet, health, and sexual behavior.

The globalizing of social life both influences and is influenced by changing patterns of urbanization, the subject of Chapter 19. This chapter also analyzes the tremendous growth in world population and the increasing threat of environmental problems.

The concluding chapter explores some of the major processes of social change from the eighteenth century to the present, offers general interpretations of the nature of social change, and considers where global change is likely to lead us in the twenty-first century.

Learning Objectives

The Sociology of the Body

Understand how social, cultural, and historical contexts shape attitudes toward "ideal" body forms. Learn about the ways that social context gives rise to two body-related social problems in the United States: eating disorders and the obesity crisis.

The Sociology of Health and Illness

Learn about functionalist and symbolic interactionist perspectives on health and illness in contemporary society. Understand the relationship between traditional medicine and complementary and alternative medicine (CAM).

Social Factors in Health and Illness

Recognize that health and illness are culturally and socially determined. Learn the social and cultural differences in the distribution of disease.

Global Health Issues

Understand the causes underlying high rates of infectious diseases in developing nations. Learn more about HIV/AIDS as a sociological phenomenon.

Human Sexuality

Learn about the debate over the importance of biological versus social and cultural influences on human sexual behavior. Explore the cultural differences in sexual behavior and patterns of sexual behavior today.

CHAPTER EIGHTEEN

THE SOCIOLOGY OF THE BODY: HEALTH AND ILLNESS AND SEXUALITY

look at the three photographs on the next page. The first two images of a sunken face and an emaciated body are almost identical. The young girl on the left is Somalian, dying from lack of food. The young woman in the middle is American, dying from anorexia—she chose not to eat or ate too little. The third photograph shows a woman who is severely overweight. Although there are very different social and physical causes of the three women's body shapes and weights, each woman is at risk for major health problems and ultimately a hastened death.

The social dynamics involved in each case are vastly different. Starvation from lack of food is caused by factors outside people's control and afflicts only the very poor. Starvation from anorexia, an illness with no known physical origin, is caused by an obsession with achieving a slim body. Anorexia and other eating disorders are illnesses of the affluent, not of those who have little or no food. It is completely unknown in developing countries where food is scarce, such as Somalia. **Obesity**, or excessive body weight, is also virtually unknown in poor countries where food is scarce and where people work at physically grueling jobs, such as herding or farming. Obesity is caused by a high-calorie, high-fat diet, accompanied by a sedentary lifestyle, such as having a desk job, or lacking the time (or economic resources) to maintain a regular exercise regime.

Anorexia and obesity are important social problems in the Western world. Although both are conditions of the body, the causes are widely believed to reflect social factors more so than

Take a look at the three women to the left: The first woman is painfully thin as a result of famine and malnutrition, sadly common problems in an area of the world plagued by frequent drought and crop failure. The second has become painfully thin by her own doing; people suffering from anorexia feel compelled by a variety of personal and social pressures to lose weight, and will often continue to view themselves as overweight even when they have reached a state of emaciation. The third woman is severely overweight and is preparing for a dangerous gastric bypass surgery.

physical or biological factors. If both conditions reflected biology alone, then we would expect that rates would be fairly constant across history—because human physiology has changed little throughout the millennia. However, both are very recent social problems, as we will see later in this chapter. Both conditions also are highly stratified by social factors such as gender, social class, and race. Women are far more likely than men to have anorexia, while economically disadvantaged persons are far more likely than their wealthier counterparts to struggle with obesity today. Both also are shaped by the cultural context. Fashion magazines today regularly show images of models who are severely underweight, yet uphold these women as paragons of beauty. The average fashion model today is 23 percent thinner than the average American woman, yet twenty-five years ago that number was 8 percent (Derenne and Beresin 2006). At the same time, our culture also promotes excessive eating; social scientists have observed that we live in an "obesogenic" environment (Brownell and Horgen 2004), where high-fat food and "supersized" meals are plentiful and cheap. A Big Mac is less expensive than a healthy salad in most parts of the country, accounting in part for the social class gradient in obesity.

The field known as **sociology of the body** investigates the ways in which our bodies are affected by our social experiences, as well as by the norms and values of the groups to which we belong. Only recently have sociologists recognized the profound interconnections between social life and the body. Therefore, this field is quite new and exciting. Sociology of the body encompasses several basic themes, which we address throughout this chapter. One theme is the effects of social change on the body. Another theme is the increasing separation of the body from "nature"—from our surrounding environment and our biological rhythms. Our bodies are affected by science and technology in ways ranging from life-sustaining machines to diets, and this is creating new dilemmas. Reproductive technologies, for example, have introduced new options but also have generated intense social controversies. We will explore two such controversies, over genetic engineering and abortion, later in the chapter. We also analyze why eating disorders and obesity have become so common in the Western world, study the social dimensions of health and illness, and examine social and cultural influences on our sexual behavior.

The Sociology of the Body

Let's now turn to two specific social problems facing Americans today: eating disorders and the obesity crisis. Both illustrate the ways that a "personal trouble" such as self-starvation or obesity-related complications such as diabetes reflect "public issues," such as a social context that promotes an unrealistic "thin ideal" for young women or the ways that poverty prevents individuals from buying costly low-fat foods or access to public parks and other spaces that allow for regular exercise.

Anorexia and Eating Disorders

Anorexia is related to the idea of dieting, and it reflects changing views of physical attractiveness in modern society. In most premodern societies, the ideal female shape was a fleshy one. Thinness was not desirable, partly because it was associated with lack of food and poverty. Even in Europe in the 1600s and 1700s, the ideal female shape was well proportioned—as evident in paintings by Rubens, for example. The notion of slimness as the desirable feminine shape originated among some middle-class groups in the late nineteenth century, but it became generalized as an ideal for most women only recently.

Anorexia was identified as a disorder in France in 1874, but it remained obscure until the past thirty or forty years (Brown and Jasper 1993). Since then, it has become increasingly common among young women. So has bulimia—bingeing on food, followed by self-induced vomiting. Anorexia and bulimia often occur in the same individual. A recent study estimates that 1.3 million women and 450,000 men suffer from anorexia, 2.25 million women and 750,000 men suffer from bulimia, and 5.25 million women and 3 million men suffer from binge eating. A total of 9 million Americans or about 3 percent of the population suffers from one or more forms of eating disorders (Eating Disorders Coalition [EDC] 2007). Anorexia has the highest mortality rate of any psychological disorder; 20 percent of anorexics will die from it (EDC 2003).

The occurrence of eating disorders in the United States has doubled since 1960 (EDC 2003). On any given day, 25 percent of men and 45 percent of women are dieting; Americans spend over $40 billion each year on dieting and dieting-related products (National Eating Disorders Association 2002). About 95 percent of U.S. college women say they want to lose weight, and up to 85 percent suffer serious problems with eating disorders during their college years. Around 25 percent experience bulimic episodes or anorexia. In American society, 60 percent of girls age thirteen have already begun to diet; this proportion rises to over 80 percent for young women of eighteen. College men also suffer similar experiences, but to a lesser extent. About 50 percent of American male college students want to lose weight, while about 30 percent are on diets (Hesse-Biber 1997). Over 80 percent of ten-year-old children are afraid of being fat (EDC 2003).

Obsession with slenderness—and the resulting eating disorders—extends beyond the United States and Europe. As Western images of feminine beauty have spread to the rest of the world, so too have associated illnesses. Eating disorders were first documented in Japan in the 1960s, a consequence of that country's incorporation into the global economy. Anorexia now occurs among 2 percent of young Japanese women (Curtin 2003). Eating problems also have surfaced among young, primarily affluent women in Hong Kong and Singapore, as well as in urban areas in Taiwan, China, the Philippines, India, and Pakistan (Efron 1997).

The rise of eating disorders in Western societies coincides with the globalization of food production, which has increased greatly in the last several decades. New modes of refrigeration and container transportation have allowed food to be stored for long periods and to be delivered from one side of the world to the other. Since the 1950s, supermarket shelves have been abundant with foods from all parts of the world (for those who can afford it—now the majority of the population in Western societies). Most foods are available all the time, not just when they are in season locally.

For the past decade or so, almost everyone in the United States and other developed countries has been on a diet. This does not mean that everyone is trying to get thin. Rather, when all foods are available all the time, we must decide what to eat—in other words, we must construct a diet, where diet means the foods we habitually consume. First, we have to decide what to eat in relation to the new medical information that science bombards us with—for instance, that cholesterol levels contribute to heart disease. Second, we worry about calorie content. In a society with abundant food, we can "design" our bodies in relation to our lifestyle habits (such as jogging, bicycling, swimming, and yoga) and what we eat. Eating disorders have their origins in the opportunities but also in the tensions that this situation produces.

Why do eating disorders affect women in particular and young women most acutely? Although roughly 10 percent of those with eating disorders are men, they don't suffer from anorexia or bulimia as often as women—partly because social norms stress the importance of physical attractiveness more for women than for men and partly because desirable body images of men differ from those of women. Anorexia and other eating disorders reflect the fact that women now play a larger part in the wider society but are still judged as much by their appearance as by their accomplishments. Eating disorders are rooted in feelings of shame and a desire to have control over one's body. The individual feels inadequate and imperfect, and her anxieties about how others perceive her become focused through feelings about her body. At that point, shedding weight becomes the means of making everything right in her world.

Once she starts to diet and exercise compulsively, she can become locked into a pattern of refusing food or vomiting up what she has eaten. As the body loses muscle mass, it loses heart muscle, so the heart gets smaller and weaker, which ultimately leads to heart failure. About half of all anorexics also have low white-blood-cell counts, and about a third are anemic. Both conditions can lower the immune system's resistance to disease, leaving an anorexic vulnerable to infections. However, these harmful patterns may be broken through psychotherapy and medical treatment.

The spread of eating disorders reflects the influence of science and technology. For example, calorie counting became possible through the advance of technology. But the effect of technology is always conditioned by social factors. The fact that we have much more autonomy over our bodies than in the past presents us with positive possibilities as well as new

Self Reflections

How many times a day do we see our own reflection? We take mirrors so much for granted that it is hard to imagine what people did before they were invented. Perhaps you could see yourself reflected in polished metal or marble, but even these are relatively recent inventions in human history. Before that there were really only two options: seeing oneself reflected in another's eyes, or in still water. Today, mirrors allow us to try and see ourselves as other's see us and to assess our standing in the world and, perhaps, do something about it by making ourselves, or some aspect of ourselves, over.

Ever since Charles Horton Cooley developed the concept of the "looking glass self," sociologists have puzzled about the role that others play in the development of our concept of self. Put simply, what we think about our self is a summary not simply of who we are but also of what we make of what others have made of us.

⬇ As mirrors became more affordable in the mid-nineteenth century, popular preoccupation with the moral corrosion of one's own reflection grew. Whereas Narcissus was male, contemporary mythology focuses on women. C. Allan Gilbert's drawing *All Is Vanity* (below) aptly illustrates apprehension about the effects that the glamour industry, and fashion in particular, have on women's self-esteem and health.

⬆ Caravaggio's late-sixteenth-century painting of Narcissus not only reflects how singular these moments of self-awareness were but also evokes the social concern that such an act could be dangerous, especially if it became a habit. After all, if you see with your own eyes that you are the fairest of them all, then why should you concern yourself with others and their concerns?

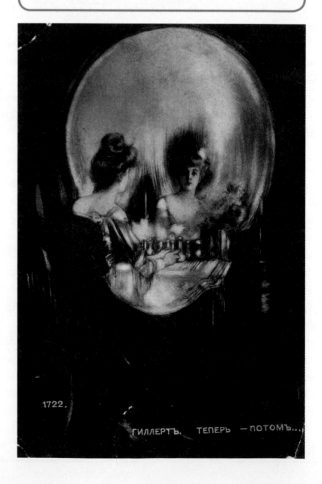

1722.

ГИЛЛЕРТЪ.   ТЕПЕРЬ — ПОТОМЪ...

Created by John Grady.

An eight-month-old baby plays in front of a mirror. Children do not recognize their own reflection until they are close to two years old. Later on in life, however, children realize that they are the image in the mirror and slowly come to understand that this is what others see.

People now use cameras to document what they see in the mirror and house them in interactive photo galleries on the Web where strangers can share their findings as a form of public art. Heather Kimber tells us what she was trying to capture:

The picture was taken in one of my bathrooms. I shot the picture because it is often how I feel about myself. I have battled weight and health issues for a good part of my adult life and I feel like the healthy part of me deep inside is laughing at me because I just can't seem to get it right on the outside.

Heather, bravely, has revealed something that most of us are too timid to admit: The self we have constructed from our experience with others may embrace different, and conflicting, values. Nevertheless, looking at ourselves in the mirror is often a far more mundane experience than the images we have been examining.

This photograph was taken in Kuwait of a thirteen-year-old African American boy. A white mother and an Arab-American father adopted him. His mother, who took the photograph, recollects:

We were at a small park outside a local Burger King for breakfast . . . when my son wandered off towards the mirrored glass. . . . My son was just starting the process of trying to find himself, something more difficult for him as an adopted child, a child with parents of other races and as an American teenager in Kuwait. That day, I'd noticed that he was wearing a bandana under his hat. I knew he had some but he'd never worn them in front of me. I saw it as an attempt to silently assert himself, of standing up to say he was American, an African American. I watched him closer that day and caught him from the corner of my eye trying out some hip-hop moves in the reflection of the glass. He's been very shy about dancing in front of the family so it was a moment I wanted to capture. . . . I took several shots of him dancing, oblivious that I'd turned the camera in his direction, but this was my favorite because of how his hand is bent. It helps to make even the reflection very clear that he was dancing and checking himself out.

"Watch Out for Fat Friends"

eware of Fat Friends!" "Fat: Can You 'Catch' It?" "Find Yourself Packing It On, Blame Friends." If these July 2007 headlines were correct, then body-conscious Americans might have started to ditch their plump pals for more svelte sidekicks. But were these headlines accurate? Does having an obese friend "make" one fat? Yes, according to the study's authors sociologist Nicholas Christakis of Harvard Medical School and political scientist James Fowler of University of California–Davis. Will dumping one's fat friend solve the problem of obesity? No, according to Christakis and Fowler.

Their study, entitled "The Spread of Obesity in a Large Social Network over 32 Years," published in the *New England Journal of Medicine* (July 26, 2007), did show that obesity was "contagious," but they also found that thinness was also

"contagious." A deeper probe behind the headlines also reveals why and how body size can "spread" across groups of friends; social norms rather than biological "contagion" are the driving force. In

How did the media interpret Christakis's findings about obesity and social networks? How do social norms affect our eating behaviors?

brief, Christakis and Fowler found that if one person becomes obese, then persons closely connected to him or her also have a greater chance of becoming obese

themselves. If a person that one considered a "friend" became obese, then one's own chances of becoming obese increase by 57 percent. However, a neighbor's weight change has no effect on one's own body weight.

One reason why the media were so eager to report the findings of the Christakis and Fowler study is that it was the first-ever study to examine the ways that one's social networks affect one's body weight. The researchers had access to a unique data source that allowed them to ask questions such as: How do one's friends affect one's weight? Does it matter if one's friends live nearby or far away? Christakis and Fowler analyzed data from a sample of 12,067 adults who were followed for a period of thirty-two years, from 1971 to 2003. These adults were participants in the renowned Framingham Heart Study. The data source revealed whom the study

anxieties and problems. All this is part of what sociologists call the **socialization of nature**: Phenomena that used to be "natural," or given in nature, have now become social—they depend on our own social decisions.

The Obesity Epidemic

Obesity is considered the top public health problem facing Americans today. Obesity, or excessive weight (see Table 18.1) increases an individual's risk for a wide range of health problems, including cardiovascular diseases, diabetes mellitus type 2, sleep apnea, osteoarthritis, and some forms of cancers (Haslam and James 2005). Yet excessive body weight also

may take a severe psychological toll. Overweight and obese Americans are more likely than their thinner peers to experience employment discrimination, discrimination by health-care providers, and daily experiences of teasing, insults, and shame (Carr and Friedman 2005). Negative attitudes toward overweight and obese persons develop as early as elementary school. In one classic sociological study (Richardson et al. 1961), a sample of ten- and eleven-year-old boys and girls were given six images of children and were asked to report how much they liked each child. The six drawings included an obese child, as well as children with various physical disabilities and disfigurements. The obese child was ranked dead last—a finding that has been replicated many times in more recent studies (e.g., Latner and Stunkard 2003).

participants were friends with, as well as who was a spouse or sibling or neighbor. It also obtained information on each person's address and body weight at each interview point.

Because of their unique data and rigorous methodology, the researchers could rule out competing explanations for their findings. For example, because they had data from many time points throughout the thirty-two-year study, they could ascertain the order in which events unfolded. It was not the case that obese people would simply seek out similar-weight people as friends. Rather, Christakis noted that there was a "direct, causal relationship." Christakis and Fowler also found that it didn't matter whether one's friend lived near or far—they found that a friend who lived five hundred miles away had just as powerful an impact on one's own weight as a friend who lived across the street.

The study also found that the "contagion" of body weight was not due to the fact that friends might share lifestyles, hobbies, and dietary choices—such as eating large meals together or discouraging one another from exercising. If it's not the "birds of a feather flock together"

explanation or "gluttony loves company" explanation, what accounts for the spread of body weight? The authors believe that their study is a testimony to the power of social norms. People develop their ideas about what is an acceptable body type by looking at the people around them. Christakis notes, "People come to think that it is okay to be bigger since those around them are bigger, and this sensibility spreads."

However, the researchers were adamant that Americans should not come away thinking that it is wise or healthy to abandon their obese friends. Rather, Christakis noted that it is good for one's health to have friends, period: "It is unlikely that severing ties with people on the basis of any of their particular traits—as some have supposed that our

results might suggest—would necessarily be beneficial." Instead, they suggest that overweight or obese people could befriend a thin person and then allow themselves to be influenced by the positive model set by the healthy-weight friend.

Questions

- What was the main finding of the Christakis and Fowler study?
- What practical recommendations might a health-care professional make after reading this study?
- Why do you think that the media were intrigued by the findings of this study?

FOR FURTHER EXPLORATION

Christakis, Nicholas A., and James H. Fowler. 2007. "The Spread of Obesity in a Large Social Network over 32 Years." *New England Journal of Medicine* 357: 370–379.

Christakis, Nicholas A., and James H. Fowler. 2007. "Letter to the Editor." *New England Journal of Medicine* 357 (18): 1868.

Kolata, Gina. 2007. "Find Yourself Packing It On? Blame Friends." *New York Times,* July 26, 2007: Page A1.

Sociologists are fascinated with the persistence of negative attitudes toward overweight and obese persons, especially because these individuals currently make up the statistical majority of all Americans. According to the Centers for Disease Control, roughly 60 percent of adults are now overweight (see Table 18.1 for technical definitions of weight categories). More than a third of American adults, 33 percent of men and 35 percent of women are obese. The proportion varies widely by race; an astounding 53 percent of non-Hispanic black and 51 percent of Mexican-American women aged 40–59 are now obese, compared to just 39 percent of non-Hispanic white women in the same age group (CDC 2007d). As the figures below reveal, the proportion of Americans struggling with weight has increased tremendously in the past two decades. An even more troubling

trend is the increase in the proportion of American children and adolescents who are overweight. Between 1976 and 1980, an estimated 6.5 percent of children ages six to eleven and 5 percent of persons ages twelve to nineteen were overweight. By contrast, in 2003–2004, 18.8 percent of children and 17.4 of adolescents were overweight (National Center for Health Statistics 2004).

The reasons behind the obesity crisis are widely debated. Some argue that the apparent increase in the overweight and obese population is a statistical artifact. The proportion of the U.S. population who are middle-aged has increased rapidly during the past two decades, as the large baby boom cohort reached middle age. Middle-aged persons, due to slowing metabolism, are at greater risk of excessive body weight.

TABLE 18.1

What Is Your Body Mass Index?

People are classified into one of six weight categories based on their body mass index (BMI), which reflects one's current height and weight. BMI can be calculated using the following formula:

$$BMI = 703 \times \frac{weight \; (lb)}{height^2 \; (in^2)}$$

WEIGHT CATEGORY	BODY MASS INDEX (BMI)
Starvation	less than 16.5
Underweight	from 16.5 to 18.5
Normal	from 18.5 to 25
Overweight	from 25 to 30
Obese	from 30 to 35
Clinically Obese	from 35 to 40
Morbidly Obese	greater than 40

SOURCE: National Heart, Lung, and Blood Institute 2008.

Others attribute the pattern—especially the childhood obesity increase—to compositional factors. The proportion of children today who are black or Hispanic is higher than in earlier decades, and both of these two ethnic groups are at a much

Why do many parents turn to fast food to feed their families? What are the consequences?

greater risk for overweight than their white peers. Still others argue that the measures used to count and classify obese persons have shifted, thus leading to an excessively high count of such persons. Finally, some social observers believe that public concern over obesity is blown out of proportion and reflects more of a "moral panic" than a "public health crisis" (Campos et al. 2006).

Most public health experts believe, however, that obesity is a very real problem caused by what Kelly Brownell calls the "obesogenic environment." Among adults, sedentary jobs have replaced physical jobs such as farming. Children are more likely to spend their afterschool hours sitting in front of a computer or television than playing tag or riding bikes around the neighborhood. Parents are pressed for time given their hectic work and family schedules and turn to unhealthy fast food rather than home-cooked meals. Restaurants, eager to lure bargain-friendly patrons, provide enormous serving sizes at low prices. The social forces that promote high fat and sugar consumption and that restrict the opportunity to exercise are particularly acute for poor persons and ethnic minorities. Small grocery stores in poor neighborhoods rarely sell fresh or low-cost produce. Large grocery stores are scarce in poor neighborhoods and in predominantly African American neighborhoods (Morland et al. 2002). High crime rates and high levels of traffic in inner-city neighborhoods make exercise in public parks or jogging on city streets potentially dangerous (Brownell and Horgen 2004).

Policy makers and public health professionals have proposed a broad range of solutions to the obesity crisis. Some have proposed (unsuccessfully) practices that place the burden directly on the individual. For example, some schools have considered having a "weight report card," where children and parents would be told the child's **body mass index (BMI)**, in an effort to trigger healthy behaviors at home. Yet most experts endorse solutions that attack the problem at a large-scale level, such as making healthy low-cost produce more widely available; providing safe public places for fitness, free exercise classes, and classes in health and nutrition to poor children and their families; and requiring restaurants and food manufacturers to clearly note the fat and calorie content of their products. Only in attacking the "public issue" of the obesogenic environment will the private trouble of excessive weight be resolved (Brownell and Horgen 2004).

☑ CONCEPT CHECKS

1. Why is anorexia more likely to strike young women than other subgroups?
2. What explanations are offered for the recent increase in obesity rates?

Percent of U.S. Adults Classified as Obese (BMI > 30)

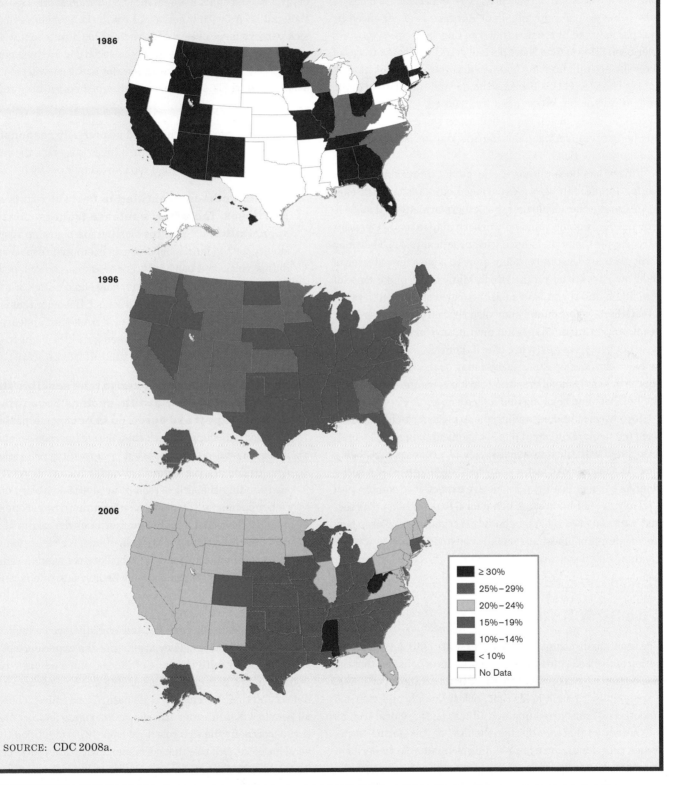

1986

1996

2006

■	≥ 30%
■	25%–29%
■	20%–24%
■	15%–19%
■	10%–14%
■	< 10%
□	No Data

SOURCE: CDC 2008a.

The Sociology of Health and Illness

One of sociologists' main concerns is the experience of illness—how being sick, chronically ill, or disabled is experienced by sick persons and by those with whom they interact. If you have ever been ill, even for a short period, you know that patterns of daily life are temporarily modified and your interactions with others change. This is because the normal functioning of the body is a vital, but often taken for granted, part of our daily lives. Our sense of self is predicated on the expectation that our bodies will facilitate, not impede, our social interactions and daily activities.

Illness has both personal and public dimensions. When we fall ill, not only do we experience pain, discomfort, confusion, and other challenges, but others are affected as well. Our friends, families, and co-workers may extend sympathy, care, support, and assistance with practical tasks. They may struggle to understand our illness or to adjust the patterns of their own lives to accommodate it. Many try to make sense of the illness and try to figure out the cause of the health problem. Others we encounter may also react to our illness; their reactions, in turn, shape our own interpretations and can pose challenges to our sense of self. For instance, a long-time smoker who develops lung disease may be made to feel guilt or shame by family members, who provide constant reminders of the link between smoking and lung disease.

Two ways of understanding the experience of illness have been particularly influential in sociological thought. The first, associated with the functionalist school, proposes that "being sick" is a social role, just as "worker" or "mother" is a social role. As such, unhealthy persons are expected to comply with a widely agreed-upon set of behavioral expectations. The second view, favored by symbolic interactionists, explores how the meanings of illness are socially constructed and how these meanings influence people's behavior.

The Sick Role

The functionalist thinker Talcott Parsons (1951) developed the notion of the **sick role** to describe patterns of behavior that the sick person adopts to minimize the disruptive impact of illness. Functionalist thought holds that society usually operates in a smooth and consensual manner. Illness is, therefore, seen as a dysfunction that can disrupt the flow of this normal state. A sick individual, for example, might be unable to perform standard responsibilities or be less reliable and efficient than usual. Because sick people cannot carry out their normal roles, the lives of people around them are disrupted: Assignments at work go unfinished and cause stress for co-workers, responsibilities at home are not fulfilled, and so forth.

According to Parsons, people learn the sick role through socialization and enact it—with the cooperation of others—when they fall ill. As with other social roles, such as gender roles, sick persons face societal expectations for how to behave, yet at the same time other members of society abide by a generally agreed-upon set of expectations for how they will treat the sick individual. The sick role is distinguished by three sets of normative expectations:

1. **The sick person is not held personally responsible for his or her poor health.** Illness is seen as the result of physical causes beyond the individual's control.

2. **The sick person is entitled to certain rights and privileges, including a release from normal responsibilities.** Since the sick person bears no responsibility for the illness, he or she is exempted from certain duties, roles, and behaviors. For example, the sick person might be released from normal household duties or a sick child is excused from attending school. Behavior that is not as polite or thoughtful as usual or an unkempt appearance might be excused. The sick person gains the right to stay in bed, for example, or to take time off from work.

3. **The sick person is expected to take sensible steps to regain his or her health, such as consulting a medical expert and agreeing to become a patient.** In order to occupy the sick role, the sick person's claim of illness should be corroborated by a medical professional who legitimates the claim. Such confirmation allows those surrounding the sick person to accept the validity of his or her claims. Without such confirmation, the sick person may be viewed as a malingerer, or one who feigns health problems to avoid his or her obligations. A sick person who refuses to consult a doctor or who does not heed the advice of a medical authority puts his or her sick-role status in jeopardy.

Over the past four decades, sociologists have refined Parsons's sick-role theory. They argue that the experience of the sick role varies with the type of illness, since people's reactions to a sick person vary according to the severity of the illness and their perception of its nature and cause. Thus not all people will uniformly experience the rights and privileges that accompany the sick role. Freidson (1970) identified three versions of the sick role that correspond with different types of illness. The *conditional* sick role applies to individuals suffering

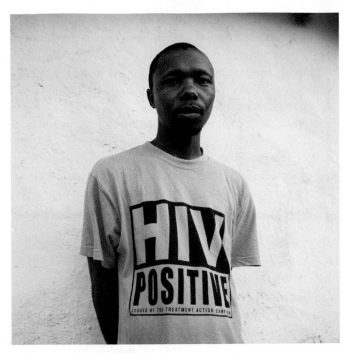

Three years after starting his antiretroviral medication, HIV-positive Bavuyisie Mbebe poses outside his home in South Africa. The HIV-Positive t-shirts are worn to challenge stigma and promote openness about HIV, and are worn by both people with the disease and their supporters.

from a temporary condition that ultimately will be cured. The sick person is expected to get well and receives some rights and privileges according to the severity of the illness. For example, someone with bronchitis would reap more benefits than someone with a common cold. The *unconditionally legitimate* sick role refers to individuals who are suffering from incurable terminal illnesses. Because the sick person cannot do anything to get well, he or she is automatically entitled to occupy the sick role. The expectation that one will seek timely medical care may be relaxed, because care seeking may be futile for some health conditions. The unconditionally legitimate role might apply to individuals with alopecia (total hair loss) or severe acne (in both cases there are no special privileges but rather an acknowledgment that the individual is not responsible for the illness), or with cancer or Parkinson's disease—which result in important privileges and the right to abandon many duties. The third sick role is the *illegitimate* role, which applies when an individual suffers from a disease or condition that is stigmatized by others. In such cases, there is a sense that the individual might be partially responsible for his or her illness; additional rights and privileges are not necessarily granted. HIV/AIDS is perhaps the most vivid example of a stigmatized illness that affects a sufferer's perceived right to assume the sick role. Some AIDS patients may be held "responsible" for

their condition and may be judged negatively for having engaged in high-risk behaviors such as unprotected sex or the use of unclean needles. Pediatric AIDS patients, those who contracted AIDS through a tainted blood transfusion, or other persons perceived to be "innocent" victims, by contrast, may be spared of stigmatization.

Evaluation

Although the sick-role model reveals how the ill person is an integral part of a larger social context, a number of criticisms can be levied against it. Some argue that the sick-role formula does not adequately capture the *lived experience* of illness. Others point out that it cannot be applied across all contexts, cultures, and historical periods. For example, it does not account for instances when doctors and patients disagree about a diagnosis or have opposing interests. It also fails to explain illnesses that do not necessarily lead to a suspension of normal activity, such as alcoholism, certain disabilities, and some chronic diseases. Furthermore, assuming the sick role is not always a straightforward process. Some individuals who suffer for years from chronic pain or from misdiagnosed symptoms are denied the sick role until they get a clear diagnosis. Other sick people, such as young women with autoimmune diseases, often appear physically healthy despite constant physical pain and exhaustion; because of their "healthy" outward appearance, however, they may not be readily granted sick-role status. In other cases, social factors such as race, class, and gender can affect whether and how readily the sick role is granted. The sick role cannot be divorced from the social, cultural, and economic influences that surround it.

The realities of life and illness are more complex than the sick role suggests. The leading causes of death today are heart disease and cancer, two diseases that are widely associated with unhealthy behaviors such as smoking, a high-fat diet, and a sedentary lifestyle. Given the emphasis on taking control over one's health and lifestyle in our modern age, individuals bear ever-greater responsibility for their own well-being. This contradicts the first premise of the sick role—that the individual is not to blame for his or her illness. Moreover, in modern societies the shift away from acute infectious disease toward chronic illness has made the sick role less applicable. Whereas it might be useful in understanding acute illness, it is less useful in chronic illness because there is no single formula for chronically ill or disabled people to follow. Moreover, chronically ill persons often find that their symptoms fluctuate, so that they feel and appear healthy on some days, yet experience disabling symptoms on other days. Living with illness is experienced and interpreted in multiple ways.

Illness as "Lived Experience"

Symbolic interactionists study the ways people interpret the social world and the meanings they ascribe to it. Many sociologists have applied this approach to health and illness and view this perspective as a partial corrective to the limitations of functionalist approaches to health. Symbolic interactionists are not concerned with identifying risk factors for specific illnesses. Rather, they address questions such as: How do people react and adjust to news about a serious illness? How does illness shape individuals' daily lives? How does living with a chronic illness affect an individual's self-identity?

One theme that sociologists address is how chronically ill individuals cope with the practical and emotional implications of their illness. Certain illnesses require regular treatments or maintenance that can affect daily routines. Undergoing dialysis or insulin injections, or taking large numbers of pills requires individuals to adjust their schedules. Other illnesses have unpredictable effects, such as sudden loss of bowel or bladder control or violent nausea. People suffering from such conditions often develop strategies for managing their illness in daily life. These include practical considerations—such as noting the location of the restrooms when in an unfamiliar place—as well as skills for managing interpersonal relations, both intimate and commonplace. Although symptoms can be embarrassing and disruptive, people develop coping strategies to live as normally as possible (Kelly 1992).

At the same time, the experience of illness can pose challenges to and changes in people's sense of self. These develop not only through the actual reactions of other people but also through the ill person's perception of those reactions. For the chronically ill or disabled, routine social interactions become tinged with risk or uncertainty, and interpretations of common situations may differ substantially. An ill person may need assistance but not want to appear dependent, for example. A healthy individual may feel sympathy for someone diagnosed with an illness but might be unsure whether to address the subject directly. The changed context of social interactions can precipitate transformations in self-identity.

Some sociologists have investigated how chronically ill individuals manage their illnesses within the overall context of their lives (Jobling 1988; Williams 1993). Illness can place enormous demands on people's time, energy, strength, and emotional reserves. Serious illness can also tax the emotional resources of loved ones. Corbin and Strauss (1985) identified three types of "work" incorporated in chronically ill people's everyday strategies. *Illness work* refers to activities involved in managing the condition, such as treating pain, doing diagnostic tests, or undergoing physical therapy. *Everyday work* pertains to the management of daily life—maintaining relationships with others, running household affairs, and pursuing professional or personal interests. *Biographical work* involves the process of incorporating the illness into one's life, making sense of it, and developing ways of explaining it to others. Such a process can help chronically ill people restore meaning and order to their lives.

Each of these processes of adaptation may be particularly difficult for ill persons who suffer from a stigmatized health condition, such as obesity, alcoholism, AIDS, or even lung cancer. Sociologist Erving Goffman (1963) developed the concept of **stigma**, which refers to any personal characteristic that is devalued in a particular social context. Stigmas typically come in one of three forms: "abominations of the body" (such as disfigurement, disability, or obesity); "tribal stigma of race, nation, or religion" (such as belonging to a historically denigrated racial or ethnic group); and "blemishes of individual character" (such as laziness, lack of personal control, or immorality). Stigmatized individuals and groups often are treated with suspicion, hostility, or discrimination. Some ill persons, particularly those marked by the stigma "abominations of the body," may arouse feelings of sympathy or compassion, especially if one is not held responsible for his or her illness. The ill person also may receive special privileges. However, when a health condition is viewed as indicative of a "character blemish," such as sexual promiscuity or gluttony, then the healthy population may reject the sufferers.

For example, one study showed that adolescents offered much less critical appraisals of overweight persons when they believed that the weight was caused by a thyroid problem, which was not in their control. As such, the weight was due to a biological factor rather than to a character flaw such as laziness or lack of self-control (Dejong 1993). Similarly, throughout history many infectious diseases, especially those contracted by the poor, often were stigmatized and viewed as indicators of shame and dishonor. This occurred in the Middle Ages with leprosy, when people were isolated in leper colonies. HIV/AIDS often provokes such stigmatization today—in spite of the fact that, as with leprosy, the risk of contracting the disease in ordinary situations is almost nonexistent. For instance, the United Nations Joint Program with the World Health Organization on HIV/AIDS reports incidences in Kerala, India, when children infected with HIV have been barred from schools and denied any interaction with other children (UNAIDS 2003). Stigmas, however, are rarely based on valid understandings or scientific data. They spring from stereotypes or perceptions that may be false or only partially correct. Further, the nature of a stigma varies widely across sociocultural context: the extent to which a trait is devalued depends on the values and beliefs of those who do the stigmatizing.

Changing Conceptions of Health and Illness

Cultures differ in what they consider healthy and normal. All cultures have known concepts of physical health and illness, but most of what we now recognize as medicine is a consequence of developments in Western society over the past three centuries. In premodern cultures, the family was the main institution for coping with sickness or affliction. There have always been individuals who specialized as healers, using a mixture of physical and magical remedies, and many such traditional systems survive today in non-Western cultures. For instance, Ayurvedic medicine (traditional healing) has been practiced in India for nearly two thousand years. It is founded on a theory of the equilibrium of psychological and physical facets of the personality, imbalances of which are treated by nutritional and herbal remedies. Chinese folk medicine similarly aims to restore harmony among aspects of the personality and bodily systems, involving the use of herbs and acupuncture for treatment.

Modern medicine sees the origins and treatment of disease as physical and explicable in scientific terms. Indeed, the application of science to medical diagnosis and cure underlay the development of modern health-care systems. Other features were the acceptance of the hospital as the setting within which to treat serious illnesses and the development of the medical profession as a body with codes of ethics and significant social power. The scientific view of disease was linked to the requirement that medical training be systematic and long term; self-taught healers were excluded. Although professional medical practice is not limited to hospitals, the hospital provided an environment in which doctors could treat and study large numbers of patients, in circumstances permitting the concentration of medical technology. On rare occasions, however, tensions may arise when physicians adhere to modern medical models and their patients adhere to folk or spiritual models of health. These cultural tensions are portrayed poignantly in the book *The Spirit Catches You and You Fall Down: A Hmong Child, Her American Doctors, and the Collision of Two Cultures* (Fadiman 1997). The book recounts the experience of the Lee family, Laotian immigrants whose infant daughter had epilepsy. The Lees believed their daughter's illness stemmed from spiritual causes, while doctors believed the condition was biological and could be alleviated with drugs. After trying to comply with a difficult medication regimen, the Lees stopped administering the drugs, and their daughter was placed in foster care, with tragic results.

Just as cultural beliefs about health and illness change across time and place, the very illnesses from which individuals suffer and both the illness causes and cures vary widely by sociohistorical context. In medieval times, the major illnesses were infectious diseases such as tuberculosis, cholera, malaria, and bubonic plague. Whereas the plague, or Black Death, epidemic of the fourteenth century killed a quarter of the population of England and devastated large areas of Europe, infectious diseases have by now become a minor cause of death in industrialized countries, replaced by noninfectious diseases such as cancer and heart disease. Although in premodern societies the highest rates of death were among infants and young children, today death rates (the proportion of the population who die each year) rise with increasing age. The leading causes of death today, heart disease and cancer, disproportionately strike persons age sixty-five and older.

In spite of the prestige that modern medicine has acquired, improvements in medical care accounted for only a minor part of the decline in death rates before the twentieth century. Effective sanitation, better nutrition, water purification, milk pasteurization, control of sewage, and improved hygiene were more consequential (Dowling 1977). Drugs, advances in surgery, and antibiotics did not significantly decrease death rates until well into the twentieth century. Antibiotics used to treat bacterial infections first became available in the 1930s and 1940s; most immunizations (against diseases such as polio) were developed later.

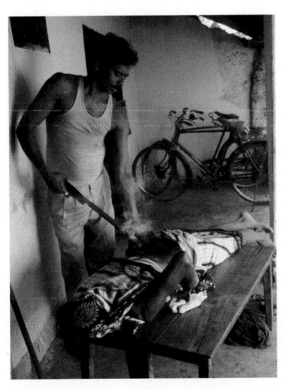

Ayurvedic treatment: Ayurvedic physician Kumar Das uses a hot iron rod and fabric soaked in herbs to heal an arthritic hip.

Alternative Medicine

Actress Jenny McCarthy was upheld as a savior by some parents of autistic children when she took on the role of an autism advocate in 2007. Several years earlier, her young son had been diagnosed with autism. Angry and frustrated with doctors' advice, she worked with nutritionists to develop her own course of treatment, placing her son Evan on a strict gluten- and casein-free diet with the hopes that it would minimize his autism symptoms. Yet other parents (and many doctors) argued that a gluten- and casein-free diet plan, such as the one McCarthy administered to her son, had not been proven to correct intestinal problems and other difficulties experienced by autistic children. McCarthy's ordeal represents an important new trend in health and health care today. Alternative therapies are being explored by a record high number of adults and are slowly gaining acceptance by the mainstream medical community. Physicians increasingly believe that such unorthodox therapies may be an important complement to (although not a substitute for) traditional medicine, provided they are upheld to rigorous scientific evaluation. Yet devoted adherents to nontraditional health regimens believe that such practices are effective and that their personal experiences are more meaningful than are the results of controlled trials.

Medical sociologists refer to such unorthodox medical practices as **complementary and alternative medicine (CAM)**. CAM encompasses a diverse set of approaches and therapies for treating illness and promoting well-being that generally fall outside standard medical practices. These approaches are usually not taught in medical schools and not practiced by physicians or other professionals trained in medical programs. However, in recent years a number of medical and nursing schools have started offering courses in alternative medicine (Fenton and Morris 2003; Wetzel, Eisenberg, and Kaptchuk 1998). Examples of common CAM therapies include chiropractic, massage, homeopathy, reflexology, herbal remedies, and acupuncture. Complementary medicine is distinct from alternative medicine in that the latter is meant to be used in place of standard medical procedures, while the former is meant to be used in conjunction with medical procedures to increase their efficacy or reduce side effects (Saks 1992). Many people use CAM approaches in addition to, rather than in place of, orthodox treatments (although some alternative approaches, such as homeopathy, reject the basis of orthodox medicine entirely).

Industrialized countries have some of the best-developed, best-resourced medical facilities in the world. Why, then, are a growing number of people exploring treatments that have not yet proven effective in controlled clinical trials, such as aromatherapy and hypnotherapy? It has been estimated that as many as one in ten Americans has ever consulted an alternative practitioner. An even larger proportion of Americans have sought out CAM treatments on their own. A recent survey found that 62 percent of all Americans said that they had used some form of CAM in 2002, where CAM was broadly defined to include prayer as well as alternative treatments (Pagan and Pauly 2005). The profile of the typical individual who seeks alternative forms of healing is female, young to middle-aged, and middle class.

There are many reasons for seeking the services of an alternative medicine practitioner or pursuing CAM regimens on one's own. Some people perceive orthodox medicine to be deficient or ineffective in relieving chronic pain or symptoms of stress and anxiety. Others are dissatisfied with features of modern health-care systems such as long waits, referrals through chains of specialists, and financial restrictions. Connected to this are concerns about the harmful side effects of medication and the intrusiveness of surgery, both staples of modern Western medicine. The asymmetrical power relationship between doctors and patients also drives some people to seek alternative medicine. Those people feel that the role of the passive patient does not grant them enough input into their own treatment and healing. Finally, some individuals profess religious or philosophical objections to orthodox medicine, which treats the mind and body separately. They believe that orthodox medicine often overlooks the spiritual and psychological dimensions of health and illness. All these concerns are critiques of the **biomedical model of health** (the foundation of the Western medical establishment), which defines disease in objective terms and believes that scientifically based medical treatment can restore the body to health (Beyerstein 1999).

The growth of alternative medicine is a fascinating reflection of the transformations occurring within modern societies. We are living in an age where much more information is available to draw on in making choices. The proliferation of health-related Web sites such as WebMD and MedicineNet provides instant access to information on health symptoms and treatments. Thus individuals are increasingly becoming health consumers, adopting an active stance toward their own health and well-being. Not only are we choosing the type of practitioners to consult, but we are also demanding more involvement in our own care and treatment. In this way the growth of alternative medicine is linked to the expanding self-help movement, which involves support groups, learning circles, and self-help books. People now want to seize control of their lives and actively manage them, rather than rely on the instructions or opinions of others.

Members of the traditional medical community, once viewed as completely resistant to the notion of alternative medicine, are increasingly taking a more open-minded approach to such therapies. Many now cautiously endorse patients' desires to consult an ever-expanding array of medical information. However, medical leaders believe that CAM should be held to the same level of scientific scrutiny as traditional medicine: It should be held up to rigorous scientific evaluation. Former editors of *New England Journal of Medicine* Marcia Angell and Jerome Kassirer (1998) have observed, "Since many alternative remedies have recently found their way into the medical mainstream [there] cannot be two kinds of medicine—conventional and alternative. There is only medicine that has been adequately tested and medicine that has not, medicine that works and medicine that may or may not work. Once a treatment has been tested rigorously, it no longer matters whether it was considered alternative at the outset. If it is found to be reasonably safe and effective, it will be accepted."

One area where CAM has worked its way into the medical mainstream is end-of-life care. Palliative care, which focuses on comfort rather than treatment, is now very common for dying adults. Pain relief regimens at the end of life often involve "traditional" medical practices such as morphine as well as complementary practices such as low-level laser therapy, meditation, aromatherapy, Chinese medicine, massage, and therapeutic touch.

Debates about complementary and alternative medicine also shed light on the changing nature of health and illness in the late modern period. Many conditions and illnesses for which individuals seek alternative medical treatment seem to be products of the modern age itself. Rates of insomnia, anxiety, stress, depression, fatigue, and chronic pain (caused by arthritis, cancer, and other diseases) are increasing in industrialized societies. Although these conditions have long existed, they are causing greater distress and disruption to people's health than ever before. Recent surveys reveal that stress has surpassed the common cold as the biggest cause of absence from work. A recent World Health Organization study reveals that depression is the most debilitating disease in the world, taking a toll on worker productivity and increasing one's risk of other serious health conditions (Moussavi et al. 2007). Ironically, these consequences of modernity are ones that orthodox medicine has difficulty addressing. Alternative medicine is unlikely to overtake mainstream health care altogether, but indications are that its role will continue to grow.

☑ CONCEPT CHECKS

1. How do functionalist theorists and symbolic interactionists differ in their perspectives on health and illness?
2. What is the biomedical model of health?
3. Compare complementary and alternative medicine.

Social Factors in Health and Illness

The twentieth century witnessed a significant increase in life expectancy for people living in industrialized countries. Diseases such as polio, scarlet fever, and diphtheria have been all but eradicated. Infant mortality rates have dropped precipitously, leading to an increase in the average age of death in the developed world. Compared with other parts of the world, standards of health and well-being are relatively high. Many advances in public health have been attributed to the power of modern medicine. It is commonly assumed that medical research has been—and will continue to be—successful in uncovering the biological causes of disease and in developing effective treatments.

Although this view has been influential, it is somewhat unsatisfactory for sociologists because it ignores the important role of social and environmental influences on patterns of health and illness. The improvements in overall public health over the past century cannot conceal the fact that health and illness occur unevenly throughout the population. Research has shown that certain groups of people enjoy much better health than others. These *health inequalities* appear to reflect larger socioeconomic patterns.

Sociologists and scientists in social **epidemiology**—the science that studies the distribution and incidence of disease and illness within the population—have attempted to explain the link between health and variables such as social class, gender, race, age, geography, and even social relationships and integration. While most scholars acknowledge the strong positive correlation between socioeconomic resources and good health, they do not agree about the nature of the connection or about how to address health inequalities. One of the main areas of debate involves the relative importance of individual variables (e.g., lifestyle, behavior, diet, and cultural patterns) versus environmental or structural factors (e.g., access to health care, income distribution, and poverty; Figure 18.1). In this section, we examine variations in health patterns in the United States according to social class, gender, race, geography, and social integration and we review some competing explanations for their persistence.

Social Class–Based Inequalities in Health

In Chapter 8, we defined *social class* as a concept that encompasses education, income, occupation, and assets. In American

FIGURE 18.1

Cultural and Material Influences on Health

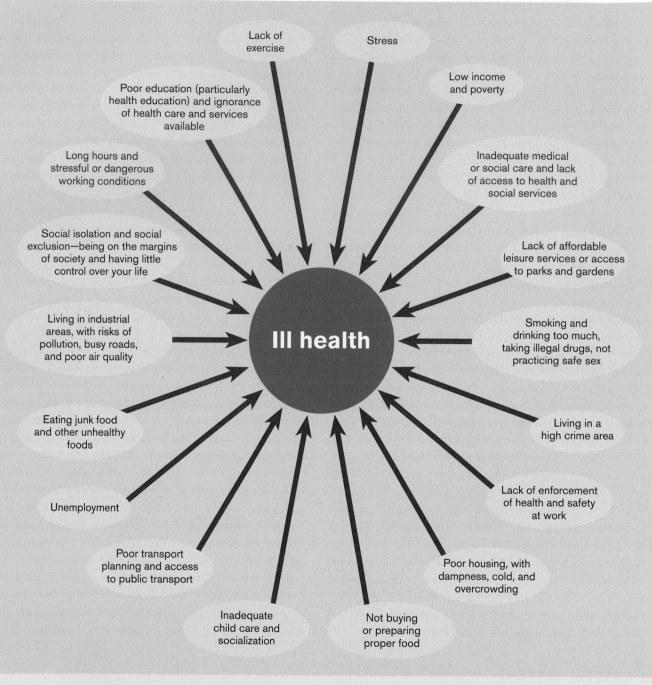

How might sociologists look at the spread of a virus differently from a medical doctor? Name three aspects of social class that affect health and how they do so. One of the contributions to ill health listed above is "Lack of affordable leisure services or access to parks and gardens." How might this affect one's health?

SOURCE: Reprinted with permission from Browne 1999. Crown copyright.

society, people with better educations, higher incomes, and more prestigious occupations have better health. What is fascinating is that each of these dimensions of social class may be related to health and mortality for different reasons.

Income is the most obvious. In countries such as the United States, where medical care is expensive and many people lack insurance, those with more financial resources have better access to physicians and medicine. But inequalities in health also persist in countries like Great Britain, which have national health insurance. For example, the landmark *Black Report* revealed that social inequalities in health and mortality in the United Kingdom had not diminished since the implementation of the National Health Service (NHS) but had instead increased (Townsend and Davidson 1982). Yet, part of this growing gap was due to improvements in mortality among the wealthier classes and not to declines among the lower socioeconomic groups. This suggested that the upper classes were making greater (or somehow "better") use of the improved access to medical resources. Thus we must think beyond income and consider the other dimensions of social class: occupational status and education.

Differences in occupational status may lead to inequalities in health and illness even when medical care is fairly evenly distributed. One study of health inequalities in Great Britain (Townsend and Davidson 1982) found that manual workers had substantially higher mortality rates than professional workers, even though Britain's health service had made great strides in equalizing the distribution of health care. Indeed, different occupations are associated with different levels of health risks. Those who work in offices or in domestic settings have less risk of injury or exposure to hazardous materials. The extent of industrial-based disease is difficult to calculate, because it is hard to determine whether an illness is acquired from working conditions or from other sources. However, some work-related diseases are well documented: Lung disease is widespread in mining, as a result of dust inhalation; work with asbestos has been shown to produce certain types of cancer.

Differences in education also are correlated with inequalities in health and illness. Numerous studies find a positive correlation between education and a broad array of preventative health behaviors. Better-educated people are significantly more likely to engage in aerobic exercise and to know their blood pressure (Shea et al. 1991) and are less likely to smoke (Kenkel, Lillard, and Mathios 2006) or be overweight (Himes 1999). By contrast, poorly educated people engage in more cigarette smoking; they also have more problems with cholesterol and body weight (Winkleby et al. 1992). More highly educated people also respond differently to health threats. One study of smokers found that after suffering a heart attack, highly educated persons were much more likely than poorly educated persons to quit smoking (Wray, Herzog, Willis, and Wallace 1998).

Most social epidemiologists view education as the most important of the three dimensions of SES in predicting health, because education is associated with a broad range of traits that promote positive health behaviors, including high levels of perceived control over one's environment (Mirowsky and Ross 2005) and **health literacy**, which refers to one's capacity to obtain, process, and understand basic health information and services needed to make appropriate health decisions (Zarcadoolas, Pleasant, and Greer 2006). Understanding one's health risks and having the means to do something about them are core components of the Health Belief Model (Becker 1974; Rosenstock 1974), which provides a framework for understanding why some individuals participate in positive health behaviors and others do not. The model proposes that individuals' decisions to engage in positive health behaviors (or to change their health behaviors) are based on their evaluation of the possible threat posed by a health condition and the perceived benefits and barriers of taking action to prevent getting the health condition. Both evaluating one's level of threat and developing a strategy to minimize risk are clearly shaped by social structural factors.

Race-Based Inequalities in Health

Life expectancy at birth in 2005 was about eighty-one years for white and Hispanic females but over seventy-six years for black females. Likewise, life expectancy at birth in 2005 was almost seventy-six years for white and Hispanic males yet less than seventy years for black males (National Center for Health Statistics 2008b). An even more startling gap emerges when early-life mortality is considered: Black infants have roughly twice the mortality rate of white babies. Roughly 14 black babies per every 1,000 born in 2005 died in their first year of life, compared to fewer than six deaths for white and Hispanic babies. Racial differences in health reveal the complex interplay among race, social class, and culture. A powerful example of the multiple ways that race affects health is the Hispanic health paradox: Although Hispanics in the United States have poorer socioeconomic resources than whites, on average, their health—and especially the health of their infants—is just as good as if not better than that of whites. Blacks, by contrast, face economic disadvantages that are similar to those of Hispanics, yet blacks do not enjoy the health benefits revealed by Hispanics. Experts attribute Hispanics' health advantage relative to blacks' to cultural factors such as social cohesion but also to methodological factors. Studies of Hispanic health in the United States focus on those who successfully migrated to the United States; as such, they are believed to be in better health, or more robust, than those Latinos who remained in their native countries (Franzini, Ribble, and Keddie 2001).

The number of people suffering from Type II diabetes, which is a chronic condition that typically develops in adults and disproportionally affects the poor and minority groups, is rapidly growing. Some research ties the onset of the disease to lifestyle choices like diet and exercise. How does the experience of diabetes patients challenge or support Parsons's three main tenets of the sick role?

A close inspection of blacks' health and mortality disadvantage further reveals the multiple ways that race matters for health. One of the main reasons—but not the only reason—for blacks' health disadvantage is that blacks as a group have less money than whites. About 58 percent of black households have no financial assets at all, almost twice the rate for white households (U.S. Bureau of the Census 2005e). And the median income of a black man is only 67 percent of that of a white man (U.S. Bureau of the Census 2005f). Yet the differences in black and white health go beyond economic causes and reflect other important aspects of the social and cultural landscape. Consider racial gaps in mortality. Young black men are more susceptible to murder than any other group. In 2005, a black person was six times more likely to be murdered than a white person, although this gap varies widely by age and gender (U.S. Bureau of Justice Statistics 2007b). Homicide victimization rates for all races have declined considerably over the past decade, yet the stark racial gap persists. The murder rate for white males between ages eighteen and twenty-four dropped from 17.8 to 12.2 per 100,000 from 1994 to 2005. During the same time period, the murder rate for young black males declined from 183.5 to 102. per 100,000. Despite this stark decline, the murder rate for young black males is still more than eight times higher than for their white peers (U.S. Bureau of Justice Statistics 2007b). This rise in violent crime has accompanied the rise of widespread crack cocaine addiction, mainly affecting poor African American neighborhoods plagued by high levels of unemployment (Wilson 1996).

Other race-based inequalities in health status, health behaviors, and health care are also stark. There is a higher prevalence of hypertension among blacks—especially black men, a difference that may be biological. There are racial differences in cigarette smoking, with blacks smoking significantly more than whites. This may be due partly to cultural differences, as well as the cigarette industry's targeting of African Americans as a market.

Despite these inequalities, some progress has been made in eradicating them. According to the National Center for Health Statistics (2005), racial differences in cigarette smoking have decreased. In 1965, half of white men and 60 percent of black men age eighteen and over smoked cigarettes. By 2006, only 24.6 percent of white men and 26.8 percent of black men smoked. In 1965, roughly equal proportions of black and white women age eighteen and older smoked (33 to 34 percent). In 2006, a smaller proportion of black women (18.6 percent) smoked than did white women (20.7 percent).

Prevalence of hypertension among blacks has been greatly reduced. In the early 1970s, half of black adults suffered from hypertension. By 1994, however, roughly 36 percent of black adults between ages twenty and seventy-four suffered from hypertension (National Center for Health Statistics 2004a). Yet, by 2004 the share of black women with hypertension had increased again to 40.3 percent (National Center for Health Statistics 2008b). This increase may reflect the currently high and rising rates of obesity among black women. Two-thirds of black women yet just one half of white women are classified as obese (Ogden et al. 2006), a pattern partly attributed to cultural differences in definitions of an attractive female physique (Hebl and Hetherton 1998). By contrast, black and white men are equally likely to be overweight or obese.

Patterns of physician visitation, hospitalization, and preventive medicine also have improved, yet racial equity still remains

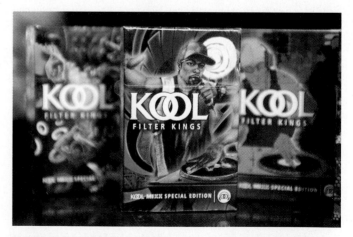

There are significant racial differences in cigarette smoking, with more blacks smoking than whites. This may be due in some measure to cultural differences, as well as the way the cigarette industry has deliberately targeted African Americans as a market.

elusive. Between 1983 and 2006, the proportion of blacks who had visited the dentist within the past year had increased from 39 percent to 59 percent, while the figure for whites increased from 57 percent to 65.7 percent (National Center for Health Statistics 2008b). In 1987, only 30 percent of white women and 24 percent of black women age forty and older reported having a mammogram within the past two years. By 2005, rates had increased substantially for both races, yet black women still lagged behind: Roughly 67.4 percent of white but just 65 percent of black women age 40 and older had received mammograms (National Center for Health Statistics 2008b). Lower rates of mammography and, more important, not receiving regular mammographies are one explanation for black women's elevated risks of breast cancer. A recent study revealed that when black women are diagnosed with breast cancer, they are diagnosed with tumors that are in more advanced stages than those of their white peers. Tumors in more advanced stages increase one's mortality risk and impede the effectiveness of potential treatments (Smith-Bindman et al. 2006).

How might the influence of poverty on health be countered? Extensive programs of health education and disease prevention are one possibility. But such programs work better among more prosperous, well-educated groups and in any case usually produce only small changes in behavior. Increased accessibility to health services would help, but probably to a limited degree. The only really effective policy option is to attack poverty itself, so as to reduce the income gap between rich and poor (Najman 1993).

Gender-Based Inequalities in Health

Women in the United States generally live longer than men—a relatively recent phenomenon. In the United States, there was only a two-year difference in female and male life expectancies in 1900. By 1940, this gap had increased to 4.4 years; by 1970, to 7.7 years. The gender gap declined to a little over five years in 2005 (Cleary 1987; National Center for Health Statistics 2008b).

The main reason for the gender gap is that the leading cause of death has changed since the turn of the century. In 1900, the leading cause of death was infectious disease, which struck men, women, and children equally. Since mid-century, however, heart disease and cancer have been the leading causes of death for American adults. Both are influenced by lifestyle, diet, and behavior—all of which are shaped by the distinctive experiences of women and men in contemporary society.

Social explanations for women's mortality advantage focus on behavioral differences between men and women, including smoking, drinking, and preventive health behaviors. Men are more likely to smoke cigarettes than are women, and smoking is associated with heart disease and various types of cancer. Likewise, higher proportions of men than women drink alcoholic beverages, binge drink, and smoke marijuana (National Center for Health Statistics 2005). Men historically have been socialized to equate risk with masculinity (Mahalik, Burns, and Syzdek 2007). Men also are less likely than women to seek regular preventative care, partly reflecting women's need for regular checkups during their reproductive years (Bertakis et al. 2000). Further, behaviors such as drinking and smoking are frowned upon for women moreso than for men (Kandall and Petrillo 1996).

Some researchers argue that male roles lead men to adopt the Coronary Prone Behavior Pattern, or Type A personality, and that Type A personalities (i.e., persons who are competitive, impatient, ambitious, and aggressive) are twice as likely as laid-back (Type B) personalities to suffer heart attacks (Spielberger et al. 1991). Indirect evidence for this hypothesis comes from examining gender differences in hypertension (i.e., elevated blood pressure). In the early 1990s, 25 percent of men and 20 percent of women age twenty to seventy-four reported having hypertension. By 2002, however, the differences between genders had been reduced to 0.7 percent (National Center for Health Statistics 2008b). This may indicate that the gender gap in Type A personalities has declined as more women have entered the workforce and pursued careers. Other factors (such as diet) may contribute to the convergence of hypertension between men and women.

Sociologists generally focus on societal factors in explaining these differences, but biological factors may also pertain. Disentangling the effects of biology from social context is very difficult, however, given that gender shapes one's social experiences from the moment of birth (see Chapter 10). One study from the 1950s used an innovative design in its attempts to discern the distinctive effects of biology and environment on mortality risk. The researchers focused on a subpopulation of men and women who were believed to have identical lifestyles, diets, and levels of stress: nuns and monks (Madigan 1957). The nuns lived longer than the monks, and both had life expectancies essentially the same as the rest of the population. Because the environment was equalized for the two groups, lifestyle factors such as diet, drinking, and stress could be ruled out as explanatory factors (Madigan 1957). However, critics note that the monks smoked more than the nuns did, so that lifestyle differences were not entirely accounted for. Further, the study could not account for the gender-related lifestyle factors that existed prior to the time persons entered the religious order.

A number of studies spanning the fields of biology and epidemiology do provide suggestive evidence that women have a biological advantage. Recent studies suggest that estrogen helps protect women against heart disease by reducing circulatory levels of harmful cholesterol, whereas testosterone increases low-density lipoprotein. Women also have stronger immune systems, in part because testosterone causes immunosuppression (Ness and Kuller 1999).

Biologists have also cited genetic factors. Humans have twenty-three pairs of chromosomes, one of which determines sex. Males have XY sex chromosomes, while females have two X chromosomes. The X chromosome carries more genetic information than the Y, including some defects that can lead to physical abnormalities. Instead of making females more vulnerable to X-linked disorders, this seems to give females a genetic advantage. A female typically needs two defective X chromosomes for most genetically linked disorders to manifest themselves; otherwise, one healthy X chromosome can override the abnormal one. A male who has a defective X chromosome will have a genetically linked disease because there is no other X chromosome to cancel it out. This may account for the higher number of miscarriages of male fetuses and for the greater ratio of male to female infant deaths and deaths at all ages due to congenital abnormalities and weaker cardiopulmonary systems (Hayflick 1994; Hill and Upchurch 1995). However, biology alone cannot explain gender difference in mortality, especially because this relationship differs substantially over time and across nations.

Despite the female advantage in mortality, most large surveys show that women more often report poor health. Women have higher rates of illness from acute conditions and nonfatal chronic conditions, including arthritis, osteoporosis, and depressive and anxiety disorders. They are slightly more likely to report their health as fair to poor, they spend about 40 percent more days in bed each year, and their activities are restricted due to health problems about 25 percent more than men. In addition, they make more physician visits each year and undergo twice the number of surgical procedures as do men (National Center for Health Statistics 2003).

There are two main explanations for women's poorer health yet longer lives: (1) Greater life expectancy and age bring poorer health, and (2) women make greater use of medical services, including preventive care (National Center for Health Statistics 2003). Men may experience as many or more health symptoms as women, but men may ignore their symptoms, underestimate the extent of their illness, or utilize preventive services less often (Waldron 1986).

Social Integration: The Key to Better Health?

A growing number of sociologists are exploring the role of social cohesion and social support in promoting good health. Social integration or solidarity is one of the most important concepts in

sociology. Durkheim (1964; orig. 1893) saw the degree and type of solidarity within a culture as one of its most critical features. In his study of suicide, for example, he found that individuals and groups who were well integrated into society were less likely to take their own lives than were others. Since that time, many studies have confirmed that social cohesion, or the degree of integration in a society, and social support, such as love and practical assistance from significant others, are associated with better physical and mental health.

Richard Wilkinson (1996) argues that the healthiest societies are not the richest ones but those in which income is distributed most evenly and levels of social integration are highest. In surveying empirical data from countries worldwide, Wilkinson notes a clear relationship between mortality rates and patterns of income distribution. Inhabitants of countries such as Japan and Sweden, which are among the most egalitarian societies in the world, enjoy better levels of health than do citizens of countries with a more pronounced gap between rich and poor, such as the United States. In Wilkinson's view, the widening gap in income distribution undermines social cohesion and makes it more difficult for people to manage risks and challenges. Heightened social isolation and the failure to cope with stress are reflected in health indicators. Wilkinson argues that social factors—the strength of social contacts, ties within communities, a sense of security—are the main determinants of the health of a society.

Wilkinson's thesis has provoked energetic responses. Some claim that his work should become required reading for policy makers and politicians. They agree that overemphasis on market relations and the drive toward prosperity has failed many

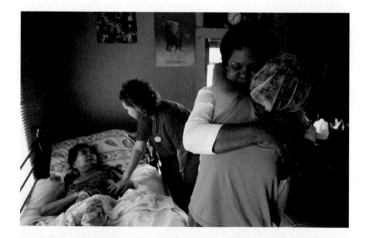

Dr. Regina Benjamin, a family physician dedicated to serving the working-class families in a small shrimping community on the Gulf Coast, visits one of her patients at home. Working-class women have less access to formal support networks in times of crisis than middle-class women. Social support—such as counseling services, hotlines, or home visits—can help patients cope with the effects of stress and illnesses.

members of society; it is time to consider more humane and socially responsible policies to support those who are disadvantaged (Kawachi and Kennedy 1997). Others criticize his study on methodological grounds and argue that he has not demonstrated a clear causal relationship between income inequality and poor health (Judge 1995). Illness, critics contend, could be caused by any number of other mediating factors. They argue that the empirical evidence for his claims remains suggestive at best.

Whereas Wilkinson investigates the links between social cohesion and health at the macro-social level, other sociologists have focused on more micro-level indicators of social support, such as the degree of emotional and practical support that one receives in one's close personal relationships. One of the strongest predictors of both physical and mental health is having a confidante with whom one can share private thoughts. Multiple studies based on large representative samples show that interpersonal support is associated with reduced risk of mortality, morbidity, and depression. Sociologists propose several explanations for the protective effects of social support (House 2001). First, isolation from others may be distressing and anxiety provoking, producing physiological changes that could produce serious health problems in the long term. Second, social relationships—especially marriage and long-term family relationships—provide social support and social control. A spouse may encourage health-promoting behaviors such as adequate sleep, diet, exercise, and compliance with medical regimes or may discourage health-damaging behaviors such as smoking, excessive eating, or substance abuse.

Third, social ties link people with broad social networks that facilitate access to a wide range of health-enhancing resources such as medical referral networks, access to others dealing with similar health problems, or opportunities to acquire needed resources via jobs, shopping, or financial institutions. Each of these forms of support may be particularly valuable to persons facing stress and adversity. For example, Ann Oakley and her colleagues (1994) studied the role of social support in the health of socially disadvantaged women and children in four English cities. They found that social support—such as counseling services, hotlines, and home visits—can act as a buffer against women's negative health consequences of stress. Other studies have shown that social support is important in helping people adjust to disease and illness (Ell 1996).

☑ CONCEPT CHECKS

1. How do social class, race, and gender affect health?
2. Describe three ways that social integration affects physical health.

Global Health Issues

The Developing World: Colonialism and the Spread of Disease

The hunting and gathering communities of the Americas, before the arrival of the Europeans, were not as susceptible to infectious disease as the European societies of the period. Many infectious organisms thrive only when human populations live above the density level that is characteristic of hunting and gathering life. Permanently settled communities, particularly large cities, risk the contamination of water supplies by waste products. Hunters and gatherers were less vulnerable in this respect because they moved continuously across the countryside.

During the colonial era, efforts to bring Western ideals to developing societies also brought certain diseases into other parts of the world. Smallpox, measles, and typhus, among other major maladies, were unknown to the indigenous populations of Central and South America before the Spanish conquest in the early sixteenth century. The English and French colonists brought the same diseases to North America (Dubos 1959). Some of these illnesses produced epidemics that ravaged or completely wiped out native populations, which had little or no resistance to them.

In Africa and subtropical parts of Asia, infectious diseases have been rife for a long time. Tropical and subtropical conditions are especially conducive to diseases such as malaria, carried by mosquitoes, and sleeping sickness, carried by the tsetse fly. Historians believe that risk from infectious diseases were lower in Africa and Asia prior to the time that Europeans tried to colonize these regions—as they often brought with them the practices that negatively affected the health of local natives. The threat of epidemics, drought, or natural disaster always loomed, but colonialism led to major unforeseen changes in the relation between populations and their environments, producing harmful effects on health patterns. The Europeans introduced new farming methods, upsetting the ecology of whole regions. For example, wide tracts of East Africa today are completely devoid of cattle owing to the uncontrolled spread of the tsetse fly, which multiplied as a result of the changes the intruders introduced. (The tsetse fly carries illnesses that are fatal to both humans and livestock.) Before the Europeans' arrival, Africans successfully maintained large herds in these same areas (Kjekshus 1977).

The most significant consequence of the colonial system was its effect on nutrition and, therefore, on levels of resistance to illness as a result of the changed economic conditions involved in producing for world markets. In many parts of Africa, the nutritional quality of native diets became substantially depressed as cash-crop production supplanted the production of native foods.

This was not a one-way process, however. Indeed, early colonialism also radically changed Western diets, having a paradoxical impact in terms of health. On the one hand, Western diets benefited from the addition of new foods, such as bananas, pineapples, and grapefruit. On the other hand, the importation of tobacco and coffee, together with raw sugar (which found uses in all manner of foods), has had harmful consequences. Smoking tobacco, especially, has been linked to cancer and heart disease.

Infectious Diseases Today in the Developing World

Although major strides have occurred in reducing, and in some cases eliminating, infectious diseases in the developing world, they remain far more common there than in the West. The most important example of a disease that has almost completely disappeared is smallpox, which as recently as the 1960s was a scourge of Europe as well as many other regions. Campaigns against malaria have been much less successful. When the insecticide DDT was first produced, it was hoped that the mosquito, the prime carrier of malaria, could be eradicated. At first, there was considerable progress, but this has slowed because some strains of mosquito have become resistant to DDT. An estimated one million deaths occur due to malaria each year; rates are highest in sub-Saharan Africa, and children are at a particularly high risk (Snow et al. 2005). Recognizing the magnitude of this global health concern, in 2005 President George W. Bush initiated the $1.2 billion, five-year President's Malaria Initiative; its goal is to reduce malaria-related deaths in fifteen African countries by 50 percent.

An obstacle to effectively fighting disease in the developing world is that basic medical resources are still lacking in many nations. The relatively few hospitals and trained doctors are concentrated in urban areas, where the affluent minority monopolizes their services. Most developing countries have introduced some form of national health service, organized by the central government, but the medical services are limited. The wealthy use private health care, sometimes traveling to the West for sophisticated medical treatment. Conditions in many developing world cities, particularly in the shantytowns, make the control of infectious diseases very difficult: Many shantytowns lack basic services such as water, sewage systems, and garbage disposal.

Water and sanitation are critical factors for public health, yet many nations fall short on both dimensions. The World Health Organization (2004) reports that in 2004, 1 billion people lacked access to improved water sources, which represented 17 percent of the global population. Further, in 2004, 2.6 billion people lacked access to adequate sanitation, which represented 42 percent of the world's population. Over half of those without improved sanitation—nearly 1.5 billion people—live in China and India. These conditions are breeding grounds for diseases such as diarrhea, malaria, and trachoma, although the means of transmission varies based on the disease. For example, trachoma—an infectious eye disease which can cause blindness—is strongly related to lack of face-washing, given the lack of water supply.

HIV/AIDS

A devastating exception to the trend of eliminating infectious diseases in the developing world is HIV/AIDS, which has become a global epidemic. Estimates of the number of people infected with HIV are between 37 million and 45 million worldwide. In 2007 alone, 2.1 million people died from AIDS-related illnesses (UNAIDS 2007b). Using middle-range estimates,

Looking AIDS in the Face: Anonymous (covering face) is a university student at Maputo University in Mozambique. Due to the extreme stigma he might face, he chose not to include any of his clothes in the photograph for fear of being identified. "I can't be identified because it may have a bad impact on my position as a university student. . . . Here in Mozambique there is discrimination promoted by the government. In one of his speeches the prime minister said Mozambique should not invest in educating people with AIDS as there is no hope for them. . . . If my faculty discovered my status . . . they would try all sorts of devious means to get rid of me."

The Number of HIV-Positive People around the World

The effect of HIV/AIDS will be greatest in sub-Saharan Africa. In 2007 alone, there were 1.7 million new HIV infections in sub-Saharan Africa; over three quarters of all AIDS-related deaths occurred there. In Botswana, Namibia, and Swaziland, nearly 40 percent of the population is infected with HIV/AIDS.

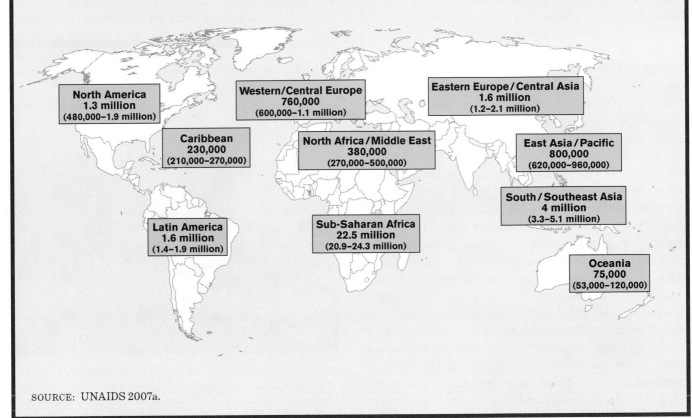

North America
1.3 million
(480,000–1.9 million)

Western/Central Europe
760,000
(600,000–1.1 million)

Eastern Europe/Central Asia
1.6 million
(1.2–2.1 million)

Caribbean
230,000
(210,000–270,000)

North Africa/Middle East
380,000
(270,000–500,000)

East Asia/Pacific
800,000
(620,000–960,000)

South/Southeast Asia
4 million
(3.3–5.1 million)

Latin America
1.6 million
(1.4–1.9 million)

Sub-Saharan Africa
22.5 million
(20.9–24.3 million)

Oceania
75,000
(53,000–120,000)

SOURCE: UNAIDS 2007a.

about 760,000 people are living with HIV/AIDS in Western and Central Europe, 1.3 million in North America, 1.8 million in Latin America and the Caribbean, and nearly 22.5 million in sub-Saharan Africa (Global Map 18.2). The main effect of the epidemic is still to come, because of the time it takes for HIV infection to develop into full-blown AIDS. The majority of people affected in the world today are heterosexuals. As of 2005, about half are women. In sub-Saharan Africa, young women are more than twice as likely as men to be infected. Worldwide, at least four HIV infections are contracted heterosexually for every instance of homosexual spread.

In high-income countries, the rate of new infections has declined, yet the demographics are striking. In the United States, there were over 43,000 new infections in 2005 and nearly half of these were in southern states (National Center for Health Statistics 2005). Of these, nearly half were in African Americans. In fact, African American women are eight times more likely to be infected with HIV than white women, and HIV/AIDS is the leading cause of death among African American women age twenty-five to thirty-four in the United States (UNAIDS 2007a). Although there was a steep drop in AIDS-related deaths after the introduction of antiretroviral therapy, African Americans are not benefiting from such life-prolonging treatments. The United Nations Joint Program on HIV and AIDS reports that African Americans are half as likely to be receiving antiretroviral treatment (UNAIDS 2005a).

Stigmatization of people with HIV/AIDS remains a major barrier to successful treatment programs. The stigma that associates HIV positive status with sexual promiscuity and

The Rise of International NGOs and Health Services

The decline of the public sector in the provision of health-care services in the 1980s in the developing world created serious gaps in health care. At the same time, these countries experienced greater health problems, including epidemics of preventable and treatable diseases. For example, the World Health Organization (WHO) reported that there were 8.8 million new cases of tuberculosis around the world in 2005, but 7.4 million of these cases were reported in Asia and sub-Saharan Africa (World Health Organization 2007b). In part because of the inability of governments to provide adequate services, health care has been one sector in which the rise of international nongovernmental organizations (INGOs) in the provision of basic social services is most apparent. Development scholars often describe this as the "NGOization" of the developing world. For example, although falling short of its goals, the Global Fund to Fight AIDS, Tuberculosis and Malaria raised $3.7 billion to fight these diseases in 2005, more than the annual gross domestic product of many of the recipient countries. Today, INGOs provide a wide range of health services to citizens of developing nations including direct health services such as disease prevention, training of medical professionals, procuring drugs, research efforts, and patient advocacy, to name a few (Mwabu, Ugaz, and White 2001).

There are advantages to nonstate provision of health services. INGOs often have more resources than governments, particularly those in the developing world. Some scholars and practitioners argue that INGOs are more efficient at providing health care than the bureaucratic structure of governments' health-care systems. For governments lacking the resources

A mother feeds her baby after an operation. Millions of people in the remote parts of India are too poor to afford healthcare. They rely on services like this hospital charity for aid.

immorality results in an avoidance of HIV/AIDS prevention and treatment programs. Clearly, the statistics cited above demonstrate that HIV/AIDS is not a "gay disease."

In the United States, a quarter of people living with HIV/AIDS do not know that they are infected (UNAIDS 2005a). Part of the reason is the high level of fear and denial associated with being diagnosed as HIV positive. The stigma of having HIV/AIDS and the discrimination against people living with these infections are major barriers to the treatment of the epidemic worldwide. A 2002 survey found that one in ten doctors and nurses in Nigeria have refused treatment to a person because of his or her HIV/AIDS status. In India, 70 percent of people living with HIV/AIDS have reported discrimination by health-care workers (UNAIDS 2003).

Discrimination also occurs in government health-care planning (UNAIDS 2003). A case in point is South Africa, where President Thabo Mbeki, in a 2001 speech justifying his government's inaction and unwillingness to finance AIDS prevention, declared that HIV did not cause AIDS and that, contrary to scientific opinion, antiretroviral medicines were ineffective (Forrest and Streek 2001). Such attitudes have slowed progress in confronting the AIDS epidemic in South Africa, where at the end of 2005 nearly 39 percent of the population were living with HIV/AIDS (UNAIDS 2005b).

Although the spread of AIDS in Western societies has slowed, the opposite has been true in the developing world, where health education is limited and the medical establishment is poor. In countries heavily affected by the HIV/AIDS

Bill and Melinda Gates seen visiting a female sex workers' self-help group, supported by the Gates Foundation, in Chennai, India.

and human capital to deliver basic health services to their citizens, INGOs provide valuable services for public health.

INGOs as the primary provider of a nation or region's health services also have their disadvantages. Namely, the priorities of a given INGO can supersede improving overall societal health. Private organizations are now in positions to dictate the health priorities for poorer regions of the world. A recent article in the *Los Angeles Times* describes the unintended consequences of health programs sponsored by the Bill and Melinda Gates Foundation (Piller and Smith 2007). The Gates Foundation has given $8.5 billion to various organizations that provide vaccines and fight AIDS, tuberculosis, and malaria. However, fighting these high-profile diseases has taken valuable medical staff away from basic care. Basic needs such as nutrition and transportation infrastructure are neglected and caregivers are instructed to ignore diseases not treatable through Gates-

sponsored NGOs. The article tells the story of Matespang Nyoba, a woman living with AIDS in Lesotho whose baby died in childbirth. Ms. Nyoba's baby did not die of complications due to AIDS. The hospital where she delivered her baby receives funding from the Gates foundation for HIV/AIDS medications but lacked stethoscope tubes, a basic piece of hospital equipment. Without oxygen delivered through these tubes, the baby asphyxiated. Ms. Nyoba's story is not uncommon. In fact, the WHO reported that the high rate of women who die in pregnancy and childbirth was a major health issue in 2007 (World Health Organization 2007a) but one that is often not a priority among international health-focused NGOs.

The priorities of INGOs are usually shaped by concerns other than the individual needs of a particular hospital or even a particular country. While very important for confronting the spread of disease, INGOs cannot yet replace national healthcare systems.

References

Mwabu, Germano M., Cecilia Ugaz, and Gordon White. 2001. *Social Provision in Low-Income Countries: New Patterns and Emerging Trends.* Oxford: Oxford University Press.

Piller, Charles, and Douglas Smith. 2007. "Unintended Victims: The Gates Foundation's Generous Gifts to Fight AIDS, TB and Malaria Have Inadvertently Put Many of Those with Other Healthcare Needs at Risk." *Los Angeles Times.*

World Health Organization. 2007a. "2007: A Review of Notable Health Issues," www.who.int/features/2007/year_review/en/index.html (accessed December 30, 2007).

World Health Organization. 2007b. "World Health Statistics 2007."

epidemic, only 5 percent of pregnant women receive healthcare services aimed at preventing mother-to-child HIV transmission (UNAIDS 2005b). Besides the devastation to individuals who suffer from it, the AIDS epidemic is creating severe social consequences, including sharply rising numbers of orphaned children. Frail older adults are increasingly called on to provide physical care to their adult children who suffer from

An eleven-year-old orphan girl sells her grandmother's brooms for 3¢ (U.S.) each in order to buy food in a shanty compound in Kitwe, Zambia. About 70 percent of the world's HIV-infected people live in sub-Saharan Africa and more than one million children in Zambia alone have been orphaned by parents who have succumbed to AIDS.

AIDS (Knodel 2006). Worldwide, the parents of an estimated fifteen million children have died as a result of HIV/AIDS; 11.4 million are in sub-Saharan Africa (Global Map 18.2). In Uganda alone, 77 percent of the population are under the age of eighteen; 30 percent of those are orphans with over 1 million AIDS orphans (AIDS Orphans Educational Trust 2003). The decimated population of working adults combined with the surging populations of orphans sets the stage for massive social instability as economies break down and governments cannot provide for the social needs of orphans, who become targets for recruitment into gangs and armies.

☑ CONCEPT CHECKS

1. Why are infectious diseases more common in developing nations than in the United States today?
2. What are three social consequences of the AIDS epidemic in developing nations?

Human Sexuality

The global AIDS epidemic and attempts to halt its spread are further examples of the socialization of nature. As with the study of health and illness, scholars differ over the importance of biological versus social and cultural influences on human sexual behavior, another important facet of the sociology of the body.

The Diversity of Human Sexuality

Judith Lorber (1994) distinguishes as many as ten different sexual identities: straight (heterosexual) woman, straight man, lesbian woman, gay man, bisexual woman, bisexual man, transvestite woman (a woman who regularly dresses as a man), transvestite man (a man who regularly dresses as a woman), transsexual woman (a man who becomes a woman), and transsexual man (a woman who becomes a man). Sexual practices themselves are even more diverse. Freud argued that human beings are born with a wide range of sexual tastes that are ordinarily curbed through socialization—although some adults may follow these even when, in a given society, they are regarded as immoral or illegal. Freud began his research during the Victorian period, when many people were sexually prudish; yet his patients still revealed an amazing diversity of sexual pursuits.

Among possible sexual practices are the following: A man or woman can have sexual relations with women, men, or both.

Sexual identities take many forms. Sexual practices are even more diverse. How do sociologists study sexuality?

This can happen with one partner at a time or with two or more partners participating. One can have sex with oneself (masturbation) or with no one (celibacy). One can have sexual relations with transsexuals or people who erotically cross-dress; use pornography or sexual devices; practice sadomasochism (the erotic use of bondage and the inflicting of pain); have sex with animals; and so on (Lorber 1994). In most societies, sexual norms encourage some practices and discourage or condemn others. Such norms, however, vary among cultures. Homosexuality is an example. As we will discuss later, some cultures have tolerated or actively encouraged homosexuality in certain contexts. Among the ancient Greeks, for instance, the love of men for boys was idealized as the highest form of sexual love.

Accepted types of sexual behavior also vary among cultures, which indicates that most sexual responses are learned. The most extensive cross-cultural study was carried out by Clellan Ford and Frank Beach (1951), using anthropological evidence from more than two hundred societies. Striking variations were found in what was regarded as "natural" sexual behavior and in norms of sexual attractiveness. For example, in some cultures, extended foreplay is desirable and even necessary before intercourse; in others, foreplay is nonexistent. In some societies, it is believed that overly frequent intercourse leads to physical debilitation or illness.

In most cultures, norms of sexual attractiveness (held by both females and males) focus more on physical looks for women than for men, a situation that may be changing in the West as women become active in spheres outside the home. The traits seen as most important in female beauty, however, differ greatly. In the modern West, a slim, small physique is admired, while in other cultures a more generous shape is attractive. Sometimes the breasts are not considered a source of sexual stimulus, whereas some societies attach erotic significance to them. Some societies value the shape of the face, whereas others emphasize the shape and color of the eyes or the size and form of the nose and lips. Although anthropologists and sociologists focus on cross-cultural differences in mate selection processes, evolutionary theorists emphasize universals, as these purportedly universal practices contribute to the continuation of the human species. For instance, research by David Buss reveals widespread male preference for a relatively low waist-hip ratio in women, as it can be seen as an indicator of a woman's reproductive fitness, or her ability to bear healthy offspring. Women, by contrast, are drawn to men with ambition and economic stability, which are considered indications of one's ability to adequately provide for their offspring (Buss 2003).

Sexuality in Western Culture

Western attitudes toward sexual behavior were for nearly two thousand years molded primarily by Christianity, whose dominant view was that all sexual behavior is suspect except that needed for reproduction. During some periods this view produced an extreme prudishness, but at other times many people ignored the church's teachings and engaged in practices such as adultery. The idea that sexual fulfillment can and should be sought through marriage was rare.

In the nineteenth century, religious presumptions about sexuality were partly replaced by medical ones. Most early writings by doctors about sexual behavior, however, were as stern as the views of the church. Some argued that any type of sexual activity unconnected with reproduction would cause serious physical harm. Masturbation was said to cause blindness, insanity, heart disease, and other ailments, while oral sex was claimed to cause cancer. In Victorian times, sexual hypocrisy abounded. Virtuous women were believed to be indifferent to sexuality, accepting their husbands' advances only as a duty. Yet in the expanding towns and cities, prostitution was rife and often tolerated.

Many Victorian men—who appeared to be sober, well-behaved citizens, devoted to their wives—regularly visited prostitutes or kept mistresses. Such behavior was accepted, whereas "respectable" women who took lovers were regarded as scandalous and shunned in polite society. The differing attitudes toward the sexual activities of men and women formed a double standard, which persists today.

Currently, traditional attitudes exist alongside much more permissive attitudes, which developed strongly in the 1960s. Some people, particularly those influenced by Christian teachings, believe that premarital sex is wrong; they frown on all forms of sexual behavior except heterosexual activity within marriage—although it is now more commonly accepted that

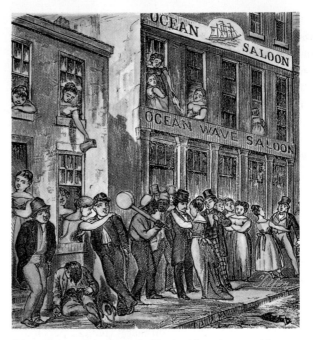

Sexual hypocrisy abounded in the Victorian era. Virtuous women were said to be indifferent to sexuality, while it was acceptable for their husbands to visit prostitutes or keep mistresses. This 1878 illustration of the St. Louis red-light district shows that prostitution was openly tolerated and "loose" women were not held to the same standards as their "respectable" sisters.

sexual pleasure is an important feature of marriage. Others approve of premarital sex and tolerate different sexual practices. Sexual attitudes have undoubtedly become more permissive over recent decades in most Western countries. Movies and plays include scenes that previously would have been unacceptable, and pornographic material is available to most adults who want it. Pornography is reportedly the predominant use for the World Wide Web. By the end of 2004, there were 420 million pages of pornography, and it is believed that the majority of these Web sites are owned by fewer than fifty companies (LaRue 2005).

Sexual Behavior: Kinsey's Study

We can speak more confidently about public values concerning sexuality than we can about private practices, for such practices have gone undocumented for much of history. When Alfred Kinsey began his research in the United States in the 1940s and 1950s, it was the first major investigation of sexual behavior. Kinsey and his co-researchers (1948, 1953) faced condemnation from religious organizations, and his work was denounced as immoral in the newspapers and in Congress. But he persisted, thus making his study the largest rigorous study of sexuality at that time, although his sample was not representative of the overall American population.

Kinsey's results were surprising because they revealed a tremendous discrepancy between prevailing public expectations of sexual behavior and actual sexual conduct. He found that almost 70 percent of men in his study had visited a prostitute and 84 percent had had premarital sexual experience. Yet, following the double standard, 40 percent of men expected their wives to be virgins at the time of marriage. More than 90 percent of males had engaged in masturbation and nearly 60 percent in oral sexual activity. Among women, about 50 percent had had premarital sexual experience, although mostly with the man whom they eventually married. Some 60 percent had masturbated, and the same percentage had engaged in oral-genital contacts.

The gap between publicly accepted attitudes and actual behavior was probably especially pronounced just after World War II, the time of Kinsey's study. A phase of sexual liberalization had begun in the 1920s, when many younger people felt freed from the strict moral codes that had governed earlier generations. Sexual behavior probably changed, but issues concerning sexuality were not openly discussed. People participating in sexual activities that were still strongly disapproved of on a public level concealed them, not realizing that others were engaging in similar practices. The more permissive 1960s brought openly declared attitudes more into line with the realities of behavior.

Sexual Behavior since Kinsey

In the 1960s, social movements that challenged the existing order, like those associated with countercultural lifestyles, also broke with existing sexual norms. These movements preached sexual freedom, and the introduction of the contraceptive pill allowed sexual pleasure to be separated from reproduction. Women's groups also started pressing for greater independence from male sexual values, rejection of the double standard, and the need for women to achieve greater sexual satisfaction in their relationships. Until recently, it was unclear to what extent sexual behavior had changed since the time of Kinsey's research.

In the late 1980s, Lillian Rubin (1990) interviewed a thousand Americans between the ages of thirteen and forty-eight to identify changes in sexual behavior and attitudes over the previous thirty years or so. Her findings indicate significant changes. Sexual activity begins at a younger age; moreover, teenagers' sexual practices are as varied and comprehensive as those of adults. There is still a double standard, but it is not as powerful as before. One of the most important changes is that women now expect, and actively pursue, sexual pleasure in relationships—a phenomenon that Rubin argues has major consequences for both sexes.

Women are more sexually available than before, which most men applaud; but women also have a new assertiveness that men find difficult to accept. The men Rubin (1990) talked to often said they "felt inadequate," were afraid they could "never do anything right," and found it "impossible to satisfy women these days."

Men feel inadequate? Doesn't this contradict much of what this textbook has said so far? After all, in modern society men still dominate in most spheres, and they are generally much more violent toward women than women are toward men. Such violence substantially seeks to control and subordinate women. Yet several authors argue that masculinity is a burden as much as a source of reward. Much male sexuality, they add, is compulsive rather than satisfying (Kimmel 2003).

In 1994, a team of researchers led by Edward Laumann published *The Social Organization of Sexuality: Sexual Practices in the United States,* the most comprehensive study of sexual behavior since Kinsey. Their findings reflect an essential sexual conservatism among Americans. For instance, 83 percent of their subjects had had only one partner (or no partner at all) in the preceding year, and among married people the figure rose to 96 percent. Fidelity to one's spouse was also quite common: Only 10 percent of women and less than 25 percent of men reported having an extramarital affair during their lifetime. According to the study, Americans average only three partners during their entire lifetime (Table 18.2). Despite the apparent ordinariness of sexual behavior, some distinct historical changes were revealed in this study, the most significant being a progressive increase in the level of premarital sexual experience, particularly among women. In fact, over 95 percent of Americans getting married today are sexually experienced.

In addition, sexual permissiveness among young people is much greater today than it was in the 1970s. According to the National Center for Health Statistics (2005), in 2003 nearly half (47 percent) of all high school students reported having had sexual intercourse; 14 percent reported having had four or more partners. Both figures represent declines from 1991, when more than 54 percent of high school students had ever had sex and nearly 19 percent had had four or more sex partners. U.S. rates are far higher than those in Japan and China (Tang and Zuo 2000; Toufexis 1993). Considering that the General Social Survey in 1994 reported that over 70 percent of American adults believed that teenage sex is "always wrong" and another 16 percent believed it is "almost always wrong," parental beliefs and adolescent behavior are clearly in conflict. One study of the sexual behavior of American middle and high school students concluded that early sexual activity was higher among students from single-parent families, from a lower socioeconomic status, who demonstrated lower school

A Southern California high school teacher leads his health class on a discussion on sexuality.

performance and intelligence and had lower religiosity—and among students with high levels of "body pride" (Halpern et al. 2000; Lammers et al. 2000).

Although documenting and monitoring the sexual behavior of young people remains a widespread concern even in the twenty-first century, researchers are increasingly documenting sexual activity among older persons. Older persons, once considered either uninterested in or physically incapable of having satisfying sexual relations, reveal high levels of both sexual activity and satisfaction. The U.S. National Health and Social Life Survey (NSHAP), a new study of sexuality among American women and men ages fifty-seven to eighty-five, reports that most married older persons have had sex in the last year. Although sexual problems do arise, they were reported by the minority of respondents. Women tended to report more sexual problems than men; commonly reported problems included lack of sexual interest, inability to climax, pain, and lack of pleasure during intercourse. Among men, by contrast, sexual problems included climaxing too early and performance anxiety (Lindau et al. 2007).

Sexual Behavior in the United States: The Sociological Debate

Sociologists frequently use survey questionnaires to gain information on human behavior. However, obtaining detailed information on sexual behavior and attitudes is difficult. The two most comprehensive studies of sexuality in the United States—the Kinsey studies (1948, 1953) and the Laumann study (1994)—offer very different portraits of sexual preferences and behaviors. Do these conflicting results reflect historical changes in sexual mores, or are the differences an outcome of methodological approaches?

In stark contrast to Kinsey's results, which found that a high proportion of men had premarital or extramarital sex, the Laumann study revealed that 83 percent of survey respondents had only one or no sexual partners in the year prior to the study. Moreover, only 10 percent of women and fewer than 25 percent of men reported ever having had an extramarital affair. It's possible that Americans have become more sexually conservative—perhaps from fear of AIDS and sexually transmitted diseases.

An alternative explanation for the discrepant findings is the researchers' different methodological approaches. Kinsey, an evolutionary biologist, first gave a questionnaire about sexual practices to students in his zoology classes. Finding this method unsatisfactory, he next conducted face-to-face interviews and then focused on specific social groups. He and his colleagues eventually interviewed nearly eighteen thousand people.

Kinsey recognized that the ideal survey would be random and thus results would represent the general population. However, he did not believe it was possible to persuade a randomly selected group of Americans to answer deeply personal questions about their sexual behavior. Consequently, his survey respondents were primarily college students living in sorority and fraternity houses, prisoners, psychiatric patients, and friends. To make his data more credible, Kinsey made every effort to interview 100 percent of the members of each group, such as all students living in a given fraternity house. Because Kinsey's data are based on a convenience sample, they are not representative of the American public. Moreover, many of his survey respondents volunteered to participate in the study. Thus they may be unique from nonvolunteers in that they have wider sexual experiences or a greater interest in sexuality. Further, many of his study questions asked about "lifetime" behavior or whether one had ever engaged in a particular practice; such a question will necessarily yield a greater number of positive responses than a question that focuses on a limited time frame, such as the past twelve months.

The Laumann study, in contrast, is based on data from the National Health and Social Life Survey (NHSLS). The NHSLS data were obtained from a nationally representative random sample of more than three thousand American men and women age eighteen to fifty-nine who spoke English. In addition, Laumann's team purposely oversampled among blacks and Hispanics so that they would have enough members of these minority groups to analyze their survey responses separately with confidence that findings were statistically reliable and valid.

Recognizing that people are often hesitant to discuss sexuality, Laumann's team paid particular attention to choosing nonjudgmental language in their questionnaire. The team also built several "checks" into their questionnaire to ensure the veracity of responses. Several questions were redundant but were asked in different ways throughout the interview to gauge whether respondents were answering truthfully. The team also included eleven questions that had been asked previously on another national random sample survey of Americans. Comparisons of responses to the two sets of questions provided Laumann's researchers with assurance that their results were consistent with others' findings.

Although the Kinsey and Laumann studies are influential works on human sexuality, they also demonstrate that the process through which sociological knowledge is obtained can be as important as the actual research findings.

Sexual Orientation

Sexual orientation involves the direction of one's sexual or romantic attraction. The term *sexual preference,* which is sometimes incorrectly used instead of *sexual orientation,* is

---

TABLE 18.2

Sex in America: Social Influences on Sexual Behavior

TOTAL	SEX PARTNERS IN THE PAST 12 MONTHS				SEX PARTNERS SINCE AGE 18						MEDIAN NUMBER OF SEX PARTNERS SINCE AGE 18
	NONE	1	2–4	5+	NONE	1	2–4	5–10	11–20	21+	
	12%	71%	14%	3%	3%	26%	30%	22%	11%	9%	3
Men	10%	67%	18%	5%	3%	20%	21%	23%	16%	17%	6
Women	14	75	10	2	3	32	36	20	6	3	2
Ages 18–24	11%	57%	24%	9%	8%	32%	34%	15%	8%	3%	2
25–29	6	72	17	6	2	25	31	22	10	9	4
30–34	9	73	16	2	3	21	29	25	11	10	4
35–39	10	77	11	2	2	19	30	25	14	11	4
40–44	11	75	13	1	1	22	28	24	14	12	4
45–49	15	75	9	1	2	26	24	25	10	14	4
50–54	15	79	5	0	2	34	28	18	9	9	2
55–59	32	65	4	0	1	40	28	15	8	7	2
Never married, not living with someone	25%	38%	28%	9%	12%	15%	29%	21%	12%	12%	4
Never married, living with someone	1	75	20	5	0	25	37	16	10	13	3
Married	2	94	4	1	0	37	28	19	9	7	2
Divorced, separated, or widowed, not living with someone	31	41	26	3	0	11	33	29	15	12	5
Divorced, separated, or widowed, living with someone	1	80	16	3	0	0	32	44	12	12	6

---

misleading and is to be avoided because it implies that one's sexual or romantic attraction is entirely a matter of personal choice. As you will see below, sexual orientation results from a complex interplay of biological and social factors not yet fully understood.

The most commonly found sexual orientation in all cultures, including the United States, is *heterosexuality,* a sexual or romantic attraction for persons of the opposite sex. Heterosexuals in the United States are also sometimes referred to as "straight." It is important to note that although heterosexuality may be the prevailing norm in most cultures, it is not "normal" in the sense of being dictated by some universal moral or religious standard. Like all behavior, heterosexual behavior is socially learned within a particular culture.

Homosexuality involves a sexual or romantic attraction for persons of one's own sex. Today, the term *gay* is used to refer to male homosexuals, *lesbian* for female homosexuals, and *bi* as shorthand for *bisexuals,* people who experience sexual or romantic attraction for persons of either sex. Although it is difficult to know for sure because of the stigma attached to homosexuality, which may result in the underreporting of sexuality in demographic surveys, estimates find that from 2 to 5 percent of all women and 3 to 10 percent of all men in the United States are homosexual or bisexual (Burr 1993; General Social Survey [GSS] 1997; Laumann et al. 1994).

The term *homosexual* was first used by the medical community in 1869 to characterize what was then regarded as a personality disorder. The American Psychiatric Association

TOTAL	SEX PARTNERS IN THE PAST 12 MONTHS				SEX PARTNERS SINCE AGE 18						MEDIAN NUMBER OF SEX PARTNERS SINCE AGE 18
	NONE	1	2–4	5+	NONE	1	2–4	5–10	11–20	21+	
Less than high school degree	16%	67%	15%	3%	4%	27%	36%	19%	9%	6%	3
High school degree or equivalent	11	74	13	3	3	30	29	20	10	7	3
Some college or vocational school	11	71	14	4	2	24	29	23	12	9	4
College graduate	12	69	15	4	2	24	26	24	11	13	4
Advanced degree	13	74	10	3	4	25	26	23	10	13	4
No religion	11%	67%	17%	6%	3%	16%	29%	20%	16%	16%	5
Mainline Protestant	11	74	13	2	2	23	31	23	12	8	4
Conservative Protestant	13	70	14	3	3	30	30	20	10	7	3
Catholic	13	72	13	3	4	27	29	23	8	9	3
Jewish	4	78	15	4	0	24	13	30	17	17	6
Other religion	15	63	15	6	3	42	20	16	8	13	3
White	12%	73%	12%	3%	3%	26%	29%	22%	11%	9%	3
Black	13	60	21	6	2	18	34	24	11	11	4
Hispanic	11	70	17	3	3	36	27	17	8	9	2
Asian	15	77	8	0	6	46	25	14	6	3	1
Native American	12	76	10	2	5	28	35	23	5	5	3

SOURCE: Laumann et al. 1994.

Sexuality and the Mass Media

What does it take to capture the imagination of the country? Information that surprises us. Information that comes from solid research and credible sources, and that bears on the way we live, our common humanity (or, more often, inhumanity), and our desire to know about how well we are doing as individuals, parents, partners, and citizens. That is why an article such as the one sociologist Diane Lye wrote on parenting gets picked up by reporters: It went beyond the intuitive and taught us something. It was news.

Lye found that there was a lower divorce rate among men who had sons. If the research had stopped there, the presumptive meaning likely would have been that men still prefer sons over daughters, and attachment to sons will keep them home. It would have been a story, but not one that hit most major newspapers in the country. But Lye went further. She had data to indicate that American men did not prefer sons over daughters, so she looked for other explanations. Her data allowed her to measure how much a father interacted with a child, and in what ways. She found that men interacted with sons more than with daughters—a fact she expected because men's traditional forms of leisure, spectator sports, and active participation in sports, might seem more appropriate for their sons than for their daughters. The next step: She decided to look at those fathers who broke the mold and did these activities with daughters and see what their rates of divorce were. She found that men who interacted with daughters in the same way as with sons also had lower divorce rates. She hypothesized that it is interaction that matters, and that men may feel they have fewer ways of interacting with a daughter, hence do less, and are thus less connected. If they do feel free to play with girl children in ways that are satisfying and comfortable, they will be equally attached to these children, creating an additional bond to support the marriage.

This finding was picked up by one reporter; again, wire services brought it to the attention of other newspapers and

Pepper Schwartz

the story was repeated throughout the United States. It had a great deal of "play" in the various kinds of media (TV shows and magazine writers also crib from each other's stories) and showed an audience how children and sex role stereotypes about children might affect marital stability.

***

What does this tell us? That sociology not only needs to be the discoverer of truths and the corrector of politically expedient dogma or common myths, but it must be the framer of questions and the deliverer of memorable books and treatises of the journals and textbooks of academia. Right now, the common wisdom is skewing toward moral frames and explanations versus socioeconomic explanations, conflict theory, or cultural explanations. *** Television programs and magazine articles have interpreted romantic and sexual patterns of today as genetic and evolutionary strategies. *** Meanwhile, the public is buying millions of books by John Gray that tell us that men are from a different planet than women—and while

did not remove homosexuality from its list of mental illnesses until 1973 or from its influential *Diagnostic and Statistical Manual of Mental Disorders* (DSM) until 1980. These long-overdue steps were taken only after prolonged lobbying and pressure by homosexual rights organizations. The medical community

was belatedly forced to acknowledge that no scientific research had ever found homosexuals as a group to be psychologically unhealthier than heterosexuals (Burr 1993). However, the DSM IV continues to classify other aspects of sexuality as "disorders," including disorders of desire (e.g., low interest in sociologists feel that his assertions are easily torn apart, they do not choose a platform that reaches the same large audience that he does.

***

Why not? The answer to that involves, at least partly, the pretensions and customs of our discipline and, perhaps ironically, our ignorance about the way the world works. ***

In general, writing about contemporary issues as they unfold is akin to being an ambulance chaser in our profession—the word "popularizer" is not an accolade. ***

Yet, despite our attempts to ghettoize 95 percent of our work, journalists find us: Desperate for "fresh" information, they slog through our prose and latch on to our books and papers. They reduce research findings to two-minute segments and use us as talking heads in news clips or as part of their documentaries. ***

***

I am asking us to package our work and to have a purpose to our work—to put it in appropriate places, in language that is compelling, and to connect it to the important events of our day. ***

There is a huge emotional payoff in reaching the public with a sociological focus. I have had a couple of experiences where I felt that I was helping create a way of looking at things as well as supporting issues that meant a lot to me with evidence I believed in. I have worked as a journalist almost as much as I have worked as a sociologist. I have been on television in the Northwest for eighteen years in various capacities—as a "relationship expert," commentator, and as on-air support for news events. I write a column with sociologist Janet Lever for *Glamour* where each month 9 to 11 million women read what we feel is interesting and important about sex and health. In our two-page column, among other things, we comb books and the research literature looking for solid information for information-hungry readers. I have done this for several other media outlets as well—the most influential of which has been the *New York Times*—and I have found our journals crammed with good research upon which I could build a thesis and an article. I have also been an expert witness in a number of trials, the most satisfying of which have

been trials involving custody cases, the right to serve in the army, and the right to marriage for gay men and lesbians. Much of the data that I used in my testimony was part of a study conducted in the late 1970s and early 1980s with my dear friend and colleague, Philip Blumstein, now deceased from AIDS. ***

Was I the only one with this kind of information? No. But my work was still in the public eye because the book Phil and I wrote, *American Couples,* was published as a trade book, had been heavily promoted, and sold well. It had reached a number of publics, remained in the collective memory, not to mention Nexus and several rolodexes, and therefore was able to be put to good use. In the end, I felt that our ten years of work counted for something.

*** If we continue to ignore the media, we can be sure that others will claim their attentions. But I believe that we need to vie for their affections. I would like us to be good citizens as well as good scholars and enter—and be powerful in—the debates and policies of our time.

***

SOURCE: Pepper Schwartz, "Stage Fright or Death Wish: Sociology in the Mass Media," *Contemporary Sociology* 27 (5) (September 1998): 439–445.

PEPPER SCHWARTZ *is Professor of Sociology at the University of Washington in Seattle. She is the author of fourteen books, including* The Gender of Sexuality, Finding Your Perfect Match, The Great Sex Weekend, The Lifetime Love and Sex Quiz Book, American Couples, *and* Everything You Know about Love and Sex Is Wrong. *She is the past president of the Society for the Scientific Study of Sexuality, past president of the Pacific Sociological Association, and the 2005 recipient of the American Sociological Association's award for the Public Understanding of Sociology. She is currently the relationship expert for Perfectmatch.com and a columnist for* Seattle Metropolitan *magazine, among others. In the past she has been the sex and health columnist for* Glamour *magazine and for* American Baby *magazine. She lectures nationally and internationally on relationship issues, women's issues, parent and child issues, communication between men and women, and maintaining personal and family well-being in the modern world.*

sex), disorders of sexual arousal (e.g., lubrication and erectile problems), and orgasmic disorders (American Psychiatric Association 2000).

In a small number of cultures, same-sex relationships are the norm in certain contexts and do not necessarily signify

what today is termed *homosexuality.* For example, the anthropologist Gilbert Herdt (1981, 1984, 1986) reported that among more than twenty tribes in Melanesia and New Guinea, ritually prescribed same-sex encounters among young men and boys were considered necessary for subsequent masculine virility

(Herdt and Davidson 1988). Ritualized male–male sexual encounters also occurred among the Azande of Africa's Sudan and Congo (Evans-Pritchard 1970), Japanese samurai warriors in the nineteenth century (Leupp 1995), and highly educated Greek men and boys at the time of Plato (Rouselle 1999).

IS SEXUAL ORIENTATION INBORN OR LEARNED?

Most sociologists believe that sexual orientation—whether homosexual, heterosexual, or bisexual—results from a complex interplay among biological factors and social learning. Since heterosexuality is the norm for most people in U.S. culture, considerable research has focused on why some people become homosexual. Some scholars argue that biological influences predispose certain people to become homosexual from birth (Bell et al. 1981; Green 1987). Biological explanations have included differences in brain characteristics of homosexuals (LeVay 1996; Maugh and Zamichow 1991) and the effect on fetal development of the mother's in utero hormone production during pregnancy (Blanchard and Bogaert 1996; Manning et al. 1997; McFadden and Champlin 2000). Such studies, which are based on small numbers of cases, give highly inconclusive (and highly controversial) results (Healy 2001). It is virtually impossible to separate biological from early social influences in determining a person's sexual orientation.

Studies of twins may shed light on any genetic basis for homosexuality, since identical twins share identical genes. In two related studies, Bailey and Pillard (1991) examined 167 pairs of brothers and 143 pairs of sisters, with each pair of siblings raised in the same family, in which at least one sibling defined himself or herself as homosexual. Some of these pairs were identical twins (who share all genes), some were fraternal twins (who share some genes), and some were adoptive brothers or sisters (who share no genes). The researchers reasoned that if sexual orientation is determined entirely by biology, then all the identical twins should be homosexual, since their genetic makeup is identical. Among the fraternal twins, some pairs would be homosexual, since some genes are shared. The lowest rates of homosexuality were predicted for the adoptive brothers and sisters.

The results seem to show that homosexuality, like heterosexuality, results from a combination of biological and social factors. Among the men and the women studied, roughly one out of every two identical twins was homosexual, compared with one out of every five fraternal twins and one out of every ten adoptive brothers and sisters (Bailey and Pillard 1991; see also Burr 1993; Maugh 1991, 1993). In other words, a woman or man is five times as likely to be lesbian or gay if her or his identical twin is lesbian or gay than if her or his sibling is lesbian or gay but related only through adoption. These results offer some support for the importance of biological factors, since the higher the percentage of shared genes, the greater the percentage of cases in which both siblings were homosexual. However, because approximately half of the identical twin brothers and sisters of homosexuals were not themselves homosexual, social learning must also be involved; otherwise one would expect all identical twin siblings of homosexuals to be homosexual as well.

Clearly, even studies of identical twins cannot fully isolate biological from social factors. It is often the case that even in infancy, identical twins are treated more like one another by parents, peers, and teachers than are fraternal twins, who in turn are treated more like one another than are adoptive siblings. Thus identical twins may have more than genes in common: They may also share a higher proportion of similar socializing experiences. Sociologist Peter Bearman has shown the intricate ways that genetics and social experience are intertwined. Bearman (2002) found that males with a female twin are twice as likely to report same-sex attractions. He theorized that parents of opposite-sex twins are more likely to give them unisex treatment, leading to a less traditionally masculine influence on the males. Having an older brother decreases the rate of homosexuality. Bearman hypothesized that an older brother establishes gender socializing mechanisms for the younger brother to follow, which allows him to compensate for unisex treatment. Bearman's work is consistent with the statements offered by professional organizations such as the American Academy of Pediatrics (AAP), which concludes "sexual orientation probably is not determined by any one factor but by a combination of genetic, hormonal, and environmental influences" (AAP 2004).

HOMOPHOBIA

Homophobia, a term coined in the late 1960s, refers to both attitudes and behaviors marked by an aversion to or hatred of homosexuals, their lifestyles, and their practices. It is a form of prejudice reflected not only in overt acts of hostility and violence toward lesbians and gays but also in forms of verbal abuse that are widespread in American culture, for example, using terms like *fag* or *homo* to insult heterosexual males or using female-related offensive terms such as *sissy* or *pansy* to insult gay men.

One recent study of homophobia in U.S. schools concluded that the estimated two million lesbian, gay, and bisexual middle and high school students are frequently the targets of humiliating harassment and, sometimes, physical abuse. Interviews with lesbian, gay, and bisexual students, as well as youth service providers, teachers, administrators, counselors, and parents in seven states, found harassment to be a common and painful experience among lesbian, gay, and bisexual students (Bochenek and Brown 2001). The study cited a CBS poll reporting that a third of eleventh-grade students knew about incidents of sexual harassment of gays and lesbians, while more than a quarter admitted to engaging in harassment.

The study also found that verbal abuse often escalated into physical abuse. In one well-publicized incident, an openly gay Wisconsin student was verbally humiliated, spat and urinated on, hit, subjected to a mock rape conducted by classmates in a science lab, and brutally beaten and seriously injured. When he complained to the school principal after the mock rape, she reportedly told him that "boys will be boys" and that his open gayness was causing the problem (Bochenek and Brown 2001). This unhappy student twice attempted suicide—a tragically common occurrence because lesbian, gay, and bisexual youths are at a four times greater risk for suicide than their straight peers (Gibson 1989). Yet the vast majority of victims of homophobic violence never report the incident, for fear of being "outed" (New York City Gay and Lesbian Anti-Violence Project 1996).

Homophobia is widespread in U.S. culture, although it is slowly starting to erode. Public figures who use homophobic language are publicly upbraided. In 2007, when actor Isaiah Washington of the popular television show *Grey's Anatomy* referred to a gay co-star as a "faggot," Washington was demonized by the national media and was released from his contract with the television show. That same year, the Gallup Poll found that 57 percent of Americans viewed homosexuality as an acceptable lifestyle (Saad 2007a). Yet social change has evolved slowly. It was in the very recent past (2003) that the Supreme Court ruled in *Lawrence v. Texas* that the state of Texas's prohibition on homosexual sex was a violation of the constitutional right to privacy; in many states homosexuality was still a legally punishable crime.

THE MOVEMENT FOR GAY AND LESBIAN CIVIL RIGHTS

Until recently, most gays and lesbians hid their sexual orientation for fear that "coming out of the closet"—or publicly revealing one's sexual orientation—would cost them their jobs, families, and friends and leave them open to verbal and physical abuse. Yet, since the late 1960s, many gays and lesbians have acknowledged their homosexuality openly, and in some cities the lives of lesbian and gay Americans have become quite normalized (Seidman et al. 1999). New York City, San Francisco, London, and other large metropolitan areas worldwide have thriving gay and lesbian communities. Coming out may be important not only for the person who does so but also for

The Stonewall Inn nightclub raid in 1969 is regarded as the first shot fired in the battle for gay rights in the United States. The twenty-fifth anniversary of the event was commemorated in New York City with a variety of celebrations as well as discussions on the evolution and future of gay rights.

others in the larger society: Previously closeted lesbians and gays discover they are not alone, while heterosexuals recognize that people whom they admire and respect are homosexual.

The current global wave of gay and lesbian civil rights movements began partly as an outgrowth of the U.S. social movements of the 1960s, which emphasized pride in racial and ethnic identity. One pivotal event was the Stonewall riots in June 1969, when New York City's gay community—angered by continual police harassment—fought the New York Police Department for two days (D'Emilio 1983; Weeks 1977). The Stonewall riots became a symbol of gay pride. In 1994, on the twenty-fifth anniversary of the Stonewall riots, one hundred thousand people attended the International March on the United Nations to Affirm the Human Rights of Lesbian and Gay People. In May 2005, the International Day Against Homophobia (IDAHO) was first celebrated, with events held in more than forty countries. Clearly, significant strides have been made, although discrimination and homophobia remain serious problems for many lesbian, gay, and bisexual Americans.

There are enormous differences among countries in the degree to which homosexuality is legally punishable. Sixty-eight countries still outlaw sex between males, and twenty-six outlaw sex between women. In Africa, male homosexual acts have been legalized in only a handful of countries, whereas female homosexuality is seldom mentioned in the law at all. In South Africa, the official policy of the former white government was to regard homosexuality as a psychiatric problem that threatened national security. Once the black government

Gay and Lesbian Rights in the World

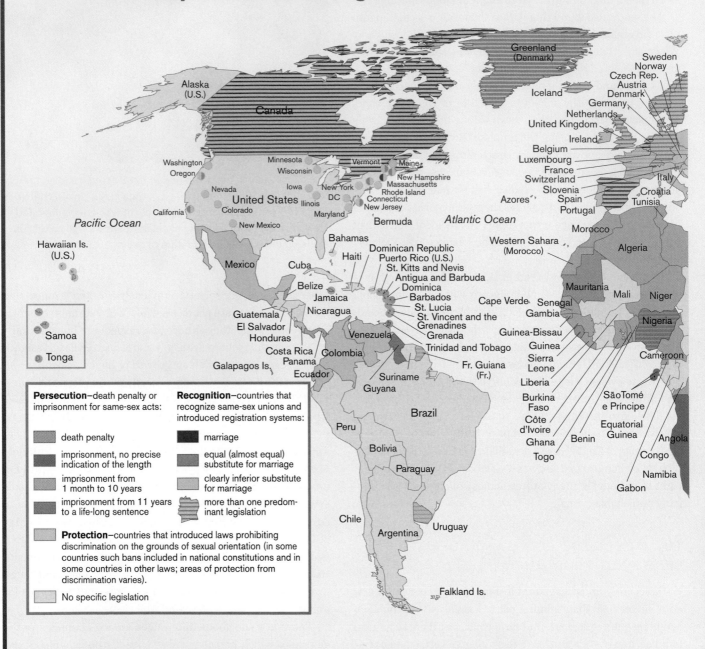

Persecution—death penalty or imprisonment for same-sex acts:

- death penalty
- imprisonment, no precise indication of the length
- imprisonment from 1 month to 10 years
- imprisonment from 11 years to a life-long sentence

Protection—countries that introduced laws prohibiting discrimination on the grounds of sexual orientation (in some countries such bans included in national constitutions and in some countries in other laws; areas of protection from discrimination varies).

No specific legislation

Recognition—countries that recognize same-sex unions and introduced registration systems:

- marriage
- equal (almost equal) substitute for marriage
- clearly inferior substitute for marriage
- more than one predominant legislation

SOURCE: International Lesbian and Gay Association 2008.

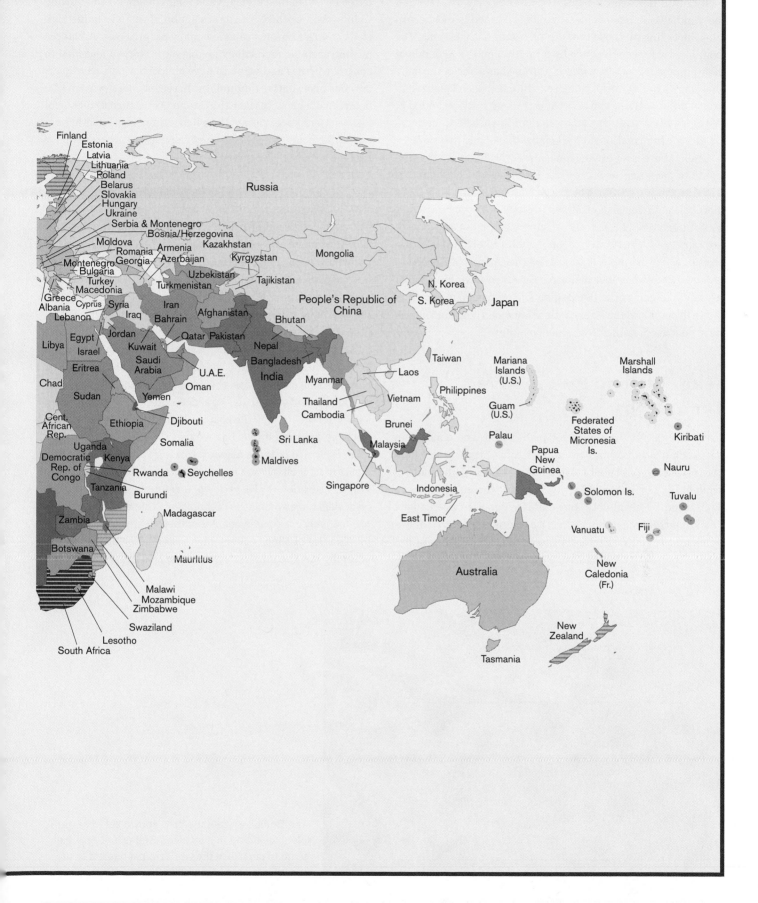

took power, however, it legislated full equality. In Asia and the Middle East, male homosexuality is banned in most countries, including all those that are predominantly Islamic. For example, Iran executed two men in 2005 on the grounds of their homosexuality. In contrast, Europe has some of the most liberal laws in the world: Homosexuality has been legalized in nearly all countries, and several European nations and U.S. states legally recognize same-sex marriages (see Chapter 15 for further information on the legalization of gay marriage).

Today there is a growing movement worldwide for the civil rights of gays and lesbians. The International Lesbian and Gay Association (2007), which was founded in 1978, has more than 600 member organizations in some ninety countries. It holds international conferences, supports lesbian and gay social movement organizations, and lobbies international organizations. For example, it persuaded the Council of Europe to require all of its member nations to repeal laws banning homosexuality. In general, active lesbian and gay social movements thrive in countries that emphasize individual rights and liberal state policies (Frank and McEneaney 1999).

Sexuality and Procreative Technology

As with most of the topics in this chapter, the concept of "the socialization of nature" applies to a better sociological understanding of sexual behavior. An example is human reproduction. For hundreds of years, most women's lives were dominated by childbirth and child rearing. In premodern times, contraception was ineffective or unknown. Even in Europe and the United States as late as the eighteenth century, women commonly experienced as many as twenty pregnancies (often involving miscarriages and infant deaths). Today, owing to improved methods of contraception, women in industrialized countries no longer have so many pregnancies. Advances in contraceptive technology enable most women and men to control whether and when to have children. Contraception is only one **procreative technology**. In recent years, women who delay childbearing to their thirties and older turn to technologies that enhance, rather than limit, their reproduction behavior. This and other areas in which natural processes have become social are described below.

CHILDBIRTH

The medicalization of pregnancy and childbirth developed slowly, as obstetric specialists replaced local physicians and midwives. Today in industrialized societies, most births occur in a hospital with the help of a specialized medical team.

In the past, new parents had to wait until the birth to learn the sex of their baby and whether it would be healthy. Today, prenatal tests such as the sonogram (an image of the fetus produced by ultrasonic waves) and amniocentesis (which samples amniotic fluid from around the fetus) can reveal structural or chromosomal abnormalities before birth. Such new technology introduces new ethical and legal decisions. For example, when a disorder is detected, the couple must decide whether to have the baby, knowing it may be seriously disabled.

Prospective parents also are turning to technologies that increase their chances of conceiving a child. Fertility drugs, in vitro fertilization (IVF), artificial insemination, and hormone treatments are among the technologies that are assisting reproductively challenged couples in their desire to start a family. The use of such technologies also is altering the nature of family life; the number of twins born in the United States

The Boniellos were the third known set of sextuplets to survive in the United States and only the tenth to survive in the world. What has led to the recent rise of multiple births?

increased by roughly 50 percent, and the number of triplet (or more) births soared by 404 percent between 1980 and 1997 (Martin and Park 1999). This rise in multiple births is partially explained by the growing popularity of fertility drugs like Clomid and procedures like in vitro fertilization, which result in multiple births more frequently than unassisted fertilizations do.

GENETIC ENGINEERING: DESIGNER BABIES

Considerable scientific endeavor is being devoted to intervening in the genetic makeup of the fetus to influence its subsequent development. The likely social effect of such genetic engineering is provoking debates almost as intense as those over abortion. According to supporters, genetic engineering will bring many benefits—for example, identifying the genetic factors that make some people vulnerable to certain diseases. Genetic reprogramming would ensure that these illnesses no longer pass from generation to generation. It would be possible to "design" our children's bodies before birth in terms of skin color, color of hair and eyes, weight, and so forth.

This issue is a prime example of the opportunities and problems that the increasing socialization of nature creates. What choices will parents make if they can design their babies, and what limits should be placed on those choices? Genetic engineering is unlikely to be cheap. Will this mean that those who can afford to pay will program out from their children any traits they see as socially undesirable? What will happen to the children of more deprived groups, who will continue to be born unaltered?

Some sociologists argue that differential access to genetic engineering might lead to the emergence of a "biological underclass." Those who don't have the physical advantages genetic engineering can bring might be subject to prejudice and discrimination and might have difficulty finding employment and life or health insurance (Duster 1990).

THE ABORTION DEBATE

The most controversial ethical dilemma created by modern reproductive technologies is this: Under what conditions should abortion be available to women? The abortion debate has become highly intense because it centers on basic ethical issues to which there are no easy solutions. Those who are "pro-life" believe that abortion is always wrong except in extreme circumstances, because it is equivalent to murder. For them, ethical issues must be subject to the value placed on human life. Those who are "pro-choice" argue that the mother's control over her own body—her own right to live a rewarding life—must be the primary consideration.

The debate has led to numerous episodes of violence, including the 1998 murder of obstetrician Barnett Slepian in Buffalo, New York. Slepian had been one of just three doctors in the area who performed abortions. Can this debate ever be resolved? One prominent social and legal theorist, Ronald Dworkin (1993), has suggested that it can. The intense divisions between those who are pro-life and those who are pro-choice, he argues, hide deeper sources of agreement between the two sides, and therein is a source of hope. In current times, we place a high value on the sanctity of human life. Each side agrees with this value but interprets it differently—the one emphasizing the interests of the child, the other the interests of the mother. If the two sides can be persuaded that they share a common ethical value, a more constructive dialogue may be possible.

☑ CONCEPT CHECKS

1. Describe several changes in sexual practices over the past two centuries.
2. What are the most important contributions of Alfred Kinsey's research on sexuality?
3. Name at least three important findings about sexual behavior discovered since Kinsey.
4. What is sexual orientation?

The Sociology of the Body

- The field of the *sociology of the body* studies how the social world affects our bodies and especially addresses processes of social change. Modern *social technologies* have managed, for instance, to separate the body from nature; an example is dieting, which involves planned interventions in bodily functioning.
- Food production in the modern world has been globalized: Owing to technologies of transportation and storage (refrigeration), now everyone in the developed world is on a diet in some sense, having to *decide* what to eat every day. Social relations influence such decisions. Women especially are judged by physical appearance, but feelings of shame about the body can lead anyone to compulsive dieting, exercising, or bodybuilding to make the body conform to social expectations.

The Sociology of Health and Illness

- Sociologists are interested in the experience of illness—how being sick, chronically ill, or disabled is experienced by the sick person and by those nearby. The idea of the *sick role*, developed by Talcott Parsons, suggests that a sick person adopts certain forms of behavior to minimize the disruptive effect of illness. A sick individual has certain privileges, such as the right to withdraw from normal responsibilities, but in return must work to regain health by following medical advice.
- Symbolic interactionists have investigated how people cope with disease and chronic illness. The experience of illness can provoke changes in individuals' self-identity and in their daily routines. Stigmatized health conditions may have a particularly powerful influence on one's daily experiences. This dimension of the sociology of the body is increasingly relevant for many societies; people are now living longer than before and suffer more from chronic debilitating conditions than from acute illnesses.

Social Factors in Health and Illness

- Health and illness are connected to population issues as well as being strongly affected by social factors such as class, race, and gender. Modern Western medicine views illness as having physical origins and hence as being explicable in scientific terms. In spite of modern medicine's importance, public health measures, such as better sanitation and nutrition, were more important in reducing infant mortality rates.

Global Health Issues

- Historians believe that risk from infectious diseases were lower in Africa and Asians prior to the time that Europeans tried to colonize these regions—as they often brought with the practices that negatively affected the health of local natives . For example, the colonial system, with its stress on cash crops, negatively affected the nutrition of developing-world people.
- Susceptibility to the major illnesses is strongly influenced by socioeconomic status. For example, people in the industrialized world live longer than those in the developing world; the richer are healthier, taller, and stronger than those from less privileged backgrounds.

Human Sexuality

- Researchers have examined both biological and cultural influences on human sexual behavior, concluding that sexuality, like gender, is mostly socially constructed. There is an extremely wide range of sexual practices, but in any society only some will be approved and reflected in social norms. Because these norms also vary widely, however, we can say that most sexual responses are learned rather than innate.

Key Concepts

biomedical model of health (p. 578)
body mass index (BMI) (p. 572)
complementary and alternative medicine (CAM) (p. 578)
epidemiology (p. 579)
health literacy (p. 581)
homophobia (p. 598)
obesity (p. 565)
procreative technology (p. 602)
sick role (p. 574)
socialization of nature (p. 570)
sociology of the body (p. 566)
stigma (p. 576)

Review Questions

1. What are two main body issues facing the United States today? Why are these public issues and not just individual problems?
2. Compare and contrast the two main approaches to thinking about health and illness in sociology.
3. Describe some of the differences between traditional systems of health care and modern medicine.

4. What is the difference between complementary and alternative medicines? How do sociologists explain widespread use of such therapies?
5. How are the various dimensions of social class related to differences of health and mortality?
6. How does race matter in health inequalities? Give an example.
7. How do biological and social factors explain gender differences in health?
8. What is the relationship between colonialism and health? How has the legacy of colonialism contributed to contemporary health disparities between the developed and developing worlds?
9. What are the sociological debates around Kinsey and Laumann's surveys of sexuality in the United States? What is your opinion?
10. What is the difference between *sexual preference* and *sexual orientation?* Why do these differences in terminology matter?

Thinking Sociologically Exercises

1. Statistical studies of our national health show a gap in life expectancies between the rich and the poor. Review all the major factors that would explain why rich people live about eight years longer than poor people.
2. This text discusses the biological and sociocultural factors associated with sexual orientation. Why are twin studies the most promising type of research on the genetic basis of sexual orientation? Summarize the analysis of these studies, and show whether it presently appears that sexual orientation results from genetic differences and/or sociocultural practices and experiences.

Learning Objectives

Living in Cities

Learn how cities have changed as a result of industrialization and urbanization.

Theories of Urbanism

Learn how theories of urbanism have placed increasing emphasis on the influence of socioeconomic factors on city life.

Rural, Suburban, and Urban Life in the United States

Learn about the recent key developments affecting American cities, suburbs, and rural communities in the last several decades: suburbanization, urban decay, gentrification, and "aging in place" of rural areas.

Cities and Globalization

See that global economic competition has a profound impact on urbanization and urban life.

Urbanization in the Developing World

Recognize the challenges of urbanization in the developing world.

World Population Growth

Learn why the world population has increased dramatically and understand the main consequences of this growth.

Population, Industrialization, and the Environment

See that the environment is a sociological issue related to urbanization and population growth.

CHAPTER NINETEEN

URBANIZATION, POPULATION, AND THE ENVIRONMENT

handan, China—When residents of this northern Chinese city hang their clothes out to dry, the black fallout from nearby Handan Iron and Steel often sends them back to the wash.

Half a world away, neighbors of ThyssenKrupp's former steel mill in the Ruhr Valley of Germany once had a similar problem. The white shirts men wore to church on Sundays turned gray by the time they got home.

These two steel towns have an unusual kinship, spanning 5,000 miles and a decade of economic upheaval. They have shared the same hulking blast furnace, dismantled and shipped piece by piece from Germany's old industrial heartland to Hebei Province, China's new Ruhr Valley.

The transfer, one of dozens since the late 1990s, contributed to a burst in China's steel production, which now exceeds that of Germany, Japan, and the United States combined. It left Germany with lost jobs and a bad case of postindustrial angst.

But steel mills spewing particulates into the air and sucking electricity from China's coal-fired power plants account for a big chunk of the country's surging emissions of sulfur dioxide and carbon dioxide. Germany, in contrast, has cleaned its skies and is now leading the fight against global warming.

In its rush to re-create the industrial revolution that made the West rich, China has absorbed most of the major industries that once made the West dirty. Spurred by strong state support, Chinese companies have become the dominant makers of steel, coke, aluminum, cement, chemicals, leather, paper, and other goods that faced high costs, including tougher environmental rules, in other parts of the world. China has become the world's factory, but also its smokestack (Kahn and Landler 2007).

China's rapid rise as an industrial power—with India not far behind—creates enormous environmental challenges, not just for these two countries, but for all of us. Their combined population of 2.4 billion people accounts for one out of every three people on the planet. They contain some of the world's largest and fastest-growing urban areas, whose population is swollen with impoverished rural migrants looking for jobs. They are seeking to achieve the same standard of living that their neighbors in Japan, Europe, the United States, and other industrial countries have come to expect as a birthright. But their combination of population growth, urbanization, and industrialization has had toxic environmental results.

China's economy, for example, has grown at nearly 10 percent a year for more than two decades. This rapid industrialization has lifted hundreds of millions of people out of poverty and into the middle class, but at a high environmental cost: Toxic chemical spills have threatened the water supply of millions of people, while the air in major cities has become so polluted that the ultramodern skyscrapers that seemingly go up overnight are often not visible. Sixteen of the most polluted cities in the world are in China (Oliver 2008).

In its rush to develop, China is building a vast network of highways across the country, much like the United States did a half century ago. The nearly 53,000 miles of new roads will connect all major cities in China, supporting (and generating) automobile use that is projected to outstrip that of the United States by the middle of the century—or earlier. For a country where as recently as twenty-five years ago the bicycle and rickshaw were the principal means of transportation, this is an enormous transformation, and one that will contribute to urban traffic congestion, along with increased levels of energy use and pollution. As China makes the transition from **rural** to urban in record time, its planners call for relocating some four hundred million people—more than the entire U.S. population—to newly built urban centers over the next twenty-five years. If achieved, this will require the construction of half of all the buildings in the world during that time (Economy 2007).

China's booming economy depends on burning coal. Every week or so a new coal-burning power plant is brought on line, most of them with outmoded technology. The sulfur dioxide from these plants is believed to contribute to nearly a half-million deaths a year in China, while causing acid rain that poisons lakes, rivers, and farmlands. Climate-changing smoke and soot from China's power plants have been detected across the Pacific Ocean in California. If China continues on

A coal miner emerges from a mine after a day's work in Shanxi Province, China.

its present course, its demand for energy will double over the next quarter century, while its increased production of global warming gases will outstrip that of all other industrial countries combined (Bradsher and Baraboza 2006; IEA 2007).

If China's environmental problems are shared by all of us, so too are its causes. The International Energy Agency estimates that as much as a third of China's carbon emissions, which contribute to the greenhouse gases that cause global warming, are the direct result of the energy consumed in making products for American, European, and Japanese consumers (Kahn and Landler 2007). The relocation of a polluting steel plant from Germany to China is just one way in which the environmental costs of a global economy have been transferred from wealthy industrial nations to poorer less developed ones. And China is quick to point out that the United States, the wealthiest industrial nation in the world, is still the world's largest contributor to greenhouse gases.

In this chapter we examine the ways in which population growth, urbanization, and the environment go hand-in-hand, against the backdrop of rapid industrialization that is transforming many parts of the world. Cities are the capitals of civilization: They are culturally lively, commercially dynamic, and alluring. They are efficient in providing for a large number of the population in a small amount of space. They are also often rife with problems of poverty, racial and ethnic exclusion and antagonism, and crime. And in the developing world, such as India and China, they are exploding in population, serving as magnets for the largest rural-urban migration in human history. At the beginning of the twentieth century, fewer than one out of every seven people on the planet lived in cities. By 2008 the number of people living in cities had surpassed the number living in rural areas, and over the next thirty years as many as two thirds of the human population may be urban.

We begin by studying the origins of cities and the vast growth in the numbers of city dwellers that has occurred over the past century. From there, we review the most influential theories of urban life. We then move on to consider patterns of urban development in North America compared with cities in the developing world. Cities in the developing world are growing at an enormous rate. We consider why this is happening and at the same time look at changes now taking place in world population patterns. We conclude by assessing the connections among urbanization, world population growth, and environmental problems.

Living in Cities

Cities in Traditional Societies

The world's first cities appeared about 3500 B.C.E., in the river valleys of the Nile in Egypt, the Tigris and Euphrates in what is now Iraq, and the Indus in what is today Pakistan. Cities in traditional societies were very small by modern standards. Babylon, for example, one of the largest ancient Near Eastern cities, extended over an area of only 3.2 square miles and at its height, around 2000 B.C.E., probably numbered no more than fifteen to twenty thousand people. Rome under Emperor Augustus in the first century B.C.E. was easily the largest premodern city outside China, with some three hundred thousand inhabitants—the population of Bakersfield, California, or Toledo, Ohio, today.

Most cities of the ancient world shared certain features. They were usually surrounded by walls that served as a military defense and emphasized the separation of the urban community from the countryside. The central area of the city was almost always occupied by a religious temple, a royal palace, government and commercial buildings, and a public square. This ceremonial, commercial, and political center was sometimes enclosed within a second, inner wall and was usually too small to hold more than a minority of the citizens. Although it usually contained a market, the center was different from the business districts found at the core of modern cities, because

the main buildings were nearly always religious and political rather than commercial (Fox 1964; Sjoberg 1960, 1963; Wheatley 1971).

The dwellings of the ruling class or elite tended to be concentrated in or near the center. Less privileged groups lived toward the perimeter of the city or outside the walls, moving inside if the city came under attack. Different ethnic and religious communities were often segregated in separate neighborhoods, where their members lived and worked. Sometimes these neighborhoods were also surrounded by walls. Communication among city dwellers was erratic. Lacking any form of printing press, public officials had to shout at the tops of their voices to deliver pronouncements. "Streets" were usually strips of land on which no one had yet built. A few traditional civilizations boasted sophisticated road systems linking particular cities, but these existed mainly for military purposes, and transportation for the most part was slow and limited. Merchants and soldiers were the only people who regularly traveled over long distances.

Although cities were the main centers for science, the arts, and cosmopolitan culture, their influence over the rest of the country was always weak. No more than a tiny proportion of the population lived in the cities, and the division between cities and countryside was pronounced. By far the majority of people lived in small rural communities and rarely came into contact with more than the occasional state official or merchant from the towns.

Industrialization and Urbanization

The contrast in size between the largest modern cities today and those of premodern civilizations is extraordinary. The most populous cities in the industrialized countries number over ten million inhabitants. A **conurbation**—a cluster of cities and towns forming a continuous network—may include even larger numbers of people. The peak of urban life today is represented by what is called the **megalopolis**, the "city of cities." The term was originally coined in ancient Greece to refer to a city-state that was planned to be the envy of all civilizations. The current megalopolis, though, bears little relation to that utopia. The term was first applied in modern times to refer to the Northeast Corridor of the United States, an area covering some 450 miles from north of Boston to south of Washington, D.C. In this region, about forty-four million people live at a density of over seven hundred persons per square mile. An urban population almost as large and dense is concentrated in the lower Great Lakes region surrounding Chicago.

Britain was the first society to undergo industrialization, beginning in the mid-eighteenth century. The process

Traffic outside of the Bank of England in the financial district of London in 1896. In only one century, the population of London grew from over one million people to over seven million.

of industrialization generated increasing **urbanization**—the movement of the population into towns and cities, away from the land. In 1800, fewer than 20 percent of the British population lived in towns or cities with more than 10,000 inhabitants. By 1900, this proportion had risen to 74 percent. London held about 1.1 million people in 1800; by the beginning of the twentieth century, it had increased in size to a population of over 7 million, at that date the largest city ever seen in the world. It was a vast manufacturing, commercial, and financial center at the heart of the still-expanding British Empire.

The urbanization of most other European countries and the United States took place somewhat later. In 1800, the United States was more of a rural society than were the leading European countries. Fewer than 10 percent of Americans lived in communities with populations of more than 2,500 people. Today, 84 percent of Americans reside in metropolitan areas (Kaiser Family Foundation 2008). Between 1800 and 1900, as industrialization grew in the United States, the population of New York City leapt from 60,000 people to 4.8 million.

Urbanization in the twenty-first century is a global process, into which the developing world is being drawn more and more (Kasarda and Crenshaw 1991). From 1900 to 1950, world urbanization increased by 239 percent, compared with a global population growth of 49 percent. The six decades have seen a greater acceleration in the proportion of people living in cities. From 1950 to 1986, urban growth worldwide was 320 percent, while the population grew by 54 percent. Most of this growth has occurred in cities in developing world societies. In 1975, 39 percent of the world's population lived in urban areas. By 2008, the proportion had increased to over 50 percent, with more than 3.3 billion persons living in urban areas worldwide. This number expected to reach 5 billion by 2030. The trend will be most marked in Africa and Asia where the urban population will double between 2000 and 2030. By 2030, the towns and cities of the developing world will account for 81 percent of the worldwide urban population (UNFPA 2008a).

Along with this worldwide urbanization come the effects of globalization. For example, the rise of urban-industrial areas in developing countries has brought intensified economic competition to industries in U.S. cities. South Korea's shoe industry has led to the impoverishment of urban areas in northeastern Massachusetts that formerly relied on that industry for their prosperity. Similarly, Pittsburgh and Baltimore have had to adjust to losing much of the market for their steel industry to Japan. We will examine later in the chapter how the global economy has influenced forms of city life in recent years.

☑ CONCEPT CHECKS

1. What are two characteristics of ancient cities?
2. What is urbanization? How is it related to globalization?

Theories of Urbanism

The Chicago School

Scholars associated with the University of Chicago from the 1920s to the 1940s—especially Robert Park, Ernest Burgess, and Louis Wirth—developed ideas that were for many years the chief basis of theory and research in urban sociology. Two concepts developed by the "Chicago School" are worthy of special attention. One is the so-called **ecological approach** to urban analysis; the other, the characterization of urbanism as a *way of life,* developed by Wirth (Park 1952; Wirth 1938). It is important to understand these ideas as they were initially conceived by the Chicago School and to see how they have been revised and even replaced by sociologists in more recent decades.

URBAN ECOLOGY

Ecology is a term taken from a physical science: the study of the adaptation of plant and animal organisms to their environment. In the natural world, organisms tend to be distributed in systematic ways over the terrain, such that a balance or equilibrium between different species is achieved. The Chicago School believed that the locations of major urban settlements and the distribution of different types of neighborhoods within them can be understood in terms of similar principles. Cities do not grow up at random but grow in response to advantageous features of the environment. For example, large urban areas in modern societies tend to develop along the shores of rivers, in fertile plains, or at the intersection of trading routes or railways.

"Once set up," in Park's (1952) words, "a city is, it seems, a great sorting mechanism which . . . infallibly selects out of the population as a whole the individuals best suited to live in a particular region or a particular milieu." Cities become ordered into "natural areas," through processes of competition, invasion, and succession—all of which occur in biological ecology. If we look at the ecology of a lake in the natural environment, we find that competition among various species of fish, insects, and other organisms operates to reach a fairly stable distribution among them. This balance is disturbed if new species invade—try to make the lake their home. Some of the organisms that used to proliferate in the central area of the lake are driven out to eke out a more precarious existence around its fringes. The invading species are their successors in the central sections.

Patterns of location, movement, and relocation in cities, according to the ecological view, have a similar form. Different neighborhoods develop through the adjustments made by inhabitants as they struggle to gain their livelihoods. According to mid-twentieth-century writings, a city can be pictured as a map of areas with distinct and contrasting social characteristics. Cities can be seen as formed in concentric rings, broken up into segments. In the center are the **inner-city** areas, a mixture of big-business prosperity and decaying private homes. Beyond these are older established neighborhoods, housing workers employed in stable manual occupations. Farther out still are the suburbs, in which higher-income groups tend to live. Processes of invasion and succession occur within the segments of the concentric rings. Thus as property decays in a central or near-central area, ethnic minority groups might start to move into it. As they do so, more of the preexisting population start to leave, precipitating a wholesale flight to neighborhoods elsewhere in the city or out to the suburbs. However, as we will see later in this chapter, these traditional patterns are starting to change—as wealthy persons and the young flood into urban areas, seeking amenities such as arts and culture, and suburban areas become more desirable (and affordable) to poor and working-class persons.

Another aspect of the **urban ecology** approach emphasized the *interdependence* of different city areas. Differentiation—the specialization of groups and occupational roles—is the main way in which human beings adapt to their environment. Groups on which many others depend will have a dominant role, often reflected in their central geographical position. Business groups, for example, such as large banks or insurance companies, provide key services for many in a community and hence are usually to be found in the central areas of settlements (Hawley 1950, 1968).

Part of what it means to think like an urban sociologist today is to ask whether and how the conditions observed in cities are socially constructed or natural. We have seen that the early Chicago School favored the idea that spatial patterns were natural outcomes. This all began to change when two black graduate students at the University of Chicago published the book *Black Metropolis* (Drake and Cayton 1945), which posed a challenge to the human-ecology framework.

Drake and Cayton's massive study, based on extensive historical and ethnographic data, showed that the black residential neighborhoods of Chicago were by no means the result of "natural forces" but were instead shaped by unnatural, social forces. These areas were called *ghettos,* a term that has come to mean many things to many people but that can be most usefully defined as a residential area where a racial or ethnic group initially comes to live as a consequence of systematic exclusion from more desirable places. Drake and Cayton showed that the poor living conditions in the ghetto were not due to the fact the people living there were black. Rather, the difficult living conditions reflected the fact that blacks were given no choice but to live in the worst areas of the city. There was nothing natural about this placement and it would not have occurred if not for social forces such as exclusion, violence, and restrictive covenants where neighborhood "improvement" associations passed laws making it illegal to sell land in a community to blacks. After the publication of Drake and Cayton's *Black Metropolis,* it was harder for sociologists to think of the distributions of populations in urban areas as natural.

URBANISM AS A WAY OF LIFE

Wirth's thesis of **urbanism** as a *way of life* (1938) is concerned less with whether cities are natural or socially constructed than with what urbanism is as a form of social existence. Urbanism focuses on the ways that life in cities is different from life elsewhere. Wirth also asserted that the effects of life in cities can be felt outside cities as well. For example, have you ever noticed that many young people today dress in garments that were once thought to be distinctive to urban minority youth? It is not uncommon to find some teenagers in suburban high schools all over America dressing in baggy pants, untucked T-shirts, and high top sneakers. If Wirth were writing today he might cite this as an example for his claim that the cultural life that begins in cities draws in the outlying population, so that urbanism is "a way of life" in many places outside cities as well.

Wirth's theory is important because it acknowledges that urbanism is not just part of a society but expresses and influences the nature of the wider social system. Aspects of the urban way of life are characteristic of social life in modern societies as a whole, not just the activities of those who happen to live in big cities.

A second aspect of Wirth's argument focused on proximity and anonymity, aspects of social life that he viewed as distinctive to cities. In cities, Wirth points out, large numbers of people live in close proximity to each other, without knowing most others personally—a fundamental contrast to small, traditional villages. Most contacts between city dwellers are fleeting and partial and are means to other ends rather than being satisfying relationships in themselves. Interactions with sales clerks in stores, baristas at coffee shops, or passengers or ticket collectors on trains are passing encounters, entered into not for their own sake but as means to other aims.

Because those who live in urban areas tend to be highly mobile, there are relatively weak bonds between them. People are involved in many different activities and situations each day—the pace of life is faster than in rural areas. Competition prevails over cooperation. Wirth accepts that the density of social life in cities leads to the formation of neighborhoods having distinct characteristics, some of which may preserve the characteristics of small communities. In immigrant areas, for example, traditional types of connections between families are found, with most people knowing most others on a personal basis. The more such areas are absorbed into wider patterns of city life, however, the less these characteristics survive.

Wirth was among the first to address the "urban interaction problem" (Duneier and Molotch 1999), the necessity for city dwellers to respect social boundaries when so many people

The "urban interaction problem" is a necessity for city dwellers—respecting social boundaries when so many people are in close physical proximity all the time. Whether listening to music on portable devices or reading magazines or newspapers, many people have strategies for distancing themselves and managing social boundaries in busy urban environments.

are in close physical proximity all the time. Wirth elaborates that "the reserve, the indifference, and the blasé outlook that urbanites manifest in their relationships may thus be regarded as devices for immunizing themselves against the personal claims and expectations of others." Many people walk down the street in cities acting unconcerned about the others near them, often talking on cellphones or listening to iPods that block out the sounds of urban life. Through such appearance of apathy they can avoid unwanted transgression of social boundaries.

Wirth's ideas have deservedly enjoyed wide currency. The impersonal nature of many day-to-day contacts in modern cities is undeniable—but to some degree this is true of social life in general in modern societies. Although one might assume that the "immunization" urban dwellers engage in to distance themselves from others is unique to city life, urban interaction may be only a subtype of the universal social condition. While the presence of strangers is more common in cities (Lofland 1973, 1998), all people must manage social boundaries in their face-to-face interactions with others—as has been found as far afield as Western Samoa (Duranti 1994) or among the African Poro people (Bellman 1984). It is always necessary to ask whether the problems one associates with cities are aspects of social life more generally. In assessing Wirth's ideas, we must also ask whether his generalizations about urban life hold true for all cities during all times.

Yet neighborhoods marked by close kinship and personal ties often are actively created by city life; they are not just remnants of a preexisting way of life that survive for a period within the city. Claude Fischer (1984) has put forward an explanation for why large-scale urbanism helps to promote diverse subcultures, rather than swamping everyone within an anonymous mass. Those who live in cities, he points out, are able to collaborate with others of like background or interests to develop local connections; and they can join distinctive religious, ethnic, political, and other subcultural groups. A small town or village does not allow the development of such subcultural diversity. Those who form ethnic communities within cities, for instance, might have had little or no knowledge of one another in their land of origin. When they arrive in a new country, they gravitate to areas where others from a similar linguistic and cultural background are living, and new subcommunity structures are formed. An artist might find few others in a village or small town with whom to associate but may find a community of like-minded artistic or intellectual peers in neighborhoods like Williamsburg in Brooklyn, New York. Likewise, some gay and lesbian young people may find more hospitable communities in cities that have large gay subcultures like San Francisco, compared to the small towns where they may have grown up.

A large city is a world of strangers, yet it supports and creates personal relationships. This is not paradoxical. We have to separate urban experience into the public sphere of encounters with strangers and the more private world of family, friends, and work colleagues. It may be difficult to meet people when one first moves to a large city. But anyone moving to a small, established rural community may find the friendliness of the inhabitants largely a matter of public politeness—it may take years to become accepted when one is "new" in town. This is not the case in the city, because cities are continually welcoming new, geographically mobile residents. Although one finds a diversity of strangers, each is a potential friend. And once within a group or network, the possibilities for expanding one's personal connections increase considerably.

Wirth's ideas retain some validity, but in the light of subsequent contributions it is clear that they are overgeneralized. Modern cities frequently involve impersonal, anonymous social relationships, but they are also sources of diversity—and, sometimes, intimacy.

JANE JACOBS: "EYES AND EARS UPON THE STREET"

Like most sociologists in the twentieth century, the Chicago School researchers were professors who saw their mission as contributing to a scholarly literature and advancing the field of social science.

At certain moments in the history of sociology, however, advances have also come from thinkers working outside universities without formal training in sociology. One such person was Jane Jacobs, who published *The Death and Life of Great American Cities* in 1961.

Jacobs was an architecture critic with a high school education, but through her own independent reading and research in the 1950s, she transformed herself into one of the most learned figures in the emerging field of urban studies. She is known as a public intellectual, because her main goal was to speak to the educated public rather than to contribute to a scholarly literature. Nevertheless, her work has had an impact on scholarship in sociology as well.

Like sociologists such as Wirth of the Chicago School before her, Jacobs noted that "cities are, by definition, full of strangers," some of whom are dangerous. She tried to explain what makes it possible for cities to meet the challenge of "assimilating strangers" in such a way that strangers can feel comfortable together. She argued that cities are most habitable when they feature a diversity of uses, thereby ensuring that many people will be coming and going on the streets at any time. When enough people are out and about, Jacobs wrote, "respectable" eyes and ears dominate the street and are fixed on

Ida Robello and her friends in Brooklyn, New York, are examples of the "eyes and ears upon the street" described in *The Death and Life of Great American Cities* by Jane Jacobs. These women have lived on their block near the Gowanus Canal for over fifty years, and they spend nearly every afternoon chatting with each other on the stoop.

strangers, who will thus not get out of hand. Underneath the seeming disorder of a busy street is the very basis for order in "the intricacy of sidewalk use, bringing with it a constant succession of eyes." The more people are out, or looking from their windows at the people who are out, the more their gazes will safeguard the street.

Although Jacobs's ideas seem to cover a broad range of urban situations, there have also been notable exceptions: Only three years after her book was published, for example, a young woman named Kitty Genovese was stabbed to death in Queens, New York, while thirty-eight people watched from their windows (Rosenthal 1999).

It is very common for people to make the mistake of believing that certain principles are natural to social life, only to discover later on that these principles hold up only under particular social conditions. The world has changed a great deal since Jacobs wrote *The Death and Life of Great American Cities*. When Jacobs was writing, most of the people on the sidewalks she discussed were similar in many respects, yet today homeless people, drug users, panhandlers, and others representing economic inequalities, cultural differences, and extremes of behavior can make sidewalk life unpredictable (Duneier 1999). Under these conditions, strangers do not necessarily feel the kind of solidarity and mutual assurance she described. Sociologists today must ask, What happens to urban life when "the eyes and ears upon the street" represent vast inequalities and cultural differences? Do the assumptions Jacobs made still hold up? In many cases the answer is yes, but in other cases the answer is no. More than four decades after her book was published, Jacobs's ideas remain extremely influential.

Joys in the Hood

In her book *The Death and Life of Great American Cities* (1961), the most influential American book ever written on urban planning, Jane Jacobs argued that the undesirable elements of city life—the noise, the energy, the crowding, the complexity—were precisely the elements that created healthy and vibrant communities. Born in Scranton, Pennsylvania, Jacobs managed to graduate high school before leaving for New York City during the Great Depression to become a writer. "Instead of listening in class, I always had something much more interesting I was reading under the desk," Jacobs recalls (Fulford 1997), betraying the rebellious streak that would characterize her future intellectual and professional life. Once in New York, she was so uninspired by coursework at Columbia University that she dropped out, devoting herself full-time to writing and social activism. Throughout her career, Jacobs has been an outspoken critic of urban policies, such as expressways and low-density housing, which speed suburban sprawl and rob communities of their vitality. For a *New York Times Magazine* issue dedicated in the spring of 2000 to exploring the rise of the "suburban nation" in America, Jacobs sat to speak with Mitchell Duneier, one of the authors of this text.

Jane Jacobs

MD: The pioneering urban sociologist says the suburbs are an interesting case study, but she still wouldn't want to live there. You're known as one of the greatest champions of New York City neighborhood life. Why did you leave Greenwich Village for Toronto?

JJ: You know, I wasn't leaving Greenwich Village for Toronto. I was leaving the United States for Canada. And it was because of the Vietnam War, which neither Greenwich Village nor Toronto had anything to do with

instigating. I'm glad I was brought up an American, but I'm not cut out to be a citizen of an empire. And I like it here. I like the civility and politeness. It's not a cruel city.

MD: Was it hard to make the adjustment after life in Greenwich Village?

JJ: It's remarkably like living in Greenwich Village. People think living in Greenwich Village is terribly exotic in some way, but actually, you raise children, you make meals, you feel very good if you can get new curtains for your windows. So the neighborhood I live in is very similar.

MD: It seems that some of the architects and developers in America today, inspired by the ideas in your book *The Death and Life of Great American Cities,* are now experimenting with new ways to build planned

Urbanism and the Created Environment

Whereas the earlier Chicago School of sociology emphasized that the distribution of people in cities occurs naturally, scholars such as Drake and Cayton have countered that this is not true with regard to the black population. They demonstrated

that blacks often did not get to live in neighborhoods they desired, even if their incomes allowed them to do so, because of most subtle and institutional forms of discrimination. More recent theories of the city have stressed that urbanism is not a natural process but has to be analyzed in relation to major patterns of political and economic change.

According to this view, it is not the stranger on the sidewalk communities—communities that look pretty suburban—yet are patterned on mixed-use urban neighborhoods.

JJ: Yeah, I see those.

MD: Have you been to any of them, like Seaside, in Florida?

JJ: No. I've just seen the pictures of them. But where I think the New Urbanism will have the most difference is in in-filling suburbs, which we've been needing to do for a long time. Here we've got all these existing suburbs that—I don't want to say they're no good. There's a lot that they offer that is good. And people are ingenious about the way that they use them.

MD: Ingenious in what ways?

JJ: Lots of people who lost their jobs earlier in the 90s were very valuable, skilled people. And lots of people today have arranged to have home offices. And one thing that has heartened me is how many women in suburbs have their own businesses, performing useful operations that just didn't exist in suburbs before. Some didn't exist anywhere. Some have to do with child care, some have to do with making houses better. Women have almost taken over the real estate business in the suburbs.

MD: And what did you mean by the in-filling of the suburbs?

JJ: There's a lot of underused land that's kind of a nuisance. For instance, all those malls. There are too many of them, and they're too boring. Really, buildings and other facilities could fit into those places. This happened in cities long ago: They had large backyards and side yards, and another house would be put into the backyard. You could get to it from the front yard with its own little walk. Some of the most charming places in Manhattan Island are like that and have been kept. It's a very old urban device. I think it will very likely become a suburban device.

MD: So you're in favor of these new suburban models?

JJ: Well, I'm in favor of lots of choices. There is no way that you can make things by one pattern and satisfy everyone's aspirations. And that's a good thing. Suburbs are among the choices, and there are people who want them. Their children may not want to stay there, but that's O.K. What I object to is that largely through the compulsion of certain financing arrangements, mainly centralized under the government, suburbs of a certain kind have taken way more than their share of choices and the market.

MD: In your new book, *The Nature of Economies,* you use the example of nature to show that diversity is an essential element of economic growth. So what do you make of the phenomenal suburban growth fueled by the relatively specialized new economy?

JJ: You mean like Silicon Valley? It really is a remarkably varied collection of services and suppliers. The businesses that make up a place like Silicon Valley are terribly diverse. The place wouldn't work if it weren't. Everything from temporary workers when places are growing up rapidly to the venture capitalists that are financing the whole thing.

MD: What would you tell people who are concerned about the effects of suburban sprawl on the life of their community?

JJ: There's no reason why anyone should listen to me on suburbs, because I don't especially like suburbs and I don't understand them the way people who live in modern suburbs understand them. And especially if I were to give any suggestions about what should be done with suburbs. That's one of the terrible things that happened to cities. People who not only didn't care about cities, but even hated them, began to prescribe for them. It was disastrous! No matter how well they meant or how much they thought they loved humankind.

SOURCE: Mitchell Duneier, "Questions for Jane Jacobs," *New York Times Magazine,* April 9, 2000.

---

who is most threatening to many urban dwellers, especially the poor; instead, it is the stranger far away, working in a bank or real estate development company, who has the power to make decisions that transform whole blocks or neighborhoods (Logan and Molotch 1987). This focus on the political economy of cities, and on different kinds of strangers, represented a new and critical direction for urban sociology.

HARVEY: THE RESTRUCTURING OF SPACE

Urbanism is one aspect of the **created environment** brought about by the spread of industrial capitalism, according to David Harvey (1973, 1982, 1985). In traditional societies, city and countryside were clearly differentiated. In the modern world, industry blurs the division between city and countryside. Agriculture becomes mechanized and is run according to considerations of price and profit, just like industrial work, and this process lessens the differences in modes of social life between urban and rural people.

In modern urbanism, Harvey points out, space is continually *restructured*. The process is determined by where large firms choose to place their factories, research and development centers, and so forth; the controls that governments operate over both land and industrial production; and the activities of private investors, buying and selling houses and land. Business firms, for example, are constantly weighing the relative advantages of new locations against existing ones. As production becomes cheaper in one area than another, or as the firm moves from one product to another, offices and factories will be closed down in one place and opened up elsewhere. Thus at one period, when there are considerable profits to be made, there may be a spate of office-block building in the center of large cities. Once the offices have been built and the central area redeveloped, investors look for the potential for further speculative building elsewhere. Often what is profitable in one period will not be so in another, when the financial climate changes.

The activities of private home buyers are strongly influenced by how far, and where, business interests buy up land, as well as by rates of loans and taxes fixed by local and central government. After World War II, for instance, there was vast expansion of suburban development outside major cities in the United States. This was partly due to ethnic discrimination and the tendency of whites to move away from inner-city areas. However, it was made possible, Harvey argues, only because of government decisions to provide tax breaks to home buyers and construction firms and by the setting up of special credit arrangements by financial organizations. These provided the basis for the building and buying of new homes on the peripheries of cities and at the same time promoted demand for industrial products such as the automobile.

CASTELLS: URBANISM AND SOCIAL MOVEMENTS

Like Harvey, Manuel Castells (1977, 1983) stresses that the spatial form of a society is closely linked to the overall mechanisms of its development. But in contrast to the Chicago sociologists, Castells sees the city not only as a distinct *location*—the urban area—but as an integral part of processes of **collective consumption**, which in turn are an inherent aspect of industrial capitalism. Homes, schools, transport services, and leisure amenities are ways in which people consume the products of modern industry. The taxation system influences who is able to buy or rent where and who builds where. Large corporations,

banks, and insurance companies, which provide capital for building projects, have a great deal of power over these processes. But government agencies also directly affect many aspects of city life, by building roads and public housing, planning parks, and so forth. The physical shape of cities is thus a product of both market forces and the power of government.

But the nature of the created environment is not just the result of the activities of wealthy and powerful people. Castells stresses the importance of the struggles of underprivileged groups to alter their living conditions. Urban problems stimulate a range of social movements, concerned with improving housing conditions, protesting against air pollution, defending parks, and combating building development that changes the nature of an area. For example, Castells has studied the gay movement in San Francisco, which succeeded in restructuring neighborhoods around its own cultural values—allowing many gay organizations, clubs, and bars to flourish—and gained a prominent position in local politics.

Cities, Harvey and Castells both emphasize, are almost wholly artificial manmade environments, constructed by people. In some ways, the views set out by Harvey and Castells and those of the Chicago School usefully complement each other and can be combined to give a comprehensive picture of urban processes. The contrasts between city areas described in the urban ecology approach do exist, as does the overall impersonality of city life. But these are more variable than the members

The Castro district in San Francisco is not only open but celebratory about its thriving gay and lesbian population.

of the Chicago School believed and are primarily governed by the social and economic influences analyzed by Harvey and Castells. John Logan and Harvey Molotch (1987) have suggested an approach that directly connects the perspectives of authors such as Harvey and Castells with some features of the ecological standpoint. They agree with Harvey and Castells that broad features of economic development, stretching nationally and internationally, affect urban life in a quite direct way. But these wide-ranging economic factors, they argue, are focused through local organizations, including neighborhood businesses, banks, and government agencies, together with the activities of individual house buyers.

Places—land and buildings—are bought and sold, according to Logan and Molotch, just like other goods in modern societies, but the markets that structure city environments are influenced by how different groups of people want to use the property they buy and sell. Many tensions and conflicts arise as a result of this process—and these are the key factors structuring city neighborhoods. For instance, an apartment house is seen as a home by its residents but as a source of income by its landlord. Businesses are most interested in buying and selling property in an area to obtain the best production sites or to make profits in land speculation. Their interests and concerns are quite different from those of residents, for whom the neighborhood is a place to live.

☑ CONCEPT CHECKS

1. How does urban ecology use physical science analogies to explain life in modern cities?
2. What is the urban interaction problem?
3. According to Jane Jacobs, the more people are on the streets, the more likely the street life will be orderly. Do you agree with Jacobs's hypothesis and her explanation for this proposed pattern?

Rural, Suburban, and Urban Life in the United States

What are the main trends that have affected city, suburban, and rural life in the United States over the past several decades? How can we explain patterns including suburban sprawl, the disappearance of traditional rural life, and population declines in central cities and older suburbs? These are

questions we will take up in the following sections. One of the major changes in population distribution in the period since World War II is the movement of large parts of city populations to newly constructed suburbs; this movement outward has been a particularly pronounced feature of American cities and is related directly to central-city decay. At the same time, rural populations have continued to decline as young people seek richer professional and personal opportunities in our nation's large and small cities. We therefore begin with a discussion of rural America and suburbia before moving on to look at the inner city.

The Decline of Rural America?

Rural life has long been the focus of romanticized images among Americans. Close-knit communities and families, stretches of picturesque cornfields, and isolation from social problems such as poverty and crime round out the stereotype of rural life. Yet these stereotypes stand in stark contrast to life in many parts of rural America today. Rural areas of the United States are defined by the Census Bureau as those areas located outside urbanized areas or urban clusters. Rural areas have fewer than 2,500 people and typically are areas where people live in open country. Rural America contains over 75 percent of the nation's land area, yet holds just 17 percent of the total U.S. population (U.S. Bureau of the Census 2004b). For most of the twentieth century, rural communities have experienced significant population losses, despite several modest short-term reversals in the 1970s and the 1990s. Of the 1,346 U.S. counties that shrank in population between 2000 and 2007, 85 percent were located outside metropolitan areas, and 50 percent rely heavily on farming, manufacturing, and mining as their main revenue sources (Mather 2008).

Population losses in rural areas are attributed to declines in farming and other rural industries, high poverty rates, scarce economic opportunities or lifestyle amenities for young people, lack of government services, and—in some regions—a dearth of natural amenities such as forests, lakes, or temperate winters. Population losses are compounded by the fact that most people leaving rural areas are young people, meaning that fewer babies are born to replace the aging population (Johnson 2006). Many rural areas have disproportionately high numbers of older adults, because young persons seek opportunities elsewhere and leave the older persons behind. This phenomenon, called **aging in place**, explains the relatively old populations in rural areas in the Rust Belt and upper Midwest (McGranahan and Beale 2002). Rural areas now face the difficult challenge of attracting and retaining residents and businesses. This is a daunting challenge, though, as many

Population Distribution by Urbanized Areas and Urban Clusters

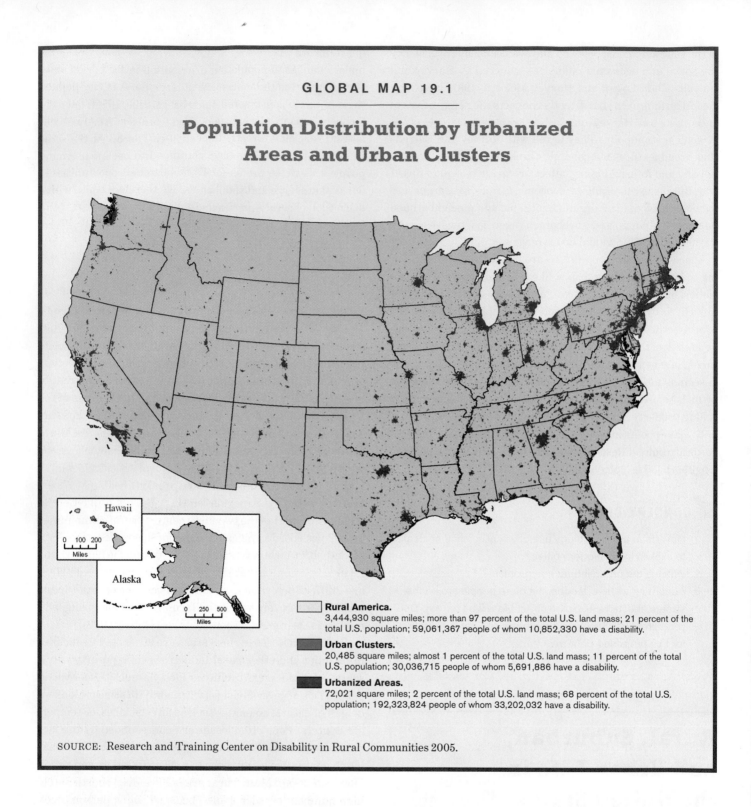

Hawaii

0 100 200
Miles

Alaska

0 250 500
Miles

☐ **Rural America.**
   3,444,930 square miles; more than 97 percent of the total U.S. land mass; 21 percent of the total U.S. population; 59,061,367 people of whom 10,852,330 have a disability.

■ **Urban Clusters.**
   20,485 square miles; almost 1 percent of the total U.S. land mass; 11 percent of the total U.S. population; 30,036,715 people of whom 5,691,886 have a disability.

■ **Urbanized Areas.**
   72,021 square miles; 2 percent of the total U.S. land mass; 68 percent of the total U.S. population; 192,323,824 people of whom 33,202,032 have a disability.

SOURCE: Research and Training Center on Disability in Rural Communities 2005.

rural areas lack the job opportunities or cultural amenities that young people desire.

Yet more troubling than the loss of population in rural areas are concerns about social problems including high levels of child poverty, high rates of motor vehicle fatalities and other accidental deaths, and low levels of health and educational services (Mather 2008). Child poverty is usually perceived as an urban problem, yet 2005 data from the U.S. Census Bureau reveal that of the one hundred counties with the highest child poverty rates, ninety-five are rural. While the national child poverty rate averaged 18.5 in 2005, rates were as high as 70.1 and 61.9 in rural Ziebach County, South Dakota, and Owsley

Joe Peterson and John Baker have coffee in Chugwater, Wyoming. To attract young families, the town is offering plots of land for just $100 to move to the small farming and ranching community.

County, Kentucky. Not all areas are equally likely to be poverty stricken, however. Child poverty rates are highest in the most remote rural counties with the lowest population densities. Race also shapes rural poverty, just as it shapes urban poverty. Rural counties with the highest child poverty rates often are "majority minority" counties, where fewer than 50 percent of the population are non-Hispanic whites. These areas include black-majority counties in the Mississippi Delta and counties in the Midwest and West that have large Native American populations, often dwelling on Indian reservations (O'Hare and Mather 2008).

Despite the challenges facing rural America, many rural sociologists are guardedly optimistic about the future of non-metropolitan life. Some surveys show that Americans would prefer to live in remote areas rather than cities. Technological innovations in transportation and telecommunications afford people flexibility to work away from their urban offices. A number of government programs offer young people financial incentives to serve as teachers or health-care professionals in remote areas, while not-for-profits like Teach for America place young teachers at schools in rural areas. However, such programs are likely to be effective only in attracting workers and businesses to rural areas that have at least some natural or recreational amenities (Johnson 2006).

Suburbanization

THE HISTORY OF SUBURBS

The word *suburb* has its origins in the Latin term *sub urbe*, or "under city control," an appropriate meaning throughout most of the history of urbanism. Suburbs were originally small pockets of dwellings dependent on urban centers for their amenities and livelihood. Today, they are any residential or commercial area adjoining a city, regardless of whether or not they are subject to central-city control. Many suburbs are effectively autonomous areas over which city administrations have little direct influence.

In the United States, **suburbanization**, the massive development and inhabiting of towns surrounding a city, rapidly increased during the 1950s and 1960s, a time of great economic growth. World War II had previously absorbed most industrial resources, and any development outside the war effort was restricted. But by the 1950s, war rationing had ended, automobiles instead of tanks were being mass produced, and people were encouraged to pursue at least one part of the "American dream"—owning a house and a piece of land. During that decade, the population in the cities increased by 10 percent, whereas in the suburban areas it grew by no less than 48 percent.

The prevailing economic scene also facilitated moving out of the city. The Federal Housing Administration (FHA) provided assistance in obtaining mortgage loans, making it possible in the early postwar period for families to buy housing in the suburbs for less than they would have paid for rent in the cities. The FHA did not offer financial assistance to improve older homes or to build new homes in the central areas of ethnically mixed cities; its large-scale aid went only to the builders and buyers of suburban housing. The FHA, together with the Veterans Administration, funded almost half of all suburban housing built during the 1950s and 1960s.

Early in the 1950s, lobbies promoting highway construction launched Project Adequate Roads, aimed at inducing the federal government to support the building of highways. President Eisenhower responded with a giant construction program for interstate roadways, and in 1956, the Highway Act was passed, authorizing $32 billion to be used for building such highways. This coincided with a period of expansion in the automobile industry such that families came to own more than one car; the result was that previously out-of-the-way suburban areas, with lower property taxes, became accessible to places of work. At the same time, the highway program led to the establishment of industries and services in suburban areas themselves. Consequently, the movement of businesses from the cities to the suburbs took jobs in the manufacturing and service industries with them. Many suburban towns became essentially separate cities, connected by rapid highways to the other suburbs around them. From the 1960s on, the proportion of people commuting between suburbs increased more steadily than the proportion commuting to cities.

Scholars are currently debating whether the divide between "suburb" and "city" is meaningful, as many older suburbs, often on the fringes of major cities, share many characteristics that were once hallmarks of city life—including racial, ethnic, and social class diversity. These "first suburbs" or "inner-ring" suburbs are home to an estimated 20 percent of all Americans and include places like Prince George's County, Maryland; Essex County, New Jersey; and Cuyahoga County, Ohio (Puentes and Warren 2006). First suburbs have pockets of poverty (despite generally high levels of household income and wealth among residents), an aging housing stock, old infrastructure, growing populations of immigrants, sizeable populations of older adults who bought their homes when housing prices were still reasonable, and little land left for new development that will generate property-tax revenue. These aging suburbs stand in stark contrast to outer suburbs that have new housing stock, expanses of open land, and populations that tend to be more racially and ethnically homogeneous. As a result, the term *urban area* or *metropolitan area* is increasingly used by researchers to describe regions that encompass central cities and their immediate outskirts.

When social scientists today talk about movement away from cities to suburbs, they are also describing the move from "first suburbs" to newer outer-ring suburbs and to smaller urban areas. A recent report by the Census Bureau found that between 2000 and 2004, eighteen of the nation's largest twenty-five metropolitan areas witnessed population declines. Outflow was heaviest from the New York, Los Angeles, Chicago, and San Francisco/Oakland metropolitan areas.

Inflow was most substantial in counties that are more than forty miles away from metropolitan areas, and to smaller cities, dubbed micropolitan areas—or areas with populations between 10,000 and 49,999 and that have strong commuting networks with neighboring counties. Movement to bedroom communities such as Stroudsburg, Pennsylvania, or retirement communities such as Traverse City, Michigan, reflect several major social forces, including rising housing prices and the aging of the baby boom population. Young families in particular are seeking out places where they can get a good home value yet still commute to their city jobs (U.S. Bureau of the Census 2006a).

Another important change in suburbs today—even outer suburbs—is that more and more members of racial and ethnic minorities are moving there. From 1980 to 1990, the suburban population of blacks grew by 34.4 percent, of Latinos by 69.3 percent, and of Asians by 125.9 percent. In contrast, the suburban white population grew by only 9.2 percent. In the following decade, from 1990 to 2000, the movement of racial and ethnic minority groups to the suburbs slowed, but it remained diverse. The suburban population of blacks grew by 14.2 percent, Latinos by 40 percent, Asians by 45 percent, and whites by 7.6 percent (U.S. Bureau of the Census 1999). This steady increase in minority suburban populations was concentrated in so-called melting-pot metros, or the metropolitan regions of New York, Los Angeles, Chicago, San Francisco, Miami, and other immigrant gateway cities (Frey 2001).

Members of minority groups move to the suburbs for reasons similar to those who preceded them: better housing, schools, and amenities. Like the people who began the exodus to suburbia in the 1950s, they are mostly middle-class professionals. According to the chairman of the Chicago Housing

Suburban Levittown, New York, in the 1950s.

A new housing development in the exurb, Highland, California.

Authority, "Suburbanization isn't about race now; it's about class. Nobody wants to be around poor people because of all the problems that go along with poor people: poor schools, unsafe streets, gangs" (DeWitt 1994).

Nevertheless, the suburbs remain mostly white. Minority groups constituted only 25 percent of the total suburban population and 27 percent of suburban populations in the nation's largest metropolitan areas in 2000, although they accounted for 30 percent of the total U.S. population that year. By contrast, whites accounted for three fourths of the suburban population in 2000 but just over half of the population in central cities (U.S. Bureau of the Census 2000a). Three out of every four African Americans continue to live in the central cities, compared with one in every four whites. Most black suburban residents live in black-majority neighborhoods in towns bordering the city.

While the last several decades saw a movement from the cities to the suburbs, they also witnessed a shift in the regional distribution of the U.S. population from north to south and east to west. As a percentage of the nation's total population, it is estimated that by 2010, the Northeast will have dropped from 25 to 18.1 percent and the Midwest from 29 to 21.8 percent. Meanwhile the population of the South would increase from 30.7 to 36.8 percent and that of the West from 15.6 to 23.4 percent (U.S. Bureau of the Census 2005d).

Urban Problems

Inner-city decay is partially a consequence of the social and economic forces involved in the movement of businesses, jobs, and middle-class residents from major cities to the outlying suburbs since the 1950s. The manufacturing industries that provided employment for the urban blue-collar class largely vanished and were replaced by white-collar service industries. Millions of blue-collar jobs disappeared, and this affected in particular the poorly educated, drawn mostly from minority groups. Although the overall educational levels of minority groups improved over this period, the improvement was not sufficient to keep up with the demands of an information-based economy (Kasarda 1993). William Julius Wilson (1991, 1996) has argued that the problems of the urban underclass grew out of this economic transformation (see Chapter 8).

These economic changes also contributed to increased residential segregation of different racial and ethnic groups and social classes, as we saw in Chapter 11. Discriminatory practices by home sellers, real estate agents, and mortgage lending institutions further added to this pattern of segregation (Massey and Denton 1993). From 1980 to 2000, the share of African Americans in the United States living in predominantly black neighborhoods decreased from 57 to 47 percent. Over the same period, the share of African Americans living in black/Hispanic neighborhoods rose from 18 to 28 percent (Orfield 2000). The decade from 1990 to 2000 has shown a modest decline in the black-white segregation, yet segregation continues to be high among lower income quartiles, the poor, those with less education, and those in service occupations (Iceland, Sharpe, and Steinmetz 2003). The social isolation of minority groups, particularly those in the underclass or "ghetto poor," can escalate urban problems such as crime, lack of economic opportunities, poor health, and family breakdown (Massey 1996).

Adding to these difficulties is the fact that city governments today operate against a background of almost continual financial crisis. As businesses and middle-class residents moved to the suburbs, the cities lost major sources of tax revenue. High rates of crime and unemployment in the city require it to spend more on welfare services, schools, police, and overall upkeep. Yet because of budget constraints, cities are forced to cut back many of these services. A cycle of deterioration develops in which the more suburbia expands, the greater the problems faced by city dwellers become.

Explaining Urban Poverty: The Sociological Debate

The plight of the American inner city has grown bleak in recent times. According to U.S. Census data, the proportion of our nation's poor who live in central cities increased from 34 percent in 1970 to 43 percent in 1990. By 2002, the proportion of the poor living in central cities had dropped slightly to 41 percent (U.S. Bureau of the Census 2003b). Not only are the poor increasingly concentrated in urban areas but the poor living in the inner city are clustered in neighborhoods overwhelmingly inhabited by other poor families. The consequences are that the urban poor—particularly the black urban poor—are living in very poor, socially isolated, racially homogeneous neighborhoods, which are increasingly plagued with troubles such as joblessness, crime, and poor quality of life.

How is it possible that the living conditions of inner-city blacks have taken such a turn for the worse—especially in the three decades that followed the civil rights movement of the 1960s and progressive public policies such as the Fair Housing Act of 1968? Two books on inner-city poverty posit distinct—yet complementary—explanations for the state of urban poverty today. In *When Work Disappears: The World of the New Urban Poor* (1996), sociologist William Julius Wilson argues, as we saw earlier in the chapter, that the loss of jobs is at the root of inner-city decline. Sociologists Douglas S. Massey and Nancy A. Denton, in their book *American Apartheid: Segregation*

Americans on the Move

How many times did your parents move from one residence to another while you were growing up? The United States has a high rate of residential mobility. In 2005–2006, 13.7 percent of Americans changed their place of residence at least once. Of these, over half (62.3 percent) moved to another home within the same county (U.S. Bureau of the Census 2007n). Although this number is no higher than the annual mobility rates of Canada, Australia, and New Zealand, Americans do tend to move more than residents of other industrially developed countries such as France, the United Kingdom, Japan, and Belgium. Yet except for a sharp increase in mobility in the mid-1980s, fueled by recovery from the recession of 1982–1983,

mobility rates in the United States are in long-term decline. In the 1950s and 1960s, approximately twenty out of every hundred Americans moved at least once every year. Mobility rates began to fall in the 1970s and, since the late 1980s, have consistently hovered around 17 percent, falling to lower levels in recent years.

Why do people move? According to a 1991 survey, the most commonly cited reason for moving was to improve one's housing situation: to buy a better home, to make the transition from renting to owning, and so on. Many respondents also cited employment factors as a reason for moving (Gober 1993).

Because many Americans move for job-related reasons, migration patterns tend to reflect regional patterns of economic development. For example, the Northeast and Midwest, long home to much of the nation's industrial manufacturing, have suffered what demographers call an "out-migration" as a result of the deindustrialization of the American economy. Much of the growth in service-sector work and high-tech production has occurred in the South and West, and millions of Americans have left the Northeast and Midwest in search of jobs in these areas. The Midwest has slowly been able to recover from this situation, shifting its economic base to more viable forms of production and thus attracting enough new residents from other regions to counter the out-migration to the South and West. But the Northeast continues to lose residents at a rapid pace. In 2005, the Northeast lost a total of 280,000 residents, while the West gained 112,000 and the South gained 303,000 (U.S. Bureau of the Census 2007n).

and the Making of the Underclass (1993), counter that the persistent poverty among urban blacks in the United States is due primarily to residential segregation.

Wilson's (1987, 1996) position can be described as the "economic restructuring" hypothesis. He argues that persistent urban poverty stems primarily from the structural transformation of the inner-city economy. The decline of manufacturing industries, the "suburbanization" of employment, and the rise of a low-wage service sector have dramatically reduced the number of entry-level jobs that pay wages sufficient to support a family. The high rate of joblessness resulting from economic shifts has led to a shrinking pool of marriageable men (those financially able to support a family). Thus marriage has become less attractive to poor women, unwed childbearing has increased, and female-headed families have proliferated. New generations of children are born into poverty, and the vicious circle is perpetuated. Wilson argues that blacks suffer disproportionately due to past discrimination and because they are concentrated in locations and occupations particularly affected by economic restructuring.

It is all too easy to view these demographic shifts as the result of natural and inevitable long-term processes: High-tech and service-sector work comes to account for a greater share of the gross national product (GNP), these industries naturally spring up in the South and West, making the regions attractive even for traditional manufacturing firms that wish to relocate, and the Northeast is depopulated.

A better explanation begins with—of all things— globalization. As globalization has proceeded, a number of important transformations have taken place in the economic sector. Changes in the financial infrastructure have made it easier for investors to put their money into enterprises anywhere on the globe, and corresponding improvements in communications technology, transportation, and managerial practices have made it more practical for businesses to move their production sites to wherever their costs will be minimized. Capital, economists and sociologists say, has become increasingly mobile under the influence of globalization.

Whereas the mobility of capital sometimes translates into American firms shifting the site of their production to the developing world, in other cases it means that firms will open in or relocate to regions of this country where their production costs will be low. All else being equal, if unions are strong in one region and weak in another, firms are more likely to do business in the region with the weak unions, because they will be able to get away with paying lower wages. Firms also prefer to operate in cities and states that are eager for new development and likely to grant substantial tax breaks. In general, state and local governments in the South and West have been more willing than governments in the Northeast to grant tax breaks to firms, and unions tend to be weaker in these regions than in the Northeast. These factors—in addition to cheaper land and energy—have helped pull some firms out of the Northeast and into the South and West, and have encouraged many startup firms to set up shop in the South and West. Although the dynamics involved are clearly complex, globalization and

the mobility of capital appear to lie behind recent trends in regional economic development and therefore underlie key patterns in regional migration.

Should attempts be made to halt these changes? What would migration patterns look like if unions were strong in all regions and if cities and states refused to grant generous tax breaks to corporate America? Is the depopulation of the Northeast a good or bad thing?

Wilson elaborated that these economic changes were accompanied by an increase in the spatial concentration of poverty within black neighborhoods. This new geography of poverty, he felt, was due in part to the civil rights movement of the 1960s, which provided middle-class blacks with new opportunities outside the ghetto. The out-migration of middle-class families from ghetto areas left behind a destitute community lacking the institutions, resources, and values necessary for success in postindustrial society. He also acknowledges that such neighborhoods lack locally available training and education and have suffered from the dissolution of government and private support of local organizations that once supplied job information as well as employment opportunities. Thus the urban underclass arose from a complex interplay of civil rights policy, economic restructuring, and a historical legacy of discrimination.

While Wilson emphasizes macro-level economic shifts as the cause underlying the concentration of urban poverty, Massey and Denton support the "racial residential segregation" hypothesis. This view holds that high levels of racial

B.W. Cooper housing residents jump rope outside their apartments in New Orleans, Louisiana. Before Hurricane Katrina, B.W. Cooper held about 1,000 families and was the city's largest housing project, but it is now more than 80 percent empty.

Massey and Wilson are two of the leading sociologists of the past fifty years. From the standpoint of many Americans who would see both of their arguments as supporting the same progressive political agenda, it would not matter whether poverty was caused by segregation or joblessness. Either cause requires a major shift in political priorities and a significant role for the U.S. government in solving the problem. In their political sympathies, Wilson and Massey have a tremendous amount in common, so why has their debate been so fierce?

The answer is that one of their highest shared priorities is the scientific goal of explanation. Each of them is trying to explain the root causes of the contemporary ghetto. But ultimately, they have a great deal in common. Both of them agree that if you are poor, the neighborhood you live in has a major effect on your life chances, above and beyond other aspects of your life. These "neighborhood effects" must be addressed, regardless of how they came into being.

The Ghetto as a Sociohistorical Problem

Thus far, we have used the word *ghetto* without defining it. What are ghettos, and how did ghettoized poverty influence the results of the disaster in New Orleans? Many people mistakenly believe that ghettos are where African Americans or Latinos live, but the word *ghetto* derives from the Italian *ghet,* and the first ghettos were in Venice and Rome in the fourteenth century. Created by Pope Paul IV and later by Pope Pius V, as a way of isolating Jews from the mainstream Christian societies in which they lived, the first ghettos were associated with the Jews, and certainly not blacks or Latinos as is the case in the contemporary United States.

Sociologists originally drew a distinction between ghettos on the one hand and slums on the other. Ghettos were residential zones where particular groups were forced to live. The people who lived in these zones were not necessarily impoverished but simply of a particular ethnic or racial group who were viewed as inferior and in need of being forcibly cordoned off by the wider society. Slums were zones inhabited by poor people, including members of a dominant, nonstigmatized race such as poor whites in the United States. In recent years, many sociologists have started using the terms *ghettos* and *slums* interchangeably, but it is better to retain the analytical clarity inherent in the former distinction.

A crucial criterion for the definition of the ghetto is that the people who live there must have been forced to do so. Indeed, this was the situation of blacks in the United States and Jews in Rome. In the United States, blacks were forced to live in certain parts of the Northern cities because of restrictive covenants

residential segregation may increase minority poverty by limiting access to employment opportunities. Segregation in ghettos exacerbates employment problems because it leads to weak informal employment networks and contributes to the social isolation of individuals and families, thereby reducing their chances of acquiring the skills, including adequate educational training, that facilitate mobility in a society. Because no other group in society experiences the degree of segregation, isolation, and poverty concentration that African Americans do, African Americans are far more likely to be disadvantaged when they have to compete with other groups in society for resources and privileges.

Massey and Denton argue further that in the absence of residential segregation, the structural and economic changes observed by Wilson would not have produced the disastrous social and economic consequences observed in inner cities during the past thirty years. Although rates of black poverty were driven up by the economic dislocations Wilson identifies, it was segregation that confined the higher levels of deprivation to a small number of densely settled, tightly packed, and geographically isolated areas.

Massey and Denton (1993) also dispute Wilson's claim that concentrated poverty arose because the civil rights revolution allowed middle-class blacks to move out of the ghetto. Their principal objection to Wilson's focus on middle-class outmigration is that focusing on the flight of the black middle class deflects attention from the "real issue, which is the limitation of black residential options through segregation."

The debate between Wilson and Massey and Denton highlights an important aspect of sociology—namely, that many of its leading practitioners are trying to think like scientists.

that made it illegal to sell them land in certain neighborhoods. Jews were forced to live in the *ghet* because of a decree by various popes. During the fourteenth century, most Jews were also forced to wear insignias when they traveled outside the zone where they lived, to indicate that they were Jews.

Force or compulsion is a historical rather than a contemporary factor in defining the idea of a ghetto. In other words, whereas the inhabitants of the original ghettos were given but little choice of where they could live, inhabitants of today's ghettos may feel that they live in their highly segregated and impoverished neighborhoods by choice. Sociological studies have demonstrated over and again that when poor people have an opportunity to move they will often resist every chance to do so. This is not because they do not want to improve their life chances, but because they do not believe their lives would be better independent of the social networks and neighborhood institutions that sustain them.

Are ghettos necessarily zones for the economically marginalized and exploited populations of stigmatized people? Whereas the U.S. ghetto was used to warehouse a significant labor supply for growing factories during the two World Wars, the Jewish ghetto of Venice did not originally seem to have such a mission. Jews were very successful, and they continued to have significant economic ties to the wider society long after they were ghettoized (Stow 2000). Ultimately, laws were enacted that made it difficult for Jews to carry on their occupations, but these were not intrinsic to ghettoization.

There have been many ghettos in the history of the world, but there are no sociological studies that compare ghettos in more than a few societies. For this reason, there is still much to know about the characteristics that would define the ghetto concept. From what we know, it is a residential zone in which stigmatized racial or religious groups are compelled to live by the wider society.

This takes us to an example in the contemporary United States. When Hurricane Katrina struck New Orleans, Louisiana, in August 2005, the victims of the floods that ravaged the city in the storm's aftermath were mainly poor blacks who lived in the poorest ghettos of the city. Why were these poor people disproportionately affected by the extreme weather conditions? The answer has mainly to do with the social and political history of these particular residential zones, which were always given fewer resources for drainage and pumping systems after past storms. It also has to do with the limited resources that poor people have to evacuate and the limited networks they have outside the zones where they live, especially consisting of people who have the resources to help them. By contrast with the poor blacks who were trapped inside the ghettos as they flooded, many middle-class whites had the resources and social connections to leave the city when warnings first appeared on the national news. The effect of Hurricane Katrina followed the fault lines of the larger urban problems associated with racial segregation and ghettoization in the inner cities today, a subject we return to later in this chapter.

Urban Renewal and Gentrification

Urban decay is not wholly a one-way process; it can stimulate countertrends, such as **urban renewal**, or **gentrification**. Dilapidated areas or buildings may become renovated as more affluent groups move back into cities. Such a renewal process is called gentrification because those areas or buildings become upgraded and return to the control of the urban "gentry"— high-income dwellers—rather than remaining in the hands of the poor.

Does gentrification of a run-down inner-city area necessarily result in the dispossession of the existing population, or do renewed interest and an infusion of money in such areas promote a revitalization that works to their advantage? Not long ago, Clinton Street was a graffiti-ridden streetscape (*top*), but it has evolved into a lively restaurant row on New York's Lower East Side (*bottom*).

"Detroit Declared Most Dangerous U.S. City"

etroit, Michigan, was named the "most dangerous" city in the United States in 2007, according to a study published by CQ Press, a unit of the Congressional Quarterly. Television news anchors announced in worried tones that the Motor City was unsafe and that it had recently surpassed St. Louis, Missouri, to earn the dubious distinction of the most crime-ridden city in the nation. City rankings have important implications for the health of American cities; families and businesses may choose to locate in—or flee—specific urban areas based on their crime statistics. For this reason, rankings are not to be taken lightly. Just days after the CQ Press study was widely reported by the media, a group of criminologists and sociologists condemned the study on methodological grounds. Michael Tonry, president of the American Society of Criminology (ASC) and professor of law and public policy at the University of Minnesota, said "these rankings represent an irresponsible misuse of data and do groundless harm to many communities" (Earthtimes.org 2007).

What exactly did the CQ Press find? Since 1994, the organization has generated an annual list of the "safest" and

"most dangerous" cities in the United States. The fourteenth annual *City Crime Rankings: Crime in Metropolitan America* calculated its rankings based on Federal Bureau of Investigation (FBI) statistics. Their analysis was limited to U.S. cities with populations of 75,000 or more and focused on the per-capita rates for homicide, rape, robbery, aggravated assault,

burglary, and auto theft. A per-capita rate means the number of crimes committed divided by the number of persons residing in that city. The study calculated crime rates for each city and assigned each a summary score, with zero representing the national average.

Based on these rankings the most dangerous cities (in order) were Detroit (with a score of 407); St. Louis (with a score of 406); Flint, Michigan; Oakland, California;

Camden, New Jersey; and Birmingham, Alabama. The five safest cities were Mission Viejo, California (scoring minus 82); Clarkstown, New York; Brick Township, New Jersey; Amherst, New York; and Sugar Land, Texas (CNN 2007).

Not surprisingly, these rankings are dismissed by the mayors and law enforcement officials of the cities topping the "most dangerous" list. Detroit police officials released a statement disputing the report, saying it failed to put general crime statistics into a proper context (CNN 2007). These criticisms are more than just sour grapes. The critiques reveal serious problems with how the statistics are calculated, according to Richard Rosenfeld, a professor of criminology and criminal justice at the University of Missouri–Saint Louis. As noted earlier, a crime rate equals the number of crime victims (numerator) divided by the city population (the denominator). If a suburban resident is a crime victim while visiting an urban area, then the victim is added to the numerator but not the denominator of the equation. This artificially inflates the crime rate in communities where the central city population is substantially smaller than its neighboring suburbs, explained Rosenfeld.

In *Streetwise: Race, Class, and Change in an Urban Community* (1990), sociologist Elijah Anderson analyzed the effect of gentrification on cities. Although the renovation of a neighborhood generally increases its value, it rarely improves the living standards of its current low-income residents, who are usually forced to move out. In the Philadelphia neighborhood that Anderson studied, close to the ghetto, many black residences

were condemned, forcing over one thousand people to leave. Although they were told that their property would be used to build low-cost housing that they would be given the first opportunity to buy, large businesses and a high school now stand there.

The poor residents who continued to live in the neighborhood received some benefits in the form of improved schools and police protection, but the resulting increase in taxes and

Rates also are misleading because they fail to consider important characteristics of a city's population, such as its age distribution. For instance, a city that has a very large number of eighteen- to thirty-four-year-old men might have a higher per-capita crime rate than a city with a very large number of sixty-five- to seventy-four-year-old women, because younger men are more likely than older women to both commit crimes and be crime victims.

The study also failed to consider the specific nature of the crimes committed in specific cities, thus sending the message that crime is random—and thus likely to strike innocent bystanders or tourists. For example, the Detroit police department noted that the vast majority of shootings in their city are drug related and not random. A further problem is that not all cities were considered in the CQ report; cities such as Chicago and Minneapolis were dropped because their data were incomplete.

Finally, the ratings do not address the critical point that cities are heterogeneous. One neighborhood may have a very high crime rate, while another has a very low crime rate. "Differences in crime rates are far greater within cities than between them," according to Rosenfeld (2007). The CQ Press rankings also suggest that all people are equally likely to be a crime victim in a given city if that city happens to have a high crime rate. Rosenfeld countered, "knowing the city in which a person lives reveals next to nothing about his or her crime risk, especially when compared with genuine risk factors such as age and lifestyle. People who spend their evenings outside of the home are at a far greater risk than the homebodies," he suggested.

Rosenfeld's critique meshes closely with that of major organizations like the ASC and the FBI. In an official statement, the ASC cautioned that the CQ Press rankings "fail to account for the main conditions affecting crime rates, the mismeasurement in crime, large community differences in crime within cities, and the factors affecting individuals' crime risk" (Earthtimes.org 2007). The ASC also approved a resolution opposing the development of city crime rankings from FBI Uniform Crime Reports (UCRs). The U.S. Conference of Mayors passed a similar measure and committed itself to working with both the FBI and the U.S. Department of Justice to "educate reporters, elected officials, and citizens on what the UCR data mean and don't mean" (Earthtimes.org 2007).

Even the FBI itself posted a disclaimer on its Web site, denouncing the CQ Press rankings. The Web site notice read, "these rough rankings provide no insight into the numerous variables that mold crime.... Valid assessments are possible only with careful study and analysis of the range of unique conditions affecting each local law enforcement jurisdiction." The ASC concurs that such rankings are not helpful and in fact may hurt already vulnerable American cities: "city crime rankings make no one safer, but they can harm the cities they tarnish and divert attention from the individual and community characteristics that elevate crime in all cities" (Earthtimes.org 2007).

Questions

- According to the CQ Press report, what are the five most dangerous cities in the United States? The five safest?
- What is a crime rate, and how is it calculated?
- What are three methodological critiques of the CQ reports?
- Do you believe city crime rankings are valuable sources of information? Why or why not?

FOR FURTHER EXPLORATION

CNN. 2007. "Experts Say 'Most Dangerous City' Rankings Twist Numbers." *CNN* (November 18, 2007). www.cnn.com/2007/US/11/18/dangerous.cities.ap/ (accessed January 21, 2008).

Earthtimes.org. 2007. "Criminologists Condemn City Crime Rankings." Earthtimes.org (November 16, 2007). www.earthtimes.org/articles/printpressstory.php?news=226260 (accessed January 21, 2008).

Federal Bureau of Investigation. 2006. Caution Against Ranking. www.fbi.gov/ucr/cius2006/rankingmessage.htm (accessed January 21, 2008).

Rosenfeld, Richard. 2007. "Why City Crime Rankings Offer a Misleading Picture." *USA Today* (November 2007). http://blogs.usatoday.com/oped/2007/11/why-city-crime.html.

USA Today. 2007. "Detroit Declared Most Dangerous U.S. City." *USA Today* (November 18, 2007). www.usatoday.com/news/nation/2007-11-18-dangerous-cities_N.htm (accessed January 21, 2008).

rents also forced them to leave for a more affordable neighborhood, most often deeper into the ghetto. African American residents Anderson interviewed expressed resentment at the influx of "yuppies," whom they held responsible for the changes that drove the poorer people away.

The white newcomers had come to the city in search of cheap "antique" housing, closer access to their city-based jobs, and a trendy urban lifestyle. They professed to be "open minded" about racial and ethnic differences; in reality, however, little fraternizing took place between the new and old residents unless they were of the same social class. Because the African American residents were mostly poor and the white residents were middle class, class differences were compounded by racial ones. Though some middle-class blacks lived in the area, most chose to live far from the ghetto, fearing that otherwise they would receive the same treatment that whites reserved for the black underclass. Over time, the neighborhood was gradually transformed into a white middle-class enclave.

It is important to note that the process of gentrification parallels another trend discussed earlier: the transformation of the urban economy from a manufacturing to a service-industries base. Addressing the concerns of the victims of these economic changes is critical for the survival of the cities.

☑ CONCEPT CHECKS

1. Describe at least two problems facing rural America today.
2. Why did so many Americans move to suburban areas in the 1950s and 1960s?
3. What is a "first" or "inner-ring" suburb? What traits does it share with urban areas? With suburbs?
4. What are the two unintended consequences of urbanization? How do they deepen socioeconomic and racial inequalities?

Cities and Globalization

In premodern times, cities were self-contained entities that stood apart from the predominantly rural areas in which they were located. Road systems sometimes linked major urban areas, but travel was a specialized affair for merchants, soldiers, and others who needed to cross distances with any regularity. Communication between cities was limited. The picture at the start of the twenty-first century could hardly be more different. Globalization has had a profound effect on cities by making them more interdependent and encouraging the proliferation of horizontal links between cities across national borders. Physical and virtual ties between cities now abound and global networks of cities are emerging.

Some people have predicted that globalization and new communications technology might lead to the demise of cities as we know them. This is because many of the traditional functions of cities can now be carried out in cyberspace rather than in dense and congested urban areas. For example, financial markets have gone electronic, e-commerce reduces the need for both producers and consumers to rely on city centers, and telecommuting permits a growing number of employees to work from home rather than in an office building.

Yet, thus far, such predictions have not been borne out. Rather than undermining cities, globalization is transforming them into vital hubs within the global economy. Urban centers have become critical in coordinating information flows, managing business activities, and innovating new services and technologies. There has been a simultaneous dispersion and concentration of activity and power within a set of cities around the globe (Castells 1996).

Global Cities

The role of cities in the new global order has been attracting a great deal of attention from sociologists. Globalization is often thought of in terms of a duality between the national level and the global, yet it is the largest *cities* of the world that make up the main circuits through which globalization occurs (Sassen 1998). The functioning of the new global economy is dependent on a set of central locations with developed informational infrastructures and a hyperconcentration of facilities. It is in such points that the "work" of globalization is performed and directed. As business, production, advertising, and marketing assume a global scale, there is an enormous amount of organizational activity that must be done in order to maintain and develop these global networks.

Saskia Sassen has been one of the leading contributors to the debate on cities and globalization. She uses the term **global city** to refer to urban centers that are home to the headquarters of large, transnational corporations and a superabundance of financial, technological, and consulting services. In *The Global City* (1991), Sassen bases her work on the study of three such cities: New York, London, and Tokyo. The contemporary development of the world economy, she argues, has created a novel strategic role for major cities. Most such cities have long been centers of international trade, but they now have four new traits:

1. They have developed into command posts—centers of direction and policy making—for the global economy.
2. Such cities are the key locations for financial and specialized service firms, which have become more important in influencing economic development than is manufacturing.
3. They are the sites of production and innovation in these newly expanded industries.
4. These cities are markets on which the "products" of financial and service industries are bought, sold, or otherwise disposed of.

New York, London, and Tokyo have very different histories, yet we can trace comparable changes in their nature over the past two or three decades. Within the highly dispersed world economy of today, cities like these provide for central control of crucial operations. Global cities are much more than simply places of coordination, however; they are also contexts of production. What is important here is not the production of material goods, but the production of the specialized services required by business organizations for administering offices and factories scattered across the world, and the production of financial innovations and markets. Services and financial goods are the "things" the global city makes.

The downtown areas of global cities provide concentrated sites within which whole clusters of "producers" can work in close interaction, often including personal contact, with one another. In the global city, local firms mingle with national and multinational organizations, including a multiplicity of foreign companies. Thus 350 foreign banks have offices in New York City, plus 2,500 other foreign financial corporations; one out of every four bank employees in the city works for a foreign bank. Global cities compete with one another, but they also constitute an interdependent system, partly separate from the nations in which they are located.

Other authors have built on Sassen's work, noting that as globalization progresses, more and more cities are joining New York, London, and Tokyo in the ranks of the global cities. Castells has described the creation of a tiered hierarchy of world cities—with places such as Hong Kong, Singapore, Chicago, Frankfurt, Los Angeles, Milan, Zurich, and Osaka serving as major global centers for business and financial services. Beneath these, a new set of regional centers is developing as key nodes within the global economy. Cities such as Madrid, São Paulo, Moscow, Seoul, Jakarta, and Buenos Aires are becoming important hubs for activity within the so-called emerging markets.

Inequality and the Global City

The new global economy is highly problematic in many ways. Nowhere can this be seen more clearly than in the new dynamics of inequality visible within the global city. The central business district juxtaposed with impoverished inner-city areas in many global cities should be seen as interrelated phenomena, as Sassen and others remind us. The growth sectors of the new economy—financial services, marketing, high technology—are reaping profits far greater than any found within traditional economic sectors. As the salaries and bonuses of the very affluent continue to climb, the wages of those employed to clean and guard their offices are dropping. Sassen (1998) argues that we are witnessing the "valorization" of work located at the forefront of the new global economy and the "devalorization" of work that occurs behind the scenes.

Disparities in profit-making capabilities are expected in market economies, but the magnitude of the disparities in the

The city of Los Angeles has taken steps to dissuade the homeless from sleeping in public places. Notice that the bench pictured here is not long enough for a person to stretch out on and that the shape and placement of the slats would make it quite uncomfortable for any extended period of time.

new global economy is having a negative effect on many aspects of the social world, from housing to the labor market. Those who work in finances and global services receive high salaries, and the areas where they live become gentrified. At the same time, orthodox manufacturing jobs are lost, and the very process of gentrification creates a vast supply of low-wage jobs—in restaurants, hotels, and boutiques. Affordable housing is scarce in gentrified areas, forcing an expansion of low-income neighborhoods. Whereas central business districts are the recipients of massive influxes of investment in real estate, development, and telecommunications, marginalized areas are left with few resources.

Within global cities, a geography of "centrality and marginality" is taking shape—as Mitch Duneier's (1999) study in New York's Greenwich Village revealed. Alongside resplendent affluence there is acute poverty. Yet although these two worlds coexist side by side, the actual contact between them can be surprisingly minimal. As Mike Davis (1990) noted in his study of Los Angeles, there has been a "conscious 'hardening' of the city surface against the poor." Accessible public spaces have been replaced by walled compounds, neighborhoods guarded by electronic surveillance, and "corporate citadels." In Davis's (1990) words:

To reduce contact with untouchables, urban redevelopment has converted once vital pedestrian streets into traffic sewers and transformed public parks into temporary receptacles for the homeless and wretched. The American city . . . is being systematically turned inside out—or, rather, outside in. The valorized spaces of the new megastructures and super-malls are concentrated in the center, street frontage is denuded, public activity is sorted into strictly functional compartments, and circulation is internalized in corridors under the gaze of private police.

According to Davis, life is made as "unliveable" as possible for the poorest and most marginalized residents of Los Angeles. Benches at bus stops are short or barrel-shaped to prevent people from sleeping on them, the number of public toilets is fewer than in any other North American city, and sprinkler systems have been installed in many parks to deter the homeless from living in them. Police and city planners have attempted to contain the homeless population within certain regions of the city, but in periodically sweeping through and confiscating makeshift shelters, they have effectively created a population of "urban bedouins."

☑ CONCEPT CHECKS

1. Discuss the effects of globalization on cities.
2. What are the four main characteristics of global cities?

Urbanization in the Developing World

Between 1920 and 2007, the world's urban population increased from about 270 million to 3.3 billion, and roughly half of the world's population now live in cities (UNDP 2008). Between 2007 and 2050, the global urban population is expected to increase as much as it has since 1920, by 3.1 billion—bringing the total urban population to more than 6 billion, or roughly 70 percent of the world population in 2050. Levels of urbanization vary by region, yet the majority of residents in all continents are expected to live in urban areas by 2050. Developed nations now have the highest levels of urbanization today, surpassing 80 percent in Australia, New Zealand, and North America in 2007. Europe is the least urbanized major area in the developed world, with just 72 percent of its population living in urban areas. Among the less developed regions, Latin America and the Caribbean each has a very high level of urbanization (78 percent)—higher than Europe. By contrast, Africa and Asia remain mostly rural, with 38 percent and 41 percent of their populations, respectively, living in urban areas. However, given the very large population of Asia, half of the world's urban population lived in Asia in 2007, while an additional 16 percent lived in Europe.

In coming decades, levels of urbanization are expected to rise even higher, with Africa and Asia urbanizing more rapidly than other nations. By 2050, an estimated 54 percent of the world's urban population will be concentrated in Asia, with 19 percent in Africa. As Global Map 19.2 shows, most of the twenty-five cities projected to have more than ten million residents in 2015 are located in the developing world. Most people in developed countries already live in cities. In 2000, 75 percent of the population of developed countries lived in cities, yet by 2030, 83 percent of people living in developed countries are anticipated to live in cities (United Nations Population Division 2002).

Manuel Castells (1996) refers to **megacities** as one of the main features of third-millennium urbanization. They are defined not by their size alone—although they are vast agglomerations of people—but also by their role as connection points between enormous human populations and the global economy. Megacities are intensely concentrated pockets of activity through which politics, media, communications, finances, and production flow. According to Castells, megacities function as magnets for the countries or regions in which they are located. People are drawn toward large urban areas for various reasons; within megacities are those who succeed in tapping into the global system and those who do not. Besides serving as nodes in the global economy, megacities also become "depositories of all these segments of the population who fight to survive." These "pulls" to urban life are supported by

The overcrowded streets of the Hong Kong–Guangdong megacity.

The Twenty-Five Urban Areas Expected to Have More Than Ten Million Inhabitants in 2015

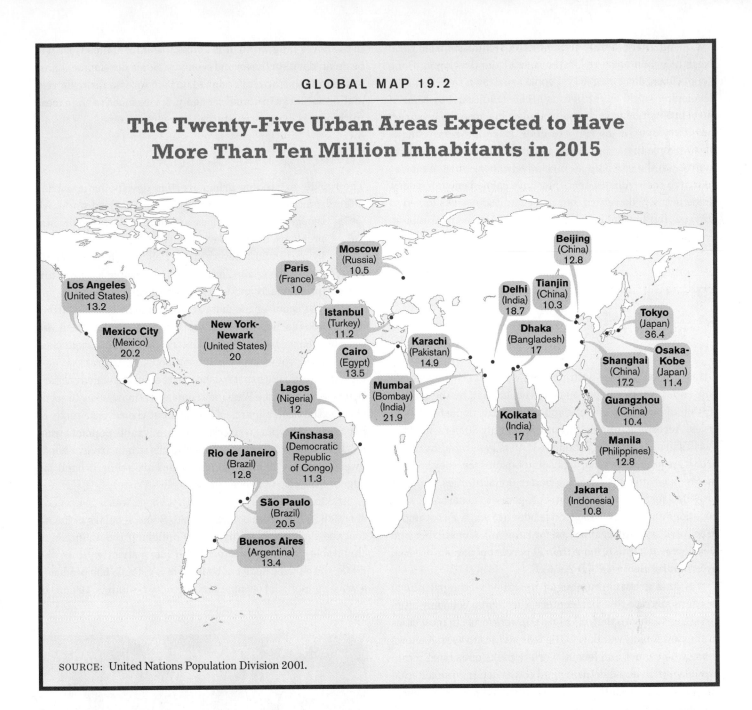

Moscow (Russia) 10.5

Paris (France) 10

Beijing (China) 12.8

Los Angeles (United States) 13.2

Delhi (India) 18.7

Tianjin (China) 10.3

Istanbul (Turkey) 11.2

Tokyo (Japan) 36.4

Mexico City (Mexico) 20.2

New York-Newark (United States) 20

Cairo (Egypt) 13.5

Karachi (Pakistan) 14.9

Dhaka (Bangladesh) 17

Osaka-Kobe (Japan) 11.4

Shanghai (China) 17.2

Lagos (Nigeria) 12

Mumbai (Bombay) (India) 21.9

Guangzhou (China) 10.4

Kolkata (India) 17

Rio de Janeiro (Brazil) 12.8

Kinshasa (Democratic Republic of Congo) 11.3

Manila (Philippines) 12.8

São Paulo (Brazil) 20.5

Jakarta (Indonesia) 10.8

Buenos Aires (Argentina) 13.4

SOURCE: United Nations Population Division 2001.

countless empirical studies. Average urban incomes are higher than those in rural areas. Urban dwellers also have better access to public services, including education, health, transportation, communication, water supply, sanitation, and waste management. Because of economies of scale, cities are better equipped to efficiently and cheaply provide such services to large, concentrated populations (UNDP 2008).

Yet why is the rate of urban growth in the world's less developed regions so much higher than elsewhere? According to United Nations projections, the urban share is likely to rise from 75 to 81 percent in more developed countries and from 44 to 56 percent in less developed countries (UNFPA 2008).

Two factors in particular must be taken into account. First, rates of population growth are higher in developing countries than they are in industrialized nations. Although fertility rates tend to be lower in urban areas than rural areas worldwide, the higher overall fertility rates in developing versus developed nations account for the more rapid urban growth in those nations. Thus, urban growth is fueled by high fertility rates among people already living in cities. In the 1980s, natural increase (or the difference between birth and death rates) accounted for more than 70 percent of all urban growth in an estimated one quarter of African nations and one half of Asian nations (UNDP 2008).

Second, there is widespread *internal migration* from rural areas to urban ones—as in the case of the developing Hong Kong–Guangdong megacity. People are drawn to cities in the developing world either because their traditional systems of rural production have disintegrated or because the urban areas offer superior job opportunities. Rural poverty prompts many people to try their hand at city life. They may intend to migrate to the city only for a relatively short time, aiming to return to their villages once they have earned enough money. Some actually do return, but most find themselves forced to stay, having for one reason or another lost their position in their previous communities.

Challenges of Urbanization in the Developing World

ECONOMIC IMPLICATIONS

Urbanization carries both positive and negative economic consequences. Urbanization is driven, in part, by the concentration of both employment and investment opportunities in cities. According to some estimates, roughly 80 percent of the world's gross domestic product (GDP) is generated by urban areas. As cities draw more jobs and businesses, they become magnets for migrants seeking better opportunities, and they provide a fertile setting for entrepreneurs to generate new innovations and use technology in productive ways. For example, in countries of the Organisation for Economic Cooperation and Development (OECD), more than 81 percent of patents are filed by urban residents (OECD 2006).

Yet as a growing number of unskilled and agricultural workers migrate to urban centers, the formal economy often struggles to absorb the influx into the workforce. In most cities in the developing world, it is the *informal economy* that allows those who cannot find formal work to make ends meet. From casual work in manufacturing and construction to small-scale trading activities, the unregulated informal sector offers earning opportunities to poor or unskilled workers.

Informal economic opportunities are important in helping thousands of families (and women, especially) to survive in urban conditions, but they have problematic aspects as well. The informal economy is untaxed and unregulated. It is also less productive than the formal economy. Countries where economic activity is concentrated in this sector fail to collect much-needed revenue through taxation. The low level of productivity also hurts the general economy—the proportion of the GDP generated by informal economic activity is much lower than the percentage of the population involved in the sector.

The OECD estimates that a billion new jobs will be needed by 2025 to sustain the estimated population growth in cities in the developing world. It is unlikely that all of these jobs will be created within the formal economy. Some development analysts argue that attention should be paid to formalizing or regulating the large informal economy, where much of the excess workforce is likely to cluster in the years to come.

ENVIRONMENTAL CHALLENGES

The rapidly expanding urban areas in developing countries differ dramatically from cities in the industrialized world. Although cities everywhere are faced with environmental problems, those in developing countries are confronted by particularly severe risks. Pollution, housing shortages, inadequate sanitation, and unsafe water supplies are chronic problems for cities in less developed countries.

Housing is one of the most acute problems in many urban areas. Cities such as Calcutta, India, and São Paulo, Brazil, are massively congested; the rate of internal migration is much too high for the provision of permanent housing. Migrants crowd into squatters' zones that mushroom around the edges of cities. In urban areas in the West, newcomers are most likely to settle close to the central parts of the city, but the reverse tends to happen in developing countries, where migrants populate what has been called the "septic fringe" of the urban areas. Shanty dwellings made of burlap or cardboard are set up around the edges of the city wherever there is a little space.

In São Paulo, it is estimated that there was a 5.4 million shortfall in habitable homes in 1996. Some scholars estimate that the shortage is as high as 20 million, if the definition of "habitable housing" is interpreted more strictly. Since the 1980s, the chronic deficit of housing in São Paulo has produced a wave of unofficial occupations of empty buildings. Groups of

Families sit on the sidewalk with their belongings after being evicted by police from a central São Paulo building. Hundreds of squatters had settled in São Paulo buildings until, facing forced eviction by riot police, they were compelled to leave.

unhoused families initiate mass squats in abandoned hotels, offices, and government buildings. Many families believe that it is better to share limited kitchen and toilet facilities with hundreds of others than to live on the streets or in *favelas,* the makeshift shantytowns on the edges of the city. Still, 40 percent of the population live in *favelas* (Barcelona Field Studies Centre 2003).

City and regional governments in less developed countries are hard pressed to keep up with the spiraling demand for housing. In cities such as São Paulo there are disagreements among housing authorities and local governments about how to address the housing problem. Some argue that the most feasible route is to improve conditions within the *favelas*—to provide electricity and running water, pave the streets, and assign postal addresses. Others fear that makeshift shantytowns are fundamentally uninhabitable and should be demolished to make way for proper housing for poor families.

Congestion and overdevelopment in city centers lead to serious environmental problems in many urban areas. Mexico City is a prime example. About 94 percent of Mexico City consists of built-up areas, with only 6 percent of land being open space. The level of green spaces—parks and open stretches of green land—is far below that found in even the most densely populated North American or European cities. Pollution is a major problem, coming mostly from the cars, buses, and trucks that pack the inadequate roads of the city, the rest deriving from industrial pollutants. It has been estimated that living in Mexico City is equivalent to smoking forty cigarettes a day. In March 1992, pollution reached its highest level ever. Whereas an ozone level of just under 100 points was deemed "satisfactory" for health, in that month the level climbed to 398 points. The government had to order factories to close down

Newspaper salesman Alvarado uses a mask to protect himself from air pollution as he sells papers at a busy crossroad in Mexico City. Behind him a screen indicates the day's pollution levels.

for a period, schools were shut, and 40 percent of cars were banned from the streets on any one day. The city did not meet acceptable air quality standards for ozone limits 209 days in 2006. Yet, this was a substantial improvement from 304 days in 1994.

SOCIAL EFFECTS

Urban areas are increasingly distinguished by a vast social and economic divide between the haves and the have nots, with poor people bearing the brunt of the negative aspects of urbanization (UNDP 2008). Overall, urban residents, even in developing nations, tend to fare better than rural dwellers along a host of outcomes, including infant and child mortality rates, adult health and mortality, and access to effective birth control and reproductive health services. Better urban public infrastructure, higher levels of maternal education, and better access to health care in cities are responsible for these health advantages. However, for poor urban dwellers, especially in developing nations, neighborhoods are overcrowded and social programs underresourced. Poverty is widespread, and existing social services cannot meet the demands for health care, family planning advice, education, and training.

Because of stark income inequalities in urban areas, especially in developing nations, the plight of the urban poor is growing worse and the size of the urban poor population is growing more rapidly than the overall urban population. Because of high housing costs, poor people in cities often have little choice but to live in overcrowded slums, where sanitation and water facilities are inadequate. The UN-Habitat estimates that more than a billion persons lived in urban slums in 2007, and every one in three city dwellers will live in inadequate housing, with no or few basic services. The largest proportion of urban slum dwellers can be found in Asia (581 million), followed by sub-Saharan Africa (199 million) and Latin America and the Caribbean (134 million) (Moreno and Waran 2006). The pressures of urban living also are associated with increasing prevalence of chronic diseases (including cardiovascular disease, cancers, and diabetes) and accidents. Traffic accidents, in particular, are growing as a cause of injury or death in cities. Unhealthy behaviors also are thriving in urban areas. Growing consumption of fats and sweeteners in the more urbanized developing countries are contributing to high levels of obesity and cardiovascular disease (UNDP 2008).

The unbalanced age distribution in developing countries adds to their social and economic difficulties. Compared to industrialized countries, a much larger proportion of the population in the developing world is under the age of fifteen. A youthful population needs support and education, and during that time its members would not be economically productive. But many developing countries lack the resources to provide

Why are obesity and cardiovascular disease on the rise in urban communities?

universal education. When their families are poor, many children must work full time, and others have to eke out a living as street children, begging for whatever they can. Poor urban children fare worse than more well-off urban children and rural children in terms of health, are more likely to be underweight, and are less likely to receive important vaccinations. These disadvantages experienced by children in urban slums set off lifelong patterns of disadvantage. When the street children mature, most become unemployed, homeless, or both.

The Future of Urbanization in the Developing World

In considering the scope of the challenges facing urban areas in developing countries, it can be difficult to see prospects for change and development. Conditions of life in many of the world's largest cities seem likely to decline even further in the years to come. But the picture is not entirely negative.

First, although birthrates remain high in many countries, they are likely to drop in the years to come as urbanization proceeds. This in turn will feed into a gradual decrease in the rate of urbanization itself. In West Africa, for example, the rate of urbanization should drop to 3.4 percent per year by 2020, down

from an annual rate of over 4.5 percent growth over the previous three decades (United Nations Population Division 2002).

Second, globalization is presenting important opportunities for urban areas in developing countries. With economic integration, cities around the world are able to enter international markets, to promote themselves as locations for investment and development, and to create economic links across the borders of nation-states. Globalization presents one of the most dynamic openings for growing urban centers to become major forces in economic development and innovation. Indeed, many cities in the developing world are already joining the ranks of the world's global cities.

Third, migrants to urban areas are often positively "selected" in terms of traits such as higher levels of educational attainment. Thus, migration may be beneficial to those persons who find better work opportunities, and for their families who benefit from remittances—or the money that the migrant workers send back home. Urban migration may also provide opportunities for educated women in developed nations who face obstacles in rural areas, thereby giving them access to jobs outside the home and contributing to their empowerment.

☑ CONCEPT CHECKS

1. Urban growth in the developing world is much higher than elsewhere. Discuss several economic, social, and environmental consequences of such rapid expansion of cities in developing nations.

World Population Growth

There are currently an estimated 6.6 billion people in the world. It was estimated that "baby number 6 billion" was born on October 12, 1999, although of course no one can know when and where this event happened. Paul Ehrlich (Fremlin 1964) calculated in the 1960s that if the rate of population growth at that time continued, nine hundred years from now (not a long period in world history as a whole) there would be 60,000,000,000,000,000 (60 quadrillion) people on the face of the earth. There would be one hundred people for every square yard of the earth's surface, including both land and water. The physicist J. H. Fremlin (1964) speculated that housing such a population would require a continuous two-thousand-story building covering the entire planet. Even such a mammoth structure would have only three or four yards of floor space per person.

Such a picture, of course, is nothing more than nightmarish fiction designed to drive home how cataclysmic the consequences of continued population growth would be. The real issue is what will happen over the next thirty or forty years, by which time, if current trends are not reversed, the world's population will already have grown to unsustainable levels. Partly because governments and other agencies heeded the warnings of Ehrlich and others twenty years ago by introducing population-control programs, there are grounds for supposing that world population growth is beginning to trail off. And population control policies, especially China's one-child policy, have been so effective in reducing birthrates that policy makers now fear that China will not have a large enough pool of young people to care for their aging parents in future decades. Estimates calculated in the 1960s of the likely world population by the year 2000 turned out to be inaccurate and highly overstated, because these estimates presumed that the high growth rates of the 1960s—topping out at 2.2 percent in 1963—would persist into future decades. The United Nations (2006) estimated the world population would be 6.7 billion in July 2007, compared with some earlier estimates of over 8 billion. Nevertheless, considering that a century ago there were only 1.5 billion people in the world, this still represents growth of staggering proportions. Moreover, the factors underlying population growth are by no means completely predictable, and all estimates have to be interpreted with caution.

Population Analysis: Demography

The study of population is referred to as **demography**. The term was invented about a century and a half ago, at a time when nations were beginning to keep official statistics on the nature and distribution of their populations. Demography is concerned with measuring the size of populations, explaining their rise or decline, and documenting the distribution of such populations both within and across continents, nations, states, cities, and even neighborhoods. Population patterns are governed by three factors: births, deaths, and migrations. Demography is customarily treated as a branch of sociology, because the factors that influence the level of births and deaths in a given group or society, as well as migrations of population, are largely social and cultural.

Much demographic work tends to be statistical and uses large sample surveys as well as official birth and death records. All the industrialized countries today gather and analyze basic statistics on their populations by carrying out censuses (systematic surveys designed to find out about the whole population of a given country). Although rigorous modes of data collection are used, and every effort is made to count each and every person in a population, censuses still are not one hundred percent accurate, nor is every individual in a given sampling frame captured in these surveys. In the United

States, for example, a comprehensive population census every ten years (i.e., the decennial census) and sample studies are regularly conducted. Yet for various reasons, many people are not counted in the official population statistics, including illegal immigrants, homeless people, transients, and others who for one reason or another either did not complete their survey or were not located by census enumerators.

In many developing countries, particularly those with recent high rates of population growth, demographic statistics are much more unreliable. For instance, some demographers have estimated that registered births and deaths in India may represent only about three quarters of the actual totals (Cox 1976). The accuracy of official statistics is believed to be even lower in parts of central Africa.

Basic Demographic Concepts

Among the basic concepts used by demographers, the most important are crude birthrates, fertility, fecundity, and crude death rates. **Crude birthrates** are expressed as the number of live births per year per thousand persons in the population. They are called "crude" rates because of their very general character. Crude birthrates, for example, do not tell us what proportions of a population are male or female, or what the age distribution of a population is (the relative proportions of young and old people in the population). For example, a population made up of only young women would have a higher birthrate than a population of older men. Where statistics are collected that relate birth or death rates to such categories, demographers speak of "specific" rather than "crude" rates. For instance, an age-specific birthrate might specify the number of births per thousand women in the twenty-five- to thirty-four-year-old age group.

If we wish to understand population patterns in any detail, the information provided by specific birthrates is normally necessary. Crude birthrates, however, may be useful for making overall comparisons between different groups, societies, and regions. The crude birthrate in the United States is fourteen per thousand. Other industrialized countries have lower rates, such as eight per thousand in Germany, and ten in Russia and Italy. In many other parts of the world, crude birthrates are much higher. In India, for instance, the crude birthrate is twenty-four per thousand; in Ethiopia it is forty per thousand (Population Reference Bureau 2008a).

Birthrates are an expression of the fertility of women. **Fertility** refers to how many live-born children the average woman has. A fertility rate is usually calculated as the average number of births per thousand women of childbearing age.

Fertility is distinguished from **fecundity**, which means the potential number of children women are biologically capable of bearing. It is physically possible for a normal woman to bear a child every year during the period when she is capable of conception. There are variations in fecundity according to the age at which women reach puberty and menopause, both of which differ among countries as well as among individuals. Although there may be families in which a woman bears twenty or more children, fertility rates in practice are always much lower than fecundity rates, because social and cultural factors limit breeding. Even women in cultures who do not use birth control fail to meet their maximum reproductive potential. For instance, breastfeeding one's newborn infant causes a woman to have amenorrhea (i.e., a cessation of menstruation), and in turn, temporary natural postpartum infertility.

Crude death rates (also called "mortality rates") are calculated in the same way as birthrates—the number of deaths per thousand of population per year. Again, there are major variations among countries, but death rates in many societies in the developing world are falling to levels comparable to those of the West. The death rate in the United States and India in 2007 was eight per thousand. In Ethiopia it was fifteen per thousand. A few countries have much higher death rates. In Sierra Leone, for example, the death rate is twenty-three per thousand due in part to AIDS, warfare, and high infant mortality rates (Population Reference Bureau 2008b). Like crude birthrates, crude death rates provide only a very general index of **mortality** (the number of deaths in a population). Specific death rates give more precise information. Crude death rates can be very misleading, however. For example, the number of deaths per thousand people can be higher for developed nations than in less developed countries, despite standards of health being better in developed countries. This is because developed countries have relatively more older people, who are more likely to die in a given year, so that the overall mortality rate can be higher even if the mortality rate at any given age is lower.

A particularly important specific death rate is the **infant mortality rate**: the number of babies per thousand births in any year who die before reaching age one. One of the key factors underlying the population explosion has been reductions in infant mortality rates. Declining rates of infant mortality are the most important influence on increasing **life expectancy**—that is, the number of years the average person can expect to live. In 1900, life expectancy at birth in the United States was about forty years. Today it has increased to seventy-eight years. This does not mean, however, that most people at the turn of the century died when they were about forty years of age. When there is a high infant mortality rate, as there is in many developing nations, the average life expectancy—which is a statistical average—is brought down by deaths that occurred at age 0 or 0.5 years, for example (Global Map 19.3). If we look at the life expectancy of only those people who survive the first year of life, we find that in 1900 the average person could expect to live

to age fifty-eight. Illness, nutrition, and the influence of natural disasters are the other factors influencing life expectancy. Life expectancy has to be distinguished from **life span**, which is the maximum number of years that an individual could live. Although life expectancy has increased in most societies in the world, life span has remained unaltered. Only a small proportion of people live to be one hundred or more.

Dynamics of Population Change

Rates of population growth or decline are measured by subtracting the number of deaths per thousand over a given period from the number of births per thousand—this is usually calculated annually. Some European countries have negative growth rates—in other words, their populations are declining. Virtually all of the industrialized countries have growth rates of less than 0.5 percent. Rates of population growth were high in the eighteenth and nineteenth centuries in Europe and the United States but have since leveled off. Many developing countries today have rates of between 2 and 3 percent (Global Map 19.4). These may not seem very different from the rates of the industrialized countries, but in fact, the difference is enormous.

The reason is that growth in population is **exponential** rather than arithmetic. An ancient Persian myth helps illustrate this concept. A courtier asked a ruler to reward him for his services by giving him twice as many grains of rice for each service as he had the time before, starting with a single grain on the first square of a chess board. Believing himself to be on to a good thing, the king commanded grain to be brought up from his storehouse. By the twenty-first square, the storehouse was empty; the fortieth square required ten billion grains of rice (Meadows et al. 1972). In other words, starting with one item and doubling it, doubling the result, and so on, rapidly leads to huge figures: 1:2:4:8:16:32:64:128, and so on. In seven operations the figure has risen by 128 percent. Exactly the same principle applies to population growth. We can measure this effect by means of the **doubling time**, the period of time it takes for the population to double. The formula used to calculate doubling time is 70 divided by the current growth rate. For example, a population growth of 1 percent will produce a doubling of numbers in seventy years. At 2 percent growth, a population will double in thirty-five years, while at 3 percent it will double in twenty-three years.

Malthusianism

In premodern societies, birthrates were very high by the standards of the industrialized world today. Nonetheless,

Passengers travel in an overcrowded train in the eastern Indian city of Patna. The Indian railroad, one of the world's largest rail networks, serves over thirteen million people a year and continues to be one of the only forms of affordable transportation available to the majority of Indians.

population growth remained low until the eighteenth century because there was a rough overall balance between births and deaths. Although there were sometimes periods of marked population increase, these were followed by increases in death rates. In medieval Europe, for example, when harvests were bad, marriages tended to be postponed and the number of conceptions fell, while deaths increased. These complementary trends reduced the number of mouths to be fed. No preindustrial society was able to escape from this self-regulating rhythm (Wrigley 1968).

During the rise of industrialism, many looked forward to a new age in which food scarcity would be a phenomenon of the past. The development of modern industry, it was widely supposed, would create a new era of abundance. In his celebrated work *Essay on the Principle of Population* (2003; orig. 1798), Thomas Malthus criticized these ideas and initiated a debate about the connection between population and food resources that continues to this day. At the time Malthus wrote, the population in Europe was growing rapidly. Malthus pointed out that whereas population increase is exponential, food supply depends on fixed resources that can be expanded only by developing new land for cultivation. Population growth therefore tends to outstrip the means of support available. The inevitable outcome is famine, which, combined with the influence of war and plagues, acts as a natural limit to population increase. Malthus predicted that human beings would always live in circumstances of misery and starvation, unless they practiced what he called "moral restraint." His cure for excessive population growth was for people to delay marriage and to strictly limit their frequency of sexual intercourse. (The use of contraception he proclaimed to be a "vice.")

For a while, **Malthusianism** was ignored, because the population development of the Western countries followed a quite different pattern from that which he had anticipated—as we shall see below. Rates of population growth trailed off in the nineteenth and twentieth centuries. Indeed, in the 1930s there were major worries about population decline in many industrialized countries, including the United States. Malthus also failed to consider that technological developments that foster increases in food production would develop in the modern era. However, the upsurge in world population growth in the twentieth century has again lent some credence to Malthus's views, although few support them in their original version. Population expansion in developing countries seems to be outstripping the resources that those countries can generate to feed their citizenry—especially in nations that suffered from natural disasters including droughts and floods that hurt local food supplies.

The Demographic Transition

Demographers often refer to the changes in the ratio of births to deaths in the industrialized countries from the nineteenth century onward as the **demographic transition**. The notion was first worked out by Warren S. Thompson (1929), who described a three-stage process in which one type of population stability would be eventually replaced by another as a society reached an advanced level of economic development.

Stage one refers to the conditions characteristic of most traditional societies, in which both birthrates and death rates are high and the infant mortality rate is especially large. Population grows little if at all, as the high number of births is more or less balanced by the level of deaths. Stage two, which began in Europe and the United States in the early part of the nineteenth century—with wide regional variations—occurs when death

Life Expectancies in Global Perspective, 2002

The United States presently ranks eighteenth in the world in life-expectancy rates—low among Western nations, but considerably higher than most Second World and developing nations. How much of a correlation do you find between life expectancy and income level?

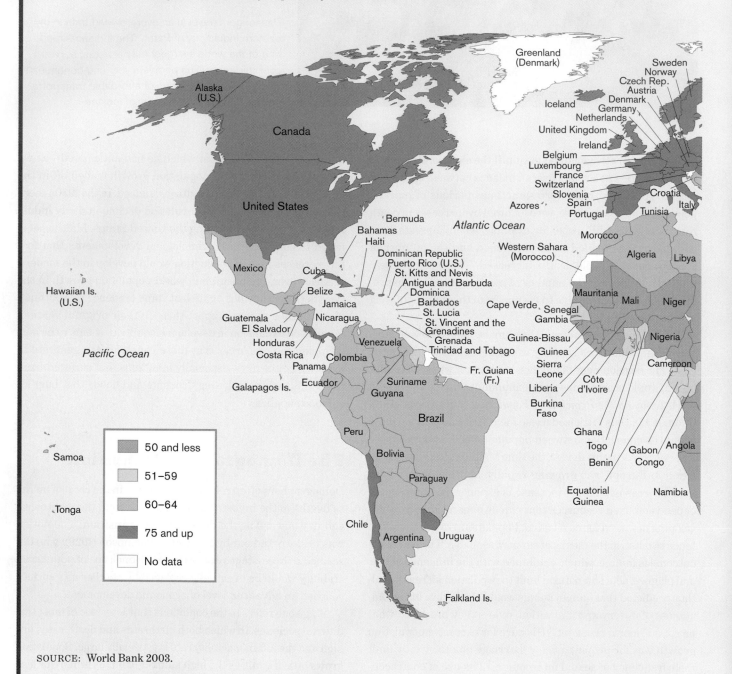

Legend:
- 50 and less
- 51–59
- 60–64
- 75 and up
- No data

SOURCE: World Bank 2003.

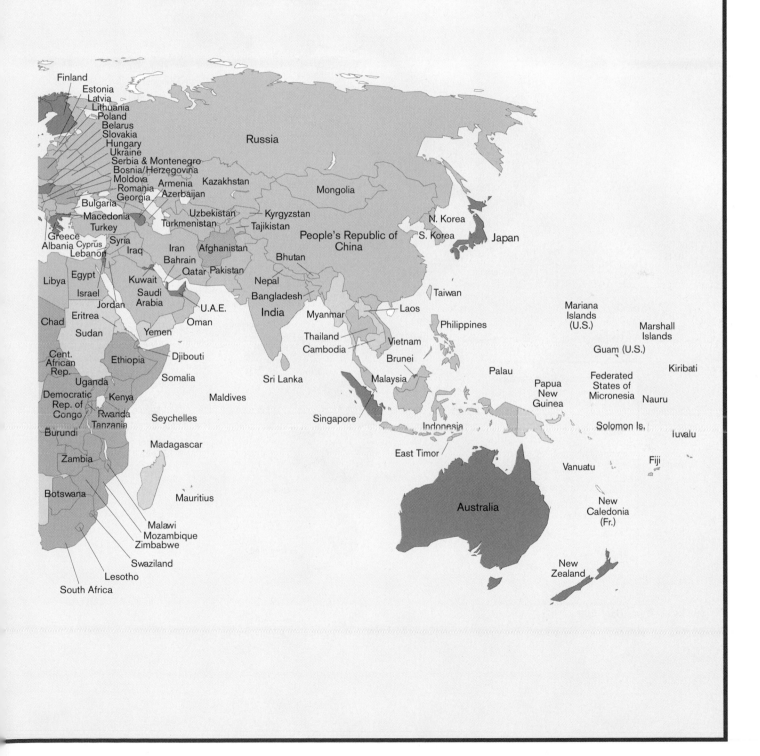

Population Growth Rate, 1980–2002

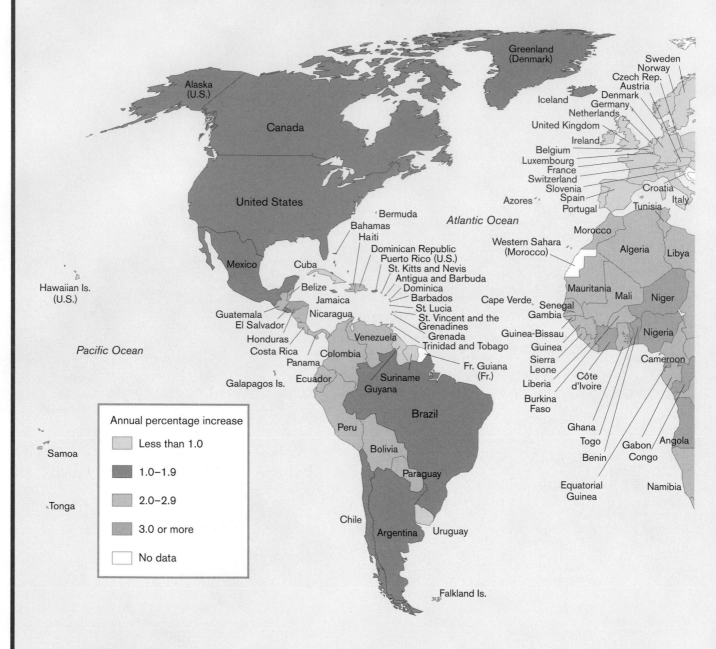

Annual percentage increase

- Less than 1.0
- 1.0–1.9
- 2.0–2.9
- 3.0 or more
- No data

SOURCE: World Bank 2003.

rates fall while fertility remains high. This is, therefore, a phase of marked population growth. It is subsequently replaced by stage three, in which, with industrial development, birthrates drop to a level such that population is again fairly stable.

Demographers do not fully agree about how this sequence of change should be interpreted, or how long lasting stage three is likely to be. Fertility in the Western countries has not been completely stable over the past century or so; considerable differences in fertility remain among the industrialized nations, as well as between classes or regions within them. Nevertheless, it is generally accepted that this sequence accurately describes a major transformation in the demographic character of modern societies.

In recent decades, demographers have debated whether a **"second demographic transition"** has begun. Under this new model, fertility rates may continue to fall because of shifts in family structure. Key influences on the second demographic transition include delayed marriage, delayed childbearing, rising rates of cohabitation, and high, steady rates of divorce. The last two patterns arguably lead to lower birthrates, because most women prefer not to conceive a child when they are cohabiting or are divorced (and thus between relationships). As a result, women may be more "vigilant" about their contraception, and thus birthrates will remain low among increasingly large numbers of unmarried persons (deKaa 2003).

The theories of demographic transition directly oppose the ideas of Malthus. Whereas for Malthus, increasing prosperity would automatically bring about population increase, the thesis of demographic transition emphasizes that economic development, generated by industrialism, would actually lead to a new equilibrium of population stability.

Prospects for Change

Fertility remains high in developing-world societies because traditional attitudes to family size have been maintained. Having large numbers of children is often still regarded as desirable, providing a source of labor on family-run farms. Some religions either are opposed to birth control or affirm the desirability of having many children. Contraception is opposed by Islamic leaders in several countries and by the Catholic Church, whose influence is especially marked in South and Central America. The motivation to reduce fertility has not always been forthcoming even from political authorities. In 1974, contraceptives were banned in Argentina as part of a program to double the population of the country as fast as possible; this was seen as a means of developing its economic and military strength.

Yet a decline in fertility levels has at last occurred in some large developing countries. An example is China, which currently has a population of about 1.3 billion people—almost a quarter of the world's population as a whole. In 1979, the Chinese government established one of the most extensive programs of population control that any country has undertaken, with the object of stabilizing the country's numbers at close to their current level. The government instituted incentives (such as better housing and free health care and education) to promote single-child families, whereas families who have more than one child face special hardships (wages are cut for those who have a third child). China's antinatal policies have effectively transformed the Chinese population. During the 1950s, China had a total fertility rate (TFR) of roughly 6 children per woman. TFR refers to the average number of babies a woman will give birth to in her life, if she conforms to current age-specific fertility rates (ASFRs) through her lifetime. China's TFR fell to about 2.4 by 1990, and demographers pin the current TFR at roughly 1.6 to 1.9.

Despite the success of the program in lowering birthrates and stemming population growth, the Chinese government and citizens have recognized the potentially harmful unintended consequences of the policy. Chinese population officials now fear that the current low birthrate means that the country will not have sufficient numbers of adult children to care for their aging parents in future decades. Low numbers of youthful workers also mean that the nation may ultimately lack the economic resources to provide formal (and costly) services for its burgeoning elderly population. The policy has had another major unintended consequence that has potentially dire implications for China's future: expectant parents who are eager to have an only son have been aborting female fetuses, or putting up their first-born infant daughters for adoption. As a result, social observers fear that a highly skewed sex ratio—where men outnumber women—will lead to low rates of marriage among the least "desirable" men and high levels of antisocial behavior among these socially unconnected men.

Furthermore, the policy is at odds with normative beliefs; most young couples in China still view a two-child family as the proper family. China's program also demands a degree of centralized government control that is either unacceptable or unavailable in most other developing countries. In India, for instance, many schemes for promoting family planning and the use of contraceptives have been tried but with only relatively little success. To date, India has maintained noncoercive policies. For example, the National Population Policy (NPP 2000) focuses on offering information, resources, and reproductive health services to citizens so that they can make informed, voluntary choices (National Commission on Population, Government of India, 2000). India in 1988 had a population of 789 million. In 2000, its population just topped 1 billion. And even if its population-growth rate does diminish, by 2050, India will be the most populous country in the world, with over 1.5 billion people.

Some claim that the demographic changes that will occur over the next century will be greater than any before in all of human history. It is difficult to predict with any precision the rate at which the world population will rise, but the United Nations (UN) has several fertility scenarios. The "high" scenario places the world's population at more than 16 billion people by 2150! The "medium" fertility scenario, which the UN deems most likely, assumes that fertility levels will stabilize at just over two children per woman, resulting in a world population of 10.8 billion people in 2150 (UN 2003).

This overall population increase conceals two distinct trends. First, most developing countries will undergo the process of demographic transition described above. This will result in a substantial surge in the population, as death rates fall. India and China are each likely to see their populations reach 1.5 billion people. Areas in Asia, Africa, and Latin America will similarly experience rapid growth before the population eventually stabilizes.

The second trend concerns the developed countries that have already undergone the demographic transition. These societies will undergo very slight population growth, if any at all. Instead, a process of aging will occur in which the number of young people will decline in absolute terms and the older segment of the population will increase markedly. This will have widespread economic and social implications for developed countries. First, the **dependency ratio** will increase; this refers to the ratio of the number of economically dependent members of the population to the number of economically productive members. Economically dependent persons are those considered too young or old to work, typically those under age fifteen and over age sixty-five. Productive members of society are those of working age, typically ages fifteen through sixty-four. As the dependency ratio increases, pressure will mount on health and social services. Yet, as their numbers grow, older people will also have more political weight and may be able to push for higher expenditures on programs and services of importance to them.

What will be the consequences of these demographic changes? Some observers see the makings of widespread social upheaval—particularly in the developing countries undergoing demographic transition. Changes in the economy and labor markets may prompt widespread internal migration as people in rural areas search for work. The rapid growth of cities will be likely to lead to environmental damage, new public-health risks, overloaded infrastructures, rising crime, and impoverished squatter settlements.

Famine and food shortages are another serious concern. There are already 842 million people in the world who suffer from hunger or undernourishment (United Nations Food and Agriculture Organization [UN FAO] 2003). In some parts of the world, more than a third of the population are undernourished (Figure 19.1). As the population rises, levels of food output will need to rise accordingly to avoid widespread scarcity. Yet this scenario is unlikely; many of the world's poorest areas are particularly affected by water shortages, shrinking farmland, and soil degradation—processes that reduce, rather than enhance, agricultural productivity. It is almost certain that food production will not occur at a level to ensure self-sufficiency. Large amounts of food and grain will need to be imported from areas where there are surpluses. According to the UN FAO (Nikos 1995), by 2010 industrialized countries will be producing 1,614 pounds of grain per person, compared to only 507 pounds per head in the developing world.

Technological advances in agriculture and industry are unpredictable, so no one can be sure how large a population the world might eventually be able to support. Yet even at current population levels, global resources may already be well below those required to create living standards in the less developed world comparable to those of the industrialized countries.

☑ CONCEPT CHECKS

1. What is the difference between fertility and fecundity?
2. Explain Malthus's position on the relationship between population growth and the food supply.
3. Describe the stages of the demographic transition.
4. What is life expectancy? How does it differ from life span?

Population, Industrialization, and the Environment

Since the beginning of the practice of agriculture thousands of years ago, human beings have left an imprint on nature. Hunting and gathering societies mainly lived from nature; they existed on what the natural environment provided and made little attempt to change the world around them. With the coming of agriculture, this situation was altered. For crops to grow, land must be cleared, trees cut down, and encroaching weeds and wild foliage kept at bay. Even primitive farming methods can lead to soil erosion. Once natural forests are cut down and clearings made, the wind may blow away the topsoil. The farming community then clears some fresh plots of land, and so the process goes on. Some landscapes that we today think

FIGURE 19.1

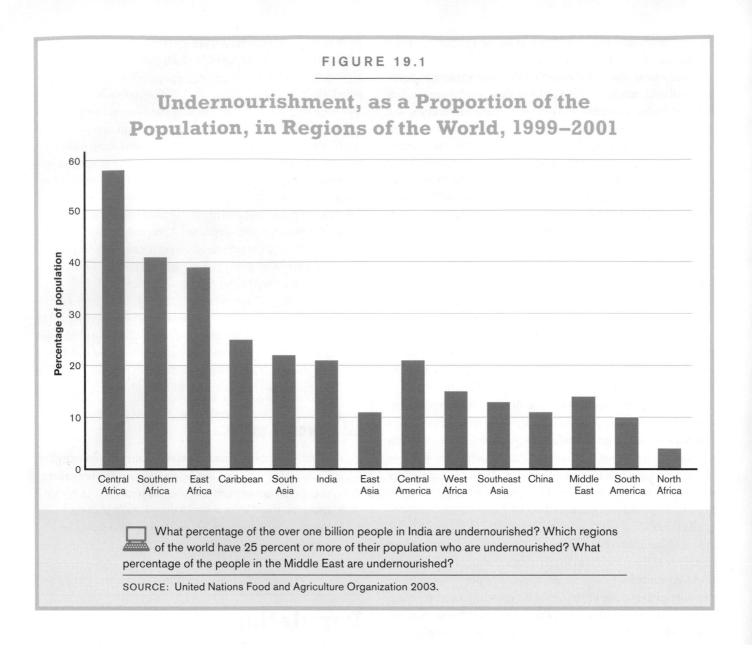

Undernourishment, as a Proportion of the Population, in Regions of the World, 1999–2001

What percentage of the over one billion people in India are undernourished? Which regions of the world have 25 percent or more of their population who are undernourished? What percentage of the people in the Middle East are undernourished?

SOURCE: United Nations Food and Agriculture Organization 2003.

of as natural, such as the rocky areas and scrubland in southwestern Greece, are actually the result of soil erosion created by farmers five thousand years ago.

Yet before the development of modern industry, nature dominated human life far more than the other way around. Today the human onslaught on the environment is so intense that few natural processes are uninfluenced by human activity. Nearly all cultivable land is under agricultural production. What used to be almost inaccessible wildernesses are now often nature reserves, visited routinely by thousands of tourists. Modern industry, still expanding worldwide, has led to steeply climbing demands for sources of energy and raw materials. Yet the world's supply of such energy sources and raw materials is limited, and some key resources are bound to run out if global

consumption is not restricted. Even the world's climate, as we shall see, has probably been affected by the global development of industry.

The Environment: A Sociological Issue?

Why should the environment be a concern for sociologists? Aren't we talking of issues that are the province purely of scientists or technologists? Isn't the effect of human beings on nature a physical one, created by modern technologies of industrial production? Yes, but modern industry and technology have come into being in relation to distinctive social institutions. The origins of our effect on the environment are social, and so are many of its consequences.

Much of the debate surrounding the environment and economic development hinges on the issue of consumption patterns. Consumption refers to the goods, services, energy, and resources that are used up by people, institutions, and societies. It is a phenomenon with both positive and negative dimensions. On the one hand, rising levels of consumption around the world mean that people are living under better conditions than in times past. Consumption is linked to economic development—as living standards rise, people are able to afford more food, clothing, personal items, leisure time, vacations, cars, and so forth. On the other hand, consumption can have negative impacts as well. Consumption patterns can damage the environmental resource base and exacerbate patterns of inequality. As we saw in Chapter 9 ("Global Inequality"), the gap between rich and poor in the world has grown during the recent decades. To take one measure, the average per-person consumption of goods and services in the world's least developed economies grew only half as fast as in advanced industrial economies between 1975 and 2005 (slightly less than one percent per year, in comparison with two percent per year). The poorest region of the world, sub-Saharan Africa, actually experienced economic decline: Per-person consumption shrank by a half a percent per year during the period. Even in East Asia, the world's fastest-growing region (where growth averaged more than six percent per year), significant inequalities emerged within countries such as China (UNDP 2007).

Finally, although the rich are the world's main consumers, the environmental damage that is caused by growing consumption has the heaviest effect on the poor. The wealthy are in a better position to enjoy the many benefits of consumption without having to deal with its negative effects. On a local level, affluent groups can usually afford to move away from problem areas, leaving the poor to bear most of the costs. Chemical plants, power stations, major roads, railways, and airports are often sited close to low-income areas. On a global level, we can see a similar process at work: Soil degradation, deforestation, water shortages, lead emissions, and air pollution are all concentrated within the developing world. Poverty also intensifies these environmental threats. People with few resources have little choice but to maximize the resources that are available to them. As a result, more and more pressures are put on a shrinking resource base as the human population increases.

Rescuing the global environment will thus mean social as well as technological change. Given the vast global inequalities that exist, there is little chance that the poor developing countries will sacrifice their own economic growth because of environmental problems created largely by the rich ones. Yet the earth does not seem to possess sufficient resources for

Kids play on a merry-go-round near an oil refinery at the Carver Terrace housing project playground in west Port Arthur, Texas. Port Arthur sits squarely on a two-state corridor routinely ranked as one of the country's most polluted regions.

everyone on the planet to live at the standard of living most people in the industrialized societies take for granted. Hence if the impoverished sectors of the world are to catch up with the richer ones, the richer ones likely will have to revise their expectations about constant economic growth. Some "green" or environmental advocates argue that people in the rich countries must react against consumerism and return to more simple ways of life if global ecological disaster is to be avoided.

Global Environmental Threats

One problem we all face concerns environmental **ecology**. The spread of industrial production may already have done irreparable damage to the environment. Ecological questions concern not only how we can best cope with and contain environmental damage but also the very ways of life within industrialized societies. According to one popular Web site, Global Footprint, if all people on earth were to somehow achieve the standard of living of the average American, it would require seven planets to feed, clothe, shelter, and provide the countless consumer items that make up what most of us consider a decent life. While such calculations are perhaps somewhat fanciful, the overall message is not: our current path—whether as a nation or as all humanity—is no longer sustainable. Technological progress is, of course, unpredictable, and it may be that the earth will in fact yield sufficient resources to permit global industrialization without resulting in irreversible ecological changes to the planet. At the moment, however, this does not seem feasible, and if the developing countries are to achieve living standards comparable to those currently enjoyed in the West, global readjustments will be necessary.

BIODIVERSITY

According to World Conservation Union (WCU), the most widely accepted authoritative source, more than 16,306 species are currently threatened with extinction. Hundreds of animal species have already become extinct even since the 1950s. On a list of 41,415 species that are being actively monitored by the WCU one out of every four mammals, one in eight birds, and nearly three quarters of all plants are endangered. From gorillas to coral, human population growth, urbanization, and industrialization are resulting in rapid deforestation, threatening biodiversity everywhere on the planet. The loss of biodiversity, in turn, means more to humans than the loss of natural habitat—although many would agree with the nineteenth-century American writer Hendry David Thoreau's spiritual musing, "In wilderness lies the preservation of the world." Biodiversity also provides humans with new medicines and sources and varieties of food and plays a role in regulating atmospheric and oceanic chemistry. The World Conservation Union, which draws on the support of the governments of 140 different countries, more than 800 nongovernmental organizations, and some 10,000 scientists and experts from around the world, concludes its 2007 report with these chilling words: "Life on Earth is disappearing fast and will continue to do so unless urgent action is taken" (International Union for Conservation of Nature 2007).

Global environmental threats are of several basic sorts: pollution, the creation of waste that cannot be disposed of in the short term or recycled, and the depletion of resources that cannot be replenished. The amount of domestic waste—what goes into our garbage cans—produced each day in the industrialized societies is staggering; these countries have sometimes been called the "throw-away societies" because the volume of items discarded as a matter of course is so large. For instance, food is mostly bought in packages that are thrown away at the end of the day. Some of these can be reprocessed and reused, but most cannot. Some kinds of widely employed plastics simply become unusable waste; there is no way of recycling them, and they have to be buried in garbage dumps. Or to take another example, the disposal of electronic waste—computers, mobile phones, MP-3 players, and the host of toys and gadgets that contain electronic circuits—is a growing problem. Discarded electronics, which contain toxins that cause cancer and

A worker at an e-waste recycling company in Bangalore, India, shows shredded pieces of printed circuit boards of obsolete electronic gadgets undergoing recycling process. E-waste is a growing environmental and public health concern as the world becomes more wired and companies introduce new products at a faster pace.

other illnesses, are routinely "recycled" to landfills in China, India, and other poor countries, where there are few if any safeguards against contaminating local watersheds, farmlands, and communities.

Global green movements and parties (such as Friends of the Earth, Greenpeace, or Conservation International) have developed in response to the new environmental hazards. Although green philosophies are varied, a common thread concerns taking action to protect the world's environment, conserve rather than exhaust its resources, and protect the remaining animal species.

GLOBAL WARMING

When environmental analysts speak of waste materials, however, they mean not only goods that are thrown away but also gaseous wastes pumped into the atmosphere. Examples are the carbon dioxide released into the atmosphere by the burning of fuels such as oil and coal in cars and power stations and gases released into the air by the use of such things as aerosol cans, material for insulation, and air-conditioning units. Carbon dioxide is the main influence on the process of global warming that many scientists believe is occurring, while the other gases attack the ozone layer around the earth.

Global warming is thought to happen in the following way. The buildup of carbon dioxide in the earth's atmosphere functions like the glass of a greenhouse. It allows the sun's rays to pass through but acts as a barrier to prevent them from passing back. The effect is to heat up the earth; global warming is sometimes termed the "greenhouse effect" for this reason. There is no longer any question but that human activities play a key role in global warming. In 2007 the Intergovernmental Panel on Climate Change (IPCC) issued its fourth assessment since 1990 on the state of the planet's climate. The IPCC—a blue-ribbon group of scientists created by the United Nations Environment Program and its World Meteorological Organization in 1988—took the planet's temperature, and found it to be rapidly rising.

The IPCC report concluded that "warming of the planet is unequivocal, as is now evident from observations of increases in global average air and ocean temperatures, widespread melting of snow and ice, and rising global average sea level" (IPCC 2007). The report noted that eleven of the last twelve years were the warmest on record, and that Northern Hemisphere temperatures during the second half of the twentieth century were likely the highest in the past thirteen centuries—or longer. Rising temperatures were resulting in the rapid shrinking of arctic icecaps, along with mountain glaciers; long-term droughts in some regions, with greater rainfall in others; an increase in hurricane activity in the north Atlantic; and in general more turbulence in global weather. Most significantly, the IPCC report stated unequivocally that human activity is the principal source of global warming, very likely causing most of the temperature increase over the last century. It found, for example, that human-caused global greenhouse gas emissions have grown since the industrial revolution, increasing 70 percent in the past several decades alone (IPCC 2007).

The U.S. government, which had generally refused to accept as conclusive the link between human activity and global warming, finally joined more than 100 other countries in accepting the report's conclusions (Rosenthal and Revkin 2007). In recognition of its work, the IPCC—along with former U.S. vice president Al Gore, whose Academy Award–winning film *An Inconvenient Truth* popularized the issue of global warming—received the 2007 Nobel Peace Prize.

Why should global warming matter? Apart from requiring American snowboarders to travel much farther north for good conditions, won't rising temperatures result in more moderate climates in most places? The IPCC report documents the many dangers that global warming will bring. Apart from severe droughts—which will turn once-fertile lands into deserts—global warming will threaten the water supplies of hundreds of millions of people, increase the danger of flooding for others, adversely affect agriculture in parts of the world, and further reduce planetary biodiversity. It will likely have devastating consequences for low-lying areas, as melting polar ice caps—particularly in Greenland and the Antarctic—lead to rising sea levels. Cities that lie near the coasts or in low-lying areas will be flooded and become uninhabitable. Under some scenarios, for example, most of Florida disappears beneath the rising seas; a number of South Sea islands have already been affected. The IPCC specifically identified the following impacts as likely:

> warming greatest over land and at most high northern latitudes and least over Southern Ocean and parts of the North Atlantic Ocean, continuing recent observed trends
>
> contraction of snow cover area, increases in thaw depth over most permafrost regions, and decrease in sea ice extent; in some projections . . . Arctic late-summer sea ice disappears almost entirely by the latter part of the 21st century
>
> *very likely* increase in frequency of hot extremes, heat waves, and heavy precipitation
>
> *likely* increase in tropical cyclone intensity; less confidence in global decrease of tropical cyclone numbers
>
> poleward shift of extra-tropical storm tracks with consequent changes in wind, precipitation, and temperature patterns
>
> *very likely* precipitation increases in high latitudes and *likely* decreases in most subtropical land regions, continuing observed recent trends. (2007)

The IPCC (2007) also offers some hope that the worst consequences of global warming can be mitigated, since it concludes that there is still time for changes to be made. But these changes will require concerted action by governments and people around the world. They include national policies that encourage water, land, and energy conservation, the development of alternative energy sources, and in general incorporating scientific thinking about global climate change into our ways of thinking about everything from tourism to transportation. While the IPCC report addresses governments, it also stands to reason that individual behavior can make a difference, even if that difference is small. Because individuals in the United States and other advanced industrial nations consume far more than the average person in developing nations, their ecological footprint is much greater. Recycling, walking or riding a bicycle rather than driving whenever possible, buying fuel-efficient cars, turning the heat down and the air conditioning off—all of these are small steps that can add up, if practiced by a large enough number of people. As the IPCC report makes clear, the time for concerted action may be running out.

ENERGY

Modern industry, still expanding worldwide, has led to steeply climbing demands for sources of energy and raw materials. Yet the world's supply of such energy sources and raw materials is limited. Even at current rates of use, for example, the known oil resources of the world will be completely consumed by the year 2050. New reserves of oil may be discovered, or alternative sources of cheap energy invented, but there plainly is a point at which some key resources will run out if global consumption is not limited.

The United States is the largest consumer of energy in the world, as well as the world's largest producer of greenhouse gases, accounting for perhaps a quarter of the world's total (although as mentioned previously, China is rapidly catching up and may have surpassed the United States by the time you read this). Most of America's energy comes from nonrenewable fossil fuels—mainly petroleum, and to a lesser degree coal and natural gas. According to U.S. government figures, the United States in 2005–2006 consumed 24 percent of the world's petroleum, 21 percent of its natural gas, 17 percent of its coal, and 24 percent of its electricity—and produced 21 percent of all carbon emissions that result from fossil fuel consumption (US EIA 2007). Since the United States has only 8 percent of the world's population, it is clearly consuming a greatly disproportionate share of global energy reserves.

The high level of U.S. consumption is partly due to the fact that, as an advanced industrial economy with a high standard of living, Americans use far more energy than people in developing countries. For example, in the United States, the per-person consumption of petroleum is nearly thirteen times greater than that of the average Chinese, thirty-one times greater than that of the average Indian, and thirty-eight times greater than that of the average Kenyan. Similar disparities exist with regard to the consumption of other energy sources, such as natural gas, coal, and electricity (Figure 19.2). By the same token, the per-person contribution to carbon dioxide (greenhouse gas) emissions in the United States is five times that of China, nineteen times that of India, and seventy-three times that of Kenya. But the fact that the United States is a highly developed economy is not the whole story. The average American also consumes twice as much petroleum—and contributes twice the amount of carbon dioxide to the atmosphere—as the average person in Germany or Japan, two equally highly developed economies. It seems clear that the United States, by international standards, is an energy hog as well as a polluter.

It is also clear that as the poor nations of the world pursue economic development, if their per-person levels of energy consumption approach that of the United States—or even that of 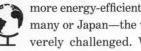 more energy-efficient developed countries such as Germany or Japan—the world's energy sources will be severely challenged. Whether or not the world's oil reserves, for example, will be greatly reduced or even depleted over the next twenty-five to fifty years is much debated, but there is little disagreement over the fact that if continued economic growth in China and India depend heavily on the use of petroleum—and if the United States and other advanced industrial countries fail to develop alternative sources of energy—the cost of oil and gasoline will greatly increase. As petroleum becomes increasingly scarce, the cost of extracting and refining it rises. Coal—one alternative energy source that remains in relative abundance—is, as we have already noted, a highly polluting source of greenhouse gases. While "clean coal" technology exists, it remains costly. Nuclear energy is another alternative to petroleum. Although widely used in Europe (more than a third of France's energy comes from nuclear plants), nuclear energy has a number of potential drawbacks: There is the fear that an accident in a nuclear plant could release the spread of deadly radiation, as happened in Chernobyl, Ukraine, in 1986, which exposed more than six million people, requiring the resettlement of some three hundred thousand; there are problems of disposing of radioactive waste from spent nuclear fuel, which remains highly toxic for thousands of years; there is the danger that nuclear fuel could be stolen and used to make nuclear weapons.

There is an emerging consensus among scientists and policy makers around the world that if economic development is to occur, it has to be concerned increasingly with conservation of scarce resources, as well as reduce the production of greenhouse gases and other pollutants.

SUSTAINABLE DEVELOPMENT

Rather than calling for a reining back of economic growth, more recent developments turn on the notion of **sustainable development**. Sustainable development means that growth should, at least minimally, be carried on in such a way as to recycle physical resources rather than deplete them and to keep levels of pollution to a minimum; ideally, development would be based largely on renewable resources such as wind, sun, and water, rather than fossil fuels that will eventually become depleted. The term *sustainable development* was first introduced in a 1987 report commissioned by the United Nations, *Our Common Future*. This is also known as the Brundtland Report, because the organizing committee that produced the report was chaired by G. H. Brundtland, at that time the

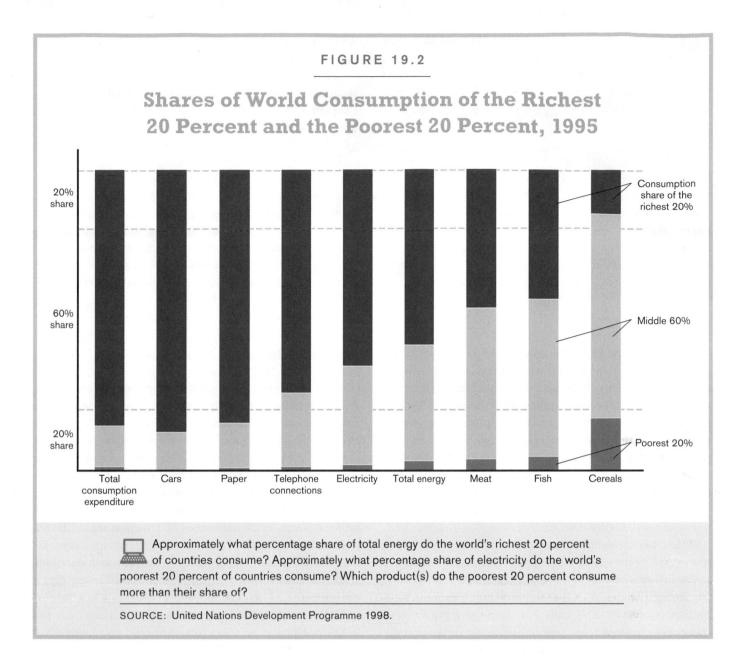

FIGURE 19.2

Shares of World Consumption of the Richest 20 Percent and the Poorest 20 Percent, 1995

20% share

60% share

20% share

Consumption share of the richest 20%

Middle 60%

Poorest 20%

Total consumption expenditure · Cars · Paper · Telephone connections · Electricity · Total energy · Meat · Fish · Cereals

Approximately what percentage share of total energy do the world's richest 20 percent of countries consume? Approximately what percentage share of electricity do the world's poorest 20 percent of countries consume? Which product(s) do the poorest 20 percent consume more than their share of?

SOURCE: United Nations Development Programme 1998.

prime minister of Norway. Sustainable development was defined as the use of renewable resources to promote economic growth, the protection of animal species and biodiversity, and the commitment to maintaining clean air, water, and land. The Brundtland Commission regarded sustainable development as "meeting the needs of the present, without compromising the ability of future generations to meet their own needs."

After the publication of *Our Common Future,* the phrase *sustainable development* came to be widely used by environmentalists and governments. It was employed at the UN Earth Summit in Rio de Janeiro in 1992 and has subsequently appeared in other ecological summit meetings organized by the United Nations.

The Brundtland Report attracted much criticism. Critics see the notion of sustainable development as too vague and as neglecting the specific needs of poorer countries. According to the critics, the idea of sustainable development tends to focus attention only on the needs of richer countries; it does not consider the ways in which the high levels of consumption in the more affluent countries are satisfied at the expense of other people. For instance, demands on Indonesia to conserve its rain forests could be seen as unfair, because Indonesia has a greater need than the industrialized countries for the revenue it must forgo by accepting conservation.

Still, the hope for globally sustainable development is far from abandoned. Despite the early criticisms of the Brundtland

Landscape of what used to be rain forest in Riau, Indonesia. In order to harvest palm oil, the rain forests are being cut down, torched and replaced with palm trees. Much of the forest is cut down illegally, and the government cannot regulate the deforestation.

Report, progress has been made in better understanding how renewable resources and conservation can—indeed, must—play a key role in any country's development strategy, for the many reasons outlined in this chapter: If the cost of development is toxic air and water, cities choked with traffic congestion, and the global depletion of key sources of energy, another path must be sought. The United Nations Division for Sustainable Development, which provides technical assistance to developing nations, in 2007 issued a report addressing such issues as energy, industrial development, air quality, and climate change (UN CSD 2007).

China, whose rapid economic growth has brought severe energy and environmental challenges, also has an emerging grassroots environmental movement (Birnbaum and Yu 2007; Wu 2007). The country's current (eleventh) Five Year Plan, for the period 2007–2012, calls for a 20 percent reduction in energy consumption in relation to the size of its economy over the plan period; the country has enacted legislation requiring far stricter fuel economy standards for cars than exist in the United States (Niederberger, Brunner, and Zhou 2007). In 2005, China's President Hu Jintao called on China's leadership to build a "harmonious society"—both among people (by addressing the growing economic inequality) and with nature. In Hu's words, "The present ecological and environmental situations in China are rather tough and grave in some places. Without a sound natural environment, people will have no clean water to drink, fresh air to breathe, healthy food to eat, which will result in serious social problems" (Xinhua 2005). Whether China is able to achieve the lofty goal of continuing rapid economic growth—including elevating hundreds of millions of people out of poverty—while at the same time achieving some sort of balance with nature remains to be seen.

Prospects for Change

Of all the environmental problems discussed in this chapter, global warming is arguably the most pressing. Greenhouse gases released in the atmosphere do not simply affect the climate of the country in which they were produced but alter climatic patterns for the entire world. For this reason, many policy makers and scientists believe that any viable solution to the problem must also be global in scale. Yet the political difficulties in negotiating an international treaty to reduce greenhouse gases are enormous and suggest that although globalization has ushered in a new era of international cooperation, the world is still far from being able to speak decisively with a unified political voice about many of the issues that it confronts.

In December 1997, delegates from 166 nations gathered in Kyoto, Japan, in an effort to hammer out an agreement to reduce global warming. The summit was the culmination of two years of informal discussion among the countries. World leaders, faced with mounting scientific evidence that global warming is indeed occurring and under pressure from voters to adopt environmentally friendly policies, clearly recognized that international action of some kind was needed. But faced as well with intense lobbying by industry, which fears it will bear the brunt of the cost for reducing fossil fuel emissions, world leaders felt compelled to balance safeguarding the environment against the threat of economic disruption.

As a result, the pollution reductions agreed to by the countries are meager. Thirty-eight of the advanced industrial nations represented at the conference agreed to reduce total emission levels by 2010 to approximately 5 percent below what they were in 1990. But different countries agreed to different specific targets: The United States agreed (upon ratification by the U.S. Congress) to reduce emission levels by 7 percent, the fifteen countries of the European Union pledged an 8 percent reduction, and Japan promised a 6 percent cut. The nations also tentatively agreed to establish an emissions "trading" system whereby a country that has reduced emissions levels beyond its target will be able to sell emissions "credits" to countries that have been unable to meet their goals. The agreement also includes commitments on behalf of the industrialized countries to assist developing countries by providing technology and funding to help overcome their limited capacity to respond to climate change.

To become an active and enforceable treaty, the Kyoto Protocol must receive support from countries that emit 55 percent of global greenhouse emissions. This finally happened in November 2004 when Russia ratified the agreement. This brought the total number of ratifying countries to 127, including China, India, Japan, New Zealand, and the European Union. Notably, Australia and the United States have refused to ratify the treaty even though, as we have noted, the United States is responsible for the largest single share of global greenhouse gases of any country, with the possible exception of China.

While politicians hailed the accord as an important first step in dealing with global warming, there are three serious problems with the Kyoto agreement. First, while many newly industrialized countries, such as China, India, and Russia, have now ratified the treaty, the terms of the agreement largely exempt them from making emission reductions. Because the reduction of greenhouse gas emissions requires expensive technology upgrades for factories and other industrial infrastructure, opponents of the agreement have argued that the exemption for developing countries gives them an unfair competitive advantage in the global market. Yet this critique fails to take into account that developed countries produce over five times more emissions per person than developing countries (UN WFP 2004). This holds true even for China, which has the largest population and has been industrializing rapidly. Second, many environmentalists warn that the reduction in greenhouse gases agreed to at Kyoto is not enough to reverse the trend toward global warming, only enough to slow its onset. Unless much greater emissions reductions are achieved, the world will still experience most of the disastrous consequences of global warming in the next century. Others, including U.S. president George W. Bush, initially suggested that the science that supports the Kyoto Protocol is inconclusive and provides insufficient evidence that the measures adopted in the agreement would have their intended effect (White House Press Office 2001). In recent years, President Bush has started to accept the scientific evidence on global warming but has nevertheless resisted committing the United States to the treaty. Third, and most problematic, the Kyoto accord, which must be ratified by the legislative bodies of all the signatory countries, faces stiff political opposition. Industry leaders and conservative politicians in the United States, for example, claim that reaching even the 7 percent reduction agreed to by the U.S. delegation would be tremendously expensive and that the environmental regulations required to achieve even this modest goal would hamstring U.S. business and retard economic growth. In 2001, in an attempt to satisfy American business interests, President Bush proposed an alternative strategy to lower greenhouse gas emissions through a system of government incentives for voluntary emission reductions by private businesses. Countries that ratified the treaty denounced the Bush plan as ineffective and openly criticized the unwillingness of the United States to ratify the Kyoto Protocol or seriously address the global problems created in no small part by American industrialism. In 2005, President Bush said that unless China and India (two of the largest emitters) would agree to be bound by the treaty, the United States would not do so. The Intergovernmental Panel on Climate Change's 2007 report has been seen as a wakeup call by many, including the U.S. government, which, as noted above, endorsed the commission's findings. Hopefully the report will lead to actions that will halt and even reverse the worst effects of global climate change. The Kyoto agreement expires in 2012, and in December 2007 environment ministers and delegates from more than 180 countries met in Bali, Indonesia, to discuss post-Kyoto efforts to combat climate change (Harris 2007). Hopefully, the shortcomings of Kyoto will be resolved, and rich and poor nations alike will be able to find common ground on a strategy that all now agree is required.

It is clear that modern technology, science, and industry are not exclusively beneficial in their consequences. Sociologists perceive a responsibility to examine closely the social relations and institutions that brought about the current state of affairs, because rectifying the situation will require a profound consciousness of human responsibility.

☑ CONCEPT CHECKS

1. Give two examples of waste materials and their sources.
2. Describe the basic processes that give rise to global warming.
3. Define sustainable development, and provide at least one critique of the concept.
4. Name one positive and one negative aspect of current consumption patterns.
5. What are the three main problems with the Kyoto agreement?

Living in Cities

- Traditional cities differed in many ways from modern urban areas. They were mostly very small by modern standards and were surrounded by walls, and their centers were dominated by religious buildings and palaces.
- In traditional societies, only a small minority of the population lived in urban areas. In the industrialized countries today, between 60 and 90 percent do so. Urbanism is also increasing very rapidly in developing countries.

Theories of Urbanism

- Early approaches to urban sociology were dominated by the work of the Chicago School. The members of this school saw urban processes in terms of ecological models derived from biology. Louis Wirth developed the conception of urbanism as a "way of life." These approaches have more recently been challenged, though without being discarded altogether.
- Later approaches to urban theory have placed more emphasis on the influence of broader socioeconomic factors—particularly those deriving from industrial capitalism—on city life.

Rural, Suburban, and Urban Life in the United States

- The expansion of suburbs—suburbanization—has contributed to inner-city decay. Wealthier groups and businesses tend to move out of the central city to take advantage of lower tax rates. This begins a cycle of deterioration, in which the more suburbia expands, the greater the problems faced by those living in the central cities. Urban renewal (also called gentrification)—the refurbishing of old buildings to put them to new uses—has become common in many large cities.

Cities and Globalization

- Urban analysis today must be prepared to link global and local issues. Factors that influence urban development locally are sometimes part of much more international processes. The structure of local neighborhoods and their patterns of growth and decline often reflect changes in industrial production internationally.

Urbanization in the Developing World

- Massive urban development is occurring in developing countries. Cities in these societies differ in major respects from those

characteristic of the West. The majority of the population live in illegal makeshift housing, in conditions of extreme poverty.

World Population Growth

- Population growth is one of the most significant global problems currently faced by humanity. About a quarter of the world's population suffer from malnutrition, and over ten million people die of starvation each year. This misery is concentrated in the developing countries.
- The study of population growth is called demography. Much demographic work is statistical, but demographers are also concerned with trying to explain why population patterns take the form they do. The most important concepts in population analysis are birthrates, death rates, fertility, and mortality.
- The changes in population patterns that have occurred in the industrialized societies are usually analyzed in terms of a process of demographic transition. Before industrialization, both birthrates and death rates were high. During the beginning of industrialization, there was population growth because death rates were reduced while birthrates took longer to decline. Finally a new equilibrium was reached with low birthrates balancing low death rates.

Population, Industrialization, and the Environment

- World resources are finite, even if the limits of what can be produced are continually revised due to technological developments. Energy consumption and the consumption of raw materials and other goods are vastly higher in the Western countries than in other areas of the world. These consumption levels depend, moreover, on resources transferred from developing regions to the industrially developed nations. If resources were shared equally, there would be a significant drop in Western living standards.
- There are few aspects of the natural world that have not been affected by human activity. The industrialization of agriculture, the depletion of natural resources, the pollution of air and water, and the creation of vast mountains of unrecyclable waste are all sources of threat to the future survival of humanity. Addressing these issues will mean, among other things, that richer nations will have to revise their expectations of persistent economic growth.

Key Concepts

aging in place (p. 617)
collective consumption (p. 616)
conurbation (p. 609)
created environment (p. 615)
crude birthrates (p. 635)
crude death rates (p. 636)

Review Questions

1. What is the theory of urban ecology? How did the research of Drake and Cayton challenge this theory?
2. What are the two aspects of Wirth's theory of urbanism as a way of life?
3. How does urban living contribute to the development of subcultures?
4. According to David Harvey, why is geographic space continually restructured?
5. Explain the concept of "aging in place." How does this affect population change and social problems in rural areas?
6. Why might the distinction between "suburb" and "city" no longer be useful today?
7. What two theories explain the concentration of poverty in urban areas? On what point do these theories disagree?
8. What explains the higher rates of urbanization in the developing world?
9. How does the theory of demographic transition challenge Malthus's ideas about population growth?
10. What trends are likely to shape world population over the next two centuries? What are the possible implications of this?

Thinking Sociologically Exercises

1. Explain what makes the urbanization now occurring in developing countries, such as Brazil and India, different from and more problematic than the urbanization that took place a century ago in New York, London, Tokyo, and Berlin.
2. Following analysis presented in this chapter, concisely explain how the expanded quest for cheap energy and raw materials and present-day dangers of environmental pollution and resource depletion threaten not only the survival of people in developed countries but also that of people in less developed countries.

Learning Objectives

Social Change and Globalization

Recognize that numerous factors influence social change, including the physical environment, political organization, culture, and economic factors.

What Comes after Modern Industrial Society?

Evaluate the notion that social change is leading into a postindustrial or postmodern stage of social organization.

Factors Contributing to Globalization

Recognize the importance of information flows, political changes, and transnational corporations.

The Globalization Debate

Understand the debates among skeptics, hyperglobalizers, and transformationalists over whether globalization differs radically from anything in human history.

The Effect of Globalization on Our Lives

Appreciate how globalization has influenced the rise of individualism, changing work patterns, popular culture, risk, and inequality in modern society.

The Need for Global Governance

Understand why new forms of global governance are needed to address the risks, challenges, and inequalities produced by globalization.

CHAPTER TWENTY

GLOBALIZATION IN A CHANGING WORLD

I magine standing before a clock that measures time on a cosmic scale, in which each second represents sixty thousand years. On such a clock it would take twenty-four hours for the five-billion-year history of our planet to unfold. Human-like apes would not even appear until the last two minutes, and human beings only in the last four seconds. Compared to us, even the dinosaurs would look like long-term residents of the planet—they roamed the earth for nearly three quarters of an hour on our twenty-four-hour clock, before disappearing forever. Will human beings—whose great civilizations appeared only in the last quarter second—do nearly as well?

Human beings are very recent residents of planet earth, yet we have unquestionably made our presence known. Our numbers have exploded to some 6.5 billion people and will probably increase by half again over the next fifty years. We have spread to every nook and cranny on the planet. Thanks to modern science and industry, each of us uses up a vastly greater amount of the planet's limited resources than did our ape-like ancestors. Indeed, the combination of population explosion and modern industrial expansion threatens both our planet and our human civilization.

Human beings have shown a unique ability to create massive problems—and then find ways to solve them. Today our problems are global, requiring global solutions. Globalization has contributed to such challenges as global warming, the worldwide spread of AIDS, conflict among nations, terrorism, and global poverty. Yet globalization can also contribute to their solution. All human beings share a common home and, therefore, a common interest in its preservation.

Globalization refers to the fact that we increasingly live in one world, so that individuals, groups, and nations become more *interdependent*—that is, what happens twelve thousand miles away is likely to have enormous consequence for our daily lives. In this chapter we examine these global processes and see what leading sociologists and other social scientists have had to say about it. We go beyond our discussions from elsewhere in the book, considering why the modern period is associated with especially profound and rapid social change. We explore how globalization has contributed to this change and consider what the future is likely to bring.

Social Change and Globalization

During a period of only two or three centuries—a sliver of time in the context of human history—human social life has been wrenched away from the types of social order in which people lived for thousands of years.

Social change can be defined as the transformation over time of the institutions and culture of a society. Globalization has accelerated these processes of social change, affecting virtually all of humanity. As a result, far more than any generation before us, we face an uncertain future. To be sure, previous generations were at the mercy of natural disasters, plagues, and famines. Yet, although these problems still trouble much of the world, today we must also deal with the social forces that we ourselves have unleashed.

Social theorists have tried for the past two centuries to develop a single grand theory that explains social change. Marx, for example, emphasized the importance of economic factors in shaping social life, including politics and culture. But no single-factor theory can account for the diversity of human social development from hunting and gathering and pastoral societies, to traditional civilizations, and to the highly complex social systems of today. In analyzing social change, we can accomplish two tasks: We can identify major factors that have consistently influenced social change, such as the physical environment, economics, political organization, and culture; and we can develop theories that explain particular periods of change, such as modern times.

The Physical Environment

The physical environment often affects the development of human social organization. This is clearest in extreme environmental conditions. For example, people in polar regions develop different practices from those living in subtropical areas. Residents of Alaska, where the winters are long and cold and the days very short, follow different patterns of social life from residents of the much warmer U.S. South. Most Alaskans spend more of their lives indoors and, except in summer months, plan outdoor activities carefully, given the inhospitable environment.

Less extreme physical conditions can also affect society. The native population of Australia has remained hunters and gatherers because the continent has hardly any indigenous plants suitable for cultivation or animals suitable for pastoral production. Most of the world's early civilizations originated in areas with rich agricultural land—for instance, in river deltas. The ease of communications across land and the availability of sea routes are also important: Societies cut off from others by mountain ranges, impassable jungles, or deserts often remain relatively unchanged over long periods.

Jared Diamond (2005) makes a strong case for the importance of environment in his book *Collapse: How Societies Choose to Fail or Succeed*. Diamond, a physiologist, biologist, and geographer, examines over a dozen past and present societies, some of which collapsed (past examples include Easter Island and the Anasazi of Southwestern United States; more recent examples include Rwanda and Haiti) and some of which overcame serious challenges to succeed. Diamond identifies five factors contributing to a society's collapse: the presence of hostile neighbors, the absence (or collapse) of trading partners for essential goods, climate change, environmental problems, and an adequate response to environmental problems. Three of these factors involve environmental conditions. The first four factors are often outside a society's control and need not always result in collapse. The final factor, however, is always crucial, as success or failure depends on the choices made by a society and its leaders.

The collapse of Rwanda, for example, is typically attributed to ethnic rivalries fueled by Rwanda's colonial past. According to some explanations of the genocide that left more than eight hundred thousand Tutsis dead after a few horrific months in 1994, much of the cause lay in the legacy of colonialism. During the first part of the twentieth century, Belgium ran Rwanda through Tutsi administrators because, according to prevailing European racial theories, the Belgians considered the Tutsis—somewhat taller and lighter-skinned than the Hutus and, therefore, closer in resemblance to Europeans—to be more "civilized." This led to resentment and hatred that boiled over in 1994, fueled by Hutu demagogues urging the killing of all Tutsis.

Diamond holds that this explanation is only part of the story. Through careful analysis of patterns of landholding, population, and killing, he argues that the root causes are found

Rwandan refugees trying to reach the United Nations camp in Tanzania. Over 800,000 Tutsis and moderate Hutus were killed during a period of 100 in 1994 days. Hundreds of thousands of Rwandans fled to neighboring countries to escape the bloodshed.

in overpopulation and resulting environmental destruction. Rwanda, he shows, was one of the fastest-growing places on earth, with disastrous consequences for its land and people, who had become one of the planet's most impoverished populations. Faced with starvation—and the absence of land to share among the growing number of (male) children—Rwanda was ripe for violence and collapse. Although ethnic rivalries may have fueled the fires of rage, Diamond also shows that in some hard-hit provinces Hutus killed other Hutus, as young men sought to acquire scarce farmland by any means.

Some have criticized Diamond for overemphasizing the environment at the expense of other factors. By itself—except perhaps for extreme circumstances, such as the extended drought that doomed the Anasazi early in the fourteenth century—the environment does not necessarily determine how a society develops. Today especially, when humans can control much of their immediate living conditions, environment seems less important: Modern cities have sprung up in the arctic cold and the harshest deserts.

Political Organization

A second factor influencing social change is the type of political organization a society has. In hunting and gathering societies, this influence is minimal because no political authorities can mobilize the community. In other types of society, however, distinct political agents—chiefs, lords, monarchs, and governments—strongly affect the course of social development. How a people respond to a crisis can determine whether they thrive or fail, and leadership is crucial to success or failure. A leader capable of pursuing dynamic policies and generating a mass following or radically altering preexisting modes

of thought can overturn a previously established order. However, individuals can reach positions of leadership and become effective only under favorable social conditions. Mahatma Gandhi, the famous pacifist leader in India, succeeded in securing his country's independence from Britain because World War II and other events had unsettled the existing colonial institutions in India.

Japan illustrates how effective leadership averted possible ecological and economic collapse (Diamond 2005). Political and military stability under the Tokugawa *shoguns* (military rulers from 1603 to 1867) ushered in a period of prosperity. This economic growth, however, contributed to massive deforestation of the island country. Its leaders (the celebrated *samurai* warriors) instituted programs of conservation and reforestation, and today—despite having one of the highest population densities of any industrial country—nearly three quarters of Japan is covered with forests (Diamond 2005).

Military strength played a fundamental part in the establishment of most traditional states, but the connections between level of production and military strength are indirect. A ruler may channel resources into building up the military, for example, even when this impoverishes the rest of the population—as happened in Iraq in the 1980s under the rule of Saddam Hussein and in North Korea during the 1990s under Kim Jong Il.

The most important political factor that has promoted change in the modern era is the emergence of the modern state, a vastly more efficient mechanism of government than those of premodern societies. Government plays a much bigger role in our lives, for better or worse, than it did before modern industrial societies arose.

Globalization today may be challenging national governments' ability to effectively exert leadership. A number of theorists argue that political power is becoming increasingly uncoupled from geography (Sassen 1996; Shaw 2000). Sociologist William Robinson (2001), for example, claims that as economic power has become deterritorialized, so too has political power: Just as transnational corporations operate across borders, with little or no national allegiances, transnational political organizations are becoming stronger as national governments are becoming weaker. Groups such as the World Trade Organization (WTO) now have the power to punish countries that violate its principles of free trade (Conti 2003). European countries have opened their borders to one another, established a common currency, and given up substantial political power to the European Union (EU), a regional form of governance.

Will the twenty-first century see new forms of political organization better suited to a world in which people, products, knowledge, religious beliefs, pop culture, and pollution all cross borders easily? Although it is too soon to tell, most likely the most important forms of political organization of this century will bear little resemblance to those of the twentieth.

Culture

The third main influence on social change consists of cultural factors, which include the effects of communications systems, religious and other belief systems, and popular culture.

A particularly important cultural influence is the nature of communications systems. The invention of writing, for instance, promoted record keeping, facilitating the control of material resources and the development of large-scale organizations. In addition, writing altered people's perception of the relationship among past, present, and future. Societies that write keep a record of past events, through which they gain a sense of their society's evolution. The existence of a written constitution and laws enables a country to have a legal system based on the interpretation of legal precedents—just as written scriptures enable religious leaders to justify their beliefs by citing chapter and verse from religious texts, like the Bible or Qur'ān.

We saw in Chapters 6, 13, and 16 how the Internet has changed our personal relationships, our forms of recreation, the ways in which we learn and work, the nature of politics and social movements—in fact, almost every aspect of modern life. These changes, among the most rapid in human history, have caused what geographer David Harvey (1989) calls the compression of time and space. And they have all occurred within a single generation.

Religion may be either a conservative or an innovative force in social life. Some forms of religious belief and practice have acted as a brake on change, emphasizing traditional values and rituals. Yet, as Max Weber held, religious convictions frequently mobilize pressures for social change. For instance, American church leaders promote attempts to reduce poverty or diminish inequalities in society. Religious leaders such as Dr. Martin Luther King Jr. were in the forefront of the American civil rights movement, and adherents to liberation theology fought for better schools, water supplies, health services, and democracy in Latin America—often at the cost of their lives.

Yet at the same time, religion today has resisted many of the cultural aspects of globalization. Islamists, fundamentalist Christians, and ultraorthodox Jewish *haredim* all reject what they regard as the corrupting influences of modern secular culture, now spreading globally through mass media and the Internet (Juergensmeyer 1993, 2000). Islamists call this "westoxification"—literally, getting drunk on the temptations of modern Western culture. While such religious communities usually embrace modern technology, which they sometimes use to disseminate their ideas, they reject the corruptions that go along with it.

An Egyptian girl walks next to the Muslim Fulla dolls at a kids shop in Cairo. Two years after she first came on the market, Fulla is now thought to be the best-selling girl's toy in the Arab world, displacing her Western rival, Barbie.

Political scientist Samuel Huntington (1993, 1998) has advanced the controversial thesis that such differences are part of seismic fault lines between entire civilizations. According to his "clash of civilizations" thesis,

> The great divisions among humankind and the dominating source of conflict will be cultural. Nation states will remain the most powerful actors in world affairs, but the principal conflicts of global politics will occur between nations and groups of different civilizations. The clash of civilizations will dominate global politics. The fault lines between civilizations will be the battle lines of the future. (1993)

Huntington identifies several major civilizations as having great potential for future conflict: Christianity, subdivided into Western Christianity and Eastern Orthodox; Islam; Hindu; Chinese; African; Buddhist; and Japanese. Although his thesis seems especially plausible after the events of September 11, 2001, it has been criticized as overly simplistic. Each of his so-called civilizations encompasses enormous differences in beliefs and practices, while old-fashioned geopolitical interests—for example, over scarce resources such as oil and water—will likely shape international conflicts well into the twenty-first century. Moreover, to the extent that national policies are influenced by a belief in the clash of civilizations, Huntington's thesis may become a self-fulfilling prophecy, as different sides square off for a cosmic war against what each believes to be the forces of unmitigated evil (Juergensmeyer 1993).

In fact, the principal cultural clashes of the twenty-first century may not be between so-called civilizations but between those who believe that truthful understanding derives from religious faith and those who find such understanding in science, critical thinking, and secular thought (Juergensmeyer 1993). Secular ideals, such as self-betterment, freedom, equality, and democratic participation, are largely creations of the past two or three centuries.

German philosopher Friedrich Nietzsche first proclaimed the death of God in 1882, arguing that absolute beliefs no longer could provide a guide to action in modern secular society. Secularism, Nietzsche believed, had won out over religious faith. It is no longer possible to make such a claim with any degree of confidence.

Economic Factors

Of economic influences, the farthest reaching is the effect of industrial capitalism. Capitalism differs fundamentally from previous production systems because it involves the constant expansion of production and the ever-increasing accumulation of wealth. In traditional production systems, levels of production were fairly unchanging because they were geared to customary needs. Capitalism requires the constant revision of the technology of production, a process that increasingly involves science. The rate of technological innovation fostered in modern industry is vastly greater than that in any previous type of economic order. And such technological innovation has helped create a global economy whose production lines draw on a worldwide workforce.

Economic changes affect other changes as well. Science and technology, for example, are driven in part by economic factors. Corporations, to remain competitive, must spend large sums on research and development to commercialize scientific insights. Governments often spend far more money than individual businesses can afford in an effort to ensure that their countries don't fall behind militarily or economically. For instance, when the Soviet Union launched the world's first satellite (*Sputnik*) in 1957, the United States responded with a massive and costly space program, inspired by fear that the Russians were winning the space race. During the 1960 presidential campaign, John F. Kennedy heightened that fear by repeatedly accusing the Republicans of being lax on Russian missile technology, suggesting that a "missile gap" made us vulnerable to nuclear attack. The arms race, fueled by government contracts with corporations, has provided major economic support for scientific research as well as more general support for the U.S. economy.

Most recently, governments worldwide are spending vast sums to win the next technological race—nanotechnology. Nanotechnology involves working with matter at the atomic scale, or "nano" scale, creating devices exhibiting properties that can exist only at such small sizes. (The nanoscale is defined as smaller than 100 nanometers; a nanometer is a billionth of a meter.) While much of this research remains in the early stages, nanotechnology has already produced such devices as:

- highly fluorescent nanocrystals ("quantum dots") that can penetrate into the tiniest blood vessels, illuminating blockages that would otherwise be undetectable and holding promise for treating heart problems
- nanoscale sensors that can detect a single molecule of a chemical warfare agent, promising highly sensitive sensors that can be used in cities or battlefields
- nanomaterials for explosives that have more than twice the energy of conventional explosives
- data storage devices based on nanoscale electronics that can store one hundred times as much data as the most powerful devices currently available
- highly efficient nanoscale filtration devices that can remove major industrial contaminants from groundwater (National Nanotechnology Initiative [NNI] 2005)

Numerous countries are investing public funds to support research and development in this promising area, hoping to profit from scientific breakthroughs. China, for example, is

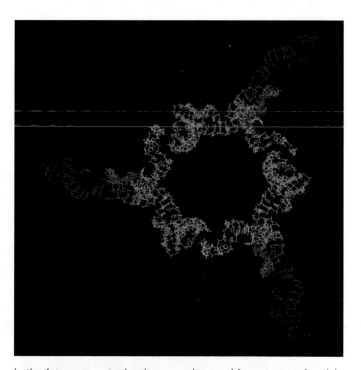

In the future, nanotechnology may be used for a range of activities, from medical applications to dealing with environmental issues. As an example, this triangular nanoparticle, developed by Purdue University, can carry anticancer treatments directly to infected cells.

training some fifty thousand engineers in advanced chip design at universities in seven cities. The U.S. government launched the NNI in 2001; today it involves twenty-six federal agencies and spends more than $1 billion yearly to foster nanoscale research and development.

☑ CONCEPT CHECKS

1. Name three examples of cultural factors that may influence social change.
2. How does industrial capitalism affect social change?
3. What are the most important political factors that influence social change?

What Comes after Modern Industrial Society?

Social theorists do not agree on where social change is leading us. In this section, we examine two perspectives: the notion that we are now a postindustrial society and the idea that we have reached a postmodern period.

Toward a Postindustrial Society?

Some observers have suggested that we are entering a phase of development beyond the industrial era altogether. A variety of new terms describe this new social order, such as **information society**, **service society**, and **knowledge society**. The most commonly used term, however—first employed by Daniel Bell (1976) in the United States and Alain Touraine (1974) in France—is **postindustrial society**, the *post* (meaning "after") suggesting that we are moving beyond old forms of industrial development.

The diversity of terms reflects the countless ideas put forward to interpret current social changes. But one consistent theme is the significance of *information* or *knowledge* in the society of the future. Our ways of life throughout the nineteenth and twentieth centuries, based largely on machine power (the manufacture of material goods in factories), is being displaced by one in which information underlies the production system.

In his now-classic *The Coming of the Post-Industrial Society,* Daniel Bell (1976) argues that the postindustrial order is distinguished by a growth of service occupations at the expense of jobs that produce material goods. The blue-collar worker is no longer the most essential type of employee. White-collar

The "Geek Squad," a company founded by Robert Stephens in Minneapolis, Minnesota, and later purchased by the Best Buy retail chain, provides consumer computer support and technical repairs. They are an example of the new types of service-sector jobs emerging in a postindustrial society.

(clerical and professional) workers outnumber blue-collar (factory) workers, with professional and technical occupations growing fastest of all.

People working in higher-level white-collar occupations specialize in the production of information and knowledge. The production and control of what Bell calls "codified knowledge"—systematic, coordinated information—is society's main productive resource. Those who create and distribute this knowledge—scientists, computer specialists, economists, engineers, and professionals of all kinds—increasingly become the leading social groups, replacing industrialists and entrepreneurs. On the level of culture, there is a shift away from the work-ethic characteristic of industrialism; people are freer to innovate and enjoy themselves in both their work and their domestic lives.

How valid is the view that a postindustrial society is replacing the old industrial order? Although the thesis has been widely accepted, the empirical assertions on which it depends are suspect in several ways.

1. The trend toward service occupations, accompanied by a decline in employment in other production sectors, dates back almost to the beginning of industrialism itself; it is not simply a recent phenomenon. From the early 1800s, manufacture and services

both expanded at the expense of agriculture, with the service sector consistently showing a faster rate of increase than manufacture. The blue-collar worker never really was the most common type of employee; a higher proportion of paid employees have always worked in agriculture and services, with the service sector increasing proportionally as the numbers in agriculture dwindled. The most important change has not been from industrial to service work but from farm employment to all other types of occupation.

2. Still, since the 1970s there has been a significant loss of factory jobs to low-wage countries, such as China, with a corresponding increase in service jobs (many of which pay far lower wages than the factory jobs that were lost). The most recent trends support the postindustrial thesis that factory employment in the United States is declining while service sector employment is increasing.

3. The service sector is very diverse. Service occupations are not identical to white-collar jobs; many service jobs (such as that of gas-station attendant) are blue collar in the sense that they are manual. Most white-collar positions involve little specialized knowledge and have become substantially mechanized. This is true of much office work today. The notion that creative and challenging white-collar work is replacing highly routinized factory work is incorrect; much service-sector employment today is just as routinized and unsatisfying as factory work was in the past (and pays less).

4. Many service jobs contribute to a process that ultimately produces material goods and, therefore, should be counted as part of manufacture. Thus a computer programmer working for an industrial firm, designing and monitoring the operation of machine tools, is directly involved in a process of making material goods.

5. The postindustrial society thesis exaggerates the importance of economic factors in producing social change. Such a society is described as the outcome of developments in the economy that lead to changes in other institutions. However, the forces behind today's changes are political and cultural as well as economic—for example, the growing importance of religious beliefs as a force for social change indicates that the production and consumption of goods and services is not the only driving force in history.

6. Finally, the very concept of *postindustrial* implies that we are somehow at the end of history—after all, what can come after "post"? Any attempt to divide history into before-and-after stages is bound to be proven wrong over time, as new (and unanticipated) technological breakthroughs, and their associated social changes, occur. Will the postindustrial stage give way to a biosocial stage, in which genetic engineering results in new human capabilities and forms of society? A nanosocial stage, in which atomic devices solve all human problems, including the need to work? Such fanciful speculations may be the realm of science fiction, but they point out the dangers of predicting the future on the basis of the most recent technological trends.

Postmodernity

Some authors believe that current developments are even more profound than signaling the end of industrialism. They claim that we are witnessing a movement beyond modernity—the attitudes and ways of life associated with modern societies, such as our belief in progress, the benefits of science, and our capability to control the modern world. A postmodern era has already arrived.

Advocates of postmodernity claim that modern societies drew inspiration from the idea that history has a shape—it "goes somewhere" and leads to progress—and that now this notion has collapsed. There are no longer any overall conceptions of history that make sense (Lyotard 1985). Not only is there no general notion of progress that can be defended, but there is no such thing as history. The **postmodern** world is thus highly pluralistic and diverse. In countless films, videos,

Fredric Jameson describes the Westin Bonaventure Hotel, located in downtown Los Angeles, as an original postmodern space. The architecture distorts viewers' sense of place—the glass exterior mirrors the building's surroundings rather than permitting a view inside.

and TV programs, images circulate worldwide. We encounter many ideas and values, but these have little connection with the history of the areas we live in, or indeed with our own personal histories. Everything seems constantly in flux. According to one group of authors:

> Our world is being remade. Mass production, the mass consumer, the big city, big-brother state, the sprawling housing estate, and the nation-state are in decline: flexibility, diversity, differentiation, and mobility, communication, decentralization and internationalization are in the ascendant. In the process our own identities, our sense of self, our own subjectivities are being transformed. We are in transition to a new era. (Hall et al. 1988)

Most contemporary social theorists accept that information technology and new communications systems, among other technological changes, are producing major social transformations. However, the majority of theorists disagree with the postmodernists, who argue that attempts to understand general processes in the social world are doomed, as is the notion that we can change the world for the better. Writers such as Ulrich Beck and Anthony Giddens (2004) claim that as much as ever, general theories of the social world allow us intervene to shape it in a positive way. Such theories have considered how contemporary societies are becoming globalized, while everyday life is breaking free from tradition and custom. But these changes should not spell the end of social and political reform. Values, such as a belief in the importance of social community, equality, and caring for the weak and vulnerable, are still very much alive worldwide.

☑ CONCEPT CHECKS

1. What is the "postindustrial society"?
2. What is the "postmodern era"? What is the main critique of this concept?

Factors Contributing to Globalization

Although globalization is often portrayed solely as an economic phenomenon, it is in fact created by the coming together of technological, political, and economic factors. It has been driven above all by the development of information and communications technologies that have intensified the speed and scope of interaction among people worldwide.

Information Flows

Important advances in technology and the world's telecommunications infrastructure have facilitated the explosion in global communications. The post–World War II era has seen a transformation in the scope and intensity of telecommunications flows. Traditional telephone communication, which depended on analog signals sent through wires and cables, has been replaced by integrated systems in which vast amounts of information are compressed and transferred digitally. Cable technology has become more efficient and less expensive. The development of fiber-optic cables, for example, has dramatically expanded the number of channels that can be carried, and even this recent technology has achieved significant advances: While the first transoceanic fiber-optic cables could carry the equivalent of thirty-five thousand telephone circuits, the most recent have ten thousand times that capacity (Hecht 2003). The spread of communications satellites has also helped to expand international communications. Today a network of more than two hundred satellites facilitates the transfer of information around the globe.

The effect of these communications systems has been staggering. In countries with highly developed telecommunications infrastructures, homes and offices have multiple links to the outside world, including telephones (both land lines and mobile phones), fax machines, digital and cable television, electronic mail, and the Internet. The Internet is the fastest-growing communication tool ever developed—more than 1.4 billion people worldwide (over one fifth of the world population) were estimated to be using the Internet at the end of June 2008, nearly twice the number of only five years earlier (Internet World Stats 2008b).

These forms of technology facilitate the compression of time and space: Two individuals located on opposite sides of the planet not only can hold a conversation in real time but also can send documents and images to each other with the help of satellite technology. Widespread use of the Internet and mobile phones is accelerating processes of globalization; more people are becoming interconnected through these technologies in places that have previously been isolated or poorly served by traditional communications (Figure 20.1). Although the telecommunications infrastructure is not evenly developed around the world (Table 20.1), a growing number of countries now have access to international communications networks.

Globalization is also being driven forward by the electronic integration of the world economy. The global economy increasingly involves activity that is *weightless* and *intangible* (Quah 1999) because products have their base in information, as with computer software, media and entertainment products, and Internet-based services. This new economic context has been

FIGURE 20.1

The Multiplication of Television Sets and Telephones in Regions of the World, 1985–2005, and the Explosion in Online Communication

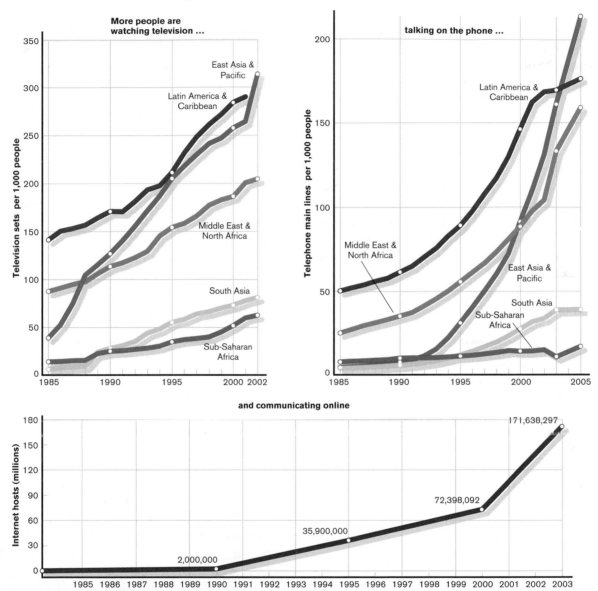

From 1985 to 2002, which region saw the greatest increase in television sets per 1,000 people? How would you describe the increase in main telephone lines per 1,000 people that Sub-Saharan Africa experienced from 1985 to 2005? What is the difference between East Asia/ Pacific and South Asia in the number of main telephone lines per 1,000 people in 1985 and in 2005? What was the approximate increase in Internet hosts in the ten years from 1990 to 2003? In the three years from 2000 to 2003? What does Figure 20.1 have to do with globalization?

SOURCE: United Nations 2003; World Bank 1999, 2002, 2005.

TABLE 20.1

Global Unevenness of Telecommunications Infrastructure and Use

COUNTRY	POPULATION (MILLIONS)	TELEPHONE MAINLINES (PER 1,000)[a]	FIXED LINE AND MOBILE PHONE SUBSCRIBERS (PER 1,000)[b]	PERSONAL COMPUTERS (PER 1,000)[b]
China	1,319.98	280	690	41
France	61.71	550	1,390	575
Germany	82.27	650	1,830	545
India	123.32	30	240	16
Japan	127.77	360	1,150	542
Sweden	9.15	590	1,650	763
United Kingdom	61.03	550	1,730	600
United States	301.62	540	1,390	762

[a] In 2006.

[b] In 2005.

SOURCES: World Bank 2008.

described in various terms, including *postindustrial society, information society,* and *knowledge society.* The emergence of the knowledge society reflects a broad base of consumers who are technologically literate and who integrate new advances in computing, entertainment, and telecommunications into their everyday lives.

The very operation of the global economy reflects the changes characteristic of the information age. Many aspects of the economy now require networks that cross national boundaries (Castells 1996). To be competitive in globalizing conditions, businesses and corporations have become more flexible and less hierarchical. Production practices and organizational patterns have become more flexible, partnering arrangements with other firms have become commonplace, and participation in worldwide distribution networks has become essential.

Whether one works in a factory or a call center, today the job can be done more cheaply in China, India, or some other developing country. The same is true for software engineers, graphic designers, and financial consultants. Of course, to the extent that global competition for labor reduces the cost of goods and services, it also provides for a wealth of cheaper

products (Roach 2005). As consumers, we all benefit from low-cost flat-panel TVs made in China or inexpensive computer games programmed in India. It is an open question, however, whether the declining cost of consumption will balance out wage and job losses due to globalization.

A call center in Gurgaon, India.

Political Changes

Political changes are driving forces behind contemporary globalization. One of the most significant is the collapse of Soviet-style communism, which occurred in Eastern Europe in 1989 and in the Soviet Union itself in 1991. Since then, countries in the former Soviet bloc—including Russia, Ukraine, Poland, Hungary, the Czech Republic, the Baltic states, and the states of the Caucasus and Central Asia—have been moving toward Western-style political and economic systems and have been integrating within the global community. In fact, the collapse of communism not only hastened processes of globalization but also was a result of it. The centrally planned communist economies and the ideological and cultural control of communist political authority ultimately could not survive in an era of global media and an electronically integrated world economy.

A second political factor leading to intensifying globalization is the growth of international and regional mechanisms of government. The United Nations (UN) and the EU are two prominent examples of international organizations that bring together nation-states into a common political forum. Whereas the UN does this as an association of individual nation-states, the EU is a form of transnational governance in which some national sovereignty is relinquished by its member states. The governments of EU states are bound by directives, regulations, and court judgments from common EU bodies, but they also reap economic, social, and political benefits from their participation in the regional union.

A third political factor is the growing importance of international governmental organizations (IGOs) and international nongovernmental organizations (INGOs; see also Chapter 6). An *international governmental organization* is a body that is established by participating governments and given responsibility for regulating or overseeing a domain of activity that is transnational in scope. Such bodies regulate issues ranging from civil aviation to broadcasting to the disposal of hazardous waste. In 1909, there were thirty-seven IGOs in existence to regulate transnational affairs; by 2005, there were more than seven thousand (Union of International Organizations 2005). INGOs differ from IGOs in that they are not affiliated with government institutions. Rather, they are independent organizations that work alongside governmental bodies in making policy decisions and addressing international issues. Some of the best-known INGOs—such as Greenpeace, Médecins Sans Frontières (Doctors without Borders), the Red Cross, and Amnesty International—are involved in environmental protection and humanitarian relief efforts. But the activities of the nearly fifty-nine thousand lesser-known groups also link countries and communities (Figure 20.2).

Finally, the spread of information technology has expanded the possibilities for contact among people worldwide. It has

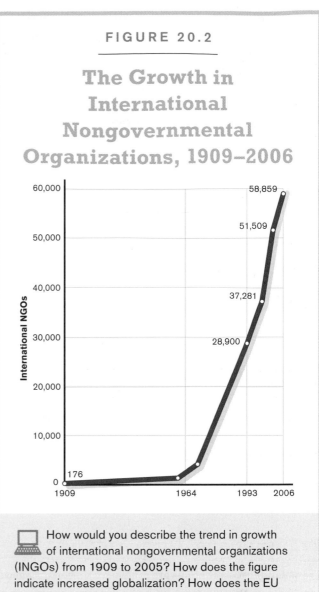

FIGURE 20.2

The Growth in International Nongovernmental Organizations, 1909–2006

How would you describe the trend in growth of international nongovernmental organizations (INGOs) from 1909 to 2005? How does the figure indicate increased globalization? How does the EU differ from the UN? Name two examples of INGOs.

SOURCE: Union of International Organizations 2005.

also facilitated the flow of information about people and events in distant places. Some of the most gripping events of recent decades—such as the fall of the Berlin wall, the violent crackdown on democratic protesters in China's Tiananmen Square, and the terrorist attacks of September 11, 2001—have unfolded through the media before a truly global audience. Such events, along with less dramatic ones, have caused a reorientation in people's thinking from the level of the nation-state to the global stage.

This shift has two significant consequences. First, as members of a global community, people increasingly perceive that social responsibility extends beyond national borders. There is a growing assumption that the international community has an obligation to act in crisis situations to protect the physical well-being or human rights of people whose lives are under threat. In the case of natural disasters, such interventions take the form of humanitarian relief and technical assistance. In recent years, earthquakes in Armenia and Turkey, floods in Mozambique, famine in Africa, hurricanes in Central America, and the tsunami that hit Asia and Africa have been rallying points for global assistance.

There have also been stronger calls for interventions in the case of war, ethnic conflict, and the violation of human rights, although such mobilizations are more problematic than with natural disasters. Yet in the case of the Gulf War in 1991 and the violent conflicts in the former Yugoslavia (Bosnia and Kosovo), military intervention was seen as justified by many people who believed that human rights and national sovereignty had to be defended.

Second, a global outlook means that people increasingly look to sources other than the nation-state in formulating their own sense of identity. This phenomenon both is produced by and further accelerates processes of globalization. Local cultural identities in various parts of the world are experiencing powerful revivals at a time when the traditional hold of the nation-state is undergoing profound transformation. In Europe, for example, inhabitants of Scotland and the Basque region of Spain might be more likely to identify themselves as Scottish or Basque—or simply as Europeans—rather than as British or Spanish.

Transnational Corporations

Transnational corporations are companies that produce goods or market services in more than one country. These may be small firms with one or two factories outside the country where they are based or gigantic international ventures whose operations crisscross the globe. Some of the biggest transnational corporations are ExxonMobil, Wal-Mart, Coca-Cola, Toyota, Ford, BMW, Nike, Disney, Google, Starbucks, and McDonald's. Even when transnational corporations have a clear national base, they are oriented toward global markets and global profits.

Transnational corporations account for two thirds of all world trade, are instrumental in diffusing new technology around the globe, and are major actors in international financial markets. As one group of writers has noted, they are "the linchpins of the contemporary world economy" (Held et al. 1999). Well over six hundred transnational corporations had annual sales of more than $10 billion in 2006, whereas only 105 countries could boast gross domestic products (GDPs) of at least that amount. In other words, the world's leading transnational corporations are larger economically than most of the

Transnational corporations such as Coca-Cola are eager to tap growing markets in countries like China and India. Corporate leaders break ground on a new plant in the Gansu province of China. The plant will be the twenty-fifth bottling plant Coca-Cola has opened in mainland China since it entered the market twenty-five years ago.

world's countries. Wal-Mart, the world's largest corporation in terms of sales, had revenues that surpassed the GDPs of all but twenty-one countries. Among the world's largest economies, fourteen are transnational corporations.

Transnational corporations became a global phenomenon after World War II. Expansion initially came from firms based in the United States, but by the 1970s European and Japanese firms also began to invest abroad. In the late 1980s and 1990s, transnational corporations expanded dramatically with the establishment of three powerful regional markets: Europe (the Single European Market), Asia-Pacific (the Osaka Declaration guaranteed free and open trade by 2010), and North America (the North American Free Trade Agreement). Since the early 1990s, countries in other areas have also eased restrictions on foreign investment. By the turn of the twenty-first century, few economies were beyond the reach of transnational corporations. Over the past decade, transnational corporations based in industrialized economies have been expanding their operations in developing countries and in the societies of the former Soviet Union and Eastern Europe.

The "electronic economy" also underpins economic globalization. Banks, corporations, fund managers, and individual investors can now shift funds internationally with the click of a mouse. This new ability carries great risks, however. Transfers of vast amounts of capital can destabilize economies and trigger international financial crises. As the global economy becomes increasingly integrated, a financial collapse in one part of the world can have an enormous effect on distant economies.

The political, economic, social, and technological factors described above are producing a phenomenon without parallel in terms of intensity and scope. Before considering the consequences of globalization, let's examine the main views about globalization that have been expressed in recent years.

☑ CONCEPT CHECKS

1. How has technology facilitated the compression of time and space?
2. What are the three causes of increasing globalization?
3. Briefly describe the history of transnational corporations since the 1970s.

The Globalization Debate

Most people accept that important transformations are occurring, but the extent to which one can explain them as "globalization" is contested. This is not surprising, given the unpredictable and turbulent process that globalization involves. David Held and his colleagues (1999) have identified three schools of thought: *skeptics, hyperglobalizers,* and *transformationalists.* These approaches to the globalization debate are summarized in Table 20.2.

TABLE 20.2

Conceptualizing Globalization: Three Tendencies

CHARACTERISTIC	SKEPTICS	TRANSFORMATIONALISTS	HYPERGLOBALIZERS
What's new?	Trading blocs, weaker geogovernance than in earlier periods	Historically unprecedented levels of global interconnectedness	A global age
Dominant features	World less interdependent than in 1890s	"Thick" (intensive and extensive) globalization	Global capitalism, global governance, global civil society
Power of national governments	Reinforced or enhanced	Reconstituted, restructured	Declining or eroding
Driving forces of globalization	Governments and markets	Combined forces of modernity	Capitalism and technology
Pattern of stratification	Increased marginalization of global south	New architecture of world order	Erosion of old hierarchies
Dominant motif	National interest	Transformation of political community	McDonald's, Britney Spears, etc.
Conceptualization of globalization	As internationalization and regionalization	As the reordering of interregional relations and action at a distance	As a reordering of the framework of human action
Historical trajectory	Regional blocs/clash of civilizations	Indeterminate: global integration and fragmentation	Global civilization
Summary argument	Internationalization depends on government acquiescence and support	Globalization transforming government power and world politics	The end of the nation-state

SOURCE: Adapted from Held et al. 1999.

Sociologists without Borders

For many studies, human suffering is a topic of study, a research problem, a set of data points abstracted from everyday experience and analyzed in offices and classrooms and computers far, far away from the "real" world. Dissatisfied with this level of detachment, Sociologists without Borders/*Sociólogos Sin Fronteras* (SSF) was founded in 2001 on the belief that poverty, disease, malnourishment, and torture are problems that sociologists should grapple with not only as analysts but as activists as well.

The "without borders" movement, according to Professor Judith Blau (2006), "was launched by professional groups from highly developed [countries] to assist peoples in poorer countries and to provide much needed services. The most famous such group is Doctors without Borders *Médecins Sans Frontières (MSF),*and others include Reporters without Borders, Architects without Borders, and Engineers without Borders. As an academic INGO [international nongovernmental organization], Sociologists without Borders works to encourage collaborative teaching across international borders." In 2004, SSF began a partnership in Kibera, a dense urban settlement just outside of Kenya's capital city.

Judith Blau

The impoverished settlement of Kibera is located three miles southeast of Nairobi, Kenya, in East Africa. There are no roads in Kibera. Families rely on craftwork and small-scale vending of used clothing, vegetables, and cassettes to generate income—typically less than $1 a day. The average family home is nine feet by nine feet. Drinking water is pumped through

The Skeptics

Skeptics in the globalization controversy believe that present levels of economic interdependence are not unprecedented. Pointing to nineteenth-century statistics on world trade and investment, they contend that modern globalization differs from the past only in the intensity of interaction among nations.

The skeptics agree that there may be more contact among countries today than in previous eras, but in their eyes the current world economy is not sufficiently integrated to constitute a truly globalized economy. This is because the bulk of trade occurs within three regional groups—Europe, Asia-Pacific, and North America. The countries of the EU, for example, trade predominantly among themselves. The same is true of the other regional groups, thereby invalidating the notion of a single global economy (Hirst 1997).

Many skeptics focus on *regionalization* within the world economy—such as the emergence of major financial and trading blocs—as evidence that the world economy has become less integrated rather than more (Boyer and Drache 1996; Hirst and Thompson 1999). Compared with the patterns of trade that prevailed a century ago, they argue, the world economy is less global in its geographical scope and more concentrated on intense pockets of activity.

Skeptics reject the view held by some, such as the hyperglobalizers (see below), that globalization is producing a world order in which national governments are less central. According to the skeptics, national governments continue to be key players because of their involvement in regulating and coordinating economic activity. Governments, for example, are the driving force behind many trade agreements and policies of economic liberalization.

plastic pipes alongside sewage trenches carrying refuse and human waste to a river at the base of the valley. Waterborne diseases such as cholera, typhoid, and worm infestations are rampant. Health services and sex education are minimal. An estimated 54 percent of people living in Kibera either are HIV positive or have AIDS.

In the United States, slums typically are found in just the poorest blocks of larger, thriving cities. But with a population of approximately eight hundred thousand, Kibera is a slum-city with more inhabitants than places like San Francisco, Detroit, or Boston all living in an area roughly the size of Central Park. Since Kibera is technically an illegal settlement, landlords are not obliged to provide any services—no toilets, no water, no electricity, no trash collection, no infrastructure, and no housing. Most Americans have no concept of what places like Kibera are really like, even though over one billion people throughout the world—about one sixth of the total human population—live under similar conditions (Van Hove 2006).

In 2004, Sociologists without Borders partnered with an organization called Carolina for Kibera, an NGO originally founded to combat ethnic violence among young people in Kibera that has now expanded its commitments to include health, sports, women's outreach, and microfinance projects. Blau (2006), a sociologist at the University of North Carolina at Chapel Hill, stresses that "in contrast with the charity model, SSF works hand-in-hand with the residents of Kibera so that they set the priorities in their own terms, and SSF tries to provide resources. It is a variation on service-learning, and it is our intent that the residents and the NGO are steering us. They are the experts."

Each year, SSF and Carolina for Kibera select one college student to serve as a Nairobi Fellow in the Kibera slums. In her 2005 field report, Lynsey Farrell, a student at Boston University, describes some of the challenges she faced jump-starting an income-generating newspaper project with local residents. Farrell's main goal was to help girls at the Binti Pamoja Centre who wanted to use writing as a tool to address the concerns of young women in Kibera. Drawing from their intimate knowledge of community life, the girls wrote articles about topics such as rape, relationships, and sexually transmitted diseases and distributed the newspaper throughout Kibera.

After almost three months living in the community, Farrell submitted her final field report to SSF. Although Kibera was often a disheartening place, she found human strength and vitality amid conditions of extreme poverty. "People in Kenya are resilient," Farrell (2005) writes. "I see in the girls' at Binti Pamoja many strengths, and see in them determination to help their community. Given the opportunity, they laugh and gossip and flirt, just like teenagers across the world. *Maisha ni ngumu* (Life is hard), but it is not impossible.... Kiberans are not poor, although they lack the resources and property that we associate with wealth. Despite the reports and surveys and experts proclaiming the horror of this growing urban slum, after a couple months working there I came away with a positive impression of their resourcefulness and determination to maintain a sense of community and normalcy that those on the outside do not imagine they have."

The Hyperglobalizers

The hyperglobalizers argue that globalization is a very real phenomenon with consequences almost everywhere. They see globalization as a process that is indifferent to national borders. It is producing a new global order, swept along by powerful flows of cross-border trade and production. Journalist Thomas Friedman (2000, 2005) portrays globalization as a juggernaut that sweeps up everything in its path, sometimes with unfortunate short-term results, but ultimately with enormous benefits for everyone.

Hyperglobalizers largely focus on the changing role of the nation-state, arguing that individual countries no longer control their economies because of the vast growth in world trade. National governments and the politicians within them have decreasing control over the issues that cross their borders—such as volatile financial markets and environmental threats. Citizens recognize that politicians' ability to address these problems is limited and, as a result, lose faith in existing systems of governance. Some hyperglobalizers believe that the power of national governments is also being challenged from above—by new regional and international institutions, such as the EU and WTO. These shifts signal the dawning of a global age (Albrow 1997) in which national governments decline in importance and influence.

More scholarly versions of a strong globalization position come from sociologists such as William Robinson (2001, 2004, 2005a, 2005b), Leslie Sklair (2002a, 2002b, 2003), and Saskia Sassen (1996, 2005). Although these scholars do not see themselves as hyperglobalists, nonetheless they argue that transnational economic actors and political institutions are challenging the dominance of national ones. Robinson has studied these changes throughout the world, with a special focus on Latin America. He argues that the most powerful economic actors today are not bound by national boundaries; they are transnational. For example, the "transnational capitalist class" is emerging out of (and is transforming) the capitalist classes of individual countries, because the transnational corporations they manage are global rather than national. By the same token, he argues that nation-states are becoming "component elements" of a transnational state—exemplified, for example, by the WTO, which serves the interests of global businesses as a whole by ensuring that individual countries adhere to the principles of free trade. Robinson (2001) concludes that "the nation-state is a historically-specific form of world social organization in the process of becoming transcended by globalization."

The Transformationalists

The transformationalists take more of a middle position. Writers such as David Held and Anthony G. McGrew (1999), as well as Anthony Giddens (1990), see globalization as the central force behind a broad spectrum of change. According to them, the global order is being transformed, but many of the old patterns remain. Governments, for instance, still retain a good deal of power in spite of global interdependence. These transformations are not restricted to economics but are equally prominent within politics, culture, and personal life. Transformationalists contend that the current level of globalization is breaking down established boundaries between internal and external, international and domestic. In adjusting to this new order, societies, institutions, and individuals must navigate contexts where previous structures have been shaken up.

Unlike hyperglobalizers, transformationalists see globalization as a dynamic and open process that is subject to influence and change. It is developing in a contradictory fashion, encompassing tendencies that frequently operate in opposition to one another. Globalization is a two-way flow of images, information, and influences. Global migration, media, and telecommunications are contributing to the diffusion of cultural influences. According to transformationalists, globalization is a decentered and self-aware process characterized by links and cultural flows that work in a multidirectional way. Because globalization is the product of numerous intertwined global networks, it is not driven from one particular part of the world.

Rather than losing sovereignty, countries are restructuring in response to new, nonterritorial forms of economic and social organization (e.g., corporations, social movements, and international bodies). Transformationalists argue that we are no longer living in a state-centric world; instead, governments must adopt a more active, outward-looking stance under the complex conditions of globalization (Rosenau 1997).

Whose view is most nearly correct? There are elements of truth in all three views, although those of the transformationalists are perhaps the most balanced. The skeptics underestimate how far the world is changing; world finance markets, for example, are organized on a global level much more than ever before. Yet at the same time, the world has undergone periods of globalization before—only to withdraw into periods when countries protected their markets and closed their borders to trade. Although the march of globalization seems inevitable, it may not continue unabated: Countries that find themselves losing out may attempt to stem the tide. Many countries in Latin America, for example, have recently elected left-wing governments that reject free trade, arguing instead for protections for their citizens.

The hyperglobalizers are correct in pointing to the current strength of globalization as dissolving many national barriers, changing the nature of state power, and creating powerful transnational social classes. However, they often see globalization too much in economic terms and as too much of a one-way process. In reality, globalization is much more complex. World-systems theorists such as Immanuel Wallerstein (2004) and Giovanni Arrighi (1994) argue that while countries remain important actors on the global field, so too are transnational corporations. National governments will neither dissolve under the weight of a globalized economy (as some hyperglobalizers argue) nor reassert themselves as the dominant political force (as some skeptics argue), but rather will seek to steer global capitalism to their own advantage. According to this argument, U.S. dominance of the world economy is seriously challenged by the rise of East Asia, and particularly China, whose economy has been expanding at more than 9 percent per year for nearly two decades.

The world economy of the future may be much more globalized than today's, with multinational corporations and global institutions playing increasingly important roles. But some countries in the world economy may still be more powerful than even the most powerful transnational actors. Clyde Prestowitz (2005), an expert on international trade, summarizes this position in his book on the rise of China and India as economic powers. He concludes that

Unless things go badly off track, the story of the next fifty years will be that of China recovering its historically central position as the Middle Kingdom [the world's center], with the world's largest population and economy. ... Its GDP in 2050 will be $45 trillion versus about $35 trillion for the United States. China will be the world's largest market for virtually everything as well as the biggest recipient of investment from, and the largest investor in, most other countries.

☑ **CONCEPT CHECKS**

1. Compare and contrast how the skeptics, the hyperglobalizers, and the transformationalists explain the phenomenon of globalization.
2. How might skeptics, hyperglobalizers, and transformationalists differently interpret the growing global prominence of China?

The Effect of Globalization on Our Lives

Although globalization is often associated with changes within big systems—such as world financial markets, production and trade, and telecommunications—the effects of globalization are felt equally strongly in the private realm. Inevitably, our personal lives have been altered as globalizing forces enter into our local contexts, our homes, and our communities through impersonal sources—such as the media, the Internet, and popular culture—as well as through personal contact with individuals from other countries and cultures.

As the societies in which we live undergo profound transformations, the institutions that underpin them have become outdated. This is forcing a redefinition of the family, gender roles, sexuality, personal identity, our interactions with others, and our relationships to work.

The Rise of Individualism

In the current age, individuals have much more opportunity to shape their own lives than previously. At one time, tradition and custom strongly influenced them. Factors such as social class, gender, ethnicity, and religious affiliation could close off certain avenues for individuals or open up others. The values, lifestyles, and ethics prevailing in one's community provided fixed guidelines for living.

Conditions of globalization, however, bring a new *individualism* in which people actively construct their own identities. The weight of tradition and established values is lessening as local communities interact with a new global order. The social codes that formerly guided people's choices and activities have significantly loosened.

Traditional frameworks of identity are dissolving; new patterns of identity are emerging. Globalization is forcing people to constantly respond and adjust to the changing environment; as individuals, we now evolve within the larger context. Even small choices in daily life—what to wear, how to spend leisure time, and how to care for our health and our bodies—are part of an ongoing process of creating and re-creating our self-identities.

Work Patterns

Although we may regard work as a chore or a necessary evil, it is undeniably a crucial element in our lives. Not only our jobs but also many other aspects of our existence—from our friends to our leisure pursuits—are shaped by our work patterns.

Globalization has unleashed profound transformations within the world of work. New patterns of international trade and the move to a knowledge economy have significantly impacted long-standing employment patterns. Many traditional industries have become obsolete or are losing their share of the market to competitors abroad. Global trade and new forms of technology have affected traditional manufacturing communities, where industrial workers have been left unemployed and without the skills required of the knowledge-based economy. These communities are facing new social problems, including long-term unemployment and rising crime rates, as a result of economic globalization.

If at one time people's working lives were dominated by employment with one employer over several decades—the so-called job-for-life framework—today more individuals are

Advancements such as laptop computers and the Internet have allowed those in remote areas, such as these Aboriginal children in rural Australia, unprecedented access to technology and the ability to communicate easily with people all around the world.

creating their own career paths. Often this involves changing jobs several times over the course of a career, building up new skills and abilities, and transferring them to diverse work contexts. Standard patterns of full-time work are dissolving into more flexible arrangements: working from home via information technology, job sharing, short-term consulting projects, flextime, and so forth (Beck 1992). While this affords new opportunities for some, for most it means greater uncertainty. Job security and attendant health-care and retirement benefits have largely become things of the past.

Women's entering the workforce in large numbers has strongly affected the personal lives of people of both sexes. Expanded professional and educational opportunities have led many women to put off marriage and children until after they have begun a career. Also, many women return to work shortly after having children, instead of remaining at home. These shifts have required important adjustments within families, in terms of the domestic division of labor, the role of men in child rearing, and the emergence of more family-friendly working policies to accommodate the needs of dual-earner couples.

Popular Culture

The cultural effects of globalization have received much attention. Images, ideas, goods, and styles are now disseminated worldwide more rapidly than ever. Trade, new information technologies, the international media, and global migration have all promoted the free movement of culture across national borders. Many people believe that we now live in a single information order—a massive global network where information is shared quickly and in great volumes. A simple example illustrates this point.

The film *Titanic,* the most popular film of all time, has grossed more than $1.8 billion since its release in 1997—two thirds of it outside the United States. The film was popular with all age groups but particularly with adolescent girls. The stars of *Titanic,* Leonardo DiCaprio and Kate Winslet, found their careers and futures utterly transformed; they had been elevated from little-known actors to global celebrities. *Titanic* is one of a handful of cultural products that has succeeded in cutting across national boundaries and creating a truly international phenomenon.

What accounts for the enormous popularity of a film like *Titanic*? And what does its success tell us about globalization? At one level, *Titanic* was popular for straightforward reasons: It combined a simple plotline (a romance against the backdrop of tragedy) with a well-known historical event (the 1912 sinking of the *Titanic,* in which more than sixteen hundred people perished). The film was also lavishly produced and included state-of-the-art special effects culminating in the spectacular

A Chinese woman buys a ticket to see *Titanic* at a Beijing theater. *Titanic* is one of the most commercially successful films ever made.

sinking of the ocean liner. Romance, drama, raw fear—all played a role in the film's success.

But another reason for *Titanic*'s popularity is that it reflected ideas and values that resonated with audiences worldwide. One of the film's central themes is the possibility of romantic love prevailing over class differences and family traditions. The success of a film like *Titanic* reflects the changing attitudes toward personal relationships and marriage, for example, in parts of the world that have favored more traditional values. Yet *Titanic,* along with many other Western films, may also *contribute* to this shift in values. Western-made films and television programs, which dominate the global media, advance political, social, and economic agendas that reflect a specifically Western worldview. Some people worry that globalization is fostering a global culture in which the values of the most powerful and affluent—in this instance, Hollywood filmmakers—overwhelm local customs and tradition. According to this view, globalization is a form of cultural imperialism in which Western values, styles, and outlooks smother individual national cultures.

Others, by contrast, have linked globalization to a growing *differentiation* in cultural traditions and forms. They claim that global society is characterized by an enormous diversity of cultures existing side by side. Local traditions are joined by a host of additional cultural forms from abroad, presenting a bewildering array of lifestyle options. Rather than a unified global culture, what we are witnessing is the fragmentation of cultural forms (Baudrillard 1988). Established identities and ways of life grounded in local communities and cultures are giving way to hybrid identities composed of elements from contrasting cultural sources (Hall 1992). Thus a black urban South African today might be strongly influenced by the traditions and cultural outlooks of his tribal roots at the same time as he adopts cosmopolitan styles and tastes—in dress, leisure pursuits, hobbies, and so forth—that have been shaped by globalizing forces.

Globalization and Risk

Because globalization is an open-ended and internally contradictory process, it produces outcomes that are difficult to predict and control. Another way of thinking of this dynamic is in terms of *risk*. Many of the changes wrought by globalization present new forms of risk. Unlike risks from the past, which had established causes and known effects, today's risks are incalculable in origin and indeterminate in their consequences.

THE SPREAD OF "MANUFACTURED RISK"

Humans have always had to face risks, but today's risks are qualitatively different from those of earlier times. Until recently, human societies were threatened by **external risk** from the natural world—dangers such as drought, earthquakes, famines, and storms. Today, however, we increasingly face various types of **manufactured risk**—risks created by the effect of our own knowledge and technology on the natural world. Many current environmental and health risks are the outcomes of our own interventions into nature.

Environmental Risks One of the clearest illustrations of manufactured risk involves threats posed by the natural environment (see Chapter 19). One of the consequences of accelerating industrial and technological development has been the steady spread of human intervention into nature—for example, through urbanization, industrial production and pollution, large-scale agricultural projects, the construction of dams and hydroelectric plants, and nuclear power. The collective outcome of such processes has been widespread environmental destruction whose precise cause is indeterminate and whose consequences are difficult to calculate.

In the globalizing world, ecological risk takes many forms. For example, concern over global warming has been mounting in the scientific community; it is now generally accepted that the earth's temperature has increased from the buildup of harmful gases within the atmosphere. If polar ice caps continue to melt as they currently are, sea levels will rise and may threaten low-lying land masses and their human populations. Changes in climate patterns may have caused the severe floods that afflicted parts of China in 1998 and Mozambique in 2000, or the record number of hurricanes that swept through the Atlantic and Gulf of Mexico in the fall of 1995 (as well as the one that devastated New Orleans in 2005).

Because environmental risks are diffuse in origin, it is unclear how to address them or who bears responsibility for remedying them. For example, although scientists have found that chemical pollution levels have harmed Antarctic penguin colonies, it is impossible to identify either the exact origins of the pollution or its possible consequences for the penguins in the future. In such an instance—and in hundreds of similar cases—action to address the risk is unlikely because the extent of both the cause and the outcome is unknown (Beck 1995).

Health Risks Lately, the dangers posed to human health by manufactured risks have attracted great attention. The media and public health campaigns, for example, urge people to limit their exposure to harmful ultraviolet rays and to apply sunscreen to prevent burning. Sun exposure has been linked to a heightened risk of skin cancer, possibly due to the depletion of the ozone layer—the layer of the earth's atmosphere that filters out ultraviolet light. Because of the high volume of chemical emissions produced by human activities and industry, the concentration of ozone in the atmosphere has been diminishing, and in some cases ozone holes have opened up.

Many examples of manufactured risk are linked to food, because advances in science and technology have heavily influenced modern farming and food production techniques. For example, chemical pesticides and herbicides are widely used in commercial agriculture, and many animals (such as chickens and pigs) are pumped full of hormones and antibiotics. Some

A farmer compares root growth of genetically modified corn, right, and unmodified corn on the left.

"Small Bird Flocks Pose Bird Flu Risk for Humans"

Does avian flu or "bird flu" pose a serious global health risk today? And if so, how severe is the risk? Although early headlines triggered tremendous fear, scientists today are arguing that the risk is modest in Europe and North America, yet more severe in Asia and Africa. In 2006 and 2007, news headlines from Indonesia, to Belgium, to the United States warned readers that "Mysterious Bird Flu Baffles . . . Scientists" and "New Avian Influenza Flareups." In response to these cautionary reports, the avian flu was recognized as a global threat for the first time in 2007. However, that same year, just 86 human cases (and 59 deaths) were confirmed, down from 115 cases (and 79 deaths) in 2006, according to the World Health Organization (WHO). On the heels of these declines, news reports have been more tempered, with headlines offering messages like "A Pandemic That Wasn't but Might Be" and "Top Expert Says Bird Flu Risk Overestimated." Although initial media reports told us that the pandemic could ultimately strike as many as 200 million people, it seemed that overnight, the virus started to fade away. What happened? And how should individuals assess their own risk of contracting this mystery illness?

Bird flu first captured the attention of the scientific and medical communities in the late 1990s, when six people in Hong Kong contracted the disease—a mysterious virus called H5N1 which jumped from birds to humans. At that time, officials called for the slaughtering of the entire local poultry population. The

disease seemed to slip away temporarily, but then re-emerged in 2003. Since that time, bird flu has spread to more than sixty countries in Africa, Asia, Europe, and the Middle East, leading to the deaths of just over 200 people as of January 2008, and hundreds of millions of birds—usually domestic poultry including chickens, turkeys, and geese (Associ-

A young girl wears a mask to protect herself from bird flu at the bird market in Hong Kong.

ated Press 2007). Although the number of cases is small compared to other pandemics through history, the risk of death is high: more than 60 percent of persons known to be infected with the disease ultimately die from it.

Health researchers say that these declining numbers don't mean that the disease is "disappearing," but rather that the world has become better prepared, and better preventions have developed. In other words, awareness of risk has triggered programs and practices that may ultimately reduce risk of the disease. Effective vaccines have been developed, and many countries, cities, companies,

and schools have official pandemic plans in place and maintain supplies of medication and masks. Testing has also improved: Results from flu tests come back faster, hospitals maintain separate wards for people who are believed to be victims of the flu, and epidemiologists try to trace and treat all potentially infected persons. Farmers are forthcoming about reporting bird deaths (and vaccinating healthy birds), and vendors and butchers—particularly in Asia—now use gloves when handling produce. In some parts of the world, such as Vietnam, school children are taught about bird flu. These actions show how mere perception of risk can trigger behaviors that ultimately reduce risk. According to Joseph Domenech, chief veterinary officer of the United Nations' Food and Agriculture Organization (FAO), "surveillance, early detection, and immediate response have improved and many newly infected countries managed to eliminate the virus from poultry" (Medical News Today 2008).

Despite these strides, scientists acknowledge that the disease is a mystery, and myriad questions about its transmission remain unanswered. For instance, the WHO is now investigating whether the disease can be transmitted person-to-person, rather than bird-to-person. Scientists also are wrestling with questions about how the virus spreads internationally and how the processes of bird migration and international trade contribute to its global transmission.

Social scientists have focused less on questions about the disease's transmission and more on the ways that people think about their risk. One reason for the vast amount of media attention, even though the death count is only a few hundred cases worldwide, is that scientists and laypersons have no way of knowing just how widespread the disease may become. Estimates of the disease's potential reach range from 2 million to 150 million (James 2005), with the WHO suggesting that anywhere from 2 million to 7 million persons could die. Projections for the United States are just as uncertain: A draft report of the U.S. government's emergency plan predicts that as many as 200 million Americans could be infected and 200,000 could die within a few months if the bird flu came to the United States and no vaccine were available. According to Harvard School of Public Health epidemiologist Marc Lipitsch, "we can't predict what a virus we've never seen will do" (James 2005).

Another factor that makes the disease risk appear high is that avian flu can strike any individual, not just those already in poor health. This factor raises fears about individuals' own vulnerability to the illness: Lubitsch observed, "It's not like a normal flu that kills primarily the elderly . . . it does so in a wide range of age groups" (James 2005).

Social scientists also observe that cautionary headlines about new diseases like bird flu raise worries about low-prevalence health conditions yet detract attention from high-prevalence (though less novel) diseases. Although 21 million Americans now have diabetes and another 45 million are at risk for developing it, many view the bird flu—which has struck no Americans—as a greater potential personal risk. Peter Sandman, a risk communications consultant in New Jersey, observes, "The risks that hurt people and the risks that upset people

A team of veterinarians completes a series of bird flu vaccinations in a rural county in China, as part of a nationwide inoculation effort.

are almost completely unconnected." Rutgers University psychologist Howard Leventhal observed that unfamiliarity also raises individuals' feelings of risk. "Prevalent events are seen as less serious than rare events." For instance, he noted that bird flu is known in the United States only through media reports, rather than personal experience. Novel or unfamiliar conditions are frightening and may lead people to imagine the worst possible outcome. By contrast, most people know someone who has had diabetes or heart disease; thus the condition—although high risk—seems more familiar and less dangerous (Fountain 2006). As a result, the threat of bird flu seems large and menacing because of its unfamiliarity. That doesn't mean that the risk of bird flu should be ignored; rather, it means that individuals should consider the prevalence and risk factors for illness before becoming excessively worried—at least in the United States.

Questions

- How many cases of bird flu deaths have been documented? What proportion of all persons contracting the disease ultimately die?
- How have high levels of perceived risk indirectly led to reductions in the risk of contracting bird flu?

- Given that no cases of U.S. deaths due to bird flu have been documented, why are fear levels so high, according to social scientists who study risk?

FOR FURTHER EXPLORATION

Associated Press. 2007. "After 10 Years, Bird Flu Still Baffles Scientists." MSNBC (December 27, 2007). www.msnbc.msn.com/id/22407411/ (accessed February 7, 2008).

Fountain, Henry. 2006. "On Not Wanting to Know What Hurts You." *New York Times* (January 15, 2006). www.nytimes.com/2006/01/15/weekinreview/15fount.html?pagewanted=print (accessed February 7, 2008).

James, Michael S. 2005. "How Many People Could Bird Flu Kill?" ABC News (September 30, 2005). http://abcnews.go.com/Health/Flu/story?id=1173856 (accessed February 7, 2008).

McNeil, Donald G. 2008. "A Pandemic That Wasn't But Might Be." *New York Times* (January 22, 2008). www.nytimes.com/2008/01/22/science/22flu.html?pagewanted=print (accessed February 7, 2008).

Medical News Today. 2008. "New Avian Influenza Flare-ups." www.medicalnewstoday.com/articles/95042.php (accessed February 7, 2008).

News-Medical.Net. 2008. "Top Expert Says Bird Flu Risk Overestimated." News-Medical.Net (January 14, 2008). www.news-medical.net/print_article.asp?id=34274 (accessed February 7, 2008).

Smith, Jeremy. 2008. "Small Bird Flocks Pose Bird Flu Risk for Humans." Reuters India (January 23, 2008). http://in.reuters.com/articlePrint?articleId=INIndia-31550220080123 (accessed February 7, 2008).

Yahoo News. 2008. "'Mysterious' Bird Flu Baffles Indonesian Scientists." Yahoo! News (February 6, 2008). http://news.yahoo.com/s/afp/healthfluindonesia;_ylt=Ar1GmBNM9evpb6vTwr.qQnWTvyIi (accessed February 7, 2008).

The Manufactured Risks of Electronic Viruses and World Climate Change

Globalization comes with many unfamiliar, manufactured risks. Among them are two that may have had a direct impact on you. On May 4, 2000, chaos engulfed the electronic world when a virus nicknamed the "love bug" succeeded in overloading computer systems worldwide. Launched from a personal computer in Manila, the capital of the Philippines, the love bug spread rapidly across the globe and forced almost a tenth of the world's e-mail servers to shut down. The virus was carried worldwide through an e-mail message with the subject heading "I Love You." When recipients opened the file that was attached to the message, they unknowingly activated the virus in their own computer. The love bug would then replicate itself and automatically send itself on to all the e-mail addresses listed in the computerized address book, before attacking information and files stored on the computer's hard drive. The virus spread westward around the globe as employees, first in Asia, then in Europe and North America, arrived to work in the morning and checked their e-mail. By the end of day, the love bug was estimated to have caused more than $1.5 billion of damage worldwide.

The love bug was a particularly fast-spreading virus, but it was not the first of its kind. Electronic viruses have become

people have suggested that such farming techniques compromise food safety and could adversely affect humans. Two particular controversies have raised widespread public concern: the debate over genetically modified foods and mad cow disease.

The saga of genetically modified foods began a few years ago when some of the world's leading chemical and agricultural firms decided that new knowledge about genes could transform the world's food supply. These companies had been making pesticides and herbicides but wanted to develop a major market for the future. The American firm Monsanto was the leader in developing much of the new technology. Monsanto bought up seed companies, sold off its chemical division, worked to bring the new crops to market, and launched a gigantic advertising campaign promoting the benefits of its genetically modified crops to farmers and consumers. The early responses were just as the company had confidently anticipated. By early 1999, 55 percent of the soybeans and 35 percent of the maize produced in the United States contained genetic alterations. It is currently estimated that between 60 and 70 percent of all produce sold in grocery stores contains some genetically modified components (Safe-food.org 2003). In addition to North America, genetically modified crops are being widely grown in China.

Since genetically modified crops are new, no one can be certain about their effects once they are introduced into the environment. Many ecological and consumer groups are concerned about the potential risks involved with the adoption of this largely untested technology.

Bovine spongiform encephalopathy (BSE), known popularly as mad cow disease, was first detected in British cattle in 1986. Scientists have linked BSE infection to the practice of raising cattle—normally herbivores—on feed containing traces of the parts of other animals. After the outbreak, the British government took steps to control the disease among cattle, but it claimed that eating beef was safe for humans. Only in the mid-1990s was it admitted that several human deaths from more common—and more dangerous—as computers and electronic forms of communication have grown in importance and sophistication. Viruses such as the love bug demonstrate how interconnected the world has become with the advance of globalization. You might think that in this particular instance global interconnectedness proved to be quite a disadvantage, since a harmful virus was able to spread so rapidly around the globe. Yet many positive aspects of globalization are reflected in this case as well. As soon as the virus was detected, computer and security experts from around the world worked together to prevent its spread, protect national computer systems, and share intelligence about the virus's origins.

Another aspect of manufactured risk and one you likely have noticed—or been directly affected by—is the unusual weather in recent years. Scientists and disaster experts have pointed out that extreme weather events—such as unseasonably hot temperatures, droughts, floods, and cyclones—have been occurring with ever-greater frequency. In 1998 alone, for example, eighty separate natural catastrophes were recorded at points around the globe, including devastating floods in China, hurricanes in Latin America, wildfires in Indonesia, and severe ice storms in North America. Since that time, drought has gripped regions as diverse as Ethiopia, southern Afghanistan, and the midwestern United States; floods have ravaged Venezuela and Mozambique; violent windstorms have battered parts of Europe; a plague of locusts has swarmed through the Australian outback; and devastating tsunamis have struck Thailand, Indonesia and neighboring nations in southeast Asia.

Although no one can be certain, many people believe that these natural disasters are caused in part by global warming (the heating up of the earth's atmosphere). If carbon dioxide emissions that contribute to global warming continue unchecked, it is likely that the earth's climate will be irreversibly harmed. Who is responsible for global warming, and what can be done to slow its progress? As with so many aspects of our changing world, the risks associated with global warming are experienced worldwide, yet its precise causes are nearly impossible to pinpoint. In an age of globalization, we are constantly reminded of our interdependence with others: The actions of individuals or institutions in one part of the world can, and do, have significant consequences for people everywhere.

Creutzfeldt-Jakob disease, a degenerative brain condition, had been linked to the consumption of beef from infected cattle. Thousands of British cattle were killed, and strict new legislation regulated cattle farming and the sale of beef products. Most recently, cattle infected with BSE have been discovered in Canada and the United States, sparking widespread fears about the safety of the food supply.

Although extensive scientific research has explored the risks to humans from BSE, the findings remain inconclusive. There is a risk that individuals who consumed British beef in the years preceding the discovery of BSE may have been exposed to infection. Calculating the risks to humans from BSE is an example of the complexity of risk assessment in the contemporary world. It is necessary to know if and when infected cattle were part of a certain food chain, the level and distribution of the infection present in the cattle, how the beef was processed, and many other details. The sheer quantity of unknown factors has complicated the task.

THE GLOBAL "RISK SOCIETY"

Global warming, the BSE crisis, the debate over genetically modified foods, and other manufactured risks present new choices and challenges. Individuals, countries, and transnational organizations must negotiate risks as they make choices about how to live and conduct business. Because there are no definitive answers about the causes and outcomes of such risks, this can be a bewildering endeavor. Should we use food and raw materials if their production or consumption might harm our health and the natural environment?

German sociologist Ulrich Beck (1992) sees these risks contributing to a global risk society. As technological change progresses and produces new forms of risk, we must constantly respond and adjust to these changes. The risk society, he argues, is not limited to environmental and health risks; it includes a series of interrelated changes within contemporary social life: shifting employment patterns, heightened job insecurity, the declining influence of tradition and custom on self-identity, the erosion of traditional family patterns, and the democratization of personal relationships. Because personal futures are much less fixed than they were in traditional societies, decisions of all kinds present risks. Getting married, for example, is a riskier endeavor today than when marriage was a lifelong institution. Decisions about educational qualifications and career paths can also feel risky: It is difficult to predict what skills will be valuable in an economy that is changing so rapidly.

According to Beck (1995), an important aspect of the risk society is that its hazards are not restricted spatially, temporally, or socially. Today's risks have global, not merely personal, consequences. Many forms of manufactured risk, such as those concerning human health and the environment, cross national boundaries. Consider the explosion at the Chernobyl nuclear power plant in Ukraine in 1986. Everyone living in the immediate vicinity—regardless of age, class, gender, or status—was exposed to dangerous levels of radiation. At the same time, the effects of the accident stretched far beyond Chernobyl itself: Throughout Europe and beyond, abnormally high levels of radiation were detected long after the explosion.

Globalization and Inequality

Beck and other scholars have identified risk as one of the main outcomes of globalization and technological advance. Yet globalization is generating other important challenges as well, because its effect is differential—and some of its consequences are not benign. Next to mounting ecological problems, the expansion of inequalities within and among societies is one of the most serious challenges today.

INEQUALITY AND GLOBAL DIVISIONS

The majority of the world's wealth is concentrated in the industrialized or developed countries, whereas developing nations suffer from widespread poverty, overpopulation, inadequate educational and health-care systems, and crippling foreign debt. The disparity between the developed and the developing world widened steadily over the course of the twentieth century and is now the largest it has ever been.

The 1999 *Human Development Report,* published by the United Nations Development Programme (UNDP), revealed that the average income of the fifth of the world's population living in the richest countries was seventy-four times greater than the average income of the fifth living in the poorest. More than one fifth of the world's population accounted for 86 percent of the world's overall consumption, 82 percent of export markets, and 74 percent of telephone lines. The combined income of the world's richest 500 people is greater than that of the poorest 416 million. The poorest 40 percent of the world's population, who live on less than $2 a day, account for 5 percent of global income, whereas the richest 10 percent account for 54 percent of global income (UNDP 2005). The 2007 report indicates that the ratio of the richest 20 percent to the poorest 20 percent ranges from 3.9 (Norway) to 57.6 (Sierra Leone) (United Nations 2008). Similarly, the percentage of population living below $2 a day ranges from nonexistent for the countries high on the human development index such as Iceland and Norway to over 70 percent in low-ranked countries such as Burkina Faso and Sierra Leone. The UNDP estimates that if wealthy countries were to stop growing and poor countries were to continue growing at the current rate, it would take over two hundred years for the poorest to catch up. The World Development Indicators (WDI) 2007 says that the number of people living on less than $1 a day declined by 260 million from 1990 to 2004 largely due to massive poverty reduction in China, but this overall decline was marred by a rise of 60 million poor people in sub-Saharan Africa (World Bank 2008).

In much of the developing world, levels of economic growth and output over the past century have not kept up with the rate of population growth, whereas the level of economic development in industrialized countries has far outpaced it. These opposing tendencies have caused a marked divergence between the richest and poorest countries. The distance between the world's richest and poorest country was approximately 3 to 1 in 1820, 11 to 1 in 1913, 35 to 1 in 1950, 72 to 1 in 1992, and 173 to 1 in 2001 (Figure 20.3). The figure for 2006 using gross national income (GNI) per capita (ATLAS Method) is 760.4 to 1 (World Bank 2008). The WDI 2007 shows that the mortality rate for children under age five is fifteen times higher in low-income countries than in high-income countries (World Bank 2008). Over the past century, among the richest quarter of the world's population, income per head has increased almost sixfold, while among the poorest quarter, the increase has been less than threefold.

Globalization seems to be exacerbating these trends by further concentrating income, wealth, and resources within a small core of countries (Figure 20.4). Indeed, the global economy is growing and integrating rapidly. The expansion of global trade has been central to this process—between 1990 and 1997, international trade grew by 6.5 percent. Since 2000, the volume of global trade has averaged an increase of about 5 percent a year (WTO 2005); the volume of exports and imports in 2005 exceeded $26 trillion, or 58 percent of total global output, up from 44 percent in 1980 (World Bank 2008). Only a handful of developing countries have managed to benefit from that rapid growth (developing countries account for only a third of global trade), and the process of integration into the global economy has been uneven. Some countries—such as the East Asian economies, Chile,

FIGURE 20.3

The Widening of the Gaps between Richer and Poorer Countries between 1820 and 1992

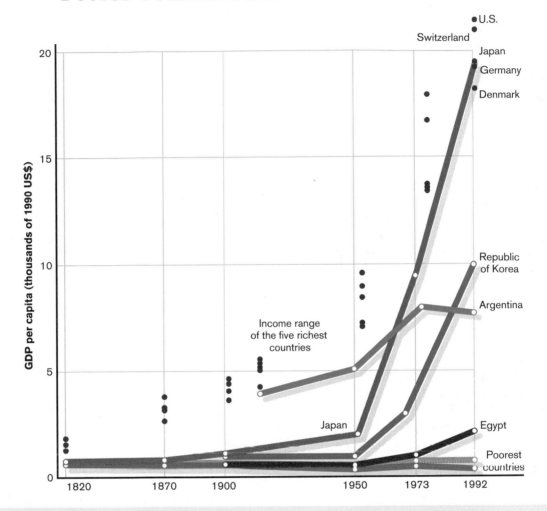

What is the approximate gap in GDP per capita between the cluster of wealthy countries and the poorest countries in 1900? What is the approximate gap in GDP per capita of the United States and poor countries in 1992? In what year was the income range of the five richest countries the most spread out? Which countries in the figure show a leveling off or decline in GDP per capita at any time since 1950?

SOURCE: United Nations Development Programme 1999.

India, and Poland—have fared well, with growth in exports of over 5 percent. Other countries—such as Russia, Venezuela, and Algeria—have seen few benefits from expanding trade and globalization (UNDP 1999). There is a danger that many of the countries most in need of economic growth will be left further behind as globalization progresses.

Many scholars see free trade as the key to economic development and poverty relief. Organizations such as the WTO work to liberalize trade regulations and to reduce trade barriers. Free trade across borders is viewed as a win–win proposition for both developed and developing countries. While the industrialized economies are able to export their products to

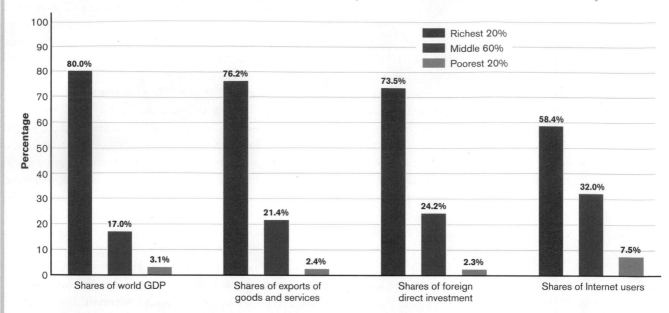

FIGURE 20.4

Shares of the Richest, Middle, and Poorest Countries in Global Income, Trade, Finance, and Communications, 2000

The richest 20 percent of countries account for what percentage of the world's GDP? The middle 60 percent of countries account for what share of exports of goods and services? The richest 20 percent and the middle 60 percent combined account for what percentage of the share of direct foreign investment? Considering that a big part of what is called globalization is an increase in the export of goods and services, based on the information in the figure, who could we say controls and benefits the most from globalization? What actions have the wealthy nations failed to take that would promote greater agricultural trade with poorer, primarily agriculture-exporting nations?

SOURCE: World Bank 2005.

markets worldwide, it is claimed that developing countries will benefit by gaining access to world markets. This, in turn, would improve their prospects for integration into the global economy.

THE CAMPAIGN FOR GLOBAL JUSTICE

Many critics argue that free trade is a one-sided affair that benefits those who are already well off and exacerbates poverty and dependency within the developing world. Recently, much of this criticism has focused around the WTO, which is at the forefront of efforts to increase global trade.

In 1999, more than fifty thousand people from around the world took to the streets of Seattle to protest during the

WTO's Millennium Round of trade talks. Trade unionists, environmentalists, human rights campaigners, antinuclear activists, farmers, and representatives from hundreds of local and international nongovernmental organizations joined forces to voice their frustration with the WTO—an organization seen by many as favoring economic imperatives over all other concerns, including human rights, labor rights, the environment, and sustainable development.

Negotiators from the WTO's 134 member states (the number of members has since risen to 151) had come together to discuss measures to liberalize conditions for global trade and investment in agriculture and forest products, among other issues. Yet the talks broke off early with no agreements reached. The organizers of the protests were triumphant—not only had the demonstrations succeeded in disrupting the talks, but internal disputes among delegates had also surfaced. The Seattle protests were heralded as the biggest victory to date for campaigners for global justice. Since that time, every ministerial meeting of the WTO has faced massive demonstrations by those excluded from the processes of setting the rules for global trade.

Does this campaign represent the emergence of a powerful antiglobalization movement, as some commentators have suggested? Protesters in other cities, such as London and Washington, D.C., argue that free trade and economic globalization further concentrate wealth in the hands of a few, while increasing poverty for the majority of the world's population. Most of these activists agree that global trade is necessary and potentially beneficial for national economies, but they claim that it needs to be regulated by *different* rules: trade rules oriented toward protecting human rights, the environment, labor rights, and local economies—not toward ensuring larger profits for already rich corporations.

The protesters claim that the WTO is an undemocratic organization dominated by the interests of the world's richest nations—particularly the United States. Although the members of the WTO include many developing nations, many have no influence over the organization's policies because the agenda is set by the richest nations. Poorer nations have fewer resources, in terms of money and trained personnel, to confront the highly complex issues related to international trade. The president of the World Bank has pointed out that nineteen of the forty-two African states that are members of the WTO have little or no representation at its headquarters in Geneva (World Bank 2000). Such imbalances have very real consequences. For example, although the WTO has insisted that developing nations open their markets to imports from industrialized countries, it has allowed developed countries to maintain high barriers to agricultural imports and to provide vast subsidies for their domestic agriculture production to protect their own agricultural sectors.

In 2005, the U.S. government spent $19 billion to boost the income of crop and livestock farmers, and European governments spent $80 billion to do the same (Walter and Palmer 2005). This means that the world's poorest (and predominantly agricultural) countries do not have access to the large markets for agricultural goods in developed countries. This issue has confounded the expansion of WTO rules covering trade in services, foreign investment, government procurement, and other areas. Beginning with the 2003 WTO ministerial meeting in Mexico, the "Group of 21" developing nations led by Brazil and India have refused to consider the expansion of WTO rules until the United States and the EU eliminate subsidies for agriculture production and allow greater access to other agriculture markets, such as cotton. The issue of agriculture

subsidies still has not been resolved. A group of developing counties, again led by Brazil, won two major disputes at the WTO over subsidies for European sugar and American cotton. Despite these rulings, the issue of illegal subsidies used by Europe and the United States to support their farmers continues to hamper WTO ministerial meetings.

A similar divide exists over the protection of intellectual property rights—an issue monitored by a WTO multilateral agreement called TRIPS (Trade-Related Aspects of Intellectual Property Rights). Industrial countries own 97 percent of all patents worldwide with only five patent offices (China, Japan, the European Patent Office, the Republic of Korea, and the United States of America) accounting for 77 percent of all patents filed and 74 percent of all patents granted (World Intellectual Property Organization 2007), but the concept of intellectual property rights is alien to the developing world. Recently there has been a significant increase in the number of patent claims as biotechnology companies and research institutes push to control and "own" more forms of knowledge, technology, and biodiversity. Many samples of plant material, for example, have been taken from biodiverse areas such as rain forests and developed by pharmaceutical companies into profitable—and patented—medicines. Local knowledge about the medicinal uses of the plants is often used in developing and marketing the medicines, yet the indigenous people receive no compensation for their contribution. As industrialized countries within the WTO push to strengthen intellectual property laws, many people in developing countries argue that such a move works against the needs of their countries. Research agendas are dictated by profit interests, not human interests, and valuable forms of technology may end up inaccessible to poorer countries that could benefit from their use.

Another criticism of the WTO is that it operates in secret and is not accountable to citizens who are affected by its decisions. In many ways, these criticisms are valid. Trade disputes between members of the WTO are decided behind closed doors by an unelected committee of "experts." When a decision is handed down, it is legally binding on all member states and enforceable through a mechanism that authorizes WTO member nations to enact punitive trade policies unless the losing nation complies with the decision. The WTO can also challenge or override laws in nations that are seen as barriers to trade. This includes national laws or bilateral agreements designed to protect the environment, conserve scarce resources, safeguard public health, or guarantee labor standards and human rights. For example, the WTO has ruled against the EU, which refused to import U.S. hormone-treated beef because of its possible links to cancer, and has challenged a law passed in Massachusetts that prohibits companies from investing in Myanmar (Burma) because of its government's human rights violations. In another instance, the United States and the EU

At a rally in Geneva, Switzerland, Oxfam members protest the trade policies of the WTO. Many protesters claim that the WTO is an undemocratic organization that is dominated by the interests of the world's richest nations—particularly the United States. Although the members of the WTO include developing nations, many of them have almost no practical influence over the organization's policies, because the agenda is set by the richest nations.

have attempted to use the TRIPS provision to block the importation of inexpensive generic HIV/AIDS medication into countries in sub-Saharan Africa, whose populations are being devastated by this epidemic. This move produced worldwide public outrage, which forced the WTO to reconsider its rules that regulate patent rights when public health is at stake.

A final concern is the undue influence wielded by the United States over the activities of the WTO and other international bodies such as the World Bank and the International Monetary Fund. With its overwhelming economic, political, and military might, the United States is able to influence debates and decision making in many international institutions. The unevenness of globalization in part reflects the fact that political and economic power is concentrated in the hands of a few core states. Even as the United States influences the WTO, the United States is also subject to the WTO's rules and decisions. In fact, the United States almost always loses when it is forced to defend its trading practices before a WTO appellate panel (Conti 2003). For example, in 2003 the WTO determined that high tariffs placed on imports of steel into the United States violated the rights of WTO member nations. Under heavy pressure from its trading partners, the United States eventually rescinded the tariffs and complied with WTO law. This example highlights a tension about the nature of power and the processes of globalization: Can we expect the world's sole superpower to play by the rules when the rules go against the interests of the superpower? What effect will this tension have on the creation of a just and equitable global legal and political system?

Protesters against the WTO and other international financial institutions argue that exuberance over global economic integration and free trade is forcing people to live in an economy rather than a society. Many are convinced that such moves will further weaken the economic position of poor societies by allowing transnational corporations to operate with few or no safety and environmental regulations. Commercial interests, they claim, are increasingly taking precedence over concern for human well-being. Not only within developing nations, but in industrialized ones as well, there must be more investment in "human capital"—public health, education, and training—if global divisions are not to deepen. The challenge for the twenty-first century is to ensure that globalization works for people everywhere, not only for those who are already well placed to benefit from it.

☑ CONCEPT CHECKS

1. What effects does globalization have on our everyday lives?
2. Why is globalization associated with new forms of risks? What are the new forms of risk?
3. Briefly describe the debate over the role that free trade plays in global inequality.

The Need for Global Governance

As globalization progresses, existing political structures and models appear unequipped to manage the risks, inequalities, and challenges that transcend national borders. Individual governments cannot control the spread of HIV/AIDS, counter the effects of global warming, or regulate volatile financial markets. In light of this governing deficit, some have called for new forms of global governance. As a growing number of challenges operate above the level of individual countries, responses must also be transnational.

Although it may seem unrealistic to speak of governance above the level of the nation-state, some steps have already been taken toward a global democratic structure, such as the formation of the United Nations and the EU. The EU in particular is an innovative response to globalization and could become a model in other parts of the world where regional ties are strong. New forms of global governance could help promote a cosmopolitan world order in which transparent rules and standards for international behavior, such as the defense of human rights, are established and observed.

The years since the end of the cold war have witnessed violence, internal conflict, and chaotic transformations in many areas of the world. Some observers have taken a pessimistic view, seeing globalization as accelerating crisis and chaos. Others see opportunities to harness globalizing forces in the pursuit of greater equality, democracy, and prosperity. The move toward global governance and more effective regulatory institutions is not misplaced at a time when global interdependence and the rapid pace of change link all people together more than ever before. It is not beyond our abilities to reassert our will on the social world. Indeed, such a task appears to be both the greatest necessity and the greatest challenge facing human societies at the start of the twenty-first century.

☑ CONCEPT CHECKS

1. What are some examples of a move toward a global democratic structure?
2. Summarize optimistic versus pessimistic views toward global governance.

Study Outline

www.wwnorton.com/studyspace

Social Change and Globalization

- *Social change* may be defined as the transformation, over time, of the institutions and culture of a society. The modern period, although occupying only a small fraction of human history, has shown rapid and major changes, and the pace of change is accelerating.
- The development of social organization and institutions, from hunting and gathering to agrarian to modern industrial societies, is too diverse to suit any single-factor theory of social change. At least three broad categories of influences can be identified: The physical environment includes such factors as climate or the availability of communication routes (rivers, mountain passes); these are important, especially as they affect early economic development, but should not be overemphasized. Political organization (especially military power) affects all societies, traditional and modern, with the possible exception of hunting and gathering societies. Cultural factors include religion (which can act as a brake on change), communications systems (such as the invention of writing), and individual leadership.
- The most important economic influence on modern social change is industrial capitalism, which depends on and promotes constant innovation and revision of productive technology. Science and technology also affect (and are affected by) political factors, especially the emergence of the modern state with its relatively efficient forms of government. Cultural influences include another effect of science and technology: the critical and innovative character of modern thinking, which constantly challenges tradition and cultural habits.

What Comes after Modern Industrial Society

- Social theorists have speculated on where social change will lead us. One influential view holds that the industrial era is being superseded by a *postindustrial society* based on the importance of information and service, rather than on manufacturing and industrialization. Some authors speak not only of the end of industrialism, but of the end of modernity itself. Our beliefs in progress, in the benefits of science, and in our ability to control the modern world are diminishing, say the *postmodernists,* and there is such a diversity and plurality of individual concerns and outlooks that it is no longer possible to have any overarching conception of history or of where we are headed.

Factors Contributing to Globalization

- Globalization is produced by the coming together of political, economic, cultural, and social factors. It is spurred mainly by advances in information and communications technologies that have intensified the speed and scope of interaction among people worldwide.
- Several factors contribute to increasing globalization. First, the end of the cold war, the collapse of Soviet-style communism, and the growth of international and regional forms of governance have drawn countries closer together. Second, the spread of information technology has facilitated the global flow of information and has encouraged people to adopt a global outlook. Third, transnational corporations have grown in size and influence, building networks of production and consumption that span the globe and link economic markets.

The Globalization Debate

- Globalization has become a hotly debated topic. Skeptics believe that the idea of globalization is overrated and that current levels of interconnectedness are not unprecedented. Some skeptics focus instead on processes of regionalization that are intensifying activity within major financial and trade groups. Hyperglobalizers take an opposing position, arguing that globalization is a powerful phenomenon that threatens to erode the role of national governments altogether. Transformationalists believe that globalization is transforming many aspects of the current global order—including economics, politics, and social relations—but that old patterns still remain. According to this view, globalization is a contradictory process, involving a multidirectional flow of influences that sometimes work in opposition.

The Effect of Globalization on Our Lives

- Globalization is not restricted to large, global systems. Its impact is felt in our personal lives, in the way we think about ourselves and our connections with others. Globalizing forces enter our local contexts and our intimate lives both through impersonal sources such as the media and the Internet and through personal contacts with people from other countries and cultures.
- Globalization is an open-ended, contradictory process—it produces outcomes that are difficult to control and predict. Globalization is presenting new forms of risk. *External risk* refers to dangers that spring from the natural world, such as earthquakes. *Manufactured risks* are those that are created by the effect of human knowledge and technology on the natural world. Some believe that we are living in a global-risk society in which human societies everywhere are faced with risks (e.g., global warming) that have been produced by our own interventions into nature.
- Globalization is proceeding rapidly but unevenly. It has been marked by a growing divergence between the richest and poorest countries. Wealth, income, resources, and consumption are concentrated among the developed societies, whereas much of the developing world struggles with poverty, malnutrition, disease, and foreign debt. Many of the countries most in need of the economic benefits of globalization are in danger of being marginalized.
- Barriers to international trade have been steadily reduced in recent decades, and many believe that free trade and open markets will allow developing countries to integrate more fully into the global economy. Opponents argue that international trade bodies, such as the WTO, are dominated by the interests of the richest countries and ignore the needs of the developing world. Opponents claim that trade rules must protect human rights, labor rights, the environment, and national economies, rather than simply ensuring larger profits for corporations.

The Need for Global Governance

- Globalization is producing risks, challenges, and inequalities that cross national borders and elude the reach of existing political structures. Because individual governments are unequipped to handle these transnational issues, there is a need for new forms of global governance. Reasserting our will on the rapidly changing social world may be the greatest challenge of the twenty-first century.

Key Concepts

external risk (p. 673)
information society (p. 660)
knowledge society (p. 660)
manufactured risk (p. 673)
postindustrial society (p. 660)
postmodern (p. 661)
service society (p. 660)
social change (p. 656)
transnational corporations (p. 666)

Review Questions

1. What is social change? What do sociologists hope to learn by studying it?
2. What are the five factors that lead to societal collapse, according to Jared Diamond? Which of these do you think is most pertinent today?
3. What are three ways that political organization shapes social change?
4. What is the idea of postmodernity as it relates to history? What is the critique of this argument?
5. Describe three political changes that have contributed to increasing globalization.
6. How has the spread of information technology challenged ideas about the nation-state?
7. Describe the transformationalist perspective on globalization. In this view, what is happening to nation-states?
8. How is globalization challenging traditional frameworks of identity?
9. What is the difference between external and manufactured risk? Which poses a greater threat?
10. What is the goal of the World Trade Organization (WTO)? What do critics have to say about it, according to the text?

Thinking Sociologically Exercises

1. Discuss the many influences on social change: environmental, political, and cultural factors. Summarize how each element can contribute to social change.
2. According to this chapter, we now live in a society where we increasingly face various types of manufactured risks. Briefly explain what these risks consist of. Do you think the last decade has brought us any closer to or further away from confronting the challenges of manufactured risks? Explain.

GLOSSARY

Words in bold type within entries refer to terms found elsewhere in the glossary.

AARP: U.S. advocacy group for people age fifty and over; formerly the American Association of Retired Persons.

absolute poverty: The minimal requirements necessary to sustain a healthy existence.

abstract and concrete attitudes: Abstract attitudes are ideas that are consistent with mainstream societal views, while concrete attitudes are ideas that are based on actual experience.

achievement gap: Disparity on a number of educational measures between the performance of groups of students, especially groups defined by **gender, race, ethnicity**, ability, and socioeconomic status.

"acting white" thesis: The thesis that black students do not aspire to or strive to get good grades because it is perceived as "acting white."

activity theory: A functionalist theory of aging which holds that busy, engaged people are more likely to lead fulfilling and productive lives.

affective individualism: The belief in romantic attachment as a basis for contracting **marriage** ties.

age-grades: The system found in small traditional cultures by which people belonging to a similar age-group are categorized together and hold similar rights and obligations.

ageism: Discrimination or **prejudice** against a person on the grounds of age.

agents of socialization: Groups or social contexts within which processes of **socialization** take place.

aging: The combination of biological, psychological, and social processes that affect people as they grow older.

aging in place: Phenomenon in which many rural areas have disproportionately high numbers of older adults, because young persons seek opportunities elsewhere and leave the older persons behind.

agrarian societies: Societies whose means of subsistence are based on agricultural production (crop growing).

alienation: The sense that our own abilities as human beings are taken over by other entities. The term was originally used by Marx to refer to the projection of human powers onto gods. Subsequently he used the term to refer to the loss of workers' control over the nature and products of their labor.

Alzheimer's disease: A degenerative disease of the brain resulting in progressive loss of mental capacity.

andragogy: Term coined by educators to refer to adult learning.

anomie: A concept first brought into wide usage in sociology by Durkheim, referring to a situation in which social **norms** lose their hold over individual behavior.

antiracism: Forms of thought and/or practice that seek to confront, eradicate and/or ameliorate racism.

apartheid: The system of racial **segregation** established in South Africa.

ascription: Placement in a particular social **status** based on characteristics such as family of origin, race, and gender.

assimilation The acceptance of a **minority group** by a majority population, in which the new group takes on the **values** and **norms** of the dominant **culture.**

authority: A **government**'s legitimate use of **power.**

automation: Production processes monitored and controlled by machines with only minimal supervision from people.

back region: Areas apart from **front region** performance, as specified by Erving Goffman, in which individuals are able to relax and behave informally.

biomedical model of health: The set of principles underpinning Western medical systems and practices. The biomedical model of health defines diseases objectively, in accordance with the presence of recognized symptoms, and believes that the healthy body can be restored through scientifically based medical treatment. The human body is likened to a machine that can be returned to working order with the proper repairs.

black feminism: A strand of **feminist theory** that highlights the multiple disadvantages of **gender, class,** and **race** that shape the experiences of nonwhite women. Black feminists reject the idea of a single, unified gender oppression that is experienced evenly by all women and argue that early feminist analysis reflected the specific concerns of white, middle-class women.

body mass index (BMI): Measure of body fat based on height and weight.

bureaucracy: A type of **organization** marked by a clear hierarchy of authority and the existence of written rules of procedure and staffed by full-time, salaried officials.

capitalism: An economic system based on the private ownership of **wealth,** which is invested and reinvested in order to produce profit.

capitalists: People who own companies, land, or stocks (shares) and use these to generate economic returns.

caste societies: Societies in which different social levels are closed, so that all individuals must remain at the social level of their birth throughout life.

caste system: A social system in which one's social status is given for life.

causal relationship: A relationship in which one state of affairs (the effect) is brought about by another (the cause).

causation: The causal influence of one factor, or **variable,** upon another. A cause and effect relationship exists whenever a particular event or state of affairs (the effect) is produced by the existence of another (the cause). Causal factors in sociology include the reasons individuals give for what they do, as well as external influences on their behavior.

charismatic: The inspirational quality capable of capturing the imagination and devotion of a mass of followers.

churches: Large bodies of people belonging to an established religious organization. The term is also used to refer to the place in which religious ceremonies are carried out.

citizens: Members of a political community, having both rights and duties associated with that membership.

civil inattention: The process whereby individuals in the same physical setting demonstrate to one another that they are aware of each other's presence.

civil religion: A set of religious beliefs through which a society interprets its own history in light of some conception of ultimate reality.

civil rights: Legal rights held by all **citizens** in a given national community.

civil society: The realm of activity that lies between the **state** and the market, including the **family,** schools, community associations, and noneconomic institutions. Civil society, or civic culture, is essential to vibrant democratic societies.

class: Although it is one of the most frequently used concepts in **sociology,** there is no clear agreement about how the notion should be defined. Most sociologists use the term to refer to socioeconomic variations between groups of individuals that create variations in their material prosperity and power.

clock time: Time as measured by the clock, in terms of hours, minutes, and seconds. Before the invention of clocks, time reckoning was based on events in the natural world, such as the rising and setting of the sun.

cognition: Human thought processes involving perception, reasoning, and remembering.

cohabitation: Two people living together in a sexual relationship of some permanence, without being married to one another.

collective action: Action undertaken in a relatively spontaneous way by a large number of people assembled together.

collective consumption: A concept used by Manuel Castells to refer to processes of urban consumption—such as the buying and selling of property.

colonialism: The process whereby Western nations established their rule in parts of the world away from their home territories.

communication: The transmission of information from one individual or group to another. Communication is the necessary basis of all social interaction. In face-to-face **encounters,** communication is carried on by the use of **language** and by bodily cues that individuals interpret. With the development of writing and electronic media such as radio, television, and computers, communication becomes in some part detached from immediate face-to-face social relationships.

communism: A set of political ideas associated with Marx, as developed particularly by Lenin and institutionalized in the Soviet Union, Eastern Europe, and some Third World countries.

community policing: A renewed emphasis on crime prevention rather than law enforcement to reintegrate policing within the community.

comparable worth: Policies that attempt to remedy the gender pay gap by adjusting pay so that those in female-dominated jobs are not paid less for equivalent work.

comparative questions: Questions concerned with drawing comparisons between different human societies for the purposes of sociological **theory** or research.

comparative research: Research that compares one set of findings on one society with the same type of findings on other societies.

complementary and alternative medicine (CAM): A diverse set of approaches and therapies for treating illness and promoting well-being that generally falls outside of standard medical practices.

compulsion of proximity: People's need to interact with others in their presence.

concrete operational stage: A stage of cognitive development, as formulated by Piaget, in which the child's thinking is based primarily on physical perception of the world. In this phase, the child is not yet capable of dealing with abstract concepts or hypothetical situations.

conflict theory: Argument that deviance is deliberately chosen and often political in nature.

conflict theories of aging: Arguments that emphasize the ways in which the larger social structure helps to shape the opportunities available to the elderly. Unequal opportunities are seen as creating the potential for conflict.

constitutional monarchs: Kings or queens who are largely figureheads. Real power rests in the hands of other political **leaders.**

contradiction: A term used by Marx to refer to mutually antagonistic tendencies in a society.

contradictory class locations: Positions in the class structure, particularly routine white-collar and lower managerial jobs, that share characteristics of the class positions both above and below them.

controls: Statistical or experimental means of holding some **variables** constant in order to examine the causal influence of others.

control theory: A theory that views **crime** as the outcome of an imbalance between impulses toward criminal activity and controls that deter it. Control theorists hold that criminals are rational beings who will act to maximize their own reward unless they are rendered unable to do so through either social or physical controls.

conurbation: An agglomeration of towns or cities into an unbroken urban environment.

conversation analysis: The empirical study of conversations, employing techniques drawn from **ethnomethodology.** Conversation analysis examines details of naturally occurring conversations to reveal the organizational principles of talk and its role in the production and reproduction of social order.

core countries: According to **world-systems theory,** the most advanced industrial countries, which take the lion's share of profits in the world economic system.

corporate crime: Offenses committed by large corporations in society. Examples of corporate crime include pollution, false advertising, and violations of health and safety regulations.

corporate culture: An organizational culture involving rituals, events, or traditions that are unique to a specific company.

corporations: Business firms or companies.

correlation: The regular relationship between two **variables,** often expressed in statistical terms. Correlations may be positive or negative. A positive correlation between two variables exists when a high rank on one variable is associated with a high rank on the other. A negative correlation exists when a high rank on one variable is associated with a low rank on the other.

correlation coefficients: The measure of the degree of **correlation** between **variables.**

created environment: Constructions established by human beings to serve their needs, derived from the use of man-made **technology**—including, for example, roads, railways, factories, offices, private homes, and other buildings.

crimes: Any actions that contravene the **laws** established by a political authority. Although we may think of criminals as a distinct subsection of the population, there are few people who have not broken the law in one way or another during their lives. While laws are formulated by state authorities, it is not unknown for those authorities to engage in criminal behavior in certain situations.

crude birthrates: Statistical measures representing the number of births within a given population per year, normally calculated in terms of the number of births per thousand members. Although the crude birthrate is a useful index, it is only a general measure, because it does not specify numbers of births in relation to age distribution.

crude death rates: Statistical measures representing the number of deaths that occur annually in a given population per year, normally calculated as the ratio of deaths per thousand members. Crude death rates give a general indication of the **mortality** levels of a community or society, but are limited in their usefulness because they do not take into account the age distribution.

cults: Fragmentary religious groupings to which individuals are loosely affiliated, but which lack any permanent structure.

cultural capital: The advantages that well-to-do parents usually provide their children.

cultural navigators: People who draw from both their home culture and mainstream culture to create an attitude that allows them to succeed.

cultural relativism: The practice of judging a **society** by its own standards.

cultural turn: **Sociology**'s recent emphasis on the importance of understanding the role of **culture** in daily life.

cultural universals: **Values** or modes of behavior shared by all human **cultures.**

culture: The **values, norms,** and **material goods** characteristic of a given group. Like the concept of **society,** the notion of culture is widely used in **sociology** and the other social sciences (particularly anthropology). Culture is one of the most distinctive properties of human social association.

culture of poverty: The thesis, popularized by Oscar Lewis, that poverty is not a result of individual inadequacies but is instead the outcome of a larger social and cultural atmosphere into which successive generations of children are socialized. The culture of poverty refers to the **values,** beliefs, lifestyles, habits, and traditions that are common among people living under conditions of material deprivation.

cybercrime: Criminal activities by means of electronic **networks** or involving the use of new information **technologies.** Electronic money laundering, personal identity theft, electronic vandalism, and monitoring electronic correspondence are all emergent forms of cybercrime.

cyberspace: Electronic networks of interaction between individuals at different computer terminals.

degree of dispersal: The range or distribution of a set of figures.

democracy: A political system that allows the **citizens** to participate in political decision making or to elect representatives to **government** bodies.

democratic elitism: A theory of the limits of **democracy,** which holds that in large-scale societies democratic participation is necessarily limited to the regular election of political **leaders.**

demographic transition: An interpretation of population change, which holds that a stable ratio of births to deaths is achieved once a certain level of economic prosperity has been reached. According to this notion, in preindustrial societies there is a rough balance between births and deaths, because population increase is kept in check by a lack of available food, by disease, or by war. In modern societies, by contrast, population equilibrium is achieved because **families** are moved by economic incentives to limit the number of children.

demography: The study of populations.

denomination: A religious **sect** that has lost its revivalist dynamism and become an institutionalized body, commanding the adherence of significant numbers of people.

dependency culture: A term popularized by Charles Murray to describe individuals who rely on state welfare provision rather than entering the labor market. The dependency culture is seen as the outcome of the "paternalistic" welfare state that undermines individual ambition and people's capacity for self-help.

dependency ratio: The ratio of the number of economically dependent members of the population to the number of economically productive members.

dependency theories: Marxist theories of economic development arguing that the poverty of low-income countries stems directly from their exploitation by wealthy countries and the **multinational corporations** that are based in wealthy countries.

dependent development: The theory that poor countries can still develop economically, but only in ways shaped by their reliance on the wealthier countries.

dependent variable: A **variable,** or factor, causally influenced by another (the **independent variable**).

developing world: The less-developed societies, in which industrial production is either virtually nonexistent or only developed to a limited degree. The majority of the world's population live in less-developed countries.

developmental questions: Questions that sociologists pose when looking at the origins and path of development of **social institutions** from the past to the present.

deviance: Modes of action that do not conform to the **norms** or **values** held by most members of a group or **society.** What is regarded as deviant is as variable as the norms and values that distinguish different **cultures** and

subcultures from one another. Forms of behavior that are highly esteemed by one group are regarded negatively by others.

deviant subculture: A **subculture** whose members hold values that differ substantially from those of the majority.

diaspora: The dispersal of an ethnic population from an original homeland into foreign areas, often in a forced manner or under traumatic circumstances.

differential association: An interpretation of the development of criminal behavior proposed by Edwin H. Sutherland, according to whom criminal behavior is learned through association with others who regularly engage in **crime.**

direct democracy: A form of **participatory democracy** that allows **citizens** to vote directly on **laws** and policies.

discrimination: Behavior that denies to the members of a particular group resources or rewards that can be obtained by others. Discrimination must be distinguished from **prejudice:** Individuals who are prejudiced against others may not engage in discriminatory practices against them; conversely, people may act in a discriminatory fashion toward a group even though they are not prejudiced against that group.

disengagement theory: A functionalist theory of **aging** which holds that it is functional for society to remove people from their traditional roles when they become elderly, thereby freeing up those roles for others.

disestablishment: A period during which the political influence of established religions is successfully challenged.

displacement: The transferring of ideas or emotions from their true source to another object.

division of labor: The specialization of **work** tasks, by means of which different **occupations** are combined within a production system. All **societies** have at least some rudimentary form of division of labor, especially between the tasks allocated to men and those performed by women. With the development of industrialism, the division of labor became vastly more complex than in any prior type of production system. In the modern world, the division of labor is international in scope.

doubling time: The time it takes for a particular level of population to double.

dyad: A group consisting of two persons.

ecological approach: A perspective on urban analysis emphasizing the "natural" distribution of city neighborhoods into areas having contrasting characteristics.

ecology: The scientific study of the distribution and abundance of life and the interactions between organisms and their natural environment.

economic interdependence: The fact that in the **division of labor,** individuals depend on others to produce many or most of the goods they need to sustain their lives.

economy: The system of production and exchange that provides for the material needs of individuals living in a given **society.** Economic institutions are of key importance in all social orders. What goes on in the economy usually influences other areas in social life. Modern economies differ substantially from traditional ones, because the majority of the population is no longer engaged in agricultural production.

egocentric: According to Piaget, the characteristic quality of a child during the early years of her life. Egocentric thinking involves understanding objects and events in the environment solely in terms of the child's own position.

emigration: The movement of people out of one country in order to settle in another.

empirical investigations: Factual inquiries carried out in any area of sociological study.

encounter: A meeting between two or more people in a situation of face-to-face interaction. Our daily lives can be seen as a series of different encounters strung out across the course of the day. In modern societies, many of these encounters are with strangers rather than people we know.

entrepreneur: The owner/founder of a business firm.

epidemiology: The study of the distribution and incidence of disease and illness within a population.

ethnic cleansing: The creation of ethnically homogeneous territories through the mass expulsion of other ethnic populations.

ethnicity: Cultural **values** and **norms** that distinguish the members of a given group from others. An ethnic group is one whose members share a distinct awareness of a common cultural identity, separating them from other groups. In virtually all **societies,** ethnic differences are associated with variations in **power** and material **wealth.** Where ethnic differences are also racial, such divisions are sometimes especially pronounced.

ethnie: A term used to describe a group that shares ideas of common ancestry, a common cultural identity, and a link with a specific homeland.

ethnocentrism: The tendency to look at other **cultures** through the eyes of one's own culture, and thereby misrepresent them.

ethnography: The firsthand study of people using **participant observation** or interviewing.

ethnomethodology: The study of how people make sense of what others say and do in the course of day-to-day social interaction. Ethnomethodology is concerned with the "ethnomethods" by which people sustain meaningful interchanges with one another.

evangelicalism: A form of Protestantism characterized by a belief in spiritual rebirth (being "born again").

exchange mobility: The exchange of positions on the socioeconomic scale such that talented people move up the economic hierarchy while the less talented move down.

experiment: A **research method** in which **variables** can be analyzed in a controlled and systematic way, either in an artificial situation constructed by the researcher or in naturally occurring settings.

exponential: A geometric, rather than linear, rate of progression, producing a fast rise in the numbers of a population experiencing such growth.

extended family: A **family** group consisting of more than two generations of relatives living either within the same household or very close to one another.

external risk: Dangers that spring from the natural world and are unrelated to the actions of humans. Examples of external risk include droughts, earthquakes, famines, and storms.

factual questions: Questions that raise issues concerning matters of fact (rather than theoretical or moral issues).

families of orientation: The families into which individuals are born.

families of procreation: The families individuals initiate through **marriage** or by having children.

family: A group of individuals related to one another by blood ties, **marriage,** or adoption, who form an economic unit, the adult members of which are responsible for the upbringing of children. All known **societies** involve some form of family system, although the nature of family relationships varies widely. While in modern societies the main family form is the **nuclear family, extended family** relationships are also found.

family capitalism: Capitalistic enterprise owned and administered by entrepreneurial **families.**

fecundity: A measure of the number of children that it is biologically possible for a woman to produce.

feminist theory: A sociological perspective that emphasizes the centrality of **gender** in analyzing the social world and particularly the uniqueness of the experience of women. There are many strands of feminist theory, but they all share the desire to explain **gender inequalities** in **society** and to work to overcome them.

feminization of poverty: An increase in the proportion of the poor who are female.

fertility: The average number of live-born children produced by women of childbearing age in a particular **society.**

field of action: The arena within which **social movements** interact with established **organizations,** the ideas and outlook of the members of both often becoming modified as a result.

first world: The group of **nation-states** that possesses mature industrialized economies based on capitalistic production.

flexible production: Process in which computers design customized products for a mass market.

focused interaction: Interaction between individuals engaged in a common activity or in direct conversation with one another.

Fordism: The system of production pioneered by Henry Ford, in which the assembly line was introduced.

formal operational stage: According to Piaget's theory, a stage of cognitive development at which the growing child becomes capable of handling abstract concepts and hypothetical situations.

formal organization: Means by which a group is rationally designed to achieve its objectives, often by means of explicit rules, regulations, and procedures.

formal relations: Relations that exist in groups and **organizations,** laid down by the **norms,** or rules, of the official system of authority.

front region: Settings of social activity in which people seek to put on a definite "performance" for others.

functionalism: A theoretical perspective based on the notion that social events can best be explained in terms of the functions they perform—that is, the contributions they make to the continuity of a **society.**

fundamentalists: A group within **evangelicalism** that is highly antimodern in many of its beliefs, adhering to strict codes of morality and conduct.

gender: Social expectations about behavior regarded as appropriate for the members of each **sex.** Gender refers not to the physical attributes distinguishing men and women but to socially formed traits of masculinity and femininity. The study of gender relations has become one of the most important areas of **sociology** in recent years.

gender gap: The differences between women and men, especially as reflected in social, political, intellectual, cultural, or economic attainments or attitudes.

gender inequality: The inequality between men and women in terms of **wealth, income,** and **status.**

gender roles: Social roles assigned to each **sex** and labeled as masculine or feminine.

gender socialization: The learning of **gender roles** through social factors such as schooling, the media, and **family.**

gender typing: Women holding **occupations** of lower **status** and pay, such as secretarial and retail positions, and men holding **jobs** of higher status and pay, such as managerial and professional positions.

generalized other: A concept in the **theory** of George Herbert Mead, according to which the individual takes over the general **values** of a given group or **society** during the **socialization** process.

generational equity: The striking of a balance between the needs and interests of members of different generations.

genocide: The systematic, planned destruction of a racial, political, or cultural group.

gentrification: A process of **urban renewal** in which older, deteriorated housing is refurbished by affluent people moving into the area.

geragogy: Term coined by educators to refer to older-adult learning.

glass ceiling: A promotion barrier that prevents a woman's upward mobility within an **organization.**

glass escalator: The process by which men in traditionally female professions benefit from an unfair rapid rise within an **organization.**

global city: A city—such as London, New York, or Tokyo—that has become an organizing center of the new global economy.

global commodity chains: Worldwide **networks** of labor and production processes yielding a finished product.

global inequality: The systematic differences in **wealth** and **power** between countries.

globalization: The development of social and economic relationships stretching worldwide. In current times, we are all influenced by **organizations** and social **networks** located thousands of miles away. A key part of the study of globalization is the emergence of a **world system**—for some purposes, we need to regard the world as forming a single social order.

global outsourcing: A business practice that sends production of materials to factories around the world. The components of one final product often originate from many different countries than the one in which the product is ultimately put together and sold. Factories from different countries must compete with each other to obtain business.

global village: A notion associated with Marshall McLuhan, who believed that the world has become like a small community as a result of the spread of electronic communication. For instance, people in many different parts of the world follow the same news events through television programming.

government: The enacting of policies and decisions on the part of officials within a political apparatus. We can speak of government as a process, or *the* government as the officialdom responsible for making binding political decisions. While in the past virtually all governments were headed by monarchs or emperors, in most modern **societies** governments are run by officials who do not inherit their positions of **power** but are elected or appointed on the basis of qualifications.

graying: A term used to indicate that an increasing proportion of a **society's** population is becoming elderly.

group production: Production organized by means of small groups rather than individuals.

groupthink: A process by which the members of a group ignore ways of thinking and plans of action that go against the group consensus.

health literacy: One's capacity to obtain, process, and understand basic health information and services needed to make appropriate health decisions.

hidden curriculum: Traits of behavior or attitudes that are learned at school but not included within the formal curriculum—for example, **gender** differences.

high-trust system: Organization or **work** setting in which individuals are permitted a great deal of autonomy and control over the work task.

historicity: The use of an understanding of history as a basis for trying to change history—that is, producing informed processes of **social change.**

homeless: People who have no place to sleep and either stay in free shelters or sleep in public places not meant for habitation.

homophobia: An irrational fear or disdain of homosexuals.

human capital theory: Argument that individuals make investments in their own "human capital" in order to increase their productivity and earnings.

human resource management: A style of management that regards a company's work force as vital to its economic competitiveness.

hunting and gathering societies: Societies whose mode of subsistence is gained from hunting animals, fishing, and gathering edible plants.

hyperreality: An idea associated with Jean Baudrillard, who argued that as a result of the spread of electronic communication, there is no longer a separate "reality" to which TV programs and other cultural products refer. Instead, what we take to be "reality" is structured by such communication itself. For instance, the items reported on the news are not just about a separate series of events, but actually define and construct what those events are.

hypotheses: Ideas or guesses about a given state of affairs, put forward as bases for empirical testing.

ideal type: A "pure type," constructed by emphasizing certain traits of a social item that do not necessarily exist in reality. An example is Max Weber's ideal type of bureaucratic organization.

identity: The distinctive characteristics of a person's or group's character that relate to who they are and what is meaningful to them. Some of the main sources of identity include **gender,** sexual orientation, nationality or **ethnicity,** and social **class.**

ideology: Shared ideas or beliefs that serve to justify the interests of **dominant groups.** Ideologies are found in all **societies** in which there are systematic and ingrained inequalities between groups. The concept of ideology connects closely with that of **power,** since ideological systems serve to legitimize the power that groups hold.

immigration: The movement of people into one country from another for the purpose of settlement.

impression management: Preparing for the presentation of one's **social role.**

income: Payment, usually derived from wages, salaries, or investments.

independent variable: A **variable,** or factor, that causally affects another (the **dependent variable**).

industrialism hypothesis: Theory that **societies** become more open to **social mobility** as they become more industrialized.

industrialization: The process of the machine production of goods. See also **industrialized societies.**

industrialized societies: Strongly developed **nation-states** in which the majority of the population work in factories or offices rather than in agriculture, and most people live in urban areas.

infant mortality rate: The number of infants who die during the first year of life, per thousand live births.

informal economy: Economic transactions carried on outside the sphere of orthodox paid employment.

informal relations: Relations that exist in groups and **organizations** developed on the basis of personal connections; ways of doing things that depart from formally recognized modes of procedure.

information poverty: The "information poor" are those people who have little or no access to information **technology,** such as computers.

information society: A **society** no longer based primarily on the production of **material goods** but on the production of knowledge. The notion of the information society is closely bound up with the rise of **information technology.**

information technology: Forms of **technology** based on information processing and requiring microelectronic circuitry.

in-groups: Groups toward which one feels particular loyalty and respect—the groups to which "we" belong.

inner city: The areas composing the central neighborhoods of a city, as distinct from the suburbs. In many modern urban settings in the **first world,** inner-city areas are subject to dilapidation and decay, the more affluent residents having moved to outlying areas.

instincts: Fixed patterns of behavior that have genetic origins and that appear in all normal animals within a given species.

institutional capitalism: Capitalistic enterprise organized on the basis of institutional shareholding.

institutional racism: Patterns of **discrimination** based on **ethnicity** that have become structured into existing social institutions.

intelligence: Level of intellectual ability, particularly as measured by **IQ (intelligence quotient)** tests.

interactional vandalism: The deliberate subversion of the tacit rules of conversation.

interest group: A group organized to pursue specific interests in the political arena, operating primarily by lobbying the members of legislative bodies.

intergenerational mobility: Movement up or down a social stratification hierarchy from one generation to another.

international division of labor: The interdependence of countries or regions that trade in global markets.

international governmental organization (IGO): An international organization established by treaties between **governments** for purposes of conducting business between the nations making up its membership.

international nongovernmental organization (INGO): An international organization established by agreements between the individuals or private **organizations** making up its membership.

intragenerational mobility: Movement up or down a **social stratification** hierarchy within the course of a personal career.

IQ (intelligence quotient): A score attained on tests of symbolic or reasoning abilities.

iron law of oligarchy: A term coined by Weber's student Robert Michels meaning that large **organizations** tend toward centralization of **power,** making **democracy** difficult.

kinship: A relation that links individuals through blood ties, **marriage,** or adoption. Kinship relations are by definition part of marriage and the **family,** but extend much more broadly. While in most modern societies few social obligations are involved in kinship relations extending beyond the immediate family, in other cultures kinship is of vital importance to social life.

knowledge economy: A **society** no longer based primarily on the production of **material goods** but based instead on the production of knowledge. Its emergence has been linked to the development of a broad base of consumers who are technologically literate and have made new advances in computing, entertainment, and telecommunications part of their lives.

knowledge society: Another common term for **information society**—a **society** based on the production and consumption of knowledge and information.

Kuznets curve: A formula showing that inequality increases during the early stages of capitalist development, then declines, and eventually stabilizes at a relatively low level; advanced by the economist Simon Kuznets.

labeling theory: An approach to the study of **deviance** that suggests that people become "deviant" because certain labels are attached to their behavior by political authorities and others.

language: The primary vehicle of meaning and communication in a society, language is a system of **symbols** that represent objects and abstract thoughts.

latent functions: Functional consequences that are not intended or recognized by the members of a social system in which they occur.

laws: Rules of behavior established by a political authority and backed by state **power.**

leader: A person who is able to influence the behavior of other members of a group.

legitimation crisis: The failure of a political order to generate a sufficient level of commitment and involvement on the part of its **citizens** to be able to govern properly.

liberal democracies: Systems of **democracy** based on parliamentary institutions, coupled to the free-market system in the area of economic production.

liberal feminism: Form of **feminist theory** that believes that **gender inequality** is produced by unequal access to **civil rights** and certain social resources, such as education and employment, based on **sex.** Liberal feminists tend to seek solutions through changes in legislation that ensure that the rights of individuals are protected.

liberation theology: An activist Catholic religious movement that combines Catholic beliefs with a passion for social justice for the poor.

life chances: A term introduced by Max Weber to signify a person's opportunities for achieving economic prosperity.

life course: The various transitions people experience during their lives.

life expectancy: The number of years the average person can expect to live

life histories: Studies of the overall lives of individuals, often based on both self-reporting and documents such as letters.

life span: The maximum length of life that is biologically possible for a member of a given species.

linguistic relativity hypothesis: A **hypothesis,** based on the **theories** of Sapir and Whorf, that perceptions are relative to **language.**

local knowledge: Knowledge of a local community, possessed by individuals who spend long periods of their lives in it.

local nationalisms: The beliefs that communities that share a cultural identity should have political autonomy, even within smaller units of a **nation-states.**

lower class: A social class comprised of those who work part time or not at all

and whose household income is typically lower than $17,000 a year.

low-trust systems: Organizational or **work** settings in which people are allowed little responsibility for, or control over, the work task.

macrosociology: The study of large-scale groups, **organizations,** or social systems.

Malthusianism: A doctrine about population dynamics developed by Thomas Malthus, according to which population increase comes up against "natural limits," represented by famine and war.

managerial capitalism: Capitalistic enterprises administered by managerial executives rather than by owners.

manifest functions: The functions of a type of social activity that are known to and intended by the individuals involved in the activity.

manufactured risk: Dangers that are created by the impact of human knowledge and **technology** on the natural world. Examples of manufactured risk include global warming and genetically modified foods.

market-oriented theories: Theories about economic development that assume that the best possible economic consequences will result if individuals are free to make their own economic decisions, uninhibited by governmental constraint.

marriage: A socially approved sexual relationship between two individuals. Marriage almost always involves two persons of opposite sexes, but in some cultures, types of homosexual marriage are tolerated. Marriage normally forms the basis of a **family of procreation**—that is, it is expected that the married couple will produce and bring up children. Some societies permit **polygamy,** in which an individual may have several spouses at the same time.

Marxism: A body of thought deriving its main elements from Marx's ideas.

mass media: Forms of communication, such as newspapers, magazines, radio, and television, designed to reach mass audiences.

material goods: The physical objects that a **society** creates, which influence the ways in which people live.

materialist conception of history: The view developed by Marx, according to which material, or economic, factors have a prime role in determining historical change.

matrilocal: A **family** system in which the husband is expected to live near the wife's parents.

mean: A statistical measure of central tendency, or average, based on dividing a total by the number of individual cases.

means of production: The means whereby the production of **material goods** is carried on in a **society,** including not just **technology** but the social relations between producers.

measures of central tendency: The ways of calculating averages.

median: The number that falls halfway in a range of numbers—a way of calculating central tendency that is sometimes more useful than calculating a **mean.**

mediated interaction: Interaction between individuals who are not physically in one another's presence—for example, a telephone conversation.

mediated quasi-interaction: Interaction that is one-sided and partial—for example, a person watching a television program.

Medicare: A program under the U.S. Social Security Administration that reimburses hospitals and physicians for medical care provided to qualifying people over sixty-five years old.

megacities: A term favored by Manuel Castells to describe large, intensely concentrated urban spaces that serve as connection points for the global **economy.** It is projected that by 2015 there will be thirty-six megacities with populations of more than 8 million residents.

megalopolis: The "city of all cities" in ancient Greece—used in modern times to refer to very large **conurbations.**

melting pot: The idea that ethnic differences can be combined to create new patterns of behavior drawing on diverse cultural sources.

microsociology: The study of human behavior in contexts of face-to-face interaction.

middle class: A social **class** composed broadly of those working in white-collar and lower managerial occupations.

minority group (or ethnic minority): A group of people in a minority in a given **society** who, because of their distinct physical or cultural characteristics, find themselves in situations of inequality within that society.

mode: The number that appears most often in a given set of data. This can sometimes be a helpful way of portraying central tendency.

modernization theory: A version of market-oriented development theory that argues that low-income societies develop economically only if they give up their traditional ways and adopt modern economic institutions, **technologies,** and cultural **values** that emphasize savings and productive investment.

monogamy: A form of **marriage** in which each married partner is allowed only one spouse at any given time.

monopoly: A situation in which a single firm dominates in a given industry.

monotheism: Belief in a single god.

mortality: The number of deaths in a population.

multiculturalism: Ethnic groups exist separately and share *equally* in economic and political life.

multinational corporations: Business corporations located in two or more countries.

multiple sovereignty: A situation in which there is no single sovereign **power** in a **society.**

nationalism: A set of beliefs and **symbols** expressing identification with a national community.

nation-states: Particular types of **states,** characteristic of the modern world, in which governments have sovereign **power** within defined territorial areas, and populations are **citizens** who know themselves to be part of single nations. Nation-states are closely associated with the rise of **nationalism,** although nationalist loyalties do not always conform to the boundaries of specific states. Nation-states developed as part of an emerging nation-state system, originating in Europe; in current times, they span the whole globe.

nations without states: Instances in which the members of a nation lack political **sovereignty** over the area they claim as their own.

neoliberalism: The economic belief that free market forces, achieved by minimizing government restrictions on business, provide the only route to economic growth.

networks: Sets of informal and formal social ties that link people to each other.

New Age movement: A general term to describe the diverse spectrum of beliefs and practices oriented on inner spirituality. Paganism, Eastern mysticism, shamanism, alternative forms of healing, and astrology are all examples of New Age activities.

new criminology: A branch of criminological thought, prominent in Britain in the 1970s, that regarded **deviance** as deliberately chosen and often political in nature. The new criminologists argued that **crime** and deviance could only be understood in the context of **power** and inequality within **society.**

newly industrializing economies (NIEs): Developing countries that over the past two or three decades have begun to develop a strong industrial base, such as Singapore and Hong Kong.

new religious movements: The broad range of religious and spiritual groups, **cults,** and sects that have emerged alongside mainstream **religions.** New religious movements range from spiritual and self-help groups within the **New Age movement** to exclusive sects such as the Hare Krishnas.

new social movements: A set of **social movements** that have arisen in Western **societies** since the 1960s in response to the changing risks facing human societies. New social movements such as **feminism,** environmentalism, the antinuclear movement, protests against genetically modified food, and antiglobalization demonstrations differ from earlier social movements in that they are single-issue campaigns oriented to nonmaterial ends and draw support from across class lines.

new-style terrorism: A recent form of **terrorism** characterized by global ambitions, loose global organizational ties, and a more ruthless attitude toward the violence the terrorists are willing to use.

nonverbal communication: Communication between individuals based on facial expression or bodily gesture rather than on **language.**

norms: Rules of conduct that specify appropriate behavior in a given range of social situations. A norm either prescribes a given type of behavior or forbids it. All human groups follow definite norms, which are always backed by **sanctions** of one kind or another—varying from informal disapproval to physical punishment.

nuclear family: A **family** group consisting of a wife, a husband (or one of these), and dependent children.

obesity: Excessive body weight indicated by a **body mass index (BMI)** over 30.

occupation: Any form of paid employment in which an individual regularly works.

oldest old: Sociological term for persons aged eighty-five and older.

old old: Sociological term for persons aged seventy-five to eighty-four.

old-style terrorism: A type of **terrorism** that is local and linked to particular states and has limited objectives, which means that the violence involved is fairly limited.

oligarchy: Rule by a small minority within an **organization** or **society.**

oligopoly: The domination of a small number of firms in a given industry.

organic solidarity: According to Émile Durkheim, the social cohesion that results from the various parts of a **society** functioning as an integrated whole.

organization: A large group of individuals with a definite set of authority relations. Many types of organizations exist in **industrialized societies,** influencing most aspects of our lives. While not all organizations are bureaucratic, there are close links between the development of organizations and bureaucratic tendencies.

organized crime: Criminal activities carried out by **organizations** established as businesses.

out-groups: Groups toward which one feels antagonism and contempt—"those people."

pariah groups: Groups who suffer from negative **status discrimination**—they are looked down on by most other members of society. The Jews, for example, have been a pariah group throughout much of European history.

participant observation: A method of research widely used in **sociology** and anthropology, in which the researcher takes part in the activities of the group or community being studied.

participatory democracy: A system of **democracy** in which all members of a group or community participate collectively in making major decisions.

pastoral societies: **Societies** whose subsistence derives from the rearing of domesticated animals.

patriarchy: The dominance of men over women. All known **societies** are patriarchal, although there are variations in the degree and nature of the **power** men exercise, as compared with women. One of the prime objectives of women's movements in modern societies is to combat existing patriarchal institutions.

patrilocal: A **family** system in which the wife is expected to live near the husband's parents.

peer group: A friendship group composed of individuals of similar age and social **status.**

periphery: Countries that have a marginal role in the world **economy** and are thus dependent on the core producing societies for their trading relationships.

personality stabilization: According to the theory of **functionalism,** the **family** plays a crucial role in assisting its adult members emotionally. **Marriage** between adult men and women is the arrangement through which adult personalities are supported and kept healthy.

personal space: The physical space individuals maintain between themselves and others.

pilot study: A trial run in **survey** research.

pluralism: A model for ethnic relations in which all ethnic groups in the United States retain their independent and separate identities, yet share equally in the rights and **powers** of **citizenship.**

political rights: Rights of political participation, such as the right to vote in local and national elections, held by **citizens** of a national community.

politics: The means by which **power** is employed to influence the nature and content of governmental activities. The sphere of the political includes the activities of those in **government,** but also the actions of others. There are many ways in which people outside the governmental apparatus seek to influence it.

polyandry: A form of **marriage** in which a woman may simultaneously have two or more husbands.

polygamy: A form of **marriage** in which a person may have two or more spouses simultaneously.

polygyny: A form of **marriage** in which a man may simultaneously have two or more wives.

polytheism: Belief in two or more gods.

population: The people who are the focus of social research.

portfolio worker: A worker who possesses a diversity of skills or qualifications and is therefore able to move easily from **job** to job.

post-Fordism: A general term used to describe the transition from mass industrial production, characterized by **Fordist** methods, to more flexible forms of production favoring innovation and aimed at meeting market demands for customized products.

postindustrial society: A notion advocated by those who believe that processes of social change are taking us beyond the industrialized order. A postindustrial society is based on the production of information rather than **material goods.** According to postindustrialists, we are currently experiencing a series of social changes as profound as those that initiated the industrial era some two hundred years ago.

postmodern: A technologically sophisticated society that is preoccupied with consumer goods and media images.

postmodern feminism: Feminist persepective that challenges the idea of a unitary basis of identity and experience shared by all women. Postmodern feminists reject the claim that there is a grand theory which can explain the position of women in society, or that there is any single, universal essence or category of "woman." Instead, postmodernism encourages the acceptance of many different standpoints as equally valid.

postmodernism: The belief that **society** is no longer governed by history or progress. Postmodern society is highly pluralistic and diverse, with no "grand narrative" guiding its development.

poverty line: An official **government** measure to define those living in poverty in the United States.

power: The ability of individuals or the members of a group to achieve aims or further the interests they hold. Power is a pervasive element in all human relationships. Many conflicts in **society** are struggles over power, because how much power an individual or group is able to achieve governs how far they are able to put their wishes into practice.

power elite: Small **networks** of individuals who, according to C. Wright Mills, hold concentrated **power** in modern **societies.**

prejudice: The holding of preconceived ideas about an individual or group, ideas that are resistant to change even in the face of new information. Prejudice may be either positive or negative.

preoperational stage: A stage of cognitive development, in Piaget's theory, in which the child has advanced sufficiently to master basic modes of logical thought.

primary deviation: According to Edwin Lemert, the actions that cause others to label one as a deviant.

primary groups: Groups that are characterized by intense emotional ties, face-to-face interaction, intimacy, and a strong, enduring sense of commitment.

primary socialization: The process by which children learn the cultural **norms** of the **society** into which they are born. Primary socialization occurs largely in the **family.**

procreative technology: Techniques of influencing the human reproductive process.

profane: That which belongs to the mundane, everyday world.

projection: Attributing to others feelings that a person actually has herself.

psychopaths: Specific personality types; such individuals lack the moral sense and concern for others held by most normal people.

public sphere: The means by which people communicate in modern **societies,** the most prominent component of which is the **mass media**—movies, television, radio, videos, records, magazines, and newspapers.

race: Differences in human physical characteristics used to categorize large numbers of individuals.

racialization: The process by which understandings of **race** are used to classify individuals or groups of people. Racial distinctions are more than ways of describing human differences; they are also important factors in the reproduction of patterns of **power** and inequality.

racial literacy: The skills taught to children of multiracial families to help them cope with racial hierarchies and to integrate multiple ethnic identities.

racism: The attribution of characteristics of superiority or inferiority to a population sharing certain physically inherited characteristics. Racism is one specific form of **prejudice,** focusing on physical variations between people. Racist attitudes became entrenched during the period of Western colonial expansion, but seem also to rest on mechanisms of **prejudice** and **discrimination** found in human **societies** today.

radical feminism: Form of **feminist theory** that believes that **gender inequality** is the result of male domination in all aspects of social and economic life.

random sampling: Sampling method in which a sample is chosen so that every member of the **population** has the same probability of being included.

rape: The forcing of nonconsensual vaginal, oral, or anal intercourse.

rational choice approach: More broadly, the **theory** that an individual's behavior is purposive. Within the field of criminology, rational choice analysis argues that deviant behavior is a rational response to a specific social situation.

rationalization: A concept used by Max Weber to refer to the process by which modes of precise calculation and organization, involving abstract rules and procedures, increasingly come to dominate the social world.

reference group: A group that provides a standard for judging one's attitudes or behaviors.

reflexivity: This describes the connections between knowledge and social life. The knowledge we gain about **society** can affect the way in which we act in it. For instance, reading a **survey** about the high level of support for a political party might lead an individual to express support for that party too.

regionalization: The division of social life into different regional settings or zones.

relative deprivation: Feelings of deprivation a person feels by comparing himself with a group.

relative poverty: Poverty defined according to the living standards of the majority in any given society.

religion: A set of beliefs adhered to by the members of a community, incorporating **symbols** regarded with a sense of awe or wonder together with ritual practices. Religions do not universally involve a belief in supernatural entities.

religious economy: A theoretical framework within the sociology of

religion, which argues that religions can be fruitfully understood as **organizations** in competition with one another for followers.

religious movements: Associations of people who join together to seek to spread a new **religion** or to promote a new interpretation of an existing religion.

religious nationalism: The linking of strongly held religious convictions with beliefs about a people's social and political destiny.

representative sample: A sample from a larger **population** that is statistically typical of that population.

research methods: The diverse methods of investigation used to gather empirical (factual) material. Different research methods exist in **sociology,** but the most commonly used are fieldwork (or **participant observation**) and **survey** methods. For many purposes, it is useful to combine two or more methods within a single research project.

response cries: Seemingly involuntary exclamations individuals make when, for example, being taken by surprise, dropping something inadvertently, or expressing pleasure.

revolution: A process of political change, involving the mobilizing of a mass **social movement,** which by the use of violence successfully overthrows an existing regime and forms a new **government.**

roles: The expected behaviors of people occupying particular **social positions.** The idea of **social role** originally comes from the theater, referring to the parts that actors play in a stage production. In every **society,** individuals play a number of social roles.

rural: The country.

sacred: Describing something that inspires attitudes of awe or reverence among believers in a given set of religious ideas.

sample: A small proportion of a larger **population.**

sampling: Studying a proportion of individuals or cases from a larger **population** as representative of that population as a whole.

sanction: A mode of reward or punishment that reinforces socially expected forms of behavior.

scapegoats: Individuals or groups blamed for wrongs that were not of their doing.

science: In the sense of physical science, the systematic study of the physical world. Science involves the disciplined marshaling of empirical data, combined with **theoretical approaches** and **theories** that illuminate or explain those data. Scientific activity combines the creation of boldly new modes of thought with the careful testing of **hypotheses** and ideas. One major feature that helps distinguish science from other idea systems (such as **religion**) is the assumption that *all* scientific ideas are open to criticism and revision.

secondary deviation: According to Edwin Lemert, following the act of **primary deviation,** secondary deviation occurs when an individual accepts the label of deviant and acts accordingly.

secondary groups: Groups characterized by large size and by impersonal, fleeting relationships.

second demographic transition: New demographic model that calls for fertility rates that may continue to fall because of shifts in family structure.

second world: Before the 1989 democracy movements, this included the industrialized Communist societies of Eastern Europe and the Soviet Union.

sects: Religious movements that break away from orthodoxy.

secularization: A process of decline in the influence of **religion.** Although modern **societies** have become increasingly secularized, tracing the extent of secularization is a complex matter. Secularization can refer to levels of involvement with religious organizations (such as rates of **church** attendance), the social and material influence wielded by religious organizations, and the degree to which people hold religious beliefs.

secular thinking: Worldly thinking, particularly as seen in the rise of **science, technology,** and rational thought in general.

segregation: The practices of keeping racial and ethnic groups physically separate, thereby maintaining the superior position of the **dominant group.**

self-consciousness: Awareness of one's distinct **social identity** as a person separate from others. Human beings are not born with self-consciousness but acquire an awareness of self as a result of early **socialization.** The learning of

language is of vital importance to the processes by which the child learns to become a self-conscious being.

self-identity: The ongoing process of self-development and definition of our personal **identity** through which we formulate a unique sense of ourselves and our relationship to the world around us.

semiotics: The study of the ways in which nonlinguistic phenomena can generate meaning—as in the example of a traffic light.

semiperiphery: Countries that supply sources of labor and raw materials to the **core** industrial **countries** and the world economy but are not themselves fully **industrialized societies.**

sensorimotor stage: According to Piaget, a stage of human cognitive development in which the child's awareness of its environment is dominated by perception and touch.

service society: A concept related to the one of **postindustrial society,** it refers to a social order distinguished by the growth of service occupations at the expense of industrial jobs that produce **material goods.**

sex: The biological and anatomical differences distinguishing females from males.

sexual harassment: The making of unwanted sexual advances by one individual toward another, in which the first person persists even though it is clear that the other party is resistant.

shaming: A way of punishing criminal and deviant behavior based on rituals of public disapproval rather than incarceration. The goal of shaming is to maintain the ties of the offender to the community.

sick role: A term associated with the functionalist Talcott Parsons to describe the patterns of behavior that a sick person adopts in order to minimize the disruptive impact of his or her illness on others.

signifier: Any vehicle of meaning and **communication.**

situational ethnicity: Ethnic identity that is chosen for the moment based on the social setting or situation.

slavery: A form of **social stratification** in which some people are literally owned by others as their property.

social age: The **norms, values,** and **roles** that are culturally associated with a particular chronological age.

social aggregate: A simple collection of people who happen to be together in a particular place but do not significantly interact or identify with one another.

social capital: The social knowledge and connections that enable people to accomplish their goals and extend their influence.

social category: People who share a common characteristic (such as **gender** or **occupation**) but do not necessarily interact or identify with one another.

social change: Alteration in basic structures of a **social group** or **society.** Social change is an ever-present phenomenon in social life, but has become especially intense in the modern era. The origins of modern **sociology** can be traced to attempts to understand the dramatic changes shattering the traditional world and promoting new forms of social order.

social closure: Practices by which groups separate themselves off from other groups.

social constraint: The conditioning influence on our behavior of the groups and **societies** of which we are members. Social constraint was regarded by Émile Durkheim as one of the distinctive properties of **social facts.**

social construction of gender: The learning of **gender roles** through **socialization** and interaction with others.

social exclusion: The outcome of multiple deprivations that prevent individuals or groups from participating fully in the economic, social, and political life of the **society** in which they live.

social facts: According to Émile Durkheim, the aspects of social life that shape our actions as individuals. Durkheim believed that social facts could be studied scientifically.

social gerontology: The study of **aging** and the elderly.

social group: A collection of people who regularly interact with one another on the basis of shared expectations concerning behavior and who share a sense of common **identity.**

social identity: The characteristics that are attributed to an individual by others.

social interaction: The process by which we act and react to those around us.

socialization: The social processes through which children develop an awareness of social **norms** and **values** and achieve a distinct sense of self. Although socialization processes are particularly significant in infancy and childhood, they continue to some degree throughout life. No individuals are immune from the reactions of others around them, which influence and modify their behavior at all phases of the **life course.**

socialization of nature: The process by which we control phenomena regarded as "natural," such as reproduction.

social mobility: Movement of individuals or groups between different **social positions.**

social movements: Large groups of people who seek to accomplish, or to block, a process of **social change.** Social movements normally exist in conflict with **organizations,** whose objectives and outlook they oppose. However, movements that successfully challenge **power,** once they become institutionalized, can develop into organizations.

social position: The **social identity** an individual has in a given group or **society.** Social positions may be general in nature (those associated with **gender roles**) or may be more specific (occupational positions).

social reproduction: The process of perpetuating **values, norms,** and social practices through **socialization,** which leads to structural continuity over time.

social rights: Rights of social and welfare provision held by all **citizens** in a national community, including, for example, the right to claim unemployment benefits and sickness payments provided by the **state.**

social roles: Socially defined expectations of an individual in a given **status,** or **social position.**

Social Security: A government program that provides economic assistance to persons faced with unemployment, disability, or agedness.

social self: The basis of **self-consciousness** in human individuals, according to the theory of G. H. Mead. The social self is the **identity** conferred upon an individual by the reactions of others. A person achieves self-consciousness by becoming aware of this **social identity.**

social stratification: The existence of **structured inequalities** between groups in **society,** in terms of their access to material or symbolic rewards. While all societies involve some forms of stratification, only with the development of state-based systems did wide differences in **wealth** and **power**

arise. The most distinctive form of stratification in modern societies is **class** divisions.

social structure: The underlying regularities or patterns in how people behave and in their relationships with one another.

society: A group of people who live in a particular territory, are subject to a common system of political **authority,** and are aware of having a distinct **identity** from other groups. Some societies, like **hunting and gathering societies,** are small, numbering no more than a few dozen people. Others are large, numbering millions—modern Chinese society, for instance, has a population of more than a billion people.

sociobiology: An approach that attempts to explain the behavior of both animals and human beings in terms of biological principles.

sociological imagination: The application of imaginative thought to the asking and answering of sociological questions. Someone using the sociological imagination "thinks himself away" from the familiar routines of daily life.

sociology: The study of human groups and **societies,** giving particular emphasis to analysis of the industrialized world. Sociology is one of a group of social sciences, which include anthropology, economics, political science, and human geography. The divisions between the various social sciences are not clear-cut, and all share a certain range of common interests, concepts, and methods.

sociology of the body: Field that focuses on how our bodies are affected by social influences. Health and illness, for instance, are determined by social and cultural influences.

source: Origin of data used by a researcher, but gathered elsewhere.

sovereignty: The undisputed political rule of a **state** over a given territorial area.

standard deviation: A way of calculating the spread of a group of figures.

state: A political apparatus (**government** institutions plus civil service officials) ruling over a given territorial order, whose **authority** is backed by **law** and the ability to use force. Not all societies are characterized by the existence of a state. **Hunting and gathering societies** and smaller **agrarian societies** lack state institutions. The emergence of the state marked a distinctive

transition in human history, because the centralization of political **power** involved in state formation introduced new dynamics into processes of **social change.**

state-centered theories: Development **theories** that argue that appropriate **government** policies do not interfere with economic development, but rather can play a key role in bringing it about.

state overload: A **theory** that holds that modern **states** face major difficulties as a result of being overburdened with complex administrative decisions.

status: The social honor or **prestige** that a particular group is accorded by other members of a **society.** Status groups normally display distinct styles of life—patterns of behavior that the members of a group follow. Status privilege may be positive or negative. **Pariah** status **groups** are regarded with disdain or treated as outcasts by the majority of the **population.**

stepfamily: A **family** in which at least one partner has children from a previous **marriage,** living either in the home or nearby.

stereotype threat: Idea that when African American students believe they are being judged not as individuals but as members of a negatively stereotyped social group, they will do worse on tests.

stereotyping: Thinking in terms of fixed and inflexible categories.

stigma: Any physical or social characteristic that is labeled by **society** as undesirable.

strike: A temporary stoppage of **work** by a group of employees in order to express a grievance or enforce a demand.

structural mobility: Mobility resulting from changes in the number and kinds of **jobs** available in a **society.**

structural strain: Tensions that produce conflicting interests within **societies.**

structuration: The two-way process by which we shape our social world through our individual actions and by which we are reshaped by **society.**

structured inequalities: Social inequalities that result from patterns in the **social structure.**

subcultures: **Values** and **norms** distinct from those of the majority, held by a group within a wider **society.**

suburbanization: The development of suburbia, areas of housing outside **inner cities.**

surplus value: The value of a worker's labor power, in **Marxist** theory, left over when an employer has repaid the cost of hiring the worker.

surveillance: The supervising of the activities of some individuals or groups by others in order to ensure compliant behavior.

surveillance society: Term referring to how information about our lives and activities is maintained by **organizations.**

survey: A method of sociological research in which questionnaires are administered to the **population** being studied.

sustainable development: The notion that economic growth should proceed only insofar as natural resources are recycled rather than depleted; biodiversity is maintained; and clean air, water, and land are protected.

symbol: One item used to stand for or represent another—as in the case of a flag, which symbolizes a nation.

symbolic ethnicity: Ethnic **identity** that is retained only for symbolic importance.

symbolic interactionism: A **theoretical approach** in **sociology** developed by George Herbert Mead, which emphasizes the role of **symbols** and **language** as core elements of all human interaction.

Taylorism: A set of ideas, also referred to as "scientific management," developed by Frederick Winslow Taylor, involving simple, coordinated operations in industry.

technology: The application of knowledge of the material world to production; the creation of material instruments (such as machines) used in human interaction with nature.

terrorism: Use of attacks on civilians designed to persuade a government to alter its policies, or to damage its standing in the world.

theism: A belief in one or more supernatural deities.

theoretical approach: A perspective on social life derived from a particular theoretical tradition. Some of the major theoretical traditions in **sociology** include **functionalism, symbolic interactionism,** and **Marxism.** Theoretical approaches supply overall perspectives within which sociologists work and influence the areas of their research as well as the modes in which research problems are identified and tackled.

theoretical questions: Questions posed by sociologists when seeking to explain a particular range of observed events. The asking of theoretical questions is crucial to allowing us to generalize about the nature of social life.

theory: An attempt to identify general properties that explain regularly observed events. Theories form an essential element of all sociological works. While theories tend to be linked to broader **theoretical approaches,** they are also strongly influenced by the research results they help generate.

third world: A term used during the cold war to describe developing nations.

time–space: When and where events occur.

timetables: The means by which **organizations** regularize activities across time and space.

total institutions: Groups who exercise control over their members by making them subsume their individual **identities** in that of the group, compelling them to adhere to strict ethical codes or rules, and sometimes forcing them to withdraw from activity in the outside world.

tracking: Dividing students into groups according to ability.

transactional leaders: **Leaders** who are concerned with accomplishing the group's tasks, getting group members to do their **jobs,** and making certain that the group achieves its goals.

transformational leaders: **Leaders** who are able to instill in the members of a group a sense of mission or higher purpose, thereby changing the nature of the group itself.

transnational corporations: Business **corporations** located in two or more countries.

triad: A group consisting of three persons.

triangulation: The use of multiple **research methods** as a way of producing more reliable empirical data than is available from any single method.

underclass: A **class** of individuals situated at the bottom of the class system, normally composed of people from **ethnic minority** backgrounds.

unfocused interaction: Interaction occurring among people present in a particular setting but not engaged in direct face-to-face **communication.**

union density: A statistic that represents the number of union members as a percentage of the number of people who could potentially be union members.

upper class: A social **class** broadly composed of the more affluent members of **society,** especially those who have inherited **wealth,** own businesses, or hold large numbers of stocks (shares).

urban ecology: An approach to the study of urban life based on an analogy with the adjustment of plants and organisms to the physical environment. According to ecological theorists, the various neighborhoods and zones within cities are formed as a result of natural processes of adjustment on the part of **populations** as they compete for resources.

urbanism: A term used by Louis Wirth to denote distinctive characteristics of urban social life, such as its impersonality.

urbanization: The development of towns and cities.

urban renewal: The process of renovating deteriorating neighborhoods by encouraging the renewal of old buildings and the construction of new ones.

values: Ideas held by individuals or groups about what is desirable, proper, good, and bad. What individuals value is strongly influenced by the specific **culture** in which they happen to live.

variable: A dimension along which an object, individual, or group may be categorized, such as income or height.

vertical mobility: Movement up or down a hierarchy of positions in a **social stratification** system.

wealth: Money and material possessions held by an individual or group.

welfare capitalism: Practice in which large **corporations** protect their employees from the vicissitudes of the market.

welfare state: A political system that provides a wide range of welfare benefits for its **citizens.**

white-collar crime: Criminal activities carried out by those in white-collar, or professional, **jobs.**

work: The activity by which people produce from the natural world and so ensure their survival. Work should not be thought of exclusively as paid employment. In traditional cultures, there was only a rudimentary monetary system, and few people worked for money. In modern **societies,** there remain types of work that do not involve direct payment (e.g., **housework**).

working class: A social **class** broadly composed of people working in blue-collar, or manual, **occupations.**

working poor: People who work, but whose earnings are not enough to lift them above the **poverty line.**

world-accommodating movements: Religious movements that emphasize the importance of inner religious life and spiritual purity over worldly concerns.

world-affirming movements: Religious movements that seek to enhance followers' ability to succeed in the outside world by helping them to unlock their human potential.

world information order: A global system of **communication** operating through satellite links, radio and TV transmission, and telephone and computer links.

world-rejecting movements: Religious movements that are exclusive in nature, highly critical of the outside world, and demanding of their members.

world-systems theory: Pioneered by Immanuel Wallerstein, this **theory** emphasizes the interconnections among countries based on the expansion of a capitalist world **economy.** This economy is made up of **core countries, semiperiphery,** and **periphery.**

young old: Sociological term for persons aged sixty-five to seventy-four.

BIBLIOGRAPHY

ABC News/Washington Post Poll. (2006). Which punishment do you prefer for people convicted of murder: the death penalty or life in prison with no chance of parole? Retrieved fall 2007, from http://www.pollingreport.com/crime.htm

Abdul-Rauf, Muhammad. (1975). *Islam: Creed and worship.* Washington, DC: Islamic Center.

Abeles, R. P., & Riley, M. W. (1987). Longevity, social structure, and cognitive aging. In C. Schooler & K. Warner Schaie (Eds.), *Cognitive functioning and social structure over the life course.* Norwood, NJ: Ablex.

Accad, E. (1991). Contradictions for contemporary women in the Middle East. In C. T. Mohanty, A. Russo, & L. Torres (Eds.), *Third world women and the politics of feminism.* Bloomington: Indiana University Press.

Ackman, D. (2004, June 23). Wal-Mart and sex discrimination by the numbers. *Forbes.* Retrieved January 9, 2007, from www.forbes.com/2004/06/23/cx_da_0623topnews.html

Adherents.com. (2007). Percentage of religious adherents worldwide. Retrieved fall 2007 from http://www.adherents.com/Religions_By_Adherents.html

Agingstats.gov. (2007). 2006 Older American update: Key indicator of wellness. Retrieved January 2008 from http://agingstats.gov/Agingstatsdotnet/Main_Site/Data/2006_Documents/OA_2006.pdf

AIDS Orphans Educational Trust. (2003). AIDS Orphans Educational Trust–Uganda. Retrieved December 28, 2004, from www.orphanseducation.org

Al Ahmad, J. (1997; orig. 1962). *Gharbzadegi: Weststruckedness.* Costa Mesa, CA: Mazda Publications.

Albrow, M. (1997). *The global age: State and society beyond modernity.* Stanford, CA: Stanford University Press.

Aldrich, H. E., & Marsden, P. V. (1988). Environments and organizations. In N. J. Smelser (Ed.), *Handbook of sociology.* Newbury Park, CA: Sage.

Ali, T. (2003, May–June). Re-colonizing Iraq. *New Left Review, 21,* 5–19.

Allen, B. (1996). *Rape warfare: The hidden genocide in Bosnia-Herzegovina and Croatia.* Minneapolis: University of Minnesota Press.

Allen, M. P. (1981). Managerial power and tenure in the large corporation. *Social Forces, 60,* 482–494.

Altman, L. K., & Oppel, R. (2008, January 10). W.H.O. says Iraq civilian death toll higher than cited. *The New York Times.* Retrieved fall 2008 from http://www.nytimes.com/2008/01/10/world/middleeast/10casualties.html?_r=1&oref=slogin

Alvarez, R., Robin, L., Tuan, M., & Huang, S-I. (1996). Women in the professions: Assessing progress. In P. J. Dubeck & K. Borman (Eds.), *Women and work: A handbook.* New York: Garland.

Amato, P., Loomis, L.S., & Booth, A. (1995). Parental divorce, marital conflict, and offspring well-being during early adulthood. *Social Forces, 73,* 895–915.

Amenta, E. (1998). *Bold relief: Institutional politics and the origins of modern American social policy.* Princeton, NJ: Princeton University Press.

American Academy of Pediatrics. (2004). Sexual orientation and adolescents. *Pediatrics, 113*(6): 1827–1832.

American Association of Retired Persons (AARP). (1997). Report of social security advisory council. Retrieved November 24, 2003, from www.aarp.org/focus/ssecure/part 2/advisory.htm

American Association of University Women (AAUW). (1992). *How schools shortchange girls.* Washington, DC: American Association of University Women Educational Foundation.

American Council on Education (ACE). (2001). The American freshman: National norms for Fall 2000. Los Angeles, CA: UCLA Higher Education Research Institute and ACE. [Results also published in: This year's freshmen at 4-year colleges: Their opinions, activities, and goals. *Chronicle of Higher Education,* January 26, 2001, p. A49.]

American Federation of Labor and Congress of Industrial Organizations (AFL-CIO). (2008). About Us. Retrieved spring 2008 from http://www.aflcio.org/aboutus/

American Psychiatric Association. (2000). *Diagnostic and statistical manual of mental disorders* (4th ed., Text rev.). Washington, DC: American Psychiatric Association.

Amin, S. (1974). *Accumulation on a world scale.* New York: Monthly Review Press.

Ammons, S. K., & Markham, W. T. (2004). Working at home: Experiences of skilled white collar workers. *Sociological Spectrum, 24*(2): 191–238.

Amsden, A. H. (1989). *Asia's next giant: South Korea and late industrialization.* New York: Oxford University Press.

Amsden, A.H., Kochanowicz, J., & Taylor, L. (1994). *The market meets its match: Restructuring the economies of Eastern Europe.* Cambridge, MA: Harvard University Press.

Anderson, B. (1991). *Imagined communities: Reflections on the origin and spread of nationalism* (Rev. ed.). New York: Routledge.

Anderson, E. (1990). *Streetwise: Race, class, and change in an urban community.* Chicago: University of Chicago Press.

Anderson, E. (1999). *Code of the street.* New York: Norton.

Angell, M. and Kassirer, J.P. (1998). Alternative medicine—the risks of untested and unregulated remedies. *New England Journal of Medicine, 339,* 839.

Angier, N. (1995, June 11). THE NATION; If you're really ancient, you may be better off. *The New York Times*. Retrieved November 7, 2008, from http://query.nytimes.com/gst/fullpage.html?res=990CE4DD1430F932A25755C0A963958260&sec=health&spon=&pagewanted=2

Anyon, J. (2006). Social class, school knowledge, and the hidden curriculum revisited. In L. Weiss & G. Dimitriadis (Eds.), *The newsociology of knowledge*. New York: Routledge.

Anyon, J., & Nolan, K. (2004). Learning to do time: Willis' cultural reproduction model in an era of deindustrialization, globalization, and the mass incarceration of people of color. In N. Dolby, G. Dimitriadis, & P. Willis (Eds.), *Learning to Labor in New Times*. New York: Routledge.

Anzaldua, G. (1990). *Making face, making soul: Haciendo caras: Creative and cultural perspectives by feminists of color*. San Francisco: Aunt Lute Foundation.

Appadurai, A. (1986). Introduction: Commodities and the politics of value. In A. Appadurai (Ed.), *The social life of things*. Cambridge, UK: Cambridge University Press.

Appelbaum, R., & Lichtenstein, N. (2006). A new work of retail supremacy: Supply chains and workers' chains in the age of Wal-Mart. *International Labor and Working-Class History 70*, 106–125.

Appelbaum, R. P. (1990). Counting the homeless. In J. A. Momeni (Ed.), *Homeless in the United States* (Vol. 2). New York: Praeger.

Appelbaum, R. P., & Christerson, B. (1997). Cheap labor strategies and export-oriented industrialization: Some lessons from the East Asia/Los Angeles apparel connection. *International Journal of Urban and Regional Research, 21, 2*.

Appelbaum, R. P., & Henderson, J. (Eds.). (1992). *States and development in the Asian Pacific Rim*. Newbury Park, CA: Sage.

Applebaum, E., Bernhardt, A., & Murnane, R. J. (Eds.). (2003). *Low-wage America: How employers are reshaping opportunity in the workplace*. New York: Russell Sage Foundation.

Apter, T. (1994). *Working women don't have wives: Professional success in the 1990s*. New York: St. Martin's Press.

Arias, E. (2007; orig. April 19, 2006). United States Life Tables, 2003. *National Vital Statistics Reports, 54*. Retrieved January 2008 from http://www.cdc.gov/nchs/data/nvsr/nvsr54/nvsr54_14.pdf

Ariès, P. (1965). *Centuries of childhood*. New York: Random House.

Arjomand, S. A. (1988). *The turban for the crown: The Islamic revolution in Iran*. New York: Oxford University Press.

Aronowitz, S., & Giroux, H. A. (1987). *Education under siege: The conservative, liberal and radical debate over schooling*. London: Routledge.

Arrighi, G. (1994). *The long twentieth century: Money, power, and the origin of our times*. New York: Verso.

Asch, S. (1952). *Social psychology*. Englewood Cliffs, NJ: Prentice-Hall.

Ashworth, A. E. (1980). *Trench warfare: 1914–1918*. London: Macmillan.

Association for Corporate Growth (ACG). (2007, July). What goes up, must come down? *Mergers and Acquisitions, 9–10*.

Atchley, R. C. (2000). *Social forces and aging: An introduction to social gerontology* (9th ed.). Belmont, CA: Wadsworth.

Attaran, M. (2004). Exploring the relationship between information technology and business process reengineering. *Information & Management, 41*(5): 585–596.

Avery, R. B., & Canner, G. B. (2005, Summer). New information reported under HMDA and its application in fair lending enforcement. *Federal Reserve Bulletin*. Retrieved spring 2006 from www.federalreserve.gov/pubs/bulletin/2005/3-05hmda.pdf

Avins, M. (2003, December 9). MoveOn redefines party politics. *Los Angeles Times*, p. A-1.

Bahrami, H., & Evans, S. (1995). Flexible recycling and high-technology entrepreneurship. *California Management Review, 37*(3):62–89

Bailey, J. M., & Pillard, R. C. (1991). A genetic study of male sexual orientation. *Archives of General Psychiatry, 48*: 1089–1096.

Bales, K. (1999). *Disposable people: New slavery in the global economy*. Berkeley: University of California Press.

Bales, R. F. (1953). The egalitarian problem in small groups. In T. Parsons (Ed.), *Working papers in the theory of action*. Glencoe, IL: Free Press.

Bales, R. F. (1970). *Personality and interpersonal behavior*. New York: Holt, Rinehart, and Winston.

Balmer, R. (1989). *Mine eyes have seen the glory: A journey into the evangelical subculture in America*. New York: Oxford University Press.

Balswick, J. O. (1983). Male inexpressiveness. In K. Soloman & N. B. Levy (Eds.), *Men in transition: Theory and therapy*. New York: Plenum Press.

Baltes, P. B., & Schaie, K. W. (1977). The myth of the twilight years. In S. Zarit (Ed.), *Readings in aging and death: Contemporary perspectives*. New York: Harper & Row.

Baltic 21 Secretariat. Passenger car density. Retrieved spring 2006 from http://www.baltic21.org/reports/indicators/tr08.htm.

Bamberger, B. J. (1992). Judaism. In the *American Academic Encyclopedia* (online edition). Danbury, CT: Grolier Electronic.

Bankoff, E. A. (1983). Aged parents and their widowed daughters: A support relationship. *Gerontologist, 38,* 226–230.

Barcelona Field Studies Centre. (2003). Sao Paulo Growth and Management. Retrieved December 28, 2004, from www.geographyfieldwork.com/SaoPauloManagement.htm

Barker, M. (1981). *The new racism: Conservatives and the ideology of the tribe*. Frederick, MD: University Press of America.

Barnet, R. J.; & Cavanagh, J. (1994). *Global dreams: Imperial corporations and the new world order*. New York: Simon and Schuster.

Bart, P. B., & O'Brien, P. H. (1985). *Stopping rape: Successful survival strategies*. New York: Pergamon Press.

Basham, A. L. (1989). *The origins and development of classical Hinduism*. Boston: Beacon Press.

Basu, A. (Ed.). (1995). *The challenge of local feminisms: Women's movements in global perspective*. Boulder, CO: Westview Press.

Baudrillard, J. (1983). *Simulations*. New York: Semiotext(e).

Baudrillard, J. (1988). *Jean Baudrillard: Selected writings*. Stanford, CA: Stanford University Press.

Baxter, J., & Kane, E. (1995). Dependence and independence: A cross national analysis. *Gender and Society, 9, 2*.

BBC News. (2001). Bin Laden's warning: Full text. Retrieved January 10, 2005, from http://news.bbc.co.uk/1/hi/world/south_asia/1585636.stm

Bean, F. D., Chanove, R., Cushing, R., de la Garza, R., Haynes, C., Freeman, G., et al. (1994). *Illegal Mexican migration and the United States/Mexico border: Operation hold-the-line and El Paso/Juarez*. Washington, DC: U.S. Commission on Immigration Reform.

Bearman, P. (2002). Opposite-sex twins and adolescent same-sex attraction. *American Journal of Sociology, 107,* 1179–1205.

Beasley, C. (1999). *What is feminism?* Thousand Oaks, CA: Sage.

Beck, U. (1992). *Risk society.* London: Sage.

Beck, U. (1995). *Ecological politics in an age of risk.* Cambridge, UK: Polity Press.

Becker, G. (1964). *Human capital.* New York: National Bureau of Economic Research.

Becker, G. (1991). *A treatise on the family.* Cambridge, MA: Harvard University Press.

Becker, H. S. (1963). *Outsiders: Studies in the sociology of deviance.* New York: Macmillan.

Becker, M. H. (Ed.). (1974). The Health Belief Model and personal health behavior. *Health Education Monographs, 2,* 324–473.

Beijing Women's Conference. (1995, September 15). Declaration and platform for action, Fourth World Conference on Women: Action for Equality, Development, and Peace, Beijing (chapter III, critical area of concern no. 43). Retrieved November 10, 2008, from http://www1.umn.edu/humanrts/instree/e5dplw.htm

Belgrave, L. L. (1988). The effects of race difference in work history, work attitudes, economic resources, and health in women's retirement. *Research on Aging, 10,* 383–398.

Bell, A., Weinberg, M., & Hammersmith, S. (1981). *Sexual preference: Its development in men and women.* Bloomington: Indiana University Press.

Bell, D. (1976). *The coming of post-industrial society: A venture in social forecasting.* New York: Basic Books.

Bellah, R. N. (1968). Civil religion in America. In W. G. McLoughlin & R. N. Bellah (Eds.), *Religion in America.* Boston: Houghton Mifflin.

Bellah, R. N. (1975). *The broken covenant.* New York: Seabury Press.

Bellman, B. (1984). *The language of secrecy: Symbols and metaphors in Poro ritual.* New Brunswick, NJ: Rutgers University Press.

Bendick, M., Jackson, C., & Reinoso, V. (1993). Measuring employment discrimination through controlled experiments. In *The review of black political economy.* Washington, DC: Fair Employment Council of Greater Washington.

Bengston, V. L., Rosenthal, C., & Burton, L. (1990). Families and aging: Diversity and heterogeneity. In R. H. Binstock & L.K. George (Eds.), *Handbook of aging and the social sciences* (3rd ed.). New York: Academic Press.

Bennet, J. (1992, September 21). The old men sit and talk of a virus within. *The New York Times.* Retrieved November 8, 2008, from http://query.nytimes.com/gst/fullpage.html?res=9E0CEFDD113DF932A1575AC0A964958260&sec=&spon=&pagewanted=2

Berenson, A. (2005, December 4). Sales of impotence drugs fall, defying expectations. *The New York Times.* Retrieved November 8, 2008, from http://www.nytimes.com/2005/12/04/business/yourmoney/04impotence.html

Berger, P. L. (1963). *Invitation to sociology.* Garden City, NY: Anchor Books.

Berger, P. L. (1967). *The sacred canopy: Elements of a sociological theory of religion.* Garden City, NY: Anchor Books.

Berger, P. L. (1986). *The capitalist revolution: Fifty propositions about prosperity, equality, and liberty.* New York: Basic Books.

Berger, P. L., & Hsiao, H. M. (1988). *In search of an East Asian development model.* New Brunswick, NJ: Transaction.

Berle, A., & Means, G. C. (1982; orig. 1932). *The modern corporation and private property.* Buffalo, NY: Heim.

Berryman, P. (1987). *Liberation theology: Essential facts about the revolutionary movement in Central America and beyond.* Philadelphia: Temple University Press.

Bertram, E., Blackman, M., Sharpe, K., & Andreas, P. (1996). *Drug war politics.* Berkeley: University of California Press.

Beyer, P. (1994). *Religion and globalization.* Thousand Oaks, CA: Sage.

Beyerstein, B. L. (1999, Fall/Winter). Psychology and "'alternative medicine": social and judgmental biases that make inert treatments seem to work. *The Scientific Review of Alternative Medicine, 3*(2).

Bielby, W. (2005). Applying social research on stereotyping and cognitive bias to employment discrimination litigation: The case of allegations of systematic gender bias at Wal-Mart stores. In R. L. Nelson & L. B. Neilsen (Eds.), *Handbook on employment discrimination research: Rights and realities.* Norwell, MA: Kluwer Academic Press.

Birnbaum, J. H. (2005, March 30). AARP leads with wallet in fight over Social Security. *Washington Post.* Retrieved December 6, 2005, from www.washingtonpost.com/wp-dyn/articles/A11076-2005Mar29.html

Birren, J. E., & Bengston, V. L. (Eds.). (1988). *Emerging theories of aging.* New York: Springer.

Birren, J. E., & Cunningham, W. (1985). Research on the psychology of aging. In J. E. Birren & K. W. Schaie (Eds.), *The handbook of aging* (2nd ed.). New York: Van Nostrand.

Blanchard, R., & Bogaert, A. F. (1996). Homosexuality in men and number of older brothers. *American Journal of Psychiatry, 153,* 27–31.

Blau, J. (2004). Internationalizing public sociologies. *Sociologists Without Borders.* Retrieved December 27, 2004, from www.sociologistswithoutborders.org

Blau, P. (1963). *Bureaucracy in modern society.* New York: Random House.

Blau, P. (1977). *Inequality and heterogeneity: A primitive theory of social structure.* New York: Free Press.

Blau, P., & Duncan, O. D. (1967). *The American occupational structure.* New York: Wiley.

Blauner, R. (1964). *Alienation and freedom.* Chicago: University of Chicago Press.

Blauner, R. (1972). *Racial oppression in America.* New York: Harper & Row.

Blech, B. (1991). *Understanding Judaism: The basics of creed and deed.* Northdale, NJ: Erlbaum.

Block, F. (1990). *Postindustrial possibilities: A critique of economic discourse.* Berkeley: University of California Press.

Blondet, C. (1995). Out of the kitchen and onto the streets: Women's activism in Peru. In A. Basu (Ed.), *The challenge of local feminisms.* Boulder, CO: Westview Press.

Blum, L. M. (1991). *Between feminism and labor: The significance of the comparable worth movement.* Berkeley: University of California Press.

Bobak, L. (1996, October 23). India's tiny slaves. *Ottawa Sun.*

Bobo, L., & Kluegel, J. R. (1991). *Modern American prejudice: Stereotypes, social distance, and perceptions of discrimination toward Blacks, Hispanics, and Asians.* Paper presented at the 1991 meeting of the American Sociological Association, Cincinnati, Ohio.

Bochenek, M. A., & Brown, W. (2001, May 30). *Hatred in the hallways: Violence and discrimination against lesbian, gay, bisexual, and transgender students in U.S. schools.* New York: Human Rights Watch. Retrieved December 28, 2004, from www.hrw.org/reports/2001/uslgbt/toc.htm

Boden, D., & Molotch, H. (1994). The compulsion of proximity. In D. Boden & R. Friedland (Eds.), *Nowhere: Space, time, and modernity*. Berkeley: University of California Press.

Bohan, S. (1999, August 2). Bohemian grove and global elite. *Sacramento Bee*. Retrieved December 28, 2004, from www.mt.net/watcher/bohemiangrove.html

Bonacich, E., & Appelbaum, R. P. (2000). *Behind the label: Inequality in the Los Angeles garment industry*. Berkeley: University of California Press.

Bonnell, V. E., & Hunt, L. (Eds.) (1999). *Beyond the cultural turn*. Berkeley: University of California Press.

Bonnett, A. (2000). *Anti-racism*. New York: Routledge.

Booth, A. (1977). Food riots in the north-west of England, 1770–1801. *Past and Present, 77,* 90.

Borjas, G. J. (1994). The economics of immigration. *Journal of Economic Literature, 32,* 1667–1717.

Bositis, D. (2001). Black elected officials: A statistical summary: 2001. *Joint Center for Political and Economic Studies*. Retrieved January 2008 from http://www.jointcenter.org/publications1/publication-PDFs/BEO-pdfs/2001-BEO.pdf.

Bosse, R., et al. (1987). Mental health differences among retirees and workers: Findings from the normative aging study. *Psychology and Aging, 2,* 383–389.

Boswell, J. (1995). *The marriage of likeness: Same-sex unions in pre-modern Europe*. London: Fontana.

Bourdieu, P. (1984). *Distinction: A social critique of judgement of taste*. Cambridge, MA: Harvard University Press.

Bourdieu, P. (1988). *Language and symbolic power*. Cambridge, UK: Polity Press.

Bourdieu, P. (1990). *The logic of practice*. Palo Alto, CA: Stanford University Press.

Bowen, K. (1996). *Evangelism and apostasy: The evolution and impact of evangelicals in modern Mexico*. Montreal, QC, Canada: McGill-Queens University Press.

Bowlby, J. (1953). *Child care and the growth of love*. Baltimore, MD: Penguin.

Bowles, S., & Gintis, H. (1976). *Schooling in capitalist America*. New York: Basic Books.

Boyer, R., & Drache, D. (Eds.). (1996). *States against markets: The limits of globalization*. New York: Routledge.

Bradsher, K. (2000, June 16). Efficiency on wheels: U.S. auto industry is catching up with the Japanese. *The New York Times*.

Braithwaite, J. 1996. Crime, shame, and reintegration. In P. Cordella & L. Siegal (Eds.), *Readings in contemporary criminological theory*. Boston: Northeastern University Press.

Bramlett, M. D., & Mosher, W. D. (2002). Cohabitation, marriage, divorce, and remarriage in the United States. *Vital Health Statistics, 23,* 22. National Center for Health Statistics.

Brass, D. J. (1985). Men's and women's networks: A study of interaction patterns and influence in an organization. *Academy of Management Journal, 28,* 327–343.

Braverman, H. (1974). *Labor and monopoly capital: The degradation of work in the Twentieth Century*. New York: Monthly Review Press.

Brekhus, W. H. (2003). *Peacocks, chameleons, centaurs: Gay suburbia and the grammar of social identity*. Chicago: University of Chicago Press.

Brennan, T. (1988). Controversial discussions and feminist debate. In N. Segal & E. Timms (Eds.), *The origins and evolution of psychoanalysis*. New Haven, CT: Yale University Press.

Bresnahan, T., Brynjolfsson, E., & Hitt, L. (2002). Information technology, workplace organization, and the demand for skilled labor: firm-level evidence, *Quarterly Journal of Economics, 117*(1), 339–376.

Brewer, R. M. (1993). Theorizing race, class and gender: The new scholarship of black feminist intellectuals and black women's labor. In S. M. James & A. P. A. Busia (Eds.), *Theorizing black feminisms: The visionary pragmatism of black women*. New York: Routledge.

Bricourt, J. C. (2004). Using telework to enhance return to work outcomes for individuals with spinal cord injuries. *Neurorehabilitation, 19*(2), 147–159.

Brimelow, P. (1995). *Alien nation: Common sense about America's immigration disaster*. New York: Random House.

Britain, S. (1975). The economic contradictions of democracy. *British Journal of Political Science, 15,* 129–159.

Brookfield, S. (1986). *Understanding and facilitating adult learning*. San Francisco: Jossey-Bass.

Brown, C., & Jasper, K. (Eds.). (1993). *Consuming passions: Feminist approaches to eating disorders and weight preoccupations*. Toronto, Canada: Second Story Press.

Brown, J. K. (1977). A note on the division of labor by sex. In N. Glazer & H. Y. Waehrer (Eds.), *Woman in a man-made world* (2nd ed.). Chicago: Rand McNally.

Brown, S. L. (2004, May). Family structure and child well-being: The significance of parental cohabitation. *Journal of Marriage and Family, 66,* 351–367.

Browne, K. (1998). An introduction to sociology (2nd ed.). *Sociology Review 9.2.*

Brownmiller, S. (1975). *Against our will: Men, women, and rape*. New York: Simon and Schuster.

Brownmiller, S. (1986). *Against our will: Men, women, and rape* (Rev. ed.). New York: Bantam.

Brownell, K. D., & Horgen, K. B. (2004). *Food fight: The inside story of the food industry, America's obesity crisis, and what we can do about it*. New York: McGraw-Hill.

Brownstein, R. (2003, June 23). Liberal group flexes online muscle in its very own primary. *Los Angeles Times,* p. A-9.

Brubaker, R. (1992). *The politics of citizenship*. Cambridge, MA: Harvard University Press.

Bruce, S. (1990). *Pray TV: Televangelism in America*. New York: Routledge.

Bryan, B., Dadzie, S., & Scafe, S. (1987). Learning to resist: Black women and education. In G. Weiner & M. Arnot (Eds.), *Gender under scrutiny: New inquiries in education*. London: Hutchinson.

Bull, P. (1983). *Body movement and interpersonal communication*. New York: Wiley.

Bullock, C., III. (1984). Equal education opportunity. In C. S. Bullock III & C. M. Lamb (Eds.), *Implementation of civil rights policy*. Monterey, CA: Brooks and Cole.

Bumpass, L., & Lu, H. (2000). Trends in cohabitation and implications for children's family context in the United States. *Population Studies, 54,* 29–41.

Bumpass, L., Sweet, J. A., & Cherlin, A. (1991, November). The role of cohabitation in declining rates of marriage. *Journal of Marriage and the Family, 53,* 913–927.

Burawoy, M. (1972). *The colour of class*. Manchester, UK: Manchester University Press [for] the Institute for African Studies, University of Zambia.

Burawoy, M. (1979). *Manufacturing consent*. Chicago: University of Chicago Press.

Burawoy, M. (1985). *The politics of production.* New York: Verso.

Burawoy, M. (2004, August 17). For public sociology. Presidential address, 2004, presented at the ASA Annual Meeting, San Francisco, California.

Burns, J. M. (1978). *Leadership.* New York: Harper & Row.

Burns, T., & Stalker, G. M. (1994). *The management of innovation* (Rev. ed.). Oxford, UK: Oxford University Press.

Burr, C. (1993, March). Homosexuality and biology. *Atlantic Monthly, 271,* 47–65.

Burris, B. H. (1993). *Technocracy at work.* Albany: State University of New York Press.

Burris, B. H. (1998). Computerization of the workplace. *Annual Review of Sociology, 24,* 141–157.

Burt, M. R. (1992). *Over the edge: The growth of homelessness in the 1980s.* New York: Russell Sage.

Business Journal. (2000). Judge tosses insurer's bid to keep redlining data secret. Retrieved January 11, 2005, from http://sanjose.bizjournals.com/sanjose/stories/2000/09/11/daily42.html*Business Week.* (1997, December 15). Good news on wage inequality.

Buss, D. M. (2003). *Evolution of desire: Strategies of human mating.* New York: Basic Books.

Butler, J. (1989). *Gender trouble: Feminism and the subversion of identity.* New York: Routledge.

Butterfield, F. (1998, December 28). Decline of violent crimes is linked to crack market. *The New York Times,* p. A18.

Bynner, J., Ferri, E., & Shepherd, P. (1997). *Twenty-something in the 1990s: Getting on, getting by, getting nowhere.* Brookfield, VT: Ashgate.

Cairncross, F. (1997). *The death of distance: How the communications revolution will change our lives.* Boston: Harvard Business School Press.

Campos, P., Saguy, A., Ernsberger, P., Oliver, E., & Gaesser, G. (2006). The epidemiology of overweight and obesity: Public health crisis or moral panic? *International Journal of Epidemiology, 35,* 55–60.

Caplow, T. (1956). A theory of coalitions in the triad. *American Sociological Review, 21,* 489–493.

Caplow, T. (1959). Further development of a theory of coalitions in triads. *American Journal of Sociology, 64,* 488–493.

Caplow, T. (1969). *Two against one: Coalitions in triads.* Englewood Cliffs, NJ: Prentice Hall.

Cardoso, F. H., & Faletto, E. (1979). *Dependency and development in Latin America.* Berkeley: University of California Press.

Carr, D., & Friedman, M. (2005). Is obesity stigmatizing? Body weight, perceived discrimination and psychological well-being in the United States. *Journal of Health and Social Behavior, 46,* 244–259.

Carrington, K. (1994). Postmodern and feminist criminologies: Disconnecting discourses? *International Journal of the Sociology of Law 22*(3), 261–277.

Carrington, K. (1998; orig. 1994) Essentialism and feminist criminologies. In M. Dragan (Ed.), *The critical criminologist.* Chicago: Northeastern Illinois University.

Castells, M. (1977). *The urban question: A Marxist approach.* Cambridge, MA: MIT Press.

Castells, M. (1983). *The city and the grass roots: A cross-cultural theory of urban social movements.* Berkeley: University of California Press.

Castells, M. (1992). Four Asian tigers with a dragon head: A comparative analysis of the state, economy, and society in the Asian Pacific Rim. In R. P. Appelbaum & J. Henderson (Eds.), *States and development in the Asian Pacific Rim.* Newbury Park, CA: Sage.

Castells, M. (1996). *The rise of the network society.* Malden, MA: Blackwell.

Castells, M. (1997). *The power of identity.* Malden, MA: Blackwell.

Castells, M. (1998). *End of millennium.* Malden, MA: Blackwell.

Castells, M. (2000). *The Rise of the network society.* Malden, MA: Blackwell.

Castells, M. (2001). *The Internet galaxy.* Oxford, UK: Oxford University Press.

Castles, S., & Miller, M. J. (1993). *The age of migration: International population movements in the modern world.* London: Macmillan.

Catalano, S. M. (2005). Criminal victimization, 2004. Retrieved October 5, 2005, from www.ojp.usdoj.gov/bjs/pub/pdf/cv04.pdf

Census of India. (2007a). Number of literates and literacy rates. Retrieved January 2008 from http://www.censusindia.gov.in/Census_Data_2001/India_at_glance/literates1.aspxm

Census of India. (2007b). Religious composition. Retrieved January 2008 from http://www.censusindia.gov.in/Census_Data_2001/India_at_glance/religion.aspx

Center for American Women and Politics (CAWP). (2007a). Facts on women in Congress, 2007. Retrieved fall 2007 from http://www.cawp.rutgers.edu/fast_facts/levels_of_office/Congress_CurrentFacts.php

Center for American Women and Politics (CAWP). (2007b). Statewide elected office. Retrieved fall 2007 from http://www.cawp.rutgers.edu/fast_facts/levels_of_office/statewide.php

Centers for Disease Control and Prevention (CDC). (2006a, July 21). Births, marriages, divorces, and deaths— Provisional data for 2005. *National vital statistics report, 54,* 20. Retrieved spring 2008 http://www.cdc.gov/nchs/data/nvsr/nvsr54/nvsr54_20.pdf

Centers for Disease Control and Prevention (CDC). (2006b). Morbidity and mortality weekly report: QuickStats: Percentage of parents who were married or cohabitating at birth of first child, by race/ethnicity and sex. Retrieved January 2008 from http://www.cdc.gov/MMWR/preview/mmwrhtml/mm5536a8.htm

Centers for Disease Control and Prevention (CDC). (2007a). Prevalence of the autism spectrum disorders in multiple areas of the United States,: Surveillance years 2000 and 2002. A report from the Autism and Developmental Disabilities Monitoring Network. Retrieved September 19, 2008, from http://www.cdc.gov/ncbddd/dd/addmprevalence.htm

Centers for Disease Control and Prevention (CDC). (2007b). Adult cigarette smoking in the United States: Current estimates. Retrieved September 19,2008, from www.cdc.gov/tobacco/data_statistics/fact_sheets/adult_data/adult_cig_smoking.htm, accessed

Centers for Disease Control and Prevention (CDC). (2007c). Births: Final data for 2005. *National Vital Statistics Report.* Retrieved January 2008 from http://www.cdc.gov/nchs/data/nvsr/nvsr56/nvsr56_06.pdf

Centers for Disease Control and Prevention (CDC). (2007d). New CDC study finds no increase in obesity among adults; Rates still high. Retrieved January

2008 from http://www.cdc.gov/nchs/
pressroom/07newsreleases/obesity.htm

Centers for Disease Control and Prevention
(CDC). (2008a). U.S. obesity trends 1986–
2007. Retrieved fall 2008 from http://
www.cdc.gov/nccdphp/dnpa/obesity/
trend/maps/

Center for Public Integrity. (2003, May
15). How the feds stack up. Retrieved
January 10, 2005, from www.
publicintegrity.org/hiredguns/report.
aspx?aid=167

Center for Responsive Politics (CRP). (2003).
2000 presidential race: Total raised and
spent. Center for Responsive Politics.
Retrieved December 29, 2004, from
www.opensecrets.org/2000elect/index/
AllCands.htm

Center for Responsive Politics (CRP).
(2007a). The dollars and cents of
incumbency. Retrieved January 2008
from http://www.opensecrets.org/
bigpicture/cost.php

Center for Responsive Politics (CRP).
(2007b). Business-labor-ideology
split in PAC & individual donations
to candidates and parties. Retrieved
January 2008 from http://www.
opensecrets.org/bigpicture/blio.
php?cycle=2006

Center for Responsive Politics (CRP).
(2008). Banking on becoming president.
Retrieved November 2008 from http://
www.opensecrets.org/pres08/index.php

Center on Education Policy (CEP). (2007).
Retrieved spring 2008 from http://www.
cep-dc.org/

Central Intelligence Agency (CIA).
(2000). CIA world factbook. Retrieved
December 29, 2004, from www.cia.
gov/cia/publications/factbook/geos/
rs.html#Econ

Chafe, W. H. (1974). *The American woman:
Her changing social, economic, and political
roles, 1920–1970.* New York: Oxford
University Press.

Chafe, W. H. (1977). *Women and equality:
Changing patterns in American culture.*
New York: Oxford University Press.

Chafetz, J. S. (1990). *Gender equity: An
integrated theory of stability and change.*
Newbury Park, CA: Sage.

Chafetz, J. S. (1997). Feminist theory and
sociology: Underutilized contributions
for mainstream theory. *Annual Review of
Sociology, 23,* 97–120.

Chaliand, G., & Ragu, J. (1992). *Strategic
atlas: A comparative geopolitics of the
world's powers.* New York: Harper &
Row.

Chambliss, W. J. (1973, November). The
saints and the roughnecks. *Society, 11,*
24–31.

Chambliss, W. J. (1988). *On the take: From
petty crooks to presidents.* Bloomington:
Indiana University Press.

Chaney, D. (1994). *The cultural turn: Scene-
setting essays in contemporary cultural
history.* New York: Routledge.

Chang, I., & Kirby, W. C. (1997). *The rape of
Nanking: The forgotten holocaust of World
War II.* New York: Basic Books.

Charleston Business Journal. (2003). Are "all-
American cars" still made in America?
Retrieved January 11, 2005, from www.
charlestonbusiness.com/pub/6_18/
news/2930-1.html

Chase-Dunn, C. (1989). *Global formation:
Structures of the world economy.*
Cambridge, MA: Basil Blackwell.

Chaves, M. (1993, July). Intraorganizational
power and internal secularization in
Protestant denominations. *American
Journal of Sociology, 99,* 1–48.

Chaves, M. (1994). Secularization as
declining religious authority. *Social
Forces, 72,* 749–774.

Cheng, L., & Hsiung, P. (1992). Women,
export-oriented growth, and the state:
The case of Taiwan. In R. P. Appelbaum
& J. Henderson (Eds.), *States and
development in the Asian Pacific Rim.*
Newbury Park, CA: Sage.

Chepesiuk, R. (1998). *Hard target: The United
States war against international drug
trafficking, 1982–1997.* Jefferson, NC:
McFarland and Company.

Cherlin, A. (1990, July). Recent changes
in American fertility, marriage, and
divorce. *Annals of the American Academy
of Political and Social Science, 510,*
145–154.

Cherlin, A. (1992). *Marriage, divorce, remarriage* (Rev. ed.). Cambridge, MA:
Harvard University Press.

Cherlin, A. (1999). *Public and private families:
An introduction* (2nd ed.). New York:
McGraw Hill.

Cherlin, A., Chase-Lansdale, P., & McRae,
C. (1998). Effects of parental divorce
on mental health throughout the life
course. *American Sociological Review, 63,*
239–249.

Chicago Tribune. (2003, August 31).
Cost of a nursing home room jumps,
study finds. Retrieved December 29,
2004, from www.chicagotribune.
com/classified/realestate/over55/
chi0308300022aug31,0,364422.story?-
coll5chi-classifiedover55-hed

China Internet Network Information Center.
(2007). Statistical survey report on the
internet development in China. Retrieved
January 2008 from http://www.cnnic.cn/
download/2007/20thCNNICreport-en.
pdf

China.org.cn. (2001). Privacy key in
marriage rule revision. Retrieved
January 13, 2006, from www.china.org.
cn/english/PMD/13226.htm

Chodorow, N. (1978). *The reproduction
of mothering.* Berkeley: University of
California Press.

Chodorow, N. (1988). *Psychoanalytic theory
and feminism.* Cambridge, UK: Polity
Press.

Chua, A. (2003). *World on fire: How exporting
free market democracy breeds ethnic
hatred and global instability.* New York:
Doubleday.

Clawson, D., & Clawson, M. A. (1999,
August). What has happened to the U.S.
labor movement? Union decline and
renewal. *Annual Review of Sociology 25,*
95–119.

Cleary, P. D. (1987). Gender differences in
stress-related disorders. In R. C. Barnett
(Ed.), *Gender and stress.* New York: Free
Press.

Cleveland, J. N. (1996). Women in high-
status nontraditional occupations. In P. J.
Dubeck & K. Borman (Eds.), *Women and
work: A handbook.* New York: Garland.

Cloward, R. A., & Ohlin, L. E. (1960).
Delinquency and opportunity. New York:
Free Press.

CNN. (2003, February 1). INS: 7 million
illegal immigrants in United States.
Retrieved January 27, 2006, from
www.cnn.com/2003/US/01/31/illegal.
immigration

CNN. (2004a, February 25). Bush calls for
ban on same-sex marriages. Retrieved
December 29, 2004, from http://edition.
cnn.com/2004/ALLPOLITICS/02/24/
elec04.prez.bush.marriage/index.html

CNN. (2004b). The outspoken Bill Cosby.
Retrieved spring 2006 from http://
edition.cnn.com/2004/SHOWBIZ/
TV/11/11/cosby/index.html

Coate, J. (1994). Cyberspace innkeeping:
Building online community. Online
paper. Retrieved December 29, 2004,
from www.well.com:70/0/Community/
innkeeping

Cohen, A. (1955). *Delinquent boys: The culture
of the gang.* Glencoe, IL: Free Press.

Cohen, J., & Langer, G. (2005, October 24).
Poll: Will you live longer and better?
ABC News. Retrieved December 6, 2005,

from http://abcnews.go.com/Health/PollVault/story?id=1232993&CMP=OTC-RSSFeeds0312

Cohen, L. E.; Broschak, J. P., & Haveman, H. A. (1998). And then there were more? The effect of organizational sex composition on the hiring and promotion of managers. *American Sociological Review, 63,* 5.

Cohen, R. (1997). *Global diasporas: An introduction.* London: UCL Press.

Coleman, J. S. (1987). Families and schools. *Educational Researcher, 16,* 6.

Coleman, J. S. (1988). Social capital in the creation of human capital. *American Journal of Sociology, 94*(supplement), S95–S120.

Coleman, J. S. (1990). *The foundations of social theory.* Cambridge, MA: Harvard University Press.

Coleman, J. S., et al. (1966). *Equality of educational opportunity.* Washington, DC: U.S. Government Printing Office.

Collins, P. H. (1990). *Black feminist thought: Knowledge, consciousness, and the politics of empowerment.* Boston: Unwin Hyman.

Collins, R. (1979). *The credential society: An historical sociology of education.* New York: Academic Press.

Collins, R., Chafetz, J. S., Blumberg, R. L., Collins, S., & Turner, J. (1993). Toward an integrated theory of gender stratification. *Sociological Perspectives, 36,* 185–216.

Coltrane, S. (1992). The micropolitics of gender in non-industrial societies. *Gender and Society, 6,* 86–107.

Combat 18. (1998). Retrieved January 10, 2005, from www.combat18.org

Common Cause. (2002). Campaign finance reform: Election 2002—incumbent advantage. Retrieved November 6, 2002, from www.commoncause.org/news/default.cfm?ArtID538

Common Cause. (2003). Spending more than a half billion on political contributions, lobbying and ad campaigns, Pharma wins big on Medicare. Retrieved July 1, 2003, from www.commoncause.org/action/070103_phrma_report.pdf

Computer Security Institute. (2007). 2007 CSI computer crime and security survey. Retrieved May 2007 from http://i.cmpnet.com/v2.gocsi.com/pdf/CSISurvey2007.pdf

Computer World. (2002). The best places to work in IT: United States. Retrieved January 20, 2005, www.computerworld.com/departments/surveys/bestplaces/bestplaces_us_region_sort/0, 10984,,00.html

Conley, D. (1999). *Being black, living in the red: Race, wealth, and social policy in America.* Berkeley and Los Angeles: University of California Press.

Connell, R. W. (1987). *Gender and power: Society, the person, and sexual politics.* Boston: Allen and Unwin.

Connelly, M. (2007, July 16). Trust in Government at a Very Low Point. *The New York Times.* Retrieved January 2008. from http://thecaucus.blogs.nytimes.com/2007/07/16/trust-in-government-at-a-very-low-point/

Conner, K. A., Dorfman, L. T., & Tompkins, J. B. (1985). Life satisfaction of retired professors: The contribution of work, health, income, and length of retirement. *Educational Gerontology, 11,* 337–347.

Conti, J. A. (2003). *Trade, power, and law: Dispute resolution in the World Trade Organization, 1995–2002.* Unpublished master's thesis, University of California, Santa Barbara.

Cooley, C. H. (1964; orig. 1902). *Human nature and the social order.* New York: Schocken Books.

Coombs, P. (1985). *The world crisis in education: The view from the eighties.* Oxford, UK: Oxford University Press.

Coontz, S. (1992). *The way we never were: American families and the nostalgia trap.* New York: Basic Books.

Corbin, J., & Strauss, A. (1985). Managing chronic illness at home: Three lines of work. *Qualitative Sociology, 8,* 224–247.

Corsaro, W. (1997). *The sociology of childhood.* Thousand Oaks, CA: Pine Forge Press

Cosmides, L., & Tooby, J. (1997). Evolutionary psychology: A primer. University of California at Santa Barbara: Institute for Social, Behavioral, and Economic Research Center for Evolutionary Psychology. Retrieved January 11, 2005, from available at www.psych.ucsb.edu/research/cep/primer.htm

Coward, R. (1984). *Female desire: Women's sexuality today.* London: Paladin

Cowgill, D. O. (1968). The social life of the aged in Thailand. *Gerontologist, 8,* 159–163.

Cowgill, D. O. (1986). *Aging around the world.* Belmont, CA: Wadsworth.

Cox, W. M., & Alm, R. (1999). *Myths of rich and poor: Why we're better off than we think.* New York: Basic Books.

Crompton, R. (1998). *Class and stratification: An introduction to current debates* (2nd ed.). Cambridge, UK: Polity Press.

Crowley, J. E. (1985). Longitudinal effects of retirement on men's psychological and physical well-being. In H. S. Parnes, J. E. Crowley, R. J. Haurin, L. J. Less, W. R. Morgan, F. L. Mott, & G. Nestel (Eds.), *Retirement among American men* (pp. 147–173). Lexington, MA: Lexington Books.

Cumings, B. (1987). The origins and development of the northeast Asian political economy: Industrial sectors, product cycles, and political consequences. In F. C. Deyo (Ed.), *The political economy of the new Asian industrialism.* Ithaca, NY: Cornell University Press.

Cumings, B. (1997). *Korea's place in the sun: A modern history.* New York: Norton.

Cumming, E. (1963). Further thoughts on the theory of disengagement. *International Social Science Journal, 15,* 377–393.

Cumming, E. (1975). Engagement with an old theory. *International Journal of Aging and Human Development, 6,* 187–191.

Cumming, E., & Henry, W. E. (1961). *Growing old: The process of disengagement.* New York: Basic.

Currie, E. (1998). *Crime and punishment in America.* New York: Henry Holt.

Curtin, J. S. (2003). Youth trends in Japan: Part four—anorexia and other teenage eating disorders on the rise. Japanese Institute of Global Communications. Retrieved December 29, 2004, from www.glocom.org/special_topics/social_trends/20030701_trends_s46

Cutler, S. J., & Grams, A. E. (1988). Correlates of everyday self-reported memory problems. *Journal of Gerontology, 43,* S82–S90.

D'Andrade, R. (1995). *The development of cognitive anthropology.* New York: Cambridge University Press.

Dahlburg, J. (1995, August 27). Sweatshop case dismays few in Thailand. *Los Angeles Times,* p. A-4.

Dannefer, D. (1989). Human action and its place in theories of aging. *Journal of Aging Studies, 3,* 1–20.

Danzger, M. H. (1989). *Returning to tradition.* New Haven, CT: Yale University Press.

Danziger, S. H., & Gottschalk, P. (1995). *America unequal.* Cambridge, MA: Harvard University Press.

David, R. (2007). Indian middle class slowly changing its ways. Retrieved fall 2007 from http://www.forbes.

com/facesinthenews/2007/11/10/india-middleclass-survey-face-markets-cx_rd_1108autofacescan01.html

Davidman, J. (1991). *Tradition in a rootless world: Women turn to orthodox Judaism.* Berkeley: University of California Press.

Davies, B. (1991). *Frogs and snails and feminist tales.* Sydney, Australia: Allen and Unwin.

Davies, J. C. (1962). Towards a theory of revolution. *American Sociological Review, 27,* 5–19.

Davies, M. W. (1983). *Women's place is at the typewriter: Office work and office workers, 1870–1930.* Philadelphia: Temple University Press.

Davis, D., & Polonko, K. (2001). Telework America 2001 summary. International Telework Association & Council. Retrieved January 20, 2005, from www.telecommute.org/telework/ twa2001.htm

Davis, K., & Moore, W. E. (1945, April). Some principles of stratification. *American Sociological Review, 10,* 242–249.

Davis, M. (1990). *City of quartz: Excavating the future in Los Angeles.* New York: Verso.

Davis, S. (1988). *2001 management: Managing the future now.* New York: Simon and Schuster.

Deacon, T. W. (1998). *The symbolic species: The co-evolution of language and the brain.* New York: Norton.

Death Penalty Information Center. (2007a). Number of executions by state and region since 1976. Retrieved fall 2007 from http://www.deathpenaltyinfo. org/number-executions-state-and-region-1976

Death Penalty Information Center. (2007b). Executions by race since 1976. Retrieved fall 2007 from http://www.deathpenaltyinfo.org/article. php?scid=5&did=184#inmaterace

de Beauvoir, S. (1974; orig. 1949). *The second sex.* New York: Random House.

Dejong, W. (1993). Obesity as a Characterological stigma: The issue of responsibility and judgments of task performance. *Psychological Reports, 73,* 963–970.

Delany, S. R. (1999). *Times square red, times square blue.* New York: New York University Press.

D'Emilio, J. (1983). *Sexual politics, sexual communities: The making of a homosexual minority in the United States, 1940–1970.* Chicago: University of Chicago Press.

DeNavas-Walt, C., Proctor, B. D., & Lee, C. H. (2005). Income, poverty, and

health insurance coverage in the United States: 2004. *U.S. Census Bureau, Current Population Reports, P60–229.* U.S. Government Printing Office, Washington, DC. Retrieved spring 2006 from www.census.gov/prod/2005pubs/ p60–229.pdf

DeNavas-Walt, C., Proctor, B. D., & Smith, J. (2007). Income, poverty, and health insurance coverage in the United States: 2006. *U.S. Census Bureau, Current Population Reports.* U.S. Government Printing Office, Washington, DC. Retrieved January 2008 from http:// www.census.gov/prod/2007pubs/p60–233.pdf

DeParle, J. (2005, September 4). What happens to a race deferred. *The New York Times.*

Department of Homeland Security. (2004). Yearbook of immigration statistics, 2004. Retrieved fall 2005 from uscis.gov/ graphics/shared/statistics/yearbook/YrBk04Im.htm

Derenne, J. L., & Beresin, E. (2006). Body image, media, and eating disorders. *Academic Psychiatry, 30,* 257–261.

de Tocqueville, A. (1969; orig. 1835). *Democracy in America.* New York: Doubleday.

Devault, M. L. 1991. *Feeding the family: The social organization of caring as gendered work.* Chicago: University of Chicago Press.

de Witt, K. (1994, August 15). Wave of suburban growth is being fed by minorities. *The New York Times,* pp. A1, B6.

Dey, A. N. (1997, July 2). Characteristics of elderly nursing home residents: Data from the 1995 national nursing home survey. *Advance Data, 289,* 1–8.

Deyo, F. C. (1987). *The political economy of the new Asian industrialism.* Ithaca, NY: Cornell University Press.

Deyo, F. C. (1989). *Beneath the miracle: Labor subordination in the new Asian industrialism.* Berkeley: University of California Press.

Diamond, J. (2005). *Collapse: How societies choose to fail or succeed.* New York: Penguin.

Dickens, W. T., & Leonard, J. S. (1985, April). Accounting for the decline in union membership. NBER Working Paper Series, 1275. *Industrial and Labor Relations Review, 38,* 323–334.

Dickman, S. (1999, June 23). Can life in nursing homes by meaningful? Warner School team studies whether changes

in organizational culture improve life. University of Rochester press release. Retrieved November 7, 2008, from http://www.rochester.edu/news/show. php?id=1139

Diekema, D. A. (1991). Televangelism and the mediated charismatic relationship. *Social Science Journal, 28*(2):143–162.

DiMaggio, P. (1997). Culture and cognition. *Annual Review of Sociology, 23,* 263–287.

Dimitrova, D. (2003). Controlling teleworkers: Supervision and flexibility revisited. *New Technology Work and Employment, 18*(3): 181–195.

DiPrete, T. A., & Nonnemaker, K. L. (1997). Structural change, labor market turbulence, and labor market outcomes. *American Sociological Review, 62,* 386–404.

DiPrete, T. A., & Soule, W. T. (1988). Gender and promotion in segmented job ladder systems. *American Sociological Review, 53,* 26–40.

Dobash, R. E., & Dobash, R. P. (1992). *Women, violence, and social change.* New York: Routledge.

Dolbeare, C. (1995). *Out of reach: Why everyday people can't find affordable housing.* Washington, DC: Low Income Housing Information.

Domhoff, G. (1974). *The bohemian grove and other retreats.* New York: Harper & Row.

Domhoff, G. W. (1971). *The higher circles: The governing class in America.* New York: Vintage Books.

Domhoff, G. W. (1979). *The powers that be: Processes of ruling class domination in America.* New York: Vintage Books.

Domhoff, G. W. (1983). *Who rules America now? A view for the '80s.* New York: Prentice-Hall.

Domhoff, G. W. (1998). *Who rules America? Power and politics in the Year 2000.* Belmont, CA: Mayfield.

Domhoff, G. W. (2005). Power in America: Wealth, income, and power. Retrieved spring 2006 from http://sociology.ucsc. edu/whorulesamerica/power/wealth. html

Dore, R. (1980). *British factory, Japanese factory: The origins of national diversity in industrial relations.* Berkeley: University of California Press.

Dowling H. F. (1977). *Fighting infection: Conquests of the twentieth century.* Cambridge, MA: Harvard University Press.

Drake, S., & Cayton, H. R. (1945). *Black metropolis: A study of negro life in a northern city.* New York: Harcourt, Brace.

Draper, P. (1975). !Kung women: Contrasts in sexual egalitarianism in foraging and sedentary contexts. In R. R. Reiter (Ed.), *Toward an anthropology of women.* New York: Monthly Review Press.

Dreier, P., & Appelbaum, R. P. (1992, Spring–Summer). The housing crisis enters the 1990s. *New England Journal of Public Policy, 8,* 155–167.

Drentea, P. (1998). Consequences of women's formal and informal job search methods for employment in female-dominated jobs. *Gender and Society, 12,* 321–338.

DrugWarFacts.org. (2005). Drug war facts: Economics. Retrieved spring 2006 from www.drugwarfacts.org/economi.htm

Du Bois, W. E. B. (1903). *The souls of black folk.* New York: Dover.

Dubos, R. (1959). *Mirage of health.* New York: Doubleday/Anchor.

Duignan, P., & Gann, L. H. (Eds.). (1998). *The debate in the United States over immigration.* Stanford, CA: Hoover Institution Press.

Duncan, G. J., Brooks-Gunn, J., Yeung, W. J., & Smith, J. R. (1998, June). How much does childhood poverty affect the life chances of children? *American Sociological Review, 63*(3): 406–423.

Duncombe, J., & Marsden, D. (1993). Love and intimacy: The gender division of emotion and "emotion work": A neglected aspect of sociological discussion of heterosexual relationships. *Sociology, 27,* 221–241.

Duneier, M. (1999). *Sidewalk.* New York: Farrar, Straus, and Giroux.

Duneier, M., & Molotch, H. (1999). Talking city trouble: Interactional vandalism, social inequality, and the urban interaction problem. *American Journal of Sociology, 104,* 1263–1295.

Dunn, D., Almquist, E. M.; & Saltzman Chafetz, J. (1993). Macrostructural perspectives on gender inequality. In P. England (Ed.), *Theory on gender, feminism on theory.* New York: Aldine DeGrutyer.

Duranti, A. (1994). *From grammar to politics: Linguistic anthropology in a western Samoan village.* Berkeley: University of California Press.

Durkheim, É. (1964; orig. 1893). *The division of labor in society.* New York: Free Press.

Durkheim, É. (1965; orig. 1912). *The elementary forms of the religious life.* New York: Free Press.

Durkheim, É. (1966; orig. 1897). *Suicide.* New York: Free Press.

Dush, C. M. K., Cohan, C. L., & Amato, P. R. (2003). The relationship between cohabitation and marital quality and stability: Change across cohorts? *Journal of Marriage and the Family, 65,* 539–549.

Duster, T. (1990). *Backdoor to eugenics.* New York: Routledge.

Dutt, M. (1996). Some reflections on U.S. women of color and the United Nations fourth world conference on women and NGO forum in Beijing, China. *Feminist Studies, 22.*

Duverger, M. (1954). *Political parties.* London: Methuen.

Dworkin, A. (1987). *Intercourse.* New York: Free Press.

Dworkin, R. M. (1993). *Life's dominion: An argument about abortion, euthanasia, and individual freedom.* New York: Knopf.

Dychtwald, K. (1990). *Age wave: How the most important trend of our time will change your future.* New York: Bantam Books.

Dye, T. R. (1986). *Who's running America?* (4th ed.). Englewood Cliffs, NJ: Prentice Hall.

E-Crime Watch. (2007). 2007 E-Crime watch survey: Survey results. Retrieved November 3, 2007, from www.cert.org/archive/pdf/ecrimesummary07.pdf

Earth Trends. (2003). Agriculture inputs, 2003. Retrieved fall 2005 from www.earthtrends.wri.org/pdf_library/data_tables/agr2_2003.pdf

Eating Disorder Coalition (EDC). (2003). Statistics. Retrieved December 29, 2004, from www.eatingdisorderscoalition.org/reports/statistics.html

Eating Disorder Coalition (EDC). (2007). Eating disorder statistics: 9 million Americans, hundreds dying each year. Retrieved January 2008 from http://www.eatingdisorderscoalition.org/reports/FactSheet9Million.pdf

Ebomoyi, E. (1987). The prevalence of female circumcision in two Nigerian communities. *Sex Roles, 17,* 3–4.

Economic and Social Research Council (ESRC). 2008. Global migration. Retrieved January 2008 from http://www.esrc.ac.uk/ESRCInfoCentre/facts/international/migration.aspx?ComponentId=15051&SourcePageId=14912

The Economist. (1996). *Pocket world in figures.* London: Profile Books.

The Economist. (2003, November 6). Survey: Therapy of the masses.

Edin, K., & Kefalas, M. (2005). *Promises I can keep: Why poor women put motherhood before marriage.* Berkeley: University of California Press.

Edin, K., & Lein, L. (1997). Work, welfare, and single mothers' economic survival strategies. *American Sociological Review, 62,* 2.

Efron, S. (1997, October 18). Eating disorders go global. *Los Angeles Times,* p. A-1.

Eibl-Eibesfeldt, I. (1972). Similarities and differences between cultures in expressive movements. In R. A. Hinde (Ed.), *Nonverbal communication.* New York: Cambridge University Press.

Eisen, A. M. (1983). *The chosen people in America: A study in Jewish religious ideology.* Bloomington: Indiana University Press.

Eisenhower Institute. (1961). Farewell address. The Dwight D. Eisenhower Institute, Gettysburg College. Retrieved December 19, 2004, http://www.eisenhowerinstitute.org/about/dwight_d_eisenhower/the_farewell_address.dot

Ekman, P., & Friesen, W. V. (1978). *Facial action coding system.* New York: Consulting Psychologists Press.

el Dareer, A. (1982). *Woman, why do you weep? Circumcision and its consequences.* Westport, CT: Zed.

Elias, N. (1987). *Involvement and detachment.* London: Oxford University Press.

Elias, N., & Dunning, E. (1987). *Quest for excitement: Sport and leisure in the civilizing process.* Oxford, UK: Blackwell.

Ell, K. (1996). Social networks, social support, and coping with serious illness: The family connection. *Social Science and Medicine, 42,* 173–183.

Elshtain, J. B. (1981). *Public man; Private woman.* Princeton, NJ: Princeton University Press.

Elwert, F. (2005). *How cohabitation does—and does not—reduce the risk of divorce.* Unpublished manuscript.

Emmanuel, A. (1972). *Unequal exchange: A study of the imperialism of trade.* New York: Monthly Review Press.

Encyclopedia Britannica. (2006). Religion. Britannica Book of the Year, 2005. Retrieved January 23, 2006, from http://search.eb.com/eb/article-9398490

England, P. (1992). *Comparable worth: Theories and evidence.* New York: Aldine de Gruyter.

Entertainment Software Association. (2007). Sales, demographic and usage data. Retrieved fall 2007 from http://www.theesa.com/facts/pdfs/ESA_EF_2007.pdf

Epstein, G. (2003). More women advance, but sexism persists. Barron's. www.collegejournal.com/successwork/work

placediversity/20030605=Epstein.html, accessed spring 2006.

Ericson, R., & Haggerty, K. (1997). *Policing the risk society.* Toronto: University of Toronto Press.

Erikson, K. (1966). *Wayward puritans: A study in the sociology of deviance.* New York: Wiley.

Erikson, R., & Goldthorpe, J. H. (1992). *The constant flux: A study of class mobility in industrial societies.* Oxford, UK: Oxford University Press.

Esposito, J. L. (1984). *Islam and politics.* Syracuse, NY: Syracuse University Press.

Estes, C. L. (1986). The politics of aging in America. *Aging and Society, 6,* 121–134.

Estes, C. L. (1991). The Reagan legacy: Privatization, the welfare state, and aging. In J. Myles & J. Quadagno (Eds.), *States, labor markets, and the future of old age policy.* Philadelphia: Temple University Press.

Estes, C. L., Binney, E. A., & Culbertson, R. A. (1992). The gerontological imagination: Social influences on the development of gerontology, 1945–present. *Journal of Aging and Human Development, 35,* 49–67.

Estes, C. L., Swan, J., & Gerard, L. (1982). Dominant and competing paradigms in gerontology: Towards a political economy of aging. *Aging and Society, 2,* 151–164.

Estes, C. L., Gerard, L., Zones, J. S., & Swan, J. (1984). *Political economy, health, and aging.* Boston: Little, Brown.

Estlund, C. L. (2006, December). The death of labor law? *Annual Review of Law and Social Science, 2,* 105–123.

Estrich, S. (1987). *Real rape.* Cambridge, MA: Harvard University Press.

Ettlinger, M., & Chapman, J. (2005, March 23). Social Security and the income of the elderly. Economic Policy Institute Issue Brief #206. Retrieved January 2008 from http://www.epi.org/content.cfm/ib206

Etzioni-Halévy, E. (1985). *Bureaucracy and democracy: A political dilemma.* New York: Routledge, Chapman and Hall.

Europa.eu. (2004). The history of the European Union. Retrieved spring 2006 from http://europa.eu/abc/history/index_en.htm

Evans, P. (1979). *Dependent development.* Princeton, NJ: Princeton University Press.

Evans, P. (1987). Class, state, and dependence in East Asia: Some lessons for Latin Americanists. In F. C. Deyo (Ed.), *The political economy of the new Asian industrialism.* Ithaca, NY: Cornell University Press.

Evans, P. (1995). *Embedded autonomy: States and industrial transformation.* Princeton, NJ: Princeton University Press.

Evans, R. J. (1977). *The feminists: Women's emancipation movements in Europe, America, and Australasia, 1840–1920.* New York: Barnes & Noble.

Evans-Pritchard, E. E. (1970). Sexual inversion among the Azande. *American Anthropologist, 72,* 1428–1434.

Fadiman, A. (2002). *The spirit catches you and you fall down.* New York: Farrar, Straus, and Giroux.

Falk, G., Falk, U., & Tomashevich, V. (1981). *Aging in America and other cultures.* Saratoga, CA: Century Twenty-One.

Fallows, D. (2005). How women and men use the Internet. Pew Internet & American Life Project. Retrieved November 17, 2008, www.pewinternet.org/pdfs/PIP_women_and_men_online.pdf

Fallows, D., & Rainie, L. (2004). The Internet as a unique news source. Pew Internet & American Life Project. Retrieved January 9, 2006, www.pewinternet.org/pdfs/PIP_News_Images_July04.pdf

Farley, M. (1998, November 22). Women in the new China. *Los Angeles Times,* p. A-1.

Farrell, L. (2005). Sociologists without borders field report. Retrieved spring 2006 from www.sociologistswithoutborders.org/essays/SSF%20Report.pdf

Featherman, D. L., & Hauser, R. M. (1978). *Opportunity and change.* New York: Academic Press.

Federal Bureau of Investigation (FBI). (2005a). Crime in the United States, 2004. *The uniform crime report.* Table 42. Retrieved November 8, 2008, from http://www.fbi.gov/ucr/cius_04/persons_arrested/table_38-43.html#table42

Federal Bureau of Investigation (FBI). (2005b). Crime in the United States, 2004. *The Uniform Crime Report.* Table 38. Retrieved November 8, 2008, from www.fbi.gov/ucr/cius_04/persons_arrested/table_38-43.html

Federal Bureau of Investigation (FBI). (2007a). Crime in the United States, 2006. Table 1, Crime in the United States. Retrieved November 3, 2007, from http://www.fbi.gov/ucr/cius2006/data/table_01.html

Federal Bureau of Investigation (FBI). (2007b). Crime in the United States, 2006. Table 38, Arrests, by Age, 2006. Retrieved fall 2007 from http://www.fbi.gov/ucr/cius2006/data/table_38.html

Federal Bureau of Investigation (FBI). (2007c). Crime in the United States, 2006. Table 2, Arrests, by Sex, 2006. Retrieved November 3, 2007, from http://www.fbi.gov/ucr/cius2006/data/table_42.html

Federal Interagency Forum on Aging-Related Statistics. (2004, November). Older Americans 2004: Key indicators of well-being. Federal Interagency Forum on Aging-Related Statistics. Washington, DC: U.S. Government Printing Office.

Federal Register. (2007). Annual update of the HHS poverty guidelines. Retrieved fall 2007 from http://aspe.hhs.gov/poverty/07fedreg.htm

Federal Reserve Board. (2006). Survey of consumer finances, 2004. Retrieved fall 2007 from http://www.federalreserve.gov/pubs/bulletin/2006/financesurvey.pdf

Fenton M. V., & Morris, D. L. The integration of holistic nursing practices and complementary and alternative modalities into curricula of schools of nursing. *Alternative Therapies in Health and Medicine, 9*(4):62–67.

Ferguson, A. (2000). *Bad boys: Public schools in the making of black masculinity.* Ann Arbor: University of Michigan Press.

Ferguson, K. E. (1984*). The feminist case against bureaucracy.* Philadelphia: Temple University Press.

FierceBiotech. (2007). Press release. Worldwide corporate investment in R&D grew by 10% last year. Retrieved fall 2007 from http://www.fiercebiotech.com/press-releases/press-release-worldwide-corporate-investment-r-d-grew-10-last-year

Filkins, D. (1998, October 22). Afghans pay dearly for peace. *Los Angeles Times,* p. A-1.

Finke, R., & Stark, R. (1988). Religious economies and sacred canopies: Religious mobilization in American cities, 1906. *American Sociological Review, 53,* 41–49.

Finke, R., & Stark, R. (1992). *The churching of America, 1776–1990: Winners and losers in our religious economy.* New Brunswick, NJ: Rutgers University Press.

Finley, N. J., Roberts, D., & Banahan, B. F. (1988). Motivators and inhibitors of attitudes of filial obligation toward aging parents. *The Gerontologist, 28,* 73–78.

Firestone, M. (2007). Women entrepreneurs outside the US. Retrieved fall 2007 from http://us.smetoolkit.org/us/en/content/en/2255/Women-Entreprenuers-Outside-the-U-S—Firestone, S. (1971). *The dialectic of sex.* London: Paladin.

Fischer, C. S. (1984). *The urban experience* (2nd ed.). New York: Harcourt Brace Jovanovich.

Fischer, C. S., Hout, M., Sánchez Jankowski, M., Lucas, S. R., Swidler, A., & Vos,K. (1996). *Inequality by design: Cracking the bell curve myth.* Princeton, NJ: Princeton University Press.

Fisher, B. S., Cullen, F. T., & Turner, M. G. (2000, December). *The sexual victimization of college women.* Washington, DC: U.S. Department of Justice, National Institute of Justice, Bureau of Justice Statistics, NCJ 182369. Retrieved December 29, 2004, from www.ncjrs.org/pdffiles1/nij/182369.pdf

Foley, D. (1990). *Learning capitalist culture: Deep in the heart of Tejas.* Philadelphia: University of Pennsylvania Press.

Foner, N. (1984). *Ages in conflict: A cross-cultural perspective on inequality between old and young.* New York: Columbia University Press.

Forbes. (2007a). Special report: The world's richest people. Retrieved fall 2007 from http://www.forbes.com/2007/03/06/billionaires-new-richest_07billionaires_cz_lk_af_0308billieintro.html

Forbes. (2007b). Special report: CEO compensation. Retrieved fall 2007 from http://www.forbes.com/2007/05/03/highest-paid-ceos-lead-07ceo-cz_sd_0503ceo_land.html

Forbes. (2007c). Profile: Mr. H. Lee Sott, Jr., CEO/President/Director at Wal-Mart Stores, Inc. Retrieved fall 2007 from http://www.forbes.com/finance/mktguideapps/personinfo/FromPersonIdPersonTearsheet.jhtml?passedPersonId=871995

Forbes. (2007d). Special report: Listing the world's billionaires. Retrieved fall 2007 from http://www.forbes.com/2007/03/07/billionaires-worlds-richest_07billionaires_cz_lk_af_0308billie_land.html

Ford, C. S., & Beach, F. A. (1951). *Patterns of sexual behavior.* New York: Harper & Row.

Forrest, D., & Streek, B. (2001, October 26). Mbeki in bizarre AIDS outburst.

Daily Mail and Guardian (Johannesburg). Retrieved December 29, 2004, www.aegis.com/news/dmg/2001/MG011021.html

Fortune. (2008). Fortune global 500. Retrieved fall 2008 from http://money.cnn.com/magazines/fortune/global500/2007/

Foucault, M. (1971). *The order of things: An archaeology of the human sciences.* New York: Pantheon.

Foucault, M. (1979). *Discipline and punish: The birth of the prison.* New York: Random House.

Foucault, M. (1988). Technologies of the self. In L. H. Martin, H. Gutman, & P. H. Hutton (Eds.), *Technologies of the self: A seminar with Michel Foucault.* Amherst: University of Massachusetts Press.

Fox, O. C. (1964). The pre-industrial city reconsidered. *Sociological Quarterly, 5.*

Frank, A. G. (1966). The development of underdevelopment. *Monthly Review, 18.*

Frank, A. G. (1969a). *Latin America: Underdevelopment or revolution.* New York: Monthly Review Press.

Frank, A. G. (1969b). *Capitalism and underdevelopment in Latin America: Historical studies of Chile and Brazil.* New York: Monthly Review Press.

Frank, A. G. (1979.) *Dependent accumulation and underdevelopment.* London: Macmillan.

Frank, D. J., & McEneaney, E. H. (1999). The individualization of society and the liberalization of state policies on same-sex sexual relations, 1984–1995. *Social Forces, 7*(3): 911–944.

Franzini, L., Ribble, J. C., & Keddie, A. M. (2001). Understanding the Hispanic paradox. *Ethnicity & Disease, 11*(3): 496–518.

Freedom House. (2005). Electoral democracies, 2005. Retrieved January 9, 2006, from www.freedomhouse.org/template.cfm?page=205&year=2005

Freedom House. (2007a). Map of freedom 2007. Retrieved January 2008 from http://www.freedomhouse.org/template.cfm?page=363&year=2007

Freedom House. (2007b). Electoral democracies 2007. Retrieved January 2008 from http://www.freedomhouse.org/template.cfm?page=368&year=2007

Freeman, R. B. (1999). *The new inequality: Creating solutions for poor America.* Boston: Beacon Press.

Freeman, R. B., & Rogers, J. (1999). *What workers want.* Ithaca, NY: ILR Press and Russell Sage Foundation.

Free the Children. (1998). Retrieved December 29, 2004, from www.freethechildren.org

Freidson, E. (1970). *Profession of medicine: A study of the sociology of applied knowledge.* New York: Dodd, Mead.

Fremlin, J. H. (1964, October 19). How many people can the world support? *New Scientist, 24,* 285–287.

French, H. W. (2001a, January 1). Diploma at hand, Japanese women find glass ceiling reinforced with iron. *The New York Times,* p. A1.

French, H. W. (2001b, April 27). Japan's new premier picks precedent-setting cabinet. *The New York Times,* p. A1.

Frey, W., & Liaw, K. (1998). The impact of recent immigration on population redistribution in the United States. In J. Smith & B. Edmonston (Eds.), *The immigration debate.* Washington, DC: National Academy Press.

Friedan, B. (1963). *The feminine mystique.* New York: Norton.

Friedlander, D., & Burtless, G. (1994). *Five years after: The long-term effects of welfare-to-work programs.* New York: Russell Sage.

Friedman, R. A., & Currall, S. C. (2003). Conflict escalation: Dispute exacerbating elements of e-mail communication. *Human Relations, 56*(11): 1325–1347.

Friedman, T. (2000). *The Lexus and the olive tree: Understanding globalization.* New York: Anchor.

Friedman, T. (2005). *The world is flat: A brief history of the twenty-first century.* New York: Farrar, Straus, and Giroux.

Fries, J. F. (1980). Aging, natural death, and the compression of morbidity. *New England Journal of Medicine, 303,* 130–135.

Fröbel, F., Heinrichs, J., & Kreye, O. (1979). *The new international division of labor.* New York: Cambridge University Press.

Fry, C. L. (1980). *Aging in culture and society.* New York: Bergin.

Fryer, D., & McKenna, S. (1987). The laying off of hands—unemployment and the experience of time. In S. Fineman (Ed.), *Unemployment: Personal and social consequences.* London: Tavistock.

Fukui, T. (2004, September 7). Investing in America. . . . 25 years of new challenges, Acura Media Newsroom, Honda News. Retrieved December 2007 from http://www.hondanews.com/search/release/2327?q=gentlemen&s=acura

Furstenberg, F. F., Jr., & Cherlin, A. J. (1991). *Divided families.* Cambridge, MA: Harvard University Press.

Gallup. (2007). Trust in the federal government. Retrieved spring 2008 from http://www.galluppoll.com/content/default.aspx?ci=28795

Gamoran, A., & Nystrand, M. (1995). An organizational analysis of the effects of ability grouping. *American Educational Research Journal, 32*(4): 687–715.

Gans, H. J. (1979, January). Symbolic ethnicity: The future of ethnic groups and cultures in America. *Ethnic and Racial Studies, 2,* 1–20.

Ganzeboom, H. B. G., Luijkx, R., & Treiman, D. (1989). Intergenerational class mobility in comparative perspective. *Research in Social Stratification and Mobility, 8,* 3–79.

Gardner, C. B. (1995). *Passing by: Gender and public harassment.* Berkeley and Los Angeles: University of California Press.

Garfinkel, H. (1963). A conception of, and experiments with, "trust" as a condition of stable concerted actions. In O. J. Harvey (Ed.), *Motivation and social interaction.* New York: Ronald Press.

Garland, D. (2002). *The culture of control: Crime and social order in contemporary society.* Chicago: University of Chicago Press.

Gavron, H. (1966). *The captive wife: Conflicts of housebound mothers.* London: Routledge and Kegan Paul.

Geary, D. (1981). *European labor protest, 1848–1939.* New York: St. Martin's Press.

Geertz, C. (1973). *The interpretation of cultures.* New York: Basic Books.

Geertz, C. (1983). *Local knowledge: Further essays in interpretative anthropology.* New York: Basic Books.

Gelb, I. J. (1952). *A study of writing.* Chicago: University of Chicago Press.

Gelles, R., & Cornell, C. P. (1990). *Intimate violence in families* (2nd ed.). Newbury Park, CA: Sage.

Gellner, E. (1983). *Nations and nationalism.* Ithaca, NY: Cornell University Press.

General Social Survey (GSS). (1997). General social surveys, 1972–1994 [Cumulative file]. Retrieved January 10, 2005, from http://webapp.icpsr.umich.edu/cocoon/ICPSR-STUDY/03728.xml

Gerbner, G., Gross, L., Morgan, M., & Signorielli, N. (1986). Television's mean world: violence profile no. 14–15. Philadelphia: Annenberg School of Communication, University of Pennsylvania.

Gereffi, G. (1995). Contending paradigms for cross-regional comparison: Development strategies and commodity chains in East Asia and Latin America. In P. H. Smith (Ed.), *Latin America in comparative perspective: New approaches to methods and analysis.* Boulder, CO: Westview Press.

Gereffi, G. (1996). Commodity chains and regional divisions of labor in East Asia. *Journal of Asian Business, 12*(1): 75–112.

Gershuny, J., Godwin, M., & Jones, S. (1994). The domestic labour revolution: A process of lagged adaptation? In M. Anderson, F. Bechofer, & J. Gershuny (Eds.), *The social and political economy of the household.* Oxford, UK: Oxford University Press.

Gershuny, J., & Miles, I. D. (1983). *The new service economy: The transformation of employment in industrial societies.* London: Francis Pinter.

Giddens, A. (1984). *The constitution of society.* Cambridge, UK: Polity Press.

Giddens, A. (1990). *The consequences of modernity.* Cambridge, UK: Polity Press.

Giddens, A. (1998). *The third way: The renewal of social democracy.* Cambridge, UK: Polity Press.

Gilligan, C. (1982). *In a different voice: Psychological theory and women's development.* Cambridge, MA: Harvard University Press.

Ginzburg, C. (1980). *The cheese and the worms.* London: Routledge and Kegan Paul.

Giuffre, P. A., & Williams, C. L. (1994). Boundary lines: Labeling sexual harassment in restaurants. *Gender and Society, 8,* 378–401.

Glascock, A., & Feinman, S. (1981). Social asset or social burden: An analysis of the treatment for the aged in non-industrial societies. In C. L. Fry (Ed.), *Dimensions: Aging, culture, and health.* New York: Praeger.

Glasius, M., Kaldor M., & Anheier, H. (Eds.). (2002). *Global civil society 2002.* Oxford, UK: Oxford University Press.

Glassner, B. (1999). *The culture of fear: Why Americans are afraid of the wrong things.* New York: Basic Books.

Glenn, E. N. (1994). Introduction. In G. Change, L. R. Forcey, & E. N. Glenn (Eds.), *Mothering: Ideology, experience, and agency.* New York: Routledge.

Glock, C. Y. (1976). On the origin and evolution of religious groups. In C. Y. Glock and R. N. Bellah (Eds.), *The new religious consciousness.* Berkeley: University of California Press.

Glueck, S. W., & Glueck, E. (1956). *Physique and delinquency.* New York: Harper & Row.

Gober, P. (1993). *Americans on the move.* Washington, DC: Population Reference Bureau.

Goffman, E. (1963). *Stigma: Notes on the management of spoiled identity.* Englewood Cliffs, NJ: Prentice-Hall.

Goffman, E. (1967). *Interaction ritual.* New York: Doubleday/Anchor.

Goffman, E. (1971). *Relations in public: Microstudies of the public order.* New York: Basic Books.

Goffman, E. (1973). *The presentation of self in everyday life.* New York: Overlook Press.

Goffman, E. (1981). *Forms of talk.* Philadelphia: University of Pennsylvania Press.

Gold, T. (1986). *State and society in the Taiwan miracle.* Armonk, NY: M.E. Sharpe.

Goldberg, C. (1997, January 30). Hispanic households struggle amid broad decline in income. *The New York Times,* pp. A1, A16.

Goldberg, C. (2001, July 27). School computer money approved. *The New York Times.*

Goldberg, D. J., & Rayner, J. D. (1987). *The Jewish people: Their history and their religion.* New York: Penguin Books.

Goldin, C. D. (1990). *Understanding the gender gap: An economic history of American women.* New York: Oxford University Press.

Goldscheider, F. K. (1990). The aging of the gender revolution: What do we know and what do we need to know? *Research on Aging, 12,* 531–545.

Goldscheider, F. K., & Goldscheider, C. (1999). *The changing transition to adulthood: Leaving and returning home.* Thousand Oaks, CA: Sage.

Goldscheider, F. K., & Waite, L. J. (1991). *New families, no families? The transformation of the American home.* Berkeley: University of California Press.

Goldstein, J., & Morning, A. (2000). The multiple-race population of the United States: Issues and estimates. *Proceedings of the National Academy of Sciences 97*(11): 6230–6235.

Goldstein, S., & Goldstein, A. (1996). *Jews on the move: Implications for Jewish identity.* Albany, NY: SUNY Press.

Gonnerman, J. (2004). *Life on the outside: The prison odyssey of Elaine Bartlett.* New York: Farrar, Straus, and Giroux.

Goode, W. J. (1963). *World revolution in family patterns*. New York: Free Press.

Goode, W. J. (1971). Force and violence in the family. *Journal of Marriage and the Family, 33*, 624–636.

Goodhardt, G. J., Ehrenberg, A. S. C., & Collins, M. A. (1987). *The television audience: Patterns of voting* (2nd ed.). London: Gower.

Gottfredson, M. R., & Hirschi, T. (1990). *A general theory of crime*. Stanford, CA: Stanford University Press.

Granovetter, M. (1973). The strength of weak ties. *American Journal of Sociology, 78*, 1360–1380.

Grant Thornton. (2007). International Business Report 2007. Retrieved fall 2007 from http://www.grantthornton.ca/resources/documents/IBR2007WomeninBusinessPressRelease.pdf

Grassroots. (1989). Why did they kill David Webster? *Grassroots, 10*(2). Retrieved spring 2006 from http://disa.nu.ac.za/articledisplaypage.asp?filename=GRMay89&articletitle=Why+did+they+kill+David+Webster%3F

Gray, J. (2003). *Al Qaeda and what it means to be modern*. Chatham, UK: Faber and Faber.

Green, F. (1987). *The "sissy boy" syndrome and the development of homosexuality*. New Haven, CT: Yale University Press.

Green, J. C. (2004). The American religious landscape and political attitudes: A baseline for 2004. The Pew Forum on Religion & Public Life. Table 1. Retrieved January 23, 2006, from http://pewforum.org/publications/surveys/green-full.pdf

Greenberg, J. S., & Becker, M. (1988). Aging parents as family resources. *Gerontologist, 28*, 786–791.

Greenfield, P. M. (1993). Representational competence in shared symbol systems. In R. R. Cocking & K. A. Renninger (Eds) *The development and meaning of psychological distance*. Hillsdale, NJ: Erlbaum.

Greenhouse, S., & Hays, C. L. (2004, June 23). Wal-Mart sex-bias suit given class-action status. *The New York Times.*

Griffin, S. (1979). *Rape, the power of consciousness*. New York: Harper & Row.

Grint, K. (1991). *The sociology of work*. Cambridge, UK: Polity Press.

Gross, J. (1992, July 13). Suffering in silence no more: Fighting sexual harassment. *The New York Times,* p. A1.

Grusky, D. B., & Hauser, R. M. (1984). Comparative social mobility revisited: models of convergence and divergence in 16 countries. *American Sociological Review, 49,* 19–38.

The Guardian. (2002). Top 1% earn as much as the poorest 57%. Retrieved January 10, 2005, from www.guardian.co.uk/business/story/0,,635292,00.html

Gubrium, J. F. (1986). *Oldtimers and alzheimer's: The descriptive organization of senility*. Greenwich, CT: JAI Press.

Gubrium, J. F. (1991). *The mosaic of care: frail elderly and their families in the real world*. New York: Springer.

Gubrium, J. F. (1993). *Speaking of life: Horizons of meaning for nursing home residents*. Hawthorne, NY: Aldine de Gruyter.

Gubrium, J. F., & Sankar, A. (Eds.). (1994). *Qualitative methods in aging research*. Newbury Park, CA: Sage.

Guibernau, M. (1999). *Nations without states: Political communities in a global age*. Cambridge, MA: Blackwell.

Guynup, S. (2004, July 28). Scarification: Ancient body art leaving new marks. National Geographic Channel. Retrieved spring 2006 from http://news.nationalgeographic.com/news/2004/07/0728_040728_tvtabooscars.html

Habermas, J. (1975). *Legitimation crisis* (T. McCarthy, Trans.). Boston: Beacon Press.

Habermas, J. (1989; orig. 1962). *The structural transformation of the public sphere: An inquiry into a category of bourgeois society*. Cambridge, UK: Polity Press.

Haddad, Y. Y. (1979, September–October). The Muslim experience in the United States. *The Link, 2*(4).

Hadden, J. (1990, March). Precursors to the globalization of American televangelism. *Social Compass, 37,* 161–167.

Hadden, J. (1997a). The concepts "cult" and "sect" in scholarly research and public discourse. New Religious Movements website. Retrieved January 10, 2005, from http://religiousmovements.lib.virginia.edu/cultsect/concult.htm

Hadden, J. (1997b). New religious movements mission statement. New Religious Movements website. Retrieved January 10, 2005, from http://religousmovements.lib.virginia.edu/welcome/mission.htm

Hadden, J. (2004). Televangelism. Religious Broadcasting website. Retrieved January 3, 2005, from http://religious broadcasting.lib.virginia.edu/televangelism.html

Hadden, J., & Shupe, A. (1987). Televangelism in America. *Social Compass, 34*(1): 61–75.

Hadden, J., & Swann, C. (1981). *Prime time preachers: The rising tide of televangelism*. Reading, MA: Addison Wesley.

Hagan, J., & McCarthy, B. (1992). Mean streets: The theoretical significance of situational delinquency among homeless youth. *American Sociological Review, 98,* 597–627.

Haggard, S. (1990). *Pathways from the periphery: The politics of growth in newly industrializing countries*. Ithaca, NY: Cornell University Press.

Hall, E. T. (1969). *The hidden dimension*. New York: Doubleday.

Hall, E. T. (1973). *The silent language*. New York: Doubleday.

Hall, S. (1992). The question of cultural identity. In S. Hall, D. Held, & T. McGrew (Eds.), *Modernity and its futures*. Cambridge, UK: Polity Press.

Hall, S., Held, D., & McGrew, T. (1988, October). New times. *Marxism Today.*

Halpern, C. T., et al. (2000). Smart teens don't have sex (or kiss much either). *Journal of Adolescent Health, 26*(3): 213–225.

Hamel, G. (1991, Summer). Competition for competence and inter-partner learning within international strategic alliances. *Strategic Management Journal, 12,* 83–103.

Hamilton, M. M. (2000, April 14). Web retailer Kozmo accused of redlining; Exclusion of D.C. minority areas cited. *Washington Post.*

Hammond, P. E. (1992). *Religion and personal autonomy: The third disestablishment in America*. Columbia: University of South Carolina Press.

Handy, C. (1994). *The empty raincoat: Making sense of the future*. London: Hutchinson.

Harknett, K., & McLanahan, S. (2004). Racial and ethnic differences in marriage after the birth of a child." *American Sociological Review, 69,* 790–811.

Harris, D. (2003). *Racial classification and the 2000 census*. Commissioned paper. Panel to Review the 2000 Census, Committee on National Statistics. University of Michigan, Ann Arbor.

Harris, D. R., & Sim, J. J. (2000). *An empirical look at the social construction of race: The case of mixed-race adolescents*. Population Studies Center Research

Report 00–452, University of Michigan, Ann Arbor.

Harris, J. R. (1998). *The nurture assumption: Why children turn out the way they do.* New York: Free Press.

Harris, M. (1975). *Cows, pigs, wars, and riches: The riddles of culture.* New York: Random House.

Harris, M. (1978). *Cannibals and kings: The origins of cultures.* New York: Random House.

Harris, M. (1980). *Cultural materialism: The struggle for a science of culture.* New York: Vintage Books.

Hartig, T., Johansson, G., & Kylin, C. (2003). Residence in the social ecology of stress and restoration. *Journal of Social Issues, 59*(3): 611–636.

Hartman, C. (2000). Facts and figures on wealth. Inequality.org. Retrieved January 3, 2005, from www.inequality.org/factsfr.html

Hartman, M., & Banner, L. (Eds.). (1974). *Clio's consciousness raised: New perspectives on the history of women.* New York: Norton.

Hartman, M., & Hartman, H. (1996). *Gender equality and American Jews.* Albany: SUNY Press.

Hartmann, H. I., et al. (1985). An agenda for basic research on comparable worth. In H. I. Hartmann, et al. (Eds.), *Comparable worth: New directions for research.* Washington, DC: National Academy Press.

Harvey, D. (1973). *Social justice and the city.* Oxford, UK: Blackwell.

Harvey, D. (1982). *The limits to capital.* Oxford, UK: Blackwell.

Harvey, D. (1985). *Consciousness and the urban experience: Studies in the history and theory of capitalist urbanization.* Oxford, UK: Blackwell.

Harvey, D. (1989). *The condition of postmodernity.* Cambridge, MA: Blackwell.

Haslam, D. W., & James, W. P. (2005). Obesity. *Lancet, 366*(9492): 1197–1209.

Hatch, N. O. (1989). *The democratization of American Christianity.* New Haven, CT: Yale University Press.

Hathaway, A. D. (1997). Marijuana and tolerance: Revisiting Becker's sources of control. *Deviant Behavior, 18*(2): 103–124.

Haugen, E. (1977). Linguistic relativity: Myths and methods. In W. C. McCormack & S. A. Wurm (Eds.), *Language and thought: Anthropological issues.* The Hague: Mouton.

Hawkes, T. (1977). *Structuralism and semiotics.* Berkeley: University of California Press.

Hawley, A. H. (1950). *Human ecology: A theory of community structure.* New York: Ronald Press Company.

Hawley, A. H. (1968). Human ecology. *International Encyclopedia of Social Science* (Vol. 4). New York: Free Press.

Hayflick, L. (1994). *How and why we age.* New York: Ballantine Books.

Hays, S. (2000). Constructing the centrality of culture—and deconstructing sociology? *Contemporary Sociology, 29*(4): 594–602.

Healthful Life Project. (2003). The world's ageing population and scientific attempts to make it an even greater problem. Retrieved December 7, 2005, from http://healthfullife.umdnj.edu/archives/aging_pop%20_archive.htm

Healy, M. (2001). Pieces of the puzzle. *Los Angeles Times.* Retrieved January 10, 2005, from http://pqasb.pqarchiver.com/latimes/results.html?RQT=511&sid=1&firstIndex=460&PQACnt=1

Hebl, M. R., & Heatherton, T. F. (1998). The stigma of obesity in women: The difference is black and white. *Personality and Social Psychology Bulletin, 24,* 417–426.

Hecht, J. (2003, May 16). New life for undersea fiber. *Technology Review.* Massachusetts Institute of Technology. Retrieved spring 2006 from www.techreview.com/NanoTech/wtr_13185,318,p1.html

Heelas, P. (1996). *The new age movement.* Oxford, UK: Blackwell.

Heidensohn, F. (1985). *Women and crime.* London: Macmillan.

Heise, D. R. (1987). Sociocultural determination of mental aging. In C. Schooler & K. Warner Schaie (Eds.), *Cognitive functioning and social structure over the life course.* Norwood, NJ: Ablex.

Held, D. (1987). *Models of democracy.* Stanford, CA: Stanford University Press.

Held, D., McGrew, A., Goldblatt, D., & Perraton, J. (1999). *Global transformations: Politics, economics, and culture.* Cambridge, UK: Polity Press.

Helm, L. (1992, November 21). Debt puts squeeze on Japanese. *Los Angeles Times.*

Henderson, J. (1989). *The globalization of high technology production: Society, space, and semiconductors in the restructuring of the modern world.* London: Routledge.

Henderson, J.; & Appelbaum, R. P. (1992). Situating the state in the Asian development process. In R. P. Appelbaum & J. Henderson (Eds.), *States and development in the Asian Pacific rim.* Newbury Park, CA: Sage.

Hendricks, J. (1992). Generation and the generation of theory in social gerontology. *Aging and Human Development, 35,* 31–47.

Hendricks, J., & Hatch, L. R. (1993). Federal policy and family life of older Americans. In J. Hendricks & C. J. Rosenthal (Eds.), *The remainder of their days: Impact of public policy on older families.* New York: Greenwood.

Hendricks, J., & Hendricks, C. D. (1986). *Aging in mass society: Myths and realities.* Boston: Little, Brown.

Henry, W. E. (1965). *Growing older: The process of disengagement.* New York: Basic Books.

Henslin, J. M., & Biggs, M. A. (1971). Dramaturgical desexualization: The sociology of the vaginal examination. In J. M. Henslin (Ed.), *Studies in the sociology of sex.* New York: Appleton-Century-Crofts.

Henslin, J. M., & Biggs, M. A. (1997). Behavior in public places: The sociology of the vaginal examination. In J. M. Henslin (Ed.), *Down to earth sociology: Introductory readings* (9th ed.). New York: Free Press.

Hentoff, N. (2002, May 24). The FBI's magic lantern: Ashcroft can be in your computer. *The Village Voice.*

Herdt, G. (1981). *Guardians of the flutes: Idioms of masculinity.* New York: McGraw-Hill.

Herdt, G. (1984). *Ritualized homosexuality in Melanesia.* Berkeley: University of California Press.

Herdt, G. (1986). *The Sambia: Ritual and gender in New Guinea.* New York: Holt, Rinehart and Winston.

Herdt, G., & Davidson, J. (1988). The Sambia 'urnim-man': Sociocultural and clinical aspects of gender formation in Papua, New Guinea. *Archives of Sexual Behavior, 17.*

Hernandez, D. J. (1993). *America's children: Resources from family, government, and economy.* New York: Russell Sage Foundation.

Herrnstein, R. J., & Murray, C. (1994). *The bell curve: Intelligence and class structure in American life.* New York: Free Press.

Hesse-Biber, S. (1997). *Am I thin enough yet? The cult of thinness and the commercialization of identity.* New York: Oxford University Press.

Hexham, I., & Poewe, K. (1997). *New religions as global cultures.* Boulder, CO: Westview Press.

Higher Education Research Institute (HERI). (1990). *The American freshman.* Los Angeles: University of California.

Hill, K., & Upchurch, D. M. (1995). Gender differences in child health: Evidence from the demographic and health surveys. *Population and Development Review, 21,*127–151.

Himes, C. L. (1999). Racial differences in education, obesity, and health in later life. In N. E. Adler, M. Marmot, B. S. McEwen, & J. Stewart (Eds.), *Socioeconomic status and health in industrial nations: Social, psychological, and biological pathways. Annals of the New York Academy of Sciences, 896,* 370–372.

Hirshci, T. (1969). *Causes of delinquency.* Berkeley: University of California Press.

Hirst, P. (1997). The global economy: Myths and realities. *International Affairs, 73,* 409–425.

Hirst, P., & Thompson, G. (1992). The problem of "globalization": International economic relations, national economic management, and the formation of trading blocs. *Economy and Society, 24,* 357–396.

Hirst, P., & Thompson, G. (1999). *Globalization in question: The international economy and the possibilities of governance* (Rev. ed.). Cambridge, UK: Polity Press.

Ho, S. Y. (1990) *Taiwan: After a long silence.* Hong Kong: Asia Monitor Resource Center.

Hochschild, A. R. (1975). Disengagement theory: A critique and proposal. *American Sociological Review, 40,* 553–569.

Hochschild, A. R. (1997). *The time bind.* New York: Metropolitan Books.

Hochschild, A. R., with Machung, Anne. (1989). *The second shift: Working parents and the revolution at home.* New York: Viking.

Hodge, R., & Tripp, D. (1986). *Children and television: A semiotic approach.* Cambridge, UK: Polity Press.

Hofstede, G. (1997). *Cultures and organizations: Software of the mind.* New York: McGraw Hill.

Hogan, B. (2000, June). U.N.: Women's conference presses for political parity. Radio Free Europe.

Holmes, S. A. (1996, November 18). Quality of life is up for many blacks, data say. *The New York Times,* p. A1.

Holmes, S. A. (1997, September 30). New reports say minorities benefit in fiscal recovery. *The New York Times,* p. A1.

Holton, R. J. (1978). The crowd in history: Some problems of theory and method. *Social History, 3,* 219–233.

Homans, G. (1950). *The human group.* New York: Harcourt, Brace.

Homans, H. (1987). Man-made myth: The reality of being a woman scientist in the NHS. In A. Spencer & D. Podmore (Eds.), *In a man's world: Essays on women in male-dominated professions.* London: Tavistock.

Hood, J. R. (2002, December 16). More abuse seen as elder population grows. Caregiver USA News. Retrieved December 7, 2005, from www.andthou shalthonor.org/news/abuse.html

hooks, b. (1996). *Bone black: Memories of girlhood.* New York: Henry Holt.

Hopkins, T. K., & Wallerstein, I. (1996). *The age of transition: Trajectory of the world-system, 1945–2025.* London: Zed Books.

House, J. S. (2001). Social isolation kills, but how and why? *Psychosomatic Medicine,* 63, 273–274.

Hout, M. (1988). More universalism, less structural mobility: The American occupational structure in the 1980s. *American Journal of Sociology, 93,* 1358–1400.

Hout, M., & Lucas, S. R. (1996). Education's role in reducing income disparities. *The Education Digest, 62*(3).

Howard, J. H., Rechnitzer, P.A., Cunningham, D.A., & Donner, A.P. (1986). Change in type A behavior a year after retirement. *Gerontologist, 26,* 643–649.

Huber, J. (1990). Macro-micro link in gender stratification. *American Sociological Review, 55,* 1–10.

Huber, J. (Ed.). (1992). *Micro-macro linkages in sociology.* Newbury Park, CA: Sage.

Hudson, T. (1995, May 20). Medicaid's new crisis: Are we pitting the elderly against the poor? Hospitals and Health Networks.

Hughes, D. M. (2001, January). The 'Natasha' trade: Transnational sex trafficking. *National Institute of Justice Journal,* 9–15.

Humphreys, L. (1970). *Tearoom trade: Impersonal sex in public places.* Chicago: Aldine.

Hunter, J. D. (1987). *Evangelism: The coming generation.* Chicago: University of Chicago Press.

Hunter, L. (1990). *After bereavement: A study of change in attitudes about life among older widows.* Unpublished Ph.D. dissertation, The Fielding Institute, Santa Barbara, California.

Huntington, S. P. (1991). *The third wave: Democratization in the late twentieth century.* Norman: University of Oklahoma Press.

Huntington, S. P. (1993, Summer). The clash of civilizations? *Foreign Affairs, 72*(3): 22–49.

Huntington, S. P. (1998). *The clash of civilizations and the remaking of world order.* New York: Simon & Schuster.

Hurtado, A. (1995). Variation, combinations, and evolutions: Latino families in the United States. In R. Zambrana (Ed.), *Understanding Latino families.* Thousand Oaks, CA: Sage.

Hurtado, S., & Pryor, J. H. (2006). The American freshman: National norms for fall 2005. Higher Education Research Institute, University of California, Los Angeles. Retrieved September 19, 2008, from www.gseis.ucla.edu/heri/PP/ Norms05-Summary.ppt

Hyman, H. H., & Singer, E. (1968). *Readings in reference group theory and research.* New York: Free Press.

Hyman, R. (1984). *Strikes* (2nd ed.). London: Fontana.

Illich, I. D. (1983). *Deschooling society.* New York: Harper & Row.

Inglehart, R. (1997). *Modernization and postmodernization: Cultural, economic and political change in 43 societies.* Princeton, NJ: Princeton University Press.

Institute of International Education (IIE). (2007a). International student enrollment in U.S. rebounds. *Open Doors Report 2007.* Retrieved fall 2008 from http://opendoors.iienetwork. org/?p=113743

Institute of International Education (IIE). (2007b). American students studying abroad at record levels: Up 8.5%. *Open Doors Report 2006.* Retrieved January 2008 from http://opendoors.iienetwork. org/?p=113744

Intelligence Report. (2001, Summer). *Reevaluating the Net,* no. 102. Montgomery, AL: The Southern Poverty Law Center.

International Campaign to Ban Land Mines. (2007). States not parties. Retrieved spring 2008 from http://www.icbl.org/ treaty/snp

International Centre for Prison Studies. (2007). Prison brief—Highest to lowest rates. Retrieved fall 2007 from http://www.kcl.ac.uk/depsta/law/research/icps/worldbrief/wpb_stats.php?area=all&category=wb_poprate

International Labor Organization (ILO). (2000, January). *Statistical information and monitoring programme on child labour (SIMPOC): Overview and strategic plan 2000–2002.* Prepared by the International Program on the Elimination of Child Labour (IPEC) and Bureau of Statistics (STAT). Geneva: ILO.

International Labor Organization (ILO). (2004a). More women are entering the global labour force than ever before, but job equality, poverty reduction remain elusive. Retrieved November 9, 2008, from http://www.ilo.org/global/About_the_ILO/Media_and_public_information/Press_releases/lang—en/WCMS_005243/index.htm

International Labor Organization (ILO). (2004b). Breaking through the glass ceiling: Women in management. Retrieved December 4, 2005, from www.ilo.org/dyn/gender/docs/RES/292/F267981337/Breaking%20Glass%20PDF%20English.pdf

International Labor Organization (ILO). (2007, March). Global employment trends for women, Brief. Retrieved fall 2007 from http://www.ilo.org/public/english/employment/strat/download/getw07.pdf

International Lesbian and Gay Association (ILGA). (2007). About ILGA. Retrieved January 2008 from http://www.ilga.org/aboutilga.asp

International Lesbian and Gay Association (ILGA). (2008). LGTBI rights in the world. Retrieved October 2008 from http://www.ilga.org/map/LGBTI_rights.jpg

International Money Fund. (2005). World economic lookout. Retrieved spring 2006 from www.imf.org/external/pubs/ft/weo/2005/01/pdf/chapter4.pdf

International Money Fund. (2006). Facts on child labor. Retrieved fall 2006 from http://www.ilo.org/dyn/declaris/DECLARATIONWEB.DOWNLOAD_BLOB?Var_DocumentID=6215

International Road Federation. (1987). United Nations annual bulletin of transport statistics, cited in *Social trends*. London: HMSO.

International Telework Association & Council (ITAC). (2004). Telework facts and figures. Retrieved January 20, 2005, from www.telecommute.org/resources/abouttelework.htm

International Union for Conservation of Nature (ICUN). (2007). Extinction crisis escalates: Red list shows apes, corals, vultures, dolphins all in danger. Retrieved spring 2008 from http://cms.iucn.org/what/species/wildlife/index.cfm?uNewsID=81

Internet World Stats. (2008a). Top 20 countries with highest number of Internet users. Retrieved fall 2008 from http://www.internetworldstats.com/top20.htm

Internet World Stats. (2008b). Internet usage stats: World Internet users and population stats. Retrieved January 2008 from http://www.internetworldstats.com/stats.htm

Interparlimentary Union. (2008). Women in national parliaments: World classification. Retrieved fall 2008 from http://www.guide2womenleaders.com/situation_statistics.htm

Iyer, P. (1989). *Video night in Kathmandu.* New York: Vintage.

Jacobs, J. (1961). *The death and life of great American cities.* New York: Random House.

Jacoby, S. (1998). *Modern manors: Welfare capitalism since the New Deal.* Princeton, NJ: Princeton University Press.

Jaher, F. C. (Ed.). (1973). *The rich, the well born, and the powerful.* Urbana: University of Illinois Press.

Janis, I. L. (1972). *Victims of groupthink.* Boston: Houghton Mifflin.

Janis, I. L. (1989). *Crucial decisions: Leadership in policy making and crisis management.* New York: Free Press.

Janis, I. L., & Mann, L. (1977). *Decision making: A psychological analysis of conflict, choice, and commitment.* New York: Free Press.

Jencks, C., Smith, M., Acland, H., Bane, M.J., Cohen, D., Gintis, H., et al. (1972). *Inequality: A reassessment of the effects of family and school in America.* New York: Basic Books.

Jensen, A. (1969). How much can we boost IQ and scholastic achievement? *Harvard Educational Review, 39,* 1–123.

Jensen, A. (1979). *Bias in mental testing.* New York: Free Press.

Jin, Ge. (2006, May). Chinese gold farmers in the game world. *Consumers, Commodities and Consumption: A Newsletter of the Consumer Studies Research Network, 7*(2). Retrieved October 26, 2008, from https://etfiles.uiuc.edu/dtcook/www/CCCnewsletter/7-2/jin.htm

Jobling, R. (1988). The experience of psoriasis under treatment. In M. Bury & R. Anderson (Eds.), *Living with chronic illness: The experience of patients and their families.* London: Unwin Hyman.

John, M. T. (1988). *Geragogy: A theory for teaching the elderly.* New York: Haworth.

Johnson, M., & Morton, J. (1991). *Biology and cognitive development: The case of face recognition.* Oxford, UK: Blackwell.

Johnson, M. P. (1995). Patriarchal terrorism and common couple violence: Two forms of violence against women in U.S. families. *Journal of Marriage and the Family, 57,* 283–294.

Johnson-Odim, C. (1991). Common themes, different contexts: Third World women and feminism. In C. Mohanty, et al. (Eds.), *Third world women and the politics of feminism.* Bloomington: Indiana University Press.

Joint Center for Housing Studies. (1994). *The state of the nation's housing.* Cambridge, MA: Harvard University Press.

Jones, E. (1998, Fall). Globalism and the American tide. *National Interest, 53,* 116–119.

Jones, J. (1986). *Labor of love, labor of sorrow: Black women, work, and the family from slavery to the present.* New York: Random House.

Jones, S. G. (1995). Understanding community in the information age. In S. G. Jones (Ed.), *CyberSociety: Computer-mediated communication and community.* Thousand Oaks, CA: Sage.

Judge, K. (1995). Income distribution and life expectancy: A critical appraisal. *British Medical Journal, 311,* 1282–1287.

Juergensmeyer, M. (1993). *The new cold war? Religious nationalism confronts the secular state.* Berkeley: University of California Press.

Juergensmeyer, M. (1995a). *Radhasoami reality: The logic of a modern faith.* Princeton, NJ: Princeton University Press.

Juergensmeyer, M. (1995b, July). The new religious state. *Comparative Politics, 27,* 379–391.

Juergensmeyer, M. (2001). *Terror in the mind of God: The global rise of religious violence.* Berkeley: University of California Press.

Kaiser Family Foundation. (2005). Trends and indicators in the changing health care marketplace. Retrieved December 7, 2005, from www.kff.org/insurance/7031/print-sec1.cfm.

Kaiser Family Foundation. (2008). State health facts: Population distribution by metropolitan status, states (2006–2007), U.S. (2007). Retrieved spring 2008 from http://www.statehealth facts.org/comparebar.jsp?cat=1&ind=18

Kandall, S., & Petrillo, J. (1996). *Substance and shadow: Women and addiction in the United States.* Cambridge, MA: Harvard University Press.

Kanellos, M. (2007, March 25). Intel to produce chips in China. CNET News.com. Retrieved fall 2007 from http://www.news.com/Intel-to-produce-chips-in-China/2100-1006_3-6170016.html?tag=ne.gall.related

Kanter, R. M. (1977). *Men and women of the corporation.* New York: Basic Books.

Kanter, R. M. (1983). *The change masters: Innovation for productivity in the American corporation.* New York: Simon and Schuster.

Kanter, R. M. (1991). The future of bureaucracy and hierarchy in organizational theory. In P. Bourdieu & J. Coleman (Eds.), *Social theory for a changing society.* Boulder, CO: Westview Press.

Kasarda, J. (1993). Urban industrial transition and the underclass. In W. J. Wilson (Ed.), *The ghetto underclass.* Newbury Park, CA: Sage.

Kasarda, J., & Crenshaw, E. M. (1991). Third world urbanization: Dimensions, theories, and determinants. In *Annual Review of Sociology 1991,* 17. Palo Alto, CA: Annual Reviews.

Katz, J. (1999). *How emotions work.* Chicago: University of Chicago Press.

Kautsky, J. (1982). *The politics of aristocratic empires.* Chapel Hill: University of North Carolina Press.

Kawachi, I., & Kennedy, B. P. (1997). Socioeconomic determinants of health: Health and social cohesion: why care about income inequality? *British Medical Journal, 314,* 1037.

Kedouri, E. (1992). *Politics in the Middle East.* New York: Oxford University Press.

Kelling, G. L., & Coles, C. M. (1997). *Fixing broken windows: Restoring order and reducing crime in our communities.* New York: Free Press.

Kelley, J., & Evans, M. D. R. (1995). Class and class conflict in six western nations.

American Review of Sociology, 60(2): 157–178.

Kelly, L. (1987). The continuum of sexual violence. In J. Hanmer & M. Maynard (Eds.), *Women, violence, and social control.* Atlantic Highlands, NJ: Humanities Press.

Kelly, M. P. (1992). *Colitis: The experience of illness.* London: Routledge.

Kemp, A., Madlala, N., Moodley, A., & Salo, E. (1995). The dawn of a new day: Redefining South African feminism. In A. Basu (ed.), *The challenge of local feminisms.* Boulder, CO: Westview Press.

Kenkel, D., Lillard, D., & Mathios, A. (2006). The roles of high school completion and GED receipt in smoking and obesity. *Journal of Labor Economics, 24*(3): 635–660.

Kenway, J., et al. (1995). Pulp fictions? Education, markets, and the information superhighway. *Australian Educational Researcher, 22.*

Kenworthy, L., & Malami, M. (1999). Gender inequality in political representation: A worldwide comparative analysis. *Social Forces, 78*(1): 235–269.

Kern, S. (1983). *The culture of time and space: 1880–1918.* Cambridge, MA: Harvard University Press.

Kerr, C., Dunlop, J., Harbison, F., & Myers, C. (1960). *Industrialism and industrial man: The problems of labor and management in economic growth.* Cambridge, MA: Harvard University Press.

Kiecolt, K. J., & Nelson, H. M. (1991, September). Evangelicals and party realignment, 1976–1988. *Social Science Quarterly, 72,* 552–569.

Kimmel, M. S. (2003). *The gender of desire: Essays on male sexuality.* Albany: State University of New York Press.

Kinder, M. (1993). *Playing with power in movies, television, and video games.* Berkeley: University of California Press.

King, N. R. (1984). Exploitation and abuse of older family members: An overview of the problem. In J. J. Cosa (Ed.), *Abuse of the elderly.* Lexington, MA: Lexington Books.

Kinsey, A. C., Pomeroy, W. R., & Martin, C. E. (1948). *Sexual behavior in the human male.* Philadelphia: Saunders.

Kinsey, A. C. (1953). *Sexual behavior in the human female.* Philadelphia: Saunders.

Kinsley, D. (1982). *Hinduism: A cultural perspective.* Englewood Cliffs, NJ: Prentice Hall.

Kjekshus, H. (1977). *Ecology, control, and economic development in East African history.* Berkeley: University of California Press.

Klasen, S., & Wink, C. (2003). Missing women: Revitalizing the debate. *Feminist Economics, 9*(2 & 3): 263–299.

Kling, R. (1996). Computerization at work. In R. Kling (Ed.), *Computers and controversy* (2nd ed.). New York: Academic Press.

Kluckhohn, C. (1949). *Mirror for man.* Tucson: University of Arizona Press.

Knodel, J. (2006, August). Parents of persons with AIDS: Unrecognized contributions and unmet needs. *Journal of Global Ageing, 4,* 46–55.

Knoke, D. (1990). *Political networks: The structural perspective.* New York: Cambridge University Press.

Knorr-Cetina, K., & Cicourel, A. V. (Eds.). (1981). *Advances in social theory and methodology: Towards an integration of micro- and macro-sociologies.* Boston: Routledge and Kegan Paul.

Kobrin, S. J. (1997). Electronic cash and the end of national markets. *Foreign Policy, 107,* 65–77.

Kohn, M. (1977). *Class and conformity* (2nd ed.). Homewood, IL: Dorsey Press.

Kollmeyer, C. (2003). Globalization, class compromise, and American exceptionalism: Political change in 16 advanced capitalist countries. *Critical Sociology, 29*(3): 369–391.

Kollock, P., & Smith, M. A. (1996). Managing the virtual commons: Cooperation and conflict in computer communities. In S. Herring (Ed.), *Computer-mediated communication.* Amsterdam: John Benjamins.

Kosmin, B. A. (1991). *Research report: The national survey of religious identification.* New York: City University of New York Graduate Center.

Kosmin, B. A., Mayer, E., & Keysar, A. (2001, December 19). American religious identification survey (ARIS). New York: CUNY Graduate Center. Retrieved January 3, 2005, from www.gc.cuny.edu/studies/aris.pdf

Kozol, J. (1991). *Savage inequalities: Children in America's schools.* New York: Crown.

Krueger, C. (1995, September 22). Retirees with company heath plans on decline. *Los Angeles Times.*

Lacayo, R. (1994, February 7). Lock 'em up! *Time.*

Laing, R. D. (1971). *Self and others.* London: Tavistock.

Lake, R. (1981). *The new suburbanites: Race and housing in the suburbs.* New Brunswick, NJ: Center for Urban Policy Research, Rutgers University Press.

Lambert, R. (1995). Foreign student flows and the internationalization of higher education. In K. Hanson & J. Meyerson (Eds.), *International challenges to American colleges and universities.* Phoenix, AZ: Oryx Press.

Lammers, C., Ireland, M., Resnick, M., & Blum, V. (2000). Influences on adolescents' decision to postpone onset of sexual intercourse: A survival analysis of virginity among youths aged 13 to 18 years. *Journal of Adolescent Health, 26*(1): 42–48.

Land, K. C., Deane, G., & Blau, J. R. (1991). Religious pluralism and church membership. *American Sociological Review, 56,* 237–249.

Landale, N., & Fennelly, K. (1992). Informal unions among mainland Puerto Ricans: Cohabitation or an alternative to legal marriage? *Journal of Marriage and the Family, 54,* 269–280.

Landry, B. (1988). *The new black middle class.* Berkeley: University of California Press.

Lane, H. (1976). *The wild boy of Aveyron.* Cambridge, MA: Harvard University Press.

Lappe, F. M., Collins, J., & Rosset, P. (1998). *World hunger: 12 Myths* (2nd ed.). New York: Grove Press.

Laquer, W. (2003). *No end to war: Terrorism in the 21st century.* New York & London: Continuum.

Lareau, A. (2003). *Unequal childhoods: Class, race, and family life.* Berkeley: University of California Press.

LaRue, J. (2005, May 19). Obscenity and the First Amendment. Summit on Pornography. Rayburn House Office Building, Room 2322.

Lashbrook, J. (1996). Promotional timetables: An exploratory investigation of age norms for promotional expectations and their association with job well-being. *Gerontologist, 36*(2): 189–198.

Laslett, P. (1991). *A fresh map of life.* Cambridge, MA: Harvard University Press.

Latner, J. D., & Stunkard, A. J. (2003). Getting worse: The stigmatization of obese children. *Obesity Research, 11,* 452–456.

Laumann, E. O., Gagnon, J. H., Michael, R. T., & Michaels, S. (1994). *The social organization of sexuality: Sexual practices in the United States.* Chicago: University of Chicago Press.

Lawrence, B. B. (1989). *Defenders of God: The fundamentalist revolt against the modern age.* San Francisco: Harper & Row.

Lazarsfeld, P. F., Berelson, B., & Gaudet, H. (1948). *The people's choice.* New York: Columbia University Press.

Leach, E. (1976). *Culture and communication: The logic by which symbols are connected.* New York: Cambridge University Press.

Lee, G. (1982). *Family structure and interaction: A comparative analysis* (2nd ed.). Minneapolis: University of Minnesota Press.

Lee, R. B., & DeVore, I. (Eds.). (1968). *Man the hunter.* New York: Aldine de Gruyter.

Lemert, E. (1972). *Human deviance, social problems, and social control.* Englewood Cliffs, NJ: Prentice-Hall.

Lenhart, A., Horrigan, J., Rainie, L., Allen, K., Boyce, A., Madden, M., et al. (2003, April 16). The ever-shifting Internet population: A new look at Internet access and the digital divide. Washington, DC: The PEW Internet and American Life Project. Retrieved November 9, 2008, from http://www.pewinternet.org/report_display.asp?r=88

Leonhardt, D. (2001, July 15). Belt tightening seen as threat to the economy. *The New York Times,* p. 1.

Lepkowsky, M. (1990). Gender in an egalitarian society: A case study from the coral sea. In P. R. Sandy & R. G. Goodenough (Eds.), *Beyond the second sex.* Philadelphia: University of Pennsylvania Press.

Leupp, G. P. (1995). *Male colors, the construction of homosexuality in Tokugawa Japan.* Berkeley: University of California Press.

Levay, S. (1996). *Queer science: The uses and abuses of research into homosexuality.* Cambridge, MA: MIT Press.

Levin, W. C. (1988). Age stereotyping: College student evaluations. *Research on Aging, 10,* 134–148.

Lewis, O. (1968). The culture of poverty. In D. P. Moyhihan (Ed.), *On understanding poverty: Perspectives from the social sciences.* New York: Basic Books.

Lichtenstein, N. (2006). Wal-Mart: A template for twenty-first-century capitalism. In N. Lichtenstein (Ed.), *Wal-Mart: The face of twenty-first-century capitalism.* New York: New Press.

Lightfoot-Klein, H. (1989). *Prisoners of ritual: An odyssey into female genital circumcision in Africa.* New York: Haworth.

Lindau, S. T., Schumm, P., Laumann, E.O., Levinson, W., O'Muircheartaigh, C. A., & Waite, L. J. (2007). A study of sexuality and health among older adults in the United States. *New England Journal of Medicine, 357,* 762–774.

Linden, G., Kraemer, K. L., & Dedrick, J. (2007). Who captures value in a global innovation system? The case of Apple's iPod. Alfred P. Sloan Foundation: Personal Computing Industry Center. Retrieved fall 2007 from http://pcic.merage.uci.edu/papers/2007/AppleiPod.pdf

Lipset, S. M. (Ed.). (1981). *Party coalitions in the 1980s.* San Francisco: Institute for Contemporary Affairs.

Lipset, S. M., & Bendix, R. (1959). *Social mobility in industrial society.* Berkeley: University of California Press.

Lipsky, D. (2003a). *Absolutely American: Four years at West Point.* Boston: Houghton Mifflin.

Lipsky, D. (2003b, August 6). After four years at West Point, David Lipsky still wants more. *Powell's Author Interviews.* Retrieved spring 2006 from http://64.233.169.104/search?q=cache:-oXEygPXnw4J:www.powells.com/authors/lipsky.html+www.powells.com/authors/lipsky.html&hl=en&ct=clnk&cd=1&gl=us

Locke, J., & Pascoe, E. (2000, March 11). Can a sense of community flourish in cyberspace? *The Guardian.*

Lofland, L. H. (1973). *A world of strangers.* New York: Basic Books.

Lofland, L. H. (1998). *The public realm: Exploring the city's quintessential social territory.* New York: Aldine de Gruyter.

Logan, J. R., & Molotch, H. L. (1987). *Urban fortunes: The political economy of place.* Berkeley: University of California Press.

Long, E. (Ed.). (1997). *From sociology to cultural studies: New perspectives.* Malden, MA: Blackwell.

Loprest, P. (1999). Families who left welfare: Who are they and how are they doing? Washington, DC: Urban Institute. Retrieved January 3, 2005, from www.urban.org/Template.cfm?NavMenuID=24&template=/TaggedContent/ViewPublication.cfm&PublicationID=7297

Lorber, J. 1994. *Paradoxes of gender.* New Haven, CT: Yale University Press.

Loury, G. (1987). Why should we care about group inequality? *Social Philosophy and Policy, 5,* 249–271.

Lowe, G. S. (1987). *Women in the administrative revolution: The feminization of clerical work.* Toronto: University of Toronto Press.

Lyon, D. (1994). *The electronic eye: The rise of surveillance society.* Minneapolis: University of Minnesota Press.

Lyotard, J. (1985). *The post-modern condition: A report on knowledge.* Minneapolis: University of Minnesota Press.

MacEnoin, D., & al-Shahi, A. (Eds.). (1983). *Islam in the modern world.* New York: St. Martin's Press.

Maddox, G. L. (1965). Fact and artifact: Evidence bearing on disengagement from the Duke Geriatrics Project. *Human Development, 8,* 117–130.

Maddox, G. L. (1970). Themes and issues in sociological theories of human aging. *Human Development, 13,* 17–27.

Madigan, F. C. (1957). Are sex mortality differentials biologically caused? *Millbank Memorial Fund Quarterly, 25,* 202–223.

Mahalik, J. R., Burns, S. M., & Syzdek, M. (2007). Masculinity and perceived normative health behaviors as predictors of men's health behaviors. *Social Science & Medicine, 64*(11): 2201–2209.

Maharidge, D. (1996). *The coming white minority.* New York: Times Books.

Malotki, E. (1983). *Hopi time: A linguistic analysis of the temporal concepts in the Hopi language.* Berlin: Mouton.

Malthus, T. (2003; orig. 1798). *Essay on the principle of population: A Norton critical edition* (Rev. Ed.; P. Appleman, Ed.). New York: Norton.

Manning, J. T., Koukourakis, K., & Brodie, D. A. (1997). Fluctuating asymmetry, metabolic rate and sexual selection in human males. *Evolution and Human Behavior, 18*(1): 15–21.

Manpower, Inc. (2008). Company overview. Retrieved spring 2008 from http://www.manpower.com/about/companyoverview.cfm

Manton, K. G., Corder, L. S., & Stallard, E. (1993). Estimates of change in chronic disability and institutional incidence and prevalence rates in the U.S. elderly population from the 1982, 1984, and 1989 National Long Term Care Survey. *Journal of Gerontology, 47,* S153–S166.

Mare, R. D. (1991). Five decades of educational assortative mating. *American Sociological Review, 56*(1): 15–32.

Marsden, P. (1987). Core discussion networks of Americans. *American Sociological Review, 52,* 122–131.

Marsden, P., & Lin, N. (1982). *Social structure and network analysis.* Beverly Hills, CA: Sage.

Marshall, T. H. (1973). *Class, citizenship, and social development: Essays by T. H. Marshall.* Westport, CT: Greenwood Press.

Martin, D. (1990). *Tongues of fire: The explosion of protestantism in Latin America.* Cambridge, UK: Blackwell.

Martin, J. A., & Park, M. M. (1999). Trends in twin and triplet births: 1980–97. *National Vital Statistics Reports, 47*(24).

Martin, R. C. (1982). *Islam: A cultural perspective.* Englewood Cliffs, NJ: Prentice Hall.

Martineau, H. (1962; orig. 1837). *Society in America.* Garden City, NY: Doubleday.

Marx, K. (1977; orig. 1864). *Capital: A critique of political economy* (Vol. 1). New York: Random House.

Marx, K. (2000; orig. 1844). The economic and philosophical manuscripts. In D. McLellan (Ed.), *Karl Marx: Selected writings.* New York: Oxford University Press.

Massey, D. S. (1996). The age of extremes: Concentrated affluence and poverty in the twenty-first century. *Demography, 33*(4): 395–412.

Massey, D. S. (2006, Winter). Blackballed by Bush. *Contexts Magazine, 5*(1): 40–42.

Massey, D. S., & Denton, N. A. (1993). *American apartheid: Segregation and the making of the underclass.* Cambridge, MA: Harvard University Press.

Matsueda, R. L. (1992). Reflected appraisals, parental labeling, and delinquency: Specifying a symbolic interaction theory. *American Journal of Sociology, 97,* 1577–1611.

Mauer, M. (2004). Hispanic prisoners in the United States. The Sentencing Project. Retrieved spring 2006 from www.sentencingproject.org/Admin%5CDocuments%5Cpublications%5Cinc_hispanicprisoners.pdf

Maugh, T. H., II, & Zamichow, N. (1991, August 30). Medicine: San Diego's researcher's findings offer first evidence of a biological cause for homosexuality. *Los Angeles Times.*

McDonough, S. (2005, April 25). U.S. prison population soars in 2003, '04. ABCNews.com. Retrieved spring 2006 from http://abcnews.go.com/US/LegalCenter/wireStory?id=699808&CMP=OTC-RSSFeeds0312.

McFadden, D., & Champlin, C. A. (2000). Comparison of auditory evoked potentials in heterosexual, homosexual, and bisexual males and females. *Journal of the Association for Research in Otolaryngology, 1,* 89–99.

McKinlay, J. B. (1975). A case for refocusing downstream: The political economy of illness. In P. Conrad & R. Kern (Eds.), *The sociology of health and illness: Critical perspectives.* New York: St. Martin's Press.

McLanahan, S., & Sandefur, G. (1994). *Growing up with a single parent: What hurts, what helps.* Cambridge, MA: Harvard University Press.

McLanahan, S., & Sandefur, G. (2004). Diverging destinies: How children are faring under the second demographic transition. *Demography, 41,* 607–627.

McLaren, P. (1985). The ritual dimensions of resistance: Clowning and symbolic inversion. *Journal of Education, 167*(2): 84–97.

McLeod, J. (1995). *Ain't no makin' it.* Boulder, CO: Westview Press.

McLuhan, M. (1964). *Understanding media.* London: Routledge and Kegan Paul.

McMichael, P. (1996). *Development and social change: A global perspective.* Thousand Oaks, CA: Pine Forge.

McNeely, C. L. (1995). *Constructing the nation-state: International organization and prescriptive action.* Westport, CT: Greenwood.

Mead, M. (1963; orig. 1935). *Sex and temperament in three primitive societies.* New York: William Morrow.

Mead, M. (1966, July). Marriage in two steps. *Redbook Magazine, 48–49,* 84–86.

Mead, M. (1972). *Blackberry winter: My earlier years.* New York: William Morrow.

Meadows, D. H., Meadows, D. L., Randers, J., & Behrens III, W. W. (1972). *The limits to growth.* New York: Universe Books.

Meatto, K. (2000, September–October). Real reformers, real results: Our seventh annual roundup of student protest. Mojo Wire Magazine. Retrieved January 3, 2005, from www.mojones.com/mother_jones/SO00/activist_campuses.html

Melton, J. G. (1989). *The encyclopedia of American religions* (3rd ed.). Detroit, MI: Gale Research Co.

Melton, J. G. (1996). *The encyclopedia of American religions* (5th ed.). Detroit, MI: Gale Research Co.

Menn, J. (2003, August 11). The "geeks" who once shunned activism amid the digital revolution are using their money and savvy to influence public policy. *Los Angeles Times,* p. A-1.

Merkyl, P. H., & Smart, N. (Eds.). (1983). *Religion and politics in the modern world.* New York: New York University Press.

Merton, R. K. (1957). *Social theory and social structure* (Rev. ed.). New York: Free Press.

Merton, R. K. (1968; orig. 1938). Social structure and anomie. *American Sociological Review, 3.*

Meyer, J. W., & Rowan, B. (1977). Institutionalized organizations: Formal structure as myth and ceremony. *American Journal of Sociology, 83,* 340–363.

Michels, R. (1967; orig. 1911). *Political parties.* New York: Free Press.

Mickelson, R. A (1990). The attitude-achievement paradox among black adolescents. *Sociology of Education, 63,* 44–61.

Migration Policy Institute. (2007a). 2006 American community survey and census data on the foreign born by state. Retrieved January 2008 from http://www.migrationinformation.org/datahub/acscensus.cfm

Migration Policy Institute. (2007b). Annual immigration to the United States: The real numbers. Retrieved January 2008 from http://www.migrationpolicy.org/pubs/FS16_USImmigration_051807.pdf

Milgram, S. (1963). Behavioral study of obedience. *Journal of Abnormal and Social Psychology, 67,* 371–378.

Mills, C. W. (1948). *The new men of power.* New York: Harcourt Brace.

Mills, C. W. (1951). *White collar.* New York: Oxford University Press.

Mills, C. W. (1956). *The power elite.* New York: Oxford University Press.

Mills, C. W. (2000; orig. 1959). *The sociological imagination.* New York: Oxford University Press.

Mills, T. J. (1967). *The sociology of small groups.* Englewood, NJ: Prentice-Hall.

Milner Jr., M. (2004). *Freaks, geeks, and cool kids: American teenagers, schools, and the culture of consumption.* New York: Routledge.

Miner, H. (1956). Body ritual among the Nacirema. *American Anthropologist, 58,* 503–507.

Mirowsky, J., & Ross, C. E. (2005). Education, cumulative advantage, and health. Ageing International, *30*(1): 27–62.

Mirza, H. (1986). *Multinationals and the growth of the Singapore economy.* New York: St. Martin's Press.

Mitchell, J. (1975). *Psychoanalysis and feminism.* New York: Random House.

Mitnick, K. (2000, February 22). They call me a criminal. *The Guardian.*

Modood, T., Berthoud, R., Lakey, J., Nazroo, J., Smith, P., Virdee, S., et al. (1997). *Ethnic minorities in Britain: Diversity and disadvantage.* London: Policy Studies Institute.

Moen, P. (1995). A life course approach to postretirement roles and well-being. In L. A. Bond, S. J. Cutler, & A. Grams (Eds.), *Promoting successful and productive aging.* Newbury Park: Sage.

Moffit, R. E. (2007). The President's Medicare budget proposal: A step forward on entitlement spending. The Heritage Foundation. Retrieved January 2008 from http://www.heritage.org/Research/HealthCare/wm1344.cfm

Moffitt, T. E. (1996). The neuropsychology of conduct disorder. In P. Cordella & L. Siegel (Eds.), *Readings in contemporary criminological theory.* Boston: Northeastern University Press.

Mohanty, C. T. (1991). Under Western eyes: Feminist scholarship and colonial discourse. In C. T. Mohanty, A. Russo, & L. Torres (Eds.), *Third world women and the politics of feminism.* Bloomington: Indiana University Press.

Molnar, A. 1996. *Giving kids the business: The commercialization of America's schools.* Boulder, CO: Westview Press.

Moore, G. (1990). Structural determinants of men's and women's personal networks. *American Sociological Review, 55,* 726–735.

Moore, L. R. (1994). *Selling God: American religion in the marketplace of culture.* New York: Oxford University Press.

Mor-Barak, M. E., Scharlach, A., Birba, L., & Sokolov, J. (1992). Employment, social networks, and health in the retirement years. *International Journal of Aging and Human Development, 35,* 145–159.

Moreno, E. L., and Warah, R. (2006). Urban and slum trends in the 21st century. UN Chronicle, Issue 2. Retrieved spring 2008 from http://www.un.org/Pubs/chronicle/2006/issue2/0206p24.htm

Morland, K., Wing, S., Diez-Roux, A., & Poole, C. (2002). Neighborhood characteristics associated with the location of food stores and food service places. *American Journal of Preventive Medicine, 22*(1): 23–29.

Morris, J. (1974). *Conundrum.* New York: Harcourt Brace Jovanovich.

Moss, M. S., Moss, S. Z., and Moles, E. L. (1985). The quality of relationships between elderly parents and their out-of-town children. *Gerontologist, 25,* 134–140.

Moussavi, S., Chatterji, S., Verdes, E., Tandon, E., Patel, V., & Ustun, B. (2007). Depression, chronic diseases, and decrements in health: Results from the World Health Surveys. *The Lancet, 370,* 851–858.

Moynihan, D. P. (1965). *The negro family: A case for national action.* Washington, DC: U.S. Government Printing Office.

Moynihan, D. P. (1993). Defining deviancy down. *American Scholar, 62*(1): 10–18.

Muncie, J. (1999). *Youth and crime: A critical introduction.* London: Sage.

Murdock, G. P. (1949). *Social structure.* New York: Macmillan.

Murray, C. A. (1984*). Losing ground: American social policy, 1950–1980.* New York: Basic Books.

Najman, J. M. (1993). Health and poverty: Past, present, and prospects for the future. *Social Science and Medicine, 36*(2): 157–166.

Narayan, D. (1999, December). *Can anyone hear us? Voices from 47 countries.* Washington, DC: World Bank Poverty Group, PREM.

National Association of Latino Elected Officials (NALEO). (2004). Latinos win big on election night. Retrieved January 27, 2006www.naleo.org/press_releases/PR_NALEO_EDay_Win_110304.pdf

National Center for Education Statistics. (2005). Digest of education statistics, 2004. Retrieved January 20, 2006, from http://nces.ed.gov/programs/digest/d04/tables/dt04_298.asp

National Center for Health Statistics. (2003). Women's health. Retrieved January 11, 2005, from www.cdc.gov/nchs/fastats/womens_health.htm

National Center for Health Statistics. (2004). Health, United States, 2004. With Chartbook on Trends in the Health of Americans. Hyattsville, Maryland. Retrieved September 10, 2005, from http://www.cdc.gov/nchs/data/hus/hus04.pdf

National Center for Health Statistics. (2005). Health, United States, 2005. Retrieved spring 2006 from www.cdc.gov/nchs/data/hus/hus05.pdf

National Center for Health Statistics. (2008a). Center for Disease Control, Fast Stats: Life Expectancy. Retrieved January 2008 from http://www.cdc.gov/nchs/fastats/lifexpec.htm

National Center for Health Statistics. (2008b). Health, United States, 2007.

Retrieved January 2008 from http://www.cdc.gov/nchs/data/hus/hus07.pdf#027

National Center on Elder Abuse. (1999). Types of elder abuse in domestic settings. Elder Abuse Information Series No. 1. Retrieved December 7, 2005, from www.elderabusecenter.org/pdf/basics/fact1.pdf

National Center on Elder Abuse. (2005). Fact sheet: Elder abuse prevalence and incidence. Retrieved December 7, 2005, from www.elderabusecenter.org/pdf/publication/FinalStatistics050331.pdf

National Coalition of Homeless Veterans. (2007). Background and statistics. Retrieved fall 2007 from http://www.nchv.org/background.cfm

National Coalition on Health Care. (2008). Facts on health insurance coverage. Retrieved January 2008 from http://www.nchc.org/facts/coverage.shtml

National Crime Record Bureau. (2006). Crime in India: 2005 annual publication. Retrieved fall 2007 from http://ncrb.nic.in/crime2005/cii-2005/CHAP5.pdf

National Eating Disorders Association. (2002). Statistics: Eating disorders and their precursors. Retrieved January 29, 2006, from www.nationaleatingdisorders.org/p.asp?WebPage_ID=286&Profile_ID=41138

National Election Studies (NES). (2003). The NES guide to public opinion and electoral behavior—Voter turnout 1948–2002. Retrieved January 3, 2005, from www.umich.edu/,nes/nesguide/toptable/tab6a_2.htm

National Heart, Lung, and Blood Institute. (2008). Aim for a healthy weight: Information for patients and the public. Retrieved spring 2008 from http://www.nhlbi.nih.gov/health/public/heart/obesity/lose_wt/risk.htm

National High-Tech Crime Unit (NHTCU). (2005). High-tech crime: The impact on UK business 2005. Retrieved , accessed October 5, 2005, from www.nhtcu.org/media/documents/publications/8817_Survey.pdf

National Immigration Forum. (2006, January 26). Facts on Immigration. Retrieved January 27, 2006, from www.immigrationforum.org/DesktopDefault.aspx?tabid=790

National Law Center on Homelessness and Poverty. (2004, July). Key data concerning homeless persons in America. Retrieved spring 2006 from www.nlchp.org/FA_HAPIA/HomelessPersoninAmerica.pdf

National Low Income Housing Coalition (NLIHC). (2000, September). Out of reach: The growing gap between housing costs and income of poor people in the United States. Washington, DC: The National Low Income Housing Coalition/Low Income Housing Information Service. Retrieved January 3, 2005, from www.nlihc.org/oor2000/index.htm

National Marriage Project. (2007). The state of our unions: The social health of marriage in America: 2007. The National Marriage Project. Retrieved fall 2007 from http://marriage.rutgers.edu/Publications/SOOU/SOOU2007.pdf

National Nanotechnology Initiative (NNI). (2005). About the NNI. Retrieved spring 2006 from www.nano.gov/html/about/home_about.html

National Opinion Research Center. (2004). General social survey. Retrieved January 2008 from http://www.norc.org/GSS+Website/Data+Analysis/

Nellie May. (2005). Undergraduate students and credit cards in 2004: An analysis of usage rates and trends. Braintree, MA: Nellie Mae. Retrieved spring 2006 from www.nelliemae.com/library/ccstudy_2005.pdf

Nelson, E. A., & Dannefer, D. (1992). Aged heterogeneity: Fact or fiction? The fate of diversity in gerontological research. *Gerontologist, 32,* 17–23.

Nesiah, D. (1997). *Discrimination with reason? The policy of reservations in the United States, India and Malaysia.* New York: Oxford University Press.

Ness, R. B., & Kuller, L. H. (1999). *Health and disease among women: Biological and environmental influences.* New York: Oxford University Press.

Neuman, J. (2003, November 30). Liberals take a cue from Republicans and turn to big donors to set up think tanks and media outlets to counter the conservative message. *Los Angeles Times,* p. A-20.

Newman, K. S. (2000). *No shame in my game: The working poor in the inner city.* New York: Vintage.

New York City Gay and Lesbian Anti-Violence Project. (1996). Project annual. Retrieved January 3, 2005, from report. www.avp.org

New York Life. (2006). Study finds that costs average $204 per day, or $74,445 for private room. Retrieved January 2008 from http://www.newyorklife.com/cda/0,3254,15833,00.html

Nie, N., & Ebring, L. (2000). Internet and society—a preliminary report. Stanford Institute for the Quantitative Study of Society (SIQSS). Retrieved September 23, 2005, from www.stanford.edu/group/siqss/Press_Release/Preliminary_Report.pdf

Nie, N., Simpser, A., Stepanikova, I., & Zheng, L. (2004). Ten years after the birth of the Internet, how do Americans use the Internet in their daily lives? Draft Report. Stanford University. Retrieved September 23, 2005, from www.stanford.edu/group/siqss/SIQSS_Time_Study_04.pdf

Niebuhr, H. R. (1929). *The social sources of denominationalism.* New York: Holt.

Nielson, F. (1994, October). Income inequality and industrial development: Dualism revisited. *American Sociological Review, 59,* 654–677.

Nielsen Media Research. (2001). Internet access for blue collar workers spikes 52 percent, according to Nielsen/Net-ratings. Retrieved May 3, 2001, from http://209.249.142.22/press_releases/PDF/pr_010412.pdf

Nien Hsing. (2007). About: Global distribution. Nien Hsing Textile Co. Ltd website. Retrieved December 2007 from http://www.nht.com.tw/en/about-2.htm

Nordhaus, W. D. (1975). The political business cycle. *Review of Economic Studies, 42,* 169–190.

Nye, J. (1997, Fall). In government we don't trust. *Foreign Policy,* 99–111.

Oakes, J. (1985). *Keeping track: How schools structure inequality.* New Haven, CT: Yale University Press.

Oakes, J. (1990). *Multiplying inequalities: The effects of race, social class, and tracking on opportunities to learn mathematics and science.* Santa Monica, CA: Rand.

Oakley, A. (1974). *The sociology of housework.* New York: Pantheon.

Oakley, A., et al. (1994). Life stress, support, and class inequality: Explaining the health of women and children. *European Journal of Public Health, 4,* 81–91.

Offe, C. (1984). *Contradictions of the welfare state.* Cambridge, MA: MIT Press.

Offe, C. (1985). *Disorganized capitalism.* Cambridge, MA: MIT Press.

Office of National Drug Control Policy. (2005). Drug control funding tables. The White House. Retrieved spring 2006 from www.whitehousedrugpolicy.gov/publications/policy/06budget/funding_tbls.pdf

Ogbu, J. U., & Fordham, S. (1986). Black students' school success: Coping with the "burden of acting White." *Urban Review, 18,* 176–206.

Ogden, C. L., Carroll, M. D., Curtin, L. R., McDowell, M.A., Tabak, C. J., & Flegal, K. M. (2006). Prevalence of overweight and obesity in the United States, 1999–2004. *JAMA, 495,*1549–1555.

Ohmae, K. (1990). *The borderless world: Power and strategy in the industrial economy.* New York: HarperCollins.

Ohmae, K. (1995). *The end of the nation-state: How regional economies will soon reshape the world.* New York: Simon & Schuster.

Oliver, M. L., & Shapiro, T. M. (1995). *Black wealth/white wealth: A new perspective on racial inequality.* New York: Routledge.

Oliver, R. (2008, March 11). All about: Developing cities and pollution. CNN.com. Retrieved spring 2008 from http://edition.cnn.com/2008/WORLD/asiapcf/03/09/eco.cities/index.html

Olson, M. H. (1989). Work at home for computer professionals: Current attitudes and future prospects. *ACM Transactions on Information Systems, 7*(4): 317–338.

Olson, M. H., & Primps, S. B. (1984). Working at home with computers. *Journal of Social Issues, 40*(3): 97–112.

Oppenheimer, V. K. (1970). *The female labor force in the United States.* Westport, CT: Greenwood Press.

Oppenheimer, V. K. (1988). A theory of marriage timing. *American Journal of Sociology, 94,* 563–591.

Organization for Economic Co-operation and Development (OECD). (1999). Technology and industry—Scoreboard 1999—Benchmarking knowledge-based economies. Retrieved 2000 from http://www.oecd.org/document/4/0,3343,en_2649_34409_2087236_1_1_1_1,00.html

Organization for Economic Co-operation and Development (OECD). (2005). Factbook: Economic, environmental, and social statistics. Retrieved spring 2006 from http://oberon.sourceoecd.org/vl=820148/cl=43/nw=1/rpsv/fact2005/

Organization for Economic Co-operation and Development (OECD). (2006). Territorial reviews; competitive cities in the global economy. Retrieved spring 2008 from http://www.oecd.org/document/2/0,3343,en_2649_34413_37801602_1_1_1_37429,00.html

Orloff, A. S. (1993). *The politics of pensions: A comparative analysis of Britain, Canada, and the United States, 1880–1940.* Madison: University of Wisconsin Press.

Ortiz, V. (1995). The diversity of Latino families. In R. Zambrana (Ed.), *Understanding Latino families.* Thousand Oaks, CA: Sage.

Ostling, R. (1993, April 5). The church search. *Time.*

Ouchi, W. (1982). *Theory Z: How American business can meet the Japanese challenge.* New York: Avon.

Packer, G. (2003, May 9). Smart-mobbing the war. *The New York Times.*

Pagan, J., & Pauly, M. V. (2005). Access to conventional medical care and the use of complementary and alternative medicine. *Health Affairs, 24,* 255–263.

Pager, D. (2003). The mark of a criminal record. *American Journal of Psychology 108*(5): 937–975.

Pahl, J. (1989). *Money and marriage.* London: Macmillan.

Palmore, E. B., Burchett, B. M., Fillenbaum, G. G., George, L. K., & Wallman, L. M. (1985). *Retirement: Causes and consequences.* New York: Springer.

Paludi, M. A., & Barickman, R. B. (1991). *Academic and workplace sexual harassment: A resource manual.* Albany, NY: SUNY Press.

Panyarachun, A. et al. (2004). A more secure world: Our shared responsibility: Report of the secretary-general's high-level panel on threats, challenges and change. New York, United Nations. Retrieved spring 2006 from www.un.org/secureworld

Park, R. E. (1952). *Human communities: The city and human ecology.* New York: Free Press.

Parkin, F. (1971). *Class inequality and political order: Social stratification in capitalist and communist societies.* New York: Praeger.

Parkin, F. (1979). *Marxism and class theory: A bourgeois critique.* London: Tavistock.

Parsons, T. (1951). *The social system.* Glencoe, IL: Free Press.

Parsons, T. (1960). Towards a healthy maturity. *Journal of Health and Social Behavior, 1,* 163–173.

Parsons, T. (1964). *The social system.* New York: Free Press.

Parsons, T., & Bales, R. F. (1955). *Family, socialization, and interaction process.* Glencoe, IL: Free Press.

Paul, D. Y. (1985). *Women in Buddhism: Images of the feminine in the Mahayana tradition.* Berkeley: University of California Press.

Pearce, F. (1976). *Crimes of the powerful: Marxism, crime, and deviance.* London: Pluto Press.

Peterson, C. C., & Peterson, J. L. (1988). Older men's and women's relationships with adult kin: How equitable are they? *International Journal of Aging and Human Development, 27,* 221–231.

Peterson, R. (1996). A re-evaluation of the economic consequences of divorce. *American Sociological Review, 61,* 528–536.

Petrovic, M., & Hamilton, G.G. (2006). Making global markets: Wal-Mart and its suppliers. In N. Lichtenstein (Ed.), *Wal-Mart: The face of Twenty-first-century capitalism.* New York: New Press

Pew Hispanic Center. (2006). Foreign born at mid-decade. Retrieved January 2008 from http://pewhispanic.org/files/other/foreignborn/Table-30.pdf

Pew Internet. (2005). Internet: The mainstreaming of online life. Pew Internet & American Life Project. Retrieved spring 2006 from www.pewinternet.org/pdfs/Internet_Status_2005.pdf

Pew Internet. (2007). Daily Internet activities. Pew Internet & American Life Project. Retrieved January 2008 from http://www.pewinternet.org/trends/Daily_Internet_Activities_8.28.07.htm

Pew Research Center for the People and the Press. (2003, November 5). The 2004 political landscape: Evenly divided and increasingly polarized. The Pew Research Center for the People and the Press. Retrieved January 3, 2005, from http://people-press.org/reports/display.php3?ReportID5196

Pew Research Center for the People and the Press. (2004). Democrats gain edge in party identification. Retrieved January 9, 2006, from http://people-press.org/commentary/display.php3?AnalysisID=95

Pillemer, K. (1985). The dangers of dependency: New findings in domestic violence against the elderly. *Social Problems, 33,* 146–158.

Pillemer, K., & Finkelhor, D. (1988). The prevalence of elder abuse: A random sample survey. *Gerontologist, 28,* 51–57.

Pine, J. (1999). *Mass customization: The new frontier in business competition.* Cambridge, MA: Harvard Business School Press.

Pinkney, A. (1984). *The myth of black progress.* New York: Cambridge University Press.

Pintor, R. L., & Gratschew, M. (2002). Voter turnout since 1945: A global report. Stockholm, Sweden: International Institute for Democracy and Electoral Assistance (International IDEA). Retrieved January 3, 2005, from http://www.idea.int/publications/vt/upload/VT_screenopt_2002.pdf

Piore, M. J., & Sabel, C. F. (1984). *The second industrial divide: Possibilities for prosperity.* New York: Basic Books.

Pitts, V. (2004). Debating body projects: Reading Tattooed. *Health: An Interdisciplinary Journal for the Social Study of Health, Illness and Medicine, 8*(4): 533–535.

Plett, P. C. 1990. *Training report: Training of older workers in industrialized countries.* Geneva: International Labor Organization.

Plett, P. C., & Lester, B. T. (1991). *Training for older people: A handbook.* Geneva: International Labor Organization.

Political Money Line. (2003, December 14). Federal lobby directory. Retrieved January 3, 2005, from www.tray.com

Pollak, O. (1950). *The criminality of women.* Philadelphia: University of Pennsylvania Press.

Polletta, F., and Jasper, J. M. (2001). Collective identity and social movements. *Annual Review of Sociology 27,* 283–305.

Popenoe, D. (1993). American family decline, 1960–1990: A review and appraisal. *Journal of Marriage and Family, 55,* 527–555.

Popenoe, D. (1996). *Life without father: Compelling new evidence that fatherhood and marriage are indispensable for the good of children and society.* New York: Martin Kessler Books.

Popenoe, D. (2005). Marriage and family: What does The Scandinavian experience tell us? The state of our unions: The social health of marriage in America: 2005. The National Marriage Project. Retrieved January 13, 2006, from http://marriage.rutgers.edu/Publications/SOOU/SOOU2005.pdf

Popenoe, D. (2007). The future of marriage in America. *The state of our unions: The Social health of marriage in America.* The National Marriage Project. Retrieved January 2008 from http://marriage.rutgers.edu/Publications/SOOU/TEXTSOOU2007.htm

Population Reference Bureau. (2008a). Birth rate (annual number of births per 1,000 total population).

Retrieved spring 2008 from http://www.prb.org/Datafinder/Topic/Bar.aspx?sort=r&order=a&variable=3

Population Reference Bureau. (2008b). Death rates (annual number of deaths per 1,000 total population). Retrieved spring 2008 from http://www.prb.org/Datafinder/Topic/Bar.aspx?sort=r&order=a&variable=3

Portes, A., & Stepik, A. (1993). *City on the edge: The transformation of Miami.* Berkeley: University of California Press.

Potter, K. H. (1992). Hinduism. *The American Academic Encyclopedia* (online edition). Danbury, CT: Grolier Electronic.

Powell, W. W., & Brantley, P. (1992). Competitive cooperation in biotechnology: Learning through networks? In N. Nohria & R. Eccles (Eds.), *Networks and organizations: Structure, form and action.* Boston: Harvard Business School Press.

Powell, W. W., Koput, K. W., & Smith-Doerr, L. (1996). Interorganizational collaboration and the locus of innovation: Networks of learning in biotechnology. *Administration Science Quarterly, 41.*

Pratt, J. H. (2003). *Teleworking comes of age with broadband.* International Telework Association & Council. Retrieved November 9, 2008, from http://www.joannepratt.com/TWA2003_Executive_Summary.pdf

Prebisch, R. (1967). *Hacia una dinamica del desarollo Latinoamericano.* Montevideo, Uruguay: Ediciones de la Banda Oriental.

Prebisch, R. (1971). Change and development—Latin America's great task. Report submitted to the Inter-American Bank. New York: Praeger.

President's Commission on Organized Crime. (1986). Records of Hearings, June 24–26, 1985. Washington, DC: U.S. Government Printing Office.

Prestowitz, C. (2005). *Three billion new capitalists: The global shift of wealth and power to the East.* New York: Basic Books.

Provenzo, E. F., Jr. (1991). *Video kids: Making sense of Nintendo.* Cambridge, MA: Harvard University Press.

Putnam, R. (1993). The prosperous community: Social capital and public life. *American Prospect, 13,* 35–42.

Putnam, R. (1995). Bowling alone: America's declining social capital. *Journal of Democracy, 6,* 65–78.

Putnam, R. (2000). *Bowling alone: The collapse and revival of American*

community. New York: Simon and Schuster.

Quadagno, J. (1989). Generational equity and the politics of the welfare state. *Politics and Society, 17,* 353–376.

Quah, D. (1999). *The weightless economy in economic development.* London: Centre for Economic Performance.

Quinn, J. F., & Burkhauser, R. V. (1994). Retirement and labor force behavior of the elderly. In L.G. Martin & S. H. Preston (Eds.), *Demography of aging.* Washington, DC: National Academy Press.

Rainie, L., Fox, S., & Fallows, D. (2003). The Internet and the Iraq war: How online Americans have used the Internet to learn war news, understand events, and promote their views. Washington, DC: The PEW Internet and American Life Project. Retrieved January 10, 2005, from www.pewinternet.org/PPF/r/87/report_display.asp

Ramirez, F. O., & Boli, J. (1987). The political construction of mass schooling: European origins and worldwide institutionalism. *Sociology of Education, 60.*

Ranis, G. (1996). Will Latin America now put a stop to "stop-and-go?" New Haven, CT: Yale University, Economic Growth Center.

Ranis, G., & Mahmood, S. A. (1992). *The political economy of development policy change.* Cambridge, MA: Blackwell.

Redding, S. G. (1990). *The spirit of Chinese capitalism.* Berlin: De Gruyter.

Reich, R. (1991). *The work of nations: Preparing ourselves for 21st-century capitalism.* New York: Knopf.

Renzetti, C., & Curran, D. (1995). *Women, men, and society* (3rd ed.). Needham Heights, MA: Allyn and Bacon.

Research and Training Center on Disability in Rural Communities. (2005). Update on the demography of rural disability part one: Rural and urban. Retrieved spring 2008 from http://rtc.ruralinstitute.umt.edu/RuDis/RuDemography.htm

Reskin, B., & Padavic, I. (1994). *Women and men at work.* Thousand Oaks, CA: Pine Forge Press.

Reskin, B., & Roos, P. A. (1990). *Job queues, gender queues: Explaining women's inroads into male occupations.* Philadelphia: Temple University Press.

Richardson, D., & May, H. (1999). Deserving victims? Sexual status and the social construction of violence. *Sociological Review, 47,* 308–331.

Richardson, S. A., Goodman, N., Hastorf, A. H., & Dornbusch, S. M. (1961). Cultural uniformity in reaction to physical disabilities. *American Sociological Review, 26,* 241–247.

Riddick, C. C. (1985). Life satisfaction for older female homemakers, retirees, and workers. *Research on Aging, 7,* 383–393.

Rieff, D. (1991). *Los Angeles: Capital of the third world.* New York: Simon and Schuster.

Riesman, D. (1961). *The lonely crowd: A study of the changing American character.* New Haven, CT: Yale University Press.

Riley, M. W., Foner, A., & Waring, J. (1988). Sociology of age. In N. J. Smelser (Ed.), *Handbook of sociology.* Newbury Park, CA: Sage.

Ringer, B. B. (1985). *"We the People" and others: Duality and America's treatment of its racial minorities.* New York: Tavistock.

Risen, J., & Lichtblau, E. (2005, December 16). Bush lets U.S. spy on callers without courts. *The New York Times.*

Ritzer, G. (1993*). The McDonaldization of society.* Newbury Park, CA: Pine Forge Press.

Roach, S. S. (2005, June 6). The new macro of globalization. *Global: Daily Economic Comment.*

Roberts, S. (1995, April 27). Women's work: What's new, what isn't. *The New York Times,* p. B6.

Roberts, S. (2005, September 4). In Manhattan, poor make 2¢ for each dollar to the rich. *The New York Times.*

Robinson, W. I. (2001, April). Social theory and globalization: The rise of a transnational state. *Theory and Society 30*(2): 157–200.

Robinson, W. I. (2004). *A theory of global capitalism: Production, class and state in a transnational world.* Baltimore: Johns Hopkins University Press.

Robinson, W. I. (2005a, July). Global capitalism: The new transnationalism and the folly of conventional thinking. *Science and Society, 69*(3): 316–328.

Robinson, W. I. (2005b, December). Gramsci and globalisation: From nation-state to transnational hegemony. *Critical Review of International Social and Political Philosophy, 8*(4): 1–16.

Rodriguez, C. D. (2004, June 11). The immigrant contribution. *La Prensa* San Diego. Retrieved spring 2006 from www.laprensa-sandiego.org/archieve/june11–04/imigrant.htm

Roof, W. C. (1993). *A generation of seekers: The spiritual journeys of the baby boom generation.* San Francisco: Harper San Francisco.

Roof, W. C. (1999). *Spiritual marketplace: Baby boomers and the remaking of American religion.* Princeton, NJ: Princeton University Press.

Roof, W. C., Carroll, J. W., & Roozen, D. A. (Eds.). (1995). *The post-war generation and establishment religion: Cross-cultural perspectives.* Boulder, CO: Westview Press.

Roof, W. C., & McKinney, W. (1990). *American mainline religion: Its changing shape and future prospects.* New Brunswick, NJ: Rutgers University Press.

Roos, P., & Reskin, B. (1992). Occupational desegregation in the 1970s—integration and economic equity. *Sociological Perspectives, 35,* 69–91.

Roscoe, W. (1991). *The Zuni man-woman.* Albuquerque: University of New Mexico Press.

Roscoe, W. (2000). *Changing ones: Third and fourth genders in native North America.* New York: Palgrave Macmillan.

Rosenau, J. N. (1997). *Along the domestic-foreign frontier: Exploring governance in a turbulent world.* Cambridge, UK: Cambridge University Press.

Rosenbaum, J. E. (1979). Organizational career mobility: Promotion chances in a corporation during periods of growth and contraction. *American Journal of Sociology, 85.*

Rosener, J. B. (1997). *America's competitive secret: Women managers.* New York: Oxford University Press.

Rosenstock, I. (1974). Historical origins of the health belief model. *Health Education Monographs, 2*(4).

Rosenthal, A. M. (1999). *Thirty-eight witnesses: The Kitty Genovese case.* Berkeley: University of California Press.

Rossi, A. (1973). The first woman sociologist: Harriett Martineau. In *The feminist papers: From Adams to de Beauvoir.* New York: Columbia University Press.

Rostow, W. W. (1961). *The stages of economic growth.* Cambridge, UK: Cambridge University Press.

Rothschild, J. (2000, January). Creating a just and democratic workplace: More engagement, less hierarchy. *Contemporary Sociology: Utopian Visions: Engaged Sociologies for the 21st Century, 29*(1): 195–213.

Rousselle, R. (1999). Defining ancient Greek sexuality. *Digital Archives of Psychohistory, 26*(4). Retrieved January 11, 2005, www.geocities.com/kidhistory/ja/defining.htm

Rowe, R. H., & Kahn, R. L. (1987, July 10). Human aging: Usual and successful. *Science, 237,* 143–149.

Rowling, J. K. (1998). *Harry Potter and the sorcerer's stone.* New York: Scholastic.

Rubin, L. B. (1990). *Erotic wars: What happened to the sexual revolution?* New York: Farrar, Straus, and Giroux.

Rubinstein, W. D. (1986). *Wealth and inequality in Britain.* Winchester, MA: Faber and Faber.

Rudé, G. (1964). *The crowd in history: A study of popular disturbances in France and England, 1730–1848.* New York: Wiley.

Ruggles, P. (1990). *Drawing the line: Alternative poverty measures and their implications for public policy.* Washington, DC: Urban Institute Press.

Ruggles, P. (1992). Measuring poverty. *Focus, 14.* University of Wisconsin-Madison, Institute for Research on Poverty.

Rusting, R. L. (1992). Why do we age? *Scientific American, 267,* 130–141.

Rutter, M., & Giller, H. (1984). *Juvenile delinquency: Trends and perspectives.* New York: Guilford Press.

Reporters Without Borders (RWB). (2003). The Internet under surveillance: 2003 Report. Paris, France: Reporters Without Borders. Retrieved January 3, 2005, from www.rsf.org/IMG/pdf/doc-2236.pdf

Ryan, T. (1985). The roots of masculinity. In A. Metcalf & M. Humphries (Eds.), *Sexuality of men.* London: Pluto.

Saad, Lydia. (2007a, May 29). Tolerance for gay rights at high-water mark. Gallup News Service. Retrieved February 17, 2008, from http://www.gallup.com/poll/27694/Tolerance-Gay-Rights-HighWater-Mark.aspx

Saad, L. (2007b, August 2). Gallup finds increase in independents, typical of off-years. Gallup News Service. Retrieved January 2008 from http://www.gallup.com/poll/28279/Gallup-Finds-Increase-Independents-Typical-OffYears.aspx

Sabel, C. F. (1982). *Work and politics: The division of labor in industry.* New York: Cambridge University Press.

Sachs, J. (2000, June 22). A new map of the world. *The Economist,* 81–83.

Sadker, M., & Sadker, D. (1994). *Failing at fairness.* New York: Scribner.

Safe-food.org. (2003). You are eating genetically engineered food. Is it good for you? Do you have a choice? Retrieved January 3, 2005, from www.safe-food.org

Sahliyeh, E. (Ed.). (1990). *Religious resurgence and politics in the contemporary world.* Albany, NY: SUNY Press.

Saks, M. (Ed.). (1992). *Alternative medicine in Britain.* Oxford, UK: Clarendon.

Salter, H. (1998, June 25). Making a world of difference: Celebrating 30 years of development progress. USAID press release.

Sampson, R. J., & Cohen, J. (1988). Deterrent effects of the police on crime: A replication and theoretical extension. *Law and Society Review, 22*(1).

Sandefur, G., & Libeler, C. (1997). The demography of American Indian families. *Population Research and Policy Review, 16,* 95–114.

Sarkisian, N., & Gerstel, N. (2004). Kin support among blacks and whites: Race and family organization. *American Sociological Review, 69,* 812–837.

Sartre, J. (1965; orig. 1948). *Anti-Semite and Jew.* New York: Schocken Books.

Sassen, S. (1991). *The global city: New York, London, Tokyo.* Princeton, NJ: Princeton University Press.

Sassen, S. (1996). *Losing control: Sovereignty in the age of globalization.* New York: Columbia University Press.

Sassen, S. (1998). *Globalization and its discontents.* New York: New Press.

Sassen, S. (2005). *Denationalization: Territory, authority and rights.* Princeton, NJ: Princeton University Press.

Sassler, S. (2004). The process of entering in cohabitating unions. *Journal of Marriage and Family, 66,* 491–505.

Savage, D. G. (1998, March 5). Same-sex harassment illegal, says high court. *Los Angeles Times.*

Sawhill, I. V. (1989). The underclass: An overview. *Public Interest, 96,* 3–15.

Sax, L. J., Lindholm, J. A., Astin, A. W., Korn, W. S., & Mahoney, K. M. (2001). The American freshman: National norms for fall 2001. Higher Education Research Institute, UCLA Graduate School of Education & Information Studies. Retrieved January 3, 2005, from http://www.gseis.ucla.edu/heri/pr-display.php?prQry=19

Sayers, J. (1986). *Sexual contradiction: Psychology, psychoanalysis, and feminism.* New York: Methuen.

Schaie, K. W. (1979). The primary mental abilities in adulthood: An exploration in the development of psychometric intelligence. In P. B. Baltes & O. G. Brim (Eds.), *Lifespan development and behavior* (Vol. 2). New York: Academic Press.

Schaie, K. W. (1983). *Longitudinal studies of adult psychological development.* New York: Guilford Press.

Schaie, K. W. (1984). Midlife influences upon intellectual functioning in old age. *International Journal of Behavioral Development, 7,* 463–478.

Schaie, K. W, & Hendricks, J. (Eds.). (2000). *The evolution of the aging self: The societal impact on the aging process.* New York: Springer.

Scheff, T. (1966). *Being mentally ill.* Chicago: Aldine.

Schiller, H. I. (1989). *Culture Inc.: The corporate takeover of public expression.* New York: Oxford University Press.

Schiller, H. I. (1991). Not yet the post-imperialist era. *Critical Studies in Mass Communication, 8,* 13–28.

Schmidt, R. (1980). *Exploring religion.* Belmont, CA: Wadsworth.

Schooler, C. (1987). Cognitive effects of complex environments during the life span: A review and theory. In C. Schooler & K. W. Schaie (Eds.), *Cognitive functioning and social structure over the life course.* Norwood, NJ: Ablex.

Schor, J. (1992). *The overworked American.* New York: Basic Books.

Schuman, H., Steel, C., & Bobo, L. (1985). *Racial attitudes in America: Trends and interpretations.* Cambridge, MA: Harvard University Press.

Schumpeter, J. (1983, orig. 1942). *Capitalism, socialism, and democracy.* Magnolia, MA: Peter Smith.

Schwartz, G. (1970). *Sect ideologies and social status,* Chicago: University of Chicago Press.

Schwarz, J. E., & Volgy, T. J. (1992). *The forgotten Americans.* New York: Norton.

Scott, S., & Morgan, D. (1993). Bodies in a social landscape. In S. Scott & D. Morgan (Eds.), *Body matters: Essays on the sociology of the body.* Washington, DC: Falmer Press.

Scott, W. R., & Meyer, J. W. (1994). *Institutional environments and organizations: Structural complexity and individualism.* Thousand Oaks, CA: Sage.

Scully, D. (1990). *Understanding sexual violence: A study of convicted rapists.* Boston: Unwin Hyman.

Sedlak, A., & Broadhurst, D. (1996). *Third national incidence study of child abuse and neglect.* Washington, DC: U.S. Department of Health and Human Services.

Seefeldt, C., & Keawkungwal, S. (1985). Children's attitudes toward the elderly in Thailand and the United States. *International Journal of Comparative Sociology, 26,* 226–232.

Segura, D. A., & Pierce, J. L. (1993). Chicana/o family structure and gender personality: Chodorow, familism, and psychoanalytic sociology revisited. *Signs, 19,* 62–91.

Seidman, S. (1997). Relativizing sociology: The challenge of cultural studies. In E. Long (Ed.), *From sociology to cultural studies: New perspectives.* Malden, MA: Blackwell.

Seidman, S., Meeks, C., & Traschen, F. (1999). Beyond the closet? The changing social meaning of homosexuality in the United States. *Sexualities, 2*(1): 9–34.

Seltzer, J. (2000, November). Families formed outside of marriage. *Journal of Marriage and the Family, 62,* 1247–1268.

Senior Journal.com. (2004, March 29). Retiring in the red: A new reality for older Americans. Retrieved spring 2006 from www.seniorjournal.com/NEWS/Money/4-03-29Retiringinred.htm

Sennett, R. (1998). *The corrosion of character: The personal consequences of work in the new capitalism.* New York: Norton.

The Sentencing Project. (2004). New incarceration figures: Growth in population continues. Retrieved spring 2006 from www.sentencingproject.org/pdfs/1044.pdf

Service Employees International Union (SEIU). (2008). About SEIU. Retrieved spring 2008 from http://www.seiu.org/about/index.cfm

Seville Statement on Violence. (1990). *American Psychologist, 45*(10): 1167–1168. Retrieved January 3, 2005, from www.lrainc.com/swtaboo/taboos/seville1.html

Sewell, W. H., Jr. (1992). A theory of structure: Duality, agency, and transformation. *American Journal of Sociology, 98,* 1–29.

Sewell, W. H., Jr. (1999). The concept of culture. In V. E. Bonnell & L. Hunt. (Eds.), *Beyond the cultural turn.* Berkeley: University of California Press.

Sewell, W. H., & Hauser, R. M. (1980). The Wisconsin longitudinal study of social and psychological factors in aspirations and achievements. In A. C. Kerckhoff

(Ed.), *Research in sociology of education and socialization* (Vol. 1). Greenwich, CT: JAI Press.

Shah, A. (2008, March 1). World military spending. *Global Issues*. Retrieved fall 2008 from http://www.globalissues.org/Geopolitics/ArmsTrade/Spending.asp

Shattuck, R. (1980). *The forbidden experiment: The story of the wild boy of Aveyron*. New York: Farrar, Straus, and Giroux.

Shaw, Martin. (2000). *Theory of the global state: Globality as an unfinished revolution*. Cambridge, UK: Cambridge University Press.

Shea, S., Stein, A. D., Basch, C. E., Lantigua, R., Maylahn, C., Strogatz, D., et al. (1991). Independent associations of educational attainment and ethnicity with behavioral risk factors for cardiovascular disease. *American Journal of Epidemiology, 134*(6): 567–582.

Sheldon, W. A. (with the collaboration of E. M. Haul and E. McDennott). (1949). *Varieties of delinquent youth*. New York: Harper & Row.

Shelton, B. A. (1992). *Women, men, and time: Gender differences in paid work, housework, and leisure*. Westport, CT: Greenwood.

Shils, E. (1972). *The intellectuals and the powers and other essays*. Chicago: University of Chicago Press

Siegel, J. (1993). *A generation of change: A profile of America's older population*. New York: Russell Sage Foundation.

Sigmund, P. E. (1990). *Liberation theology at the crossroads: Democracy or revolution?* New York: Oxford University Press.

Simmel, G. (1955). *Conflict and the web of group affiliations* (Kurt Wolff, Trans.). Glencoe, IL: Free Press.

Simon, J. (1981). *The ultimate resource*. Princeton, NJ: Princeton University Press.

Simon, J. (1989). *The economic consequences of immigration*. Cambridge, MA: Basil Blackwell.

Simpson, G. E., & Yinger, J. M. (1986). *Racial and cultural minorities: An analysis of prejudice and discrimination*. New York: Plenum Press.

Simpson, J. H. (1985). Socio-moral issues and recent presidential elections. *Review of Religious Research, 27*, 115–123.

Sjoberg, G. (1960). *The pre-industrial city: Past and present*. New York: Free Press.

Sjoberg, G. (1963). The rise and fall of cities: A theoretical perspective. *International Journal of Comparative Sociology, 4*, 107–120.

Sklair, L. (2002a). Democracy and the transnational capitalist class. *Annals of the American Academy of Political and Social Science, 581*, 144–157.

Sklair, L. (2002b). *Globalization: Capitalism and its alternatives* (3rd ed.). New York: Oxford University Press.

Sklair, L. (2003). Transnational practices and the analysis of the global system. In A. Hulsemeyer, *Globalization in the twenty-first century*. New York: Palgrave Macmillan.

Sklar, H. (1999, December). Brother, can you spare a billion? *Z Magazine*. Retrieved January 3, 2005, from www.zmag.org/ZNET.htm

Skocpol, T. (1979). *States and social revolutions: A comparative analysis of France, Russia, and China*. New York: Cambridge University Press.

Skocpol, T. (1992). *Protecting soldiers and mothers: The political origins of social policy in the United States*. Cambridge, MA: Harvard University Press.

Slapper, G., & Tombs, S. (1999). *Corporate crime*. Essex, UK: Longman.

Slevin, P. (2005, July 26). Prison experts see opportunity for improvement. *Washington Post*. Retrieved spring 2006 from www.washingtonpost.com/wpdyn/content/article/2005/07/25/AR2005072501484.html

Smart, N. (1989). *The world religions*. Englewood Cliffs, NJ: Prentice Hall.

Smedley, A. (1993). *Race in North America: Origin and evolution of a world view*. Boulder: Westview Press.

Smeeding, T. M. (2000, March). Changing income inequality in OECD countries: Updated results from the Luxembourg income study (LIS). Luxembourg Income Study Working Paper #252. Syracuse, NY: Maxwell School of Citizenship and Public Affairs, Syracuse University. Retrieved January 11, 2005, from www.lisproject.org/publications/liswps/252.pdf

Smeeding, T. M., Rainwater, L., & Burtless, G. (2000, September). United States poverty in a cross-national context. Luxembourg Income Study Working Paper #244. Syracuse, NY: Maxwell School of Citizenship and Public Affairs, Syracuse University. Retrieved January 11, 2005, from www.lisproject.org/publications/liswps/244.pdf

Smelser, N. J. (1963). *Theory of collective behavior*. New York: Free Press.

Smith, A. (1776). *An inquiry into the nature and causes of the wealth of nations*. London: Methuen & Co., Ltd.

Smith, A. (1988). *The ethnic origins of nations*. Boston: Blackwell.

Smith, P., & West, B. (2000). Cultural studies. In *Encyclopedia of Naturalism* (Vol. 1). San Diego, CA: Academic Press.

Smith, T. W. (1998). American sexual behavior: Trends, socio-demographic differences, and risk behavior. In J. Garrison, M. D. Smith, & D. Bersharov (Eds.), *The demography of social behavior*. Menlo Park, CA: Kaiser Family Foundation.

Smith-Bindman, R., et. al. (2006, April 18). Does utilization of screening mammography explain racial and ethnic differences in breast cancer? *Annals of Internal Medicine, 144*(8): 541–553.

Smolowe, J. (1994, February 7). . . . and throw away the key. *Time*.

Snow, R. W., Guerra, C. A., Noor, A. M., Myint, H. Y., & Hay, S. I. (2005). The global distribution of clinical episodes of Plasmodium falciparum malaria. *Nature, 434*(7030): 214–217.

So, A. (1990). *Social change and development: Modernization, dependency, and world-systems theories*. Newbury Park, CA: Sage.

Social Security Administration (SSA). (1997, October). Highlights of social security. SSA website. Retrieved October 28, 1997, from www.ssa.gov/statistics/highlite.html

Social Security Administration (SSA). (2005a, March 23). 2005 annual report of the board of trustees of the federal old-age and survivors insurance and disability insurance trust funds. Retrieved December 6, 2005, from www.ssa.gov/OACT/TR/TR05/index.html

Social Security Administration (SSA). (2005b). Frequently asked questions about social security's future. Retrieved December 7, 2005, from www.ssa.gov/qa.htm

Social Security Administration (SSA). (2008). Social security basic facts. Retrieved fall 2008 from http://www.ssa.gov/pressoffice/basicfact.htm

Sokolovsky, J. (Ed.). (1990). *The cultural context of aging: Worldwide perspectives*. New York: Bergin and Garvey.

Solomon, R. P. (1992). *Black resistance in high school: Forging a separatist culture*. Albany: SUNY Press.

Sorokin, P. A. (1927). *Social mobility*. New York: Harper.

Soumerai, S. B., & Avorn, J. (1983). Perceived health, life satisfaction, and activity in urban elderly: A controlled study of the impact of part-time work. *Journal of Gerontology, 38,* 356–362.

Southwick, S. (1996). Liszt: Searchable directory of e-mail discussion groups. Retrieved January 3, 2005, from www.liszt.com

Spain, D., & Bianchi, S. M. (1996). *Balancing act: Motherhood, marriage, and employment among American women*. New York: Russell Sage Foundation.

Spenner, K. (1983). Deciphering Prometheus: Temporal change in the skill level of work. *American Sociological Review, 48,* 824–837.

Spilerman, S. (1977). Careers, labor market structure, and socioeconomic achievement. *American Journal of Sociology, 83,* 551–593.

Sreberny-Mohammadi, A. (1992). Media integration in the third world. In B. Gronbeck, et al. (Eds.), *Media, consciousness, and culture*. London: Sage.

Stacey, J. (1990). *Brave new families: Stories of domestic upheaval in late twentieth century America*. New York: Basic Books.

Stacey, J. (1993). Good riddance to "the family": A response to David Popenoe. *Journal of Marriage and Family, 55,* 527–555.

Stacey, J. (1996). *In the name of the family: Rethinking family values in a postmodern age*. Boston: Beacon Press.

Stack, C. B. (1997). *All our kin: Strategies for survival in a black community*. New York: Harper Calophon.

Stampp, K. (1956). *The peculiar institution*. New York: Knopf.

Stark, R., & Bainbridge, W. S. (1980). Towards a theory of religious commitment. *Journal for the Scientific Study of Religion, 19,* 114–128.

Stark, R., & Bainbridge, W. S. (1985). *The future of religion, secularization, revival, and cult formation*. Berkeley: University of California Press.

Stark, R., & Bainbridge, W. S. (1987). *A theory of religion*. New Brunswick, NJ: Rutgers University Press.

Starrs, P. F. (1997). The sacred, the regional, and the digital. *Geographical Review, 87*(2): 193–218.

Statham, J. (1986). *Daughters and sons: Experiences of non-sexist childraising*. New York: Basil Blackwell.

Statistical Office of the European Communities. (1991). *Basic statistics of the community*. Luxembourg: European Union.

Steele, C. M., & Aronson, J. (1995). Stereotype threat and the intellectual test performance of African-Americans. *Journal of Personality and Social Psychology, 69,* 797–811.

Steele, C. M., & Aronson, J. A. (2004). Stereotype threat does not live by Steele and Aronson alone. *American Psychologist, 59,* 47–48.

Steinberg, R. J. (1990). Social construction of skill: Gender, power, and comparable worth. *Work and Occupations, 17,* 449–482.

Steinmetz, S. K. (1983). Family violence toward elders. In S. Saunders, A. Anderson, & C. Hart (Eds.), *Violent individuals and families: A practitioner's handbook*. Springfield, IL: Charles C. Thomas.

Stetz, M., & Oh, B. (Eds.). (2001). *Legacies of the comfort women of world war II*. Armonk, NY: M.E. Sharpe.

Stillwagon, E. (2001, May 21). AIDS and poverty in Africa. *The Nation*.

Stinner, W. F. (1979). Modernization and the family extension in the Philippines: A social-demographic analysis. *Journal of Marriage and the Family, 41,* 161–168.

Stone, L. (1980). *The family, sex, and marriage in England, 1500–1800*. New York: Harper & Row.

Stone, M. (1993). *Shelter poverty: New ideas on affordable housing*. Philadelphia: Temple University Press.

Stop Violence Against Women. (2006). Prevalence of domestic violence. Retrieved fall 2007 from http://www.stopvaw.org/Prevalence_of_Domestic_Violence.html

Stow, K. (2000). *Theater of acculturation: The Roman ghetto in the sixteenth century*. Seattle: University of Washington Press.

Stryker, R. (1996). Comparable worth and the labor market. In P. J. Dubeck & K. Borman (Eds.), *Women and work: A handbook*. New York: Garland.

Sullivan, O. (1997). Time waits for no (wo)man: An investigation of the gendered experience of domestic time. *Sociology, 31,* 221–239.

Sutherland, E. H. (1949). *Principles of criminology*. Chicago: Lippincott.

Swidler, A. (1986). Culture in action: Symbols and strategies. *American Sociological Review, 51,* 273–286.

Swidler, A. (2001). *Talk of love: How culture matters*. Chicago: University of Chicago Press.

Tabor, J. D., & Gallagher, E. V. (1995). *Why Waco? Cults and the battle for religious freedom in America*. Berkeley: University of California Press.

Tan, A., & Ramakrishna, K. (Eds.). (2002). *The new terrorism*. Singapore: Eastern Universities Press.

Tang, S., & Zuo, J. (2000). Dating attitudes and behaviors of American and Chinese college students. *Social Science Journal, 37*(1): 67–78.

Taylor, P., Funk, C., & Clark, A. (2007). As marriage and parenthood drift apart, public is concerned about social impact. A social and demographic trends report. Retrieved January 2008 from http://pewresearch.org/assets/social/pdf/Marriage.pdf

Teachman, J. (2003). Premarital sex, premarital cohabitation, and the risk of subsequent marital dissolution among women. *Journal of Marriage and the Family, 65,* 444–455.

Telework Coalition. (2004). Telework facts. Retrieved September 23, 2005, from www.telcoa.org/id33.htm

Tempest, R. (1996, September 22). Barbie and the world economy. *Los Angeles Times*.

Thomas, G. M., Meyer, J., Ramirez, F., & Boli, J. (1987). *Institutional structure: Constituting state, society and the individual*. Newbury Park, CA: Sage.

Thomas, W. I., & Znaniecki, F. (1966; orig. 1918–1920). *The Polish peasant in Europe and America: Monograph of our immigrant group* (5 vols.). New York: Dover.

Thompson, B. (2001). *A promise and a way of life*. Minneapolis: University of Minnesota Press.

Thompson, E. P. (1971). The moral economy of the English crowd in the eighteenth century. *Past and Present, 50,* 76–136.

Thompson, J. B. (1990). *Ideology and modern culture*. Cambridge, UK: Polity Press.

Thompson, J. B. (1995). *The media and modernity: A social theory of the media*. Cambridge, UK: Polity Press.

Thompson, W. S. (1929). Population. *American Journal of Sociology, 34,* 959–975.

Thorne, B. (1993). *Gender play: Girls and boys in school*. New Brunswick, NJ: Rutgers University Press.

Tilly, C. (1978). *From mobilization to revolution*. Reading, MA: Addison-Wesley.

Tilly, C. (1992). How to detect, describe, and explain repertoires of contention. Working Paper No. 150. Center for the Study of Social Change. New York: New School for Social Research.

Tilly, C. (1996). The emergence of citizenship in France and elsewhere. In C. Tilly (Ed.), *Citizenship, identity, and social history*. Cambridge, UK: Cambridge University Press.

Tkaczyk, C. (2008). 2007 Fortune 500: The Top 50. Retrieved spring 2008 from http://money.cnn.com/galleries/2007/fortune/0704/gallery.500top50.fortune/index.html

TNS. (2007). TNS Financial services affluent market research program, 2007: TNS reports record breaking number of millionaires in the USA. Retrieved fall 2007 from http://www.tns-us.com/press/millionaires.pdf

Totti, X. F. (1987, fall). The making of a Latino ethnic identity. *Dissent, 34*.

Toufexis, A. (1993, May 24). Sex has many accents. *Time*.

Touraine, A. (1974). *The post-industrial society*. London: Wildwood.

Touraine, A. (1977). *The self-production of society*. Chicago: University of Chicago Press.

Touraine, A. (1981). *The voice and the eye: An analysis of social movements*. New York: Cambridge University Press.

Townsend, E. (2002, December 4). E-activism connects protest groups. *The Hartford Courant*. Retrieved September 23, 2005, from www.globalpolicy.org/ngos/advocacy/protest/iraq/2002/1204activism.htm

Townsend, P., & Davidson, N. (Eds.). (1982). *Inequalities in health: The black report*. Harmondsworth, UK: Penguin.

Toyota Corporation. (2001). 2001 number and diffusion rate for motor vehicles in major countries. Retrieved spring 2006 from www.toyota.co.jp/IRweb/corp_info/and_the_word/pdf/2003_c07.pdf

Toyota Corporation. (2008). Engineering and manufacturing plants. Retrieved fall 2008 from http://www.toyota.com/about/our_business/operations/manufacturing/index.html

Treas, J. (1995). Older Americans in the 1990s and beyond. *Population Bulletin, 5*.

Treiman, D. (1977). *Occupational prestige in comparative perspective*. New York: Academic Press.

Troeltsch, E. (1931). *The social teaching of the Christian churches* (2 vols.). New York: Macmillan.

Truman, D. B. (1981). *The governmental process*. Westport, CT: Greenwood Press.

Tumin, M. M. (1953, August). Some principles of stratification: A critical analysis. *American Sociological Review, 18*, 387–394.

Turnbull, C. (1983). *The human cycle*. New York: Simon and Schuster.

Turowski, J. (1977). Inadequacy of the theory of the nuclear family: The Polish experience. In L. L. Otero (Ed.), *Beyond the nuclear family model: Cross-cultural perspectives*. Beverly Hills, CA: Sage.

Tuttle, L. (1986). *Encyclopedia of feminism*. New York: Facts on File.

Twine, F. W. (1991). *Just black? Multiracial identity* [Motion picture; color, 57 minutes]. (Available from Filmmakers Library, New York)

Twine, F. W. (1997). *Racism in a racial democracy: The maintenance of white supremacy in Brazil*. New Brunswick, NJ: Rutgers University Press.

Twine, F. W. (2003, Fall). Racial literacy in Britain: Antiracist projects, black children, white parents. *Contours: A Journal of the African Diaspora, 1*(2): 129–153.

Twine, F. W. (2004, November). A white side of black Britain: The concept of racial literacy. *Ethnic and Racial Studies (a Special Issue on Racial Hierarchy), 27*(6): 1–30.

U.K. Statistics Authority. (2001). Ethnicity and identity: Inter-ethnic marriage. Retrieved spring 2008 from http://www.statistics.gov.uk/CCI/nugget.asp?ID=1090&Pos=1&ColRank=2&Rank=416

UN Chronicle. (1995). *32*(4): 29.

UNICEF. (1997). *The state of the world's children, 1997*. New York: Oxford University Press.

UNICEF. (2000). *State of the world's children, 2000*. New York: United Nations Children's Fund.

UNICEF. (2005). Female genital mutilation/cutting: A statistical exploration. Retrieved fall 2007 from http://www.unicef.org/publications/files/FGM-C_final_10_October.pdf

UNICEF. (2007). The state of the world's children, 2007. Retrieved fall 2007 from http://www.unicef.org/sowc07/docs/sowc07_figure_3_1.pdf

Union of International Associations. (2005). Statistics on international organizations and NGOs. Retrieved spring 2008 from http://www.uia.org/statistics/organizations/types-2004.pdf

United Nations (UN). (2003). Table 26. United Nations human development report, 2003. Retrieved January 3, 2005, from http://hdr.undp.org/en/reports/global/hdr2003/

United Nations (UN). (2005). Population challenges and development goals. Retrieved January 2008 from http://www.un.org/esa/population/publications/pop_challenges/Population_Challenges.pdf

United Nations (UN). (2006). World population prospects: The 2006 revision. Retrieved September 18, 2008, from http://www.un.org/esa/population/publications/wpp2006/wpp2006.htm

United Nations (UN). (2008). Human development report 2007/2008. Retrieved fall 2008 from http://www.weforum.org/pdf/gendergap/report2007.pdf

United Nations Conference on Trade and Development (UNCTAD). (2004, March 24). UN report says world urban population of 3 billion today expected to reach 5 billion by 2030. Press release. Retrieved September 25, 2005, from www.un.org/esa/population/publications/wup2003/pop899_English.doc

United Nations Conference on Trade and Development (UNCTAD). (2005). *World investment report 2005: Transnational corporations, extractive industries and development*. New York: United Nations Conference on Trade and Development.

United Nations Conference on Trade and Development (UNCTAD). (2007). *World investment report 2007: Transnational corporations and the internationalization of R&D*, Annex Table A.1.5. New York: United Nations Conference on Trade and Development.

United Nations Development Programme (UNDP). (1998). *Human development report 1998*. New York: Oxford University Press.

United Nations Development Programme (UNDP). (1999). *Human development report 1999*. New York: Oxford University Press.

United Nations Development Programme (UNDP). (2005). Human development report, 2005. Retrieved September 28, 2005, http://hdr.undp.org/en/reports/global/hdr2005/

United Nations Development Programme (UNDP). (2007). Human development report: Inequality in income or expenditure, Table 15. Retrieved fall 2007 from http://hdrstats.undp.org/indicators/146.html

United Nations Economic Commission for Europe. (2003). Ireland. Retrieved spring 2006 from www.unece.org/stats/trend/irl.pdf

United Nations Educational, Scientific, and Cultural Organization (UNESCO). (2003). Institute for statistics. Retrieved January 3, 2005, from www.uis.unesco.org/ev.php?URL_ID54926&URL_DO5DO_TOPIC&URL_SECTION5201

United Nations Educational, Scientific, and Cultural Organization (UNESCO). (2006). *Education for all: Global monitoring report, 2006*. Paris, France: United Nations Educational, Scientific and Cultural Organization. Retrieved spring 2006 from www.unesco.org/education/GMR2006/full/chapt2_eng.pdf

United Nations Food and Agriculture Organization (UN FAO). (2001). The impact of HIV/AIDS on food security. United Nations Food and Agriculture Organization, Conference on World Food Security, May 28–June 1.

United Nations Food and Agriculture Organization (UN FAO). (2003). The state of food insecurity in the world, 2003. Retrieved January 3, 2005, from www.fao.org/docrep/006/j0083e/j0083e00.htm

United Nations Food and Agriculture Organization (UN FAO). (2004). The state of food insecurity in the world, 2004. United Nations Food and Agriculture Organization. Retrieved November 30, 2005, from www.fao.org/documents/show_cdr.asp?url_file=/docrep/007/y5650e/y5650e00.htm

United Nations Food and Agriculture Organization (UN FAO). (2005). Armed conflicts leading cause of world hunger emergencies. Retrieved December 1, 2005, from www.fao.org/newsroom/en/news/2005/102562/index.html

United Nations Food and Agriculture Organization (UN FAO). (2007). Hunger facts. Retrieved fall 2007 from http://www.wfp.org/aboutwfp/facts/hunger_facts.asp

United Nations Joint Programme on HIV/AIDS (UNAIDS). (2002). Impact of AIDS on older populations. Retrieved January 10, 2005, from http://data.unaids.org/publications/Fact-Sheets02/fs_older_en.pdf

United Nations Joint Programme on HIV/AIDS (UNAIDS). (2003). AIDS epidemic update, December 2003. Retrieved January 10, 2005, from http://data.unaids.org/Publications/IRC-pub06/JC943-EpiUpdate2003_en.pdf

United Nations Joint Programme on HIV/AIDS (UNAIDS). (2005a). Global summary of the AIDS epidemic, December 2005. Retrieved spring 2006 from www.unaids.org/epi/2005/doc/EPIupdate2005_pdf_en/Epi05_02_en.pdf

United Nations Joint Programme on HIV/AIDS (UNAIDS). (2005b). AIDS epidemic update, December 2005. Retrieved spring 2006 from www.unaids.org/epi/2005/doc/EPIupdate2005_pdf_en/Epi05_10_en.pdf

United Nations Joint Programme on HIV/AIDS (UNAIDS). (2007a). Press release: Global HIV prevalence has leveled off; AIDS is among the leading causes of death globally and remains the primary cause of death in Africa. Retrieved fall 2007 from http://data.unaids.org/pub/EPISlides/2007/071119_epi_pressrelease_en.pdf

United Nations Joint Programme on HIV/AIDS (UNAIDS). (2007b). 07 AIDS epidemic update. Retrieved January 2008 from http://data.unaids.org/pub/EPISlides/2007/2007_epiupdate_en.pdf

United Nations Office on Drugs and Crime. (2005). World drug report, 2005. Retrieved spring 2006 from www.unodc.org/unodc/en/world_drug_report.html

United Nations Population Division. (2001). World urbanization prospects: The 2001 revision. Retrieved spring 2006 from www.un.org/esa/population/publications/wup2001/wup2001dh.pdf

United Nations Population Division. (2002). World urbanization prospects, 2001 revision—Data tables and highlights. Retrieved January 3, 2005, from www.un.org/esa/population/publications/wup2001/wup2001dh.pdf

United Nations Population Fund (UNFPA). (1998). *The state of world population, 1998.* New York: United Nations.

United Nations Population Fund (UNFPA). (2005a). Violence against women fact sheet. Retrieved December 4, 2005, from www.unfpa.org/swp/2005/presskit/factsheets/facts_vaw.htm

United Nations Population Fund (UNFPA). (2005b). Gender-based violence: A price too high. *State of the World Population, 2005.* Retrieved December 4, 2005, from www.unfpa.org/swp/2005/english/ch7/index.htm

United Nations Population Fund (UNFPA). (2008). State of world population 2007: Unleashing the potential of urban growth. Retrieved spring 2008 from http://www.unfpa.org/swp/2007/english/introduction.html

United Nations World Food Program (UNWFP). (2001, January 8). News release: WFP head releases world hunger map and warns of hunger "hot spots" in 2001. New York: UNWFP.

United Nations World Food Program (UNWFP). (2004). Paying the price of hunger: The impact of malnutrition on women and children. Retrieved December 1, 2005, from http://documents.wfp.org/stellent/groups/public/documents/newsroom/wfp076313.pdf

Urban Institute. (2005, August 25). Low-income working families: Facts and figures. Retrieved spring 2006 from www.urban.org/UploadedPDF/900832.pdf

U.S. Bureau of Justice Statistics. (2005a). Press release: Violent crime rate unchanged during 2005, theft rate declined. Retrieved fall 2007 from http://www.ojp.usdoj.gov/bjs/pub/press/cv05pr.htm

U.S. Bureau of Justice Statistics. (2005b). National crime victimization survey: Criminal victimization, 2005. Retrieved fall 2007 from http://www.ojp.usdoj.gov/bjs/pub/pdf/cv05.pdf

U.S. Bureau of Justice Statistics. (2005c). Justice expenditure and employment extracts: Direct expenditure by level of government, 1982–2005. Retrieved fall 2007 from http://www.ojp.usdoj.gov/bjs/glance/tables/expgovtab.htm

U.S. Bureau of Justice Statistics. (2007a). Prison and jail inmates at midyear 2006. Retrieved fall 2007 from http://www.ojp.gov/bjs/abstract/pjim06.htm

U.S. Bureau of Justice Statistics. (2007b). Homicide victimization rates per 100,000 population by age, race and gender. Retrieved January 2008 from http://www.ojp.usdoj.gov/bjs/homicide/tables/varstab.htm

U.S. Bureau of Labor Statistics. (2005a). Women in the labor force: A databook. Table 11. Retrieved December 3, 2005, from www.bls.gov/cps/wlf-table11-2005.pdf

U.S. Bureau of Labor Statistics. (2005b). Contingent and alternative employment arrangements. Retrieved March 13, 2006, from www.bls.gov/news.release/conemp.toc.htm

U.S. Bureau of Labor Statistics. (2007a). Prison statistics. Retrieved November 3, 2007, from http://www.ojp.gov/bjs/prisons.htm#findings

U.S. Bureau of Labor Statistics. (2007b). Data annual averages: Table 37, Median weekly earnings of full-time wage and salary workers by selected characteristics. Retrieved fall 2007 from http://www.bls.gov/cps/cpsaat37.pdf

U.S. Bureau of Labor Statistics. (2007c). Employment status by sex, presence or age of children, race, or Hispanic or Latino ethnicity: March 2006. Retrieved fall 2007 from http://www.bls.gov/cps/wlf-table5-2007.pdf

U.S. Bureau of Labor Statistics. (2007d). Employment status of the civilian noninstitutional population, by age and sex, 2006 annual averages. Retrieved fall 2007 from http://www.bls.gov/cps/wlf-table1-2007.pdf

U.S. Bureau of Labor Statistics. (2007e). Median usual weekly earnings of full time wage and salary workers by detailed occupation and sex, 2006 annual averages. Retrieved fall 2007 from http://www.bls.gov/cps/wlf-table18-2007.pdf

U.S. Bureau of Labor Statistics. (2007f). Employed persons by detailed occupation and sex, 2006 annual averages. Retrieved fall 2007 from http://www.bls.gov/cps/wlf-table11-2007.pdf

U.S. Bureau of Labor Statistics. (2007g). Median usual weekly earnings of full time wage and salary workers in current dollars by race, Hispanic or Latino ethnicity, and sex, 1979-2006 annual averages. Retrieved fall 2007 from http://www.bls.gov/cps/wlf-table16-2007.pdf

U.S. Bureau of Labor Statistics. (2007h). Highlights of women's earnings in 2006. Retrieved January 2008 from http://www.bls.gov/cps/cpswom2006.pdf

U.S. Bureau of Labor Statistics. (2008a). Economic news release; Union members summary. Retrieved spring 2008 from http://www.bls.gov/news.release/union2.nr0.htm

U.S. Bureau of the Census. (1996). *65+ in the United States.* Current Population Reports: Special Studies: P23-190. Washington, DC: U.S. Government Printing Office.

U.S. Bureau of the Census. (1998). World population profile, 1998—Highlights. Retrieved January 3, 2005, from http://64.233.169.104/search?q=cache:sPI1fpSZgOUJ:www.census.gov/ipc/www/wp98001.html+World+population+profile,+1998%E2%80%94Highlights&hl=en&ct=clnk&cd=1&gl=us

U.S. Bureau of the Census. (1999). Population profile of the United States, chapter 2. Retrieved January 4, 2005, from www.census.gov/population/pop-profile/1999/chap02.pdf

U.S. Bureau of the Census. (2000a). The changing shape of the nation's income distribution. Retrieved January 4, 2005, from www.census.gov/prod/2000pubs/p60-204.pdf

U.S. Bureau of the Census. (2000b). Census 2000 special tabulation. Profile of selected demographic and social characteristics for the foreign born population who entered the United States 1990-2000. Retrieved January 2008 from http://www.census.gov/population/cen2000/stp-159/1990-2000.pdf

U.S. Bureau of the Census. (2001). Asset ownership of households: 1995. Retrieved January 4, 2005, from www.census.gov/hhes/www.wealth/1995/wlth95-1.html

U.S. Bureau of the Census. (2002). Geographical mobility: Population characteristics. Current population reports, PS20-538. Retrieved January 4, 2005, from www.census.gov/prod/2001pubs/p20-538.pdf

U.S. Bureau of the Census. (2003a). Asset ownership of households: 2000. Retrieved January 4, 2005, from www.census.gov/hhes/www.wealth/1998_2000/wlth00-1.html

U.S. Bureau of the Census. (2003b). Number in poverty and poverty rate by race and Hispanic origin: 2001 and 2002. Retrieved January 4, 2005, from www.census.gov/hhes/poverty/poverty02/table1.pdf

U.S. Bureau of the Census. (2003c). People and families by selected characteristics: 2001 and 2002. Retrieved January 4, 2005, from www.census.gov/hhes/poverty/poverty02/table2.pdf

U.S. Bureau of the Census. (2003d). Poverty status: Status of families, by type of family, presence of related children, race, and Hispanic origin: 1959 to 2002. Retrieved January 4, 2005, from www.

census.gov/hhes/poverty/histpov/hstpov4.html

U.S. Bureau of the Census. (2004a). Current population survey, annual social and economic supplement, 2004, Ethnicity and Ancestry Statistics Branch, Population Division. Table 1.2. Retrieved spring 2006 fromwww.census.gov/population/socdemo/hispanic/ASEC2004/2004CPS_tab1.2a.html

U.S. Bureau of the Census. (2004b). American community survey: Selected social characteristics, 2004. Table DP-2. Retrieved December 7, 2005, from http://factfinder.census.gov/servlet/ADPTable?_bm=y&-geo_id=01000US&-qr_name=ACS_2004_EST_G00_DP2&-ds_name=ACS_2004_EST_G00_&-redoLog=false&-_scrollToRow=46&-format

U.S. Bureau of the Census. (2004c). U.S. interim projections by age, race, sex, and Hispanic origin. Retrieved January 2008 from http://www.census.gov/population/www/projections/usinterimproj/natprojtab01a.pdf

U.S. Bureau of the Census. (2005a). Statistical abstract of the United States, 2004-2005. Table No. 297. Homicide victims by race and sex: 1980 to 2001. Retrieved spring 2006 from www.census.gov/prod/2004pubs/04statab/law.pdf

U.S. Bureau of the Census. (2005b). Table 4. Poverty status of families, by type of family, presence of related children, race and Hispanic origin, 1959-2004. Retrieved spring 2006 from www.census.gov/hhes/www.poverty/histpov/hstpov4.html

U.S. Bureau of the Census. (2005c). Table H-3. Mean household income received by each fifth and top 5 percent, all races, 1967 to 2004. Retrieved spring 2006 from www.census.gov/hhes/www.income/histinc/h03ar.html

U.S. Bureau of the Census. (2005d). America's families living arrangements: 2004. Current population survey. Retrieved January 12, 2006, from www.census.gov/population/www.socdemo/hh-fam/cps2004.html

U.S. Bureau of the Census. (2005e). Asset ownership rates for households, by selected characteristics: 2000. Table 2. Retrieved January 29, 2006, from www.census.gov/hhes/www.wealth/1998_2000/wlth00-2.html

U.S. Bureau of the Census. (2005f). Race and Hispanic origin of people by median income and sex: 1947 to 2004. Table P-2. Retrieved January 29, 2006, from www.census.gov/hhes/www.income/histinc/p02.html Accessed January 29, 2006.

U.S. Bureau of the Census. (2006a). Statistical abstract of the United States. Retrieved January 9, 2006, from www.census.gov/statab/

U.S. Bureau of the Census. (2006b). 2006 American community survey: Race—Total population. Retrieved January 2008 from http://factfinder.census.gov/servlet/MetadataBrowserServlet?type=DTtable&id=ACS_2006_EST_G00_&table=ACS_2006_EST_G2000_B02003&_lang=en

U.S. Bureau of the Census. (2006c). 2006 American community survey: Hispanic or Latino origin by specific origin—Total population. Retrieved January 2008 from http://factfinder.census.gov/servlet/MetadataBrowserServlet?type=DTtable&id=ACS_2006_EST_G00_&table=ACS_2006_EST_G2000_B03001&_lang=en

U.S. Bureau of the Census. (2006d). 2006 American community survey: Asian alone by selected groups—Total population. Retrieved January 2008 from http://factfinder.census.gov/servlet/MetadataBrowserServlet?type=DTtable&id=ACS_2006_EST_G00_&table=ACS_2006_EST_G2000_B02006&_lang=en

U.S. Bureau of the Census. (2007a). The 2007 statistical abstract, the national data book. Table 296, Table 303. Retrieved fall 2007 from www.census.gov/prod/2007pubs

U.S. Bureau of the Census. (2007b). Historical income inequality tables. Table H-2 Retrieved fall 2007 from http://www.census.gov/hhes/www/income/histinc/h02ar.html

U.S. Bureau of the Census. (2007c). Historical income inequality tables. Table H-13. Retrieved fall 2007 from http://www.census.gov/hhes/www/income/histinc/h13.html

U.S. Bureau of the Census. (2007d). Educational attainment in the United States: 2006. Retrieved fall 2007 from http://www.census.gov/population/www/socdemo/education/cps2006.html

U.S. Bureau of the Census. (2007e). Historical income inequality tables. Table H-3. Retrieved fall 2007 from http://www.census.gov/hhes/www/income/histinc/h03ar.html

U.S. Bureau of the Census. (2007f). Historical income inequality tables. Table H-9. Retrieved fall 2007 from http://www.census.gov/hhes/www/income/histinc/h09ar.html

U.S. Bureau of the Census. (2007g). Income, poverty, and health insurance coverage in the United States: 2006. Retrieved fall 2007 from http://www.census.gov/prod/2007pubs/p60-233.pdf

U.S. Bureau of the Census. (2007h). Historical poverty tables, Table 4. Retrieved fall 2007 from http://www.census.gov/hhes/www/poverty/histpov/hstpov4.html

U.S. Bureau of the Census. (2007i). America's families living arrangements: 2007. Current population survey. Table A1. Retrieved September 19, 2008, from www.census.gov/population/www/socdemo/hh-fam/cps2007.html

U.S. Bureau of the Census. (2007j). 2006 American community survey: Sex by Age—Total population. Retrieved January 2008 from http://factfinder.census.gov/servlet/MetadataBrowserServlet?type=DTtable&id=ACS_2006_EST_G00_&table=ACS_2006_EST_G2000_B01001&_lang=en

U.S. Bureau of the Census. (2007k). Age and sex of all people, family members, and unrelated individuals iterated by income-to-poverty ratio and race. Current population survey. Retrieved January 2008 from http://pubdb3.census.gov/macro/032007/pov/new01_100.htm

U.S. Bureau of the Census. (2007l). America's families and living arrangements: 2006. U.S. Census Bureau, Housing and Household Economic Statistics Division, Fertility & Family Statistics Branch. Retrieved January 2008 from http://www.census.gov/population/www/socdemo/hh-fam/cps2006.html

U.S. Bureau of the Census. (2007m). 2006 American community survey. Retrieved January 2008 from http://factfinder.census.gov/servlet/DatasetMainPageServlet?_program=ACS&_submenuId=&_lang=en&_ts=

U.S. Bureau of the Census. (2007n). Geographical mobility; 2005 to 2006, detailed tables. Retrieved November 10, 2008, from www.census.gov/population/www/socdemo/migrate/cps2006.html

U.S. Bureau of the Census. (2008a). The 2008 statistical abstract, the national data book: Table 217—Educational attainment by race and Hispanic origin: 1960 to 2006. Retrieved January 2008 from http://www.census.gov/compendia/statab/tables/08s0217.pdf

U.S. Bureau of the Census. (2008b). The 2008 statistical abstract, the national data book: Table 598—employed civilians by sex, race, and Hispanic origins: 2006. Retrieved January 2008 from http://www.census.gov/compendia/statab/tables/08s0598.pdf

U.S. Bureau of the Census. (2008c). The 2008 statistical abstract, the national data book: Table 609—Unemployed and unemployment rates by educational attainment, sex, race and Hispanic origin: 1992 to 2006. Retrieved January 2008 from http://www.census.gov/compendia/statab/tables/08s0609.pdf

U.S. Bureau of the Census. (2008d). The 2008 statistical abstract, the national data book: Table 679—Median income of people with income in constant (2005) dollars , sex, race and Hispanic origin: 1990 to 2005. Retrieved January 2008 from http://www.census.gov/compendia/statab/tables/08s0679.pdf

U.S. Bureau of the Census. (2008e). The 2008 statistical abstract, the national data book: Table 674—Median income by race and Hispanic origin by current and constant (2005) dollars: 1980 to 2005. Retrieved January 2008 from http://www.census.gov/compendia/statab/tables/08s0674.pdf

U.S. Bureau of the Census. (2008f). American community survey 2007. Retrieved January 2008 from http://factfinder.census.gov/servlet/DatasetMainPageServlet?_program=ACS&_submenuId=&_lang=en&_ts=

U.S. Bureau of the Census. (2008g). The 2008 Statistical Abstract. Table 602: Employment by industry: 2000 to 2006. Retrieved spring 2008 from http://www.census.gov/compendia/statab/tables/08s0602.pdf

U.S. Bureau of the Census. (2008h). The 2008 Statistical Abstract. Table 600: Employment projections by occupation: 2004 and 2014. Retrieved spring 2008 from http://www.census.gov/compendia/statab/tables/08s0600.pdf

U.S. Census Bureau News. (2007). Household income rises; poverty rate declines, number of uninsured is up. Retrieved fall 2007 from http://

www.census.gov/Press-Release/www/releases/archives/income_wealth/010583.html

U.S. Department of Education, National Center for Education Statistics. (1993). *Adult literacy in America: A first look at the results of the national adult literacy survey.* Washington, DC: U.S. Government Printing Office.

U.S. Department of Health and Human Services. (2004). Indicators of welfare dependence: Annual report to Congress, 2004, Table 2. Retrieved spring 2006 from aspe.hhs.gov/hsp/indicators04

U.S. Department of Health and Human Services. (2006a). 2006 National survey on drug use & health: National results. Section 3: Alcohol use. Retrieved fall 2007 from http://www.oas.samhsa.gov/nsduh/2k6nsduh/2k6Results.cfm#Ch3

U.S. Department of Health and Human Services. (2006b). Summary: Child Mistreatment 2005. Retrieved January 2008 from http://www.acf.hhs.gov/programs/cb/pubs/cm05/summary.htm

U.S. Department of Health and Human Services. (2007b). Health, United States, 2006. Table 27: Life expectancy at birth, at 65 years of age, and at 75 years of age, by race and sex: United States, selected years, 1900-2004. Retrieved January 2008 from http://www.cdc.gov/nchs/data/hus/hus06.pdf#027

U.S. Department of Housing and Urban Development. (2007). Annual homeless assessment report. Retrieved fall 2007 from http://www.hud.gov/offices/cpd/homeless/ahar.cfm

U.S. Department of Justice. (2003). Budget Trend data 1975 through the president's 2003 request to the Congress. Retrieved fall 2007 from http://www.usdoj.gov/jmd/budgetsummary/btd/1975_2002/2002/html/page117-119.htm

U.S. Department of Labor. (2007). History of federal minimum wage rates under the Fair Labor Standards Act, 1938-2007. Retrieved fall 2007 from www.dol.gov/esa/minwage/chart.htm

U.S. Equal Employment Opportunity Commission. (2005). Sexual harassment charges EEOC & FEPAs combined: FY 1992-FY 2004. Retrieved December 2, 2005, from www.eeoc.gov/stats/harass.html

U.S. Equal Employment Opportunity Commission. (2007). Sexual harassment charges EEOC & FEPAs combined: FY 1997-FY 2004. Retrieved fall 2008 from http://www.eeoc.gov/stats/harass.html

United Steel Workers. (2008). Who we are. Retrieved spring 2008 from http://www.usw.org/our_union/who_we_are

Valenzuela, A. (1999). *Subtractively schooling: U.S. Mexican youth and the politics of caring.* Albany: State University of New York Press.

Vallas, S., & Beck, J. (1996). The transformation of work revisited: The limits of flexibility in American manufacturing. *Social Problems, 43*(3): 339-361.

van der Veer, P. (1994). *Religious nationalism: Hindus and Muslims in India.* Berkeley: University of California Press.

van Gennep, A. (1977; orig. 1908). *The rites of passage.* London: Routledge and Kegan Paul.

Vaughan, D. (1986). *Uncoupling: Turning points in intimate relationships.* New York: Oxford University Press.

Vaughan, D. (1996). *The challenger launch decision: Risky technology, culture, and deviance at NASA.* Chicago: University of Chicago Press.

Viorst, J. (1986). And the prince knelt down and tried to put the glass slipper on Cinderella's foot. In J. Zipes (Ed.), *Don't bet on the prince: Contemporary feminist fairy tales in North America and England.* New York: Methuen.

Vogel, E. F. (1979). *Japan as number one: Lessons for America.* New York: Harper Colophon.

Wacquant, L. J. D. (1993). Redrawing the urban color line: The state of the ghetto in the 1980s. In C. Calhoun & G. Ritzer (Eds.), *Social problems.* New York: McGraw-Hill.

Wacquant, L. J. D. (1996). The rise of advanced marginality: Notes on its nature and implications. *Acta Sociologica, 39*(2): 121-139.

Wacquant, L. J. D. (2002, May). Scrutinizing the street: poverty, morality, and the pitfalls of urban ethnography. *American Journal of Sociology, 107,* 1468-1532.

Wacquant, L. J. D., & Wilson, W. J. (1993). The cost of racial and class exclusion in the inner city. In W. J. Wilson (Ed.), *The ghetto underclass: Social science perspectives.* Newbury Park, CA: Sage.

Wagar, W. (1992). *A short history of the future.* Chicago: University of Chicago Press.

Wajcman, J. (1998). *Managing like a man: Women and men in corporate management.* Cambridge, UK: Polity Press.

Waldron, I. (1986). Why do women live longer than men? In P. Conrad & R. Kern (Eds.), *The sociology of health and illness.* New York: St. Martin's.

Wallerstein, I. (1974a). *Capitalist agriculture and the origins of the European world-economy in the sixteenth century.* New York: Academic Press.

Wallerstein, I. (1974b). *The modern world-system.* New York: Academic Press.

Wallerstein, I. (1979). *The capitalist world economy.* Cambridge, UK: Cambridge University Press.

Wallerstein, I. (1990). *The modern world-system II.* New York: Academic Press.

Wallerstein, I. (1996a). *Historical capitalism with capitalist civilization.* New York: Norton.

Wallerstein, I. (Ed.). (1996b). World inequality. St. Paul, MN: Consortium Books.

Wallerstein, I. (2004). *World-system analysis: An introduction.* Durham, NC: Duke University Press.

Wallerstein, J. S., & Kelly, J. B. (1980). *Surviving the break-up: How children and parents cope with divorce.* New York: Basic Books.

Wallis, R. (1984). *The elementary forms of new religious life.* London: Routledge and Kegan Paul.

Walmart Class. (2005). Case Developments. Retrieved December 4, 2005, from www.walmartclass.com/public_home.html

Walum, L. R. (1977). *The dynamics of sex and gender: A sociological perspective.* Chicago: Rand McNally.

Warner, S. (1993). Work in progress toward a new paradigm for the sociological study of religion in the United States. *American Journal of Sociology, 98,* 1044-1093.

Warren, B. (1980). *Imperialism: Pioneer of capitalism.* London: Verso.

Waters, M. C. (1990). *Ethnic options: Choosing identities in America.* Berkeley: University of California Press.

Wattenberg, M. P. (1996). *The decline of American political parties, 1952-1994* (Rev. ed.). Cambridge, MA: Harvard University Press.

Waxman, L., & Hinderliter, S. (1996). *A status report on hunger and homelessness in America's cities.* Washington, DC: U.S. Conference of Mayors.

Weber, M. (1947). *The theory of social and economic organization.* New York: Free Press.

Weber, M. (1963; orig. 1921). *The sociology of religion*. Boston: Beacon Press.

Weber, M. (1977; orig. 1904). *The Protestant ethic and the spirit of capitalism*. New York: Macmillan.

Weber, M. (1979; orig. 1921). *Economy and society: An outline of interpretive sociology* (2 vols.). Berkeley: University of California Press.

Weeks, J. (1977). *Coming out: Homosexual politics in Britain, from the nineteenth century to the present*. New York: Quartet.

Weihau, C. (2006, February 15). Divorce rate surges across China. *China Daily*. Retrieved January 2008 from http://www.chinadaily.com.cn/english/doc/2006-02/15/content_520204.htm

Weiss, R. (1997). Aging: New answers to old questions. *National Geographic, 192*(5): 2–31.

Weitzman, L. (1985). *Divorce revolution: The unexpected social and economic consequences for women and children in America*. New York: Free Press.

Weitzman, L., et al. (1972). Sex-Role socialization in picture books for preschool children. *American Journal of Sociology, 77*, 1125–1150.

Wellman, B. (1994). I was a teenage network analyst: The route from the Bronx to the information highway. *Connections, 17*(2): 28–45.

Wellman, B., Carrington, P. J., & Hall, A. (1988). Networks as personal communities. In B. Wellman & S. D. Berkowitz (Eds.), *Social structures: A network approach*. New York: Cambridge University Press.

Wellman, B., Salaff, J., Dimitrova, D., Garton, L., Gulia, M., & Haythornthwaite, C. (1996). Computer networks as social networks: Collaborative work, telework, and virtual community. *Annual Review of Sociology, 22*, 213–238.

Wellman, D. T. (1987). *Portraits of white racism*. New York: Cambridge University Press.

West, C., & Fenstermaker, S. (1995). Doing difference. *Gender and Society, 9*(1): 8–37.

West, C., Fenstermaker, S., & Zimmerman, D. (1987, June). Doing gender. *Gender and Society, 1*, 125–151.

Western, B. (1997). *Between class and market: Postwar unionization in the capitalist democracies*. Princeton, NJ: Princeton University Press.

Western, B., & Beckett, K. (1999). How unregulated is the U.S. labor market? The penal system as a labor market institution. *American Journal of Sociology, 104*(4): 1030–1060.

Wetzel, M. S., Eisenberg, D. M., & Kaptchuk, T. J. (1998). Courses involving complementary and alternative medicine at US medical schools. *JAMA, 280*(9): 784–787.

Wheatley, P. (1971). *The pivot of the four quarters*. Edinburgh: Edinburgh University Press.

Wheeler, D. L. (1998). Global culture or culture clash: New information technologies in the Islamic world—a view from Kuwait. *Communication Research, 25*(4): 359–376.

White, C. (2003, June 27). China is top of the gaggers. Dot Journalism. Retrieved January 4, 2005, from www.journalism.co.uk/news/story673. html

White, M., & Trevor, M. (1983). *Under Japanese management: The experience of British workers*. New York: Gower.

White House Press Office. (2001, June 11). President Bush discusses global climate change.

White, L. K. (1990, November). Determinants of divorce: A review of research in the eighties. *Journal of Marriage and the Family, 52*, 904–912.

Whitman, D. (1994, July 25). The poor aren't poorer. *U.S. News and World Report, 117*, pp. 33, 36, 38.

Widom, C. S., & Newman, J. P. (1985). Characteristics of non-institutionalized psychopaths. In D. P. Farrington & J. Gunn (Eds.), *Aggression and dangerousness*. Chichester, UK: Wiley.

Wilkinson, R. (1996). *Unhealthy societies: The afflictions of inequality*. New York: Routledge.

Will, J., Self, P., & Datan, N. (1976). Maternal behavior and perceived sex of infant. *American Journal of Orthopsychiatry, 46*, 135–139.

Williams, C. L. (1992). The glass escalator: Hidden advantages for men in the "female" professions. *Social Problems, 39*, 253–267.

Williams, S. J. (1993). *Chronic respiratory illness*. London: Routledge.

Willis, P. (1977). *Learning to labour*. Lexington, MA: Lexington Books.

Wilson, B. (1982). *Religion in sociological perspective*. New York: Oxford University Press.

Wilson, E. O. (1975). *Sociobiology: The new synthesis*. Cambridge, MA: Harvard University Press.

Wilson, J., & Sherkat, D. E. (1994). Returning to the fold. *Journal for the Scientific Study of Religion, 33,* 148–161.

Wilson, J. Q., & Kelling, G. (1982, March). Broken windows. *Atlantic Monthly*.

Wilson, W. J. (1978). *The declining significance of race: Blacks and changing American institutions*. Chicago: University of Chicago Press.

Wilson, W. J. (1987). *The truly disadvantaged: The inner city, the underclass, and public policy*. Chicago: University of Chicago Press.

Wilson, W. J. (1991, February). Studying inner-city social dislocations: The challenge of public agenda research. *American Sociological Review, 56*, 1–14.

Wilson, W. J. (1996). *When work disappears: The world of the new urban poor*. New York: Knopf.

Winkleby, M. A., Jatulis, D. E., Frank, E., & Fortmann, S. P. (1992). Socioeconomic status and health: How education, income, and occupation contribute to risk factors for cardiovascular disease. *American Journal of Public Health, 82*, 816–820.

Wirth, L. (1938, July). Urbanism as a way of life. *American Sociological Review, 44*, 1–24.

Witkowski, S. R., & Brown, C. H. (1982). Whorf and universals of color nomenclature. *Journal of Anthropological Research, 38*, 411–420.

Wolf, N. (1992). *The beauty myth: How images of beauty have been used against women*. New York: Anchor Books.

Wolff, E. N. (2000). Recent trends in wealth ownership, 1983–1998. Tables 8 and 9. Jerome Levy Economic Institute. Retrieved January 4, 2005, from www.levy.org/default.asp?view5publications_view&pubIDf73a204517

Women's Policy, Inc. (2008). Election 2008 wrap-up: Record number of women to serve in the House, Senate. Retrieved November 2008 from http://www.womenspolicy.org/site/DocServer/election_2008.pdf?docID=1341

Wong, S. (1986). Modernization and Chinese culture in Hong Kong. *Chinese Quarterly, 106*, 306–325.

Woodrum, E. (1988). Moral conservatism and the 1984 presidential election. *Journal for the Scientific Study of Religion, 27*, 192–210.

World Bank. (1997). *World development report 1997: The state in a changing world*. New York: Oxford University Press.

World Bank. (1999). *International bank for reconstruction and development, world development indicators 1999*. Washington, DC: World Bank.

World Bank. (2000). *World development report*. New York: Oxford University Press.

World Bank. (2000–2001). World development indicators. In World Development Report 2000–2001: Attacking Poverty. Retrieved January 4, 2005, from http://poverty.worldbank. org/library/topic/3389/

World Bank. (2003). World development indicators 2003. Retrieved January 4, 2005, from www.worldbank.org/ data/onlinedatabases/onlinedatabases.html

World Bank. (2005). World development indicators 2005. Retrieved spring 2006 from http://devdata.worldbank.org/ wdi2005/cover.ht

World Bank. (2007a). Gross national income 2007. Retrieved fall 2007 from http://siteresources.worldbank.org/ DATASTATISTICS/Resources/GNI.pdf

World Bank. (2007b). Country classification. Retrieved fall 2007 from http:// go.worldbank.org/K2CKM78CC0

World Bank. (2007c). Country groups. Retrieved fall 2007 from http:// go.worldbank.org/D7SN0B8YU0

World Bank. (2007d). Gross national income per capita, 2007. Retrieved fall 2007 from http://siteresources.worldbank.org/ DATASTATISTICS/Resources/GNIPC. pdf

World Bank. (2007e). Key development data and statistics. Retrieved fall 2007 from http://web.worldbank.org/WBSITE/ EXTERNAL/DATASTATISTICS/0,,con tentMDK:20535285-menuPK:1192694-p agePK:64133150-piPK:64133175-theSiteP K:239419,00.html

World Bank. (2007f). World development indicators, 2006. Retrieved fall 2007 from http://devdata.worldbank.org/ wdi2006/contents/TOC.htm

World Bank. (2007g). Data and statistics— Quick reference tables: Total GDP 2006. *World Bank Indicators*. Washington, DC: World Bank. Retrieved fall 2007 from http://siteresources.worldbank.org/ DATASTATISTICS/Resources/GDP.pdf

World Bank. (2008). World development indicators, 2007. Retrieved fall 2008 from http://go.worldbank. org/1SF48T40L0

World Health Organization. (2004). Water, sanitation and health: the current situation. Retrieved January 2008 from http://www.wssinfo.org/en/142_ currentSit.html

World Intellectual Property Organization. (2007). WIPO patent report. Retrieved spring 2008 from http://www.wipo.int/ ipstats/en/statistics/patents/patent_ report_2007.html#P143_10808

Worldsteel.org. (2008). Major steel producing countries, 2005 and 2006. Retrieved spring 2008 from http://www.worldsteel.org/?action= storypages&id=195

World Trade Organization (WTO). (2005). *International trade statistics, 2005*. Table IV.22. Geneva: The World Trade Organization.

World Trade Organization (WTO). (2007). International trade statistics, 2007: Share of manufactures in total merchandise trade by region. Table 11.6. Retrieved fall 2007 from http://www. wto.org/english/res_e/statis_e/its2007_e/ section2_e/ii06.xls

World Wide Guide to Women in Leadership. (2008). The situation of female membership of governments by 2008. Retrieved fall 2008 from http://www. grantthornton.ca/resources/documents/ IBR2007WomeninBusinessPressRelease. pdf

Worrall, A. (1990). *Offending women: Female lawbreakers and the criminal justice system*. London: Routledge.

Wray, L. A., Herzog, A. R., Willis, R. J., & Wallace, R. B. The impact of education and heart attack on smoking cessation among middle-aged adults. *Journal of Health and Social Behavior, 39*(4): 271–294.

Wright, E. O. (1978). *Class, crisis, and the state*. London: New Left Books.

Wright, E. O. (1985). *Classes*. New York: Shocken.

Wright, E. O. (1997). *Class counts: Comparative studies in class analysis*. New York: Cambridge University Press.

Wright, E. O. (2000). *Class counts: Student edition*. New York: Cambridge University Press.

Wrigley, E. A. (1968). *Population and history*. New York: McGraw-Hill.

Wrigley, J., & Dreby, J. (2005). Fatalities and the organization of U.S. child care 1985–2003. *American Sociological Review, 70*, 729–757.

Wrigley, J., & Dreby, J. (2006, January 29). Keeping kids safe, to prevent more Nixzmary Brown cases, the state must regulate informal day care. *Newsday*, p. A.42.

Wuthnow, R. (1976). *The consciousness reformation*. Berkeley: University of California Press.

Wuthnow, R. (1978). *Experimentation in American religion*. Berkeley: University of California Press.

Wuthnow, R. (1988). Sociology of religion. In N. J. Smelser (Ed.), *Handbook of sociology*. Newbury Park, CA: Sage.

Wuthnow, R. (1990). Improving our understanding of religion and giving: Key issues for research. In R. Wuthnow & V. A. Hodgkinson (Eds.), *Faith and philanthropy in America*. San Francisco: Jossey-Bass.

Wuthnow, R. (2005, February 4). Hanging in the balance: Sociology and theology. Lecture.

Yankelovich, C. S. (1991, May 8). What's OK on a date. Survey for Time and CNN.

Young, I. M. (1990). *Throwing like a girl and other essays in feminist philosophy and social theory*. Bloomington: Indiana University Press.

Young, J. (1998). Breaking windows: Situating the new criminology. In P. Walton and J. Young (Eds.), *The new criminology revisited*. London: Macmillan.

Young, J. (1999). *The exclusive society: Social exclusion, crime, and difference in late modernity*. London: Sage.

Young, M., & Willmott, P. (1973). *The symmetrical family: A study of work and leisure in the London region*. London: Routledge and Kegan Paul.

Yue Yuen. (2007). Yue Yuen Industrial (Holdings) Ltd: About us: Corporate profile. Retrieved December 2007 from http://www.yueyuen.com/about_ corporateProfile.htm

Zammuner, V. (1986). Children's sex-role stereotypes: A cross-cultural analysis. In P. Shaver & C. Hendrick (Eds.), *Sex and gender*. Beverly Hills, CA: Sage.

Zarcadoolas, C., Pleasant, A., & Greer, D. (2006). *Advancing health literacy: A framework for understanding and action*. San Francisco: Jossey-Bass.

Zerubavel, E. (1979). *Patterns of time in hospital life*. Chicago: University of Chicago Press.

Zerubavel, E. (1982). The standardization of time: A sociohistorical perspective. *American Journal of Sociology, 88*, 1–23.

Zhang, N., & Xu, W. (1995). Discovering the positive within the negative: The women's movement in a changing China.

In A. Basu (Ed.), *The challenge of local feminisms*. Boulder, CO: Westview Press.

Zimbardo, P. G. (1969). The human choice: Individuation, reason, and order versus deindividuation, impulse, and chaos. In W. J. Arnold & D. Levine (Eds.), *Nebraska symposium on motivation, 17*. Lincoln: University of Nebraska Press.

Zimbardo, P. G. (writer) (1992). *Quiet rage: The Stanford prison experiment* [Documentary]. (Available from http://www.prisonexp.org/)

Zimbardo, P. G , Ebbesen, E. B., & Maslach, C. (1977). *Influencing attitudes and changing behavior*. Reading, MA: Addison-Wesley.

Zuboff, S. (1988). *In the age of the smart machine: The future of work and power.* New York: Basic Books.

CREDITS

Text

Gregory Dicum and Nina Luttinger, © 2006 by Nina Luttinger and Gregory Dicum. This piece originally appears in *The Coffee Book: Anatomy of an Industry from Crop to the Last Drop* by Nina Luttinger and Gregory Dicum. Reprinted by permission of The New Press.

Mitchell Duneier: "Questions for Jane Jacobs," *New York Times Magazine,* April 9, 2000. Copyright © 2000, Mitchell Duneier. Reprinted by permission.

Robert Hauser: "What If We End Social Promotion?" by Robert Hauser from *Education Week,* April 7, 1999. Reprinted by permission of the author.

Brooke Kroeger: Excerpts from "When a Dissertation Makes a Difference," *The New York Times,* March 20, 2004, p. B9. Copyright © 2004 The New York Times. All rights reserved. Used by permission and protected by the Copyright Laws of the United States. The printing, copying, redistribution, or retransmission of the Material without express written permission is prohibited. www.nytimes.com.

Pepper Schwartz: "Stage Fright or Death Wish: Sociology in Mass Media" by Pepper Schwartz from *Contemporary Sociology,* Vol. 27, No. 5 (Sept., 1998), pp. 439–445. Reprinted by permission of the author and the American Sociological Association.

Diane Vaughan: "How Theory Travels: A Most Public Public Sociology" by Diane Vaughan from *ASA Footnotes, Nov. 2003.* Reprinted by permission of the author.

Robert Wuthnow: Reprinted by permission of the author.

Figures

Page 38: (left) "Diamonds *Were* a Girl's Best Friend" page 34, Edward R. Tufte, *Envisioning Information* (Cheshire, Connecticut, Graphics Press LLC, 1990). Reprinted by permission; (right) "Napoleon's March to Moscow" by C. J. Minard, page 41, Edward R. Tufte, *The Visual Display of Quantitative Information* (Cheshire, Connecticut, Graphics Press LLC, 1983). Reprinted by permission; page 77: Income Per Person, GNI per capita 2003, World Bank Atlas. © The International Bank for Reconstruction and Development/ The World Bank. Reprinted with permission; page 102: Christopher Swiszcz, "Map of Dorm Room, Wheaton College, Male Student, Class of 2000." Reprinted by permission of Christopher Swiszcz; page 103: Siri Ammentorp Dumont, "Map of Dorm Room, Wheaton College, Female Student, Class of 2000." Reprinted by permission of Siri Ammentorp Dumont; p. 580: Ken Pyne, Figure: Cultural and material influences on health, *An Introduction to Sociology,* 3rd Edition, by Ken Browne, Fig. 16.4, p. 410. Reprinted by permission of the artist; page 618: Brandt and Enders, Map: Population Distribution by Urbanized Areas and Urban Clusters, Update of the Demography of Rural Disability Part One, RTC: Rural, University of Montana, 2005. Reprinted by permission of Alexandra Enders.

Photos

Frontmatter: page v: (top) Ed Kashi/Corbis; (bottom) Bettmann/Corbis; page vi: (top) AP Photo; (center) Photofest; (bottom) Alex di Suvero/The New York Times/Redux; page vii: (top) Tim Fadek/Polaris; (bottom) Henry Diltz/Corbis; page viii: (top) Ruth Fremson/The New York Times; (center) AP Photo; (bottom) Monica Almeida/The New York Times/Redux; page ix: Courtesy of France Winddance Twine. Photo by Michael Smyth; Ruth Fremson/New York Times/Redux; page x: (top) Reuters/Corbis; (center) Jeff Zelevansky/Bloomberg News/Landov; (bottom) Micah Walter/Reuters; page xi: (top) Ed Kashi/Corbis; (bottom) Getty Images; page xii: (top) Howard Schatz/IPN Stock; (bottom) Wu Hong/epa/Corbis; page xiii: David Butow/Redux.

Part One: page 1: (from left to right) Ed Kashi/Corbis; Pablo Corral V/Corbis; Gavriel Jecan/Corbis; Bettmann/Corbis; Picture Contact/Alamy; Philip G. Zimbardo/Stanford Prison Experiment.

Chapter 1: page 2: Ed Kashi/Corbis; page 4: AP Photo; page 5: Ricco Torres/Epsilon/20th Century Fox/The Kobal Collection/WireImage.com; page 6: (left) Bo Zaunders/Corbis; (right) Bettmann/Corbis; page 7: The New Yorker Collection 1969 Dana Fradon from cartoonbank.com; page 8: Pablo Corral V/Corbis; page 9: Thomas Hoeker/Magnum/PNI; page 11: (left) Corbis; (right) Bettmann/Corbis; page 12: (top) Bettmann/Corbis; (bottom) Granger Collection; page 13: Bettmann/Corbis; page 14: Warder Collection; page 15: Granger Collection; page 16: Getty Images; page 18: Courtesy Michael Burawoy; page 20: AP Photo; page 22: (left) Kevin Dodge/Corbis; (right) Gavriel Jecan/Corbis.

Chapter 2: page 26: Bettmann/Corbis; page 28: Aldine de Gruyter; page 30: Staatliche Museen zu Berlin; page 32: Picture Contact/Alamy; page 34: Photograph Courtesy © Laura Tillman; page 36: Jason Lindsey/Alamy; page 40: Philip G. Zimbardo/Stanford Prison Experiment; page 41: Imperial War Museum, London; page 42: Getty Images.

Part Two: page 51: (from left to right) AP Photos; AP Photo; Photofest; Alex di Suvero/The New York Times/Redux; Tim Fadek/Polaris; Henry Diltz/Corbis.

AP Photo; page 375: Karen Kasmauski/Corbis; page 377: AP Photo.

Chapter 13: page 380: Reuters/Corbis; page 386: Danny Lehman/Corbis; page 389: Ted Soqui/Corbis; pages 390–391: AP Photo; 392: STR/AFP/Getty Images; page 393: AP Photo; page 394: Bettmann/Corbis; page 395: Joe Skipper/Reuters/Corbis; page 396: AP Photo; page 399: Randy Snyder/epa/Corbis; page 405: Réunion des Musées Nationaux/Art Resource; pages 406–407: Courtesy David Cunningham; page 408: AFP/Getty Images; page 409: Polaris; page 411: Hulton-Deutsch Collection/Corbis; page 413: Jewel Samad/AFP/Getty Images; page 415: AP Photo; page 417: Reuters/Corbis.

Part Four: page 421: (from left to right) Jeff Zelevansky/Bloomberg News/Landov; AP Photo; Reuters; Ed Kashi/Corbis; Douglas R. Clifford/St Petersburg Times/Zuma Press; Getty Images.

Chapter 14: page 422: Jeff Zelevansky/Bloomberg News/Landov; page 425: (left) AP Photo; (right) Newscom; page 427: Bettmann/Corbis; page 429: AP Photo; page 432: Courtesy William Bielby; pages 435–437: AP Photo; page 438: Peter Parks/AFP/Getty Images; page 441: AP Photo; page 445: Gideon Mendel/Corbis; page 446: Reuters; page 448: Getty Images; page 449: Courtesy of Dell Inc.; page 451: John N. Gress/Reuters/Corbis; page 453: William Perlman/Star Ledger/Corbis; page 455: Bill Pugliano/Getty Images.

Chapter 15: page 460: Micah Walter/Reuters; page 463: (left) Hamid Sardar/Corbis; (right) Kazuhiro Nogi/AFP/Getty Images; page 464: Karen Kasmauski/Corbis; page 466: Ariel Skelly/Corbis; page 467: Philip Rostron/Masterfile; page 468: (top) © The New Yorker Collection 1934 Don Herold from cartoonbank.com. All Rights Reserved; (bottom) © The New Yorker Collection 1937 Richard Taylor from cartoonbank.com. All Rights Reserved; page 469: (clockwise from left) © The New Yorker Collection 2003 Barbara Smaller from cartoonbank.com. All Rights Reserved; © The New Yorker Collection 1994 Bernard Schoenbaum from cartoonbank.com. All Rights Reserved; © The New Yorker Collection 1998 Harry Bliss from cartoonbank.com. All Rights Reserved; page 476: David Butow/Corbis Saba; page 477: (top) Melanie Stetson Freeman/The Christian Science Monitor/

Getty Images; (bottom) Getty Images; page 478: Monica Almeida/The New York Times/Redux; page 481: Newscom; page 482: Everett Collection; page 486: Courtesy Julia Wrigley; page 489: Corbis; page 490: Kimberly White/Reuters/Corbis.

Chapter 16: page 494: Ed Kashi/Corbis; page 496: The Sacramento Bee/Hector Amezcua/Zuma Press; page 497: Douglas R. Clifford/St Petersburg Times/ZUMA Press; page 499: J.A. Giordano/Corbis; page 502: Gary Connor/PhotoEdit/PNI; page 503: Matt Eich/The New York Times/Redux; page 506: Courtesy Robert Hauser; page 507: Will & Deni McIntyre; page 508: Ted Streshinsky/Corbis; page 510: Mary Knox Merrill/The Christian Science Monitor/Getty Images; page 512: AP Photo; page 516: Granger Collection; page 518: Bill Nation/Corbis; page 519: © 1997, Lloyd Dangle; page 521: Second Life is a trademark of Linden Research, Inc. Certain materials have been reproduced with the permission of Linden Research, Inc. COPYRIGHT © 2001–2008 LINDEN RESEARCH, INC. ALL RIGHTS RESERVED; page 522: Pal Pillai/AFP/Getty Images.

Chapter 17: page 526: Getty Images; page 529: AP Photo; page 530: Courtesy Robert Wuthnow; page 532: Bennett Dean/Eye Ubiquitous/Corbis; page 534: Joseph Sohm: ChromoSohm Inc./Corbis; page 535: © 1999 Joel Gordon; page 537: (clockwise from top left) Photo © Marrie Bot, 1982; Reuters; Cristian Baitg Reportage/Alamy; Ian McAlpine/Kingston Whig Standard/The Canadian Press; pages 538–539: AP Photo; page 541: Siewert Falko/dpa/Corbis; page 543: © Raffi Alexander/Spiderbox; page 547: World Religions Photo Library/Photos12.com; page 552: Bettmann/Corbis; page 554: AP Photo; page 556: Catherine Karnow/Corbis; pages 557–558: AP Photo; page 559: Reuters/Landov.

Part Five: page 563: (from left to right) Howard Schatz/IPN Stock; Gideon Mendel/Corbis; Wu Hong/epa/Corbis; Manjunath Kiran/epa/Corbis; David Butow/Redux; Khaled Desouki/AFP/Getty Images.

Chapter 18: page 564: Howard Schatz/IPN Stock; page 566: (from left to right) Chris Steele-Perkins/Magnum Photos; Ed Quinn/Corbis; Karen Kasmauski/Corbis; 568: (left) Alinari/Art Resource; (right) Rykoff Collection/Corbis; page 569: (top) Laura Dwight/

Corbis; (center) Photography by Tammy Ali; (bottom) © Heather Kimber; page 570: Gabriela Hasbun/Redux; page 571: Sandy Huffaker/The New York Times/Redux; page 572: Mark Peterson/Corbis; page 575: Gideon Mendel/Corbis; page 577: Lindsay Hebberd/Corbis; page 582: (top) Vincent Laforet/The New York Times/Redux; (bottom) Getty Images; page 584: Jeffery Allan Salter/Corbis; page 586: Gideon Mendel/Corbis; page 588: Fredrik Renander/Redux; page 589: (top) AP Images/James Nachtwey/VII; (bottom) Louise Gubb/Corbis Saba; page 590: Donna Connor/Sygma/Corbis; page 591: Granger Collection; page 593: Marmaduke St. John/Alamy; page 596: Courtesy Pepper Schwartz; page 599: New York Daily News; page 602: AP Photo.

Chapter 19: page 606: Wu Hong/epa/Corbis; page 608: Natalie Behring/Bloomberg News/Landov; page 610: Getty Images; page 612: David Brabyn/Sipa; page 613: Andrew Lichtenstein/Corbis; page 614: AP Photo; page 616: Kat Wade/Corbis; page 619: AP Photo; page 620: (left) Hulton Archive/Getty Images; (right) David McNew/Getty Images; page 622: Philippa Lewis/Corbis; page 623: AP Photo; page 624: Mario Tama/Getty Images; page 625: (top) Arlene Gottfried/The Image Works; (bottom) Nicole Bengiveno/The New York Times; page 626: Reuters/Rebecca Cook/Landov; page 629: Dvir Bar-Gal/Zuma Press; page 630: Giry Daniel/Corbis Sygma; pages 632–633: AP Photos; page 634: Mario Tama/Gettty Images; page 637: Reuters/Krishna Murari Kishan: page 645: AP Photo; page 646: Manjunath Kiran/epa/Corbis; page 650: Orjan F. Ellingvag/Dagens Naringsliv/Corbis.

Chapter 20: page 654: David Butow/Redux; page 657: Getty Images; page 658: Khaled Desouki/AFP/Getty Images; page 659: Reprinted with permission from Nano Letters Vol. 5, No. 9, pg. 1768. Copyright 2005 American Chemical Society. Permission granted by author Peixuan Guo; page 660: Getty Images; page 661: Carl & Ann Purcell/Corbis; page 664: Zack Canepari/The New York Times/Redux; page 666: AP Photo; page 668: Courtesy Judith Blau; page 671: Robert Essel NYC/Corbis; page 672: AP Photo; page 673: Jim Richardson/Corbis; page 674: Ted Aljibe/AFP/Getty Images; page 675: Ryan Pyle/The New York Times/Redux; page 676: AFP/Corbis; page 677: AP Photo; page 682: Martial Trezzini/epa/Corbis.

INDEX

AARP, 167, 371, 372
abolitionism, 340, 410
abortion
    antiabortion activists, 412, 556
    debate over, 603
    right to, 399, 412
Abraham, 546
absenteeism, 429, 430
absolute poverty, 229
abstract attitudes toward schooling, 505
achievement gap in educational outcomes, 502
acid rain, 608
acquisitions and mergers, corporate, 162, 228
"acting white" thesis, 505
activity theory, 362
adoption law, 491
adult education, 371
advertisements
    gender norms in, 284–85
    white racial attitudes, 322–23
affective individualism, 466
affiliative speech, 126, 127
affirmative-action programs, 321, 339
Afghanistan, 558, 559
    drought-related deaths in, 255, 258
    infant mortality rates, 259
    Taliban rule of, 5, 81–82, 543, 559
    terrorism and, 418
    women's rights in, 543
AFL-CIO, 434
Africa
    colonialism in, 416, 586
    democracy's spread in, 390
    food production in, 260
    HIV/AIDS in, 255, 259, 587, 589, 590, 669
    homosexual rights in, 599–602
    infant mortality rates, 259

infectious disease in, 585
Internet access in, 523
low-income countries of, 250
nationalism and conflicts in, 82, 416
poverty in, 77
African Americans, 339–41
    aging and, 364
    "black codes," 340
    black feminism, 308–9
    caste in the United States, 208–9
    child-raising responsibilities, kinship and neighborhood networks utilized for, 312
    civil rights movement, 340–41, 407, 409, 623, 658
    civil rights of, 386
    as crime victims, 184, 186
    with criminal records, effect on employment of, 196, 199
    discrimination against, 208–9, 223
    "double consciousness" of, 14
    economic divide among, 349
    education and, 214, 344, 345, 501
    families, 475
    health and illness, 581–83
    HIV/AIDS among, 587
    incarceration rates, 171, 194
    income inequality, 223, 224, 346, 348
    infant mortality rates, 259, 346, 581
    internal migration from South to North, 340
    marriage and, 17, 312, 471, 475, 622
    murder rate for young black males, 582
    obesity among, 572
    political power of, 348
    poverty among, 79, 232, 233, 366

remarriage by, 479
    segregation, 14, 208, 318, 321, 328, 340, 615
        residential, 343, 347–48, 611, 621, 622, 623–25
    social interaction on urban streets between whites and, 130–31
    in the suburbs, 620–21
    support networks, 475
    underclass and, 220, 341
    unemployment rate, 346
    urban poverty and, 621–24
    voter turnout, 393
    wealth gap between whites and, 212–13
    women's movement and, 410
    see also race
African Methodist Episcopal Church, 543
African National Congress (ANC), 140, 208
afterlife, 548
age-grades, 90–91, 100
ageism, 368
agents of socialization, 89–93
    the family, 89–90, 306
    mass media, 92–93
    peer relationships, 90–92
    work, 93
aggressive behavior
    biological view of deviance, 177–78
    gender and biology's role in, 280, 281
    male teenage athletes and, 20–21
aging and seniors, 355–78, 643
    biological, 357, 358–59
    categories of, 364
    credit card debt, 213
    global perspective on, 375–78
    graying of industrial societies, 356–57, 376–77
    prejudice and, 368

psychological, 357, 359, 360–61
    redefining retirement, 372–73
    roles associated with, 360
    social, 357, 359–60
    sociological definition of, 357
    sociological explanations of, 360–63
        functionalism, 361–62
        self-concept, 363
        social conflict theories, 362–63
    telecommuting and older workers, 161
    in the U.S.
        baby boomers, 359
        expectations of, 364–65, 366
        fears about, 370
        graying of society, 356–57, 361
        growth of elderly population, 365
        health problems, 369–70
        lifelong learning, 370–71
        median age of U.S. population, 1850–2050, 356, 357
        physical abuse, 369
        politics of, 371–74, 394
        poverty and, 365–66, 367
        race and, 364
        social isolation and, 366–68
    aging in place, 617
    agrarian societies, 9, 71, 73, 77
        low-income countries, 250, 252
        social stratification in, 207
    agriculture, 8, 643
        manufactured risk and, 673–77
        soil erosion and, 643–44
        WTO and agricultural subsidies, 681
        see also food production

marijuana, 192
  labeling theory, 181
  social acceptability of, 9
  narcotics trade,
    international, 192–93
  teenagers and, 190
  war on drugs, 190, 192–93
Druids, 552
Du Bois, W. E. B., 14
Dukes, Betty, 296, 432–33
Dukes v. Wal-Mart Stores, Inc.,
  432–33
Duke University, 144
  lacrosse team, 20
Duncan, Otis Dudley, 228
Duneier, Mitchell, 614, 629
Dunne, Kieran, 486
Durand, Jorge, 342
Durenberger, Dave, 374
Durkheim, Émile, 11, 13, 16, 54
  on anomie, 11, 179
  on conformity, 57
  on deviance, 176, 179
  first principle of sociology, 11
  on religion, 11, 16, 532, 533
  on social constraint, 11
  on suicide, 11, 32, 584
Dutt, Mallika, 311
Dworkin, Ronald, 603
dyads, 138–39
dysfunctions, 16

Eappen, Matthew, 486
Early Childhood Longitudinal
  Study, 554
East Asian newly
  industrializing
  economies, 75, 78,
  260–62, 270, 271, 274
  corporate investment in, 440
  global trade and, 678–79
Eastern Europe
  democratization of, 382, 388,
    390, 416, 665
  economic future of, 275
  religion in former socialist
    countries, 557
  revolutions of 1989, 408
  women in professional
    positions in, 305
Eastern Orthodox Church,
  546
eating disorders, 565–70
Eckankar, 552
ecological approach to urban
  analysis, 610–11
economic capital, 215
economic deprivation, social
  movements and, 404–5

economic interdependence, 426
Economic Policy Institute
  (EPI), 365
economic restructuring
  hypothesis, 622
"Economics of Immigration,
  The," 335
economy
  defined, 424
  informal, 426
  the modern, 435–44
ecstasy (MDMA), 190
Edin, Kathryn, 237, 476–77
Edison Project, 509–10, 512
education and literacy, 213–14,
  495–513
  academic achievement and
    differential outcomes
    achievement gap, 502
    gender and, 505–7
    intelligence, 502–5
    race and the "acting white
      thesis," 505
    school discipline, 507–8,
      509
    stereotype threat, 507
  in the developing world,
    512–13, 514–15, 633–34
  in East Asian newly
    industrializing
    economies, 271
  gender inequality in, 299–
    300, 313, 505–6
  global economic inequality of
    women and, 304
  health and illness,
    inequalities in, 581
  hidden curriculum, 497, 522
  historically, 516
  inequality and, 213–14,
    498–501
    "between school effects,"
      499–500
    gender inequality, 299–
      300, 313, 505–6
    global inequality, 251, 254,
      260
    "within school effects,"
      500–501
  internationalization of,
    502–3
  knowledge economy in
    investments in, 453
  lifelong learning, 370–71,
    523
  in math and science, 510–11
  new communications
    technology and, 521–23
  No Child Left Behind
    (NCLB) Act, 509, 512

occupation and, 213
  open admissions to college,
    512
  politics and, 5112
  privatization of, 509–12
  race and, 213–14, 344–46
  reform in the U.S., 508–9
  social exclusion and, 239
  social mobility and, 226–27,
    228
  social promotion, 506–7
  sociological theories of,
    496–98
    assimilation perspective,
      496–97
    credentialism, 497
    schools as contested
      spaces, 498
    social reproduction,
      497–98
  technological change, media,
    and, 520–23
  tracking, 500–501
  in the U.S., 498–512
  voting behavior and, 394
"edutainment," 522
egocentrism, 88–89
Egypt, 547, 558, 559
Ehrlich, Paul, 634, 635
Eil-Eibesfeldt, I., 109–10
Eisenhower, Dwight D.,
  401–2
  highway system and, 619
Ekman, Paul, 109, 110
elderly, *see* aging and seniors
electoral college, 392–93
electronic communications
  emotional expression in,
    110–11
  face-to-face communications
    replaced by, 124–27
  global culture and, 80
  impression management
    and, 114–15
  interactional vandalism and,
    118
  loneliness and, 144–45
  work and the workplace,
    160–61
  see also cell phones;
    e-mail; information
    technology; Internet;
    telecommunications
    technologies
electronic data interchange
  (EDI) software, 448
"electronic economy," 666
Elementary and Secondary
  Education Act of 1965,
  509

*Elementary Forms of the
  Religious Life, The*
  (Durkheim), 532
Ellington, Andrea, 279–80,
  289, 309–12
Ellis, Cheryl, 481
El Salvador, 79
e-mail
  audience segregation and,
    114–15
  "Autofill" features, 114
  emotional expression in,
    110–11
  face-to-face contact replaced
    by, acceptability of, 125
  embarrassment and "saving
    face," 111–12
  emigration, 330
Eminem, 64
empirical (factual) questions,
  29
Employee Free Choice Act, 434
employment, *see*
  unemployment; work
  and the workplace
encounter, 113
*End of Child Labor within Reach,
  The* (ILO), 264
End of Millennium (Castells),
  191–92
energy consumption and
  environmental issues,
  648
Engineers without Borders,
  668
England, *see* Britain
English language
  American "cultural
    imperialism" and, 53
  "English-only" movement,
    68
  the Internet, as primary
    language of, 53, 124
Enron scandal, 191
entrepreneurs, 437
environment, 402, 403, 669
  adaptation of humans to
    physical, 58–59
  China industrialization and
    the, 607–8
  corporate crime and, 191
  global warming, 269
  manufactured risk, 673
  nature/nurture debate, *see*
    nature/nurture debate
  new social movements and,
    413
  population growth and, *see*
    population growth, the
    environment and

North American Free Trade Agreement (NAFTA), 414

North Atlantic Treaty Organization (NATO), 165
  Kosovo bombing campaign, 327

North Korea, 657

Norway
  politics, women in, 305
  poverty rate in, 231

nuclear energy, 648

nuclear family, 461, 462, 463, 470
  decline in the U.S., 471–72
  defined, 462
  historical perspective, 465

nuclear weapons, 659

nursing homes, 370, 374

N.W.A., 64

Nyoba, Matespang, 589

Oakes, Jeannie, 501

Oakley, Ann, 585

Obama, Barack, 341, 348, 389, 396

obedience to authority, Milgram's research on, 141–42, 163

obesity, 565–66, 570–73
  social networks and, 570–71
  stigma of, 576

O'Brien, Patricia, 301

occupations
  contingent workforce, 454–55
  defined, 424
  division of labor, see division of labor
  education and, 213
  family background and, 500
  gender typing or sex segregation, 290–91, 292, 293–96, 304
  health and illness, inequalities in, 581
  job satisfaction and, 436–37
  knowledge economy, 453, 454
  manufacturing, see manufacturing
  portfolio worker, 453–54
  service sector, see service sector
  status and, 214, 216
  trends in the occupations structure, 451–55, 622

Odle, Stephanie, 296

Office of Faith-Based and Community Initiatives, 530

Office of Management and Budget, 320

Office of Refugee Resettlement, 336

Ogbu, John, 505

Ohlin, Lloyd E., 180

Ohmae, Kenichi, 391, 416

oil companies, 437–38

oil consumption, 648

old age, as stage of life course, 101–4

oldest old, 364

old old, 364, 369–70, 375

old-style terrorism, 417

oligarchy, 155

oligopolies, 438

Oliver, Melvin, 212, 223

Omar, Mullah, 559

one-person households, 471, 491

One Tree Hill, 190

Ontario, Family Law Act, 490

open admissions to colleges, 512

open-ended questionnaires, 35

Operating Engineers Union, 397

opinion leaders, 36

optimism, life-extending effect of, 360–61

Oregon, domestic partnerships in, 491

organic organizations, 150–51

organic solidarity, 11, 13

Organisation for Economic Cooperation and Development (OECD), 453, 510, 511, 632

organizations, 147–58, 157
  bureaucracy, see bureaucracy
  corporations, see corporations
  decentralization of, 160, 162
  defined, 147
  formal, 147
  gender and, 155–58
  influence over everyday life, 166–67
  information technology's effects on, 160–61
  international, 164–66
  mechanistic, 150, 151
  modern alternatives to traditional, 158–64
  as networks, 161–63
  organic, 150–51
  physical settings of, 151–54

social capital and membership in, 166–67
  surveillance in, 151–54, 161
  theories of, 148–64

organized crime, 191–92

Ottoman Empire, 560

Ouchi, William, 158

Ouellette, Ryan, 63

Our Common Future (Brundtland Commission), 648–50

out-groups, 137

overweight, *see* obesity

Overworked American, The (Schor), 466

Oxfam, 418

ozone layer, depletion of, 673

paganism, 541

Pager, Devah, 195–96, 198–99

Pahlavi, Mohammad Reza, shah of Iran, 558–59

Paine, Alice, 411

Pakistan, 77, 558
  Islamic socialists in, 557
  Kashmir and, 415
  slavery in, 207

Palestine, 388, 547, 558

Palestinians, 415, 558, 560

Palin, Sarah, 300

palliative care, 579

Pankhurst, Emmeline, 411

Panopticon, 154

Parent-Teacher Association (PTA), 166

pariah groups, 241

Park, Robert, 610, 611

Parkin, Frank, 243

Parkinson's disease, 575

Parks, Rosa, 340, 409

Parsons, Talcott, 16, 306, 307, 361–62, 463–64, 574

participant observation, 34

participatory democracy, 387, 400

part-time workers, 454–55

Passing By: Bender and Public Harassment (Gardner), 130

pastoral societies, 71, 73

patents, 632, 681

patriarchy, 308, 464

patrilocal family, 463

Paul IV, Pope, 624

Pediatrics, 174, 175

peer group as socializing agency, 90–92

Pelosi, Nancy, 300

Pentecostalism, 541

"People's Choice," 35–36

periphery countries, in world-systems theory, 267

Perkins, James, 407

per-person gross national income (GNI), 248, 251, 254

Persian Gulf War, 165, 382, 518, 560, 666

personality stabilization, 463–64

personal space, 107–8, 119
  iPod use and, 121

Peru, 310

pesticides, 673

Pew Research Center, 489, 560

Pfizer, 275

pharmaceutical industry
  corporate crime and, 191
  Medicare Reform Act of 2003 and, 397–99

Philippines, 271
  child labor in, 264
  eating disorders in, 567
  family patterns, changes in, 470
  women in management in, 304

physical abuse of the elderly, 369

physicians, asymmetrical power relations between patients and, 578

Piaget, Jean, 88–89

pilgrims, religious, 536, 537

pilot study, 35

"Pink & Blue" project, 96

Piore, Michael, 447

Pitts, Victoria, 62–63

Pius V, Pope, 624

play, role in child development of, 88

Pledge of Allegiance, 549

pluralism, 328
  pluralist theories of democracy, 400–401

Poland, 305, 382, 390, 665
  family patterns, changes in, 470
  global trade and, 679
  Solidarity movement, 557
  transnational corporations and, 440

police and policing, 196–99
  broken windows theory, 183
  community policing, 200
  crime rates and, 196, 197
  as knowledge workers, 197–99

sociologists, role of, 24
Sociologists without Borders/
    Sociólogos Sin Fronteras
    (SSF), 668–69
sociology
    Comte's role in investing
        field of, 10–11
    influence of sociological
        research, 44
    practical implications of,
        23–24
    public, 18–19, 42
    as restatement of the
        obvious, 23
    as a science, 11, 13, 22–23
sociology of the body, 566
    see also health and illness
soil erosion and degradation,
    643–44, 645
Sojourner Truth, 410
Solidarity movement, 557
Somalia, 165
sonograms, 602
Sorokin, Pitirim, 225
Soros, George, 389
South Africa
    apartheid in, 140, 207, 208,
        272, 310, 318, 321, 324,
        327, 343
    as caste society, 207, 208
    HIV/AIDS in, 588
    homosexual rights in,
        599–602
    Internet access in, 523
    liberal democracy in, 388,
        390
    public sociology in, 272–73
    women's movement in, 310
Southern Baptists, 550, 551
South Korea, 260
    as newly industrializing
        economy, 78, 260, 261,
        274, 440
sovereignty, 383
Soviet Union, former
    collapse of communism, 41,
        274, 416, 558, 665
    creation of, 41
    economic future republics
        of, 275
    middle-income countries
        of, 250
    nationalism and conflicts
        in, 82
    Sputnik, 659
    women in professional
        positions in, 305
space program, 659
Spain, 402–3
    Basques and, 415, 666

marriage in, 489
Spain, Daphne, 466
specialization in corporations,
    decreased, 158, 159–60
Spectrem Group, 218
speech, 69
    affiliative, 126, 127
    assertive, 126
    see also talk, social rules and
Spencer, Christopher, 444
Spenner, Kenneth, 446
*Spirit Catches You and You Fall
    Down: A Hmong Child,
    Her American Doctors,
    and the Collision of Two
    Cultures, The* (Fadiman),
    577
Spitzer, Elliot, 111
spousal abuse, *see* domestic
    violence
"Spread of Obesity in a Large
    Social Network over 32
    Years," 570–71
Sputnik, 659
Sri Lanka, Buddhist socialists
    in, 557
Stacey, Judith, 461, 462
Stack, Carol, 475
Stalker, G. M., 150–51, 158
stalking, 301, 302
standard deviation, 45
standardized questionnaires,
    35
Stanton, Elizabeth Cady, 542
staring, 108, 129–30
Stark, Rodney, 538, 555
starvation, *see* famine, global
    hunger, malnutrition
    and
state
    defined, 383
    nation-states, *see* nation-
        states
state-centered theories of
    global inequality,
    270–71, 274
State Farm Insurance, 295
State in a Changing World, The
    (World Bank), 271
State of the World's Mothers
    report, 258
state overload, 403
States and Social Revolutions
    (Skocpol), 41
statistical terms, 45
status (social position), 111
    occupation and, 214, 216
    teenage behavior and, 206,
        209
    Weber's views on, 241–42

Steele, Claude, 507
steel industry, 607–8
stepfamilies, 472, 482–83
Stepik, Alex, 350
stereotype threat, 507
stereotyping, 324
    gender, 433
Stern, Andy, 434
Stevenson, Anne, 477
stigma, 576
    illnesses carrying, 575, 576,
        587–88
Stone, Lawrence, 465–66
Stonewall Inn, 599
stoppage of work, 429, 430
storybooks, gender
    socialization from,
    95–96
stratification, social, *see* social
    stratification
Straus, Murray, 485
Strauss, Anselm, 575
*Streetwise: Race, Class, and
    Change in an Urban
    Community* (Anderson),
    130–31, 626
stress, 579, 585
strikes, labor, 428–29, 430
"striking a pose" (impression
    management), 111–12
structural mobility, 224–25
structural strain, 408–9
structuration of human
    societies, process of, 7
structured inequalities, 216
Student Non-Violent
    Coordinating
    Committee, 407
subcultures, 63–65
    deviant behavior and, 176,
        180
    differential association and,
        181
    labeling theory and, 181–82
    norms of, 177, 180
    in urban areas, 612
subprime mortgages, 212–13,
    219
suburbanization, 614–15, 619–21
    of employment, 622
    evolving suburbs in the 21st
        century, 620–21
    history of, 619
Sudan, 258, 416, 558, 559
    Azande of, 598
    genocide in Darfur region
        of, 327
Sudhest Island, gender roles in
    Vanatinai society, 286
suffragettes, 411

Suharto, 328, 390
suicide, 23
    in China, female, 304
    Durkheim on, 11, 32, 584
Suicide (Durkheim), 32
Sunni Muslims, 547
support systems, health and,
    585
Supreme Court
    Brown v. Board of Education,
        208, 340
    female justices, 300–301
    Lawrence v. Texas, 599
    Roe v. Wade, 399
    on same sex harassment,
        297
    *Webster v. Reproductive
        Health Services,* 399
Surgenson, Patricia, 296
surplus value, 241
surveillance, 152
    crime prevention and, 196
    on the Internet, 389–92
    limits of, 154
    in organizations, 151–54, 161
    in prisons, 154
    types of, 152–53
surveillance society, 154
Survey of Consumer Finances,
    212
surveys, 34, 35–37, 36–37,
    42–43
    advantages and
        disadvantages of, 36–37
    Humphreys's "tearoom
        trade," 42–43
Survivor (TV program), 139
sustainable development, 271,
    648–50
Sutherland, Edwin H., 181, 190
Swaziland, life expectancy in,
    356
sweatshops, 264–65, 270, 355
Sweden, 403
    cohabitation in, 471, 489
    constitutional monarchy in,
        388
    education and knowledge
        economy, 453
    health and illness in, 584
    labor unions in, 430
    politics, women in, 305
    poverty rate in, 231
    social mobility in, 225
Swidler, Ann, 58
Swift Vets and POWs for
    Truth, 399
Switzerland, civil unions in,
    491
symbolic ethnicity, 319

symbolic interactionism, 15, 16, 28, 88
  on gender and housework, 299
  illness as "lived experience," 574, 576
symbols, 15, 69
  semiotics and material culture, 69–70
symmetrical family, 464

tables, reading, 46–47
Taiwan
  caring for elderly in, 377
  eating disorders in, 567
  as high-income country, 250, 260
  as newly industrializing economy, 78, 260, 261, 274, 440
Tajikistan, 258
Taliban, 5, 81–82, 543, 559
talk, social rules and, 116–19
  gender and talkativeness, 126–27
  interactional vandalism, 116–18
  personal space, 119
  response cries, 118–19
Tanzania, 77
  al Qaeda attack of U.S. embassy in, 527
  child labor in, 264
"Tapping the Mood Gene," 60–61
target hardening, 182, 183, 196
Tasago, Wirat, 248
Tatas of Togo, 101
tattoos, 63, 180
taxes
  property, to fund schools, 239
  urbanism and, 616, 621
  welfare systems and, 403
Taylor, Frederick Winslow, 427
Taylor, Verta, 288–89
Taylorism, 427
Tearoom Trade (Humphreys), 27–28, 42–43, 44
technological determinists, 446
technology
  defined, 424
  eating disorders and, 567
  global inequality and, 274–75
  information, see information technology
  media, education, and, 520–23

rate of innovation, 659
social movements and, 413–14
telecommunications, see telecommunications technologies
transnational corporations of the twenty-first century and, 444
technology adopters, 274
technology disconnected, 274–75
technology innovators, 274, 275
teenagers
  conformity among, 140–41
  consumerism, 206
  crime rates, 189–90
  drug use by, 190
  Japanese and American, comparison of, 98–99
  juvenile delinquency, see juvenile delinquency
  male teenage athletes and aggressive behavior, 20–21
  pregnancies among, 259
  sexual behavior of, 592–93
  as stage of life course, 100
  status consciousness, 205–6, 209
telecommunications technologies, 441, 444, 662–64
telecommuting, 160–61, 446
telephones, 662, 663
  cell phones, 122–23
televangelists, 538, 556
television, 517, 518, 663
  gender socialization from, 95
  global culture and, 79
  violence studies, 92
  see also mass media
Telework Coalition, 160
Temporary Assistance for Needy Families (TANF) program, 236
temporary workers, 454–55, 457
terrorism, 5, 417–18, 655
  defining, 417
  new-style, 417–18
  old-style, 417
  war and, 418
  war on, 402
Terrorism Awareness Information Program, 389
testosterone, 281, 584
texts, 69

Thailand
  challenge to democracy in, 390, 391
  as newly industrializing economy, 260, 274
  reverence of elderly in, 376
  sex slaves in, 207
theism, 528
theoretical questions, 29
theories and theoretical approaches in sociology, 10–21
  early theorists, 10–13
    Auguste Comte, 10–11
    Émile Durkheim, 11
    Karl Marx, 11–12
    Max Weber, 12–13
  factual research, relationship to, 10
  middle-range theories, 19–21
  modern approaches, 15–19
    feminism and feminist theory, 17
    functionalism, 15–16
    Marxism and class conflict, 16–17
    postmodern theory, 17–19
    rational choice theory, 17
    symbolic interactionism, 15
  modern world, sociological debate about, 14–15
  neglected founders, 13–14
    W. E. B. Du Bois, 14
    Harriet Martineau, 13–14
  theory defined, 10
third parties, 396
third world, 75, 76
  see also developing world
Thomas, Justice Clarence, 297
Thompson, Becky, 321
Thompson, John, 518–19
Thompson, Warren S., 637
Thompson Products, 439
Thoreau, Henry David, 646
Tibetan Buddhism, 535
Tibetans, 415
Tilly, Charles, 405–8, 410, 411
Time Bind, The (Hochschild), 467
time-space social interaction, 119–28
  clock time, 121
  compulsion of proximity, 121, 126–27
  iPod use and, 120
  regionalization, 119–21
  social life and, 121
timetables, 153–54
Time Warner, 162, 438

Titanic, 672
TNS Financial Services, 218
Tocqueville, Alexis de, 340
Tokyo, Japan, 628
Tonry, Michael, 626
Torah, 547
Toshiba, 450
total institutions, 541
totemism, 532
Touraine, Alain, 409–10, 660
Towey, Jim, 198
toys
  Barbie, manufacturing of, 267–70
  gender learning and, 94–95
  gender stereotyping and, 281
  toxic, from Chinese factories, 450
trachoma, 586
tracking in schools, 500–501
trade, 263, 679–81, 682
traditional societies or civilizations, 71, 73–74
transactional leaders, 140, 403
transformationalists, 667, 670–71
transformational leaders, 140
transnational corporations, 274, 391, 423–24, 438, 439–44, 449, 657, 666–67, 670, 682
  colonialism's lasting effects for, 266
  global supply chains, 424
  international character of products of, 443, 444
  largest, 439–40, 441
  twenty-first century, 442–44
triads, 139
Triangle Shirtwaist Factory fire, 355
triangulation, 42
Tricky, 64
Tripp, David, 92
TRIPS (Trade-Related Aspects of Intellectual Property Rights), 681, 682
Troeltsch, Ernst, 538
Truman, Harry S., 394
tsetse fly, 585
tsunamis, 666, 677
tuberculosis, 588, 589
Tufte, Edward, 38–39
Tumin, Melvin, 242
al-Turabi, Hassan, 559
Turkey, 388
  Armenian genocide, 327
  earthquakes in, 666

vertical mobility, 225, 226
veterans, homeless, 240
Veterans Administration, 619
Viacom, 438
Victorian family, 467
    sexuality and, 590, 591
video games, social
        and intellectual
        development of children
        and, 92–93
Video Kids (Provenzo), 92
Vietnam, 274, 557
Vietnam War, 554
violence
    crimes of, 184, 185, 186,
        188–89, 194
    within families, 484–85
    male teenage athletes and
        aggressive behavior,
        20–21
    murder rate for young black
        males, 582
    religious nationalism and,
        560
    social movements and, *see*
        revolution
    television and, 92
    against women, 188–89,
        301–3, 308, 464
viruses, electronic, 676–77
*Visual Display of Quantitative
    Information* (Tufte), 38
Visual Explanations (Tufte), 38
Vodafone Airtouch, 438
Voigy, Thomas, 229
volunteer work, 426
Voter News Service (VNS),
        395
voting, 516
    voter registration, 396
    voter turnout, 167, 371,
        393–96, 402, 403
    women's right to vote, 399,
        411, 412

Waco, Texas, 539, 541
Wadhwa, Vivek, 511
Wajcman, Judy, 156–58
Wales, 415
Wall, Jeff, 113
Wallerstein, Immanuel, 266,
        670
Wallerstein, Judith, 481
Wall Street Journal, 438, 510
Wal-Mart, 223, 295, 296, 423–
        24, 434, 438, 442–43,
        447–48
    *Dukes v. Wal-Mart Stores,
        Inc.,* 432–33

flexible business structure
        of, 447–48
    supply chain management,
        448
*"Wal-Mart: A Template for
    Twenty-First Century
    Capitalism,"* 423–24
warfare
    food shortages and, 258
    terrorism and, 418
war on terrorism, 402
Washington, domestic
        partnerships in, 491
Washington, George, 393
Washington, Isaiah, 599
Washington University in
        Saint Louis, 43
waste disposal, environmental
        challenge of, 646
water resources, 586, 632, 643,
        645
Watts, Duncan, 162
Wayward Puritans (Erikson),
        176
wealth, 212–13
    cultural capital and, 227–28
    defined, 212
    privilege and, 213
    race and, 212–13
    in the U.S., concentration of,
        212, 213
Web Camera, 110
Weber, Max, 12–13, 16, 17, 209
    bureaucracy and
        organizations, study of,
        12–13, 15, 147, 148–49,
        155, 161, 400
    on capitalism, 12, 14–15, 261,
        532
    on religion, 12, 14, 532–33,
        533, 538, 540, 658
    on social stratification,
        241–42
WebMD, 578
Webster, David, 272–73
*Webster v. Reproductive Health
    Services,* 399
Weitzman, Lenore, 95, 479
welfare capitalism, 439
welfare reform, 220–21, 236–
        38, 387
welfare state, 386–87, 402–3
welfare system, 236–38, 312,
        386–87, 403
    immigrants to the U.S. and,
        337, 338
    percentage of U.S.
        population on welfare,
        1960–2002, 237
    "welfare dependency," 236

welfare-to-work programs,
        236–38
Wellman, Barry, 145
Wellman, David, 351
West Point, 135–36
"Weststruckendness" and
        "Westoxification," 559,
        560, 658
Wheeler, Deborah, 81
*When Work Disappears: The
    World of the New Urban
    Poor* (Wilson), 621
Where the Blame Lies (cartoon),
        335
White, Merry, 98–99
White Collar (Mills), 42
white-collar crime, 190–91
White House Office of Faith-
        Based and Community
        Initiatives, 198
Whorf, Benjamin Lee, 68
Wiccan rituals, 541, 552
"Wild Boy of Aveyron," 86, 87
Wilkinson, Reginald, 199
Wilkinson, Richard, 584–85
Williams, Christine, 296–97
Williams, Jody, 165, 166
Williamsburg, Brooklyn, 612
Willis, Paul, 498, 508
Wilson, Edward O., 59
Wilson, William Julius, 351,
        621, 622–23, 624
Winfrey, Oprah, 341
Wirth, Louis, 610, 611–13
Woman's Bible, The (Stanton),
        542
women
    birth control, access to, 304,
        306
    crime and, 187–89
        crimes against women,
            188–89
    division of labor, gender and,
        298–99, 306, 307, 464,
        672
    housework and, 298–99, 303,
        426, 464
    interactional vandalism,
        117–18
    Martineau's sociological
        focus on, 14
    migration, feminization of,
        332
    political participation of,
        300, 305–6, 399–400,
        411, 412
    poverty and, 78, 233
    religious images and, 542
    religious organizations, role
        in, 542–43

social mobility and, 225
    Social Security benefits,
        372–73
    violence against, 188–89,
        301–3, 308, 464
    in the workplace, 155–58,
        228, 287–97, 455,
        467–70, 572
    age at first marriage and,
        471, 672
    balancing family and
        work, 279–80, 290,
        297–98, 303, 309–12,
        466–67
    comparable-worth
        policies, 293, 296, 462
    downward mobility of,
        228–29
    gender pay gap, 291–97,
        303, 432–33
    gender typing or sex
        segregation, 290–91,
        292, 293–96, 304,
        432–33
    glass ceiling, 296, 304
    glass elevator, 296–97
    globally, 303–5, 313
    historically, 287–90
    human capital theory,
        294–96
    in management, 156–58,
        291, 304, 400
    networking and, 144
    as percentage of the total
        labor force, 287, 288,
        290
    "second shift," 303, 465
    sexual harassment, 297,
        298
    social mobility and,
        228–29
    telecommuting, 161
    urban women out earning
        male peers, 294–95
Women's Environment
        and Development
        Organization, 313
women's movement, 399,
        410–12
    educational achievement
        and, 505–6
    international, 310–11, 313, 411
Woodward, Louise, 486
work and the workplace,
        423–58
    alienation and, 428, 445
    balancing family and, 279–
        80, 290, 297–98, 303,
        309–12, 466–67
    career paths, 671–72